NOTABLE
SPORTS
FIGURES

NOTABLE
SPORTS
FIGURES

Dana Barnes, Editor

VOLUME 1 • A-E

GALE®

Detroit • New York • San Diego • San Francisco • Cleveland • New Haven, Conn. • Waterville, Maine • London • Munich

Notable Sports Figures

Project Editor
Dana R. Barnes

Editorial
Laura Avery, Luann Brennan, Frank Castronova, Leigh Ann DeRemer, Andrea Henderson, Kathy Nemeh, Angela Pilchak, Tracie Ratiner, Bridget Travers

Research
Gary J. Oudersluys, Cheryl L. Warnock, Kelly Whittle

Editorial Support Services
Charlene Lewis, Sue Petrus

Editorial Standards
Lynne Maday

Permissions
Lori Hines

Imaging and Multimedia Content
Randy Basset, Dean Dauphinais, Leitha Etheridge-Sims, Lezlie Light, Dan W. Newell, Dave G. Oblender

Product Design
Jennifer Wahi

Manufacturing
Evi Seoud, Rhonda Williams

Library of Congress Cataloging-in-Publication Data

Notable sports figures / project editor, Dana R. Barnes.
    p. cm.
Includes bibliographical references and index.
ISBN 0-7876-6628-9 (Set Hardcover) -- ISBN 0-7876-6629-7 (Volume 1)
--ISBN 0-7876-6630-0 (Volume 2) -- ISBN 0-7876-6631-9 (Volume 3) --
ISBN 0-7876-7786-8 (Volume 4)
1. Sports--Biography. 2. Athletes--Biography. 3. Sports--History.
I. Barnes, Dana R.
GV697.A1N68 2004
796'.092'2--dc21

2003011288

Contents

Introduction

Notable Sports Figures provides narrative biographical profiles of more than 600 individuals who have made significant contributions to their sport and to society. It covers sports figures from the nineteenth, twentieth, and twenty-first centuries who represent a wide variety of sports and countries. Lesser-known sports such as cricket, equestrian, and snowboarding are featured alongside sports like baseball, basketball, and football. *Notable Sports Figures* includes not only athletes, but also coaches, team executives, and media figures such as sportscasters and writers.

Notable Sports Figures takes a close look at the people in sports who have captured attention because of success *on* the playing field or controversy *off* the playing field. It provides biographical coverage of people from around the world and throughout history who have had an impact not only on their sport, but also on the society and culture of their times. Each biography features information on the entrant's family life, early involvement in sports, career highlights, championships, and awards. *Notable Sports Figures* also examines the impact that the subject had and continues to have on his or her sport, and the reasons why the individual is "notable." This includes consideration of the successes and failures, on the field and off, that keep the person in the public eye.

The biographies in *Notable Sports Figures* profile a broad variety of individuals. Athletes such as **Babe Ruth, Michael Jordan,** and **Martina Navratilova** are featured for their record-breaking accomplishments. **Jackie Robinson** and **Janet Guthrie** remain in the public consciousness because of their determination to cross racial and gender boundaries. Other sports figures have captured our attention by their controversial activities. Skater **Tonya Harding** continues to hold public interest not because of any medals won, but because of the scandalous attack on **Nancy Kerrigan**. Baseball player **"Shoeless" Joe Jackson** was one of the greatest players of his era, but he is remembered more for his complicity in the **"Black Sox"** scandal of 1919 than for his accomplishments on the field. Their lives, accomplishments, and reasons for the public's ongoing fascination with them are examined in *Notable Sports Figures*.

SELECTION PROCESS AND CRITERIA

A preliminary list of athletes, team executives, sportswriters, broadcasters, and other sports figures was compiled from a wide variety of sources, including Hall of Fame lists, periodical articles, and other biographical collections. The list was reviewed by an advisory board, and final selection was made by the editor. An effort was made to include athletes of varying nationalities, ethnicities, and fields of sport as well as those who have contributed to the success of a sport or team in general. Selection criteria include:

- Notable "first" achievements, including those who broke racial or gender barriers and paved the way for others

- Impact made on the individual's sport and on society as a whole

- Records set and broken

- Involvement in controversial or newsworthy activities on and off the playing field

FEATURES OF THIS PRODUCT

For easy access, entries are arranged alphabetically according to the entrant's last name.

- **Timeline**—includes significant events in the world of sports, from historic times to the present.

- **Entry head**—lists basic information on each sports figure, including name, birth and death years, nationality, and occupation/sport played.

- **Biographical essay**—offers 1,000 to 2,500 words on the person's life, career highlights, and the impact that the individual had and continues to have on his or her sport and on society. Bold-faced names within entries indicate an entry on that person.

- **Photos**—provide a portrait for many of the individuals profiled. Several essays also include an action photo.

- **Sidebars**—present a chronology of key events in the entrant's life, a list of major awards and accomplishments, and, as applicable, career statistics, brief biographies of important individuals in the entrant's life, "where is s/he now" information on previously popular sports figures, and excerpts from books and periodicals of significant events in the entrant's life and career.

• **Contact Information**—offers addresses, phone numbers, and web sites for selected living entrants.

• **Selected Writings**—lists books and publications written or edited by the entrant.

• **Further Information**—provides a list of resources the reader may access to seek additional information on the sports figure.

• **Appendix**—offers a glossary of commonly used sports abbreviations.

• **Indices**—allow the reader to access the entrants by nationality or sport. A general subject index with cross-references offers additional access.

We Welcome Your Suggestions. Mail your comments and suggestions for enhancing and improving *Notable Sports Figures* to:

The Editors
Notable Sports Figures
Gale Group
27500 Drake Road
Farmington Hills, MI 48331-3535
Phone: (800) 347-4253

Advisory Board

Robert Kirsch

Reference Librarian
Lake Forest High School
Lake Forest, Illinois

William Munro

Manager
Ponce de Leon Branch, Atlanta-Fulton Public Library
Atlanta, Georgia

Alan Nichter

Branch Librarian
Seffner-Mango Branch Library
Hillsborough County Public Library Cooperative
Seffner, Florida

Mila C. Su

Reference Coordinator
Robert E. Eiche Library, Penn State Altoona
Altoona, Pennsylvania

Contributors

Don Amerman, Julia Bauder, Cynthia Becker, David Becker, Michael Belfiore, Kari Bethel, Michael Betzold, Tim Borden, Carol Brennan, Gerald Brennan, Paul Burton, Frank Caso, Gordon Churchwell, Gloria Cooksey, Andrew Cunningham, Lisa Frick, Jan Goldberg, Joyce Hart, Eve Hermann, Ian Hoffman, Syd Jones, Wendy Kagan, Aric Karpinski, Christine Kelley, Judson Knight, Eric Lagergren, Jeanne Lesinski, Carole Manny, Paulo Nunes-Ueno, Patricia Onorato, Tricia Owen, Kristin Palm, Mike Pare, Annette Petruso, Ryan Poquette, Susan Salter, Brenna Sanchez, Lorraine Savage, Paula Scott, Pam Shelton, Ken Shepherd, Ann Shurgin, Barbra Smerz, Roger Smith, Janet Stamatel, Jane Summer, Erick Trickey, Amy Unterburger, Sheila Velazquez, Bruce Walker, Dave Wilkins, Kelly Winters, Rob Winters, Ben Zackheim

Acknowledgments

Photographs and illustrations appearing in *Notable Sports Figures* have been used with the permission of the following sources:

AP/WIDE WORLD PHOTOS:
1980 U.S. Olympic hockey team, photograph. AP/Wide World Photos./ Aamodt, Kjetil Andre, photograph. AP/Wide World Photos./ Aaron, Hank, photograph. AP/Wide World Photos./ Abbott, Jim, photograph. AP/Wide World Photos./ Abdul-Jabbar, Kareem, photograph. AP/Wide World Photos./ Abdul-Jabbar, Kareem, photograph. AP/Wide World Photos./ Agassi, Andre, photograph. AP/Wide World Photos./ Aikman, Troy, photograph. AP/Wide World Photos./ Akers, Michelle, photograph. AP/Wide World Photos, Inc./ Albert, Marv, photograph by Ron Frehm. AP/Wide World Photos./ Albright, Tenley, photograph. AP/Wide World Photos./ Alexander, Grover Cleveland, photograph. AP/Wide World Photos./ Allison, Davey, photograph. AP/Wide World Photos./ Alamo, Roberto, photograph. AP/Wide World Photos./ Anderson, George "Sparky," photograph. AP/Wide World Photos./ Andretti, Mario, photograph. AP/Wide World Photos./ Anthony, Earl, photograph. AP/Wide World Photos./ Armstrong, Lance, photograph. AP/Wide World Photos./ Armstrong, Lance, photograph. AP/Wide World Photos./ Ashe, Arthur, photograph. AP/Wide World Photos./ Ashford, Evelyn, photograph. AP/Wide World Photos./ Auerbach, Red, photograph. AP/Wide World Photos./ Autissier, Isabelle, photograph. AP/Wide World Photos./ Bailey, Donovan, photograph. AP/Wide World Photos./ Banks, Ernie, photograph. AP/Wide World Photos./ Bannister, Roger, photograph. AP/Wide World Photos./ Barton, Donna, photograph. AP/Wide World Photos./ Baugh, Sammy, photograph. AP/Wide World Photos./ Baumgartner, Bruce, photograph. AP/Wide World Photos./ Baylor, Elgin, photograph. AP/Wide World Photos./ Beckenbauer, Franz, photograph. AP/Wide World Photos./ Becker, Boris, photograph. AP/Wide World Photos./ Bedard, Myriam, photograph by Roberto Borea. AP/Wide World Photos./ Bell, Bert, photograph. AP/Wide World Photos./Bell, James "Cool Papa," photograph by Leon Algee. AP/Wide World Photos./ Bench, Johnny, photograph. AP/Wide World Photos./ Berra, Yogi, photograph. AP/Wide World Photos./ Biondi, Matt, photograph. AP/Wide World Photos./ Bird, Larry, photograph. AP/Wide World Photos./Bjoerndalen, Ole Einar, photograph. AP/Wide World Photos./ Blair, Bonnie, photograph. AP Wide World Photos./ Blair, Bonnie, portrait. AP/Wide World Photos./ Blake, Sir Peter, photograph. AP/Wide World Photos./ Bogues, Tyrone, "Muggsy," photograph. AP/Wide World Photos./ Bonds, Barry, photograph. AP/Wide World Photos./ Bonds, Barry, photograph. AP/Wide World Photos./ Borders, Ila, photograph by Nick Ut. AP/Wide World Photos./ Borg, Bjorn, photograph. AP/Wide World Photos./ Bossy, Michael, photograph. AP/Wide World Photos./ Bradley, William Warren, photograph. AP/Wide World Photos./ Bradman, Don, photograph. AP/Wide World Photos./ Bradshaw, Terry, photograph. AP/Wide World Photos./ Brock, Lou, photograph. AP/Wide World Photos./ Brock, Lou, photograph. AP/Wide World Photos./ Brooks, Herb, photograph by Gene J. Puskar. AP/Wide World Photos./ Brown, Jim, photograph. AP/Wide World Photos./ Brown, Jim, photograph. AP/Wide World Photos./ Brown, Mordecai, "Three Finger," photograph. AP/Wide World Photos./ Brown, Tim, photograph. AP/Wide World Photos./ Bubka, Sergei, photograph. AP/Wide World Photos./ Budge, Don, photograph. AP/Wide World Photos./ Butcher, Susan, photograph. AP/Wide World Photos./ Button, Dick, photograph. AP/Wide World Photos./ Campanella, Roy, photograph. AP/Wide World Photos./ Campbell, Earl, photograph. AP/Wide

World Photos./ Canseco, Jose, photograph. AP/Wide World Photos./ Capriati, Jennifer, photograph. AP/Wide World Photos./ Capriati, Jennifer, photograph. AP/Wide World Photos./ Carter, Cris, photograph by Michael Conroy. AP/Wide World Photos./ Carter, Vince, photograph by Chuck Stoody. AP/Wide World Photos./ Carter, Vince, photograph. AP/Wide World Photos./ Cartwright, Alexander Joy, photograph. AP/Wide World Photos./ Caulkins, Tracy, photograph. AP/Wide World Photos./ Chamberlain, Wilt, photograph. AP/Wide World Photos./ Chelios, Chris, photograph. AP/Wide World Photos./ Chun, Lee-Kyung, photograph. AP/Wide World Photos./ Clark, Kelly, photograph. AP/Wide World Photos./ Clark, Kelly, photograph. AP/Wide World Photos./ Clemens, Roger, photograph. AP/Wide World Photos./ Clemens, Roger, photograph. AP/Wide World Photos./ Clemente, Roberto Walker, photograph. AP/Wide World Photos./ Coachman, Alice, photograph. AP/Wide World Photos./ Coleman, Derrick, photograph. AP/Wide World Photos./ Colorado Silver Bullets (Samonds, Shereen, and former major league pitcher Phil Niekro), photograph. AP/Wide World Photos./ Comaneci, Nadia, photograph. AP/Wide World Photos./ Connors, Jimmy, photograph. AP/Wide World Photos./ Conradt, Jody, photograph. AP/Wide World Photos./ Cooper, Cynthia, photograph by David J. Phillip. AP/Wide World Photos./ Cosell, Howard, photograph. AP/Wide World Photos./ Courier, Jim, photograph. AP/Wide World Photos./ Cousy, Bob, photograph. AP/Wide World Photos./ Daly, Chuck, photograph. AP/Wide World Photos./ Davis, Terrell, photograph by Ed Andrieski. AP/Wide World Photos./ Dawes, Dominique, photograph by John McConnico. AP/Wide World Photos./ Dean, Dizzy, photograph. AP/Wide World Photos./ Decker-Slaney, Mary, photograph. AP/Wide World Photos./ Deegan, Brian, photograph. AP/Wide World Photos./ DeFrantz, Anita, photograph by Douglas C. Pizac. AP/Wide World Photos./ De La Hoya, Oscar, photograph. AP/Wide World Photos./ Dickerson, Eric, photograph by Bill Janscha. AP/Wide World Photos./ Dimaggio, Joe, photograph. AP/Wide World Photos./Disl, Uschi, photograph. AP/Wide World Photos./ Ditka, Mike, photograph. AP/Wide World Photos./Doby, Larry, photograph. AP/Wide World Photos./ Dolan, Tom, photograph. AP/Wide World Photos./ Dorsett, Tony, photograph by Bruce Zake. AP/Wide World Photos./ Dravecky, Dave, photograph. AP/Wide World Photos./ Durocher, Leo, photograph. AP/Wide World Photos./ Dyroen, Becky, photograph. AP/Wide World Photos./ Earnhardt, Dale, photograph. AP/Wide World Photos./ Edwards, Teresa, photograph. AP/Wide World Photos./ Egerszegi, Krisztina, photograph. AP/Wide World Photos./ Elway, John, photograph. AP/Wide World Photos./ Erving, Julius, photograph. AP/Wide World Photos./ Esposito, Phil, photograph by Kevin Frayer. AP/Wide World./ Evans, Janet, photograph. AP/Wide World Photos./ Ewbank, Weeb, photograph. AP/Wide World./ Fangio, Juan Manuel, photograph by Eduardo DiBaia. AP/Wide World Photos./ Faulk, Marshall, photograph. AP/Wide World Photos./ Favre, Brett. AP/Wide World Photos./ Fernandez, Lisa, photograph. AP/Wide World Photos./ Figo, Luis, photograph. AP/Wide World Photos./ Fisk, Carlton, photograph. AP/Wide World Photos./ Fittipaldi, Emerson, photograph. AP/Wide World Photos./ Fleming, Peggy, photograph. AP/Wide World Photos./ Flowers, Vonetta, photograph by Darron Cummings. AP/Wide World Photos./ Foreman, George, photograph by Charles Rex Arbogast. AP/Wide World Photos./ Forsberg, Magdalena, photograph. AP/Wide World Photos./ Foyt, A.J., photograph. AP/Wide World Photos./ Foyt, A. J., photograph by Dave Parker. AP/Wide World Photos./ Freeman, Cathy, photograph. AP/Wide World Photos./ Gable, Dan, photograph. AP/Wide World Photos./ Galindo, Rudy, photograph by Craig Fujii. AP/Wide World Photos./ Garcia, Sergio, photograph by Beth A. Keiser. AP/Wide World Photos./ Garnett, Kevin, photograph. AP/Wide World Photos./ Gehrig, Lou, photograph. AP/Wide World Photos./ Gibson, Althea, photograph. AP/Wide World Photos./ Gibson, Josh, photograph. AP/Wide World Photos./ Gonzales, Richard "Pancho," photograph. AP/Wide World Photos./Goolagong, Evonne, photograph. AP/Wide World Photos./ Goosen, Retief, photograph. AP/Wide World Photos./ Gordeeva, Ekaterina, photograph. AP/Wide World Photos./ Graf, Steffi, photograph. AP/Wide World Photos./ Granato, Cammi, photograph. AP/Wide World Photos./ Grange, Harold "Red," photograph. AP/Wide World Photos./ Grange, Red, photograph. AP/Wide World Photos./ Graziano, Rocky, photograph. AP/Wide World Photos./ Greenberg, Hank, photograph. AP/Wide World Photos./ Greene, Joe, photograph. AP/Wide World Photos./ Griese, Bob, photograph. AP/Wide World Photos./ Griffey, Jr., Ken, photograph. AP/Wide World Photos./ Griffey, Ken, Jr., photograph by Jay Drowns. AP/Wide World Photos./ Griffin, Archie, photograph. AP/Wide World Photos./ Gwynn, Tony, portrait. AP/Wide World Photos./ Hackl, Georg, photograph. AP/Wide World Photos./ Halas, George, photograph. AP/Wide World Photos./ Hall, Glenn, photograph. AP/Wide World Photos./ Hamilton, Scott, photograph. AP/Wide World Photos./ Hamm, Mia, photograph. AP/Wide World Photos./ Hardaway, Afernee, photograph. AP/Wide World Photos./ Hardaway, Tim Duane, photograph by Lee Wilfredo. AP/Wide World Photos./ Harding, Tonya, photograph. AP/Wide World Photos./ Harkes, John, photograph. AP/Wide World Photos./ Harwell, Ernie, photograph. AP/Wide World Photos./ Heiden, Eric, photograph. AP/Wide World Photos./ Henderson, Rickey, photograph by Kevork Djansezian. AP/Wide World Photos./ Henie, Sonja, photograph. AP/Wide World Photos./ Henie, Sonja, photograph. AP/Wide World Photos./ Hernandez, Luis, photograph. AP/Wide World Photos./ Hill, Grant, photograph. AP/Wide World Photos./ Hirsch, Elroy Leon, photograph. AP/Wide World Photos./ Hogan, Ben, photograph. AP/Wide World Photos./ Holdsclaw, Chamique, photograph. AP/Wide World Photos./ Holmgren, Mike, photograph. AP/Wide World Photos./ Hornsby, Rogers, photograph. AP/Wide World Photos./ Hornung, Paul, photograph. AP/Wide World Photos./ Howe, Gordie, photograph. AP/Wide World Photos./ Howe, Gordie, photograph by Dawn Villella. AP/Wide World Photos./ Hughes, Sarah, photograph. AP/Wide World Photos./ Hull, Brett, photograph. AP/Wide World Photos./ Indurain, Miguel, photograph. AP/Wide World Photos./ Irvin, Michael, photograph AP/Wide World Photos./ Jackson, Bo (Vincent), photograph. AP/Wide World Photos./ Jackson, Joseph "Shoeless Joe," photograph. AP/Wide World Photos./ Jackson, Phil, photograph by Tim Boyle. (c) Tim Boyle of AP/Wide World Photos./ Jackson, Reginald Martinez, photograph by Ray Stubblebine. AP/Wide World Photos./ Jansen, Dan, photograph. AP/Wide World Photos./ Jenner, Bruce, photograph. AP/Wide World Photos./ Johnson, Earvin "Magic", photograph. AP/Wide World Photos./ Johnson, Junior, photograph. AP/Wide World Photos./ Johnson, Michael, photograph. AP/Wide World Photos./ Johnson, Randy, portrait. AP/Wide World Photos./ Jones, Kevin, photograph. AP/Wide World Photos./ Jones, Marion, photograph by Michael Probst. AP/Wide World Photos./ Jones, Robert Tyre, Jr., photograph. AP/Wide World Photos./ Joyce, Joan, photograph. AP/Wide World Photos./ Joyner, Florence Griffith, photograph. AP/Wide World Photos./ Joyner-Kersee, Jackie, photograph. AP/Wide World Photos./ Kaline, Al, photograph. AP/Wide World Photos./ Karelin, Alexander, photograph. AP/Wide World Photos./ Kariya, Paul, photograph. AP/Wide World Photos./ Karsten, Ekaterina, photograph. AP/Wide World Photos./ Kelly, Jim, photograph. AP/Wide World Photos./ Kemp, Shawn, photograph. AP/Wide World Photos./ Kidd, Jason, photograph. AP/Wide World Photos./ Killebrew, Harmon, photograph. AP/Wide World./ Killy, Jean-Claude, photograph. AP/Wide World Photos./ Killy, Jean-Claude, photograph. AP/Wide World Photos./ King, Billie Jean, photograph. AP/Wide World Photos./ King, Don, photograph. AP/Wide World./ Kiraly, Karch, photograph. AP/Wide World Photos./ Kirvesniemi, Harri, photograph. AP/Wide World Photos./ Klug, Chris, photograph. AP/Wide World Photos./ Klug, Chris, photograph. AP/Wide World Photos./ Knight, Bobby, photograph. AP/Wide World Photos./ Koch, Bill, photograph. AP/Wide World Photos./ Korbut, Olga, photograph. AP/Wide World Photos./ Kostelic, Janica, photograph. AP/Wide World Photos./ Kournikova, Anna, photograph by Bill Kostroun. AP/Wide World Photos./ Kronberger, Petra, photograph by Michel Lipchitz. AP/Wide World Photos./ Krone, Julie, photograph. AP/Wide World Photos./ Kuerten, Gustavo, photograph. AP/Wide World Photos./ Kummer, Clarence, photograph. AP/Wide World Photos./ Kwan, Michelle, photograph. AP/Wide World Photos./ Ladewig, Marion, photograph. AP/Wide World Photos./ Lalas, Alexi, photograph. AP/Wide World Photos./ Lambeau, "Curley," photograph. AP/Wide World Photos./ LaMotta, Jake, photograph. AP/Wide World Photos./ Largent, Steve, photograph. AP/Wide World Photos./ Lasorda, Tommy, photograph. AP/Wide World Photos./ Latynina, Larisa, photograph. AP/Wide World Photos./ Laver, Rod, photograph. AP/Wide World Photos./ Lemieux, Mario, photograph. AP/Wide World Photos./ Lemon, Meadowlark (George), photograph. AP/Wide World Photos./ Leonard, Sugar Ray, photograph by Eric Risberg. AP/Wide World Photos./ Leonard, Sugar Ray, photograph. AP/Wide World Photos./ Leslie, Lisa, photograph. AP/Wide World Photos./ Lewis, Carl, photograph. AP/Wide World Photos./ Lewis, Lennox, photograph by Adam Nadel. AP/Wide World Photos./

AP/Wide World Photos./ Rheaume, Manon, photograph. AP/Wide World Photos./ Rice, Jerry, photograph. AP/Wide World Photos./ Richard, Maurice, photograph. AP/Wide World Photos./ Richardson, Dot, photograph. AP/Wide World Photos./ Riddles, Libby, photograph. AP/Wide World Photos./ Rigby, Cathy, photograph. AP/Wide World Photos./ Riley, Pat, photograph by Mark Lennihan. AP/Wide World Photos./ Ripken, Calvin, photograph. AP/Wide World Photos./ Roba, Fatuma, photograph. AP/Wide World Photos./ Robertson, Oscar, photograph. AP/Wide World Photos./ Robinson, David, photograph. AP/Wide World Photos./ Robinson, Jackie, photograph. AP/Wide World Photos./ Rocker, John, photograph. AP/Wide World Photos./ Rodman, Dennis, photograph. AP/Wide World Photos./ Rodriguez, Alex, photograph. AP/Wide World Photos./ Roy, Patrick, portrait. AP/Wide World Photos./ Rubin, Barbara Joe, photograph. AP/Wide World Photos./ Ruud, Birger, photograph. AP/Wide World Photos./ Rudolph, Wilma, photograph. AP/Wide World Photos./ Russell, Bill, photograph. AP/Wide World Photos./ Ruth, Babe, photograph. AP/Wide World Photos./ Ryan, Lynn Nolan, photograph by Tim Sharp. AP/Wide World Photos./ Sabatini, Gabriela, photograph. AP/Wide World Photos./ St. James, Lyn, portrait. AP/Wide World Photos./ Sale, Jamie, and David Pelletier, photograph by Lionel Cironneau. AP/Wide World Photos./ Sampras, Pete, photograph. AP/Wide World Photos./ Sampras, Pete, photograph. AP/Wide World Photos./ Samuelson, Joan Benoit, photograph. AP/Wide World Photos./ Sanders, Barry, photograph by Rusty Kennedy. AP/Wide World Photos./ Sanders, Deion, photograph. AP/Wide World Photos./ Sanders, Deion, photograph by Rusty Kennedy. AP/Wide World Photos./ Sawchuk, Terry, photograph. AP/Wide World Photos./ Sayers, Gale, photograph. AP/Wide World Photos./ Schayes, Dolph, photograph. AP/Wide World Photos./ Schilling, Curtis Montague, photograph by Lenny Ignelzi. AP/Wide World Photos./ Schmeling, Max, photograph. AP/Wide World Photos./ Schmidt, Mike, photograph. AP/Wide World Photos./ Schmirler, Sandra, photograph. AP/Wide World Photos./ Schramm, Tex, photograph. AP/Wide World Photos./ Schumacher, Michael, photograph. AP/Wide World Photos./ Scott, Wendell Oliver, photograph. AP/Wide World Photos./ Scurry, Briana, photograph. AP/Wide World Photos./ Selanne, Teemu, photograph. AP/Wide World Photos./ Seau, Junior, photograph. AP/Wide World Photos./ Seaver, Tom, photograph. AP/Wide World Photos./ Secretariat, photograph. AP/Wide World Photos./ Secretariat, photograph. AP/Wide World Photos./ Seles, Monica, photograph. AP/Wide World Photos./ Selig, Bud, photograph. AP/Wide World Photos./ Sharp, Sterling, photograph. AP/Wide World Photos./ Shea, Jack, photograph. AP/Wide World Photos./ Sheffield, Gary, photograph. AP/Wide World Photos./ Shula, Don, photograph. AP/Wide World Photos./ Simpson, O. J., photograph. AP/Wide World Photos./ Smith, Tommie, photograph. AP/Wide World Photos./ Sosa, Sammy, photograph by Gary Dineen. AP/Wide World Photos./ Spinks, Michael, photograph. AP/Wide World Photos./ Spitz, Mark (Andrew), photograph. AP/Wide World Photos./ Sprewell, Latrell, photograph by John Dunn. AP/Wide World Photos./ Staley, Dawn, photograph by Rusty Kennedy. AP/Wide World Photos./ Starr, Bart, photograph. AP/Wide World Photos./ Staubach, Roger, photograph. AP/Wide World Photos./ Steinbrenner, George, photograph. AP/Wide World Photos./ Stengel, Casey, photograph. AP/Wide World Photos./ Stenmark, Ingemar, photograph. AP/Wide World Photos./ Stewart, Jackie, photograph. AP/Wide World Photos./ Stewart, Jackie, photograph. AP/Wide World Photos./ Stewart, Kordell, photograph. AP/Wide World Photos./ Stockton, John, photograph. AP/Wide World Photos./ Stojko, Elvis, photograph. AP/Wide World Photos./ Strawberry, Darryl, photograph. AP/Wide World Photos./ Strawberry, Darryl, photograph by Ron Frehm. AP/Wide World Photos./ Street, Picabo, photograph by David Longstreath. AP/Wide World Photos./ Street, Picabo, photograph. AP/Wide World Photos./ Strug, Kerri, photograph. AP/Wide World Photos./ Strug, Kerri, photograph. AP/Wide World Photos./ Suleymanoglu, Naim, photograph. AP/Wide World Photos./ Summitt, Pat, photograph. AP/Wide World Photos./ Suzuki, Ichiro, photograph by Eliane Thompson. AP/Wide World Photos./ Suzuki, Ichiro, photograph. AP/Wide World Photos./ Swoopes, Sheryl, photograph. AP/Wide World Photos./ Tarkanian, Jerry, photograph. AP/Wide World Photos./ Tarkanian, Jerry, photograph. AP/Wide World Photos./ Tarkenton, Fran, photograph. AP/Wide World Photos./ Taylor, Lawrence, photograph. AP/Wide World Photos./ Tendulkar, Sachin, photograph. AP/Wide World Photos./ Thomas, Frank, photograph. AP/Wide World Photos./ Thomas, Isiah, photograph by

Michael Conroy. AP/Wide World Photos./ Thomas, Isiah, photograph. AP/Wide World Photos./ Thomas, Thurman, photograph. AP/Wide World Photos./ Thompson, Jenny, photograph by Paul Sakuma. AP/Wide World Photos./ Thorpe, Ian, photograph by Russell McPhedran. AP/Wide World Photos./ Tomba, Alberto, photograph. AP/Wide World Photos./ Tomba, Alberto, photograph. AP/Wide World Photos, Inc./ Torrence, Gwen, photograph. AP/Wide World Photos./ Torvill, Jayne, and Christopher Dean, photograph. AP/Wide World Photos./ Trottier, Brian, photograph. AP/Wide World Photos./ Tunney, Gene, photograph. AP/Wide World./ Turner, Cathy, AP/Wide World Photos./ Tyson, Mike, photograph by Lennox McLendon. AP/Wide World Photos./ Tyus, Wyomia, photograph. AP/Wide World Photos./ Unitas, Johnny, photograph. AP/Wide World Photos./ Unitas, Johnny, photograph. AP/Wide World Photos./ Unser, Al, photograph. AP/Wide World Photos./ Vaughn, Mo, photograph. AP/Wide World Photos./ Ventura, Jesse, photograph. AP/Wide World Photos./ Vicario, Arantxa Sanchez, photograph. AP/Wide World Photos./ Vitale, Dick, photograph. AP/Wide World Photos./ Wagner, Honus, photograph. AP/Wide World Photos./ Waitz, Grete, photograph. AP/Wide World Photos./ Waitz, Grete, photograph. AP/Wide World Photos./ Walcott, Joe, photograph. AP/Wide World Photos./ Waldner, Jan Ove, photograph. AP/Wide World Photos./ Walton, Bill, photograph. AP/Wide World Photos./ Warne, Shane, photograph. AP/Wide World Photos./ Warner, Kurt, photograph by James A. Finley. AP/Wide World Photos./ Watters, Ricky, photograph. AP/Wide World Photos./ Webb, Anthony, "Spud," photograph. AP/Wide World Photos./ Webb, Karrie, photograph. AP/Wide World Photos./ Webber, Chris, photograph. AP/Wide World Photos./ Weber, Dick, photograph. AP/Wide World Photos./ Wehling, Ulrich, photograph. AP/Wide World Photos./ Weihenmayer, Erik, photograph. AP/Wide World Photos./ Weishoff, Paula, photograph. AP/Wide World Photos./ Weissmuller, Johnny, photograph. AP/Wide World Photos./ West, Jerry, photograph. AP/Wide World Photos./ West, Jerry, photograph. AP/Wide World Photos./ White, Reggie, photograph. AP/Wide World Photos./ Whitworth, Kathy, photograph. AP/Wide World Photos./ Wigger, Deena, photograph. AP/Wide World Photos./ Wilkens, Lenny, photograph. AP/Wide World Photos./ Wilkens, Lenny, photograph. AP/Wide World Photos./ Wilkins, Dominique, photograph. AP/Wide World Photos./ Wilkinson, Laura, photograph. AP/Wide World Photos./ Williams, Serena, photograph. AP/Wide World Photos./ Williams, Serena, photograph. AP/Wide World Photos./ Williams, Ted, photograph. AP/Wide World Photos./ Williams, Venus, photograph. AP/Wide World Photos./ Williams, Venus, photograph. AP/Wide World Photos./ Winfield, Dave, photograph. AP/Wide World Photos./ Witt, Katarina, photograph. AP/Wide World Photos./ Wooden, John, photograph. AP/Wide World Photos./ Wooden, John, photograph. AP/Wide World Photos./ Woods, Tiger, photograph by Dave Martin. AP/Wide World Photos./ Woods, Tiger, photograph by Diego Giudice. AP Wide World Photos./ Woodson, Charles, photograph. AP/Wide World Photos./ Woodson, Rod, photograph. AP/Wide World Photos./ Woodward, Lynette, photograph by Orlin Wagner. AP/Wide World Photos./ Wright, Mickey, photograph. AP/Wide World Photos./ Yamaguchi, Kristi, portrait. AP/Wide World Photos./ Young, Cy, photograph. AP/Wide World Photos./ Young, Sheila, photograph. AP/Wide World Photos./ Young, Steve, photograph. AP/Wide World Photos./ Zaharias, Babe (Mildred Ella) Didrikson, photograph. AP/Wide World Photos./ Zidane, Zinedine, photograph. AP/Wide World Photos./

ASSOCIATED FEATURES, INC.:
Dryden, Ken, photograph. Associated Features, Inc./ Esposito, Tony, photograph. Associated Features, Inc./ Hasek, Dominik, photograph. Associated Features./ Plante, Jacques, photograph. Associated Features./ Sakic, Joe, photograph. Associated Features.

BRUCE BENNETT STUDIOS, INC.:
Belfour, Ed, photograph. Courtesy of Bruce Bennett./ Bowman, Scotty, photograph. John Giamundo/B. Bennett./ Gretzky, Wayne, photograph. Courtesy of Bruce Bennett./ Gretzky, Wayne, photograph. Courtesy of Bruce Bennett./ Lefleur, Guy, photograph. Courtesy of Bruce Bennett./ Lemieux, Mario, photograph. Michael DiGirolamo/B. Bennett./ Lindros, Eric, photograph. Courtesy of B. Bennett./ Lindros, Eric, photograph. Courtesy of Bruce Bennett.

CORBIS:
Alexander, Grover Cleveland, photograph by George Rinhart. (c)Underwood & Underwood/Corbis./ Ali, Muhammad, photograph. UPI/Corbis-Bettmann./ Ali, Muhammad, photograph. (c) Bettmann/Corbis./ Allen, Marcus, photograph. (c)Bettmann/Corbis./ Ashe, Arthur, photograph. (c)Hulton-Deutsch Collection/Corbis./ Auerbach, Arnold, photograph. (c)Bettmann/Corbis./ Bench, Johnny Lee, photograph. (c)Bettmann/Corbis./ Benoit, Joan, photograph. Corbis-Bettmann./ Berra, Yogi, photograph. (c)Bettmann/Corbis./ Bird, Larry Joe, photograph. (c) Reuters New Media Inc./Corbis./ Blake, Hector "Toe", photograph. (c) Bettmann/Corbis./ Brisco-Hooks, Valerie, photograph. Corbis-Bettmann./ Brown, Paul, photograph. Corbis/ Bettmann./ Caray, Harry, photograph. UPI/CORBIS-Bettmann./ Carter, Don, photograph. (c) Bettmann/Corbis./ Chamberlain, Wilt, photograph. UPI/Corbis-Bettmann./ Chang, Michael, photograph. Reuters/Bettmann./ Clemente, Roberto, photograph. UPI/Bettmann./ Conner, Bart, photograph. (c)Bettmann/Corbis./ Connolly, Maureen, photograph. UPI/Corbis- Bettmann./ Corbett, James John, photograph. (c)Bettmann/Corbis./ Costas, Bob, photograph by Wally McNamee. Wally McNamee/Corbis./ Court, Margaret Smith, photograph. UPI/Corbis-Bettmann./ Court, Margaret Smith, photograph. UPI/Corbis-Bettmann./ Davis, Al, photograph. (c)AFP/Corbis./ De Varona, Donna, photograph. (c) Bettman/Corbis./ Devers, Gail, photograph. Reuters/Bettmann./ Faldo, Nick, photograph. Reuters/Bettmann./ Fleming, Peggy, photograph. Corbis./ Frazier, Joe, photograph. (c) Hulton-Deutsch Collection/Corbis./ Furtado, Julie, photograph. (c) Ales Fevzer/Corbis./ Gibson, Althea. Portrait. UPI/Bettmann./ Gifford, Frank, photograph. (c)Mitchell Gerber/Corbis./ Graf, Steffi, photograph. (c) Dimitri LundtCorbis./ Graham, Otto, photograph. Bettmann/Corbis./ Guthrie, Janet, photograph. Corbis-Bettmann./ Halas, George Stanley "Papa Bear," photograph. (c) Bettmann/Corbis./ Hamill, Dorothy, photograph. UPI/Bettmann./ Hamill, Dorothy, photograph. (c) Corbis./ Hawk, Tony, photograph by Jason Wise. (c) Duomo/Corbis./ Hayes, Robert, photograph. (c)Bettmann/Corbis./ Heisman, John, photograph. (c) Bettmann/Corbis./ Heisman, John, photograph. (c) Bettmann/Corbis./ Hill, Lynn, photograph. UPI/Corbis-Bettmann./ Hingis, Martina, photograph. (c) Torsten Blackwood/Corbis./ Hogan, Ben, photograph. (c) Bettmann/Corbis./ Holyfield, Evander, photograph. UPI/Corbis Bettmann./ Holyfield, Evander, photograph. Reuters/Bettmann./ Hornsby, Rogers, photograph. Bettmann/Corbis./ Hunter, Catfish, photograph. (c)Bettmann/Corbis./ Jagr, Jaromir, photograph. (c) Reuters NewMedia Inc./Corbis./ Jenner William Bruce, photograph Neal Preston. Corbis./ Johnson, Earvin "Magic," photograph. Bettmann Newsphotos./ Johnson, Jack, photograph. (c) Bettmann/Corbis./ Jordan, Michael, photograph. Reuters/Corbis-Bettmann./ Jordan, Michael, photograph. Reuters/Corbis-Bettmann./ Joyner-Kersee, Jackie, photograph. Reuters/Bettmann./ Kahanamoku, Duke, photograph. The Bettmann Archive./ King, Billie Jean, photograph. (c) Bettmann/Corbis./ Knight, Bobby, photograph by Gary Hershorn. NewMedia Inc./Corbis./ Korbut, Olga, photograph. Corbis./ Koufax, Sanford (Sandy), photograph. (c)Bettmann/Corbis./ Kwan, Michelle. Reuters/Corbis-Bettmann./ Landry, Thomas, photograph. (c)Bettmann/Corbis./ Laver, Rod, photograph. UPI/Corbis-Bettmann./ Lemon, Meadowlark, photograph. (c)Bettmann/Corbis./ Liston, Sonny, photograph. (c)Bettmann/Corbis./ Lombardi, Vince, photograph. Corbis/Bettmann./ Louis, Joe, photograph. Corbis-Bettmann./ Madden, John, photograph. (c) Bettmann/Corbis./ Maris, Roger (Eugene), photograph. (c)Bettmann/Corbis./ McEnroe, John, photograph. UPI/Corbis-Bettmann./ Mikan, George, photograph. (c)Bettmann/Corbis./ Miller, Shannon, photograph. (c)Mike King/Corbis./ Mirra, Dave, photograph. (c) Duomo/Corbis./ Moise, Patty, photograph. UPI/Corbis-Bettmann./ Montana, Joe, photograph. (c)Bettmann/Corbis./ Moody, Helen F., photograph by George Rinhart. (c)Underwood & Underwood/Corbis./ Moore, Archie Lee, photograph. (c)Bettmann/Corbis./ Olajuwon, Akeem, photograph. UPI/Corbis-Bettmann./ O'Neal, Shaquille, photograph. (c) Reuters NewMedia Inc./Corbis./ Orr, Bobby, photograph. (c) Bettmann/Corbis./ Owens, Jesse, photograph. UPI/Corbis-Bettmann./ Payton, Walter, photograph. (c)Bettmann/Corbis./ Piazza, Mike, photograph. (c)Reuters NewMedia Inc./Corbis./ Reeves, Dan, photograph. (c) Bettmann/Corbis./ Robinson, Brooks Calbert, Jr., photograph. (c)Bettmann/Corbis./ Robinson, Shawna, photograph. UPI/Corbis-Bettmann./ Robinson, Sugar Ray, photograph. (c) Bettmann/Corbis./ Rozelle, Pete, photograph by Sande. (c) Bettmann/Corbis./

Ryan, Nolan, photograph. UPI/Corbis-Bettmann./ Salming, Borje. (c) Bettmann/Corbis./ Sanders, Summer, photograph. UPI/Corbis-Bettmann./ Schott, Marge, photograph. (c) Bettmann/Corbis./ Seles, Monica, photograph. Reuters/Bettmann./ Shoemaker, Willie, photograph. (c) Bettmann/Corbis./ Simpson, O.J., photograph. (c) Bettmann/Corbis./ Smith, Emmitt, photograph. Rueters/Corbis-Bettmann./ Spitz, Mark, photograph. (c) Bettmann/Corbis./ Thorpe, Jim, photograph. Corbis./ Tilden, Bill, photograph. UPI/Corbis-Bettmann./ Tretiak, Vladislav, photograph. (c) Bettmann/Corbis./ Tyson, Michael, photograph. (c) Bettmann/Corbis./ Unser, Bobby, photograph. (c) Bettmann/Corbis./ Ventura, Jesse "The Body," photograph. (c) Corbis./ Williams, Esther, photograph. UPI/Bettmann./ Williams, Esther, photograph. (c) Bettmann/Corbis./ Williams, Ted, photograph. (c)Bettmann/Corbis./ Zaharias, Babe Didriksen. Portrait. UPI/Bettmann.

FISK UNIVERSITY LIBRARY:
Owens, Jesse, photograph. Fisk University Library./ Robinson, Sugar Ray, photograph. Fisk University Library.

THE GALE GROUP:
Earnhardt, Dale, photograph by Dennis Winn. The Gale Group.

GETTY IMAGES/ARCHIVE PHOTOS, INC.:
Aaron, Hank, photograph. Archive Photos, Inc./ Andretti, Mario, photograph. Archive Photos, Inc./ Aparicio, Luis, photograph. Archive Photos, Inc./ Bannister, Roger, photograph. Liaison Agency/Hilton Get./ Barclay, Charles, photograph by Sue Ogrocki. Archive Photos./ Beard, Amanda, photograph. Reuters/Gary Hershorn/Archive Photos./ Beckham, David, photograph. Anthony Harvey/Getty Images./ Belle, Albert, photograph by Scott Olson. Reuters/Archive Photos./ Bradshaw, Terry, photograph. Sporting News/Archive Photos, Inc./ Butkus, Dick, photograph. Sporting News/Archive Photos, Inc./ Campanella, Roy, photograph. Archive Photos./ Carter, Don, photograph. Archive Photos./ Casals, Rosemary, photograph. Archive Photos, Inc./ Cawley, Evonne, photograph. (c) Hulton Archive/Getty Images./ Chastain, Brandi, photograph. (c) Scott Harrison/Getty Images./ Cobb, Ty, photograph. Archive Photos, Inc./ Cobb, Ty, photograph. Archive Photos./ Connors, Jimmy, photograph. (c) Hulton Archive/Getty Images./ Cosell, Howard, photograph. Archive Photos, Inc./ Cousy, Bob, photograph. Archive Photos, Inc./ Dempsey, Jack, photograph. Archive Photos, Inc./American Stock./ DiMaggio, Joe, photograph. Archive Photos/Agip./ Duncan, Tim, photograph by Bob Padgett. Archive Photos./ Evert, Chris, photograph. Archive Photos, Inc./ Evert, Chris, photograph. Clive Brunskill/Allsport/Getty Images./ Federov, Sergei, photograph by Peter Jones. Reuter/Archive Photos./ Flutie, Doug, photograph by Brendan McDermid. Archive Photos, Inc./ Gehrig, Lou, photograph. Archive Photos, Inc./ Greenspan, Bud, photograph. (c) Matthew Stockman/Getty Images./ Hamm, Mia, photograph by Tony Quinn. ALLSPORT Photography USA Inc./ Havlicek, John, photograph. Archive Photos, Inc./ Hoffman, Mat, photograph. (c) J. Emilio Flores/Getty Images./ Iverson, Allen, photograph by Tom Mihalek. Hulton/Archive./ Johnson, Michael, photograph by Wolfgang Rattay. Reuter/Archive Photos./ Johnson, Rafer, portrait. (c) Getty Images./ Kirby, Karolyn, photograph. (c) Jonathan Ferrey/Getty Images./ Lipinski, Tara, photograph. Reuters/Str/Archive Photos./ Lombardi, Vince, photograph. Archive Photos, Inc./Sporting News./ Mack, Connie, photograph. APA/Archive Photos./ Maradona, Diego, photograph by S. Bruty. Allsport Photography (USA) Inc./ Marciano, Rocky, photograph. Archive Photos, Inc./ Martinez, Pedro, photograph. (c) Reuters/Colin Braley/Getty Images./ Mays, Willie, photograph. Archive Photos, Inc./ Meagher, Mary T., photograph. (c) Tony Duff/Getty Images./ Miller, Reggie, photograph by Ray Stubblebine. Reuter/Archive Photos./ Moon, Warren, photograph Susumu Takahashi. Archive Photos./ Nicklaus, Jack, photograph. Archive Photos, Inc./ Nomo, Hideo, portrait. Reuter/Archive Photos./ Palmer, Arnold, photograph. Archive Photos, Inc./ Pele, photograph. Archive Photos./ Petrenko, Viktor, photograph. (c) Pascal Rondeau/Getty Images./ Pierce, Mary, photograph by Jack Dabaghian. Reuter/Archive Photos./ Rickey, Branch, photograph. Archive Photos, Inc./Sporting News./ Ripken, Cal, Jr., photograph. Archive Photos, Inc./ Robinson, Frank, photograph. Archive Photos./ Robinson, Jackie, photograph. Archive Photos./

Rose, Pete, photograph. (c) Stephen Dunn/Getty Images./ Russell, Bill, portrait. (c) Sporting News/Getty Images./ Sayers, Gale, photograph. Sporting News/Archive Photos, Inc./ Shoemaker, Willie, photograph. APA/Archive Photos, Inc./ Shriver, Eunice, photograph. Archive Photos, Inc./ Skobilikova, Lydia, photograph. (c) Hulton Archive/Getty Images./ Sorenstam, Annika, photograph by Steve Marcus. Archive Photos./ Starr, Bart, photograph. Sporting News/Archive Photos, Inc./ Sullivan, John Lawrence, photograph. (c) Hulton Archive/Getty Images./ Swann, Lynn, photograph. Sporting News/Archive Photos./ Thomas, Derrick, photograph by Susumu Takahashi. Reuters/Archive Photos, Inc./ Torre, Joe, photograph. Reuters/Ray Stubblebine/Archive Photos./ Tretiak, Vladislav, photograph. (c) Getty Images./ Trinidad, Felix Tito, photograph. (c) Gary M. Williams/Liaison Agency/Getty Images/ El Neuvo Dia./ Turner, Ted, photograph. Archive Photo/Malafronte./ Van Dyken, Amy, photograph. Reuters/Eric Gailard/Archive Photos./ Wenzel, Hanni, photograph. (c) Tony Duffy/Getty Images./ Williamson, Alison, photograph. (c) Mark Dadswell, Getty Images./

HOCKEY HALL OF FAME:
Blake, Hector, photograph. Courtesy of Hockey Hall of Fame./ Vezina, Georges, photograph. Courtesy of Hockey Hall of Fame.

THE LIBRARY OF CONGRESS:
Dempsey, Jack, photograph. The Library of Congress./ Rockne, Knute, photograph. The Library of Congress. Rudolph, Wilma, photograph. The Library of Congress./ Ruth, Babe, photograph. The Library of Congress.

BILLY MILLS:
Mills, Billy, photograph. Courtesy of Billy Mills./ Mills, Billy, photograph. Courtesy of Billy Mills.

NATIONAL ARCHIVES AND RECORDS ADMINISTRATION:
Thorpe, Jim, photograph. National Archives and Records Administration.

NATIONAL BASEBALL LIBRARY & ARCHIVE:
Chicago White Sox team, photograph. National Baseball Library & Archive, Cooperstown, NY.

NEW YORK KNICKS
Ewing, Patrick, photograph by George Kalinsky. The New York Knicks.

THE NEW YORK PUBLIC LIBRARY:
Washington, Ora, photograph by D. H. Polk. Photographs and Prints Division, Schomburg Center for Research in Black Culture, The New York Public Library, Astor, Lenox and Tilden Foundations.

PENSKE MOTORSPORTS, INC.:
Jackson, Joe, photograph. From The Image of Their Greatness: An Illustrated History of Baseball from 1900 to the Present, revised edition, by Lawrence Ritter and Donald Honig. Crown Trade Paperbacks, 1992. Copyright (c) 1992 by Lawrence S. Ritter and Donald Honig./ Penske, Roger. Photo courtesy of Penske Motorsports, Inc.

POPPERFOTO:
Patterson, Floyd, photograph. Popperfoto/Archive Photos./ Retton, Mary Lou, photograph. Popperfoto.

MITCHELL B. REIBEL:
Borg, Bjorn, photograph. Mitchell Reibel.

SPORTSPICS:
Petty, Richard, photograph. SportsPics.

UNITED PRESS INTERNATIONAL:
U. S. Olympic Hockey team, 1980, photograph. Courtesy of United Press International.

WIREIMAGE.COM:
Bryant, Kobe, photograph. Steve Granitz/WireImage.com.

Entry List

VOLUME 4

T

Timeline

776 B.C.
Greece's first recorded Olympic Games. Only Greeks are allowed to compete, and the games are limited to foot races of approximately 200 yards.

490 B.C.
According to Greek satirist Lucian, a courier named Pheidippides runs from the plains of Marathon to Athens, a distance of about 22 miles, with news of a Greek victory over the Persians. This becomes the inspiration for modern-day "marathon" races.

1457
Scotland's Parliament forbids "futeball and golfe" as their popularity is distracting men from practicing archery which is required for military training.

1552
Scotland's Royal Golf Club of St. Andrews begins. Its official founding comes 200 years later in 1754.

1702
Queen Anne of England gives approval for horseracing and introduces the idea of sweepstakes.

1744
First recorded cricket match in England. Rules of the game are codified in 1788.

1842
Alexander Cartwright invents baseball. Although the game has been played for many years, Cartwright writes down rules of play.

1863
The official rules for soccer are established by the Football Association in England.

1869
Princeton and Rutgers play the first college football game. Rutgers wins 6-4.

1874
British sportsman Walter Clopton Wingfield codifies the rules for lawn tennis.

1875
First running of the Kentucky Derby, won by Aristides.

1876
The National League (NL) is formed. The NL becomes the first stable baseball major league.

1877
The first Wimbledon tennis championship is won by Spencer Gore.

1891
Basketball invented by **James Naismith,** a physical education instructor at Springfield Men's Christian Association Training School. Naismith wrote the first 13 rules for the sport.

1892
"Gentleman Jim" Corbett defeats **John L. Sullivan** to win the first boxing championship fought with padded gloves and under the Marquis of Queensberry Rules.

1896
First of the "modern" Olympics are held in Athens, Greece. Competing are 311 athletes from 13 countries.

1900
The American League (AL) is formed. It soon joins the National League as a baseball major league.

Britain's Charlotte Cooper wins the first women's Olympic gold medal in women's tennis. Margaret Abbott wins the nine-hole golf competition, becoming the first American woman to win Olympic gold.

1903
The National Agreement calls an end to the war between the American and National baseball leagues. The agree-

ment calls for each league to be considered major leagues, the same alignment as today.

The first World Series is played. It features the Pittsburgh Pirates of the National League and the Boston Pilgrims of the American League. Boston wins the series 5-3.

1908
Jack Johnson defeats Tommy Burns to become the first African American to hold the world heavyweight boxing championship.

1911
First Indianapolis 500 is run.

Cy Young retires with a career record 511 wins. The trophy given annually to the best pitcher in each league is named after Young.

1912
Jim Thorpe wins three Olympic medals, one of them a gold medal in the decathlon. The medals are stripped from him in 1913 when it is discovered that he accepted a token sum of money to play baseball. The medals are restored and returned to his family in 1982.

1917
The National Hockey League (NHL) is formed. The new league contains only four teams.

1919
The **Chicago "Black Sox"** throw the World Series against the Cincinnati Reds in the biggest sports gambling incident of all-time. Eight players, including the great **"Shoeless" Joe Jackson,** are banned from baseball by commissioner Kennesaw Mountain Landis.

1920
The New York Yankees purchase the contract of **Babe Ruth** from the Boston Red Sox. "The Curse of the Bambino" prevents the Red Sox from winning a World Series since.

The National Football League (NFL) forms in Canton, Ohio. The original league has 14 teams.

1926
Gertrude Ederle becomes the first woman to swim the English Channel. Her time is nearly five hours faster than the previous five men who made the crossing.

1927
Babe Ruth of the New York Yankees hits 60 home runs in one season, breaking his own single-season record.

His total is more than 12 *teams* hit during the season. Ruth retires with 714 career home runs, also a record at the time.

1928
Ty Cobb retires from baseball with a lifetime .366 average that still stands as a record today. Cobb also retired with the career record for hits (4,189) and runs (2,246).

1930
Uruguay hosts and wins the first soccer World Cup. The event has been held every four years since.

Bobby Jones wins "Grand Slam" of golf by capturing the U.S. and British Opens and Amateurs.

1931
Knute Rockne dies in a plane crash. He finishes with a 121-12-5 record, a winning percentage of .881. Rockne led Notre Dame to five unbeaten and untied seasons.

1932
The Negro National League is formed. This is the first "major" league set up for African-American players.

Babe Didrikson Zaharias wins three gold medals at the Summer Olympics in Los Angeles, California. She sets new world records in the javelin throw and 80-meter hurdles.

1936
Sonja Henie wins the Winter Olympics gold medal for women's figure skating for the third consecutive time.

Jesse Owens wins four gold medals in track and field at the Summer Olympics in Berlin, Germany. Owens' feat comes as a shock to German dictator Adolf Hitler.

1937
Don Budge wins tennis's "Grand Slam." He is the first player to win Wimbledon and the Australian, French, and U.S. championships in the same calendar year.

1938
Helen Wills wins the final of her 19 "Grand Slam" singles tennis titles. She wins eight Wimbledons, seven U.S. Opens, and four French Opens.

The great **Joe Louis** knocks out German fighter **Max Schmeling.** The victory carries extra meaning as it also marks a win against Nazi Germany.

1939
The first baseball game is televised. The game features Cincinnati and Brooklyn.

On July 4, **Lou Gehrig** gives his famous farewell speech. He dies soon after from Amyotrophic Lateral Sclerosis (ALS), now called Lou Gehrig's Disease.

1941

Ted Williams of the Boston Red Sox hits .406. He is the last player to hit over .400 for an entire season.

Joe DiMaggio of the New York Yankees hits safely in 56 consecutive games. He breaks the record of 44 set by Wee Willie Keeler.

1943

The All American Girls Professional Baseball League is formed. At its peak in 1948 the league boasts 10 teams.

1945

Brooklyn Dodgers' executive **Branch Rickey** signs **Jackie Robinson** to a minor league contract.

1946

The color line in football is broken. Woody Strode and Kenny Washington play for the Rams and Marion Motley and Bill Willis join the Browns.

The Basketball Association of America is founded. Within three years it becomes the National Basketball Association (NBA).

1947

Jackie Robinson breaks the color barrier in baseball. This heroic ballplayer is subjected to harsh treatment from fans, fellow ballplayers, and even teammates.

1949

The Ladies' Professional Golf Association (LPGA) forms. **Babe Didrikson Zaharias** is a co-founder.

1957

Althea Gibson becomes the first African American to win Wimbledon and U.S. tennis championships. She repeats her feat the next year.

1958

Baseball's Brooklyn Dodgers move to Los Angeles and New York Giants move to San Francisco. The moves devastate long-time fans of each team.

What is now called the "greatest game ever played" is won by the Baltimore Colts in sudden-death overtime over the New York Giants 23-17. The game is widely televised and has much to do with the growth in popularity of football.

1959

Daytona 500 is run for the first time. It now is one of the most watched sporting events in the United States.

The American Football League (AFL) is founded. The league brings professional football to many new markets.

1960

Sugar Ray Robinson retires from boxing. During his career he wins the welterweight title once and holds the middleweight title five times. His lifetime record is 182-19.

Cassius Clay wins a gold medal in the light-heavyweight class at the Summer Olympics in Rome, Italy. Later, Clay throws his medal into the Ohio River as a reaction against the racial prejudice with which he is forced to contend.

Wilma Rudolph becomes the first American woman to win three gold medals in one Summer Olympics in Rome, Italy. She wins the 100- and 200-meter dashes and is a part of the winning 4 x 100 relay team.

1961

Roger Maris of the New York Yankees hits a single-season record 61 home runs. His record is tarnished by some observers because Maris plays a 162 game schedule while **Babe Ruth,** whose record he broke, played only 154 games in 1927.

1962

Wilt Chamberlain of the Philadelphia Warriors scores 100 points in a single game. He accomplishes this feat on March 2 against the New York Knicks. Chamberlain goes on to set another record when he averages 50.4 points per game during the same season and also leads the NBA in rebounding with 25.7 boards per game.

Oscar Robertson averages a triple double for an entire NBA season. He averages 30.8 points, 12.5 rebounds, and 11.4 assists per game.

1964

Cassius Clay scores a technical knockout of **Sonny Liston** to win the heavyweight championship. The victory is seen as a gigantic upset at the time. The day after his victory over Liston, Clay announces that he is a member of the Nation of Islam. He also announces that he is changing his name to **Muhammad Ali.**

1965

Star running back of the Cleveland Browns, **Jim Brown,** retires to pursue an acting career. He leaves the game holding the record for most career rushing yards, 12,312, in only eight seasons.

1966

The Boston Celtics win their eighth consecutive championship. No other major sports franchise has won this many consecutive titles.

Texas Western beats Kentucky 72-65 for the NCAA basketball championship. The champions feature an all-African American starting five while Kentucky starts five white players.

1967

First Iditarod dog sledding race held. The race begins as a 56 mile race, but by 1973 it evolves into a 1,152 mile trek between Anchorage and Nome, Alaska.

Charlie Sifford becomes the first African American to win on the PGA golf tour when he captures the Greater Hartford Open.

The first Super Bowl is played between the Green Bay Packers and Kansas City Chiefs. It is originally called the AFL-NFL World Championship Game.

1968

Bill Russell becomes the first African-American coach in any major sport. He leads the Boston Celtics to two championships as player-coach.

Americans **Tommie Smith** and John Carlos protest racism in the U.S. by raising black glove-clad fists on the medal stand after finishing first and third in the 200-meters at the Mexico City Olympics. The two are suspended from competition.

Eunice Kennedy Shriver begins the Special Olympics. The program grows into an international showcase for mentally challenged athletes.

The "Heidi" game becomes a piece of sports history as fans in the East miss the Oakland Raiders's thrilling comeback against the New York Jets. NBC decides to leave the game with 50 seconds left to start the movie *Heidi* on time at 7:00 p.m. ET. The network is barraged with calls complaining about the decision.

The American Football League (AFL) and National Football League (NFL) merge. The league retains the NFL name and splits teams into American and National conferences.

1969

Rod Laver of Australia wins the tennis "Grand Slam" for the second time in his career. He also won the Slam in 1962 as an amateur.

1970

Pele plays in fourth World Cup for his home country of Brazil.

On September 21, ABC's Monday Night Football debuts. The game features a contest between the Cleveland Browns and New York Jets. **Howard Cosell** and Don Meredith are the commentators.

1971

Gordie Howe, "Mister Hockey," retires from the NHL. At the time he holds career records for goals (801), assists (1,049), and points (1,850). Howe goes on to play seven more seasons in the World Hockey Association (WHA).

1972

Congress passes the Education Amendment Act, which includes Title IX. Title IX bans sex discrimination in federally funded schools in academics and athletics. The new law changes the landscape of college athletics, as more playing opportunities and scholarships are open to women.

Secretariat wins horse racing's Triple Crown, setting records for every race. He is the only horse to run under two minutes in the Kentucky Derby and wins the Belmont Stakes by a record 31 lengths.

Mark Spitz wins seven Olympic swimming gold medals. He sets the record for most medals won at a single Olympic Games.

Black September, an Arab terrorist group, kills eleven Israeli athletes held captive in the Olympic Village. The Games are suspended the following morning for a memorial service, after which, with the approval of the Israelis, they reconvene.

Out of respect to the Native American population, Stanford University changes its nickname from Indians to Cardinals. Other schools do the same, but professional teams do not.

1973

UCLA wins its seventh consecutive NCAA basketball championship. Coached by the legendary **John Wooden,** the Bruins during one stretch win 88 games in a row. UCLA goes on to win three more titles under Wooden.

Billie Jean King defeats Bobby Riggs in a "Battle of the Sexes" tennis match. Riggs, a self-proclaimed "male chauvinist," is 25 years older than King.

Running back **O.J. Simpson** of the Buffalo Bills becomes the first NFL player to ever rush for over 2,000 yards in a season. Simpson is the only player to accomplish this feat in 14 games.

The Miami Dolphins finish the NFL season with a perfect 17-0 record. The Dolphins close out their season with a 14-7 victory over the Washington Redskins in

Super Bowl VII. No NFL team before or since has finished a season with a perfect record.

1974

Hank Aaron breaks **Babe Ruth**'s career home run record. Aaron has to overcome not only history but racist attacks as he hits number 715 in Atlanta.

Muhammad Ali stuns the world with his eighth round knockout of **George Foreman** in "The Rumble in the Jungle." Ali uses the "rope-a-dope" strategy to wear out the much more powerful Foreman.

1975

Muhammad Ali defeats **Joe Frazier** in the "Thrilla in Manila." The victory was Ali's second in three fights with Frazier.

Pitchers Dave McNally and Andy Messersmith win their challenge to baseball's "reserve clause." Arbitrator Peter Seitz rules that once a player completes one season without a contract he can become a free agent. This is a landmark decision that opens the door to free agency in professional sports.

1976

Romanian **Nadia Comaneci** scores perfect 10s seven times in gymnastics competition at the Summer Olympics in Montreal, Quebec, Canada. This marks the first time that a 10 has ever been awarded.

Kornelia Ender of East Germany wins four Olympic gold medals in swimming. Her time in every one of her races breaks a world record.

1977

Janet Guthrie qualifies on the final day for a starting spot in the Indianapolis 500. She becomes the first woman to compete in the Memorial Day classic.

A.J. Foyt wins the Indianapolis 500 for a record-setting fourth time.

1978

Nancy Lopez wins a record-breaking five LPGA tournaments in a row during her rookie season. She goes on to win nine tournaments for the year.

1979

ESPN launches the first all-sports television network. The network now carries all the major professional and college sports.

1980

The **U.S. men's Olympic ice hockey team** defeats the heavily favored team from the Soviet Union, 4-3, in what becomes known as the "Miracle on Ice." The Americans go on to win the gold medal.

Eric Heiden of the U.S. wins five individual gold medals in speed skating at the Winter Olympics in Lake Placid, New York. No one before or since has won five individual events in a single Olympic Games. No other skater has ever swept the men's speed skating events.

The U.S. and its allies boycott the Summer Olympics in Moscow, USSR. The Americans cite the Soviet invasion of Afghanistan as the reason for their action.

1981

Richard Petty wins the Daytona 500. His win is his record-setting seventh victory in the big race.

1982

Louisiana State defeats Cheney State for the title in the first NCAA women's basketball championship.

Wayne Gretzky, the "Great One," scores 92 goals in a season. He adds 120 assists to end the season with 212 points, the first time anyone has scored over 200 points in one season.

Shirley Muldowney wins last of three National Hot Rod Association (NHRA) top fuel championships. Muldowney won 17 NHRA titles during her career.

1983

Australia II defies the odds and wins the America's Cup after 132 years of domination by the U.S. defenders. The New York Yacht Club had won 24 straight competitions.

1984

The Soviet Union and its allies (except Romania) boycott the Summer Olympics held in Los Angeles, California. Many believe this is in response to the U.S. boycott of Moscow Games in 1980.

Carl Lewis repeats **Jesse Owens**'s feat of winning four gold medals in track and field at the Summer Olympics in Los Angeles, California. Lewis wins the same events as Owens: the 100- and 200-meters, the long jump, and the 4 x 100m relay.

Joan Benoit Samuelson wins the first ever Olympic marathon for women. Her winning time over the 26.2 mile course is 2:24.52.

Dan Marino of the Miami Dolphins throws for 5,084 yards and 48 touchdowns, both NFL single-season records.

1985

On September 11, **Pete Rose** breaks **Ty Cobb**'s record for career hits when he gets his 4,192nd hit. Rose finishes his career with 4,256 hits. Unfortunately, Rose is banned from baseball after allegations of his gambling on the sport come to light.

1986

Nancy Lieberman is the first woman to play in a men's professional league - the United States Basketball League.

Jack Nicklaus wins his record 18th and final major championship at the Masters. During his illustrious career he wins 6 Masters, 4 U.S. Opens, 3 British Opens, and 5 PGA Championships.

1988

Greg Louganis wins gold medals in both platform and springboard diving. He is the first person to win both diving medals in two consecutive Olympics. Louganis wins despite hitting his head on the board during the springboard competition.

Florence Griffith-Joyner sets world records in both the 100- and 200-meter dashes.

Steffi Graf of Germany wins the "Golden Slam" of tennis by winning each of the "Grand Slam" events in addition to the Olympic gold medal. Graf retires with a record 22 victories in "Grand Slam" events.

1992

Jackie Joyner-Kersee establishes herself as the most dominant athlete in the five-event heptathlon, winning her second consecutive Summer Olympics gold medal in the event. Joyner-Kersee had set the world record at 7,291 points and held the next five highest scores.

Cito Gaston becomes the first African-American manager to take his team to the World Series. He is also the first to manage the world champions as his Blue Jays win the title the same year.

1993

Michael Jordan retires from basketball after leading the Bulls to three consecutive NBA championships. He says he is retiring to try to play professional baseball.

Julie Krone becomes the first woman jockey to win a Triple Crown horse race. She rides Colonial Affair to victory in the Belmont Stakes.

The Miami Dolphins defeat the Philadelphia Eagles 19-14, giving Dolphins coach **Don Shula** his 325th win. The victory moved Shula into first place on the all-time list, beating the record held by **George Halas** of the Chicago Bears.

1994

The husband of figure skater **Tonya Harding** hires two men to attack Harding's rival, **Nancy Kerrigan.** The men strike at the U.S. Figure Skating Championships in Detroit, Michigan. Kerrigan is knocked out of the competition, but still qualifies for the Olympic team.

Speedskater **Bonnie Blair** wins her fifth Winter Olympic gold medal, the most by any American woman. She won the 500-meters in 1988 then won both the 500- and 1000-meters in 1992 and 1994. Blair won a total of seven Olympic medals.

Pole-vaulter **Sergei Bubka** of the Ukraine sets the world record in the pole vault with a jump of 6.14 meters. Bubka holds the top 14 jumps of all-time in the event.

A baseball player's strike wipes out the end of the regular season and, for the first time since 1904, the World Series. The strike hurts baseball's popularity for years to come.

1995

Michael Jordan returns to the Chicago Bulls. He leads Chicago to three consecutive championships then retires again in 1998. Jordan retires as a five-time winner of the NBA Most Valuable Player Award and six-time winner of the NBA Finals MVP.

Extreme Games (X Games) are held for first time in Rhode Island and Vermont. The X Games and Winter X Games have been held every year since.

1996

Sprinter **Michael Johnson** wins a rare double at the Summer Olympics in Atlanta, Georgia. He wins both the 200- and 400-meter races, the first man ever to accomplish this feat at the Olympics.

Carl Lewis wins the long jump gold medal at the Summer Olympics in Atlanta, Georgia. It is the athlete's ninth gold medal, tying him for the most all-time with Finnish track legend Paavo Nurmi and Soviet gymnast **Larisa Latynina.**

Jackie Joyner-Kersee wins a bronze medal in the long jump at the Summer Olympics in Atlanta, Georgia. This brings her medal total for three Olympic Games to six, making her the most decorated female track and field athlete in U.S. history.

U.S. women capture the first-ever women's soccer Olympic gold medal.

Dan Marino retires. He leaves the game holding the NFL career record for yards (51,636) and touchdown passes (369).

1997

The Women's National Basketball Association (WNBA) is formed.

Tiger Woods is only 21 when he wins the Masters by a record-shattering 12 strokes. He also sets a record by shooting 18 under par.

1998

Team USA captures the first women's ice hockey gold medal at the Winter Olympics in Nagano, Japan.

Cal Ripken, Jr. breaks **Lou Gehrig**'s iron man record when he plays in his 2,632nd game on September 19.

1999

Vote-buying scandal rips the International Olympic Committee (IOC). Several IOC members are forced to quit because they took bribes from cities hoping to host the Olympics.

Wayne Gretzky retires with NHL records that may never be broken. He holds or shares 61 single-season and career records including the career records for most goals (894), most assists (1,963) and points (2,857). Gretzky also holds the single-season records for goals (92), assists (163), and points (215).

2000

New York Yankees win their 26th World Series. The win makes the Yankees the winningest organization in sports history.

2001

Tiger Woods becomes the first golfer to hold the championship for all four professional "Grand Slam" events when he wins the Masters. His accomplishment is not called a "Grand Slam" because all his victories do not occur in the same calendar year.

Roman Sebrle of the Czech Republic earns the title of "world's greatest athlete" by setting a world record in the 10-event decathlon. His final score is 9,026 points, making him the first man to surpass the 9,000 barrier.

Barry Bonds of the San Francisco Giants hits 73 home runs, a new major league single-season record. The next season he becomes only the fourth major leaguer to hit over 600 career home runs.

Michael Jordan returns to the NBA, this time playing for the Washington Wizards, a team in which he holds partial ownership. His 30.4 career scoring average is the highest of all-time.

2002

Brazil wins record fifth World Cup championship.

Coach **Phil Jackson** of the Los Angeles Lakers sets a record by coaching his ninth NBA champion. He won six titles as coach of the Chicago Bulls and three with Los Angeles. Jackson also tied **Scotty Bowman** of the NHL for most professional titles won as coach.

Hockey coach **Scotty Bowman** retires. He holds career records for most regular season (1,244) and playoff (223) wins.

Lance Armstrong wins the Tour de France cycling race for the fourth straight year. His victory comes only six years after doctors gave him little chance of surviving testicular cancer that had spread to his lymph nodes and brain.

Pete Sampras breaks his own record by winning his 14th Grand Slam tournament, the U.S. Open. He defeats rival **Andre Agassi** in the final.

Emmitt Smith of the Dallas Cowboys sets a new NFL career rushing record with 17,162 yards. Smith passes the great **Walter Payton** of the Chicago Bears.

Jerry Rice scores the 200th NFL touchdown of his remarkable career, the only man to reach this plateau. He ends the 2002 season holding the records for receptions (1,456), yards receiving (21,597), and touchdowns (202).

2003

Serena Williams wins four "Grand Slam" tennis championships in a row. She defeats her sister, **Venus Williams,** in the final of every event.

Kjetil Andre Aamodt
1972-

Norwegian alpine skier

K jetil Andre Aamodt of Norway, nicknamed "Baby Shark," won two gold medals in Alpine skiing at the 2002 Winter Olympic Games in Salt Lake City, Utah. These were his second and third Olympic gold medals, and they brought his Olympic medal total to seven—more than any other Alpine skier in history. Aamodt has won top honors at both the Olympics and in international championships in five skiing events— slalom, giant slalom, downhill, combined, and super-G, for 17 medals overall.

Growing up in Oslo, Aamodt (pronounced "AH-mott") idolized the great Swedish skier **Ingemar Stenmark**, whose 86 World Cup race victories stand alone. Young Aamodt would hurry home after school to watch Stenmark's races on television.

Aamodt's father, Finn Dag, is one of the most highly regarded Alpine ski instructors in Norway; Aamodt, not surprisingly, was an accomplished skier by age seven. He also played many other sports and he has continued to play golf, soccer, and ice hockey as adult.

Aamodt first came to prominence as a skier in 1990 when he became a junior world champion. He skied in his first World Cup in 1989-90, in time to meet his idol, Stenmark, who was still ranked No. 1 in the world. "I did not know him very well," Aamodt told the *Houston Chronicle*'s John P. Lopez. "I was usually in the second (slower) group. When I met him, I thought he would be taller."

Aamodt enjoys a special rivalry with one of his peers, Lasse Kjus. They are the same age, attended the same skiing school and frequently compete in the same races. The childhood friends also roomed together for 10 years. "We have a great rivalry, a great friendship and we help each other," Aamodt told the *Salt Lake Tribune*'s Tom Wharton. Kjus was the world's first skier to win five medals at a world championship, which he did at Vail, Colorado in 1999.

Aamodt, after finishing 34th overall in the 1989-90 World Cup, improved his standing each year. He moved

Kjetil Andre Aamodt

up to 17th and 13th, then finished in second place in 1992-93 in second place after Marc Girardelli of Luxembourg edged him out for his fifth title, despite Aamodt's end-of-the-season surge. The season, Aamodt said, was "kind of up and down." Aamodt finally took the gold at the World Cup in 1993-94, at age 22.

First Olympic Gold

In 1992, Aamodt won the gold medal in the super-G and a bronze in the giant slalom at the Olympics in Albertville, France. That year he also won the gold medal for the giant slalom in the world championships. The following year, he won gold medals in the slalom and the giant slalom, as well as a bronze in the combined at the world championships.

In 1994, Norway hosted the Winter Olympics at Lillehammer, and Aamodt took home two silver medals,

Chronology	
1972	Born in Oslo, Norway
1989	Begins rookie season in World Cup competition
1998	Shut out of medals Winter Olympics at Nagano, Japan

Awards and Accomplishments	
1990	Wins junior world championship
1991	Silver medal, super-G event, World Championships
1992	Gold medal, super-G, bronze in giant slalom, Olympics
1993	First place, giant slalom, World Cup
1993	First place, super-G, World Cup
1993	Third place, combined skiing and second place, overall, World Cup
1993	Gold medal, slalom and giant slalom and silver medal, combined skiing, World Championships
1994	First place, combined skiing, second place, giant slalom and first place, overall, World Cup
1994	Silver medal, downhill skiing and combined skiing, and bronze medal, super-G, Olympics
1996	Bronze medal, super-G, World Championships
1997	First place, combined skiing and second place, overall, World Cup
1997	Gold medal, combined skiing, World Championships
1998	Second place, combined skiing, World Cup
1999	First place, combined skiing and sec ond place, overall, World Cup
1999	Gold medal, combined skiing and bronze medal, downhill, World Championships
2000	First place, combined skiing and slalom, second place, overall, World Cup
2001	Third place, combined skiing, World Cup
2001	Gold medal, combined skiing and silver medal , giant slalom, World Championships
2002	Gold medal super-G event and combined skiing, Olympics; wins seventh overall medal, world record for Alpine skier
2003	12th world Alpine championship medal

one in the combined, and one in the downhill event, as well as a bronze medal in the super-G. In 1996, Aamodt won a bronze medal in the super-G at the world championships, and in 1997, took home a gold medal in the combined at the world championships.

But he fared poorly at the 1998 Olympics in Nagano, Japan, winning no medals. He told the Associated Press, "I felt like I hadn't done my job, and failed totally in both the super-G and combined. But I took the experiences from Nagano with me."

The following year, Aamodt redeemed himself by winning the gold in the combined and the bronze in the downhill at the world championships. He again won gold in the combined in the 2001 world championships, as well as a silver medal in the giant slalom.

Aamodt, at age 30, clinched his Alpine-record seventh Olympic medal at the 2002 Olympics in Salt Lake City by mastering the most difficult section of the super-G course. It was called the Buffalo Jump, because, as local legend had it, Native American hunters would chase buffalo over the precipice to certain doom at the bottom. The Olympians also had to make a hairpin left turn afterwards to avoid leaving the course. Although all the skiers survived Buffalo Jump, the turn forced many, including four of the top favorites, off the course. Of the 56 starters, 21 could not complete the course.

Aamodt, the third skier out of the gate, won his second gold medal of the Olympiad by completing the course one-tenth of a second better than runner-up Stephan Eberharter of Austria. Aamodt's winning time was 1 minute, 21.58 seconds.

Eberharter complained that he was insuffiently warned about that sharp turn after the Buffalo Jump. "I lost by a tenth of a second," Eberharter said. "That could have been the difference." Aamodt, unsympathetic, told reporters that super-G competitors get only one walk-through. "In the super-G," he said, "you inspect the course once and then you have a go at it. You make quick, good early decisions or you don't."

It was Aamodt's second gold of the Olympiad. Four days earlier, he won the men's Alpine combined. "To win [another] Super G after 10 years in the Olympics is just a dream come true," Aamodt told the *Edmonton Journal*'s Rob Gloster. "I've worked hard all my life. I love skiing. I love competition. That's the secret of my success."

What's Next?

Aamodt has no plans to slow down, telling reporters at the Olympics he felt he could continue to compete at world-class levels for at least the next four years. "I've made my mark in the Olympics, but I still feel like I have a lot to prove," he said. Besides, he said, with "only" 20 World Cup victories, he had a lot of catching up to do if he wanted to approach Stenmark's record of 86.

In February, 2003, Aamodt earned a record 12th world Alpine championship medal, finishing second, 49-hundredths of a second behind Michael Walchhofer of Austria. "He has not been as consistent a World Cup force as greats like Ingemar Stenmark, **Alberto Tomba** and **[Hermann] Maier**, but he has clearly mastered the art of peaking for the big race," Christopher Clarey of the *New York Times* wrote of Aamodt in February, 2003.

Aamodt lives in Monaco, where he mostly stays out of the media spotlight, training in relative seclusion.

FURTHER INFORMATION

Periodicals

Chamberlain, Tony. "Medaling Is His Business: Aamodt Earns Record Seventh." *Boston Globe* (February 17, 2002): D2.

Clarey, Christopher. *International Herald Tribune* (February 15, 2002): Sport, 18.

Gloster, Rob. "Baby Shark Bites into Super-G: Norway's Aamodt Kills Medal Hopes of Several Favourites." *Edmonton Journal* (February 17, 2002): C5.

"Kjetil Andre Aamodt Factfile." *Agence France Presse*(February 16, 2002): Sports.

Lopez, John P. "'Baby Shark' Aamodt Captures Second Event After Failing to Strike Gold for 10 Years." *Houston Chronicle* (February 17, 2002): Special, 6.

Mellgren, Doug. "Norwegian Star Seeks Missing Medals at Olympics." *Associated Press* (February 2, 2002): Sports News.

Nasstrom, Stephan. "Norway's Aamodt Shows Steady Improvement." *Associated Press*(November 21, 1993): Sports News.

Pennington, Bill. "Olympics: Alpine; Aamodt Makes a Precision Turn, Then Makes History." *New York Times* (February 17, 2002): section 8, page 9.

Spencer, Clark. "King of the Hill Wins Again; Aamodt Runs Medal Total to Seven." *Ottawa Citizen* (February 17, 2002): B5.

Wharton, Tom. "Norwegian Pals Still Top Ski Contenders." *Salt Lake Tribune* (February 25, 2001): C6.

Other

Clarey, Christopher. "Early American Promise Is Unfilfilled in Downhill." *New York Times*, http://www.nytimes.com/2003/02/09/sports/ (February 8, 2003).

Sketch by Michael Belfiore

Hank Aaron
1934-

American baseball player

The baseball legend Hank Aaron holds the major league record for the most career home runs (755) and made his way into the record books with 12 other career firsts, including most games, at-bats, total bases, and runs batted in (RBI). "Hammerin' Hank" made history on April 8, 1974, when he surpassed **Babe Ruth**'s home run record of 714; he went on to outdo Ruth by 42 home runs. Throughout his long, decorated career as a player for the Indianapolis Clowns, Milwaukee Braves, Atlanta Braves, and Milwaukee Brewers, Aaron played a record number of All-Star Games and won three Golden Glove Awards for his performance in right field. As the last Negro League player to have also played in the major leagues, Aaron was a bridge between two worlds, facing and speaking out against racial discrimination, particularly toward the end of his career. He was inducted into the Baseball Hall of Fame in 1982.

Hank Aaron

Born in Mobile, Alabama, in 1934, Henry Louis Aaron was the third of eight children of Herbert and Estella Aaron. Nicknamed "Man" by his parents and siblings, young Aaron lived with his family in a poor, predominantly black area of town called Down the Bay. The family later moved to an area known as Toulminville, where the young athlete was raised in the midst of the Great Depression. He fell in love with baseball at an early age, taking his first swings with broomsticks as bats and bottle caps as balls. His boyhood idol was the first African American major league player, **Jackie Robinson**.

A star athlete in high school, Aaron played shortstop and third base; despite the fact that he batted crosshanded, he was a powerful hitter. By his junior year he was playing semiprofessional baseball with the Mobile Black Bears, who paid him ten dollars a game. A distinguished football player as well as a baseball star, he attended Mobile's Central High School and later transferred to the Josephine Allan Institute. Although he received several football scholarship offers, he turned these down to pursue a career in major league baseball.

Played in Negro League and Major League

On November 20, 1951, 18-year-old Aaron was signed by scout Ed Scott to play shortstop for the Negro League team the Indianapolis Clowns. Leaving home for the first time, he relocated to the Midwest, where he helped the Clowns to a 1952 Negro League World Series victory. Yet

Chronology

1934	Born on February 5, 1934, in Mobile, Alabama
1951	Signed by the Indianapolis Clowns
1952	Helps lead Clowns to victory in Negro World Series
1952	Signed by Milwaukee Braves; wins Northern League Rookie of the Year
1953	Plays for Jacksonville Tars; named South Atlantic League's Most Valuable Player
1953	Marries Barbara Lucas
1954	Joins Milwaukee Braves as outfielder
1955	Plays in first of 24 All-Star Games
1956	Leads league in batting average
1962	With teammates Eddie Matthews, Joe Adcock, and Frank Thomas, becomes first of four players ever to hit consecutive home runs in a game
1966	Moves with Braves to Atlanta; leads league in home runs
1968	Hits 500th home run
1971	Divorces Barbara Lucas
1972	Hits 649th home run, tie with Willie Mays for second place in career home runs
1973	Marries Billye Williams
1974	Hits 715th home run, surpassing Babe Ruth to take first place in career home runs
1975	Transfers to Milwaukee Brewers
1975	Sets record for baseball's highest-ever RBI (2,212)
1976	Retires from playing career; rejoins Atlanta Braves as coach and manager
1990	Becomes senior vice president and assistant to president of Atlanta Braves
1991	Publishes autobiography *I Had a Hammer*

Awards and Accomplishments

1955-76	Played in All-Star Games
1956, 1959	Won National League batting title
1957	Won Most Valuable Player Award
1957, 1960, 1963, 1966	Named leader of league in RBI
1957, 1963, 1966-67	Named leader of league in home runs
1958-60	Won Golden Glove Award
1974	Broke Babe Ruth's career home run record
1976	Awarded Spingarn Medal from the National Association for the Advancement of Colored People (NAACP)
1982	Inducted into Baseball Hall of Fame

Aaron was with the Negro League for only about six months before he received two telegram offers from major league teams—one from the San Francisco Giants and one from the Milwaukee Braves. Thinking he'd have a better chance to make the team, Aaron chose the Braves over the Giants, who had star player **Willie Mays**.

Sold to the Milwaukee team for $10,000, Aaron signed with Braves' scout Dewey Griggs on June 14, 1952. His first assignment was to the team's farm club in Eau Claire, Wisconsin. Playing second base in the farm club, Aaron was named Northern League Rookie of the Year in 1952. "[I]t wasn't too much of a transition from playing the type of baseball that we played in the Negro League to playing professional baseball," Aaron

Hank Aaron: Chasing the Dream

Director Mike Tollin's 1995 television documentary *Hank Aaron: Chasing the Dream* was a paean to the legendary baseball player, celebrating his life with archival film footage, photographs, re-creations of events, and present-day interviews. The documentary positioned Aaron as a major player in the American civil rights movement, the seeds of which were planted as early as the 1940s, and which came to fruition in the 1970s, at the end of Aaron's career. Some critics questioned the filmmaker's decision not to include Aaron as a narrator or even as an interviewee; Tollin chose instead to create a mystique about the athlete. Nonetheless, *Chasing the Dream* received a 1996 Academy Award nomination. The documentary aired on TBS on April 12, 1995, four days after the 20-year anniversary of Aaron's home run title.

told Tavis Smiley of National Public Radio (NPR). "The difference, of course, was that instead of making $400 a month, I was making $600 a month. Instead of getting $2 a day meal money, I was getting $3 a day meal money. So it wasn't that much of a difference."

The following year Aaron played for the Braves' affiliate team in the South Atlantic League, the Jacksonville Tars. As one of the first five African Americans to play in the "Sally League," Aaron faced racial discrimination in the segregated South. He was separated from his teammates while traveling by bus, and often had to make his own arrangements for housing and meals. Despite these indignities, Aaron helped lead Jacksonville to a pennant win and was named the league's Most Valuable Player. He had led the league in everything from batting average (.362) and RBI (125) to runs (115) and hits (208).

While playing winter ball in Puerto Rico in 1953, Aaron learned to play the outfield. This new skill would come in handy the following spring, when an injury sidelined Braves left fielder Bobby Thomson. Aaron stepped in to take his place in the outfield, making his major league debut at age 20. In March 1954 he hit his first major-league home run during spring training. He made his official debut at the Braves' April 13 game against the Cincinnati Reds. Ten days later he hit his first major league home run. Aaron stopped just short of completing his first season with the Braves, breaking his ankle in early September and sitting out the rest of the year.

It did not take Aaron long to regain his footing. In 1955 he moved to right field, where he would remain for most of his career and earn three Golden Glove Awards; in batting, he averaged .314 and hit 27 home runs. In July he played in his first All-Star Game. The following season his batting average edged up to .328, leading to his first of two National League batting titles. By 1957 the 23-year-old player seemed at the peak of his powers, leading the league with his batting prowess. In a game that led the Braves to a pennant win, Aaron scored a heroic home run in the eleventh inning and was carried off the field by his teammates. He went on to average .393 and hit three home runs in the 1957 World Series, helping the Braves to victory over the New York Yan-

Hank Aaron, swinging bat

kees. In October he was named the league's Most Valuable Player for the first and only time of his career.

Now a full-fledged baseball superstar, Aaron began racking up home runs. The six-foot, 180-pound player took his power not from his heft but from his strong, supple wrists and his deft swing. "I looked for one pitch my whole career, a breaking ball," he told David Hinckley of the New York *Daily News*. "I never worried about the fastball. They couldn't throw it by me, none of them."

In June 1959, after hitting three homers in a single game against the San Francisco Giants, Aaron was paid $30,000 to appear on the television show *Home Run Derby*. After this experience, which earned him nearly as much as his annual salary, Aaron altered his hitting style to bring in even more home runs. Defending this choice, he once said, "I noticed that they never had a show called 'Singles Derby,'" according to the *Sporting News*. In June 1962 he and teammates Eddie Matthews, Joe Adcock, and **Frank Thomas** became the first four players ever to hit consecutive home runs in a game.

Became America's Home Run King

In 1966 the Braves moved to Atlanta, giving the American South its first major league baseball team. That year and the following, Aaron led the league in home runs. Soon baseball fans began to recognize that

the slugger had a chance at breaking Babe Ruth's home run record. In July 1968 he had hit his 500th homer, and a year later he took the 3,000th hit of his career.

The more home runs Aaron hit, the more mail he received—and not all of it was fan mail. By the early 1970s Aaron was receiving an estimated 3,000 letters a day, most of it from racists who warned the player against beating Ruth's record. "Dear Henry," read one such letter as quoted by Larry Schwartz of ESPN.com. "You are (not) going to break this record established by the great Babe Ruth if I can help it."

The experience changed the soft-spoken player, who became more forthright on racial issues. "When people ask me what progress Negroes have made in baseball, I tell them the Negro hasn't made any progress on the field," he said in 1970 according to BaseballLibrary.com. "We haven't made any progress in the commissioner's office.... I still think it's tokenism. We don't have Negro secretaries in some of the big league offices, and I think it's time that the major leagues and baseball in general just took hold of themselves and started hiring some of these capable people."

On June 10, 1972, Aaron hit his 649th home run, tying with Willie Mays for second place in career home runs. His quest for Ruth's record had officially begun, and the following year and a half was the most difficult period in

Career Statistics

Yr	Team	AVG	GP	AB	R	H	HR	RBI	BB	SO	SB
1954	MIL	.280	122	468	58	131	13	69	28	39	2
1955	MIL	.314	153	602	105	189	27	106	49	61	3
1956	MIL	.328	153	609	106	200	26	92	37	54	2
1957	MIL	.322	151	615	118	198	44	132	57	58	1
1958	MIL	.326	153	601	109	196	30	132	59	49	4
1959	MIL	.355	154	629	116	223	39	123	51	54	8
1960	MIL	.292	153	590	102	172	40	126	60	63	16
1961	MIL	.327	155	603	115	197	34	120	56	64	21
1962	MIL	.323	156	592	127	191	45	128	66	73	15
1963	MIL	.319	161	631	121	201	44	130	78	94	31
1964	MIL	.328	145	570	103	187	24	95	62	46	22
1965	MIL	.318	150	570	109	181	32	89	60	81	24
1966	ATL	.279	158	603	117	168	44	127	76	96	21
1967	ATL	.307	155	600	113	184	39	109	63	97	17
1968	ATL	.287	160	606	84	174	29	86	64	62	28
1969	ATL	.300	147	547	100	164	44	97	87	47	9
1970	ATL	.298	150	516	103	154	38	118	74	63	9
1971	ATL	.327	139	495	95	162	47	118	71	58	1
1972	ATL	.265	129	449	75	119	34	77	92	55	4
1973	ATL	.301	120	392	84	118	40	96	68	51	1
1974	ATL	.268	112	340	47	91	20	69	39	29	1
1975	MIL-B	.234	137	465	45	109	12	60	70	51	0
1976	MIL-B	.229	85	271	22	62	10	35	35	38	0

ATL: Atlanta Braves; MIL: Milwaukee Braves; MIL-B: Milwaukee Brewers.

Aaron's life. While many fans cheered him on, others continued to threaten the African American player. The Federal Bureau of Investigation was called in, and security was tightened at the Braves' ballpark. The 39-year-old player had to travel with Secret Service agents protecting him. Even worse, his college-student daughter had received threats as well. Separated from his teammates, Aaron often slept at the ballpark, in a room reserved for him, so that he did not have to go out into the public. Throughout this period he drew strength from his strong Christian faith and did not waver from his principles of hard work and self-discipline. He ended the 1973 season with 713 home runs—just one shy of tying Ruth's record.

The 1974 baseball season began with much anticipation; fans wondered not if but when Aaron would break Ruth's record. The answer was not long in coming, as Aaron hit a homer in his first at-bat of the season. His eyes teared as he rounded third base; he was now tied for the record. That night, according to Schwartz, he called his mother, saying, "I'm going to save the next one for you, Mom." Four days later, on April 8, 1974, the largest crowd in Braves history (53,775) filled the Atlanta-Fulton County Stadium. Aaron hit the record-breaking homer in the fourth inning, off a fastball from Los Angeles Dodgers pitcher Al Downing. The ball sailed over the left-center field wall and into the Braves bull pen, where it was caught by relief pitcher Tom House. As Aaron rounded the bases, two college students leaped onto the field to run with him before security guards stepped in. Aaron's excited teammates mobbed him at home base, and the crowd went wild.

Aaron's feat came more than two years before his retirement as a major league ballplayer. He hit his last home run as a Braves player, his 733rd, on October 2, 1974. In November Aaron squared off with Japanese home run king **Sadaharu Oh** in a home run contest, beating Oh 10-9 (the Japanese slugger would go on to break Aaron's record, however). By the following season Aaron had been traded to the Milwaukee Brewers; in Wisconsin, he was able to end his career where he began it. He hit his first home run for the Brewers on April 18, and by May 1 he had set another record: baseball's highest-ever RBI (2,212). Aaron took his final at-bat, hitting a single, on October 3, 1976, in Milwaukee County Stadium. He was 42 years old. Six years later he was inducted into the National Baseball Hall of Fame, receiving 97.83 percent of the votes cast. Only **Ty Cobb** has received a higher percentage of votes.

Immediately after his retirement, Aaron rejoined the Atlanta Braves—this time as a player-development manager in the team's minor-league farm system. American media mogul **Ted Turner**, who had purchased the Braves in 1976, had invited Aaron to take the job. Here he helped develop such Braves talent as Tom Glavine and David Justice. It was not long before Aaron was asked to manage the major league team. In 1990 he became a baseball executive, named senior vice president and assistant to the president of the Braves. A budding businessman, Aaron also served as a board member for the Braves and for Turner Broadcasting System (TBS), and as vice president of business development for the CNN Airport Network.

Throughout the 1990s and into the 2000s, Aaron has been very active in community services and philanthropy; his partner in these ventures is his wife, Billye Aaron (his marriage to first wife Barbara Lucas ended in divorce in 1971). Aaron's 1991 autobiography, *I Had a Hammer,* made the *New York Times* bestseller list, while *Hank Aaron: Chasing the Dream,* a 1995 TBS documentary about the player's life, received an Academy Award nomination. In 1999, at a celebration marking Aaron's 65th birthday, Major League Baseball introduced the Hank Aaron Award, presented annually to the best hitters in the American League and the National League. Also in the late 1990s, Aaron and his wife established the Hank Aaron Chasing the Dream Foundation, to help boys and girls ages 9 to 12 pursue their dreams. A statue of Aaron, cast in the mid-1990s, graces the courtyard at the entrance to Turner Field, home of the Atlanta Braves.

SELECTED WRITINGS BY AARON:

(With Lonnie Wheeler) *I Had a Hammer.* New York: HarperCollins, 1991.

FURTHER INFORMATION

Books

"Hank Aaron." *Notable Black Men.* Detroit, MI: Gale Research, 1998.

Periodicals

Hinckley, David. "Hank Did More Than Hit Homers." (New York) *Daily News* (July 7, 2002): 10.

Sandomir, Richard. "Of Home Runs and History." *New York Times* (April 12, 1995): C24.

Other

"Hank Aaron." BaseballLibrary.com. http://www.pubdim. net/baseballlibrary/ballplayers/A/Aaron_Hank.stm (November 13, 2002).

"Hank Aaron." National Baseball Hall of Fame. http:// www.baseballhalloffame.org/hofers_and_honorees/ hofer_bios/aaron_hank.htm (November 12, 2002).

"Hank Aaron Statistics." Baseball Almanac. http:// www.baseball-almanac.com/players/player.php? p=aaronha01 (November 19, 2002).

"The Hank Aaron Timeline." *Sporting News.* http://www. sportingnews.com/archives/aaron/timeline.html (November 14, 2002).

Schwartz, Larry. "Hank Aaron: Hammerin' Back at Racism." ESPN.com. http://espn.go.com/sports century/features/00006764.html (November 12, 2002).

Tavis Smiley. National Public Radio (October 30, 2002).

Sketch by Wendy Kagan

Jim Abbott
1967-

American baseball player

With 95-mph fastballs, Jim Abbott would be considered a gifted pitcher by any standard. What made Abbott stand out during his amateur and professional career was the challenge he overcame to deliver his strikeouts. Abbott was born with a deformed right arm, and played baseball virtually one-handed.

A product of Flint, Michigan, Abbott was brought up by his father, Mike (a sales manager), and mother Kathy (a lawyer) to live independently. The Abbotts tried using a prosthetic device when Jim was very young, but the boy hated the artificial hand and learned to do without it. Abbott's parents encouraged their son to play soccer, a game in which the legs, not the arms, prevail. Jim, however, was enamored of baseball. His father taught the boy a move— it would become known as the Abbott switch—that would stay with the ballplayer through his career. When pitching, Abbott would balance his glove on his right wrist, where the arm ends. For fielding, the boy learned to quickly switch the glove to his strong left hand.

The Abbott Switch

To perfect his signature move, Abbott spent countless hours pitching against a brick wall and seamlessly transferring his glove to catch the ball. The boy was equally attentive to his studies, though, showing the motivation that would carry him into adulthood. He chose as his role model pitcher **Nolan Ryan**, a strikeout leader during the 1970s.

Even when he entered Little League, Abbott never felt different regarding his physical condition. At age eleven, he threw a no-hitter that ended after five innings citing the mercy rule (when one team is many runs ahead of the other). The press quickly took notice of this unusual talent, sparking public interest in Abbott that continued for the next two decades. Opposing coaches who tried to take advantage of Abbott's perceived handi-

Jim Abbott

cap soon learned that the young man would not be intimidated: as a high-school freshman, Abbott once faced a string of batters who had been ordered to bunt. The first got on using that strategy; Abbott then threw the following seven out.

By the time he enrolled at the University of Michigan, Abbott was respected for his talent as much as his inspirational value. He pitched for the Wolverines with a six-win, two-loss freshman record that helped win the school the Big Ten title for 1986. In his sophomore year, Abbott rose to an 11-3 record, but got an even bigger thrill when he carried the flag for Team USA at the Pan American Games, held in Havana. He threw his way to a win for the U.S. over Cuba—the first such victory in twenty-five years. A year later, Abbott appeared on the international stage again, this time with the U.S. Olympic Team at the 1988 summer games in Seoul, South Korea. In Seoul, Abbott made possible a defeat against defending champion Japan and helped clinch the gold medal for Team USA in what was then an Olympic demonstration sport.

Into the Majors

Abbott finished his junior year at the University of Michigan by garnering honors including the Golden Spikes Award as outstanding amateur baseball player in the United States; and the Sullivan Memorial Trophy as America's outstanding amateur athlete. It was only a matter of time before the Major Leagues came calling. Abbott

decided to forego his senior year in favor of a spot on the California Angels roster. When he reported for practice in March, 1989, however, the first-round draft choice was discouraged to learn that there was some lingering doubt about his ability to hold his own in big-league ball. "There are times it hurts," he told *Sport* reporter Johnette Howard. "Especially when you work as hard and do as much as anybody else has done, you feel maybe there's not much more to prove, and yet, there's still that skepticism."

Still, Abbott's debut against the Seattle Mariners in April, 1989, drew enormous press coverage. The pitcher rose to the occasion, striking out four batters and giving up no runs and just two singles. He followed that up by what was considered an outstanding rookie season, with an 8-5 win-loss record, all while under heavy scrutiny. No doubt, Abbott's one-handed game contributed to the constant barrage of reporters and photographers. So in-demand was the young star that Angels manager Doug Rader told *Sports Illustrated* writer Bruce Anderson that Abbott "had to answer some of the dumbest, most undignified questions I've ever heard, but he's handled everything with dignity and grace. And he's one helluva pitcher."

Beyond the limelight, Abbott faced the realities of professional baseball. "It's hard work," he admitted to Rob Brofman in a 1989 *Life* interview. "It's hard sitting there in the dugout for nine innings every day doing nothing. It's boring but the worst part is the insecurity—never knowing exactly where you're supposed to be, what's going on." On the other hand, "the best part of being a rookie is the newness of things," Abbott added. "You look in the locker and there's something new every day—a new jacket, new spikes, a new glove."

By 1991 Abbott was no longer seen as a novelty, but as a hardworking professional—the best pitcher in the American League in September of that year. But as with the case of all athletes, his performance waxed and waned with the advancing years. After a poor 1992 season (7-15), Abbott was traded to the New York Yankees. In 1993-94 he contributed a nearly equal won-loss record (11-14, and 9-8) while his Earned Run Average

Career Statistics

Yr	Team	W	L	ERA	GS	CG	SHO	IP	H	HR	BB	SO
1989	CAL	12	12	3.92	29	4	2	181.3	190	13	74	115
1990	CAL	10	14	4.51	33	4	1	211.7	246	16	72	105
1991	CAL	18	11	2.89	34	5	1	243.0	222	14	73	158
1992	CAL	7	15	2.77	29	7	0	211.0	208	12	68	130
1993	NYY	11	14	4.37	32	4	1	214.0	221	22	73	95
1994	NYY	9	8	4.55	24	2	0	160.3	167	24	64	90
1995	CHW	6	4	3.37	17	3	0	112.3	116	10	335	45
1995	CAL	5	4	4.15	13	1	1	84.7	93	4	29	41
1996	CAL	2	18	7.48	23	1	0	142.0	171	23	78	58
1998	CHW	5	0	4.55	5	0	0	31.7	35	2	12	14
1999	MIL	2	8	6.91	15	0	0	82.0	110	14	42	37
TOTAL		87	108	4.25	254	31	6	1674.0	1779	154	620	888

CAL: California Angels; CHW: Chicago White Sox; MIL: Milwaukee Brewers; NYY: New York Yankees.

rose to 4.55. Abbott played for the Chicago White Sox before returning to the Angels in 1995. The following year the one-time sensation posted a disastrous season— 2 wins, 18 losses, and a 7.48 ERA.

Down, But Not Out

"Baseball can be cruel," wrote *Sporting News* reporter Steve Marantz in 1997, "even to its most admirable player." Abbott took that year off to recoup and reenergize, then accepted a minor-league contract with the White Sox for the 1998 season. He endured half a season "riding buses around North Carolina," according to a *Sports Illustrated* article, "pitching in the Alabama humidity … and toiling in an old stadium in rodeo-rabid Alberta." When the White Sox called him up in September 1998, added the reporter, "almost no one noticed."

But Abbott made them notice, wrapping up the season with a 5-0 record against such formidable foes as the Cleveland Indians and Abbott's former team, the New York Yankees. But the winning streak did not last. A 2-8 season with the Milwaukee Brewers in 1999 marked the end of Abbott's Major League play. His career won-loss record stood at 87-108, with a 4.25 ERA. But his influence lived on through the positive and inspirational image he invoked for the public, particularly the disabled.

With his Major League career ended, Jim Abbott left the spotlight of professional sports. The husband and father continued to provide inspiration off the field by working with physically challenged children. Though he's been known to shy away from television or film depictions of his life, the left-hander has been the subject of several biographies, including *Nothing to Prove: The Jim Abbott Story.*

If Abbott's "glory days are gone," Marantz noted in the *Sporting News* in 1997, "it is perhaps because we have come to take his uniqueness for granted. Against what standard should a pitcher with one hand be measured? The only standard is Abbott's and he would have

Awards and Accomplishments

1978	Pitched first no-hitter at age eleven
1985	Baseball scholarship to University of Michigan
1986	University of Michigan Wolverines win Big Ten title
1987	Silver medal for Team USA, Pan-American Games, Havana, Cuba
1987	Golden Spikes Award
1987	Sullivan Memorial Trophy
1988	Gold medal for Team USA at summer Olympic games, Seoul, South Korea
1988	First-round draft choice, California Angels
1991	Named to American League All-Star team

us measure him against pitchers with two hands. Such is his illusion, art and greatness."

FURTHER INFORMATION

Books

Bernatos, Bob. *Nothing to Prove: The Jim Abbott Story.* New York: Kodansha International, 1995.

Contemporary Heroes and Heroines, Book II. Detroit: Gale, 1992.

Johnson, Rick L. *Jim Abbott: Beating the Odds.* Dillon Press, 1991.

Newsmakers. Detroit: Gale, 1988.

Reiser, Howard. *Jim Abbott: All-American Pitcher.* Danbury, CT: Children's Press, 1993.

Savage, Jeff. *Sports Great Jim Abbott.* Springfield, NJ: Enslow, 1993.

White, Ellen Emerson. *Jim Abbott: Against All Odds.* New York: Scholastic, Inc., 1990.

Periodicals

Anderson, Bruce. "No More Doubts." *Sports Illustrated.* (July 24, 1989).

"Back in the Game." *Sports Illustrated.* (October 5, 1998).

Brofman, Rob. "One for the Angels." *Life.* (June, 1989).

Hersch, Hank. "Ace of the Angels." *Sports Illustrated.* (September 9, 1991).

Marantz, Steve. "Time Is Throwing a Curve to Heroic Jim Abbott." *Sporting News.* (March 31, 1997).

Sketch by Susan Salter

Kareem Abdul-Jabbar
1947-

American basketball player

Kareem Abdul-Jabbar

More than a decade after his retirement, Kareem Abdul-Jabbar at 7-feet-2-inches tall remains one of the tallest men ever to play professional basketball. Despite his 267-pound frame, he was never awkward and was known in fact for his grace and flexibility—a rare talent among very large men. Powerful yet smooth in his playing style, he left his mark on the game with his signature shot, the skyhook. Goggle-eyed, but never gawky, he led two teams—the Bucks and later the Lakers—to a total of six championship titles, taking six most valuable player (MVP) awards in the process. With 38,387 career points, Jabbar retired as the all-time leading scorer in the history of professional basketball. Highly religious and introspective, he is remembered not only for his outstanding performance as a player but also for his politically aware persona. While many professional athletes go to great lengths to maintain their personal privacy, few have created an aura of inner depth as has been achieved by Jabbar.

Childhood of a Big Man

Kareem Abdul-Jabbar was born Ferdinand Lewis Alcindor Jr. on April 16, 1947, in New York City, the only child of Lewis Sr. and Cora Alcindor. As a child and as a young man Jabbar went by the name of Lew Alcindor. Jabbar was 22" inches long at birth, and even as a very young boy he seemed to be following in the much larger footsteps of his forefathers. His grandfather, a native of Trinidad, was 6-feet-8-inches tall. Lewis Sr., at 6-feet-2-inches tall, went by the nickname "Big Al." Even Jabbar's mother, who was of Cherokee descent, was herself 5-feet-11-inches tall.

Lewis Sr., a Julliard-trained symphony conductor, supplemented the family income as a bill collector and worked also for the New York Transit Authority Police. Jabbar was born in Harlem where the family lived at 111th Street and Seventh Avenue. They later moved to Inwood, a diverse section of Manhattan. Jabbar was raised in the Catholic Church and attended parochial schools. In grade school he was one of only two African American students enrolled at St. Jude's Elementary. Outside of school he spent his time with his friends, shooting baskets at a playground called the Battlegrounds at Amsterdam and 151st street.

In the fourth grade Jabbar transferred to Holy Providence Boarding School in Cornwells Heights, Pennsylvania, where the student population numbered 40 boys, all of whom were African American. It was a motley crowd at Holy Providence, which was mainly a reform school. Jabbar, who was an honor student, hardly fit with the crowd, and when he completed the school year his parents brought him back to New York City.

The year at Holy Providence was not a total loss, however, because recess periods and free time there were spent in playing peach-basket basketball. He developed new skills during his year in Pennsylvania, and four years later when he finished eighth grade he was well-honed in the sport. What is more, he stood a most impressive 6-feet-8 inches tall by that time. Not surprisingly he was widely recruited by high school basketball coaches.

On scholarship at Power Memorial High School from 1962-66, he played with the varsity team for four years.

Chronology

1947	Born in New York City on April 16
1966	Leads UCLA freshman team to a 21-0 record, averages 33 points per game
1967	Leads UCLA varsity to NCAA championship
1968	Leads UCLA to a back-to-back NCAA titles; converts from Catholic to Muslim
1969	Leads UCLA to a third straight NCAA title; drafted by the Milwaukee Bucks as the first pick in the first round of the NBA draft
1969-70	Leads Bucks to a 29 victory increase from previous season
1970-71	Leads Bucks to NBA championship; marries Janice "Habiba" Brown; makes legal name change to Kareem Abdul-Jabbar
1972	Studies Arabic at Harvard; a daughter, Habiba, is born
1973	Separates from wife Habiba in December
1975	Goes to the Los Angeles Lakers in a trade for four players
1976	A son, Kareem, is born
1977	Leads Lakers to a league-best 53-29 record; divorces Habiba
1978	Becomes the captain of the Lakers
1979	A daughter, Sultana, is born
1980	Leads Lakers to NBA championship
1982	Leads Lakers to NBA championship
1983	Averages 27 points per game for playoffs; loses Bel-Air home in a fire
1985	Leads Lakers to championship; publishes *Giant Steps*, an autobiography
1986	Signs one-year contract extension for unprecedented 18th season; surpasses 35,000-point milestone
1987	Scores 32 points in the deciding game of the NBA finals; Lakers take the championship
1988	Leads Lakers to a repeat championship
1989	Retires from professional play leaving nine NBA records: 38,387 points scored, 20 seasons played, 5,762 playoff points, 6 MVP awards, 57,446 minutes played, 1,560 games played, 15,837 field goals made, 28,307 field goal attempts, and 3,189 blocked shots
1990	Publishes a memoir, *Kareem;* Lakers retire Jabbar's jersey, Number 33.
1996	Publishes *Black Profiles in Courage*
2000	Works at the White Mountain Apache reservation and documents the experience in *Season on the reservation : my sojourn with the White Mountain Apache*
2000-01	Coaches for NBA
2002	Coaches for the USBL

Kareem Abdul-Jabbar

Abdul-Jabbar's personal life remained unsettled during and after his Los Angeles playing years. He was always uncomfortable with reporters, describing them as "scurrying around like cockroaches after crumbs." Fans, especially white, found it difficult to understand his conversion to Islam; his attitudes towards race; and his shy, introverted personality. Abdul-Jabbar's Islamic faith also estranged him from his parents, although they eventually reconciled.

Source: "Kareem Abdul-Jabbar." *St. James Encyclopedia of Popular Culture.* 5 vols. St. James Press, 2000.

Under the direction of coach Jack Donahue Jabbar led his team to a 78-1 record and two national championships. He lettered and made the all-city team for each of his four years of high school, and set a New York City record for the most points scored by a high school player. He set a record also for the most rebounds.

Although a war raged in Vietnam and a draft was in force for U.S. males, Jabbar received a 4-F status from the draft board because he was far too tall for the military to accommodate. With his choice of college scholarships available he accepted an offer to play for Coach **John Wooden**'s Bruins at the University of California at Los Angeles (UCLA). While still on the freshman team, in 1966 Jabbar immediately attracted a great deal of attention by averaging 33 points per game and leading the team to an undefeated season with a record of 21-0. As a sophomore he was offered a lifetime contract with the Harlem Globetrotters a professional exhibition team—but turned it down.

On the UCLA varsity squad Jabbar brought the school to three consecutive national championships, from 1967 until he graduated in 1969. He was named College Player of the Year in 1967 and again in 1969. Jabbar's unusual height advantage caused the National College Athletic Association (NCAA) to institute a ten-year ban on the dunk shot in college basketball, beginning with Jabbar's junior year at UCLA. Not to be quashed, Jabbar perfected a variety of the dunk, a new straight-armed shot called the skyhook, which became his signature shot for the duration of his career.

Spiritual Journeys

While in college during the 1960s, Jabbar's interest in humanity and in his own spirituality matured along with his basketball skills. It was a time of social change and sometimes of civil unrest, when African Americans in the United States spoke out and demanded proper equality. In 1968 many African American athletes refused to participate in the Olympic games in Mexico City as a way of protesting for civil rights. Jabbar, searching for peace of soul, turned to the Islamic religion of the Middle East. Around that same time He took part in a ceremony called Shahada by which he adopted an Islamic name, calling himself Kareem. He spent the summer of 1968 working with a youth program in Harlem, and at the end of the season he embraced Islam one step further by adopting Jabbar as his surname.

Jabbar's journey of personal growth followed other avenues as well after he made the acquaintance of the late actor Bruce Lee who was also a renowned marital arts experts. Jabbar met Lee through a studio called the New York Akikai. Beginning in 1967 Jabbar began to train with Lee, and the two worked together until Lee's untimely death in 1973. The two had also started shooting a movie, called *Game of Death*, but the shooting was suspended when Lee died. Jabbar's life was enriched in many ways by his association with Lee, both spiritually and professionally. The speed and flexibility that he developed in working with such a masterful martial artist went a long way in expanding the impact of Jabbar's game skills.

Career Statistics

Yr	Team	GP	PTS	FG%	3P%	FT%	RPG	APG	SPG	BPG	TO	PF
1969-70	MIL	82	2361	—	51.8	65.3	14.5	4.1	—	—	—	283
1970-71	MIL	82	2596	—	57.7	69.0	16.0	3.3	—	—	—	264
1971-72	MIL	81	2822	—	57.4	68.9	16.6	4.6	—	—	—	235
1972-73	MIL	76	2292	—	55.4	71.3	16.1	5.0	—	—	—	208
1973-74	MIL	81	2191	—	53.9	70.2	14.5	4.8	1.4	3.5	—	238
1974-75	MIL	65	1949	—	51.3	76.3	14.0	4.1	1.0	3.3	—	205
1975-76	LAL	82	2275	—	52.9	70.3	16.9	5.0	1.5	4.1	—	292
1976-77	LAL	82	2152	—	57.9	70.1	13.3	3.9	1.2	3.2	—	262
1977-78	LAL	62	1600	—	55.0	78.3	12.9	4.3	1.7	3.0	208	182
1978-79	LAL	80	1903	—	57.7	73.6	12.8	5.4	0.9	4.0	282	230
1979-80	LAL	82	2034	0.0	60.4	76.5	10.8	4.5	1.0	3.4	297	216
1980-81	LAL	80	2095	0.0	57.4	76.6	10.3	3.4	0.7	2.9	249	244
1981-82	LAL	76	1818	0.0	57.9	70.6	8.7	3.0	0.8	2.7	230	224
1982-83	LAL	79	1722	0.0	58.8	74.9	7.5	2.5	0.8	2.2	200	220
1983-84	LAL	80	1717	0.0	57.8	72.3	7.3	2.6	0.7	1.8	221	211
1984-85	LAL	79	1735	0.0	59.9	73.2	7.9	3.2	0.8	2.1	197	238
1985-86	LAL	79	1846	0.0	56.4	76.5	6.1	3.5	0.8	1.6	203	248
1986-87	LAL	78	1366	33.3	56.4	71.4	6.7	2.6	0.6	1.2	186	245
1987-88	LAL	80	1165	0.0	53.2	76.2	6.0	1.7	0.6	1.1	159	216
TOTAL		1560	38387	5.6	55.9	72.1	11.2	3.6	0.7	2.0	2527	4657

LAL: Los Angeles Lakers; MIL: Milwaukee Brewers.

Professional Big Man

After a winning college career at UCLA with only one loss to mar his record, Jabbar signed in 1969 with the Milwaukee Bucks. The Bucks was a one-year-old expansion team with a losing season to its credit. Jabbar would have preferred to go to New York to play with the Knicks, but Milwaukee had first pick in the draft that year, and Milwaukee picked Jabbar. There was a another professional team in New York at that time, called the Nets. The Nets, a part of the American Basketball Association, offered Jabbar a contract, but he turned it down because the Bucks offered him much more money.

According to Jabbar, his first season with the National Basketball Association (NBA) was bittersweet. He enjoyed playing ball and excelled as a defensive player. Equally skilled on offense, he averaged about 29 points per game at center and was named Rookie of the Year. The Bucks finished second in the division and went to the playoffs that season. Overall, they realized an increase of 29 victories over the previous season.

The 1970-71 NBA season for Jabbar was more exciting than even his rookie year. He topped the list of scorers in the NBA and was named MVP of the NBA. Milwaukee went into the playoffs and then to the finals where they won the league championship.

The 1971-72 season for Jabbar was an instant replay of the previous year, as he led the league in scoring and collected a second MVP award. At the end of the 1972-73 season the Bucks made NBA history when they emerged with more than 60 wins for the third time since the 1970-71 season. It was the first time that an NBA team had won so many games for three years in a row.

Amid the newness and excitement of joining the NBA, Jabbar learned very quickly that the reporters had few good things to say about celebrities who kept to themselves. Although he liked to be a loner, Jabbar learned quickly that some reporters were pushy and rude and posed an unpleasant annoyance for professional athletes. Another new experience for Jabbar was the way the officials in the league seemed to tolerate players who poked and jabbed him just because of his great size. Some players even gouged his eyes while game officials looked the other way. In order to protect himself Jabbar began to wear goggles on the court. The glasses quickly became a part of the big man's image.

The Los Angeles Lakers

Jabbar, who won a third MVP award in 1974, asked to be traded after the 1974-75 season. The Bucks honored his request and traded him to the Los Angeles Lakers in return for four players in 1975. After six seasons with the Bucks, he was entering the peak of his career as he made the move to Los Angeles. He recorded his highest statistics ever during the 1975-76 season and won a fourth MVP award with the Lakers in 1976. He made history as the first Lakers player ever to be honored as MVP, and in 1976-77 he walked away with a fifth MVP award.

Although the Lakers had a 53-29 record that year—the best in the league—the team failed to win the conference title. The 1979-80 season brought a new team owner, Dr. Jerry Buss, to the Lakers. Jabbar re-negotiated his contract to a generous advantage. A new player, a phenomenal 20-year-old rookie named **Magic Johnson**, joined the Lakers that year. The Lakers won the championship, and Jabbar won a record-breaking sixth MVP award.

Awards and Accomplishments

1962-66	Sets a record for most points (2,067) and most rebounds (2,002) by a high school player in New York City
1966	Receives a New York State Regents' scholarship; accepts a scholarship to UCLA
1967-69	Named to first team, All-America; named most outstanding player, National College Athletic Association tournament
1967, 1969	Named college player of the year by *Sporting News,* United Press International, Associated Press, and U.S. Basketball Writers Association; named national player of the year
1969	Received Naismith Award; graduated as the leading scorer in the history of University of California at Los Angeles
1970	Named National Basketball Association Rookie of the Year
1970-77, 1979-89	Played in National Basketball Association All-Star Games
1971-72	Led National Basketball Association in scoring
1971-72, 1974, 1976-77, 1980	Named league's most valuable player
1971, 1985	Named most valuable player of National Basketball Association playoffs
1971-77, 1980-81, 1984, 1986	Named to All-NBA First Team
1974-75, 1979-81	Named to All-Defensive First Team
1975-76, 1979-80	Led National Basketball Association in blocked shots
1976	Led National Basketball Association in rebounds
1980	Named to the National Basketball Association thirty-fifth anniversary all-time team
1984	Broke Wilt Chamberlain's career scoring record of 31,419 points; broke Jerry West's all-time playoff scoring record
1985	Named *Sports Illustrated* Sportsman of the Year
1989	Retired with National Basketball Association career records for most minutes (57,446), most points (38,387), most field goals, and first player to play for 20 seasons
1996	Named to the National Basketball Association fiftieth anniversary all-time team
1995	Enshrined in the Naismith Memorial Basketball Hall of Fame on May 15

Kareem Abdul-Jabbar, right

As the Lakers collected more championships—in 1982, 1985, and 1987—the team in 1988 became the first in nearly 20 years to win back-to-back NBA championships. In 1989, after 20 seasons of professional play, Jabbar retired from the NBA. The Lakers retired his jersey, Number 33, in 1990. Likewise, the Bucks retired his jersey.

Family Life

Soon after the Bucks won the NBA championship in 1971, Jabbar donned the white robes of a Muslim groom for his wedding to Janice Brown. In recognition of her new life with Jabbar, Brown adopted the Muslim name Habiba. Jabbar, who was known professionally as Lew Alcindor during his first two seasons with the Bucks, changed his name legally to Kareem Abdul-Jabbar at that time.

The ceremony, which took place in Washington, D.C, was held at dawn, according to Muslim custom. When mosque officials refused to allow Jabbar's parents to wit-

ness the ceremony because of their Catholic faith they were understandably offended. They had traveled all the way from New York to see their only child get married, and the incident caused a serious rift between the Alcindors and their son. Jabbar felt badly; he had not been told until after the ceremony that his parents were barred from entering the mosque. The rift between him and his parents was slow to heal, and nearly ten years passed before he made amends with his family. After that time Jabbar always made sure to point to the camera and say, "Hi to Moms and Pops in New York," whenever he appeared on national television. His marriage to Habiba, however, did not fare as well, and the couple was divorced in 1977.

Jabbar spent the summer of 1972 at Harvard studying the Arabic language, and that year Habiba gave birth to the couple's first child, a daughter also named Habiba. Jabbar, who was raised as an only child, had difficulty conforming his life to accommodate a significant other person and a child. The union between Jabbar and his wife had weakened early in the marriage. He and Habiba separated permanently in December of 1973.

Separation notwithstanding, Jabbar and his wife remained close with one another. Their son, Kareem, was

Where Is He Now?

After retiring from the NBA Jabbar took a ten-year hiatus from basketball, returning in 1999. Among his more visible projects during that time, in 1995 he researched and published a book, *Black Profiles in Courage.* In it he documented the stories of inspirational African Americans: Harriet Tubman of the Underground Railroad, a Moorish slave named Estevanico who discovered Arizona and New Mexico, and others. In the course of his research he spent time at the Fort Apache Indian Reservation near White River, Arizona. He returned to White River in 1999-2000 season to serve as an assistant coach, at Alchesay High School on the reservation. Jabbar accepted only one dollar in compensation for the five-month assignment. He documented the experience in 2000 in a book with Stephen Singular, called *Season on the reservation: my sojourn with the White Mountain Apache.*

Jabbar, who contributes color commentary to ESPN in Bristol, Connecticut, rejoined the NBA briefly as a coach with the Los Angeles Clippers in 2000. He coached a training session with the Indiana Pacers in 2001, and in 2002 joined the United States Basketball League as the head coach of the Oklahoma Storm. He led the Storm to its first league championship but resigned just a few days later without explanation. Observers suggested that he wished to return to coaching in the NBA.

born in 1976. In 1977, the year of Jabbar's divorce, he met Cheryl Pistono, and she later gave birth to their son Amir. A second daughter, Sultana, was born to Jabbar and Habiba in 1979, two years after their divorce. A third son, Adam, was born to Jabbar and an unnamed woman.

Although Jabbar's luxurious Bel-Air home was destroyed by a fire early in 1983, he found his faith in Islam and took a philosophical approach. In December of the year he published an autobiography, *Giant Steps,* with Peter Knobler. Jabbar's later memoir, *Kareem,* was written with Mignon McCarthy and published in 1990. This book documents his final season with the NBA.

Between 1979 and 1998 Jabbar made ten film appearances. Most of them were as himself, including his roles in *Fletch* and *Forget Paris.* He served as the executive producer of *The Vernon Johns Story,* a made-for-television movie about a civil rights pioneer.

CONTACT INFORMATION

Address: c/o Amsel Eisenstadt & Frazier, 5757 Wilshire Blvd., Suite 510, Los Angeles, CA 90046. Phone: (323) 939-1188.

SELECTED WRITINGS BY ABDUL-JABBAR:

(With Peter Knobler) *Giant Steps,* New York: Bantam Books, 1983.
(With Mignon McCarthy) *Kareem,* New York: Random House, 1990.
(With Alan Steinberg) *Black Profiles in Courage: A Legacy of African American Achievement,* New York: William Morrow and Co., 1996.
(With Stephen Singular) *Season on the Reservation: My Sojourn with the White Mountain Apache,* New York: W. Morrow and Co., 2000.

FURTHER INFORMATION

Books

Abdul-Jabbar, Kareem, and Mignon McCarthy, *Kareem,* New York: Random House, 1990.
Abdul-Jabbar, Kareem, and Peter Knobler, *Giant Steps,* New York: Bantam Books, 1983.
Cobourn, R. Thomas, *Kareem Abdul-Jabbar: Basketball Great,* New York: Chelsea House Publishers, 1995.

Periodicals

Jet, July 22, 2002, p. 51.

Online

"Kareem Abdul-Jabbar Biography," http://www.hoophall.com/halloffamers/Abdul-Jabbar.htm (January 7, 2003).
"stormmenu2," *Oklahoma Storm,* http://www.theoklahomastorm.com/index.htm (January 7, 2003).

Sketch by G. Cooksey

Andre Agassi
1970-

American tennis player

In the 1980s America's tennis fans took to heart a new kind of player, one without the disciplined control of a **Boris Becker** or the tantrums of a **John McEnroe.** "To see him is to think of MTV," wrote a *Sports Illustrated* reporter when Agassi burst onto the scene in 1987. "The kid … has a teenager hipster's style and swagger.… He looks like he might arrive for matches by skateboard." At the same time, the same observer noted, he showed both good manners and old-fashioned enthusiasm. "Remember when tennis players expressed joy instead of fist-pumping intensity?… Remember when they smiled? Agassi does all that. He's a throwback." It was a powerful combination, and Agassi picked up endorsement contracts from Nike and Canon. But for a long time, critics wrote him off because he couldn't seem to win any of the Grand Slam tournaments. Finally, in 1992, counted out as a serious contender, he won Wimbledon, the most important of the tournaments. He followed this up with wins at the U.S. and Australian Opens that finally silenced his critics.

Tennis Prodigy

In 1974, Agassi's hometown of Las Vegas hosted the Alan King tennis tournament, attracting a number of big names. But spectators were even more attracted to a four-year-old Andre Agassi hitting topspin forehands. Even

Andre Agassi

Jimmy Connors came by to witness the young prodigy and hit a few balls with him. In fact, Agassi had started much younger. His father, Emmanuel "Mike" Agassi, an Iranian immigrant, determined to raise a champ, had hung a ball and racquet over Andre's crib and by the age of two, young Agassi could use that racquet to serve the ball.

At age 13, with his father's encouragement, Andre Agassi left regular schooling and moved to Bandentown, Florida, to attend the renowned tennis academy run by Nick Bollettieri, who became Agassi's coach. Despite his early promise, Agassi actually proved to be an average player among the budding stars at the academy, and he began to turn to beer and marijuana to dull some of the frustration. "While he foundered mid-ladder at the academy for three years, trying to live up to the expectations of a father who was disappointed if he didn't win every match, Agassi did distinguish himself in the burgeoning ranks of racket-smashers," according to a *Sports Illustrated* reporter. Instead of kicking him out, Bollettieri taught him to refocus his energy into his game, channeling his anger into more power on the court.

This seemed to work. By the time Agassi was 16, he had won five United States Tennis Association (USTA) national junior titles. Understandably bored with the junior leagues, Agassi turned pro two days after his 16th birthday. In fact, he'd already signed a contract with Nike, a sign of his appeal to fans and sponsors alike. About this time, he also became a born-again Christian, a decision that caused him to question whether he should abandon his tennis career and focus on something more spiritual. In the end, another player in his bible-study group convinced him to stick with tennis, and Agassi credits his conversion with giving him a more relaxed personality that has actually enhanced his game and his career.

A Different Kind of Pro

Agassi's more relaxed style appealed to a number of fans. Instead of moodiness, they saw enthusiasm. Instead of someone throwing racquets after missing shots, they saw Agassi throwing kisses to the crowd after winning shots. His flashy clothes and long hair just added to this feeling of a fresh, young face in the tennis world, and the crowds took to him easily. Not that everyone was cheering. "God help him when he really starts losing," Ion Tiriac, Boris Becker's manager, told *Sports Illustrated*. "You can prance around like an idiot when you're on top, but whatever seems funny now will be seen as obscene or disastrous or a calculated disturbance as soon as you stop winning."

But for Agassi, the early years were winning years. He won his first pro tournament in 1987 and rose from a 41 ranking to 24. The next year turned out even better. He won six tournaments in 1988, including four in a row. Overall, he garnered a very impressive 63-11 record that year, and reached the semi-finals of both the French and U.S. Opens. He also helped carry the U.S. team to victory in the Davis Cup, crushing his Argentine opponent 6-2, 6-2, 6-1, "a victory which had the rest of the American team shaking their heads in disbelief," according to sports journalist and Agassi biographer Robert Philip. That year he went to number three in the rankings. He also became the second youngest player (after Boris Becker) to pass the $1 million mark in career prize money.

Difficult Years

The next year was a disappointment. Agassi won only one tournament, and when he again lost the semifinals at the U.S. Open, critics began to wonder if he was just a flash in the pan. Fulfilling Tiriac's prophecy, they began to question his seriousness, calling him spoiled and overrated. As in 1988, he refused to play Wimbledon, citing among other things their refusal to let him wear his brightly colored tennis outfits.

The next few years were not much better. He did win four tournaments in 1990 and made it to the finals of the French Open, the first time he had gotten that far in a Grand Slam tournament. And at the end of the year, he won the first ever Association of Tennis Professionals World Tour Championship, beating other top-seeded players. But in 1991, he won only two tournaments and once again lost the French Open, this time to an old rival from his days at the Bollitieri Academy, **Jim Courier**. What made it harder was that he was poised to win toward the end of their final match, but he lost both of the final sets. Critics said Agassi would always "choke"

Chronology

1970	Born April 29 in Las Vegas, Nevada
1974	Exhibits tennis skills at Alan King Tennis Tournament
1983	Enters Bollettieri Tennis Academy in Bradenton, Florida
1986	Turns pro, signs endorsement contract with Nike
1988	Ranked number 3, with 63-11 record; reaches semifinals at U.S. and French Opens
1988	Passes $1 million mark in prize winnings, becoming second youngest player to do so
1990	Helps U.S. team win Davis Cup; reaches finals in U.S. and French Opens
1992	Wins Wimbledon, first "Grand Slam" victory
1993	Coach and mentor, Nick Bollettieri, announces he is leaving Agassi team
1994	Hires Brad Gilbert as coach
1994	Wins U.S. Open; ranked number 2
1995	Wins Australian Open; ranked number 1 men's tennis player in world
1995	Founds Andre Agassi Foundation to help at-risk children
1996	Wins gold medal, 1996 Summer Olympics
1997	Marries actress Brooke Shields, April 19
1997	Falls to number 101 in tennis rankings
1999	Divorces Brooke Shields
1999	Wins French Open
1999	Learns that both sister Tami and mother have breast cancer
1999	Begins dating Steffi Graf
2000	Wins Australian Open
2001	Wins Australian Open (first back-to-back Grand Slam victory)
2001	Marries Steffi Graf, October 22; four days later she gives birth to their son, Jaden Gil

Born to Serve

Really now. Can Andre Agassi, whose self-contradictions force tennis observers to question whether he's the game's new savior or just another infantile twerp, actually be unique?...

Bottom line: Agassi ... is still a teenager. End of puzzle. See ya when you're 20 and back from the ozone, dude. He's got rock 'n' roll hair. Big deal. The last close-clipped, white American idol ... may have been Pat Boone. But just because Agassi is No. 4 in the world; just because he has the speed, eyes and hands of a tennis genius; just because he hits the ball on the rise as well and as true and as hard as any human could possibly hit it—whew, man, and much harder than you would ever suspect a 5 ft. 11 in., 155-pound, spare-looking spider boy could—doesn't mean we should rush him into understanding geography, or acting less like a showboating nincompoop on the court or ... or playing Wimbledon or something.

So, could Agassi, with his sidewinding howitzer forehand, his exotic, Middle Eastern surf-rat looks and that come-hither grin that melts all the girls, truly be the swirl of fresh air that tennis has been longing for? Or is he merely a chic bundle of cynical contrivances, a marketeer's dream package with a streak of show-biz evangelism, a veritable "Wayne Newton in denim"...?

Source: Curry Kirkpatrick, *Sports Illustrated*, March 13, 1989, p. 64.

when the pressure was on, and by early 1992, he had dropped out of the Top 10 rankings. He was suffering a loss of confidence, as he himself noted. At age 22, he worried that he might be a has-been.

A Rebirth

Things began to change in 1992. Agassi had ended his boycott of Wimbledon in 1991, and he reportedly found the grass difficult to play on. In 1992, he began training with Wimbledon legend John McEnroe to overcome this handicap, and his hard work paid off when he beat Boris Becker and McEnroe himself to make it to the Wimbledon finals, against Goran Ivanisevic, a player famed for his hard serve. After losing the first match, Agassi came back to defeat Ivanisevic in the next two matches, but lost the next match. This time, Agassi did not choke. Instead, he went on to win in a hard-fought final match by a 6-4 score. In his excitement, he fell to his knees and screamed with joy.

By winning Wimbledon, Agassi had put to rest the myth that he could not win the big ones. But it was not all smooth sailing. The next year, bronchitis and a sprained wrist caused him to skip the Australian and French Opens. Still bothered by his wrist injury, and out of shape, he lost his Wimbledon title to **Pete Sampras** in the quarterfinals. Perhaps the highlight of that tournament was when Barbra Streisand showed up in the stands to support Agassi. For a time there was specula-

tion of a romantic involvement, but neither party has confirmed them, and at the time Agassi was still very much with his long-time girlfriend Wendy Stewart.

In late 1993, Agassi's mentor and coach, Nick Bollittieri, announced that he was leaving to pursue other interests, a move that hurt him and may have contributed to his first-round loss in the U.S. Open a short time later. Agassi then missed the 1994 Australian Open, complaining of the same wrist injury that had troubled him at Wimbledon. Again, it seemed that he might be on his way out.

New Coach, New Triumphs

In the summer of 1994, Agassi hired former player Brad Gilbert to be his new coach, citing Gilbert's reputation for winning matches he was expected to lose. Gilbert convinced him to focus on winning smarter, and outthinking his opponents. The new strategy paid off when he won the 1994 U.S. Open, his second Grand Slam win. "Agassi is suddenly the biggest thing in tennis because he proved himself serious at last, and an Agassi with purpose is simply gigantic," wrote a *Sports Illustrated* reporter. Agassi was back in the top ranks, this time at number two in the rankings. Perhaps to mark this new seriousness, he shaved off his trademark long hair shortly before the Australian Open, where he reached the finals without losing a match and then defeated old rival Pete Sampras to take the title. It was a delicious revenge, and the sweeter because it made Andre Agassi the number one men's tennis player for the first time in his life.

Agassi would not remain number one for long. He lost at Wimbledon to Boris Becker and then to Sampras at the U.S. Open. By November of 1995, Sampras was back at number one, and in 1996, Agassi lost early rounds at the Australian and French Opens and at Wimbledon. He did win a gold medal at the 1996 Summer Olympics, but there was not much to celebrate the next year.

Awards and Accomplishments

1988	Named Association of Tennis Professionals' "Most Improved Player of the Year"
1990	Wins first ever Tennis Professionals World Tour Championship
1990	Reaches finals, French Open and U.S. Open
1990	On victorious U.S. team, Davis Cup (vs. Australia)
1991	Reaches finals, French Open
1992	Wins Wimbledon, first "Grand Slam" victory
1992	On victorious U.S. team, Davis Cup (vs. Switzerland)
1994	First place, U.S. Open; ranked number 2
1995	First place, Australian Open; ranked number 1 men's tennis player in world
1996	Gold medal, 1996 Summer Olympics
1999	First place, French Open
2000	First place, Australian Open
2001	First place, Australian Open (first back-to-back Grand Slam victory)
2001	Second place, U.S. Open

The next few years were a rollercoaster. He won no tournaments in 1997, and by the end of that year he was ranked a dismal 122. Off the court, his personal life was also trying. In May of 1997 he married his long-time fiancée, actress Brooke Shields, but by April 1999, they were divorced. By that time, he had begun yet another comeback. In 1998 he won five tournaments, and reaching the finals in five others. He ended the year ranked number six. Then he won the U.S. Open and the French Open in 1999. He had now won each of the Grand Slam tournaments. To top it off, he won the Australian Open again in early 2000, and once again in 2001—his first back-to-back victories in a Grand Slam tournament.

Agassi ended 2002 with a ranking of second and a record of 53-12. In October of 2001 he married fellow tennis great **Steffi Graf**, whom he started dating when both won the French Open in 1999, shortly after his divorce from Shields. Four days after their marriage, Graf gave birth to a baby boy, named Jaden Gil. From teenage hipster to family man, Andre Agassi had come a long way, and through it all he has retained a wicked tennis arm that attracted spectators when he was four, and continues to surprise opponents long after he has been counted out from serious competition.

FURTHER INFORMATION

Books

Bauman, Paul. *Agassi and Ecstasy: The Turbulent Life of Andre Agassi.* New York: Basic Books, 1997.

Philip, Robert. *Agassi: The Fall and Rise of the Enfant Terrible of Tennis.* London: Bloomsbury, 1993.

Periodicals

Dellapina, John. "Agassi pulls off the improbable in U.S. Open." *Knight Ridder/Tribune News Service* (September 7, 2002): K5764.

Jenkins, Sally. "Image is not everything." *Sports Illustrated* (March 11, 1992): 34.

Jenkins, Sally. "Beauty and baldy." *Sports Illustrated* (February 6, 1995): 46.

Jenkins, Sally. "Love and love (tennis star Andre Agassi)." *Sports Illustrated* (March 13, 1995): 52.

Jensen, Mike. "Sampras stops Agassi, wins 5th U.S. Open title." *Knight Ridder/Tribune News Service* (September 7, 2002): K5764.

Kirkpatrick, Curry. "Born to serve: Andre Agassi was recently born again. Now, if he can only grow up." *Sports Illustrated* (March 13, 1990): 64.

Kirkpatrick, Curry. "Agassi's ecstasy." *Sports Illustrated* (September 30, 1991): 12.

Kirkpatrick, Curry. "Back from exile." *Sports Illustrated* (August 1, 1988): 40.

"The many faces of Agassi." *Time* (September 6, 1999): 66.

McEnroe, Patrick. "Are you tough enough?"*Tennis* (September 1999): 135.

Price, S. L. "Anarchy and Agassi." *Sports Illustrated* (September 19, 1994): 34.

Price, S. L. "Lawnmower man." *Sports Illustrated* (July 12, 1999): 28.

Price, S. L. "A grand occasion." *Sports Illustrated* (September 16, 2002): 52.

Roessing, Walter. "Andre Agassi: From hot shot to top shot." *Boys' Life* (June 1996): 6.

Sullivan, Robert. "The teen dream who could wake up U.S. tennis." *Sports Illustrated* (October 26, 1987): 36.

Wertheim, L. Jon. "What a racket!" *Sports Illustrated for Kids* (June 1, 2000): 36.

Sketch by Robert Winters

Troy Aikman
1966-

American football player

Star quarterback of the Dallas Cowboys for more than a decade, Troy Aikman led "America's team" to three Super Bowl victories before the toll of multiple injuries finally took him out of the game. In April 2001, rather than risk a potentially disabling injury, Aikman at the age of thirty-four left professional football to launch a new career as a sports broadcaster. Although he expressed regret at leaving the game that had been his the focus of his life for more than half his years, Aikman told the Associated Press (AP): "I know it's the right thing for me because of my health, concussions, the back problems I've had. It took its toll." He recalled fondly being linked with wide receiver **Michael Irvin** and running back **Emmitt Smith**

Troy Aikman

as one of "The Triplets." Of their association, Smith said, "All three of us stepped up. We all pushed one another. He [Aikman] probably was the laid-back one, but he was the stubborn one, too. His stubbornness was really his way of showing that losing was not an option."

Born in West Covina, California

He was born Troy Kenneth Aikman in West Covina, California, on November 21, 1966. The youngest of the three children of Ken and Charlyn Aikman, he grew up in Cerritos, a suburb of Los Angeles. Because of congenital problems with his feet, he was forced to wear casts up to his knees until he was fourteen months old. His foot problems as an infant, however, did nothing to slow Aikman's development as an athlete. As a boy, he was most interested in baseball. When Troy was twelve, the Aikmans moved to a farm near Henryetta, Oklahoma, and he soon found himself focusing less on baseball and more on football, which was particularly popular in the Sooner State. Aikman quarterbacked his Henryetta High School football team, as a junior leading the Fighting Hens to their first state playoffs in thirty years and to a 6-4 record in his senior year. Although Henryetta never became a football power during his years there, Aikman managed to earn all-state honors his senior year, and word filtered out about his brilliance on the gridiron. As a result, he was heavily recruited by some of the top colleges in the country. Impressed by its football coach, Barry Switzer, Aikman finally decided on the University of Oklahoma.

As impressed as he had been with Switzer as a person, Aikman found that the Oklahoma coach's strategy made little use of his quarterbacking skills. He soon realized that Switzer didn't plan to alter his offensive strategy to accommodate him. Aikman later told *Sports Illustrated*: "He changed . . . [the offense] a little bit, but the only real difference when I played was that we threw the ball 12 times a game instead of seven." A crushing lost to archrival Kansas further eroded Aikman's confidence. After a disappointing freshman season, Aikman returned for his sophomore year and led the Sooners to victory in their first three games of the season, only to have his ankle broken in the team's face-off with the University of Miami. Switzer tapped Jamelle Holloway as the new starting quarterback, and Aikman despaired of regaining the job. In the end, he decided to transfer to UCLA, where he was confident he would get more of an opportunity to play. He was forced to sit out his first season at UCLA after the transfer but won the starting quarterback job in 1987, finishing his debut season with the team as the second highest rated college passer in the country. Aikman led UCLA to records of 10-2 in both his junior and senior years, winning All-American honors and finishing his college career as the third-ranked passer in National Collegiate Athletic Association (NCAA) history.

Drafted by Dallas Cowboys

The Dallas Cowboys, who had fallen on hard times in the late 1980s, made no secret of the fact that they wanted to tap Aikman in the 1989 NFL draft. Dallas drafted Aikman first overall in the draft. In his first year with the Cowboys, Aikman found himself in competition with Steve Walsh, another rookie, for the job of starting quarterback. Although Aikman eventually won the job, the Cowboys suffered through a disastrous season, ending with a record of 1-15. In 1990, things improved, but only slightly. The Cowboys improved their record to 7-9. However, Aikman performed well, as he did again in 1991, leading the Cowboys to the playoffs with an 11-5 record in the regular season. The quarterback was injured in the twelfth game of the regular season and rode the bench for the remainder of the season and the playoffs. Aikman's brilliance on the gridiron was not to be denied in 1992. With a pass-completion rate of sixty-four percent, he threw for 3,445 yards and twenty-three

Career Statistics

Yr	Team	GP	ATT	COM	YDS	COM %	Y/A	TD	INT
1989	DAL	11	293	155	1749	52.9	6.0	9	18
1990	DAL	15	399	226	2579	56.6	6.5	11	18
1991	DAL	12	363	237	2754	65.3	7.6	11	10
1992	DAL	16	473	302	3445	63.8	7.3	23	14
1993	DAL	14	392	271	3100	69.1	7.9	15	6
1994	DAL	14	361	233	2676	64.5	7.4	13	12
1995	DAL	16	432	280	3304	64.8	7.6	16	7
1996	DAL	15	465	296	3126	63.7	6.7	12	13
1997	DAL	16	518	292	3283	56.4	6.3	19	12
1998	DAL	11	315	187	2330	59.4	7.4	12	5
1999	DAL	14	442	263	2964	59.5	6.7	17	12
2000	DAL	11	262	156	1632	59.5	6.2	7	14
TOTAL		165	47	15	2898	32942	61.5	7.0	165	141

DAL: Dallas Cowboys.

touchdowns, leading the Cowboys to the NFC Championship. Facing off against the Buffalo Bills in the Super Bowl, Aikman led Dallas to a one-sided 52-17 victory.

The Cowboys got off to a shaky start in 1993, losing the first two games of the season. But the team bounced back to finish the year with a 12-4 record and making it into the playoffs once again. With a pass-completion rate of sixty-nine percent, Aikman led the Cowboys to the NFC East Division championship. Although Aikman was injured in the NFC Championship Game against the San Francisco 49ers, he was back in action for the Super Bowl, which featured a rematch with the Bills. Once again, Dallas prevailed, winning the NFL Championship with a 30-13 victory over Buffalo.

Dreams of 'Three-Peat' Dashed

The Cowboys' dreams of a Super Bowl "three-peat" were dashed in 1994. Although the team played once again to a 12-4 record, the Cowboys fell to the 49ers in the NFC Championship Game. Determined to return to the Super Bowl, the Cowboys battled their way to a 12-4 record again in 1995. After defeating the Green Bay Packers 38-27 in the NFC Championship Game, the Cowboys found themselves facing off against the Pittsburgh Steelers in Super Bowl XXX. Each team had won four previous Super Bowls, and the winner of Super Bowl XXX would become the winningest team in the history of the big game. Aikman became the first quarterback in NFL history to lead his team to three Super Bowl victories before the age of thirty as the Cowboys battled to a 27-17 win over the Steelers.

Injury and growing disenchantment with Cowboys coach Switzer took its toll on Aikman in 1996. He nevertheless turned in an impressive performance for the season with a pass-completion rate of 63.7 percent and total passing yardage of 3,126. The Cowboys made it into the playoffs but lost their second-round game to the Carolina Panthers, 26-17. Things got worse for the

Awards and Accomplishments

1982-83	Named to Oklahoma All-State High School Football Team
1987	Led UCLA Bruins to Aloha Bowl victory over Florida Gators
1988	Named quarterback on all college All-American teams
1993	Led Dallas Cowboys to Super Bowl victory over Buffalo Bills
1993	Named Super Bowl's Most Valuable Player
1994	Led Cowboys to Super Bowl victory over Bills
1996	Led Cowboys to Super Bowl victory over Pittsburgh Steelers
1997	Named NFL Man of the Year by True Value

Cowboys in 1997. The team ended the season with a losing 6-10 record, and Aikman's pass-completion rate fell to 56.4 percent. In 1998, Aikman missed five of the Cowboys' regular season games and threw for only 2,330 yards and five touchdowns. He was also successfully treated for skin cancer during the year. The Cowboys made it into the playoffs once again but lost their first-round game to the Arizona Cardinals. This scenario was repeated in 1999 when the Cowboys lost their first-round game in the playoffs to the Minnesota Vikings.

Retires from Pro Football

In April 2001, shortly after being waived by the Cowboys, Aikman announced his retirement from professional football. In the end, it was concern over a potentially disabling injury that forced him from the game. In his last twenty starts with the Cowboys, through the end of the 2000 season, Aikman had suffered four concussions. He told the AP: "I wanted to play. I just can't do that anymore. I think when all things are considered, it was the right thing for me and my family."

Aikman, who in April 2000 married former Cowboys public relations staffer Rhonda Worthey, lives with his wife in Plano, Texas, a suburb of Dallas. He's traded his helmet for a microphone and now works as a member of the FOX Sports broadcasting team. Former Cowboys coach Jimmy Johnson summed up Aikman's brilliant

Related Biography: Coach Jimmy Johnson

One of only five NFL head coaches to lead a team to back-to-back Super Bowl victories, Jimmy Johnson came to the Dallas Cowboys the same year as Aikman and exerted a profound influence on the future direction of the quarterback's career. It was Johnson and Cowboys owner Jerry Jones who rebuilt the Cowboys offensive line around the talent of Aikman, running back Emmitt Smith, and wide receiver Michael Irvin, who came to be known as "The Triplets."

Rarely has a coach had to assume a new post under more daunting circumstances than Johnson experienced in 1989, when Jones named his old college roommate to succeed the legendary Tom Landry as coach of the Cowboys. Fans, stunned and angry by the abrupt removal of Landry, initially gave Johnson the coldest reception imaginable. But Johnson proved himself, coaching the Cowboys to two consecutive Super Bowl victories in his four years at the helm of the team.

He was born James Craig Johnson in Port Arthur, Texas, on July 16, 1943. Although he was not particularly big or strong, Johnson proved himself a competitive scrapper, winning all-state football honors in high school and a football scholarship to the University of Arkansas. He began his coaching career as a defensive line coach at Louisiana Tech and worked at a number of high schools and colleges in the region before landing the head coaching job at Oklahoma State. During his four years at Oklahoma State, Johnson twice coached his team to bowl games. From Oklahoma State, Johnson moved to head coach at the University of Miami, which he guided to a phenomenal 52-9 record over four seasons.

career as well as anyone when he told the *Dallas Morning News*: "He's the greatest big-game quarterback you could find. It's like he trained his whole life to perform in the spotlight."

CONTACT INFORMATION

Address: Troy Aikman, c/o Fox Sports West, 10000 Santa Monica Blvd., Los Angeles, CA 90067-7002. Phone: (310)286-3800.

SELECTED WRITINGS BY AIKMAN:

(With Greg Brown) *Things Change,* Taylor Publishing, 1995.
Aikman: Mind, Body, and Soul, Benchmark Press, 1998.
(With Brian Jensen) *Where Have All Our Cowboys Gone?* Taylor Publishing, 2001.

FURTHER INFORMATION

Books

"Jimmy Johnson." *Newsmakers 1993,* Issue 4. Detroit: Gale Group, 1993.
"Troy Aikman." *Newsmakers 1994,* Issue 4. Detroit: Gale Research, 1994.
"Troy Aikman." *Sports Stars,* Series 1-4. U•X•L, 1994-1998.

Periodicals

Aron, Jaime. "Dallas QB Troy Aikman Retires." Associated Press (April 10, 2001).

Other

"Aikman, Troy K." HickokSports.com. http://www.hickoksports.com/biograph/aikmantr.shtml (December 21, 2002).
"Troy Aikman Biography." http://wv.essortment.com/troyaikmanbiog_rmho.htm (December 21, 2002).
"Troy Aikman, Quarterback." Pro-Football-Reference.com. http://www.football-reference.com/players/AikmTr00.htm (December 17, 2002).

Sketch by Don Amerman

Michelle Akers
1966-

American soccer player

Michelle Akers led the United States to an Olympic gold medal and two World Cup championships in women's soccer, and has drawn acclaim for her successful battle against chronic fatigue immune dysfunction syndrome. "If I hadn't had the illness, I would've thought soccer, trophies, World Cups and scoring goals would've been the best thing about my life," Akers said of her battles with her condition. "But it's not. I consider this illness a blessing. And, that has helped me get through each day and through the tough times when this illness is really an anchor, dragging me down day to day."

Akers, who scored 136 goals and is one of only four players, male or female, to score more than 100 goals in international competition. She sparked the United States to arguably its most shining moment in women's team sports-the 1999 World Cup. And while many consider the choreographed, made-for-television clip of **Brandi Chastain** ripping off her jersey as the signature moment of the American victory over China at the Rose Bowl, Akers embodied the U.S. grit during the 90 minutes of regulation before succumbing to fatigue in the 110-degree heat at Pasadena, California. "Want to know a secret? Brandi wasn't the only player who lost her shirt when we won the World Cup," Akers wrote on the *Sports Illustrated for Women* Web site in September, 1999. "I lost mine, too: Team doctors had to cut it off me after I got knocked out late in the game and staggered off the field. All I remember was lying in the fetal position in a Rose Bowl exam room while they snipped off my jersey and attached me to two IVs, an oxygen mask and an EKG machine."

"Girls Don't Play Football"

Akers, born in Santa Clara, California, grew up in Seattle. She had dreamed of being a wide receiver for the Na-

Chronology

1966	Born in Santa Clara, California
1986	Graduates from University of Central Florida
1990	Marries Roby Stahl, professional soccer player
1991	Begins struggles with health problem later diagnosed as CFIDS—chronic fatigue immune dysfunction syndrome (Epstein-Barr virus).
1994	Akers and Stahl file for divorce
1995	Injured as U.S. loses to eventual champion Norway in women's World Cup
2001	Lends name to high school girls tournament in Florida, the Michelle Akers Soccer Classic

tional Football League's Pittsburgh Steelers and, in fact, had practiced catching "Hail Mary" passes during recess. She cried when an elementary school teacher told her, "Michelle, girls can't play football." Soccer, however, was a more than adequate fallback and she became a three-time All-American at Seattle's Shorecrest High School. Akers credits religion, which aroused her interest when she was a high school sophomore, as turning around her life. While acknowledging her successes, she added, "Unfortunately, I had also become the epitome of the rebellious teenager. Skipping school. Dating older guys. Experimenting with drugs. Lying. You name it. I was putting my family, and everyone around me through the test of true love."

At the University of Central Florida, in Orlando, Akers was a four-time All-American, won the first Hermann Trophy as national player of the year and was offensive MVP in the 1987 NCAA Final Four. She was also Central Florida's Athlete of the Year in 1988-89.

Embarks on Pro Career

In 1989, Akers met pro soccer player Roby Stahl and they married within six months. Shortly after the honeymoon, she left for Sweden to play for the semi-pro club Tyreso, in the first of three stops with that team. In 1991 came the World Cup in China. Akers scored 10 goals in that tournament. "I fell into a fantasy world—a quick engagement, a house, a wedding, a World Cup. It all happened too fast," said Akers. People frequently mispronounced the hyphenated name—the lack of publicity women's sports received at the time didn't help. "Once a P.A. (public-address) announcer at a game introduced her as Michelle Aerosol," says longtime national squad teammate Julie Foudy. "Another time I was at a camp and someone said, 'Oh, you play with that girl … um … Michelle Anchor-Steam!' Yeah, right, Mich is a beer." However, Akers' life "turned upside down" shortly thereafter, Kelly Whiteside wrote on the Sports Illustrated-CNN Web site. The Epstein-Barr virus hit full force, producing chronic fatigue, and in 1994 she and Stahl filed for divorce. "But amid such traumatic events, one thing has remained constant: Akers's status as the best woman player in the world," Whiteside wrote.

Michelle Akers

Glory at the Rose Bowl

Akers sparked the Americans to a gold medal in the 1996 Olympics, and the United States team aimed for their second World Cup title in 1999. Much had changed in the American sports landscape since the previous Cup victory in China eight years earlier. Women's sports were now more in the spotlight, and the soccer talent pool was deeper. As more girls in elementary, middle and high school levels were opting for soccer as their outdoor sport of choice instead of field hockey and track, dividends were paid for the national soccer program. "Now there are players on the national team who, as they were growing up, dreamed of being like Mich," Whiteside wrote.

With visibility, however, came pressure to succeed, both on the field and off. "As they were constantly reminded, the pressure on the U.S. players was far more than just a desire to win the World Cup," the *Washington Post*'s William Gildea wrote. "This event was seen by some as a bellwether of women's sports in America. Could women's teams fill stadiums, draw advertisers and attract television viewers in a non-Olympic event?"

The team proved that they could, largely due to its high-drama victory over China in the title game at the Rose Bowl on a Saturday afternoon in July, before a crowd of more than 90,000 that included President Clinton and scores of celebrities, as well as a national television audience. The 5-foot-10 Akers, known largely for her scoring prowess—her late penalty kick had sealed a

Awards and Accomplishments

1985	Scores goal against Denmark in first game with U.S. national team
1985	ESPN Athlete of the Year
1988	Inaugural winner of Hermann Award for national women's soccer collegiate player of the year, while at Central Florida
1990	U.S. Olympic Committee Soccer Player of the Year
1990-91	Soccer Federation Female Player of the Year
1991	Scores winning goal late in championship game as U.S. wins inaugural women's World Cup, 2-1 over host China; Akers receives Silver Ball award as second-best player
1991	U.S. Olympic Committee Athlete of the Year
1991	First female American soccer player to sign shoe endorsement deal
1995	Named to U.S. Women's Cup all-tournament team
1996	Member of the gold medal-winning national team at Centennial Olympic Games, scoring pivotal goal in 2-1 semifinal victory over Norway
1996	Most Valuable Player in U.S. Women's Cup
1999	Leads U.S. to World Cup victory despite injury against China in title game in Pasadena, California
2000	Voted FIFA (Federation of International Football Associations) Women's Player of the Century in joint poll of FIFA committee and FIFA Magazine readers
2001	Receives Wilma Rudolph courage award

Where Is She Now?

Akers retired as a player shortly after the 1999 World Cup, opting out of the 2000 Olympics. She is pursuing a medical career and recently began a physician's assistant school in Florida following a stretch as a technical assistant to the former women's national team doctor. She had intended to play for the Orlando franchise of the newly formed women's pro league, the WUSA, in its inaugural 2001 season, but withdrew, citing a shoulder injury. The franchise moved from Orlando, Akers' hometown, to North Carolina.

Akers founded a sports ministry, Soccer Outreach International, in 1997. She belongs to the FIFA Soccer Committee, the NSCAA Women's Subcommittee, and the Sports Outreach America board and teaches at soccer camps. She also lent her name to a high school girls soccer tournament whose 20-year run was in danger after such corporate sponsors as Burger King and Target had withdrawn. It has been renamed the Michelle Akers Soccer Classic, held at Lake Mary High School, near Orlando.

In a commentary for *USA Today,* Akers, in advance of the 2003 World Cup, warns against the "flameout" that beset her defending champion team in the mid-1990s. "Coach April Heinrichs will need to take it down a notch or this could be a repeat of 1995," she wrote. "By the time the World Cup came in '95-the player roster pretty much remained the same from the '91 squad-overwhelming demands from team sponsorships, player endorsements, media and an outrageous game and travel schedule drained everyone.... There are danger signs of this happening at the 2003 Cup."

2-0 semifinal win over Brazil—was a defensive standout that day, neutralizing star Chinese forward Jin Yan. She had at least three collisions and banged into an advertising board outside the playing field. Neither teams scored in regulation time and Akers, one of the world's most durable athletes, could hardly play in the sweltering heat, estimated at 110 degrees Fahrenheit on the field that day. "Finally, as time expired in regulation, she could go no farther, collapsing in front of the goal she was defending," Steven Goff wrote in the *Washington Post.* "It took about five minutes for her to stand, braced by two trainers who kept her from falling over. As the team gathered before the start of overtime, Akers sat slumped on the bench, her head covered with a wet towel. As the match proceeded, few of the 90,185 in attendance noticed her being taken to the locker room for further examination."

Neither team scored during overtime play and penalty kicks would settle the championship. Rules prohibited Akers, a logical choice for a shootout, from re-entering the game. Chastain's goal following a pivotal save by the U.S. goalkeeper, **Briana Scurry**, gave the Americans the title as bedlam erupted in the Rose Bowl. "I'll never know how I made it to the podium for the trophy presentation, but I'm glad I did," Akers wrote in *Sports Illustrated for Women.* "Standing there with the team was such an intense moment, and so was the scene afterward when I wobbled off the stage and the crowd started chanting 'Akers! Akers! Akers!'" Coach Tony DiCicco had this to say about Akers, "Michelle Akers inspires me and I know she does the same for everybody on the U.S. team."

The entire tournament had worn on Akers. "The grueling schedule and physical battering of the tournament tested her growing faith," author Judith A. Nelson wrote. "Michelle required two liters of intravenous fluid fol-

lowing each game. Her right knee troubled her; and, in a freak accident, a fan grabbed her hand and yanked her shoulder out of the socket." Too drained to join her teammates in a whirlwind publicity tour, Akers relaxed on a Santa Monica beach with a friend, former teammate Amanda Cronwell the following day. The salt water soothed Akers, but the dining out provided no reprieve. Fans besieged her in a Mexican restaurant.

Mainstream Heroes

Despite her celebrity status, Akers still maintains a person-next-door persona. *Sports Illustrated* columnist Rick Reilly noted that the winter before the 1999 World Cup, a youngster knocked on the door of Akers' home outside Orlando, Florida and said, "Can you come out and kick the ball with us?" Now, if this were the door of most American male professional athletes, the kid would've been: 1) escorted away by security, 2) rolled away by paramedics or 3) simply trying to make contact with her biological father," Reilly explained further. "What did Akers do? She went out and kicked with her, but only after bringing out an armful of pictures, books and pins. Ain't it great? Ten-year-old girls all over the country are taking down their Backstreet Boys posters and putting up the Goal-Goal Girls."

Said Akers, who rejoined her parents in Seattle shortly after the World Cup and worked at a nearby soccer camp: "Offers rolled in: Book proposals, movie deals, speaking engagements, endorsements. One of my biggest tasks will be to decide which ones I have the energy, and the desire, to do." During the middle of the World Cup Akers summed her determination: "You get to the point where you get so beat up that another ding is not going to stop you. I've learned how to kind of just put it behind me and focus on the job at hand."

SELECTED WRITINGS BY AKERS:

Akers, Michelle et. al. *Standing Fast: Battles of a Champion,* Singapore: JTC Sports, 1997.

Akers, Michelle and Judith A. Nelson. *Face to Face with Michelle Akers,* Integrated Resources, 1998.

Akers, Michelle and Greg Lewis. *The Game and the Glory: An Autobiography,* Grand Rapids: Zondervan, 2000.

FURTHER INFORMATION

Other

Akers, Michelle. "Cup Gold No Sure Thing for U.S. Women." *USA Today,* http://www.usatoday.com/sports/soccer (November 25, 2002).

Akers, Michelle. "Still Crazy after the World Cup." USA Women's World Cup '99 Online, http://www.womensoccer.com/wwcup99 (December 17, 2002).

Akers, Michelle. "A Welcome Timeout." *Sports Illustrated for Women,* http://sportsillustrated.cnn.com/siforwomen/ (September 13, 1999).

Bamberger, Michael. "Women of Destiny: World Cup Champs:" *CNN-Sports Illustrated,* http://sports illustrated.cnn.com/features/1999/sportsman (December 20, 1999).

Gildea, William. "U.S. Effort Nets Second World Cup Title." *Washington Post,* http://www.washingtonpost.com/wp-srv/sports/soccer/longterm/worldcup99/articles/cup11.htm (July 11, 1999).

Goff, Steven. "Akers's Gritty Play Is Inspirational to U.S. Squad." *Washington Post,* http://www.washingtonpost.com/wp-srv/sports/soccer/longterm/worldcup99/articles/cupside11.htm (July 11, 1999).

Langdon, Jerry. "Akers, Scurry Have Been Dominant Forces, but They Need Help." Gannett News Service, http://www.soccertimes.com/langdon (July 6, 1999).

"Michelle Akers: Just The Basics." Elaine's Team USA Webpage, http://www.geocities.com/teamusasoccer/akers.html (December 17, 2002).

Nelson, Judith A. "Michelle's Higher Goal: A World Cup and Olympic Gold Medal are only the beginning for a determined Michelle Akers." *Pentacostal Evangel,* http://pentecostalevangel.ag.org/pentecostal-evangel/articles/Olympics/Akers.cfm#author (March-April, 2000).

People Just Like Us: Michelle Akers, Olympic Soccer, http://www.peoplejustlikeus.org/Sports/Michelle_Akers.html (December 23, 2002).

Reilly, Rick. "The Goal-Goal Girls!" CNN-Sports Illustrated, http://sportsillustrated.cnn.com/inside_game/magazine/lifeofreilly/1999/0705 (July 6, 1999).

Schorr, Andrew. "Celebrity Pathfinder: Michelle Akers." http://www.healthtalk.com/celeb/makers/01.html (December 17, 2002).

Women's Soccer World, http://womensoccer.com/biogs/akers.html, Michelle Akers biography (December 17, 2002).

Whiteside, Kelly. "World Beater: Michelle Akers Is Ready to Lead the U.S. to Another Title." *CNN-Sports Illustrated,* http://sportsillustrated.cnn.com/soccer/world/1999/womens_worldcup/news/1999/02/12 (February 12, 1999).

Sketch by Paul Burton

Marv Albert
1941-

American sportscaster

Marv Albert was well respected in the sports realm until the skeletons in his closet came tumbling out in 1997. Since then it has been a long road for him to pick himself up and dust himself off. Albert is slowly working his way back into the world of sportscasting, but he will never be like he was before his fall from glory. He was known for his passion for sports and how this enthusiasm came through on his broadcasts. Albert was also known for his hectic schedule, covering any game he could possible make it to. Apparently his chaotic career took a toll on his personal life.

Early Broadcasts

Albert started early in his pursuit of a career in broadcasting, with his first play by plays being about the performances of his hamsters. In the third grade, when assigned to write an essay about what he would like to be when he grew up, he wrote about his aspirations to become a broadcaster. Albert's teacher, who commented that being a broadcaster was a lofty ambition, did not appreciate that enthusiasm. Years later the teacher wrote a note to Albert congratulating him on proving her wrong.

Albert knew what he wanted and went for his goals with a vengeance. He was able to secure a position as the New York Dodger's office boy at the age of about fifteen. With that position Albert was able to use the press box whenever there was a game. He would cart his reel to reel on the subway to the ballpark each game and would do his own announcing of the games. Marv also earned an opportunity to work with the infamous **Howard Cosell**.

Albert's first big break was in 1963. He worked along side announcer Marty Glickman, doing the statistics for him. Albert would drive Glickman crazy because he would emulate everything he did, writes Albert in his book *I'd Love to But I Have a Game.* One night Glickman was unable to make it to the game due to a snow-

Marv Albert

Chronology

1941	Born in Brooklyn, New York
1950	Writes essay explaining how he would become a broadcaster when he grows up
1958	Begins working as the Brooklyn Dodger's office boy
1961	Becomes an announcer for WOLF radio in Syracuse, New York
1963	Announces his first Knicks game
1964	Earns Bachelor of Arts degree from New York University
1965	Marries Benita Caress
1967	Becomes the Knicks regular announcer
1967	Starts position as Sports Director for WHN Radio New York, New York
1975	Publishes his first book on sports trivia
1977	Signs to broadcast games with NBC
1979	Writes his second book on broadcasting
1993	Publishes an autobiography
1994	Writes a book about Knicks Championship season
1997	Charged with assault and battery by Vanessa Perhach
1997	Resigns from Madison Square Garden Network after being fired from NBC
1998	Rehired by Madison Square Garden Network and Turner
1998	Marries Heather Faulkner
1999	Rehired by NBC

storm, and that was when Albert was able to do his first broadcast for the Knicks. Two years later he became the regular play-by-play announcer.

Sportscaster Extraordinaire

"Marv's career took off…thanks to his distinctive style and Herculean work ethic, he was soon a household name, at least in the New York metropolitan area," said Steve Wulfe for *Sports Illustrated*. In 1977 he was recruited by NBC to broadcast and shortly after this he was called on to broadcast all kinds of national sports programs. Albert also developed a reputation as being the fill in for anyone who wouldn't show up for *The David Letterman Show*. David would call up Albert and ask him to put together some of his sports bloopers.

Skeletons in the Closet

Albert's days in the limelight were numbered as a dark cloud would overshadow his accomplishments. In 1997 Vanessa Perhach accused him of assault and battery. Albert vehemently denied the charges. Formal charges of assault and battery were entered against Albert. His defense was that this woman was upset because he was attempting to break off his ten-year affair with her. Many of Albert's fetishes, such as wearing women's lingerie, came out at the trial.

Apparently Perhach had pursued similar accusations with other men who attempted to break up with her as well, but that information was not allowed in the trial.

Albert wanted to save face before any more skeletons came tumbling out of his closet. On September 25, 1997 he entered a plea bargain of guilty to the misdemeanor of assault and battery. He never had to serve time in jail, but was court ordered to attend therapy to ensure he addressed the serious sexual issues he had.

Leaving it Behind

Albert was fired from NBC the day of his guilty plea. The following day he tendered his resignation from Madison Square Gardens Network. Albert's life was in total upheaval. Everything he had worked so hard for since he was a boy seemed to have slipped out of his hands, never to be retrieved again. Not only that but Albert had to endure the shame and humiliation, as well as the numerous jibes that were being taken at him right and left. "Marv Albert last week was booted out of the broadcast booth and into his worse nightmare…Albert was chewed up and spit out, which, some would say, means justice prevailed," reported Gerry Callahan for *Sports Illustrated*. Although most other reporters were not quite as harsh as Callahan, all had a hay day with the particulars of the case.

It was Albert's humble attitude and obvious remorse for his actions that brought him back to the Madison Square Garden company. In an interview with David Kindred for the *Sporting News,* MSG president Dave Checketts stated, "We think of ourselves as a family, and Marv is a member of the family. We told him at the start of this, if he did his part, we'd take him back." It was this opportunity that allowed Marv to slowly rebuild the life he had worked so hard to create for himself. Chris Bellard wrote in *Sports Illustrated:* "That his comeback has been so complete…is a testament not only to his skill as an announcer but also to the respect he has earned in more than 35 years in the industry."

SELECTED WRITINGS BY ALBERT:

Marv Albert's Sports Quiz Book. Price Stern Sloan Publishing, 1975.

(With Hal Bock Albert) *Yesss:Marv Albert on Sportscasting.* New American Library, 1979.

(With Rick Reilly) *I'd Love to But I Have a Game: 27 Years Without a Life.* New York, NY: Doubleday, 1993.

(With Phil Berger) *Miracle on 33rd Street: The New York Knickerbocker's Championship Season, 1969-70.* McGraw/Hill/Contemporary Books, 2001.

FURTHER INFORMATION

Books

"Marv Albert." *Newsmakers 1994.* Issue 4. Farmington Hills, MI: The Gale Group. Gale Research, 1994.

"Marv Albert." *St. James Encyclopedia of Popular Culture.* 5 vols. St. James Press, 2000.

Periodicals

"Albert Receives a 12-Month Suspended Sentence." Court TV Online. http://www.courttv.com/casefiles/marv/marvalbert.html. (January 3, 2003).

Ballard, Chris. "Yesss! He's Back." *Sports Illustrated.* (March 26, 2001):28.

Callahan, Gerry. "The Dirt Under the Rug." *Sports Illustrated,* (October 6, 1997): 128.

Kindred, David. "A Second Chance, Absent of Joy." *Sporting News,* (July 27, 1998): 63.

"Marv Albert Biography." *Washington Post,* (September 25, 1997).

Neill, Michael. "What, Me Guilty?." *People Weekly,* (December 1, 1997): 197.

"Personal foul? A Virginia Woman Charges NBC Basketball Announcer Marv Albert with Sexual Assault." *People Weekly,* (June 2, 1997): 94.

Reilly, Rick. "One Step Out of the Doghouse." *Sports Illustrated,* (July 27, 1998): 94.

Schneider, Michael. "Albert Returns to Lead NBA on NBC." *Variety,* (December 20, 1999): 24.

Wulf, Steve. "Bonus Piece: As Harry Caray Often Says, 'it might be....it could be....'" *Sports Illustrated,* (November 2, 1992): 74.

Wulf, Steve. "Oh, No! For the Yes Man." *Time,* (October 6, 1997): 44.

Sketch by Barbra J Smerz

Tenley Albright
1935-

American figure skater

A pioneer on and off the ice, Tenley Albright was the first American woman to win a gold medal in ladies singles figure skating at the Olympics and the first American woman to win a world championship. Albright's strengths were her figures, and graceful free skates. She was as technically proficient as women figure skaters were in her day, and her success marked the beginning of America's powerful presence in figure skating. After her skating career ended, Albright attended Harvard Medical School and became a surgeon.

Albright was born on July 18, 1935, in Newton Center, Massachusetts, the only daughter of Hollis and Elin Albright. Albright's father was a surgeon, and the family was one of privilege. Her father was a lover of sports, and encouraged his daughter. Albright began skating when she was eight or nine years old on a backyard skating rink her father created for her because of her interest in skating.

Began Skating

Albright later told Hali Helfgott of *Sports Illustrated,* "What attracted me to skating was that I wanted to fly. I broke umbrellas trying to jump off the garage roof when I was little." Within a year of pond skating, she moved to the Skate Club of Boston for lessons. Albright had not planned to skate seriously, but Maribel Vinson Owen, who had won U.S. championships in the late 1920s and early 1930s, noticed her abilities. Owen later coached Albright.

One initial problem for Albright was her disinterest in compulsory figures, which were certain moves, such as figure eights, created on the ice. Albright found them boring, but later became skilled at them. She preferred the free skate, a program set to music. Skating was not her only talent. She was also very academically talented, attending the Winsor School in Boston, and the Manter Hall School in Cambridge, Massachusetts.

Developed Polio

When Albright was 11 years old, she developed non-parlytic polio (also known as poliomyelitis or infantile paralysis), which put her in the hospital for three weeks. She could not use her leg, back, or neck. Many people suffering from the viral disease became paralyzed because it attacked motor nerve tissues. Albright's doctors urged her to begin skating soon after her illness was over because it would help work her back muscles, which had been weakened by the illness. Albright soon began taking skating very seriously.

Tenley Albright

Within a few months of recovering from her illness, Albright won the under 12 category at the Eastern Regional Championship. Albright won a number of titles over the next few years. She was the National Ladies Novice Singles Championship title winner in 1949, and then the National Junior Champion in 1950. In 1951, she won the U.S. Ladies Senior Eastern Championship and finished second at the U.S. Championship behind Sonya Klopfer.

While Albright was serious about skating—to the point that she would spend summers practicing at locations with indoor rinks —academics remained important to her as well. She wanted to be a surgeon like her father, and would study between practice sessions and skates, even at competitions. Her hard work would pay off when she succeeded in both areas of her life.

Won First U.S. Women's Title

In 1952, when she was 16, Albright won her first U.S. women's singles championship. Albright would repeat as U.S. singles champion every year through 1956. This victory led to Albright qualifying to represent the United States at the Winter Olympics in Oslo, Norway. Though she was not expected to win a medal, she ended up winning a silver medal in women's singles figure skating. Jeanette Altwegg from England won the gold medal. This was the first time an American woman had won a medal in figure skating since Beatrix Loughran in

1924. An injury prevented Albright from going to the World Championship that year.

Albright did even better in 1953, when she became the first triple crown winner. In addition to the U.S. title in women's singles figure skating, she also won the North American Championship and the World Championship. This was also the first time an American had won the World Championship. Despite her success, Albright had a reserved personality and her coaches often had to remind her to smile.

Entered Radcliffe College

To achieve her goal of being a surgeon, Albright entered Radcliffe College in the fall of 1953. Balancing school and skating was difficult. She practiced figure skating daily from four to six o'clock in the morning before classes and related studies. Albright also studied ballet during the day to supplement her skating.

Albright continued to compete internationally while attending school, although she did not match her 1953 success. In 1954, she could not defend her title at the World Championship. During her free skate Albright fell and came away with only second to West German Gundi Busch.

To prepare for the 1956 Olympics, Albright took a leave of absence from Radcliffe in the fall term of 1955. She had already attended summer term so she could keep up with her class. She garnered her second triple crown in 1955, winning the World, U.S. and North American Championships.

Won Gold Medal at Olympics

Because of her stature in world figure skating, Albright was a favorite going into the 1956 Winter Olympics in Cortina, Italy. In the days before the competition, Albright suffered an injury that nearly put an end to her chances at a medal. While practicing, her skate blade hit a groove and she fell, her left skate blade slicing her right ankle to the bone, slashing a vein. The incident hospitalized Albright, and was front page news in Boston.

Awards and Accomplishments

1949	Won Ladies Novice Championship
1950	Won Ladies Junior Championship
1951	Won Eastern Senior Ladies Championship; finished second at the U.S. Championship
1952	Won silver medal at Winter Olympics in Oslo, Norway
1952, 1956	Won U.S. Championship
1952-56	Won U.S. women's singles title
1953, 1955	Won North American Championship
1953, 1955	Won World Championship
1954, 1956	Placed second at World Championship
1956	Won gold medal at Winter Olympics in Cortina, Italy
1974	Inducted into the Ice Skating Hall of Fame
1975	Received honorary degree of science from Russell Sage College
1976	Inducted into the U.S. Figure Skating Hall of Fame; awarded Golden Plate Award by the American Academy of Achievement
1983	Inducted into the International Women's Sports Hall of Fame
1988	Inducted into the Olympic Hall of Fame
1999	Inducted into the Scholar-Athlete Hall of Fame

Albright's father came to Italy and took charge of his daughter's medical care. Although in pain and needing to wear a bandage outside of the competition, Albright resumed practicing. The day before the competition, Albright was still unable to do many of her jumps; but she pulled it together and won the gold medal for her graceful free skate with ten of eleven judges giving her first place.

Albright landed all of her jumps, including her single axel (which was the most difficult jump women were expected to complete at the time). She defeated 21 other competitors, including 16 year-old Carol Heiss Jenkins, a fellow American. Of her performance, she told Dick Heller of the *Washington Times,* "I was skating to 'The Bacarolle' from 'Tales of Hoffman.' Suddenly, the audience began to sing the words, and their voices just thrilled me. Chills were going up and down my spine. I forgot about the injury and just skated."

Albright followed up her Olympic gold with another spectacular performance, finishing second a short time later at the World Championship in Garmisch-Partenkirchen, Germany. Heiss Jenkins, who finished second at the Olympics, finished first at the World Championship. Albright went on to defeat Jenkins at the U.S. championship.

Retired from Competitive Figure Skating

In January 1957, Albright retired from competitive figure skating. Although she had an offer to join the Ice Capades, the leading professional ice show of the day that many figure skaters of her stature joined when they retired, she continued with her education instead. She graduated from Radcliffe in 1957 and then entered Harvard Medical School. Albright was never paid to skate.

Years after her victory, Albright's importance as a figure skater remained. Ten years later, Barbara La Fontaine remembered in *Sports Illustrated,* "Tenley re-

Where Is She Now?

Albright completed her medical training at Harvard Medical School, graduating in 1961. While she still skated for her own enjoyment, her focus for many years was on her surgical career. She began by joining her father's practice and was also a general surgeon at Boston's Deaconess Hospital. Albright's skating career was definitely linked to her medical career. She told Gary Klein of the *Los Angeles Times,* "When I was competing, we were outdoors. So despite all my preparation, I never knew whether I would be skating in a snowstorm or whether it would be raining or windy. I've learned to expect the unexpected. You don't always know what you'll find when you open a patient, and you have to be prepared."

Later in her medical career, Albright had a solo practice, in affiliation with New England Baptist Hospital. She also developed an interest in research, working at the Harvard Medical School and Massachusetts Institute of Technology's Whitehead Institute studying how to prevent and detect diseases early in their progression, researching drug delivery systems, and fundraising for human-genome research. She also founded Sports Medicine Resource in Brookline, Massachusetts.

Sports medicine was not her only link to skating. She skated for charity performances like the United States Figure Skating Memorial Fund, and taught underprivileged children how to skate. In 1976, she was the first woman named to the U.S. Olympic Committee and served as chief physician for the U.S. Winter Olympic team. Albright also served on the International Olympic Committee.

Albright married Tudor Gardiner in 1962, and had three daughters: Lilla, Elin, and Elee Emma. She divorced, and later married Gerald Blakeley, her second husband.

mains in the minds of many people our most accomplished and impressive champion. A well-bred young lady, she was nevertheless, a real competitor, as steely as she was gracious. Her style was distinguished, a technical proficiency rounded by a dancer's training and sensitivity and marked by taste and intellect."

CONTACT INFORMATION

Address: 25 Shattuck St., #316, Boston, MA 02115-6092. Phone: 617-247-8202.

FURTHER INFORMATION

Books

Hickok, Ralph. *A Who's Who of Sports Champions: Their Stories and Records.* Boston: Houghton Mifflin Company, 1995.

Johnson, Anne Janette. *Great Women in Sports.* Detroit: Visible Ink Press, 1996.

Layden, Joe. *Women in Sports: The Complete Book on the World's Greatest Female Athletes.* Santa Monica, CA: General Publishing Group, 1997.

Malone, John. *The Encyclopedia of Figure Skating.* New York: Facts on File, Inc., 1998.

Porter, David L., editor. *Biographical Dictionary of American Sports: Basketball and Other Indoor Sports.* New York: Greenwood Press, 1989.

Sherrow, Victoria. *Encyclopedia of Women and Sports.* Santa Barbara,CA: ABC-CLIO, 1996.

Woolum, Janet. *Outstanding Women Athletes: Who They Are and How they Influenced Sports in America.* Phoenix: Oryx Press, 1998.

Periodicals

"Formula for Titles." *Newsweek* (April 6, 1953): 76.

Helfgott, Hali. "Catching Up With … Tenley Albright, Figure Skater January 30, 1956." *Sports Illustrated* (January 30, 1956): 16.

Heller, Dick. "Albright Overcame Polio, Ankle Injury to Win Gold in Skating." *Washington Times* (February 11, 2002): C7.

Klein, Gary. "Most of Her Breaks Have Been Good Ones." *Los Angeles Times* (February 21, 2002): U7.

La Fontaine, Barbara. "There is a Doctor on the Ice." *Sports Illustrated* (February 8, 1965): 28.

Matson, Barbara. "Albright Was First, Foremost." *Boston Globe* (September 25, 1999): F7.

Rosen, Karen, and Joe Drape. "Notebook: '56 Skater Golden Despite Late Injury." *Atlanta Journal and Constitution* (January 16, 1994): E14.

Other

"Athlete Profile: Tenley Albright." U.S. Olympic Team. http://www.usolympicteam.com/athlete_profiles/t_albright.html (January 13, 2003).

Sketch by A. Petruso

Grover Cleveland Alexander

Grover Cleveland Alexander
1887-1950

American baseball player

Grover Cleveland Alexander serves as an icon for his generation of professional baseball players. While perhaps not the model or disciplined athlete—in fact, by most accounts, he was far from that—Alexander was a product of the times in which he lived. His adult years spanned two World Wars, the first, in which he served as an army sergeant in France. He lived through Prohibition, two marriages and divorces from the same woman, the Great Depression, and ill health due to epilepsy, alcoholism, and in later life, cancer. He was described as a soft-spoken yet cantankerous man who did not appreciate having rules dictated to him. Above all, Alexander was a phenomenal pitcher with an attitude, who, despite personal demons that haunted him throughout most of his adult life, established major-league records, many of which still stand today. He was a personality on and off the field, and until age, poor health, and his way of living took their toll, Alexander was a force to be reckoned with.

Alexander was born on February 26, 1887, in Elba, Nebraska, a rural community just outside of St. Paul, Nebraska. He was the youngest of thirteen children (twelve boys and one girl). According to Jack Kavanagh, author of *Ol' Pete: The Grover Cleveland Alexander Story,* the famous pitcher's father, William, attributed his son's skill with deadly curveballs to "his great ability as a corn husker," bragging that "Dode," as Alexander was known at home, husked as many as 1,300 bushels of corn in thirteen days. It was from such ambitious corn-husking that Alexander developed his ability to pitch effortlessly and tirelessly, suggested Mr. Alexander.

Baseball, however, was mostly an interesting past time for Alexander until 1909. He intended to follow his parents' dream for him to attend law school like his namesake, the former president. Although Alexander worked for a time as a telephone lineman for the Howard Telephone Company, he managed to play on local teams for the fee of five silver dollars. He then began playing baseball for independent clubs nearby. His abilities were quickly noted, and he signed his first contract in 1909 with the Galesburg Boosters, in Central City, Nebraska. Alexander demonstrated his talent by pitching a no-hitter against Pekin and a 1-0 shutout that first year. He made $50 a month—not a bad salary for a former telephone lineman. Apparently, however, it was not a much safer vocation; Alexander received a nearly fatal baseball beaning to the head that left him unconscious for two days. Alexander recovered from the injury, but he suffered dou-

Grover Cleveland Alexander

ble vision for many months afterwards, making him a liability as a pitcher. Galesburg soon sold the afflicted player to the Indianapolis Indians, but this relationship ended almost before it began when the vision-challenged pitcher accidentally broke three of the manager's ribs with his first pitch. He then was sold to the Syracuse Chiefs, but by the time the season began, Alexander's vision was clear. In that 1910 season, Alexander had twenty-nine wins along with fifteen shutouts for the Chiefs.

Alexander was twenty-four when the Philadelphia club bought his contract in 1911. The freshman pitcher from rural Nebraska wasted no time wowing his teammates, his opponents, or his fans. His first season, Alexander set a major-league record. His twenty-eight wins set a record for a rookie pitcher, a record that stood untouched for sixty years.

Alexander continued to play well for Philadelphia, and over the next six years pitched a total of 329 games, of which 219 were complete games. Baseball is a business, however, and team owner William Baker traded both Alexander and his personal catcher and close friend, "Reindeer" Bill Killefer, for $55,000—this, after Alexander had led the Phillies to their first pennant and World Series in 1915. Baker admitted that the trade was purely a business transaction rather than a strategic move. Killefer and Alexander made their new home in the windy city, playing for the Chicago Cubs in the 1918 season. In June of that year, Alexander married Aimee Arrant.

Fate forced Alexander to take a slight detour from his career that same year. Alexander was drafted into the Army after only playing three games for the Cubs. He served in France as a sergeant for the 342nd Artillery. According to Kavanagh, the shelling Alexander was exposed to during his service and which caused Alexander to lose his hearing in one ear was possibly the trigger of his epilepsy, which showed its first symptoms shortly thereafter. Another theory suggested that it was the serious head injury Alexander incurred early in his career that was to blame. Whatever the cause, Alexander's life was forever changed. After Alexander's death, his ex-wife Aimee defended Alexander's seemingly wild behavior while promoting *The Winning Team,* a film based on Alexander's life, starring Ronald Reagan and Doris Day.

Mrs. Alexander attributed the pitcher's wild reputation to a misunderstanding of her former husband's physical illnesses, which included "spells of epilepsy" and shell shock (now known as Post-Traumatic Stress Disorder). Claimed the widow, Alexander's drinking "was just an outlet for his physical miseries." In fairness,

Career Statistics

Yr	Team	W	L	ERA	IP	H	R	ER	BB	SO	SV	SHO
1911	PHI	28	13	2.57	367.0	385	133	105	129	227	3	7
1912	PHI	19	17	2.81	310.1	289	133	97	105	195	3	3
1913	PHI	22	8	2.79	306.1	288	106	95	75	159	2	9
1914	PHI	27	15	2.38	355.0	327	133	94	76	214	1	6
1915	PHI	31	10	1.22	376.1	253	86	51	64	241	3	12
1916	PHI	33	12	1.55	389.0	323	90	67	50	167	3	16
1917	PHI	30	13	1.83	388.0	366	107	79	56	200	0	8
1918	CHI	2	1	1.73	26.0	19	7	5	3	15	0	0
1919	CHI	16	11	1.72	235.0	180	51	45	38	121	1	9
1920	CHI	27	14	1.91	363.1	335	96	77	69	173	5	7
1921	CHI	15	13	3.39	252.0	286	110	95	33	77	1	3
1922	CHI	16	13	3.63	245.2	283	111	99	34	48	1	1
1923	CHI	22	12	3.19	305.0	308	128	108	30	72	2	3
1924	CHI	12	5	3.03	169.1	183	82	57	25	33	0	0
1925	CHI	15	11	3.39	236.0	270	106	89	29	63	0	1
1926	CHI	3	3	3.46	52.0	55	26	20	7	12	0	0
1926	STL	9	7	2.91	148.1	136	57	48	24	35	2	2
1927	STL	21	10	2.52	268.0	261	94	75	38	48	3	2
1928	STL	16	9	3.36	243.2	262	107	91	37	59	2	1
1929	STL	9	8	3.89	132.0	149	65	57	23	33	0	0
1930	PHI	0	3	9.14	21.2	40	24	22	6	6	0	0
TOTAL		373	208	2.56	5190	4868	1852	1476	951	2198	32	90

CHI: Chicago Cubs; PHI: Philadelphia Phillies; STL: St. Louis Cardinals.

Alexander did struggle with epilepsy, and due to the lack of effective drugs of those days, the disease was nearly impossible to control. There were a few tricks to staving off seizures, however. As Kavanagh put it, "Alexander was subject to seizures during a ballgame as well as away from the field. He discovered that by sipping ammonia from a small bottle, he could forestall a pending attack." In *Alexander the Great: The Story of Grover Cleveland Alexander,* Jerry E. Clark and Martha E. Webb wrote that Alexander also used alcohol in an attempt to control his disease: "To compensate for the seizures, he drank alcohol to excess, and this itself became a debilitating weakness."

Alexander was discharged in 1919, and he returned to Chicago to pick up from where he'd left off. Alexander's year away from the sport that he loved and his new physical challenges seemed to have little effect on the pitcher's skill, and he continued to devastate the hitters who faced him. Alexander's first season back was a warm-up, and he pitched twenty complete games out of thirty games played, and had sixteen wins with eleven losses.

By 1921, it was fairly common knowledge that Alexander had a serious drinking problem. Alexander's drinking began to affect his performance on the field, and it exacerbated his already rebellious and moody nature. Still, Alexander played better than most, and he continued to play for Chicago until his addiction and ill health became troublesome.

Alexander was admitted into a sanitarium for dual treatment of the effects of alcoholism and epilepsy after the season in 1925. He would be admitted again in 1929

as his career and personal life began to fall apart, and from this, he would not recover as well. The 1926 season rolled around, and the club's new manager, Joe McCarthy, "had strict rules against the consumption of alcohol on the team," wrote Clark and Webb. Alexander's drinking was a problem. Alexander's attitude, his consistent violation of training rules, and his addiction to alcohol overrode the pitcher's asset to the team, and the choice became clear for McCarthy. Alexander remained with the Cubs until mid-season, 1926. Ironically, the fans, who adored the troubled pitcher, presented Alexander with a car just prior to Alexander's final game with Chicago. He then was waived to the St. Louis Cardinals.

Any baseball fan familiar with the important games of 1926 has to wonder if Chicago regretted its decision. Alexander played extremely well for the Cardinals for the first two seasons. Perhaps the shock of being traded was just what he needed. The Cardinals were the third major-league team Alexander played for, but they would not be the last team. Although Alexander only played a little over three seasons with the Cardinals, it is the team with which his name will always be most associated. On Oct. 10, in the seventh inning of the seventh and deciding game of the 1926 World Series, a great pitcher sometimes dubbed "Old Pete" or "Alex the Great" became a legendary, baseball folk-hero. Despite any past or future feats Alexander achieved or would achieve, it was that day that defined him in the history books and baseball stories.

The game itself had all the quality ingredients for myth making. The opposing team was the New York

---

Related Biography: Catcher "Reindeer" Bill Killefer

No movie captured his life story. He was never inducted into the Hall of Fame. But, "Reindeer" Bill Killefer was an integral key to Alexander's success and was a good friend to the famous pitcher on and off the field.

William Killefer was born the same year as Alexander, 1887, in Bloomingdale, Michigan. Soon after he began his major league career (1909 with the Browns), he was dubbed Reindeer because of his amazing running speed. The match up with Alexander was one of the most successful battery matches there ever was; Killefer was well tuned to Alexander's every move and responded accordingly.

Killefer was a master at mediation and at getting along well with others. Killefer also was a team player, and he remained loyal to the talented men he called his friends such as Rogers Hornsby and Alexander. Killefer's teammates were also loyal to him, and he was known as a player's manager. While Killefer looked out for the good of the team, he knew that the team's success depended on the wellbeing of its individual players as well as its staff. He more likely was remembered for his coaching and management than for his playing.

He joined the Phils in 1911, where he was first paired up with Alexander in what would become a legendary battery. Killefer also was a playing manager for the Cubs, from 1921-1925, and for the Browns, from 1930-1933. According to Killefer's obituary in the *New York Times*, July 3, 1960, Killefer's career spanned more than forty-five years, when he finally retired in 1955 after scouting for Cleveland. He died in Elsmere, Delaware, on July 2, 1960, at the age of 72.

The Winning Team

Two years following Grover Cleveland Alexander's death, Warner Brothers released *The Winning Team,* a movie portrayal of Alexander's personal and professional tragedies and triumphs. Directed by Lewis Seiler, the film starred Ronald Reagan and Doris Day, and also featured several major-league baseball players of the 1950s such as "Peanuts" Lowrey, Jerry Priddy, and George Metkovich.

Hollywood took certain liberties, rearranging some chronological events and romanticizing the great pitcher's life. It did, however, emphasize the troubled and passionate relationship between Alexander and Aimee, and while perhaps downplaying the seriousness of Alexander's drinking, the movie shed more light on the pitcher's other health problems that resulted from his experiences in World War I and from his uncontrollable epilepsy. Because of the film's removal from close adherence to the facts, it received sharp criticism.

Yankees, who had already lost to the Cardinals the previous day, with Alexander pitching. The Yankees featured players who were already legendary themselves, such as **Lou Gehrig** and **Babe Ruth**, and neither team was giving an inch. This was, after all, the deciding game. The score was 3-2, with the Cardinals leading. The bases were loaded, and power-hitter Tony Lazzeri was up next. At this point, Alexander was roused from his nap in the bullpen and told to warm up; he was coming in as a relief pitcher. Alexander struck out Lazzeri in four pitches, and then he held the Yankees scoreless for the rest of the game, thus winning the Series for the Cardinals. It was the Cardinals' first World Championship.

Alexander had one more good season with the Cardinals. The following season was perhaps the pinnacle of achievement for Alexander. He received a raise to $17,500, his top salary. Also in 1927, Alexander's twenty-first win made him the second player in National League history to win twenty games for three different teams. This would not occur again until 1978, when **Gaylord Perry** would be named the third. Ironically, while setting a record, the 1927 season would also mark the end of an era for Alexander, as he never topped the twenty-win mark again.

The following season in 1928, Alexander had only sixteen wins and played his final World Series. The year 1929 was the beginning of the end for Alexander professionally and personally. It was this year that he and Aimee first divorced, and drinking became increasingly problematic. Alexander was traded back to the Phillies, but his glory days were clearly over. For the first time in the pitcher's career, he had more losses than wins.

Alexander officially was released by the club on June 3, 1930, bringing his major-league career to a sad end.

In 1938, Alexander was notified by the Baseball Writers Association of America (BBWAA) that he'd been selected for the Baseball Hall of Fame in Cooperstown, New York. According to Charles C. Alexander, author of *Breaking the Slump: Baseball in the Depression Era,* when Alexander was informed that he been selected, he was quoted as saying, "The Hall of Fame is fine, but it doesn't mean bread and butter. It's only your picture on the wall."

The Baseball Hall of Fame is a sign of outstanding achievement in a player's career and is taken a bit more seriously by today's members than by its earlier inductees. Sports writer Bud Poliquin commented that Alexander "grudgingly participated in Cooperstown's first induction ceremony." However, Alexander was not the only player of his day to feel little sentimentality about the honor. **Ty Cobb**, for instance, "boycotted that inaugural induction ceremony in '39 because of a feud with the commissioner," stated Poliquin. Poliquin also recounted when Mickey Cochrane, Frankie Frisch, Lefty Grove, and Carl Hubbell were all inducted in 1947 at the same ceremony, none of them showed up.

This attitude was not as ungracious as it might seem, but merely reflected the reality of the times. By this time Alexander had been away from the majors for nearly eight years. He continued to pitch for a time, and played very briefly for Dallas, a semiprofessional club of the Texas League. Alexander also pitched for the well-known House of David club (Benton Harbor, MI), from 1931-35. Ever the rebel, the Baseball Hall of Fame's "Alexander" web page revealed that "a clean-shaven 'Pete' Alexander pitched for the House of David baseball club comprised of players whose religion dictated that men neither shave nor cut their hair." Alexander pitched as long as he could find a team to take him and as long as he was able. When he could no longer pitch, Alexander worked a variety of odd jobs, includ-

Awards and Accomplishments

1911	Major League record for a rookie pitcher of twenty-eight wins
1911-30	Major League record: 373 wins
1911-30	Most National League games pitched (696)
1911-30	Most National League wins (373)
1911-30	Led League in complete games pitched six times
1916	Major League record: sixteen shutouts in one season
1916	Major League record of a 1.22 earned-run average
1927	Second player in National League history to win twenty games for three different teams with twenty-one wins for the Cardinals
1939	Hall of Fame induction

Alexander set over twenty National League records, many of which were not tied or broken until the modern baseball era.

ing selling tickets at a racetrack and working as a greeter in a bar. While working in a sideshow on 42nd Street in New York City, in a low, soft voice, Alexander would captivate his audiences with tales of the glory days of baseball.

That a former professional baseball player would work at such seemingly demeaning jobs was not so unusual for retirees of Alexander's generation. Unlike today, baseball in those days offered little if any retirement security. Pensions were unheard of in Alexander's day. Some players like Waite Hoyt were fortunate enough to become sports announcers or radiocasters. Others became managers or coaches if possible. But a greater number of former players had to take what they could find. Charles C. Alexander quoted Hoyt as stating that one of the downsides of choosing baseball as a career was that "it takes the player's best years and trains him for nothing else."

Kavanagh and others have described Alexander's glory days, but there is a strong undercurrent of sadness as the increasing obscurity that defined Alexander's post-National League years becomes apparent. When he could no longer play baseball due to his health, Alexander took what odd jobs he could find. During the war years of the 1940s, Alexander worked for a time in a Cincinnati airplane factory. When his health worsened to a nearly disabling degree, a small pension was arranged by the Baseball Commission at the urging of Aimee Alexander. Towards the end of his life, Alexander's health problems increased, adding heart disease and cancer to his list of ailments. On Nov. 4, 1950, the once-great pitcher was found dead of heart failure in a small room he rented from Mrs. Josie Nevrivy, in St. Paul, Nebraska. The fact that he died alone, suffered from poor health, and was nearly destitute seems to permanently seal his status as tragic baseball hero. However, Alexander's personality and career achievements, despite his unlucky personal circumstances, also bespeak an irrepressible spirit that is the stuff of which baseball legends are made.

FURTHER INFORMATION

Books

Alexander, Charles C. *Breaking the Slump: Baseball in the Depression Era*. New York: Columbia University Press, 2002.

Clark, Jerry E., and Martha Ellen Webb. *Alexander the Great: The Story of Grover Cleveland Alexander*. Omaha: Making History, 1993.

Kavanagh, Jack. *Ol' Pete: The Grover Cleveland Alexander Story*. South Bend, IN: Diamond Communications, Inc., 1996.

Thorn, John, and John Holway. *The Pitcher*. New York: Prentice Hall, 1987.

Periodicals

Poliquin, Bud. "Hall More than just Pictures Hanging on the Wall." *Post-Standard* (Syracuse, NY) (July 27, 2002): B1.

Other

"Grover Alexander Career Pitching Statistics." *Baseball Almanac,* http://baseball-almanac.com/players/p_galex2.htm (October 23, 2002).

Grover Cleveland Alexander Biography. *HickokSports.com,*http://www.hickoksorts.com/biograph/alexangc.shtml (October 14, 2002).

Grover Cleveland Alexander Chronology. *BaseballLibrary.com,* http://www.pubdim.net/baseballlibrary/ballplayers/A/Alexander_Grover_Cleveland.stm (October 14, 2002).

Neyer, Rob. "MLB: Phillies History Littered with Losses." *ESPN.com,* http://espn.go.com/mlb/columns/neyer_rob/1376775.html (October 30, 2002).

Seymour, Harold. "Grover Cleveland Alexander." *Biography Resource Center.* Gale Group, http://www.galenet.com/servlet/BioRC (October 15, 2002).

Sketch by Tricia R. Owen

Muhammad Ali
1942-

American boxer

His nickname, "The Greatest," almost says it all. The fact that it was self-anointed says the rest. Today, Muhammad Ali is the universally admired three-time heavyweight champion, lauded by boxing fans and civil rights leaders, both in America and throughout the world. He is remembered respectfully as the man of

principle who threw away his Olympic medal in disgust
at racism and who almost threw away his career when
he refused to fight an unjust war in Vietnam. He is remembered fondly for his prowess in the ring and his
consummate showmanship before the matches. He is an
authentic American hero, struggling valiantly in his
greatest battle, against Parkinson's Disease. When he
was in his prime, he sparked as much controversy as affection. He was an angry Black Muslim and student of
the radical Malcolm X, who was almost sent to jail for
his views. The transformation of Ali is a remarkable testament to the man and his inner strength.

A Stolen Bicycle

Muhammad Ali was born Cassius Marcellus Clay on
January 17, 1942, in Louisville, Kentucky. Unlike most
future champions, his parents, Cassius and Odessa
(Grady) Clay, were middle-class and he lived in the respectable part of town. His father was a sign and mural
painter, and his mother was a domestic. Sundays, the
family, including younger brother Rudolph (now Ra-
haman Ali), would troop to the Mount Zion Baptist
Church, and weekdays he attended DuValle Junior High
School, and then Central High School. Ali was never a
good student, and he confessed in later years that he has
always been a slow reader.

At the age of 12, a curious incident set young Cassius
Clay on a new path. On an October afternoon he rode his
new bike to the Columbia Auditorium. Later, when he
went back to get it, it had been stolen. Someone told him
there was a police officer in the basement, so Clay went
down there. The basement turned out to be a boxing
gym—the officer, Joe Martin, was a boxing enthusiast
with his own gym. After listening to his volley of threats
against whoever stole the bike, Martin invited him to come
around to his gym and learn something about boxing.

Six weeks after he started training with Joe Martin,
Clay fought and won his first bout. Over the next few
years of his training, Martin became more and more impressed, not only with Clay's speed and strength, but
even more by his mental quickness and his ability to take
a punch without the twin dangers of getting mad or going
into a panic. In high school, Clay became a very successful amateur boxer, winning six Kentucky Golden Gloves
Championships and two nationals. By the time he graduated, he had 100 wins and only 8 losses. Throughout the
1950s, he also appeared on a local television program *Tomorrow's Champions*. He was paid four dollars for each
televised match. Then, shortly after graduation, he won a
gold medal at the 1960 Rome Olympics in light-heavyweight boxing. He decided to turn pro.

The Louisville Lip

Almost immediately, Clay signed one of the most lucrative contracts in boxing history, which guaranteed a
50/50 split in his earnings with eleven Kentucky mil-

Muhammad Ali

lionaires known as the Louisville Sponsoring Group. He
hired Angelo Dundee as his first professional trainer,
and easily dispatched his opponent, Tunney Hunsacker,
in his first professional match, on October 29, 1960. The
purse was $2,000. Over the next 4 years he fought and
won 19 professional matches, but it wasn't this alone
that made him a heavyweight contender.

Early on, Cassius Clay mastered the fine art of publicity. At the Olympics he began inventing rhymes that
predicted how he would do in a match, and he brought
this skill home with him. Before long he was something
of a media darling, dismissed by some as "The
Louisville Lip," but always good for sports copy. He understood the value of that attention, and as he told *Sports
Illustrated* in 1964, "If you wonder what the difference
between [other boxers] and me is, I'll break the news:
you never heard of them. I'm not saying they're not
good boxers.... I'm just saying you never heard of
them." Before long, people were clamoring for a Cassius
Clay shot at the heavyweight title.

Before long, **Sonny Liston** bowed to the pressure and
agreed to fight Clay in Miami. In the weeks leading up to
the match, Clay turned up the volume on the traditional
hype, rhyming and hurling insults at Liston. About this
time, he began using the chant "float like a butterfly,
sting like a bee." And on February 25, 1964, backed up

Chronology

1942	Born Cassius Marcellus Clay, January 17, in Louisville, Kentucky
1954	Begins boxing
1960	Wins gold medal, Rome Olympics, light-heavyweight boxing
1960	First professional boxing match, defeats Tunney Hunsacker, October 29
1963	Converts to Islam, inspired by Malcolm X
1964	Takes World Heavyweight Championship from Sonny Liston
1964	Announces name change, to Muhammad Ali
1964	Marries Sonji Roi
1966	Divorces Sonji
1966	Refuses to go to Vietnam
1967	Stripped of boxing license and heavyweight title by New York State Athletic Commission and World Boxing Association, May
1967	Convicted of draft-dodging, sentenced to five years in prison (but released on appeal)
1967	Marries Belinda Boyd
1970	Conviction overturned
1970	Returns to the ring, against Jerry Quarry, November
1971	Loses to Joe Frazier in title match, February
1974	Beats Joe Frazier in rematch, becomes World Heavyweight Champion again
1974	Defeats George Foreman in "Rumble in the Jungle" to become World Heavyweight Champion again
1975	Defeats Joe Frazier again in "Thrilla in Manilla," often considered the greatest boxing match ever
1976	Divorces Belinda
1977	Marries Veronica Proche
1978	Loses title to Leon Spinks
1978	Reclaims title from Leon Spinks in rematch
1979	Retires from professional boxing
1980	Returns to professional boxing, loses to Larry Holmes in WBC title match
1981	In last professional boxing match, loses to Trevor Berbick
1982	Diagnosed with Parkinson's Disease
1985	Visits Lebanon in attempt to secure release of hostages, February
1985	Founds World Organization for Right, Liberty and Dignity (WORLD)
1985	Divorces Veronica
1986	Marries Yolanda "Lonnie" Williams
1990	Visits Iraq in successful attempt to secure release of American hostages
1996	Chosen to light Olympic Torch in Atlanta
2000	Wins WBA title from John Ruiz
2001	Establishes Muhammad Ali Center, Louisville, Kentucky

Awards and Accomplishments

1959	National Golden Gloves Light Heavyweight Champion
1959	National Amateur Athletic Union champion
1960	National Golden Gloves Light Heavyweight Champion
1960	National Amateur Athletic Union champion
1960	Gold medal, Rome Olympics, light-heavyweight boxing
1964-67	World Heavyweight Champion
1970	Dr. Martin Luther King Memorial Award
1974	Sportsman of the Year, *Sports Illustrated*
1974	Fighter of the Year, Boxing Writers Association
1974-78	World Heavyweight Champion
1978-79	World Heavyweight Champion
1979	Honorary Doctorate of Humane Letters, Texas Southern Univesity
1979	Street named after him in Louisville, Kentucky
1985	Recognized for long, meritorious service, World Boxing Association
1987	Elected to Boxing Hall of Fame
1990	Inducted into International Boxing Hall of Fame
1996	Lights Olympic torch, Atlanta
1997	Arthur Ashe Award for Courage, ESPN
1997	Essence Living Legend Award

his talk by defeating the "unbeatable" Sonny Liston. At 22, Cassius Clay was the World Heavyweight Champion

A Controversial Champ

Something else happened in Miami in 1964. Inspired by Malcolm X, Cassius Clay joined the Nation of Islam, and renounced his "slave name" in favor of Muhammad Ali, "Beloved of Allah." The name had been personally bestowed upon him by Elijah Muhammad, founder of the Nation of Islam. Realizing how this would affect people's view of him, he kept his conversion secret before the match, fearing the news might cost him his shot at the title. But soon after the fight, he went public with the news.

For many Americans this seemed like some kind of betrayal. Black Muslims were often feared and hated, as radicals, as dangerous, as un-American. And now the heavyweight champ, the beloved Cassius Clay was one of them. Or rather Muhammad Ali, a name that sounded foreign, maybe subversive, to Americans in the 1960s. And then Muhammad Ali came out against the Vietnam War, refusing to even consider going over there if he was drafted.

Ali's remarks caused a national uproar. In April of 1967, when he refused induction into the U.S. Army, on religious grounds, politicians and veterans groups called for his imprisonment. In fact, he was arrested and ultimately sentenced to five years in prison, but he was freed pending appeal. Then boxing officialdom stepped in. The World Boxing Association stripped him of his heavyweight title, and the New York State Athletic Commission banned him from boxing. Every other state commission soon joined them. Muhammad Ali was suddenly out of a title and out of a job.

In and Out of the Wilderness

For three-and-a-half years, Muhammad Ali endured the public outcry and the loss of his livelihood, and numerous death threats, while his case wound through the courts. He managed to support himself by public speaking engagements on college campuses. Finally, in June of 1970, the Supreme Court reversed his draft-dodging conviction on a technicality. In September of that same year the NAACP successfully sued the New York State Athletic Commission for the restoration of Ali's boxing license.

It was a heady victory, and the beginning of a long climb that would make Muhammad Ali a national hero once again. In November, 1970, in Atlanta, he fought his first professional match in almost four years, knocking out Jerry Quarry in the third round. In March of 1971,

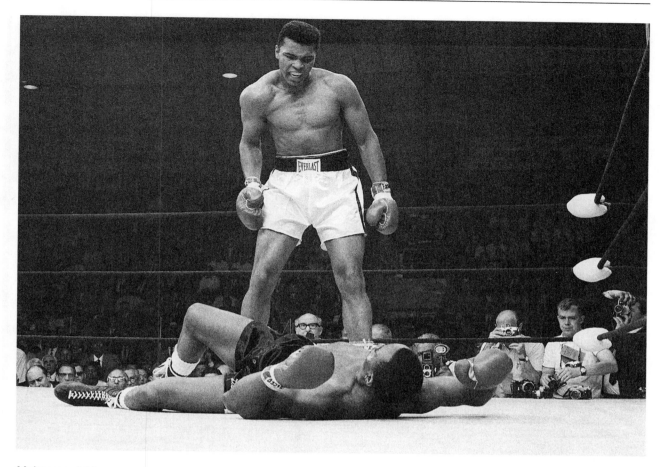

Muhammad Ali

he returned to New York to fight **Joe Frazier**, who had risen to the world heavyweight championship in Ali's absence. The fight between the two "champions" was long anticipated, and both were promised an unprecedented $2.5 million. After a long and bruising battle, Joe Frazier knocked Muhammad Ali down in the fifteenth round. Ali managed to get up from the staggering blow, but he lost the match on points. It was Ali's first defeat as a professional boxer.

On January 28, 1974, Ali returned to Madison Square Garden for a rematch with Joe Frazier. By this time, Frazier had lost the crown and Ali had been beaten once again, by Ken Norton. But the fight was highly anticipated by boxing fans. Again, it was a grueling match, with both men taking a lot of punishment. But this time the decision went to Muhammad Ali, who had earned his shot against the new champion, **George Foreman**.

In one of the biggest spectacles in boxing history, Muhammad Ali and George Foreman met in Kinshasha, Zaire, for the "Rumble in the Jungle." The very air of Africa seemed to give Ali a lift, and wherever he went, enthusiastic crowds followed him. The setting had the opposite effect on George Foreman, in those days known as "the surly champ." The fight took place on October 30, 1974, before 60,000 spectators and millions of pay-per-view customers. Most experts expected Ali to fall to the legendary Foreman punch, but after absorbing blows for six rounds, Muhammad Ali sent an exhausted George Foreman to the mat in the eighth round. Muhammad Ali was back on top.

The next year, in September of 1975, after easily besting such lesser lights as the "Bayonne Bleeder," Ali met Frazier one last time, for the "Thrilla in Manilla." Many look back on this as the finest boxing match in history. As Gerald Suster wrote in *Champions of the Ring,* "In the first five rounds, Ali did enough to stop or even kill any strong heavyweight. In the succeeding five rounds, Frazier broke through Ali's guard to pound him to the body and whack him to the head, in turn doing enough to stop or even kill any strong heavyweight." Finally, in the 11th round, Frazier's trainer, Eddie Futch, threw in the towel. Afterwards, a number of fans signed a petition asking that these two never fight each other again, so brutal had it been.

Later Years

Although this moment might have been a good time to retire, Ali soldiered on. In 1978 Leon Spinks took the

Where Is He Now?

Today, Muhammad Ali is a world-renowned celebrity, who has weathered the storms of terrible controversies and emerged as a national icon. Even the greatest modern boxers live in his shadow. At the same time, he stands as a symbol of principle in the face of adversity, a crusader for civil rights who risked everything to maintain his religious freedom and his right to dissent from U.S. government policy. Even while struggling against Parkinson's Disease, which plays havoc with his speech and coordination, he continues to travel around the world, most recently as a UN peace envoy to Afghanistan. He has also worked at establishing the Muhammad Ali Center in Louisville, a non-private community center, which is scheduled to open in 2003.

title away, but later that year Ali reclaimed it, making him a three-times champion. Finally, on June 26, 1979, Ali retired from professional boxing at the age of 37. His retirement did not last long. Ali had grown used to a very lavish and lifestyle and within a few years his fortune had dwindled. So in 1980 Ali returned to the ring, battling Larry Holmes for the World Boxing Council title with a guaranteed purse of $8 million. Holmes won a technical knockout in the eleventh round. A year later, Ali lost to Trevor Burdick. This time he retired for good, at the age of 40.

By this time, Ali was suffering from Parkinson's Disease. After the Holmes fight, people had noticed a change in Ali's health. At first he'd been misdiagnosed with a thyroid condition, but in 1982, the Parkinson's diagnosis was confirmed by medical tests. Doctors speculated that he might have contracted the illness from too many blows to the head. It was a sad revelation for Ali, but he was grateful that the disease was not contagious, so he could continue to have contact with his many fans throughout the world.

Ali's other interests have included painting, originally inspired by his father, and in 1979 he put on a one-man show of his works. He has also been called upon to perform diplomatic missions—in 1980, he toured Africa in an attempt to drum up support for President Carter's boycott of the Moscow Olympics. In 1985 he traveled to Lebanon in an unsuccessful attempt to secure the release of U.S. hostages, and in 1990 he traveled to Baghdad, Iraq, on a similar mission, this time successfully. In 1996, he was chosen to light the torch at the Atlanta Olympics, after carrying it for the last lap.

With so much focus on his boxing career and the pressures of his public life, Ali has not always had the calmest private life. He has been divorced three times, and he currently lives with his fourth wife, Lonnie. Much to her father's displeasure, his daughter Leila has followed Ali's footsteps into the boxing ring.

CONTACT INFORMATION

Address: P.O. Box 187, Berrien Springs, MI 59103.

SELECTED WRITINGS BY ALI:

(With Richard Durham) *The Greatest: My Own Story,* New York: Random House, 1975.

FURTHER INFORMATION

Books

Ali, Muhammad and Richard Durham. *The Greatest: My Own Story.* New York: Random House, 1975.
Cottrell, John. *The Story of Muhammad Ali, Who Once Was Cassius Clay.* London: Muller, 1967.
Hauser, Thomas. *Muhammad Ali: His Life and Times.* New York: Simon and Schuster, 1992.
Olsen, Jack. *Black is Best: The Riddle of Cassius Clay.* New York: Putnam, 1967.
Remnick, David. *King of the World.* New York: Random House, 1998.
Suster, Gerald. *Champions of the Ring.* London: Robson Books, 1994.

Sketch by Robert Winters

Marcus Allen
1960-

American football player

Heisman Trophy winner Marcus Allen came to be admired for his intelligence and quiet determination as much as for his skill in gaining yardage. An all-around athlete with a winning smile and boyish charm, Allen's appearance concealed a mature team player. As a senior at the University of Southern California (USC), he was a first-round draft pick, taken by the Raiders under the shadow of that team's move from Oakland to Los Angeles, California. In 1984 Allen was named the most valuable player of Super Bowl XVIII. A Pro Football Hall of Fame enshrinee, he has been quoted, "There is absolutely nothing that compares with winning."

Born in San Diego, California, on March 16, 1960, Marcus LaMarr Allen is the second of six siblings, the children of Gwen, a licensed vocational nurse, and Harold "Red" Allen, a construction foreman. As a child Allen played little league along with his four brothers. Later, at San Diego's Lincoln High School from 1975-78, he lettered in baseball, basketball, track, and football. He was named to the all-city and all-league football teams and remained strong in academics. Although he played quarterback in high school, he preferred to play running back and opted to attend the University of Southern California (USC) because of the school's history of Heisman Trophy winning running backs.

Marcus Allen

College Career

After some special team experience as a freshman at USC, Allen spent his sophomore year playing fullback. The switch happened early in the season when tailback Charles White injured a shoulder during the first game, and Allen filled in as the sole fullback offense. He logged more than 100 yards rushing during that first game and spent the rest of the 1979 season at fullback, blocking for White, who won the Heisman Trophy easily that year. The Trojans went 10-0-1 and beat Ohio State University at the Rose Bowl, 17-16. Allen contributed a total of 649 yards rushing, 314 yards in receptions caught, and eight touchdowns scored that season.

For the 1980 season Allen moved into the starting tailback position. It was a demanding position to play and an eye-opening experience. As tailback he was preceded in the job by such USC legends as **O.J. Simpson**. Allen performed admirably, racking up 1,563 yards that season.

With the Trojans ranked at Number 1, Allen set a personal goal of rushing for 2000 yards during his senior year; it was an unprecedented benchmark. After logging 210 yards in the season opener against Tennessee, he rushed for 274 yards against Indiana the following week. In the third game, a win against the Sooners of Oklahoma, Allen made 208 yards on 39 carries. He made 233 yards against Oregon the following week a the Trojans triumphed 56-22.

The crushing blow of a mid-season loss to the University of Arizona was softened for Allen by the satisfaction of rushing for 211 yards, including a 74-yard touchdown run. Two low-yardage games of 153 and 143 against Stanford and Notre Dame respectively were cause for celebration regardless, as USC won both games. He rushed for 289 and 243 yards against Washington State and the University of California at Berkeley respectively and faced his last two regular season games with a running total of 1,968 yards.

In a freezing rain at Washington that season, he surpassed the 2000-yard rushing mark. He ended his college career with 2,342 yards and won the Heisman Trophy that year.

Allen went to **Al Davis**'s Raiders in the first round of the 1982 National Football League (NFL) draft. With a whirlwind of agents offering contracts, Allen hired attorney/agent Ed Hookstratten who negotiated a $150,000 contract for Allen's first year, plus a $400,000 signing bonus.

The Raiders

Hookstratten arranged also for Allen to train with Olympic track and field coach Jim Bush, who also trained record-breaking Olympic sprinter Quincy Watts during his 20-year career at the University of California. The training program with Bush helped Allen to improve his endurance and strength as he entered his rookie year with the NFL. One week prior to the season opener against San Francisco Allen moved into the starting lineup. In that game he gained more than 100 yards rushing. A second game against Atlanta was followed by an eight-week (57-day) players' strike, the longest in NFL history.

The Raiders returned from the strike with a win in a Monday-night home game against the San Diego Chargers. When the shortened season had ended, Allen had rushed for 697 yards and 11 touchdowns. His 401 receptions that season included three touchdowns. At the Tampa Bay stadium for Super Bowl XVIII in 1984, Allen broke loose for a 74-yard touchdown run after the

Career Statistics

Yr	Team	GP	Rushing					Receiving			
			ATT	YDS	AVG	TD		REC	YDS	AVG	TD
1982	RAI	9	160	697	4.4	11		38	401	10.6	3
1983	RAI	15	266	1014	3.8	9		68	590	8.7	2
1984	RAI	16	275	1168	4.2	13		64	758	11.8	5
1985	RAI	16	380	1759	4.6	11		67	555	8.3	3
1986	RAI	13	208	759	3.6	5		46	453	9.8	2
1987	RAI	12	200	754	3.8	5		51	410	8.0	0
1988	RAI	15	223	831	3.7	7		34	303	8.9	1
1989	RAI	8	69	293	4.2	2		20	191	9.6	0
1990	RAI	16	179	682	3.8	12		15	189	12.6	1
1991	RAI	8	63	287	4.6	2		15	131	8.7	0
1992	RAI	16	67	301	4.5	2		28	277	9.9	1
1993	KAN	16	206	764	3.7	12		34	238	7.0	3
1994	KAN	13	189	709	3.8	7		42	349	8.3	0
1995	KAN	16	207	890	4.3	5		27	210	7.8	0
1996	KAN	16	206	830	4.0	9		27	270	10.0	0
1997	KAN	16	124	505	4.1	11		11	86	7.8	0
TOTAL		221	3022	12243	4.1	123		587	5411	9.2	21

KAN: Kansas City Chiefs; RAI: Los Angeles Raiders.

Awards and Accomplishments

1981	Heisman Trophy; College Player of the Year: Walter Camp, Maxwell Club, and *Football News*
1982	Rookie of the Year; Pro-Bowl
1984	Most Valuable Player, Super Bowl XVIII
1993	NFL Comeback Player of the Year
2000	College Football Hall of Fame

Raiders took possession of the ball on their own 26-yard line in the last 12 seconds of the third quarter. The score by Allen turned the tide for the Raiders, and the team won the Super Bowl for the third time in franchise history. He wrote of the experience later, "There are those moments in life that simply defy proper explanation, so magical that they beg a poet's talent for description. They pass all too soon, a blur in time so quickly gone that there is not ample opportunity to fully appreciate them as they occur. Such a moment for me began when [Jim] Plunkett called the play."

During the 1985 season, Allen injured his ankle at the home opener against the New York Giants. It was the team's third game—and their third straight loss. The injury—although nothing appeared broken—plagued Allen for some time. Although he was named to the Pro Bowl that year, the doctors refused to release him to play, and his stats sagged in 1986.

After a lackluster 1987 season, and another player's strike delay, Allen led the Raiders on the rebound in 1988, for the seventh time in his career. He re-signed with the Raiders in 1989 but played only sporadically through 1991. The 1992 football season marked Allen's eleventh and last with the Raiders. He signed with Kansas City and played out his career with the Chiefs until retiring from professional play in 1997.

When he retired after 221 games played, Allen had logged 145 career touchdowns including 123 rushing touchdowns. His NFL record of 11 consecutive games with 100 or more rushing yards stood from 1986 until 1997. Third in pass receptions, with 587, and seventh on the all-time rushing list with 12,243 career yards, he was a six-time Pro Bowler. His 1985 single season mark of 2,314 combined rushing and receiving yards is the third-highest in the NFL.

Allen, who married Kathryn Eickenstadt on June 26, 1993, lives in Montecito, California. In retirement he works as a sports analyst for the CBS television network's NFL broadcast team.

CONTACT INFORMATION

Address: c/o CBS Sportsline.com, 2200 West Cypress Creek Road, Ft. Lauderdale, FL 33309. Fax: (954) 351-8823. Phone: (954) 351-2120.

SELECTED WRITINGS BY ALLEN:

(With Carlton Stowers) *Marcus*, St. Martin's Press, 1997.

FURTHER INFORMATION

Books

Allen, Marcus with Carlton Stowers, *Marcus*, New York: St. Martin's Press, 1997.

Leder, Jane Mersky, *Marcus Allen,* Mankato, MN:
    Crestwood House Inc., 1985.

Online

"CBS Sportsline.com," http://cbs.sportsline.com/u/cbs/
    mallen.html (December 26, 2002).
"Jim Bush, Physical Fitness Consultant," *USTCA Coaches Diploma Program,* http://www.ustrackcoaches.org/
    HURDLES/Courses/jim_bush_resume.htm (December 18, 2002).

Sketch by G. Cooksey

Davey Allison

Davey Allison
1961-1993

American race car driver

Davey Allison was a champion stock-car driver, with major race wins; he captured the Daytona 500, stock-car racing's most important event, in 1992. His winnings on the Winston Cup circuit, the major league of the sport, totaled $6.7 million. Allison came from a family of race car drivers that included his father, Bobby, his uncle, Donnie, and his younger brother, Clifford. In 1993, the helicopter he was piloting to the Talladega Superspeedway to see a friend practice spun out of control and went down in a parking lot where he was attempting to land. He died at age 32 the next day of head injuries.

Allison's first job in the business was working for his father's company, Bobby Allison Racing, ate age 12. He swept garage floors and sorted parts for 50 cents an hour. In 1979, the year he graduated from high school, he completely rebuilt a 1967 Chevy Nova. Also that year, he started his career as a racer.

Allison entered his first NASCAR Winston Cup race in 1985, at Talladega Superspeedway. Allison won three Winston 500 titles—in 1987, 1989, and in 1992. Before competing in the Winston Cup races, Allison won eight Automobile Racing Club of America (ARCA) races, in a three-year span.

Big Moments at Daytona

In 1988, Allison was in second place, behind his father, in the Daytona 500. He treasured the moment more than his victory on the same track four years later. "Since I was a kid, I've dreamed about battling to the wire, finishing 1-2 with my dad," Davey Allison said. "The only difference was, I wanted him to finish second." Bobby Allison pulled away at the finish line, his Buick beating Davey's Ford by two lengths. Bobby, 50 at the time, became the oldest driver to win the 500.

"I saw the nose of Davey's car coming up, out of the corner of my eye," Bobby Allison said. "But I felt I had the horsepower to beat him." His son added: "I've worked for this guy all my life. At the finish today, I knew he'd make it awful tough on me."

Davey Allison would finally capture Daytona in 1992. He ran a patient race that day, and avoided a 14-car accident on lap 92 that effectively eliminated Allison's principal competition, Sterling Marlin, Bill Elliott and Ernie Irvan. Ironically, Allison smashed his primary car in a collision with Marlin in practice four days earlier. Racing with a different car, Allison felt he had to run smarter. "In a 200-lap race, there's no need to stick your neck out and take a chance," he said. "A couple of cars were faster than us, but they ended up a bunch of sheet metal in the garage." Allison, fourth at the time of the crash, led the final 102 laps. "I saw it coming," he said. "They ran out of room, I picked which way to go and Morgan (Shepherd) followed me, then all hell broke loose."

Allison's maturity clearly emerged. He admitted that had he been in that position a year earlier, he might not have had the presence of mind to avoid the crash. "When he graduated in 1985 to the Winston Cup tour," *Joseph Siano* wrote in the New York Times, "he arrived with a reputation as a fast driver, but one who needed to get his competitive fires—and the frustration that came with losing—under better control." Allison once injured his hand punching the transporter that carried his car. Siano cited the arrival of Larry McReynolds as crew

Chronology

1961	Born in Hollywood, Florida
1979	Graduates from high school
1979	Begins racing career
1985	Makes NASCAR Winston Cup debut
1988	Loses out on Winston Cup championship after collision with Ernie Irvan on final race of year
1993	Dies after a helicopter crash at the Talladega Superspeedway

Related Biography: Race Car Driver Bobby Allison

Davey Allison's father, Bobby Allison, was also a champion race car driver and an avid private airplane pilot. Born on December 3, 1937, Bobby Allison began racing in the 1950s. He moved to Alabama in 1959, where he joined with his brother, Donny Allison, and friend Red Farmer as the original members of the celebrated "Alabama Gang" of racers. In 1983, after four attempts, Bobby Allison won the Winston Cup. He stopped racing for several years after being involved in a near-fatal crash on the track in 1988, but he returned to race on the senior circuit in the early 1990s. Bobby and his wife, Judy, lost two sons, Davey and Clifford, to accidents. They also have two daughters, Carrie and Bonnie.

chief on Allison's team as a turning point. He then won 11 of his 19 victories, "and more important, he became less headstrong behind the wheel."

The Allisons joined Lee and **Richard Petty** as father-and-son winners at Daytona.

Allison was also on his way to his first Winston Cup championship in 1992, when, in the last race of the Cup season, in Hampton, Georgia, a crash caused by Irvan eliminated him. Allison had needed only to finish in sixth place to win the Winston Cup standings and was, in fact, sixth when he encountered trouble on lap 253. "Ernie Irvan's Kodak Chevrolet had a tire go down and he lost control directly in front of Rusty Wallace and Allison," the Web site *NASCAR.com* wrote in its recap of 1992. "Wallace miraculously avoided the spinning Irvan, but Allison was not so lucky. Allison T-boned Irvan, ending his day." Allison settled for third in the standings, behind Alan Kulwicki and Elliott. But he was philosophical about his setback, noting to reporters that his father finished in second place in the Winston Cup standings four times before finally winning in 1983 at age 46.

No Strangers to Tragedy

Tragedy ran in the Allison family. In 1988, Bobby Allison nearly was killed when his car crashed at Pocono, Pennsylvania. He suffered permanent damage to his memory and his balance, and had to stop racing, although he stayed in the sport as an owner. At the time of his death, Davey Allison had only recently returned to racing as a driver, having suffered a concussion and broken an arm and ribs a year earlier, also in Pocono. Almost a year before Allison's helicopter crash, his younger brother, racer Clifford Allison, then 27, died in a car crash during practice in Brooklyn, Michigan. And Donnie Allison, Davey's uncle, was in a life-threatening crash in 1981 that ended his career.

Allison had purchased the ill-fated helicopter less than a month before he died. If there was one passion he had besides auto racing, it was flying airplanes. He obtained his private pilot's license in 1987, and subsequently received night and instrument ratings. He became certified to fly helicopters in 1992.

It was not unusual for a stock-car driver to also be a private pilot. As Darrell Waltrip, a star driver explained

to *USA Today's* Dick Patrick, "We have a lot of places to go, and we try to make it easy as we can. It's just a way of life. It's part of our business."

At the time of the crash, Allison was headed from his home in Hueytown, Alabama to the Talladega Superspeedway, to watch driving friend David Bonnett practice. Bonnet, along with his father Neil Bonnett and Allison himself, were all part of a tight-knit racing cadre led by Bobby Allison and dubbed the Alabama Gang.

Witnesses said Allison was guiding the aircraft in for a landing in a small parking lot adjacent to the speedway. Only a foot off the ground, and seemingly about to touch down, the machine leapt back into the air, and 25 feet up, spun out of control. It crashed to the blacktop on its left side, where its full weight came down on Allison.

Fellow driver and longtime family friend Red Farmer, 60, was also on board. He suffered broken bones but survived the crash probably, he later told reporters, because his racing instincts kicked in and he braced himself just before impact. Allison was still wrestling with the controls as the helicopter went down.

Allison underwent surgery to relieve pressure on his brain, but to no avail. The official cause of death was acute subdural hematoma—severe bruising of the brain and the resulting swelling of the brain's delicate tissues.

Allison's father suffered the same injury in the auto accident that ended his career. After Bobby Allison's accident, he joined the board of directors of the National Head Injury Foundation. This nonprofit group's mission is to help victims of traumatic brain injury (TBI) and the families of victims. After Allison's death, the National Head Injury Foundation established a fund in Allison's name to educate people about TBI.

Allison left behind his wife, Liz, their daughter Krista Marie, then 3 years old, and their son Robert Grey, who was 23 months old at the time of Allison's death, as well as his parents, Bobby and Judy, and two sisters.

Allison Legacy

Davey Allison was part of a famed racing family with a legacy for excellence—and tragedy. He knew the dan-

Awards and Accomplishments

1987	Becomes first Winston Cup series rookie to qualify to start in the front row at the Daytona 500.
1987	Wins his first Winston 500 race
1987	Named NASCAR rookie of the year
1989	Wins his second Winston 500 race
1991	Leads in more races (23) than any other driver
1992	Wins his third Winston 500 race
1992	Leads in more laps (1,377) than any other driver
1992	Wins Daytona 500
1993	Wins International Race of Champions at the Talladega Superspeedway in Alabama
1996	Inducted into the National Motorsports Press Association's Stock Car Hall of Fame (posthumous)
1997	Inducted into the Bristol (TN) Motor Speedway's Heroes of Bristol Hall of Fame (posthumous)
1998	Inducted into the International Motorsports Hall of Fame (posthumous)

gers of his sport, as did the other Allisons. "Through this whole thing, nobody ever heard me say, 'why me?'" he said after his brother, Clifford's death. "The thing to do is retain the memories and prepare to live every day the best I can, on and off the track."

"Davey Allison grew up in this sport and, from a small child into adulthood, dedicated his life to it," NASCAR president Bill France, Jr., said upon Allison's death.

"There are no guarantees in life," John Sonderegger wrote in the *St. Louis Post-Dispatch*. "Davey Allison knew all too well how precarious this world can be. . . . Davey once said that if he were killed in a racing crash, 'I'd die with a smile on my face.' That pretty much is the way race-car drivers accept the risk. But Allison didn't die on the track."

Noting Kulwicki's death in a plane crash three months earlier, Sonderegger wrote, "That's one reason there is so much pain in the NASCAR family. Two of the sport's brightest young stars died in accidents that had nothing to do with racing cars."

FURTHER INFORMATION

Books

Allison, Liz. *Davey Allison: A Celebration of Life*. Charlottesville, VA: Howell Press, 1995.

Periodicals

Fachet, Robert. "Allison's Passenger Discusses Crash." *Washington Post* (July 15, 1993): D2.

Patrick, Dick. "Severe Head Injury Caused Death." *USA Today* (July 14, 1993): 7C.

Siano, Joseph. "Davey Allison, Stock-Car Driver, Dies at 32 After Helicopter Crash." *New York Times* (July 14, 1993): D20.

Sonderegger, John. "Mourning Allison; Pain Flares as Drivers Race at Talladega." *St. Louis Post-Dispatch* (July 25, 1993): 1F.

Tuschak, Beth. "Copter Crash Is Latest Tragedy to Hit Allisons." *USA Today* (July 13, 1993): 13C.

Other

"1988: Father Before Son." Nascar.com. http://www.nascar.com/2003/kyn/history/daytona/01/31/daytona_1988/ (February 11, 2003).

"1992: Davey's Day." Nascar.com. http://www.nascar.com/2003/kyn/history/daytona/02/05/daytona_1992/ (February 5, 2003).

"Bobby Allison." Infoplease.com. http://www.infoplease.com/ipsa/A0108963.html (January 14, 2003).

"Bobby Allison." BobbyAllison.com. http://www.bobbyallison.com/ (January 14, 2003).

"Davey Allison" NASCAR.com. http://www.nascar.com/2002/kyn/history/races/02/02/dallison/ (December 16, 2002).

"History60-69." ARCA Online. http://www.arcaracing.com/Remax/history60-69.html (January 13, 2003).

Sketch by Michael Belfiore

Roberto Alomar
1968-

American baseball player

Roberto Alomar, arguably the best second baseman in the major leagues, has rarely been given the same sort of recognition that other superstar players, like first baseman **Mark McGwire** or center fielder **Ken Griffey, Jr.**, have received. Alomar, one of only four players ever to have both ten career Golden Glove awards and a lifetime batting average of over .300, currently plays for the New York Mets.

Baseball in the Blood

The game of baseball runs in Alomar's family. Alomar's older brother, Sandy Jr., is currently a catcher for the Colorado Rockies, and their father, Sandy Sr., played in the major leagues for fifteen years. When the younger Alomars were first signed into the major leagues, they found themselves playing in Charleston, S.C., for a Class A team in the San Diego Padres organization that featured their father as a coach. Although Sandy Jr. was older, Alomar was the first of the two to break into the major leagues, becoming a regular figure in the Padres lineup in 1988. In 1989, the twenty-one-year-old Alomar became the youngest player to take the field for a National League team on opening day. That same year Sandy Jr. was trad-

Roberto Alomar

ed to the Cleveland Indians, where he would become the American League's Rookie of the Year in 1990.

Although Alomar had some freshman jitters in his first full year in the major leagues, committing eleven errors in the month of April, 1989, by the end of the season he had proved himself to be an excellent player. He finished that year with the sixth-highest batting average in the league and the third-highest number of hits, including the most sacrifice hits of any player. Alomar was traded to the Toronto Blue Jays for the 1991 season, and it was there that, at the age of twenty-three, he first became a true star. He won his first Golden Glove award that year and placed sixth in the Most Valuable Player voting.

"For [Alomar] to have accomplished what he has at this age is really mind-boggling," Blue Jays' hitting coach Larry Hisle said to Bruce Newman of *Sports Illustrated* early in the 1992 season. "You have to remember that most players that age are just making it to the big leagues. Robbie has already been an All-Star twice." But the best was yet to come: Toronto won the World Series that year and again in 1993, and Alomar was named the Most Valuable Player of their 1992 American League Championship Series win over the Oakland Athletics.

An Unfortunate Incident

Alomar was traded to the Baltimore Orioles after the 1995 season. He remained an excellent player and continued to rack up Golden Glove awards and annual All-

Star designations, but his career was marred by an unfortunate incident late in 1996. In one of the final games of the regular season, umpire John Hirschbeck mistakenly called a far outside pitch that should have been a ball a third strike. Alomar and Hirschbeck exchanged words at the plate. Alomar returned to the dugout peaceably, but once there he continued to complain about the unfairness of the call. Hirschbeck then threw Alomar out of the game, at which point Alomar and Orioles' manager Davey Johnson ran out onto the field to contest the call. The exchange that followed was very heated. Hirschbeck allegedly insulted Alomar in profane terms, but the cameras that were filming the game could not capture those words. What the cameras did capture, the image that was broadcast across the country in the days that followed, was Alomar spitting at Hirshbeck.

Alomar immediately regretted his behavior, but it was too late. The incident, and the league's handling of it, provoked a storm of controversy. Many people, including the umpires' union, said that Alomar's five-game suspension, which he would not have to serve until the beginning of the next season, was too light. The umpires threatened to go to strike over their perception that the league was not taking an assault on one of their own seriously, and it took a court order to get them to keep officiating. In the meantime, the day after Alomar spat at Hirschbeck he hit a home run in the tenth inning to win a spot in the playoffs for Baltimore.

Career Statistics

Yr	Team	AVG	GP	AB	R	H	HR	RBI	BB	SO	SB
1988	SD	.266	143	545	84	145	9	41	47	83	24
1989	SD	.295	158	623	82	184	7	56	53	76	42
1990	SD	.287	147	586	80	168	6	60	48	72	24
1991	TOR	.295	161	637	88	188	9	69	57	86	53
1992	TOR	.310	152	571	105	177	8	76	87	52	49
1993	TOR	.326	153	589	109	192	17	93	80	67	55
1994	TOR	.306	107	392	78	120	8	38	51	41	19
1995	TOR	.300	130	517	71	155	13	66	47	45	30
1996	BAL	.328	153	588	132	193	22	94	90	65	17
1997	BAL	.333	112	412	64	137	14	60	40	43	9
1998	BAL	.282	147	588	86	166	14	56	59	70	18
1999	CLE	.323	159	563	138	182	24	120	99	96	37
2000	CLE	.310	155	610	111	189	19	89	64	82	39
2001	CLE	.336	157	575	113	193	20	100	80	71	30
2002	NYM	.266	149	590	73	157	11	53	57	83	16
TOTAL		.304	2183	8386	1414	2564	201	1071	959	1032	462

BAL: Baltimore Orioles; CLE: Cleveland Indians; NYM: New York Mets; SD: San Diego Padres; TOR: Toronto Blue Jays.

A New Team

Alomar played in Baltimore for two more seasons before being traded to the Cleveland Indians, where his brother Sandy was still playing. The Indians were glad to have him: they had not had a solid second baseman since trading Carlos Baerga away in 1996, and they needed a good player to complement their star shortstop Omar Vizquel. The Alomar-Vizquel combination succeeded better than anyone could have hoped, and the two were widely considered to be the best second base-shortstop duo in the major leagues in the late 1990s. "I can't be with anyone better than [Alomar] at second base," Vizquel told John Kuenster of *Baseball Digest* in 2000. "We are like family."

"Married to Baseball"

Many of Alomar's teammates over the years, from the Padres to his current team, the New York Mets, have commented about how dedicated he is to the game. "He said he is married to baseball and I didn't understand what that meant until I played with the guy," Vizquel once commented to *Baseball Digest* reporter T. J. Quinn. "Every day he pointed out to me something I didn't know or something I didn't see." As Alomar explains it, he brings the same attitude to baseball that he did to his Catholic school in Puerto Rico as a child. "It's like how you go to school and you study and get good grades," he told Quinn. "That's how I study baseball."

FURTHER INFORMATION

Periodicals

Bloom, Barry M. "Roberto Alomar." *Buffalo News* (February 25, 2002): S7.

Deacon, James. "Dropping the Ball: Baseball's Playoffs Are All Spit and No Shine." *Maclean's* (October 14, 1999): 74.

"Hot Pursuit." *The Sporting News* (June 10, 1996): 9-10.

Kaplan, David A. "When the Spit Hits the Fan: Crying 'Remember the Alomar!' Umpires Try to Walk." *Newsweek* (October 14, 1996): 96.

Kuenster, John. "Vizquel and Alomar Rated as Best Middle Infield Duo in Majors." *Baseball Digest* (November, 2000): 19.

Kurkjian, Tim. "Do Not Disturb." *Sports Illustrated* (January 29, 1996): 142-145.

Kurkjian, Tim. "Public Enemy No. 1." *Sports Illustrated* (October 14, 1996): 28-31.

Kurkjian, Tim. "Ready to Leap?" *Sports Illustrated* (August 14, 1995): 58-59.

Newman, Bruce. "Home Suite Home." *Sports Illustrated* (June 8, 1992): 36-39.

Quinn, T. J. "Roberto Alomar of the Mets: An All-Around Performer." *Baseball Digest* (July, 2002): 24-27.

Suttell, Scott. "All Eyes on Alomar." *Crain's Cleveland Business* (March 29, 1999): T14.

Verducci, Tom. "Scoring Machine." *Sports Illustrated* (May 24, 1999): 48.

Verducci, Tom. "Tribal Warfare." *Sports Illustrated* (October 20, 1997): 46-51.

Wulf, Steve. "The Spit Hit the Fan." *Time* (October 14, 1996): 82.

Other

"Roberto Alomar." Baseball-Reference.com. http://www.baseball-reference.com/a/alomaro01.shtml (November 25, 2002).

"Roberto Alomar." CNN/Sports Illustrated. http://sports illustrated.cnn.com/baseball/mlb/players/2035/ (November 15, 2002).

"Roberto Alomar." ESPN.com. http://sports.espn.go.com/mlb/players/stats?statsId=4189 (November 15, 2002).

Sketch by Julia Bauder

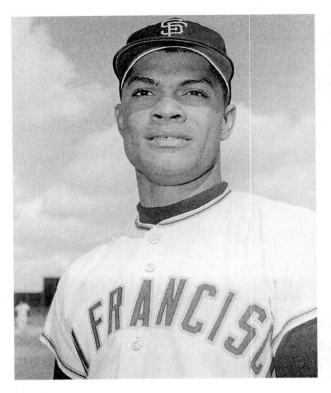

Felipe Alou

Felipe Alou
1935-

Dominican baseball player

Felipe Alou is the second Dominican in the history of major league baseball to become a major league player. His career as a player spanned 17 years starting in 1958, and afterwards he switched to managing and managed a total of 1,635 minor league games, as well as many games in the Latin American leagues during the off-seasons. He also spent brief periods as a major league coach before becoming the first Dominican major league manager in the history of the game at the age of 57, in May of 1992, when he began managing the Montreal Expos. He left the Expos in 2001 and signed on as manager with the San Francisco Giants in 2002.

Son of a Carpenter

Felipe Alou was born in 1935 in the Dominican Republic town of Haina, the son of a black carpenter and blacksmith father, and a Caucasian mother. "I knew a bit about the history of the slaves," he later told Jeff Blair in the *St. Louis Post-Dispatch,* "but I thought it (racism) was just a baseball thing. I had white aunts and uncles. We still have family with green eyes and blond hair. I get relatives who come and visit me in Florida, and nobody thinks we're related." Still Alou first became fully aware of racism in the United States when he made a brief stopover in Miami in 1954 on the way to the Pan-Am Games in Mexico City. There, Alou was informed that he would be required by racist laws to ride at the back of city buses. The Dominican team won the gold metal at the Pam-Am games, and this directly led to Alou's signing with the San Francisco Giants baseball team.

Although baseball was his first love, Alou first trained to become a doctor and a carpenter. As he later explained to *Ebony*'s Walter Leavy, "I was a student at the University of Santo Domingo, with the idea of becoming a doctor. At the same time, I was working with my father as a carpenter, which was great because most of the homes on the island were made of wood. I just loved baseball best."

He started in the Giants' minor league teams, playing in Southern American towns like Lake Charles, Louisiana and Cocoa, Florida. He had as a guide, teammate Julio Navarro, a white Puerto Rican, who could order food at restaurants where Alou was not allowed to eat, and bring it back to his black teammates.

A Player in the Major Leagues

Alou made his major league debut with the San Francisco Giants in 1958. Through a 17-year major league playing career, he played as both an outfielder and first-baseman with the Giants (1958-63), the Braves (1964-69), the Althetics (1970-71), the Yankees (1971-73), the Expos (1973), and finally the Brewers for one year before retiring as a player in 1974. At the end of his playing career, Alou had a .286 career batting average, 206 home runs to his credit, along with 852 runs batted in, over a career that including 2,082 games. Named to the National League All-Star team three times, Alou also made it to the World Series with the Giants in 1962 (his team lost the to Yankees). While playing for the Giants, Alou played on the same team as his younger brothers, Matty and Jesus.

Alou's best year as a player came in 1966. That year, he hit 31 home runs, batting .327 with the Braves. His 218 hits and 122 runs gave him the best record in the league that year. Also in this year, his brother, fellow major leaguer Matty Alou, averaged .342, the year's best batting average.

As a player, Alou often spoke out against what he felt were below-standard working conditions for Latin Ameri-

Related Biography: Baseball Players Matty and Jesus Alou

Felipe Alou's two younger brothers, Matty and Jesus both played major league baseball at the same time as Felipe. All three brothers played together on the same team briefly in 1963, when Jesus joined the Giants. During one memorable game, the three of them comprised the only outfield to be made up entirely of brothers.

Matty is the second-oldest of the Alou brothers, born in 1938. He began his major league career in 1960, two years after Felipe, when he joined Felipe's team, the Giants. He hit his stride in 1966, the year he moved from the Giants to the Pirates, that year leading the National League in batting, with an average of .342. In 1969, he led the league in hits and doubles. Jesus is the youngest of the brothers, born in 1942. He was called "Jay" by sportscasters who didn't want to seem blasphemous by using the name "Jesus.

can baseball players. He held that he and his fellow Latino players were not paid as much as white players, and that they were more often subjected to criticism. As he later told *Ebony,* "It was not until I managed my first game that I realized the responsibility that goes with being a manager. As a minority, I have to be a good example. Those of us [minority managers] who are in eminence now have to show people that we are capable of controlling a game, handling players and the media, and can have a [good] relationship with the fans and the city in which we manage. If we don't manage well or mix well with the fans, the next minority guy isn't going to have much of a chance." Alou retired as a player in 1974, and moved on to managing and coaching. He started his managing career in the minor leagues with the Expos organization.

A New Career as Manager

In 1976, Alou's son Felipe Jr. drowned. This had a profound impact on Alou's outlook on his career and his life. As he told Blair in the *St. Louis Post-Dispatch,* "I have to say that it was after Felipe's death that I changed. Before that, I was like anyone else and took things for granted. I still thought like a major leaguer, because I was only a couple of years out of the game as a player, and was going to get back into it as a coach, or something. But you lose your first-born son, and you don't take anything for granted anymore. For there can be nothing worse than that. Nothing.... For a while I wanted to be left alone."

With Felipe Jr., gone, Alou is left with ten surviving children, the products of four marriages. The eldest is Maria Jimenez, in her early forties as the 1990s drew to a close. Alou's first wife was Maria, with whom he had daughter Maria, and sons Moises, and Jose. Next he married Beverley Martin, who hailed from Atlanta, and with whom he fathered Christia, Cheri, and Jennifer. His next wife was a Dominican named Elsa Brens, and with her, Alou had Felipe Jose and Luis Emilio. Alou's fourth marriage was to Canadian Lucie Gagnon in 1985. By 1998, the couple had two children, Valerie and Felipe Jr.

Alou became manager of the Montreal Expos in 1992. Alou's goals as manager was to develop younger, less well-paid players into outstanding ballplayers, since, throughout the 1990s, the Expos cut costs by trading higher-paid players to other teams. His strategy paid off; by 1994, the Expos had the best win-loss record in major league baseball, and Alou was named Manager of the Year. By the end of his tenure with the Expos, Alou had brought his team to victory more times than any other manager in the history of the team. This was especially remarkable considering that the Expos had the second-lowest payroll in the National League at the time of Alou's recognition as Manager of the Year, with only two players over the age of 30.

A Giant at Heart

Alou was dismissed as Expos manager in 2001. After spending a season as a bench coach for the Detroit Tigers, he was hired in September, 2002 to manage the San Francisco Giants starting in 2003. With this appointment, his career came full circle; he had started his major league career as a player for the Giants in 1958. "I'm going back home to where I started and, hopefully, I'm going to end it right there," he told Janie McCauley of the *UAS Today.* At 67 years old, he also became the oldest major league manager. Giants general manager Brian Sabean told McCauley at the time of Alou's hiring, "We're obviously thrilled we're able to welcome Felipe back. Everyone in baseball realizes what he's done in the game. It's thrilling because he's a Giant at heart. He calls himself a baseball soldier in conversation. He's more like baseball royalty to us."

Career Statistics

Yr	Team	AVG	GP	AB	R	H	HR	RBI	BB	SO	SB
1958	SF	.253	75	182	21	46	4	16	19	34	4
1959	SF	.275	95	247	38	68	10	33	17	38	5
1960	SF	.264	106	322	48	85	8	44	16	42	10
1961	SF	.289	132	415	59	120	18	52	26	41	11
1962	SF	.316	154	561	96	177	15	98	33	66	10
1963	SF	.281	157	565	75	159	20	82	27	87	11
1964	MILB	.253	121	415	60	105	9	51	30	41	5
1965	ATL	.297	143	555	80	165	23	78	31	63	8
1966	ATL	.327	154	666	122	218	31	74	24	51	5
1967	ATL	.274	140	574	76	157	15	43	32	50	6
1968	ATL	.317	160	662	72	210	11	57	48	56	12
1969	ATL	.282	123	476	54	134	5	32	23	23	4
1970	OAK	.271	154	575	70	156	8	55	32	31	10
1971	OAK	.250	2	8	0	2	0	0	0	1	0
1971	NY	.289	131	461	52	133	8	69	32	24	5
1972	NY	.278	120	324	33	90	6	37	22	27	1
1973	NY	.236	93	280	25	66	4	27	9	25	0
1973	NY	.208	19	48	4	10	1	4	2	4	0
1974	MILW	.000	3	3	0	0	0	0	0	2	0
TOTAL		.286	2082	7339	985	2101	206	852	423	706	107

ATL: Atlanta Braves; MILB: Milwaukee Braves; MILW: Milwaukee Brewers; NY: New York Yankees; OAK: Oakland Athletics; SF: San Francisco Giants.

Baseball continues to run in Alou's family; son Moises signed with the Astros as a player, and Jose started his work life as a minor league player for the Expos before trading his baseball uniform for that of a police officer. Alou's sons Felipe and Luis were working their way up to the major leagues as players as the 20th century drew to a close, and his nephew, Mel Rojas, became a pitcher for the New York Mets. Alou's daughter, Christia, also works in baseball, although in a very different capacity; she is a lawyer working for the law firm that represents the Major League Baseball Players Association. Said Christia of her father to Jeff Blair of the *Toronto Globe and Mail* in the *St. Louis Post-Dispatch,* he is "a man who has lived his life through baseball." She said of her job that it was her way of keeping the family business of baseball going.

FURTHER INFORMATION

Periodicals

Blair, Jeff. "Alou Excels at Longevity in Montreal." *St. Louis Post-Dispatch* (August 29, 1998): Sports, 6.

Leavy, Walter. "Baseball's Minority Managers; Taking Charge on the Field." *Ebony* (May, 1993): 110.

Massarotti, Tony. "Baseball; Red Sox Skip to Alou— Kelly Could Be on Deck." *Boston Herald* (March 10, 2002): B18.

Other

"Felipe Alou." BaseballLibrary.com. http://www.pubdim. net/baseballlibrary/ballplayers/A/Alou_Felipe.stm (December 2, 2002).

"Felipe Alou Statistics." Baseball Almanac. http://www. baseball-almanac.com/players/ player.php?p=aloufe01 (December 2, 2002).

"Felipe Alou Statistics." Baseball-Reference.com. http:// www.baseball-reference.com/a/aloufe01.shtml (December 2, 2002).

"Felipe Alou Welcomed in San Francisco." WinterBase ball.com. http://www.latinobaseball.com/articles/ index.php?section=Feature&articleid=94 (December 2, 2002).

"Giants Name Felipe Alou Manager." USAToday.com. http://www.usatoday.com/sports/baseball/nl/giants/ 2002-11-13-alou_x.htm (December 2, 2002).

"Jesus Alou." BaseballLibrary.com. http://www.pubdim. net/baseballlibrary/ballplayers/A/Alou_Jesus.stm (December 2, 2002).

"Matty Alou." BaseballLibrary.com. http://www.pubdim. net/baseballlibrary/ballplayers/A/Alou_Matty.stm (December 2, 2002).

Sketch by Michael Belfiore

Sparky Anderson
1934-

American baseball manager

George "Sparky" Anderson became a big league manager at the age of thirty-five and left the game with

Chronology

1934	Born February 22 in Bridgewater, South Dakota
1942	Moves to Los Angeles
1953	Marries Carol Valle
1959	Makes major league debut with Philadelphia
1964	Becomes minor league manager in Toronto
1969	Accepts managerial position with the Cincinnati Reds
1970	Gets first win as a major league manager
1970	Makes first trip to the World Series
1972	Wins National League Manager of the Year
1975	Wins first World Series with the Reds
1975	Named National League Manager of the Year
1978	Fired by Cincinnati
1979	Named Detroit Tigers' new manager
1984	Wins World Series with the Tigers
1987	Wins a division title with the Tigers
1993	Gets his 2,000 career win
1995	Retires from baseball
2000	Inducted into Baseball Hall of Fame

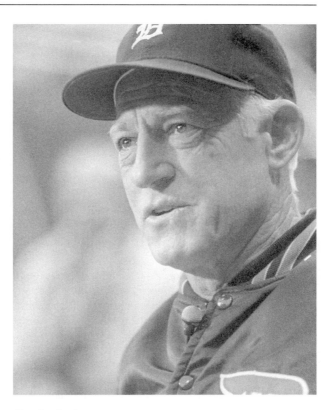

Sparky Anderson

2,228 victories after twenty-six years running the Cincinnati Reds and the Detroit Tigers. Although there are only two managers in baseball that have won more games, **Connie Mack** and John McGraw, Anderson is the last person to take credit for his success. His modesty is almost as astonishing as his record. Even with seven division titles, five pennants and three World Series' on his resume, Sparky Anderson has always insisted his success was due largely to luck and the players he had the honor of managing. His unusual manner of speech and penchant for exaggeration made Anderson a lovable throwback to the golden age of baseball. But what made the Hall of Fame skipper one of the games' great ambassadors, however, was his commitment to principle and his belief in treating everyone—from the ballpark's elevator operator to his star players—with the same generosity and respect.

The Early Years

George Lee Anderson was born February 22, 1934 in Bridgewater, South Dakota. The family had little money and moved to Los Angeles in 1942 in search of work in the shipyards. Anderson's interest in baseball was first sparked by his father, who played catcher on a semipro team and encouraged his son's interest in the sport. After hanging around the baseball field at the University of Southern California, Anderson was offered a job as the team's batboy and formed a lifelong relationship with their coach, Rod Dedeaux. The world revolved around baseball for Anderson and his friends. It was the only thing that caught his attention other than Carol Valle. Valle, a girl he met in the fifth grade, would become his wife in 1953.

Anderson took two buses to attend Dorsey High because the school he was supposed to attend didn't offer baseball. Playing shortstop for Dorsey, he was recognized for his enthusiasm for the game more than his tal-

ent. "There were some guys with much greater ability," remembered Dedeaux in Anderson's book *They Call Me Sparky.* "But they played to maybe 80% of their ability. Georgie always gave you 110%. That pushed him past guys who had more natural talent than him." His drive is what initially caught the interest of Lefty Phillips, a part-time scout for the Cincinnati Reds. When Anderson graduated from high school Phillips was then a full-time scout for the Brooklyn Dodgers and quickly signed Anderson to play for Santa Barbara in the California State League. He would toil in the Dodgers' farm system until 1959 when he was traded to the Philadelphia Phillies. He then played one season with the Phillies, his only season in the major leagues. He soon moved to the International League in Toronto and played second base until he became the team's manager in 1964.

The Big Leagues

Anderson spent the next six years bouncing around the minor leagues learning his craft and passing on his knowledge and enthusiasm. He was hired by the Cincinnati Reds in 1970. He immediately recognized the difference between the minor and major leagues. The stakes were higher and so were the salaries, but Anderson felt the real fun was in the minor leagues and told his team shortly after his arrival. The Reds were far from the minors, however, with **Johnny Bench**, Tony Perez and **Pete Rose** on the roster. The Reds were a team loaded with young talent and on the verge of domination. Al-

Awards and Accomplishments

1971, 1973, 1976-77	Named manager for National League at the All-star game
1972, 1975	Named National League Manager of the Year
1975	Wins World Series
1976	Wins second World Series
1984	Wins first World Series with Detroit Tigers
1985	Named American League manager at the All-star game
2000	Inducted into Baseball Hall of Fame

though Anderson was relatively unknown it didn't take long before his enthusiasm and their talent turned the team into "The Big Red Machine."

Anderson's feisty attitude immediately made headlines. Before his first season, he claimed the Reds would win the division by ten games. Later in his career he would become famous for such predictions but in this particular case he was rewarded by his talented young team. The Reds won the division by 13 1/2 games and went to the World Series where they lost to Baltimore in five games. After the team matured—they featured eight rookies in 1970—they became one of the seventies most dominate teams. In his nine seasons in Cincinnati, Anderson's teams would average ninety-six wins a season and win their division in five of his first seven years. They capped their back to back World Series' victories in 1976. Over the next two years "The Big Red" started to dismantle and although Sparky was an extremely popular figure in Cincinnati, he was fired in 1978.

The age of free-agency had arrived in baseball and while baseball was changing, Anderson's old fashioned values weren't. Among the many rumored reasons floated in the wake of his firing was that his style had supposedly fallen out of favor with the new crop of wealthy young players. Anderson had always demanded a certain amount of discipline from his players on and off the field. He insisted his players look like major leaguers, always clean shaven and well dressed. He wanted his teams to look, act and play with the same amount of excellence and passion. Whatever the reasons for his firing, Sparky Anderson would prove them wrong in Detroit.

Sparky in Detroit

Sparky Anderson left Cincinnati and became manager of the Detroit Tigers in 1979. Anderson's ability to level with his players as people and not as personalities would ultimately prove more powerful than the politics of major league baseball. His teams in Detroit would never be as powerful or talented as those in Cincinnati, but his message would take them to the top and make him the only manager to win a World Series in both the National and American leagues.

The 1984 Tigers won the World Series in convincing fashion. They led the race from the beginning of the sea-

Sparky Anderson Hall of Fame Induction Speech

I want all of you at this moment—and it's a must for me, 'cause this will be the last time I ever get to speak, 'cause when I walk away from here today, I'll never win another game, and I'll never lose another game, and I know that; so in that respect it's a sad moment for me, knowing I will never get to get up in front of a group—but, I want you to take a look at the people behind me and put it in your brain, when you look at 'em. The people that came before them, and these people, and the people that will come after them. That is baseball. All the other stuff you've heard about baseball is just makeup. Those people made this game, and they will protect this game. And when you set in a room with the, and you look around, you say to yourself, "My goodness, George Sugar, how could we come from the streets of Santa Barbara to Cincinnati, Ohio? That's impossible. How could a young man from Bridgewater, South Dakota, 600 people, and couldn't play ever be in front of a microphone, and they're talking about the third winningest manager?"

Well let me tell you this, and get it straight, and I hope every manager that follows me will listen very carefully: Players earn this, by their skills. Managers come here, as I did, on their backs, for what they did for me. I never believed different, I will never believe different, and I think that's what made my career so lucky. I was smart enough to know the people that were doing the work, and I could never under any circumstances ever thank 'em.

My father never got past the third grade, but there ain't a guy that ever went to Harvard as smart as my Daddy. My Daddy said this. He said, "I'm gonna give you a gift. It's the greatest gift to take all the way through your life. And if you live with this gift, everything will work perfect." And he said, "Son, I'm gonna give you a gift that will never cost a dime, and that gift is this: If everyday of your life, and every person you meet, you will just be nice to that person, and treat that person like they are someone." And, you know, I can tell you this. I have tried as hard as I could, and there's no way you can try any harder than I have. My Daddy was all man. He didn't need no big degrees to walk tall. He could walk tall just from the way he handled himself.

I'm not gonna mention players individually or coaches individually. But I'll tell you this: No coach ever worked for me in my whole career. I worked with coaches, and that was the thing I think I enjoyed so much. We were together. We worked together. They told me many times what to do and I listened. 'Cause you know something? It's a funny thing. There are other people besides the manager that are smart. You know, a manager has that above his door. He can be the dumbest moron there ever was, but as long as he's manager he's got "Manager" above his door. That don't work. There's two kind of managers. One that ain't very smart. He gets bad players, loses games, and gets fired. Then there was somebody like me that was a genius. I got good players, stayed out of the way, let 'em win a lot, and then just hung around for 26 years. It was a lot of fun.

Source: Induction Speeches: Sparky Anderson. "Baseball Hall of Fame." http://baseball halloffame.org/hof_weekend/2000/speeches/anderson_sparky.htm (November 24, 2002).

son until the last out of the Series. He would ultimately spend seventeen seasons with the Tigers and claim that the 1987 season was his most satisfying of his career. In 1987, his Tigers were overachievers that made it to the playoffs without the talent of the top clubs but with a feisty determination that reflected Anderson's personality perfectly. During Sparky's years in Detroit he would endure only five losing seasons and make a very public stand against the baseball strike before retiring.

Retirement

He left the Tigers in 1995, resisting a rebuilding project that he and the owners felt he shouldn't have to endure. After flirting with the idea of managing somewhere else, however, Anderson decided he was no longer afraid of the prospect of being out of baseball. He retired to California, the father of three, grandfather of 14 and loving husband of the girl he met in the fifth grade.

Sparky Anderson never strayed from the small town values he learned from his father as a child. He applied the same principles on the field as he did in his personal life. He became one of the most successful managers in baseball history without ever incurring a single smudge on his reputation or straying very far from his roots. "The biggest thing I'll miss," he said during his last days as a big league manager. "Is all the BS I've thrown out."

SELECTED WRITINGS BY ANDERSON:

(With Dan Ewald) *They Call Me Sparky,* Sleeping Bear Press, Chelsea, MI, 1998.

FURTHER INFORMATION

Books

Anderson, Sparky, and Dan Ewald. *They Call Me Sparky.* Chelsea, MI: Sleeping Bear Press, 1998.

Periodicals

"Anderson has Plenty to Talk About as he Returns to Tigers." *Detroit Free Press* (April 5, 1995).
"Fisk, Big Red Machine Meet Again at Cooperstown." *New York Daily News* (July 23, 2000).
"He'll Be Missed, but Time is Right For Sparky's Exit." *Detroit Free Press* (September 21, 1995).
"Managing His Way to Fame." *Baseball Digest* (June, 2000): 46.
"The New Perfesser." *Sports Illustrated* (June 28, 1993): 54.
"A Nice Guy Finishes First." *U.S. News & World Report* (March 13, 2000): 12.
"A Not-So-Classic Fall Classic." *Time* (October 22,1984): 82.
"Sparky's Big Day." *Detroit Free Press* (July 23, 2000).
"Sparky, McGraw to be Neighbors." *Detroit Free Press* (July 20, 2000).
"Sparky Anderson: A Manager Without a Team." *Detroit Free Press* (November 14, 1995).
"Sparky Anderson Exits Walking Tall." *New York Daily News* (February 20, 1995).
"Sparky's Finest Move." *The Sporting News* (July 10, 1995): 8.
"Sparky Says He'd Avoid Spotlight." *Detroit Free Press* (October 14, 2002).
"Will Home Finale Be Triple Play with Sparky Anderson?" *Detroit Free Press* (September 20, 1995).

Sketch by Aric Karpinski

Mario Andretti

Mario Andretti
1940-

American race car driver

Mario Andretti was named Driver of the Century for his distinguished racing career that spanned five decades. Andretti earned his reputation with Championship cars. He won a total of 52 Championship car races, including the prestigious Indianapolis 500 in 1969. He is also the all time leader of Championship car pole position wins with 67 and the all time lap leader with 7,587 laps. Andretti is the all time record holder for Champion car starts with 407 and he is the only driver to ever win Championship car races in four decades. In addition to a remarkable career with Championship cars, Andretti had distinguished himself as a driver who can win on any kind of track and in any kind of car. Andretti has also won races on the sprint, midget, and Formula One circuits. This kind of versatility has put Andretti into a class by himself.

Began Racing in Italy

Mario Gabriele Andretti was born on February 28, 1940 in Montona, Italy (currently Montovun, Croatia).

Chronology

Year	Event
1940	Born on February 28, 1940 in Montona, Italy
1948	Family relocates to a refugee camp in Lucca, Italy following World War II
1955	Andretti family immigrates to the United States
1959	Mario and Aldo Andretti begin driving at the Nazareth Speedway
1959	Aldo Andretti is seriously injured in a racing accident
1961	Marries Dee Ann Hoch
1962	Son Michael is born
1963	Enters first United States Auto Club race in Allentown, Pennsylvania
1964	Wins first United States Auto Club Championship race in Salem, Indiana
1964	Becomes United States citizen
1964	Son Jeff is born
1965	Begins driving for Dean Van Lines
1965	Finishes third in Indianapolis 500 and wins Rookie of the Year award
1965	Wins United States Auto Club National Championship
1966	Wins United States Auto Club National Championship
1969	Wins Indianapolis 500
1969	Wins United States Auto Club National Championship
1969	Daughter Barbara Dee is born
1971	Wins first Formula One race
1978	Wins Formula One World Championship
1981	Comes in second in controversial Indianapolis 500
1984	Wins United States Auto Club National Championship
1985	Finishes second in Indianapolis 500
1992	Four Andrettis (Mario, Michael, Jeff, and John) compete in Indianapolis 500
1993	Wins final Indy car race
1993	Sets fastest qualifying speed at Michigan International Speedway
1994	Retires from open-wheel racing
2002	Joins board of directors for Championship Auto Racing Teams

His father, Alvise Luigi (known as "Gigi") was a farm administrator, while his mother, Rina, raised Mario, his twin brother Aldo, and his older sister Anna Maria. They were a well off family in this small town on the Istrian Peninsula until World War II broke out in Europe. Italy had joined the Axis nations of Germany and Japan and was defeated by the Allied forces. As part of the surrender agreement, the Istrian Peninsula was given to Yugoslavia. In 1948 the Andrettis and many other Italian families left their homes on the Istrian Peninsula and moved to other parts of Italy.

The Andrettis relocated to a refugee camp in Lucca, Italy. It was there that Mario and Aldo began driving their uncle's motorcycle and wooden derby car. At age 13 the boys got their first jobs parking cars for a garage. "The first time I fired up a car, felt the engine shudder and the wheel come to life in my hands, I was hooked. It was a feeling I can't describe. I still get it every time I get into a race car," explained Andretti in *What's It Like Out There*. The Andretti brothers idolized Italian race legend Alberto Ascari, but they had to hide their passion from their father because he disapproved of the sport. Without their parents' knowledge or permission, the boys began racing for a new youth racing league in Italy called Formula Junior.

Due to the difficult economic conditions in post-war Italy, the Andretti family immigrated to the United States in 1955 and they settled in Nazareth, Pennsylvania. The 15-year-old Andretti twins did not speak English so they were placed in the seventh grade in school, much to their embarrassment. In order to catch up with their classmates, they enrolled in correspondence courses. Through these courses Mario met Dee Ann Hoch, who would eventually become his wife.

Became a Professional Racecar Driver in America

Racing in America was quite different than that in Europe. In particular, Americans favored stock cars, while Europeans raced sports cars. In addition, Americans raced on oval tracks, while Europeans raced on winding roads. The Andretti boys learned everything they could about American racing and saved money to build a car. They eventually managed to rebuild a 1948 Hudson Hornet, which they debuted on the Nazareth Speedway in 1959. The brothers took turns racing their Hornet and borrowed other cars to race. They quickly established themselves as winners at the speedway. However, during the final race of 1959 Aldo crashed the Hornet and was seriously injured. He was in a coma for two weeks. Gigi Andretti discovered his sons' racing escapades because of this accident and he was extremely upset with the twins.

Neither Aldo's accident nor Gigi's disapproval stopped Mario from racing. During the next two years he won 21 of 46 stock car races. He also began racing in the United Racing Club sprint car circuit and the indoor midget car winter circuit to gain driving experience. In 1963 Andretti entered his first United States Auto Club (USAC) race, a sprint car race, in Allentown, Pennsylvania. This race allowed him to compete against some of the champions of racing, including **A.J. Foyt**. Although Andretti was a fairly successful driver, he was not yet able to support his young family on racing alone so he also worked as a foreman for Motorvator, a company that manufactured golf carts.

In April of 1964 Andretti entered his first USAC Championship race and in October of the same year he won his first USAC victory in Salem, Indiana. In 1965 Andretti became the lead driver for the Dean Van Lines team, which was owned by Al Dean. In this position, Andretti earned $5,000 a year plus 40 percent of his winnings. Andretti was now a full-time professional driver. With the support of Al Dean and chief mechanic Clint Brawner, Andretti was now in a position to win big races. In particular, 1965 was the first year that Andretti entered the Indianapolis 500. "The start of the 500 Mile Race is something else," Andretti explained in his autobiography *What's It Like Out There?* "The pace car pulls off the track, the green flag is dropped, and 33 drivers push their accelerators to the floor. It looks as if all 33 are trying to hit the first turn at once. Dust comes from all over. The sound alone is enough to drive the timid to

Awards and Accomplishments

1964	First United States Auto Club Championship in Salem, Indiana
1965	Won two United States Auto Club races
1965	Voted Rookie of the Year at the Indianapolis 500
1965	Championship Auto Racing Teams National Champion
1966	Championship Auto Racing Teams National Champion
1966	Won 14 United States Auto Club races
1967	Won nine United States Auto Club races
1967	Won the 12 Hours of Sebring race
1967	Daytona 500 Champion
1967	Driver of the Year
1968	Won three United States Auto Club races
1969	Indianapolis 500 Champion
1969	Won eight United States Auto Club races
1969	Championship Auto Racing Teams National Champion
1970	Won the 12 Hours of Sebring race
1971	First Formula One victory in South Africa
1972	Won the 12 Hours of Sebring race
1974	United States Auto Club National Dirt Track Champion
1978	Driver of the Year
1978	Formula One World Champion
1979	International Race of Champions titlist
1984	Championship Auto Racing Teams National Champion
1984	Driver of the Year
1985	Electrolux Clean Sweep Award for having won pole and race on five different occasions
1985	Driver of the Year
1987	Won 50th Championship car race at Phoenix
1991	One of four Andrettis to race in the Indianapolis 500
1992	Driver of the Quarter Century
1993	Oldest winner in Championship car history at age 53 at the Phoenix Indy
1999	Named Driver of the Century by the Associated Press (tied with A.J. Foyt)
2000	Named Driver of the Century by *RACER* magazine

Related Biography: Race Car Driver Michael Andretti

Michael Andretti, the oldest child of Mario and Dee Ann Andretti, is a racing champion in his own right. He was born on October 5, 1962 in Bethlehem, Pennsylvania. When he was only four years old he saw the Indianapolis Speedway for the first time. When he was seven years old his father won the coveted Indianapolis 500 race. Just 15 years later Michael Andretti competed in his first Indianapolis 500 along with his father. He was the fastest rookie in that race and earned the Indianapolis 500 Rookie of the Year Award.

Like his father, Michael Andretti became a successful driver early in his career. When he was 19 years old he won his first professional championship in the Northeast Formula Ford Division. Two years later, in 1983, he debuted in the Indy Car World Series and the International Motor Sports Association. In addition to his first Indianapolis 500 start in 1984, Michael Andretti also had his first Sports Car Club of America Trans-am event. He has been a versatile driver like his father.

Michael Andretti has been racing on the CART circuit for 18 seasons and he has finished in the top ten of the championship in 17 of those years. He has won 42 Champ car races, which is the most of any active driver. He is also the Champ car leader in pole positions with 32, and laps led with 6,564. The one title that is noticeably missing from Michael Andretti's collection is the Indianapolis 500. Although he has competed in the race 13 times, he has not yet won there.

In addition to racing, Michael Andretti, like his father, has a number of other business interests. He is the owner of Michael Andretti Powersports, and vice president of Andretti Enterprises and Andretti Global Development Corporation. His 15-year-old son, Marco, has already been racing karts and he seems poised to continue the Andretti family legacy.

---

the edge of panic." Andretti, however, was not timid and he finished the race in third place and won the Indianapolis Rookie of the Year Award. Although Andretti only won one USAC race that year, he finished well in several other races and earned enough points in the season to win the USAC National Championship, which was unusual for a rookie.

The Family Business

Andretti's racing career has always been a family business. Although his twin brother, Aldo, was not able to continue racing after two serious crashes in 1959 and 1969, he still remained involved in the sport and in his brother's career. During the peak of his racing career, Andretti became a family man. He married his English tutor, Dee Ann Hoch, on November 25, 1961. Their first child, Michael, was born in 1962, followed by Jeff in 1964, and Barbara Dee in 1969. The Andretti children were exposed to racing from an early age and were subjected to the lifestyle imposed by such a career. For example, the family spent every May living in Indianapolis, Indiana because of the Indianapolis 500, even though Nazareth, Pennsylvania was their hometown. The Andretti children also occupied themselves

with their own racing vehicles and motorized toys, including dirt bikes, go-karts, motorcycles, snowmobiles, and jet skis.

The love for speed was shared by all of the children, even Barbara Dee. The only Andretti daughter loved to race dirt bikes as a child, although she would later pursue a career in singing and songwriting. Both Andretti sons, however, became racecar drivers, as did Aldo's oldest son, John. Andretti claims that he did not plan for his sons to follow in his footsteps. "These kids didn't grow up with me mapping their careers," Andretti told Ed Hinton of *Sports Illustrated* in 1992. "I think it was just a matter of being exposed to it." Andretti did not push his children into the sport, because he recognized that not everyone was capable of racing. "You have to be a dedicated person," Andretti explained to Lyle Kenyon Engel in *Mario Andretti: The Man Who Can Win Any Kind of Race.* "You have to want to do it more than anything else. You have to want to be Number One. Then you have to have the ability. You must be brave, but also have common sense." In 1992 the Andretti family made history when all four racers Mario, Michael, Jeff, and John, drove in the Indianapolis 500. While Jeff's career was cut short because of a serious accident that damaged his legs, Michael and John continue the Andretti racing legacy.

Won the Indianapolis 500

Andretti's success continued throughout the rest of the 1960s. In particular, he repeated the USAC National

Mario Andretti, sitting in car

Championship in 1966 and he won the prestigious Daytona 500 in 1967, as well as the 12 Hours of Sebring endurance race. In 1967 Andretti won eight races but he came in second place in the USAC championship behind A.J. Foyt, another legend in racing who often challenged Andretti on the track. "He and I always respected one another because neither one wanted to settle for second," Foyt told Dave Caldwell of *Knight Ridder/Tribune News Service* in 1994. In 1968 Andretti again came in second place in the USAC championship to another racing rival, **Bobby Unser**. Andretti solidified his power as a racing champion by clinching the 1969 Indianapolis 500. He also won the Pike's Peak Hill Climb in Colorado, a race that had been dominated by Bobby Unser and his family. Andretti topped off 1969 with his third USAC National Championship.

The Indianapolis 500 is the most popular auto race among the general public and one of the most coveted championships among drivers. The track is called "The Brickyard" because it was paved with bricks when it was first built. In 1969 Andretti made his fifth appearance at the Indianapolis 500. During a practice session before the qualifying race, Andretti's car spun out of control and hit the concrete retaining wall. The car flew apart and began to burn. Andretti was lucky to walk away from the crash, although he suffered second-degree burns on his face.

During the qualifying run, Andretti placed second. A.J. Foyt, who had already won three Indianapolis 500

titles, won the pole position. Andretti knew that his car had mechanical problems and tended to overheat, so he did not expect to win the race. He decided to just run the car as hard as he could until it gave out. Although the car did start to overheat, Andretti learned that he could control the problem if he kept his speed at about 165 miles per hour. Several times he had wanted to go faster because of the tense competition around him, but he restrained himself to preserve his car. His strategy paid off. As other drivers fell out of the race due to mechanical problems, Andretti took the lead. In the end, he won his first and only Indianapolis 500 championship in three hours, 11 minutes, and 41 seconds.

A Versatile Driver

In the 1970s Andretti focused on Formula One racing on the international Grand Prix circuit. This consisted of 16 races held on four continents. Andretti's first Formula One race came in 1971 at the South African Grand Prix. He won several other Formula One races over the next few years. In 1978 he won the Formula One World Championship and a year later he won the International Race of Champions title.

Andretti's ability to be a successful racer in different cars and on different tracks is what has made him a truly exceptional driver. "Mario has a combination of various important factors that few of his fellow drivers in USAC share; a burning desire to prove his talents in all fields of racing," wrote Lyle Kenyon Engel in his 1970 book *Mario Andretti: The Man Who Can Win Any Kind of Race.* "He's not satisfied in topping the list in his major racing area of interest, championship cars, but also he wants to excel in sports cars, stockers and Formula cars."

Andretti continued to race both Formula One and Indy cars throughout the 1980s and half of the 1990s. "I have won on 127 different kinds of tracks, clockwise and counterclockwise. I have experienced the passing of the engine from the front to the back. I have raced with the greats who have since retired, and in places that are now parking lots," G.S. Prentzas quoted Andretti from a 1978 interview in the book *Mario Andretti.* In 1984 he won the Championship Car National Championship for the fourth time. He was also named Driver of the Year for the third time, becoming the first driver to receive the award in three different decades. Unfortunately, Andretti was never able to repeat his win at the Indianapolis 500. He came close in 1981 when he placed second to Bobby Unser. After the race was over, Unser was penalized one lap for passing illegally and Andretti was declared the winner. However, Unser protested the penalty, the decision was overturned, and Unser was reinstated as the champion.

Although Andretti continued to drive when many of his contemporaries retired, his victories became sparser as he got older. Andretti won his last Indy car race in Phoenix in

1993. It was the 52nd of his career. That same year, he set the highest qualifying speed at the Michigan International Speedway at 234.275 miles per hour, proving that age had not slowed him down. Andretti decided to retire at the end of the 1994 season. "There's no question that I've driven past my prime, but realistically, I'm still capable of bringing home results," Andretti told Bruce Newman of *Sports Illustrated* in 1994. Even after his retirement, Andretti continued to race in the 24 Hours of LeMans, the one international motor racing title that had eluded him.

CONTACT INFORMATION

Address: Andretti Enterprises, 3310 Airport Rd, Allentown, PA 18109-9302. Phone: (610) 266-0264.

SELECTED WRITINGS BY ANDRETTI:

(With Bob Collins) *What's It Like Out There,* Regnery, 1970.

FURTHER INFORMATION

Books

The Complete Marquis Who's Who. Marquis Who's Who, 2001.

Encyclopedia of World Biography. Farmington Hills, MI: Gale Research, 1998.

Engle, Lyle Kenyon. *Mario Andretti: The Man Who Can Win Any Kind of Race.* New York: Arco Publishing Company, Inc., 1970.

Prentzas, G.S. *Mario Andretti.* New York: Chelsea House Publishers, 1996.

St. James Encyclopedia of Popular Culture. St. James Press, 2000.

Periodicals

Caldwell, Dave. "Mario Andretti to Give His Best Shot in His 29th and Final Indy 500." *Knight Ridder/Tribune News Service* (May 28, 1994).

Cote, Greg. "Name Says It All: Andretti." *Knight Ridder/Tribune News Service* (March 2, 1997).

Hinton, Ed. "Duel with Time." *Sports Illustrated* (June 26, 1995): 50-53.

Hinton, Ed. "Inherit the Wind." *Sports Illustrated* (May 11, 1992): 78.

Honeycutt, Dean. "On the Fast Track with Mario Andretti." *The Washington Times* (January 22, 1998): 8.

Kallmann, Dave. "Andretti Moving Too Fast for Talk About Family 'Curse.'" *Milwaukee Journal Sentinel* (May 31, 2002).

Long, Gary. "Mario Remains in a Class by Himself." *Knight Ridder/Tribune News Service* (May 26, 1994).

Meacham, Jody. "Andretti's Career Comes to an Anticlimax." *Knight Ridder/Tribune News Service* (October 10, 1994).

Myslenski, Skip. "Meet the Next Potentially Great Andretti." *Knight Ridder/Tribune News Service* (August 16, 2002).

Nagy, Bob. "Return of the Master: Mario Andretti Still Winning After All These Years." *Motor Trend* (March 1985): 121-123.

Newman, Bruce. "Arrivederci, Mario." *Sports Illustrated* (October 17, 1994): 88.

Shaw, Bill. "A Driver Divided, Mario Andretti Wants the Indy 500 for Both Himself and His Son." *People Weekly* (May 28, 1984): 60-61.

Stone, Matt. "Like Fathers, Like Sons." *Motor Trend* (September 2001): 116.

Other

Motorsports Hall of Fame. http://www.mshf.com/hof/andretti_mario.htm (December 18, 2002).

Official Andretti Family Website. http://www.andretti.com (December 31, 2002).

Sketch by Janet P. Stamatel

Earl Anthony
1938-2001

American bowler

Utterly without personal flash or pyrotechnics, Earl Anthony became the overwhelmingly dominant professional bowler of the twentieth century. Sporting a crewcut and horn-rimmed glasses in an age of permed hair and gold chains, Anthony was "Square Earl" to some. But the near-mechanical consistency of his form and the deadly accuracy of his shots earned him a more fitting tag: "The Machine." There was no better bowler in the 1970s and early 1980s than Earl Anthony. He was

Earl Anthony

Chronology

1938	Born April 27, in Kent Washington
1960	Offered baseball contract by Baltimore Orioles
1962	Bowls for the first time
1963	Bowls seven events on the PBA Tour
1969	Joins PBA Tour for second time
1970	Wins first PBA tournament
1974	Wins PBA Nationals and the Tournament of Champions back-to-back
1975	Becomes first bowler to win $100,000 on the PBA Tour
1976	Passes Dick Weber on all-time tournament victory list
1978	Suffers heart attack
1982	Becomes first bowler to pass $1 million in career winnings
1983	Retires from PBA Tour
1986	Briefly rejoins to PBA Tour
1990	Joins PBA Seniors Tour for one year
1996	Rejoins Seniors Tour for one year
1997	Wins last PBA tournament
2001	Dies in New Berlin, Wisconsin

named Bowler of the Year from 1974 through 1976, and again from 1981 through 1983. He led the Professional Bowlers Association (PBA) Tour in scoring in five separate years. Over the course of his stop-and-start career—he retired four times—he won an unequalled forty-one titles on the regular PBA Tour, including six PBA national championships and two Tournament of Champions titles; he reached the championship round—the so-called top five—in PBA tournaments 144 times, more than anyone else. He later added seven wins in the PBA Seniors Tour. He was the first pro bowler to amass more than $1 million in career winnings. "He was a tremendous guy," **Dick Weber** told Harry Page of the *San Antonio Express-News*. "He was a fierce, fierce competitor and everybody feared him. He had a simple game, and he could adjust to anything on the left side. I really admired what he did with a bowling ball. There was none like him. He was the greatest speed-control bowler ever to play the game."

Early Life

Earl Anthony grew up in Tacoma, Washington and entered the U.S. Air Force just before he was due to graduate from high school. His first sport was baseball, and he was a good enough pitcher to be offered a $35,000 signing bonus by the Baltimore Orioles. The deal fell through, however, on the very next day at an Orioles training camp when Anthony tore the rotator cuff muscle in his throwing arm. His baseball career was

over and it was a year before he could raise his arm above his shoulder. The injury apparently did not affect his bowling prospects. "I'm not sure bowling and pitching have a lot in common. It's two different deliveries," Anthony told the *Toronto Star*'s Jim Proudfoot. "But you're talking hand-and-eye co-ordination and making a ball do certain precise things. Those are similarities."

Returning to Tacoma, a 21-year-old Anthony took a job as a forklift driver for a grocery store chain. Encouraged by co-workers, he joined the company bowling team. Ironically, although Anthony had, as a boy, worked as a pinsetter at a local bowling alley, he had never bowled. He was *very* good, however. By the season's end his average was 217, up at the rarefied level of professional bowlers. In 1963 he turned pro. He joined the PBA Tour long enough to bowl in seven events without winning a cent in any of them. For the next seven years he satisfied himself bowling at local tournaments in Tacoma, winning about $8,000 in the process.

Rejoins PBA Tour

Anthony returned to the PBA Tour in 1969 and had an encouraging second-place finish in his first tournament. He won his first event 1970 in Seattle, and another one the following year in New York City. It was in 1974, however, that Earl Anthony began establishing himself as the world's best pro bowler. After a slow start—he missed winning his first thirteen tournaments—he won two of the biggest events on the Tour, the Tournament of Champions and the PBA National Championship back-to-back. Before the season was over, he won four more events and set records for season average with 219.34 and season winnings with over $90,000. In 1975 he became the first pro bowler to win over $100,000 in a single season. In 1976 with his 27th title he passed Dick Weber as the leader on the career victory list. His success was due, in part at least, to knowing what he wanted. "I set goals throughout the years," he was quoted in the *New York Times*. "I wanted to win 40 tournaments and I won 45. I wanted to the first bowler to win $100,000 in a year and I did that. I wanted to win $1 million and I did that."

In 1978 Anthony suffered a serious heart attack, but made an astonishing comeback, leading the PBA in scoring in 1980 and 1983, and being named Bowler of the Year from 1981 through 1983. In February 1982 he became the first bowler in history to win more than $1 million in his career, rolling five straight strikes to take a national championship in Toledo Ohio. However, by 1983 the constant life on the road had worn Anthony down and, with $1,216,421 in career winnings and forty-one PBA Tour wins, he announced his retirement. At the request of friends he made a brief comeback in 1986. "I absolutely hated it. My concentration was gone. I'd get out there and forget what I was trying to do. I'd start thinking about whether my lawn needed mowing. So that was it for me," he told the *Toronto Star*.

Joins Seniors Tour

He became a commentator on televised bowling events and a representative of the makers of Ebonite bowling balls. He joined the PBA Seniors Tour in 1990 but, wracked by arthritis, he retired from that a year later. When alternative medical treatments relieved the arthritis substantially, Anthony returned to the Seniors in 1996. The public loved having him back, enthusiastically cheering every strike and moaning every pin left standing. "Such respect is saved for the few great athletes who have transcended their sports. Anthony is one," wrote the *Milwaukee Journal Sentinel*'s Paul Drzewiecki. He retired from bowling for the final time at the end of the 1997 season.

Earl Anthony died in August 2001 after falling down the stairs at a friend's home in New Berlin Wisconsin. The official cause of death was head trauma. He was survived by his wife, Susie, his son, Mike, and his daughters Tracy Nelson and Jeri.

With his thick glasses and deadpan expression, Earl Anthony looked like the most improbable of athletic champions. His record though speaks for itself. He was the only pro bowler to win at least one title fourteen years in a row—despite his mid-career heart attack. He rolled more than 600 perfect games in his career. He was named to the Professional Bowlers Association Hall of Fame in 1981 and the American Bowling Congress Hall of Fame in 1986. What's more, bowlers loved him. In 1985 the readers of *Bowling Magazine* voted him the greatest bowler of all time, an honor that was reiterated in 1995 when American Bowling Congress members voted him the "best bowler ever," giving him well-over three times the number of votes garnered by the runner-up, Dick Weber. It is unlikely Bowling will ever see the likes of Earl Anthony again.

Awards and Accomplishments	
1973-75, 1980, 1983	George Young High Average Award
1974-76, 1981-83	Leading money winner on PBA Tour
1974-76, 1981-83	Bowler of the Year, Bowling Writers Association
1977, 1984	ABC Masters winner
1986	Inducted into PBA Hall of Fame
1986	Inducted into American Bowling Congress Hall of Fame
1997	AMF Grand Prix of Bowling winner

FURTHER INFORMATION

Periodicals

"Anthony Says Goodbye To Career of Fast Lanes." *New York Times*. June 20, 1991.

"Anthony Quitting Tour." *New York Times*. October 16, 1983.

Drzewiecki, Paul. "Anthony gets his due from fans: Respect and admiration follow legendary bowler." *Milwaukee Journal Sentinel*. April 8, 1997.

Fuller, Tom. "Anthony Hopes To Return To The Top At The Seattle Open." *Seattle Times*. July 5, 1997.

Klein, Tom. "Runner-Up Anthony Goes Out On A Roll." *St. Louis Post-Dispatch*. June 21, 1991.

Proudfoot, Jim. "Out of baseball, Anthony became No. 1 in bowling." *Toronto Star*. August 26, 1989.

Smith, Craig. "Legendary Anthony Still Bowls 'Em Over—Hall Of Famer On Mission For Sport." *Seattle Times*. June 30, 1996.

Smith, Craig. "Tacoma bowler became a legend." *Seattle Times*. August 15, 2001.

Sonderegger, John. "Rolling On: Anthony Still Likes To Compete." *St. Louis Post-Dispatch*. June 20, 1990.

Sketch by Gerald E. Brennan

Luis Aparicio
1934-

Venezuelan baseball player

Most will agree that in the game of baseball, power is king. However, one individual who did not fit this mold, yet achieved star status, is Luis Aparicio. "Little Looie" set an example of skill, strength, and dexterity that seized the spotlight usually afforded to power hitters. While home runs were not his specialty, Aparicio's physical prowess and multi-faceted assets as a baseball player in the 1950s, 1960s, and 1970s are well recorded in baseball history. In fact, many consider Luis Aparicio to be baseball's best all-around shortstop.

Luis Aparicio

Growing up in Venezuela

Luis Aparicio was born in Maracaibo, Venezuela, on April 29, 1934. It's not surprising that he became enraptured with baseball at a very early age. His father, Luis E. Aparicio Sr., a tractor driver for an oil company, was an avid baseball player and the very first Venezuelan to ever be offered a major league contract to play baseball. Playing the game he loved in the Venezuelan league (with the Caracas Club) to the age of 41, Aparicio Sr. passed along his considerable knowledge, teaching his son the "ins" and "outs" of the game and the particulars involved in becoming an effective and valuable team player.

Attending public schools in Maracaibo, Aparicio grew to his 5'9" height, and 155-160 pound weight by high school. In fact, his slight stature later earned him the recognizable nickname of "Little Looie." Deciding that baseball was his destiny, Aparicio left high school after completing two years and began playing with an amateur team in Caracas, Venezuela. Incredibly, he batted .350, which helped to propel his team into the Latin American World Series. Later, he played for the Barquismeto Cardinals.

Following in his father's image, Aparicio became a shortstop—assuming the position he would continue to play for his entire professional career. In fact, in 1953, he took his father's place as shortstop for the Maracaibo Gavilanes.

Chronology

1934	Born April 29 in Maracaibo, Venezuela
1950-53	Plays with amateur teams in Venezuela
1953	Replaces his father as shortstop for the Maracaibo Gavilanes in Venezuela
1954	Plays in the minor leagues on Waterloo, a White Sox farm team
1955	Moves to Southern Association; plays with Memphis
1956	Debuts in majors; named Rookie of the Year
1956	Marries Sonia Llorente on October 1
1956-62	Plays with Chicago White Sox
1956-64	American League stolen base leader 9 consecutive years
1959	Helps Chicago White Sox win the pennant
1963-67	Plays with Baltimore Orioles
1968-70	Plays with Chicago White Sox
1971-73	Plays with Boston Red Sox
1984	Named to Baseball Hall of Fame (first Venezuelan player)

"Discovered" that same year, Aparicio was offered a contract to play for the Chicago White Sox. Moving to the United States, he played with Waterloo, a White Sox farm team in 1954. The following year, he joined the Southern Association, playing for Memphis. He was a standout—leading the league in stolen bases, assists, and total putouts—though he also led in errors.

Major League Career

Nineteen fifty-six was a banner year for Aparicio. He joined the Chicago White Sox, replacing fellow Venezuelan Chico Carrasquel as the starting shortstop, married Sonia Llorente (and later had five children), and was named the American League's Rookie of the Year. He remained with the White Sox for the next seven years, from 1956 to 1964, during which time he established his dominance at shortstop.

Nineteen fifty-nine was also a magical year for the starting shortstop and his close friend and fielding partner, second baseman, Nellie Fox. Second-baseman Nellie Fox paired with Aparicio for seven consecutive seasons (1956-1962) to form a defensive duo of great distinction. With Aparicio as the lead-off man for the White Sox and Fox batting second, the two earned considerable respect from fans and competitors alike. Opposing teams were well aware of the threat these two posed both on the field and at the plate. Many times players were "cheated" out of hits because of the exacting field chemistry displayed by these two Hall of Famers.

This strong pair were instrumental in helping the White Sox overcome their rivals, the New York Yankees, and go on to win the American League pennant. In fact, Aparicio made the final "out" of that season and Nellie Fox was named Most Valuable Player that year (with Aparicio coming in second). It was the first pennant win for the White Sox in forty years.

Career Statistics

Yr	Team	AVG	GP	AB	R	H	RBI	SO	SB	SB%
1956	CWS	.266	152	603	69	142	56	63	21	.840
1957	CWS	.257	143	605	82	148	41	55	28	.778
1958	CWS	.266	145	569	76	148	40	38	29	.829
1959	CWS	.257	152	585	98	157	51	40	56	.812
1960	CWS	.277	153	625	86	166	61	39	51	.864
1961	CWS	.272	156	579	90	170	45	33	53	.803
1962	CWS	.241	153	529	72	140	40	36	31	.721
1963	BAL	.250	146	34	73	150	45	35	40	.870
1964	BAL	.266	146	49	93	154	37	51	57	.770
1965	BAL	.225	144	452	67	127	40	56	26	.788
1966	BAL	.276	151	563	97	182	41	42	25	.694
1967	BAL	.233	134	600	55	127	31	44	18	.783
1968	CWS	.264	155	573	55	164	36	43	17	.607
1969	CWS	.280	156	567	77	168	51	29	24	.857
1970	CWS	.313	146	250	86	173	43	34	8	.727
1971	BOS	.232	125	3	56	114	45	43	6	.600
1972	BOS	.257	110	84	47	112	39	28	3	.500
1973	BOS	.271	132	550	56	135	49	33	13	.929
TOTAL		.262	2599	10230	1335	2677	791	742	506	.788

BAL: Baltimore Orioles; BOS: Boston Red Sox; CWS: Chicago White Sox.

Traded to the Baltimore Orioles in 1963, Aparicio was a strong addition to his team, with his usual fielding skills. In 1968, Aparicio returned to the White Sox and remained there for the next three seasons. Two of these years were strong batting years for him. In 1969, he hit .280 and in 1970, he achieved his career high .313 batting average.

Establishes Many Records

"Little Looie" earned many honors during his career and established many new records. For the nine years between 1956 and 1964, he was the leader in stolen bases (reaching his highest number of fifty-six in 1959). Further, he earned the honor of being the first major league player since **Ty Cobb** to steal fifty or more bases three years in a row.

Aparicio was an outstanding fielder and earned great distinction as a Gold Glove winner every year from 1958 to 1962 and then in 1964, 1966, 1968, and 1970. (Gold Gloves are presented to honor the best fielders at their positions.) In addition, Aparicio led all American League shortstops in fielding for eight consecutive years, led five times in games played, seven times in assists, four times in putouts, twice each in total chances per game and double plays, and only once in errors. The American League at-bats leader in 1966, Aparicio ranks first among all shortstops in lifetime games (2,581), double plays (1,553), chances (12,564), and assists (8,016).

Aparicio's high level of performance won him a place on the All-Star team as shortstop from 1958-1964 and 1970-1972—a total of ten times. He also ranked as the Sporting News All-Star shortstop every other year from 1964 to 1972.

Moving on After Professional Baseball

With his professional baseball career behind him, Aparicio moved back to his home country, Venezuela, assuming co-ownership of a baseball club there. In 1984, he achieved the highest honor in baseball when he was inducted into the Baseball Hall of Fame in Cooperstown, New York. In another honor, his number was retired by the White Sox the same year.

Aparicio presented the ultimate baseball package—exceptional fielding skills, amazing base running abilities, and fairly good batting numbers. His exceptional base stealing and fielding prowess created a level of fan excitement that was usually only reserved for home run hitters. "Little Looie" truly proved that size is only one measure of an individual's excellence.

FURTHER INFORMATION

Books

Frommer, Harvey. *Baseball's Hall of Fame.* New York: Franklin Watts, 1985.

"Luis Aparicio." *St. James Encyclopedia of Popular Culture.* five volumes. Detroit: St. James Press, 2000.

"Luis Aparicio." *Discovering Multicultural America.* Detroit: Gale, 1996.

"Luis Ernesto Aparicio, Jr." *Dictionary of Hispanic Biography.* Detroit: Gale, 1996.

Skipper, John C. *A Biographical Dictionary of the Baseball Hall of Fame.* Jefferson, NC: McFarland & Company, 2000.

Awards and Accomplishments

1956	American League Rookie of the Year
1958-64, 1970-72	All-Star Team
1958-62, 1964,1966, 1968,1970	Gold Glove Winner
1984	Elected to Hall of Fame
1984	Number retired by White Sox

At the time of his retirement, Aparicio held the major-league record for most games at short (2,581), and American League marks for assists (8,016), double plays (1,553), chances (12,564), and putouts (4,548). He also led the league in stolen bases nine consecutive times (1956-64).

Other

BaseballAlmanac-Gold Glove Award: Shortstops. http://www.baseball-almanac.com/awards/aw_ggss.shtml (November 19, 2002).

HickokSports.com-Biography-Luis Aparicio. http://www.hickoksports.com/biograph/aparicio.shtml (November 19, 2002).

Luis Aparicio-Strength Down the Middle. http://www.1959whitesox.com/cgi/player.cgi?player=Aparicio_Luis (November 19, 2002)

Luis Aparicio-BaseballLibrary.com. http://www.pubdim.net/baseballlibrary/ballplayers/A/Aparacio_Luis.stm (November 19, 2002)

Luis Aparicio. http://sportsillustrated.cnn.com/baseball/mlb/stats/alltime/player/batting/5870.html (November 19, 2002)

Luis Aparicio. http://sports.espn.go.com/mlb/alltime/playercard?playerId=300=0 (November 19, 2002).

Luis E. Aparicio, Jr. http://www.hickoksports.com/biograph/aparicio.shtml (November 19, 2002).

Luis Aparicio. http://brsmith.mybravenet.com/History/400Pages/al1959.html (November 19, 2002).

National Baseball Hall of Fame - Luis Aparicio's Plaque. http://www.baseballhalloffame.org/hofers_and_honorees/plaques/aparicio_luis.htm (November 19, 2002).

National Baseball Hall of Fame-Nellie Fox. http://www.baseballhalloffame.org/hofers_and_honorees/hofer_bios/fox_nellie.htm (November 19, 2002).

Nellie Fox/BaseballLibrary.com. http://www.pubdim.net/baseballlibrary/ballplayers/F/Fox_Nellie.stm (November 19, 2002).

Player Pages—Nellie Fox. http://www.thebaseballpage.com/past/pp/foxnellie/default.htm (November 19, 2002).

Player Pages—Luis Aparicio. http://www.thebaseballpage.com/past/pp/aparicioluis/default.htm (November 19, 2002).

Player Profile: Luis Aparicio. http://www.diamondfans.com/profile-aparicio.html (November 19, 2002).

Sketch by Jan Goldberg

Lance Armstrong
1971-

American cyclist

Cancer was arguably the best thing that ever happened to Lance Armstrong. The world champion cyclist's career can be divided into two distinct periods: pre- and post-cancer. In the first, he was a brash young rider who won by sheer force and drive, but who did so arrogantly and without respect for his sport. After beating the odds and surviving testicular cancer, Armstrong came back to racing a humbled and thoughtful rider who channeled his energies, learned to depend on his team, and won an astonishing four grueling Tour de France races.

Armstrong was born September 18, 1971 near Dallas, Texas. His mother Linda, a secretary, was just seventeen years old when he was born, and her husband, Gunderson, left the family when Lance was two. When Linda got a better job, mother and son moved from a low-income suburb of Dallas and bought a home in Plano, Texas. Linda's second husband, Terry Armstrong, was a born-again Christian and strict disciplinarian who could not tolerate the rambunctious nature of a growing boy. Lance never bonded with his adoptive father. His mother, with whom he remains very close, was always his greatest influence.

In addition to an adversarial relationship with his stepfather, Armstrong did not fit in in Plano, where kids who were football players and whose parents had money were in favor, and he was neither. In fifth grade, he found a way to channel some of his energy and angst when he won a distance-running race at school. He then started swimming at the City of Plano Swim Club, where, after a rocky start, he found a place where he fit in. Because of his lack of skill the twelve-year-old was assigned to a class of seven-year-olds, but Armstrong swallowed his pride and soon began to swim quite well. Under the guidance of coach Chris MacCurdy, he started to train, swim, and win competitively. At age thirteen, he was riding his bike twenty miles every day to and from school and swim practice, which started at 5:30 in the morning and met again after school.

Saw His Future in Grueling Race

Hanging out at the local bike shop, the Richardson Bike Mart, Armstrong saw an ad for a competition called a triathlon, which was a combination swim, bike, and running race. The event, a junior triathlon called IronKids, seemed like a natural fit for Armstrong. His mother encouraged him and saved money to buy him the racing clothes and bike he needed. He easily won the race, and soon signed up for another. He had discovered something that he could excel at; he found he thrived at

Chronology

1971	Born September 18 in Texas
1984	Wins his first triathlon, a junior event called IronKids
1987	Enters his first non-junior triathlon
1987	Competes as a professional triathlete
1989	Qualifies to train with the U.S. Olympic developmental team in Colorado Springs, Colorado
1989	Competes in the Junior World Championships in Moscow
1992	Turns pro after Olympics in Barcelona, Spain
1992	Finishes first professional race dead last—27 minutes behind the winner
1993	Becomes youngest world road-racing champion
1993	Wins first stage in the Tour de France, but drops out
1993	Is member of first U.S. team, Team Motorola, to be ranked top-five in the world
1994	Fails to win a single race
1995	Finishes Tour de France with one stage win
1996	Drops out of Tour de France in July with a cold
1996	Is diagnosed with advanced testicular cancer in October
1996	Undergoes operations to remove affected testicle and lesions in his brain
1997	Cancer goes into remission in January
1997	Signs modest contract with U.S. Postal Team after being dropped by French Cofidis team
1998	Marries Kristin "Kik" Richard and returns to racing

Lance Armstrong

suffering through the grueling competitions. When his mother told Armstrong she was divorcing his stepfather, the boy was ambivalent; it would be a relief to be rid of him, but it also meant his mother would have to struggle to support them on her own.

In 1987, at age fifteen, Armstrong entered his first non-junior triathlon, the President's Triathlon. He finished the course a respectable 32nd in a field of much older, more experienced athletes. He declared his intentions to be the best in ten years time, which was a clear indication of his natural cockiness. In 1988, he placed fifth in the event. He entered as many triathlons as he could, often lying about his age to qualify. The older athletes called him Junior. He soon started entering cycling contests as well, and winning against more experienced riders. His prize winnings made Armstrong a contributor to the family income, which also motivated him. At age sixteen, he was earning about $20,000 a year in race money. After an astonishing cycling race win in New Mexico in 1989, Armstrong was invited by the U.S. Cycling Federation to train with the U.S. Olympic developmental team in Colorado Springs, Colorado, and to compete at the Junior World Championships in Moscow.

Armstrong found in Moscow that he had a lot to learn about the tactical aspects of European racing, but his natural talent and competitive drive was clear to both European and American officials and team managers. When he returned home from Moscow, Armstrong, who was set to graduate in a few weeks, found out that the administrators of Plano East High were counting his time away as unexcused and were not going to let him graduate. Frantic but determined, Armstrong and his

mother found a private school that would let him transfer and graduate on time, if he made up his work over the summer. Soon after graduation, Armstrong was invited to join the U.S. national team.

Coach Tried to Rein Him In

The U.S. team coach, Chris Carmichael, recognized Armstrong's aggressive, headstrong nature and sought to rein it in and teach him the skills of international cycling competition. At the 1990 World Championships, his first race with the national team, Armstrong ignored Carmichael, who had instructed him to pace himself and remain with the "peloton," or pack of cyclists, on the 115-mile course. Armstrong went full force, and pulled far ahead of the peloton. As he tired though, the pack caught up with him and the riders who had conserved their energy pulled ahead. Still, Armstrong finished a respectable 11th, the best finish ever for an American in the race. Armstrong, who was nicknamed the Texas Bull, had many similar experiences, but never seemed to be able to learn from them.

In 1992, Armstrong won his first two major races, the First Union Grand Prix in Atlanta and Thrift Drug Classic in Pittsburgh. He also raced on the U.S. Olympic team at the Games in Barcelona, Spain, finishing 14th in the road race. Soon after, he entered his first professional European race, a tough, one-day race called the San Sebastian Classic, which was also held in Spain. The

Awards and Accomplishments

1984	First place, Iron Kids Triathlon
1991	First place, U.S. National Amateur Championships
1992	First place, First Union Grand Prix
1992	First place, Thrift Drug Classic
1992	14th place in road race, Olympic Games in Barcelona, Spain
1992	Second place, World Cup race in Zurich, Switzerland
1993	Thrift Drug Triple Crown: first place in Thrift Drug Classic, K-Mart Classic, and CoreStates
1993	First place, U.S. Pro Road Race
1993	Second place, Tour DuPont
1993	World road-racing champion
1995-96	First place, Tour DuPont
1996	12th place, Olympic Games in Atlanta, Georgia
1998	Fourth place, U.S. Pro Championships
1998	Fourth place, World Championships
1998	First place, Tour of Luxembourg
1998	First place, Sprint 56K Criterium
1998	First place, Cascade Classic
1998	First place, Rheinland Pfafz Rundfahrt
1998	Second place, First Union International
1999-2002	First place, Tour de France
2000	Third place in time trial, Olympic Games in Sydney, Australia

Sportsman of the Year

The man doesn't sit still. His wife knows why, too.

She met him when he was a pale-yellow version of himself, half gone from chemo and scared to die. "I got to know Lance when he was standing on the edge between life and death," Kristin says. "It was awesome to be part of. I felt like he showed me the view from that cliff. That bonds two people. And if you get to come back down from that edge, it changes your life. You never want to miss out on anything fun or beautiful or scary again."

So he does his Texas Tornado thing. He motocrosses Baja with Lyle Lovett. He drives like he's racing Steve McQueen. He wakes the kids up to play. He puts Luke in one of those little trailers behind his bike. (O.K., Luke, we're going to take this downhill at about 70 miles per hour! Hang on!) He pounds out a hand-cramping number of letters to cancer patients and learns to surf in Hawaii. Anything to prove he'll never waste that second chance.

Source: Reilly, Rick. *Sports Illustrated,* December 16, 2002, p. 52.

crowd laughed at him as he finished last, 27 minutes behind the winner, in the driving rain. Two weeks later, he took second place in a World Cup race in Zurich, Switzerland. Armstrong plowed ahead in the international circuit, competing well in races, but not winning favor. His brash and disrespectful attitude offended many European riders and fans. "I raced with no respect. Absolutely none," he admitted in his autobiography. "I paraded, mouthed off, shoved my fists in the air. I was still the kid from Plano with a chip on my shoulder, riding headlong, pedaling out of anger." In 1993, he won the Thrift Drug Triple Crown: first place in Thrift Drug Classic, K-Mart Classic, and CoreStates and took first place in the U.S. Pro Road Race.

Armstrong was becoming proficient in daylong events, and had placed second in the eleven-day Tour DuPont. With this respectable but meager experience behind him, Armstrong plowed into his first Tour de France. The 21-year-old, first-year pro had no concept of the respect that the grueling, 21-day, 2,300-plus-mile race through the French and Belgian countryside and mountains deserved. He lasted eleven days, dropping out in 62nd place. He came back one month later to win the 1993 World Championships in Oslo, Norway. At the awards ceremony, he pulled his mother up onto the podium with him. His first big, international win fueled Armstrong to work harder. His team, Team Motorola, finished the season ranked in the top five in the world—a first for an American team.

Cocky But Unable to Go the Distance

A powerful, muscular rider, he continued to excel in one-day races, but usually faded early in multi-day competitions, though he placed second again in the Tour DuPont,

the biggest race in America, and almost a prerequisite to the Tour de France. He did not win a single race in 1994.

Competitive road-racing cyclists must be multi-talented. Riders must be able to endure long stretches of paced cycling, and also be able to power up steep mountains. Most cyclists are better at one or the other, but to ever compete in the Tour de France, he must be a master of both. Armstrong trained in the Rocky Mountains and European Alps to make him more proficient at the climbing portions of multi-stage races. Armstrong finally proved himself in the Tour DuPont in 1995 by finishing in first place.

Armstrong finished his first Tour de France, in 1995, a humbled man. His Motorola teammate, Fabio Casartelli, was killed in a crash in the 15th stage of the race. Armstrong dedicated his 18th-stage win to Casartelli, but admitted after the race that he had learned more about life and death on this Tour than he had about cycling. At this point, he was ranked seventh in the world and was making about $750,000 per year. After the season ended, he trained harder than ever to come back even stronger for the 1996 season.

An early season crash set Armstrong back in his training, and he was finishing second in races he'd expected to win. Then, Team Motorola announced it was quitting its sponsorship, leaving the Motorola riders teamless. This season would be key for Armstrong if he expected to land a contract with another team. The pressure made him perform well at the European spring races, and he won the Tour DuPont for the second year in a row. When he crossed the finish line, exhausted rather than exalted, he should have known something was wrong.

Armstrong was ranked fourth in the world at the start of the 1996 Tour de France but feeling sick and out of breath, pulled himself out of the race by the sixth day. He refocused his energies to finding a new sponsor and preparing for the 1996 Olympics, held on home turf in Atlanta, Georgia. He finished a disappointing 12th in At-

Lance Armstrong

lanta, but managed to sign a two-year, $2.5 million contract with French team Cofidis. His performance in the fall World Cup season was disappointing, as well, and he retreated to his new home in Austin, Texas to rest.

Pain Tolerance Delayed Cancer Diagnosis

Armstrong noticed swelling in his right testicle but did not seek medical attention until he started coughing up blood. What he thought would be a routine visit turned on him when he was diagnosed with testicular cancer. Accustomed to enduring pain, Armstrong had ignored his discomfort for so long that the cancer had spread to his abdomen and lungs. At the time, he was most concerned with not being able to race again.

Doctors removed the testicle, and Armstrong began aggressive chemotherapy treatment. The situation turned critical when doctors found the cancer had spread to his brain, and on October 25, 1996, he underwent brain surgery to remove two tumors. His tolerance for pain served him well through his battle with cancer, and he was given a 40-percent chance of survival. Luckily, his sponsors and the Cofidis team remained behind him, though legally they did not have to. After a while, Cofidis started to back away from Armstrong and, while he lay sick and curled up in his bed, renegotiated his contract.

After a few short months of surgery and aggressive and debilitating chemo, Armstrong's cancer was in remission. He returned home bald, scarred, weak, but alive. His doctors were cautiously optimistic about his recovery and possible return to racing, but Armstrong found himself, for the first time in his life, looking at life as more than a race to win, and did some soul searching. He then founded the Lance Armstrong Foundation to help cancer patients and survivors. He met Kristin "Kik" Richard working with the foundation. The two were married in 1998 and have three children.

Armstrong's doctors cautioned him to train slowly, and it became clear he would not ride in the 1997 season; they would not allow him to race until his cancer had been in remission for a full year. Dropped from the Cofidis team, Armstrong resolved to come back stronger than ever. The U.S. Postal Team took a risk on Armstrong by signing him when he was unable to race, but for it he took a drastic cut in pay. Armstrong placed 14th in his first race back, Spain's Ruta del Sol, a remarkable finish considering he had also just beaten cancer. In France soon after, he dropped out of a race midway and returned to Texas in an inexplicable funk. After watching Armstrong languish in front of the TV for weeks, his coach, Chris Carmichael, told him to announce his retirement or get back to training. After an intensive train-

Related Biography: United States Postal Service Pro Cycling Team

No cyclist wins the Tour de France on his own. On each team, there is an arrangement of cyclists who strategize to bring the team leader to the finish line. At times, the leader will ride behind a teammate, "drafting," and cyclists often flank their leader to protect him from collisions with other riders. "An individual can make a silly mistake, but when he's got a great team around him, it's hard to make a mistake," Armstrong admitted to Bonnie DeSimone of the *Chicago Tribune*. The United States Postal Service Pro Cycling Team consists of twenty riders from around the world. Seventeen of the twenty riders, including second-place Tour of Spain winner Roberto Heras, must have Grand Tour experience. Armstrong's 2003 team includes Viatcheslav Ekimov, George Hincapie, Benoit Joachim, Floyd Landis, Pavel Padrnos and Victor Hugo Pena, who raced with him in the 2002 Tour de France. Each must be talented enough to win, but who forfeit their own glory for that of their team and leader.

ing camp in the Appalachians, Armstrong recovered his will to race.

A Most Remarkable Recovery

Armstrong finished fourth in the U.S. Pro Championships in June 1998. After a first place finish in the Tour of Luxembourg and taking fourth in the World Championships, Armstrong was back in full force. Wisely, he avoided the 1998 Tour de France, which was plagued by a doping scandal. 1999 was going to be his year.

On July 4, 1999 Armstrong, leaner and stronger than ever, started the Tour de France with force. After taking the lead early on—and donning the race leader's yellow jersey—competitors were sure he would drop back. He hung back for a few stages, but regained his lead on the ninth day, where the race entered the grueling Alps region. Speculation of performance-enhancing drug use dogged him, but his drug tests came up clean. The race was his when he crossed the finish line in Paris on July 25, 1999. He was only the second American to win the Tour de France. The first was Greg Le Mond. His repeat 2000, 2001, and 2002 wins of the Tour de France were nothing short of miraculous. The "Golden Boy of American Cycling" amazed his friends, family, and fans by first conquering cancer, and then the world's toughest race. In 2003, he'll set out to tie Spaniard **Miguel Indurain**'s record of five Tour de France wins.

SELECTED WRITINGS BY ARMSTRONG:

(With Sally Jenkins) *It's Not About the Bike,* Berkley Books, 2001.

FURTHER INFORMATION

Books

Armstong, Lance (with Sally Jenkins). *It's Not About the Bike*. New York: Berkley Books, 2001.

Thompson, John. *Lance Armstrong*. Philadelphia: Chelsea House Publishers, 2001.

Periodicals

Abt, Samuel. "Armstrong completes a tour de force." *New York Times* (July 29, 2002): D1.

Abt, Samuel. "The French (mostly) adore Armstrong." *New York Times* (July 30, 2002): D5.

Abt, Samuel. "Getting things right, so no one can follow." *New York Times* (July 29, 2002): D5.

Anderson, Kelly. "King of the hill." *Sports Illustrated* (July 29, 2002): 32.

Brown, Justin. "Cycling is all pumped up about its doping problem." *Christian Science Monitor* (July 26, 2002): 12.

DeSimone, Bonnie. "Armstrong hasn't hit his finish line yet." *Chicago Tribune* (July 29, 2002): 3.1.

"Easiest rider." *People* (August 12, 2002): 68.

"Pedaling to the top." *Christian Science Monitor* (July 30, 2002): 10.

Pugh, Tony. "Postal service bets on a winner with Lance Armstrong." Knight Ridder Tribune Business News (July 29, 2002): 1.

Reilly, Rick. "Lance Armstrong: For his courage and commitment—not to mention his fourth straight Tour de France victory—SI salutes the ultimate road warrior." *Sports Illustrated* (December 16, 2002): 52.

Richburg, Keith. "Moving to the four; leg-strong Armstrong wins another Tour de France." *Washington Post* (July 29, 2002): D1.

Ruibal, Sal. "Once again, it's Tour de Lance." *USA Today* (July 29, 2002): C1.

Ruibal, Sal. "Tour course for 2003 OK with Armstrong." *USA Today* (October 25, 2002): C3.

Other

Lance Armstrong Official Web site. http://www.lance armstrong.com (January 15, 2003).

Lance Armstrong Foundation. http://www.laf.org (January 15, 2003).

Sketch by Brenna Sanchez

Arthur Ashe
1943-1993

American tennis player

Arthur Ashe's 1993 memoir, aptly titled *Days of Grace,* is a reflection on his brief but rich life as a champion tennis player, a father, an African-American man, and a compassionate and courageous human being. As the first African American to win a major men's tennis title and to be ranked number one internationally, Ashe used his position and reputation to speak out against inequities not only in the world of professional sports, but also against injustices wherever he saw them. That would prove to be a sacrifice more than simply a good deed. Ashe himself admitted in 1989 that had he focused only on tennis he could have been a better competitor. At the same time, it was clear by his words and actions that he didn't want to be remembered only for all his "firsts" as a black athlete but also as an African-American man who had fulfilled his "duties as a citizen," as he noted in his memoir. When he died at age 49 of AIDS-related pneumonia, thousands of mourners from all over the world attended his funeral.

Growing Up

Arthur Robert Ashe Jr. was born on July 10, 1943, near Richmond, Virginia, in one of the local hospitals that cared for black citizens. The hospitals in much of the U.S. were not integrated; segregation was the rule for medical care. Integrated schools were also unheard of in the South, so Ashe attended an all-black school. Even the playgrounds of his childhood years were segregated, and he watched from a distance as white children played tennis, a game that immediately fascinated him. In 1947, his father was made superintendent of the blacks-only Brook Field, a public park with a pool, tennis courts, basketball courts and baseball fields. The Ashes moved to the caretaker's cottage in the center of Brook Field, which soon became young Arthur's entire universe.

Ashe was a sickly kid who suffered from measles, chickenpox, mumps, whooping cough, and diphtheria, among other illnesses, which left him thin and weak. He'd always been interested in sports but, with arms and legs "thin as soda straws," as he described himself in his 1967 autobiography, *Advantage Ashe,* he was too light for football and too slow for track. He began to hit tennis balls. Then, in 1950, about a year after he'd first picked up a tennis racquet, his mother, Mattie Cordell Cunningham Ashe, died unexpectedly. Mattie Ashe had gone to the hospital for a minor surgery but succumbed to toxemia, a poisoning of the blood. The seven-year-old Ashe was devastated and refused to attend her burial. In order to cope, he grew somewhat emotionally distant and poured his energy into his schoolwork and tennis, and excelled at both.

By channeling his grief into his tennis game, Ashe had found a way to make adversity work in his favor. He did the same with his schoolwork. Attending a segregated elementary school in Richmond, he and his classmates were always taught they had to work harder than white children in order to succeed. "Discrimination plus the bias women faced in the job market combined to provide us with some truly remarkable teachers," he told the *Chicago Tribune.*

Arthur Ashe

"Every day we got the same message drummed into us. 'Despite discrimination and lynch mobs,' teachers told us, 'some black folks have always managed to find a way to succeed. Okay, this may not be the best-equipped school; that just means you're going to have to be a little bit better prepared than white kids and ready to seize any opportunity that comes your way.'" Ashe was further encouraged by his father, a strict but loving disciplinarian who steeped in his son the virtues of morality.

Early Lessons

A student at Virginia Union University and part-time tennis teacher at Brook Field, Ronald Charity, soon recognized Ashe's natural talent. Charity began to coach Ashe, and encouraged him to enter his first tournament, at the Brook Field courts, which he lost to a boy three years his elder. But Ashe was not at all discouraged. By the time he was ten, Ashe was competing against—and defeating—older, stronger boys, but the most important lesson he learned from Charity wasn't about shot-making; it was about sportsmanship. Charity had taught the young phenomenon not to gloat, as did his next instructor, Dr. Walter Johnson.

Johnson was a physician in Lynchburg, Virginia, who in his spare time coached African-American tennis players during summers at his home. His protégé, **Althea Gibson,** was the first to break the color barrier of the American Lawn Tennis league in 1956, after which she won the

Chronology

1943	Born July 10 in Richmond, Virginia
1950	Mother dies of complications from surgery
1957	Plays his first integrated event, becoming first African American to play in the Maryland boys' championships
1959	Debuts at U.S. National Championships
1963	First African American ever picked for U.S. Davis Cup team
1963	Debuts at Wimbledon
1964	First major grass-court title at Eastern Grass Court Championships
1965	Wins National Collegiate Athletic Association singles and doubles title
1966	Earns his bachelor of science degree in business administration from UCLA; inducted into Army
1968	As America's top-ranked amateur player, wins first of seven Davis Cups as member of U.S. team
1969	Wins U.S. Open and Davis Cup
1970	Wins Australian Open
1970	Lobbies to have South Africa expelled from International Lawn Tennis Federation; serves as U.S. Goodwill Ambassador to Africa
1973	First visit to South Africa; becomes first black professional to play in its national championships
1974	Elected President of Association of Tennis Professionals
1975	Wins World Champion Tennis Championships
1975	Wins Wimbledon
1975	Becomes top-ranked player in the world
1977	Weds photographer Jeanne Marie Moutoussamy
1978	Last tournament win of career, Pacific Southwest Championships in Los Angeles
1979	Suffers heart attack and undergoes quadruple-bypass surgery
1980	Retires from competitive tennis
1981-85	Named captain of U.S. Davis Cup team
1983	Undergoes second bypass surgery and receives blood transfusion
1985	Arrested in anti-apartheid demonstration outside South African embassy in Washington
1986	Daughter Camera is born in New York
1988	Hospitalized for bacterial infection, leading to HIV diagnosis
1991	Returns to South Africa with U.S. delegation as observer of political changes
1992	Arrested for demonstrating in front of White House on behalf of Haitian refugees
1992	Announces he has AIDS
1992	Founds Arthur Ashe Foundation for the Defeat of AIDS
1993	Dies of AIDS-related pneumonia on February 6
1996	Arthur Ashe monument erected in Richmond
1997	Main stadium at site of U.S. Open in New York City named Arthur Ashe Stadium

French and Italian titles, and numerous wins at Wimbledon and the U.S. Open. From the summer of 1953 to the summer of 1960, Ashe worked with Dr. Johnson, who not only fine-tuned Ashe's game but also his conduct, the etiquette and composure that would become an Ashe hallmark. It was still prior to the civil-rights movement in America, and whenever black players were allowed to compete against whites, they were too aware that they had to be on their best behavior on the court. Ashe, like Johnson's other students, was schooled in the courteous acceptance of defeat and the humble pride of victory.

From 1955 to 1963, Ashe won titles in American Tennis Association (ATA) competitions. (The ATA was the African-American equivalent of the United States Lawn Tennis Association.) In 1960 and 1961, Ashe took the U.S. Junior Indoor singles title, which got him noticed by a Missouri coach, Richard Hudlin, a friend of Johnson's. It soon became apparent that if Ashe was to pursue tennis, he'd have to leave Richmond, a racially-segregated city that precluded Ashe from playing whites. With winter approaching and the city's indoor courts closed to blacks, Ashe took Hudlin up on his suggestion that he spend his senior year in St. Louis. Once there, Ashe learned to leave his solid baseline game and became one of the original serve-and-volley players. He graduated from Sumner High School with the highest grade point average. But what gave him the greatest happiness was the realization of Dr. Johnson's dream that an African-American player would oppose a white player in a major United States Lawn Tennis Association (USLTA; now the USTA) competition. Though it had denied him access to competition several times on account of his race, the USLTA listed Ashe as the fifth-ranked junior player in the country and a Junior Davis Cup team member.

The Amateur Years

Numerous universities offered the young athlete and scholar a place in their freshman class. Ashe chose UCLA, which boasted one of the country's best collegiate tennis programs, and intended to study architecture or engineering. However, Ashe's coach urged him to major in business administration so he could better balance his studies, tennis practice and travel, ROTC, and the 250 hours of work his scholarship required he give to the college. The strategy paid off. When Ashe entered UCLA he was twenty-eighth in the U.S. amateur rankings. Two years and numerous tournaments later, Ashe was ranked sixth.

Under the tutelage of coach J. D. Morgan, who'd scouted Ashe, and **Pancho Gonzalez**, Ashe honed his aggressive court style, with a powerful backhand and speed-of-light serve. This was the ammunition that made him such a success on the faster grass and hard court surfaces. By the time he graduated from UCLA, he'd captured the NCAA singles and doubles (with Ian Crookenden) titles, played on the U.S. Davis Cup team, won the Johnston Award for his contribution to the sport, and was the country's number-one collegiate competitor. But perhaps most satisfying was the naming of February 4 as Arthur Ashe Day in the city of Richmond. "Ten years ago," Ashe said in a speech that day, "this would not have happened. It is as much a tribute to Richmond and the state of Virginia as it is to me."

Ashe was inducted into the army in 1966, the year he graduated from UCLA. During the two years Ashe served in the army, first as deputy brigade commander in Fort Lewis, Washington, and then as a second lieutenant, his tennis career stalled somewhat. After boot camp, he was offered the position of assistant tennis coach at the United States Military Academy at West Point, New York, which he accepted, but it still didn't leave him much time to develop his game. He did reach the U.S. Indoor Championship finals in 1966, won the U.S. Clay Court Championship the following year, and at one point had a 9-0 singles Davis Cup record, but he missed a number of major tournaments and lost in the third round in straight sets to Australian John Newcombe at the U.S. Nationals.

Ranked Number One

Professional tennis players who'd experienced Ashe's topspin backhand or powerhouse serve knew he was a competitor with the makings of a champion. Though still an amateur, he'd won numerous tournaments against the sport's best players, and his Davis Cup team performance was admirable. But he hadn't taken a single Grand Slam event. No one knew better than Ashe himself that in 1968-his college years behind him, his two years of army service complete-he would have to put everything he had into tennis if he wanted to be successful as a professional.

Upon leaving the military Ashe was in excellent physical condition, and he was mentally prepared to be a winner. That summer he played well at Wimbledon, though he fell to **Rod Laver** in the semi-finals. But he was victorious in both the U.S. Nationals men's singles title and the first U.S. Open, a feat no man had ever accomplished. In addition, his Davis Cup team took the title from the Australians, a win Ashe cherished above all others. He once said he never lost sleep over any tournament other than the Davis Cup. To Ashe, there was an enormous difference between losing as an individual and losing as a representative of the United States.

The first black man to win a Grand Slam title and now the top-ranked player in America, Arthur Ashe had achieved true celebrity status. Photographs of him appeared on magazine covers, his name appeared on tennis-related products, major corporations signed him on as spokesman, and he offered tennis clinics for American Express and Coca-Cola. He was appointed tennis director at the Doral Resort and Country Club in Miami, Florida, and even made the tabloid gossip pages when he dated fashion models and stars such as singer Diana Ross.

Ashe put his hard-won fame to use. He turned professional in 1969 and immediately began to work to protect players' rights and interests. With his colleagues he created the International Tennis Players Association, acting first as treasurer and later as the union's vice-president. (The association was renamed the Association of Tennis Professionals in 1972, and two years later Ashe was elected ATP president.) He repeatedly spoke out against the apartheid policies of the South African government and succeeded in having South Africa expelled from Davis Cup competition. With his stature, Ashe's public

Awards and Accomplishments	
1955	ATA 12-and-under singles; ATA 12-and-under doubles
1956	ATA 15-and-under doubles
1957	ATA 15-and-under singles
1958	15-and-under singles; ATA 15-and-under doubles
1960	18-and-under singles; ATA men's singles; U.S. Junior Indoors singles
1961	ATA men's singles; ATA men's doubles; U.S. Junior Indoors singles; U.S. Interscholastics singles
1962	ATA men's singles
1963	ATA men's singles; U.S. Hard Courts singles
1964	Eastern Grass Court Championship; sixth-ranked amateur in nation
1964	Received Johnston Award for contributing the most to the growth of tennis while exhibiting good sportsmanship
1965	NCAA singles; NCAA doubles
1967	U.S. Clay Courts singles
1968	U.S. National singles; U.S. Open singles
1970	U.S. Indoors doubles; Australian Open singles
1971	French Open doubles
1975	World Championship Tennis singles; Wimbledon singles
1975	Named Association of Tennis Professionals (ATP) Player of the Year
1977	Australian Open doubles
1985	Inducted into International Tennis Hall of Fame
1992	Named *Sports Illustrated* Sportsman of the Year

American Tennis Association (ATA) is the oldest African-American sports organization in the United States.

Davis Cup: (as player) 1963, 1965-70, 1975, 1977-78, won 27 singles; (as captain) 1981-85, won 1981, 1982.

Ashe retired in 1980 with a career record of 818 wins, 260 losses, and 51 titles.

outcry garnered world attention to the oppressive rule of apartheid, and in 1970 Ashe was selected to act as good-will ambassador to Africa. The U. S. Department of State sent him to Kenya, Nigeria, Tanzania, and Uganda, where he met with government leaders, students, and diplomats. The following year, as a member of a delegation of tennis players, Ashe visited Cameroon, Gabon, Senegal, and Cote d'Ivoire. It was at a tennis club in Cameroon where Ashe noticed the young, talented Yannick Noah, who he arranged to have sent to France for tutelage under the care of the French Tennis Federation.

Center Court

Over the course of the next few years, Ashe's game seemed to stagnate. A new generation of competitors, such as **Bjorn Borg** and **Jimmy Connors**, were testing his dynamic serve-and-volley game with power, precision, and an almost appalling sense of confidence. By 1975, Ashe's ranking had sunk to fifth place. Some blamed his political activism for his deteriorating game, others his age (he was 31). Ashe steeled himself, determined to win the World Champion Tennis title that spring in Dallas, Texas. He did. But an even bigger victory was in sight.

When Arthur Ashe stepped onto the grass at Wimbledon and bowed to the Royal Box, the last thing on his

Arthur Ashe

mind was the fact that he was the first African American to compete in the exclusive court of the world's oldest tennis tournament. The date was July 5, 1975, and Ashe was playing for the men's singles title. The challenge would require his complete concentration. His opponent was one of the top-seeded players, twenty-two-year-old fellow American Jimmy Connors. The two had battled before and in all three of their matches, Ashe had been the loser. Sports fans on both sides of the Atlantic expected the brash and self-taught Connors to "slaughter" Ashe, as Ashe noted in his memoir *Days of Grace*.

In addition, only days before Wimbledon, Connors had filed a lawsuit against Ashe for libel. Ashe was not intimidated. He'd stood by his principles, having accused Connors of playing matches for big purses while refusing to join the United States squad for the international Davis Cup competition, where players are paid in the currency of patriotic honor, not hard cash. Despite the lawsuit, Ashe retained his cool and even demeanor.

Ashe won Wimbledon by finessing the hard-hitting Connors with a brilliantly strategic game of defensive tennis. He played conservatively, hitting balls deep then rushing the net, keeping Connors off balance. Also, Ashe had decided that rather than try to outpower the south-paw, he'd hit the ball softly, breaking Connors' rhythm. It would also force Connors to generate his own power, rather than simply redirect the ball using Ashe's velocity. Ashe's plan for the historic match would later help some

of the decade's best players—Bjorn Borg, Ivan Lendl, and **John McEnroe**—undercut Connors' phenomenal, dominating power game. With a 6-1, 6-1, 5-7, 6-4 victory at Wimbledon, he not only obtained the number-one ranking in the world that year but saw the culmination of a lifetime of struggle. "When I took the match point, all the years, all the effort, all the support I had received over the years came together," he later reflected.

Back to Business

During a benefit tournament in 1976 for the United Negro College Fund at New York's Madison Square Garden, a professional photographer stepped up to Ashe to take his picture. By the day's end, Ashe had a date with the photographer, the stunning Jeanne Marie Moutoussamy. Four months later, Ashe—in a cast having recently undergone heel surgery-and Moutoussamy were married in New York City by Reverend Andrew Young, U.S. Ambassador to the United Nations.

Ashe's heel surgery had been successful, but another injury followed, and, compounded with recurrent eye inflammations, he decided to lay low for the year. Though he took the Australian Open doubles title, with his partner Tony Roche, he was forced to skip Wimbledon and the U.S. Open in 1977. This caused his ranking to fall, which in turn led the sportswear company Catalina to drop Ashe as a key endorser. Ashe was forced to come up with other means of providing an income.

Ashe's academic background in business and his real-life experience with some of the largest corporations in America made him comfortable acting as a consultant and entrepreneur. During the course of his life, he had a business relationship with Head USA, a manufacturer of sports gear that kept Ashe on board even though it lost accounts in the South due to Ashe's race. Doral Resort and Country Club maintained its association with Ashe, which had special meaning for Ashe since the nearby Admiral Hotel refused to accommodate him during a 1961 tournament in Miami, yet housed all the other junior players, who were white. In addition, Ashe became a columnist with *Tennis* magazine and the *Washington Post,* and was a consultant with clothing manufacturer Le Coq Sportif. "The longevity and human quality of these connections mean far more to me than the money they bring," he wrote in *Days of Grace.* Ashe also acted as consultant with the Aetna Life and Casualty Company, where he had been in charge of minority recruitment, and would later be honored by the offer of a seat on their board of directors.

The Greatest Burden

By 1979 Ashe still wasn't ready to give up tennis. He played thirteen tournaments but reached the finals in only two. Then, on July 30, a tremendous pain in his chest woke the athlete from a sound sleep. Within an hour, the pain would recur twice. Each time it subsided he went back to sleep. The next day, Ashe gave two tennis clinics in New York and while signing autographs, was struck again. Arthur Ashe had had a heart attack. In December he underwent a quadruple bypass surgery. He would never play tennis again.

But Ashe was optimistic and tried to get back into competition shape. It was not to be. On April 16, 1980, Ashe announced his retirement from competitive tennis. Yet he remained actively involved in the sport. That year he was made captain of the U.S. Davis Cup team, whose members included the mercurial John McEnroe, Peter Fleming, and Vitas Gerulaitis, and led the team to victory in 1981 and 1982. He worked as a sports commentator for ABC and HBO television, gave innumerable clinics to inner city children, wrote articles and books on the sport, made a tennis video, and in 1985 was inducted into the International Tennis Hall of Fame in Newport, Rhode Island.

In 1983, Ashe underwent a second bypass operation. Weak from the procedure, he was given a blood transfusion to try to bolster his strength and speed his recovery. In 1988, Ashe needed an operation on his brain, and tests following that surgery were positive for the virus that causes AIDS. Doctors concluded that Ashe had contracted HIV from the transfusion he was given following his second heart surgery. At the time the news was a death sentence. However, this did not stop Ashe from struggling for social justice. In 1985 he was arrested outside the South African embassy in Washington, DC, while protesting against the country's institutionalized racism. A few years later he was arrested again, for speaking out against President Bush's policy regarding the treatment of Haitian refugees with HIV/AIDS.

In 1992, *USA Today* threatened to run a story announcing that Ashe had AIDS. He talked it over with his wife and decided to scoop the paper. In a public press conference, Ashe not only admitted that he had AIDS but kicked off his campaign to educate the public about the disease and set up a foundation to defeat the disease. He spoke out against discrimination against homosexuals in general and AIDS sufferers for the remainder of his life. But he never asked for pity. When a well-meaning reporter for *People* magazine suggested that having AIDS must be the greatest burden Ashe had ever had to bear, he corrected her. "No, it isn't," he wrote in his memoir. "Being Black is the greatest burden I've had to bear.... Having to live as a minority in America. Even now it continues to feel like an extra weight tied around me."

Ashe completed his final memoir, *Days of Grace,* just two days before he died. The book concludes with an open letter to his daughter, Camera, then only six years old (she was born December 21, 1986), whom he wrote was a "daily affirmation of the power of life." That spirit kept Ashe active and outspoken throughout his fatal illness. "He was out doing things, making his point, and taking care of business right up until the end,"

Related Biography: Tennis Player Yannick Noah

Yannick Simon Camille Noah was born on May 18, 1960, in Sedan, France, and at the age of three he moved with his family to his father's native country of Cameroon. In 1971, while attending a tennis clinic at a local club, Noah was given the chance to play with Ashe, who was making his second goodwill tour of Africa. Ashe, moved by the youngster's plight and his talent, arranged to have Noah enrolled at the French Tennis Federation (FTF) training center in Nice, France, where he trained for five years. One year short of graduation, Noah left school to focus exclusively on tennis. In 1977, Noah won the French junior title and the Wimbledon junior title, after which he went professional.

In 1978, Noah took the Australian Open and U.S. Open singles titles, and in 1979 made it to the semis and finals at the French Open and Wimbledon. His Grand Slam performances earned him the top ranking in France in 1980. At age twenty-three he won the French Open, and a year later he and partner Henri Leconte won the doubles title there.

Noah stayed off the tennis circuit for a year to recover from injuries and the devastating death of his grandfather. He came back to his game to win the Italian Open in 1985, but what looked like an auspicious return to the game was only transitory. He played his way to the finals of many tournaments and achieved the ranking in 1986 of third in the world in singles play and first in doubles, yet the more prestigious titles eluded him. After pursuing a music career for a few years, he trained the French team in 1996 for the Davis Cup and the Fed Cup, the premier international team event for women. In both events, France was victorious.

Noah lives in Montreux, Switzerland, and often participates in the charitable tennis tournaments and the ATP Senior Tour tournaments in Switzerland.

---

former competitor Jimmy Connors recalled in *Sports Stars*. "I guess that sums up everything he stood for."

Ashe's Legacy

Arthur Ashe's legacy is manifold. Rarely have sports celebrities taken on social issues with such passion and commitment as did Ashe. He broke color barriers both in his own country and abroad, and fought tirelessly for social justice, founding the African American Athletic Association to mentor student athletes and helping preserve the history of African-American athletes with his contributions to the 1988 *A Hard Road to Glory.* He helped erase the stigma of having AIDS, raised public awareness of this devastating epidemic, and spoke to the United Nations General Assembly in an effort to get more funds devoted to AIDS research. In 1990, when President Nelson Mandela, freed from his South African jail after twenty-seven years, was asked which American he'd most like to meet, his immediate response was "Arthur Ashe." Tennis champion **Martina Navratilova** characterized Ashe, as reported in the *Washington Post* (and quoted in *Newsmakers 1993),* as "an extraordinary human being who transcended his sport, his race, religion and nationality and in his own way helped to change the world."

Increasing minority presence in all sectors of society was a vision to which Arthur Ashe dedicated his life. "I know I could never forgive myself," Ashe wrote in his memoir, "if I elected to live without human purpose, without trying to help the poor and unfortunate, without recognizing that perhaps the purest joy in life comes from trying to help others." Ashe was adamant about the necessity of increasing minority participation throughout society, not just in the sports arena. "We deify black athletes," the *Houston Chronicle* quoted Ashe as saying in 1992. "Black families are eight times more likely to push youngsters into athletics than are white families.... The disparity is glaring." Shortly after his retirement, Ashe said (according to an article on About.com), "We have been on the same roads-sports and entertainment-too long. We need to pull over, fill up at the library, and speed away to Congress and to the Supreme Court, the unions and the business world."

SELECTED WRITINGS BY ASHE:

(With Clifford Gewecke, Jr.) *Advantage Ashe,* Coward, McCann, 1967.

(With Frank DeFord) *Arthur Ashe: Portrait in Motion,* Houghton Mifflin, 1975.

(With Louie Robinson, Jr.) *Getting Started in Tennis,* Atheneum, 1977.

Mastering Your Tennis Strokes, Macmillan, 1978.

(With Neil Amdur) *Off the Court,* New American Library, 1981.

Arthur Ashe's Tennis Clinic, Golf Digest/Tennis Inc., 1981.

(With Kip Branch, Oceana Chalk, and Francis Harris) *A Hard Road to Glory: A History of the African-American Athlete,* Warner, 1988.

(With Arnold Rampersad) *Days of Grace,* Knopf, 1993.

FURTHER INFORMATION

Books

Ashe, Arthur and Arnold Rampersad. *Days of Grace.* New York: Knopf, 1993.

The Complete Marquis Who's Who. Marquis Who's Who, 2001.

Contemporary Black Biography, Vol. 18. Farmington Hills, MI: Gale Research, 1998.

Newsmakers 1993. Farmington Hills, MI: Gale Research, 1993.

Weissberg, Ted. *Arthur Ashe: Tennis Great.* New York: Chelsea House, 1991.

Periodicals

"Arthur Ashe's Widow Says She's Not in Agreement with Husband's Statue Being Erected amid Civil War Heroes." *Jet* (January 22, 1996): 34.

Bruning, Fred. "How a Private Citizen Lost His Privacy Rights." *Maclean's* (May 4, 1992): 13.

Chicago Tribune (November 28, 1988).

"France's Davis Cup Captain Yannick Noah Remembers Big Help from U.S. Davis Cup Captain Arthur Ashe." *Jet* (February 27, 1995): 48.

Johnson, Robert E. "Arthur Ashe's New Book, *Days of Grace,* Tells of His Three Burdens: Race, AIDS, and Davis Cup." *Jet* (July 26, 1993): 34.

Leavy, Walter. "Arthur Ashe: The Gentle Warrior 1943-1993." *Ebony* (April 1993): 110.

Lipper, Bob. "Arthur Ashe." *Richmond Times Dispatch* (February 1, 2002).

Review of *Days of Grace. Ebony* (September 1993): 18.

Other

"1998 Racial and Gender Report Card." Center for the Study of Sport in Society, Northeastern University. http://www.sportinsociety.org/ (July 5, 2002).

About.com. http://racerelations.about.com (July 10, 2002).

American Tennis Association. http://www.atanational.com (July 22, 2002).

"Arthur Ashe: Much More Than Tennis." About.com. http://tennis.about.com/ (July 7, 2002).

"Ashe's Impact Reached Far Beyond the Court." ESPN Classic. http://espn.gp.com/classic/biography/s/Ashe_Arthur.html (July 10, 2002).

Celebrities in Switzerland. http://switzerlandisyours.com/ (July 10, 2002).

Contemporary Authors Online. http://galenet.galegroup.com/ (July 4, 2002).

Fed Cup. http://216.239.37.120/ (July 19, 2002).

"Fête Le Mur." BNP Paribas. http://tennis.bnpparibas.com / (July 10, 2002).

Internet Movie Database. http://www.imdb.com/ (July 5, 2002).

"Marvelous Messenger: Ashe stressed importance of striving for excellence outside sports." *Houston Chronicle.* http://www.houstonchron.com/ (July 5, 2002).

MCM.NET. http://www.mcm.net/ (July 19, 2002).

Sports Illustrated/CNN. http://sportsillustrated.cnn.com/tennis/features/1997/arthurashebiography.html (July 4, 2002).

"Women and Minorities in Tennis." Tennis Industry. http://www.tennisindustry.com/ (July 10, 2002).

Sketch by Jane Summer

Evelyn Ashford
1957-

American track and field athlete

Recognized as one of track and field history's most accomplished sprinters, Evelyn Ashford is the only woman in U.S. track history to win four Olympic gold medals—one in the 100-meter sprint and three as part of

Evelyn Ashford

Chronology

1957	Born April 15 in Shreveport, Louisiana
1972-75	Defeats star male football runner in race at Roseville High School (Roseville, California) and becomes only female on school track team; serves as co-captain during senior year
1975	Accepts a full athletic scholarship to the University of California at Los Angeles
1976	Competes in Olympic Games in Montreal, Canada, finishing fifth in the 100-meter dash
1978	Leaves college to train full-time for the 1980 Olympics
1980	U.S. President Jimmy Carter boycotts Olympics in Moscow to protest Soviet invasion of Afghanistan; Ashford is devastated that she will not get to compete
1981	Competes in World Cup championships
1983	Pulls right hamstring and falls during finals at World Cup
1984	Competes in Olympic Games in Los Angeles, California, winning two gold medals and setting an Olympic record in sprinting
mid-1980s	Serves as reporter for cable TV program *World Class Woman*
1986	Gives birth to daughter, Raina Ashley Washington
1987	Misses most of track season because of troublesome hamstring muscle
1988	Competes in Olympic Games in Seoul, South Korea, winning a gold medal for 4 x 100 relay and a silver in sprinting after finishing second to Florence Griffith-Joyner
1992	Competes in Olympic Games in Barcelona, Spain, winning gold medal as leader of 4 x 100 relay team, at age 35
1992	Retires after Olympics; devotes time to raising her daughter and serves as public speaker and track-and-field commentator
1999	Participates in U.S. Olympic Committee's worldwide Olympic Day on June 23

4 x 100-meter relay teams. Two years after giving birth to her daughter, she won a silver medal for the 100-meter in the 1988 Olympics, finishing second to the great U.S. sprinter **Florence Griffith-Joyner**, and a gold medal in the 4 x 100 relays. Ashford twice broke the world record for the 100-meter sprint and broke the American record five times. She broke the American record for the 200-meter sprint three times. A U.S. national champion five times in the 100-meter and five times in the 200-meter, Ashford won the World Cup a total of four times and won the Pan-Am Championship in each race in 1979. Still running in top form at age thirty-five, she won a gold medal in the 4 x 100 relays in the 1992 Olympics.

Racing the Boys

Evelyn Ashford was born April 15, 1957, in Shreveport, Louisiana, but grew up in the Sacramento, California, area. One day as she was running during physical education class at Roseville High School, the football coach pulled her aside and asked if she would race his fastest player. "I think you can beat him," the coach said. Evelyn did, and from then on she began to win little prizes and big popularity for running faster than the male athletes. Because girls did not yet have their own track team at Roseville, Evelyn became the only female member of the boys' team in the early 1970s. By her senior year in high school, she had won numerous state and regional track meets, racing against other girls.

During her senior year, Ashford became one of the first women to be offered a full athletic scholarship to the University of California at Los Angeles (UCLA). She accepted the scholarship and began training for the 1976 Olympics during her freshman year. She qualified for the 100-meter sprint but came in fifth place at her first Olympic Games, in Montreal, Canada, at age nineteen. A taste of the Olympics and a drive to win a gold medal, inspired by the great African-American woman athlete **Wilma Rudolph**, gave Ashford the impetus she needed to train hard for the 1980 Olympics. She left UCLA in 1978 to focus on her training full time.

Bitter Disappointment

Ranked number one in the world in the 100-meter dash at age twenty-three, Ashford believed she was in the prime of her career as the time neared for the 1980 Olympic Games in Moscow, USSR. However, along with dozens of other American athletes, Ashford was devastated when President Jimmy Carter announced a U.S. boycott of the Olympics in protest of the Soviet invasion of Afghanistan. Ashford abandoned her training, and she and her husband, Ray Washington, spent the summer traveling around the United States and visiting relatives. However, Ashford soon set her sights on the 1984 Games. She took first place in the 1981 World Cup in both 100- and 200-meter races and was the U.S. National Champion in 1983, in both sprints. However,

---

The Fastest Doubleheader Ever

Ashford isn't the fastest starter, but ... she caught a good one. Then she just tore on down the track. "I wasn't thinking about anything; I just ran," she said. "I didn't seem to wake up until the last 20 meters. When I crossed the line, I thought, 'That was nothing special. Maybe 11.1'." Her "nothing special" was 10.79, a world record. Her wind was a legal .56 mps. When she heard the time, she collapsed. "I'm stunned," she said. "Just stunned . . . stunned."

Source: Moore, Kenny. *Sports Illustrated* (July 11, 1983): 28.

Awards and Accomplishments

1976	Qualified for U.S. Olympic team and placed fifth in 100-meter sprint
1977	Won Association of Intercollegiate Athletics for Women (AIAW) championships in 100-meter and 200-meter dashes and 800-meter relay
1977, 1979, 1981-83	U.S. National Champion in 100-meter sprint
1977-79, 1981, 1983	U.S. National Champion in 200-meter sprint
1978	Won AIAW 200-meter dash and finished second in 100-meter dash
1979	Broke American record for 200-meter sprint three times; Pan-Am Champion in both 100-meter and 200-meter sprint
1979, 1981	World Cup Champion in 100-meter and 200-meter sprint
1979, 1981, 1983-84	Broke American record for 100-meter sprint a total of five times
1983-84	Broke world record for 100-meter sprint
1984	Olympic Gold Medal for 100-meter sprint
1984, 1988, 1992	Won Olympic Gold Medals for 4 x 100-meter relay
1988	Olympic Silver Medal for 100-meter sprint; first black woman to carry American flag during an Olympic opening ceremony
1989	Won Flo Hyman Award, given by Women's Sport Foundation
1993	Won ESPY Award as Outstanding Women's Track Performer of the Year
1994	Inducted into Mt. San Antonio College Relays Hall of Fame
1997	Inducted into U.S. Track & Field Hall of Fame; inducted into Women's Sports Hall of Fame

As of the end of 2002, Ashford was the only woman in U.S. track-and-field history to win four Olympic gold medals. She won two of those medals, and her Olympic silver medal, after the birth of her daughter.

The Flo Hyman Award, established in 1987, commemorates the All-World Cup volleyball team player, who died at age 31. It is given by the Women's Sports Foundation to a woman athlete who over her career has exemplified Hyman's "dignity, spirit and commitment to excellence."

The ESPY Award is given by ESPN television for excellence in sports performance.

---

after winning her first two 100-meter races in the 1983 World Championships, she pulled her right hamstring muscle and fell in the final race. The injury stayed with her into 1984 and was still bothering her as the Olympics began.

Double Gold

Her determination and training paid off, however. The 1984 Olympics were held in her college town, Los Angeles, and this time the Soviets led a boycott. Ashford withdrew from the 200-meter race to rest her hamstring and focus on the 100-meter. In that race she defeated Heike Drechsler of Germany to win her first Olympic gold medal. In tears as she finished the race and throughout the medal ceremony, Ashford said she couldn't believe it was over and that she had won. Yet, the 27-year-old runner had another gold medal coming, in the 4 x 100-meter relay. It was the first of three consecutive gold medals she would bring home in that event.

Ashford's critics claimed that her 1984 Olympic win was not decisive because East German champion Marlies Gohr had not raced due to the Communist boycott. However, soon after the Olympics, Ashford and Gohr competed in the 100-meter in a Zurich, Switzerland, meet. Ashford was slightly behind Gohr for ninety meters but gathered speed during the last ten to beat the German champion and set a world-record time of 10.79 seconds, Ashford's career personal best. This victory silenced her critics, and another Olympic win four years later proved she was the best in the 4 x 100 relay as well.

Gold and Silver

Ashford gave birth to her daughter, Raina Ashley, in 1986 and went back to training shortly afterward. By 1988 she had won the 100-meter at the Goodwill Games and had qualified for the Olympics, although still battling the troublesome hamstring injury throughout 1987. At the 1988 Olympics in Seoul, South Korea, Ashford finished second in the 100-meter race, narrowly losing to the celebrated American runner Florence Griffith-Joyner. Teaming up with Griffith-Joyner, Alice Brown, and Sheila Echols for the 4 x 100 relay, however, Ashford won her third Olympic gold medal, to go with her silver.

In the relay, she and Griffith-Joyner fumbled the baton exchange, leaving Ashford with the task of catching up to and beating Russian runner Natalya Pomoshchnikova and then her old opponent Marlies Gohr. Ashford passed them both for the win, wiping out any vestige of criticism that she was a second-place runner to the East German. However, Ashford was angry with herself for some time over losing the 100-meter to Griffith-Joyner, even though experts have said that "Flo-Jo" could not have been beaten by anyone that year.

"I'm Excited!"

Instead of retiring after her 1988 Olympic victories, Ashford continued to train and by 1992 had qualified for the Olympic Summer Games in both the sprint and the 4 x 100 relay. On learning of her qualification, she told the press, "I don't know about you guys, but I'm excited! I'm 35. I'm not supposed to be running like this." At the 1992 Games in Barcelona, Spain, where she was referred to as "the grand old lady of track," Ashford won her fourth gold medal, in the 4 x 100 relay.

Retirement

Since retiring after the 1992 Olympics, Ashford has served as a public speaker and has done Olympic advisory work for General Motors. She has also been a track and field commentator and has made public appearances for the U.S. Olympic Committee, although most of her time is devoted to being a mother to her daughter, Raina. She told Don Bosley of the *Sacramento Bee* in April 2000, "This is as close as I need to be to track and field. I am very satisfied with where I left the sport, what I accomplished in the sport." She also said that Wilma Rudolph was her inspiration as a girl. "I just wanted to get some Olympic gold medals," said Ashford. "I thought that was the highest accomplishment anybody could have was to get a gold medal. Even one."

Evelyn Ashford has been one of the most successful women sprinters in history, overcoming the obstacles of a lack of support for women in the sport during the early 1970s as well as the lost opportunity to participate in the 1980 Olympics. At only 5'5" tall, she was fiercely competitive on the track but warm and personable to everyone. Ashford has proved that being a wife and mother can be compatible with sustaining a record-breaking career in sports.

CONTACT INFORMATION

Address: 818 Plantation Lane, Walnut, CA 91789.

FURTHER INFORMATION

Books

Great Women in Sports. "Evelyn Ashford." Detroit: Visible Ink Press, 1996.

Who's Who among African Americans, 14th ed. "Evelyn Ashford." Detroit: Gale Group, 2001.

Periodicals

Bosley, Don. "Golden Memories: Ashford Content with Her Medals, Doesn't Begrudge Jones' Fortunes." *Sacramento Bee* (April 2, 2000).

Harvey, Randy. "Ashford's Extra Gear Made Her a Racing Machine." *Los Angeles Times* (December 3, 1997): 3.

Moore, Kenny. "The Fastest Doubleheader Ever: Evelyn Ashford, Calvin Smith Set World Records at National Sports Festival." *Sports Illustrated* (July 11, 1983): 28.

Other

All-Star Agency. "Evelyn Ashford." http://www.allstar agency.com/ (January 8, 2003).

ESPN. "ESPY Awards Past Winners." http://espn.go.com/ (January 9, 2003).

Hickok Sports.com. "Ashford, Evelyn; Flo Hyman Award." http://www.hickoksports.com/ (January 8, 2003).

Infoplease. "Evelyn Ashford." http://www.infoplease. com/ (January 8, 2003).

International Medalist Association. "Olympic Day 1999." http://www.internationalmedalist.org/ (January 8, 2003).

Mt. San Antonio College Relays Hall of Fame. "Evelyn Ashford." http://vm.mtsac.edu/relays/HallFame/ Ashford.htm (January 8, 2003).

Sketch by Ann H. Shurgin

Arnold "Red" Auerbach
1917-

American basketball coach

As a coach and executive, Arnold "Red" Auerbach has directed the Boston Celtics to sixteen National Basketball Association (NBA) championships, the third most in North American professional team sports. Auerbach, inducted into the Basketball Hall of Fame, coached the Celtics to nine titles, including eight straight from 1959-66, and oversaw seven others as general manager and president. The NBA Coach of the Year trophy bears his name. Auerbach, whose Celtics coaching won-loss record was 1,037-548, is renowned for his headstrong personality, shrewd personnel moves and such strategic innovations as the "sixth man." He has survived transient and sometimes meddlesome ownership, and even coups within the Celtics organization.

Auerbach also selected the league's first African-American player (Chuck Cooper), appointed the first black coach in pro sports (**Bill Russell**) and fielded the first all-black starting five. Auerbach often baited referees, and even got into a fistfight with an opposing team's owner. He celebrated his wins by lighting up a victory cigar. Auerbach also wrote several books, and was a frequent motivational speaker. He was stripped of his title as team president in 1997 when the Celtics named Rick Pitino head coach and chief of basketball operations, but the organization restored it in 2001 when Pitino left. In 2002, an 84-year-old Auerbach saw the Celtics reach the NBA's Eastern Conference playoff finals after having missed postseason play the previous six seasons. Bill Simmons, who interviewed Auerbach for *ESPN.com* in February, 2002, described Auerbach as "looking like a cross between the Celtics leprechaun, Yoda and God."

Born in Brooklyn

Auerbach grew up in the Williamsburg section of Brooklyn, New York, where football and baseball, he said, were too expensive. At Eastern District High

Arnold "Red" Auerbach

School, he made the All-Brooklyn second team his senior year. After one season at Seth Low Junior College in Brooklyn, Auerbach transferred to George Washington University. Auerbach lettered at GWU for three seasons, then coached in the Washington, D.C., area and served in the U.S. Navy.

Auerbach coached the Washington Capitals of the Basketball Association of America (precursor to the NBA), which began play in 1946. One year later, Auerbach coached in his first NBA championship, the Capitals losing 4 games to 2 to the Minneapolis (now Los Angeles) Lakers. He left Washington after a contract dispute and quit the Tri-Cities Blackhawks after only one season because the owner traded a player without consulting him.

Boston Era Begins

Celtics founder and owner Walter Brown named Auerbach coach for the 1950-51 season. Led by guard **Bob Cousy**, the Celtics improved from 22-46 to 39-30 in Auerbach's first year. Throughout the 1950s, Boston fielded winning teams but not a champion. The Celtics lacked a big man in the middle. Then, Auerbach made his first major personnel move. Coveting 6-foot-9 center Bill Russell, who led the University of San Francisco to back-to-back NCAA titles, Auerbach in 1956 traded all-star forward Ed Macauley and guard Cliff Hagan to St. Louis for the rights to draft Russell.

Trading two established players, one a star, for a collegiate prospect was a gamble. But the Celtics dynasty began with that deal. Russell's presence gave Boston a balanced lineup. The Celtics won their first championship the following season, defeating St. Louis, ironically, in a climactic seventh game in Boston, 125-123 in double overtime. After falling to the Hawks in the 1958 Finals with Russell injured, the Celtics won the next eight championships, still the record in pro sports. Auerbach gave up coaching in 1966 to become general manager and named Russell player-coach—the first African-American sports coach.

Other crafty deals by Auerbach included picking journeyman forward Don Nelson off the waiver wire for $100 in 1966 (Nelson helped the Celtics win five titles); trading the NBA rights to guard Charlie Scott of the rival American Basketball Association for power forward Paul Silas, only to reacquire Scott three years later (Silas and Scott were teammates on the 1976 title team); drafting Indiana State star **Larry Bird** in 1978, a year before Bird was available for the pros (Bird, who became one of basketball's all-time greats, carried Boston to three titles); and trading the unwanted Bob McAdoo to the Detroit Pistons in 1979 for two draft picks and the rights to M. L. Carr. (Boston sent those draft picks to the Golden State Warriors for center Robert Parish and a draft choice, which turned out to be Kevin McHale. Parish and McHale helped anchor the Celtics championship teams in the Bird era.)

Celtics Mystique

Auerbach, who espoused the team-first concept, realized synergies long before the word was in vogue. "He was known for picking the right players, coaching them and keeping them in line with his system," Lisette Hilton wrote on the *ESPN Classic* Web site.

For instance, **Wilt Chamberlain** of the Philadelphia Warriors and 76ers (and later the Los Angeles Lakers), Russell's longtime rival at the center position, often outscored Russell head-to-head and had better individual statistics. But under Russell, the Celtics won eleven titles in thirteen years; Chamberlain was a champion but twice, and only once while Russell played.

"Our pride was never rooted in statistics," Auerbach once said. He would on occasion, however, play the numbers game as a form of one-upmanship. In the mid-1960s he announced the signing of Russell to a contract that paid $1 more than Chamberlain (and enabled Russell to talk his way out of a $2 fine for arriving late to a practice).

Auerbach also mixed in the likes of gritty forwards Tom Heinsohn and Jim Loscutoff; guard K.C. Jones, a college teammate of Russell's who became one of the NBA's premier defensive guards; and backcourt man Sam Jones (no relation to K.C.) out of unheralded North

Chronology

1917	Born September 20 in Brooklyn, New York
1932-35	Attends Eastern District High School, Brooklyn, New York; named all-Brooklyn second team as a senior
1936-37	Attends Seth Low Junior College, New York
1937-40	Earns three letters in basketball at George Washington University, Washington, D.C.
1941	Marries Dorothy Lewis
1941-43	Coaches Roosevelt High School, Washington, D.C.
1942	Plays for Harrisburg Senators, American Basketball League/Eastern Basketball League
1943-46	Serves in United States Navy
1946-49	Coaches Washington Capitals of the Basketball Association of America (precursor to National Basketball Association)
1949-50	Coaches Tri Cities Blackhawks of NBA and assistant coach, Duke University, Durham, North Carolina
1950	Named head coach of NBA's Boston Celtics
1956	Traded Ed Macauley and Cliff Hagan to St. Louis Hawks for the right to draft Bill Russell out of college
1957	Wins first NBA championship as Celtics defeat Hawks in seven-game final
1959-66	Coaches Celtics to eight consecutive NBA championships; retires in 1966 to focus on general manager duties
1978	Drafts Larry Bird while Bird was still a college junior
1979	Considers and rejects offer from New York Knicks
1997	Stripped of team president's title as Celtics name Rick Pitino chief of basketball operations and head coach
2001	Auerbach restored as team president

Awards and Accomplishments

1962	Arch McDonald Achievement Award
1965	NBA Coach of the Year
1968	Inducted into National Basketball Hall of Fame and Naismith Memorial Hall of Fame
1969	Elected to International Jewish Sports Hall of Fame
1971	Selected NBA's 25th anniversary All-Time Team Coach
1980	Named greatest coach in NBA history by Professional Basketball Writers Association of America; named NBA Executive of the Year
1995	Inducted into Sport in Society Hall of Fame, Northeastern University, Boston

Carolina A&T, referred to Auerbach by word of mouth. Cerebral forward-guard **John Havlicek** and forward Tom Sanders integrated nicely with Auerbach's system; Havlicek, best known for stealing the ball to save a playoff series against Philadelphia in 1965, achieved legendary status over his sixteen years.

Auerbach's "sixth man" was first substitute. He did not always start the best five players; the most suitable five, however, finished, the first reserve often among them. Frank Ramsey was the first sixth man—later, Havlicek, McHale and **Bill Walton** filled those roles capably under Auerbach and subsequent coaches.

"When I came to the Celtics there was this Celtic mystique. And I was one of the few skeptics," said Silas, who came to Boston in 1973 and played on two champions (and a third in Seattle). "I went up to Red and said, 'Now I understand what the Celtic mystique is.'"

"Hey, I made my share of mistakes," Auerbach told Simmons. "One time I drafted a kid named Bill Green, helluva player … but he wouldn't fly! There was no way he could play in the league."

Russell First Black Coach

Though Russell's appointment as coach in 1966 broke pro sports' coaching racial barrier, Auerbach didn't see it that way. "When I retired, I said there is no better man to coach Russell than Russell," Auerbach told *USA Today* in February, 2002. "He was given the job strictly because of merit. Him being black or white was

never thought of, hinted at or discussed." Still, Auerbach opened the door for a black to coach, and at the beginning of the 2002-03 season, there were 13 black coaches in the 29-team league.

Naming Russell was more Auerbach's way of staying internal. Auerbach or one his former players coached all Boston's championships, except Bill Fitch in 1981. Russell, after the Philadelphia 76ers broke Boston's string of eight straight titles in 1967, led the Celtics back to supremacy the following two years before retiring. Heinsohn and K.C. Jones also coached them to a pair of titles apiece. "I needed Red to push me back sometimes," Russell said. "But he did it in a way I could understand, and I wasn't offended by it."

Abrasive Personality

Auerbach guided the team during a simpler era. "When Red ran the Celtics in the '50s and '60s, he was head coach, director of basketball operations, general manager, team president, head scout … he did *everything*," wrote Simmons, a Boston native. He was a constant amid transient ownership. Walter Brown died in 1964 and control of the team frequently changed hands. Rumors occasionally had the team moving to such places as Providence, Hartford, or Long Island. Auerbach even says he had to reach into his own checkbook to get the team out of town for road games.

"(Woody) Erdman was a thief," Auerbach told the *Boston Globe*'s Dan Shaughnessy of a team owner in the early 1970s. "He had a company in New York and when we played there, he used to take the gate receipts and never pay any bills. I once put out six or seven thousand dollars of my own money so that we could make a road trip. We were on a COD basis with the phone company and the airlines. The guy was an out-and-out thief."

Running a team, however, became more complex in the 1980s and 1990s, and Auerbach gradually withdrew from basketball operations. "Years ago, let's say I want to trade Mike for Ike—you call someone and say you want to make a trade, you say 'Give me a big guy, I got a big guy, you got a guard I can use, let's make a deal,' and then see ya, it's over."

Arnold "Red" Auerbach

Auerbach amassed $17,000 in fines during his coaching career. And, before a playoff game at St. Louis, he flattened Hawks owner Ben Kerner during an argument over the height of the basket. "So we're having a rhubarb with the refs," Auerbach told Simmons. "Finally, they bring out the (measuring) stick. So Kerner comes out of the stands, and he starts cussing me, and he takes a step toward me ... so I hit him."

Pat Riley, who coached the Lakers against the Celtics during the Bird-**Magic Johnson** showdowns of the 1980s and had played for the Lakers in the late 1960s, accused the Celtics of shutting off the hot water to the visiting locker rooms of ancient Boston Garden, the Celtics' home until 1995. Auerbach has vehemently denied the charge. (The Celtics now play at the FleetCenter.)

Auerbach's testy side also emerged in 1984, when, as team president, he upbraided Brent Musburger, then of CBS, before a national audience while accepting the league championship trophy. "Whatever happened to the Laker dynasty?" he said, waving his cigar after Boston beat Los Angeles in a bitter, seven-game series.

Boston had long embraced hockey and baseball while the Celtics, in their early glory years, often did not sell out Boston Garden. They even had some radio broadcasts in the mid-1960s relegated to FM, when they shared the same station with the Bruins—even when the Bruins were perennially in last place in the National Hockey League (NHL). Auerbach did little to promote the team in a marketing sense, feeling a winning team sells itself. And the aloof Russell, who refused to sign autographs, drew some negative public and press reaction because of his stridence on civil-rights issues.

"The Boston Celtics and Russell owned the NBA in their heyday, but they were always a backroom act in Boston—poor cousins to the ever popular Red Sox in baseball and NHL Bruins," Peter J. Bjarkman wrote in *The Biographical History of Basketball.*

Internal Battles

Following the Celtics' thirteenth championship in 1976, the team struggled for three seasons, and worse, Auerbach had major problems with owner John Y. Brown (no relation to Walter Brown). Brown, who later became governor of Kentucky, was highly intrusive and even sarcastically addressed Auerbach as "Living Legend" during staff meetings.

The tension escalated in February, 1979, when Brown, reportedly without Auerbach's consent, obtained the talented but troublesome McAdoo from the New York Knicks. Auerbach then considered the unthinkable to Boston fans—an offer as Knicks general manager. "We had a collective heart attack," Simmons wrote. "Red was leaving? He's leaving??? Everywhere he went, people urged him to stay: cab drivers, waiters, gas station attendants, people on the street. He stayed."

Brown's sale of the team to Harry Mangurian made the decision easier. Then, in October, 1979, Larry Bird began another glorious Celtics era, Boston winning championships in 1981, 1984 and 1986.

But after the third championship of the Bird era, tragedy befell the Boston organization. The Celtics drafted Len Bias from the University of Maryland in 1986—Auerbach and Maryland coach Charles "Lefty" Driesell were close friends and Bias had worked as a counselor in Auerbach's summer camp in Marshfield, Mass.—and two days after Boston drafted him second overall, Bias died in Washington, D.C. of a cocaine overdose. Another Celtic would die seven years later when star guard Reggie Lewis collapsed with a heart problem during a playoff game and died during the summer while working out.

Pushed Aside for Pitino

The Celtics in 1996-97 won only fifteen games, their worst season ever, and owner Paul Gaston summoned Pitino, who had coached Kentucky to the 1996 NCAA title and had revived the Knicks in the late 1980s. Pitino demanded control of team operations and Gaston demoted Auerbach to executive vice president. Pitino, meanwhile, was on billboards and bank commercials.

But the team, which hadn't made the playoffs since 1995, continued to falter and Pitino left in 2001. Gaston reinstated Auerbach as team president. "The mere fact that the Celtics had to trumpet his return speaks volumes about the damage incurred by Pitino's regime," Stringer wrote.

Auerbach's Legacy

That the Celtics sold for $360 million in September, 2002, reflects the market value of their legacy, of which Auerbach is the architect. "While the leprechaun may represent them in their logo, (Auerbach) is the true icon of the Boston Celtics," Peter Stringer wrote on the *New England Sports Network* Web site.

His impact also transcends sports. After the November, 2002, off-year congressional elections, Kevin Merida of the *Washington Post* interviewed Auerbach about the psychology of winning and losing. "You see, it's too easy to lose," he said of the Democratic Party's setbacks. "Sometimes you've already lost before you play—you've made your excuses ahead of time. "For instance, you have an injury, so you're expected to lose. This guy is hurt, blah, blah. See what I mean? ... So you go in there with a defeatist complex.

"You show me a guy who loses an election and he's happy, he's an idiot. If you lose, you have to go out and say, 'I'm the unhappiest person in the world.' When you lose, I want you to be unhappy, I want you to be miserable."

SELECTED WRITINGS BY AUERBACH:

(With Paul Sann) *Auerbach: Winning the Hard Way*, Little Brown, 1966.
Basketball for the Player, the Fan and the Coach, Simon & Schuster, 1975.
(With Joe Fitzgerald) *Red Auerbach: An Autobiography*, Putnam, c. 1977.
(With Sandy Grossman) *Red on Roundball*, RCA SelectaVision, 1982.
Athletes: The Paintings of Joe Wilder, M.D. With essays by Red Auerbach, H. N. Abrams, 1985.
(With Joe Fitzgerald) *On and Off the Court*, Macmillan, 1985.
(With Ken Dooley) *MBA: Management by Auerbach*, Macmillan, 1991.

FURTHER INFORMATION

Books

Bjarkman, Peter C. *Biographical History of Basketball*. Lincolnwood, IL: Masters Press, c2000.

Other

"Arnold (Jacob) Auerbach." Biography Resource Center. http://galenet.galegroup.com, (November 6, 2002).
"Auerbach, Red." Jews in Sports. http://www.jews insports.org, (October 31, 2002).
"Auerbach in the Saddle." NESN.com. http://www.nesn.com, (October 4, 2001).
"Auerbach's Celtics Played as a Team." ESPN Classic. http://espn.go.com, (November 1, 2002).
"Deadline Dealings." Boston Celtics Web Site. http://www.nba.com/celtics, (November 4, 2002).

"Hall of Famers: Arnold 'Red' Auerbach." Basketball Hall of Fame. http://www.hoophall.com (November 6, 2002).

"More Black Coaches Guide NBA Than Ever Before." BET.com. http://www.bet.com (February 14, 2002).

"Phil Jackson vs. Red Auerbach." CNN/Sports Illustrated. http://cnnsi.com, (June 18, 2002).

"Red Auerbach." Biography Resource Center. http://galenet.galegroup.com, (November 6, 2002).

"Russell Sees Life Lessons in Basketball." Christian Science Monitor. http://www.csmonitor.com (June 15, 2001).

"Seeing Red After All These Years." ESPN.com. http://www.espn.go.com (March 22, 2002).

"Straighten Up and Fly Right." Boston Globe. http://www.boston.com (September 28, 2002).

"The No-Pity Party." Washington Post. http://www.washingtonpost.com/wp-dyn/articles/A20166-2002 Nov6.html (November 7, 2002).

"Titles Prove That He's The Won." Boston Globe. http://www.boston.com/sports (December 30, 1999).

Sketch by Paul Burton

Isabelle Autissier
1956-

French yacht racer

During a decade of competitive marathon sailing, Isabelle Autissier demonstrated nearly supernatural sailing prowess and unmitigated bad luck. She is the first woman to sail around the world alone and she piloted a yacht from New York to San Francisco by way of Cape Horn in world-record time. She also capsized and barely eluded death—twice—in violent, remote seas near Antarctica. Autissier retired from the sport as a national heroine in her native France and is widely regarded as the best woman ocean racer ever. "When you get down to it," *Cruising World* magazine concluded, "there is no one else on the planet like Isabelle Autissier."

Passion for the Sea

Autissier grew up in a sailing family in the French coastal town of LaRochelle. Her father, Jean, owned a succession of cruising boats and encouraged his five daughters to sail. Isabelle began sailing when she was six years old and started planning her first solo voyage around the world when she was twelve. "As a child, I was never told that something was impossible," she once told the *Charlotte Observer*. "I was only taught that everything had a price."

After graduating from college in 1978 with a degree in nautical engineering, Autissier taught at "fishing schools" in France where local fishermen learned better techniques and gained a background in research and marine sciences. For three years, she spent her nights and weekends welding together a 30-foot, steel-hulled cruising boat called Parole. In 1986, she sailed Parole across the Atlantic single-handedly. "When I returned to France," Autissier recalled, "I decided to try racing, just to see what it was like, to have the experience. I thought it would help me know more about the sea and sailing." In 1987, she won her class and finished third overall in the Mini Transat, a solo race across the Atlantic. She finished fourth in La Solitaire du Figaro in 1989. "In the beginning, I said I would race just for the experience and then go back to my job, (but) racing and trying to go fast in a small boat was such fun."

Around the World

Autissier entered the 1990-91 running of the BOC around-the-world yacht race, the first woman to compete in the contest. The grueling race, which has been renamed Around Alone, is run every four years and requires sailors to travel 27,000 miles over eight months. It begins and ends on the East Coast of the United States, with stops in South Africa, Australia, and Uruguay. During the second leg of the race, Autissier's 60-foot yacht, named Ecureuil Poitou-Charentes, lost its mast in rough seas and high winds as she neared Australia. She fashioned a makeshift rig, limped into port, made repairs, and set out again. She completed the voyage, finishing seventh. It was the first time a woman sailor had circumnavigated the globe alone. "It was wonderful because I discovered everything: I discovered sailing alone for a long time, the Southern Ocean, everything," Autissier said in a Knight Ridder/Tribune News Service article. "It was really a wonderful experience.... I came back to Newport (Rhode Island) and ... I thought: I did what I have wanted to do in life. Since I was a little girl, I wanted to sail around the world, and now I have done it. The rest of my life is extra."

Autissier again displayed her sailing prowess—including expert understanding of weather patterns, currents, and navigation—while setting a world record in the spring of 1994. She and a three-man crew piloted her new yacht, the Ecureuil Poitou-Charentes 2, around Cape Horn from New York to San Francisco in just sixty-two days, five hours, and fifty-five minutes—beating the old record by two weeks.

Capsized

Nineteen yachts raced in a southerly direction from Charleston, South Carolina, at the start of the 1994-95 Around Alone Race—and Isabelle Autissier, following a hunch about Atlantic weather patterns, sailed north and east. Her instincts were correct. Autissier easily tri-

Chronology

1956	Born October 18 in Brittany, France
1978	Graduates from college with a degree in nautical engineering
1987	Finishes third in the Mini Transat, a solo race across the Atlantic
1989	Finishes fourth in La Solitaire du Figaro competition
1991	Finishes seventh in the BOC yacht race (later renamed Around Alone) to become the first woman sailor to circumnavigate the planet
1994	Sets world record sailing around Cape Horn from New York to San Francisco in sixty-two days, five hours, and fifty-five minutes—beating the old record by two weeks
1994	Capsizes in the Indian Ocean during the Around Alone Race and spends four days adrift before being rescued by the Australian military
1996	Disqualified from the Vendee Globe race when she requires assistance to repair a broken rudder
1999	Capsizes midway between New Zealand and Cape Horn during her third Around Alone race; rescued by rival Giovanni Soldini
1999	Announces retirement from solo marathon racing

Isabelle Autissier

umphed in the first leg of the race, arriving in Cape Town, South Africa, five days before her nearest competitor. Race director Mark Schrader called her 1,200-mile lead "incomprehensible."

Her luck would soon change, however. During the second leg, the Ecureuil Poitou Charentes 2 lost its 83-foot mast in a gale on the Indian Ocean. Autissier jury-rigged a new mast, as she had four years earlier, and traveled to Kerguelen Islands. Repairs were made and she set out for Sydney, but halfway between Australia and the Antarctic her boat was hit by a monumental wave, rolled a full 360 degrees, and lost its rigging and part of its deck. The wave would have washed Autissier away had she been on deck when it hit. She activated her electronic positioning beacons, which signaled race officials in Charleston. The Australian Navy rescued Autissier from her listing ship four days later. The Ecureuil Poitou Charentes 2 was never recovered.

Autissier returned to France and built a new 60-foot racing ship for the 1996 Vendee Globe competition in which racers must sail around the world alone—and, unlike the Around Alone, without stopping. She was disqualified when the boat, named PRB after the French building-products company sponsoring her, lost a rudder and she needed help replacing it. Autissier completed the race anyway, her second solo trip around the planet.

Averting Disaster—Again

Two years later, Autissier entered the Around Alone for the third time. She was leading the race in its third leg when—halfway between New Zealand and Cape Horn—a huge wave hit PRB and caused its autopilot to malfunction. The boat capsized. She had only enough time to slam the waterproof hatch behind her to prevent the cabin from flooding. Autissier activated her emergency beacons, but she was far from shipping lanes and out of

the range of the rescue services. Race officials directed one of her competitors, Giovanni Soldini of Italy, to go to her aid. Soldini piloted his boat through fierce conditions for more than twenty hours to reach Autissier's coordinates. "The problem is that these positions aren't precise, and it won't be easy to see Isabelle's boat," Soldini e-mailed to his Milan-based racing team. "Visibility is always poor, and in any case I'll need some luck."

Two and a half hours later, Soldini saw the upturned hull of Autissier's boat being pummeled by enormous waves. Twice he steered close to PRB and called for her, but there was no sign of Autissier. On his third pass, Soldini threw a hammer at the hull. It struck forcefully. An escape hatch opened, and Autissier crawled out. She had been sleeping.

Weeks after being rescued from the raging, frigid Southern seas for the second time in her larger-than-life career, Isabelle Autissier had this to say about racing around the world alone: "No more. . . . This has been my crazy job for 10 years. I had 10 wonderful years doing that, maybe the best years of my life—great adventures, great friends, great feelings. It has been a wonderful story for me. But now it's time to do something else."

Since that time, in 1999, the quiet, modest Frenchwoman has kept a low profile and avoided media coverage. She lives near the coast of France, in the region where she was born and learned, as a child, to sail.

Awards and Accomplishments

1991	First woman ever to sail alone around the world
1994	Sailed from New York harbor to San Francisco's Golden Gate Bridge by way of Cape Horn in fastest time ever
1996	Sailed around the world alone for the second time
2002	Inducted into the Museum of Yachting's Single-Handed Sailors' Hall of Fame

FURTHER INFORMATION

Periodicals

Fisher, Bob. "Sailing: French Leader Saved by Rival." *Guardian* (London, England) (February 17, 1999).

Gorman, Edward. "Autissier Pays Tribute to Rescuer Soldini." *The Times* (London, England) (March 4, 1999).

Gorman, Edward. "Race Rival Turns Back to Rescue Stricken Sailor." *The Times* (London, England) (February 17, 1999).

Gorman, Edward. "Autissier Sails Close to the Wind." *The Times* (London, England) (February 17, 1999).

Manly, Chris. "Ocean Ordeal: High Seas Triumph: Lone Yachtswoman 'Never in Doubt' About Rescue." *The Advertiser* (Adelaide, Australia) (February 18, 1999).

Meade, Tom. "Solo Sailor Prepares for Next Trip Around Globe." Knight Ridder News Service (August 19, 1998).

McCormick, Herb. "A Woman of Singular Disposition." *Cruising World* (January, 1999).

McCormick, Herb. "Isabelle Airlifted to Safety After Rollover—Auguin wins Leg II." *Cruising World* (March 1995)

Mossop, Brian. "Waves of Disaster." *Gold Coast Bulletin* (September 18, 2002).

"Rescue at Sea." *Sports Illustrated* (January 9, 1995).

Stinemetz, Morgan. "Autissier Showed Courage in Solo Effort." *Sarasota Herald Tribune* (March 13, 1999).

Time. "The Deep End of the Sea: Capsized in Round-the-World Boat Race, France's Most Beloved Female Sailor is Saved by a Rival." (March 1, 1999).

Sketch by David Wilkins

Donovan Bailey
1967-

Canadian sprinter

Canadian sprinter Donovan Bailey set the world record in a 100-meter race in 1996, earning the distinction of "world's fastest man." At his peak during the 1996 Summer Olympic Games in Atlanta, the Jamaican-born Bailey ran a record-setting, gold-medal-winning time of 9.84 seconds. With three teammates, he also captured the gold in the 4x100-meter relay. In Canada, his home since age 13, Bailey became a star, if not a national hero. The outspoken athlete gained a reputation for bluntness and bravado, often publicly ridiculing his rivals. He retained his world record until 1999, when American sprinter Maurice Greene outstripped him by 5-100ths of a second. By then Bailey had sustained a nearly career- ending Achilles tendon injury; he went on to recover and return to sprinting, retiring in 2001 before his 34th birthday.

Bailey, one of five sons born in Manchester, Jamaica to George and Daisy Bailey, would wake at dawn to help tend to the family's chickens, goats, and pigs before going to school. He moved with his family to the Toronto suburb of Oakville in 1981. Here Bailey attended Queen Elizabeth Park High School, becoming a track and basketball standout. "I could have left high school and run track right away, but that wasn't what I wanted," he told Michael Farber of *Sports Illustrated*. "I wanted a nice house, money, fast cars. I was taught to work real hard, to work on my own."

Bailey attended Sheridan College in Oakville, playing forward for one season on the basketball team. Graduating with a degree in economics, he set out to accomplish his material goals. A self-made businessman, Bailey worked as a marketing and property consultant, and ran a business importing and exporting clothing. At 22 he bought a house in Oakville and drove a Porsche 911 convertible. But track and field still lured him, and in 1991 he began to train seriously as a sprinter.

Hones Sprinting Skills

At one of his first major competitions, the 1991 Pan-American Games, Bailey made the finals. But he still had

Donovan Bailey

to prove himself. Athletics Canada, his sport's governing body, overlooked him for the 1991 world championships and the 1992 Olympics. In 1993 he made the world championships in Stuttgart, Germany; to his disappointment, however, he was dropped from the relay race. While in Stuttgart, Bailey met Dan Pfaff, a track coach at Louisiana State University. Seeing promise in Bailey, Pfaff invited the sprinter to train with him in Baton Rouge.

In March 1994 he began intensively training with Pfaff, who corrected Bailey's running form and put him on a program of sprinting, lifting weights, and better diet. Pfaff also helped the Canadian sprinter improve his attitude, which had soured after his disappointments. After three months, Bailey had pared his 100-meter sprinting time from 10.36 to 10.03 seconds. These three-tenths of a second had made a world of difference, putting Bailey into an elite class of sprinters.

Bailey had captured the attention of the track world, but still had work to do. Improving his starting techniques, he managed to trim his sprinting time by tenths and hundredths of seconds. By spring of 1995 he was running under 10 seconds, at 9.99, and by June had clocked 9.91, a Canadian record. At the world championships in Goteborg, Sweden, he captured the title with a winning time of 9.97, clinching the title of "world's fastest man."

Captures Olympic Gold

Bailey peaked as a sprinter in 1996, during the Olympic Games in Atlanta. Taking the gold medal in 100 meters, he set a world-record time of 9.84 seconds, becoming the fastest man in history. In his signature style, Bailey started at the back of the pack before overtaking his competitors in a dramatic mid-race surge.

Although he became a star in Canada, Bailey did not become the fully-embraced national hero he had envisioned. Canada was still reeling from its 1988 Olympic disappointment, when **Ben Johnson** had captured the gold, only to forfeit it after the sprinter tested positive for steroids. Like Bailey, Johnson was a Jamaican-born Canadian, and Bailey was haunted by the media's frequent comparisons between him and the disgraced Johnson. Bailey, nonetheless, took pride in being a "clean" runner who never touched steroids or other drugs.

Bailey's next significant victory came in Toronto in 1997, when he beat American sprinter **Michael Johnson** (the Olympic 200- and 400-meter champion) in a one-to-one race to 150 meters. In mid-race, Johnson had clutched his thigh in pain, leaving Bailey to take the $1.5 million reward—the biggest athletic prize in history. Calling Johnson "a faker and a chicken," as Mike Rowbottom of the *Independent* quoted him, Bailey reveled in his win. Yet fans decried the brash sprinter's lack of sportsmanship.

Two months later, Bailey lost his world-championship title to another American, Maurice Greene. Bailey blamed his loss on his recent obsession over Johnson. "I found it was impossible to peak twice," he told Rowbottom. In 1999 Greene went on to break Bailey's world-record time, clocking 9.79 seconds in 100 meters.

Calls It Quits

Meanwhile, the Canadian sprinter was struggling to overcome a nearly career-ending injury. In September, 1998, he had ruptured his Achilles tendon while playing basketball with friends. After surgery to the tendon, he could not walk. Despite expectations, he went on to recover and resume his career. By 2000, he was again ranked Canada's No. 1 sprinter. But he would not again clinch an international title. In 2001 he announced his retirement at the end of the season. He ran his final race in August at the world track-and-field championships in Edmonton, Alberta.

After receiving a standing ovation during a farewell lap, Bailey spoke with the media about his plans. "I came from corporate Canada, and I don't think it'll be a big problem going back," he told George Johnson of the Montreal *Gazette*. Bailey added that he'd also like to help coach Canada's new young sprinters. He lives in Oakville, Ontario, with his girlfriend, Michelle Mullin, and daughter, Adrienna.

The Canadian network VisionTV had planned to air an interview with Bailey on its show, "Credo," in late February, 2003, in conjunction with Black History Month. The show features Canadian newsmakers discussing faith and values.

FURTHER INFORMATION

Books

"Maurice Greene." *Contemporary Black Biography,* Volume 27. Edited by Ashyia Henderson. Gale Group, 2001.

Periodicals

Buffery, Steve. "Donovan Bailey Has Quietly Become One of the World's Fastest Men." *Toronto Sun* (August 6, 1995).

Cole, Cam. "Ghost of Johnson Finally Laid to Rest." *Gazette* (Montreal; July 28, 1996): B1.

Farber, Michael. "Blast from the North." *Sports Illustrated* (July 22, 1996): 142.

Johnson, George. " I'll Stay in Sport'." *Gazette* (Montreal, August 7, 2001): C5.

Ralph, Dan. "Donovan's Done Dashing." *Calgary Herald* (May 26, 2001): C1.

Rowbottom, Mike. "Bailey Banks on Record Return after Dash for Cash Furore." *Independent* (London, January 26, 1998): S1.

Rowbottom, Mike. "Bailey Has the Twinkle of a Star." *Independent* (London, June 28, 1997): 25.

Todd, Jack. "Taking the Fast Lane to Atlanta." *Gazette* (Montreal, July 6, 1996): C1.

Sketch by Wendy Kagan

Garnet "Ace" Bailey
1948-2001

Canadian hockey player

Hockey player Ace Bailey played for five seasons with the Boston Bruins in the National Hockey League (NHL), then played in Detroit, St. Louis, Washington, and Edmonton before becoming a scout for Edmonton and then director of pro scouting for the Los Angeles Kings. As a Bruin, he was on the teams that won the Stanley Cup in 1970 and 1972. According to Matt McHale in the Los Angeles *Daily News,* although Bailey was not a superstar skater or top scorer, "He had an engaging personality that produced a thousand stories and hundreds of friends."

Son of a Hockey Player

Born Garnet Bailey in Lloydminster, Saskatchewan, Bailey grew up playing hockey. His father, Irvine Bailey, was a star forward for Toronto in the 1920s and 1930s. Irvine Bailey's career ended when he was thirty, when a cross-check from behind, administered by Boston player Eddie Shore, almost killed him in December of 1933. The resulting head injury was almost fatal. Irvine Bailey's father was so angry that he took a train from Toronto to Boston, a pistol in his pocket, intending to kill Shore. He was picked up by police at the Boston train station before he could do any shooting.

When he was seventeen, Bailey was selected 13th overall in the amateur draft, ironically by the Boston Bruins, the team whose player had almost killed his father. Bailey joined the team in the 1968-69 season after scoring twenty-four goals and fifty-six points for a Bruins farm team, the Hershey Bears of the American Hockey League.

In 1969-70, Bailey scored eleven goals in fifty-eight games; in that season, the Bruins won the Stanley Cup. They won the Cup again in 1972.

Bailey's most famous play occurred in Game 1 of the 1972 Stanley Cup finals against the New York Rangers. Late in the game, with both sides in balance, Bailey skated down the left side of the rink around Ranger Brad Park, who had the puck. Bailey, who had only scored nine times in that entire year, kicked Park's stick, and flipped the puck over Rangers goaltender Ed Giacomin and into

Chronology	
1948	Born June 13, in Lloydminster, Saskatchewan, Canada
1966	Selected 13th overall in the amateur draft by Boston Bruins and begins playing with the Hershey Bears, a Bruins farm team
1968-73	Plays with the Boston Bruins
1969-70	Scores 11 goals in 58 games; Bruins win Stanley Cup
1971-72	Bruins win Stanley Cup
1972-74	Plays with Detroit Red Wings
1973-75	Plays with St. Louis Blues
1974-78	Plays with Washington Capitals
1978-79	Plays with Edmonton Oilers
1979-80	Coaches with Houston Apollos
1980-81	Coaches with Wichita Wind
1981-94	Scout for the Edmonton Oilers; during his time with the team, they win five Stanley Cups
1994-2001	Director of pro scouting for the Los Angeles Kings
2001	Dies while en route from Boston to Los Angeles on United Airlines Flight 175; on September 11, 2001, the plane is hijacked by terrorists and crashes into the South Tower of the World Trade Center, killing everyone on board

the net. Bailey's teammate at the time, **Phil Esposito**, told a reporter for the *Tampa Tribune,* "I mean, Ace roofed it. We were so . . . happy for Ace. We loved that guy."

Bailey met his wife, Kathy, on a plane while he was playing for the Boston Bruins. As a member of the team, he frequently flew to away games and Kathy was a flight attendant for Eastern Airlines.

According to McHale, Bailey treated his wife "like a princess, handling all the cooking, shopping and laundry." Kathy Bailey told McHale that he often called her when he was out of town to remind her of what was in the refrigerator that needed to be eaten.

"Coach, I Used It Every Day"

In 1973, Bailey was traded to the Detroit Red Wings. According to Bernie Czarniecki in the *Detroit Free Press,* Red Wings coach Johnny Wilson said that Bailey "gives us muscle" and praised Bailey for helping the team win in a game against the New York Islanders. Wilson also noted, "He was a very enthusiastic player. He played extremely well for us. He was a fast skater and challenged the opposition, home or road." Bailey played with the Red Wings for two seasons, then moved on to the St. Louis Blues, where he played another two seasons.

From 1974 to 1978, Bailey played with the Washington Capitals, then spent a year with the Edmonton Oilers. His playing career ended in 1979. Over his eleven seasons with the National Hockey League, he had 107 goals, 171 points, and 278 assists.

Bailey was known for his lighthearted approach to life, as well as to his sport. After being selected to play for Washington, Bailey received a four-inch-manual from Washington coach Tom McVie, telling him how to get into condition to play. Bailey used the manual to prop up a beer

Career Statistics

Yr	Team	League	GP	G	AST	PTS	PIM
1967-68	OKL	CHL	34	8	13	21	67
1968-69	HER	AHL	60	24	32	56	104
1968-69	BOS	NHL	8	3	3	6	10
1969-70	BOS	NHL	58	11	11	22	82
1970-71	OKL	CHL	11	3	8	11	28
1970-71	BOS	NHL	36	0	6	6	44
1971-72	BOS	NHL	73	9	13	22	64
1972-73	BOS	NHL	57	8	13	21	89
1972-73	DET	NHL	13	2	11	13	16
1973-74	DET	NHL	45	9	14	23	33
1973-74	STL	NHL	22	7	3	10	20
1974-75	STL	NHL	49	15	26	41	113
1974-75	WAS	NHL	22	4	13	17	8
1975-76	WAS	NHL	67	13	19	32	75
1976-77	WAS	NHL	78	19	27	46	51
1977-78	WAS	NHL	40	7	12	19	28
1978-79	EDM	WHA	38	5	4	9	22
1979-80	HOU	CHL	7	1	0	1	0
1980-81	WCH	CHL	1	0	0	0	2
WHA Totals			38	5	4	9	22
NHL Totals			568	107	171	278	633

BOS: Boston Bruins; DET: Detroit Red Wings; EDM: Edmonton Oilers; HOU: Houston Apollos; HRS: Hershey Bears; OKL: Oklahoma City Blazers; STL: St. Louis Blues; WAS: Washington Capitals; WCH: Wichita Wind.

keg in his bar. On the first day of training camp, according to Tom FitzGerald in the *San Francisco Chronicle,* Bailey beat several other players in a footrace, and McVie said approvingly, "Ace, I can see you used your book this summer." Bailey replied, "Coach, I used it every day."

In the Los Angeles *Daily News,* a reporter told another story that showed Bailey's quirky humor and quick thinking. Late in his playing career, when he was a left wing with the Edmonton Oilers, Bailey shared a room with rookie **Wayne Gretzky** while the team was on the road. One day Gretzky and Bailey woke up only an hour before a game, and missed the team bus to the stadium. Bailey got Gretzky a taxi, then packed their suitcases and arrived at the stadium late. He put on his hockey gear and jumped into the shower. When the other teammates came back into the dressing room after the warmup, they found Bailey sitting in front of his locker, dripping wet, apparently from sweat. "Great warmup, Ace," some players said to Bailey, assuming that he had been out there playing with them.

Becomes a Hockey Scout

After ending his playing career, Bailey coached with the Houston Apollos and Wichita Wind for a year each, then became a scout for the Oilers. He was an Oilers scout for thirteen years and helped the team to five Stanley Cups before becoming director of pro scouting for the Los Angeles Kings in 1994.

On September 11, 2001, Bailey was on United Airlines Flight 175, en route from Boston to Los Angeles, when the plane was hijacked by terrorists and crashed into the south tower of the World Trade Center in New York City. All on board were killed in the resulting fireball, which destroyed the tower. In his memory, his family established the Ace Bailey Children's Fund, which benefits children who need medical care.

Bailey was admired and respected by his colleagues. The *Dailey News* of Los Angeles reported the feelings of Ray Bennett, the assistant coach of the Kings, after his death. "Ace, if you were introduced to him, you knew him. He didn't just shake your hand. He grabbed your arm. He slapped you on the back. . . . He understood that this game is really about relationships and the people you meet." In an article on the International Ice Hockey Federation Web site, a reporter quoted Wayne Gretzky, who said, "Ace may not have been the greatest hockey player to play in the NHL, but he taught many players how to win championships and more importantly, he was a winner as a person. We will all miss him greatly."

FURTHER INFORMATION

Periodicals

"Espy Recalls His Friend Acer." *Tampa Tribune* (September 15, 2001): 1.

FitzGerald, Tom. "Coach's Manual Handy." *San Francisco Chronicle* (September 18, 2001): D2.

McHale, Matt. "One Hard Year Mending Continues for Families of Kings Scouts Killed in Attacks." *Daily News* (Los Angeles, CA) (September 11, 2002): S1.

Politi, Steve. "Soul on Ice." *Star-Ledger* (Newark, NJ) (February 11, 2001): 5.

"Remembering Ace." *Daily News* (Los Angeles, CA) (September 13, 2001): S1.

Wheatley, Tom. "Bailey is Remembered as Fun-Loving, But Tough on Ice." *St. Louis Post-Dispatch* (September 13, 2001): C3.

Other

Czarniecki, Bernie. "Garnet (Ace) Bailey: Left Wing A Jewel on the Ice in 1973." *Detroit Free Press* (November 7, 2002), http://www.freep.com/ (November 11, 2002).

"Garnet 'Ace' Bailey." *Hockeydb.com,* http://www.hockeydb.com/ (November 17, 2002).

Moharib, Nadia. "Canadian Killed in Terrorist Attack." *Canoe* (September 12, 2001), http://www.canoe.ca/ (November 11, 2002).

"Stanley Cup Winner and LA Kings Scout Bailey Perished." *IHHF.* http://www.iihf.com/news/iihfpr5701.htm (November 11, 2002).

"Stanley Cup Winners." *Wikipedia,* http://www.wikipedia.org/wiki/Stanley_Cup (November 17, 2002).

Sketch by Kelly Winters

Ernie Banks
1931-

American baseball player

Hall of Famer Ernie Banks was the greatest and most popular player in the history of the Chicago Cubs, a man so closely associated with the franchise both during and after his playing days that he was known as Mr. Cub. Over the course of 19 seasons, he played 2528 games in which he got 2583 hits, 512 home runs, and 1636 runs batted in. He turned in such an awesome performance in 1958 (.313, 47 home runs, and 129 RBI) and 1959 (.304, 45 home runs, and 143 RBI) that he was named the National League's Most Valuable Player both years. Banks was the shining star of a team that was mediocre for most of his career, and his one great regret was that he never played in the World Series. Nonetheless losing never dampened his optimism which was so legendary that when he was elected to Baseball's Hall of Fame in his first year of eligibility, Thomas Boswell of the *Washington Post* called

Ernie Banks

him "the only man in baseball history better known for his good spirits than for his achievements."

Childhood in Texas

Ernest Banks, born in Dallas, Texas in 1931, was his family's first son and second born child. Ernie was an introverted, good hearted child, devoted to helping around the house, and attending church and Sunday School, and for a time his mother thought he would follow in his grandfather's footsteps and become a minister. Growing up, he participated in a number of sports. He was a talented basketball player, averaging 20 points per game in high school, and a high jumper who could clear nearly six feet. In summers and fall, when he wasn't working in the cotton fields near Dallas for $1.75 a day, he played pick-up softball. Banks' father played for the Dallas Green Monarchs and the Black Giants, two teams in the Negro Leagues that existed while major league ball was still segregated. Ernie served as batboy on his father's teams, but he did not play baseball himself until well he was into his teens.

In 1947 William Blair, a black newspaper publisher and ex-Negro League pitcher, saw a softball game in which the sixteen-year-old Banks slugged a long homer off an established pitcher named Brannon. "Brannon was the fastest pitcher I had ever seen," Blair recalled to the *St. Louis Post-Dispatch*'s Barry Horn. "I never saw anyone who could throw like him. I never saw anyone get the solid licks off him. And here was this willowy kid walloping ball after ball off him. Ernest, I could tell

Chronology

1931	Born in Dallas, Texas
1946	Joins black barnstorming team in Amarillo, Texas
1950	Signs with Kansas City Monarchs of the Negro National League
1951-52	Serves in U.S. Army
1953	Signs with Chicago Cubs for $2,000 bonus
1955-60	Hits more home runs than any other major leaguer
1958-59	Named National League's MVP in two consecutive years
1962	Switches from shortstop to first base
1969	Cubs lose pennant after leading NL for most of the season
1970	Gets 500th home run and 1600th RBI on same day
1971	Retires as an active player after 19 seasons with Cubs
1977	Elected to National Baseball Hall of Fame

Awards and Accomplishments

1955-62, 1965, 1967, 1969	National League All-Star team
1958-59	National League Most Valuable Player; *Sporting News* Player of the Year
1958, 60	National League Home Run leader
1960	Rawlings Gold Glove shortstop
1967	Lou Gehrig Memorial Award
1977	Inducted into National Baseball Hall of Fame

right away, was going to be something special." With Blair's help, Banks joined a black baseball team from Amarillo that barnstormed from New Mexico up to Nebraska. He played that one summer at shortstop and learned rapidly. "You had to show Ernest everything one time, and he learned it," Blair told Horn.

Enters Negro Leagues

That summer, when Amarillo played the Kansas City Monarchs, one of the premier teams in black baseball, Banks caught the eye of Monarchs's manager **James 'Cool Papa' Bell**. Bell brought Banks onto the Monarchs after he graduated from high school in 1950. At the end of the season, he barnstormed on a team with **Jackie Robinson**, who said he thought Banks could make it in the majors. Although Robinson had integrated baseball two years earlier, the thought of playing with a big league ball club had never entered Banks' mind. He spent the 1951 and 1952 seasons in the U.S. Army. When he returned to the Monarchs in 1953 the Negro Leagues were on their last legs. Most of their best players had jumped to the majors. An ankle injury led Banks to give up baseball in the middle of the 1953 season, but days later Monarchs manager Buck O'Neil persuaded him to finish the season with the team. Banks did not know it, but the Chicago Cubs-and several other teams-had told the Monarchs they were interested in his services. After a game in Chicago, O'Neil took Banks to Wrigley Field, the Cubs' ballpark. There Cubs general manager Wid Matthews informed Banks he would be joining the team. The Cubs had bought Banks' contract from the Monarchs for $10,000.

Banks played 10 games with the Cubs at the end of the 1953 season, hitting .314 and getting 2 home runs. Another black player, Gene Baker, had joined the Cubs before Banks. But Banks got into a game first and became the first African-American to play for the team. Even with his sunny disposition, it was not easy for Banks as the first black on a team in the early 1950s. "For awhile, it was like I was there, but I wasn't there," Banks revealed to the *Post-Dispatch*. "I was there to play and do what I had to do on the field. We talked and laughed on the train rides and we played together, but we lived apart. When games were over, me and Gene headed home to the [black] south side of the city and the other players all went north."

"Mr. Cub"

Banks made the team as the Cubs' starting shortstop in 1954 and stayed with the team until he retired in 1971. For most of those 19 years he was among the most potent offensive threats in baseball. From 1955 to 1960 he was the most prolific home run hitter in the game, hitting more than either **Hank Aaron**, **Willie Mays** or **Mickey Mantle** hit during the same period. During that six year period he averaged more than 115 runs batted in and over 41 homers a year. In the 1958 and 1959 seasons he went on such a tear that he was named the National League's Most Valuable Player both years. It was achievement enough winning two MVPs in a row. Doubly impressive was the fact that, while MVPs are usually selected from pennant winning clubs, the Cubs finished *fifth* both years.

Banks was also a durable player. Beginning his first day with the Cubs he played 424 games straight, a record for a player just breaking into baseball. After a minor injury he played another 717 without an interruption. In the 1960s, Banks-already in his 30s-slowed down a bit. Still he continued to hit between 20 and 30 homers a year with good RBI production. In 1961 after a failed experiment in left field, Banks was shifted from shortstop to first base where he remained until his retirement.

Banks had impressive numbers, but unfortunately for most of his career he was the Cubs *only* impressive player. In the 1950s and for the first half of the 1960s, the club lived in the National League's second division. To the club's perennially bad record, Banks owes another of his claims to fame: He holds the record for the most games played with a single team, 2528, without ever playing in the World Series. The closest Banks came to post-season play was the infamous 1969 season. It was the best Cubs team in years, featuring stars such as Billy Williams, Ferguson Jenkins, Ron Santo and Glenn Hundley. However after leading the league the entire season, the Cubs collapsed completely in September and were overtaken by the New York Mets who went on to win the World Series.

Career Statistics

Yr	Team	AVG	GP	AB	R	H	HR	RBI	BB	SO	SB	E
1953	CHI	.314	10	35	3	11	2	6	4	5	0	1
1954	CHI	.275	154	593	70	163	19	79	40	50	6	34
1955	CHI	.295	154	596	98	176	44	117	45	72	9	22
1956	CHI	.297	139	538	82	160	28	85	52	62	6	25
1957	CHI	.285	156	594	113	169	43	102	70	85	8	14
1958	CHI	.313	154	617	119	193	47	129	52	87	4	32
1959	CHI	.304	155	589	97	179	45	143	64	72	2	12
1960	CHI	.271	156	597	94	162	41	117	71	69	1	18
1961	CHI	.278	138	511	75	142	29	80	54	75	1	21
1962	CHI	.269	154	610	87	164	37	104	30	71	5	11
1963	CHI	.227	130	432	41	98	18	65	39	73	0	9
1964	CHI	.264	157	591	67	156	23	95	35	84	1	10
1965	CHI	.265	163	612	79	162	28	106	55	64	3	15
1966	CHI	.272	141	511	52	139	15	75	29	59	0	10
1967	CHI	.276	151	573	68	158	23	95	27	93	2	10
1968	CHI	.246	150	552	71	136	32	83	27	67	2	6
1969	CHI	.253	155	565	60	143	23	106	42	101	0	4
1970	CHI	.252	72	222	25	56	12	44	20	33	0	4
1971	CHI	.193	39	83	4	16	3	6	6	14	0	0
TOTAL		.274	2528	9421	1305	2583	512	1636	763	1236	50	261

CHI: Chicago Cubs.

At 38 years old, Banks had played in nearly every game that season, and second-guessers speculated after the fact that if manager **Leo Durocher** had rested Banks more over the course of 1969, he could have helped the team more in the closing weeks. For years Banks deeply rued having never played in a Series, telling *USA Today*'s Greg Boeck in 1990 that "It's a hole in my life."

Positive Attitude

Despite his years with also-ran Cubs teams, Ernie Banks became famous for his infectiously positive attitude toward baseball and life. It was typified by the slogan "Let's play two" that has been associated with him since July 1969. "It was about 105 degrees in Chicago," Banks told the *Houston Chrinicle*'s Richard Dean. "And that's a time when everybody gets tired. I came into the clubhouse and everybody was sitting around and I said, 'Beautiful day. Let's play two.' And everybody looked at me like I was crazy. There were a couple of writers around and they wrote that and it stayed with me." Banks parlayed his optimism into a part-time profession after he retired as a player, giving motivational talks at companies around the country.

In 1970, a year before Banks hung up his spikes, he entered two elite baseball clubs on the same day. On May 12 at Chicago's Wrigley Field he hit his 500th home run; it also happened to be his 1600th run batted in. After his retirement, he coached with the Cubs and worked with their minor league hitters. He worked in insurance and banking for much of the 1980s and 1990s. Banks was voted into the National Baseball Hall of Fame in the first year of his eligibility, an indicator not only of his formidable statistical legacy but also of his enduring popularity with the media and the public.

Although he hasn't set foot in a major league batter's box in more than 30 years, "Mr. Cub" Ernie Banks continues to be among the most beloved sports celebrities in the country. His popularity has but little to do with the fact is among the all-time leaders in with 2,528 games, 9,421 at-bats, 4,706 total bases, 1,009 extra-base hits and 512 home runs. It rests instead with the heartfelt smile that never seems to leave his face and his openness to friend and stranger alike. His Hall of Fame status seems to extend into the realm of living itself. Banks summed up his philosophy for Mark Potash of the *Chicago Sun-Times*: "My theme is, 'The spirit of friendship is the balance of life.' Not money. Not the World Series. It's friendship. The relationships I have with people, that's enough to keep me happy."

CONTACT INFORMATION

Address: Ernie Banks International, Inc., 520 Washington Blvd., Suite 284, Marina Del Rey, CA 90292-5442. Online: http://www.letsplaytwo.com/.

SELECTED WRITINGS BY BANKS:

(With Enright, Jim) *Mr. Cub*. Chicago: Follett Publishing Company, 1971.
"Take it From Mr. Cub - Time is Right." *Chicago Sun-Times*. October 4, 1989.

FURTHER INFORMATION

Books

Allen, Maury. *Baseball's 100*. New York: A&W Library, 1981.

Dewey, Donald, and Nicholas Acocella. *The Biographical History of Baseball.* New York: Carroll & Graf, 1995.

Enright, Jim. *Baseball's Great Teams: The Chicago Cubs.* New York: Macmillan, 1975.

Periodicals

Berkow, Ira. "'Cubs Family' Minus Banks." *New York Times,* June 14, 1983.

Boeck, Greg. "For Banks, Lack of Postseason Play 'a Hole in My Llife'." *USA Today,* October 16, 1990.

Bonk, Thomas. "Mr. Cub Not Feeling His Years at 61." *Chicago Sun-Times,* February 9, 1992.

Boswell, Thomas. "Banks, 5 Others Join Hall." *Washington Post,* August 9, 1977.

Dean, Richard. "Still Mr. Cub." *Houston Chronicle* June 22, 1997.

Horn, Barry. "At 66, Banks Recalls Texas Roots." *St. Louis Post-Dispatch,* October 5, 1997.

Potash, Mark. "Mr. Cub's Latest Slogan: Great To Be Alive at 65." *Chicago Sun-Times,* March 8, 1996.

Stone, Larry. "Cubs Legend Taps Memory Bank." *Seattle Times,* June 9, 2002.

Weir, Tom. "Friendly Confines Beckon 'Mr. Cub'." *USA TODAY.* July 9, 1990.

Zwecker, Bill. "Ernie Banks Takes a Look at His Past," *Chicago Sun-Times.* October 23, 1994.

Sketch by Mike Pare

Roger Bannister

Roger Bannister
1929-

English track and field athlete

In 1954, Roger Bannister became the first person to run a mile in under four minutes. A noted British runner, he won the British mile championships in 1951, 1953, and 1954, and also won the Empire championship in 1954. In addition, he won the European 1,500 meter championship in 1954.

"I Just Ran Anywhere and Everywhere"

Bannister was born in 1929 in Harrow, England. As a child, he loved to run. According to Cordner Nelson and Roberto Quercetani in *The Milers,* he once said, "I just ran anywhere and everywhere—never because it was an end in itself, but because it was easier for me to run than to walk"

He won his school's cross-country meet for three years in a row when he was 12, 13, and 14. When he was 16, he decided to become a runner, but when he began studying medicine at Oxford University in 1946, he had never run on a track or worn running shoes with spikes. In 1946, Bannister began medical school in Oxford, where he had won a scholarship. Every day, during his lunch hour, he paid threepence to enter Paddington Park, near the hospital where he worked, so that he could practice running.

At the time, Bannister was not obviously talented as a runner; he had an ungainly walk, and barely made Oxford University's third track team. On March 22, 1947, however, he was running as a pacer for members of Oxford's first team in a mile race against Cambridge. Instead of stopping, as a pacer was supposed to, he kept on running, not only completing the course but winning by 20 yards with a time of 4:30.8. According to Frank Deford in *Sports Illustrated,* Bannister later said, "I knew from this day that I could develop this newfound ability." He still did not think of athletics as a career, but simply as something one did in order to be well-rounded.

In June of 1948, Bannister ran his first big race, the Kinniard Cup, and came in fourth. His time was 4:18.7. In the same year, he came in fifth in the Amateur Athletic Association Race with a time of 4:17.2. The Olympics were held in London that year, and Bannister was fascinated and inspired by the athletes. He decided to set his sights on competing at the Helsinki Olympics in 1952.

In 1949, Bannister won races in the United States with times of 4:11.1 and 4:11.9. After taking six weeks off, he came in third in another race with a time of 4:14.2. In 1950, he ran a mile in 4:13, not an impressive time compared to some of his earlier efforts. However, his last lap was an amazing 57.5, indicating that he was capable of greater speed, and that he had the ability to push for a burst of speed at the end of a race.

In 1951, he ran in the Penn Relays, starting out slowly but then taking the lead after two and a half laps. He won with a time of 4:08.3, and his last lap was 56.7. He knew from this performance that he could probably run a mile in 4 minutes, 5 seconds. At the time, no one had ever run a mile in less than four minutes, and most observers of track and field believed it could not be done.

1952 Olympics

Bannister won the British mile championships in 1951 and 1953. He competed in the 1500 meters in the 1952 Helsinki Olympics. In the semifinal, he came in fifth, but the next day, in the final, his legs were tired and heavy. Fourth place was the best he could do. Although he was initially disgusted with his performance, he later was proud that he had made it to the Olympics.

After the Olympics, Bannister spent some time deciding whether or not he wanted to continue running. He decided to devote himself to breaking the four-minute barrier for the mile. He trained for half an hour each day; this does not seem like much time, but Bannister spent it doing arduous speed workouts. To help him track his timing and set the pace, he recruited a friend, Chris Chataway. On June 27, 1953, he ran 4:02 with the help of two other friends, Chris Brasher and Don Macmillan, as pacers. Although the time was a British record, the authorities would not allow it to be placed in the record books because Bannister had used pacers. At the time, runners were supposed to run on their own, and pace themselves.

In the winter and spring of 1954, Bannister was so busy with his studies that he did not have time to run much. He would soon start his medical residency, which would leave him with even less free time. He was further frustrated by the knowledge that Australian miler John Landy was aiming to break the four-minute barrier, and that Landy might do it by spring. Bannister decided that he would try to break the record on May 6, in his first race of 1954, at a small meet. And, in order to relax, he went rock-climbing in Scotland.

Chronology	
1929	Born in Harrow, Middlesex, England
1945	Decides to become a runner
1946	Begins medical studies at St. Mary's College, Oxford University
1947	Shows talent while running as a pacer in a mile race at Oxford
1948	Is inspired by the Olympics, held in London, to try and compete in 1952 Olympics
1952	Competes in Helsinki Olympics
1954	Becomes first person to run a mile in less than 4 minutes
1954	Graduates from St. Mary's College, continues medical studies
1955	Publishes *The Four-Minute Mile*
1963	Earns medical degree from Oxford University, becomes a neurologist
1975	Is involved in an automobile crash; knighted by Queen Elizabeth II
1975- present	Continues working in neurology, writing scientific papers, and conducting research

Bannister knew he would have the best chance at breaking the record if the weather was perfect. When May 6 dawned with rain and win, he went to his job at St. Mary's Hospital Medical School in London, knowing as he made his rounds that he might lose his chance at the meet later that day.

"A Scene of the Wildest Excitement"

After his work, Bannister took the train from London to Oxford. On the train he met Franz Stampfl, who coached Bannister's teammate Chris Brasher. Stampfl told Bannister that despite the weather, he should give it his best try, saying, according to Deford, "If you don't take this opportunity, you may never forgive yourself." Bannister remained undecided through lunch and teatime later that day. As the race began at the Iffley Road track in Oxford, only about 1,100 spectators had showed up. Among them were Bannister's parents, who had been told by a friend that something special might happen that day.

As Bannister warmed up on the track, he kept looking toward the church of St. John the Evangelist, where a flag flying straight out above the steeple showed the strength of the wind. A few minutes before the race started at 6:10 p.m., the flag began to drop, and Bannister told himself that if everyone in characteristically rainy and windy England waited for good weather before doing anything, nothing would ever be done. He told Chataway and Brasher he was going to make the attempt on the record.

The gun sounded, and the runners took off. Brasher was in the lead until the end of the third lap, when Chataway took over the pace. On the backstretch Bannister passed him, moving ahead of all the other runners, into a new pace, never run before. On the stretch, a gust of wind pushed him sideways, stealing valuable fractions of seconds, but Bannister kept going, hitting the tape at 3:59.4. According to Nelson and Quercetani, he later

Related Biography: Miler John Landy

John Landy was Roger Bannister's closest competitor; if Bannister had not broken the four-minute barrier, Landy would have been the first person to do so. The two men spurred each other on, gaining strength and determination from each other's presence.

Born April 12, 1930 in Melbourne, Australia, Landy attended the University of Melbourne, where he ran on the track team and studied agricultural science. From 1954 to 1956, he taught biology and science at a grammar school in Geelong, Australia. In 1955, Landy was made a Member of the Order of the British Empire. The following year Landy was a member of the Australian Olympic track and field team and won a bronze medal in the 1,500 meters.

Landy married Lynn Catherine Fisher, a journalist, in 1971; they have two children. He has devoted most of his career to agriculture, and the development of his family's farm. He was also deeply interested in natural history and nature photography, and in 1985 published a book, *Close to Nature*, featuring the flora and fauna on his family property.

From 1985 to 1989, Landy was a consultant to the Australian Department of Sport, Recreation, and Tourism, and from 1988 to the present he has worked as a consultant to the Commonwealth Scientific and Industrial Organization. In 2002, Landy was Governor General of Victoria, Australia. He told Robert Phillips in the London, England *Daily Telegraph*, "Roger got the four-minute mile first and he got to the tape first in Vancouver. He deserved them both."

Awards and Accomplishments

1948	Wins Kinniard Cup
1951	Wins mile race in Penn Relays
1951, 1953-54	Wins British mile championships
1954	Wins Empire mile championship
1954	Wins European 1,500 meter championship
1954	Becomes first person to run a mile in less than 4 minutes, setting new world record of 3:59.4
1954	Wins Empire mile championships, setting new world record of 3:58.9
1954	*Sports Illustrated* Sportsman of the Year; Pears Trophy
1975	Knighted by Queen Elizabeth II

said of those last few seconds of the race, "I felt that the moment of a lifetime had come. There was no pain, only a great utility of movement and aim. The world seemed to stand still or did not exist, the only reality was the next two hundred yards of track under my feet." As he crossed over the finish line, he was so spent that he collapsed, almost passing out.

The crowd went wild, rushing onto the track and surrounding Bannister. A report in the London *Times* on the following day noted, "There was a scene of the wildest excitement—and what miserable spectators they would have been if they had not waved their programmes, shouted, even jumped in the air a little."

The Miracle Mile

At the end of that summer, Bannister was due to compete in the mile race on August 7 at the Empire Games in Vancouver, Canada. By then, Landy had already broken Bannister's mile record with a time of 3:58.0, and the contest between the two men to see who would be the world's fastest miler was billed as "The Miracle Mile." Thirty-five thousand spectators attended, and the race was broadcast live throughout North America—a highly unusual event, since the two lead runners were not Americans. It was the first international sporting event to be broadcast live to all of North America. The event was also the lead story in the first issue of *Sports Illustrated*.

At first Landy was boxed in by other runners, but he took the lead at the second bend. Bannister was fifth. At the first quarter mile, the time was 58.2. Landy remained in the lead for the second and third laps, but Bannister

worked his way up from the back. With one lap to go, he was just behind Landy. Landy, knowing that Bannister liked to save a burst of speed for the end of a race, ran has fast as he could. With 90 yards to go, Landy looked over his shoulder to see where Bannister was, and at that moment, Bannister passed him, running to victory with a Commonwealth record time of 3:58.8. Landy's final time was 3:59.6. It was the first time two runners had broken the four-minute barrier in the same race. According to a reporter in the Melbourne, Australia *Sunday Herald Sun*, Bannister felt pushed and inspired by Landy's ability, and the competition between the two men fueled Bannister's desire to win. Bannister said, "John Landy had shown me what a race could really be at its greatest."

The people of Vancouver were so excited by the race that they commissioned a statue of the two men, depicting the moment when Landy looked over his shoulder and Bannister passed him, and erected it outside Empire Stadium, where the Commonwealth Games were held. In honor of his achievements, Bannister was named the 1954 *Sports Illustrated* Sportsman of the Year. He also received the Silver Pears trophy, awarded for outstanding British achievement in any field.

After the Commonwealth Games race, Bannister retired from competition. He graduated from St. Mary's College in Oxford and devoted himself to his medical training, although he did take the time to write a book, *The Four Minute Mile,* which described his training and the record-breaking race.

Bannister the Neurologist

Bannister earned his medical degree from Oxford in 1963, and became a neurologist. When asked why he did not become a neurosurgeon, he said, according to Deford, "The interesting thing for me was deciding where the tumor was—rather than taking it out." Beginning in 1969, he served as the editor of a textbook, *Brain's Clinical Neurology*. In 1990 it was retitled *Brain and Bannister's Clinical Neurology.*

In 1975, Bannister was involved in a head-on automobile crash that almost killed him. Although he recovered from his severe injuries, he has been unable to run

Roger Bannister, crossing finish line

since then, although he still bicycles. After his crash, he spent his enforced period of rest thinking about his work and what he wanted to do, and became involved in medical research; he set up a laboratory to study the part of the brain that controls blood pressure.

Also in 1975, Bannister was knighted by Queen Elizabeth, receiving the title "Sir Roger Bannister." The honor was not in recognition of his running, but of his life's work as a runner and a physician. Bannister has written hundreds of scholarly papers, and has edited medical textbooks. During the 1970s he was chair of the British Sports Council, and he helped design urine tests that would detect athletes who used performance-enhancing drugs.

In 1996, speaking at the Cincinnati Heart Mini-Marathon Clinic, Bannister said that he believed the next time barrier for the mile is 3:30, according to Bob Queenan in the *Cincinnati Post*. He noted that Algerian athlete Noureddine Morceli had run 3:44.29 on July 3, 1995.

In 2001, Bannister's breaking of the four-minute barrier was chosen as the Greatest British Sports Performance of the Century, according to Alison Kervin in the London *Times*. Bannister told Kervin that he was "very flattered indeed," especially since his performance was placed above that of five-time Olympic gold-medal winner, **Steve Redgrave**, an athlete whom Bannister had long admired.

SELECTED WRITINGS BY BANNISTER:

The Four-Minute Mile, Lyons and Burford, 1955.

FURTHER INFORMATION

Books

"Roger Bannister," *Encyclopedia of World Biography Supplement, Vol. 21,* Gale Group, 2001.

Nelson, Cordner, and Roberto Quercetani, *The Milers,* Tafnews Press, 1985.

Periodicals

"Bannister Breaks Magical Barrier: Times Past" (reprint of May 7, 1954 article), *Times* (London, England), (September 28, 2001): 8.

"Bannister's Tactics Best by a Mile," *Sunday Herald Tribune* (Melbourne, Australia), (April 28, 2002): 63.

Berry, Kevin, "Race Turned Two Athletes into Legends," *Sunday Mail* (Adelaide, Australia), (April 28, 2002): 48.

Deford, Frank, "Pioneer Miler Roger Bannister and Everest Conqueror Edmund Hillary Became, at Mid-century, the Last Great Heroes in An Era of Sea Change in Sport," *Sports Illustrated,* (December 27, 1999): 102.

Jackson, Tony, "A Four-Midable Feat: Britain's Bannister Took 3 Minutes, 59.4 Seconds to Shock Athletic World," *Rocky Mountain News* (Denver, CO), (August 29, 1999): 32C.

Kervin, Alison, "Winner by a Mile: Bannister's Historic Run the Best of British Athletics," *Times* (London, England), (September 28, 2001): 1.

Philip, Robert, "Landy Second to None Among Nice Guys of Sport," *Daily Telegraph* (London, England), (July 29, 2002): NA.

Queenan, Bob, "Bannister Sees 3 1/2-Minute Mile as Next Great Barrier to Break," *Cincinnati Post,* (March 23, 1996): 7B.

Other

"A Brief Chat with Roger Bannister," Runner's World Daily. http://www.runnersworld.com/ (January 14, 2003).

"John (Michael) Landy," *Contemporary Authors Online,* http://www.galenet.com/servlet/BioRC (January 17, 2003).

Sketch by Kelly Winters

Charles Barkley
1963-

American basketball player

During a sixteen-year career in the National Basketball Association (NBA), forward Charles Barkley proved himself to be one of best basketball players of all

Charles Barkley

time, as well as one of the more controversial. An excellent rebounder despite his generous girth and unexceptional height, he was dubbed "The Round Mound of Rebound" while a player at Auburn University. As a pro, he became "Sir Charles" and was named league MVP for the 1992-1993 season, became a perennial member of the All-Star Team, and was rated as one of the top fifty players of all time by the NBA. None of these rewards, however, lessened his desire to play for a championship team, a goal that sent him from the Philadelphia 76ers to the Phoenix Suns to the Houston Rockets. Off the court, Barkley often made news with his verbal and physical sparring. After retiring in 2000, he became an analyst for TNT's *Inside the NBA,* where his wit and willingness to criticize make for lively viewing.

Growing Up

Born February 20, 1963 in Leeds, Alabama, Barkley weighed just six pounds at birth and suffered from anemia to the degree that he required a complete blood transfusion at six weeks. His parents Frank and Charcey Glenn Barkley divorced when he was still a baby. He was raised by his mother and grandmother. By the tenth grade, when he was a chubby five feet-ten inches and not yet a varsity player, Barkley had decided he was going to play in the NBA and make a great deal of money. His prospects improved when a growth spurt pushed him to six feet-four inches prior to his senior year. Subsequently, he starred on the Leeds High varsity team, averaging 19.1 points and 17.9 rebounds per game. When an Auburn University assistant coach saw Barkley score twenty-six points in the state semifinals, he recommended him to head coach Sonny Smith as fat but decidedly fast and talented.

At Auburn, Barkley broke the university record for blocked shots with 145. During his junior year he was named the Southeastern Conference Player of the Year. Barkley also came close to joining the U.S. Olympic team in 1984, being one of the last four players eliminated. Coach **Bobby Knight** of Indiana University was not a fan of Barkley's showy style of play, which included 360-degree spinning dunks. Shortly thereafter, the young player left Auburn a year early to join the NBA. He was the fifth player selected in the 1984 draft, behind **Hakeem Olajuwon** and **Michael Jordan**, and signed with the Philadelphia 76ers.

Dominant Rebounder

In Philadelphia, Barkley joined established stars **Julius Erving** and **Moses Malone**. He did well in his first season, averaging fourteen points and 8.6 rebounds per game. During the next two seasons, he evolved into a starter for Philadelphia and became the shortest player to lead the NBA in rebounding. In 1987 Barkley was named to the All Star team for the first time. Some analysts have connected Barkley's playing success with his unusual physique, saying that he was able block with his wide body and outrun bigger opponents. Barkley, however, credits his success to his greater competitiveness and emotion on the court.

Emotion, however, would sometimes get Barkley in trouble. He began to complain about his teammates, whom he lumped together as "a bad team that has to play perfect to win." The comment resulted in a $3,000 fine. During the 1991-1992 season, Barkley tried to spit on a heckler who sat court-side, but missed and hit a little girl. He apologized to the girl and gifted her family with season tickets, and was fined again. That same year, he was arrested for punching a man in Milwaukee, but was acquitted when a jury decided that the other

man had started the fight. Amidst media coverage of such events, Barkley was chastised for not serving as a better role model for children. He responded that playing basketball well does not automatically make someone a hero. Felons and drug addicts can dunk, he pointed out. His own heroes were his mother and grandmother, whom he credited with showing him how to work hard.

Barkley continued to improve his game, but the Philadelphia team often struggled. In 1989 former Detroit Piston "Bad Boy" Rick Mahorn joined the 76ers and became part of a "Bump and Thump" partnership with Barkley. They helped the 76ers win the Atlantic division title, but the team lost to the Chicago Bulls and Michael Jordan in the second round of the finals. When Barkley missed fifteen games in 1990-1991 season, the team fizzled and missed the playoffs.

In 1992 Barkley was named to the "Dream Team" representing the United States in the Olympics, when the rules were changed to allow professional players. At the competition in Barcelona, Spain, he led the U.S. team in scoring but was also a source of embarrassment when he elbowed a thin player from Angola and then threatened to boycott the awards ceremony. Along with Michael Jordan, he objected to wearing uniforms made by Reebok when he was a paid spokesman for Nike.

Heads to Phoenix

After campaigning to be traded, Barkley became a member of the Phoenix Suns beginning with the 1992-1993 season. That year, the Suns had the best record in the NBA and Barkley won the MVP award. The team met the Chicago Bulls in the NBA finals, where they lost the series in Game six. The next year, Barkley considered retiring when he hurt his back in training camp. But the idea of trying again for the NBA title lured him back. However, the Suns would lose to Houston in the Western Conference semi-finals. During the 1995-96 season, Barkley experienced regular knee pain, but still managed to average 23.2 points and 11.6 rebounds per game. When the Suns lost in the first round of the playoffs, Barkley was outspoken about his desire to play for a better team.

Career Statistics

Yr	Team	GP	PTS	FG%	3P%	FT%	RPG	APG	SPG
1984-85	PHI	82	1148	.545	.167	.733	8.60	1.9	1.16
1985-86	PHI	80	1603	.572	.227	.685	12.80	3.9	2.16
1986-87	PHI	68	1564	.594	.202	.761	14.60	4.9	1.75
1987-88	PHI	80	2264	.587	.280	.751	11.90	3.2	1.25
1988-89	PHI	79	2037	.579	.216	.753	12.50	4.1	1.59
1989-90	PHI	79	1989	.600	.217	.749	11.50	3.9	1.87
1990-91	PHI	67	1849	.570	.284	.722	10.10	4.2	1.64
1991-92	PHI	75	1730	.552	.234	.695	11.10	4.1	1.81
1992-93	PHO	76	1944	.520	.305	.765	12.20	5.1	1.57
1993-94	PHO	65	1402	.495	.270	.704	11.20	4.6	1.55
1994-95	PHO	68	1561	.486	.338	.748	11.10	4.1	1.62
1995-96	PHO	71	1649	.500	.280	.777	11.60	3.7	1.61
1996-97	HOU	53	1016	.484	.283	.694	13.50	4.7	1.30
1997-98	HOU	68	1036	.485	.214	.746	11.70	3.2	1.04
1998-99	HOU	42	676	.478	.160	.719	12.30	4.6	1.02
1999-00	HOU	20	289	.477	.231	.645	10.50	3.2	.70
TOTAL		1073	23757	.541	.266	.735	11.7	3.9	1.54

HOU: Houston Rockets; PHI: Philadelphia 76ers; PHO: Phoenix Suns.

Reluctantly Retires

The last three years of Barkley's career were spent with the Houston Rockets. He was happy with the change, but would spend less time playing because of injuries. During the 1996-1997 season he was named one of the NBA's top fifty players of all time. Not only was he near the top of the NBA's all-time scoring list, he was one of only four players in league history to accumulate at least 20,000 points, 10,000 rebounds, and 3,500 assists. A torn quadriceps tendon reinforced Barkley's decision to retire in 2000. It was a difficult parting for the player, who would later be tempted to follow the example of Michael Jordan coming out of retirement.

In 2000, Barkley found an arena where his strong opinions and often humorous style of expressing himself were quite welcome. He became a commentator for TNT's *Inside the NBA,* working with co-analyst Kenny Smith and host Ernie Johnson. In his opinion, the job required little more than being himself. "Prepare for my work? ... Hell, I played sixteen years. I can tell you who can play and who can't," he remarked in *Time.* His contributions helped make the program one of the most highly regarded studio sport shows and earned him a contract extension in 2002 that was reported to be worth 1.5 million per year.

Barkley for Governor

Barkley's new contract also gives him a spot on CNN's *Talkback Live,* where he comments on current news issues during the NBA season. The assignment reflects Barkley's strong interest in social and political issues. He said in the *Milwaukee Journal Sentinel* that he would not represent a Republican or Democratic viewpoint, but rather would express his own opinions. However, for several years he has talked about running for governor of Alabama as a Republican. Barkley has al-ways been outspoken on the subjects of race and class. He hates the commonly held idea that sports are the only route to success for young blacks. In *Sports Illustrated* he summarized his political motivation by saying, "I want to be able to tell people that there's no difference between white folks and black folks." Barkley has criticized other black athletes, including his friends Michael Jordan and **Tiger Woods**, for not speaking out. He says he is different because he is willing to be ridiculed.

Barkley manages to be entertaining, maddening, and thought-provoking all at once. His super-sized persona matches both his figure and his phenomenal career in professional basketball. Standing half-a-foot shorter than many of his adversaries on the court, he became a leading rebounder. While struggling to keep his weight under 300 pounds, he nevertheless outpaced them as well. A tiny handful of players have better records in rebounding, scoring, and assists. The NBA star has explained that his accomplishments come from being willing to work hard and truly wanting to succeed. Barkley joked at his retirement from basketball, "Just what the country needs: another unemployed black man." But with his growing presence on television and political aspirations, it should be fascinating to see what Charles Barkley does next.

CONTACT INFORMATION

Address: Turner Broadcasting System Inc., 1 CNN Ctr., Atlanta, GA, 30348. Phone: (404) 827-1700.

SELECTED WRITINGS BY BARKLEY:

(With Roy S. Johnson) *Outrageous!: The Fine Life and Flagrant Good Times of Basketball's Irresistible Force,* Simon & Schuster, 1992.

(With Rick Reilly) *Sir Charles: The Wit and Wisdom of Charles Barkley,* Warner Books, 1994.

(Michael Wilson, editor) *I May Be Wrong, But I Doubt It: Some Things I've Learned So Far,* Random, 2002.

FURTHER INFORMATION

Books

Sports Stars, series 1-4. U•X•L, 1994-98.

Periodicals

McCallum, Jack. "Citizen Barkley." *Sports Illustrated* (March 11, 2002): 32.

Tyrangiel, Josh. "It's Charles in Charge." *Time* (November 26, 2001): 94.

Wolfley, Bob. "CNN Offers Sir Charles and the World." *Milwaukee Journal Sentinel.* (July 26, 2002): 02C.

Other

Platt, Larry. "Charles Barkley." Salon.com. http://dir.salon.com (May 30, 2000).

Sketch by Paula Pyzik Scott

Rick Barry
1944-

American basketball player

Rick Barry, at six-foot-seven-inches, was one of the most entertaining and talented forwards to play in the National Basketball Association (NBA) during the 1970s. Averaging 24.8 points per game over the course of his fourteen seasons of play, Barry was famous for his deadly accurate underhanded free throws (.900). He was

Rick Barry

equally famous among other players for his difficult personality and harsh demeanor.

Super Scorer

Rick Barry was born on March 28, 1944 in Elizabeth, New Jersey. He enrolled at the University of Miami in 1961, but did not play basketball for the Hurricanes during his freshman year. Averaging an impressive 19.0 points per game during his sophomore year, Barry exploded during his junior season, averaging 32.2 points per game, and went on to earn the National Collegiate Athletic Association (NCAA) scoring title in 1965, scoring an average of 37.4 points per game. Barry's superstar performance at the University of Miami earned him a top spot in the 1965 National Basketball Association (NBA) draft, and he was selected in the first round by the San Francisco Warriors. Barry married Pam Hale, the daughter of the University of Miami coach, in 1965.

During his rookie season, Barry took the NBA by storm, averaging 25.7 points and 10.6 rebounds per game and becoming only the fourth player in NBA history to score more than 2,000 points in his first year of league. Barry, who also became famous for his accurate, underhanded free throws, shot better than 86 percent from the foul line. Barry played in the NBA All-Star game and was named the game's most valuable player. He was also selected as the NBA Rookie of the Year.

If his rookie season was spectacular, his sophomore season was sensational. During the 1966-67 season Barry led the league in scoring, averaging 35.6 points per game. He also averaged 9.2 rebounds and 3.6 assists per game. With no other superstars on the Warriors' team, Barry was still able to carry his team into the NBA championship series in 1966, but the Warriors lost to the Philadelphia 76ers, led by center **Wilt Chamberlain**.

Joins American Basketball Association (ABA)

Following his sophomore season in the NBA, Barry became the first superstar to abandon the NBA and join the fledgling ABA, a smaller league that was struggling to attract larger audiences. Barry's decision to make the jump was based on several key factors. First, his father-in-law, Bruce Hale, was the one offering Barry a spot on his ABA team, the Oakland Oaks. Second, and perhaps more important, the Oaks were offering him a contract that, at the time, was unheard of. On June 20, 1967, Barry signed a three-year contract worth $500,000. Plus, Barry was awarded fifteen percent stock in ownership of the team and promised five percent of ticket sales that exceeded $600,000. The deal made Barry, who had been making $30,000 a year as a Warrior, one of the highest paid players in the game.

There was only one flaw Barry's plan: he was bound to the Warriors for one more year under the option clause of his contract. According to the agreement, common to the times, although Barry's two-year contract with San Francisco had expired, Warriors' management reserved a one-year option that obligated Barry to remain with the team even though a new contract had not been formulated. As a result, when Barry announced his departure from San Francisco, Warriors owner Franklin Mieuli, filed a $4.5-million lawsuit against Oakland Oaks owner, singer Pat Boone. When a federal judge ruled that the option clause was valid, Barry decided to sit down for the 1968-69 season rather than return to the Warriors.

Following his one-year, self-imposed exile from the game, Barry finally joined the Oakland Oaks. During the 1968-69 season, Barry, as expected, immediately became the ABA's hottest drawing card. He averaged 34.0 points, 9.4 rebounds, and 3.9 assists per game. He became the only player in history to win scoring titles in the NCAA, NBA, and ABA. After the season's end the Warriors filed suit to force Barry to return to the team, but failed to convince a lower court or the California State Court of Appeals that their claim to Barry was valid. The Warriors also lost their bid to collect $350,000 in damages from the Oaks.

With one legal battle over, it wasn't long before Barry found himself embroiled in another. Just days after the final judgment in the previous lawsuit, Boone sold the Oaks to Earl Foreman, who immediately announced that the team would be moved to Washington, D.C. and become the Washington Capitals. Barry, who insisted that he had an oral agreement with the Oaks that he would not have to leave the area, believed that such a move voided his contract. Wanting to stay in the San Francisco Bay Area, where he was settled with his wife and sons, on August 28, 1969, Barry negotiated with his old team, the Warriors, for a five-year contract.

Barry was thrown back into the courts when the now-Washington Capitals sued the Warriors for $10 million and the Warriors, in turn, counter sued the Capitals for $8 million. Ultimately the judge in the case ruled that Barry was still committed to the Capitals. Barry was required to join the team in Washington, and the Warriors revised the pending contract so that Barry would rejoin the Warriors after he had fulfilled his obligation to the ABA. Despite being required to move with his team, Barry managed to continue his performance on the floor, averaging 27.7 points per game during the 1970-71 season with the Capitals.

When the Capitals became the Virginia Squires following the 1969-70 season, Barry grew more unhappy and more vocal about his dissatisfaction with playing in Virginia. Finally the Squires sold the remainder of Barry's contract to the New York Nets. Barry played for the Nets for two seasons. During the 1970-71 season he averaged 29.4 points, 6.8 rebounds, and 5.0 assists per game. The following year he averaged 31.5 points, 7.5 rebounds, and 4.1 assists per game.

Returns to the Warriors

Finding the New York area and the Nets organization to his liking, Barry re-signed with the Nets following the 1971-72 season, but this move prompted yet another series of lawsuits. The Warriors sued for Barry based on the contract he had signed in 1969, which stipulated Barry's return to the Warriors after he had fulfilled his commitment with his present ABA team. Barry claimed that the contract should be void because the NBA had broken antitrust laws by pooling money among teams to pay his contract.

Career Statistics

Yr	Team	GP	PTS	P/G	FG%	3P%	FT%	RPG	APG	SPG
1966	SF	80	2059	25.7	.439	—	.862	10.6	2.2	—
1967	SF	78	2775	35.6	.451	—	.884	9.2	3.6	—
1969	OAK	35	1190	34.0	.514	.300	.888	9.4	3.9	—
1970	WASH	52	1442	27.7	.561	.205	.864	7.0	3.4	—
1971	NY	59	1734	29.4	.486	.221	.890	6.8	5.0	—
1972	NY	80	2518	31.5	.479	.308	.878	7.5	4.1	—
1973	GS	82	1832	22.3	.452	—	.902	8.9	4.9	—
1974	GS	80	2009	25.1	.456	—	.899	6.8	6.1	2.1
1975	GS	80	2450	30.6	.464	—	.904	5.7	6.2	2.9
1976	GS	81	1701	21.0	.435	—	.923	6.1	6.1	2.5
1977	GS	79	1723	21.8	.440	—	.916	5.3	6.0	2.2
1978	GS	82	1898	23.1	.451	—	.924	5.5	5.4	1.9
1979	HOU	80	1082	13.5	.461	—	.947	3.5	6.3	1.2
1980	HOU	72	866	12.0	.422	.330	.935	3.3	3.7	1.1
TOTAL		1020	25279	24.8	.461	.273	.893	6.7	4.9	2.0

GS: Golden State Warriors; HOU: Houston Rockets; NY: New York Nets; OAK: Oakland Oaks; SF: San Francisco Warriors; WASH: Washington Capitals.

Although several years later he was proven right regarding the league's misuse of pooled money, in 1972 a federal judge ruled that Barry owed the Warriors three years.

Faced with sitting out for three years or joining his old team, now renamed the Golden State Warriors, Barry decided to return to the Bay Area. During his first two years back with the Warriors, Barry averaged 22.3 and 25.1 points per game, respectively. In 1974-75 he carried the team to the NBA championship, averaging 30.6 points per game on the season. With a NBA title in hand, Barry re-signed with the Warriors for another three years in 1975. Then in 1979 he exercised his rights as a free agent and accepted a bid from the Houston Rockets. After playing two years off the bench, Barry, one of the games most prolific scorers, retired.

In 1979 Barry walked out on his wife and five children. He remarried but then divorced, and later married Lynn Norenberg. After retiring in 1980, Barry moved about the country, hoping to eventually land a coaching job in the NBA. Barry became the coach of the United States Basketball League's team in Cedar Rapids, Iowa. Other coaching stops included teams in Fort Wayne, Indiana, Asbury Park, New Jersey, and Fort Myers, Florida. His reputation as an intolerant arrogant bully on the court continues to shadow his life two decades later. A very public plea to fill the coaching vacancy at Golden State in 1997 ended without even an interview. In 2001 KNBR, a local radio station in San Francisco, hired Barry as a sports talk show host. Barry, who fills the noon-to-three slot, does interviews and sports analysis.

Much has been made of Barry's four sons, Scooter, Jon, Brent, and Drew (he and his first wife also have an adopted daughter). All four have had different levels of success as college and professional basketball players. It is the father, though, that has his name written in the history books as one of the most spectacular players of his day.

CONTACT INFORMATION

Address: KNBR, 55 Hawthorne Street, San Francisco, California 94105. Fax: (415)995-6867. Phone: (415) 808-KNBR. Email: rbarry@susqsf.com.

SELECTED WRITINGS BY BARRY:

(With Jordan Cohn) *Rick Barry's Pro Basketball Scouting Report,* Bonus Books, 1989.

(With Jordan Cohn) *Rick Barry's Pro Basketball Bible, 1996-1997.* 8th ed., Basketball Books Ltd., 1996.

FURTHER INFORMATION

Periodicals

"Captain Barry." *Newsweek* (January 6, 1975): 34.

Cote, Greg. "Barry, Whose Goal is to Coach in the NBA, May Wait in Vain." Knight Ridder/Tribune News Service (May 25, 2000).

Lawrence, Mitch. "Waiting for His Chance: Rick Barry Paying His Dues in Fort Wayne, Hoping for Opportunity to Coach in NBA." Knight Ridder/Tribune News Service (January 20, 1994).

"One-man Bandwagon." *Sports Illustrated* (May 12, 1997): 18.

Newman, Bruce. "Daddy Dearest." *Sports Illustrated* (December 2, 1991): 74-77.

Roessing, Walter. "The Barry Bunch." *Boys' Life* (March 1997): 14-16.

Other

"NBA Legends: Rick Barry." National Basketball Association. http://www.nba.com/history/barry_bio.html (December 11, 2002)

Awards and Accomplishments

1965	First Team All American; led the nation in scoring with 37.4 points per game; selected in the first round of the National Basketball Association (NBA) draft by the San Francisco Warriors
1966	Selected Rookie of the Year and All Rookie Team; named Most Valuable Player of the NBA All Star Game
1966-67	Named First Team All NBA and NBA All Star
1967	Led league in scoring with 35.6 points per game
1969-72	Named First Team All American Basketball Association (ABA) and ABA All Star
1973-78	Named NBA All Star
1974-76	Named First Team All NBA
1975	Selected as Most Valuable Player of the NBA Championship Series
1986	Inducted into the Basketball Hall of Fame
1996	Named one of the 50 Greatest Players in NBA History

"Richard Francis Barry, III." *Biography Resource Center Online.* Gale Group, 1999. http://www.galenet.com/servlet/BioRC/ (December 11, 2002).

"Rick Barry." Sports Stats.com. http://www.sportsstats.com (December 7, 2002).

Sketch by Kari Bethel

Donna Barton

Donna Barton
1966-

American jockey

American Donna Barton, considered among the most successful female jockeys of all time, is one of only a handful of female jockeys to ride in a Breeders' Cup event. Barton took on her first job as a jockey as a way to earn enough money to attend college. Second only to top-ranked Judy Krone in wins among female jockeys, she had won $4.6 million in purse earnings by 1998.

Born to Ride

Born in New Mexico in 1966, Barton had riding in her blood. Her mother, Patti Barton Browne, raced over 1,200 thoroughbred winners during her pioneering 15-year career as a woman jockey that began in 1969 after the job of jockey was made open to female equestrians. Barton's younger brother Jerry and older sister Leah also worked as jockeys. While growing up, Barton and her family were often on the road because her mother worked as a truck driver and trick rider and her father, Charlie Barton, rode the rodeo circuit. She attended seven schools, then completed high school in three years by taking correspondence courses.

Continuing her education by attending college was a bigger goal for Barton than following the family tradition, and at age 18 she left home and moved to Louisville to see what she could make of her life. As a teen she had worked as a groom at local stables, and realized that she would never be able to earn the money for college tuition unless she could find a job that would pay well. Barton thought she had found that job exercising horses for Kentucky trainer Jack van Berg, but found that even on a trainer's salary she would never be able to afford school.

Barton almost considered working as a trainer, but decided that work as a jockey would provide the opportunity to make big money—jockeys are paid ten percent of the purse winnings. With her experience and diminutive stature, the five-foot-three-inch, 102-pound Barton knew she had what it would take. She decided to take on a few races, figuring she'd make some quick money and then quit.

Barton began her career on May 30, 1987, when she steered Bold Splinter to fifth place in a race in Birmingham, Alabama. She rode Discover Acro to her first win weeks later, July 9, 1987 at the Birmingham Race Course. Still, times were lean, as the competition among jockeys for jobs from trainers pitted Barton against experienced, proven jockeys of both sexes. In 1993 she rode her first major race, and finally drew the attention of respected horse trainer D. Wayne Lukas. Lukas took the young jockey under his wing, coaching her and providing her with the horsepower that enabled her to build a strong record of wins.

Chronology

1987	Begins working as jockey
1988	Achieves first win in Birmingham, Alabama race
1993	Begins riding professionally
1995	Finishes second in her first Breeders' Cup race
1998	Announces retirement from racing
1998	Marries trainer Frank Brothers in November
1999	Enrolls as a freshman at University of Louisville

Awards and Accomplishments

1995	Finishes second on Hennessy in Breeders' Cup Juvenile.
1996	Sets three meet records for women jockeys at Churchill Downs.
1997	On February 1 wins the 1,000th race of her career.
1997	Honored by Louisville Thoroughbred Club with Courage, Spirit & Triumph Award.

Barton's success as a jockey propelled her into a career that swept her into the world of competitive horse racing, the only major professional sport in the United States in which women and men compete on equal terms. Still, she encountered sexism, one instance being at the 1996 Kentucky Derby when she was refused the opportunity to race the horse Honor and Glory by owner Michael Tabor. *Cincinnati Enquirer* contributor Neil Schmidt quoted Lukas's take on the situation: "Donna was the perfect fit for this horse in a lot of ways . . . (but) was eliminated on the basis of her gender."

For over a decade Barton's dreams of attending college were overshadowed by the excitement of life at the track, the constant upheaval of living out of a suitcase while working seven meets each year, and her ambition of riding in the Kentucky Derby. Frustrating this goal was the fear among owners of sending a horse out with a female rider. In several cases Barton was pulled off of horses at the last minute due to owner fears, and watched as those mounts went on to win, their male jockeys collecting both their share of the purse and the congratulations. As Lukas wryly observed, Barton is "very personable and charismatic—but that will only take you so far."

One of the first big races of Barton's career was in 1995, her first Breeders' Cup, in which she rode Hennessy in the Juvenile division and finished a close second. Pairing with the colt Boston Harbor earned Barton three more wins in 1996. Still, she was pulled from the saddle later in the season and replaced by winning jockey Jerry Bailey. Ironically for Barton, Boston Harbor would end the season as the Two-Year-Old Champion Colt.

Despite being denied a shot at the major races, by the mid-1990s Barton had no problem finding steady work, adding trainer Ken McPeek and others to her stable of employers. Her 1,000th win—considered a milestone in the racing world—came in early February of 1997, when Barton rode Primistal to victory in the sixth race at Kentucky's Turfway Park. In 1997 alone she won 136 races for $4.5 million in prize money.

On Sunday, September 27, 1998, just prior to riding Hidden Pleasure in the eighth race at Turfway Park in Henderson, Kentucky, Barton announced to the media that this race would be her last. Finishing her last race in eighth place, she retired with 1,131 wins from 9,234 starts and earnings of $18,661,388. Her final words to the media:

"This is one of the happiest and saddest days of my life." Barton retired as the second winningest female jockey of all time. She also retired having amassed a riding-related injury list that included several broken ribs, cracked neck vertebrae, a broken collarbone, four broken noses, and six concussions. Asked two years into retirement whether she missed racing, Barton told Neil Schmidt of the *Cincinnati Enquirer:* "No I don't. . . . As far as having to sell myself and prove myself every single day [as a jockey], that's a lot of pressure on any person. Twelve years was enough."

After retiring in the fall of 1998 at age 32, Barton enrolled at the University of Louisville to begin work on her college degree. Accepting an offer to provide television network horseracing coverage, she has since served as co-host of the *Paddock Preview Show* at Churchill Downs and covered several major race telecasts as a reporter for NBC. Married two months after retirement to 52-year-old noted horse trainer Frank Brothers, she moved to her husband's farm, where she helps exercise and train the stable's young thoroughbreds every morning. "She's a luxury to have at the barn," Brothers was quoted as saying on the Kneeland Race Track Web site. "That's when she isn't working for NBC or Churchill Downs or TVG, though."

CONTACT INFORMATION

Address: c/o Churchill Downs, 700 Central Ave., Louisville, KY 40208.

FURTHER INFORMATION

Books

Davidson, Scooter Toby, editor. *Great Women in the Sport of Kings*. Dimensions Press, 1999.

McEvoy, John, and Julie McEvoy. *Women in Racing: In Their Own Words*. Eclipse Press, 2001.

Sammy Baugh
1914-

American football player

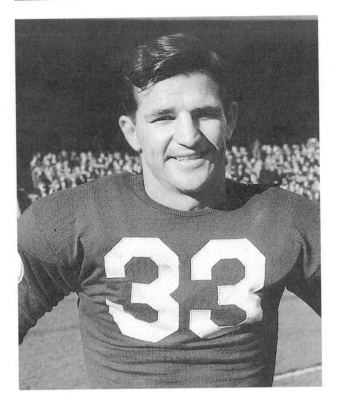

Sammy Baugh

ple was Ki Aldrich, who later became Baugh's college and professional football teammate.

Moves to Sweetwater, Texas

Baugh played one year of high school football in Temple before his family moved to Sweetwater, Texas, where Baugh joined the football team. Aiming for the opening in a used automobile tire swinging from a tree limb, he practiced pinpoint accurate passing as he moved around his backyard.

A letterman in three sports, baseball was Baugh's long suit. Because Sweetwater High School did not field a baseball team, Baugh played semi-pro ball for the Abilene Oilers. When the Oilers played a game against Texas Christian University (TCU) in Fort Worth, Baugh's talent caught the eye of TCU athletic director Leo "Dutch" Meyer.

Recruited for College Career at TCU

In 1933, Meyer recruited Baugh to TCU to play baseball. When Meyer became the TCU football coach in 1934, he recruited Baugh to play as a single-wing tailback. By the end of the season, which TCU finished 8-4, Meyer saw Baugh's leadership with the team and moved him to a T-formation quarterback. College quarterbacks handed the ball to running backs who advanced the ball. In 1935, TCU went 12-1 and captured the national championship.

According to folk lore, sports writer Pop Boone of the *Fort Worth Press* named him "Slingin" Sammy. Baugh became the first great passer in college history. In his three seasons at TCU (1934-1936) he completed 285 passes (out of 597) for 3,471 yards. He scored thirty-nine career Horn Frog touchdowns.

Sports Illustrated writer and novelist, Dan Jenkins, recalled Baugh's powerful arm and intensity of play. "In Sam's three seasons at TCU, he beat at least seven teams that were ranked in the nation's top 10 at the time—Rice in 1934; Baylor, Rice and LSU (in the Sugar Bowl) in 1935; Arkansas, Santa Clara and Marquette (in the Cot-

The first superstar passer in college football, Sammy Baugh held every National Football League (NFL) passing record and was chosen for the charter classes of both the college (1951) and professional (1963) football halls of fame. Many of his records stood for fifty years and others will never be broken. The college All-American became a six-time NFL All-Pro. He coached college football and was the first head coach of the American Football League's (AFL) New York Titans (now the New York Jets).

Samuel Adrian Baugh was born March 17, 1914 on a farm outside Temple, Texas, a town of 10,000 people halfway between Austin and Waco. Recruited to play baseball at Texas Christian University (TCU), his coaches saw raw athletic talent when he tried out for football in the off-season. Nicknamed "Slinging Sammy" because of his rifle accuracy passing skills, he went on to break every record in Southwest Conference football (1934-1936) and play professional football for the Washington Redskins (1937-1952).

Discovers Sports in Temple, Texas

Football in Texas is a big-time sport, even for youngsters. Baugh started playing when he was eight years old. Beyond the Temple bantam leagues, junior high kids competed with youngsters from other towns. Baugh remembers playing the Cisco Lobos for the Texas state junior high championship. Texas football is also a small and insular world. Watching from the sidelines in Tem-

Awards and Accomplishments

1935	Named to All-Southwest Conference Team
1936	Named to All-American Team; All–Southwest Conference Team
1937, 1940, 1943, 1945, 1947, 1949	Named NFL All-Pro
1943	Only NFL player ever to lead league in passing, punting and interceptions
1951	Inducted College Football Hall of Fame
1963	Inducted Pro Football Hall of Fame
1999	Inducted Cotton Bowl Hall of Fame

ton Bowl) in 1936." Jenkins was only seven years old when he first saw Baugh play in Fort Worth.

Baugh did more than just lead the team on offense. He was also an outstanding TCU defensive back and punter. Dutch Meyer called him "the greatest athlete I ever saw." As a punter, he averaged 40.9 yards for 198 tries. One punt went eighty-five yards.

Leads Frogs to Bowl Game Wins

In 1936, the Horn Frogs played LSU in the Sugar Bowl in New Orleans. In a cold New Years Day fog, TCU won the game 3-2. Even though he was unable to score an offensive touchdown, Baugh intercepted two LSU passes and made a spectacular forty-four yard run across the icy field to set up a field goal. He punted the ball fourteen times with a forty-eight yard average. He was named an All-Southwest Conference player in 1935 and 1936, and an All-American in 1936.

In the 1937 Cotton Bowl, the first one played in Dallas, Baugh led the Horn Frogs to a 16-6 victory over Marquette. In the fourth quarter of this battle between Baugh and Buzz Buivid, the two best passers in college football, "Slingin Sammy" stayed on the sidelines. Couch Meyer wanted his quarterback for the 1938 season, Davey O'Brien, to get some playing time. Because it was Baugh's final college football game, the crowd chanted his name until he returned for a few last plays of the game. The next year O'Brien won the Heisman Trophy.

Becomes Redskins First Round Draft Pick

Selected by the Washington Redskins in the first round of the 1937 college football draft, Baugh felt he would warm the bench. There were no passing quarterbacks in pro football and he doubted any team would take a chance with him. When baseball scout, **Rogers Hornsby**, came calling, Baugh signed on to play third base for the St. Louis Cardinals. The Cardinals changed

him to shortstop and sent him to their minor league franchise in Columbus, Ohio. Subsequently, the Cards sent Baugh to their Rochester, New York farm team where he played shortstop behind Marty Marion. Marion became a Cardinal regular while Baugh looked at changing sports.

Baugh called Redskins owner George Preston Marshall and told him he decided to try pro ball for one year. The Redskins had moved from Boston to Washington in 1937 and sought novel ways to recruit new fans. Marshall thought it was a great gimmick to bring a Texas cowboy quarterback to play in the nation's capital so he gave Baugh a shot. Those were the days of leather cap helmets that offered little protection. It was not until the John T. Riddell Company, researching using plastics for army helmets, developed a prototype for football players that evolved into standard headgear in the 1940s.

Marshall paid Baugh $8,000, but he got his money's worth. After practicing for only a week with the Redskins, he led the team to a 13-3 victory over the powerhouse New York Giants. In their inaugural season in Washington, Baugh led the Redskins to a National Football League (NFL) championship over the heavily favored Bears at Wrigley Field in Chicago. Each Bears player in the championship game received $122.78.

Baugh played a full sixty minutes of football, seeing action both as an offensive quarterback and defensive back. His professional football record for best career punting average (41.1 yards) and best single season punting average (51.4 yards in 1940) remain unbroken today. His pass completion average of 70.3% stood from 1945 until 1982. In 1943, he became the only NFL player to lead the league in passing, punting and interceptions.

The Washington Redskins was Baugh's only professional team. He played in the nation's capital from 1937 until 1952. Baugh was selected as an NFL All-Pro in his rookie year, 1937, and in five later years: 1940, 1943, 1945, 1947 and 1949.

Career Statistics

| | | Passing | | | | | | Punting | | | |
Yr	Team	ATT	COM	YDS	TD	INT	Punts	YDS	AVG	LNG
1937	WASH	171	81	1127	8	14	—	—	—	—
1938	WASH	128	63	853	5	11	—	—	—	—
1939	WASH	96	53	518	6	9	26	—	38.0	69
1940	WASH	177	111	1367	12	10	35	—	51.3	85
1941	WASH	193	106	1236	10	19	30	—	48.7	75
1942	WASH	225	132	1524	16	11	37	—	46.6	74
1943	WASH	239	133	1754	23	19	50	—	45.9	81
1944	WASH	146	82	849	4	8	44	—	40.6	76
1945	WASH	182	128	1669	11	4	33	—	43.3	57
1946	WASH	161	87	1163	8	17	33	—	45.1	60
1947	WASH	354	210	2938	25	15	35	—	43.7	67
1948	WASH	315	185	2599	18	14	0	0	0.0	0
1949	WASH	255	145	1903	18	14	1	53	53.0	53
1950	WASH	166	90	1130	10	11	9	—	39.1	58
1951	WASH	154	67	1104	7	17	4	—	55.3	58
1952	WASH	33	20	152	2	1	1	48	48.0	48
TOTAL		2995	1693	21886	187	203	338	101	45.1	85

WASH: Washington Redskins.

Turns to Coaching

After leaving the Redskins, Baugh coached college and professional football. He was elected to the College Football Fall of Fame in 1951. In 1952, he became an assistant coach at Hardin-Simmons University in Abilene (TX) to be near his beloved Double Mountain Ranch in Rotan, Texas, eighty miles away. He became the head coach in 1955. During his four year stint Hardin-Simmons claimed a 23-28 record. The Texas Sports Hall of Fame installed him as a member in 1954.

In December 1959, Baugh accepted a job in the newly organized American Football League as head coach of the New York Titans (now the Jets). He had a 14-14 record in his two-year tenure. He returned home to West Texas until he was lured out of retirement in 1963 by owner Bud Adams, to become head coach of the Houston Oilers. That same year Baugh was named to the Pro Football Hall of Fame. He lasted just one season as head coach but stayed on until 1966 to coach the backfield offense. He joined the coaching staff of the Detroit Lions in 1966 on a six-month contract so he could tend his 500 head of cattle in Texas during the rest of the year. He retired to his ranch permanently in 1968.

Receives Honors In Retirement

Baugh's college football feats had not been forgotten. In 1993 Texas Christian University retired his Number 45 jersey and in 1999 he was elected to the Cotton Bowl Hall of Fame in 1999.

The Touchdown Club of Columbus, Ohio annually honors the best passing quarterback in college football with the Sammy Baugh Trophy. During the last forty-two years, winners include Duante Culpepper (1998),

Steve Young (1983), John Elway (1982) and Bob Griese (1966).

College Hall of Fame sportswriter Grantland Rice was no slacker of hyperbole. During the Golden Age he immortalized Notre Dame's "Four Horsemen." The best team in college football today is awarded the Grantland Rice Trophy. He said of Sammy Baugh's passing, "He hurled the ball with as much speed as [professional baseball] player Dizzy Dean ever knew." That was an understatement.

Historians say that Sammy Baugh was the first great passer in the National Football League. He played as an offensive quarterback and punter. On defense, Baugh was a safety. In 2002, he still held records in five NFL categories and was tied for first in five more. Baugh's jersey number (#33) is the only one ever retired by the Washington Redskins.

FURTHER INFORMATION

Other

"100 Greatest Players of All-Time, #3 Sammy Baugh." http://www.collegefootballnews.com/Top_100_Players/Top_100_Players_3_Sammy_Baugh.htm (November 15, 2002).

"Hall of Famer Sammy Baugh Reflects 50 Years After Career Ends." http://ca.sports.yahoo.com/020816/6/odz.htm (November 15, 2002)

"Professional Football Hall of Fame." http://www.profootballhof.com/players/enshrinees/sbaugh.cfm (November 15, 2002)

Sketch by David Becker

Bruce Baumgartner
1960-

American wrestler

Bruce Baumgartner

Amateur freestyle wrestler Bruce Baumgartner won the U.S. national championship seventeen times in as many years. An eight-time Midlands Champion, he medalled at four Olympic Games, from 1984-96, earning gold medals in two. After winning the World Cup Championship in 1997 for the eighth time, he retired from competition. In 2002 Baumgartner was named to the National Wrestling Hall of Fame.

Bruce Robert Baumgartner was born on November 2, 1960, the second son of Robert Sr., a diesel mechanic, and Lois Baumgartner of Haledon, New Jersey. A late bloomer by some standards, Baumgartner was a humdrum athlete and an unimpressive student at Haledon's Manchester Regional High School. As a child he was not much interested in watching television and was too large to play peewee football. Disinterested in Little League, he finally turned to wrestling for lack of other options. At 190 pounds in the ninth grade, his exceptional size worked to his advantage on the mats, and by senior year he had progressed to third place in the statewide freestyle wrestling standings.

Collegiate Wrestler

Because wrestling is not a lucrative sport, Baumgartner had little trouble dodging college recruiters and their scholarship offers. Free to choose any college, he enrolled at Indiana State University (ISU) at Terre Haute in 1978, where he joined the wrestling team and competed for four years of college. By his senior year, he had suffered only twelve losses over four seasons, for a won-loss record of 134-12 matches. He earned his first of seventeen U.S. national freestyle titles in 1980.

In addition to winning his second national title in 1981, Baumgartner prevailed internationally at the World University Games in Bucharest, Romania. 1981 proved to be a landmark year for Baumgartner when he lost to Dan Cook, at the Amateur Athletic Union (AAU) national championship. The loss was significant because it would be the last time Baumgartner would realize defeat at the hands of an American for the duration of his seventeen-year wrestling career.

In 1982 as a senior in college, Baumgartner won the National College Athletic Association (NCAA) heavyweight wrestling championship after an undefeated season of 44-0. Furthermore, having won the Midland Tournament Championships in Chicago in 1980 and again in 1981, he went on to repeat that victory seven times over, winning consecutive Midland titles every year through 1987.

While proving himself as an outstanding athlete, Baumgartner sharpened his academic skills, earning a B.S. in 1982 with a 3.77 average. He won a spot on the World Team that year and moved from Indiana to Oklahoma where from 1982-84 he worked as a graduate assistant wrestling coach at Oklahoma State University.

After winning three silver medals a one bronze in international competition in 1983, Baumgartner sought the gold in 1984. He won the AAU nationals, the World Cup, and a gold medal at the Tiblisi Tournament in the former Soviet Union. He earned a spot on the U.S. Olympic team also that year, winning a gold medal at the games in Los Angeles. Baumgartner's Olympic gold medal was a national milestone at that time—a first-ever accomplishment for a U.S. wrestler.

Perennial Champion

Armed with a master's degree from Oklahoma State, in 1984 Baumgartner moved to Pennsylvania where he settled into a paid position as a wrestling coach at Edinboro University. With limited funding from USA Wrestling, the New York Athletic Club, and an athletic shoe manufacturer, he continued to train and compete. By the time the Olympics came around in Seoul, South Korea, in 1988, Baumgartner had prevailed in a second and third World Cup in 1985 and 1986 respectively. He took a bronze at the 1987 World Championship, and a silver at the World Cup in 1988. Also in 1987 he won an unprecedented eighth consecutive Midlands Championship.

Chronology	
1960	Born November 2 in Haledon, New Jersey
1978	Graduates from Manchester Regional High School
1978	Enrolls at ISU at Terre Haute
1980	Is named as an alternate to the Olympic team
1980-81	Achieves runner-up at NCAA Division I heavyweight finals
1982	Concludes collegiate career with a 134-12 record and 73 pins; is named to the World Team; earns a B.S. degree in industrial arts education; marries Linda Hochman on June 6.
1982-84	Attends Oklahoma State University as a graduate assistant wrestling coach
1984	Earns an M.S. degree in industrial arts education
1984-97	Serves as wrestling coach (later head wrestling coach) at Edinboro University
1996	Is named captain and flag bearer of U.S. Olympic team
1997	Retires from amateur competition
1998	Is named athletic director at Edinboro University

Awards and Accomplishments	
1980	Midlands Tournament Champion
1980-96	National Freestyle Champion
1981	World University Champion; Midlands Tournament Champion
1982	National College Athletic Association Division I champion, heavyweight; Midlands Tournament Champion
1983	Bronze medal at the World Championships; silver at the World Cup Championships; silver at Tiblisi Tournament; silver at Pan-American Games; Sports Festival Champion; Midlands Tournament Champion
1984	Gold medal at the Olympic games; gold medal at Tiblisi Tournament; won Amateur Athletic Union National Championship; Midlands Tournament Champion
1984-86, 1989-91, 1994, 1997	Won World Cup
1985	Gold medal at World Superchampionships; bronze at World Championships; silver at Tiblisi Tournament; Sports Festival Champion (Baton Rouge, Louisiana); Midlands Tournament Champion
1986	Won World Championship; gold medal at Goodwill Games; Sports Festival Champion (Chapel Hill, North Carolina); Midlands Tournament Champion
1987	Bronze medal at World Championships; gold at Pan-American Games; Midlands Tournament Champion
1988	Silver medal at the Olympic games; silver at World Cup Championships; Pan-American Champion
1989	Pan-American Champion; silver medal at World Championships; won World Wrestling Grand Championship
1990	Silver medal at Goodwill Games; silver at World Championship; Grand Masters Champion
1991	Gold medal at Pan-American Games
1992	Gold medal at the Olympic games; won U.S. Grand Prix Championship
1993	Won World Championship; won U.S. Grand Prix Championship; silver medal at World Cup
1994	Bronze medal at Goodwill Games; silver at World Championship
1995	Won World Championship; gold medal at Pan-American Games; won silver at World Cup; won James E. Sullivan Award
1996	Bronze medal at the Olympic games
2000	Named a Legend of the Century by the New York Athletic Club
2001	Inducted into the Sports Hall of Fame in New Jersey
2002	Inducted into the National Wrestling Hall of Fame and Museum

First United States wrestler to win three Olympic medals. One of only five U.S. athletes to win medals at four Olympic competitions.

Winning everything—and winning all the time—Baumgartner's unbroken string of victories at the national freestyle championship would endure from 1980-96. For good measure he won gold medals at the World Superchampionships in Tokyo in 1985, at the Goodwill Games in Moscow in 1986, and at the Pan American Games in 1987. Although he missed the gold at Seoul, he returned from his second Olympic competition with a very respectable silver medal.

Most significant in the mid 1980s was his gold medal win at the World Championships in Budapest. There, Baumgartner prevailed over the Russian David Gobedjichvili and became the first American to win a gold medal at the World Amateur Heavyweight competition. Although the tables turned at the Seoul Olympics when Baumgartner settled for silver while Gobedjichvili took the gold, Baumgartner's revenge would come at the 1992 Olympics in Barcelona, where he defeated Gobedjichvili for the gold. Baumgartner, in fact, at Barcelona became the first American wrestler to win medals in three Olympic competitions.

In 1993 Baumgartner entered his fourteenth year of competition since winning the national finals for the first time. That year he won a gold medal for the second time at the World Amateur Heavyweight competition. He won his fifteenth national title in 1994 and took a gold medal in the World Championships again in 1995. That year he slowed his pace to undergo surgery to his left shoulder to repair a torn rotator cuff.

Athletic Honors

Baumgartner, who was nominated for the AAU's James E. Sullivan Award in 1986, and from 1992-94, captured the elusive honor on a fifth nomination in 1995. He bested an impressive field of competition for the award that year, including golfer **Tiger Woods**. Baumgartner was only the second wrestler to receive the Sullivan since its inception in 1930.

At his fourth Olympic competition, in Atlanta in 1996, Baumgartner was named U.S. team captain and carried the national flag into the ceremonies. He returned from the games with a bronze medal that year, thus joining an elite field of only four other U.S. athletes who had won medals at four different Olympic competitions.

In 1997, after winning his eighth World Cup Championship, Baumgartner retired from competition. He was named to the Sports Hall of Fame in New Jersey in 2001 and was enshrined at the National Wrestling Hall of Fame in Stillwater, Oklahoma, as a member of the inaugural class of 2002. Since 1988 Baumgartner has served as athletic director at Edinboro University where his wife, the former Linda Hochman, is also on staff as a sports trainer. In 2000 Baumgartner was honored as a Legend of the Century by the New York Athletic Club.

At 6-feet-2-inches tall and 286 pounds Baumgartner's physical strength is anchored largely in his 18-inch biceps and 52-inch chest. Regardless, his training partners and opponents counter that mental fortitude, maturity, and introspection have played a significant role toward the longevity and magnitude of his amateur career.

CONTACT INFORMATION

Address: 12765 Forrest Drive, Edinboro, PA 16412. Fax: (814) 734-4475. Phone: (814) 732-2776. Email: bruce@brucebaumgartner.com. Online: www.bruce-baumgartner.com/.

FURTHER INFORMATION

Books

"Bruce Baumgartner." *Contemporary Newsmakers 1987,* Issue Cumulation. Detroit: Gale Group, 1988.

Periodicals

Christian Science Monitor (March 8, 1996): 13.
Christian Science Monitor (July 23, 1996): 12.
Sports Illustrated (October 20, 1986): 78.
Sports Illustrated (July 22, 1997): 118.
Time (Summer 96 Special Issue): 80.

Sketch by G. Cooksey

Elgin Baylor
1934-

American basketball player

He never played a championship team or won a scoring title; he played well before the made-for-video era and disdained self-promotion. But teammates, opponents and longtime observers of the game eagerly proclaim forward Elgin Baylor as one of pro basketball's greats.

Baylor was an All-NBA First Team choice 10 times in his career, and he participated in 11 All-Star games, sharing the MVP award in the 1959 classic with Bob Pettit of St. Louis. In his 14 NBA seasons, he scored 23,149 points, averaging 27.4 per game. Baylor also had 11,463 rebounds and 3,650 assists.

Named after Watch

Baylor was born in Washington, D.C., and named Elgin after the watch his father, John, was looking at the

Elgin Baylor

moment Baylor was born. He didn't play basketball until about age 14, but as a senior at the all-black Spingarn High School in Washington, he became the first African-American named to the all-metropolitan team.

Baylor struggled academically, however, and enrolled at the College of Idaho on a football scholarship. He played no football there, but averaged 31.3 points per game in basketball and transferred to Seattle University, at the urging of Seattle auto dealer Ralph Monroe. College transfer rules required him to sit out one year. When Baylor returned to the court, he led the country in rebound point (20.3 per game) and earned a second-team All-America status. One year later, he was a first-team All-American as the Chieftains (now the Redhawks) reached the NCAA championship game, losing to Kentucky 84-72 in the final. Baylor scored 25 points and pulled down 19 rebounds, but the game was a lost. However, he did achieved a rarity in the NCAA tournament when he became one of the few players on a non-winning championship team to receive the most outstanding player award.

Revives Lakers

Baylor left after his junior season when the Minneapolis Lakers made Baylor their first overall draft choice; they signed him in 1958. The Lakers, led by Hall of Famer **George Mikan**, had been the league's first dynasty, winning five championships in six years from 1949-1954, but had fallen on hard times, financially as well as in the standings. Its record in 1957-58 was 19-

Chronology

1934	Born in Washington, D.C.
1950-54	Attended Spingarn High School, Washington
1954-55	Attended College of Idaho on football scholarship; played basketball instead and averaged 31.3 points per game.
1955-58	Enrolled at Seattle University; played two seasons after sitting out one year due to transfer rules
1958	Drafted by Minneapolis Lakers; left Seattle University after junior season
1960	Lakers move to Los Angeles
1971	Retires after playing only nine games that season
1974	Named assistant coach of New Orleans Jazz
1976	Named Jazz head coach
1979	Resigns as Jazz head coach
1986	Los Angeles Clippers name him vice president of basketball operations
1995	Voted NBA's worst general manager by Athlon Sports Pro Basketball Edition.

NBA Legends: Elgin Baylor

Had Elgin Baylor been born 25 years later, his acrobatic moves would have been captured on video, his name emblazoned on sneakers, and his face plastered on cereal boxes. But he played before the days of widespread television exposure. All we have now to showcase his prowess are the words of those who saw one of the greatest player that ever played basketball. Baylor's longtime teammate Jerry West told HOOP magazine in 1992 that Baylor "was one of the most spectacular shooters the game has ever known,. I hear people talking about forwards today and I haven't seen many that can compare with him."

Source: *NBA.com*

53. Season ticket sales spiked when Minneapolis signed Baylor for $20,000, a hefty sum at the time. "If he had turned me down, I'd have been out of business," owner Bob Short said. "The club would have been bankrupt."

Baylor made an impact immediately, earning the Rookie of the Year while leading the Lakers to the NBA Finals. Boston won the series in four straight games. Baylor averaged 24.9 points per game, fourth in the league and ranked third in rebounds (15). Minneapolis won 14 games more than the previous season. One year later, the team's last in Minnesota, he set an NBA record with a 64-point game, which he broke the next season with 71 against the New York Knicks. It stood as the league record until Philadelphia's **Wilt Chamberlain** scored 100 in 1962.

Off to Los Angeles

When the Lakers started the 1960-61 season in Los Angeles, **Jerry West** joined Baylor and the two would form a potent, outside-inside tandem. Baylor averaged about 35 points per game during the team's first three seasons on the West Coast, including 38.3 in 1961-62. During that time, men were expected to perform military duty. Baylor missed 40 percent of his team's regular-season games in the 1960-61 season because of military service. "For most of his career, Baylor was the team leader off the court," Larry Schwartz wrote on the Web site *ESPN.com*. "He was the focus of most conversations. He was the one who began discussions, turned them joyfully into arguments and then made the final judgment of the disputes-whether whimsical or serious. Would a lion whip a tiger? No, Baylor decided. It was Baylor who disciplined the rookies, who decided when it was time for a pre-game meal, who decided when it was time to play poker."

The Lakers dominated the Western Conference, reaching the NBA Finals eight times in 12 years. Unfortunately they lost all eight. In three of the seven championship finals in which Baylor played (he missed the 1965 championship round, having ripped his kneecap in the Western Conference final), Los Angeles came tantalizingly close to winning only to lose to Boston in the climactic seventh game by less than 4 points each game. In two of those series, Los Angeles led the best-of-7 series in games, 3-2.

Baylor, nicknamed the "Big E," scored 61 points in Game five of the 1962 Finals in Boston Garden to spark Los Angeles to a 3-2 series advantage; it was then a single-game playoff record and remains a Finals record. But in Game seven that year, Frank Selvy missed a short jump shot at the end of regulation that would have given the Lakers the title. Boston, with the home court advantage, prevailed 110-107 in overtime. Four years later, a late Los Angeles rally fell short and the Celtics won another seventh game at home with a score of 95-93. In 1969, this time with Wilt Chamberlain joining Baylor and West, Boston won another Game seven with a score of 108-106 in Los Angeles. One year later, with the Celtics out of the way, the Lakers faced the New York Knicks in the Finals. That series went seven games as well, but in the finale, a badly injured Willis Reed hobbled onto the court unexpectedly and led New York to an easy 113-99 win. During Baylor's era, the Lakers lost six games in which they were one win short from a title.

Years later, recalling the 1962 seventh game, Baylor insisted both he and Selvy were fouled at the end of regulation. "Selvy thought **Bob Cousy** fouled him," Baylor said. "I thought Cousy fouled him. He took the shot from a spot where he was very proficient. Cousy said he never fouled him. I was in a position to get the offensive rebound. But somebody behind me shoved me out of bounds right into the referee. There was no foul call there, either. I looked around and saw (Bill) Russell and Sam Jones behind me."

"Some years later Baylor got a copy of the game's film and confirmed what he had suspected," the *NBA.com* wrote on its Web site. "Sam Jones had shoved him out of bounds, away from the rebound. Jones later joked about it with him and admitted pushing him."

Knee injuries and a torn Achilles' tendon plagued Baylor from the mid-sixties through the end of his career. Longtime Lakers announcer Chick Hearn said ob-

Career Statistics

Yr	Team	GP	PTS	FG%	FT%	RPG	APG	PF
1958-59	MIN	70	1742	40.8	77.7	15.0	4.1	270
1959-60	MIN	70	2074	42.4	73.2	16.4	3.5	234
1960-61	LAL	73	2538	43.0	78.3	19.8	5.1	279
1961-62	LAL	48	1836	42.8	75.4	18.6	4.6	155
1962-63	LAL	80	2719	45.3	83.7	14.3	4.8	226
1963-64	LAL	78	1983	42.5	80.4	12.0	4.4	235
1964-65	LAL	74	2009	40.1	79.2	12.8	3.8	235
1965-66	LAL	65	1079	40.1	73.9	9.6	3.4	157
1966-67	LAL	70	1862	42.9	81.3	12.8	3.1	211
1967-68	LAL	77	2002	44.3	78.6	12.2	4.6	232
1968-69	LAL	76	1881	44.7	74.3	10.6	5.4	204
1969-70	LAL	54	1298	48.6	77.3	10.4	5.4	132
1970-71	LAL	2	20	42.1	66.7	5.5	1.0	6
1971-72	LAL	9	106	43.3	81.5	6.3	2.0	20
TOTAL		846	23149	43.1	78.0	13.6	4.3	2596

LAL: Los Angeles Lakers; MIN: Minneapolis Lakers.

serving Baylor in 1965-66 "was like watching (race horse) Citation run on spavined legs." He played merely two games in 1970-71. Nine games into the 1971-72 season, Baylor announced his retirement. Ironically, the Lakers immediately reeled off a 33-game winning streak and won their first title in Los Angeles, the one Baylor had coveted. Baylor, inducted into the Basketball Hall of Fame in 1977. He was also named to the NBA's 35th and 50th anniversary teams.

Struggles as coach, executive

The expansion team New Orleans Jazz(now Utah) named Baylor an assistant coach in their first season in 1974. He became head coach in December 1976, replacing Butch van Breda Kolff. He left after the 1978-79 season, compiling an 86-135 record.

In 1986, Baylor became vice president of basketball operations for the Los Angeles Clippers. The Clippers, who were considered a second-fiddle to their city rival the Lakers both on and off the court, have mostly struggled, reaching the playoffs sparingly. Some NBA observers blame frugal and meddlesome owner Donald Sterling more than Baylor. "To be fair, Baylor has one of the toughest jobs in the NBA, working for the most notoriously stingy owner in the league, if not in the annals of sports. It could make anyone sensitive," Bob Laws wrote in the *Santa Monica Mirror*. "There's no doubt that Sterling should bear the brunt of the blame for the Clippers' ongoing woes," he explains.

Laws, however, does not spare Baylor. "But maybe it's time to take a closer look at 'Teflon' Baylor, beloved in this town for his heroics while playing for that other L.A. hoop team. The man is seemingly beyond reproach with the local media, who are happy to just blame it on Sterling. I guess this will always be a Laker town. Lucky for Elgin Baylor."

Baylor legacy

"Because his career had paralleled the succession of the juggernaut Boston Celtics teams in the 1950s and 1960s, Baylor never played on a club that won an NBA championship," the *NBA.com* wrote on its Web site. "His best years as a scorer coincided with Wilt Chamberlain's peak years, and Baylor never captured a scoring title." Some of Baylor's most acrobatic moves never made film. It was well before the home video era and television coverage of the NBA was sparse during his prime. "It is possible that no forward ever performed with the offensive proficiency and flair that Elgin Baylor showed for the Lakers during the late 1950s and throughout the '60s," Schwartz wrote. "It wasn't just the number of points he scored; it was the way he got them, thrilling fans with the remarkable variety of his elegant actions."

FURTHER INFORMATION

Other

"Celtics, Lakers Work OT to Start Rivalry." NBA.com, http/www.nba.com:/history/finals/19611962.html, (December 23, 2002).:

"Hall of Famers: Elgin Baylor." Basketball Hall of Fame Web site, http://www.hoophall.com/hallof-famers/Baylor.htm (December 16, 2002).

Laws, Bob. "Clippers Beat Themselves—Again." Santa Monica Mirror, http://www.smmirror.com/volume3/issue44/clippers_ beat_themselves.asp, (April 17-23, 2002).

"NBA Legends: Elgin Baylor." NBA History, http://www.nba.com/history/baylor_bio.html (December 22, 2002).

Schwartz, Larry. "Before Michael, There Was Elgin." ESPN.com, http://espn.go.com/sportscentury/features (December 16, 2002).

Awards and Accomplishments

1954	Named to Washington, D.C. all-metropolitan team as a senior at Spingarn High School
1958	Most outstanding player of NCAA men's basketball tournament as Seattle University reaches title game, losing 84-72 to Kentucky
1959	NBA Rookie of the Year
1959	NBA All-Star Game Co-MVP with Bob Pettit, St. Louis Hawks
1960	Scored 71 points against New York Knicks
1962	Scored 61 points against Boston Celtics, still a record for most points in an NBA Finals game
1977	Enshrined in Basketball Hall of Fame
1980	Named to NBA's 35th Anniversary Team
1996	Named to NBA's 50th Anniversary Team

"Sports Biographies: Baylor, Elgin." Hickok Sports http://www.hickoksports.com/biograph/baylorel. shtml (December 16, 2002).

Stevens, Joe. "Clippers' Goal: Make Playoffs." Island Valley Bulletin, www.dailybulletin.com, (October 30, 2002).

Sketch by Paul Burton

Amanda Beard

Amanda Beard
1981-

American swimmer

Amanda Beard, the youngest swimmer on the 1996 U.S. Olympic team, became a national hero when she captured one gold and two silver medals at the Summer Games in Atlanta. Fans adored the spunky 14-year-old from California, who clutched a lucky teddy bear on the medal stand, and who swam to greatness with a youthful innocence. Although her swimming career slumped just following the 1996 Olympics, Beard made a comeback. After winning a bronze medal in the 200-meter breaststroke at the 2000 Olympics in Sydney, Australia, Beard won an NCAA championship and again became a top contender in professional women's swimming. In 2002 she broke the American record in the 200-meter breaststroke, and collected several medals in national and international swimming competitions.

Beard was the youngest of three daughters born in Irvine, California. Beard's older sisters, Leah and Taryn, had joined a local swim program, piquing their little sister's interest. When five-year-old Beard told her family she would swim in the Olympics one day, her parents just smiled. "There wasn't exactly a swimming gene pool here," her father, Dan Beard told Leigh Montville of *Sports Illustrated*. "We weren't setting out to make

champions. We just liked the benefits of the sport, the competition, the fact that it makes kids schedule their time, the friendships that it brings." Beard also played soccer and softball, took jazz and tap-dancing lessons, and cared for the family's many pets.

Trained for Olympics

Beard started swimming for the Colony Red Hots; at age 13 she joined the Irvine Novaquatics. Upon Novaquatics' coach Dave Salo's recommendation, Beard's parents agreed to let their daughter start training full-time in swimming. She would swim five afternoons and three early mornings a week.

Initially, Beard disliked the breaststroke, preferring the vigorous butterfly. But training with Brian Pajer, an Olympic breaststroke finalist, changed her. In January, 1994, she clocked 1:33 in 100 meters; by August, she had pared to 1:15. At age 13, Beard skipped the junior national competition and went straight to the senior nationals, competing in faraway cities. She swam against the country's best at the 1995 Phillips 66 Spring Nationals, finishing third in the 200-meter breaststroke and fifth in the 100-meter breaststroke. Internationally, she swam in the 1995 Pan Pacific Competition, capturing bronze medals in the 100 and 200 breaststroke finals, and a silver in the 400 medley relay. By the following year, at the Olympic trials in Indianapolis in March, Beard sailed to first place in the 100 with 1:08.36, the second-fastest time in women's breaststroke history. At the press conference afterwards, the small, Olympic-bound swimmer held the teddy bear.

Captures Three Olympic Medals

Beard became a media darling. She was the youngest member of the 1996 Olympic swim team, and the youngest Olympic swimmer since Nicole Kramer in 1976. Sports reporters regaled fans with stories about Beard's love for animals and her dream of pursuing an adult career as an interior decorator. "She likes to race and she refuses to be beaten," Olympic team coach Don Wagner told Johnny Ludden of the *Washington Post*. "I think her innocence in the sport is one of the things that makes her so good. She's not intimidated by anyone."

At the Atlanta Games, Beard was the Americans' best shot for a medal in the women's breaststroke. South Africa's Penny Heyns, the world-record holder in the 100-meter breaststroke, was another favorite. Beard had beaten Heyns in a pre-Olympic race, and she aimed to win again.

In the 100-meter Olympic final, Beard and Heyns squared off with six other swimmers. Off to a slow start, Beard, who did not wear goggles, had something in her eye early in the race. She started slowly, yet halfway through the race began passing her competitors. She finished second, just behind Heyns, who became South Africa's first Olympic gold medalist in 55 years. Beard, the silver medalist, was happy to learn she had set an American record at 1:08.09.

The 200-meter final was a replay of the 100: Beard started off slowly, then caught up to every other swimmer except Heyns, the former University of Nebraska star. "I just wanted a medal," Beard told the *Detroit Free Press*. "I didn't care what color it was. I'm happy with silver." Yet Beard would also take home a gold. Swimming in the 400-meter individual medley relay, she and Beth Botsford, Angel Martino, and **Amy Van Dyken** finished first.

Beard continued to train after the Olympics, but in 1997, she grew four inches, and her changing body perhaps affected her performance. In the 1997 U.S. Swimming national championships, she finished ninth in the 100-meter breaststroke. By 1998 her world ranking had dropped to 53rd in the 200 breaststroke. She quit swimming briefly, then returned as a college student.

Peaked Again

When Beard attended the 2000 Olympic trials, she no longer carried her lucky teddy bear. Instead, the sophomore-to-be from the University of Arizona showed up with two tattoos and a pierced tongue. Though considered a long shot, she made the team, finishing second in the 200 breaststroke. "I saw the '2' by my name," she told the Associated Press. "Take 1996 and times it by 100, and that's how I was feeling."

At the 2000 Olympics, Beard captured the bronze medal in the 200 breaststroke. Her teammate, Kristy

Chronology	
1981	Born October 29 in Irvine, CA
early 1990s	Swims with Colony Red Hots youth swim team
1994	Joins Irvine Novaquatics swim club; begins training seriously and competing nationally
1996	Wins two silver and one gold medal in Olympic Games in Atlanta, GA
1998	Drops in women's swimming rankings; retires briefly from professional swimming
1999–2003	Attends University of Arizona
2002	Breaks American record in 200m breaststroke

Kowal, took the silver. "My coach told me, 'You're in eighth. All you can do is move up,'" Beard told Harris. "I decided to go out there and give it a shot. I went all out and told myself I've got to do it."

Beard then competed as the University of Arizona's top breaststroker, winning the NCAA 200-yard championship in 2001. Later that year she decided to accept endorsements, making her ineligible for collegiate swimming. Her 2002 achievements included first place in the 100- and 200-meter breaststrokes at the Pan Pacific Championships. That year, she broke the American record in the women's 200-meter breaststroke.

Beard plans to compete in the world championships in July, 2003, in Barcelona, Spain.

Beard's Impact

Beard gambled at a young age, devoting herself exclusively to swimming, and it paid off in a successful career. "It's all great, but it's scary, too," her mother, Gayle Beard told Montville. "You have to put your trust in a lot of people, some of whom you really don't know very well."

Even after stumbling in the late 1990s, Beard had earned enough respect within swimming that people were still pulling for her. "No matter how old you are, what size you are, it's the heart that matters," said Staciana Stitts, a 2000 Olympic teammate. "Amanda had a lot of heart in that (trial) race. She really wanted it."

FURTHER INFORMATION

Books

"Amanda Beard." *Sports Stars*. Series 1–4. U•X•L, 1994–98.

Periodicals

Harris, Beth. "Beard Defies Doubters for Second Olympic Berth." Associated Press (August 15, 2000).

Harris, Beth. "Krayzelburg Wins Second Olympic Gold." Associated Press (September 21, 2000).

Ludden, Johnny. "Beard's Pet Project Is '96 Olympic Games," *Washington Post* (July 24, 1995): C7.

Montville, Leigh. "'Kid Stuff." *Sports Illustrated* (July 22, 1996): 104.

Other

"Amanda Beard." USA Swimming Official Website. http://www.usa-swimming.org/superstars/template. pl?opt=biosearch&name=226 (January 17, 2003).

Sketch by Wendy Kagan

Franz Beckenbauer

Franz Beckenbauer
1945-

German soccer player

Franz Beckenbauer is the only person who has won soccer's World Cup as team captain and as coach. Beckenbauer captained the former West Germany to the championship in 1974, and coached it to the top in 1990. Beckenbauer, who also played for the New York Cosmos when soccer interest in the United States began to rise in the mid-to-late seventies, is now president of one of Europe's top teams, Bayern Munich, after a successful stretch for that team as player, coach and general manager. He is also president of the organizing committee for the 2006 World Cup to be hosted in Germany.

Beckenbauer, credited with popularizing the "sweeper" defensive position and using it as a mode of counterattack, was also captain of the former West Germany's national team when it won the European Championship, and led Bayern Munich to three successive European Cups and the European Cup Winners' Cup. But there was an air about Beckenbauer that transcended championships. "Every movement he made on the pitch bristled with elegance," the International Football Hall of Fame wrote of Beckenbauer. "There was an arrogance in his

play that suggested he was always in command- 'Emperor Franz' and 'The Kaiser," they called him. But more than that, he was a great thinker about the game and brought about a revolution in the way it is played by inventing the role of the attacking sweeper." Keir Radnedge wrote in *The Ultimate Encyclopedia of Soccer*. "He was the puppet master, standing back and pulling the strings which earned West Germany and Bayern Munich every major prize," he explains further.

Joined Bayern as a Teen

Beckenbauer was born in war-torn Munich in 1945, and joined with the youth team at Bayern Munich at age 14. Within three years, he surrendered his job as an insurance salesman trainee to pursue professional soccer. His arrival at the parent Bayern Munich club coincided with its ascension into the German elite league. The Bundesliga-Bayern had not been admitted when the Bundesliga (German soccer league) was formed in 1963. Beckenbauer started at the outside left forward position, but soon moved to midfield, and his play helped spark the West Germans to a 2-1 qualifying victory in the 1966 World Cup over Sweden.

First World Cup Final

During the World Cup in 1966, which England hosted, Beckenbauer scored four goals. He struck twice in a 5-0, early-round pasting of Switzerland, then scored the winner against the Soviet Union winning 2-1 in the semifinals, circling a shot around a Soviet defensive wall. In the finals, against England at historic Wembley Stadium in London, West German coach Helmut Schön had Beckenbauer play out of position, assigning him to mark British standout Bobby Charlton. For years, Schön has endured criticism for West Germany's 4-2 overtime defeat. "Experts felt that had he not been designated to mark Bobby Charlton, West Germany would have won that World Cup, as it was Charlton and Beckenbauer cancelled each other out and the rest is history," analyst Brian Beard wrote on the Web site *givemefootball.com*. Beckenbauer successfully stalked Charlton, who had scored two goals against Portugal in the semifinal, which took him out of the game offensively. England's Geoffrey Hurst, who scored three goals that day, had both in overtime after Wolfgang Weber tied the game for the Germans on a penalty kick late in regulation.

West Germany and England were not done with each other. They met again four years later, in the 1970 World Cup in Mexico. This time the British were wide open to criticism. "With England leading 2-0, (Coach) Alf Ramsey inexplicably took Bobby Charlton off," Beard wrote. "Freed from the constraints of marking Charlton, Franz inspired a German comeback. He reduced the arrears with a long-range shot and, given fresh hope, West Germany went on to win 3-2." Italy eliminated the West Germans, 4-3 in the semifinal.

On Top of the World

West Germany, the host nation in 1974, overcame a bitter loss to East Germany in the first meeting between the two rival countries. Both teams were assured of advancing under the new tournament format, but the defeat prompted Beckenbauer to hold a team meeting, suggest lineup and strategy changes to Schön and even appear on national television to calm a skittish public. "When you are hosts, there is obviously twice the pressure, because everybody expects you to win," Beckenbauer said. In the final, at Olympic Stadium in Munich, West Germany drew powerful Holland, led by Johan Cruyff and Johann Neeskens. The Dutch scored before the Germans could even touch the ball-Neeskens converted a penalty kick two minutes into the contest. But West Germany rallied on first-half goals by Paul Breitner and Gerhard Müller for a 2-1 victory and its first World Cup championship since 1954. They were the only goals the Dutch allowed in the tournament. Beckenbauer and goalkeeper Sepp Maier effectively throttled the "Clockwork Orange," once Germany took the lead.

Sixteen years later, Beckenbauer coached the West Germans to another World Cup. By then the Berlin Wall had fallen and the 1990 tournament in Rome would feature the last pre-unification national team. Andreas Brehme's penalty kick gave the Germans a 1-0 win over Argentina in the title game after they eliminated England in a shootout in the semifinals. Beckenbauer joined Brazil's Mario Zagalo as having played for and coached a World Cup champion. (Beckenbauer was a captain, Zagalo wasn't.)

Across the Atlantic

In 1977, Beckenbauer signed with the New York Cosmos of the North Atlantic Soccer League. His teammates included the redoubtable **Pele** of Brazil and Giorgio Chinaglia of Italy, each of whom had achieved his own World Cup fame. Attendance soared as the Cosmos, playing in Giants Stadium at the Meadowlands sports complex, achieved worldwide recognition. Beckenbauer, who split his playing duties between midfield and defense, was the league's MVP in 1977 and the Cosmos were league champions in 1977, 1978 and 1980. He played one final season in New York in 1982 after returning to Germany and leading SV Hamburg to Bundesliga and German Cup titles.

Beckenbauer, as coach and later an executive with Bayern Munich, has helped the team retain its status among the European elites. He was also an effective power broker as Germany landed the 2006 World Cup. "Beckenbauer's charisma and political skills were instrumental in the triumph of the German bid," the news service Reuters wrote in 2000, when Germany edged South Africa in the voting.

Chronology

1945	Born in Munich, Germany
1959	Begins playing for the Bayern Munich youth team
1966	Plays in first World Cup final as West Germany loses 4-2 in overtime to host England
1977-79	Plays for New York Cosmos of North American Soccer League
1982	Plays one final season for Cosmos after leading SV (Sport Verein-sport club) Hamburg to Bundesliga and German Cup titles
1986	Coaches West Germany to World Cup title game, won by Argentina
2000	Beckenbauer named chairman of 2006 World Cup organizing committee as Germany named host nation

SELECTED WRITINGS BY BECKENBAUER:

Dirigent im Mittelfeld. (Title means "Conductor in the Centre Zone"), Munich, Germany: Copress-Verlag, 1966.

Gentleman am Ball (Title means "Gentleman on the Ball"), Rosenheim, Germany: Komar-Verlag, 1968.

Halbzeit: Eine Zwischen-Bilanz (Title means "Halftime: A Trial Balance"), Hannover, Germany: Strohte, 1971.

Einer Wie Ich (Title means "One Like Me"), Munich, Germany: Bertelesmann, 1975.

Franz Beckenbauer's Soccer Power: Techniques, Tactics, Training, New York, NY: Simon & Schuster, 1978.

Awards and Accomplishments

1966	Named West German footballer of the year after scoring four goals in World Cup tournament
1969	Bayern Munich wins Bundesliga and German Cup titles
1972	European Footballer of the Year as Bayern Munich wins European championship; Bayern also wins Bundesliga and German Cup titles
1973	Bayern wins Bundesliga and German Cup titles
1974	Leads West Germany, host nation that year, to first World Cup title; Germans defeat Holland 2-1 in final
1976	European Footballer of the Year
1977	North American Soccer League Most Valuable Player as member of New York Cosmos, who win NASL title in 1977 and 1978
1982	Hamburg wins Bundesliga and German Cup titles

FURTHER INFORMATION

Books

Hahn, James. *Franz Beckenbauer: Soccer Superstar.* St. Paul, Minn.: EMC Corp., 1978.

LeGoulven, Francis and Robert Ichah. *Franz Beckenbauer: l' homme qui vaut 2 milliards (title means "Franz Beckenbauer: The Man Worth Two Billion.").* Paris: PAC, 1977.

Radnedge, Keir. *The Ultimate Encyclopedia of Soccer: The Definitive Illustrated Guide to World Soccer.* Rocklin, CA: Prima, 1994.

Thibert, Jacques. *Beckenbauer: Kaiser Franz* Paris: Calmann-Lévy, 1975.

Other

Beard, Brian. "The Greatest Ever, World Cup XI." Givemefootball.com, http://www.givemefootball.com/html/WC_11_beckenbauer.STM, (December 17, 2002).

"Franz Beckenbauer: West Germany," Xtratime.com, http://www.worldcuparchive.com/LEGENDS/beckbaur.html (December 22, 2002).

"Holland 1974 Home Page," http://easyweb.easynet.co.uk/~goldkeep/Holland74, (December 17, 2002)

International Football Hall of Fame: Franz Beckenbauer Profile, http://www.ifhof.com/hof/beckenbauer.asp, (December 15, 2002).

Sketch by Paul Burton

Boris Becker
1967-

German tennis player

In 1985, Boris Becker became the youngest player to win the men's singles championship at Wimbledon. He

Boris Becker

was also the first German to do so, and the first unranked player. In truth, Becker was used to being the youngest. He had started playing when he was only eight years old, and by age 11 he was playing in adult divisions. Still, it was a grand moment, and turned Becker into an international sensation, and a national hero. While Becker continued to find success on the court, winning four more Grand Slam tournaments and an Olympic gold medal, he also weathered difficult slumps and at times found himself the object of controversy and contempt. Through it all, however, he has remained Germany's most famous athlete, and a symbol of grace and good manners in a sport that has not always been known for either.

Young Champion

Boris Becker was born in Liemen, West Germany, to Karl-Heinz and Elvira Becker. His father, an architect, saw an early promise in his son and was active in constructing a tennis center near their home. Young Boris began playing competitively at the age of 8. Actually, Boris was not the best boy at the center, and at one point he was relegated to hitting with the girls, including a young **Steffi Graf**. But at age 11, he was good enough to start competing in the adult divisions. By that time he had acquired a coach, Gunther Bosch, who would one day take him to Wimbledon. In 1984, he also acquired a manager, Ion Tiriac, also a world-renowned coach. He too played a large role in Becker's future success.

In 1984 Becker entered his first Wimbledon competition, but a torn ligament soon ended his chances. The next year things went considerably better. At age 17, he appeared at Wimbledon again, alongside such established figures as **Jimmy Connors**, **John McEnroe**, and **Rod Laver**. To universal amazement, Becker found himself facing Kevin Curren in the finals. After beating Curren, 6-3, 6-7, 7-6, and 6-4, Boris Becker became the youngest champion in Wimbledon history.

The result was electric, creating an international sensation. Back in West Germany, Becker became a national idol. As he told a *New York Times* reporter, "I'm the first German, and I think this will change tennis in Germany. They never had an idol, and now maybe they have one." While some felt Becker's was overstating the case, there was no doubt that Germans were delighted, and thousands of them turned out to welcome him back to Leiman to the sounds of "Boom Boom Boris," a hit rock song based on Becker's nickname. At the same time, Becker was developing a reputation for coolness under pressure, in contrast to some of his more volatile colleagues on the court. One Wimbledon victim summed it up: "He just plays, hits the ball, wins, says thank you and goodbye."

Ups and Downs

In 1986, Becker successfully defended his title against Ivan Lendl, efficiently knocking him off in three sets: 6-4, 6-3, 7-5. "I saw a little bit in Ivan's face that he didn't know what to do with me," Becker told a *Sports Illustrated* reporter. At that point, reporters could still write that no mortal man could beat Becker, who had only lost his first Wimbledon competition because of an injury. He was still the golden boy of modern tennis.

The next year, 1987, put a little tarnish on the Becker shine. In January, he lost to Wally Masur, ranked 71st, at the Australian Open. An unusually bitter Becker hit balls toward the umpire and out of the stand, broke three rackets, and even spat water toward the umpire, earning $2,000 in fines. Two days after the match, he fired his coach, Gunther Bosch, who had been with him since childhood—an emotional breakup that left him feeling drained and bitter. Bosch began speaking to the press, often casting Becker in a negative light. At the same time, he took up with 22-year-old Benedicte Courtin, hiding out with her at a $2,600-a-night villa that caused some grumbling in the press about his high-flying lifestyle. Then the unthinkable: he lost in the second round at Wimbledon to an unknown, Peter Doohan. The press began to savage him. "I didn't lose a war. Nobody died. Basically, I just lost a tennis match," commented Becker, but he was shaken by the harshness of the attacks.

The next couple of years were somewhat better. Becker took seven titles, and captained Germany to their first Davis Cup victory. 1989 was even more satisfying. In July, he reclaimed his Wimbledon title, knocking off

Chronology	
1967	Born November 22, in Liemen, West Germany
1975	Begins playing competitive tennis
1976	Begins training with Gunther Bosch
1984	Begins working with Ion Tiriac
1984	Enters Wimbledon competition for first time; leaves due to injury
1985	Becomes youngest player to win Wimbledon championship
1986	Wins Wimbledon again
1987	Fires Gunther Bosch
1988	Helps win West Germany's first Davis Cup victory
1989	Reclaims Wimbledon title; hires Bob Brett as new trainer
1991	Begins dating Barbara Feltus
1993	Marries Barbara Feltus, December 17
1994	Son, Noah Gabriel, born
1997	Retires from Grand Slam tournament competition
1999	Retires from professional tennis
1999	Son, Elias Balthasar, born
1999	Father dies
1999	Russian model gives birth to Anna, illegitimate daughter of Boris Becker; subsequent paternity test proves he is the father
2000	In December, separates from wife, Barbara Feltus; later files for divorce
2002	Is convicted of tax evasion, given two-year suspended sentence, in October

defending champ Stefan Edberg 6-0, 7-6, 6-4. That same month he helped the German team take another Davis Cup win in Munich by beating **Andre Agassi**, the man who had blatantly insulted Becker's beloved Wimbledon. To top it all off, in September Becker won the U.S. Open for the first time, besting rival Ivan Lendl. The International Tennis Federation awarded Becker the title of World Champion that year.

Controversy Finds the Wunderkind

Having regained his championship status, Becker seemed to gain a newfound confidence. To replace Bosch he hired an unknown Australian named Bob Brett, saying he was not interested in finding another mentor or father figure. He also began speaking out more to the press about public issues, saying that the West German government was spending too much on armaments and not enough on the homeless, and saying that reunification with East Germany was progressing a little too quickly. Then in 1992 he declined to help Berlin in its bid for the 2000 Olympics, saying he feared it might revive his fellow citizen's fantasies about a master race. German fans were sometimes stunned at the views of the man who had waved the German flag at the Davis Cup and had been marketed as a clean-cut, patriotic German youth.

In another area of his life, the controversy turned truly ugly. Since Courtin, Becker had been linked with a number of women, including Olympic skater **Katarina Witt**. But in 1991 he met and fell in love with Barbara Feltus, a beautiful German-American model who also happened to be black. Hate mail and ugly taunts from

Awards and Accomplishments

1984, 1986, 1990	Quarterfinals, Australian Open
1985-86, 1989	First place, Wimbledon
1986, 1990	Semifinals, U.S. Open
1987, 1989, 1991	Semifinals, French Open
1988-89	Co-victor, Davis Cup
1988, 1990-91	Finals, Wimbledon
1989	Finals, U.S. Open
1989	Awarded title of World Champion, International Tennis Federation
1991	First place, Australian Open
1991	Semifinals, French Open
1991	Finals, Wimbledon
1992	Quarterfinals, Wimbledon
1992	Gold medal, Barcelona Olympics (with Michael Stitch)
1993-94	Semifinals, Wimbledon

Where Is He Now?

The new millennium has not been very kind to Boris Becker. In late 2000, his marriage fell apart in a very public way, just as Germans had grown to accept, and even admire it. After the outcry in the late 1990s, Boris and Barbara had emerged as a glamour couple, a visible symbol of tolerance and racial accord in a country sometimes plagued by racist violence. But in November of 2000, Becker told his wife he wanted a separation. A week later, she flew to Miami, where she filed for custody of the children and a generous financial settlement. The reason was a Russian model by the name of Angela Ermakova who claimed to have given birth to Becker's daughter, named Anna, a charge soon confirmed by a paternity test. Then in 2002, Becker was convicted of tax evasion for keeping an apartment in Munich while claiming exclusive residence in the tax haven of Monaco. He was given a suspended sentence of two years, and a fine of 500,000 euros, which left him a free man, but with a criminal record.

It was a bleak moment for the man who'd burst onto the scene as a 17-year-old with a winning smile and composure well beyond his years. Friends said that for the first time, Becker had been able to live the high life, after retiring from tennis, and that he was going through a kind of delayed adolescence. While it was clearly a darker side to Becker, some would always remember the bright lad who showed up the giants at Wimbledon when he was only 17. Even now, he remains the most famous sports name in Germany—a hero in a country that often was short on them.

neo-Nazis sometimes forced the couple to flee Germany and hide out in Monaco. "Sometimes within 15 minutes I am someone who cannot get served because I'm black," Feltus told a German reporter. "The next minute I'm Frau Becker, treated like a queen. Sometimes, I find both awful." When the couple appeared nude on the cover of *Stern* magazine, as a protest against racism, many in the staid German public were appalled. Despite these pressures, the couple married on December 17, 1993. Together they have two sons, Noah Gabriel, born in 1994, and Elias Balthasar, born in 1999.

While Becker was finding love off the court, his career on it was suffering. "After '91 I was tired of tennis," Becker acknowledged to a *Sports Illustrated* reporter in 1993. "I was tired of all the straining and the doing. I had all the success I wanted." The tiredness showed, and in 1992 he'd slipped to a number 10 ranking before rallying at the end of the year. He did rally enough to win the Australian Open and to take a gold medal in doubles tennis at the 1992 Olympics, with an old rival, Michael Stitch. But after 1991 Grand Slam tournament titles continually eluded him, and in 1997, after losing a quarterfinal match at Wimbledon, he announced that he was retiring from tournament competition. "I feel very relieved," he said. "I had a great run here. I won a number of Grand Slams … and now that I've made my decision, I feel very comfortable." Two years, later he retired from professional tennis altogether.

FURTHER INFORMATION

Periodicals

"Becker visits illegitimate daughter for first time." *Europe Intelligence Wire* (October 29, 2002)

"Boris made it a Boom town." *Sports Illustrated* (July 22, 1985): 20.

Chapman, Doug. "Boris Becker's hopes end with injured wrist." *Knigh Ridder/Tribune News Service* (June 28, 1996): 628.

Chapman, Doug. "Boris Becker announces his last match at Wimbledon." *Knigh Ridder/Tribune News Service* (July 3, 1997): 703.

"Convicted tax evader Becker gets two-year suspended sentence." *Europe Intelligence Wire* (October 25, 2002)

Deford, Frank. "Summer reruns." *Sports Illustrated* (July 14, 1986): 14.

Diaz, Jaime. "The trials of a phenom." *Sports Illustrated* (March 2, 1987): 50.

"A fallen idol." *Asia Africa Intelligence Wire* (October 30, 2002)

Iyer, Pico. "Hero in a land of few heroes." *Time* (June 30, 1986): 60.

Jenkins, Sally. "The burden of being Boris." *Sports Illustrated* (June 21, 1993): 44.

Kirkpatrick, Curry. "Das Wunderkind: Boris Becker, a 17-year-old from West Germany." *Sports Illustrated* (July 15, 1985): 18.

Kirkpatrick, Curry. "A smash hit on his home court." *Sports Illustrated* (August 12, 1985): 28.

Kirkpatrick, Curry. "Boris the Yankee wrecker." *Sports Illustrated* (July 31, 1989): 56.

Kirkpatrick, Curry. "Boom Boom." *Sports Illustrated* (September 18, 1989): 56.

Kirkpatrick, Curry. "Eye of the tiger." *Sports Illustrated* (August 27, 1990): 64.

Lambert, Pam. "The course of true love: an interracial romance makes Boris Becker a target of bigots in Germany." *People Weekly* (August 30, 1993): 105.

Price, S.L. "Broken promise." *Sports Illustrated* (May 28, 2001): 82.

Schickel, Richard. "Everyone's wild over Bobele." *Time* (July 22, 1985): 60.

Sullivan, Robert. "Woes of the wunderkind." *Sports Illustrated* (December 14, 1987): 38.

Wolff, Alexander. "Wunderbar!" *Sports Illustrated* (July 17, 1989): 14.

Sketch by Robert Winters

David Beckham
1975-

British soccer player

D avid Beckham is more than one of England's best soccer player. He is a celebrity, treated as near-royalty, hounded by the press who dwell on his every move. During his career as a member of the Manchester United, and also playing for the England in the World Cup, Beckham has been both villain and hero. Lauded, vilified, bemoaned, worshipped, and ridiculed–few professional players of any sport have undergone the constant barrage of attention on and off the field as Beckham. Handsome, with a quick eye to where the cameras are placed, he has both benefited and suffered from a life lived in the public arena.

Joins Manchester United

David Beckham was born in Leytonstone, London, on May 2, 1975 to Ted, a repair man, and Sandra Beckham. He started dreaming about playing soccer professionally when he was eight years old as he watched the sport on television. Beckham played youth soccer, and when he was eleven he won the Bobby Charlton Soccer Skills Competition, which judged ball control skills. The win earned Beckham a trip to Barcelona, where he drew the attention of a Manchester United soccer talent scout. His parents insisted that Beckham finish his schooling at Chingford High before he could join a professional team.

At the age of sixteen, Beckham signed on as an apprentice for Manchester United and the team won the Football Association (FA) Youth Cup in 1992. On April 2, 1995, Beckham made his Premier League debut at home in a match against Leeds United. During the following season, 1995-96, he began making an impact on his team from the midfield position. He was slowly growing a reputation for his ability to execute free kicks and score goals, often times in sensational fashion or at critical moments of the game. His performance during the season caught the attention of England's national team manager, who capped Beckham (named him to the national team). He made his national debut on September 1, 1996, against Moldova.

Manchester United won the Premier League championship both in 1996 and 1997. In 1997 Beckham was

David Beckham

voted the Young Player of the Year and finished second in voting for the overall Player of the Year award. Despite failing to retain the Premiere League title in 1998, Beckham was named to England's World Cup squad, and he signed a five-year, $12.5 million contract with Manchester United.

1998 World Cup Fiasco

Beckham's 1998 World Cup experience became a turning point in his career. In the match against Columbia Beckham scored a spectacular game-winning free kick. However, he went from national hero to national villain in a heartbeat when, in the next match against Argentina, he was given a red card (which means expulsion from the game) for kicking Argentina's Diego Simeone just minutes into the second half with the score tied 2-2. Argentina went on to win on penalty kicks, eliminating England in the second round. Simeone had flattened Beckham from behind and, in response, Beckham flung his leg out, grazing Simeone who fell dramatically hard. Simeone's infraction merited a yellow card (a warning), but Beckham, given the first red card of his career, was booted from the match.

In the aftermath of England's loss, Beckham was vilified. The *Daily Mirror's* headline read "10 Heroic Lions, One Stupid Boy," and the *Daily Star's* banner read "What an Idiot." Beckham was hung in effigy outside a London pub, and a Baptist church message board read "God Forgives Even David Beckham." He received

<table>
<tr><td colspan="2">

Chronology

1975	Born in Leytonstone, London, England
1991	Joins Manchester United as a trainee
1995	Makes debut in Premier League match
1996	Becomes starting midfielder
1998	Gets ejected from World Cup game against Argentina; vilified in England; signs five-year, $12.5 million with Manchester United
1999	Marries Victoria Adams, also known as Posh Spice
2000	Publishes autobiography
2001	Named team captain
2002	Scores free kick goal in the World Cup against Argentina

</td></tr>
</table>

History of the Manchester United Soccer Team

Manchester United came into existence in 1878, under the name Newton Health. In 1909 the team began playing in the newly built arena, Old Trafford, where the team continues to play today. The team had moments of glory and dismal failure during its first decades. League play was suspended during World War II, and Old Trafford suffered damage from bombings, but the team quickly rebuilt it when play resumed in 1946. During the next twelve years Manchester United built a successful program, but a plane crash in 1958 that claimed the lives of eight players severely affected the team.

The Reds, as the team is known, careened through the 1960s and 1970s, matching great winning streaks with equally impressive slumps. In 1986 the team hired Sir Alex Ferguson, a seasoned and successful manager, to rebuild the Reds into a top-ranked organization. Between 1992 and 2001, the team claimed seven FA Premiere League titles.

Manchester United is a popular team in England, with the biggest payroll and the most media exposure. The team grossed nearly $140 million in 2000, more than any other team in the world. Comparable to the one-time stature of the Dallas Cowboys or the New York Yankees, fans tended to either love them or hate them. For his part, Beckham is the highest paid player on the United team, earning some $13 million a year from salary and endorsements, and he, like his team, tends to inspire a strong reaction among fans who defend or distain him.

death threats and was continually booed the following season each time he touched the ball. Beckham was not immune to the constant criticism, and publicly apologized, saying, according to *Sports Illustrated,* "I will always regret my actions. I want every fan to know how deeply sorry I am."

Celebrity Status

Beckham, known as Beck by his fans, was quickly becoming more than a soccer player; he was a national celebrity. He is also the pretty boy, the national and international heart throb, and as much was written about his hairstyle and his choice of clothes as his soccer abilities. When Beckham began dating Victoria Adams, also known as Posh Spice from the pop group Spice Girls, in 1997, he and Adams became daily fodder for the tabloid press. Much of the media's attention was initially encouraged by the couple, who tossed tidbits of personal information to the tabloids and could be seen out and about wearing matching designer outfits. In 1998 the couple announced that Adams was pregnant, which once again added fuel to the media fire. Tabloid reporting intermixed true stories with false to further hype the couple. Much like Princess Diana before them, Beckham and Adams are reviled in the press as much as they are praised. Yet the more the press deems them uninteresting, tac! ky, and glamour hounds, the more obsessed England becomes in following their every move.

The media was in a frenzy in July 1999 when Beckham and Adams married in Luttrellstown Castle, eight miles west of Dublin. The daylong gala reportedly cost $800,000. Adams wore a diamond-encrusted crown, and Beckham wore an ivory suit. After the nuptials, the newlyweds sat in gilded, red-velvet thrones, with their young son Brooklyn between them, watching their guests mingle under live potted apple trees and fluttering doves. The night, which the *National Post* noted would be long remembered "for its monumental tackiness," included an 18-piece orchestra playing old Spice Girl tunes, footmen, fireworks, and a cake topped with an edible, nearly nude figure of Beckham and Adams embracing. Beckham and Adams appeared at the end of the affair in matching pur-

ple outfits. The couple sold the pictures of their wedding to *OK!* magazine for $2.2 million.

On-field Redemption

Beckham started the 1998-99 soccer season on a mission to redeem himself for his grave error at the World Cup. Despite playing under constant pressure and ongoing booing from the crowd, Beckham had an excellent year and lead Manchester United to an unprecedented triple crown, winning the Premier League championship, the FA Cup, and the European Cup. Beckham had another good year during the 1999-2000 season, winning his fourth Premier League championship. He was runner-up in the voting for both best player in Europe and the best player in the world, and was second in voting for the BBC Sports Personality of the Year (which was won by **Lennox Lewis**). Although he scored his fiftieth goal during the season, more press was given to his new mohawk haircut.

Beckham's play on the soccer field went a long way to redeem his image after the World Cup fiasco. Despite a slump early in 2001 that had critics grumbling about his true value, Beckham remained focused and returned to form. By the end of the 2000-01 season, having been named the team's captain, he was receiving high praise for his new-found leadership, maturity, and wisdom. Often knocked as a footballer with exceptional skills that did not necessarily come through in the clutch, Beckham quieted his critics by proving himself on the field.

Beckham's moment of supreme redemption came during the World Cup in 2002, when England once again faced Argentina. Stalled at 0-0, England was awarded a penalty kick. Although he was coming off a broken foot and was not one-hundred percent healthy, Beckham lined up to take the shot. With the Argentinean

<table>
<tr><td colspan="2">Awards and Accomplishments</td></tr>
<tr><td>1992</td><td>Wins Football Association (FA) Youth Cup</td></tr>
<tr><td>1996-97,
2000-01</td><td>Wins Premier League championship</td></tr>
<tr><td>1997</td><td>Voted Young Player of the Year</td></tr>
<tr><td>1998, 2002</td><td>Plays in World Cup</td></tr>
<tr><td>1999</td><td>Wins European Cup, Premier League, and FA Cup championships</td></tr>
</table>

players doing their best to distract him, Beckham, the master of the penalty kick, put the ball in the back of the net. England defended its 1-0 lead to advance in the World Cup. He was once again the hero.

The Beckham Phenomenon

Beckham's life on and off the field have inspired so much curiosity in England that Staffordshire University began offering a twelve-week course on Beckham and the sociological implication of his career. The course is founded on the presupposition that Beckham's 1998 World Cup mishap defined an era in England similar to the way the assassination of John F. Kennedy did in the United States. Beckham's undeniable talent to score on free kicks drew a team of international researchers to study how he literally bends the plane of the ball over defenders and into the goal. A great footballer with an even greater public persona, Beckham continues to fuel the frenzy through his rich-and-famous lifestyle and his exceptional play on the field.

CONTACT INFORMATION

Address: Manchester United Football, Sir Matt Busby Way, Manchester, M16 ORA, England.

FURTHER INFORMATION

Books

The Complete Marquis Who's Who. New York: Marquis Who's Who, 2001.

Periodicals

Barnes, Simon. "Banishment of Beckham." *The Spectator,* (February 26, 2000): 63.

Barnes, Simon. "Football's Osric." *The Spectator,* (September 8, 2001): 63.

Barnes, Simon. "Sublime and Ridiculous." *The Spectator,* (October 9, 1999): 79.

Barnes, Simon. "Triumph and Disaster." *The Spectator,* (June 5, 1999): 71.

Blonska, Joanna, and Jeffrey Klinke. "How Posh?" *People Weekly,* (July 19, 1999): 58-59.

Brownell, Ginanne. "The New Royal Couple." *Newsweek,* (October 16, 2000): 64.

Lawton, James. "Beckham has Only Himself to Blame—and Posh." *Daily Express,* (January 1, 2000): B4.

"Posh 'N Becks." *National Post,* (October 28, 2000): W6.

Thomsen, Ian. "Scourge of a Nation: England is Still Lambasting David Beckham." *Sports Illustrated,* (September 7, 1998): 10.

Other

"Beckham's Biography." *Magnificent7: The Online David Beckham Magazine.* http://www.beckham-magazine.com (January 8, 2003).

"Beck's Dad Slams MP over Call to Ban Star from Road." Manchester Online, February 10, 2001. http://www.manchesteronline.co.uk (January 8, 2003).

"David Beckham: Bio." Manchester United. http://www.manutd.co.uk (January 8, 2003).

"England Fans Salute New Captain Marvel." Manchester Online, September 9, 2001. http://www.manchester online.co.uk (January 8, 2003).

"Giles: Beckham a Parody of a Great Player." Manchester Online, December 4, 2001. http://www.manchester online.co.uk (January 8, 2003).

"More Millions for Beckham: In His Own Words." Manchester Online, August 22, 2002. http://www.manchesteronline.co.uk (January 8, 2003).

"Profile: World Cup Euphoria in England Surrounding Star David Beckham." National Public Radio, June 2, 2002. http://npr.org (January 22, 2003).

Sketch by Kari Bethel

Myriam Bedard
1969-

Canadian biathlete

Although men have competed in the biathlon at the Olympics for many years, women did not compete until the early 1990s. Canadian Myriam Bedard won some of the first Olympic medals given in the biathlon, which is a combination of cross-country skiing and marksmanship with a .22-calibre rifle that is measured by time and accuracy. (Missed targets add time to the score or length to the course.) When Bedard won two gold medals at the 1994 Winter Olympics, it marked the first time a Canadian woman had won two gold medals in one game. She was also the first North American to win a World Championship in the biathlon.

Myriam Bedard was born on December 22, 1969, one of four children born to Pierre and Francine Bedard. Her father was an electrician, while her mother was a child-care worker. Bedard was a very athletic child, playing basketball, doing gymnastics, and, more seri-

Myriam Bedard

ously, training as a figure skater. She skated from age six to age 12, but her family could not afford the kind of coaching she needed so she quit.

Introduced to Biathlon

When Bedard was 14 years old, she joined the Canadian Army cadets with a group of friends. It was there that she learned to shoot. She put this skill to work in 1985 when she was asked to be part of a mixed relay team race at the regional cadet winter games. Bedard was teamed with three men and played with borrowed equipment. Though she did not know how to cross-country ski, her shooting skills were superior. Her team won the race, and Bedard found a new sport.

Although Bedard's parents did not support her at first, she could compete because the cadets provided equipment while she was part of the group. In 1986, she used her own money so she could compete in the sport without the cadets. Bedard's first order of business was learning to ski. Though it was initially difficult, she joined a cross-country ski club and loved it. She told Hal Quinn of *Maclean's,* "I love the challenge. While physically demanding, it is such a mental sport. You must study each course and plan every part of the race ahead of time." Bedard proved to have much natural ability, though this did not guarantee success as a biathlete. Winning a biathlon is unpredictable because it depends on the weather and how the athlete feels on that day, both mentally and physically.

Won First Championships

Within a short time, Bedard was doing well at women's biathlon competitions. In 1987, she won a first and a second at the first Canadian Junior Biathlon competition. In 1988, she won a Canadian junior title, two North American championship races, and had a first and second in Canada Cup tests. Bedard competed at the World Junior Championship in 1989, finishing fourth in sprints. She also won a Canadian senior title that year.

Bedard's experiences at the worlds in 1989, more than anything else, proved to her how much harder she had to train. Part of the problem was that she did not own her own rifle until 1989, which was an expensive $2700. By this time, her training became supported by an annual grant of $7000 from Sport Canada. She also had a job in public relations for a real estate company, Le Permanent, and an endorsement deal with Duofold for long underwear.

With training Bedard improved her fitness, especially in her upper body. She was of very small stature compared to most who competed in the sport, standing only five feet, three inches tall and 115 lbs. Her ace in the hole came for her uncommon ability to recover every second stride. Bedard also had an odd shooting style that seemed to work in her favor; shooting on instinct, she did not pause to steady herself before making a shot.

Won Big Competitions

The training paid off when, in 1991, Bedard won a World Cup Biathlon gold medal. In the 1991 biathlon season, she won medals in five of six competitions, including two golds, two silvers, and one bronze. Bedard finished the season ranked second overall, the highest ranking ever for a biathlete from North America. She was often used to promote the sport for women in Canada.

The first women's biathlon events at the Winter Olympic Games were held at the 1992 Games in Albertville, France. Bedard represented Canada in both the 7.5-km and 15-km races, and as part of a team event for three women on the 7.5-km course. She was expected to medal, as she was still ranked number two in the world, but some questioned if she had participated in enough races that season to win. Bedard also faced tremendous pressure, primarily from Team Canada's coaches and officials, which made it tough on her. Despite the problems, Bedard pulled it together to win bronze in the 15-km event.

These perceived failures at the Olympics gave Bedard new goals. She told Christine Rivet of the *Ottawa Citizen,* "For me, (keeping motivated) will be easy. I know what my goals are. I know I have to improve my skiing. I know in shooting, I'm OK. I want to have the best skiing time in the world. I'm almost there."

Problems still remained for Bedard. Funding was an issue, until her agent negotiated a partnership deal with

Chronology

1969	Born on December 22
1985	Competes in first biathlon, a mixed relay team race
1986	Buys her own equipment to compete in biathlon
1992	Competes in Winter Olympics
1994	Sponsorship contract with Metropolitan Life is not renewed; marries Jean Paquet in March; daughter Maude is born on December 22
1995	Signs sponsorship deal with Canadian National Railways
1997	Is diagnosed with hypothyroidism
1998	Finishes 33rd in the 7.5-km event and 50th in the 15-km at the Olympic Games in Nagano, Japan; switches to long-track speed skating, leaving biathlon behind
1999	Competes in first race as a speed skater, at the Canadian Long-track Sprint Championship; competes in last biathlon at the World Cup

Awards and Accomplishments

1987	Won first and second Canadian Junior Biathlon Championship
1988	Won first at Canadian Junior Biathlon Championship; won two North American championship races; won first and second at Canada Cup tests
1989	Won Canadian Senior Championship; competed in World Junior Championship, finishing fourth in a sprint
1991	Won gold medal at the World Cup Biathlon; won medals in five of six biathlon competitions; finished biathlon season ranked second overall
1992	Won bronze in 15-km event at Winter Olympics in Albertville, France
1993	Won gold and silver at the World Biathlon Championship; placed second in World Cup standings
1994	Won gold medals in the 7.5-km and 15-km event at the Winter Olympics, Lillehammer, Norway; won silver in the 15-km event at the World Cup; won Bobbie Rosenfeld Award as Canada's female athlete of the year; won Lou Marsh Trophy as Canadian athlete of the year; awarded the Meritorious Service Cross
1995	Received the Velm Springstead Award for being athlete of the year in 1994
2001	Received Olympic Order from the International Olympic Committee

Metropolitan Life. The deal funded her training and offered the promise of a job after her retirement. This deal allowed Bedard to buy her own custom rifle. She trained hard (six days a week, 11 months a year) on her own with her own staff, including non-Canadian coaches in some areas. Bedard's independence made for a strained relationship with Biathlon Canada, but she was the best in the country at this point.

Bedard bounced back to do well in the 1993 season. At the World Biathlon Championship, she won gold medal in the 7.5-km race and silver in the 15 km. She became the first North American to accomplish this goal. She finished the season placed second in World Cup standings. In her training, she worked hard to increase her aerobic skills and strength, so she would peak for the 1994 Olympic Games in Lillehammer, Norway.

Won Olympic Gold

At the 1994 Olympics, Bedard finally fulfilled her promise, winning gold medals in both the 15-km race and in the 7.5-km event. This marked the first time a Canadian woman won two gold medals at the Winter Olympics. Bedard's second gold, in the 7.5-km event, was even won on two different skis. After the Olympics, she competed in the World Cup, winning silver in the 15-km event.

In the spring of 1994, Bedard received some bad news when her two-year deal with Metropolitan Life expired without renewal. This happened because of a rift between the company and her agent, Jean-Marc St. Pierre. Still, Bedard was named the Canadian Female Athlete of the Year. She also married Jean Paquet in the spring, and gave birth to her daughter, Maude, in December.

The birth of her child only slowed Bedard down temporarily. She found another sponsorship deal, a three-year pact with Canadian National Railways. Bedard also had other, smaller endorsement deals as well. She trained to be ready for some events in March during the 1995 biathlon season, but did not do well.

Could Not Return to Form

For several years, Bedard fought to be one of the best biathletes, but she could not match the times she had posted before giving birth. Her endurance had changed. In 1997, she finished 28th in a World Cup Biathlon event, her best finish in years.

In trying to prepare for the 1998 Winter Olympics at Nagano, Japan, Bedard over-trained for the 1997 season. She consulted doctors and was found to have hypothyroidism and a number of severe food allergies. To regain her health, Bedard had to account for her new medication and diet in her training. In December 1997 World Cup competition, Bedard finished 15th in the 15-km event, her best results since 1994.

Competed at Nagano

As the Olympics grew closer, Bedard believed she was regaining her form, until she suffered a lower back injury in early 1998. She wanted to compete, though she did not need to do so for a living. She told Dave Stubbs of the Montreal *Gazette,* "I'm a competitor, a perfectionist. Every race I do I really want to do well. I'm not satisfied just being here. With all I've been through the past few years, this is the way I probably should feel. But I don't. It's against my nature."

In Nagano, Bedard was one of the oldest competitors in the women's biathlon. She finished 33rd in the 7.5-km event and 50th in the 15-km event. Although after the Olympics she said she would still compete, Bedard's last event in biathlon was in March 1999, a World Cup event that was on the Val Cartier military base where she first learned the sport. As Stubbs wrote in the Montreal *Gazette,* "Bedard sees only straight ahead, enjoying life without benefit of a rear-view. And it's plain to see she has discovered something that pleases her every bit as much as did biathlon when she came to it as a teenaged army cadet, wearing rented, ill-fitting equipment."

FURTHER INFORMATION

Periodicals

Beamish, Mike. "Bedard Shoots to the Top of the Olympic Hero List." *Vancouver Sun* (February 24, 1994): D1.

"Bedard to Receive Olympic Order." *Calgary Herald* (June 20, 2001): C4.

Came, Barry. "Taking Her Best Shot." *Maclean's* (February 9, 1998): 62.

Clarey, Christopher. "A Biathlon First for a Canadian Who Wouldn't Quit." *New York Times* (February 19, 1994): section 1, p. 27.

Cleary, Martin. "Bedard Uses Time Wisely to Prepare for '94 Games." *Ottawa Citizen* (May 29, 1993): G2.

Cleary, Martin. "Shooting to the Top." *Ottawa Citizen* (February 19, 1992): B3.

Ewing, Lori. "Bedard's Back on Track." *Calgary Herald* (March 10, 1995): C3.

Ewing, Lori. "Bedard Has Silver Touch." *Calgary Herald* (March 18, 1994): D1.

Ewing, Lori. "Bedard's Picking Up Speed." *Calgary Herald* (August 15, 1998): C11.

Ewing, Lori. "Bedard Trading Rifle for Skates." *Calgary Herald* (August 6, 1998): F1.

Nemeth, Mary. "Pursuing the Agony of Victory." *Maclean's* (February 14, 1994): 58.

Quinn, Hal. "A Clear Sight on the Gold." *Maclean's* (December 2, 1991): 20.

Rivet, Christine. "Bedard Finds Riding Wave of Success Toughest." *Ottawa Citizen* (February 21, 1992): B4.

Starkman, Randy. "Biathlon: Bedard's Gold Mine." *Ottawa Citizen* (February 24, 1994): D1.

Starkman, Randy. "Biathlete Bedard Is Suffering from Hypothyroidism." (Montreal) *Gazette* (January 29, 1997): B8.

Stevens, Neil. "Bedard Named Top Female Athlete." *Ottawa Citizen* (December 20, 1994): F1.

Stubbs, Dave. "Bedard Facing Another Hurdle." (Montreal) *Gazette* (February 3, 1998): B5.

Stubbs, Dave. "Bedard Gilds the Silly." (Montreal) *Gazette* (February 26, 1994): C2.

Stubbs, Dave. "Bedard Innocent Bystander as Met Life Takes Run at Agent." (Montreal) *Gazette* (June 2, 1994): C3.

Stubbs, Dave. "Bedard Says Farewell to Career 1." (Montreal) *Gazette* (March 1, 1999): C2.

Stubbs, Dave. "Bedard Set to Embrace All Canada." *Gazette* (March 1, 1994): D8.

Stubbs, Dave. "Bedard's Indomitable Olympic Spirit." (Montreal) *Gazette* (January 6, 1998): F1.

Stubbs, Dave. "Gritty Bedard Shines Through." *Gazette* (March 2, 1992): C1.

Stubbs, Dave. "In the Spotlight: Olympics Changed Bedard's Life." *Gazette* (November 8, 1992): C1.

Stubbs, Dave. "More Honors for Bedard at Awards Gala." (Montreal) *Gazette* (March 29, 1995): E5.

Stubbs, Dave. "Railway Puts Bedard on the Fast Track." (Montreal) *Gazette* (July 19, 1995): E3.

Stubbs, Dave. "A Sight to See." (Montreal) *Gazette* (January 11, 1992): F1.

Stubbs, Dave. "Taking a Shot at Speed Skating." (Montreal) *Gazette* (January 16, 1999): G1.

Stubbs, Dave. "What Bedard Wants, She Gets." (Montreal) *Gazette* (February 5, 1994): C1.

Todd, Jack. "Bedard Battling Back." (Montreal) *Gazette* (November 5, 1997): B4.

Todd, Jack. "Bedard 33rd in 7.5-km Biathlon." (Montreal) *Gazette* (February 15, 1998): B1.

Sketch by A. Petruso

Ed Belfour
1965-

Canadian hockey player

Ed Belfour has earned a reputation throughout his career for his hot temper. His ability to be rattled at the drop of a hat was common knowledge and was used against him by opposing teams. Although he has recently subdued his temperament, many people still believe he has many demons to overcome. He is not just a goalie with a temper though. There is much more to the man behind the mask. He is "Technically strong. Extremely quick.... Aggressive and very acrobatic," and "has an undeniable belief in himself," according to D. T. Norris writing on his goalie homepage. What is often overlooked is his compassionate side, having worked with organizations benefiting children.

Little Eddie

Belfour was born in Manitoba, where hockey is a mainstay in life. He received his first pair of hockey skates at the age of five. It was at that point that he began to spend every possible moment at the skating rink. On his official Web site he explained how he became goalie simply due to the cold conditions on the ice. Apparently the temperatures would sometimes dip to quite frigid levels and while the linesmen were warming up in the dressing room, the goalie was stuck in position for the entire game and would leave the ice nearly frozen. He was the back up for the goalie and as the main goalie tired of being constantly cold, Belfour got more and more attempts at playing the position. Soon he became the main goalie and loved playing every second of the game, regardless of the conditions. Belfour's coach was glad to have him in a position that was less interactive, because even early on Belfour had quite a temper and was a penalty waiting to happen when he was a center.

In high school it was required that students try out for hockey. There were three people vying for the two positions of goaltender on the varsity team and he was the one who was cut. This was a devastating blow to Belfour and he commented, "I was so disappointed I almost decided to quit, but instead I played a year of JV. That decision changed my life." The coach of the hockey team left the school, so the principal of the high school stepped in as coach. He knew of Belfour's frustration with not making the varsity team, and would allow him to play games with the varsity team here and there. It was at one of those games he was able to vindicate himself, showing his true ability. He was not dressed for the game, but was asked to suit up for the third period, where he truly shined. Belfour recalled, "I had a very strong game, helping us spoil the sweep and extend the series." He knew his hard work had paid off. It was this experience that showed everyone that Belfour was willing to work hard to make things happen.

American Dreams

Belfour worked hard honing his goaltending skills, and intended to use these skills to create a career in hockey. Unfortunately he was not drafted for any junior hockey leagues in Canada, so he chose to accept an offer he received for a full scholarship to the University of North Dakota. Although he was quite successful throughout his college career, he was not drafted by the National Hockey League upon graduation. A year later he was signed as a free agent by the Chicago Blackhawks. His first year was unremarkable and he decided to spend a year with the Canadian Hockey League to fine-tune his skills, with the approval of the Blackhawks. He improved during that year and upon returning to the Blackhawks he was able to win their confidence. During the regular season Belfour showed the mental acuity needed to be a goalie, but all of that would unravel in the playoffs. "Teams also learned that this intensity could be played upon to get Belfour off his game," according to a writer for *Biography Resource Center Online*. It was not until Belfour met the great Russian goalie, **Vladislav Tretiak,** at a Hawks train-

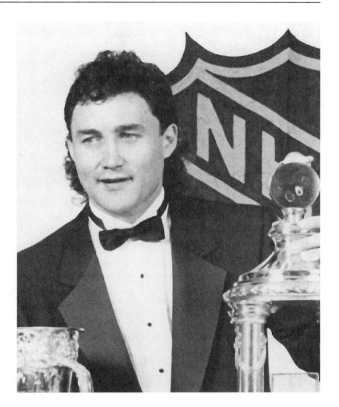

Ed Belfour

ing camp that he began to change his performance. Vlady, as Belfour calls him, became his friend as well as his mentor, and has made an impact on who Belfour is to this day. Although Belfour was improving, his time with the Hawks was to be short.

He was traded to the San Jose Sharks shortly before he was to become a free agent, but ended up signing with the Dallas Stars. This move angered many Shark fans, but it was a prudent career decision for him. Larry Wigge with the *Sporting News* stated, "Now it looks like he has joined a group that was made for him." During his tenure with the Dallas Stars he was able to overcome his mental rigidity during high stakes games. He proved this when he led the Stars to winning the Stanley Cup in the 1998-99 season. Wigge went on to say, "Belfour silenced his critics last year by winning his first Stanley Cup, staying focused and poised on the job, something he couldn't do in Chicago." Belfour says of himself, "I've learned not to be as maniacal as I used to be. When you are focused and in control, that's when you play your best." Doug Weight said in the same article, "He's definitely been a hot-tempered guy, one you could try to take him off his game. Keep running him. Keep trash-talking, and we still hope he might snap like he used to."

Still hot off the ice

Although it has seemed he has conquered his temperament on the ice, it appears that it has resurfaced in his personal life. While intoxicated, he started a fight

Chronology

1965	Born in Manitoba
1970	Receives first pair of hockey skates
1972	Begins playing goalie part time
1977	Begins playing goalie position full time
1980	Fails to make varsity team
1981	Gets his big chance in a varsity game leading team to victory
1982	Joins Winkler Flyers of Manitoba Junior Hockey League
1986	WCHA All-Star
1986	Named to NCAA All-American West second team
1986	Named to NCAA All-tournament Team
1987	Signs as free agent with Chicago Blackhawks
1987	Turns pro with Saginaw Hawks (International Hockey League)
1988	Named to IHL All-Star first team
1988	Plays in first National Hockey League game
1990	Sets the Chicago Blackhawk's record for wins in a single season.
1993	Becomes fifth goaltender to record two 40-win seasons
1997	Traded from Blackhawks to San Jose Sharks
1997	Signs with Dallas Stars
1997	Set Dallas Stars record for shut outs
1999	Beats personal best unbeaten game streak
1999	Wins Stanley Cup
2000	Arrested for public intoxication as well as several other charges
2000	Ties NHL record and sets new franchise record for shutouts in one playoff year
2000	Becomes one of four goalies to post ten 40-game seasons with a goals against average under 3.00 in each year
2000	Makes first on Dallas Stars' all-time list for goals against average with 1.99
2000	Appears in third Stanley Cup final series.
2001	Records Stars longest shut out streak
2001	Becomes one of three goalies in NHL history to post eleven 40-game seasons with a goals against average under 3.00 in each game
2001	Finishes season first among active NHL goaltenders in career shut outs
2001	Finishes season with 343 career wins
2001	Ties for first for Stars' all-time list for shut outs
2001	Sets franchise record for minutes played
2002	Destroys $5000 worth of equipment in visitors locker room after being pulled in first period game
2002	Walks out on team heading back to Dallas when he is benched in favor of rookie Marty Turco
2002	Traded to Toronto Mapleleafs
2002	Plays against Stars for first time since traded

Awards and Accomplishments

1986	Named top goaltender in Manitoba Junior Hockey League
1986	Named to Manitoba Junior Hockey League All-Star First Team
1987	First-Team Western Collegiate Hockey Association All-Star Goaltender
1987	Named to National Collegiate Athletic Association All-America West second team
1987	Member of National Collegiate Athletic Association Division I champion University of North Dakota
1987	Named to National Collegiate Athletic Association All-Tournament team
1987	Named International Hockey League Player of the Month, December
1988	Led International Hockey League Goaltenders in Minutes Played (3446)
1988	Named to International Hockey League All-Star first-team
1988	Shared (with John Cullen) Garry F. Longman Memorial Trophy (International Hockey League Top Rookie)
1991	Led National Hockey League Goaltenders in Games Played (74), Wins (43), Minutes Played (4127), Goals Against Average (2.47), Save Percentage (0.910)
1991	Named to National Hockey League All-Rookie team
1991	Named Rookie of the Year by *Sporting News*
1991	Named to *Sporting News* All-Star first team
1991	Calder Memorial Trophy
1991	Trico Goaltender Award
1991	Member, National Hockey League/Upper Deck All-Rookie Team
1991, 1993	Named to National Hockey League All-Star first team
1991, 1993	Vezina Trophy
1991, 1993	William M. Jennings Trophy
1992	Tied for National Hockey League lead in goaltender Shutouts (5)
1992	Led National Hockey League goaltenders in Playoff Goals Against Average (2.47)
1992	Shared National Hockey League single-season playoff record for most consecutive wins by a goaltender (11)
1992-93, 1996, 1998-99	Played in National Hockey League All-Star Game
1993	Leads league, games played (71), shutouts (7)
1993	Named to *Sporting News* All-Star second team
1993	Rated #12 in *Hockey Stars Presents* "The Top 50 Netminders in Pro Hockey"
1994	Ties for league lead, shutouts (7)
1995	Rated #10 in *Hockey Stars Presents* "The Top 50 Netminders in Pro Hockey"
1995	Named to National Hockey League All-Star second team
1995	Rated #11 in *Hockey Stars Presents* "The Top 50 Netminders in Pro Hockey"
1997	Named National Hockey League Player of the Week, December 1
1998	Named to The *Hockey News'* mid-season Second All-Star Team
1999	Member of Stanley Cup-champion Dallas Stars
2002	Member of gold medal-winning Canadian Olympic Team

with a security guard at a hotel in Dallas, who maced him. The police were called to the scene and Belfour was arrested for disorderly conduct as well as for resisting arrest. He was even said to have bribed a police officer to not arrest him. He became the talk of the town, as well as the hockey arena. The incident was made jest at the playoff game in Edmonton. Belfour's reputation as a hothead continued, and it was quite clear he did not want to accept the responsibility for his actions. An article in the Houston Chronicle stated Belfour had "a bad back, a worse temper and a knack for doing the wrong thing at the wrong time (and blaming everybody but himself)." His anger got the best of him in January of 2001 when he was asked to play goal in practice and sit on the bench for that night's game in favor of rookie

back-up Marty Turco. "Belfour blew up, left the team, and returned to Dallas," according to a writer for *Biography Resource Center Online*. Many believe that he was given the boot when his contract was up due to this event. "Crazy Eddie's" temper had finally gotten the best of him.

Belfour does have a soft side, when it comes to children. He has been avidly involved in the Make-a-Wish program for years now, a tradition he started when playing for the Chicago Blackhawks. When he is with children he becomes a completely different person. When in

Career Satistics

Yr	Team	GP	W	L	T	GAA	TGA	SV%	TSA	SHO
1988-89	CHI	23	4	12	3	3.87	74	.877	605	0
1990-91	CHI	74	43	19	7	2.47	170	.910	1883	4
1991-92	CHI	52	21	18	10	2.70	132	.894	1241	5
1992-93	CHI	71	41	18	11	2.59	177	.906	1880	7
1993-94	CHI	70	37	24	6	2.67	178	.906	1892	7
1994-95	CHI	42	22	15	3	2.28	93	.906	990	5
1995-96	CHI	50	22	17	10	2.74	135	.902	1373	1
1996-97	CHI	33	11	15	6	2.69	88	.907	946	1
1996-97	SJ	13	3	9	0	3.41	43	.884	371	1
1997-98	DAL	61	37	12	10	1.88	112	.916	1335	9
1998-99	DAL	61	35	15	9	1.98	117	.915	1373	5
1999-00	DAL	62	32	21	7	2.10	127	.919	1571	4
2000-01	DAL	63	35	20	7	2.34	144	.905	1509	8
2001-02	DAL	60	21	27	11	2.66	153	.895	1304	1
TOTAL		735	364	242	100	2.45	1743	.906	18273	58

CHI: Chicago Blackhawks; DAL: Dallas Stars; SJ: San Jose Sharks.

Dallas he worked with the North Dallas chapter of Make-a-Wish. During the play-offs one year he bought a section of seats and donated them to the Make-a-Wish foundation for each game. He called it the "Eagle's Nest." It was such a hit with the children, he continued the tradition into succeeding years. Jenny Wolfe, Director of Development for the North Texas chapter stated, "We are extremely grateful to Ed Belfour for his constant support of the children of Make-a-Wish."

Belfour also wanted to contribute to those who are interested in becoming hockey players, by setting up the "Ed Belfour High Performance Award" for the Manitoba Junior Hockey League. The criteria for the award was Hockey involvement including Statistics, achievements, and team participation; Academic achievements including grade point average, awards and classes; Community involvement including volunteer work, job and non-school related activities; and finally other school involvement including school sports, committee and clubs. Of course, the winning player must strive to be the best in the Manitoba Junior Hockey league. Because of Ed's generous spirit he was nominated USA Weekend's "Most Caring Athlete Award."

An Eagle with a Big Heart

Belfour is now playing with the Toronto Maple Leafs. A writer for the Chronicle states "Eddie is no longer Ed-eeeee. The numbers say Ed Belfour hasn't been for quite some time." The Maple Leafs were glad to welcome him to their team nonetheless. Belfour said, "I am more motivated than ever to prove to those people and all the doubters how wrong they are." There is still a lot of pride in Belfour. But in Belfour's heart there is still room for love and compassion as proven by his work with charities. Belfour has learned through the years that he is not the only player on the team. He is much more aware that he is an instrument—a part of the whole orchestra. In the article for the Houston Chronicle he said about his play with the Maple Leafs, "I have to step up and do more and I have to do a lot better job when the game is on the line." It is clear that Belfour has learned many lessons in his years.

FURTHER INFORMATION

Books

Biography Resource Center OnLine. Detroit: Gale Group, 2001.

Periodicals

Blackstone, Kevin. "Belfour deserving of ex-hero's welcome." *Dallas Morning News* (November 9, 2002): 1B

"Goalie Belfour goes full circle." *Houston Chronicle* (November 10, 2002): 7B

Koshan, Terry. "No sour grapes/Belfour isn't bothered by Don Cherry's remarks." *Ottawa Sun* (November 15, 2002): 74

Verdi, Bob. "Belfour never masks his feelings." *Sporting News* (January 24, 1994): 9

Wigge, Larry. "On-ice restraint has Stars' Belfour playing like a saint." *Sporting News* (June 5, 2000): 28

Other

Associated Press. FOXSports http://foxsorts.lycos.com/content/view?contentID=745392. (November 11, 2002).

Complete Ed Belfour. http://www.belfour.com/complete/influence.htm. (November 18, 2002).

Norris, Doug. The Goaltender Homepage. http://ucsu.colorado.edu/~norrisdt/bio/belfour.html. (November 18, 2002).

Sketch by Barbra J Smerz

Bert Bell
1895-1959

American football commissioner

Although he never played football professionally, DeBenneville "Bert" Bell brought the game to unprecedented heights of popularity with his revolutionary ideas and hardball style of business. An unsuccessful coach, Bell shined as the National Football League's second commissioner in the 1950s. During his 13-year reign, he created the amateur collegiate draft, established strong anti-gambling controls, instituted television blackouts for home games, and oversaw the merger of the NFL and the All-American Football Conference. Bell rooted for the underdog, and always acted for the good of the game.

Bert Bell was born in the Main Line section of Philadelphia to a wealthy family with real estate holdings and political clout. His grandfather was a congressman, his father served as a Pennsylvania attorney general, and his brother was a state governor. Bell attended Haverford Prep high school and played football at Franklin Field.

At the University of Pennsylvania, Bell played quarterback for the Penn Quakers from 1915-19. In 1916, he helped Penn to a 7-6-1 record and its first appearance at the Rose Bowl. A four-year letterman, Bell captained the team in 1919 to a 6-2-1 record, which included an 89-0 win over Delaware.

As Coach and Unsuccessful Owner

Never having played football professionally, Bell put his interest into coaching then later owning football teams. He served as an assistant or part-time coach at Penn and at Temple Universities, at one point serving under legendary coach **John Heisman**.

Bell married Ziegfeld Follies stage star Frances Upton. In 1933, since his wealthy father had cut him off from the family fortune, Bell borrowed $2,500 from his wife to buy the National Football League franchise Frankford Yellow Jackets. With co-owner Lud Wray, Bell renamed the team the Philadelphia Eagles and moved them to Center City where they played at Memorial Field and Franklin Field.

During the time he was owner of the Eagles, Bell made one of his most important contributions to football. In 1935, noticing that he was not attracting top talent to his team, Bell proposed an annual draft for selecting top-ranked college players. His strategy of allowing the teams who finished last the season before to have first selection of skilled players was made to continue the survival of the teams and the league.

Bert Bell

According to *The History of the National Football League*, "Bell's most notable achievement as an owner was convincing his fellow owners to adopt a draft of college players beginning in 1936. Without a doubt, it was one of the most important ideas ever adopted by the NFL because, when used intelligently, it has maintained the NFL's competitiveness throughout the last six decades."

Left with the old Yellow Jackets' debts, Bell was known to run the team out of a downtown restaurant and give the bartender tickets to sell. Bell ardently promoted the team in sports departments of the city's newspapers and by personally selling tickets. The unsuccessful team lost its first three games and never won more than five games in a season. By the end of its first three seasons, the team racked up financial losses of $80,000 and was put up for auction. Bell bought sole rights to the Eagles from Wray for $4,500, then became its coach.

In 1940, Art Rooney, a Pittsburgh native who had played professional baseball, became co-owner of the Eagles with Bell. In a franchise switch, the Steelers moved to Philadelphia to become the Eagles, and the Bell-Rooney Eagles went to Pittsburgh to become the Steelers. Bell remained head coach of the Steelers until 1941 when he resigned after two games.

The Commissioner

Bell continued to demonstrate his staunch character when he was unanimously elected on January 11, 1946 to succeed Elmer Layden to become the second NFL commissioner. In his first year as commissioner, Bell faced the problem of gambling in professional football. As the 1946 NFL title game between the New York Giants and the Chicago Bears was about to begin, Bell received word that Giants quarterback Frank Filchock and halfback Merle Hapes had been approached by gamblers to fix the score. Although neither player agreed to the fix, Bell suspended both players for not reporting the incident to authorities.

Another show of Bell's strength and determination was his negotiation of the NFL merger with the AAFC in 1949. The two organizations had been vying for a share of football's top talent and fans. The rivalry hurt the game as players' salaries rose and both sides lost millions of dollars. Bell successfully negotiated a merger of the two leagues to stop the fighting and help the game of football to prosper again. He oversaw other decisions under the merger, such as admittance of new members, divisions within the NFL, reassignment of AAFC players, and fair handling of the college draft.

The Impact of Television

In the 1950s, Bell faced the impact of the new medium of television with broad new policies. In 1952, he suggested that television coverage of home games be blacked out within 75 miles of that city's stadium. This would persuade residents to purchase stadium tickets rather than expect to watch the game at home for free. The ban was upheld by a federal court, and the blackout stayed in effect until 1973. Today, a blackout is lifted if a game is sold out 72 hours before kickoff.

In another move, so that televised games could air at least one commercial break per game's half, Bell created the automatic time out with two minutes to play in each half—the two-minute warning. He also invented sudden-death overtime and suggested televising night games. By 1958, Bell's innovative policies on television had propelled football to become America's most popular sport.

Bell left his mark on football through other achievements. He confronted angry team owners when he formally recognized the NFL Players Association as the organization's legitimate bargaining agent. Bell also created the "option" clause in a player's contract and ended the practice of stronger teams loading their schedules with weaker teams to guarantee wins. Bell also coined the phrase, "On any given Sunday, any team can beat any other team."

As befitting such a lover of football, Bell died at a game. At the age of 64, he suffered a fatal heart attack on October 11, 1959 while watching a football game at Philadelphia's Franklin Field. The two teams playing were the team he founded, the Eagles, and the team he co-owned, the Pittsburgh Steelers.

In the same year of Bell's death, the Maxwell Club of Philadelphia in 1959 created the Bert Bell Trophy to

Chronology	
1895	Born February 25, in Philadelphia, Pennsylvania
1915-19	Quarterback of the Penn Quakers of University of Pennsylvania football team
1919	Captain of the Penn Quakers
1933	Marries Ziegfeld Follies star Frances Upton
1933	Buys the Philadelphia Eagles with Lud Wray
1936	Creates college draft
1941	Sells the Philadelphia Eagles, becomes part owner and coach of Pittsburgh Steelers
1946-59	National Football League Commissioner
1950	Negotiates the merger with the All-American Football Conference (AAFC)
1952	Institutes TV blackout of home games
1959	Dies October 11, 1959 in Philadelphia, Pennsylvania

recognize its most valuable players. The football community also honored Bell in 1963 by choosing him as the first person to be inducted to the Pro Football Hall of Fame. In 1998, the Pennsylvania Museum Commission erected the Bert Bell Historic Marker in front of Mapes Store on Haverford Avenue in Narberth, Pennsylvania, and in December 2001, the cable channel HBO aired *The Game of Their Lives* focusing on Bert Bell and his contributions to football.

As a team owner and the second NFL commissioner, Bert Bell dedicated his life to the game he loved so much. Many of his contributions to the development of American football have lasted through the decades. Never afraid of being unpopular and generating criticism, he always strove to make the institution of football the best it could be.

FURTHER INFORMATION

Books

Caroll, Bob, and Michael Gershman, David Neft, John Thorn. *Total Football—Official Encyclopedia of the National Football League*. New York: HarperCollins, 1997.

Harrington, Denis J. *The Pro Football Hall of Fame*. Jefferson, NC: McFarland & Co., 1991

Hickock, Ralph. *Encyclopedia of North American Sports History*. New York: Facts on File, 1992.

Other

"Bert Bell: The Commissioner." Professional Football Researchers Association. http://www.football research.com/articles/frpage.cfm?topic=bell-bert (September 27, 2002).

Get Ahead Pro Speakers Bureau. http://www.getahead pro.com/upton.html (September 27, 2002).

"Hall of Fame Class III—Inducted November 11, 2000 Biographies." Official Web Site of the University of Pennsylvania's Athletic Department. http://

Awards and Accomplishments	
1959	Maxwell Club of Philadelphia establishes the Bert Bell Trophy for its most valuable player
1963	First person inducted to Pro Football Hall of Fame (charter member)
1998	Bert Bell Historic Marker erected in Narberth, Pennsylvania
2001	Featured in The Game of Their Lives HBO special

pennathletics.com/hall-of-fame/penn-hof-class3-bios. html (September 27, 2002).

Philly Burbs. http://209.71.42.240/eagles/Game_History. shtml (September 27, 2002).

"Bert Bell" Wikipedia. http://www.wikipedia.com/wiki/ Bert_Bell (September 27, 2002).

Sketch by Lorraine Savage

James "Cool Papa" Bell

James "Cool Papa" Bell
1903-1991

American baseball player

Negro league baseball lore is full of colorful tales, several of which revolve around the exploits of speedster James "Cool Papa" Bell. Teammate **Satchel Paige** once claimed that Bell was so fast that he could switch the light in their hotel room and jump into bed before the light went out. Rumor also had it that Bell had once been called out because he got hit by his own drive while rounding second base. Like many legends, these tales contain kernels of truth. Clocked at running the bases in thirteen seconds, Bell routinely stretched singles into doubles or triples; he stole bases at will and he covered centerfield with ease, taking away base hits from many batters. Bell played ball with a handful of Negro league teams in the United States and several teams in Cuba, Mexico, and the Dominican Republic, where African American players were heartily welcomed. Although Bell retired shortly before **Jackie Robinson** broke the color barrier in Major League Baseball, he accepted his role in history. Even so, he was among the African American ball players who measured themselves against white Major Leaguers in exhibition games. When asked on what level he thought most Negro league teams were compared with the Major Leagues, he did not hesitate. "We could have played right along with them," he replied in a video clip at the Major League Baseball Web site.

James Thomas Nichols was born May 17, 1903, in Starkville, Mississippi, to Jonas Bell and Mary Nichols. Bell grew up playing sandlot baseball and in 1920, he moved to St. Louis, Missouri, and took his father's name. He found work at the Independent Packing Company (later renamed Swift), and when not working he played semiprofessional baseball with the Compton Hill Cubs, part of the St. Louis City League. In this auspicious year he also married Clarabelle Thompson, with whom he would share more than fifty years of marriage. Two years later when the Compton Hill Cubs played an exhibition game against the St. Louis Stars of the Negro National League (NNL), Bell was too good of a prospect for the Stars to resist. With his left-handed curve and fade-away knuckle balls, he could dominate batters.

He snapped up the chance to pitch for the Stars, and at age nineteen made his professional baseball debut as a pitcher. The slender six foot tall youngster took the mound with rare poise for one so young and made a name for himself when he struck out slugger Oscar Charleston at a crucial point in a game. The name was "Cool Papa." Bell recalled at *MLB.com,* "They thought I was going to be afraid of the crowds. We had eleven, twelve, fifteen thousand people—more than the Major League had. I went out there like a veteran. I was a pitcher then and so like nothing is exciting, nothing like that. So they said you're looking cool out there. They started to call 'Hey Cool, Hey Cool.' So our manager [Bill Gatewood] said this 'Cool' isn't enough of a name for you, so he added 'Papa.' So that's how that was born."

After Bell injured his pitching arm, he moved to center field. With his speed and agility, he covered the often

Chronology

1903	Born May 17 in Starkville, Mississippi, to Jonas Bell and Mary Nichols
1920	Moves to St. Louis, Missouri to attend high school, work, and play semiprofessional baseball; marries Clarabelle Thompson
1922-28	Plays center field for the St. Louis Stars in the Negro National League
1933-37	Plays center field for the Pittsburgh Crawfords in the Negro National League
1938-42	Plays in the Mexican League
1942	Plays with the Chicago American Giants in the Negro National League
1943-45	Plays center field for the Homestead Grays in the Negro National League
1948-49	Plays and manages the Kansas City Monarchs in the Negro National League
1951	Scout for St. Louis Browns (now Baltimore Orioles)
1951-60	Custodian for St. Louis City Hall
1961-73	Night watchman for St. Louis City Hall
1974	Elected to the Major League Baseball Hall of Fame
1991	Dies March 7 at St. Louis University Hospital; buried in St. Peter's Cemetery, in St. Louis

Awards and Accomplishments

1928, 1930-31	Negro League championship with St. Louis Stars
1933	Named 11 times to East-West All-Star teams, beginning this year
1940	Triple Crown in Mexican Leagues
1943-44	Wins World Series with Homestead Grays
1974	Inducted into the Major League Baseball Hall of Fame

irregularly shaped playing fields with ease. He stole base hits and sacrifice flies from batters. He could compensate for his weakened arm with a quick release and accurate throw that prevented runners from trying for an extra base. Bell was also Cool Papa at the plate, but he was always ready to explode on the base paths.

Negro league pitchers took great liberties with the ball, causing it to fly in unpredictable ways. "In our league they threw the spitter, the screw ball, the emery ball, shine ball—that means Vaseline ball: there was so much Vaseline on it, it made you blink your eyes on a sunny day. Then they threw the mud ball—the mud on its seams made it sink. The emery ball would break either up or down, but if a sidearmer threw it and didn't know what he was doing, it could sail right into a hitter," Bell told John Holway in *Voices from the Great Black Baseball Leagues.* Even so, Bell often made contact, and not just contact—he knew how to place the ball where he wanted it. His lifetime batting average was an impressive .343.

Bell's speed—he could round the bases in a mere thirteen seconds—made him extra dangerous at the plate and on base. He could run out the bunt; he could get extra bases on slapped hits that for most players would be a single. In almost every game he played he stole at least one base. In 1933 Pittsburgh Pirate star Paul Waner told this story about his experience with Bell's speed, printed in Phil Dixon's *The Negro Baseball Leagues: A Photographic History,* "He was on first base and the next batter hit a single to center. This fellow Bell by that time was rounding second base and watching me as I ran. He never stopped. I made a motion, thinking to get him at third. As I started the throw I saw I was going to be too late. So I stopped ... but he didn't. He kept on for home plate. By the time I could get the ball away, he had

slid in there, was dusting himself off and walking calmly away." Satchel Paige's catcher Frazier Robinson in *Voices from the Negro Leagues* described Bell's base-stealing ability. "The only way I threw him out, he would telegraph when he was gonna steal. I knowed when he was goin'. If he'd take a big lead he wasn't goin' nowhere, but the minute he stood on that base—didn't take no lead—you better hurry up and get rid of that ball. And he could run! A lot of times he'd be thrown out but he knew how to slide. He'd trick the second baseman or the shortstop. ... He didn't hit the long ball but he could get on that base—bunt and drag the ball. He'd run over you if you get in his way." Run over opponents he did. During the ten years that the switch-hitting Bell played with the St. Louis Stars, he led the team to league titles in 1928, 1930, and 1931.

"Plays for Love of Game"

Bell played baseball almost continuously for thirty-four years, playing in both summer leagues in the United States and winter leagues in California, Cuba, Mexico, and the Dominican Republic. "It was good times," Bell recalled to Fallstrom. "I just played for the love of the game. I didn't intend to play that long, it just happened." When the NNL fell prey to the Great Depression, Bell joined the Detroit Wolves, an East-West League team, but the team disbanded before the season was over. Bell then played the remainder of the season with the St. Louis Monarchs and played winter ball in Mexico in 1933. The lure of Mexico was strong for several reasons. Though Bell had been paid $90 per month to play for the St. Louis Stars, playing south of the border was even better. He played winter baseball in Cuba from 1928 to 1930, the Dominican Republic in 1937, and in Mexico from 1938 to 1941. Not only did Bell earn a high of $450 per month touring Mexico with the Tampico, Torreon, Veracruz, and Monterrey clubs, he received the respect that black players lacked in the United States. In Cuba, Mexico, and the Dominican Republic, dark-skinned and light-skinned players played on the same teams and against other "integrated teams." It was the norm, as were good accommodations and interracial socializing. "Everyone was the same down there. We could go in any restaurant, stay in hotels, and oh, the fans? They loved us," Bell remarked in *Black Diamond: The Story of the Negro Baseball Leagues,* by Patricia C. McKissack and Frederick McKissack, Jr. Blacks also got the chance to

Career Statistics

Yr	Team	Avg	GP	AB	H	2B	3B	HR	SB
1922	STL	.417	22	60	25	3	1	3	0
1923	STL	.297	34	74	22	5	1	1	0
1924	STL	.310	59	216	67	15	1	0	9
1925	STL	.354	89	362	128	29	7	11	24
1926	STL	.362	85	370	134	24	7	15	23
1927	STL	.319	93	401	128	18	3	5	13
1928	STL	.332	72	310	103	16	6	4	7
1929	STL	.312	89	359	112	25	6	4	28
1930	STL	.332	62	264	93	17	6	7	15
1931	STL	.322	17	59	19	0	1	0	0
1932	DET/KC	.384	37	138	53	7	3	2	3
1933	PIT	.299	37	137	41	6	6	1	6
1934	PIT	.317	50	199	63	4	1	1	8
1935	PIT	.341	53	214	73	7	8	1	4
1936	PIT	.268	21	82	22	1	1	0	1
1942	CHI	.370	14	73	27	3	0	0	0
1943	WAS	.356	44	163	58	4	4	0	10
1944	WAS	.379	51	206	78	10	2	1	10
1945	WAS	.298	48	188	56	8	3	1	10
1946	WAS	.429	25	77	33	1	1	0	2
TOTAL		.338	1002	3952	1335	203	68	56	173

CHI: Chicago Giants; DET: Detroit Wolves; KC: Kansas City Monarchs; PIT: Pittsburgh Crawfords; STL: St. Louis Stars; WAS: Washington Homestead Grays.

measure their skills against those of white players when exhibition teams of players from the Major Leagues, often organized by star players, came south. Bell accumulated impressive statistics in the Latin American leagues as well. According to Negro League player Buck Leonard, as quoted in *Black Diamond*, "He was a hero down there. He did so well, a lot of the boys thought they'd take a look for themselves."

When Bell came back to the United Sates in 1942 he joined the Chicago American Giants. The following year he began a rewarding stint with the Homestead Grays. With Bell in centerfield, the Grays twice won the World Series championship against the Birmingham Black Barons, in 1943 and 1944. At age forty-three, Bell retired from professional baseball. For a short time he played semiprofessional baseball with the independent Detroit Senators. Then in 1948 he hired on to coach the B team of the Kansas City Monarchs (also called the Kansas City Stars or Travelers). Thus Bell passed on his knowledge to future generations of players, some of whom (such as **Ernie Banks**) would eventually join integrated Major League Baseball teams after Jackie Robinson broke the color barrier in 1947.

Inducted into Hall of Fame

After retiring from baseball, Bell received offers to play with Major League teams, but he declined them. "I got letters from everybody, every team," Bell told *Associated Press* reporter R.B. Fallstrom. "I said, 'I'm through.' I broke every record there was and I still could hit but my legs were gone. I used them up." Bell worked at St. Louis City Hall as a custodian and security guard for twenty-one years and he and his wife lived on Cool Papa Bell Av-

enue in north St. Louis for more than thirty-five years. There the Bells kept a collection of Negro league memorabilia and Cool Papa was happy to regale visitors with stories of old-time baseball. In 1974 Bell was inducted into the Major League Baseball Hall of Fame, one of the first players to be so honored in a belated effort to recognize the ability of deserving Negro league players. "Contemporaries rated him the fastest man on the base paths," reads Bell's plaque in the Hall of Fame. Indeed. Bell once explained that in a match-up against Olympic sprinter **Jesse Owens**, Owens could win the straight one-hundred yard dash, but it was he, Bell, who was the faster rounding the bases. Once the two sprinters were supposed to race between games of a doubleheader in Cleveland, Ohio, but when the time came, Owens declined. "He said he left his track shoes at home," Bell said in a video clip at the Major League Baseball Web site. "I didn't have any track shoes." When Bell learned that he was to be inducted into the Hall of Fame, he said that his election was his highest honor, but his biggest thrill "was when they opened the door in the majors to black players," wrote Robert McG. Thomas, Jr. of the *New York Times*.

In his later years, Bell suffered from glaucoma. Clara preceded him in death on January 20, 1991, and Bell suffered a heart attack in February and passed away at University Hospital in St. Louis on March 7. He was interred at St. Peter's Cemetery in St. Louis. Yet Bell's feats linger still. In 1996, to commemorate the seventy-fifth anniversary of Negro league baseball, Bell and two other Hall of Fame players from the Negro leagues were featured on limited edition boxes of Wheaties cereal and on "historic" baseball trading cards. Many baseball fans were pleased to see even such late recognition. For his part, the unassuming Bell had simply played the game he loved within the confines society placed on him. "When I was young, all I wanted to do was play," Bell is quoted as saying by Dixon. "And, thank the Lord, I got the chance to play for half my life, even if it wasn't in the majors. ... I didn't think about major league baseball. It wasn't just baseball then; it was everywhere. I don't feel regrets. That's how it was when I was born. I had to live in that time."

FURTHER INFORMATION

Books

Clark, Dick and Larry Lester, Eds. *The Negro Leagues Book*. Birmington, AL: Society for American Baseball Research/EBSCO Media, 1994.

Dixon, Phil with Patrick J. Hannigan. *The Negro Baseball Leagues: A Photographic History*. Mattituck, NY: Amereon House, 1992.

Gardner, Robert and Dennis Shortelle. *The Forgotten Players: The Story of Black Baseball in America*. New York: Walker & Company, 1993.

Holway, John. *The Complete Book of Baseball's Negro Leagues: The Other Half of Baseball History*. Fern Park, FL: Hastings House Publishers, 2001.

Holway, John B. *Blackball Stars: Negro League Pioneers*. New York: Carroll & Graf, 1988.

Holway, John B. *Voices from the Great Black Baseball Leagues*. New York: Dodd, Mead, 1975.

Kelley, Brent. *Voices from the Negro Leagues: Conversations with Fifty-two Baseball Standouts of the Period 1924-1960*. Jefferson, NC: McFarland & Company, 1998.

McKissack, Patricia C. and Frederick McKissack, Jr. *Black Diamond: The Story of the Negro Baseball Leagues*. New York: Scholastic, 1994.

McNeil, William F. *Baseball's Other All-Stars: The Greatest Players from the Negro Leagues, the Japanese Leagues, the Mexican League, and the Pre-1960 Winter Leagues in Cuba, Puerto Rico and the Dominican Republic*. Jefferson, NC: McFarland & Company, 2000.

McNeil, William F. *Cool Papas and Double Duties: The All-Time Greats of the Negro Leagues*. Jefferson, NC: McFarland & Company, 2001.

Ribowsky, Mark. *A Complete History of the Negro Leagues, 1884-1955*. New York: Birch Lane Press, 1995.

Periodicals

Banks, James. "Flying Feet: The Life and Times of Cool Papa Bell, the Fastest Runner Baseball Has." *Baseball History* (fall, 1996).

Fallstrom, R.B. "James 'Cool Papa' Bell Takes Things as They Come." *Associated Press* (February 10, 1990).

Fallstrom, R.B., "Cool Papa Bell." *Associated Press* (March 8, 1991).

"James 'Cool Papa' Bell Still Keeps Cool at 86." *Jet* (March 5, 1990): 48.

"Profiles of Prominent Negro-Leaguers: James 'Cool Papa' Bell." *St. Louis Post-Dispatch* (February 4, 2001): D10.

Rhoden, William C. "Cool Papa's Legacy Lives with a Statue in St. Louis." *New York Times* (September 17, 2001): C18.

Thomas, Robert McC., Jr. "James (Cool Papa) Bell, 87, Dies; Legendary Star of the Negro Leagues." *New York Times* (March 9, 1991): 11.

Other

"Speed to Burn: Bell Was the Fastest Player Ever." Major League Baseball. http://www.MLB.com/ (October 1, 2002).

Sketch by J. Lesinski

Albert Belle
1966-

American baseball player

Albert Belle, known for his outstanding power as a hitter, is also one of baseball's most enigmatic characters. S.L. Price, writing in *Sports Illustrated*,

Albert Belle

Chronology

1966	Born August 25 in Shreveport, LA
1984	Begins playing for Louisiana State University
1987	Benched for College World Series for attacking spectator
1987	Drafted by Cleveland Indians in second round
1989	Plays first major-league game in July
1990	Checks into Cleveland Clinic for drinking problem
1991	Suspended for throwing ball at fan
1992	First full season in major leagues
1994	Suspended after being charged with using a corked bat
1995	Sets record as first major leaguer to have 50 home runs and 50 RBIs in one season
1995	Leads Indians to the World Series
1995	Lashes out at the media before game, fined $50,000
1995	Starts in All-Star game
1996	Signs 5-year, $55 million contract with Chicago White Sox
1997	Faces civil suit for gambling on football and basketball
1998	Signs 5-year, $65 million contract with Baltimore Orioles
2001	Permanently injures hip

called Belle "the game's most dependable and unpredictable talent." While Belle's talent is undeniable—his career batting average is .295—he is known for his quick temper and his impatience with both the media and his many fans. Belle's hot-headedness is speculated to have been the source of his drive in the game, but that same quality cost him numerous suspensions and his chance at the Most Valuable Player Award.

"Joey Belle"

Albert Jojuan Belle was born on August 25, 1966 in Shreveport, Louisiana. Growing up, Belle's family, friends, and coaches called him "Joey," a shortened version of his middle name. Belle's family lived in a middle-class section of Shreveport, and his parents were both educators. Albert, Belle's father, was a high school football coach and a teacher; Belle's mother Carrie was a math teacher. Both parents, but particularly Carrie, pushed Belle to succeed in everything he did. This was a lesson Belle would take with him into adulthood, as he continued to set high standards for himself.

Belle's twin brother, Terry, stayed by Belle's side throughout career. A businessman, Terry assisted Belle with public relations and his relationship with the media.

Belle was an outstanding figure in high school. He was an Eagle Scout, a regular attendee of the Galilee Baptist Church, and an all-state baseball player. Belle was also a high achiever as a student, graduating sixth in

his class of 266 at Huntington High. Belle even took college courses in high school, learning computer programming languages. But as early as high school, Belle's temperament was a problem: the outstanding athlete would have fits when he didn't perform at his best, throwing bats, balls, helmets.

Belle and his family hoped for a minor league contract right out of high school, but no offers were forthcoming. The most prestigious college teams overlooked him, too; while his talent was indisputable, Belle's attitude was problematic. He did get an offer to attend Louisiana State University and play for the LSU Tigers; brother Terry was drafted along with Belle. Belle excelled as a Tiger, setting university records in seven categories (including home runs and runs batted in). He was twice named to the All-Southeast Conference. But Belle also had some setbacks in college: one incident involved a spectator yelling a racial slur; Belle dove into the stands trying to identify the man, and teammates had to tackle him. He was benched for the 1987 College World Series because of his temper.

Drafted to the Big Leagues

Belle finally got his break after his junior year in college in the second round of the 1987 draft. Several teams refused to consider Belle in any round based on his temperament, but the Cleveland Indians picked him up. He started with the Indians' minors team, and played his first major league game in July 1989. That game was a stunning success for Belle: he got a hit at his first at-bat, and hit a grand slam against the Yankees. Belle did have some trouble during those first years with the Indians, though, and was demoted to the minors a few times following outbursts.

"Snapper"

Belle's temper earned him the nickname "Snapper" among his teammates. In one incident, Belle used a bat

Career Statistics

Yr	Team	AVG	GP	AB	R	H	HR	RBI	BB	SO	SB
1989	CLE	.225	62	218	22	49	7	37	12	55	2
1990	CLE	.174	9	23	1	4	1	3	1	6	0
1991	CLE	.282	123	461	60	130	28	95	25	99	3
1992	CLE	.260	153	585	81	152	34	112	52	128	8
1993	CLE	.290	159	594	93	172	38	129	76	96	23
1994	CLE	.357	106	412	90	147	36	101	58	71	9
1995	CLE	.317	143	546	121	173	50	126	73	80	5
1996	CLE	.311	158	602	124	187	48	148	99	87	11
1997	CHW	.274	161	634	90	174	30	116	53	105	4
1998	CHW	.328	163	609	113	200	49	152	81	84	6
1999	BAL	.297	161	610	108	181	37	117	101	82	17
2000	BAL	.281	141	559	71	157	23	103	52	68	0
TOTAL		.295	1539	5853	974	1726	381	1239	683	961	88

BAL: Baltimore Orioles; CHW: Chicago White Sox; CLE: Cleveland Indians.

to destroy a porcelain sink in the clubhouse; his temper was out of control. Belle later reflected to *Sports Illustrated*, "I was sure I'd be a superstar by the time I was 21 . When I fail, I get upset. Sometimes I get upset too quickly, without thinking of the consequences."

In 1990, Belle checked himself into the Cleveland Clinic for help with a drinking problem. After a two-month leave, Belle issued a statement indicating he had received the help he needed. He signed this statement "Albert Belle," perhaps reflecting a new, more mature identity than the old "Joey."

Outstanding Hitter

During his time with the Indians, Belle consistently was one of the leaders in the American League in home runs and runs batted in (RBI). While his temper and his refusals to talk with the press were still problematic, he became one of Cleveland's most popular players, and even had a candy bar named after him. He played in two All-Star games, and despite several suspensions, amassed an impressive record. General manager John Hart was one of Belle's most committed supporters. He commented to the *New York Times*, "He is a folk hero. We brought him up. He struggled as a young player. They've [the fans have] seen him mature as a human being. Albert does more community things behind the scenes than anyone we have. The community just threw themselves behind him."

In 1995, Belle's power at bat led the team through a phenomenal season. Belle himself hit 50 home runs and had 52 doubles becoming the first major league player to top 50 in both categories in one season. Enjoying tremendous fan support and their new stadium, the Indians went to the World Series for the first time since 1954. The Indians lost that series to the Atlanta Braves, but Belle emerged from the 1995 season a hero. While he lost the Most Valuable Player award that year to **Mo**

Vaughn (members of the press vote on this award), Belle's fans voted him to start in the All-Star game for the first time.

In 1996, Belle signed a five-year, $55 million contract to play for the Chicago White Sox. This briefly made him the highest paid baseball player of all time, and certainly proved his status as one of the best players in the game. Belle used the team change as another chance for him to change his pattern of angry outbursts; the press, though, was not willing to let go of Belle's "bad boy" image. In 1997, Belle was in the spotlight for gambling on football, basketball, and, some alleged, baseball. He was also accused of hitting ex-girlfriend Stephanie Bugusky, but all charges in this matter were dropped.

In December 1998, Belle signed a 5-year contract with the Baltimore Orioles worth $65 million dollars. He jumped on another opportunity to change his image, and even began signing autographs and speaking with the press. Belle's reinvention of himself was cut short, though. An inflamed bursa sac in his right hip made 2001 a grueling season for Belle, and he sat out the 2002 season with what appears to be a permanent injury.

Bad Boy Reputation

Although he was loved by teammates and fans alike, throughout his career Belle maintained the reputation of a hot-head. He seemed to need this anger to propel him to perform, and former teammates and coaches have talked about waiting for Belle to get angry so that he would begin a hitting streak. Like **Ty Cobb** before him, Belle was one of baseball's bad boys, and his image is tainted with stories of corked bats, accosting journalists, and even running down Halloween trick-or-treaters with his truck. Belle's unflinching quest for perfection had the paradoxical effect of making him one of the game's best players and one of its most troubled, and troubling, characters.

Awards and Accomplishments

1987	Sets school records at LSU in 7 offensive categories
1993	Selected to the American League All-Star Squad
1993-95, 1998	Silver Slugger Award
1993-94	Nominee for Roberto Clemente Award
1994	Nominee for Branch Rickey Award
1994	Elected to All-Star Team
1994	Season batting average was .357, career high
1995	First Major League player to collect 50 HR and 50 2R in a season
1995	Named "Major League Player of the Year" by *Sporting News* and *Baseball Digest*
1995	Played in World Series
1995	Started in All-Star game
1996-97	Named to All-Star team

The Roberto Clemente and Branch Rickey awards are for community service.

CONTACT INFORMATION

Address: Albert Belle, Baltimore Orioles, Oriole Park at Camden Yards, 333 West Camden St., Baltimore, MD 21201. Phone: (410) 685-9800.

FURTHER INFORMATION

Periodicals

Bamberger, Michael. "He Thrives on Anger," *Sports Illustrated* (May 6, 1996): 72-82.

Bodley, Hal. "Orioles stockpiling millions for rebuilding," *USA Today* (June 22, 2001): C7.

Chass, Murray. "Belle is all business, on and off the field." *New York Times* (July 29, 1994): B9.

Leavy, Walter. "Albert Belle: A new beginning for baseball's $55 million man." *Ebony* (May 1997): 28-32.

Nightengale, Bob. "Belle is the Victim Now: You Can Bet on That." *Sporting News* (February 24, 1997): 36.

Price, S.L. "The Belle of Baltimore." *Sports Illustrated* (March 8, 1999): 48-49.

Weinstock, Jeff. "Get Smart About Dennis Rodman vs. Albert Belle." *Sport* (January 1997): 22.

Sketch by Christine M. Kelley

Johnny Bench
1947-

American baseball player

The name Johnny Bench is synonymous with baseball catcher. When Bench came on the Major League Baseball scene in 1968 with the Cincinnati Reds, he be-

Johnny Bench

came the first catcher ever to win the National League Rookie of the Year award by showing fans what a good catcher can be both behind the plate and at bat. With his keen eyesight, strong throwing arm, great agility, and savvy working relationship with pitchers, Bench was a defensive force who set records for playing a hundred or more games in thirteen consecutive seasons. Although he developed new catching and throwing postures that made him very effective and helped prevent injury, he still played with injuries to his feet, hands, and back. On the other side of the plate, cleanup hitter Bench could muscle the ball into the outfield and over the fence. Bench finished his career with a then record (for a catcher) 389 home runs. All told, Bench was a pivotal cog in the workings of what became known as Cincinnati's Big Red Machine.

Growing Up

Johnny Lee Bench was born on December 7, 1947, in Oklahoma City, Oklahoma, and raised nearby in the small town of Binger. With his father, a truck driver and one-time semiprofessional baseball player, homemaker mother, two older brothers and a younger sister, Bench formed a close-knit family. Like many boys around Binger, he picked cotton, delivered newspapers, and played sandlot baseball. Unlike the other boys, though, Bench consistently expressed his desire to play ball professionally, a revelation that earned guffaws from his classmates. Yet his father took him seriously. He coached and financially supported Binger's Little League team for several years. The Bench family liked to watch "Game of the Week" on Saturdays. Johnny listened to players give tips and dreamed about being a professional ballplayer like Oklahoma native **Mickey Mantle**.

Bench was a serious student, earning good grades in high school, and he played both baseball and basketball, for a time preferring basketball. He had big hands and feet, and was able to palm a basketball or hold seven baseballs in one hand. As a teen, hefting 100-pound bags of peanuts onto trucks built up his muscles without needing a weight room. Bench was known as a fastball pitcher, but he also learned the role of catcher as his father advised. "When I wasn't playing I was watching games, just eating and living and breathing sports," Bench recalled in his autobiography, *Catch You Later*. At age fifteen he was competing against boys several years older in American Legion baseball. In 1965 on a return trip from an out-of-town baseball game, the breaks on the Binger Bobcat team bus failed. At an intersection the bus jumped flipped over the rail and rolled down an incline toward a ravine. Bench hit floor and held on to the bottom of the seat. When the bus stopped rolling, his feet were hanging out the back door, and two teammates lay dead on the hill. This event sobered Bench and he attributed to it a reticence in making friends later in life.

Even so, the seventeen-year-old was about to see a dream come true. He was offered college scholarships to play both basketball or baseball—and he was drafted by the Cincinnati Reds organization. Bench played in the minor leagues in Tampa, Florida and the following year played Class A ball in the Carolina League. At this time he started wearing his batting helmet backwards while he caught to protect his head from foul tips and back swings. Unfortunately he couldn't protect his right hand from a foul tip in Buffalo, and his season ended with a broken thumb. While recuperating in Binger, Bench was in a serious automobile accident when a drunk entered the highway on an exit ramp.

Despite being so beaten up, he was ready to play the next spring, and by August of 1967 he was called up to the Cincinnati Reds. Again, this season ended with a split thumb for Bench, who realized that even though he had a great throwing arm, it wasn't any good unless he could handle the ball well. So taking a cue from Cubs receiver Randy Hundley, Bench started hiding his right hand behind him and caught one-handed. "I also creased the catcher's glove diagonally instead of using it like a saucer. That way I could catch more with one hand. My hands are big enough to control the catcher's glove, so the technique was a natural for me," he recalled in his autobiography. By using the batting helmet and the new one-handed technique, Bench was able to spend less time thinking about his safety and more time thinking about the batter, pitcher, and base runners. Bench caught 154 games in 1968, setting a record for a rookie catcher, earning the first of his ten Gold Glove awards, and winning the Rookie of the Year honor.

Chronology	
1947	Born December 7 in Oklahoma City, Oklahoma, to Ted and Katie Bench
1965	Selected during amateur draft by Cincinnati Reds
1966	Plays in Carolina League (minor leagues)
1967-83	Plays catcher for the National League Cincinnati Reds
1983	Bench retires from Major League Baseball
1984-93	Works as broadcaster for CBS Radio

Drives the "Big Red Machine"

During the 1970s the Cincinnati Reds were one of the dominant teams in baseball, reaching the postseason six times and ending their seasons in second place three other years. Bench was an important gear in that machine. Behind the plate, he took charge of the game. Bench made it a point to know well the ability of his pitchers and the favored pitches of the opposing batters. As Bench noted in his autobiography, "A catcher has to learn how to get the best out of a pitcher, to let him be himself, go to his strengths, and yet still be effective." He continued, "I try to get along personally with pitchers, but the most important thing is to somehow get them to have faith in you in not only receiving but calling the pitches."

According to Bench, part of a catcher's role is to "negotiate umpires," that is, tell them when they could do better, but in a respectful way so as not to get thrown out of the game. "I have a guarded respect for them. I live with them every day and we get along," he once said. "I'll argue because it is essential to beef about bad calls. You cannot feel intimidated or threatened by an umpire. He's human and will use his leverage against you. Getting your say, and keeping an umpire thinking is important for the pitcher and everybody else." Because Bench was so effective in calling the pitches, signaling defensive positions to fielders, and dealing with umpires, he earned the moniker "Little General." Even so, when new manager **Sparky Anderson** came on board in 1970, he made **Pete Rose** the team captain, which at first irked the cocky Bench.

Bench's defensive skills awed fans. Photographers snapped pictures of him holding seven baseballs in one hand. Bench made the oversized glove and backwards batting helmet regular parts of catcher apparel. His posture insured that he could quickly adjust to block an otherwise wild pitch and also minimized the motion needed before he could release a throw. Bench was fond of telling how his father had made him practice throwing twice the distance that a catcher would have to throw from home plate to any base. With his powerful arm, he could and often did throw out runners trying to steal. "Everyone marveled at his arm," Anderson recalled in *Sparky*. "It was a cannon but others threw harder. What made him so deadly were his quick feet. He got into position to throw faster than a dancer. If he was in a throwing contest, Bench would have the ball on its way to

Awards and Accomplishments

1967	Named Minor League Player of the Year by *Sporting News*
1968	Named Rookie of the Year by *Sporting News* and Baseball Writers' Association of America
1968-77	Earned ten Gold Glove awards
1968-80	Named to All-Star team fourteen times
1970	Named National League Most Valuable Player and Major League Player of the Year
1972	Named National League Most Valuable Player
1975-76	Cincinnati Reds World Series Champions
1976	World Series Most Valuable Player
1983	Cincinnati Reds establish Johnny Bench Scholarship Fund
1989	Elected to the Baseball Hall of Fame
1996	His No. 5 jersey is retired by the Cincinnati Reds
1998	Named greatest catcher ever by *Sporting News*
1999	Selected by fans to the All-Century team

Catch You Later

Strength alone is no real indicator of anything. You must have the reflexes, the agility, the coordination to go along with it. The Reds were once tested on reflex action and I scored the highest on every exercise. That and the size of my hands have helped me a lot. My strength came, I think, from some of the work I did back in Oklahoma. I still remember throwing 100-pound sacks of peanuts onto the trucks until I was ready to drop. . . .

But there have been a lot of strong catchers who have also been bad ones. It takes a lot more than beef. One thing that never fails to make a catcher look bad is the fact that he has to deal with pitchers. That takes a lot more than big hands and a mask. Pitchers are a breed unto themselves.

A catcher has to learn how to get the best out of a pitcher, to let him be himself, go to his strengths, and yet still be effective. . . .

Source: Johnny Bench (with William Brashler). *Catch You Later: The Autobiography of Johnny Bench,* Harper, 1979, p. 124.

second while the other guys were just cocking their arms." An indicator of his phenomenal defensive skills is this statistic: Bench put out 9,260 runners out of 10,110 chances. For ten years running, Bench won the National League's Gold Glove award. "When we got into a tight game, we never worried about the other team running on us," Anderson revealed. "They had to hit the ball to beat us. Do you realize the edge that gave us over a 162-game season?"

In the lineup Bench rose to the cleanup position, batting fourth or fifth, along with other productive hitters Pete Rose, **Joe Morgan**, Tony Perez, George Foster, and Dave Conception. During the regular season, he was often a slow starter and streaky batter—either he had it or he didn't—but in post-season games his batting average jumped. According to Anderson, "Bench was a catcher with the batting stats of an outfielder. ... He had so much power he looked like a man playing against little boys." Even in their new, more spacious ballpark, Riverfront Stadium, in 1970, Bench hit forty-five home runs and batted in 148 runs, leading the Reds to 102 wins for the season and victory in the National League West by fourteen and a half games—and earning a league Most Valuable Player award. "I had a season I previously only dreamed about," Bench recalled, adding, "It was the kind of year where everything fell in place. I was strong, injury-free, and helping the team in almost every way." Although the Reds swept the Pittsburgh Pirates in the National League playoffs, they lost the World Series to the Baltimore Orioles.

Matures as Player

Bench and the entire team suffered from a slump in 1971, dropping to fourth place in their only losing season of the 1970s. Like all professional athletes, baseball players have to deal with injuries, particularly muscle pulls, strains, and tears from quick sprints, awkward slides, collisions, and getting hit by the ball. Catchers get often get nicked by foul tips and block pitches and throws with their bodies. Bench spent most of the 1971

season playing injured. While his defense was sound, his offense was dismal. Frustrated, he analyzed his batting stance, tried new techniques, changed helmets, and changed grips. Nothing helped. The team heard jokes about the Big Red Machine turning into an Edsel, and the formerly confident Bench searched his soul. He remembered in *Catch You Later,* "Going from MVP to MDP [Most Disappointing Player] was a crucial period for me, the closest thing to anything like an identity crisis kids my age had in college or thereabouts." Yet he suffered through this drought and doubt period

The following year, Bench recovered his hitting power with a vengeance. He led the National League in home runs with forty and runs batted in with 125, earning another league Most Valuable Player award. Ironically, during the last months of the 1972 season, a routine physical turned up a spot on Bench's lung. He kept his condition a secret until the end of the season. He even hit a crucial home run to tie the pivotal game of the league championship series against the Pittsburgh Pirates, which was then won on a run scored from a wild pitch. After the Reds lost the World Series 4 to 3 to Oakland, Bench had what turned out to be a benign tumor removed from his lung. "I was a new man," Bench recalled in *Catch You Later.* "The weight of that September diagnosis had been removed. I had a lot of years left."

Reds Pick Up Steam

During the 1973 and 1974 seasons, the Reds worked their way to the top. In 1973 they overtook the front-running Los Angeles Dodgers in September but lost the Pennant to the New York Mets, 3 to 2. In 1974 they ended the season in second place behind the Dodgers. Then years 1975 and 1976 were stellar for the Reds as they won back-to-back world titles. However, Bench suffered a shoulder injury in mid-April when a player collided with him at home plate. Even though he had severely damaged cartilage at the top of his shoulder, Bench played hurt until the end of the season. The Reds

Career Statistics

Yr	Team	AVG	GP	AB	R	H	HR	RBI	BB	SO	SB
1967	CIN	.163	26	86	7	14	1	6	5	19	0
1968	CIN	.275	154	564	67	155	15	82	31	96	1
1969	CIN	.293	148	532	83	156	26	90	49	86	6
1970	CIN	.293	158	605	97	177	45	148	54	102	5
1971	CIN	.238	149	562	80	134	27	61	49	83	2
1972	CIN	.270	147	538	87	145	40	125	100	84	6
1973	CIN	.253	152	557	83	141	25	104	83	83	4
1974	CIN	.280	160	621	108	174	33	129	80	90	5
1975	CIN	.283	142	530	83	150	28	110	65	108	11
1976	CIN	.234	135	465	62	109	16	74	81	95	13
1977	CIN	.275	142	494	67	136	31	109	58	95	2
1978	CIN	.260	120	393	52	102	23	73	50	83	4
1979	CIN	.276	130	464	73	128	22	80	67	73	4
1980	CIN	.250	114	360	52	90	24	68	41	64	4
1981	CIN	.309	2	178	14	55	8	25	17	21	0
1982	CIN	.258	119	399	44	103	13	38	37	58	1
1983	CIN	.255	110	310	32	79	12	54	24	38	0
TOTAL		.267	2158	7658	1091	2048	389	1376	891	1278	68

CIN: Cincinnati Reds.

ended the 1975 season with 108 wins and a winning margin of twenty games, a club record. In the post-season the Big Red Machine beat the Pittsburgh Pirates in three games to win the National League Pennant and triumphed over the Boston Red Sox in seven games to win the World Series. It was the Reds' first world title in thirty-five years and the third in franchise history. Yet, while winning the world title was satisfying for Bench, his several painful injuries hurt his performance, particularly at the plate, and made him question the wisdom of playing hurt. "I came to realize that the Iron Man philosophy is filled with holes, that today's injured hero doesn't play tomorrow. The body must be understood and catered to. In pro sports, it's all you really have," he explained in his autobiography. After this experience, he determined that he'd no longer play injured.

In 1976 the Reds won 108 games in the regular season. Then they won seven consecutive games in the playoffs and World Series—against Philadelphia, and the New York Yankees. The Reds became the only team in history to sweep the playoffs and World Series. Plagued with muscle spasms in his back, Bench had an off year during the regular season, batting only .234. Yet after discovering that the spasms were linked to a deficiency in potassium, he began taking salt tablets. His performance improved by September and during the National League playoffs and the World Series he rose to the occasion. All told, during the playoffs he batted .333. In the World Series, he went eight for fifteen, with four extra base hits, two of which were home runs, earning six RBIs in four games. Longtime Reds skipper Sparky Anderson has more than once called Bench the best catcher in the business. "Bench was the greatest catcher that ever lived," Anderson wrote in *Sparky*. "No one ever played his position better than he did. He also delivered key hits all the time."

Winding Down

Of all the positions in baseball, the catcher's is the most physically demanding, so their longevity is limited. Bench suffered from various injuries throughout his career. "I had 15, 16 broken bones and seven broken cups," he once told a *Houston Chronicle* reporter. In 1978 Bench suffered another back injury at home plate and a few days later broke a bone in his foot. For several years, he played in constant pain and his numbers showed it. The team's fortunes dimmed too as key players became free agents and left the team. In 1981 Bench asked to be moved to another position. For awhile he played first base, then third. Finally, when the Reds finished in last place in 1983, the Big Red Machine ground to a halt and Bench retired.

Can't Take the Game Outta the Man

Although Bench retired from Major League baseball, the sport has continued to be an important part of his life. Over the years he has appeared on numerous television programs for the ESPN and Fox Sports networks. For nine years he worked for CBS Radio, broadcasting the National Game of the Week, the All-Star Game, and the League Championship Series. He has also served as a consultant to the Reds, when their catchers need help with their technique. He is the longtime spokesman for Cincinnati-based Fifth Third Bank and national retailer S&K Menswear. Using his celebrity status to help others, Bench has also often supported medical causes, such as the Heart Association, the American Cancer Society's Athletes vs. Cancer, the Kidney Foundation, and

Johnny Bench

the American Lung Association. The Johnny Bench Scholarship Fund, which was instituted by the Reds in 1983 to honor Bench's contributions to the team, supports scholar-athletes from Binger, Oklahoma, and from Southwestern Ohio.

In 1989, on the first ballot in which he was eligible, Johnny Bench was elected to the Baseball Hall of Fame. When Bench was a rookie, he had gotten a baseball signed by the famed hitter **Ted Williams**. "To Johnny Bench, a Hall of Famer for sure." Williams didn't need a crystal ball to make this prediction—he knew talent when he saw it. Bench's plaque in the Hall of Fame succinctly summarizes his achievements: "Johnny Lee Bench, Cincinnati. N.L., 1967-1983, redefined standards by which catchers are measured during 17 seasons with 'Big Red Machine.' Controlled game on both sides of plate with his hitting (389 homers—record 327 as a catcher, 1,376 RBI's), throwing out opposing base runners, calling pitches and blocking home plate. N.L. MVP, 1970 and 1972. Won 10 Gold Gloves. Last game, 9th inning homer led to 1972 Pennant."

Bench likes to share the secrets of his success. As a public speaker, he promotes the formula for success that has worked so well for him on and off the ball field, which he calls the Vowels of Success: "A is the ATTITUDE that you have to have. The attitude you take to your job. E is the EFFORT and the ENERGY that you have to put into something. You know it really is not that hard to give somebody an honest effort. I is for you as

an INDIVIDUAL. Each individual has to have their own responsibility. Even as individuals, we must work together as a team. O is the OPPORTUNITY. The opportunities that will come your way. U is the YOU. You are very special and you always have to treat yourself that way." Bench honed his natural talent through hard work and took advantage of the opportunities that came along, in the process becoming the best catcher of his time and making innovations in catching technique that have served other receivers well to this day.

CONTACT INFORMATION

Address: Johnny Bench, P.O. Box 5377, Cincinnati, OH 45201.

SELECTED WRITINGS BY BENCH:

From Behind the Plate, Prentice-Hall, 1972.
Catching and Power Hitting, Viking, 1975.
(With William Brashler) *Catch You Later: The Autobiography of Johnny Bench,* Harper, 1979.
(With Larry Burke) *The Complete Idiot's Guide to Baseball,* Alpha Books, 1999.
(With Rich Pilling and Paul Cunningham) *Major League Baseball's Best Shots,* Dorling Kindersley, 2000.

FURTHER INFORMATION

Books

Anderson, Sparky, with Dan Ewald. *Sparky!* New York: Prentice-Hall, 1990.
Bench, Johnny, and William Brashler. *Catch You Later: The Autobiography of Johnny Bench.* New York: Harper, 1979.
Owens, Thomas S. *Great Catchers.* New York: Metro Books, 1997.
Rhodes, Greg, and John Erardi. *Big Red Dynasty.* Cincinnati: Road West Publishing, 1997.
Vancil, Mark, and Peter Hirdt, editors. *The All-Century Team.* Chicago: Rare Air Books, 1999.

Other

Baseball Hall of Fame. http://baseballhalloffame.org/ (October 10, 2002).
JohnnyBench.com. http://johnnybench.com/ (October 10, 2002).

"Johnny Bench Bibliography." Baseball Library. http://www.baseballLibrary.com/ (October 10, 2002).

Major League Baseball. *World Series Videos: 1970: Baltimore 4, Cincinnati 1; 1972: Oakland 4, Cincinnati 3; 1975: Cincinnati 4, Boston 3; 1976: Cincinnati 4, NY (AL) 0.*

"Player Pages: Johnny Bench." The Baseball Page. http://www.thebaseballpage.com/ (October 10, 2002).

Sketch by Jeanne Lesinski

Joan Benoit Samuelson

Joan Benoit Samuelson
1957-

American marathon runner

Distance runner Joan Benoit Samuelson broke the female course record for the Boston Marathon in 1979, then went on to set a record for both the historic New England race and the world in 1983 by running the 26.2-mile marathon distance in a record two hours 22 minutes, 43 seconds. Samuelson's other achievements, including winning the gold medal as part of the U.S. team in the 1984 Summer Olympics in Los Angeles, California, have caused many to consider her perhaps the greatest female marathoner of the twentieth century.

A Born Athlete

Samuelson was born Joan Benoit on May 16, 1957, in Cape Elizabeth, Maine. Although women athletes were almost unheard of during Samuelson's childhood, the athletic Samuelson excelled at sports, particularly skiing, and showed herself to be a fearless competitor. After breaking her leg during a slalom race at age fifteen, she was encouraged to incorporate running as part of her rehabilitation program. Surprisingly, running quickly replaced skiing as the young Samuelson's passion, and after the passage of Title IX opened up more athletic opportunities for U.S. public school students in 1972 she became a star on her high school's newly formed girls' track team. Despite her obvious talent for running the mile, Samuelson recognized that off the track a girl runner might not be accepted by everyone in her community. As she recalled in an interview with *Runner's World,* on long training runs along the roads near her small town, "I'd walk when cars passed me. I'd pretend I was looking at the flowers."

The five-foot-three-inch, 105-pound Samuelson eventually got over her fear of running in public; as she told *Runner's World,* she was inspired by a college friend she saw running by on the road one day. "From that point on I decided I didn't care what other people thought. I decided that if I believe in myself, and I'm happy doing what I'm doing, I'm going to go for it." With little outside coaching assistance, she began an intensive training regime, and began to build her running base from short 5K and 10K races to include the long runs that would prepare her to not only run but race the grueling 26.2-mile marathon distance. Like most marathoners, Samuelson incorporated several runs of 20 or more miles into her weekly regime, and logged as many as 200 miles a week while at the height of her training.

Samuelson's first encounter with the historic Boston Marathon came in April of 1979, as she made a two-mile cross-country sprint to the starting line in Hopkinton, Massachusetts after becoming stuck in the traditional traffic jam outside of town. Although she started in the back of the pack, by mile 19 Samuelson had gained the lead and had mastered the most challenging parts of the course; she crossed the finish line in two hours, 35 minutes, and 15 seconds to set a women's course record.

After her spectacular debut at Boston, Samuelson returned to Maine to finish out her senior year at Bowdoin College. Now somewhat of a celebrity due to her accomplishment in Boston, the shy twenty-something Samuelson found herself drawing the unwanted attention of everyone from race directors wishing to feature her in their starting lineups to manufacturers requesting her endorsement of their running-related product. Avoiding

Chronology

1957	Born in Cape Elizabeth, Maine
1972	Begins running while recovering from a skiing accident
1979	Sets women's record in her first Boston Marathon.
1979	Graduates from Bowdoin College.
1981-84	Coaches Boston University women distance runners.
1983	Set women's world record of 2:22:43 at Boston Marathon.
1984	Set women's world record for marathon at Olympic Games.
1984	Marries Bowdoin graduate Scott Samuelson.
1987	Runs Boston Marathon while three months pregnant with first child.
1989	Finishes ninth among women runners at Boston Marathon.
1991	Finishes fourth among women runners at Boston Marathon.
1991	Diagnosed with asthma.
1996	Places 13th at 1996 Olympic Trials.

Awards and Accomplishments

1979	Breaks women's record during first-place win at Boston Marathon.
1984	First place in U.S. women's Olympic marathon trials.
1984	Gold medal for record-breaking finish at women's marathon, Summer Olympics.
1984	Named among *Ms.* magazine's women of the year.
1984	Co-recipient, Women's Sports Foundation amateur sportswoman of the year award.
1985	Vitalis Award for sports excellence.
1985	Clocks record time of 2:21:21 at Chicago's America's Marathon.
1986	Sullivan Award for best amateur athlete in the United States from Amateur Athletic Union.
1994	2:37:09 finish at Chicago Marathon qualifies her for Olympic trials.
2000	Places in top ten in Olympic Trials, her 25th career marathon.

such attention, she disappeared onto the roads around her house and logged more miles training for New England races of a variety of distances and terrains. The punishing training required for Samuelson to race distance well—which included logging many miles per week and sustaining a race pace of six minutes per mile during runs of up to three or more hours—eventually took its toll, and in 1981 she was forced to have surgery on both Achilles tendons to cure her chronic heel pain. Ignoring her physician's advice to take time off from her training to recover, Samuelson showed her determination to excel at her sport: within a month of her surgery she was back on the roads running distance. In the fall of 1982 she won a New England marathon in 2:26:11, breaking the record for U.S. women by almost two minutes.

For three years beginning in 1981, Samuelson supplemented her training by working as women's long-distance coach at Boston University, taking time out in 1983 to once again compete in Boston's historic race. Unlike her previous performance in 1979, she arrived in Hopkinton in plenty of time to warm up and after the gun she took the women's lead of the Boston Marathon quickly. At five miles Samuelson was one minute ahead of her closest female competitor, Allison Roe, who was favored to win. Unfortunately, leg cramps forced Roe to drop out at mile 17, allowing Samuelson some breathing room. Slowing her pace near mile 20, she maintained her lead to clock a finishing time of 2:22:43, shattering the world's record by two minutes and 47 seconds.

Nineteen eight-four proved to be a banner year for women's distance running: it was the first year a women's marathon would be included at the Olympic Summer Games scheduled for 1984 in Los Angeles, California. Samuelson's record-breaking finishing time at Boston in April of 1983 more than qualified her for the marathon trials scheduled for May 12, 1984, in Olympia, Washington Samuelson was thrilled at the opportunity to participate in the world games. She returned to her home state of Maine to train for the trials,

avoiding all but a few interviewers and spending hours running the back roads near her home. "One of the things I like best about Maine," she disclosed to *Runner's World,* "is that I'm no big deal up here. No one bats an eyelash. They accept me for who I am and not what I've accomplished."

To qualify for the Olympic marathon Samuelson would have to finish in the top three at the trials, no easy task considering that she would be competing against the world's fastest women. Her training went well until mid-March when her right knee became injured during a 20-mile training run. By mid-April it had become clear that the injury was one that would require surgery, and on April 25 Samuelson underwent arthroscopic surgery on her right knee. When she hobbled from the operating room that day her Olympic aspirations seemed all but futile to many in the press: after all, just 17 days remained until the trials, and Samuelson's injury had totally derailed her training program.

While many in the running world bemoaned Samuelson's likely inability to qualify for the Olympic Summer Games in the wake of such an invasive surgical procedure, they didn't factor in the runner's resolve. With less than three weeks available to regain her former strength, Samuelson focused on rebuilding her speed and endurance. Four days after surgery she was once again running, and was able to complete 17 miles by May 3. Such ambitious training proved harmful; two days after this long run Samuelson was in too much pain to run, having developed a muscle pull in her left leg due to her tendency to compensate for the instability of her right knee. Despite the pain, she was soon out on the roads again, and stood proudly among the Olympic's women's marathon trials starting line-up on race day, May 17th.

By mile two of the 1984 Olympic trials Samuelson was already fighting for the lead, and had gained the frontrunner position by mile 17. Through an outstanding effort she finished first with a time of 2:31:04, one of the

The Marathon's Maine Woman

At the gun Benoit bolted out with reckless swiftness. . .

She led by a minute at five miles, which she reached so quickly that race officials missed her completely. At 10 miles her time was 51:38, shattering her American record at that distance by a gaudy minute and 40 seconds. Noting her pace, an experienced male runner near Benoit had already told her, "You better watch it, lady."

Source: *Sports Illustrated,* May 2, 1983: 54.

Joan Benoit Samuelson

most stunning athletic achievements many running enthusiasts could recall. Samuelson now found herself embarking on a new training program in preparation for her trip to the Los Angeles Olympics. She trained throughout the Maine summer, conditioning herself to run efficiently during the hottest part of the day in preparation for an August 5th race. Her most formidable challenge was going up against Norwegian runner **Grete Waitz**, who had never lost a competitive marathon.

When the starting gun of the Olympic Summer Games women's marathon went off on August 5, 1984, Samuelson set out to win the gold. Taking a fast pace, she had wrestled the front spot from the rest of the pack by mile three. Keeping ahead of Waitz, the Maine runner kept an easy lead while the rest of the pack, including Waitz, drafted behind her waiting for Samuelson's injury to her knee to cause her to crumple to the ground. However, Samuelson had found her groove, and with enough reserve energy to make a strong "kick" at the finish line, she broke the tape in the Olympic Coliseum in 2:24:52—the third-fastest marathon finish ever for a woman runner. Waitz crossed the finish line a minute and a half later for the silver, while Portuguese runner Rosa Mota followed for the bronze.

The victorious Samuelson married her college sweetheart the September after returning home from Los Angeles. A year after her Olympic victory she went on to run a record-breaking America's Marathon in Chicago, clocking a record time of 2:21:21 and defeating top runners Mota and Ingrid Kristiansen. In 1987 she returned to Boston, losing first place to Mota but logging an incredible time for a woman three months' pregnant with her first child. Samuelson's continued appearance on the starting line at the Boston Marathon, as well as her ability to qualify for the Olympic trials in both 1996 and 2000—at age forty, now a master's runner—maintained her high profile and her status as a legend and a role model among women runners of all ages. Her qualifying time at the 1996 Olympic trials—2:36:54—put her in 13th place, itself an indication of how strong the field of women runners had become in the decade since Samuelson first ran in Boston. Despite the many setbacks that dogged her athletic career—ankle and knee surgery in the 1980s, two pregnancies, and then a diagnosis of asthma in 1991—Samuelson

has continued to exemplify the qualities that make a true athlete: perseverance and determination. "I see myself as having a responsibility to lead as strong a life as I possibly can," she told *Runner's World.* "In my life as a role model, I try to lead as good and clean a life as I can, so that children out there can aspire to do the things I've been able to do."

Although never comfortable as a media celebrity, Samuelson used her high profile as an Olympic gold-medalist and world-class distance runner to benefit several charities, including the Special Olympics, Multiple Sclerosis, and the Big Sisters of Boston. Married to fellow Bowdoin graduate Scott Samuelson in 1984, she decided to race more selectively after deciding to start a family. "If I'm not ready, I won't run," she told a contributor to the *New York Times.* Her running career since the late 1980s has indeed been redefined by motherhood. As she told *Runner's World* interviewer Amby Burfoot, "Motherhood is the hardest marathon but also the most rewarding marathon I have ever run. It never stops, whereas 26 miles has a beginning and an end."

As she has for most of her career, Samuelson often runs solo, particularly during long runs, and continues to log an average of more than 100 miles per week around Freeport, Maine, including distance training runs of 15 and 20 miles at a time. In addition to being a devoted mother, her hobbies include lobstering, skiing, stamp collecting, knitting, sewing, and canning preserves.

CONTACT INFORMATION

Address: c/o Roadrunner's Club of America, 1150 South Washington St., Suite 205, Alexandria, VA 22314-4493.

FURTHER INFORMATION

Periodicals

Boston Globe, December 6, 1999: D2.

Ms., January, 1985.

New York Times, April 20, 1983; April 25, 1984; August 7, 1984; February 7, 1985; April 27, 1986;

Runner's World, July, 1983; March, 1984; May, 1988; December, 1991; February, 1992; February, 1996; September, 2000.

Sports Illustrated, May 2, 1983; June 27, 1983; August 13, 1984; December 3, 1984; April 29, 1985; June 10, 1985; July 4, 1988.

Time, May 7, 1984; July 30, 1984; August 20, 1984.

Other

Women in Sports, http://www.makeithappen.com/wis/ (January 15, 2003).

Ultramarathon World, http://www.ultramarathonworld. com (February 26, 2000).

Sketch by Pamela L. Shelton

Senda Berenson Abbott
1868-1954

American physical education teacher

Known as the mother of women's basketball, Senda Berenson Abbott, in 1893, recognized the potential of the sport for women. An advocate of physical education for women and a physical education teacher at Smith College in Northampton, Massachusetts, she re-

vised the rules the men played by. Her modifications to the rules were meant to shield her female students from overexertion and the competitive nature of team sports. The rules she created remained in use until the 1960s.

Need for Physical Education for Women

One of five children, Senda Valvrojenski was born March 19, 1868, in Biturmansk, Lithuania. Her parents, Albert, a seller of pots and pans, and Julie Mieliszanki, were Jewish immigrants who arrived in Boston, Massachusetts, in 1875 when Senda was seven. In America, her family changed its name to Berenson.

A weak child, Berenson studied piano at the Boston Conservatory of Music and attended the Girls' Latin School in Boston. To improve her physical abilities, she enrolled in 1890 in the newly established women's teaching college, the Boston Normal School of Gymnastics. There, she studied physical education under Amy Morris Homans and the philanthropist Mary Hemenway. Hemenway had introduced Swedish gymnastics to Boston public schools in the 1880s. Soon Berenson developed strength and stamina.

In January, 1892, Berenson left the Boston Normal School for a position in Northampton, Massachusetts, at Smith College, becoming the first director of physical education at the all-women's institution. Not long after she arrived, she learned of a game called "basket ball" invented only one month earlier by **James Naismith** from the nearby International Young Men's Christian Association (YMCA) Training School in Springfield, Massachusetts. Berenson read Naismith's article about the game in the YMCA publication *Physical Education.* Intrigued that the game could have potential for her students, she visited Naismith to learn more.

Back at Smith College, Berenson organized a trial game with the women using the same rules as the men. In March 1893, one year after basketball was invented, Berenson held the first collegiate game of women's basketball featuring teams from her freshmen and sophomore classes. Men were prohibited from watching the women play.

Although she recognized that the game provided a vigorous activity for women, Victorian propriety at the time would not allow women to behave so energetic and competitively. Newspaper articles commented on the loud and wild behavior of the women. In those days, women did not play team sports or participate in activities that allowed physical contact.

Different Rules for Women

Berenson set out to modify the 13 rules the men played by to make the game less strenuous and more inclusive for all players, not just the most skilled. She advocated traits like cooperation and socialization over competition, and was opposed to women's intercollegiate games, preferring instead intramural athletics. Berenson's new rules concentrated on orderly play that prevented women from getting over excited.

To begin with, she allowed only six team members to play on the court at one time. She also divided the court into three sections from which players were assigned and remained throughout the game. This, she reasoned, prevented the women from overexerting themselves running all over the court and prevented exceptional players from dominating the game.

To eliminate physical contact, her rules disallowed players from grabbing the ball from another player's hands. Players could not dribble more than three times before passing or shooting the ball, nor could players hold the ball for more than three seconds. Balls had to be shot with only one hand, as using two hands was believed to flatten the chest and restrict breathing. Guarding was forbidden and falling down was a foul.

In John Sippel's article, "WNBA Notes Smith's Role in Women's Basketball," he wrote that Berenson modified the rules "to prevent a young lady from developing 'dangerous nervous tendencies and losing the grace and dignity and self-respect we would all have her foster.'" Sippel added, "Berenson was among those who recognized 'that if the game did not improve its reputation for womanliness, [women] might not be allowed to play it.'"

At Smith College, Berenson's interests expanded beyond basketball. She also introduced fencing and folk dancing into the school's physical education curriculum and brought remedial gymnastics to students with special physical needs. In 1901, she arranged for field hockey to debut at Smith and helped to organize Smith College's Gymnastics and Field Association. In her continuous search for new activities, she was the second American woman to attend the Royal Central Institute of Gymnastics in Stockholm, Sweden, where she studied advanced fencing.

Wrote the Definitive Rules Book

Very soon after women began playing basketball, schools throughout the country adopted the game for their women's physical education classes. Each school had developed its own style or modified the game to suit its students. In 1899, the American Association for the Advancement of Physical Education (AAAPE) formed the Women's Basketball Rules Committee to create official rules for women players based on Berenson's modifications.

Two years later, in 1901, the rules were first published by sporting goods company A.G. Spalding in the *Women's Basketball Guide,* which continued to edit and revise until 1917. Berenson's rules for women's basketball remained in use until the 1960s.

Also in 1901, Berenson wrote *Line Basket Ball for Women,* which provided not only rules for playing the

Chronology	
1868	Born March 19 in Biturmansk, Lithuania, to Albert and Julia Valvrojenski
1890	Enrolls in the Boston Normal School of Gymnastics
1892	Begins teaching physical training at Smith College
1892	Introduces basketball to female students at Smith College
1893	Organizes the first women's basketball match. Helps to organize Smith College's Gymnastics and Field Association
1895	Introduces fencing to Smith College
1897	Becomes the second American woman to attend the Royal Central Institute of Gymnastics in Stockholm, Sweden
1899	Member of Women's Basketball Rules Committee, which writes rules for women playing basketball
1899	Chairs the American Association for the Advancement of Physical Education Committee on Basketball for Girls
1905	Chief organizer of the Basketball Committee for Women
1911	Marries Smith College English professor Herbert Vaughn Abbott
1911	Directs physical education at Mary A. Burnham School
1921	Retires from teaching and travels to Europe to study art and music
1929	Moves to Santa Barbara, California
1954	Dies on February 16 in Santa Barbara

game but Berenson's philosophy about the sport's psychological and physiological effects on women. Not long after, in 1905, Berenson organized the AAAPE's Basketball Committee for Women and chaired the organization until 1917. This committee later became known as the National Association for Girls and Women in Sport.

On June 15, 1911, Senda Berenson married Smith College English professor Herbert Vaughn Abbott. That same year she resigned from the college and spent the next decade as director of physical education at the private Mary A. Burnham School for girls in Northampton, Massachusetts. In 1921, she retired and traveled to Europe to study art and music. Her brother, Bernard Berenson, was an authority on Italian Renaissance art. After Herbert Abbott died in 1929, Berenson moved to Santa Barbara, California, where she lived with her sister until her death in 1954.

Berenson's Legacy

Berenson's legacy has not been forgotten. Since her death she has been honored for her valuable role in creating and promoting women's basketball. In 1984, she was inducted into the Naismith Memorial Basketball Hall of Fame and International Women's Sports Hall of Fame for her many contributions to the game. In the same year, Berenson and women's basketball coach Margaret Wade were the first two women elected to the Basketball Hall of Fame.

The Women's Basketball Coaches Association in 1984 created the Jostens-Berenson Service Award to recognize those who are committed to women's basketball. The Women's Basketball Hall of Fame in Knoxville, Tennessee, inducted Berenson in 1999 and erected a lifelike animatronic figure of her. The WNBA honored her for her commitment "to providing women with the same opportunities that were available to men." Her alma mater Smith College dedicated the Berenson Dance Studio in her honor and maintains an archive of her writings.

Women's basketball has become one of the most popular team sports for women in the United States. Today more than 1,000 colleges sponsor women's basketball teams.

Although by today's standards, Senda Berenson needlessly restricted the roughness of play and competitive nature of basketball for women, she still must be credited for single-handedly introducing the sport to a segment of the population that might otherwise not have considered daring to participate in it. She inspired young women to be athletic at a time when they were told they should have been dainty. Berenson committed her life to training women in sport and earned her place in the history of women's athletics.

SELECTED WRITINGS BY BERENSON:

Line Basket Ball for Women, New York: A. G. Spaulding, 1901.

FURTHER INFORMATION

Books

Hickok, Ralph. *Encyclopedia of North American Sports History.* New York, NY: Facts on File, 1992

Sherrow, Victoria. *Encyclopedia of Women & Sports.* Santa Barbara, CA: ABC-CLIO, 1996

Sparhawk, Ruth M, et al. *American Women in Sports 1887-1987.* Metuchen, NJ: Scarecrow Press, 1989

Woolum, Janet. *Outstanding Women Athletes.* Phoenix, AZ: Oryx Press, 1992

Other

International Sports Hall of Fame. http://www.internationalsports.com/sa_hof/hof_inductees.html (September 27, 2002).

"Senda Berenson Asserts the Value of Adapted Women's Basketball, 1901." Barnard College. http://www.barnard.columbia.edu/amstud/resources/women/berenson.htm (September 27, 2002).

"Senda Berenson; Papers, 1875-1996." Five College Archives Digital Access Project. http://clio.fivecolleges.edu/smith/berenson (September 27, 2002).

"WNBA Notes Smith's Role in Women's Basketball." Smith College. http://www.smith.edu/newssmith/NSFall97/WNBA.html (September 27, 2002).

Sketch by Lorraine Savage

Yogi Berra
1925-

American baseball player

As a player, manager, and linguist of sorts, Yogi Berra has endeared himself to baseball fans since World War II as a hard-working, rough-edged original. As a New York Yankee he developed into a masterful catcher as well as an outstanding hitter. He won the Most Valuable Player (MVP) award in 1951, 1954, and 1955, and was elected to the Baseball Hall of Fame in 1972. Including his work as a coach and manager, Berra has been involved in a record twenty-one World Series. His influence on the sport is reflected by a list of "25 Greatest Moments" in baseball compiled by *The Sporting News* in 1999: Berra figures in ten of the moments in one fashion or another. Throughout his career, Berra has also been famous for uttering "Yogi-isms," which pass as malapropisms except for their often strange, but persuasive logic. His best-known utterance is probably the assertion "It ain't over till it's over." He now appears in *Bartlett's Familiar Quotations,* has published several books of his own, and is quoted in many contexts other than baseball.

Childhood in St. Louis

Yogi Berra grew up wanting to be a ballplayer, but first had some serious obstacles to overcome. Born Lawrence Peter Berra and raised in St. Louis, Missouri by his parents Pietro and Paulina Berra, he had three older brothers who also were passionate about baseball. However, they were all needed to help support the family. Berra left school after the eighth grade and worked in a coal yard, drove a delivery truck, and pulled tacks in a shoe factory. But the Berra boys also found time to play baseball, roller hockey, soccer, and football together. With others from the "Dago Hill" neighborhood, they formed a YMCA team called "The Stags." Berra has described his brothers as talented athletes and explained that he was lucky to be the youngest boy. Since they had improved the family's economic situation, he was able to get his father's permission to try for a baseball career. One of Berra's friends, Joe Garagiola, went on to become a catcher for the St. Louis Cardinals and a broadcaster.

Yogi Berra

Signed with Yankees

Berra polished his skills on the diamond playing for the Stockham Post American Legion Junior team beginning at age fourteen. He most often played left field for the team. In 1942 he and Garagiola tried out for the St. Louis Cardinals, who were then managed by Branch Rickey. Garagiola was signed, but Berra turned down a $250 signing bonus, half of what his friend had been given. Rickey is reported to have said that Berra wouldn't make it out of Triple A baseball. When Berra signed with the New York Yankees, he received $500 to play for the Norfolk, Virginia Tars in 1943. During his first season playing catcher, he made sixteen errors but showed promise as a hitter. In one two-day period the left-hand hitting and right-hand throwing novice batted in twenty-three runs. Berra's season average however, was just .253.

The next year Berra was advanced to the Yankees' Kansas City farm team, but did not play. Now eighteen, he joined the Navy and trained as a gunner. During the D-Day invasion of Normandy, Berra was part of the fighting for fifteen consecutive days serving as a Seaman 1st Class on the Coast Guard transport Bayfield. When he returned to the United States, Berra played on a Navy baseball team in Connecticut. He showed exceptional batting skills in an exhibition game against the New York Giants, which led to that team offering the Yankees $50,000 for his contract. The Yankees refused the offer, despite the fact that Yankee General Manager Larry MacPhail didn't know who Berra was. After his

discharge from the Navy, Berra was assigned to the Bears, the club's Newark, New Jersey farm team. In 1946 Berra batted .314 and hit fifteen home runs for the Bears before being called up to the majors at the end of season. He made a big impression in a short period of time, hitting a home run in his first major league at bat, and another in his second game.

During his first years with the Yankees, Berra struggled with his habit of swinging at bad pitches and a wild arm behind the plate. When **Casey Stengel** began managing the team in 1949, he put Berra to work with former catcher Bill Dickey, who found fault with the young player's flatfooted style of throwing but also valued his speed, strength, and agility. Soon his student was showing improvement on offense and defense. In 1949 Berra became the starting catcher for the Yankees, a position he would hold until 1959. Behind the plate, he earned a reputation as a talker who tried to distract batters from the task at hand. Berra has said that **Ted Williams** was the only player who told him shut up, which he declined to do. Berra also gained greater ease when he was at bat. While he would still go for pitches outside the strike zone, Berra proved to be hard to strike out; in 1950 he was called out on strikes only twelve times in 597 at bats.

Developed Star Qualities

Playing for Stengel, Berra became a star on the Yankees team and was, in the manager's opinion, second only to **Joe DiMaggio** among the best players he had ever managed. Berra's awards and statistics bear this out. In addition to his three MVP awards, he was voted to the All-Star team fifteen times. During a nineteen-year playing career he hit over .300 in four seasons, had more than twenty home runs eleven times, and had five 100-plus runs-batted-in (RBI) seasons. His best season at the plate was 1956, when he hit .298, had thirty home runs, and batted in 105 runs. Berra played in fourteen World Series and accumulated several championship records, including the most games as catcher, at sixty-three; most hits, at seventy-one; appearances on a winning team, at ten; and the distinction of hitting the first pinch-hit home run in World Series history. When he was elected to the Baseball Hall of Fame, the former Yankee claimed 339 out of 396 ballots cast.

Arguably the best catcher in the American league during the 1950s, Berra called three no-hitters. The most famous of these was Don Larsen's perfect game in the 1956 World Series. In *The Sporting News* Berra reminded readers forty years later of the game's special drama: "You knew that he was pitching a no-hitter, but the game was so close you couldn't worry about anything but winning the game," he said. The Yankees were more concerned about going ahead in the Series than achieving a perfect game. When the game ended with a called strike three and a score of 2-0, Berra ran to the mound and jumped into Larsen's arms. A photograph capturing this moment is one of the most famous in baseball history.

Coach and Manager

After retiring as a player at the end of 1963, Berra was introduced to the tumultuous existence of major league managers as head of the Yankees. He took the team to the 1964 world championship, but was fired after losing the seven-game series to the Cardinals. He then accepted a coaching job with the New York Mets under Casey Stengel, who called Berra his "assistant manager." In 1972 he was promoted to manager, replacing Gil Hodges. The next year he led the team to a National League pennant, but would not last through his three-year contract. According to writer Joseph Durso in the *New York Times,* Berra was fired after two-thirds of the 1975 season because of a conflict with management. In Durso's words, Berra was "gunned down after a se-

ries of reverses that were not altogether his fault." The writer named a huge drop in attendance over the previous four years, poor trading results, and grumbling players, as among the team's pre-existing problems.

Berra quickly went back to coaching, taking a job with the Yankees before year's end. In 1984 he was again elevated to manager, this time under the supervision of owner **George Steinbrenner**. Berra had reportedly turned down the job twice before and was now replacing the temperamental **Billy Martin**. He was surely entering rocky waters here: Steinbrenner had made eleven management changes in the last eleven years. Berra's continued public appeal and potential in the manager's seat were noted in the *New York Times* by George Vecsey, who enthused: "Berra is one of a kind, a national institution.... Nobody is hiring him for his value as a glib motivator of young millionaires. He is Yogi Berra, the man who knows all the secrets of the clubhouse, the man the players trusted during the turmoil [with Martin], the former manager whose mind never stopped churning with baseball details."

When Berra was sacked sixteen games into the 1985 season, it was a bitter parting. He had butted heads with Steinbrenner, including a 1984 squabble over the roster that ended with him throwing a pack of cigarettes at the owner. **Lou Piniella**, Berra's replacement as manager, asked him to return as dugout coach but was refused. Instead Berra accepted a job with the Houston Astros, a team owned by his friend John McMullen. The switch and Berra's model behavior during it were considered newsworthy. Steve Jacobson commented in *The Los Angeles Times,* "Yogi Berra is a breath of fresh air. I don't think I ever quite appreciated that before. He's a relief from the lies and the posturing and the greed of today's sports."

Berra reported for duty with the Astros after he took his first summer vacation in forty-three years. He laughed in the *New York Times* that his wife Carmen had objected, "Now I'm going to have to cook for you." Berra has, however, long been known as a family man, someone who scoffed at the idea of playing around on road trips and who is devoted to his grandchildren. He and Carmen have three sons: Lawrence Jr., Timothy, and Dale. In 1985 Berra had looked forward to managing

Career Statistics

Yr	Team	AVG	GP	AB	R	H	HR	RBI	BB	SO	SB	E
1946	NYY	.364	7	22	3	8	2	4	1	1	0	0
1947	NYY	.280	83	293	41	82	11	54	13	12	0	9
1948	NYY	.305	125	469	70	143	14	98	25	24	3	9
1949	NYY	.277	116	415	59	115	20	91	22	25	2	7
1950	NYY	.322	151	597	116	192	28	124	55	12	4	13
1951	NYY	.294	141	547	92	161	27	88	44	20	5	13
1952	NYY	.273	142	534	97	146	30	98	66	24	2	6
1953	NYY	.296	137	503	80	149	27	108	50	32	0	9
1954	NYY	.307	151	584	88	179	22	125	56	29	0	8
1955	NYY	.272	147	541	84	147	27	108	60	20	1	13
1956	NYY	.298	140	521	93	155	30	105	65	29	3	11
1957	NYY	.251	134	482	74	121	24	82	57	24	1	4
1958	NYY	.266	122	433	60	115	22	90	35	35	3	2
1959	NYY	.284	131	472	64	134	19	69	43	38	1	4
1960	NYY	.276	120	359	46	99	15	62	38	23	2	5
1961	NYY	.271	119	395	62	107	22	61	35	28	2	2
1962	NYY	.224	86	232	25	52	10	35	24	18	0	6
1963	NYY	.293	64	147	20	43	8	28	15	17	1	3
1965	NYM	.222	4	9	1	2	0	0	0	3	0	1
TOTAL		.285	2120	7555	1175	2150	358	1430	704	414	30	125

NYM: New York Mets; NYY: New York Yankees.

Dale, an infielder who had been traded to the Yankees. But the situation soured with Berra's firing and with Dale's involvement in a drug trial in Pittsburgh. Berra's son admitted to using cocaine and received legal immunity in exchange for his testimony.

Laughing with Yogi

Firings and personal dramas have little to do with public interest in Berra. At five feet, eight inches and 185 pounds, Berra was teased about his physique as a player; he also attracted attention with his love of comic books, movies, and ice cream. But by far the greatest source of amusement has been Berra's verbal inventions, which have been remarked on since the beginning of his career. Some are simply examples of the ballplayer saying the wrong thing with comic effect, while others require more careful consideration. His now famous statement "It ain't over till it's over" has been quoted and copied countless times. Berra first said it in 1973, when he was managing the Mets. His team had been nine games out of first place in September before going on to win the division and the pennant, proving the appropriateness of the comment.

The popularity of Yogi-isms might even overshadow his fame on the baseball field. All kinds of public figures like to quote Berra, including George Bush, who borrowed his line "We made too many wrong mistakes" in a televised debate. Others admire the philosophical implications of his comment "If the world was perfect, it wouldn't be" and the wisdom of "Always go to other people's funerals. Otherwise they won't go to yours." On the subject of baseball, Berra is famous for saying, "Ninety percent of the game is half mental" and "If peo-

ple don't want to come out to the ballpark, nobody's going to stop them." According to Berra, he is unable to identify a Yogi-ism himself and has to be told when he has just said something remarkable. But that hasn't prevented him from publishing several books on the subject, including *The Yogi Book* and *When You Come To a Fork in the Road, Take It*.

In 1989 Berra retired from the Astros. He has since been involved with several major projects, including the creation of the Yogi Berra Museum and Learning Center at Montclair State University. The museum was the site of the 1999 reconciliation between Berra and George Steinbrenner. For fourteen years Berra had not stepped foot in Yankee Stadium, even when Steinbrenner had put up a plaque in his honor. The Yankees' owner now apologized, saying that firing Berra was "the worst mistake I've ever made in baseball," according to *Time*. Certainly, he could hardly have fired a nicer guy. Berra has become a perennial favorite, even a baseball legend, as someone who has been cheered for his athletic prowess, admired for his baseball know-how, and enjoyed for his quirky humor.

CONTACT INFORMATION

Address: Yogi Berra Museum and Learning Center, Montclair State University, 8 Quarry Rd., Little Falls, NJ 07424-2161.

SELECTED WRITINGS BY BERRA:

(With Ed Fitzgerald) *Yogi: The Autobiography of a Professional Baseball Player*, Doubleday, 1961.

Yogi Berra, crossing home plate

Vecsey, George. "Yogi's Back in Style." *New York Times* (December 17, 1983): 19.
"Where's Yogi? Everywhere, It Seems." *The Sporting News* (October 25, 1999): 68.

Sketch by Paula Pyzik Scott

(With Til Ferdenzi) *Behind the Plate*, Argonaut, 1962.
(With Tom Horton) *Yogi: It Ain't Over*, McGraw-Hill, 1989.
The Yogi Book: I Really Didn't Say Everything I Said! Workman, 1998.
(With David Kaplan and Dale Berra) *When You Come to a Fork in the Road, Take It!: Inspiration and Wisdom from One of Baseball's Greatest Heroes*, Hyperion, 2001.
(With Dave Kaplan) *What Time Is It? You Mean Now?: Advice for Life from the Zennest Master of Them All*, Simon & Schuster, 2002.

FURTHER INFORMATION

Periodicals

Bortstein, Larry. "The Closer." *The Sporting News* (October 7, 1996): 54.
Durso, Joseph. "Yogi and the Snipers." *New York Times* (August 12, 1975): 23.
Jacobsen, Steve. "For Yogi Berra, It Still Ain't Over, And That's Refreshing." *Los Angeles Times* (April 2, 1989).
Kreiter, Ted. "Yogi Speaking." *Saturday Evening Post* (July-August, 2002): 48.
Taaffe, William. "Joe Garagiola: no longer TV's most happy fella." *Sports Illustrated* (October 3, 1988): 5.
Time (January 18, 1999): 97.

Matt Biondi
1965-

American swimmer

Matt Biondi is one of the greatest competitive swimmers in history. Over the course of his career, he earned dozens of national, international, and collegiate titles and set twelve world records. He reached his zenith at the 1988 Olympic Games in Seoul, South Korea, where he won seven medals to tie the record set by swimming legend **Mark Spitz** in 1972. Biondi, Spitz, and shooter Carl Osburn are the only U.S. athletes to win eleven Olympic medals overall. Biondi also was the first swimmer ever to win seven medals at a World Championship tournament, and he and Tom Jager were the first American swimmers to capture gold in three Olympiads. While attending the University of California—Berkeley, Biondi became the first swimmer in more than a half-century to sweep the 50, 100, and 200-yard freestyle races in the NCAA Championships. He repeated the feat a year later—another first. "He has the ability to feel the water, much like an artist feels the canvas and a pianist feels the keys," said Nort Thornton, Biondi's coach at UC Berkeley. "Those are things you just don't teach people."

Collegiate Champion

Biondi is a product of the San Francisco area—born in Palo Alto, raised in the town of Moraga, an alumni of the University of California-Berkeley. In high school, he was so skinny he was called Spiderman and derided on the basketball court. As a result, he turned to the pool at age 15—much later than most serious competitive swimmers. "I took practice very seriously," Biondi has said. "I was always conscious of every lap and every

Matt Biondi

stroke. I was thinking about what I was doing and about how I could make it better."

Hard work and natural ability combined to make Biondi one of the greatest swimmers ever at Berkeley, where he was a four-time All-American in both swimming and water polo, NCAA Swimmer of the Year three times in row, and a member of three NCAA Champion water polo squads. In 1985, Biondi was the NCAA Champion in two individual and two team events—the 100 and 200-yard freestyle races and the 4x100 yard and 4x200 yard freestyle relays. In 1986, he won those again and added the 50-yard freestyle crown—to become the first swimmer in fifty-six years to capture the 50, 100 and 200-yard freestyle championships in the same year. In 1987, he became the first person ever to repeat the feat two years in a row.

Olympic Pressures

Biondi won the first of his eight Olympic gold medals as an eighteen-year-old novice on the United States' 4x100 meter freestyle relay team at the 1984 Olympic Games in Los Angeles. Two years later, he was dominating the collegiate swimming world—with five NCAA championships—and exploding onto the international stage. In Madrid, Spain, in 1986, Biondi became the first swimmer ever to win seven medals at the World Championships. This unprecedented accomplishment would create intense pressure at the 1988 Olympics, however, where Biondi was expected to match the seven gold medals claimed by legendary U.S. swimmer Mark Spitz sixteen years earlier.

Biondi alluded to the pressure—and tried to temper expectations—in a journal he kept for *Sports Illustrated* during the '88 Olympiad. "Everyone will be counting the medals and the times and the world records, and making this big judgment: Is Matt a success or a failure?" Biondi wrote. "It seems there's so much emphasis put on that stuff and so little on how a person grows as he works his way toward the Olympics. To me, it's the path getting there that counts, not the cheese at the end of the maze. . . . People don't seem to realize that I'm coming here with only one world record, in the 100 free. Spitz had world records in all of his individual events going into the 1972 Olympics. And mostly he was swimming against just Americans. Nowadays you've got East and West Germans, Swedes, Australians, Soviets—and they're all great. Times have changed."

The '88 Games

The 1988 Olympics started with a bump for Biondi, when he finished third in the 200-meter freestyle behind Anders Holmertz of Sweden and Duncan Armstrong of Australia. Biondi chafed at a news coverage depicting his performance as disappointing. "The press always throws stuff at you," he wrote in his *Sports Illustrated* diary. "Like tonight I heard (NBC commentator) **Bob Costas** say on TV, 'Matt Biondi isn't going to win his seven gold medals. Today he had to settle for bronze.' But I feel good about the bronze. My most difficult event is over and I still have a chance to walk away with seven medals. I think that would be a hell of a performance."

Two days later, Biondi won the silver medal in the 100 meter butterfly, one-hundredth of a second behind Anthony Nesty of Suriname. He also captured gold and helped set a world record time in the 4x200 freestyle relay. Four more gold medals followed—in the 50-meter freestyle, 100-meter freestyle, 4x100 freestyle relay, and the 4x100 medley relay. Biondi ended the Games with five gold medals, one silver, and one bronze and set or contributed to four world records. He defeated his friend and rival Tom Jager in the 50-meter freestyle for the first time in two years and broke Jager's record time in the event.

In and Out of Retirement

Biondi announced his retirement from competitive swimming in 1988 and went to work on the "celebrity circuit," giving motivational speeches in as many as twenty cities a month, endorsing swimsuits and sunglasses, opening supermarkets, giving instructional clinics. He and Jager competed in a series of lucrative exhibition races. Biondi generated a six-figure income, but it was a difficult existence for someone who is shy and protective of his privacy.

At the same time, limitations were relaxed on payments amateur athletes could receive from endorsement and from their national federations, and U.S. Swimming increased its stipends to potential Olympians. This made

Chronology

1965	Born October 8 in Palo Alto, California
1984	Earns Olympic gold medal
1985	Named American Swimmer of the Year and nominated for the Sullivan Award, which goes to America's outstanding amateur athlete
1986	Becomes first swimmer ever to win seven medals at the World Championships
1987	Graduates from University of California—Berkeley, where he was four-time All-American in both swimming and water polo, played on three NCAA Champion water polo teams, and was NCAA Swimmer of the Year three years in a row
1988	Wins seven Olympic medals, tying record set by Mark Spitz in 1972
1990	Wins five medals at Goodwill Games
1991	Wins four medals at World Championships
1992	Wins three more Olympic medals and ties Spitz and shooter Carl Osburn with total of 11
1994	Donates Olympic medals—eight gold, two silver, one bronze—to the National Italian American Sports Hall of Fame in Chicago
1995	Marries Kirsten Metzger in Hawaii, her home state
1998	First son, Nathaniel, is born
2000	Earns master's degree in education from Lewis & Clark College in Portland, Oregon
2001	Begins teaching high school math in Hawaii
2002	Second son, Lucas, is born

Awards and Accomplishments

1983	Member of NCAA Champion water polo team
1984	All-American in swimming and water polo; member of NCAA Champion water polo team
1984	Gold medal (4x100 meter freestyle relay), Olympic Games, Los Angeles
1985	NCAA Swimmer of the Year; American Swimmer of the Year; All-American in swimming and water polo
1985	NCAA champion in 100 yard freestyle, 200 yard freestyle, 4x100 yard freestyle relay, 4x200 yard freestyle relay
1986	U.S. Olympic Committee Male Athlete of the Year; NCAA Swimmer of the Year; All-American in swimming and water polo
1986	NCAA champion in 50 yard freestyle, 100 yard freestyle, 200 yard freestyle, 4x100 yard freestyle relay, 4x200 yard freestyle relay
1986	Three gold medals (100 meter freestyle, 4x100 meter freestyle relay, 4x100 meter medley relay), one silver medal (100 meter butterfly); and three bronze medals (50 meter freestyle, 200 meter freestyle, 4x200 meter freestyle relay), World Championships, Madrid, Spain
1987	NCAA Swimmer of the Year; All-American in swimming and water polo; member of NCAA Champion water polo team
1987	NCAA champion in 50 yard freestyle, 100 yard freestyle, 200 yard freestyle, 4x100 yard freestyle relay
1988	U.S. Olympic Committee Male Athlete of the Year
1988	Five gold medals (50 meter freestyle, 100 meter freestyle, 4x100 meter freestyle relay, 4x200 freestyle relay, 4x100 medley relay), one silver medal (100 meter butterfly), and one bronze medal (200 meter freestyle), Olympic Games, Seoul, South Korea
1990	Four gold medals (50 meter freestyle, 100 meter freestyle, 4x100 meter freestyle relay, 4x100 meter medley relay) and one silver (100 meter butterfly), Goodwill Games, Seattle
1991	Three gold medals (100 meter freestyle, 4x100 meter freestyle relay, 4x100 meter medley relay) and one silver medal (50 meter freestyle), World Championships, Perth, Australia
1992	Two gold medals (4x100 meter freestyle relay, 4x100 meter medley relay) and one silver medal (50 meter freestyle), Olympic Games, Barcelona, Spain

it viable for Biondi and other veteran swimmers to compete in the 1992 Games in Barcelona, Spain. The United States fielded its oldest Olympic swim team in history. Biondi, 26, and Jager, 27, would become the first American swimmers to win gold medals in three Olympiads and Biondi would become one of the most decorated U.S. Olympic athletes in history. Biondi captured gold medals in the 4x100 meter freestyle relay and the 4x100 meter medley relay and a silver in the 50-meter freestyle. He did not swim in the 4x100 medley relay final, but alternates share in the award if they compete in qualifying heats. The event gave Biondi the 11th medal of his Olympic career, tying the U.S. record shared by Spitz and Osburn.

Out of the Pool

Biondi had lost his trademark competitive zeal even before the Barcelona Olympics. "I can't tell you how many mornings I got to the pool and stood over the cold water and just had to force myself to drop in," he told *Sports Illustrated*. Biondi "was thrilled with his achievements, but the intense push toward medals and records had worn on him," *Portland Oregonian* reporter Katy Muldoon wrote in a feature story in 2000. "And even though he sometimes sought it out, he says, the spotlight traumatized him. Shy by nature, Biondi found the near-constant attention from the news media and the public emotionally difficult."

Biondi met Kirsten Metzger after the '92 Games at a University of California football game where he and other Cal Olympians were honored during a halftime ceremony. A few months later, they bumped into each other on the street in Berkeley. Two years later, they married in

Hawaii, Kirsten's home state. The couple lived in northern California and Biondi, who had returned to the motivational speaking circuit, was drifting and directionless. "He would cross-country ski in winter and spend long summer afternoons sailing on San Francisco Bay with his father," Muldoon wrote. Biondi told her that he "felt like life was getting too easy, too soft. I had my speech down. I could make ends meet by working once a month."

Biondi's wife convinced him to return to college. He enrolled at Lewis & Clark College in Portland, where Kirsten had earned a graduate degree in public administration, and graduated with a master's degree in teaching in 2000. "I want to make a difference by being in a profession where I can spend a lot of time with kids," Biondi said. "And I would like to work with one group all year - not just come in . . . traveling around with my gold medals, all sensational."

CONTACT INFORMATION

Address: Office, USA Swimming, One Olympic Plaza, Colorado Springs, CO, 80909.

FURTHER INFORMATION

Periodicals

Bailey, Sandra. "Treading Water and Juggling Jobs." *The New York Times* (August 1, 1992).

Biondi, Matt. "Diary of a Champion." *Sports Illustrated* (October 3, 1988).

Litsky, Frank. "The Duel in the Pool Goes to Biondi." *The New York Times* (March 6, 1992).

Litsky, Frank. "Biondi Stays in Form Despite a Busy Agenda." *The New York Times* (March 23, 1990).

Litsky, Frank. "Otto Takes 6th Gold; One More for Biondi." *The New York Times* (September 26, 1988).

Litsky, Frank. "Biondi On Course with Butterfly Victory." *The New York Times* (August 10, 1988).

Litsky, Frank. "Biondi is Learning to Set his Pace." *The New York Times* (March 25, 1988).

Litsky, Frank. "Biondi is Trying to do Better than his World-Record Year." *The New York Times* (April 6, 1986).

Litsky, Frank. "Biondi, Jager Better Olympians' Marks." *The New York Times* (March 30, 1985).

Montville, Leigh. "Silver Threads Among the Gold." *Sports Illustrated* (July 22, 1992).

Muldoon, Katy. "Out of the Pool, and Out of the Spotlight." *Sunday Oregonian* (April 9, 2000).

"Out of Retirement and Into Careerism." *Time* (July 27, 1992).

Syken, Bill. "Catching Up With Matt Biondi, Swimmer." *Sports Illustrated* (October 28, 2002).

Sketch by David Wilkins

Larry Bird
1956-

American basketball player

By the time he joined the Boston Celtics in the National Basketball Association (NBA) in 1979, Larry Bird was already a basketball hero in his home state of Indi-

Larry Bird

ana. After a brief stay at Indiana University, he transferred to Indiana State University (ISU) and led the men's basketball team to thirty-three consecutive wins in his senior year. The perfect 1978-79 season for the Sycamores ended with a dramatic loss in the NCAA finals to Michigan State University, led by **Earvin "Magic" Johnson**. Forever linked in the annals of college sport, the two players became friendly rivals during their NBA careers and helped the league soar to new heights of popularity in the 1980s. Bird also reversed the fortunes of the Boston Celtics, a team that had gone 29-53 the year before he joined the roster. With the addition of Bird, the Celtics made the biggest turnaround in NBA history, winning sixty-one games after he joined the team. The Celtics went on to win three NBA championships with Bird, who retired in 1992. After working for the Celtics as a special assistant for five years, Bird returned to Indiana to coach the Indiana Pacers. Although he won NBA Coach of the Year honors in 1998 and took the Pacers to the NBA championship in 2000, Bird decided to retire from coaching after just three seasons. In characteristically modest fashion he told *Indianapolis Monthly* in March 2000, "I'm not great at coaching. I came in here really raw, and I didn't know what was going on. I thought I did, but there's a lot more to it than I thought there was."

"Hoosier Hysteria"

Larry Joe Bird was born in the small, southern Indiana town of West Baden on December 7, 1956. His fa-

Chronology

1956	Born December 7 in West Baden, Indiana to Claude Joseph and Georgia (Kerns) Bird
1971	Begins playing basketball at Springs Valley High School in French Lick, Indiana
1974	Enters Indiana University, but departs before school begins
1975	Enters Indiana State University in Terre Haute
1975	Marries Janet Condra on November 8
1979	Receives John Wooden Award as Collegiate Player of the Year from the Los Angeles Athletic Association
1979	Completes B.S. degree in physical education
1979	Signs contract with Boston Celtics
1980	Named NBA Rookie of the Year
1984-86	Named NBA Player of the Year
1989	Marries Dinah Mattingly on September 30
1992	Retires as professional athlete
1997	Becomes coach of Indiana Pacers

Awards and Accomplishments

1979	John Wooden Award as Collegiate Player of the Year, Los Angeles Athletic Association
1980	Named NBA Rookie of the Year
1981, 1984, 1986	NBA championship (with Boston Celtics)
1984-85	NBA Most Valuable Player in Playoffs
1984-86	Named NBA Player of the Year
1985	Man of the Year, *Sporting News*
1985	*Associated Press* Male Athlete of the Year
1992	Olympic Gold Medal (U.S. men's basketball team)
1998	Inducted into Basketball Hall of Fame
1998	Named NBA Coach of the Year

ther, Claude, worked as a laborer, often taking jobs at the local Kimball Piano and Organ Company, while his mother, Georgia (Kerns) worked as a waitress. The Birds had three children before the arrival of Larry—sons Mike and Mark and daughter Linda—and two more sons afterwards—sons Jeff and Eddie. His parents struggled throughout Bird's childhood to make ends meet, and Bird and his brothers were often sent to live with his grandmother, Lizzie Kerns, while the family shuffled between West Baden and the adjacent town of French Lick. "I just never realized how poor we were," Bird wrote in his 1989 memoir *Drive: The Story of My Life,* "Nobody in French Lick is wealthy. Everyone makes basically the same amount of money and everyone has basically the same values. It's the kind of small town where everyone stands up for his rights." Remembering his small-town roots, Bird would later jokingly refer to himself as "the hick from French Lick" when he first arrived in Boston as an NBA player, and the phrase became his nickname.

With little in the way of financial resources, the Bird children amused themselves with intra-family sporting events, especially basketball. Bird later recalled that his older brothers were fearsome competitors against their younger brother, which spurred him on to practice his skills in order to beat them. Bird was also profoundly shaped by his community's love of sports. "Sports are big, always have been," he recalled in his autobiography, "Especially basketball—giving rise to the term 'Hoosier Hysteria' to describe Indiana's fascination and support of basketball. *Everyone* knows what's going on in sports and everyone who plays sports is extremely competitive." Upon entering Springs Valley High School in 1971, Bird played football, baseball, and basketball. A broken ankle curtailed his activity in his sophomore year, but Bird returned to the basketball team as a six-foot, four-inch junior (he would eventually top out at six-feet, nine inches) and helped his team go to the sectional finals. The Spring Valley team made it to the regional finals in Bird's se-

nior year, but the squad's lack of confidence betrayed it. Even with the loss, Bird learned to keep practicing his basic skills, including his free throws and passes, that would later make him one of the most consistent players in the NBA.

Standout Player at Indiana State

In 1974 Bird headed to Indiana University, where he intended to play for legendary coach **Bobby Knight**. Before the season began, however, Bird felt so intimidated by the school's large size that he decided to drop out. After working for a year on the city's road crew in French Lick, Bird enrolled at nearby Indiana State University (ISU) in Terre Haute. On November 8, 1975 he entered into a brief marriage with Janet Condra, whom he had known since childhood. The couple divorced in 1976 but had a daughter, Corrie, born during a brief reconciliation in 1977. Bird's personal life was also marked by the suicide of his father in 1975. Now divorced, Claude Bird was depressed about his inability to make child support payments to his family and took his life in the hope that they would benefit from the Social Security payments available after his death.

NCAA rules forced Bird to refrain from playing for ISU during his first year there. When he joined the team for the 1976-77 season, he helped the Sycamores to a 25-3 record and created phenomenal interest in ISU's basketball team, with home games selling out as soon as tickets became available. Although he was drafted by the Boston Celtics when he was a junior at ISU, Bird insisted on completing his senior year. The Sycamores ended up winning thirty-three straight games and would have had an undefeated season had it not been for the 75-64 loss to Michigan State University (MSU) in the 1979 NCAA finals. The game received some of the highest-ever ratings for a college sporting event and made media stars out of Bird and his MSU rival, Earvin "Magic" Johnson, who dropped out of college to play for the Los Angeles Lakers. Bird finished his B.S. degree in physical education at ISU in 1979 and also received the **John Wooden** Award as Collegiate Player of the Year from the Los Angeles Athletic Association.

Career Statistics

Yr	Team	GP	PTS	FG%	3P%	FT%	RPG	APG	SPG	BPG	TO	PF
1979-80	BC	82	1745	.474	.406	.836	10.4	4.5	1.74	.65	3.2	279
1980-81	BC	82	1741	.478	.270	.863	10.9	5.5	1.96	.77	3.5	239
1981-82	BC	77	1761	.503	.212	.863	10.9	5.8	1.86	.86	3.3	244
1982-83	BC	79	1867	.504	.286	.840	11.0	5.8	1.87	.90	3.0	197
1983-84	BC	79	1908	.492	.247	.888	10.1	6.6	1.82	.87	3.0	197
1984-85	BC	80	2295	.522	.427	.882	10.5	6.6	1.61	1.23	3.1	208
1985-86	BC	82	2115	.496	.423	.896	9.8	6.8	2.02	.63	3.2	182
1986-87	BC	74	2076	.525	.400	.910	9.2	7.6	1.82	.95	3.2	185
1987-88	BC	76	2275	.527	.414	.916	9.2	6.1	1.64	.75	2.8	157
1988-89	BC	6	116	.474		.947	6.2	4.8	1.00	.83	1.8	18
1989-90	BC	75	1820	.473	.333	.930	9.5	7.5	1.41	.81	3.2	173
1990-91	BC	60	1164	.454	.389	.891	8.5	7.2	1.80	.97	3.1	118
1991-92	BC	45	908	.466	.406	.926	9.6	6.8	.93	.73	2.8	82
TOTAL		897	21791	.496	.376	.886	10.0	6.3	1.74	.84	3.1	2279

BC: Boston Celtics.

When he completed his college athletic career, Bird ranked fifth on the NCAA list of all-time scorers. Before leaving ISU, Bird also began dating Dinah Mattingly. The couple would marry on September 30, 1989 and have two children, Connor and Mariah.

Signs with Boston Celtics

Bird signed a $3.25 million, five-year contract with the Celtics in 1979. With an abysmal record of 29-53 the prior year, Bird joined a team at the bottom of the NBA. Along with Robert Parrish and Kevin McHale, Bird turned the team around in dramatic fashion. The Celtics went 61-21 in Bird's first season in Boston, an accomplishment that helped him win NBA Rookie of the Year honors in 1980. The following year the Celtics beat the Chicago Bulls and Philadelphia Seventy-Sixers on their way to the NBA finals, where they faced the Houston Rockets. The Celtics took the series, the first of its three NBA championships in the 1980s.

Along with Magic Johnson's Los Angeles Lakers, Bird's Celtics were the dominant team in the NBA in the 1980s. The two stars greatly increased the popularity of professional basketball during the decade, with Johnson epitomizing the glamour of a sports superstar and Bird demonstrating the value of hard work and endless practicing. Although the two players were a study in contrasts, they maintained a friendly relationship off the court and a sportsmanlike rivalry on the court. Between 1983 and 1988, either the Celtics or Lakers emerged as NBA champions. When the two teams met up in the finals in 1984, the Celtics came out on top with four games in the seven-game series. The following year the Lakers won the championship in six games over the Celtics and in 1986 Boston won the finals for a third time with Bird. It was the last championship Bird claimed; in 1987 the Lakers beat the Celtics again in six games.

In addition to his three NBA championships with the Celtics, Bird also earned Most Valuable Player awards for the playoffs in 1984 and 1985 and was named the NBA's Player of the Year three consecutive times, from 1984-86. In 1985 he also picked up Man of the Year honors from the *Sporting News* and was named Male Athlete of the Year by the *Associated Press*. Bird's humble nature, his emphasis on teamwork, and his sportsmanlike conduct also made him a favorite with basketball fans, who routinely made Celtics home games a sold-out event.

Coaches Indiana Pacers

In February 1982 Bird suffered a broken zygomatic arch in his face; it was the first of numerous injuries that plagued him in his NBA career. In 1988 he underwent surgery to remove bone spurs on his feet and he played the following season with severe back pain. In 1991 he had back surgery during the off season and returned to the Celtics lineup for only half of the 1991-92 season. After playing for the U.S men's basketball team at the Barcelona Summer Olympic Games in 1992, where the "Dream Team" won the Gold Medal, Bird announced his retirement as a professional basketball player. For the next five years, he remained on the staff of the Celtics as a special assistant.

In 1997 Bird received an offer to join the Indiana Pacers as the team's head coach. Based on Magic Johnson's experience as the coach of the Lakers after his retirement, some observers predicted that Bird would find the role of a coach to be unsatisfying. Bird proved them wrong by taking the Pacers to their best-ever season with fifty-eight wins. At the end of the season Bird claimed NBA Coach of the Year honors. In 1998 he was also inducted into the Basketball Hall of Fame.

Retires from Basketball in 2000

As he had in Boston, Bird raised the profile of the Pacers as he made the team into title contenders. In

Larry Bird

2000 the Pacers faced the Los Angeles Lakers in the NBA finals, a series that the Lakers took in six games. Despite the success of the team, however, Bird decided that he did not have enough experience to continue on as the Pacers' coach and announced his retirement. The owner of a car dealership in Martinsville, Indiana and a hotel and restaurant in Terre Haute, Bird also retained an endorsement deal with Heinz foods that kept him in the public spotlight. Along with their two children, Bird and his wife Dinah divided their time at homes in Indiana and Florida.

Bird's consistency—most evident in his career free-throw average of 88.6 percent—and commitment to team work made the Boston Celtics into perennial championship contenders in the 1980s. Bird himself emerged as one of the league's most popular players in an era often dominated by the flashy style of superstars such as Magic Johnson. As a standout collegiate and professional player, then, Larry Bird helped to make basketball into one of the most popular mass-spectator sports in North America and abroad. Despite his fame, Bird remained resolutely down-to-earth about his accomplishments. "Basketball has been my life," he wrote in *Indianapolis Monthly* in 2000, "Everything I got has been through basketball. Our family never owned our own home. We never had a car. . . . Every material thing I have is through basketball. Every piece of clothes I have is through basketball. That's the way it's been."

SELECTED WRITINGS BY BIRD:

(With Bob Ryan) *Drive: The Story of My Life,* Doubleday, 1989.

(With Jackie MacMullan) *Bird Watching: On Playing and Coaching the Game I Love,* Warner Books, 1999.

FURTHER INFORMATION

Books

Bird, Larry, with Bob Ryan. *Drive: The Story of My Life.* New York: Doubleday, 1989.

Bird, Larry with Jackie MacMullan. *Bird Watching: On Playing and Coaching the Game I Love.* New York: Warner Books, 1999.

Hubbard, Jan, ed. *The Official NBA Encyclopedia.* New York: Doubleday, 2000.

Periodicals

Bird, Larry, and Dan Shaughnessy. "Why I Love This Game." *Indianapolis Monthly* (March 2000).

Looney, Douglas S. "Larry Bird: Doer and Teacher." *Christian Science Monitor* (May 22, 1998).

MacMullan, Jackie. "Bird Meets Magic for the NCAA Title" *Sports Illustrated* (November 29, 1999).

McGraw, Dan. "The Ghost of Larry Bird." *U.S. News and World Report* (October 12, 1998).

Reyes, Sonia. "Heinz Drafts Bird Again to Score Points as Boston Market Rolls Out Pot Pies." *Brandweek* (September 9, 2002).

Taylor, Phil. "It's a Wrap." *Sports Illustrated* (June 26, 2000).

Wahl, Grant et al. "Paternity Ward." *Time* (May 18, 1998).

Other

"Larry Bird." Celtic Stats Web site. http://www.celticstats. com/player/larrybird.html (December 4, 2002).

"Larry Bird." NBA Web site. http://www.nba.com/ history/bird_bio.html (December 2, 2002).

Sketch by Timothy Borden

Ole Einar Bjoerndalen

Ole Einar Bjoerndalen
1974-

Norwegian biathlete

Ole Einar Bjoerndalen listened to a vacuum cleaner salesman, then cleaned up at the 2002 Winter Olympic Games in Salt Lake City. Bjoerndalen, from Norway, won four gold medals in the biathlon, an event that combines cross-country skiing with target shooting. Amid an Olympiad that featured the stunning success of American figure skater **Sarah Hughes**, an enthralling gold-medal hockey game and a judging scandal in ice dancing, Bjoerndalen drew attention to an event many consider on the far fringe of sport.

Bjoerndalen took the gold in the 10-kilometer sprint, 20-kilometer individual, 12.5 km pursuit, and the 4x7.5 km relay. He became only the third person to win at least four gold medals in one winter Olympiad; speed skaters **Eric Heiden** of the United States and **Lydia Skoblikova** of Russia won five and four in 1980 and 1964, respectively. He credits Oyvind Hammer, a **Dick Vitale**-style pitchman for Filter Queen vacuums and motivational speaker on the side, for elevating his confidence and consistency.

Liked Target Shooting

Bjoerndalen was adept at cross-country skiing while growing up in the small Norwegian town of Simostranda, but opted for biathlon because he enjoyed target shooting. "Often ridiculed in the United States as a freak sport, the biathlon has its roots in Nordic warfare," Charlie Leduff wrote in the *New York Times*. The event surfaced in the Olympics in 1928 as a demonstration sport, called military patrol, and became a medal event in 1960, at Squaw Valley, California.

"Biathlon is the sport of the lean and the long," Greg Baum wrote in the *Sydney Morning Herald*. "The skis are skinny, the skiers more so. Bjoerndalen is 179 cm (about 5-foot-10) and just 66kg (about 146 pounds).... Protagonists skate up hill and down dale, stopping twice to shoot at a set of five targets, once from the prone position and once upright. For each missed target, com-

petitors must do a 150m 'penalty loop,' costing up to 20 seconds, depending on skiing ability."

Bjoerndalen, who could have made Norway's powerhouse cross-country team on skiing skills alone, introduced the speed element to biathlon. He competed in the 1994 Winter Olympics, which Norway hosted in Lillehammer. He won no medals, but in World Cup competition improved to fourth and second in 1995 and 1997, respectively. In the 1998 Games at Nagano, Japan, Bjoerndalen won the gold medal in a10km event interrupted for a day by heavy snow and fog. "I was really angry," Bjoerndalen said, according to the *Anchorage Daily News*. "But five minutes later I was ready for the new race." He was also part of a silver medalist 4x7.5km team in Nagano.

Power of Positive Thinking

Bjoerndalen, however, was inconsistent. Hammer, who came along to help him in the mid-1990s, provided Bjoerndalen with a sense of stability. "He was considered a rock of talent with pebbles for nerves," Leduff wrote. Hammer, according to Leduff, "has become Rasputin in Bjoerndalen's court."

Even critics who call the biathlon a marginal event acknowledge its demands on athletes. One must ski fast on a cross-country course, then settle down at a firing range and hit a target 50 meters (about 165 feet) away with a heart rate at about 180 to 190 beats per minute. Skiing too quickly can be detrimental in biathlon, as

Chronology

1974	Born January 24 in Drammen, Norway
1994	Competes in Winter Olympic Games at Lillehammer, Norway
2002	Signs clothing deal with Odlo, in conjunction with the Norwegian Biathlon Association; extends deal with French ski equipment company Rossignol
2003	Winning streak of four straight World Cup biathlons ends as Vladimir Dratchev of Belarus defeats him in Anterselva, Italy

Awards and Accomplishments

1993	Three gold medals, junior world championships
1995	Finishes fourth in World Cup biathlon ski standings
1997	Finishes second in World Cup standings
1998	World Cup overall champion
1998	Wins gold medal in men's 10km and silver medal in men's 4x7.5km relay at Winter Olympic Games in Nagano, Japan
2001	Wins two World Cup gold medals

2002 Wins four gold medals, only third Winter Olympics athlete to do so, winning 12.5km pursuit, 10km sprint, 20km individual, and 4x7.5km relay

competitors must slow their heart rate to where they are as motionless as possible while shooting. Bjoerndalen is in such strong shape that his heart rate can drop quickly; he can also make up for missing a target by skiing faster.

Supreme at Soldier Hollow

To prepare for the thin air of Salt Lake City, home of the 2002 Olympics, Bjoerndalen trained in other high-altitude regions. The Soldier Hollow course, the biathlon site in Salt Lake, was 6,000 feet above sea level. Soldier Hollow, according to Baum, posed a special challenge. "It is a hillier course at a higher elevation than all others, which puts an enormous cardiovascular strain on competitors. Upon passing the finish line yesterday, most collapsed to the snow, though we hesitate to say 'as if shot.' Not that they complain. 'It's all hills,' (British veteran Mike) Dixon said. 'And the altitude... it's really hard. It's great.'"

Bjoerndalen began his medals run with a victory in the 20 km. Later in the same week, he was one of only nine competitors to hit every target while winning the 10 km by 29 seconds. After finishing first in the men's 12.5 km pursuit, he secured his fourth gold by anchoring Norway's 4x7.5 km relay team despite falling on a downhill stretch and missing three shots in a snowfall that made shooting difficult. "Norway, despite Bjoerndalen's formidable presence, looked to have a weaker team than the Germans and the Russians," the *British Broadcasting Corporation* wrote on its web site. "But Bjoerndalen set off for the final leg with a minute's cushion after his three teammates (Halvard Hanevold, Frode Andresen and Egil Gjelland) all produced fine performances."

"Bjoerndalen's skiing is so superior that when teammate Egil Gjelland tagged off to him with Norway in the lead by almost a minute, Bjoerndalen could've lost a pole and still won," Beth Bragg wrote in the *Anchorage Daily News*. Bjoerndalen did in fact break a pole on the course as well as tumbling downhill and missing three targets. Despite the fifteen-second penalty Norway incurred because of those errors, the Norwegian team placed first in the competition. After securing his fourth gold of the Olympiad and Norway's first gold ever in the relay, Bjoerndalen raised his arms, hugged his teammates and embraced his fiancee, Natalie Santer.

"A workmanlike approach—and exquisite skiing—made Bjoerndalen a champion for the ages," Bragg wrote. "A vocal and visible contingent of flag-waving Norwegian fans cheered his every shot and every kilometer here at Soldier Hollow, and Bjoerndalen promised there would be a big party Wednesday night."

Elevates Biathlon Status

Bjoerndalen's success has brought international media attention to a sport many consider more appropriate for the ESPN Xtreme Games. And, of course, he is a hero in Norway, which takes its winter sports seriously. Bjoerndalen's performance, Leduff wrote, "has elevated him to rock-star status in his home country, where the combined art of skiing and shooting ranks second only to soccer."

With success came sponsor deals. Bjoerndalen, who competed in World Cup events during the winter of 2002-03, signed a clothing deal with Odlo worth about $300,000. Hoping to shake off the burdens of celebrity status, he trained with fewer people during the offseason. As of late January, 2003, Bjoerndalen was second in the World Cup standings to Raphael Poiree of France. Vladimir Dratchev of Belarus snapped a Bjoerndalen winning streak of four biathlons by beating him in the 20 km individual.

FURTHER INFORMATION

Periodicals

"Bjoerndalen Wins 4th Gold; U.S. vs. Canada for Bronze in Women's Curling." *Chicago Tribune*(February 21, 2002): 8.

Leduff, Charlie. "Fourth Gold Medal for a Positive Thinker." *New York Times*(February 21, 2002): D1.

Other

Baum, Greg. "Bjoerndalen a Hot Shot in the Snow." Sydney Morning Herald, http://old.smh.com.au/news/0202/15/sport/sport14/html, (February 15, 2002).

Biography Resource Center, Ole Einar Bjoerndalen profile, http://galenet.galegroup.com, (January 31, 2003).

"Bjoerndalen Takes Fourth Gold." BBC Sport, http://news.bbc.co.uk/winterolympics2002, (February 20, 2002).

Bragg, Beth. "Simply Unbeatable: Unassuming Norwegian Quietly Earns Fourth Gold of Games," Anchorage Daily News, http://anchorage.com/sports/olympics/story/767739p-819629c.html, (February 21, 2002).

Johansen, Robert Veiaaker. "Lone Wolf Bjoerndalen Cleaning Out Pack." Translation by Brian Olsen. Frozenbullet.com, http://www.frozenbullet.com, (July 19, 2002).

Olsen, Brian. "Bjoerndalen: Sponsor Deals, Hunting Trips, and Bad News." Frozenbullet.com, http://www.frozenbullet.com, (July 2, 2002).

Sketch by Paul Burton

Bonnie Blair

Bonnie Blair
1964-

American speed skater

American speed skater Bonnie Blair won six medals competing in three Winter Olympics Games, the second most medals won by a woman in the Winter Olympic Games (the first was **Lydia Skoblikova**). Of the six, five were gold, making Blair the only American woman to ever win five gold medals in the games. Blair was also the first American speed skater to win in more than one Olympic Games (1988, 1992, and 1994). As a speed skater, Blair had exemplary technique which contributed to her success.

Blair was born on March 18, 1964, in Cornwall, New York, the youngest of six children. She was the daughter of Charlie and Eleanor Blair, who raised their large Catholic family in Champaign, Illinois. All of Blair's two sisters and three brothers speed skated competitively because of their father. In fact, Charlie Blair had his children at a competition while his youngest child was being born. Though four of Blair's other siblings went on to win national championships, it was Blair who did the best as a competitive speed skater. Professionally, Charlie Blair was an engineer while Eleanor Blair worked in real estate.

Began Skating

Blair first donned skates at the age of two, and was competing as a speed skater by the age of four. She won a number of races as a child, including the Illinois state championship when she was seven. While Blair focused on speed skating, she also competed in other sports and activities. When she was attending Centennial High School, she competed in track and field events, including 100 meter to 800 meter races, long jump, and triple jump. She also was a cheerleader and on student council.

By the time Blair was fifteen, she decided to make speed skating her sole sport, training in a vigilant and dedicated fashion. At fifteen, Blair was named to the U.S. speed skating team. She began training with Cathy Priestner, who had won a silver medal in speed skating for Canada in the 1976 games, at the University of Illinois rink.

Priestner profoundly affected Blair's direction as a speed skater. Before Priestner, Blair only competed in short-track, pack-style racing. That is, races that were conducted with a number of skaters competing against each other in a pack. Olympic speed skating competitions were conducted differently. In Olympic style, skaters skated in pairs against the clock. Priestner had Blair train in the Olympic style on both short and long-track races. The Olympic style favored Blair's small stature and emphasis on technique. From early in her career, Blair's father was convinced that she would win Olympic Gold.

Related Biography: Coach Cathy Priestner

One of Blair's most influential coaches was Cathy Priestner (later known as Cathy Priestner-Allinger when she married Todd Allinger in 1986). Priestner had been a speed skater since her teen years, winning a national championship within a year of taking up the sport. Priestner had been an Olympic medalist herself, winning silver when she represented Canada at the Winter Olympics in Innsbruck, Austria, in 1976. She was the first Canadian woman to win a medal in speed skating. She also represented Canada in speed skating in the 1972 games in Sapporo, Japan. After a decade in the broadcast booth working as a commentator for the Olympics for the CBC and CTV, Priestner later became associated with the Olympics as a member of the organizing committee for the Calgary games in 1988, Salt Lake City in 2002, and Turin, Italy in 2006. She also managed the oval built for the Calgary games after the Olympics ended for a number of years.

Competed at Olympic Trials

When Blair was sixteen, she competed at her first Olympic trials for the 1980 Winter Olympics. Though she did well at the meet, she did not make the team. Blair wanted to continue to train for the 1984 Olympics and beyond, but had problems getting funding for her training. She received help from the local Champaign community. Fundraising was spearheaded by the Champaign police force in 1982, and Blair received support from such disparate sources as one of her brother's college fraternity brothers, professional basketball player Jack Silma who played with the Milwaukee Bucks. This allowed Blair to train seriously, including one stint with the U.S. men's speed skating team in Butte, Montana. Blair remained a popular figure in Champaign for many years, and was even given the key to the city. She graduated from Centennial High School, and later took some courses at Parkland Junior College in Champaign.

Blair had more success in 1984, making the U.S. women's speed skating team for the Winter Olympics in Sarajevo, Yugoslavia. She did not medal, but finished eighth in the 500-meter race. When Blair returned to the United States, she increased the intensity of her training, including weight training, running, biking, and rollerblading in addition to skating. Her hard work paid off when in 1985, she won the U.S. sprint championship. She would win this championship every year through 1994. In 1986, Blair set her first world's record in the 500 meters. Blair would also hold a number of world's and American records over the course of her speed skating career.

Blair's success came despite the fact that she was smaller and lighter than an average female speed skater. She was only 5'5" and 125-130 lbs. Blair was forced to rely on superior technique and a ferocious will to win because of her physical limitations. Blair knew how to win and took advantage of it. She used a low crouch and had a solid stroke. Speed skating coach Bob Fenn told Angus Phillips of *Washington Post* in 1992, "From a technical standpoint, she's the most efficient skater in the whole world. And as far as skating goes, she's got a lot of class."

Won Olympic Gold

Blair began to succeed on the international speed skating stage. In 1987, she won the World Cup in both the 500 and 1000 meter races. By the time of the 1988 Winter Olympic Games in Calgary, Alberta, Blair was regarded as one of the hopes for the future of American speed skating. She lived up to the hype by winning a gold medal in the 500 meters and a bronze in the 1000 meters. During her gold medal-winning race, she also set a world's record with a time of 39.1 seconds. (She finished fourth in the 1500 meter race.) Blair was the only American to win two medals at these games, and was given the honor of carrying the American flag at the closing ceremonies.

During the Olympics, Blair was given the nickname "Bonnie the Blur." After the games ended, she received a number of commercial endorsements that funded her training, including Disney World and other commercials, though these opportunities were not as numerous or long-lived as originally hoped. Though Blair briefly considered not competing in the 1992 games, she told Douglas S. Looney of *Sports Illustrated,* "Skating has always been a pleasure and a joy. I love to go fast and create the wind. It's fun to set goals, reach goals, reset goals. I don't see any torture in this at all."

Lost Focus as a Skater

After the Olympics, Blair continued her education, studying physical education at Montana Tech University. In 1989, she won the World Sprint Championships, though she did not train as hard as she had for the Olympics. Blair lost focus for a while after the death of her father on December 25, 1989. She stopped training as a skater for a brief period, spending four months training as a cyclist. Blair finished fourth in a national sprint competition for cyclists.

Another problem for Blair was the lack of competition among the American women speed skaters in the late 1980s and early 1990s. The trials were a breeze for her. The only real competition came internationally, but because of her lack of training in 1989-91, she did not have much success in races in 1990-91. For example, Blair finished fifth in the 1991 World Sprint Championships, though she was also suffering from bronchitis at the time.

Bonnie Blair

Won Two More Golds

As the 1992 Winter Olympic Games in Albertville, France, approached, Blair regained her focus on speed skating. She was considered the best American hope for a medal, and did not disappoint. She won the first American gold of the games when she won the 500 meter race. Though the race was not great, in part because the ice surface was too warm, the victory made Blair the first woman to win gold in consecutive Winter Olympic games. Blair also won gold in the 1000 meter race. In both races, she was pushed by Ye Qiaobo of China who earned two silver medals. Blair won the 1000 meter race by only .02 seconds. Ye trained by watching tapes of Blair. Blair's only disappointment was finishing 21st in the 1500 meter race.

After the Albertville games ended, Blair again took the opportunity created by her celebrity. She signed with Advantage International, a sports marketing group, and did a number of commercials endorsements including Jeep, Evian, National Frozen Foods, and Rollerblades. She also began serving on the board for U.S. Speed skating. Training remained her focus, however. Because an indoor training oval, Pettit National Ice Center, opened in Milwaukee, Wisconsin, Blair moved there from Champaign.

Blair continued to have success on the international level, though she also challenged herself to find ways to win. In 1993 and 1994, she won gold medals at the World Championships in 500 meters. Still Blair changed her training a bit. She hired a different coach, Nick Thometz, who emphasized something different for Blair: explosive drills over strength and distance training. Blair also continued to improve her already great technique. Blair told Brian Cazeneuve of *The Sporting News,* "I'm the one who puts pressure on myself. I just want to go fast. When the gun goes off, I don't worry about the person next to me. This is an individual sport."

Competed in Last Olympics

When the 1994 Winter Olympics at Lillehammer, Norway, came around, Blair was again favored to win. She continued to compete in part because there were only two years between these Olympic Games. (The International Olympic Committee wanted Summer and Winter Olympic Games to alternate every two years.) Though Blair trained for the Olympics like they were any other meet, she dominated the trials in the 500, 1000, and 1500 meter races.

At the Olympic Games, Blair had the support of her family, the so-called "Blair Bunch" which consisted of immediate and extended family members who attended

Awards and Accomplishments

c. 1971	Won Illinois state championship in speed skating for age group
1985-94	U.S. sprint champion
1986	Set world's record in 500 meters
1987	Won World Cup in 500 meters and 1000 meters
1988	Won gold medal in Olympics speed skating in 500 meters—set world's record—and won bronze in 1000 meters
1989	Won the World Sprint Champions
1992	Won gold medals in 500 meter and 1000 meter at Olympics in speed skating
1993	Won gold in 500 meters at World Championships
1994	Won gold medals in 500 meters and 1000 meters at Winter Olympic Games in speed skating; won gold in 500 meters and 1000 at World Sprint Championships and World Cup; named Babe Zaharis Female Amateur Athlete of the Year; named Sportswoman of the Year by Women's Sports Foundation
1995	Set 500 meters speed skating world record at Calgary; retired in March as speed skater; named Sportswoman of the Year by Women's Sports Foundation; won world sprint championship
1997	Given Sports Humanitarian Award, World Sports Humanitarian Hall of Fame

Where Is She Now?

After retiring from skating, Blair had two children (son Grant and daughter Blair), worked as a motivational speaker, and wrote a book about her accomplishments, *A Winning Edge* (1996). She remained connected to speed skating by serving as a coach and conducting clinics. Her husband, Dave Cruikshank, was also a speed skater and she served as his technical consultant. Blair continued to serve on the board for U.S. Speed skating and also worked for the Olympic Committee. She did some television commentary for speed skating. In addition, Blair was active in charity work and continued to do some commercial endorsements for companies like General Mills products at the 2002 Winter Olympic Games.

a number of her more important races en masse. They saw Blair win two more golds. She won the 500 meters with a time of 39.1 seconds and the 1000 meters with a time of 1:18.74. For her success, Blair was named the Babe Zaharis Female Amateur Athlete of the Year and sportswoman of the Year by *Sports Illustrated* for 1994. The victories led to more endorsements, and even more important to Blair, the popularity of speed skating.

Blair's last year as a competitive speed skater was 1995. Though she knew she was retiring, she left on top. In early 1995, she set another world's record in the 500 meters skating on the Olympic oval in Calgary where she won her first medal. Blair broke the 39-second mark by skating it in 38.13 seconds. She also set a record in the 1000 meters with a time of 1:19.3. Blair won the World Sprint Championships, then retired on March 18, 1995, after the competition held on her home ice in Milwaukee. Blair said she quit because there was nothing left for her to prove. As Jere Longman wrote in the *New York Times*, "Blair has no mountains to climb. Many athletes wait too long, until their skills have begun to melt and slide like snow from a roof. But Blair is going out on top." At her peak, she considered the fastest woman in the world in speed skating. Blair told Shannon Brownlee of *Sports Illustrated,* "Skating is a joy. It's a solitary sport, one in which you can claim all the rewards as your own. Nobody makes you do it. It's just you."

CONTACT INFORMATION

Address: c/o 306 White Pine Rd., Delafield, WI 53018-1124.

SELECTED WRITINGS BY BLAIR:

(With Greg Brown) *A Winning Edge,* Taylor, 1996.

FURTHER INFORMATION

Books

Christensen, Karen, et al., eds. *International Encyclopedia of Women and Sports.* New York: Macmillan Reference USA, 2001.

Johnson, Anne Janette. *Great Women in Sports.* Detroit: Visible Ink Press, 1996.

Parry, Melanie, ed. *Chambers Biographical Dictionary.* Chambers, 1997.

Sherrow, Victoria. *Encyclopedia of Women and Sports.* ABC-CLIO, 1996.

Periodicals

Brand, David. "Bonnie the blue." *Time* (March 7, 1988): 69.

Brownlee, Shannon. "Yanks on the move." *Sports Illustrated* (January 27, 1988): 236.

Cazeneuve, Brian. "Skating first." *Sporting News* (February 14, 1994): S15.

Janofsky, Michael. "Olympic Profile: Bonnie Blair; A Life of Skating Leads to Calgary." *New York Times* (February 9, 1987): 166.

Janofsky, Michael. "Repeat for Blair." *New York Times* (February 11, 1992): B11.

Jeansonne, John. "Blair Has a Flair—For Gold." *Newsday* (February 6, 1994): 16.

Jenkins, Sally. "A Bonnie blare." *Sports Illustrated* (February 17, 1992): 38.

Jenkins, Sally. "Glory and gloom." *Sports Illustrated* (February 24, 1992): 18.

Longman, Jere. "Retiring at Top Speed." *New York Times* (February 19, 1995): section 8, p. 1.

Looney, Douglas S. "Bring back Bonnie." *Sports Illustrated* (March 6, 1989): 32.

Looney, Douglas S. "Sprinting to Calgary." *Sports Illustrated* (December 6, 1987): section 2, p. 10.

Matson, Barbara. "Blair has not Slowed Down: Family is her Life, Not Speed skating." *Boston Globe* (January 9, 2002): F7.

Noden, Merrell. "Catching up with … Bonnie Blair and Johann Olav Koss." *Sports Illustrated* (January 20, 1997): 4.

Noden, Merrell. "One-woman ice show." *Sports Illustrated* (January 15, 1990): 92.

Parrish, Paula. "History (Never) Lessens: Bonnie Blair was textbook good, and her legacy still is quoted chapter and verse." *Denver Rocky Mountain News* (February 15, 2002): 23S.

Phillips, Angus. "Bonnie Blair is a 5-4 Colossus on Skates." *Washington Post* (January 2, 1992): D3.

Phillips, Angus. "Introspective Blair Rebuffs Outside World in Pursuit of Gold." *Washington Post* (February 11, 1994): H5.

Reilly, Rick. "To mettle the medal." *Sports Illustrated* (March 7, 1988): 50.

Rushin, Steve. "Child of innocence." *Sports Illustrated* (December 19, 1994): 72.

Rushin, Steve. "The last lap." *Sports Illustrated* (February 27, 1995): 52.

Rushin, Steve. "Time after time." *Sports Illustrated* (February 7, 1994): 90.

Williams, Lena. "Blair Enjoys Being Olympic Spectator." *New York Times* (January 16, 2002): D7.

Witteman, Paul A. "Blades of gold." *Time* (February 24, 1992): 54.

Wolff, Alexander. "Bonnie's bounty." *Sports Illustrated* (March 7, 1994): 42.

Wolff, Alexander. "Whooosh!." *Sports Illustrated* (February 28, 1994): 18.

Other

Imperial Oil Web Site. http://www.imperialoil.ca/thisis/publications/review/2001q4 (January 5, 2003).

Sketch by A. Petruso

Sir Peter Blake

Peter Blake
1948-2001

New Zealander yachtsman

Sir Peter Blake, perhaps more than any other sailor, was responsible for changing the public perception of ocean yacht racing from a daring adventure sport practiced by a few foolhardy souls, into an avidly followed professional sport whose top players are internationally acclaimed. Blake first made headlines in 1993, when he set a world record for the fastest circumnavigation of the globe under sail (in about 75 days). Then, in 1995, the New Zealand sailing team that he headed bested the Americans at their own game in the 144-year-old America's Cup race. This was only the second time in the history of the race that the trophy had been won from the Americans. In 2000, Blake led the New Zealand team in a successful defense of the trophy, forever changing the tenor of the event, and firmly establishing Blake as an international celebrity.

Blake retired from racing following Team New Zealand's second America's Cup victory, and founded blakexpeditions, an nonprofit organization whose purpose is to help protect the world's oceans through scientific sailing voyages and educational programs. In 2001, while captaining one of his organization's first voyages, Blake was shot and killed by pirates off the coast of Brazil.

Knighted in 1995, Blake was a national hero in his homeland of New Zealand, on a par with the great New Zealand mountain climber Sir Edmund Hillary, who, along with his Napali guide, Tenzing Norgan, was the first to scale Mt. Everest. Blake was known for his fairness and his straightforward desire to avoid politics and simply enjoy his chosen sport for its own sake. After Blake's death, his friend and frequent sailing partner, Sir Robin Knox-Johnston, told the *Independent* of London, "Peter will be remembered as a giant in sailing over the last 20 years. He was a consummate seaman, excellent tactician, brilliant organizer, a natural leader and great company. He will be sorrowfully missed by all of us who had the pleasure to know and sail with him."

Raised on the Seashore

Peter James Blake was born in Auckland, New Zealand, on October 1, 1948. His father worked as an

Chronology

1948	Born in Auckland, New Zealand, on October 1
1956	Given his first boat, by his father
1968	Builds his first boat, wins New Zealand Junior Offshore championship
1970	Finishes degree in mechanical engineering, moves to England
1971	Competes in his first major race, the Cape Town to Rio de Janeiro race, aboard *Ocean Spirit*
1973-74	Competes in the first Whitbread Round the World race as a crewmember aboard *Burton Cutter*
1978-79	Competes in the second Whitbread Round the World race, as a watch leader on *Heath Condor*
1979	Marries Pippa Glanville
1979	Wins Fastnet race on *Condor*
1980	Wins Sydney-Hobart race aboard *Ceramco New Zealand*
1981-82	Competes in the third Whitbread race aboard *Ceramco New Zealand*
1985-86	Competes in the fourth Whitbread race, as captain of *Lion New Zealand*
1988	Wins the Two-man Round Australia race aboard *Steinlager I*
1989	Wins Whitbread Round the World Race as captain of *Steinlager II*
1992	Competes for the America's Cup
1993	Wins Trophee Jules Verne by setting a world record for sailing around the world in 74 days, 22 hours, 17 minutes, and 22 seconds, aboard *ENZA New Zealand*
1994	Becomes Chief Executive Officer, Team New Zealand Ltd, New Zealand's America's Cup racing team
1995	Head of New Zealand team that wins America's Cup, taking the trophy from the American team
1997	Asked to head the management of the Cousteau Foundation
1998	Heads ecological expedition in the Caspian Sea
2000	Leads New Zealand in its second victory in the America's Cup
2000	Steps down as CEO of Team New Zealand to found blakexpeditions, a nonprofit organization dedicated to ecological research and education through ocean voyages
2000	Named special envoy to the United Nations Environment Program
2000	Makes first ecological voyage to South America
2001	Killed by pirates near Macap, Brazil, at the mouth of the Amazon River

advertising salesman, after having served on gunboats off the British coast during World War II. Blake's childhood home was on the seashore, and his introduction to sailing came at the age of five, when he first took to the water in a dinghy that had been constructed especially for children.

Blake attended Takapuna Grammar School, and it was there that he learned to sail, aboard a P Class dinghy. He was just 16 years old when he entered his first long-distance sailing race, sailing from New Zealand to the Pacific Islands—a distance of 1,200 miles. At 18, he built his first boat, a 23-foot keelboat.

After high school, Blake attended Auckland's Technical Institute and studied mechanical engineering. Although this schooling would later help him build racing boats, he told the *Times* of London that he "hated every minute of it." When he was 23 years old, he relocated to England, planning to design yachts for a living. But he soon found that he enjoyed sailing more than engineering.

A Life at Sea

In 1973, the first Whitbread Round the World Race was launched, and the race gave Blake, then 25 years old, his chance to realize his dream to race yachts professionally; he was invited to join the crew of Less Williams, the captain of one of the racing yachts. The ship was a British boat, 80 feet long, called the *Burton Cutter*. The boat's interior was still being finished as the boat launched on its first leg of the race, and it began to fall apart on the second leg.

Although the ship lost the race, Blake had set firmly forth in his chosen career, and for him there was no turning back. Whitbread races followed every four years, and Blake eventually sailed in a total of five consecutive Whitbreads, becoming the first person to do so. The next race was in 1978-79, also aboard a ship commanded by Williams. On this voyage, Blake served as a watch leader. This boat was called *Heath's Condor*, and Blake and Williams were joined by Robin Knox-Johnston, with whom Blake was to have a long-standing friendship and partnership. Built with a new-type carbon-fiber mast, the ship ran into trouble during the second week of the race, when the mast collapsed.

After the race, Blake and his crew pulled into the port town of Emsworth, on the south coast of England, to have their boat refitted at the sailing club there. While they were there, Blake met his future wife, Pippa Glanville. Emsworth was Pippa's hometown, and as she later told the *Sunday Telegraph* of London, "I was in the club having a drink when Peter walked in. I'd never met anyone from the Antipodes before, and he was very tall and very striking, with very, very blond hair and blue eyes. I thought, 'Wow!' No one had ever made such an impression on me."

World Champion Yacht Racer

Less than three months later, Blake asked Pippa to marry him. They were married the same year, 1979. "He proposed to me in a marina in Miami in Florida," Pippa told the *Sunday Telegraph*, "and I just said yes straight away. I didn't hesitate. I think I'd passed a test. I knew right from the start that I was sort of sharing Peter with the team. Right up to the moment he was killed, there was always a team around Peter. For our honeymoon we sailed from here [Emsworth] to New Zealand—me and seven guys!"

In 1981-82, Blake competed in the third Whitbread race, this time as captain. The boat was called *Ceramco New Zealand*, and this one, too lost its mast during the race. But Blake and his resourceful crew managed to build a make-shift mast and get underway again within 24 hours of the mishap. They made it to Cape Town, where they put in a new mast, and went on to finish second in the race.

Blake entered the fourth Whitbread race in 1985 as captain of the *Lion New Zealand*, and again did not win. But the fifth Whitbread race, in 1989, was a charm for

Blake; his boat, *Steinlager II,* won all six legs of the race, winning the overall race by only minutes.

Blake described life aboard the *Steinlager II,* on which there were no showers, and few changes of clothes for the crew of 15, to the BBC: "You don't notice the smells or whatever that develop because everyone's the same. But when you get into port and you go away for 24 hours and come back, well you see the look on people's face when they come down below for the first time, they just about fall over backwards, the stench is just terrible. You don't wash, see, in the southern ocean, you might not change your underwear for three weeks, and you get a bit of a layer of grease and goo that builds up over you, and you seem to be just fine."

In 1993, Blake sailed around the world with crewmate Robin Knox-Johnson. The voyage broke the record for the fastest non-stop voyage around the world, and the pair won the Jules Verne trophy for sailing around the world in under 80 days. They circled the globe in 74 days, 22 hours, 17 minutes, and 30 seconds, in 1993.

Wins America's Cup—And Keeps It

Blake and Knox-Johnston again teamed up in 1995 in New Zealand's bid to wrest the America's Cup from the United States. In charge of the New Zealand America's Cup team in 1995, Blake had only a limited budget to work with. It was his outstanding leadership and organizational skills that won the race for Team New Zealand, not superior financing. Blake started by breaking his team into five groups, each responsible for a separate specialty: sailing, boatbuilding, design, administration, and public relations, and he mortgaged his house to pay for the entry fee. At the end, when funds ran dry, Blake and his team were supported by the proceeds of sales of Blake's trademark red socks, a pair of which Blake wore throughout the race, and which New Zealanders bought by the thousands.

Blake and his team won the America's Cup on the doorstep of defending champion, Dennis Connor, when they finished the race off San Diego. Team New Zealand dealt the Americans a humiliating defeat, winning the race 5-0, and the New Zealanders returned home national heroes. (The Americans had kept the Cup for 132 years, from the first race in 1851 until 1983, when it was finally won by a team of Australian sailors. However, the Americans won it back in the next race, in 1987.) Both Blake and Robin Knox-Johnston were knighted that same year, 1995, for their contributions to the sport of yachting. Team New Zealand, again with Blake in charge, though not as his ship's captain, went on to successfully defend the Cup in 2000.

Blake told the *Herald* of Glasgow about preparations for the 2000 race, "We have had a tight budget—but I believe firmly that if you have too much money you look at aspects of research and development that do not matter. Having to mind the dollars makes you focus on those

Origin of the America's Cup

One of the oldest and most prestigious prizes awarded in international yacht racing, the America's Cup was originally an 100-guinea silver trophy offered by the Royal Yacht Squadron to the winner of a race around the Isle of Wight on August 22, 1851. John Cox Stevens, a wealthy New Jersey real estate broker and founder of the New York Yacht Club, organized a syndicate of five other club members that commissioned William H. Brown in 1850 to construct a yacht "to race against the best the British had to offer." Following the design by George Steers, Brown finished *America* in 1851, in time for Stevens to accept an invitation from the Royal Yacht Squadron to enter its race around the Isle of Wight. Pitted against seventeen seasoned British boats, *America* started poorly but finished with a commanding lead and won the cup. In response to the win by *America*, the *Spirit of the Times* observed that "old England was no match for young America." Stevens accepted the cup, naming it after his yacht, and kept it on display at his Annandale, New Jersey estate. After his death in 1857, it became a trust of the New York Yacht Club "as a permanent challenge cup, open to competition by any organized yacht club of any foreign country."

areas likely to be the most productive. Money does not buy the America's Cup. In the final analysis you have to get all the little things right, and that comes down to the talent and commitment of the people on the team."

Blake cited small improvements in every aspect of the design, construction, and sailing of the boat as the contributing factors to winning the race. "Every damn thing matters," he told the *Herald,* "and if you add up the seconds here and there you end up with the difference between success and failure."

In 2000, Blake founded a nonprofit organization called blakexpeditions, whose purpose was to sail around the world in the cause of environmental conservation, and to, according to Blake's statement on the organization's web site, "convey our experiences, and what we find, through inspirational television, an exciting web site, stimulating educational programmes and informative media and publishing agendas."

Killed by Pirates

Blake was 53 years old when he was killed by pirates in 2001. At the time, he was exploring the Amazon River in Brazil with his yacht *Seamaster* and crew. Their purpose, specifically, was to study global warming. The attack came as *Seamaster* was anchored off the Brazilian coast, near the town of Macapa, at the mouth of the Amazon River. Blake and his seven crewmates were relaxing before a planned sail the next day to Venezuela. They were playing Scrabble when a row boat pulled soundlessly beside *Seamaster.* and several armed men wearing masks climbed aboard.

Blake's crew dove to the deck, but not Blake. Determined to defend his ship, he went below deck to retrieve a rifle he had stored there for defense against wild animals. By the time he came back on deck, one of the pirates was pointing a gun at the head of one of Blake's crew. Blake shouted at the pirates to get off his boat, and the pirate holding the gun began to back away, now aiming his gun at Blake. Shots were fired, and Blake's rifle jammed. Before he could bring it to bear again, he was shot two times in the back by the fleeing pirates, and killed almost instantly. One of Blake's crewmates was grazed by a bullet, but the rest escaped unscathed. The pirates were arrested in the hours following the attack, and each of them was sentenced to up to 37 years in jail.

Blake was buried in a simple grave just steps from the ocean in the small English hamlet of Warblington, where he and his family had made their home since the 1970s. The prime minister of New Zealand, Helen Clark, spoke at the funeral, saying, according to the BBC, "Peter Blake was a living legend. I believe that Peter was held in high esteem for many reasons—for his achievements, for his courage, for the causes he espoused, and for being a decent human being."

Blake is survived by his wife Pippa, their daughter, Sarah-Jane, and son, James. "He had this amazing strength," Blake's widow told the *Sunday Telegraph* of London. "He was 6ft 4in and he had this amazing strength. Yes, we've lost a husband and a father—but it's like we've also lost the backbone to our whole existence. You were always safe with Peter. And that could be at home or at sea."

A consummate sailor, a man admired for his kindness and sense of fair play, and a loving husband and father, Sir Peter Blake will perhaps best be remembered as the man who was most responsible for transforming ocean yacht racing into a sport avidly followed by millions of people around the world.

FURTHER INFORMATION

Periodicals

Alexander, Stuart. "Obituary: Sir Peter Blake." *Independent* (December 10, 2001): 6.

de Bertodano, Helena. "I'm Not Angry, Just Sad." *Sunday Telegraph* (June 30, 2002): 3.

Gold, Scott. "The World; America's Cup Winner Slain by Pirates in Brazil" *Los Angeles Times* (December 7, 2001): A1.

"Obituary of Sir Peter Blake." *Daily Telegraph* (December 7, 2001): 29.

"Sir Peter Blake." *Times* (December 7, 2001).

"Sir Peter Blake; Yachtsman Who Masterminded New Zealand's America's Cup Wins and Broke Round-the-World Record." *Herald* (December 8, 2001): 14.

Other

blakexpeditions. http://www.blakexpeditions.com (October 1, 2002).

"Hillary & Norgay." Time.com. http://www.time.com/time/time100/heroes/profile/hillary_norgay01.html (October 3, 2002).

"Laureus Sports Awards—Winners 2002." Laureus Sports Awards. http://www.laureus.com/awards/winners/index.php (October 1, 2002).

"The Life of Yachtsman and Ecologist Peter Blake." Agence France Presse. (December 6, 2001).

"More About the History of the Americas Cup." Official site of the America's Cup. http://www.americascup.com/historymore.aspx (September 27, 2002).

"Mourners Pay Tribute to Blake." BBC. http://news.bbc.co.uk/sport1/hi/other_sports/sailing/1710559.stm (December 14, 2001).

"Sir Peter Blake." BBC. http://newssearch.bbc.co.uk/olmedia/1695000/video/_1696261_blake_vi.ram (October 1, 2002).

"Sir Peter's Final Log." BBC. http://news.bbc.co.uk/sport1/hi/other_sports/sailing/1710559.stm (December 14, 2001).

Sketch by Michael Belfiore

Toe Blake
1912-1995

Canadian hockey player

Hector "Toe" Blake was one of the most influential hockey coaches in the history of the National Hockey League. He won eight Stanley Cups as a coach, five of them in consecutive seasons, with the Montreal Canadiens. He had a .634 winning percentage as a coach, and was a mentor to **Scotty Bowman**, the only man to win more Cups as a coach, with nine. Many consider Blake to be one of the best coaches in any sport. In addition to his coaching career, Blake had a Hall of Fame playing career as left wing, primarily with the Montreal Canadiens, for twelve seasons.

Toe Blake

Blake was born on August 21, 1912, in Victoria Mines, Ontario, Canada. He was given his nickname, "Toe," by which he was commonly known, by a younger sister who could not pronounce his first name. While hockey was already an important part of Canadian culture, Blake's mother did not want him to play hockey, but instead get a steady job in one of the local mines. Thus, before the age of 12, Blake played hockey as a goalie. In this time period, it was common for goalies to not wear skates to play the position. After getting a job hitching horses for a milk company to make their rounds, he bought own skates and began playing as a skater. Hockey soon became the focus of his life.

By the time he was seventeen, Blake began his playing career in the Sudbury-Nickel Belt League, first with the Cochrane Dunlops, then for the Sudbury Industries. From 1930-32, he played for the Sudbury Cub Wolves of the Northern Ontario Hockey Association. While playing for one of the Sudbury-based teams, Blake drew attention from NHL scouts. Blake then played in the Ontario Hockey Association Senior's League for the Hamilton Tigers from 1932-34. During this time period, Blake would play hockey in the winter and baseball in the summer.

Chronology

1912	Born in Victoria Mines, Ontario, Canada
1934	Appears in three games with the Montreal Maroons
1936	Traded to the Montreal Canadiens as a player, for which he played until retirement
1943-44	Put with Maurice "Rocket" Richard and Elmer Lach to form the "Punch Line"
1944	Sets Stanley Cup record by scoring five assists in one game
1948	Forced to retire as a player on the Canadiens because of injury; becomes minor league coach in Houston, Texas
1948	Works as coach for the Buffalo (New York) Bisons in the American Hockey League
1949	Becomes coach of the Valleyfield (Quebec) Braves in the Quebec Senior League
1955	Becomes coach of the Montreal Canadiens on June 8
1968	Retires as coach of Montreal Canadiens
1995	Dies of Alzheimer's on May 17 in Montreal

Signed with Montreal

In 1934, Blake was signed by the Montreal Maroons, but only appeared in three games before being sent to the minor leagues, again with Hamilton. He was on the bench when the Maroons won the Stanley Cup in 1935. At the time, Blake was considered a fighter. Blake began the 1935-36 season in the minor leagues, playing for the Providence Reds in the Can-Am League, but was traded in February 1936 to the Montreal Canadiens with Bill Miller for goalie Lorne Chabot.

It was with the Canadiens that Blake developed his scoring ability, earning the nickname "Old Lamplighter." He still retained his toughness, however, and never backed down from a fight, no matter what the situation, even if losing. By 1937, Blake was playing in the All-Star Game. In 1939, he was the leading scorer in the National Hockey League. He also won the Hart Trophy that year as the league's most valuable player. Yet the Canadiens finished sixth in the league. It was not until the 1940s that the Canadiens began to win.

When Dick Irvin was hired as coach in 1941, Montreal began to rebuild and Irvin put Blake at the center of the process. But it took several seasons for Irvin to find the right linemates for him. Because Blake spoke both French and English, and was partially French Canadian, which earned the respect of other Quebecois players, he could play with both types of players. The most dominant line he played on was the "Punch Line" with **Maurice Richard**, a prolific scorer, on right wing and Elmer Lach at center. Blake made the line run, and the trio often led the team in scoring.

Won Stanley Cups

The Punch Line was put together during the 1943-44 season, when Montreal finished first in the regular season and won the Stanley Cup. In 1944 playoffs, Blake himself set an NHL record by scoring five assists in one game against Toronto. Blake followed up this accomplishment by scoring a career high sixty-seven points in the 1944-45 season.

In the 1945-46 season, Blake again showed scoring prowess during the regular season with twenty-nine goals. During the playoffs, he added seven more, again playing primarily with the Punch Line. The Canadiens won their second Stanley Cup in three years when they defeated the Boston Bruins in five games in the finals. In addition to winning the Stanley Cup, Blake also won the Lady Byng Trophy that year. The Lady Byng is given to the player who demonstrates the most gentlemanly play. This was considered somewhat ironic as Blake was known as a hard-nosed player who had numerous run-ins with referees throughout his career.

Retired as a Player

Blake's scoring numbers went down in the 1947-48 season, when he scored only nine goals. His season, and career, were cut short that year. On January 11, 1948, a hit to Blake's body resulted in a broken ankle and forced his retirement. The Canadiens did not make the playoffs in his absence. Over the course of his thirteen seasons as a professional player in the NHL, Blake scored 235 goals and 292 assists in the regular season, plus twenty-five goals and thirty-seven assists in fifty-seven playoff games. It was hard for Blake to retire. He missed the camaraderie and the games, but found a way to stay involved with the game.

Began Coaching Career

Before the 1947-48 season ended, Blake found employment as a minor league hockey coach. Though still on crutches because of his broken ankle, he coached a team in Houston, Texas, in the United States Hockey League to a championship in 1948. The next season Blake was hired to coach on a higher level in the minor leagues. He coached the American Hockey League's Buffalo (New York) Bisons, and appeared in eighteen games as a player, during the 1948-49 season. However, he quit in a disagreement with management. In the 1949-50 season, Blake coached the Valleyfield (Quebec) Braves in the Quebec Senior League for several seasons. He also played in forty-three games for them as a player in the 1949-50 season. These experiences led to Blake becoming a savvy coach.

Hired as Coach of the Canadiens

When Irvin, Blake's old coach, retired as head coach of the Canadiens after the 1954-55 season, Blake was the only man really considered to replace him. Blake had the support of Frank Selke, Sr., the managing director of the Canadiens. He was officially hired on June 8, 1955. As Robert McG. Thomas, Jr. wrote in the *New York Times,* "But for all his acclaim as a player, no one was quite prepared for what happened when Blake, his signature fedora on his head, took his place behind the Canadien bench for the first time in 1955 and found his true calling."

One immediate problem that Blake had to face was taking charge of a team consisting of many players he had played with before his retirement. Another issue was managing former linemate Richard, who, at 35, still had a tendency to lose his temper and fight instead of do what he did best: score. Blake convinced him that he did not need to prove himself in any way but winning the Stanley Cup. This helped form Richard's legacy. In turn, Richard fully supported Blake as a coach, which influenced the entire team's attitude towards Blake.

Blake inherited a team with a good, young goalie, great scorers, and a smart defense. With this core, Blake created a dynasty and won eight Stanley Cups over the course of his 13 year coaching career. Many believe these were some of the best teams in the history of the NHL. He had the respect of his players, but used a dictatorial style of coaching and would not coddle them. While he used humor and had the ability to motivate, he also had a temper. Blake would never call out a single

Career Statistics

Yr	Team	GP	G	AST	PTS	PIM
1934-35	Maroons	8	0	0	0	0
1935-36	Canadiens	11	1	2	3	28
1936-37	Canadiens	43	10	12	22	12
1937-38	Canadiens	43	17	16	33	33
1938-39	Canadiens	48	24	23	47	10
1939-40	Canadiens	48	17	19	36	48
1940-41	Canadiens	48	12	20	32	49
1941-42	Canadiens	48	17	28	45	19
1942-43	Canadiens	48	23	36	59	26
1943-44	Canadiens	41	26	33	59	10
1944-45	Canadiens	49	29	38	67	25
1945-46	Canadiens	50	29	21	50	2
1946-47	Canadiens	60	21	29	50	6
1947-48	Canadiens	32	9	15	24	4
TOTAL		577	235	292	527	272

Canadiens: Montreal Canadiens; Maroons: Montreal Maroons.

player by name in front of the team and embarrass them. He got everyone to play better, to push themselves. Blake put as much into coaching as his players did into playing.

Won Stanley Cups

It took two seasons for the Canadiens to gel under Blake. Blake led the Canadiens to their first Stanley Cup as coach in 1956. They won the Cup each year through 1960. With each Cup, Blake was harder on himself and his players and others around him.

The team did not do well in the early 1960s, making the playoffs but not winning the Cup. While a master strategist as a coach, Blake still had the temper of a player. During a 1961 semi-final game, after losing to the Chicago Blackhawks, Blake hit referee Dalton McArthur after the game. McArthur had waved off two Montreal goals in overtime. Blake was fined the next day by the NHL. By the 1963-64 season, the Canadiens finished in first place again.

While Canadiens won Stanley Cups in the 1964-65, 1965-66 seasons, and 1967-68 seasons, Blake's temper became more evident. He was charged with attacking a fan in a game in Los Angeles on November 19, 1967. Blake was later acquitted of the charges.

Retired as Coach

Blake cut his coaching career short, retiring right after winning his eighth Stanley Cup in 1968. His Canadiens defeated the St. Louis Blues (coached by former protégé Bowman) that year. This eight Cup record stood until 2002, when his Bowman won his record ninth, and like Blake, promptly retired. As a coach, Blake had a record of 500 wins, 255 losses, and 159 ties. His playoff record was eighty-two wins, thirty-seven losses, with a series record of 18-5. Claude Ruel replaced him behind the Canadiens' bench.

Blake's reasons for retiring were complex. As the NHL expanded, there was more travel, more media to deal with, changing player attitudes, and little details like ticket demands that did not agree with the hard-lined Blake. In Bill Libby's *The Coaches,* Blake was quoted as saying "I had to quit. It's not that I had no new worlds to conquer. Every game, every season is a new challenge. But I'd been meeting these challenges as coach of the Canadiens for thirteen years. ... The pressure was getting to be unbearable. On the day of the game I was getting to be unbearable. The afternoons were the worst. All the thinking. And then the waiting, waiting, waiting. I was no good to anyone, not even my family. ... I had to quit."

Even after retiring, Blake remained with the Canadiens in some capacity, traveling with the team. He missed coaching, but never coached a team again. He remained in Montreal, and had a bar, Toe Blake's Tavern, for a number of years. This was a men's only bar near the Montreal Forum where the Canadiens played.

By 1989, Blake was in a nursing home in Montreal with Alzheimer's disease, and within a short time, he could barely recognize anyone. Many of his former players, family and friends helped raise awareness of the disease in Canada, which led to a number of fundraising activities. Blake died of the disease on May 17, 1995. His funeral was at Montreal's St. Ignatius Loyola.

Blake's legacy as a player resulted in his election to Hockey's Hall of Fame in 1966, but it was his legacy as a coach that was longer lasting. He was the model for many a coach who followed him in the NHL. As Red Fisher wrote in the *Montreal Gazette,* "He was rough, gruff, intimidating, wise, compassionate, unforgiving, scheming and hard-working—all of it dedicated to winning his eight Stanley Cups as a coach ... . Winning wasn't merely a worthwhile target—it was

Toe Blake, held up by players

everything. It was life itself. Blake wore his strengths as a coach on his sleeve: the dedication, the humor, and the violent temper." To Blake, hockey was everything. He was quoted by Fisher in the *Montreal Gazette* as saying, "Hockey has been my life. I never had the opportunity of getting one of those million-dollar contracts, but hockey was worth more than $1 million to me in plenty of ways."

FURTHER INFORMATION

Books

Diamond, Dan and Joseph Romain. *Hockey Hall of Fame: The Official History of the Game and Its Greatest Stars*. New York: Doubleday, 1988.

Fischler, Stan. *The All-New Hockey's 100*. Toronto: McGraw-Hill Ryerson Limited, 1988.

Fischler, Stan and Shirley. *Fischlers' Hockey Encyclopedia*. New York: Thomas Y. Crowell, 1975.

Hickok, Ralph. *A Who's Who of Sports Champions: Their Stories and Records*. Boston: Houghton Mifflin Company, 1995.

Kariher, Harry C. *Who's Who in Hockey*. New Rochelle: Arlington House, 1973.

Libby, Bill. *The Coaches*. Chicago: Henry Regnery Company, 1972.

Periodicals

Allen, Kevin. "Bowman acknowledges Blake's coaching legend." *USA Today* (June 9, 1998): 10C.

"Blake's legacy." *Sporting News* (May 29, 1995).

Fisher, Red. "Canadiens' greatest coach dies; Death of a hockey legend; Toe Blake was a star as a player and a coach." *Gazette* (May 18, 1995): G1.

Fisher, Red. "A final farewell to Toe; Blake was the greatest of all hockey coaches." *Gazette* (May 21, 1995): E1.

Fisher, Red. "He loved to win." *Ottawa Citizen* (September 28, 1999): B4.

Fisher, Red. "Toe Blake: From Champion Coach to Being Locked in Alzheimer's." United Press International (December 26, 1991).

Hickey, Pat. "Blake tournament creates awareness; Alzheimer's a growing problem." *Gazette* (May 15, 1994): D6.

Stinson, Thomas. "Blake's old time hockey set the standard for today's NHL." *Atlanta Journal and Constitution* (May 20, 1995): 2D.

Thomas, Robert McG, Jr. "Hector (Toe) Blake, 82, Is Dead; Coach of the Canadiens Title Teams." *New York Times* (May 18, 1995): B15.

Other

"Hector 'Toe' Blake." http://www.hockeysandwich.com/tblake.html (November 2, 2002).

Iovino, Jim. "Hector 'Toe' Blake." LCS Hockey. http://www.lcshockey.com/archive/greats/blake.asp (November 2, 2002).

"The Legends of Hockey: Players: Toe Blake: Biography." Legends of Hockey. http://www.legendsof hockey.net:8080/LegendsOFHockey/jsp/Legen (November 2, 2002).

"The Legends of Hockey: Players: Toe Blake: Career Statistics." Legends of Hockey. http://www.legendsof hockey.net:8080/LegendsOFHockey/jsp/Legen (November 2, 2002).

Sketch by A. Petruso

Tyrone "Muggsy" Bogues

Tyrone "Muggsy" Bogues
1965-

American basketball player

Finding his niche and filling it remarkably well is what made point guard Tyrone "Muggsy" Bogues a dominant player in the National Basketball Association (NBA). A superior athlete, he left his mark in the NBA, ranking among the top 20 players in career assists. He was easily recognizable on the court because he stood more than two feet shorter than other players. Because his hands were too small to palm a basketball he could never dunk the ball, but he was able to jump more than 44 inches into the air. During his career he was also known for his spirit and showmanship, traits that contributed to his ultimate success. Largely because of his outstanding leadership qualities he became one of finest point guards to play the game. "The ball's on the floor more than it's in the air. And down there is Muggsyland. That's where I rule. Put the ball on the floor, and you gotta watch out for the little fella," he wrote in his autobiography.

City Kid

Born Tyrone Curtis on January 9, 1965, in Baltimore, Maryland, Bogues was the youngest child of Richard and Elaine Bogues. He grew up along with his two brothers and one sister in the Lafayette public housing project on the city's east side. There he earned his nickname Muggsy from his neighborhood playmates.

Bogues's father was a stevedore, but scarcity of work left him with little choice but to supplement the family income with ill-gotten gains. When Bogues was 12 years old, his father was arrested, convicted, and sentenced to 20 years in federal prison for strong armed robbery. It was a difficult burden for the Bogues family, as was dodging bullets in the inner city ghetto. On one unlucky day Bogues, mistaken for a vandal, caught some buckshot in his arms and legs.

By age nine, Bogues began to frequent Lafayette Courts Community Recreational Center where he became totally absorbed with basketball. As he entered his teens he was noticeably smaller than most boys his age, but with encouragement from neighborhood coaches he learned the fine points of the game. He joined a city league team and at age 13 he was named most valuable player (MVP) in a tournament

After junior high school, Bogues enrolled at Southern High School for one year, then transferred to Dunbar High School where for the next two years—wearing jersey number 14—he played on an undefeated team. In

Career Statistics

Yr	Team	GP	PTS	FG%	3P%	FT%	RPG	APG	SPG	BPG	TO	PF
1987-88	WAS	79	393	39.0	18.8	78.4	1.7	5.1	1.6	0.0	101	138
1988-89	CHA	79	423	42.6	7.7	75.0	2.1	7.8	1.4	0.1	124	141
1989-90	CHA	81	763	49.1	19.2	79.1	2.6	10.7	2.0	0.0	146	168
1990-91	CHA	81	568	46.0	0.0	79.6	2.7	8.3	1.7	0.0	120	160
1991-92	CHA	82	730	47.2	7.4	78.3	2.9	9.1	2.1	0.1	156	156
1992-93	CHA	81	808	45.3	23.1	83.3	3.7	8.8	2.0	0.1	154	179
1993-94	CHA	77	835	47.1	16.7	80.6	4.1	10.1	1.7	0.0	171	147
1994-95	CHA	78	862	47.7	20.0	88.9	3.3	8.7	1.3	0.0	132	151
1995-96	CHA	6	14	37.5	0.0	100.0	1.2	3.2	0.3	0.0	6	4
1996-97	CHA	65	522	46.0	41.7	84.4	2.2	7.2	1.3	0.0	108	114
1997-98	CHA	2	6	40.0	0.0	100.0	0.5	2.0	1.0	0.0	1	2
1997-98	GSW	59	341	43.7	25.0	89.4	2.2	5.5	1.1	0.1	104	56
1998-99	GSW	36	183	49.4	0.0	86.1	2.0	3.7	1.2	0.0	47	44
1999-00	TOR	80	410	43.9	33.3	90.8	1.7	3.7	0.8	0.1	59	119
2000-01	TOR	3	0	0.0	0.0	0.0	1.0	1.7	0.7	0.0	4	3
TOTAL		889	6858	45.8	27.8	82.7	2.6	7.6	1.5	0.0	1433	1582

CHA: Charlotte Hornets; GSW: Golden State Warriors; TOR: Toronto Raptors; WAS: Washington Bullets.

his first year there he was named MVP of the Baltimore City Public Schools Tournament as Dunbar took its sixth consecutive championship.

College Recruit

By senior year of high school, few college coaches were anxious to take on a five-foot-three basketball player. Bogues nonetheless was being recruited by both Georgetown and Wake Forest. He accepted an offer to play with the Wake Forest Demon Deacons.

Bogues survived a turbulent freshman year after a difficult start in the affluent environment at Wake Forest. He accumulated playing time very slowly until his junior year, when a new head coach, Bob Staak, took over the Deacons. With better player-coach chemistry Bogues excelled under Coach Staak's guidance. He averaged 11.6 points for 22 games that year, led the Atlantic Coast Conference (ACC) in steals, and ranked among the top ten players nationwide for assists. He set a conference record of 17 assists in a single game, while averaging 8.4 overall. His rebounding that season ranked among the top three point guards in the ACC.

Bogues was named to the U.S. National Team in 1986, and after playing in exhibition games throughout Europe, the team went to the world championships in Malaga, Spain. With Bogues at point guard, the United States won the world title for the first time in more than 30 years.

In January of 1987, as a senior at Wake Forest, Bogues set an all-school assist record of 579. Just weeks later, in an emotional ceremony at the final home game of his career, the school retired his jersey, Number 14. He was named to the all-ACC team that year and left a conference record of 781 career assists. He led the league in steals and minutes played, and led his team in scoring. In all he left seven school records at Wake Forest.

College Draft

With the 1986-87 college season drawing to a close, Bogues joined the ACC senior tour. He played with the U.S. Basketball League and, as anticipated, was picked in the first round of the NBA draft. Also picked were two of his Dunbar teammates: Reggie Williams and Reggie Lewis. Bogues went to the Washington Bullets on the twelfth pick, signing for $1 million over four years.

With his career on track, Bogues bought a Mercedes. He bought a house for his mother, then hired a lawyer to extricate his father from prison.

Expansion Draft

As a rookie, Bogues started in the Bullets' first preseason game, but the season fizzled with time. The Bullets allowed Bogues to be drafted in 1988, when expansion brought the Hornets of Charlotte, North Carolina, and the Miami Heat into the NBA. He went to Charlotte in the third round of the expansion draft.

After a losing season in Charlotte, the Hornets nonetheless led the league in attendance, drawing near-capacity crowds for home games. In January, 1990, Gene Littles replaced Dick Harter as coach, and Allen Bristow assumed the post of general manager. Unlike Harter, Littles and Bristow accepted Bogues without hesitation, "I love guys who can press, who can make things happen," said Bristow in praise of Bogues.

By the mid 1990s Bogues had achieved average points per game in the doubles range, with a season total of 862 for the 1994-95 season, his highest on record. His assist-per-turnover ratio of 4.34 for the 1996-97 regular season ranked highest in the league. He was traded to the Golden State Warriors on November 7, 1997 and played a total of 71 games for that team over two seasons before going to the Toronto Raptors for the 1999-

Chronology

1965	Born on January 9 in East Baltimore, Maryland, to Richard and Elaine Bogues
1974	First plays basketball with a hometown rec league
1981-83	Wins back-to-back championships playing with the Dunbar High School Poets
1983-87	Attends Wake Forest University on a basketball scholarship
1986	Plays with the U.S. National Team at the World Games in Barcelona, Spain
1987	Goes to the Washington Bullets as the number 12 pick in the first round of the NBA draft
1988	Goes to the Charlotte Hornets in an expansion draft
1999	Goes to the Toronto Raptors in a trade and helps bring that organization to the playoffs for the first time in the history of the team
2000	Is traded to the New York Nicks and retires

Awards and Accomplishments

1987	Arnold Palmer Award from Wake Forest; Frances Pomeroy Naismith Award from Basketball Hall of Fame; team leader in scoring; left seven school records at Wake Forest; jersey number retired; all-ACC; set league record with 781 assists, league leader in steals and minutes played for each of three years
1989-90	Player of the Year, Charlotte Hornets
1995	Jim Thorpe Award for Special Inspiration

2000 season. After taking the Raptors to their first playoff series ever in 2000, Bogues was traded to the New York Knicks on February 22, 2001.

Due to chronic injuries, Bogues never played for the Knicks. He retired from professional play ranking at number 16 among all-time assist leaders in the NBA. Bogues was recognized for his speed and agility on many occasions, yet because of his lack of height he remained one of the most underrated players of his era.

Other Points of Interest

Early year in his career with the Charlotte Hornets, Bogues married his college sweetheart, Kimberly (Lee) Bogues, The couple has two daughters, including Bogues's daughter from a high-school relationship. Their son, Tyrone Jr., was born on March 30, 1991.

Of greater importance than his career statistics is the legacy of hope that he left with the league, and which he continues to spread through the charitable programs that he founded. In his retirement he is chairman of both Bogues Enterprises and of the Always Believe Foundation.

CONTACT INFORMATION

Address: c/o Tony Jones, Trust Marketing, 44 N. Second Street Suite 800, Memphis, TN 38103. Fax: (901) 521-0901. Phone: (901) 521-1300. Email: janis@trustmkt.com. Online: http://www.muggsy.com/.

SELECTED WRITINGS BY BOGUES:

Bogues, Tyrone "Muggsy," *In the Land of Giants: My Life in Basketball,* Boston, MA: Little, Brown & Co., 1994.

FURTHER INFORMATION

Books

Bogues, Tyrone "Muggsy," *In the Land of Giants: My Life in Basketball,* Little, Brown & Co., 1994.

Periodicals

Jet, July 31, 1995, p. 48.

Online

"Infoplease.com," http://www.infoplease.com/ipsa/A0760477.html (December 15, 2002).

"Reggie Lewis' Life," http://www.learntoquestion.com/vclass/seevak/groups/1998/sites/lewis/life.html (December 16, 2002).

Sketch by G. Cooksey

Brian Boitano
1963-

American figure skater

Brian Boitano transformed professional figure skating by both forcing his fellow skaters to excel in order to match his true technical mastery, as well as by his tireless outside of the rink, becoming one of figure skating's true ambassadors. Boitano captured six world professional titles during his career and has set standards that may never be matched. He is the first American Athlete to have his own network television special, and won an Emmy for his role in *Carmen on Ice* which aired in 1990. With over 50 titles to his name—including 23 international gold medals, two World titles, two Pro/Am titles, 16 professional titles and four U.S. National titles—Boitano also captured Olympic gold in 1988.

Growing Up

Brian Boitano was born on October 22, 1963, in Mountainview, California. His brother and two sisters were never interested in skating, but young Brian, when he was eight, attended an "Ice Follies" show with his parents and subsequently fell in love with figure skating. With his parents supporting his ambition, he soon had Linda Leaver as a coach, which proved to be a wise choice—Linda has remained Brian's coach and personal manager through the

Chronology

1963	Born October 22, in Mountainview, California
1972	Sees the "Ice Follies" when he's 8 and gets hooked on skating. Parents hire Linda Leaver, who remains with him as coach and manager throughout his career
1976	Begins winning regional titles
1978	Wins the United States Junior Men's Championship
1983	Debuts at World Figure Skating Championships and becomes 1st skater to land all six jumps in that competition
1984	Finishes fifth in his first Olympics
1986	Wins his first world title
1987	Hires Sandra Bezic to choreograph new routine for him. This propels him to victory in 1988 at U.S. Figure Skating Championship
1988	Turns professional; teams with Katarina Witt to do *Carmen on Ice*, and Boitano wins an Emmy for his performance
1992	Fights to represent the United States in the 1994 Olympics as a professional. Boitano prevails
1998	Unable to represent U.S. in Winter Olympics. International Olympic Committee forbids professionals from competing in this year's events
1998	Funds "Youth Skate," a San Francisco charity that teaches inner-city kids how to skate
2000	Third and final *Brian Boitano Skating Spectacular* airs
2002	Undergoes appendectomy in February and arthroscopic knee surgery in May

Awards and Accomplishments

1978	First place, United States Junior Men's Championship
1983-84	Second place, Nationals
1985-88	First place, Nationals
1986, 1988	First place, Worlds
1988	Gold Medal, Olympic Games
1988	Named Young Italian-American of the Year
1988	First place, World Challenge of Champions
1988-92, 1994	First place, World Professional Championship
1994	First place, U.S. Senior Men's Championship
1996	Inducted into U.S. Figure Skating Hall of fame; also inducted into World Fisgure Skating Hall of Fame
1999	Receives Gustave Lussi Award from Professional Figure Skaters Association
2000	First place, Goodwill Games
2000	Named one of major skaters of the century by *Blade* magazine

Boitano has won over 50 titles, including 23 international gold medals, two World titles, two Pro/Am titles, 16 professional titles, four U.S. National titles, as well as an Olympic Gold Medal.

nearly three decades of Brian's ice-skating career. "I thought he'd be great right away," Leaver told *Sports Illustrated.* "I used to keep charts on every student, with my predictions and expectations for them. Though Boitano was only eight, I went home and told my husband that one day he'd be the world champion."

Leaver was right. After winning nearly twenty regional medals by the time he hit his teens, Boitano captured the U.S. junior men's championship in 1978. As an amateur he competed in the World Figure Skating Championships throughout the early and mid-1980s. Then, in 1986, Brian won his first world title, defeating Canadian skater Brian Orser. That year he also won the United States Senior Men's Championships as well as taking first at the Olympic Festival.

In spite of the phenomenal success, however, Boitano felt his artistry was not up to par with his technical ability, and in 1987 he hired Sandra Bezic to coach him in this area. He introduced his new style in 1988 at the U.S. Figure Skating Championships, collecting a fourth men's single title, going on to capture gold in the Winter Olympics (held in Calgary, Alberta, Canada) later that same year and fulfilling a personal goal. He returned to the winter Olympics in 1994, but finished a disappointing sixth.

Champion of the Sport

Boitano would involve others in his pursuits to bring the sport to a new level. Following his Olympic gold he joined **Katarina Witt** to film a television special that won Brian an Emmy. Throughout the nineties he continued to produce—and often star in—programs for television,

including *A Skating Romance,* and two equally successful sequels. His book, *Boitano's Edge: Inside the Real World of Figure Skating,* published in 1997, is currently in its third printing and considered by many to be one of the great books on figure skating.

Brian Boitano lives in San Francisco, where he is artistic director of his own company, White Canvas Productions (which he founded in 1995). He spends his time working for the betterment of professional figure skating, as well as working with his Youth Skate program, which provides skating lessons and scholarships to local children. He can also be heard occasionally as a skating commentator for PBS and ABC. In February of 2002, Boitano underwent an appendectomy, from which it took him some time to recover. That operation was followed by arthroscopic knee surgery in May of 2002.

CONTACT INFORMATION

Address: c/o Keith Sherman & Associates, 234 W. 44th Street, Suite 1004, New York, New York, 10036.

SELECTED WRITINGS BY BOITANO:

(With Suzanne Harper) *Boitano's Edge: Inside the Real World of Figure Skating,* Simon & Schuster, 1997.

FURTHER INFORMATION

Books

Boitano, Brian and Suzanne Harper. *Boitano's Edge: Inside the Real World of Figure Skating,* New York: Simon & Schuster, 1997.

"Brian Boitano." *Newsmakers,* Issue Cumulation. Farmington Hills, MI: Gale Research, 1988.

"Brian Boitano." *Sports Stars,* Series 1-4. U•X•L, 1994-98.

Periodicals

Chapin, Dwight. "Where Are They Now? Brian Boitano: Nailing the Landing." *San Francisco Chronicle* (August 18, 2002): B2.

Knoell, D. "A Conversation With Brian Boitano." *Blades on Ice* (July/August 2002).

Newsweek (February 21, 1994).

People (February 15, 1988; February 19, 1996).

Sports Illustrated (February 16, 1997; January 27, 1988; February 29, 1988).

Swift, E.M. "Brian Boitano: the champion skater of '88 claims he has been forced to the Olympic sidelines by an unfair ruling." *Sports Illustrated* (February 10, 1992).

Time (February 15, 1988; February 29, 1988).

Other

"Brian Boitano," online biography at *The Skating Source.* http://www.skatingsource.com/boitano.shtml (January 29, 2003).

"Brian Boitano," http://www.geocities.com/brianboitano fan/Home.html (January 29, 2003).

"Brian Boitano Repository," http://members.tripod.com/ ~MystiD/ (as of January 29, 2003).

Sketch by Eric Lagergren

Barry Bonds
1964-

American baseball player

Professional baseball player Barry Bonds may be the sports world's most vivid study in contrasts. Revered for his practically unmatched athletic prowess—he appears poised to break Hank Aaron's record of 755 career home runs—he is, at the same time, despised by many for his aloof, or even downright rude, behavior both on- and off-field. He has been described by a former teammate as "the greatest player I have ever played with, or will ever play with" and by other commentators as a "prima donna," "a cancer" and a "spiritual drain" on his sport. Whether a hero or quite the opposite, one fact is for certain: Bonds has not only taken his sport to new levels of athletic achievement but he has raised the financial stakes for players of his caliber as well. The left-fielder was already one of the highest-paid players in

Barry Bonds

Major League Baseball (MLB), when he signed a five-year, $90 million contract with the San Francisco Giants in February 2002, tying Chicago Cubs powerhouse **Sammy Sosa** for the fourth-largest paycheck in baseball. In commanding such an increasingly large salary, Bonds has also become part of an ever-growing group of players who are overcoming the financial barriers that have historically been levied against minority baseball players. In 1997, *Jet* reported that Bonds and three other minority players commanded five of the highest salaries in the history of professional baseball.

Family Tree

Bonds came to baseball with an unparalleled pedigree. The oldest son of three-time Golden Glove winner and former San Francisco Giant Bobby Bonds and his wife, Pat, the younger Bonds began hanging around the Giants' locker room as a child. But he spent as much time out on the field, chasing fly balls with his father and godfather, the legendary **Willie Mays**. Another baseball great, **Reggie Jackson**, is a distant cousin, and Olympic sprinter Rosie Bonds is his aunt. Bonds has claimed that, even before kindergarten, he could hit a whiffle ball so hard it could break glass.

By the time he entered Serra Juniperro High School in San Mateo, California, Bonds was an all-around athlete, playing baseball, basketball and football. His big-league talent already evident, Bonds was offered a $75,000 contract when he graduated in 1982. Equally

Chronology

1964	Born July 24 in Riverside, California
1978	Enters Serra Juniperro High School where he plays baseball, basketball, and football
1982	Turns down $75,000 offer from San Francisco Giants and opts to play baseball for Arizona State University
1985	Chosen to *Sporting News* college All-Star team
1985	Drafted by Pittsburgh Pirates and plays in minor leagues
1986	Called up to major leagues
1988	Marries first wife
1990	Son Nikolai is born
1990	Wins first league Most Valuable Player (MVP) award and first of eight Gold Glove awards
1991	Daughter Shikari is born
1992	Wins second MVP award
1992	Becomes a free agent and signs with San Francisco Giants, commanding a salary making him the highest-paid baseball player in history
1993	Wins third MVP award
1994	Divorces wife
1996	Surpasses 300 home runs and 300 stolen bases
1998	Marries Elizabeth Watson
2000	Daughter Aisha is born
2001	Hits 73 home runs in the season, breaking Mark McGwire's record, and hits 500th career home run
2001	Awarded unprecedented fourth MVP award
2002	Hits 600th home run and leads Giants to the World Series
2002	Fifth MVP award

evident was Bonds' belief that baseball is first and foremost a business, an ethos he would continue to espouse throughout his career. When the Giants turned down his request for more money, he opted to buy time playing college ball at Arizona State University where, by his junior year he had been named to the All-Pac 10 team three years running. In 1985, after hitting twenty-three home runs and compiling a .347 career average, he was named to the *Sporting News* All-American Team. But it was not just the seeds of Bonds' athletic ability that were beginning to show at ASU. Already, the standout was gaining a reputation as off-putting and self-absorbed. "I liked the hell out of Barry Bonds. Unfortunately, I never saw a teammate care about him," his former coach, Jim Brock, told *Sports Illustrated*. "Part of it would be his being rude, inconsiderate and self-centered. He bragged about the money he turned down, and he popped off about his dad. I don't think he ever figured out what to do to get people to like him."

Big League Numbers, Big League Attitude

In 1985, Bonds was offered a professional contract that suited him, and he joined the Pittsburgh Pirates as the sixth pick in the first round. He spent his first season in the minor leagues, batting .299, hitting thirteen home runs and being named July's league player of the month for the Prince William (Virginia) Pirates in the Carolina League. After batting .311 in just forty-four games the following season, where he played in Hawaii, Bonds was called up to the majors at the age of twenty-one. Before long, he be-

came the Pirates' starting centerfielder and leadoff hitter. He hit a double his second day with the team and nailed his first home run less than a week later. Bonds finished the season leading the National League's (NL) rookies in home runs, runs batted in, stolen bases, and walks.

Bonds continued to shine the following year, when he was moved to left field and fifth in the batting order, finishing the season with a .261 batting average, twenty-five home runs and thirty-two stolen bases. The next year he battled a knee injury, but still raised his batting average to .283 and hit twenty-four home runs. He came back with a vengeance in 1990, earning the National League Most Valuable Player (MVP) title during a season in which he hit thirty-three home runs, 114 runs batted in (RBI), and stole fifty-two bases. He was awarded the first of eight Gold Glove awards this year as well, and became the only player in the history of the major leagues to bat .300 (his average was .301), hit over 30 home runs, drive in 100 runs, score 100 runs (he scored 104) and steal 50 bases. These amazing feats helped the Pirates claim the National League East division championship that year. In 1991 Bonds batted .292 with twenty-five home runs and 116 RBIs. He finished second to the Atlanta Braves' Terry Pendleton for the league MVP award and the Pirates lost the league championship series to the Braves. Bonds boasted stellar numbers again in 1992 and was named league MVP for the second time, but his team again lost the league championship to the Braves.

The self-indulgent, sometimes downright disrespectful, demeanor Bonds had begun to exhibit at ASU only became more visible as Bonds recognized his overall importance to the Pirates organization. He asked for salary arbitration after winning his first MVP award, but was turned down. The following year, he engaged in a heated, and well-publicized altercation with coach Bill Virdon and Pirates manager Jim Leyland at spring training. It was also reported that, during a Goodwill tour of Japan, he quit an exhibition game early and insulted his hosts by tossing aside a token gift during a post-game ceremony.

Professional and Personal Moves

While with the Pirates, Bonds met and married his wife, Sun, a cosmetologist from Sweden. The pair eloped in Las Vegas in February 1988. Their sun Nikolai, now a batboy for the Giants, was born in 1990 and their daughter Shikari a year later.

Bonds was gearing up for changes in his professional life as well. Despite his talent, the Pirates opted to let Bonds walk when he became a free agent at the end of the 1991-1992 season, and he was signed by his hometown team, the San Francisco Giants. Although he had once told *Sport* magazine, "I want to play for any California team except the Giants because it's cold and they need a new stadium," Bonds claimed he was thrilled to be playing for the same team as his father and godfather, and he wore his father's number, 25. "I will look just

Awards and Accomplishments

1985	College All-Star team
1990	Named Baseball Writers' Association of America league MVP
1990	Named *Sporting News* National League and Major League Player of the Year
1990, 1992-98, 2000-01	All-Star Team
1990-94, 1996-98	Golden Glove Award
1990-94, 1996-97, 2000-02	Silver Slugger Award
1991	*Sporting News* National League Player of the Year
1992-93, 2001-02	Named Baseball Writers' Association of America league MVP
2001	Set MLB home run single season record with 73

Barry Bonds

like my dad out in the field, with the same genes, same body, but left-handed in left field with Willie's sign on the fence. That's generation to generation. It's almost scary. It's fun, I love it. I have never been more excited to play in a city in my entire life than I am now, because I see the whole picture," he told *Sport* in 1993.

The deal the Giants offered Bonds likely struck the player as equally exciting. He would be the highest-paid player in baseball, his father would be hired on as a hitting coach and Bonds would have his own private hotel suite on the road. Bonds gave the Giants their money's worth, batting .336, hitting forty-six home runs and accumulating 123 RBIs in his first year with the team, earning him a third MVP title. The following year the Giants seemed poised for a World Series bid when an August players' strike forced cancellation of the remainder of the season. While Bonds performed expertly the following season, becoming only the sixth player in major league history to hit 250 home runs and steal 300 bases in his career, his team finished last in the National League West. The team fared no better in 1996, when Bonds joined his father, godfather and Andre Dawson as one of only four major league players to hit 300 home runs and steal 300 bases. The Giants' luck took a turn in 1997, the same year the team secured an $11.45 million contract with Bonds. Ironically, despite his powerhouse abilities, Bonds was not able to contribute to the team as much as he would have liked, as pitchers began to regularly walk him. This practice became so routine over the years, that Bonds' children have begun to hold up signs reading, "Please pitch to my Daddy, Number 25." Still, Bonds contributed largely to the pennant victory, batting .344 in the team's last eleven games.

Critical as he was to the Giants' success that year, Bonds in no way developed a reputation as a team player—not among teammates, fans or the media. The separate hotel suite was only the beginning, and Bonds has since acquired his own public relations representative, masseur and weight trainer, as well as a private enclave in the Giants clubhouse where he keeps a recliner and a large-screen television which nobody else can see. He does not stretch with the team, eat with the team, or pose for team pictures, and rarely sticks around for interviews. "Barry does a lot of questionable things. But you get used to it," former teammate Jeff Kent told *Sports Illustrated*. "You just hope he shows up for the game and performs. I've learned not to worry about it or think about it or analyze it. I was raised to be a team guy, and I am, but Barry's Barry."

As for the fans, Bonds has said he appreciates their support but once, when criticized for failing to move on a fly ball, he remarked to *The Sporting News*, "I don't care what (the fans) think. They ain't out here. . . . If you're better than me, you can come out here and put my uniform on and do it." While Bonds has never tried to justify his attitude toward his teammates or fans, he did explain his testy relationship with the media to *Sport*. "It's sickening for you to throw stones at me and then want to take them back," he told a reporter. "I do it every year, that's what (motivates) me my whole year, for you to slap me across the face and then have to come back at the end of the year and kiss me and say, 'I'm sorry.'"

Bonds has received negative publicity for his personal affairs as well. After he and Sun divorced in 1994, she sued him for half of his baseball earnings, despite having signed a prenuptial agreement. The case dragged on for years and was eventually settled in Bonds' favor by the California Supreme Court. In 1998, Bonds was married again, to Elizabeth Watson, and two years later the pair had a daughter, Aisha.

Career Statistics

Yr	Team	Avg	GP	AB	R	H	HR	RBI	BB	SO	SB	E
1986	PIT	.223	113	413	72	92	16	48	65	102	36	5
1987	PIT	.261	150	551	99	144	25	59	54	88	32	5
1988	PIT	.283	144	538	97	152	24	58	72	82	17	6
1989	PIT	.248	159	580	96	144	19	58	93	93	32	6
1990	PIT	.301	151	519	104	156	33	114	93	83	52	6
1991	PIT	.292	153	510	95	149	25	116	107	73	43	3
1992	PIT	.311	140	473	109	147	34	103	127	69	39	3
1993	SF	.336	159	539	129	181	46	123	126	79	29	5
1994	SF	.312	112	391	89	122	37	81	74	43	29	3
1995	SF	.294	144	506	109	149	33	104	120	83	31	6
1996	SF	.308	158	517	122	159	42	129	151	76	40	6
1997	SF	.291	159	532	123	155	40	101	145	87	37	5
1998	SF	.303	156	552	120	167	37	122	130	92	28	5
1999	SF	.262	102	355	91	93	34	83	73	62	15	3
2000	SF	.306	143	480	129	147	49	106	117	77	11	3
2001	SF	.328	153	476	129	156	73	137	177	93	13	6
2002	SF	.370	143	403	117	149	46	110	198	47	9	8
TOTAL		.295	2439	8335	1830	2462	613	1652	1922	1329	493	84

PIT: Pittsburgh Pirates; SF: San Francisco Giants.

Still, Bonds continues to lead his team and break records on a regular basis. While berated by fans and the media for a lackluster performance in a wild card play-off bid in 1998 and hampered by an elbow injury in 1999, when the team missed the playoffs altogether, he maintained his enviable batting average. The team's poor overall performance underscored just how much they relied on Bonds, who returned to the team early following surgery in an effort to help salvage the season. The team made it to the playoffs the following year, but were eliminated early by the New York Mets.

The Giants failed to make the playoffs in 2001, but Bonds had a watershed season. That year, he hit seventy-three home runs, breaking **Mark McGwire**'s season record of seventy and also hit his 500th career home run, arousing speculation that he will break **Hank Aaron**'s all-time record of 755. For his efforts, Bonds became the first player in major league history to be named MVP four times and he was also voted Player of the Year for the second time by his peers. He also began to break down the wall between himself and the fans, tearfully thanking them for their support in a post-game ceremony after his record-breaking seventy-first home run. Still, Bonds' reputation preceded him. When he became a free agent at the end of the season, not a single team expressed interest.

In 2002, with a .370 average, Bonds became the Giants' first batting champion since Willie Mays in 1954. On August 9, he hit his 600th home run—a feat realized by only Hank Aaron, Willie Mays and **Babe Ruth** before him and, in the postseason he finally realized his dream of playing in a World Series. The Giants eventually lost to the Anaheim Angels in a seven-game series. Still, Bonds was named league MVP for an astounding fifth time. While besting Hank Aaron's home run record

would be a phenomenal achievement, Bonds indicated mid-season that the days left to reach that goal are numbered. "At the end of this contract, I'll be 42 and my kids will be in high school," he told *Ebony*. "It doesn't matter how close I am to Hank's record, when this contract ends, it's over! You get me for four more years, and after that, this old guy is going home."

CONTACT INFORMATION

Address: c/o San Francisco Giants, Candlestick Point, 24 Willie Mays Plaza, San Francisco, CA 94107-2199.

FURTHER INFORMATION

Books

Sports Stars Series 1-4, U•X•L, 1994-98.

Periodicals

Elliot, Josh. "Would You Believe 80?." *Sports Illustrated* (April 15, 2002): 42.

Grann, David. "Baseball Without Metaphor." *New York Times Magazine* (September 1, 2002): 36.

"King of Swing: Barry Bonds Aims at Baseball's Home-Run Record, and at His Old Reputation As a Hard Man to Warm Up To." *People* (July 9, 2001): 63.

Leavy, Walter. "Death Threats, Hate Mail and Personal Losses: Everything You Always Wanted to Know About Barry Bonds' Record-Breaking Home Run Chase." *Ebony* (July 2002): 116+.

Lupica, Mike. "A Tragedy of Errors." *Sporting News* (June 19, 1995): 7.

Ila Borders

Related Biography: Baseball Player Bobby Bonds

Bobby Bonds secured himself a spot in the annals of baseball history early in his career. In only his second year in the major leagues, as a San Francisco Giant, he became the first player in league history to hit thirty home runs and steal thirty bases in a single season. Over a fourteen-year career, Bonds achieved this feat four more times, a still-standing record.

Bonds honed his skills at Polytechnic High School in Riverside, California, where he also excelled on the football team. He was not the only athlete in the family; his brother, Robert, was a 13th-round draft pick for the Kansas City Chiefs and his sister, Rosie, was a world-class hurdler who earned a place on the 1964 Olympic track team. Bobby was signed by the Giants in 1965 and was promoted to the majors in 1968. In his first major-league game, facing the Los Angeles Dodgers, he hit a grand slam home run, becoming the first major leaguer to do so in his first game since the Phillies' Bill Dugglesby in 1898.

Bonds became the Giants' leadoff hitter and he did not disappoint. During his first full season in 1969 he hit thirty-two home runs, stole forty-five bases, drove in ninety runs and scored 120 runs, leading the National League. Bonds was named to the All-Star Team twice when he was with the Giants, in 1971 and 1973. In 1973 he also led the National League with 131 runs and thirty-nine homers. He was traded to the New York Yankees after the 1974 season and he again made the All-Star Team in 1975. Following that season, he was traded to the California Angels. An injured finger hindered his 1976 season, but the following year he hit thirty-seven home runs, had 115 RBIs, 103 runs and forty-one stolen bases. He was traded to the Chicago White Sox prior to his becoming a free agent in 1978.

Bonds was traded to the Texas Rangers mid-season and his last few years as a player were marked by numerous subsequent trades and an alcohol problem. He played for the Cleveland Indians, the St. Louis Cardinals and the Chicago Cubs before retiring in 1981. He returned to Cleveland as a first-base coach and hitting instructor from 1984-1987 and in 1989 acted as player-manager to the St. Lucie Legends of Florida's short-lived Senior League. He returned to San Francisco in 1993, signing on as a hitting coach as part of son Barry's lucrative deal with the team. Father and son had a shot at sharing a World Series victory in 2002, but, after a promising start, the Giants lost the seven-game series to the Anaheim Angels.

Mariotti, Jay. "The Rebirth of Barry Bonds." *Sporting News* (June 4, 2001): 8.

Reilly, Rick. "He Loves Himself Barry Much." *Sports Illustrated* (August 27, 2001): 102.

Schulman, Henry. "Bonds Takes a High-Five for NL MVP." *San Francisco Chronicle* (November 12, 2002): C1.

Verducci, Tom. "600 and Counting." *Sports Illustrated* (August 19, 2002): 42.

Weinstock, Jeff. "Barry Bonds (Q&A)." *Sport* (April, 1993): 60.

Sketch by Kristin Palm

Ila Borders
1975-

American baseball player

The pitcher Ila Borders broke baseball's gender barrier in 1997, when she became the first woman to pitch in the men's minor leagues. Accomplishing a goal she had set since girlhood, Borders pitched her first professional game, for the Northern League's St. Paul Saints, on May 31, 1997. In her three years in the minor leagues, earning from $700 to $1,000 a month, Borders played for the St. Paul Saints, the Duluth-Superior Dukes, the Madison Black Wolf, and the Zion Pioneerzz. She had her share of victories—including 12 scoreless innings during her 1998 season with the Dukes—and her share of defeats. When she retired in 2000, Borders left an important legacy as baseball's first professional female player, and as a hero and role model for other women who aspire to play the men's sport.

Ila Borders was born on February 18, 1975, in Downey, California. One of four children, she was raised in La Miranda, a suburb of Los Angeles. Her father, Phil, was a former minor league baseball player who painted cars; her mother ran a preschool. Baseball was a family pastime that grew into a passion for the little girl. "Every Saturday and Sunday, from the time I was 5, my whole family would play ball," Borders told Larry Oakes of the Minneapolis *Star Tribune*. "My dad basically taught me everything: the mental part, the control, how to call a game, how to take care of my arm."

Dreamed of Pitching Professionally

When ten-year-old Borders announced her goal of becoming a professional baseball player, her father only

Chronology

1975	Born on February 18 in Downey, California
mid-1980s	Pitches for boys' Little League baseball teams
1989	Plays with men's semipro league
1994	Attends Southern California College on a baseball scholarship; pitches for the SCC Vanguards
1996	Transfers to Whittier Christian College; pitches for team
1997	Graduates from Whittier Christian College with degree in kinesics
1997	Pitches for minor league baseball team, the St. Paul Saints
1997	Traded to Duluth-Superior Dukes
1998	Becomes first female pitcher to win a game (July 24)
1999	Traded to the Madison Black Wolf
2000	Traded to the Zion (Utah) Pioneerzz
2000	Retires from baseball at age 26

encouraged her. With his help, she joined a local boys' Little League. It was here that Borders first faced resistance to crossing baseball's gender barrier. She felt that the Little League tried to keep her out by changing the sign-up times. Borders managed to join nevertheless, and in her first game she proved her mettle by striking out the first six batters.

It was Phil Borders who encouraged his daughter to play in a men's semipro league, and who forged an ID so the 14-year-old girl could play with men in their 20s. In junior high school, she sued for the right to play with the boys. She also played in high school, though she had to switch schools when one coach wouldn't let her join the boys' team. Upon graduating from high school at Whittier Christian College, Borders became the first woman to receive a college baseball scholarship.

Borders attended Southern California College (SCC), a small Christian college in Costa Mesa, on a baseball scholarship from 1994 to 1996. Playing for the SCC Vanguards, she became the first woman to pitch, and to win, in a National Association of Intercollegiate Athletics (NAIA) game. The five-foot-ten player pitched a 70-mile-per-hour fastball, lagging a little behind other college pitchers' speeds. She slowly gained more speed, but compensated in the meantime with changeups and curveballs. But improving her game was not the only challenge; Borders also faced sexism and discrimination, especially from opposing teams. "I've been spit on, had beer thrown on me and been sworn at, and was hit 11 times out of 11 at bats while in college," she told *Seattle Times*. Meanwhile, the sports media had gotten wind of the ponytailed pitcher's goal to play professional baseball, and journalists began following her unusual career with fascination. When throngs of journalists showed up at her games, she warned them to treat her as a pitcher first, and not as a female.

In her final year of college, Borders left SCC because she felt her teammates did not support her. She completed her degree at Whittier College, where she became the

first woman to pitch in National Collegiate Athletic Association (NCAA) Division III baseball. Borders received her bachelor's degree in kinesics, the study of the body's movements. Later she would pursue a master's degree that would qualify her for a career in either sports psychology or sports management.

Played in Men's Minor League

Just out of college, Borders reached her goal of playing professional baseball. In 1997 the St. Paul Saints invited the 22-year-old player to try out. Her 80-mile-per-hour fastball fell short of the league's average by five or six miles-per-hour, but the Saints took a chance, making Borders the first woman pitcher to sign with a men's minor league team. In her rookie year she participated in only seven games for the Saints, and was brought in mainly as a relief pitcher. As a lefty, she was occasionally called in as a foil for left-handed batters. She ended her first season with a 7.5 earned-run average (ERA) and a 0-0 record. "If I'm out to prove anything to the world, it's not that a female can do it, but that I can do it—me," she told Oakes. "I'm not out her to educate anybody; I'm out here because I love the game and want to get ahead."

On June 25, 1997, the Saints traded Borders to the Duluth-Superior Dukes. In her first year, the Dukes called her in for only 13 games. Her ERA rose to 8.53, and many sports critics thought the Dukes would not keep her. "There were pitchers with worse statistics," Borders told Neal Karlen of the *New York Times*. "I wasn't embarrassed."

During the 1998 season Borders would make some strides. On July 9 she was brought in for the first time as the starting pitcher. On July 24 she became the first female pitcher to win a men's minor league game. While she had drawn fans all along, the size of these crowds began to increase, as did the media parade that followed her. Among those running stories on Borders were the *New York Times* and *Newsweek* magazine, while television's *60 Minutes* and the *Tonight* show clamored for interviews. The buzz about Borders was mostly positive, but there were exceptions. Some baseball managers questioned whether the female player had been chosen for her pitching ability or as a crowd-drawing novelty. Yet Borders used such critiques as provocation to improve. By August of 1998 she had lowered her ERA to 4.88.

After starting the 1999 season with Duluth, Borders was traded to the Madison Black Wolf on June 10. On June 17 she pitched her second winning game in the minor leagues. She would finish the year with her best professional performance yet, with a season record of 1-0 and an ERA of 3.64. Yet the following season was not as successful for Borders. Traded to the Western League's Zion Pioneerzz, she appeared in only five games, and her ERA climbed to 9.35. In her final game, against the Feather River Mudcats, she gave up five hits and three runs. After the game, she told Mike Littlewood, the Pioneerzz's manager, that she would call it quits. "She said she thought she had her best stuff and still got hit hard," Littlewood told the Associated Press as reported on the Baseball Glory Web site. "She said she wanted to go in another direction."

On June 30, 2000, 26-year-old Borders announced her retirement from professional baseball. After she retired in the summer of 2000, Borders returned to her native California. She told the press that she would pursue a career in broadcasting, teaching, or coaching. After widespread media coverage of her retirement at age 26, Borders disappeared from the press spotlight. Her jersey, mitt, and baseball from her first minor league baseball game remain on display at the National Baseball Hall of Fame in Cooperstown, New York.

Although she had dreamed of pitching in the major leagues, she was able to appreciate how far she had come. "I'll look back and say I did something nobody ever did," she told the *Seattle Times*. "I'm proud of that. I wasn't out to prove women's rights or anything. I love baseball."

FURTHER INFORMATION

Periodicals

Ardell, Jean Hastings. "On a Dream and a Prayer." *Sporting News* (April 4, 1994): 8.

Charland, William. "A Pitcher Defies Baseball's Gender Borders." *Christian Science Monitor* (August 31, 1999): 4.

Hughes, John. "Female Prospect Keeps Making Her Pitch." *St. Louis Post-Dispatch* (May 23, 1998): 9.

Karlen, Neal. "Diamonds Are a Girl's Best Friend." *New York Times* (September 6, 1998): 6.

Oakes, Larry. "Borders Continues Crashing Barriers." (Minneapolis) *Star Tribune* (August 6, 1998): 1C.

Perry, Dwight. "Pioneering Pitcher Crossed the Gender Border." *Seattle Times* (July 3, 2000): D2.

Other

Ardell, Jean Hastings. "Ila Borders Retires." Baseball Glory.com. http://www.baseballglory.com/History%20of%20Borders.html (November 26, 2002).

Sketch by Wendy Kagan

Bjorn Borg

Bjorn Borg
1956-

Swedish tennis player

One of the best all-time performers in tennis history, Swedish player Bjorn Borg won 62 singles titles, including 11 Grand Slam titles, and was ranked number one in the world in 1979 and 1980. With his powerful two-handed backhand, menacing topspin, and balletic footwork, he challenged the chief rivals of his day, **John McEnroe** and **Jimmy Connors**. And with his flowing blond locks and soft-spoken mystique, he won over audiences around the world—and stole the hearts of many a teenage admirer. Yet the tennis legend's career was as brief as it was bright, as he announced his retirement to a shocked tennis world in 1983, at age 26.

Gift of a Tennis Racquet

Bjorn Rune Borg was born on Sweden's Flag Day, June 6, 1956, in Sodertalje, a manufacturing town about 35 minutes from Stockholm. He was the only child of Rune and Margerethe Borg, who owned a grocery store. One of Sweden's leading table-tennis players, Rune Borg captured first prize in his city's championships in the summer of 1965, and was awarded a tennis racquet. He gave that racquet to his nine-year-old son, launching in the boy a lifelong passion.

Chronology

1956	Born June 6 in Sodertalje, Sweden, to Rune and Margarethe Borg
1965	Father wins tennis racquet in table-tennis tournament, and gives racquet to Borg
1965	Takes first tennis lessons
1966	Meets Percy Rosberg, top coach in Sweden; trains with Rosberg in Stockholm
1967	Wins first junior tournament
1970	Represents Sweden in junior tournament, Berlin
1972	Scores first major win, against national tennis star Jan Erik Lundquist
1972	Qualifies for Davis Cup team; meets coach Lennart Bergelin
1973	Debuts at Wimbledon
1974	Turns pro; becomes youngest player to win French Open
1975	Sets Davis Cup record winning streak of 19 singles matches, lifting Sweden to first Cup win against Czechoslovakia
1976	Wins second of six consecutive French Open titles
1976	Wins first of five consecutive Wimbledon titles
1977	Becomes number one player in world, August 23; holds ranking for two weeks
1979-80	Begins and ends year with number one ranking
1980	Marries Romanian tennis player Mariana Simionescu
1981	Loses Wimbledon and U.S. Open titles to John McEnroe
1983	Retires at age 26
1984	Divorces Simionescu
1987	Creates sports-apparel company, Bjorn Borg Design Groups
1989	Marries Italian rock singer Loredana Berte
1990	Begins training for tennis comeback
1991	Attempts comeback unsuccessfully
1992	Separates from Berte
1993	Joins over-35 circuit
2000	Retires from senior circuit; begins training young Swedish players
2002	Marries real-estate broker Patricia Ostfeldt

Yet tennis was not the young athlete's first love. Like many other Swedish boys, Borg was a passionate ice-hockey player. At nine years old, he played starting center for his town's junior team. Making the national team was a dream he shared with many of his teammates and peers.

Borg picked up his first tennis racquet in the summertime, when there was no ice for hockey playing. He approached the new sport with zeal—though at first he was turned away from the overcrowded beginners' course at the Sodertalje Tennis Club. Undeterred, he endeavored to teach himself how to play, using his garage wall as a backboard. Soon a vacancy opened at the tennis club, and the young player spent the rest of his summer there, honing his new skills from 7 a.m. until dusk.

Trained with Sweden's Best

The following summer, his playing caught the eye of Sweden's leading tennis coach of the day, Percy Rosberg. Rosberg was in Sodertalje to observe the skills of two 13-year-olds, Peter Abrink and Leif Johansson. Borg took the opportunity to hit for half an hour with Rosberg, who noted the young player's ability to return the ball consistently—and who invited the boy to train with him at the Salk Club in Stockholm.

For the next five years, young Borg stuck with a rigorous after-school schedule of commuting to Stockholm and training at the Salk Club. His parents supported their son's pursuit, even though his devotion to tennis was taking a toll on his schoolwork. Instead of studying for his classes, he was improving his shots.

In his first two years of playing, Borg held the racquet with both hands—even when he hit forehand shots—simply because the racquet was too heavy. As he continued playing, he grew stronger, and he also discovered that it was easier to hit the ball with topspin if he adopted a one-handed forehand. Yet he would keep the two-handed backhand for his entire tennis career, and this grip would become his signature style.

Borg won his first tournament at age 11, beating Lars Goran Nyman in the Sormland County championships. Over the next four years, he swept every junior championship in his age division. At 14, Borg was selected to represent Sweden in his first international tournament, a junior championship in Berlin, Germany. The same year, he gave up ice hockey and committed himself completely to tennis.

In March 1972, when Borg was 15, he took a leave from school to compete in the Madrid Grand Prix. The tournament was a turning point for Borg, who upset Jan Erik Lundquist, a Swedish tennis legend nearing the end of his career. The win qualified Borg for the Davis Cup team, which faced New Zealand in May. On the courts in the seaside resort town of Bastaad, Borg became the youngest player ever to win a Davis Cup match, triumphing over New Zealand's top player, Onny Parun. Although he was down in the first two sets, Borg took his captain's advice to switch to a lighter racquet mid-match. The result was a triumphant upset, 4-6, 3-6, 6-3, 6-4, 6-4.

It was at the Davis Cup games that Borg gained his reputation for remaining cool under pressure—so cool and reserved that he would earn the nickname "Ice Man." While most players argued with referees when they received bad calls, Borg let the calls pass and concentrated instead on the next point. The Swedish press declared that he had *is i magen,* "ice in the stomach." As Borg's career progressed, the press alternately chided him for what seemed like his stony lack of emotion, and praised him for his good sportsmanship. Yet this stoic athlete commanded respect, and he would receive it in excess from both the press and his fans.

The Rise to the Top

Borg debuted at Wimbledon in the summer of 1973—the year of an infamous player boycott carried out by the Association of Tennis Professionals (ATP). Since he was not an ATP member, Borg was free to participate in the games, and he made a good showing. He won his first match against Indian player Prem Lall, then defeated German player Karl Meiler and Hungarian player Szabolcs Baranyi, advancing to the quarterfinals. The press took notice, with the *Daily Mirror* running the eye-catching headline A STAR IS BJORN. Borg exited after the quarters, however, losing to Roger Taylor in five sets.

If he wasn't winning championships yet, Borg was gaining experience and logging victories against highly ranked players in the championship circle. In the third round of the 1973 U.S. Open, he upset **Arthur Ashe** at the peak of the American tennis great's career. (Two years later, Ashe would get his comeuppance with a win over Borg at Wimbledon.)

A turning point for Borg came in 1974, the year he turned pro at age 17. For the first time in his career, Borg was a presence at every major tournament. In May he became the youngest player ever to win the Italian Championships, and a week later he became the youngest player ever to win the French Open. He ended the year with a full purse of prize money, earning $215,569 on the court. Even more compensation came to him from off-court activities—especially from product endorsements. The demand for Borg products became so intense that the player hired an agent, American manager Mark McCormack, of International Management Group (IMG). In order to avoid the 90 percent tax bite that Sweden took from his earnings, 18-year-old Borg relocated with his parents to Monaco—a move that angered his compatriots and led to accusations from the Swedish press that he was unpatriotic and greedy.

It was also in 1974 that Borg met the Romanian tennis player Mariana Simionescu, who would become his wife. At the time, Borg was involved in an on-again, off-again relationship with the Swedish player Helena Anliot. It was not until 1975 that Borg and Simionescu started dating. They soon became inseparable, and married on July 24, 1980.

A banner year came for the Swedish player in 1975, when he set a Davis Cup record winning streak of 19 singles matches, escorting Sweden to its first Cup win against Czechoslovakia. It was during these games that Borg met Lennart Bergelin, who would later become his trainer and one of his closest confidantes. The following year, Borg developed a powerful new serve. "I shifted the position to my left foot, so my toss wouldn't shoot all over the place," he recalled in his 1980 memoir *Bjorn Borg: My Life and Game*. "Now I had to hit the ball out in front. I gained rhythm, consistency and power."

Indeed, the new serve was perhaps what it took to raise Borg to number two in the world that year, and to win him the Wimbledon title for the first of five consecutive times. After winning his second Wimbledon title in August 1977, a hard-won five-set victory over American tennis star Jimmy Connors, 18-year-old Borg became the number one player in the world. Yet he would hold the ranking for only two weeks, slipping after a loss at the U.S. Open—the one championship tournament that Borg would never win, and that would become a kind of jinx for the Swedish tennis star.

Bjorn Borg

A Legendary Rivalry

Happily for tennis fans, who enjoy the great playing that comes hand in hand with strong competition, Borg was not the only player at the peak of his game in the late 1970s and early 1980s. Right up there with him at the top of the rankings were two other tennis giants: Americans Jimmy Connors and John McEnroe. The three powerhouses together created one of tennis history's greatest rivalries. But the rivalry between Borg and McEnroe—magnified by the players' contrasting temperaments—was perhaps the most memorable of all.

Steely nerved and seemingly emotionless on court, the Swedish tennis star had garnered the nickname "Ice Borg." Meanwhile, openly emotional McEnroe became infamous for his courtside tantrums, which led the press to dub him "McBrat." Tennis writers also pointed out the various pros and cons of beging a right-handed player (Borg) or a lefty (McEnroe), comparing the strengths and weaknesses of the great rivals. But mostly, both fans and critics loved to watch these well-matched athletes play against each other. "McEnroe was more aggressive than any other player I have ever played, the greatest fighter on a tennis court," Borg reminisced to interviewer Faisal Shariff, of Rediff Sports, in 2001. "He never gave you a free point, you had to earn every point, squeeze it out of him."

Nineteen seventy-nine was Borg's year. For the first time, he both began and ended the year with a number one ranking. He swept a string of tournaments, and became the first player ever to win the French Open and Wimbledon two years in a row. Yet rising-star McEnroe took the U.S. Open, with Borg losing in a quarterfinal night game to powerful server, Roscoe Tanner.

The following year, Borg faced McEnroe at Wimbledon, where he successfully defended his title in a classic, tooth-and-nail final match, 1-6, 7-5, 6-3, 6-7, 8-6. It was Borg's fifth straight Wimbledon win. Just a few weeks later, the rivals faced each other again at the finals of the 1980 U.S. Open, and this time McEnroe had his day in the sun. The Swedish player, still number one in the world, blamed the loss on a weak serve. "I think I lost the match because I never served so bad in a final," he told the *New York Times.* "Once in a while something is not working out well in your game. You just have one of those days."

Yet Borg would not always take such a loss in stride. In 1981, he lost to McEnroe in the finals of both Wimbledon and the U.S. Open. It was the crushing U.S. Open defeat, 4-6, 6-2, 6-4, 6-3, that some say effectively ended the Swede's career.

Retired at Age 26

Before his 1981 U.S. Open upset, Borg had won 11 Grand Slam titles and had compiled a record of the most consecutive wins in tennis history. He was a legend in his own time. But after his loss to the seemingly indefatigable McEnroe, the Swedish tennis star would win only two more matches, reaching the quarterfinals in Monte Carlo in 1982. Something had changed internally

for Borg, and by late 1982 he announced to his family, coach, and friends that tennis was no longer fun. The 26-year-old star wanted to retire.

Yet Borg did not make a public announcement of his decision until February 1983. "I was hoping this feeling I had inside would change in January, that I would say, 'O.K., I enjoy this again,'" he told Neil Amdur of the *New York Times.* "When you go out on the court, you should say this is great, I'm going to hit the tennis ball, I'm going to try to win every point, and I like to make a good shot. If you don't think and feel that, it's very difficult to play."

In retiring, Borg left his fans and fellow tennis players shocked and disappointed. Many believed he could have kept on top for several years to come. "I think Bjorn could have won the U.S. Open," Arthur Ashe told *Sports Illustrated..* "I think he could have won the Grand Slam. But by the time he left, the historical challenge didn't mean anything. He was bigger than the game. He was like Elvis or Liz Taylor or somebody. He'd lost touch with the real world."

After he retired, Borg set his sights on the world of business, starting with promotion work for the Swedish tourist board and SAS. Next came a series of his own ventures in real estate and other areas, under the umbrella group of Bjorn Borg Enterprises. In 1987 Borg created his own sports-apparel venture, Bjorn Borg Design Group, but only two years later the business faced major financial difficulties.

Pulling away from the world of tennis, he divorced his wife, Mariana, in 1984, and grew estranged from coach-mentor Lennart Bergelin. In 1985 he had a son, Robin, with the Swedish model Jannike Bjorling, but the pair never married. Although they initially agreed to share custody of the child, when Borg took up with Italian rock star Loredana Berte in 1988, Bjorling had a change of heart. Not only did she wage a custody battle, but Bjorling told a Swedish magazine that the tennis star had abused cocaine during their relationship. Borg denied any drug use, sued the magazine for defamation, and won.

It seemed that the game of life had become harder for Borg than a Grand Slam tennis match. The Swedish tabloids eagerly pursued stories about his tempestuous romantic life, his predilection for wild parties, and his business failures. Perhaps the lowest point came in February 1989, when a trip to a Milan hospital led to press reports that the tennis great had attempted suicide. Borg scoffed at the media, and denied stories that he had swallowed 60 sleeping pills. "I got sick, very sick from eating," he explained to Cindy Shmerler of the *New York Times*. "They pumped my stomach. I was out of the hospital in two hours, feeling very good."

The scandalous rumors did not end there, though. The press dug up more stories while following Borg's relationship with the raucous Loredana Berte, whom Borg married in 1989. Known for her flamboyant stage presence, tough-girl attitude, and hit song "Non Sono una Signora" (I'm Not a Lady), Berte loved to shock audiences. By 1991 her marriage to Borg had begun to sour, and in May of that year, journalists published stories about Berte's attempted suicide. These stories were real. The 40-year-old pop singer had written a suicide note and swallowed two bottles of sedatives; she, too, had her stomach pumped. The couple separated a year later.

Attempted a Comeback

Amid the turbulence in his personal life, Borg made a startling decision. He would return to tennis. In August 1990 he started practicing seriously in diverse locations, including Milan, Buenos Aires, and London. Just a year earlier he had told the *New York Times* that he had no regrets about retiring ("I don't really miss [tennis]," he said). Rumors flew that Borg needed money, since his apparel company was having financial difficulties and he had recently sold his Stockholm apartment and Vikingshill estate. The tennis star explained that he sold the properties simply to be rid of Sweden. "For six years they [the Swedish media] tried

to destroy me," he told the press in Monte Carlo, where he had relocated (quoted in *Sports Illustrated*). "I am happy to be out of Sweden."

Meanwhile, Borg had taken up with a new coach, 79-year-old Welshman Ron Thatcher, also known as Tia Honsai. A self-described martial arts master and mind-body fitness guru, Thatcher claimed to know nothing about tennis and seemed an odd choice for Borg's mentor. In another ill-fated decision, Borg stuck with his old Donnay wooden tennis racquet instead of switching to one of the lighter, wider, high-tech graphite models—the new racquets of choice for tennis stars of the 1990s.

Borg's return to the tour was to begin with the 1991 Monte Carlo Open, where he faced Spain's Jordi Arrese in the first round of play. The crowd, clearly moved to have the Swedish star back, roared welcomingly when Borg stepped onto the court. But the match was short-lived, as 26-year-old Arrese, then ranked only 52nd in the world, made quick work of Borg in a straight-set victory, 6-2, 6-3. Undeterred, Borg attempted another comeback the following year, to the same effect. In eight tournament tries in 1992 and three the following year, he was ousted in the first round. He played his last pro game at Moscow's Kremlin Cup in 1993, losing a close match to Aleksandr Volkov, 4-6, 6-3, 7-6 (9-7).

In May 1993 Borg relinquished his desire to play the Grand Slams again. But he had found a new way to enjoy tennis—by joining the senior circuit. "Senior" meant over 35 years old, and the new Nuveen Tour, created by Jimmy Connors, was attracting large crowds. Borg happily revived his rivalry with both Connors and McEnroe, and the threesome attracted hordes of fans nostalgic for tennis stars of the 1970s and '80s. "Playing the senior circuit is fun," he told Robin Finn of the *New York Times*. "The other stuff isn't; the atmosphere really is not the same anymore. It just seems like the players are out there doing a job, like machines. There isn't the connection like I have with these other guys."

Borg retired from the circuit in late 2000, at 44, but he did not retire completely from tennis. By 2001, he was training a group of promising young Swedish players aged 14 to 17. "I hope to have some of them playing [professionally] next year," he told Rediff Sports. "I hope to give Swedish tennis some good players."

In the end, it is Borg's contribution to tennis, and not the tumult of his personal life, that sports fans will remember. With his contemporaries McEnroe and Connors, Borg lifted tennis to a higher level of play—and he remains one of the sport's most inspirational, larger-than-life heroes.

CONTACT INFORMATION

Address: Bjorn Borg, Association of Tennis Professionals, Monte Carlo Sun, 74 Boulevard D'Italie, 98000 Monaco.

SELECTED WRITINGS BY BORG:

(With Eugene L. Scott) *Bjorn Borg: My Life and Game.* Simon and Schuster, 1980.

FURTHER INFORMATION

Books

Borg, Bjorn, and Eugene L. Scott. *Bjorn Borg: My Life and Game.* New York: Simon & Schuster, 1980.

Periodicals

Amdur, Neil. "Borg Says Tennis Is No Longer Fun." *New York Times* (February 3, 1983): B9.

Cohen, Charles E. "An Iceborg's Meltdown." *People Weekly* (May 13, 1991): 92.

Finn, Robin. "Borg Comeback II: A Passion Play Rewritten." *New York Times* (March 1, 1992): sec. 8, p. 1.

"For Borg, Joy Is Back but Intensity Is Gone." *New York Times* (May 5, 1993): B17.

"Into the Volley Strides the 36-Year-Old Borg. *New York Times* (July 15, 1992): B11.

Gross, Jane. "Borg on the Morning After." *New York Times* (September 9, 1980): C14.

Kirkpatrick, Curry. "UnBjorn: After Myriad Personal Setbacks, a Changed Bjorn Borg Made a Sad Return to Tennis." *Sports Illustrated* (May 6, 1991): 32.

"Love Match for Tennis Ace Borg." Agence France Press (June 8, 2002).

People Weekly (June 24, 2002): 135.

Rieger, Nancy. "Borg Realizes Dream in Running His BBDG Firm." *Footwear News* (October 24, 1988): 2.

Shmerler, Cindy. "Borg Still Boasts That Calm Exterior." *New York Times* (August 22, 1989): B7.

Time (June 1, 1992): 27.

Other

Association of Tennis Professionals. http://www.atptour.com (October 5, 2002).

"Bjorn Borg." BBC Sport. http://news.bbc.co.uk/sport/hi/english/static/in_depth/tennis/2002/wimbledon/legends/borg.stm (September 25, 2002).

"Bjorn Borg." International Tennis Hall of Fame. http://www.tennisfame.org/enshrinees/bjorn_borg.html (September 25, 2002).

"Bjorn Borg Finally Lets the Good Times Roll." Christian Science Monitor. http://www.csmonitor.com/durable/1997/08/18/feat/sports.1.html (September 25, 2002).

"The Rediff Interview: Bjorn Borg." Rediff.com. http://www.rediff.com/sports/2001/may/12borg.htm (September 25, 2002).

"Sports Icons of the 20th Century." Terra.com. http://www.terra.com/specials/sportsicons/borg_en.html (October 1, 2002).

Sketch by Wendy Kagan

Mike Bossy

Mike Bossy
1957-

Canadian hockey player

A member of the New York Islanders Stanley Cup-winning dynasty (1980-83), right wing Mike Bossy was a scoring machine. A pure scorer, Bossy had a great shot, and was an excellent shooter and skater. He matched **Maurice Richard**'s record of scoring fifty goals in fifty games. He went on to score at least fifty goals in his first nine seasons, and at least sixty in five seasons. Bossy accumulated much hardware over the course of his career, winning the Calder Trophy as rookie of the year, Conn Smythe Trophy as playoff most valuable player, and three Lady Byng Trophies for most gentlemanly play. Though Bossy's career was cut short by back problems, his contributions to the game remain important.

Bossy was born on January 22, 1957, in Montreal, Quebec, Canada, the sixth of ten children born to Borden Bossy and his British-born wife, Dorothy. Bossy learned to skate when he was three, and often played on a backyard rink his father constructed. He also played street hockey. From an early age, Bossy had the scoring touch. He was the best player for his age as a six-year-old in St. Alphonse Parish in Montreal. Family lore has Bossy scoring twenty-one goals in his first game.

Chronology

1957	Born on January 22, in Montreal, Quebec, Canada
1973-77	Leaves high school to play junior hockey for Laval Nationals in the Quebec Major Junior Hockey League
1977	Drafted by the New York Islanders with the fifteenth pick
1977-78	Joins the New York Islanders; becomes first rookie to score 50 goals in a season
1987	Plays in last game for the Islanders on May 2 because of back pain
1988	Retires from professional hockey; returns to Laval, Quebec
1992	Number retired by the New York Islanders in March
1993-96	Works in radio in Quebec
1999	Works in public relations

Awards and Accomplishments

1975, 1977	Quebec Major Junior Hockey League All-Star (first team)
1976	Quebec Major Junior Hockey League West All-Star (first team)
1978	Won the Calder Trophy as rookie of the year
1978-79, 1985	All-Star (second team)
1980-83	Won the Stanley Cup with the New York Islanders
1981-84, 1986	All-Star (first team)
1982	Won the Conn Smythe Trophy as playoff MVP
1991	Inducted into the Hockey Hall of Fame

In 1973, Bossy left high school after the 11th grade to play junior hockey. For the next four years, he played for the Laval Nationals in the Quebec Major Junior Hockey League. While in the league, Bossy scored 309 goals in 240 games. Not all of those goals were easy. He was a marked man, on the receiving end of many cheap shots. Bossy also had two qualities that detracted from his appeal to NHL clubs. He was admittedly unconcerned about defense, never fought, and did not check other players much. This affected where he was drafted in 1977.

Drafted by the Islanders

Because of his problematic qualities in juniors, plus his high salary demands and relatively small stature (only 6' and 185 lbs.), Bossy was not chosen until the 15th pick of the 1977 draft. Six other right wings were chosen ahead of him. The New York Islanders picked him because they believed he could be a good two-way player. Bossy himself was hurt that he dropped to 15th and had something to prove. While his defensive play improved, Bossy would never fight.

When Bossy joined the New York Islanders at the beginning of the 1977-78 season, the team was only five years old and very bad. Coach Al Arbour teamed Bossy with another young player, center and complete player **Bryan Trottier**, and left wing Clark Gillies to form what came to be called the Trio Grande line. Over the course of the next 11 years, the line scored many goals for the Islanders and were the primary key to their success.

Bossy showed his scoring prowess from the beginning. He scored fifty goals that season, the first rookie to accomplish this feat. He also won the Calder Trophy as rookie of the year. The Islanders also made it to the quarterfinals of the Stanley Cup, where they lost to the Toronto Maple Leafs.

During his sophomore season, 1978-79, Bossy did not slump. He had thirty-five goals by mid-season, greatly contributing to making the Islanders the highest scoring team in the league. He ended the season with sixty-nine goals, and New York won the President's Trophy for having the most points on the season. The Islanders continued to struggle in the post-season however.

Though Bossy only scored fifty-one goals in the 1979-80 season, the Islanders won the first of four Stanley Cups in 1980. The team finally gelled when they won the Cup, and Bossy was an important component to the team's success. His greatest contribution remained his scoring. By November 1980, Bossy had scored 181 goals in his first 239 games, a record high scoring percentage.

Tied Rocket's Record

During the 1980-81 season, Bossy tied a long-standing record in the NHL. In the 1944-45 season, Maurice "Rocket" Richard scored fifty goals in fifty games. Richard had been a hero of Bossy's from childhood, and Richard had watched Bossy play as a kid in Montreal. Though he was a team player, this was a goal of Bossy's that he announced publicly, putting much pressure on himself. Greatly targeted by opponents, especially by the end, Bossy tied the record by getting two goals in his fiftieth game at home against the Quebec Nordiques.

Though the team goal of winning remained Bossy's focus, he enjoyed scoring and had a number of skills that contributed to his success. He had the ability to get open and shot the puck when he got it. He was also a better skater than most people realized, with good passing and stickhandling skills. As his coach explained to E. M. Swift of *Sports Illustrated,* "Boss is not overpowering. Boss'll get the odd goal from far out, but his main strength is that he's exceptionally quick and accurate. He's the quickest I've ever seen at getting a shot off."

In 1981, when the Islanders won their second Stanley Cup, Bossy had a record in the playoffs with nine power play goals, proving his scoring touch. One of Bossy's best seasons was in 1981-82, when he scored sixty-four goals and eighty-three assists. During the playoffs, he had a bad leg injury which affected his ability to play the way that he wanted to. Yet in the playoffs, he scored seven goals in a four-game sweep over the Vancouver Canucks. Bossy won the Conn Smythe Trophy as most valuable player.

Bossy had sixty goals and fifty-eight assists in the 1982-83 season, the last of the Islanders' four cups. In

Career Statistics

Yr	Team	GP	G	AST	PTS	+/−	PIM
1977-78	Islanders	73	53	38	91	+31	6
1978-79	Islanders	80	69	57	126	+63	25
1979-80	Islanders	75	51	41	92	+28	12
1980-81	Islanders	79	68	51	119	+37	32
1981-82	Islanders	80	64	83	147	+69	22
1982-83	Islanders	79	60	58	118	+27	20
1983-84	Islanders	67	51	67	118	+66	8
1984-85	Islanders	76	58	59	117	+37	38
1985-86	Islanders	80	61	62	123	+30	14
1986-87	Islanders	63	38	37	75	−7	33
TOTAL		752	573	553	1126		210

Islanders: New York Islanders (NHL).

the early rounds of the playoffs, Bossy struggled, putting up a minus in his plus/minus rating, but the team went on to win. Bossy contributed in another way, however, and was rewarded. In 1983, Bossy won the first of his three Lady Byng Trophies, given for most gentlemanly play. Bossy had been a vocal proponent of clean hockey. He publicly stated he would never drop the gloves to fight.

Back Problems Affect Play

Until the 1986-87 season, Bossy scored at least fifty goals a season. That season, back problems deeply affected his ability to do what he did best: score. His back bothered him from the first day of training camp, and got worse as the season moved forward. He could barely bend over to tie his skates. He lost his mobility, which resulted in him taking more penalties. Bossy only played in 63 games that season, and he was not always effective in the ones he did play in. He scored only thirty-eight goals on the season. Bossy did not know it at the time, but he played last game on May 2, 1987.

Forced to Retire

Bossy hoped to go to training camp in the fall of 1987, but no medical therapy had changed his condition. He then took the 1987-88 season off to try different treatments for his back. Nothing worked, and no one could figure out what exactly was wrong. Though only thirty-one years old, Bossy was forced to officially retire in October 1988. After his playing days were over, he was unable to play hockey or even work out because of his back and knees.

After his retirement, Bossy returned to Laval, in the suburbs of Montreal, with wife Lucie and two daughters, Josiane and Tanya. His first post-hockey project involved going into business with Pierre LaCroix, his agent, and working at Titan, a hockey stick manufacturer, as vice president. He was also a broadcaster for the Quebec Nordiques. By the early 1990s, he represented Karhu,

another stick manufacturer, and Cumis, an insurance agency, in public relations positions. He also played golf and gave speeches. In 1993, Bossy broke into radio, and by 1994, he had a regular job on early morning talk radio in Quebec. There he displayed his comic abilities until he left in 1996. By 1999, Bossy was doing public relations for Humpty Dumpty potato chips and other firms. He also remained connected to hockey by serving as the ambassador for Chevrolet Safe & Fun Hockey.

At the end of his shortened playing career, Bossy had impressive numbers. He scored 573 goals and 553 assists in only 752 games. In 129 playoff games, he had eighty-five goals and seventy-five assists. When he retired, he held the record for most goals per season average with 57.3. While he wanted to be considered a great overall player, he was basically known for his impressive scoring output. Even he did not completely understand how he did it. As he was quoted as saying by Stan Fischler in *The All-New Hockey's 100,* "About 90 percent of the time I don't aim: I just try to get my shot away as quick as possible as a surprise element. I just try to get the puck on net."

CONTACT INFORMATION

Address: c/o Hockey Hall of Fame, BCE Place, 30 Yonge St., Toronto, Ontario M53 1X8 Canada; 3080 Carriefour, Laval, Quebec H7T 2K9 Canada. Online: www.mikebossy.net.

FURTHER INFORMATION

Books

Fischler, Stan. *The All-New Hockey's 100.* Toronto: McGraw-Hill Ryerson Ltd., 1988.

Hickok, Ralph. *A Who's Who of Sports Champions: Their Stories and Records.* Boston: Houghton Mifflin Company, 1995.

McGovern, Mike. *The Encyclopedia of 20th Century Athletes*. New York: Facts on File, Inc., 2001.

Periodicals

Anderson, Dave. "Bossy: Scorer with Touch of an Artiste." *New York Times* (May 17, 1981): section 5, p. 3.

Brooks, Larry. "It was a 50-50 proposition." *Sports Illustrated* (February 2, 1981): 64.

Brooks, Larry. "The Phantom of the Rinks." *Sports Illustrated* (January 19, 1981): 37.

Cazeneuve, Brian. "Catching Up With …: Mike Bossy, Islanders Sharpshooter May 14, 1984." *Sports Illustrated* (October 4, 1999): 18.

Dalla Costa, Morris. "Bossy Passionate from a Distance." *London Free Press* (January 22, 2002): D6.

Finn, Robin. "Bossy Can't Bear to Watch." *New York Times* (September 12, 1987): section 1, p. 52.

Finn, Robin. "Bossy's Desire to Play Defeated by Pain." *New York Times* (October 25, 1988): B11.

Finn, Robin. "Bossy's Stoicism Is Showing Cracks." *New York Times* (March 24, 1987).

Finn, Robin. "Future at Risk, Bossy Battles Pain." *New York Times* (February 4, 1987): A23.

Kirshenbaum, Jerry. "Three Islanders Unto Themselves." *Sports Illustrated* (December 12, 1977): 20.

"A Segue from Blues Lines to Punch Lines." *New York Times* (December 16, 1994): B17.

Swift, E. M. "Bossy showed 'em who's boss." *Sports Illustrated* (May 16, 1983): 72.

Swift, E. M. "This Man is an Islander unto Himself." *Sports Illustrated* (January 22, 1979): 20.

Vecsey, George. "Bossy Left His Numbers Behind Him." *New York Times* (March 4, 1992): B7.

Vecsey, George. "Bossy: A Search for Perfection." *New York Times* (November 2, 1980): section 5, p. 1.

Other

"Biography." http://www.mikebossy.net/bio.asp (November 2, 2002).

Feete, David A. "Mike Bossy." LCS Hockey. http://www.lcshockey/com/archive/greats/bossy.asp (November 2, 2002).

"The Legends: Players: Mike Bossy: Biography." The Legends of Hockey. http://www.legendsofhockey.net:8080/LegendsOfHockey/jsp/Legen. (November 2, 2002).

"The Legends: Players; Mike Bossy: Career Statistics." LCS Hockey. http://www.legendsofhockey.net: 8080/LegendsOfHockey/jsp/Legen. (November 2, 2002).

"Mike Bossy." http://www.hockeysandwich.com/bossy.html (November 2, 2002).

Rumble, Eric. "Interview with Mike Bossy." Chevrolet Safe & Fun Hockey. http://www.gmcanada.com/english/special/chev_safeandfun/saf_coac (November 2, 2002).

Sketch by A. Petruso

Scotty Bowman

Scotty Bowman
1933-

Canadian hockey coach

Scotty Bowman is the most successful professional hockey coach in history, winning an unprecedented nine Stanley Cup Championships in a career that spanned thirty-four years. It is a record that may never be surpassed. Bowman, who retired at age sixty-eight after the 2001-02 season, also holds records for the most regular-season games coached (2,141); most wins in the regular season (1,244); and most wins in the playoffs (223). He is the only NHL coach to lead three different teams to the Stanley Cup. Bowman's success reaches beyond hockey and the NHL, however. He is one of the best coaches of any sport or any era—in a class with football's **George Halas** and **Vince Lombardi**, basketball's **Arnold 'Red' Auerbach**, and baseball's **Casey Stengel** and **Connie Mack**. *Sports Illustrated* took that a step further in 1998, proclaiming Bowman the best coach ever in any of North America's major professional sports. The magazine noted that no other coach has been as successful with as many teams or as many generations of athletes. Bowman's ability to adapt—to both the conditions of a particular game and to changing times—was remarkable given his demanding, churlish nature. "He started coaching guys who had summer jobs and crew cuts, and now he's

Chronology

1933	Born September 18 in Montreal, Quebec
1951	Head injury ends playing days, launches coaching career
1954	Briefly attends Sir George Williams Business School
1956	Becomes assistant to the coach and general manager of the Junior Canadiens
1958	Junior Canadiens win the Memorial Cup, the top prize in junior hockey
1958	Begins coaching Junior A team in Peterborough, Ontario
1961	Becomes scout for the Montreal Canadiens
1963	Returns to coaching with the Junior Canadiens, meets the legendary Toe Blake
1966	Joins the NHL's St. Louis Blues, an expansion team, as assistant coach for the upcoming 1967-68 hockey season
1967	Takes over as Blues' head coach and leads team to 1968 Stanley Cup finals, where they lose four straight games to Blake's Montreal Canadiens
1969	Marries Suella Belle Chitty on August 16; they will have five children
1969	Bowman-led Blues win Western Division title and advance to the Stanley Cup finals, but lose
1970	Blues again win division title but lose Stanley Cup championship
1970	Takes over as general manager of the Blues, in addition to coaching
1971	Becomes coach of the Montreal Canadiens
1973, 1976-79	Wins five Stanley Cups with the Canadiens
1977	Wins the Jack Adams Award for Best Coach
1979	Becomes head coach and general manager of the Buffalo Sabres
1987	Leaves the NHL
1987	Begins three-year stint as analyst on Hockey Night in Canada on CBC, the Canadian television network
1990	Joins Pittsburgh Penguins as director of player personnel and recruitment
1991	Penguins win the Stanley Cup
1991	Penguins' head coach Bob Johnson is diagnosed with brain cancer; Bowman is selected to succeed him
1991	Inducted into Hockey Hall of Fame
1992	Wins sixth Stanley Cup as head coach with Penguins
1993	Becomes coach of the Detroit Red Wings
1995	Coaches his 1,607th game on December 29, setting the NHL record.
1996	Wins the Jack Adams Award for Best Coach
1997	Wins seventh Stanley Cup with Red Wings
1997	Records his 1,000th career win on February 8
1998	Wins eighth Stanley Cup with Red Wings
1998	Undergoes heart angioplasty and knee reconstruction surgeries
2001	Wins the Lester Patrick Award for outstanding service to hockey in the United States
2002	Wins record ninth Stanley Cup with the Red Wings
2002	Retires from coaching; signs three-year contract to work for the Red Wings as a consultant

coaching guys with Ferraris, earrings, blond streaks and agents," said Brendan Shanahan, who played for—and won three Stanley Cups with—Bowman in Detroit.

Influences and injury

William Scott Bowman was born September 18, 1933, in Montreal, Quebec, the second of John and Jane Bowman's four children. The Bowmans emigrated to Canada from Scotland and raised their family in a tenement in Verdun, a working-class Montreal suburb. Scotty inherited a relentless work ethic from his father, who never took a sick day in the thirty-one years he toiled as a blacksmith for the railroad. And he acquired a fiercely competitive nature from his mother, who would throw her cards in the fire when she lost a hand of euchre.

Verdun had dozens of skating rinks where, as a boy, Bowman learned to play hockey. By the age of seventeen, he was a promising forward with the Montreal Canadiens' junior team and a pro prospect. His dream of playing professional hockey was not to be, however. The end came during the final minutes of a Junior A playoff game at the Montreal Forum in 1951. Bowman was on a breakaway toward the opposing goal with a defenseman named Jean-Guy Talbot in pursuit. Talbot, his team on the verge of elimination from the playoffs, swung his stick twice at Bowman in frustration. Bowman was struck in the head—none of the players wore helmets in those days—and lost a piece of his skull. He required a metal plate in his head. His playing days were over. He understood hockey's intense, sometimes violent nature, however, and never held a grudge. A few years later, Bowman was coaching the St. Louis Blues when the team added Talbot to its roster. Bowman coached him for three years.

From player to coach

After his injury, Bowman turned to the job that would consume him for the next half-century—coaching. He proved to be a prodigy. Starting in the youth leagues, Bowman coached twelve- and thirteen-year-old players, then quickly advanced to fourteen- and fifteen-year-olds. By the time he was twenty-one, Bowman was coaching twenty-year-old players at the Junior B level. The job paid only $250 a year, so he also worked for a paint company. On his lunch hour he walked five minutes to the Forum to watch the Montreal Canadiens practice—and to learn. The Junior Canadiens moved to Ottawa in 1956 and Sam Pollack, the coach and general manager, asked the 23-year-old Bowman to come along as his assistant. The team won the 1958 Memorial Cup, the top prize in junior hockey, and Bowman, just twenty-five years old, was named head coach of a Junior A team in Peterborough. After three years he became the Canadiens' head scout for eastern Canada, but found he missed being with a team. In 1963 he was back on the bench, coaching the Junior Canadiens. His office in the Forum was down the hall from the office occupied by legendary Canadiens coach **Toe Blake**, who would become Bowman's mentor. Blake led the Canadiens to eight Stanley Cups in thirteen seasons from 1955 to 1968—a record that would stand until Bowman won his ninth cup as head coach in 2002.

Learning from a legend

Under Blake's tutelage, Bowman became a master of hockey strategy. "He knew how each of his players did against everyone else," Bowman told E.M. Swift of *Sports Illustrated*. "Certain guys do well against one team but not another. He was a good strategist and a good matchup man and wasn't afraid to sit guys out to change his ammunition." It was a lesson Bowman employed throughout his career. Another of Bowman's trademark tactics came from Blake, as well. He constantly changed lineups and on-ice schemes to slow down the opposition and keep them off balance. Bowman's unpredictability allowed him to stay one or two moves ahead of the opposing coach and control the game.

Bowman was only thirty-three when he rose to the pro ranks as assistant coach with the expansion St. Louis Blues, which entered the NHL in 1967. Sixteen games into the season, Blues coach and general manager Lynn Patrick asked Bowman to take over head coaching duties. The team was 4-12 when Bowman stepped in; they finished the season 23-21-14, good enough for third place and a playoff berth. Bowman orchestrated two seven-game upsets to lead the Blues to the 1968 Stanley Cup finals. They lost four straight one-goal games to Canadiens. It was Blake's final season and eighth Stanley Cup. Bowman and the Blues won the Western Division and advanced to the finals the next two years—but failed to win the Cup.

Five cups in Montreal

In 1971, Bowman was selected to coach the Canadiens by his old boss Sam Pollack, who had become Montreal's general manager. In the next eight years, Montreal racked up a remarkable 419-110-105 record for a .742 winning percentage and, more importantly, five Stanley Cups. Bowman was intense, demanding, unpredictable, and brilliant. He was respected by his players, but not liked. Montreal goalie **Ken Dryden**, in his excellent 1983 book *The Game*, wrote this: "Scotty Bowman is not someone who is easy to like. . . . Abrupt, straightforward, without flair or charm, he seems cold and abrasive, sometimes obnoxious, controversial but never colorful. He is not Vince Lombardi, tough and gruff with a heart of gold. His players don't sit and tell hateful-affectionate stories about him. . . . He is complex, confusing, misunderstood, unclear in every way but one. He is a brilliant coach, the best of his time." Canadiens star Steve Shutt put it this way: "You hated him 364 days years, and on the 365th day you got your Stanley Cup ring."

The road turns rocky

Bowman left the Canadiens in 1979 to become coach and general manager of the Buffalo Sabres. The team struggled during the seven years Bowman was there, never advancing beyond the conference finals in the playoffs. In his dual role, Bowman was spread too thin and grew tired of coaching. Three times he hired coaches to take over on the bench—Roger Neilson in 1981, Jimmy Roberts in '82, Jim Schoenfeld in '86—and three

Awards and Accomplishments	
1958	Memorial Cup, the top prize in junior hockey (as member of Junior Canadiens' coaching staff)
1969-70	Western Division title (St. Louis Blues)
1973, 1976-79	Stanley Cup (Montreal Canadiens)
1977	Jack Adams Award for Best Coach
1991	Stanley Cup (as director of player personnel with the Pittsburgh Penguins)
1991	Hockey Hall of Fame inductee
1992	Stanley Cup (as Penguins' head coach)
1993, 1996	Victor Award for NHL Coach of the Year
1996	Jack Adams Award for Best Coach
1997-98, 2002	Stanley Cup (Red Wings)
2001	Lester Patrick Award for outstanding service to hockey in the United States
2002	Retired from coaching with records for most Stanley Cup Championships as head coach (nine); most regular season wins (1,244); most playoff wins (223); most regular season games coached (2,141); and only coach to lead three different teams to the Stanley Cup.

times he replaced them. In late 1986, he again gave up the coaching duties to focus on the general manager's job, but was fired soon after that.

For the next three years, Bowman worked as an analyst on Hockey Night in Canada. In 1990, he became director of player personnel for the Pittsburgh Penguins—a job that allowed him to stay in Buffalo with his family. He had married Suella Belle Chitty in 1969, and they had five children. Their second-oldest, David, was born with hydrocephalus and spent most of his life in an institution for the mentally handicapped.

Adapting to the modern game

Bowman worked well with Pittsburgh coach Bob Johnson, who was as upbeat and outgoing as Bowman was aloof and non-communicative. Johnson led the Penguins to the Stanley Cup in 1991, but the following summer he was diagnosed with brain cancer. Bowman was named interim coach and quickly realized that his demanding, disciplinarian style would not work with a team accustomed to Johnson's positive, laid back, non-confrontational ways. The game had changed in the two decades since Bowman began his reign with the Canadiens, and he would have to change, as well. "I was aware that if I coached the way I had in the past it wouldn't have had the same results," he said. "I knew I had to be different." In the '92 playoffs, the Penguins won eleven straight games, a post-season record, and claimed their second straight Stanley Cup. It was Bowman's sixth as head coach.

The greatest ever

In 1993, Bowman became head coach of the Detroit Red Wings, a team that had not won a championship since 1955. That would change. The Wings won back-to-back titles in 1997 and 1998—and Bowman tied Blake with eight Stanley Cups. The record-breaking ninth title would be elusive, however, as the Wings struggled for the next three years. For the 2001-02 season, the team signed veteran superstars **Dominik Hasek**, **Brett Hull**, and Luc Robataille to a roster that already included future Hall-of-Famers Steve Yzerman, **Sergei Federov**, Brendan Shanahan, and **Chris Chelios**. It was arguably the most talented hockey team ever assembled—and unquestionably the oldest with six players 35 or older. Bowman expertly blended these mammoth talents and led the Wings to their third cup in six years. "He has such a command of the game, and such a great command of his team that you are in awe," coach Paul Maurice said after Bowman beat his Carolina Hurricanes in the finals. Minutes after winning his ninth Stanley Cup and surpassing his old friend and teacher Toe Blake, Bowman announced his retirement.

Scotty Bowman was the first coach to use videotape to scout opposing teams. He was the first to demand his players track their plus-minus statistics to gauge their effectiveness on the ice. He was unsurpassed at mixing and matching his lineups. He made strategic changes at dizzying speed to keep the other team guessing. "Bowman's the best," Scott Andrea wrote for the Knight Ridder News Service, "because he was able to adapt his game to the different era, teams, players and styles so well." Brett Hull paid this tribute to Bowman: "It's like being coached by Red Auerbach or Bear Bryant. These are people who only came along once in a lifetime and to say he was your coach . . . it's hard to put into words."

CONTACT INFORMATION

Address: c/o Detroit Red Wings, Joe Louis Arena, 600 Civic Center Drive, Detroit, MI 48226-4419. Phone: (313) 396-7444.

FURTHER INFORMATION

Periodicals

Albom, Mitch. "Why Scotty Finally Decided to Retire." *Detroit Free Press* (June 15, 2002).

Andera, Scott. Service "Bowman Leaves NHL with a Crown." Knight-Ridder News (June 14, 2002).

Farber, Michael. "Reign Men." *Sports Illustrated* (June 24, 2002): 42.

Farber, Michael. "That's Scotty!" *Sports Illustrated* (June 29, 1998): 64.

Gave, Keith. "Back Where He Belongs." *Sporting News* (November 2, 1998): 69

Lapointe, Joe. "Red Wings Win Back Stanley Cup." *New York Times* (June 14, 2002): D1.

Lapointe, Joe. "Bowman's Last Substitution? A Smile for a Scowl." *New York Times* (June 15, 2002): D4

Matheson, Jim. "The Wings After Scotty." *Edmonton Journal* (October 6, 2002): D10

Niyo, John. "Bowman Still Makes History." *Detroit News* (June 13, 2002): 8B

Swift, E. M. "Super Conductor." *Sports Illustrated* (May 10, 1993): 58

Other

Hradek, E. J. "A Perfect Ending to a Perfect Career." *ESPN The Magazine online* (June 13, 2002) http://msn.espn.go.com/nhl/playoffs2002/s/hradek0613.html

Sketch by David Wilkins

Bill Bradley
1943-

American basketball player

Bill Bradley has found fame in two very different careers, one on the basketball court and one in politics, by applying similarly high levels of determination and skill. Having opted not to play for a basketball powerhouse because of his academic interests, he made headlines as a standout on the Princeton team. As a dazzling shooter and deft freethrower, he led the Tigers to the NCAA finals and set two tournament records during the mid-1960s. Bradley went on to play with the New York Knickerbockers for ten years, becoming an important part of a star-studded team that won two NBA championships. He made a quick transition to politics in 1978, when he was elected U.S. Senator for New Jersey. Bradley later unsuccessfully challenged then-Vice President Al Gore for the Democratic nomination in the 2000 presidential election in a campaign focused on principles and policies.

Privileged Childhood

Growing up in Crystal City, a small town near St. Louis, Missouri, Bradley was relatively privileged among his peers, who mostly came from working-class families.

Bill Bradley

His father Warren was a banker and his mother Susan had worked as a teacher. They provided their only child with many material advantages and encouraged him to excel at school and in extracurricular activities. When he began playing basketball at age nine, Bradley was happy to have found a common interest with his classmates. He would skip the family's annual winter stay in Palm Springs, Florida and began pouring his energies into basketball.

Crystal City High School's Coach Popp broke with tradition when he put Bradley on the varsity team as a freshman in 1959. This earned his player some resentment, but it was soon dissipated by his contributions on the court. Not only had Bradley almost reached his full height of six feet, five inches, he showed exceptional shooting skills and a willingness to pass the ball. With a total of 3,068 points over the course of four years, he became known as the best high school basketball player in Missouri history, was twice named as an All-American, and led the Crystal City team to the Missouri State Final Four three times.

Picks Princeton

Basketball, however, did not eclipse Bradley's interest in his studies, or his parents' determination that he would succeed in other areas. A straight A student, he put academics first when choosing a college. Having received more than seventy-five scholarship offers, Bradley turned them all down to enroll at Princeton,

Chronology

1943	Born July 28 in Crystal City, Missouri
1959-62	Stars in basketball at Crystal City High School
1963-65	Stars in basketball at Princeton University
1965-66	Plays professional ball with Simmenthal of Milan
1965-67	Earns masters degree studying at Oxford on Rhodes Scholarship
1967	Begins NBA career with the New York Knickerbockers
1974	Marries Ernestine Schlant on January 14
1976	Publishes *Life on the Run*
1977	Retires from professional basketball
1978	Elected to the U.S. Senate
1995	Announces he will not seek re-election to Senate
1996	Declares candidacy seeking the Democratic presidential nomination
2000	Drops out of presidential race in March

where he majored in history and wrote a senior thesis on Harry Truman's Senate re-election campaign of 1940.

Bradley's priorities were not evident on the basketball court, where he had an enormous influence on the Princeton team. During his three years as a varsity player, the Tigers claimed the Ivy League championship. As a sophomore he averaged 27.3 points per game and hit 89.9 percent of his freethrows. During his senior year, he helped the team reach the No. 3 spot among 551 NCAA teams, overcoming the fact that Princeton had not been ranked during the season. Nor had any Ivy League team made it past regional competition during the previous twenty-one years. When the Tigers played No. 1-ranked Michigan, a spectacular drama developed. With just under five minutes left in the game, Bradley fouled out with the Tigers leading, 75-63. Forty-one of those points had been made by Bradley. Michigan went on to win by two points, but Bradley was named Most Valuable Player of the tournament. In a consolation game against Wichita the next day, a disconsolate Bradley had to be pressed into shooting the ball. The result was his breaking the NCAA record for most shots scored in a single game, with fifty-eight points.

Off the court, Bradley earned a reputation for gentlemanly, modest behavior. In a 1965 feature story for *Life,* Paul O'Neil noted that the young man's intensity, self-possession, and strictly model behavior had initially inspired a few sneers from his classmates, but that "a certain baffled pride" had since developed at Princeton. After graduating with honors in 1965, Bradley turned down an offer to play for the Knicks in order to get his masters degree at Oxford. When he returned to the United States, Bradley was on active duty with the U.S. Air Force Reserve for six months before he joined the Knicks mid-season in 1967.

Highly-paid Rookie

With a contract worth half a million dollars, Bradley became one of the best-paid rookies in the NBA. He would not, however, repeat the leading role of his col-

Awards and Accomplishments

1960-61	Named *Scholastic* All-American
1963	NCAA tournament record for best free throw percentage: 90.6
1964	Captain of gold medal-winning U.S. Olympic team in Tokyo
1964	Named NCAA Tournament Most Valuable Player
1964-65	Named to First Team All-America
1965	Named Player of the Year by the Associated Press United Press International
1965	Named to First Team All-Academic
1965	Sullivan Award for top amateur athlete
1965-67	Rhodes Scholar, Oxford University
1970, 1973	Member of NBA championship team
1978	Elected to first of three terms as U.S. Senator for New Jersey
1983	Elected to Basketball Hall of Fame
1996	Truman Award for public service

Career Statistics

Yr	Team	GP	PTS	FG%	FT%
1967-68	NYK	45	360	41.6	73.1
1968-69	NYK	82	1020	42.9	81.4
1969-70	NYK	67	971	46.0	82.4
1970-71	NYK	78	970	45.3	82.3
1971-72	NYK	78	1177	46.5	84.9
1972-73	NYK	82	1319	45.9	87.1
1973-74	NYK	82	1150	45.1	87.4
1974-75	NYK	79	1048	43.6	87.3
1975-76	NYK	82	914	43.3	87.8
1976-77	NYK	67	288	46.4	81.0
TOTAL		742	9217	44.8	84.0

NYK: New York Knickerbockers.

lege days, but rather served as an important contributor among a team of stars. Playing with starters Dave De-Busschere, Willis Reed, Walt Frazier, and Dick Barnett, as well as with reserves Jerry Lucas and **Phil Jackson**, he was part of a team that twice defeated the Los Angeles Lakers to earn the NBA championship, first in 1970 and again in 1973. Bradley's demeanor and lifestyle once again set him apart from his teammates, who gave him the nickname "Dollar Bill" because of his frugality, saying that he probably had the first dollar he ever earned. Avoiding the notorious Manhattan nightlife that was enjoyed by so many players, Bradley used his spare time to support social and environmental causes.

Senator Bradley

Bradley retired from basketball in 1976 and was elected to the basketball Hall of Fame in 1983. But when he decided to run for public office, the former NBA star downplayed his professional sports background. To the surprise of some, he did not begin his political career at the local level. In 1978, running as a Democrat, he was elected U.S. senator for the state of New Jersey. When Bradley took office in 1979, he was the youngest sitting U.S. senator, at just thirty-five years old. During three terms in the Senate he took special interest in the issues of Third World debt, race relations, tax policy, and the Soviet Union. Having published a tax reform treatise in 1982, he played an important role in creating the 1986 tax reform bill. His other accomplishments include expanding the Earned Income Tax Credit and giving Medicaid benefits to more women and children.

In 1990 Bradley was shocked when political newcomer Christine Todd Whitman came close to unseating him. The experience challenged the senator's perception of American politics and led to his retirement in early 1996. Subsequently, Bradley served as a contributor to the CBS news division and as a visiting scholar at Stanford, the University of Notre Dame, and the University of Maryland. He also wrote *Time Present, Time Past: A Memoir,* reflecting on both of his careers.

Presidential Candidate

After initially denying his interest in running for president, Bradley became a candidate in 1999. He acknowledged that the timing of his decision had hinged on both political goals and personal circumstances. His wife, Ernestine Schlant, a professor of comparative literature at Montclair State College, had finished writing a book and their daughter Theresa Anne was graduating from college. He wanted to prove himself as the best candidate for president, in terms of both policy and ethics, and presented himself as a markedly different choice from Al Gore. In the words of a *Newsweek* writer, he was "a kind of Anti-Clinton: a legendary jock who doesn't crave approval, an intellectual who's not afraid to think big, a grown-up with nothing to hide." But Bradley had not won a primary when he withdrew from the presidential race in March 2000. He credited his loss in part to the interest voters showed in a Republican rival, John McCain.

The 2000 presidential campaign amplified an image that Bradley initially developed on the basketball court. In his dedication to his teams and his country, he is known as a diligent worker, a leader as well as a team player, and as someone who keeps his own counsel and lives by his own high standards. While Bradley does not often draw attention to his achievements on the court, his collegiate performance, including the standing record for most points in a Final Four game, still places him among the best in the sport. In a post-election interview, *Sporting News* writer Jeff D'Alessio asked Bradley to comment on changes in the sport of basketball. He suggested that college players be kept out of competition as freshmen and said that players no longer know how to shoot. The remarks reinforce the idea that while Bradley may have changed careers, his interests and values have stayed the same.

CONTACT INFORMATION

Address: Allen & Company, 711 Fifth Ave., New York, NY 10022. Phone: (212) 832-8000.

SELECTED WRITINGS BY BRADLEY:

Life on the Run, Quadrangle, 1976.
The Fair Tax, Pocket Books, 1982.
Time Present, Time Past: A Memoir, Knopf, 1996.
Values of the Game, Artisan, 1998.
CSIS Task Force on the Multilateral Development Banks, CSIS, 1998.
The Journey From Here, Artisan, 2000.

FURTHER INFORMATION

Books

Newsmakers 2000. Detroit: Gale Group, 2000.

Periodicals

"Bradley's Game." *Newsweek* (November 15, 1999): 37.
"Bradley After the Buzzer." *Newsweek* (March 20, 2000): 29.
O'Neil, Paul. "Bradley-Good Man and True." *Life* (April 2, 1965): 93-98.
"The Art of Being Bradley." *Time* (October 4, 1999): 44.

Other

D'Alessio, Jeff. "Before he became a political name, Bradley had game." SportingNews.com. http://www.sportingnews.com. (November 6, 2002).

Sketch by Paula Pyzik Scott

Don Bradman
1908-2001

Australian cricket player

Sir Donald Bradman was widely regarded as the greatest batsman ever to play the game of cricket. Scoring an average of 99.94 runs in Test matches over the course of his 20-year career from 1928 to 1948,

Don Bradman

Bradman far outshone players who were considered great if they averaged fifty runs. He scored more triple centuries (6) and more double centuries (37) than any other batsman in the history of the game. On average, he scored a century in every three innings he played.

"I Was Just Enjoying Myself"

Born in the small Australian town of Cootamundra in New South Wales in 1908, Bradman grew up in an agricultural family. When he was two years old his parents, tired of attempting to scratch out a living on difficult land, moved Bradman, his brother, and his three sisters to Bowral, a small town in the southern highlands of New South Wales, where the climate and soil were more hospitable. Bradman was a quiet child, with few friends, and often entertained himself by tossing a golf ball against a brick water tank near his house, rebounding it and hitting it again, hour after hour.

A cricket stump is used much like a bat is used in baseball, but is much narrower than a bat—only an inch in diameter, so this was a difficult feat. As Dave Kindred noted in *Sporting News,* Bradman said many years later, "I was just enjoying myself. It never entered my head that I was training my eyesight and movements."

Later, Bradman received a cricket stump from his father, a battered and repaired hand-me-down. He was delighted with it. His mother told him that if he played well in an important game and scored more than 100, he

Chronology

1908	Born in Cootamundra, Australia
1927	Begins playing for New South Wales, completes the first of his 117 first-class centuries
1928	Begins playing for Australia
1930	Scores an average of 139.14 and becomes a hero to fans
1932	Marries Jessie Menzies
1935	Moves to Adelaide, works as a stockbroker
1935	Chosen as captain of South Australia team
1938	Breaks ankle, spends much of the season out of play
1939	Volunteers for Royal Australian Air Force at outbreak of WWII
1941	Discharged from service
1945	Founds his own brokerage company
1946	Returns to cricket and leads Australia to victory
1948	Retires from play after a whole season without a loss
1949	Becomes first cricketer to be knighted before retirement
1960-63, 1969-72	Chair of Board of Control
1970	Is made a Companion of the Order of Australia
2001	Dies at his home in Adelaide, Australia.

Awards and Accomplishments

1928-1948	Scores average of 99.94 runs in Test matches
1928-1948	Scores more triple centuries (6) and more double centuries (37) than any other batsman in cricket history
1949	Becomes first Australian cricketer to be knighted
1979	Becomes a Companion of the Order of Australia

could have a brand-new bat. Instead of 100, he scored 300, so he got three bats.

Bradman left intermediate high school when he was fourteen, but he played on local cricket teams, and was soon noticed by scouts for the New South Wales team. In 1927, when he was nineteen, he was invited to play for New South Wales. In his first match with the team, he scored 118, the first of his 117 first-class centuries.

Five-feet-seven and lightly built, Bradman made up for his lack of brute strength with speed, footwork, timing, and strong wrists, as well as stamina and a determination to keep scoring runs. Other batters might be content to score one century; Bradman kept batting, aiming for two, or even three.

In 1928, Bradman moved to Sydney and was chosen to play for Australia against England in a Test match at Brisbane. Although he failed and was dropped, he returned to play in the third Test at Melbourne. He made 79 and 112, and finished that Test series with an average of 66.85.

"A Beacon of Hope"

In the following year, Bradman scored an average of 139.14, and was widely praised as a hero of the sport. According to Kindred, sportswriter E.W. Swanton wrote of Bradman in 1930, "The stranger seeing him for the first time must have noticed the exceptional quickness of his reactions, his speed between the wickets and the lithe fitness that enabled him to take the longest innings in stride.... If perfect balance, coordination and certainty of execution be accepted as the principal ingredients of batsmanship, we who watched Don in his early manhood will not hope or expect ever to see its art displayed in a higher form."

In those days of the Great Depression, Bradman was such a hero in his native Australia that when he was batting, avid fans following the game on the radio would stop driving in order to hear the plays; people would not catch a train or a tram home from work or to do errands until he had finished batting. Outside the offices of newspapers in Sydney, Adelaide, Melbourne, and Brisbane, crowds gathered to watch the scoreboards that the papers sponsored and cheer for every run Bradman scored. As a reporter for the London *Times* wrote in Bradman's obituary, "He was, for the army of the unemployed, their beacon of hope."

All this praise led some other players to be jealous of him, and some criticized his self-assured manner. Others, playing on the English team against Australia, developed a strategy of "bodyline" bowling, which involved deliberately throwing the cricket ball at the batsman's unprotected body and head. The tactic, which was legal at the time, was successful in intimidating many players and securing wins for England, but ultimately led to injuries, bad feeling between the two nations, and even threats of canceling the competition. Bradman disliked being the target of bodyline bowling as much as any player, but when asked about it, only said coolly, "It was not, you might say, in the spirit of the game," according to Kindred. The practice of bodyline bowling was soon made illegal.

In April of 1932, Bradman married Jessie Menzies, whom he had known since childhood. They would eventually have one daughter and one son. In the ensuing years, he suffered bouts of illness, culminating in appendicitis and peritonitis; his condition was so grave that the Australian press reported that he had died.

While recovering, Bradman did not play. He and Jessie moved to Adelaide in 1935, where he had been offered a job as a stockbroker; he accepted it, believing that he should not rely on cricket alone to provide an income. However, as soon as he moved to Adelaide, he was chosen as captain of the South Australia team, and then as captain of the Australian team for the Test series against England in 1936-1937. Although Australia ultimately won the series, the competition was marred by various rifts between factions on the team, and by the fact that players' wives could not accompany them to competition. In the 1938 season, Bradman broke his ankle in the final test, which Australia lost to England, and spent the rest of the season out of play.

In 1939, when World War II broke out, Bradman volunteered for the Royal Australian Air Force, but was assigned to teach physical education in the Army. However, various injuries led the authorities to discharge him from service in 1941. He returned to the stockbroker's firm, but by 1945 it was bankrupt and his employer was arrested for fraud. Bradman founded his own company and did well.

He was back in play for the first postwar tour in 1946-1947, and led Australia to victory. His presence in the game became for many Australians a reminder of "normal," pre-war life, as well as a reminder of Australia's cultural and historic links to the British Empire.

"I Don't Laugh Much About It"

In 1948, his final year of play, he vowed that he would go the whole season without losing a match, and he did. His triumph was only marred by the events of his last game. As Kindred noted, Bradman needed only four runs in that game to reach a 100-run average for his entire 20-year career. Surprisingly, he did not score at all, an event known as a "duck." In an interview in 1996, a television reporter asked Bradman if he ever laughed to think his duck was the most famous one in the history of the game. Although forty-eight years had passed since that day, and although he had received a standing ovation from the English fans when he left the crease for the last time, Bradman said seriously, "No, I don't laugh much about it."

Bradman was knighted in 1949, the first Australian cricketer to receive this honor. He continued to work as a stockbroker until the mid-1950s, when poor health forced him to sell the business. After this, he became involved in the administrative levels of Australian cricket, working as a Test selector. He was also chair of the Board of Control from 1960 to 1963 and from 1969 to 1972.

In 1979, Bradman was made a Companion of the Order of Australia.

Bradman's wife Jessie died in 1997, and grief struck him hard. He died at his home in Adelaide, Australia, in 2001, after suffering poor health for some time. He was ninety-two. In summing up Bradman's popularity, a reporter in the London *Times* wrote that Bradman was so admired by Australians that "for most of the second half of the [twentieth] century, he would have been the people's choice as President of Australia." And as former England captain Brian Close told a reporter in the *Coventry Evening Telegraph,* "He gave Australia a lot to live for and I doubt he will ever be surpassed."

FURTHER INFORMATION

Periodicals

"Don Bradman: Obituary." *Times* (London, England) (February 26, 2001): 21.

Kindred, Dave. "A Bat, a Ball and a Ruthian Legend." *Sporting News* (April 23, 2001): 70.

"Sport Mourns for Sir Don: Cricket." *Coventry Evening Telegraph* (Coventry, England) (February 26, 2001): 43.

Sketch by Kelly Winters

Terry Bradshaw
1948-

American football player

The Steel Curtain. Franco Harris. **Lynn Swann**. Mean **Joe Greene**. These names are all indelibly imprinted in the psyches of football fans who lived through the early 1980s, as well as struck a special fear into the Dallas Cowboy fans who lost not one, but two Super Bowls to the Pittsburgh Steelers. But there is one name who stands behind them all. A small-town boy with a cannon for an arm who overcame his inner demons and media discrimination, and who's religious conversion experience not only transformed himself, but a young struggling team into a football dynasty. That man was Terry Bradshaw.

Bradshaw's career statistics—two Super Bowl MVPs, 27,989 yards gained, 212 touchdowns passed, and thirty-two touchdowns rushed—place him near the top as one of the greatest quarterbacks in National Football league (NFL) history. But unlike most sports superstars, Bradshaw has drawn on other talents as well as his folksy, country-bred, down-home, All-American personality to extend his career into media stardom as a sports commentator, as well as the author of five books. Not bad for someone once branded as the Bayou Bumpkin.

Born to Work

Bradshaw was born in 1948 into a Shreveport, Louisiana farming family, the son of William and Novis Bradshaw. The work ethic was there from the beginning. "I was born to work, taught to work, love to work." Early on he developed his skills on the football field, honing a pinpoint, accurate passing that would become his trademark. As a college football player he made all-American, an unusual honor since he didn't attend one of the football powerhouses, but instead played for Louisiana Technical University (not even a Division I school). In fact, Bradshaw's discovery by the Pittsburgh Steelers—who made him the number one pick in the 1970 football draft—started a tradition of college football powerhouses looking to Louisiana for their talent.

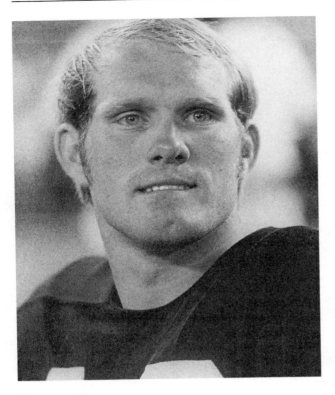

Terry Bradshaw

Number One Pick

The 1970 version of the Steelers that Bradshaw joined were a hapless team. Their number one pick in the draft was made possible by their dismal record, finishing last in the previous season with only one win to fourteen losses. Bradshaw came with high expectations attached to him, with the Steelers expecting their new phenom to help turn around the franchise. Despite his talent, the big league pressure was too much for the young rookie. His first three seasons with the Steelers were unremarkable. Their record improved but not enough to make them contenders, and questions were beginning to be raised about Bradshaw's potential to contribute to the team.

Part of the problem may have been psychological. Among the many pressures that Bradshaw had to live with was absurd claim that he was "dumb." This rumor started with trash talking from opponents like Cowboy linebacker "Hollywood Henderson" who said Bradshaw "couldn't spell 'cat' if you spotted him the 'c' and the 't.'

In actuality, Bradshaw was later diagnosed with having Attention Deficit Disorder. Schoolwork, especially reading, was always an enormous challenge for him. But nonetheless, the media rumors circulating around him were especially hurtful because it belied the obvious brilliance of his generalship on the playing field.

Bradshaw told a *New York Times* reporter: "I was a home boy raised on my mother's arm, at Louisiana Tech the same thing. If you talk slow, you're stupid. If you're clean cut, you're square. It's ridiculous. . . . I must have

Chronology

1948	Born September 12 in Shreveport, Louisiana
1970	Graduates from Louisiana Technical University and is drafted number one by the Pittsburgh Steelers
1974	Victory in Super Bowl IX over the Minnesota Vikings
1975	Victory in Super Bowl X over the Dallas Cowboys
1978	Victory in Super Bowl XI over the Dallas Cowboys
1980	Victory in Super Bowl XIII over the Los Angeles Rams
1984	Retires from Steelers and joins CBS Sports as a game analyst
1989	Inducted into NFL Hall of Fame
1995	Joins Fox NFL Sunday as host

been a showcase to look at—the comic-strip kid, the country bumpkin, the savior of the team. It was too much for a 21-years-old kid, too much for me." Bradshaw fought a seemingly futile battle to win the respect of his teammates, his fans, and the press. "If we have a bad game, it's because I'm dumb. If we have a good game, it's because everybody else played well and I got caught up in the action."

Born Again

As he acknowledged in his first autobiography, *Man of Steel,* by 1974 Bradshaw felt like he was bottoming out. His first marriage to Melissa Babish had failed, his shoulder had been injured, and he was often sullen and depressed. The turnaround came when, according to his memoir, Bradshaw, already a born-again Christian, had a revelation: "I had separated myself from God. I lived only for Terry Bradshaw, not for God. I tried to be one of the boys and went to every honky-tonk I could find and chased women and behaved in a way that was totally alien to anything I had ever known before … my whole life was out of control … I was trying to be someone else and was doing a rotten job of it."

What happened to Bradshaw amounted to a second "conversion" experience. "I just put my head in my hands and began to cry and tremble all over and finally I blurted out, 'Here I am, God. I've tried to handle it all by myself and I just can't get the job done. So I'm placing my life in Your hands. I need some peace of mind and I know You can give it to me.'" The quarterback recalls feeling suddenly "stronger mentally and physically.... Being a starting quarterback didn't matter.... What mattered was that I was myself again and I was determined to stay that way."

Team of Dynasty and Destiny

Bradshaw, benched for the first six games of the 1974 season, was finally put back into the starting quarterback slot by coach Chuck Noll. This gesture of confidence finally turned things around permanently. The Bradshaw that returned to the field was a professionally and spiritually renewed man and athlete. His level of play surpassed anything he had shown before, and culminated in the Steelers's 16-6 win over the

Career Statistics

		Passing						Rushing			
Yr	Team	ATT	COM	YDS	COM%	TD	INT	ATT	YDS	TD
1970	PIT	218	83	1410	38.1	6	24	32	233	1
1971	PIT	373	203	2259	54.4	13	22	53	247	5
1972	PIT	308	147	1887	47.7	12	12	58	346	7
1973	PIT	180	89	1183	49.4	10	15	34	145	3
1974	PIT	148	67	785	45.3	7	8	34	224	2
1975	PIT	286	165	2055	57.7	18	9	35	210	3
1976	PIT	192	92	1177	47.9	10	9	31	219	3
1977	PIT	314	162	2523	52.6	17	19	31	171	3
1978	PIT	368	207	2915	56.3	28	20	32	93	1
1979	PIT	472	259	3724	54.9	26	25	21	83	0
1980	PIT	424	218	3339	51.4	24	22	36	111	2
1981	PIT	370	201	2887	54.3	22	14	38	162	2
1982	PIT	240	127	1768	52.9	17	11	8	10	0
1983	PIT	8	5	63	62.5	2	0	1	3	0
TOTAL		3901	2025	27989	51.9	212	210	444	2257	32

PIT: Pittsburgh Steelers.

Minnesota Vikings in Super Bowl IX. After this triumph, his teammates truly embraced him for the first time. "I was starting to fit in with the team. I've never been what you'd call a joiner, but the pieces started fitting together and the players started being more friendly with me and making me part of the locker-room jokes. . . . Through the confidence I was developing and a little taste of success, I started being myself and quit worrying so much."

The Steelers of the mid and late 1970s were perhaps football history's most dominating dynasty. As Gordon Forbes of *USA Today* commented on December 29, 1988, quarterback Bradshaw and running back Franco Harris provided one of the most explosive pass-rush combos ever, on par with Joe Theisman-John Riggins, **Troy Aikman-Emmitt Smith**, or **John Elway-Terrell Davis**. Balletic wide receiver Lynn Swann and speedster John Stallworth represented two of the best deep pass reception threats. And when the Steeler offense wasn't running rampant, the defense consisting of defensive end Mean Joe Greene and bone-crushing linebacker Jack Lambert of The Steel Curtain shut their opponents down.

In 1975, Bradshaw and the Steelers repeated their triumph with another championship victory over the "America's Team" Dallas Cowboys in Super Bowl X. Bradshaw took the Steelers to another Super Bowl win in 1978 against Dallas, beating the Cowboys 35-31. He was chosen Super Bowl MVP and NFL Player of the Year. He also set team and personal records for pass attempts (472), completions (259), and yards gained (3,724) during the season. Steve Cady, writing for the *New York Times Magazine*, said: "Going into his 11th season [1980], he will have passed almost 12 miles, and the Bayou Bumpkin label has been left in the dust of the most impressive quarterbacking record in football today."

But Bradshaw wasn't done. He had one more big year in him. In 1980, he led the Steelers to a fourth Super Bowl victory over the Los Angeles Rams.

Early Retirement

By 1982 over a decade of hard professional knocks had taken it's toll, and Bradshaw's amazing passing arm began to show signs of damage with the diagnosis being chronic muscle deterioration around his right elbow. After toughing it out for the season he underwent surgery in March of 1983. Unfortunately, at Coach Chuck Noll's urging, he returned to play too early. After playing only a few games during the 1983 season, he damaged his elbow permanently and had to retire prematurely, a turn of events for which he never forgave Noll.

Bradshaw officially retired from the Pittsburgh Steelers just before the 1984 season, after fourteen years in the NFL. Despite his bitterness at having to retire early, Bradshaw left the game with the legendary status of having been the best big-game quarterback of all time. He had been one of the most prolific quarterbacks in history, leading the Steelers to four Super Bowl championships, six AFC championship games and eight straight playoff appearances (1972-79). He was at his best in post-season games. Not only was he a perfect 4-0 in Super Bowl play, in those four outstanding performances, he completed forty-nine of eighty-four attempted passes (nine for touchdowns) for 932 yards (second all-time), with just three interceptions. He still holds the Super Bowl passing records for average gain per attempt in career (11.10 yards) and average gain in a game (14.71 yards in Super Bowl XIV versus Los Angeles, in which he completed twenty-one passes for 309 yards). Bradshaw, a two-time Super Bowl MVP (Super Bowls XIII and XIV), was a four-time All-Pro.

Terry Bradshaw

Hall of Fame

After Bradshaw retired from football, he began a career in television. He had worked as a guest commentator for CBS Sports while playing for the Steelers, and in 1984 he joined the network as an NFL game analyst. He formed a famous collaboration with play-by-play announcer Verne Lundquist. So close was the relationship and so bitter was Bradshaw over his premature retirement that he chose Lundquist to introduce him at his NFL Hall of Fame induction in 1989 over his former coach, Chuck Noll. With his career statistics, four Super Bowl victories and two Super Bowl MVPs, Bradshaw was a shoo-in for the Hall of Fame and was inducted as soon as he became eligible. In his acceptance speech, Bradshaw with typical humility, thanked his teammates: "…it takes people. All our careers, we were blessed with great people around me. I'm a fortunate quarterback to have so much beautiful talent. So many wonderful athletes to go out and get the job done. Allowed me to be the kind of person I was. Go out and be aggressive and to attack. And have fun and to lie and to tell jokes and to cut up with the reporters who still hadn't figured me out yet. That was fun. I enjoyed that. I got a kick out of that."

America's Favorite Sportscaster

After ten years with CBS, including four years as sports analyst for the program The NFL Today, Bradshaw joined Fox Sports in 1995 with great fanfare, as Fox had wooed the NFL away from CBS. As co-host of the popular program Fox NFL Sunday, he has made the most of his country upbringing and has realized how much he loves to make people laugh. The show takes a lighter approach to professional football, one that new fans find as entertaining as the game itself. In fact to signify the beginning of a new style in football showmanship, Fox had Bradshaw dress in cowboy gear and ride in on a horse in its premiere show.

After an illustrious career as one of football history's greatest quarterbacks, as well as one of the game's best commentators, Bradshaw has beaten the Bayou Bumpkin label. Fox NFL Sunday is America's most-watched NFL pregame show, and has won three Emmy Awards. Bradshaw has emerged as today's preeminent NFL studio personality and in 2002 was voted America's Favorite Sportscaster in a TV Guide Reader's Poll.

Given his accomplishments it's a wonder that Bradshaw was ever tagged with the Southern simpleton stereotype. During his years with the Steelers, Bradshaw called all of his own plays. CBS play-by-play announcer Pat Summerall in his 1997 book *Pat Summerall's Sports in America,* declared Bradshaw to be one of the sharpest minds he had ever encountered. Bradshaw has shown himself to be incredibly versatile and savvy as an all-around media personality. He has co-authored five memoirs on his career. Bradshaw's interests are in no way limited to football. He is a devoted father to his daughters Erin and Rachel. He raises and breeds Simmental cattle and quarter horses on his ranch. He gives motivational speeches to corporate and other groups and endorses products. He occasionally appears in motion pictures and records gospel and country/western songs. Bradshaw, far outgrowing the Bayou Bumpkin, has shown himself to be a modern Man for All Seasons.

CONTACT INFORMATION

Address: Terry Bradshaw, Circle 12 Ranch, 1905 Pearson Lane, Westlake, TX 76262. Fax: (817) 379-5140. Phone: (817) 379-5083.

SELECTED WRITINGS BY BRADSHAW:

(With Charles Paul Conn) *No Easy Game*, 1973.

(With David Diles) *Terry Bradshaw: Man of Steel*, Zondervan, 1979.

(Author of foreword) *Pro Football's Ten Greatest Games*, Four Winds Press, 1981.

(With Buddy Martin) *Looking Deep*, Contemporary Books, 1989.

(With David Fisher) *It's Only A Game*, Pocket Books, 2001.

(With David Fisher) *Keep It Simple*, Pocket Books, 2002.

FURTHER INFORMATION

Books

Benagh, Jim David Fisher. *Terry Bradshaw: Superarm of Pro Football*. New York: Putnam, 1976.

Chass, Murray. *Power Football*. New York: Dutton, 1973.

Gutman, Bill. *Football Superstars of the '70s*. New York: Messner, 1975.

Rubin, Bob. *All-stars of the NFL*. New York: Random House, 1976.

St. James Encyclopedia of Popular Culture, five volumes. Detroit: St. James Press, 2000

Periodicals

Baily, Budd. "Bradshaw, after the Game." *Buffalo News* (August 19, 2001): F7.

Bumgarner, Bill. "Savvy recruiters don't bypass Louisiana: State's high school talent rates near top." *Times-Picayune* (January 26, 1997).

"Ex-Footballer Bradshaw Enters the Talk-Show World." *Seattle Times* (October 28, 1997): E6.

Forbes, Gordon. "Broncos tough to beat when Davis, Elway click." *USA Today* (December 29, 1998).

Interview with Terry Bradshaw. *Vanity Fair* (September, 2001): 418.

Lomartire, Paul. "Bradshaw as Clownish on Tape as He Is on TV." *Palm Beach Post* (September 16, 2001): 5J.

Mowitz, David. "His Home Is on the Range among Cattle." *Successful Farming* (October, 1997): 40-41.

Mule, Marty. "Summerall's book puts Bradshaw on pedestal." *Times-Picayune* (February 16, 1997).

Newsweek (September 8, 1980).

New York Times (January 9, 1975).

New York Times Magazine (January 9, 1980).

Nidetz, Steve. "Down-home Bradshaw has the last laugh." *Chicago Tribune* (December 8, 1995).

Ostler, Scott. "Crazy Glue: The Anchor of Fox's Increasingly Silly NFL Studio Show, Terry Bradshaw, Makes No Apologies for His Unique Brand of Tomfoolery." *Sport* (February, 1999): 28.

People (June 18, 1979).

Phillips, Carole L. "Terry Bradshaw: Gospel Singer." *Cincinnati Post* (November 21, 1996): p.2.

Review of *It's Only a Game*. *Publishers Weekly* (August 6, 2001): 80.

Spelling, Ian. "Time-Out with Terry." *Smoke* (spring, 1998).

Sport (February, 1979).

Sport (May, 1979).

Sports Illustrated (December 18, 1978).

Stewart, Larry. "Bradshaw rides to the fore in Fox's grand opening." *Los Angeles Times* (September 5, 1994).

Stuttaford, Genevieve. Review of *Looking Deep*. *Publishers Weekly* (July 14, 1989): 67.

Sumrau, Dennis. "Terry Bradshaw's Career Not Just Passing Fancy." *Capital Times* (Madison, WI) (August 10, 2001): 9A.

Time (January 22, 1979).

Weisman, Larry. "Bradshaw finally at ease with NFL: Ex Steeler warms up Fox pregame." *USA Today* (January 20, 1997).

Wineke, William R. "Terry Bradshaw Pays a Visit." *Wisconsin State Journal* (August 12, 2001): F3.

Other

"Terry Bradshaw Hall of Fame Induction Speech." *McMillen & Wife.* http://www.mcmillenandwife.com/bradshaw_speech.html.

"Terry Bradshaw's Fox Bio." *McMillen & Wife.* http://www.mcmillenandwife.com/bradshaw_fox_bio.html.

Sketch by Gordon Churchwell

Valerie Brisco-Hooks

Valerie Brisco-Hooks
1960-

American sprinter

Like a shooting star, sprinter Valerie Brisco-Hooks shone for a brief, glorious moment in the public's eye before speeding away, never to reach the same vaunted height. While she shone, however, Brisco-Hooks burned especially bright. In the 1984 Olympic Games in Los Angeles, Brisco-Hooks accomplished what no other athlete, man or woman, had ever done by winning gold medals in 200- and 400-meter races in the same Olympic Games. She capped her starring performance by running a leg on the United States women's 4x400 meter relay team and capturing her third gold medal of the games.

Brother's Death Shaped Her Life

Though she was born in the heart of the rural South in Greenwood, Mississippi, Brisco-Hooks moved with her family to an urban ghetto—the Watts neighborhood of Los Angeles—before she entered elementary school. Brisco-Hooks was one of ten children. Her father was a metal worker and her mother taught school. One of

Brisco-Hooks's older brothers, Robert, was a star runner at Locke High School in Los Angeles. When she was fourteen, Robert and another brother Melvin were finishing a workout at the Locke High School track when a stray bullet struck Robert. He died later that day.

When the police eventually learned who fired the gun, they did not prosecute the shooter because he was only in the ninth grade. He did not have to live with his guilt long, however, as one year and a day later, the boy who shot Robert Brisco was himself shot and killed.

Until her brother's death, Brisco-Hooks was known as an undisciplined and unruly child. The loss of Robert helped her set personal goals and dedicate herself to achieving them. Urged by her high school's track coach to come out for the team, Brisco-Hooks proved to be a standout runner on the same track where her brother was slain. As she said afterwards, "Someone has to carry on the family name, so they chose me."

Pregnancy Impeeds Performance

Brisco-Hooks continued to excel in her track career at the collegiate level while she attended California State-Northridge. In 1979 she won 200-meter final in the Association of Intercollegiate Athletics for Women (AIAW) championships. In that same year she represented the United States and the Pan-American Games in San Juan, Puerto Rico, winning a gold medal as a member of the United States's 4x400 meter relay team.

Brisco-Hooks continued to run, and in 1981 she married a former standout on the Cal State Northridge men's track team, Alvin Hooks. Now known as Valerie Brisco-Hooks, she gave birth to a son, Alvin, Jr., the next year. The birth of her child almost proved to be the death of her running career. For the nine months of her pregnancy and the nine months that followed, Brisco-Hooks was physi-

Awards and Accomplishments

1979	Gold medal in Pan American Games on 4x400 meter relay
1981	Set national junior college records at 200 meter and 400 meter distances
1984	Won national indoor title at 200 yards
1984	Won national outdoor title in 400 meters in 49.83 becoming first American woman to break 50 seconds in that event
1984	Ran anchor leg on 4x400 meter relay setting American record (3:19.60)
1984	Won two gold medals in 200-meter (21.81 seconds), 400-meter races (48.83 seconds) setting American and Olympic records in both. Won third gold medal in the 4x400-meter relay (3:18.29)
1985	Set world indoor record of 52.99 in 400-meter run
1986	Won national outdoor title in 400-meter run
1987	Gold medal in Pan American Games on 4x400 meter relay
1987	Bronze medal at 400 meters in World Championships
1988	Won fourth Olympic medal of career, a silver, with leg on United States 4x400 meter relay (3:15.51) in Seoul, South Korea
1995	Inducted into USA Track & Field Hall of Fame

cally inactive, preferring to watch soap operas. At her heaviest, Brisco-Hooks topped the scales at 198 pounds, almost 70 pounds above her competitive weight of 130.

When Brisco-Hooks finally became restless herself, her husband Alvin and her former coach Bobby Kersee persuaded her that she could compete again at a world class level. With Kersee as her coach and Alvin taking care of the baby (Alvin was cut from the Los Angeles Express of the United States Football League at the end of the 1983 season), slowly but surely Brisco-Hooks dropped weight and picked up her speed. Said Brisco-Hooks of her comeback, "I was really big. It took me a while to really believe in myself and want to run," but "Bobby kept coming to my house and saying, 'Valerie, I know you have it in you.'"

An Unprecedented Olympic Achievement

By early 1984, Brisco-Hooks was back in better form than she had ever been before. She won the national 200-yard indoor crown and that summer captured the 400-meter outdoor title. At the Olympic trials, Brisco-Hooks qualified to represent the United States in the individual 200- and 400-meter races and the 4x400-meter relay.

When the 1984 Olympics began Brisco-Hooks aimed to do what no athlete had ever done—win both the 200-meter and 400-meter races in the same Olympic games. Going into the competition she had two factors working in her favor: first, the games were being held in her hometown of Los Angeles; second, and most important, the Soviet-led boycott of the 1984 Olympics meant most of the world's best female best sprinters would be at home, rather than challenging their underdog American foes.

In the end, Brisco-Hooks left no doubt about who was the best sprinter in Los Angeles. She dominated her com-

petition in both the 400- and 200-meter races. She dedicated the former victory to her slain brother Robert and the latter to the rest of her family. After Brisco-Hooks won the 400, Bobby Kersee eluded security and tackled her to offer his unique congratulations. The two rolled around on the Coliseum ground in one of the great moments of the Games. Brisco-Hooks capped her performance later in the meet by running a leg on the United States women's victorious 4x400-meter relay team.

Another Olympic Medal

Though much was written about her failure to win lucrative endorsements following the 1984 Olympics, Brisco-Hooks repeatedly told reporters that she was not upset that her athletic success did not translate financially. Free from the time constraints of making commercials, in 1985 Brisco-Hooks used her new-found celebrity to lecture to Los Angeles-area school children about the dangers of drug abuse.

Brisco-Hooks continued to compete on the international track and field scene setting a world indoor record in 400-yard run in 1985, and winning a world outdoor title in 400-meter run in 1986. She finished her accolade-heavy career in the 1988 Olympic Games in Seoul, South Korea. Brisco-Hooks ran a leg on the United States women's 4x400-meter relay that finished second to the Soviet team and set an American record in the process. The performance earned her her first Olympic silver medal and fourth Olympic medal of her career.

A Life of Triumph and Tragedy

Brisco-Hooks's life has not been without tragedy since the death of her older brother Robert. In 1985, Valerie's brother Melvin, who was at the track the day his brother Robert was shot, tried to cross a Los Angeles freeway when his car broke down. Melvin was hit by a passing car and suffered two broken legs. In 2002, Valerie's nephew Amar Brisco, a former University of Nevada-Las Vegas football player was shot and killed outside a Las Vegas nightclub, after arguing about a valet parking space.

Despite the family tragedies she endured and the physical hurdles she overcame, Valerie Brisco-Hooks will be remembered primarily for her one great achievement. In 1984, she became the first athlete, male or female, to win the 200- and 400-meter races in the same Olympic Games.

FURTHER INFORMATION

Periodicals

"College Football."*Seattle Post-Intelligencer* (August 7, 2002).

Fish, Mike. "Brisco-Hooks Sprints Into Hall." *Atlanta Journal-Constitution* (November 30, 1995).

Horn, Barry. "A Mother Who Knows Best." *Dallas Morning News* (March 10, 1985).

Kornheiser, Tony. "Brisco-Hooks Running Shows Relative Success." *Washington Post* (August 11, 1984).

"Three golds, Olympic records marked legacy of Brisco-Hooks." *Bay State Banner* (February 15, 1996).

Wheatley, Tom. "Kersee's Regimen Toughens Pat's Law." *St. Louis Post Dispatch* (February 1, 2002).

Other

Hickok Sports.com Sports Biographies. http://www. hickoksports.com/biograph/briscohv.shtml (January 24, 2003).

USA Track & Field. http://www.usatf.org/athletes/hof/ brisco.shtml (January 24, 2003).

Sporting-heroes.net. http://www.sporting-heroes.net/ athletics-heroes/displayhero.asp?HeroID=1448 (August 6, 1984).

Sketch by Ian David Hoffman

Lou Brock

Lou Brock
1939-

American baseball player

During the 1970s, Lou Brock did for base-stealing what slugger **Mark McGwire** did for the homerun in the 1990s: Brock turned the pursuit of the stolen base into a national pastime. In the history of baseball, few players have covered the 90 feet between the bases more productively. During his 19-year career, Brock stole 938 bases, making him the most prolific base-stealer in the history of baseball to that time. Most notable was his 1974 season, when Brock stole 118 bases, setting a new single-season base-stealing record. Though Brock's name is most often associated with stealing bases, he was also a formidable hitter, with 3,023 hits. Brock was the 14th player in baseball history to pass the coveted 3,000 mark. As Cardinal pitcher John Curtis once told *Baseball Digest,* "He's the greatest single offensive force I've seen." Throughout his life, Brock has been a force off the field as well. He spent much of his time raising funds for his scholarship foundation, so he can offer young adults a chance at a college education. Brock knows if no one had taken a chance on him, he wouldn't have had the career he did.

Reared in Small Southern Town

Brock was born on June 18, 1939, in El Dorado, Arkansas, to Maud and Paralee Brock. He was raised in nearby Collinston, Louisiana. His family relocated there after his father, Maud, left when he was two. Brock de- scribed his hometown in an issue of *Sports Illustrated,* "It was a farm community, in the heart of what you might call the Bible Belt. Playing baseball on Sunday was considered taboo.... Our house was typical of down there-a four-bedroom shack with a porch and a swing."

After Brock's parents split up, his mother remarried. She married three times and had nine children. To help support her large family, Paralee Brock did domestic work. The family also farmed, raising everything from cotton and corn, to cows and pigs.

As a youngster, Brock wasn't much interested in baseball. It was actually a bit of childhood mischief that got Brock involved in the game. One day in school, the rebellious Brock let loose a spit wad aimed at the girl in front of him. Brock missed his target and ended up hitting the teacher. As a punishment, the teacher sent Brock to the library. Once there, he was asked to research some sports figures like **Joe DiMaggio** and **Jackie Robinson** and compose a report for the class. The teacher wanted to make Brock and his classmates more aware of what was happening in the world outside of Collinston. When Brock presented the report, his classmates sneered at him and called him the teacher's pet. Presenting the report was difficult for the shy youngster, but in the end, it changed his life.

As Brock told *Sports Illustrated,* "The most intriguing thing to me was that big league players got $8 a day for meal money. All I could think of was of how much penny candy that would buy." From then on, Brock was hooked on baseball.

Chronology

1939	Born June 18 in El Dorado, Arkansas
1957	Graduates from Union High School, Mer Rouge, Louisiana
1957	Enters college at Southern University, Baton Rouge, Louisiana
1958	Becomes member of Southern University baseball team
1959	Represents the United States at the Pan-American Games in Chicago
1961	Signs with the Chicago Cubs, spends one season in the minor leagues
1961	Makes major league debut as a Chicago Cub
1964	Traded to the St. Louis Cardinals
1964	Plays in first World Series, comes away a champion
1967	Smacks 206 hits and 21 home runs to help his team become the divisional champs; advances to World Series and helps team win
1974	Divorces his wife
1974	Sets single-season stolen bases record at 118
1979	Connects for his 3,000th hit
1979	Retires from baseball
1994	Becomes base-running and outfield instructor for St. Louis Cardinals
1995	Marries for third time, this time to Jacqueline Brock

Awards and Accomplishments

1964, 1967	Won World Series ring as member of the St. Louis Cardinals
1966	Led league with most stolen bases (74)
1967	Led league with most at-bats (689), most runs (113) and most stolen bases (52)
1967, 1971-72, 1974-75, 1979	Selected for All-Star Game
1968	Led league with most doubles (46), most triples (14) and most stolen bases (62)
1969	Led league with most stolen bases (53)
1971	Led league with most runs (126) and most stolen bases (64)
1972	Led league with most stolen bases (63)
1973	Led league with most stolen bases (70)
1974	Set major league record for most steals in a season (118)
1974	Named *The Sporting News'* Player of the Year
1975	Earned the Jackie Robinson Award
1975	Earned the Roberto Clemente Award
1977	Broke Ty Cobb's career stolen bases record of 892
1979	Became 14th player in baseball to achieve more than 3,000 hits
1979	Earned the Hutch Award, which honors former Cincinnati Reds manager Fred Hutchinson
1979	Retired with career record of 938 stolen bases, a record at the time
1985	Inducted into the Baseball Hall of Fame
2002	Earned the Horatio Alger Association of Distinguished Americans Award

By his freshman year at Union High School in Mer Rouge, Louisiana, Brock was playing baseball. His senior year, he batted over .500. He graduated in 1957, third in his class of 105.

Slugged Way onto College Baseball Team

Following high school, Brock decided he needed a college education in order to leave behind the sharecropper's life. The family didn't have a phone, which prevented Brock from calling any colleges, so he took matters into his own hands and caught a ride to Southern University in Baton Rouge, Louisiana, because he had heard that the college offered a work-study scholarship program.

School officials were so impressed by Brock's determination that they found a job for him mowing grass and offered him a work-study scholarship. The deal, however, stipulated that Brock maintain a B average. Brock ended his first semester with a C+ average and was booted from the work-study program.

Not wanting to return home a failure, Brock decided to try out for the baseball team. For days, he parked himself in the bleachers and watched the Southern University team practice. "I sat there scared to death," Brock recalled to the *St. Louis Post-Dispatch*. "The players paraded in front of me with muscles. They looked like athletes. I wasn't sure I belonged on the field with them."

Finally, Brock joined the players on the diamond and spent several days chasing fly balls, running as fast as he could, hoping the coach would notice him. Because Brock was broke at this time, he couldn't afford to eat properly and collapsed on the field one day.

Passing out got Brock noticed, and in the spirit of goodwill, the coach decided to let him bat a few balls.

Brock realized he had just a few minutes—just a few pitches—to prove himself. "I told myself, 'This is it. This is the moment,'" he recalled to the *St. Louis Post-Dispatch*. "'Either you hit this ball and stay or miss it and be gone.'" Brock impressed the coach by hitting several pitches out of the park. He was offered an athletic scholarship and was able to continue his college education.

During Brock's sophomore season, he received the attention of some scouts when they came to observe Wiley College pitcher Johnny Berry. Brock's team was playing Wiley's team at the time. During the game, Berry gave up only two hits-both homers to Brock.

That same season, Brock hit .545. With Brock in the lineup, Southern College become the first black college to win the baseball championship of the National Association of Intercollegiate Athletes.

In 1959, Brock was selected to play on the U.S. baseball team at the Pan-American Games in Chicago. During the games, Brock befriended a runner named Charles Deacon Jones, who helped Brock improve his speed by offering a few lessons in technique. A few years later, after Brock joined the Cubs, the two worked out together in Chicago as Jones continued helping Brock improve his form.

Got Dismal Start with the Cubs

Before he could complete his senior year of college in 1961, Brock signed with the Chicago Cubs and left school. His signing bonus was $30,000. Though Brock

Lou Brock, left

was sorry to leave school, the chance to help his family financially was appealing. Brock spent one brief season in the minor leagues, playing for the Cubs' farm team in St. Cloud, Minnesota, where he batted .361 and stole 38 bases. He also led the team in hits and was soon called up to the majors, where he appeared in four games in 1961.

Unfortunately, Brock's time with the Cubs proved dismal. Aspiring to be a power-hitter, Brock struck out often. He whiffed 96 times in 434 at-bats in 1962 and 122 times in 547 at-bats in 1963. His batting average wasn't that impressive either. He hit .263 in 1962, his first full season in the majors.

Besides his mediocre performance at the plate, Brock took a lot of flack for his fielding. With every game at the gusty Wrigley Field played in the afternoon, Brock had trouble tracking the ball in sunny right field. Brock had only spent one season in the minors and had not learned how to cope with the sun. He made a spectacle of himself as he dropped balls; even when he caught them, his struggle was evident. The coaches never realized that Brock played better at night and on the road.

Cubs fans—and local sportswriters in particular—poked fun at Brock. Bob Smith of the *Daily News* was brutal in his characterizations of Brock. According to David Halberstam's book *October 1964,* Smith wrote in 1963, "If you have watched all the Cub home games thus far you probably had come to the conclusion that Lou Brock is the worst outfielder in baseball history. He really isn't, but he hasn't done much to prove it."

By 1964, Brock's rage to succeed was getting the better of him. Cub roommate **Ernie Banks** recalled that Brock had trouble eating and sleeping. Banks told Brock he needed

to loosen up and let his natural ability pull him through. Brock, however, was too antsy to relax. He scribbled reports after every game he played in, making notes about the pitchers he faced, what kind of pitches they threw at him, and how well he had responded. Before games, Brock plotted how many hits he thought he should deliver and how many runs he should smack in. According to Halberstam's book, Brock told teammates over and over, "I've got to make it here. I just can't go back to Louisiana and Arkansas. I've been there, and I know what's there."

By June 1964, the Cubs were ready to drop Brock. At the time, Brock was hitting .251 and showed no signs of promise. Since the Cubs rarely gave him the green light to steal, no one knew about Brock's hidden talent for stolen bases.

Came Alive with the Cardinals

In mid-June 1964, the Cubs dealt Brock to the St. Louis Cardinals in exchange for pitcher Ernie Broglio, who'd won 18 games the prior season, and two other players. In exchange, the Cardinals got Brock and two pitchers.

"None of us liked the deal," Cardinals first baseman Bill White recalled to Peter Golenbock in his book, *The Spirit of St. Louis.* "[We'd] say we did, but we didn't like that deal. In my opinion, Lou had a lot of talent, but he didn't know anything about baseball.... But somehow, when he came to us, he turned everything around."

The Chicago papers proclaimed the trade a steal for the Cubs, believing they had traded an iffy outfielder for a strikeout king. Sportswriter Bob Smith, who'd been so critical of Brock, wrote, "Thank you, thank you, oh, you lovely St. Louis Cardinals," according to Halberstam's book. In the end, however, the Cardinals were the ones thanking the Cubs for the deal as Brock went down in Hall of Fame history. (Broglio, incidentally, injured his arm after the trade and won only seven more games, while losing 19. By 1967, he had retired.)

The day following the trade, Brock took a plane from Chicago to Houston to join the Cardinals, who were playing that day. Late in the game against the Astros, Brock entered as a pinch-hitter and struck out. According to *The St. Louis Cardinals Encyclopedia,* Cardinals general manager Bing Devine, who had brokered the deal, took some heckling from a fan, who asked him, "Who could have made that deal?"

But for Brock, the trade was rejuvenating. He thrived as a Cardinal. He left behind the sun-drenched right side of Wrigley Field and took up left field. Coaches gave Brock the go-ahead to steal. Soon, fans caught a glimpse of his potential.

For the remainder of the 1964 season, Brock batted .348 and stole 33 bases. He also provided the spark that helped the team win the National League pennant and defeat the New York Yankees in the World Series.

Career Statistics

Yr	Team	AVG	GP	AB	R	H	HR	RBI	BB	SO	SB	E
1961	CHI	.091	4	11	1	1	0	0	1	3	0	2
1962	CHI	.263	123	434	73	114	9	35	35	96	16	9
1963	CHI	.258	148	547	79	141	9	37	31	122	24	8
1964	CHI	.251	52	215	30	54	2	14	13	40	10	4
1964	STL	.348	103	419	81	146	12	44	27	87	33	10
1965	STL	.288	155	631	107	182	16	69	45	116	63	12
1966	STL	.285	156	643	94	183	15	46	31	134	74	19
1967	STL	.299	159	689	113	206	21	76	24	109	52	13
1968	STL	.279	159	660	92	184	6	51	46	124	62	14
1969	STL	.298	157	655	97	195	12	47	50	115	53	14
1970	STL	.304	155	664	114	202	13	57	60	99	51	10
1971	STL	.312	157	640	126	200	7	61	76	107	64	14
1972	STL	.311	153	621	81	193	3	42	47	93	63	13
1973	STL	.297	160	650	110	193	7	63	71	112	70	12
1974	STL	.306	153	635	105	194	3	48	61	88	118	10
1975	STL	.309	136	528	78	163	3	47	38	64	56	9
1976	STL	.301	133	498	73	150	4	67	35	75	56	4
1977	STL	.272	141	489	69	133	2	46	30	74	35	9
1978	STL	.221	92	298	31	66	0	12	17	29	17	3
1979	STL	.304	120	405	56	123	5	38	23	43	21	7
TOTAL		.293	2616	10332	1610	3023	149	900	761	1730	938	196

CHI: Chicago Cubs; STL: St. Louis Cardinals.
Post-season play: Appeared in 21 games in three World Series-1964, 1967, 1968. World Series statistics include a .391 batting average, 34 hits and 14 stolen bases.

In 1967, Brock had 206 hits, 21 home runs, and stole 52 bases, helping the Cardinals become the National League champs. They faced the Boston Red Sox in the World Series. In seven games, Brock had 12 hits, scored eight runs, and stole seven bases. His series batting average of .414 led the Cardinals to victory.

Brock continued his offensive onslaught in 1968, leading the National League in doubles with 46, triples with 14, and stolen bases with 62. Once again, the Cardinals landed in the World Series. Brock batted .464 during the series, though the Detroit Tigers defeated the Cardinals to win the title.

Over the next few years, Brock kept stealing, leading the league in stolen bases in 1969, 1971, 1972, 1973, and 1974. In 12 consecutive seasons (1965-1976) he stole more than 50 bases.

Turned Base-Stealing into an Art

By 1970, Brock was known for his basepath escapades. In the decades before Brock joined the major leagues, the stolen base had become a lost art as players concentrated more on swinging for power. The decline in the stolen base was notable. In 1930, there were 1,079 stolen bases in the league. By 1950, that number had dwindled to 650. Most people assumed **Ty Cobb**'s 1915 record of 96 stolen bases in a single season was untouchable.

Then came Brock, who elevated base-stealing to an art. He scrutinized pitchers, hoping to learn their cadence and rhythm. He wanted to be able to recognize the split-second the pitcher had committed himself to throw

home. Brock also studied a pitcher's habits, hoping to find a pattern so he would know when a curve was coming. Since curves take a second of a fraction longer to reach home plate, Brock preferred to run on a curveball.

Brock didn't just watch pitchers, he filmed them on an eight-millimeter camera. At home, he studied the films, watching for signs, twitches, anything that might help him read a pitcher better.

A former math major in college, Brock calculated that there were 3.5 seconds between the time the ball left the pitcher's hand, landed in the catcher's mitt, and ended up back at second base. Brock outlined his base-stealing strategy in a 1974 *Newsweek* article.

"I can't run from first to second in 3.5 seconds," he admitted. "I don't think I could when I was younger, and I'm slower now. So the key is that instant when the shift of the pitcher's anatomy tells me he can't come to first. He has to go to the plate. I go on that shift. That extra instant is all I need to make it safely."

Brock also got some help from teammates along the way. Batters who followed Brock often stood deep in the batter's box, forcing the catcher back farther.

Brock's base-stealing tactics turned him into an offensive machine. In effect, any single Brock hit could be turned into a double through his base-stealing prowess. Once on second, Brock could score easily if the ball was hit into the outfield.

For Brock, baseball became all about stealing bases. In an issue of *Time,* Brock expressed his thoughts this

Where Is He Now?

After the renowned base stealer retired from baseball in 1979, Brock remained close to the Cardinals organization and in 1994 began working as a base-running and outfield instructor for the team, particularly helping out during spring training.

When he's not busy with baseball, Brock tends to the company he founded, Brockworld Products, Inc. Brock is president of the St. Louis-based company, which is a marketing and promotional ventures firm. He is also involved with raising funds for the Lou Brock Scholarship Foundation, which helps students who can't afford college.

Brock and his wife, the Rev. Jacqueline Brock, live in St. Charles, Missouri, and are involved with area charitable and civic efforts, mostly those aimed at helping youth. They also serve as elders to the Abundant Life Fellowship Church near Black Jack, Missouri.

way: "Stealing is the most dramatic moment of the game. The pitcher knows you're going, the crowd knows you're going, you know you're going. When you succeed it's a great feeling. Nothing upsets the other team as much as a stolen base."

As Brock perfected his stealing strategies, he also perfected his slide. Brock preferred a straight, "pop-up" slide, instead of the traditional hook slide, which starts 15 feet out from the base and wears the body. Brock's signature pop-up slide allowed him to accelerate full-speed into the bag. Because he ended his slides by popping up, if there was an error in the throw, he could take third as well.

Before Brock came along, there was a player named Maury Wills who helped rejuvenate the stolen base. In 1962, Wills stole 104 bases, breaking Ty Cobb's record. No one imagined it could be topped again. But that was before Brock. In 1974, Brock broke Wills' stranglehold on the single-season steal mark of 104 by grabbing 118 stolen bases. That same season, he also scored 105 runs and batted .306.

Three years later, Brock broke Ty Cobb's career stolen-base record. It happened on August 29, 1977, when Brock entered the game one shy of Cobb's record of 892. As a leadoff batter, the eager Brock drew a walk and trotted to first. The Padres were nervous to have Brock on base and the pitcher, Dave Freisleben, stared at Brock, then briefly walked off the mound. On the next pitch, Brock took off and safely made it to second. He was now tied with Cobb.

In the seventh inning, Brock was on base once again with a chance to steal. Though the Cardinals were playing in San Diego, the fans were rooting for Brock. According to the *St. Louis Post-Dispatch,* they chanted, "Lou … Lou … Lou. Go! Go!" Freisleben was still on the mound. He threw to first, trying to get Brock to stick close to the bag.

Freisleben finally threw home, and Brock took off. Handily, he stole No. 893, setting a new major league

baseball record. The game came to a halt as the crowd rose for a standing ovation. The base was dug up and ceremoniously presented to Brock. It was a historic moment, and even Freisleben, who'd given away the stolen base, remarked, "I kind of got goosebumps," according to the *Post-Dispatch.*

It is also interesting to note that Brock's stealing pace was much quicker than Cobb's. Cobb spread his 892 stolen bases out over 24 seasons and 3,033 games. Brock, however, broke the record in only 2,376 games over 17 seasons. Brock also picked up the pace as he got older and was 38 years old when he broke Cobb's record. The record stood until 1997, when **Rickey Henderson** of the Oakland A's ended the season with 1,231.

Brock's feat, however, was soon forgotten after he fell into a slump during the 1978 season, hitting only .221.

Joined Elite "3,000 Hits" Club

At the start of the 1979 season, Brock announced that it would be his last. Fans may have thought him washed up, but Brock had unfinished business. There was still one record Brock was chasing-he wanted to get 3,000 hits so he could be remembered as a hitter and not just a base-stealer.

Brock's goal worried teammates. *The St. Louis Cardinals Encyclopedia* quoted teammate Ken Boyer as saying: "I want very much to see Lou get 3000 hits, but I can't lose ball games or my job if he can't deliver."

Brock had spent the off-season building up the muscles in his legs and watching tapes of himself at bat. He was ready to make his mark in 1979. That season, Brock smacked 123 hits for a .304 batting average. He ended the season with 3,023 career hits, making him the 14th player to reach the hallowed 3,000th mark. It took 20 years before another National League player, **Tony Gwynn**, did it in 2000.

Along the way, Brock married three times. He divorced his high school sweetheart, Katie, in 1974. The couple had two children, Wanda, and Lou Brock, Jr., who played football for the San Diego Chargers. Brock later married and divorced Virgie Brock. In 1995, he married Jacqueline Brock, a special education teacher from the St. Louis area.

Still King in St. Louis

When Brock retired after the 1979 season, the August Busch family, which owned the St. Louis Cardinals, gave Brock a pleasure boat named "King Louie of St. Louie." Today, Brock still rules his hometown, just as he ruled the basepaths and the record books during his baseball career. Though more than 20 years have passed since Brock retired, he remains a local legend and still works as an instructor for the Cardinals organization. He also lends his name and efforts to many local charities and was added to the St. Louis Walk of Fame in 1994. When Brock appears at Busch Stadium at Cardinals games, the crowd still chants, "Lou … Lou … Lou," in honor of the man who taught a whole city—a whole nation in fact—how to be a winner.

SELECTED WRITINGS BY BROCK:

(With Fran Schulze) *Stealing Is My Game*. Prentice Hall Press, 1976.

FURTHER INFORMATION

Books

Broeg, Bob and Jerry Vickery. *The St. Louis Cardinals Encyclopedia*. Chicago: NTC/Contemporary Publishing Group, 1998.

The Cardinals. New York: Macmillan Publishing Co., Inc., 1983.

Golenbock, Peter. *The Spirit of St. Louis: A History of the St. Louis Cardinals and Browns*. New York: Avon Books, Inc., 2000.

Halberstam, David. *October 1964*. New York: Villard Books, 1994.

Honig, Donald. *The St. Louis Cardinals: An Illustrated History*. New York: Prentice Hall Press, 1991.

Kuenster, John, ed. *From Cobb to "Catfish."* New York: Rand McNally & Co., 1975.

Periodicals

"At Age 60, Lou Brock is Ambassador for Baseball." *The Virginian Pilot* (February 5, 2000): C1.

Bonventre, Peter. "Grand Larceny." *Newsweek* (September 12, 1977): 78-79.

Dorr, Dave. "Southern U. Took a Chance On Lou Brock in 1957." *St. Louis Post-Dispatch* (February 8, 1999): E3.

Dorr, Dave. "The Base Burglar Gives Something Back." *St. Louis Post-Dispatch* (February 8, 1999): E1.

Eisenbath, Mike. "Brock Keeps on Smiling." *St. Louis Post-Dispatch* (June 13, 1999): D4.

Harris, Mikal J. "King's Legacy Is Living Without Fear, Brock Proclaims." *St. Louis Post-Dispatch* (January 23, 2002).

Kaegel, Dick. "Brock Steals Base No. 893." *St. Louis Post-Dispatch* (August 30, 1977): 1.

Kaplan, Jim. "Brock Still Has the Old Sock." *Sports Illustrated* (May 21, 1979): 50.

Kelley, Robert. "The Premier Pilferer." *Time* (July 15, 1974): 84.

"Lou Brock Wins Baseball's Coveted 1979 Hutch Award." *Jet* (January 10, 1980: 47.

"Make Way for the Sultan of Swipes." *Sports Illustrated* (August 22, 1977): 24-30.

"The Thief." *Newsweek* (September 16, 1974): 61.

Other

"Lou Brock Statistics." Baseball-Reference.com. http://www.baseball-reference.com/b/brocklo01.shtml (October 8, 2002).

"Louis C. Brock." Horatio Alger Association. http://www.horatioalger.com/member/bro02.htm (October 6, 2002).

Sketch by Lisa Frick

Herb Brooks
1937-

American hockey coach

Herb Brooks is best known for his role as coach of the **1980 U.S. Men's Olympic Hockey Team** that won the gold medal at the Winter Olympic games in Lake Placid, New York, in 1980, the so-called "Miracle on Ice." Brooks had previously played for the U.S. team himself, before starting a coaching career in which he coached on the college, national, European professional, and National Hockey League (NHL) levels.

Brooks was born on August 5, 1937, in St. Paul, Minnesota, the oldest of three children. Growing up in St. Paul, hockey was a focus of Brooks' young life. He attended public schools in St. Paul, winning the MSHS hockey championship as a senior at Johnson High School. A great high school player, Brooks later said that this one of the biggest events in his life.

Played College Hockey

Because of high school hockey accomplishments, Brooks was offered a scholarship to play hockey at the University of Michigan. Instead, he chose to stay in his home state and play college hockey at the University of Minnesota. At the time, he was known as the fastest skater in college hockey. Brooks graduated from there in 1959 (some sources say 1962) with a degree in psychology.

In 1960, Brooks tried out for the Olympic team. The 1960 Winter Games were being held in Squaw Valley, California. Brooks was the last player cut from the team. Team USA went on to defeat Russia, Canada, and Czechoslovakia in upset victories and take home a medal.

Played on USA national team

Though Brooks missed out on an Olympic medal, he did make the U.S. national team as a player. He played with the team in 1961, 1962, 1965, 1967, and 1970. He also played on the 1964 and 1968 Olympic squads.

Herb Brooks

1937	Born August 5 in St. Paul, Minnesota
1959	Graduates from the University of Minnesota
1960	Is last player cut from U.S. Olympic squad
1961	Named to the U.S. national team
1962	Member of U.S. national team
1964	Plays for Team USA at the Winter Olympics
1965	Member of U.S. national team
1967	Member of U.S. national team; plays for Team USA at the Winter Olympics
1968	Member of U.S. national team
1969	Serves as assistant coach at the University of Minnesota
1970	Member of U.S. national team; coaches the Minnesota Junior Stars
1972-79	Coaches the University of Minnesota team
1980	Coaches the U.S. hockey team to the "Miracle on Ice"— winning gold medal at the games in Lake Placid, New York
1980-81	Coaches Daro in the Swiss Elite League
1981	Hired as coach of the New York Rangers (NHL)
1985	Fired in January as coach of the New York Rangers
1986-87	Coaches St. Cloud State College, a Division III college hockey team
1987-88	Coaches the Minnesota North Stars (NHL)
c. 1988-90	Works as commentator for SportsChannel America
1991-92	Coaches the Utica Devils (AHL)
1992-93	Coaches the New Jersey Devils (NHL)
c. 1993-99	Works as scout for the Pittsburgh Penguins (NHL)
1998	Coaches Team France at the Winter Olympics
1999-2000	Coaches the Pittsburgh Penguins (NHL)
2002	Coaches Team USA at the Winter Olympics, winning silver medal; awarded the Lester Patrick Award for his contributions to hockey; named director of player development for the Pittsburgh Penguins

Though Brooks had a limited playing career, he did serve as captain of the 1965, 1967, 1968, and 1970 teams. During this time period, Brooks worked at a St. Paul insurance agency, which allowed him to continue to play hockey as an amateur.

Began Coaching Career

While still playing for Team USA, Brooks began his coaching career. In 1969, he became an assistant coach for his alma mater, the University of Minnesota. In 1970, he coached the Minnesota Junior Stars. Brooks first real success as a coach came in 1972 when he became the head coach at the University of Minnesota. The team won the NCAA Division I championships in 1974, just two years after Brooks took over. It was the first time a team made up completely of players developed in America had won the NCAA championship. They also won the WCHA title in 1975, and two more NCAA championships in 1976 and 1979.

Coached to Olympic Gold

In 1979, Brooks left the University of Minnesota to become coach of the U.S. national team which finished seventh in the world championships. The following year, he was named the coach of the U.S. Olympic team. At the time, players still had to be amateurs, so many of his players were college hockey players. Brooks picked twenty-six players to play the sixty exhibition games in the ten months prior to the Olympic games.

Brooks used this time to develop them into a team, as well as mold them for future professional careers. He also had to figure out which six to drop from the squad as only 20 would play in the Olympics. A demanding coach, he expected much from his players. Brooks also introduced them to a new system of hockey than had previously played in the United States. Brooks was inspired by Europeans to develop "American hockey." It used an aggressive forecheck with a puck possession strategy. While it was good for international play, it was hard to learn.

Though Team USA lost to the U.S.S.R. team in one of the last exhibition games 10-3 in New York City, Brooks' squad beat them when it mattered in tournament play. Team USA won 4-3 in an upset victory dubbed the Miracle on Ice. The Americans went on to defeat Finland 4-2 to win the gold medal. These victories made Brooks and his team heroes in the United States. However, Brooks declined to capitalize on his success right away. Brooks could have coached in the NHL right away, but he chose to go to Switzerland. He coached there for one season, for Daro in the Swiss Elite League, but it did not work out.

Became NHL Coach

In 1981, Brooks took his first job in the NHL. He was hired by Craig Patrick to apply his innovative coaching methods to the New York Rangers, a mediocre team. The Rangers did well in its first season under Brooks, posting a record of 39-27-14 and making the playoffs. He was named the coach of the year by the *Sporting News*. The team did not fair as well other years, and Brooks was fired in January 1985. The team's record was 15-28-8, in part because of injuries to many key players and others not playing to their potential. In his three and a half years with the team, Brooks had a record of 131-113-41.

Brooks found employment with Jostens, the ring company, but soon returned to the coaching ranks. He went back to college hockey, coaching St. Cloud State College in the 1986-87 season. The team turned around under him, finishing in third place in NCAA Division III tournament.

Returned to Coach in NHL

In 1987, Brooks returned to coach on the professional level when he was hired as coach of the Minnesota North Stars. Brooks had been offered the job three previous times, but turned it down. He did not have an immediate effect on the team, which was not great. The North Stars only had a record of 19-48-13, and Brooks was forced out, though he had a two-year contract. Brooks then spent two years doing television commentary for SportsChannel America, and working as a salesman for the Turnquist Paper Company, selling industrial paper products.

In July 1991, Brooks was named the head coach of the Utica Devils in the American Hockey League. This was the primary affiliate of the NHL's New Jersey Devils. Brooks used his teaching skills to develop the young pros. In June 1992, Brooks was picked to coach the New Jersey Devils themselves. Again, Brooks only lasted one year. The team posted a record of 40-37-7, and lost in the first round of the playoffs. Brooks resigned because of his dispute with management after his first year, though he had a three-year deal. He did not like the direction of the team.

Brooks connection to professional and international hockey was much less in the 1990s. While he went back to Turnquist Paper Company as a salesman, he also worked as a scout for the Pittsburgh Penguins for much of the 1990s. He submitted two plans to coach Team USA in the 1992 and 1994 Olympic games, but his ideas were rejected as being too costly and/or unacceptable. Brooks did coach on the international stage once in the 1990s,

guiding the French hockey team in the 1998 Winter Olympics. They did not make the playoff round in Japan.

Returned to NHL Again

Still a member of the Penguins' staff, Brooks was asked to coach the team by the same Craig Patrick who had hired and fired him from the Rangers in the 1980s. Patrick had fired the Penguins' coach Kevin Constantine, who was rigid, in favor of the more flexible Brooks. The Penguins had many European players who played his style of hockey: with creativity and taking chances, but in a disciplined way. Brooks got the team into the playoffs and nurtured Ivan Hlinka, a Czech national coach, who took over in the 2000-01 season. Brooks left his coaching position after the 1999-2000 season.

Coached USA Team at Olympics

In 2002, Brooks was selected to coach the U.S. Olympic hockey team again. The challenges he faced this time were much different than in 1980. By this time, professionals were allowed to play in the Olympics, so his team was primarily composed of older NHL veterans. Brooks' job focused on getting the Americans to adjust to the wider ice surface and different style of play. He let them play their own game, but got them to play together. However, there was no miracle this time. Team USA won the silver medal, losing to the Canadian team 5-2 in the gold medal game. As Karen Guregian of the *Boston Herald* wrote, "He commands a certain respect for being able to do the unthinkable. Even Team Canada coach Pat Quinn talked this week about 'Herbie magic'. Brooks is that rare X-Factor."

CONTACT INFORMATION

Address: c/o Pittsburgh Penguins, Mellon Arena, 66 Mario Lemieux Place, Pittsburgh, PA 15219.

FURTHER INFORMATION

Books

Fischler, Stan. *Golden Ice*. Scarborough, Ont., 1990.
Hickok, Ralph. *A Who's Who of Sports Champions: Their Stories and Records*. Boston: Houghton Mifflin Company, 1995.

Wendel, Tim. *How the U.S. Won at Lake Placid: Going for the Gold.* Westport, CT: Lawrence Hill & Company, 1980.

Periodicals

Allen, Kevin. "1980 'Miracle on Ice' wasn't first." *USA Today* (January 15, 2002): 3C.

Bradley, Jeff. "Ambitions on Ice." *Sports Illustrated* (February 10, 1992): 12.

Dupont, Kevin Paul. "Brooks Hoping to Stay Involved." *Boston Globe* (February 25, 2002): D7.

Campbell, Steve. "Brooks not living in glory daze." *Times Union* (February 15, 2002): C1.

Diamos, Jason. "Rangers Lean to Brooks as Robinson Steps Away." *New York Times* (May 10, 2002): D2.

Dupont, Kevin Paul. "Everything's Still Flowing for Brooks: Placid Atmosphere Suits Him Just Fine." *Boston Globe* (February 17, 2002): D4.

Dupont, Kevin Paul. "His Fire Still Burns: Brooks Coaching Whole New Game." *Boston Globe* (February 22, 2002): E6.

Glasser, Jeff. "Hockey." *U.S. News & World Report* (January 28, 2002): 59.

McGuire, Pierre. "In the Crease." *Sports Illustrated* (March 11, 2002): 73.

Guregian, Karen. "Brooks' magic fits Bill." *Boston Herald* (February 20, 2002): 98.

Jaffe, Michael. "Hired." *Sports Illustrated* (July 22, 1991): 77.

Kennedy, Kostya. "Inside the NHL." *Sports Illustrated* (December 27, 1999): 128.

Kovacevic, Dejan. "Brooks to Oversee Player Development for Penguins." *Pittsburgh Post-Gazette* (August 15, 2002): D7.

Kovacevic, Dejan. "Rangers Can Talk to Brooks." *Pittsburgh Post-Gazette* (April 18, 2002): D1.

McGuire, Pierre. "In the Crease." *Sports Illustrated* (April 17, 2000): 83.

Molinari, Dave. "Brooks Spurns Rangers." *Pittsburgh Post-Gazette* (May 18, 2002): B1.

Murphy, Austin. "Mellow time for a miracle man." *Sports Illustrated* (January 11, 1988): 34.

Wilbon, Michael. "With Brooks at the Helm, U.S. Is Showing Its Mettle." *Washington Post* (February 24, 2002): D15.

Wolff, Craig. "Brooks is Replaced by Patrick as Rangers' Coach." *New York Times* (January 22, 1985): B7.

Yannis, Alex. "Brooks Named to Coach Top Devils Affiliate." *New York Times* (July 12, 1991): B13.

Yannis, Alex. "Brooks Takes a Walk as the Devils Jog in Place." *New York Times* (June 1, 1993): B13.

Yannis, Alex. "Devils Hope Brooks Spins Meadowlands Miracle." *New York Times* (June 6, 1992): section 1, p. 31.

Sketch by A. Petruso

Jim Brown

Jim Brown
1936-

American football player

Hall-of-Fame running back, Jim Brown, was recognized during his football career for his dominance on the playing field. In the years following his early retirement, that same strength and determination led to success in Hollywood and social activism. With the Cleveland Browns from 1957 through 1966, Brown rewrote the record books and then left the game to pursue avenues that would challenge him more than his gridiron contemporaries ever could. He was one of the first professional football players to parlay his fame into success off the field and in doing so he not only set a precedent for all the running backs that followed but for every athlete that had aspirations beyond athletics.

The Early Days

Born James Nathaniel Brown in 1936 on St. Simons Island off the coast of Georgia, he was raised primarily by his great-grandmother after his father, a professional boxer, left the family. His mother moved North in search of work and eventually would send for her son. It was after moving north to be with his mother that Brown first encountered the barriers he would so easily break throughout his life. Finding it hard to acclimate to his

Chronology

1936	Born February 17 on St. Simons Island, Georgia
1956	Named All-America at Syracuse University
1956	Qualifies to attend the Olympic Games
1957	Named to the 1957 College All-Stars
1957	Drafted by the Cleveland Browns
1957	Named NFL Rookie of the Year
1958, 1963, 1965	Named league's Most Valuable Player
1963	Sets single season rushing record with 1,863 yards
1965	Organizes the Black Economic Union
1966	Stars in hit movie, *The Dirty Dozen*
1966	Announces retirement from NFL
1969	Breaks ground with interracial love scene in *100 Rifles*
1971	Inducted into the Pro Football Hall of Fame
1986	Starts Vital Issues program
1989	Stars Amer-I-Can
2002	Serves jail time for domestic dispute

Awards and Accomplishments

1956	Named All-American at Syracuse
1958	Named NFL Rookie of the Year
1958, 1963, 1965	Named NFL Most Valuable Player
1959	Wins the Jim Thorpe Trophy
1959, 1964	Named NFL Player of the Year
1964	Wins Bert Bell Memorial award
1964	Wins Hickok Belt Athlete of the Year
1971	Inducted into Pro Football Hall of Fame

new surroundings, Brown found his way through athletics. The ease with which he excelled in nearly every available sport impressed his coaches and gave him the drive to continue. In high school, Brown became so popular that he was elected chief justice of the high school court and was a member of the honor society for scholastic achievement. Although he was a model student, his childhood was not without temptation. Brown admits to being involved in gangs as a teenager but never enough to interfere with his lofty ambitions.

After high school, Brown was a highly sought-after recruit for many colleges and universities. He chose New York's Syracuse University and hoped to earn a full athletic scholarship. His freshman year, on both the basketball and football teams, he was benched in favor of less talented white players. It was not until an injury on the football team that Brown was given his chance to shine. Taking full advantage of the opportunity, Brown soon became a star and earned ten varsity letters at Syracuse. He even qualified for the Olympic Games after placing fifth nationally in the 1956 decathlon competition. That year he led his team to the Cotton Bowl and finished with impressive numbers.

Brown and the Browns

He was drafted in the first round of the 1957 NFL draft by the Cleveland Browns. Starting at fullback, Brown was immediately effective in his role with the team. After only the fifth game of the season, he had already set a team record for touchdowns in a single season. The team would eventually win the Eastern Division championship and Brown was unanimously voted Rookie of the Year. The following year he again won the rushing title, with 1,527 yards and tied his single-season touchdown record with eighteen.

Between the years of 1958 and 1965, Brown was voted onto every All-Pro team and was a superstar in the

league and overwhelmingly so in Cleveland. His popularity proved so powerful that he led a player revolt against the coaching staff and in particular against his role in **Paul Brown**'s offense. The revolt would result in the firing of coach Brown. Under new coach, Blanton Collier, Brown again set records in 1963 gaining 1,863 yards. At the end of that year Brown was invited to Lyndon Johnson's White House.

After blazing a definitive trail on the field, Brown began setting precedent outside the NFL. He became interested in Hollywood and in product endorsement. A new phenomenon, his Pepsi Cola contract had him traveling in the off-season as an executive and spokesperson. His role in *Rio Conchos*, a film about the U.S. Cavalry in the 1800s, led to more movie roles and farther away from his still flourishing career with the Browns.

Hollywood and Retirement

In 1966, he accepted a role in the hit movie *The Dirty Dozen*. The scheduling conflict between the film and the beginning of football training camp led to Brown's abrupt retirement from football. At thirty-years-old and still in his prime, he left football and never looked back. Brown told *Sports Illustrated*, "I quit with regret but not sorrow. I've been able to do all the things I wanted to do, and now I want to devote my time to other things. And I wanted more mental stimulation than I would have had playing football." He left the game with, among others, the leagues' rushing record which would stand until **Walter Payton** broke it in 1984.

The year Payton broke the record in a mad dash with Franco Harris, who also coveted the accolade, Brown threatened to come back to football at the age of forty-seven. "He can break the record at his convenience because he has the cooperation of his organization," Brown said of Harris. "That's not a feat by my standards. It has nothing to do with overall performance. It has to do with specialized circumstances to break a record. You want to give me those circumstances, I'll come back and break any record they set." Whether making a statement about the state of the NFL in the middle eighties or having an actual desire to play again, Brown's willingness to risk public spectacle never came to fruition.

Career Statistics

		Rushing				Receiving			
Yr	Team	ATT	YDS	AVG	TD	REC	YDS	AVG	TD
1957	Cleveland	202	942	4.7	9	16	55	3.4	1
1958	Cleveland	257	1,527	5.9	17	16	138	8.6	1
1959	Cleveland	290	1,329	4.6	14	24	190	7.9	0
1960	Cleveland	215	1,257	5.8	9	19	204	10.7	2
1961	Cleveland	305	1,408	4.6	8	46	459	10.0	2
1962	Cleveland	230	996	4.3	13	47	517	11.0	5
1963	Cleveland	291	1,863	6.4	12	24	268	11.2	3
1964	Cleveland	280	1,446	5.2	7	36	340	9.4	2
1965	Cleveland	289	1,544	5.3	17	34	328	9.6	4
TOTAL		2,359	12,312	5.2	106	262	2,499	9.5	20

Cleveland: Cleveland Browns.

The mental stimulation that Brown sought would come in the form of many film roles including, *Dark of the Sun, Ice Station Zebra* and *100 Rifles*. He also broke ground in Hollywood after being the first to portray an interracial love scene with co-star Raquel Welch. Although an important cinematic moment, Brown later blamed his screen persona on his waning popularity in Hollywood. Brown believed that his portrayal of desirable and strong characters on screen made white mainstream America nervous and led to a lack of work in years to follow. "I went from a major star to basically nothing," he said. "I think Hollywood just got tired of a big 'ol black Negro kissin' all their women."

Troubles with the Law

By the beginning of the eighties, with his movie career all but over, Brown's image began to take a beating for his continuing problem with domestic violence. Several women had brought him up on battery charges over the years, and although the charges were typically dropped, there were two notable convictions. Including an incident in 1968 where a girlfriend was found semi-conscious under his apartment's balcony. Plagued by the negative publicity, an unrenewed Pepsi endorsement contract and a dried up movie career, he would once again search for mental stimulation. It would come in the form of social activism.

Social Consciousness

His first step was to start his own production company, Ocean Productions, an attempt to provide minorities with a greater role in cinema. Not an overwhelming success, it was the first step in what would be the third phase of his life and career. As the founder of the Black Economic Union during his football days, Brown had the ambition and intelligence to use his influence to help those less fortunate and continues to today. It was rap music that awakened Brown's consciousness. "I said, 'Damn, these young brothers have got some conscious-

ness.' I started hooking into this energy," Brown said of the music of Public Enemy.

Using his celebrity to call attention to the problems of the inner city, Brown founded Amer-I-Can in 1987. Amer-I-Can attempts to instill personal growth techniques and life management skills in gang members and prison inmates. With his powerful presence, Brown often conducts seminars with Los Angeles' gang members in his house in the Hollywood Hills. Granted money to move into other cities, his is a continuing struggle that he feels could use even more help. Feeling that more popular athletes could contribute to these problems, Brown has said: "They are the beneficiaries of our struggle. But they don't recognize that because they're inundated with agents, managers, lawyers and owners who don't want them to do anything but play ball and be physical freaks of nature with no awareness." Brown's call to arms hasn't led to an increase in superstar athletes lending their skills but on his own he has made an impact. "So far I'm very encouraged," said Las Vegas Mayor Jan Jones in 1991, of the decrease in gang violence in the city. "It's the most satisfying time of my life," Brown has said. "I get a phone call from some dangerous kid on the street—and I answer my own phone, no middlemen—who wants to change his life. He'll come up here I show him a little respect, trust and without much help he can change his life."

Brown's social activity harkens back to an era when athletes used their platform to try and strike change in their communities. "In the 60's when I called athletes to come and talk to [Muhammad] Ali, they didn't bring their agents, managers and lawyers. They came because they thought it was worthwhile. We athletes were just like normal citizens in those days, fighting for our rights," he said in a recent interview. "We didn't put our sport before our manhood." Brown's commitment to giving back to his community even extended to a threat to pull out of the Pro Football Hall of Fame, to which he was elected in 1971, because he believes the board that elects its members is racist. "I don't want to become a white black man

Jim Brown

and forget my brothers," Brown has said, of his outspokenness on civil rights issues. "If black people don't get my helping hand, there won't be any helping hand."

Throughout his record setting football career with the Cleveland Browns, Jim Brown had a fearless approach to the game and in taking on Hollywood and the problems of the inner city he has displayed the same gritty determination. His example is part modern day superstar and part throwback to a more socially conscious era but either way it has kept him a successful and contributing member of society long after his gridiron glory had become a memory. He had the courage to walk away from the game before he became a shadow of himself and in the aftermath continues to hurdle over obstacles well into his sixties.

FURTHER INFORMATION

Books

Contemporary Black Biography, Vol. 11. Detroit: Gale, 1996.

Periodicals

"Arrested. Jim Brown." *Time* (March 4, 1985): 80.
"As Time Passes, Public Perceptions of Jim Brown, O.J. Simpson Change." *New York Daily News* (February 9, 1995).
"Call Him to Canton." *Sports Illustrated* (February 26, 1990): 14.
"Excellence by the yard; Franco Harris and Walter Payton: Doing it to Brown." *Time* (October 1, 1984): 84.
"Going the Extra Yard." *People* (November 25, 1991): 105.
"I'll do it Again; Gridiron Legend Jim Brown Hopes to Return to the Field and Show the Pros of Today How to Play Football." *People* (January 9, 1984): 22.
"Jim Brown." *Sports Illustrated* (September 19, 1994): 56.
"Jim Brown Begins Jail Term." *Jet* (April 1, 2002): 32.
"Prisoner of Conscience." *Sports Illustrated* (April 15, 2002): 54.
"Something of Value: Jim Brown Hits the Mean Streets to do the Right Thing." *Sport* (June, 1993): 85.
"Pete, the Way they Play Today Stinks." *Sports Illustrated* (December 12, 1983): 30.

Sketch by Aric Karpinski

Mordecai Brown
1876-1948

American baseball player

Of all the young men in history who aspired to play professional baseball, Mordecai Brown wished it perhaps most of all. After a childhood accident left him with a badly mangled right hand, he learned to throw a natural sinker ball despite the handicap. He spent fourteen years in the major leagues and was enshrined in the Baseball Hall of Fame, as one of the most successful right-handed pitchers in the history of the game.

Born Mordecai Peter Centennial Brown in Nyesville, Indiana, he was one of five children of Peter P. Brown, a farmer, and Jane Marsh, a homemaker. Brown's parents embellished his given name with a second middle name of Centennial, in honor of his birth year, which marked the first American Centennial.

As a child of six or seven, Brown became engrossed one day by the workings of a threshing machine at his

Mordecai Brown

uncle's farm and, against the warnings of his elders, put his hand too close to the blades. The index finger of his right hand was severed, leaving a misshapen stump. The odd-looking digit was barely on the mend when Brown reinjured the same hand while chasing a pig, breaking the two middle fingers and injuring the pinky finger. The broken fingers healed badly, and the pinky finger remained permanently paralyzed. The hand was crippled for the rest of his life. Years later, as a professional baseball player, the deformity earned him the nickname "Three-Finger Brown." He was known also by the nickname of "Miner" because as a teenager he went to work in the mines around Nyesville before turning to professional baseball for his livelihood.

It was while working in the mines that Brown decided to become a baseball player. With the encouragement of a co-worker—a former minor leaguer named Legs O'Connell—Brown mustered his determination and learned to grip and toss the baseball with his injured hand. With O'Connell's help Brown overcame the pain of handling the ball, yet time and again when he tossed it, the ball curved and jumped stubbornly, landing with an awkward twist. Brown was frustrated by this inability to control the ball, until O'Connell convinced him to turn the odd throwing style into an advantage. With practice and perseverance, Brown learned to pitch a natural curve ball with a special flair made possible only by the mass of crippled fingers on his right hand. In pursuing a goal of playing professional baseball he had never held hope of becoming a pitcher until he came to appreciate his own uncanny ability to throw a sinker ball.

Pitched in as a Pitcher

In his first excursion into semi-professional ball in 1898, Brown played third base for a team out of Coxville, Indiana. One day, at O'Connell's urging, the team manager allowed Brown to pitch in a pinch. When Brown stepped onto the mound, the game was thought to be hopelessly lost, but Brown pitched one strike after another—for five innings. He allowed only one hit, a weak grounder, and his team won 9-3. Brown received an offer to play for the defeated team from Brazil, Indiana.

He took his first professional job in baseball for $40.00 a month, in 1901 as a pitcher for the Terre Haute Three-I League team. In his first season, he pitched thirty-one games and won twenty-three. He won twenty-seven out of forty-two games for Omaha in 1902. Because of his deformed pitching hand, Brown threw curve balls that were difficult to hit, and his maniacal sinker ball was punctuated by a fiendish dip. Reluctant batters had no choice but to swing at Brown's sinkers, very low to the ground as they were. Right-handed batters sent Brown's pitches down and out, and left-handed batters sent them down and in. Either way Brown's pitching more often than not allowed the fielding team led by Brown to clinch an easy out.

The St. Louis Cardinals purchased Brown from Omaha in 1903, bringing him into the National League (NL). With his career on track, he married Sallie Burgham that year. A lackluster 9-13 season sent him to the Chicago Cubs in 1904, as part of a double trade with

Career Statistics

Yr	Team	W	L	GS	CG	SH	SV	IP	H	R	BB
1903	StL-N	9	13	24	19	1	0	201	231	7	59
1904	Chi-N	15	10	23	21	4	1	212.1	155	1	50
1905	Chi-N	18	12	24	24	4	0	249	219	3	44
1906	Chi-N	26	6	32	27	9	3	277.1	198	1	61
1907	Chi-N	20	6	27	20	6	3	233	180	2	40
1908	Chi-N	29	9	31	27	9	5	312.1	214	1	49
1909	Chi-N	27	9	34	32	8	7	342.2	246	1	53
1910	Chi-N	25	14	31	27	6	7	295.1	256	3	64
1911	Chi-N	21	11	27	21	0	13	270	267	5	55
1912	Chi-N	5	6	8	5	2	0	88.2	92	2	20
1913	Cin-N	11	12	16	11	1	6	173.1	174	7	44
1914	StL-F	12	6	18	13	2	0	175	172	7	43
	Bro-F	2	5	8	5	0	0	57.2	63	1	18
1915	Bro-F	17	8	25	17	3	4	236.1	189	2	64
1916	Chi-N	2	3	4	2	0	0	48.1	52	0	9
TOTAL		239	130	332	271	55	49	3172.1	2708	43	673

Bro-F: Brooklyn Feds; Chi-N: Chicago Cubs; Cin-N: Cincinnati Reds; StL-F: St. Louis Terriers; StL-N: St. Louis Cardinals.

Mike O'Neill. During his first season with the Cubs, he led the league with ten shutouts. In 1906 he finished the season 26-6, leading the league with nine shutouts and an earned run average (ERA) of 1.04.

Brown pitched for the Cubs for nine years. Between 1906 and 1910 he won 127 games, and in six separate seasons he won more than twenty games. With Brown on the mound the Cubs won the pennant four times: in 1906, 1907, 1908, and 1910. He pitched World Series shutout games in 1906, 1907, and 1908. In 1907 he pitched a no-hitter that won the series. From 1908-11, Brown led the league in saves.

Later Career

As Brown's reputation grew, a rivalry brewed with Christy "Matty" Mathewson, the pitcher for the New York Giants. In a now famous game on October 8, 1908, the two opposed each other in a replay for the National League title. It was an error by the Giants' Fred Merkle that had forced the Giants to relinquish an earlier victory on September 23, and both teams were poised for a battle. Brown pitched from early in the first inning of the makeup game, after Jack Pfeister—the Cubs' starting pitcher—allowed one run. By the final inning, Brown had ceded only one run to the Giants during the entire contest. Mathewson, by allowing four runs in the seventh inning, delivered a 4-2 victory to the Cubs. Chicago took home its third consecutive pennant that year.

Brown played for the Cincinnati Reds in 1913. He spent 1914-15 playing for the Federal League, with the St. Louis Terriers and the Brooklyn Feds. He returned to the Cubs for a final season of play in 1916. At the end of that season both he and Mathewson retired simultaneously from major league play after one final dual on September 4. Although Mathewson won that day by a score of 10-8, Brown retired with a career record of 239-130, an ERA of 2.06, and fifty-seven National League shutouts.

Brown was a sturdy man who stood five-feet-ten-inches tall and weighed 175 pounds. Despite his right-handed pitch, he batted both ways. In retirement he played for two years in the International League, then managed the Terre Haute Three-I team through 1920.

Brown operated a filling station until suffering a stroke in 1945. He died on February 14, 1948. His remains are interred at Rose Lawn Cemetery in Terre Haute.

In 1949 Brown was inducted into the Professional Baseball Hall of Fame in Cooperstown, New York. His 1.04 season ERA for 1906 stood as the number two all-time record into the twenty-first century. During his career he pitched five complete winning games in the World Series, including the winning game in 1907. In 1908 Brown became the first pitcher to record four consecutive shutouts. Long-time Cubs second-baseman Johnny Evers in discussing Brown with Hall of Fame historian Ernest J. Lanigan said, "You haven't space enough to tell of all the grand deeds of Brownie on and off the field. Plenty of nerve, ability and willingness to work at all times under any conditions.... There never was a finer character-charitable and friendly to his foes and ever willing to help a youngster breaking in." Evers was quoted by Lee Allen and Tom Meany in *Kings of the Diamond*.

FURTHER INFORMATION

Books

Allen, Lee, and Tom Meany. *Kings of the Diamond.* New York: G. P. Putnam's Sons, 1965.

Paul Brown

Awards and Accomplishments

1906	Leads the NL with 10 shutouts; records #2 all-time earned run average of 1.04
1949	Induction into the Baseball Hall of Fame, Cooperstown, New York

Retires in 1916 with a career win-loss record of 239-130, earned run average of 2.06, 57 National League shutouts, and six seasons with over 20 wins.

Garraty, John A., and Mark C. Carnes, Eds. *American National Biography.* New York: Oxford University Press, 1999.

Schoor, Gene. *Courage Makes the Champion.* Princeton: Van Nostrand Company, Inc,, 1967.

Sketch by Gloria Cooksey

Paul Brown
1908-1991

American football coach

Paul Brown was the first head coach of the Cleveland Browns football team. He played a major role in the evolution of the modern day game, devising detailed game plans, playbooks, and classroom learning techniques. He was also the first coach to hire a full-time coaching staff, as well as instituting the practice of analyzing game films. He coached with the Browns from 1946-62, and then with the Cincinnati Bengals from 1968-1975.

Growing Up

Paul Brown was born on September 7, 1908, in Norwalk, Ohio, a small town north of Canton (home of the Football Hall of Fame and where the National Football League was founded in 1920). Brown's father, Lester, was a railroad dispatcher and responsible for split-second switching of trains from one track to another. This precision rubbed off on the young Paul Brown, and decades later Coach Brown would leave nothing to chance in his football programs.

As a young man, Paul Brown played football when it was only beginning to emerge in America as a sport with a following. When Brown entered Massillon High School, he was skinny, but would earn the right to play quarterback, learning early that his true passion was in overseeing the game.

He graduated from Massillon in 1926. From there he went on to play at Miami University in Ohio. Although he saw some success on the playing field, it was dictating

what should happen and controlling all aspects of the game that truly resonated in Paul Brown. He aspired to a coaching position, and the decades he spent at the helm of football programs would change the game of football forever.

A Storybook Beginning

Brown returned to Massillon as a football coach, and turned the club around. The school was seriously in debt, and less than 3,000 fans were attending each game. Although thousands of fans at a football game in the 1930s might seem like a lot, this was Ohio, where high school football is king. Had Brown remained only at the high school level, his reputation in Ohio lore would have remained solid. But he didn't stop there.

After nine years of high school coaching, and much to the relief of most every other high school coach in Ohio, Brown left. But he left having lost only one game in sixty as a coach at Massillon. There were now over 22,000 people coming to each home game. His legacy was not only with the football program. The money generated by the popularity of football helped build a new swimming pool and observatory, and it allowed the school to offer classes in speech and drama.

On to OSU

Brown moved on to take the head coaching position with Ohio State University. Francis Schmidt had resigned as coach and the people of Ohio wanted Paul Brown.

Chronology

1908	Born September 7 in Norwalk, Ohio
1932-40	Leads Massillon (OH) High School football team to 59 wins and 1 loss in his tenure there
1940	Becomes head coach of Ohio State Buckeyes
1942	Wins national championship with Buckeyes
1944	Stationed as a lieutenant at the Great Lakes Naval Training Center outside of Chicago
1946	Hired by owner Mickey McBride, Paul Brown puts all pieces in place for a successful Cleveland Browns football team
1950	Transfers from AAFC to the NFL, plays first game against Eagles on September 16
1950	Leads Cleveland to a 10-2 season and beats L.A. Rams to win the NFL championship
1951-55	Leads the Browns to the championship game for five straight years, winning it all in 1954 and 1955
1956	Brown suffers his first losing season as coach
1961	Advertising executive Art Modell buys the Browns for $4 million
1962	Makes famous trade, sending Browns running back Bobby Mitchell to Washington for Ernie Davis (would eventually lead to his firing as head coach)
1962	Browns finish 7-6-1
1963	Released from coaching duties of the Cleveland Browns by team owner Art Modell
1967	Inducted into Professional Football Hall of Fame
1968	Starts coaching again, this time with an expansion team—the Cincinnati Bengals
1975	Retires from coaching
1991	Dies on August 5, in Cincinnati, Ohio, following complications from pneumonia

Awards and Accomplishments

1942	Coached Ohio State University to national title
1946-49	Led team to #1 finishes and titles in All American Football Conference (AAFC)
1950-55, 1957	Finished in first place in his NFL division
1950, 1954-55	Won NFL Championship Game
1967	Inducted into National Football Hall of Fame

Many of the high school coaches, according to Mark Bechtel in *Sports Illustrated,* wanted this dominating presence out of their ranks. "[They] made it known that if Brown did not get the Ohio State job, they would encourage their star players to matriculate out of state." Within two years after his hiring at OSU, Brown took the Buckeyes, who had been blown out in many of their games prior to Brown's arrival, to the national championship.

But his tenure at Ohio State would be short-lived. After only a few years, Brown was drafted and stationed as a lieutenant at the Great Lakes Naval Training Center, outside Chicago. There, he initiated a football program, and asked **Weeb Ewbank** to be one of his assistants.

Though Brown had been promised that his job at OSU would be waiting for him when he returned, his successor also happened to be a friend of his, Carroll Widdoes, and Brown didn't want to put him out of a job. So he looked for gainful football employment elsewhere.

The Pro Ranks

In 1946, the city of Cleveland had been awarded one of eight franchises in the All-America Football Conference (AAFC). In his article, Bechtel wrote that Mickey McBride, owner of a cab company in Cleveland, bought the rights to the new team. But the catch was that McBride, regardless of how much money he could spend, had no clue about what to do with a football team. He knew of only one coach in all of football, Notre Dame's Frank Leahy, whom he was going to hire. But *Cleveland Plain Dealer* Sportswriter John Dietrich encouraged McBride to look elsewhere, and persuaded him that hiring Paul Brown would be the best choice. Thus, Paul Brown took over as part owner, general manager, and head coach for the new Cleveland Browns.

With McBride's ignorance of the game, Brown had total control over the team. He had an amazing ability to spot talent, and as he formed the team, he wasn't looking for known stars. Brown sought men who would be a proper fit into the boot camp he was going to run. He intentionally went looking for obscure players, but chose **Otto Graham** as his quarterback. Brown would hire Bill Willis of Kentucky State College as an assistant coach, one of the few African Americans participating in a major college program. When all was said and done, Brown brought forty-six players to the Cleveland training camp on the campus of Bowling Green State University.

Gridiron Success

In their first season as a team, the Cleveland Browns won their first five games by a combined score of 142-20. They ended up at 12-2 on the year, winning the franchise's first AAFC Championship over New York at Cleveland Municipal Stadium. Brown coached Cleveland to championships the next three seasons, as well.

In 1949, the NFL took the Browns into the league (along with the Baltimore Colts and the San Francisco 49ers). It was the end of AAFC, but the beginning of more success for Coach Brown. The Commissioner of the National Football League (NFL), **Bert Bell**, always aware of marketing strategies, wanted to pit the best teams from both leagues against one another. So in the first game of the season, the Browns played the defending champion Philadelphia Eagles. The Cleveland Browns dominated the contest, emerging with 35-10 rout. The Browns' precision passing game was awesome, and the Eagles' coach didn't know how to defense it.

Paul Brown would coach in Cleveland until 1963. In 1968, he became the first coach of a new team in Ohio, the Cincinnati Bengals. But his success in Cincinnati didn't come close to his prior successes. He finished his tenure as coach of the Bengals with a 55-59-1 record. He retired from coaching in 1975.

Paul Brown ended his career with a 222-112-9 record in professional football. He won four All-American Football Conference titles and three NFL titles. With the Cleveland Browns, he compiled a record of forty-seven wins, four losses and three ties in the AAFC, and the move to the NFL would garner almost as much success.

Brown's Impact on Football

The list of people Paul Brown had a direct influence on is long and prestigious. A few among the many are defensive back and later Miami Dolphins head coach **Don Shula**, Bill Walsh, and offensive guard Chuck Noll. Cincinnati coach Sam Wyche learned from Brown. And **Weeb Ewbank**, who coached the Baltimore Colts and New York Jets to championships, had known Paul Brown almost from the beginning. Bud Grant and Bill Walsh, like Ewbank, also coached directly beneath Brown.

Brown's coaching style was new to all who came across it. When his players showed up for their first practice, he handed out notebooks and made them write their assignments for each play. He insisted they commit football quotations to memory. Brown is probably the single biggest influence on the modern day style of coaching. At mid-century, he was analyzing game film, using diagrams of pass patterns, and sending in guards to deliver plays to the quarterback. The current earpiece that coaches use to talk to their quarterbacks is a also brainchild of Brown's. Even the facemask, which was designed by Brown's equipment manager.

His success was won with military rigor. Brown was once quoted in the Washington Post as saying that, "The history of all successful teams shows authority concentrated in the coach. The players can't go beyond me. That's the way it should be." His players were expected to study nightly. He saw it as a classroom, just like when he was coaching high school or at the Great Lakes Naval Academy. "I've never changed my approach," he said. "I talk to them exactly as I lectured college students, and I expect them to respond as students."

The Brown System Finds An Adversary

Brown developed an incredibly complex offensive system. Contrary to closed lineups previously used,

Paul Brown

Brown opened up the field, spreading his receivers and utilizing the whole field. And he ran his team with precision, so much so that he needed assistants in his chain of command. One such assistant, Fritz Heisler, said, "He reminds me of a surgeon. He's impersonal, analytical, always studying and icy cold in doing his job. He's a perfectionist in every detail."

Paul Brown would not suffer a losing season until 1956, but the poor record gave him the pick he'd wanted in the draft. He took Syracuse fullback **Jim Brown**. One more "Brown" into the mix, however, upset the balance. In drafting Jim Brown, Coach Brown had gotten hold of a man who refused to take many orders, which in turn opened up the controversy that would ultimately cost Paul Brown his job in Cleveland.

In 1961 a flashy advertising executive named Art Modell bought the Cleveland Browns for $4 million. Modell loved Jim Brown's play, and envisioned Brown as a marketable commodity. But this was directly against Paul Brown's wishes, who wanted the ship he ran kept tight. Football players were football players. Modell, however, got Jim Brown a radio show and a newspaper column in an attempt to increase his visibility.

The battering of horns hit a fever pitch in 1962, when Paul Brown, who prior to Modell's tenure as owner always conducted the trades himself, traded, without Modell's permission, future Hall of Famer Bobby Mitchell away to the Washington Redskins. In the trade, Brown picked up

Ernie Davis, whom Brown wanted to put in his backfield for an unstoppable two back combination. Yet in an unfortunate circumstance, Davis was soon diagnosed with leukemia, and he would die before ever playing a game with the Browns. Modell, who liked Davis, was nonetheless angered over being left out of the decision-making process, and when, in 1962, the Browns finished the season only one game over .500, Modell fired Paul Brown.

Who's to Blame?

Some apologists for Modell claim he didn't have a chance, that Paul Brown lost touch with the changing times. The new generation of players were different than those who first adhered to Brown's militaristic style. Yet it is difficult to deny the success that came with his method, for better or worse. In seventeen seasons with the Cleveland Browns, Paul Brown coached the team to a .760 winning percentage, with the team making thirteen post season appearances.

Paul Brown died on August 5, 1991, in Cincinnati, Ohio, from complications following pneumonia. Upon his death, Modell, with whom he had so many disagreements, called Brown a "pioneer, an innovator. The game we have today—players, coaches, owners and fans—can be traced back to the many things he started doing in the 1950s."

In the years before his death, Paul Brown was the only voice of dissent against the expansion that has taken the NFL by storm. And he hated instant replay, saying, "It just adds another layer of error" to the game. He was never one to hold back on his opinions. And he had plenty of those. "Working under Paul Brown is like living next to a library," said Sam Wyche in a *Sports Illustrated* obituary shortly after Paul Brown died. "I'd be crazy not to take out a book."

Paul Brown was the first head coach of the Cleveland Browns football team. He played a major role in the evolution of the modern day game, devising detailed game plans, playbooks, and classroom learning techniques. He was also the first coach to hire a full-time coaching staff, as well as instituting the practice of analyzing game films. He coached with the Browns from 1946-62, and then with the Cincinnati Bengals from 1968-1975.

SELECTED WRITINGS BY BROWN:

(With Jack T. Clary) *Paul Brown: The Paul Brown Story,* MacMillan, 1979.

FURTHER INFORMATION

Books

Brown, Paul, and Jack T. Clary. *Paul Brown: The Paul Brown Story.* New York: MacMillan, 1979.

Long, Tim. *Browns Memories: The 338 Most Memorable Heroes, Heartaches and Highlights from 50 Seasons of Cleveland Browns Football.* Cleveland, OH: Gray and Company, 1996.

Moon, Bob. *The Cleveland Browns: The Great Tradition.* Sportradition Publishers, 1999.

"Paul Brown." *Newsmakers 1992*. Issue Cumulation. Detroit: Gale, 1992.

St. James Encyclopedia of Popular Culture. Detroit: St. James Press, 2000.

Sullivan, George. *Pro Football's All-Time Greats: The Immortals in Pro Football's Hall of Fame,* New York: Putnam Publishers, 1968.

Periodicals

Bechtel, Mark. "Legends By The Lake." *Sports Illustrated* (September 1, 1999).

Chicago Tribune (August 6, 1991).

King, P. "Coach of coaches: Paul Brown dies at 82, leaving behind a legacy of innovation and inspiration." *Sports Illustrated* (August 12, 1991).

Lamb, K. "Paul Brown: in the beginning there were balls and helmets and stripes. Brown made it football." *Sport-New-York* (December 1986).

New York Times (August 6, 1991).

Quarterback (November, 1969): 24-29.

Time (August 19, 1991): 54.

Washington Post (August 6, 1991).

Williams, Marty. "First Came George Halas, Then Paul Brown." *Football Digest* (April, 1976): 50-54.

Younkers, Bob. "The Man from Massillon." *Sport Life* (fall, 1950): 12-13.

Other

Mann, Frank D. "The Greatest Coach in Bengals' History." from *Browns History* Web site. http://www.brownshistory.com/ (November 2, 2002).

Sketch by Eric Lagergren

Tim Brown
1966-

American football player

A standout at Notre Dame and one of the best wide receivers in National Football league (NFL) history, Oakland Raider Tim Brown continues to break records and propel his team to the top of the standings. Though not without some rocky times with team management, he's the only Raider who has scored points four different ways: on a pass reception, on a rush, and by running back a kickoff

Tim Brown

Chronology

1966	Born July 22 in Dallas, Texas
1984	Graduates from Woodrow Wilson High School with over 4,000 all-purpose yards
1984	Chooses to go north to University of Notre Dame for college
1988	Graduates from Notre Dame as one of the best players to ever go through the famed program
1988	Drafted by Oakland Raiders
1988	Rookie selection to Pro Bowl as kick returner
1989	Out for season with injury in first game of the year
1991	Named to Pro Bowl as kick returner after sharing AFC lead in punt returns (11.4 yard average)
1992	Leads Raiders in receiving yards and touchdowns
1993	Leads AFC with 1,180 receiving yards
1997	Becomes Raiders all-time leading receiver and Raiders all-time total yardage record holder
1997	Marries Sherice Weaver
2000	Surpasses 1000-yard receiving mark for eighth straight year; has career-best 11 touchdown receptions
2001	Becomes all-time Raider leader for Pro Bowl appearances with ninth selection
2001	Becomes Raiders all-time scoring leader in touchdowns, reaching 100 touchdown mark (first Raider to do so)
2002	Begins season having caught at least two passes in 140 straight games
2002	Surpasses 1000 catches mark for his career, becoming only third receiver in NFL history to do so; later in same game goes over 14,000 yards receiving, tying him for second all-time
2002	Selected to his 10th Pro Bowl at the conclusion of 2002 season

return and a punt return. He is the Raiders all-time scoring leader and has been selected to ten pro bowls. In 2002, Brown entered the record books as only the third receiver in NFL history to have over 1000 career catches.

Growing Up

Tim Brown was born on July 22, 1966, in Dallas, Texas, to Josephine and Eugene Brown. He was a child gifted in many areas, possessing athletic prowess as well as brains, dedication, and determination. During his high school years, he was an all-around outstanding student and athlete, and according to his NFL.com biography, was named a Prep All-American and was twice an All-District running back for Woodrow Wilson High School in Dallas.

Brown developed into a great leader, and by his senior season was the team captain in football, basketball, and track, as well as being the sports editor for the school paper. By the time he graduated, he had over 4,000 all-purpose yards and was a prodigy at returning punts and kickoffs for touchdowns.

Though Tim Brown is known today for his excellence on the football field, like many great athletes he could have easily gone to another sport. His NFL.com biography lists him as All-District guard in basketball his senior year, and his senior spring he set a district record with a 24 foot 3 inch long jump. He was also one of the fastest quarter-milers in the country.

Despite not having racked up many victories in high school football (in his last three years at Woodrow Wilson, the team won only four games), Brown chose to continue his football career at Notre Dame, where he became one of the most outstanding players in Notre Dame history.

While at the school he played for both Gerry Faust and Lou Holtz. His junior season he earned his national reputation as a standout player, hauling in 45 receptions for 910 yards and five touchdowns, rushing the ball fifty-nine times for two touchdowns. But Brown's speed and versatility transferred to special teams, as well, where, in his junior year he had twenty-five kickoff returns for 698 yards, averaging just under twenty-eight yards per return. In all, he averaged 176.1 yards per game, a school record.

He would be just as impressive in his senior season at Notre Dame, and by the time he left, he was regarded as one of "most explosive all-around talents in Notre Dame History," and culminating a phenomenal college career by winning the Heisman trophy (1987). He also won the Walter Camp Trophy, a Timmie award, and was the *Sporting News* College Football Player of the Year. Tim Brown's name tops the Notre Dame record books in many categories, among them receiving yardage, kickoff returns, and kickoffs and punts returned for touchdowns.

From Irish Gold to Silver and Black

The then-Los Angeles Raiders selected Tim Brown in the 1988 NFL draft as the sixth pick overall, and Brown

Career Statistics

Yr	Team	Receiving				Rushing				Fumbles	
		REC	YDS	AVG	TD	ATT	YDS	AVG	TD	FUM	LST
1988	LA	43	725	16.9	5	14	50	3.6	1	5	0
1989	LA	1	8	8.0	0	0	0	0.0	0	1	0
1990	LA	18	165	14.7	3	0	0	0.0	0	3	0
1991	LA	36	554	15.4	5	5	16	3.2	0	1	0
1992	LA	49	693	14.1	7	3	−4	−1.3	0	6	0
1993	LA	80	1180	14.8	7	2	7	3.5	0	1	0
1994	LA	89	1309	14.7	9	0	0	0.0	0	1	1
1995	OAK	89	1342	15.1	10	0	0	0.0	0	0	0
1996	OAK	90	1104	12.3	9	6	35	5.8	0	1	0
1997	OAK	104	1408	13.5	5	5	19	3.8	0	1	1
1998	OAK	81	1012	12.5	9	1	−7	−7.0	0	3	0
1999	OAK	90	1344	14.9	6	1	4	4.0	0	0	0
2000	OAK	76	1128	14.8	11	3	12	4.0	0	0	0
2001	OAK	91	1165	12.8	9	4	39	9.8	0	0	0
2002	OAK	81	930	11.5	2	6	19	3.2	0	0	0
TOTAL		1018	14167	13.9	97	50	190	3.8	1	27	3

LA: Los Angeles Raiders; OAK: Oakland Raiders.

quickly made an impact with the team, setting a Raider rookie record for all purpose yards (2,317). But after his first season he would face disappointment. In the first game of his second year, Brown suffered a knee injury, keeping him on the sidelines for the rest of the season.

He returned for his third season a strong player, dominating the team's receiving statistics and embarking upon a string of Pro Bowl appearances. Beginning with a game against the Kansas City Chiefs in 1993, Brown would not miss a game for the next nine seasons.

He became the Raiders' all-time scoring leader in 2001, the first player for that franchise to surpass the 100 touchdown mark. He consistently excels on the field, and at the beginning of the 2002 season held the second-longest streak among active NFL players by having caught at least two passes in 140 straight games.

Hall of Fame Bound

During a Monday Night Football game on December 2, 2002, Brown become only the third player in NFL history to surpass 1000 catches. It was an appropriate national spotlight for this milestone, as he joined Raiders teammate **Jerry Rice**, who has over 1400 receptions, and Miami's **Cris Carter**. When he made the famous catch, the game was stopped and a brief celebration took place on the field.

Trailing 10-6, Brown's momentous [1,000th career] 6-yard catch across the middle set up the Raiders' first touchdown, a 26-yard pass from Rich Gannon to Jerry Rice. Was it the kind of catch Brown dreamed it would be? "Nah, not at all," he told the *San Francisco Chronicle* with a laugh. "I was like, 'No, not one this one!' But hey, I'll take it." Brown also reached another milestone

that evening. In the second half of the game he surpassed 14,000 yards receiving, moving into second place (again behind Rice, who has over 21,000 career yards).

Loyalty in the Face of Adversity

In this day and age it is impressive for one player to remain with the same team for his whole career. But Tim Brown doesn't appear to be the average NFL player. He doesn't jump to the next best offer, choosing instead to bide his time as he seeks the coveted Super Bowl Ring. During his career he has had substantial offers from the Denver Broncos and the Dallas Cowboys. But Brown remains faithful to his club, even though he often thinks he's not utilized enough—a feeling recently brought to the surface when the Raiders acquired Jerry Rice from the 49ers. *Sports Illustrated* noted that "while other receivers of his caliber have game plans built around them, [Brown] has been, for much of his career… someone to go to in case of emergency." He doesn't like feeling like a last-chance guy, and though his numbers don't indicate that this is the case, some of the maneuverings of the front office suggest otherwise.

Though he has weathered some rocky times with the Raiders franchise and club owner **Al Davis**, Brown seems to have come through the adversity a stronger and more devoted Raider. Nancy Gay wrote in *Sports Illustrated* that Brown "remains an anomaly in the transient world of today's NFL." Brown wants a Super Bowl victory. His team has made it into the AFC playoffs with the best record in the league. "I just didn't want to be known as the guy who ran out of the burning house and left everybody behind," he told *Sports Illustrated*. His loyalty may yet pay off.

Awards and Accomplishments

1983	Voted high school All-American at Woodrow Wilson High School
1986	Voted consensus All-American
1987	Winner of United Press International and *The Sporting News* and *Football News* College Player of the Year; voted a consensus All-American
1987	Named College Player of the Year by the Walter Camp Foundation
1987	Named winner of Heisman Trophy
1990	Selected to Pro Bowl for 1st time
2002	Selected to 10th Pro Bowl

CONTACT INFORMATION

Address: Tim Brown, c/o The Oakland Raiders, 1220 Harbor Bay Parkway, Alameda, CA 94502.

FURTHER INFORMATION

Books

"Tim Brown." *Almanac of Famous People,* 6th ed. Detroit: Gale Group, 1998.

Periodicals

Gay, Nancy. "Brown goes for 1,000th catch; One of Davis' favorite Raiders twice considered leaving team." *San Francisco Chronicle* (December 2, 2002).

Knapp, Gwen. "Brown's major milestone was no time for a party." *San Francisco Chronicle* (December 4, 2002).

Murphy, Austin. "Sweet Moves." *Sports Illustrated* (July 6, 1998): 89.

Reilly, Rick. "Mister T. (Notre Dame's Tim Brown)." *Sports Illustrated* (August 31, 1987): 67.

Other

Irish Legend. http://www.irishlegends.com/Pages/calendar/0702.asp (December 15, 2002).

NFL.com. http://www.nfl.com/players/1267_bios.htm (December 15, 2002).

Sketch by Eric Lagergren

Kobe Bryant

1978-

American basketball player

One of basketball's biggest talents, Kobe Bryant rose to fame as a guard for the Los Angeles Lakers in the

Kobe Bryant

late 1990s and early 2000s. Together with his superstar teammate, the center **Shaquille O'Neal**, Bryant led the Lakers to their consecutive 2000, 2001, and 2002 National Basketball Association (NBA) Championship titles. One of the NBA's youngest players, the 6-foot-6, 220-pound Bryant caused a stir by skipping college and turning pro just out of high school at age eighteen. By 1998 he made history as basketball's youngest All-Star player, and by the early 2000s sports critics and fans were comparing him to two legendary guards: **Michael Jordan** and **Magic Johnson**. A rap singer as well as a basketball star, Bryant released a single, *K.O.B.E.* (Sony Records), in 2000.

Born in Philadelphia, Pennsylvania, on August 23, 1978, Kobe Bryant was the son of basketball star Joe "Jellybean" Bryant and his wife, Pamela. His parents named their son after a type of steak they had seen on a menu before his birth. When he was five years old, Bryant moved with his family to Italy, where his father played professional basketball after retiring from the NBA. Bryant and his two older sisters, Sharia and Shaya, attended parochial schools in Italy and learned to speak Italian.

From as early as he could remember, Bryant wanted to become a basketball player. With a toy hoop in his living room, he played with his father, an eight-year veteran of the NBA with the 76ers, the Clippers, and the Rockets. Every summer his parents took the family back to Philadelphia, where Bryant played basketball on American playgrounds.

Chronology

1978	Born on August 23 in Philadelphia, PA
1984	Moves with family to Rieti, Italy
1991	Moves back to United States; attends high school in Lower Merion, PA
1996	Leads Lower Merion High School to Class AAAA state championships
1996	Selected by Charlotte Hornets in NBA draft; traded to Los Angeles Lakers
1996	Becomes youngest player to debut in an NBA game
1998	Becomes youngest player to appear in an NBA All-Star game
1999	Signs six-year contract extension with Lakers, valued at about $71 million
2000	Helps Lakers to NBA Championship title
2000	Releases rap single *K.O.B.E.* (Sony Records)
2001	Helps Lakers to second consecutive NBA Championship title
2001	Marries Vanessa Laine
2002	Helps Lakers to third consecutive NBA Championship title

Awards and Accomplishments

1996	National High School Player of the Year (*USA Today* and *Parade* magazine)
1996	Naismith Player of the Year
1996	Gatorade Circle of Champions High School Player of the Year
1996	McDonald's All-America Team member
1996	Youngest player (age 18) to debut in NBA league
1997	Nestle Crunch Slam Dunk competition winner at NBA All-Star Weekend
1997	Set new record with 31 points and 8 rebounds in Schick Rookie Game
1998	Youngest player to appear in an NBA All-Star game
1998-99	Only Lakers' player to start all 50 games
1998-99	All-NBA Third Team
1999-2000	All-NBA Second Team; NBA All-Defensive First Team; NBA All-Interview Second Team
2001-02	All-NBA First Team; All-Defensive Second Team
2002	MVP of 2002 All-Star Game

At age fourteen, upon his father's retirement from the European leagues, Bryant moved with his family back to the United States. When he started the eighth grade at a Philadelphia school, he could not understand his peers' slang. "The way I was able to make friends is that we played basketball during lunch and after school, and basketball's a universal language," Bryant told Charlie Rose of CBS-TV's *60 Minutes II*.

Went Pro after High School

At Lower Merion High School, Bryant became a basketball star, breaking records and collecting trophies and honors. As a senior he was voted National High School Player of the Year by *USA Today* and *Parade* magazine. He had helped his team win a Class AAAA state title, and had ended his high school career with a total of 2,883 points—more than any other player in the history of Southeastern Pennsylvania, which had produced such NBA greats as **Wilt Chamberlain** and Carlin Warley. Bryant also boasted a record-breaking average of 30.8 points, 12 rebounds, 6.5 assists, 4.0 steals, and 3.8 blocked shots per game.

In an unusual move, Bryant skipped college and went directly into a career as a professional basketball player. Picked 13th overall in the 1996 NBA draft, Bryant was originally selected by the Charlotte Hornets. Yet before the season began he was traded to the Los Angeles Lakers in exchange for the center Vlade Divac. At eighteen years, two months, and eleven days old, he became the youngest player ever to make an NBA debut. Donning a number 8 on his uniform, he appeared in his first game against the Minnesota Timberwolves on November 3, 1996.

Bryant made his first career start on January 28, 1997, scoring twelve points in a game against the Dallas Mavericks. In 1997's Schick Rookie Game, Bryant set a new record with a top score of thirty-one points and eight rebounds. Participating in that year's NBA All-Star

Related Biography: Basketball Player Joe "Jellybean" Bryant

Born c. 1955, Joe "Jellybean" Bryant excelled in basketball as a high school student in his native Philadelphia. He went on to play college basketball at La Salle University, making First Team honors in the 1974-75 season. In his junior year, Bryant left La Salle to join the NBA, where he played for eight seasons. As a journeyman forward, he averaged 8.7 points per game in 606 career NBA games with the Philadelphia 76ers, Los Angeles Clippers, and Houston Rockets. In 1984, retiring from the NBA, Bryant moved to Rieti, Italy, where he would play professional basketball in the Italian league. He later played in Switzerland and France as well, taking his family with him. Bryant returned to the United States after eight years in Europe, and later took a job as an assistant coach at La Salle. He remains very close to his son, Kobe. "He's always been there for me," Kobe told Dick Weiss of the New York *Daily News* in 1996. "We can talk about anything. I love him to death."

Weekend in Cleveland, he won the Nestle Crunch Slam Dunk Competition. Averaging 7.6 points per game and 15.5 minutes per game in seventy-one games during his debut season, Bryant was named to the 1996-97 NBA All-Rookie Second Team. Already sports critics were focusing in on the young player.

Bryant doubled his points-per-game in his sophomore season, ending with an average of 15.4 in seventy-nine games. He started only one game with the Lakers that season, scoring seventeen points and four rebounds against the Portland Trail Blazers in February. Voted a starter in the 1998 All-Star Game, Bryant made history as the youngest NBA All-Star player. In that year's All-Star Game in New York, he led his team with eighteen points and six rebounds.

By the 1998-99 season, Bryant was regarded as one of the sport's most promising rising stars. He was the only Lakers player to start all fifty games, and was the team's second-highest scorer with 19.9 points per game. Leading the Lakers in steals (1.44 per game), Bryant was chosen for the 1998-99 All-NBA Third Team. In January of 1999, he signed a six-year contract

Career Statistics

Yr	Team	GP	PPG	FG%	3P%	FT%	RPG	APG	SPG	BPG	TO	PF
1997	LAL	71	7.6	.417	.375	.819	1.9	1.3	.69	.32	1.58	1.4
1998	LAL	79	15.4	.428	.341	.794	3.1	2.5	.94	.51	1.99	2.3
1999	LAL	50	19.9	.465	.267	.839	5.3	3.8	1.44	1.0	3.14	3.1
2000	LAL	66	22.5	.468	.319	.821	6.3	4.9	1.61	.94	2.76	3.3
2001	LAL	68	28.5	.464	.305	.853	5.9	5.0	1.68	.63	3.24	2.9
2002	LAL	80	25.2	.469	.250	.829	5.5	5.5	1.48	.44	2.79	2.7
TOTAL		414	19.85	.452	.309	.826	4.7	3.8	1.31	.64	2.58	2.6

LAL: Los Angeles Lakers.

extension with the Lakers, believed to be worth about $71 million.

The next season, in a game against the Sacramento Kings on March 3, 2000, Bryant netted a career-high of forty points, with ten rebounds and four assists. That year would be a turning point for the Los Angeles team, which, with the help of Bryant and his powerhouse teammate Shaquille O'Neal, would take the NBA Championship title.

Became a Team Player

While praise abounded for the young player, Bryant did receive his share of criticism on one account: he was regarded by many as a "selfish" player. Perceived as a loner, Bryant rarely socialized with his party-going teammates, preferring to work out and study game tapes. Some sports writers pointed to his tendency to strive for individual distinctions rather than for team victories. And many journalists criticized Bryant in particular for often wresting control of the game from the Lakers' biggest star, O'Neal, the 7-foot-1, 330-pound center known affectionately as "Shaq." In these instances, the Lakers nearly always lost.

The end of the 1999-2000 season heralded a change in Bryant's attitude. When he jumped into Shaq's arms upon the Lakers' championship victory over the Indiana Pacers, the media took notice, pointing to a new camaraderie between the star players. Bryant's new emphasis on teamwork helped the Lakers to dominate the game throughout the early 2000s. Once considered Shaq's inferior, Bryant was beginning to rise to the superstar's level.

Another change arrived simultaneously: In 2000 the 21-year-old player became engaged. He had met 18-year-old Vanessa Laine a year earlier at a music-video shoot where she was working as a background dancer. Laine was still in high school when she and Bryant became engaged, and the media scoffed the pair for being too young to marry. "You just try to forget [the criticism] and enjoy the moment," Bryant told Karen Crouse of the *Palm Beach Post*. "I'm very fortunate to have found my life mate at such an early age." The couple married in 2001, just before the playoffs began.

Meanwhile the Lakers continued to lead the NBA. In the 2000-01 season, Bryant averaged 28.5 points per game. In the 2001 finals against the Philadelphia 76ers, he averaged 24.6 points and 5.8 assists per game in five playoff matches, helping to lift the Lakers to another championship victory. The sports media focused in on Bryant and Shaq as the NBA's most powerful duo.

The pair helped the Lakers to their third consecutive championship in 2001-02, when the team defended its title against the New Jersey Nets. In January of 2002, Bryant scored a career high of fifty-six points against the Memphis Grizzlies. He ended the season with averages of 25.5 points, 5.5 rebounds, and 5.5 assists per game, and was selected to the 2001-02 All-NBA First Team and the All-Defensive Second Team. In the 2002 All-Star Game, Bryant received Most Valuable Player distinction, netting thirty-one points, five rebounds, and five assists.

By age twenty-four, Bryant had surpassed the talents of many basketball players in the peaks of their careers. While it is likely that he has many more years ahead of him in the NBA, sports writers cannot predict when Bryant's own peak will come and go. But most agree that the Philadelphia native is destined to become one of basketball's great legends.

FURTHER INFORMATION

Periodicals

Crouse, Karen. "Bryant: 'We've Come a Long Way' on and off Court." *Palm Beach Post* (April 7, 2002): 1B.

Moore, David Leon. "Bryant Comes of Age." *USA Today* (June 6, 2001): 1A.

Weiss, Dick. "Pride of the Family." *Daily News* (New York; May 5, 1996): E1.

Other

60 Minutes II, CBS News Transcripts, May 29, 2001.

"Kobe Bryant." AskMen.com. http://www.askmen.com/
men/sports/33c_kobe_bryant.html (December 2,
2002).

"Kobe Bryant." CNN/Sports Illustrated Online. http://
sportsillustrated.cnn.com/basketball/nba/features/
2000/kobe_bryant/kobe_timeline (December 3, 2002).

"Kobe Bryant." NBA.com. http://www.nba.com/
playerfile/kobe_bryant/printable_player_files.html
(December 2, 2002).

Sketch by Wendy Kagan

Sergei Bubka
1963-

Ukrainian pole vaulter

In his 18-year career, pole vaulter Sergei Bubka set the world record 35 times, won gold medals at six consecutive world championships, and won an Olympic gold medal in Seoul in 1988. He is widely considered to be the greatest pole vaulter in history, and is the only person ever to clear a bar 20 feet overhead.

"One of Athletics' Most Anticipated Events"

Bubka was born to a working-class family in Voroshilovgrad in what was then the Soviet Union in 1963. His father, Nazar, was a member of the Soviet Army, and expected military-style discipline from Bubka and his brother, Vasily. Bubka's mother, Valentina, worked in a hospital.

Bubka's first exposure to pole vaulting came when he was nine years old; a friend invited him to join a vaulting club. Coaches there noted that he had talent, and he soon began training with coach Vitaly Petrov. Although Bubka's father tried to force him to quit, he continued to train.

Bubka's parents divorced when he was 15, and he went to live with Vasily in a factory dormitory in Donetsk, a manufacturing city. In Donetsk, Bubka continued to train with Petrov and went to school. In 1983, Bubka won his first world championship, beginning a long reign as the best in the sport. Before he entered the field, pole vaulting was a relatively obscure sport, like many other field events, and was rarely broadcast or publicized. However, according to Kevin B. Blackistone in the *Knight Ridder/Tribune News Service,* Bubka "transformed the pole vault into one of athletics' most anticipated events.... a raucous, hand-clapping, crowd-energizing event."

Blackistone noted that at a meet in London in 1984, the bar was set at 18-8. Bubka soared over it by a foot

Sergei Bubka

and a half. It was moved to 19-4. Bubka cleared it by eight inches. Polish vaulter Tadeusz Slusarski, who had won an Olympic gold medal in 1976 and a silver in 1980, watched this and predicted to American vaulter Larry Jessee that they were seeing the beginning of a great athletic career. Bubka had arrived, and no one could beat him.

At the Seoul Olympics in 1988, Bubka won a gold medal in the pole vaulting event. Bubka went to the Olympics again in 1992, at the Barcelona Games, but did not clear a single bar in the final competition. On his first try, he went under the bar, and on his second, he knocked it over. He passed on his third try, gaining time to get himself together. On his fourth try, knowing it was his last chance, he tested the wind and changed poles when he felt a gust. However, when he started down the runway, he felt the wind die: he had chosen the wrong pole. On the way up, his shins slammed into the bar: he had just lost his Olympic chance.

In May of 1996, Bubka traveled to Brazil to compete, inadvertently setting off a chain of events that may have prevented the city of Rio de Janeiro from making a successful bid to host the Olympics in 2004. As he entered Brazil, suspicious customs officials sawed his poles in half, saying that they might contain smuggled items. The poles did not, but they were ruined, and Bubka had to compete in a Rio de Janeiro meet using borrowed equipment. Embarrassed Brazilian officials apologized, according to a report in the Adelaide, Australia *Advertiser.*

Chronology

1963	Born in Voroshilovgrad, Soviet Union
1972	Begins pole vaulting
1978	Parents divorce; moves to Donetsk with his brother; continues to train
1983	Wins the first of six consecutive world championships in pole vaulting; other wins occur in 1987, 1991, 1993, 1995, and 1997
1988	Wins gold medal at Seoul Olympics
1992	Competes in Barcelona Olympics
1996	Misses Atlanta Olympics due to injury
2000	Competes in Sydney Olympics
2001	Retires from competition; becomes member of Ukraine Parliament

Awards and Accomplishments

1983, 1987, 1991, 1993, 1995, 1997	World Champion, pole vault
1988	Gold medal, Olympic Games

"The Olympic Games Are Not Meant for Me"

In July of 1996 Bubka was scheduled to compete in the Atlanta Olympic Games, but was forced out by an injury to his right Achilles tendon. Of his inability to compete in Atlanta, he told Duncan Mackay Athens in the London *Observer,* "That was a sad day in my career. I wanted to win in Atlanta because I have only one Olympic gold medal and I wanted one more." He told Ian O'Connor in the *Knight Ridder/Tribune News Service* that his injury, which began in April of 1996, "is proof that the Olympic Games are not meant for me." He took time off from training for surgery on his Achilles tendon, not returning to his sport until the summer of 1997.

At the world championships in 1997, Bubka was taken aback when Russian athlete Maksim Tarasove cleared 5.69 meters. Bubka, taking a risk, did not even try to jump that height, but had the bar raised to 6.01 meters, a height only he and two other athletes had ever cleared. It was a dangerous bluff: if he failed, he would lose. The 80,000 spectators waited tensely as he sprinted down the runway, planted his pole, and flew over the bar, winning the gold medal and setting a new championship record.

In 1998, Bubka underwent surgery on his Achilles tendon, which had bothered him for some time. By the following year he was still recovering from the surgery, and did not participate in that year's world championships. Although he was able to swim in order to retain his fitness, he could not put weight on his foot without agonizing pain, his manager Andrzej Kulikovsky told a reporter for the Adelaide, Australia *Advertiser.*

In 2000, Bubka was reluctant to participate in the pole-vaulting competition in the Olympics in Sydney, Australia, because of the strong and unpredictable winds. According to a report in the Adelaide, Australia *Advertiser,* Bubka predicted that the competition would be "a nightmare" and that the winner would be "whoever lives."

Bubka didn't enter the qualifying round until the competition had already been underway for three hours, and he missed all three tries at his opening height of 5.7 meters. He failed to qualify for the Olympic final, and did not compete.

"Bubka Does Not Jump, He Flies"

Belarussian pole vaulter Dmitriy Markov told Warren Partland in the Adelaide, Australia *Advertiser,* "Bubka does not jump, he flies. Everyone else jumps but if you want to match him you must be prepared to fly." A risk-taker, Bubka used poles that some thought were too large for him in his quest for greater and greater height. He made his run dramatically, bending his pole and soaring over the bar with spectacular style.

Part of Bubka's success at breaking the world record so many times was his tactic of raising the bar by a tiny amount each time, setting new world records in one-centimeter increments. Each time he set a record, he received bonuses, endorsements, and appearance fees, so this tactic earned him a great deal of money as well as more notoriety than anyone had ever enjoyed in his previously obscure sport. O'Connor noted that each time he broke a record, Bubka received $40,000 from the Nike company, and commented, "Bubka is no fool. He doesn't smash his own records, but nibbles at them, replacing them a fraction at a time. Since taking the Nike deal, Bubka has taken 15 nibbles, good for a $600,000 bonus." Although some observers criticized Bubka as calculating and mercenary, Blackistone noted that Bubka was simply doing what star athletes in most other sports did: "Set records. Earn bonuses. Garner greater appearance fees for the next big meet." And, Blackistone wrote, "Bubka just proved that a pole vaulter could do the same if he was as spectacular and spell-binding in his performance."

Bubka lived the high life, buying expensive cars and moving to a $2 million apartment in Monte Carlo. His riches were noted by members of the Russian mafia, which issued death threats and threats to kidnap him if he did not hand over some of the money. As a result, since the mid-1990s he has traveled with a bodyguard.

Retires from Competition

In February of 2001, at age 37, Bubka retired from competition. At a lavish party in his hometown of Donetsk, he thanked the crowd of 6,000 of his home fans for supporting him. After retiring, he continued to teach at a pole-vaulting school he founded in Ukraine, and served as the Ukrainian representative to the International Olympic Committee. American vaulter Jeff Hartwig told

Blackistone, "The sport will certainly miss Sergei. For years, we'll always be measured by what he did."

FURTHER INFORMATION

Periodicals

Athens, Duncan Mackay, "Thirty-Five World Records at Dollars 100,000 a Time. No Wonder the Russian Mafia Wants a Piece of the Action," *Observer* (London, England), (August 10, 1997): 13.

Blackistone, Kevin B., "Bubka Raised Bar High, and Few Cleared," *Knight Ridder/Tribune News Service,* (February 8, 2001): K1836.

"Bubka Has Poles Cut by Customs Officers," *Advertiser* (Adelaide, Australia), (May 9, 1996): 28.

"Bubka in a Breeze," *Advertiser* (Adelaide, Australia), (September 15, 2000): 26.

"Bubka Out of World Championships," *Birmingham Evening Mail* (Birmingham, England), (August 10, 1999): 44.

"Bubka's World Title Agony," *Advertiser* (Adelaide, Australia), (August 13, 1999): 84.

"Grand End for Bubka," *Advertiser* (Adelaide, Australia), (February 6, 2001): 69.

Mackay, Duncan, "Athletics: World Championships: There's Only One Bubka," *Guardian* (London, England), (August 11, 1997): 6.

Mackay, Duncan, "Olympic Games: Pole Vault: Bubka Bows Out Without a Vault and Brits Fails Too," *Guardian* (London, England), (August 1, 1996): 24.

O'Connor, Ian, "Sergei Bubka Denied a Chance at Olympic Gold," *Knight Ridder/Tribune News Service,* (July 31, 1996): 731K1297.

"Olympic Games: Athletics: Bubka Shock," *Birmingham Evening Mail* (Birmingham, England), (September 27, 2000): 93.

Partland, Warren, "Markov Aims for Stars," *Advertiser* (Adelaide, Australia), (March 5, 1998): 96.

Other

"Bubka and Son ... Poles Apart," *The Age,* January 21, 2003, http://www.theage.com.au/ (January 27, 2003).

Sketch by Kelly Winters

Don Budge
1915-

American tennis player

Don Budge dominated the world of tennis throughout most of his career. His lightning quick return and

Don Budge

flawless backhand made him nearly unbeatable at his prime. Yet he will forever be known for two crowning achievements: completing the first ever "Grand Slam" in 1938 by winning at Wimbledon, the U.S., French and Australian national championships, and his victory in what many call the most exciting Davis Cup match in history.

Baseball leads to Tennis

Sports were a family affair in the Budge home. Budge's father was a professional soccer player in Scotland. Suffering from respiratory problems he settled in California hoping the warmer climate would help his condition. John Donald Budge was born in California on June 13, 1915 and took to sports at a young age. While his older brother, Lloyd, excelled at tennis, Don chose baseball as his primary pursuit. Ironically, some attribute his early experience with baseball as key to his tennis success. "From the very first, Don's money-stroke was his backhand which grew directly out of his almost-perfect, left-handed batting swings," wrote E. Digby Baltzell in his book *Sporting Gentlemen.*

After honing his skills on the hard public courts of California, Budge entered the state's Fifteen-and-Under Championships just before his fifteenth birthday. At the tournament, he met Perry T. Jones, a prominent coach. Beating the top contender in the first round, Budge looked to Jones awaiting a compliment. What he received instead left a mark on him for his entire career. "With a distinct frown, he looked me up and down," Budge told

Chronology

1928	Begins to play tennis
1930	Enters and wins California State Fifteen-and-Under Championship
1933	Wins National Junior's Championship
1937	Ranked number-one amateur player in the world
1937	First man to win Wimbledon's men's singles, men's doubles, and mixed doubles
1937	Leads U.S. team to victory Davis Cup after breaking an 11 year losing streak
1938	Wins the sport's first "Grand Slam"
1939	Becomes pro
1940, 1942	Wins U.S. Professional Title
1942	Joins Air Force
1946-47, 1949, 1953	Plays and loses in U.S. Professional Finals
1953	Retires from professional tennis
1964	Voted into the Tennis Hall of Fame

Baltzell years later. "These are the dirtiest tennis shoes I ever saw in my life. Don't you ever-don't you ever-show up again on any court anywhere wearing shoes like that. I know he made an impression on me, for I've never gone on court since that day with scruffy shoes." Dirty footwear aside, Budge went on to win the tournament.

The early victory encouraged him to put aside baseball and dream of tennis success. At the age of 18 he won the National Junior Championships by beating Gene Mako, the top contender, in the fifth set, rallying from a two set deficit. Budge and Mako became life long friends and went on to make a formidable doubles team, winning the doubles at Wimbledon in 1937 and both the U.S. and Wimbledon doubles in 1938.

Budge enrolled at the University of California at Berkeley but quickly withdrew during his first year to play the Emerson Grass Court Circuit as part of an auxiliary Davis Cup Team. After losing in the fourth round at Forest Hills he was ranked in the top ten U.S. players.

Honing His Skills

Budge clearly showed early prowess, but his technique was unrefined. Frank Perry, the celebrated tennis great, called Budge's undisciplined grip style a "Wild Western" grip and took the young player under his wing to coach him. Budge also worked on his game under Coach Tom Stowe, who focused on changing his grip to an "Eastern" grip and improving his volley.

By the following spring his technique was beginning to match his imposing physical strength. Frank V. Phelps wrote in *The Biographical Dictionary of American Sports*, "Budge exhibited power, consistency, and no weaknesses at his peak. He devastated opponents by serving and smashing with a slight slice, stroke-volleying deep and hard, and driving hard with minor over spin."

Budge surprised the tennis world at Wimbledon in 1935 by beating the heavily favored Bunny Adams and advancing to a semifinal match against the renowned Baron Gottfried Von Cramm. Von Cramm won the match and so impressed Budge with his courteous manners and steadfast morals that the two became fast friends. The following year, Budge lost at Wimbledon and at the U.S. Nationals to Fred Perry, the number one ranked amateur. He tenaciously hung to the very end at the Forrest Hills match finally losing in 5 sets, including a 10-8 fifth set.

Imposing at 6-foot-1, 160 pounds, the red-haired Budge brought awesome power to bear on his opponents, but ultimately it was his drive to improve his game that made him a champion. Alan Transgrove remarked in *The Story of the Davis Cup*, "Don Budge's greatness was as much the result of his eagerness to learn and adjust his technique as to his natural talent." Indeed, in January of 1937, when he was already an accomplished player, Budge made a crucial adjustment to his game that paved the way for his incredible domination of the sport. While umpiring a match between two world-class players, he observed that one of the players hit the ball quite hard while his opponent hit very early while the ball was just inches off the ground. The unbeatable combination, Budge mused, would be a player that could hit the ball both hard and early. Working with Coach Stowe, he put his theory into practice.

A Historic Davis Cup Match

When Fred Perry turned pro in 1937, Budge became No. 1 in the amateur ranks. Armed with his newly developed hard and early stroke, the 22 year-old had perhaps the best month in tennis history. He dominated Wimbledon in 1937 becoming the first man to win the men's singles, men's doubles, and mixed doubles (playing with Gene Mako and Alice Marbles.) Along the way, he beat his friend and rival Von Cramm in three straight sets.

Just a couple of weeks later, at the Davis Cup, the rivalry with Von Cramm produced one of the most storied matches in tennis history. Needing a win to guarantee the U.S. a spot in the challenge round, Budge stepped onto the court the underdog. He lost the first two sets, came back for the next two and finally won the fifth set 8-6. Queen Mary of England was in attendance and so many Americans watched the match that activity on Wall Street slowed down. The match even attracted the attention of German dictator Adolph Hitler who listened intently to the radio broadcast.

Budge called it "the greatest match in which I ever played. It was competitive, long and close. It was fought hard but cleanly by two close friends. It was cast with the ultimate in rivals, the number-one ranked amateur player in the world and against the number two. I never played better and never played anyone as good as Cramm." Allison Danzig later wrote in the book *Budge on Tennis*, "The brilliance of the tennis was almost unbelievable. In game after game they sustained their amazing virtuosity without the slightest deviation or faltering on either side. Gradually, inch by inch, Budge picked up."

After that match, the following weekend's Challenge Round against England almost came as an after thought. Budge won three matches, ushering the U.S. to victory in the Davis Cup for the first time since 1926.

For his achievements that year, Budge won the Sullivan Award for most outstanding amateur athlete and was named Associated Press Athlete of the Year. "Playing tennis against him was like playing against a concrete wall," said Sidney Wood, a player who often faced Budge in competition, "There was nothing to attack."

Won the Grand Slam

The time was ripe to turn professional. Budge was at the top of the sport and could command the highest fees. Yet he turned down the professional offers to defend the Davis Cup for the U.S. team one more time. Few could expect that in 1938 he would turn in an even more spectacular performance than the previous year.

That year Budge demolished every obstacle in his way to win the first ever tennis Grand Slam. At the Australian competition he lost only one set the entire tournament and handily beat John Bramwich 6-4, 6-2, 6-1 at the final. Budge was just as unstoppable in the French championship only dropping three sets and defeating Roderich Menzel of Czechoslovakia 6-3, 6-2, 6-4. At Wimbledon Budge won every set he played, routing Bunny Austin of Britain, 6-1, 6-0, 6-3 for the championship.

Six days of rain pushed the final match of the U.S. championship back to September 24. But neither weather nor his friend Gene Mako could deter Budge. He took the first set 6-3 before losing his first set of the competition 6-8. Then he came back to flatten Mako 6-2, 6-1 and complete the Grand Slam.

After the historic sweep of the Australian, French, Wimbledon and U.S. championships Budge led the U.S. to victory in the Davis Cup over Australia, overpowering Adrian Quist and Bramwhich. He posted a 42-2 record in 1938, capturing six of eight tournaments. From January of 1937, Budge won an amazing 92 consecutive matches until Adrian Quist finally broke the winning streak in late 1938. Again, Budge was named best athlete of the year by the Associated Press.

The Professional Years

Ranked the number one amateur in 1937-38, Budge finally turned professional in 1939 after having spent four years in the world top ten and, five years in the U.S. top ten. In his professional debut at Madison Square Garden in New York, Budge beat Ellsworth 6-3, 6-4, 6-2 while 16,725 fans watched. On the professional tour, he beat Vines 21 to 18 matches and went 18 to 11 against his former coach, the celebrated Fred Perry. The flamboyant **Bill Tilden**, a formidable player in earlier years, joined the tour in 1941, but he was well past his prime at 48 years old and Budge handily beat him, 51-7.

Related Biography: Tennis Player Gottfried Von Cramm

Gottfried Von Cramm, born on July 7, 1908, in Nettlingen, Hanover, Germany, into an aristocratic family, was one of the world's premier tennis players. Known on the court as "The Baron" for his good looks and courtesy, he won the French Cup in 1934 and 1936. Von Cramm played a total of 111 Davis Cup matches and won six German titles, the last of which, in 1948, at the age of 40.

With his tall Aryan good looks and his record as a champion, Von Cramm would have been an ideal standard bearer for the Nazi party. However, he made the courageous choice not to endorse Nazism during World War II.

Von Cramm never won at Wimbledon. In 1935 and 1936 he was runner-up to Fred Perry and in 1937 Don Budge bested him. He and Budge enjoyed a friendship and on-court rivalry that spanned many years and included the historic Davis Cup match of 1937.

Due to his defiance of the Nazi party Von Cramm was accused of homosexuality and spent most of 1938 in prison. Budge appealed to other professional athletes, gathering 25 signatures in protest.

Upon his release in May of 1939, the management of both Wimbledon and the Queens Tournament refused to allow Von Cramm to compete, being that he was a player recently released from prison and surrounded by the stigma of homosexuality. Finally, he was permitted to play and won the Queens Tournament, beating the man who would eventually win at Wimbledon. Many believe that had he been allowed to play he might have won Wimbledon.

After the war, Von Cramm began a successful cotton import business, in his native Hanover, and served as president of the Lawn Tennis Rot-Weiss in Berlin. He died in a car accident in Cairo, Egypt, in November of 1975 and was inducted into the Tennis Hall of Fame the next year.

Budge won the U.S. pro title in 1940 defeating Perry 6-2, 5-7, 6-4, 6-3 and again in 1942 over Bobby Riggs, 6-2, 6-2, 6-2. In 1942 he left the pro tour to join the Air Force. After the war, Budge's performance was affected by a shoulder injury suffered while in military training. Nevertheless, he made it to the U.S. professional finals in 1946, '47, '49, and '53, losing the first three matches to Riggs and the last to 25 year-old **Pancho Gonzalez**. Budge retired in 1938 and in 1964 he was inducted into the Tennis Hall of Fame.

Budge will forever be remembered as the first man to win all four major tennis championships completing the first ever tennis Grand Slam in 1937. However, those who watched him play or faced him in competition hold him in an even higher regard. Fred V. Phelps recapped Budge's career in the *Biographical Dictionary of American Sports* by writing, "Many experts have called this popular, skilled sportsman the greatest player since [Bill] Tillden, and some have ranked him the greatest. " Apparently, Tillden himself was among the latter group, calling Budge "the finest player 365 days a year who ever lived."

FURTHER INFORMATION

Books

"Don Budge." *Encyclopedia of World Biography* Supplement, Vol. 21.

Awards and Accomplishments

1936, 1938	U.S. doubles champion
1937	Sullivan Award For most outstanding amateur athlete
1937	Associated Press Athlete Of The Year
1937, 1938	Wimbledon singles, doubles and mixed doubles champion
1937, 1938	U.S. singles and mixed doubles champion
1938	Australian singles champion
1938	French singles champion
1938	Associated Press Athlete Of The Year
1964	Inducted into International Tennis Hall of Fame

Other

BBC Sport. http://www.bbc.com/sport/tennis : French Open (May 23, 2002).

"Don Budge. Class of 1964." International Tennis Hall of Fame http://www.tennisfame.com/ (2002): .

"Gottfried Von Cramm Class of 1977." International Tennis Hall of Fame. http://www.tennisfame.com/ (October 30, 2002).

Les heros du grand chelem. http://www.histoiredutennis.com/Lalegende du grand chelem/ (April 25, 2001).

Schwartz, Larry. "In Big Matches, He Wouldn't Budge." ESPN.com. http://www.espn.com/ (October 30, 2002).

"Tennis great Don Budge Dead at 84." CNN/Sports Illustrated. http://www.cnnsi.com/ (January 26, 2000):.

Sketch by Mike Pare

Susan Butcher

Susan Butcher
1954-

American dogsledder

Sled-dog racer Susan Butcher's aversion to civilization and love of dogs drew her from Boston to Alaska when she was twenty years old. The former city girl embraced the Alaskan wilderness, and tested herself against it, as she learned the art of mushing, or driving a sled led by a team of three to twenty dogs. She became one of only two people to win the Iditarod Trail Dog Sled Race four times, and was the first to win three in a row.

Loved Animals, Hated the City

Butcher was born December 26, 1954, in Cambridge, Massachusetts, a college town near Boston. She is the youngest of two daughters of Charles, a chairman of his family's chemical company, and Agnes Butcher, a psychiatric social worker. Both parents were progressive thinkers who encouraged their daughters to achieve whatever they set their hearts on, and to be self-sufficient. Charles bought his daughters carpentry tools and taught them basic building skills. He spent years with his daughters teaching them to sail and trying to restore an old sailboat. Early on, the urban bustle of Cambridge did not agree with Susan Butcher, who began a school essay with "I hate the city" when she was eight. She always preferred animals and nature. Her Labrador dog, Cabee, was her best friend.

Butcher's parents divorced when she was eleven, and her world was torn apart. She and her sister remained with their mother, but the situation was rocky and both girls left home in their teens. Butcher also was diagnosed with dyslexia, a learning disability, which explained her struggles in school. She was a natural at sports, and played softball, basketball, field hockey, and loved to swim and row. She excelled at math and science and, with the help of a tutor, she made it through her English classes. Cabee died when she was fifteen, and her aunt gave Butcher a husky, Manganak. It was love at first sight, and she soon got a second dog.

After high school, Butcher and her dogs left for Colorado, where her father and stepmother lived. She found work for a woman who bred and raced sled dogs, and borrowed her dogs to learn how to mush. She quickly learned the important voice commands—like "all right" for "go," "gee" for "turn right," and "haw" for "turn left"—and found she had the physical endurance necessary to thrive in the sport, and found she was good at it.

Began Preparing for the Iditarod

The first Iditarod Trail Sled Dog Race was run in 1973 in Alaska, and when she read about it in a dog-mushing magazine, Butcher knew Alaska is where she wanted to be. At age twenty, Butcher found work in Alaskan canneries and as a veterinary technician. She bought three husky puppies and added to her pack whenever she had a little extra money. To learn self-reliance, she went into the Alaskan wilderness with her dogs and lived in a small cabin with no electricity or plumbing. Fifty miles from the nearest road, she brought all her supplies in with her and killed a moose or caribou to feed herself and her dogs. In the wild, dogs live in packs, with one "alpha" or leader dog. Butcher is extraordinary in care and training of her dogs and bonds with each of them, becoming in essence their alpha dog.

On the way across the wilderness to a friend's house for Thanksgiving dinner, Butcher fell into icy water while mushing her team of twelve dogs. She and the dogs survived -25-degree temperatures because Butcher found a cabin and tore up the floor to use for firewood. They arrived to dinner a day late. After three winters in the Wrangell Mountains, Butcher traveled to Knik, Alaska, to meet Joe Redington, the man who started the Iditarod. She worked for him, training his young dogs, and learned from a master. When Redington predicted Butcher would one day win the Iditarod, the men who heard him laughed. For practice, Butcher entered shorter mushing races like the Kobuk 220, the Norton Sound 250, Kusko 300, the Coldfoot Classic, the John Beargrease race, and the Yukon Quest International Sled Dog Race. She set records in many of them.

Butcher entered her first Iditarod in March 1978, at age twenty-three. The race starts in Anchorage, and travels 1,049 miles across the Alaskan tundra, forests, sea ice, and tiny communities to finish in Nome, usually in eleven to thirty-two days. Teams stop at dozens of checkpoints, and dogs typically get more rest than mushers on the trail. Each dog requires 8,000 calories a day, and Butcher cooked rich meals of beef, beaver, liver, fish, bacon, and seal blubber for them over a campfire. After a grueling sixteen days, Butcher crossed the finish line in Nome in 19th place. She used her $600 prize money to buy another dog, Granite. Butcher finished the 1979 Iditarod in ninth place, one spot ahead of her mentor, Joe Redington. Butcher worked cannery jobs to support her dogs, and went into debt to feed and care for them, even when she was forced to sleep in her car. Butcher finished fifth in both the 1980 and 1981 Iditarods.

A Dangerous Run-in With a Moose

Butcher met David Monson after she charged $6,000 worth of dog food with him that she thought she could pay for, but couldn't. The two were married in 1985, with Monson moving 100 miles south of the Arctic Circle to Eureka, Alaska, to live with Butcher at her Trail Breaker Kennels, where she bred and kept over 100 huskies. Butcher loves every aspect of dog breeding, from giving them affection to tending to their veterinary care herself. Too far from a vet, she gives shots, draws blood, and births her own dogs. She trains them daily to run in teams and pull a nearly 500-pound load up to seventy miles.

More than sixty mushers and 1,000 dogs started the 1982 Iditarod. An hour into the race, Butcher's fifteen-dog team—led by Granite—slid off the trail into a tree, injuring three dogs. A violent snowstorm followed and Butcher strayed ten miles off course in whiteout conditions. She dropped the injured dogs off at a checkpoint and forged ahead in 60- to 80-mph winds. She had to drop two more dogs, and Butcher coaxed her nine-dog team into Nome just three minutes, 43 seconds behind the winner, her friend Rick Swenson.

After finishing ninth in 1983 and second again in 1984, Butcher went into the 1985 feeling at the top of her game. Just after the fifth checkpoint, however, she and her team were charged by a pregnant moose, who

---

Related Biography: Dogsledder Joe Redington

Born in Oklahoma in 1917, Joe Redington is known as the "Father of the Iditarod." He moved to Knik, Alaska in 1948 and made a career of raising sled dogs after receiving one as a gift. He initially used his dogs in military search and recovery missions in Alaska from 1949 to 1957. He founded the Iditarod Trail Dog Sled Race in 1973. The race follows the actual trail that was used in the early 1900's during the gold rush to deliver supplies and mail to mining camps. A 1925 outbreak of diphtheria challenged a group of mushers to a "race against death" to cross Alaska and deliver life-saving medicine to Nome. Redington died of cancer in June 1999. Per his wishes, he was buried in his favorite dogsled in a specially made vault. A life-size, bronze memorial statue of Redington was unveiled in 2003.

---

became tangled in the team's harnesses. The moose killed two dogs and injured thirteen more before another musher shot it. Butcher dropped out of the race.

Four Time Iditarod Celebrity

After a crash early in the race, Butcher was the first to pull into Nome after eleven days on the trail in the 1986 race. She put her $50,000 prize money back into her kennel, which now housed more than 150 dogs. She raises each dog herself and sells them to mushers for $1,000 to $11,000 each—but only if they do not meet standards for her own team. Granite led Butcher's team to the win again in 1987. Her back-to-back win stirred up a furor over men and women competing together. Her longtime friendship with Rick Swenson ended because of it.

Warm temperatures wreaked havoc at the start of the 1988 Iditarod. Butcher spent twenty-four hours repairing her sled with duct tape and a pocket knife after crashing in muddy conditions. She ran next to the sled, which could not carry her, for three days until she could exchange it for another one. Butcher finished the race in first place, despite gale-force winds and cold. She was the first musher to win Iditarod three times in a row. Millions of T-shirts have been sold that read: "Alaska. Where the men are men and women win the Iditarod."

An intestinal virus plagued Butcher's dogs on the 1989 Iditarod trail, and she finished second. She set a course record of eleven days, one hour, fifty-three minutes, and twenty-three seconds to win in 1990. Now, she and her old friend Swenson were the only two mushers to win the race four times. She finished second in 1992, fourth in 1993, and did not place in 1994. She retired from racing to start a family, but her Trail Breaker Kennels remains one of the most respected in mushing.

Butcher's history-making accomplishments made her a celebrity in the lower forty-eight states. She traveled during the summer, giving speeches, signing autographs, and appearing on *Good Morning America, Today,* and the *Tonight Show.* When she took Granite to the White House to meet President George Bush, the dog got his own hotel room, ate beef from a silver platter, and was addressed as "Mr. Granite."

CONTACT INFORMATION

Address: Susan Butcher, Trail Breaker Kennel, P.O. Box 60249, Fairbanks, AK 99706. Email: sbutcher@trailbreaker.alaska.com.

FURTHER INFORMATION

Books

Dolan, Ellen M. *Susan Butcher and the Iditarod Trail.* New York: Walker and Company, 1993.

Johnson, Anne Jeanette. *Great Women in Sports.* Detroit: Visible Ink Press, 1996.

Littlefield, Bill. *Champions.* Boston: Little, Brown, and Company, 1993.

Wadsworth, Ginger. *Susan Butcher: Sled Dog Racer.* Lerner Publications, 1994.

Sketch by Brenna Sanchez

Dick Butkus
1942-

American football player

Dick Butkus, in his nine seasons as a linebacker for the Chicago Bears of the National Football League (NFL), came to epitomize his position, team and community. His on-field meanness and loyalty to his team and native city reflected football of the 1960s. Butkus was elected to the pro and college football Halls of Fame, and the award for the top college linebacker in the United States bears his name. High school and college linebacking standouts are known to wear Butkus's pro number (51), which the Bears retired.

"More than a quarter of a century after his retirement, there remains the Butkus image: the middle linebacker wrapping up a running back and viciously slamming him to the ground like an unwanted toy," Larry Schwartz wrote on the *ESPN Classic* web site. "If I had a choice," said MacArthur Lane, a running back for the rival Green Bay Packers, "I'd rather go one-on-one with a grizzly bear. I pray that I can get up every time Butkus hits me."

Yearned for Football Career

Butkus, who grew up with his blue-collar, Lithuanian family on the South Side of Chicago, wanted to play pro football by the fifth grade. He traveled out of the way to attend Chicago Vocational High School because its football coach, Bernie O'Brien, was a University of Notre Dame graduate. He was an all-state fullback on offense

Chronology

1942	Born December 9 in Chicago, Illinois
1962-64	Two-time All-America in three seasons at the University of Illinois.
1964	Helps lead Illinois to 17-7 Rose Bowl victory over the University of Washington.
1965	Chicago Bears of National Football League draft him in first round (third overall); Denver Broncos of American Football League also draft him in second round. Butkus signs with Bears.
1965	Makes 11 unassisted tackles in NFL debut against San Francisco 49ers.
1970	Panel of NFL coaches vote Butkus as player they would start with if they were building a team from scratch.
1973	Retires as player; was named all-NFL in seven of nine seasons and played in eight Pro Bowls
1974	Sues Chicago Bears, alleging mistreatment of his knee injury; eventually settles out of court for $600,000
1997	Undergoes knee reconstruction surgery
2002	San Diego Chargers sign Butkus's nephew, Luke, who also played at the University of Illinois

Dick Butkus

and downright nasty on defense. "He learned to strip the ball from runners while making a tackle, an art that served him well in the pros," Larry Schwartz wrote for the *ESPN.com* Web site.

Enamored as Butkus was with Notre Dame, however, he opted instead for the University of Illinois. Notre Dame at the time banned married players, and he was considering marriage to his high school sweetheart, whom he eventually married. In Illinois, Butkus saw an up-and-coming program run by new coach Pete Elliott. Butkus made clear why he was at Illinois. "If I was smart enough to be a doctor, I'd be a doctor," he said. "I ain't, so I'm a football player. They got me in P.E. (physical education)."

All-American at Illinois

Butkus made first-team All-America his final two college seasons. In 1963, he made 145 tackles and forced ten fumbles as Illinois won the Big Ten championship and earned a No. 3 ranking nationally after a 17-7 victory over Washington in the Rose Bowl. In 1964, the National Football Coaches Association honored Butkus as the best player in the country; Butkus also finished third in the voting for the prestigious Heisman Trophy.

"If every college football team had a linebacker like Dick Butkus, all fullbacks would soon be three feet tall and sing soprano," Dan Jenkins wrote in *Sports Illustrated.* "Dick Butkus is a special kind of brute whose particular talent is mashing runners into curious shapes."

The Bears, selecting third, took Butkus in the first round of the 1965 National Football League draft while the Denver Broncos of the upstart American Football League made Butkus their second pick. (The AFL and NFL merged a few years later). Playing in his hometown, in the more established NFL and with four-year,

$200,000 contract was too much for Butkus for refuse. It was a vintage draft for Chicago, which also had the fourth overall pick and took running back **Gale Sayers**, who also had a Hall of Fame career.

Ferocious Fixture for Bears

Butkus wasted no time making an impact. In his NFL debut in September, 1965, Butkus made eleven unassisted tackles against the San Francisco 49ers. Veteran Bill George, the Bears' middle linebacker the previous thirteen seasons, knew his Chicago days were numbered. "The second I saw him the field (at training camp), I knew my playing days were over," said George, who played but two games that season and ended his career with the Los Angeles Rams a year later.

The Bears in 1965 rebounded from three straight season-opening losses to win nine of their last eleven and finish 9-5. Butkus led Chicago in tackles, fumbles recovered and pass interceptions as the Bears allowed 104 fewer points over fourteen games than in 1964. Butkus's coach, **George Halas**, was one of the NFL's founders and liked the young player's primitive style.

He led Chicago in tackles for eight consecutive seasons, averaging 120 tackles and fifty-eight assists a year. He registered a career-best eighteen sacks in 1967. Over his nine seasons, he earned forty-seven takeaways-twenty-five fumble recoveries and twenty-two interceptions. Butkus even caught two extra points on offense after

Career Statistics

Yr	Team	FR	INT	TD
1965	CHI	6	5	0
1966	CHI	3	1	0
1967	CHI	3	1	0
1968	CHI	1	3	0
1969	CHI	2	2	0
1970	CHI	2	3	0
1971	CHI	3	4	0
1972	CHI	4	2	0
1973	CHI	1	1	1
TOTAL		25	22	1

CHI: Chicago Bears.

Awards and Accomplishments

1963	Silver Football Award as Big Ten Conference Most Valuable Player after leading Illinois to conference championship
1963-64	College All-America at linebacker position while playing for University of Illinois; all Big-Ten selection as linebacker and center
1964	Selected National Football Player of the Year by National Football Coaches Association
1965	Selected NFL Rookie of the Year
1971	In rare offensive play, caught leaping pass for winning extra point as Bears defeated Washington Redskins, 16-15
1979	Selected to Pro Football Hall of Fame
1983	Selected to College Football Hall of Fame
1985	Downtown Athletic Club of Orlando establishes Butkus Award for nation's top college football linebacker
1986	University of Illinois retires his jersey number (50)
1994	Chicago Bears retire his jersey number (51)
1995	Selected to Rose Bowl Hall of Fame

bungled snaps, one of them the winning play, a diving reception of a pass as Chicago defeated the Washington Redskins 16-15 in 1971. Butkus calls that the favorite play of his career. He never appeared in an NFL playoff game; the Bears were rebuilding during that era after their 1963 championship team had aged.

But ferocity, not statistics, defined Butkus, who stood at 6-foot-3, 240 pounds. "When I went out on the field to warm up, I would manufacture things to make me mad," he said. "If someone on the other team was laughing, I'd pretend he was laughing at me or the Bears. I'd find something to get mad about. It always worked for me." "Butkus was in the eye of the football hurricane on every play, and his primary intention was barbaric, but simple: Hurt somebody, anybody," Anthony Holden wrote on the Web site CBS SportsLine.com. "As long as Butkus gave you a teeth-rattling shot, he was happy." Butkus cashed in on his tough-guy image, endorsing antifreeze and shaving cream, among other products, on national TV.

Sues Former Team

Injuries took their toll on Butkus later in his career. After surgery on his right knee following the 1970 season, he played painfully for two years. In a 1973 game against the Atlanta Falcons, Butkus took himself out of the game. Several weeks later, he retired, having earned 1,020 tackles, 489 assists and twenty-two interceptions.

In 1974, Butkus sued the Chicago Bears' team doctor, alleging mistreatment of his injuries, and settled for $600,000, according to *Gannett News Service*. He underwent knee reconstruction surgery in 1997.

In 1985, the Downtown Athletic Club of Orlando (Florida) established the Butkus Award for the best college football linebacker. Butkus presents the award annually.

Butkus's nephew, Luke Butkus, was an offensive center at the University of Illinois from 1998-2001, earning honorable mention All-Big Ten honors. He signed with the San Diego Chargers in November, 2002, after they had cut him earlier in the fall.

Butkus's 1974 lawsuit against the Bears resurfaced in the news in November, 2002, when the media refocused on the treatment of injured football players after Philadelphia Eagles star quarterback Donovan McNabb reportedly played part of a game with a broken ankle. "Almost 30 years after Dick Butkus sued the Bears over the damage caused when his knees were treated as pincushions for pain shots, it is time for the league and the union to revamp the system," Selena Roberts wrote in the *International Herald Tribune*.

Butkus Legacy

While other linebackers such as **Lawrence Taylor** of the New York Giants and Jack Lambert of the Pittsburgh Steelers have been dominant in their eras, Butkus is still the measuring stick at that position. Promising players are described as "a high school Butkus," "a Canadian Butkus," "an Ivy League Butkus."

Butkus and his wife, Helen, live in Malibu, California. They have three children: Rick, Mathew and Nikki. He still does television commercials and small movie parts, often reflecting his "tough-guy" persona, and manages the Dick Butkus Football Network, a Web site. He also announced for the National Broadcasting Corporation during its XFL telecasts. That league folded after one season, in the winter of 2002.

"I want to be recognized as the best—no doubt about it," Butkus once said. "When they say all-pro middle linebacker, I want them to mean Butkus!" Still, Butkus, for all his talents, might have trouble in today's NFL, which often fines and suspends players for extreme hits. "Headhunting is declasse in the NFL these days," Charles Bricker wrote in the *South Florida Sun-Sentinel*. Miami Dolphins linebacker Zach Thomas said he grew up enjoying Butkus on television, but added, "Nowadays, the NFL doesn't want to show that. They just want to show all the touchdowns."

SELECTED WRITINGS BY BUTKUS:

(With Bob Billings) *Inside Defensive Football,* Regnery, 1971.
(With Robert W. Billings) *Stop-Action* Dutton, 1972.
(With Pat Smith) *Butkus: Flesh and Blood,* Doubleday, 1997.

FURTHER INFORMATION

Other

"Athletes Behind the Tradition: Butkus Award." http://graphics.fansonly.com/photos/schools/ill/sports/m-footbl/auto_pdf/butkus-award.pdf. (November 30, 2002).
"Butkus Was One Mean Bear." ESPN.com, http://espn.go.com/sportscentury/features/00014131.html (November 30, 2002).
"Chicago Bears Tradition/51: Dick Butkus." www.chicagobears.com/history , (November 30, 2002).
"Despite League's Crackdown on Illegal Hits, Trend Increasing in NFL," Sun-Sentinel.com. http://www.sun-sentinel.com/ (November 23, 2002).
"Middle Linebackers." SportsLine.com, http://www.sportsline.com (December 2, 2002).
Pro Football Hall of Fame, Butkus profile, http://www.profootballhof.com/players/mainpage.cfm?cont_id=100177 (November 30, 2002).

Sketch by Paul Burton

Dick Button
1929-

American figure skater

Ranked as one of the greatest figure skaters of all time—perhaps second only to **Sonja Henie** in terms of his impact on the sport—Dick Button remains an influential force on the contemporary scene more than fifty years after he won his second of two Olympic Gold Medals. In addition to his Olympic triumphs, Button was the reigning U.S. men's champion from 1946 to 1952 and claimed the World Championship titles from 1948 to 1952. Honored with the James E. Sullivan Award in 1949 as the country's Best Amateur Athlete, Button finished his B.A. at Harvard University in 1952 and followed it with a law degree in 1956. A regular commentator on *ABC's Wide World of Sports* since 1962, Button won an Emmy Award as Best Sports Personality in 1981. He also heads Candid Productions, a television production company that he founded in 1959, and is instrumental in

Dick Button

sponsoring several professional skating competitions that have expanded the range of opportunities available to figure skaters after their amateur careers end.

Sixteen-Year-Old U.S. Champion

Richard Totten Button was born in Englewood, New Jersey on July 18, 1929, to businessman George Button and his wife, the former Evelyn Bunn Totten. He was the youngest of three boys and at first did not appear to possess any special athletic ability. Button started skating at the age of six with his school friends and enjoyed the sport enough that he later traded in a pair of hockey skates that he had received as a Christmas present for figure skates. Button's family was wealthy enough that he could take private lessons with coach Gustav Lussi at the Philadelphia Skating and Humane Club and in Lake Placid, New York. The lessons paid off and in 1943, when Button entered his first competition at the Eastern States Novice Championship, he skated away with the silver medal.

Just weeks after that second-place finish, fourteen-year-old Button won the gold medal at the Middle Atlantic Novice Championship in April 1943, which began a string of victories. In 1944 he took first place at the Eastern States Junior and United States Novice Championships; the following year, Button won the gold medal at Junior Championships. In 1946 the United States Figure Skating Association (USFSA) resumed its men's senior competition, which had not been held for the prior two years because of World War II. Sixteen-year-old Button won the event and became the youngest men's champion in U.S. figure skating history. He repeated as champion every year through 1952. With seven championships, Button shared the honor of holding the most U.S. men's titles with Roger Turner, who reigned from 1928 to 1934.

Olympic Gold Medalist

In his climb to the top of the U.S. field, Button earned a reputation for innovation, often combining moves that highlighted the control and power of his skating. In his first International Skating Union (ISU) World Championship appearance in 1947 (the first time the event was held since 1939), Button introduced the flying (or "Button") camel, in which he jumped into the traditional camel spin with one leg stretched out parallel to the ice. Button finished second in the championship, even though he earned the most points of any skater in the competition.

Button began the 1948 season with his second victory in the U.S. Championship, followed by a victory in the European Championship (which North Americans were allowed to enter at that time). In his first Olympic appearance at the 1948 St. Moritz Games, Button built a solid lead through the first two stages of the competition, compulsory (or school) figures and the technical program. In the free skate, Button amazed the audience by performing a double axel jump, requiring two-and-one-half turns in the air. It was the first time the jump had been completed in competition and it helped Button win the gold medal. In doing so, he became the first American to claim the men's title at the Olympic Games.

Entering Harvard University in 1948, Button continued to reign as men's U.S. champion while he completed his bachelor's degree, which he received in 1952. Button was also honored with the James E. Sullivan Award, given by the Amateur Athletic Union to the best amateur athlete in the United States. Until **Michelle Kwan** won the award in 2002, Button was the only figure skater to earn such a distinction. In 1952 Button returned for his second Olympics, this time in Oslo, Norway. As the current U.S. and World Championship titleholder, Button was the favorite entering the competition. Button again made Olympic history by completing a triple-loop jump in the free skate—the first triple jump

of any kind ever completed in competition—and claimed his second gold medal. Ever the perfectionist, Button was dissatisfied with his performance; as he recalled in a profile on the U.S. Olympic Committee's Web site, "I overtrained for the second [Olympic Games] and made some errors and that has always bugged me more than the fact that I won the Olympics." Button followed the Olympic victory with a final win at the World Championship in Paris, France and then retired from amateur ranks. Throughout the 1950s he skated with the Ice Capades, a popular skating program that toured the country; Button also entered Harvard Law School, where he completed his law degree in 1956.

Sportscaster and Producer

In 1959 Button formed Candid Productions, a television production company that later presented many professional skating competitions and other sports programs such as *The Battle of the Network Stars*. In 1962 Button began appearing on *ABC's Wide World of Sports* as a commentator on figure skating; the association has lasted more than forty years and led to an Emmy Award from the National Academy of Television Arts and Sciences as Outstanding Sports Personality in 1981. After marrying skating coach and choreographer Slavka Kohout in March 1973, the couple had two children, Edward and Emily, before divorcing in 1984.

In his role as a *Wide World of Sports* analyst, Button remains one of the most familiar figure skaters to the American public decades after his retirement as an athlete. He is also regarded as a leading authority on the sport. When figure skating underwent one of its biggest changes in 1990, dropping the compulsory figures from the men's and women's competitions, Button was a leading critic of the move. "The skating of figures is an art form in itself," he told *Sports Illustrated*, "it has nothing to do with free skating." When

Where Is He Now?

More than fifty years after his second Olympic gold medal, Button remains an important force in contemporary figure skating. In the wake of the judging controversy in the pairs' competition at the 2002 Salt Lake City Winter Olympic Games, Button was one of the most vocal critics of the ISU's unwillingness to reform its practices. Using his forum as a commentator on *ABC's Wide World of Sports*, Button was particularly critical of the ISU's continuing accreditation of judges who had been found guilty of cheating at past events.

In January of 2001 Button suffered a head injury when he fell during a rehearsal of a skating performance to be included in a *Wide World of Sports* segment. The mishap required several weeks of rehabilitation before Button could return to the air. On the U.S. Olympic Committee's Web site Button said, "I'm fine, I'm here, and I'm wreaking havoc as usual." Button continues to serve as an analyst for about ten USFSA and ISU events each year. He lives in Manhattan and owns a fifty-acre farm in Old Salem, New York.

the **Tonya Harding-Nancy Kerrigan** controversy erupted in 1994 over Harding's attempt to force Kerrigan out of the Olympics with an injury, however, Button refrained from commenting. "I found it disgusting, especially the shark-feeding media," he later told Mark Leibovich of the *Knight-Ridder/Tribune News Service* in a 1996 interview.

Remained a Force in Figure Skating

Although a leading advocate in popularizing figure skating, Button does not hesitate to critique trends that he thinks are harmful to the sport. Reviewing the competitive pressures that young figure skaters endure, Button is apprehensive at the toll such demands take on the young athletes' lives, particularly in terms of their schooling. "I have an interest in the sport, but I also have an interest in the people who do it," he explained in a 1998 interview with Mark Kram of the *Knight-Ridder/Tribune News Service,* "The problem is, the people who do it are just so overloaded." He added, "What it comes down to is that there is so much money to be made, it doesn't seem to matter if [the skaters] are educated or not." Button is also critical of the ISU's refusal to adopt fundamental reforms in the judging process, even after a scandal erupted at the 2002 Olympics over the initial second-place finish of **Jamie Sale and David Pelletier** in the pair's competition. Sale and Pelletier were later awarded a gold medal, but the ISU continued to drag its feet on reforming its practices.

A legend in his sport, Button continues to be one of the most influential persons in figure skating more than half a century after his Olympic triumphs. Not only has he educated the American public on the finer points of skating, he has also managed to popularize the sport as a mass-media spectator event. Although his appreciation for the sport is obvious, however, Button does not shy away from expressing his frank assessment over the sport's shortcomings. In doing so, he remains an influential, if sometimes contentious, authority in the world of figure skating.

SELECTED WRITINGS BY BUTTON:

Dick Button on Skates. Englewood Cliffs: Prentice-Hall, 1955.
Instant Skating. New York: Grosset and Dunlap, 1964.

FURTHER INFORMATION

Books

Brennan, Christine. *Edge of Glory: The Inside Story of the Quest for Figure Skating' Olympic Gold Medals*. New York: Scribner, 1998.
Brennan, Christine. *Inside Edge: A Revealing Journey into the Secret World of Figure Skating*. New York: Scribner, 1996.
Fleming, Peggy with Peter Kaminsky. *The Long Program: Skating Toward Life's Victories*. New York: Pocket Books, 1999.
Smith, Beverley. *Talking Figure Skating: Behind the Scenes in the World's Most Glamorous Sport*. Toronto: McClelland & Stewart, 1997.
U.S. Figure Skating Association. *The Official Book of Figure Skating*. New York: Simon & Schuster Editions, 1998.

Periodicals

Kram, Mark. "Dick Button Is a Pioneer, Educator of Figure Skating." *Knight Ridder/Tribune News Service* (January 2, 1998): 102.
Leibovich, Mark. "TV's Guru of Skating Still Knows How to Navigate Around Thin Ice." *Knight Ridder/Tribune News Service* (January 26, 1996): 126.
Wulf, Steve. "Disfigured." *Sports Illustrated* (June 20, 1988): 13.

Other

"Dick Button." ESPN Web site. http://espn.go.com/abcsports/columns/button_dick/bio.html (December 8, 2002).
"Flashback . . . Figure Skating's Dick Button." United States Olympic Committee. http://www.olympic-usa.org/news/020902figure.html (February 9, 2002).

Sketch by Timothy Borden

Roy Campanella
1921-1993

American baseball player

K nown as "Campy" by his friends, colleagues, and fans, Roy Campanella is considered by many to be the best baseball catcher in the history of the game. He is often mentioned in the same breath as the great catcher **Yogi Berra**, who played for the opposing professional league, the American League. Named the National League's Most Valuable Player three times in the 1950s, Campanella was a pioneering African American player at a time of deep racial prejudice that had prevented blacks from playing in the major leagues until only a year before Campanella joined the Brooklyn Dodgers in 1948. Campanella played on the same team as the first African American major leaguer, **Jackie Robinson**, who broke the color barrier in 1947.

Not only was Campanella one of the first African Americans to play in the major leagues, he also paved the way for other blacks to play in the position of catcher, a spot until then still off-limits to non-white players. As former fellow Dodger Dusty Baker later told Larry Whiteside of the *Boston Globe,* "In the days when he caught, catching was basically a white position. . . . Catching was a thinking position that most of America didn't think people like Campanella could handle. He broke the mold. Because of the mentality of the country, the mentality of baseball, to be black and an MVP meant he had to be head and shoulders above anybody else in the league."

Campanella's career lasted until 1958, when he was paralyzed in an automobile accident. From then on, a total of 35 years until his death, he was confined to a wheelchair. He managed to stay in the game of baseball, however, as a coach and advocate for young baseball players. He was inducted into the Baseball Hall of Fame in 1969, and he died of a heart attack in 1993.

A Born Catcher

Roy Campanella was born in Homestead, Pennsylvania on November 19, 1921. His mother, Ida, was African

Roy Campanella

American, while his father, John, was an immigrant from Italy. As a boy, Campanella worked in his father's produce business and also helped his brother to deliver milk. He first seriously played the game that was to make him famous while still in high school. The position of catcher was a natural for him even then, since at five feet, nine and one half inches, he was relatively short, and at 190 pounds, was fairly heavy. Also, he discovered when trying out for the Simon Gratz High School team, no one else wanted to play catcher.

Campanella was just 15 years old in 1937 when he first played professional baseball. This was when he dropped out of school to become a member of the Bacharach Giants, based in Brooklyn, New York. Not long after, he joined the Baltimore Elite Giants, a team of the Negro National League. He remained with the Negro Leagues for nine years, playing each season for

It's Good to Be Alive

Roy Campanella's autobiography, *It's Good to Be Alive* became the basis of a television movie in 1974. Directed by noted television actor Michael Landon (perhaps best known for his starring role on the *Little House on the Prairie* TV series), the 100-minute movie was broadcast for the first time on February 22, 1974. This first showing featured an introduction by Campanella and his family.

Paul Winfield plays the part of Campanella, and the movie opens with the 1958 auto accident that ended Campanella's career as a baseball player. Focusing more on the remarkable process by which Campanella created a new life for himself than on the baseball career that made him famous, the film chronicles the collapse of Campanella's marriage as a direct result of the accident, his physical rehabilitation, and his return to a productive life as a baseball coach and inspirational speaker. *It's Good to Be Alive* remains available on both videocassette and DVD from larger video outlets.

$3,000 a season. He played an often-grueling schedule with the Elite Giants, once playing four games in a single day. Also in the Negro League, Campanella learned to play in spite of injuries that would have stopped a lesser player. "You didn't get hurt when you played in the Negro league," he was later quoted as saying by Robert McG. Thomas Jr. of the *New York Times*. "You played no matter what happened to you because if you didn't play, you didn't get paid." During the off-seasons, in the winter, Campanella played for Latin league baseball teams in Latin America. His ability to speak Spanish was a major asset there, and he was often called upon to manage the teams on which he played.

Campanella advanced to the major leagues in 1948, when he began playing for the Brooklyn Dodgers' major league team. This was only a year after Jackie Robinson joined the Dodgers, becoming the first African American to play in the major leagues. Campanella had actually been approached by Dodgers president **Wesley Branch Rickey** about joining the team in 1945. But Campanella had refused the offer, thinking that Rickey was trying to recruit him for a Negro League team he was said to be putting together. In reality, the supposed Negro League team was a cover masking Rickey's efforts to recruit black players for the Dodgers. Rickey made his offer a little more plain the following season, and this time Campanella accepted.

The year was 1946, and Campanella's first assignment with the Dodgers was on the organization's minor league Class B farm team in Nashua, New Hampshire, where he was paid about $200 a month. This represented a drastic cut in pay, but the chance it gave him to play for the major leagues was too good to pass up. Campanella quickly became one of the team's top players, and a favorite of local fans, who often presented him with gifts of chickens when he pitched winning games.

Campanella played a total of 113 games with the Nashua Dodgers, scoring a .290 batting average. Dodger president Rickey moved Campanella up to the Class AAA team in Montreal, where, in 1947, he played

catcher for 135 games, hit 13 home runs, and scored a .273 batting average. This was the same year that Jackie Robinson became the first black player to play in the major leagues. Campanella was following in Robinson's footsteps; Robinson had only the year before played on the Montreal team.

An African American First

After a brief stint on the St. Paul, Minnesota Class AA team, Campanella was finally moved up to the Brooklyn Dodgers' major league team in 1948. This made him the first African American catcher in major league baseball, and the fourth African American player in the major leagues. Jackie Robinson had preceded Campanella the year before as the first African American major league baseball player. Robinson was then followed by two other African American players, **Larry Doby** and Dan Bankhead, before Campanella joined the major leagues.

Wearing the number 39 that he was to bear throughout his career, Campanella stepped up to the plate his first night playing as a Brooklyn Dodger, and hit a home run. Also that night, he hit a double and two singles, firmly establishing himself as a force to be reckoned with. Just as he had in the Negro Leagues, Campanella grit his teeth and played through numerous potentially serious injuries during his nine seasons with the Brooklyn Dodgers. For instance, in 1954, an injury rendered two fingers on his left hand immobile, and he played anyway. "I can grip a bat and I can grip a ball, and that's all that counts," said Campanella, according to Thomas.

In 1951, Campanella was honored with Most Valuable Player status, a designation that was again bestowed upon him in 1953, when he had what some commentators thought of as his best year. In that year, Campanella had a .312 batting average, and broke three records for a catcher. These were: most putouts in a single season (807), most home runs for a catcher in a single season (41), and most runs batted in within a single season (142). Campanella was named Most Valuable Player a final time in 1955. By the end of his career, Campanella

Career Statistics

Yr	Team	AVG	GP	AB	R	H	HR	RBI	BB	SO	SB
1948	Brooklyn	.258	83	279	32	72	9	45	36	45	3
1949	Brooklyn	.287	130	436	65	125	22	82	67	36	3
1950	Brooklyn	.281	126	437	70	123	31	89	55	51	1
1951	Brooklyn	.325	143	505	90	164	33	108	53	51	1
1952	Brooklyn	.269	128	468	73	126	22	97	57	59	8
1953	Brooklyn	.312	144	519	103	162	41	142	67	58	4
1954	Brooklyn	.207	111	397	43	82	19	51	42	49	1
1955	Brooklyn	.318	123	446	81	142	32	107	56	41	2
1956	Brooklyn	.219	124	388	39	85	20	73	66	61	1
1957	Brooklyn	.242	103	330	31	80	13	62	34	50	1

Brooklyn: Brooklyn Dodgers.

had played in five World Series, and had been named a National League All-Star a total of eight times.

A Career Cut Short

Even at the height of his career, however, Campanella realized that he could not play baseball indefinitely, and so he opened a Harlem, New York liquor store with which he planned to support his family after his retirement from playing baseball. The store was a success, and was soon a prosperous business. The day he was forced to retire from baseball came sooner than Campanella planned, however. Early in the morning of January 28, 1958, as he was driving back to his Glen Cove, Long Island home from the liquor store, the car he was driving skidded on a slick road, crashed into a telephone pole, and overturned.

Campanella described the crash in a *Los Angeles Times* interview that was later quoted by the *St. Petersburg Times*. "It had snowed a little that night, and the roads were a little wet and icy. I was about five minutes from my house when I hit some ice driving around a curve. I hit my brakes and the car slid across the road, hit a pole and turned over. I tried to reach up to turn the ignition off because I thought the car would catch fire, but I couldn't move my arm."

Although he survived the crash, he suffered two fractured vertebrae. Five surgeons at Glen Cove Community Hospital worked four and a half hours to save his life. They succeeded in this, but his spine was permanently damaged; he remained paralyzed from the shoulders down. He would never be able to walk or swing a bat again.

At the time of his accident, Campanella held a .276 batting average in the major leagues. His major league career total was 1,161 hits in 1,215 games, including 627 runs and 242 home runs, and 856 runs batted in. Many later speculated that, had it not been for the racism that had kept Campanella out of the major leagues until he was 26 years old, and for the auto accident that ended his career prematurely at the age of 36, those numbers would have been much higher.

A New Life

After a ten-month hospitalization, Campanella underwent rehabilitation at New York University-Bellevue Medical Center's Rusk Institute—a process as grueling as any training in his baseball career. At the end of it, he was able to move his arms, and regained partial use of his hands.

The worst was not yet over. Campanella's wife Ruthie, unable to cope with the loss of physical intimacy imposed by the accident, left him. Campanella was also forced to sell his house to cover debts incurred as a result of the accident. Only three months after Campanella's accident, his team moved from Brooklyn to Los Angeles, California, to become the Los Angeles Dodgers. Campanella said many years later that his one regret in life was that he wasn't able to go with the Dodgers to their new home.

But Campanella persevered, never flagging in his optimism. He rebuilt his life, eventually marrying his nurse, and building up his liquor store business and his career as a television and radio personality. In the process of putting his life back together, Campanella became a tremendous source of inspiration to handicapped and other people around the country. As Thomas of the *New York Times* wrote, "his gritty determination to make a life for himself in a wheelchair won him even more fame and admiration than he had enjoyed as a baseball star."

Campanella's many fans showed their appreciation of him on May 8, 1959 at an exhibition game at the Los Angeles Coliseum between the Dodgers and the Yankees dedicated to the former star. Over 93,000 spectators showed up, a baseball attendance record that remained unbroken at the time of Campanella's death, more than 30 years later. At one point during the proceedings, Campanella was wheeled to home plate, the stadium's lights were dimmed, and the fans lit matches in Campanella's honor. More importantly to the star who had fallen on hard times, he netted $75,000 from that night's proceeds.

Roy Campanella, right

Campanella stayed active in baseball by coaching teenagers; in 1967, he took a job coaching boys from housing projects in New York City. Many of those he coached went on to play for college and professional teams. In 1969, Campanella, again following in Jackie Robinson's footsteps, became the second African American to be inducted in the Baseball Hall of Fame. In a speech on the occasion, he thanked Branch Rickey for starting his major league career. The *Chicago Sun Times* quoted Campanella, "Mr. Rickey is the one I owe everything to. This election completes my baseball career, and there's nothing more I can ask in life."

But Campanella's career in baseball was not over. In 1978, Campanella went back on the Dodgers payroll, selling his liquor store and moving to Woodland Hills, California to rejoin his old team. Among his duties at his new job was coaching Dodgers catchers at spring training in Vero Beach, Florida, and working for the organization's Community Services department.

He remained in the public eye with these activities, and remained beloved of Dodgers fans and players who recognized his positive outlook and ongoing contributions to the sport of baseball. Most of all, he was seen to epitomize the spirit of fun that he felt was essential to playing an organized sport. "It's a man's game," said Campanella, according to the *St. Petersburg Times*, "but you have to have a lot of little boy in you to play it."

Gone But Not Forgotten

Roy Campanella died of a heart attack near his home in Woodland Hills, California, on June 26, 1993. "As well as being a great baseball player," said Dodger manager **Tommy Lasorda** in *Jet* magazine, "he was a great human being." And, as former Dodger player and later San Francisco Giants manager Dusty Baker recalled in the *Boston Globe*, Campanella "was a guy who motivated me. He never complained. He would never alibi. Even though his body didn't function well, he was mentally as sharp as a tack. You could listen to him for hours and hours telling stories about baseball and life. Stories about Jack Robinson and Jim Gilliam and the Negro Leagues. He was just fascinating to be around." Campanella is survived by his wife Roxie and five children: Roy Jr., Anthony, John, Joni Roan, and Ruth Effort.

SELECTED WRITINGS BY CAMPANELLA:

It's Good to Be Alive. Boston: Little Brown & Company, 1959.

FURTHER INFORMATION

Periodicals

"Dodgers Legend Campanella Dies." *Chicago Sun Times* (June 27, 1993): Sports Sunday, 3.

Awards and Accomplishments

1949-56	Named to the Major League All-Star Team
1951, 1953, 1955	Named National League Most Valuable Player
1953	Set major league record for most home runs by a catcher in a season (41)
1953	Set major league record for most runs batted in by a catcher in a season (142)
1959	Published book *It's Good to Be Alive*
1969	Inducted as the second African American baseball player into the Baseball Hall of Fame

Earl Campbell

Donnelly, Joe. "Courage in Dodger Blue; Baseball Mourns Campanella, 71." *Record* (June 28, 1993): D1.

"Greatest Dodger of Them All." *St. Petersburg Times* (June 28, 1993): 1C.

"Hall of Fame Catcher Roy Campanella Dies at 71." *Jet* (July 12, 1993): 14.

Pearson, Richard. "Famed Dodgers Catcher Roy Campanella Dies." *Washington Post* (June 28, 1993): D8.

Thomas Jr., Robert McG. "Roy Campanella, 71 Dies; Was Dodger Hall of Famer." *New York Times* (June 28, 1993): B8.

Whicker, Mark. "Campy: Simply One of the Best." *Buffalo News* (June 28, 1993): Sports, 2.

Whiteside, Larry. "Campanella Broke Mold; Apprciation." *Boston Globe* (June 28, 1993): Sports, 25.

Other

"Biography: Roy Campanella." HickokSports.com. http://www.hickoksports.com/biograph/campanel. shtml (November 13, 2002).

"It's Good to Be Alive." All Movie Guide. http://www. allmovie.com (November 19, 2002).

"Roy Campanella." cnnsi.com. http://sportsillustrated. cnn.com/baseball/mlb/all_time_stats/players/c/43016 / (November 20, 2002).

Sketch by Michael Belfiore

Earl Campbell
1955-

American football player

Earl Campbell's professional career was marked by his ability to sustain a hit. He was known for his strength and the fearlessness of his play. He rose out of the ashes of poverty to become a force on the football field. He won the Heisman trophy and restored the hopes of Houston football fans when he joined the Oil-

ers in 1978. A small town hero in Tyler, Texas, Campbell had a very successful NFL career during which he amassed 9,407 rushing yards. Although he never played on a championship team or went to the Super Bowl, Campbell remains one of the best to ever play the game.

Born March 29, 1955 in Tyler, Texas, Campbell was the sixth of eleven children born to Bert and Ann Campbell. His father picked roses, worked in a convenience store and died when Earl was eleven years old. Raised by his mother, Earl was counted on, along with his siblings, to carry a greater responsibility within the family. He discovered a love of football in the fifth grade. He was bigger and faster than the kids that he played with and idolized linebacker **Dick Butkus**. It wasn't until high school that Campbell became a running back, a switch he was unhappy with at first. When his coach promised him he could play both sides of the ball, Campbell embraced his new position and led his team to an undefeated season and a state championship in 1973.

Campbell went on to the University of Texas in 1974. During his freshman season, he rushed for 928 yards and received the Southwest Conference Newcomer of the Year Award. He became close to his coach and mentor, Darrell Royal, and worked as hard academically as he was athletically. "He don't take no prisoners," said Royal of his star running back's style. In his sophomore

Career Statistics

Yr	Team	Rushing				Receiving			
		Att	Yds	Avg	TD	Rec	Yds	Avg	TD
1978	HOU	302	1450	4.8	13	12	48	4.0	0
1979	HOU	368	1697	4.6	19	16	94	5.9	0
1980	HOU	373	1934	5.2	13	11	47	4.3	0
1981	HOU	361	1376	3.8	10	36	156	4.3	0
1982	HOU	157	538	3.4	2	18	130	7.2	0
1983	HOU	322	1301	4.0	12	19	216	11.4	0
1984	HOU/NO	146	468	3.2	4	3	27	9.0	0
1985	NO	158	643	4.1	1	6	88	14.7	0
TOTAL		2187	9407	4.3	74	121	806	6.7	0

HOU: Houston Oilers; NO: New Orleans Saints.

Chronology

1955	Born March 29 in Tyler, Texas
1973	Leads high school team to a state championship
1974	Enrolls at the University of Texas
1977	Wins Heisman Trophy
1978	Drafted by the Houston Oilers
1984	Traded to the New Orleans Saints
1985	Retires from football
1990	Inducted into the College Football Hall of Fame
1991	Enshrined in Pro Football Hall of Fame

Awards and Accomplishments

1974-75, 1977	Named First Team All Southwestern Conference
1977	Wins Heisman Trophy
1978	Top pick in NFL draft
1978-81, 1983	Named All-Pro
1990	Inducted into College Football Hall of Fame
1991	Inducted into Pro Football Hall of Fame

season, he rushed for over 1,000 yards and was voted the Bluebonnet Offensive Player of the Game after Texas' win over Colorado in the annual Bluebonnet Bowl game. The following year was a disappointment to the university and Campbell. Campbell suffered a hamstring injury that affected his production and after a mediocre season coach Royal stepped down. The new coach, Fred Akers, challenged Campbell to lose weight and increase his production. In 1977, Campbell won the Heisman trophy after racking up an impressive 1,744 yards rushing.

The Tampa Bay Buccaneers had the first pick in the NFL draft in 1978 but traded the pick to Houston. Houston then chose Campbell as their number one pick. The Oilers at the time were a talented team that had never lived up to their expectations. Campbell soon made a name for himself in Houston and after a 199-yard night on Monday Night Football in 1978, his reputation was solidified. Although he enjoyed his reputation as one of the best in the game, Campbell's Oilers never had much success. Campbell spent most of his career in Houston until coach Bum Phillips was fired; Phillips traded for Campbell when he was hired by the New Orleans Saints in 1984. It was in New Orleans that Campbell would retire in 1985 after Phillips was fired.

After retiring Campbell went back to Texas and accepted a position with the University of Texas. He became president of Earl Campbell Meat Products and opened an Austin-based barbecue restaurant in 1999. The restaurant was closed down in 2001. "I don't know that business," Campbell said in a *Texas Monthly* article. "This was the first time in my life I ran up against a wall, that I ran up on something I just couldn't do." Known in football for being able to take a hit without going down, Campbell continued to push his brand of meat products while remaining an active presence at his alma mater.

Earl Campbell's rise out of the small Texas town of Tyler to the National Football League and beyond, was helped by his ability to keep moving forward despite the many obstacles that lay in his path. Whether on the football field or in the highly competitive food business, Campbell has had success based on his resilience. He remains married to a woman he met in the ninth grade and has two sons. Campbell's career landed him in the Pro Football Hall of Fame and in the hearts of many diehard Texas football fans.

FURTHER INFORMATION

Periodicals

"Football Star Seeks to Keep Creditors at Bay." *Austin Business Journal* (June 15, 2001).

"Where Are They Now?" *Texas Monthly* (September, 2001): 106.

Other

"The College Years." Earl Campbell. http://www.earl campbell.com/college_years/index.html (January 6, 2003).

"The Early Years." Earl Campbell. http://www.earlcamp bell.com/early_years/index.html (January 6, 2003).

"The Oilers." Earl Campbell. http://www.earlcampbell. com/oilers/index.html (January 6, 2003).

www.earlcampbell.comlife_after_football/index.html (January 6, 2003).

Sketch by Aric Karpinski

Jose Canseco
1964-

Cuban baseball player

Jose Canseco

Sportswriters once chronicled Jose Canseco's exploits both on and off the baseball diamond with a mix of reverence and disbelief. The Oakland Athletics (A's) outfielder hit impressive home runs, helped take his team to three American League pennants and a World Series win, and was the first baseball player in history to achieve the "40-40" record: 40 home runs and 40 bases stolen in a season. Canseco attained a certain notoriety off the field as well, running into trouble with the law over fast cars and guns, and was accused of using steroids. Canseco denied this last charge vehemently, but after his career ended, he made headlines once again by claiming that a large percentage of players, perhaps as high as 85 percent, used the illicit substances to improve their performance.

Cuban-Born

Canseco and his fraternal twin Oswaldo were born in Havana, Cuba, on July 2, 1964, to Jose and Barbara Canseco. In December of 1965, the family, which included an older sister, left Cuba and settled in Opa-Locka, Florida. At Coral Park High School, Canseco was a talented, if somewhat slight of frame ball player who did not make the varsity team until his senior year. A scout for the Oakland A's, a fellow Cuban, discovered him, and he was a 15th-round draft pick in 1982. He first played for the Rookie League or farm teams in several states before making his major-league debut in September of 1985 in an A's game against Baltimore.

By 1986, Canseco's impressive hitting power had earned him the American League (AL) Rookie of the Year title. Two years later, he declared his intention to set a baseball first, the 40-40, and did it on September 23, 1988, in an A's game against the Milwaukee Brewers. He was named the AL's Most Valuable Player (MVP) that season, and often earned comparisons to **Reggie Jackson**, who praised his talents. Canseco was famous for his at-bat twitches, but the quirk only seemed a warm-up to the real stunt: soaring home runs. At Game 4 of the American League Championships in Toronto in 1989, Canseco hit the ball into the fifth deck of the vast new Toronto SkyDome that estimates pegged as a 540-foot hit.

Starred on Star Team

The A's won that Series against Toronto, and took the World Series title that year against Bay Area rivals the San Francisco Giants. Canseco ended the season with a .269 average. He was signed to a record-setting five-year, $23.5 million contract, but injuries hampered his 1990 season. Though the A's made it into the next World Series, they lost to the Cincinnati Reds. In 1991, the A's failed to make the playoffs.

At the height of his career, Canseco was inarguably baseball's biggest celebrity. He was swarmed by fans everywhere he went, and was once even spotted leaving the apartment of sexy pop-singer Madonna. Several run-ins with authorities added to his cultivated bad-boy image: he racked up speeding tickets in the Porsches and Lamborghinis he collected, kept a pet cougar at his

Career Statistics

Yr	Team	AVG	GP	AB	R	H	HR	RBI	BB	SO	SB	E
1985	Oak	.302	29	96	16	29	5	13	4	31	1	—
1986	Oak	.240	157	600	85	144	33	117	65	175	15	—
1987	Oak	.257	159	630	81	162	31	113	50	157	15	7
1988	Oak	.307	158	610	120	187	42	124	78	128	40	7
1989	Oak	.269	65	227	40	61	17	57	23	69	6	3
1990	Oak	.274	131	481	83	132	37	101	72	158	19	1
1991	Oak	.266	154	572	115	152	44	122	78	152	26	9
1992	Oak/Tex	.244	119	439	74	107	26	87	63	128	6	3
1993	Tex	.255	60	231	30	59	10	46	16	62	6	3
1994	Tex	.282	111	429	88	121	31	90	69	114	15	—
1995	Bos	.306	102	396	64	121	24	81	42	93	4	0
1996	Bos	.289	96	360	68	104	28	82	63	82	3	0
1997	Oak	.235	108	388	56	91	23	74	51	122	8	5
1998	Tor	.237	151	583	98	138	46	107	65	159	29	5
1999	TB	.279	113	430	75	120	34	95	58	135	3	0
2000	NYY/TB	.252	98	329	47	83	15	49	64	102	2	2
2001	CWS	.258	76	256	46	66	16	49	45	75	2	0
TOTAL		.266	1887	7057	1186	1877	462	1407	906	1942	200	45

Bos: Boston Red Sox; CWS: Chicago White Sox; NYY: New York Yankees; Oak: Oakland Athletics; TB: Tampa Bay Devil Rays; Tex: Texas Rangers; Tor: Toronto Blue Jays.

Miami home, and was once arrested for carrying a loaded semiautomatic pistol. Promoters of a baseball-card show sued him for being a no-show, and Canseco even had a "1-900-234-JOSE" hotline, which cost fans $2 during the first minute and $1 minute thereafter. Through it all Canseco had a problematic relationship with sports journalists, who were awed by his innate talents but put off by his ego. "Canseco is a baseball virtuoso, an athletic flower that blooms once a century," wrote Rick Reilly in *Sports Illustrated*. "We know this because he mentioned it the other day."

Surprise Trade

Canseco, who had bulked up considerably since his high-school days, was also rumored to be a steroid user. He categorically denied the charges. "No. 1, I take it as a personal attack on me and my race," Canseco fumed about the matter in a 1995 interview with Barry M. Bloom in *Sport*. Between the 1991 and 1992 seasons, Canseco seemed to lose his edge. At the time, his marriage to Esther Haddad, Miss Miami 1986, was disintegrating, and in February of 1992 he was arrested after chasing and hitting Haddad's car on the highway with his Porsche. He avoided jail by agreeing to court-ordered psychiatric treatment, and later said that the therapy had helped him immensely in dealing with some of the issues in his life.

At the time, however, Canseco also had a troubled relationship with A's manager Tony LaRussa that was often hinted at in veiled comments each made to the press. On August 31, 1992, after a dismal summer, Canseco was traded two hours before the season trading deadline. He was actually in the on-deck circle at the

Oakland-Alameda Coliseum, about to go to bat, when he was called in and told the news. To be traded in itself was a shocking way to end his career with the A's, but its suddenness seemed designed to humiliate Canseco. A's general manager Sandy Alderson discussed the matter with Bloom, in the *Sport* article, a few years later. "Jose had lost his desire to be a player," Alderson asserted. "He had adopted a wish to be an entertainer in a broader sense without regard to being a baseball player. That didn't work anymore."

Years after A's management had made the infamous Canseco trade, emotions still ran high over LaRussa's role in it. Neither had spoken to one another since, though LaRussa did tell Barry M. Bloom in *Sport* that he still believed Canseco was "the most talented player I have ever managed." He also reflected back on comments Canseco had made at the time, specifically those in which the athlete asserted that the A's would have never traded a player like **Cal Ripken, Jr.** or **Kirby Puckett** so ignominiously. "If Jose would have taken care of his business like Puckett and Ripken, which is be there every day and care about teammates and the outcome of the game and personal performance, we would have never traded Jose either," LaRussa told Bloom. "He stopped caring. We couldn't get him back on track."

Traded for three players to the Texas Rangers, Canseco had another bad season in 1992 and an even worse year the next, when he was mocked by fans after a fly ball bounced off his head and over the fence. After two seasons with the Rangers, he was traded to the Boston Red Sox before the start of the 1995 baseball year, and went back to Oakland in 1997 for a season. He performed well for the Toronto Blue Jays in 1998, enjoying his best season in several years, but the Tampa Bay Devil Rays were the only team to bid for him at the close of the year. The Anaheim Angels signed him in late 2000, but released him from his contract before the season began. He was the Yankees' designated hitter for a time, but did not play in the pennant race that brought the famed post-season "Subway Series" against the New York Mets.

Canseco still told sportswriters that he hoped to hit 500 career home runs, which he believed would be the ticket to a spot in the Baseball Hall of Fame in Cooperstown, New York. He spent what would be his final season with the Chicago White Sox, where his uneven hitting of the past few seasons continued (at one point in the season, he struck out 15 times in just nine games). What would become his last career home run, No. 462, came on October 3, 2001, in a Sox-Yankees game in New York. His future was uncertain, but he vowed never to retire. "One thing is I'm not a quitter. I never have been and never will be," Canseco told *Chicago Tribune* sportswriter Paul Sullivan, even as news hit that the Sox's **Frank Thomas** would return for the team's final outing against Minnesota, making Canseco "expendable," as Sullivan wrote. Yet Canseco remained optimistic. "It's going to take a lot more than that to get me out of the game."

Announced Retirement

On May 13, 2002, Canseco announced his retirement. His agent, Alan Nero, issued a statement that explained Canseco was quitting the Charlotte Knights, a farm team in the Chicago White Sox organization, for personal reasons, including a desire to spend more time with his five-year-old daughter, Josie, from his second marriage in 1996. (The union with Jessica Seikaly, a former waitress at a Hooters restaurant, had also ended in divorce.)

Canseco's 462 home-run total stood, 38 short of his oft-stated career goal. In an ESPN Radio interview, he claimed to have been blackballed by the major-league team owners, and hinted that he would expose baseball's seamier side in a tell-all autobiography. A *Miami Herald* writer, Greg Herald, asserted that Canseco should exit the game more gracefully. "Get out with a little class," Herald urged. "Retire right. Instead, inadvertently, Canseco is giving a public seminar on how not to make that ego-defying leap from star to ex/former/used-to-be."

Few sports pundits believed that Canseco would, in the end, be admitted to the Hall of Fame, despite his impressive 40-40 first. Gary Peterson, summarizing Canseco's early promise and tragic decline in a *Contra Costa Times* article published by Knight Ridder/Tribune News Service, recalled that Canseco "arrived in the major leagues at the speed of sound…. He wasn't the architect of the A's revival, but he did a lot of the heavy lifting." Peterson noted that it was at the start of the

Chronology	
1964	Born in Havana, Cuba, on July 2
1965	Emigrated to United States from Cuba with family
1982	Drafted by Oakland A's
1985	Makes major-league debut
1988	Marries Esther Haddad on November 5
1988	Becomes first player to hit 40 home runs and steal 40 bases in a single season
1989	Oakland A's win World Series
1990	Signs record $23.5 million contract
1992	Arrested in February and charged with aggravated battery
1992	Traded to Texas Rangers
1995-2001	Plays for Boston Red Sox, Oakland A's, Toronto Blue Jays, Tampa Bay Devil Rays, New York Yankees, and Chicago White Sox
1996	Marries Jessica Seikaly on August 26
2002	Announces retirement from baseball and plans to write autobiography

1990s that the gifted player, who "seemed to have an intuitive feel for the game," began to lose his focus. "Ten years ago Canseco seemed on the fast track to Cooperstown," Peterson wrote. "Five years ago you could incite a spirited debate by questioning his candidacy for the Hall of Fame. Now? It's not even a discussion."

Made Claims of Steroid Use

Within a week of retiring, Canseco was back in the news after declaring in a Fox Sports Net interview that steroid use, contrary to his past assertions, was rampant in major-league baseball. "Steroids completely changed baseball," Knight Ridder/Tribune News Service writer Skip Bayless quoted him as saying. "That's why guys are hitting 50, 60, 75 home runs." When pressured for more specifics, Canseco declared that his forthcoming book would provide details about his own steroid use and that of other players. Bayless also wrote that Canseco had often asserted that he "could have hit 600 if I could have stayed healthy," and theorized that because of steroid abuse, the player "got too big and strong for his frame. His joints and connective tissue couldn't bear up under his rippled bulk and the unnatural power it could unleash. So one reason Canseco was able to hit 462 homers was also a reason he couldn't stay healthy enough to hit 600."

A similar charge regarding the widespread steroid use was made by former National League MVP Ken Caminiti just days later in the press. Caminiti claimed that as many as 50 percent of all players used performance-enhancing drugs, thought to cause testicular cancer, heart disease, infertility, and the mood swings known as "'roid rage," while Canseco's claims pegged the number at 85 percent. An onslaught of stories in the media centering on the ethics of steroid use followed. Many sportswriters noted that while a drug-testing policy was sometimes called for in professional baseball, it was thought that the powerful players' union would categorically reject any such changes.

Arrested for Nightclub Brawl

On Halloween of 2001, Canseco and his brother Ozzie were involved in a Miami nightclub brawl and were arrested. They later rejected plea agreements on the felony charges and the cases were slated to go to trial in November of 2002. If convicted, Canseco could receive a maximum sentence of 31 years. The charges seemed to further doom his goal of entering the Baseball Hall of Fame.

When Canseco retired, he was one of just nine major-league players who had hit 400 home runs and stolen 200 bases or more as well. Seven of the other eight had been inducted into the Baseball Hall of Fame already, and though Canseco was the first to ever make the 40-40 mark, many sportswriters noted that his contributions to baseball were overshadowed by the controversies he instigated. As Herald wrote, "Everybody discounts his chances to be voted into the Hall of Fame because nobody seems able to stay focused on the talent that otherwise would make Cooperstown a logical destination.... The injuries, the speeding tickets, the steroid rumors, the divorces (and Madonna!), that fly caroming off his cap, the dark paranoia-all that static obscuring all that skill."

CONTACT INFORMATION

Address: Jose Canseco, c/o Major League Baseball, 75 Ninth Ave., New York, NY 10011. Fax: (212) 485-3456. Phone: (212) 485-3182.

FURTHER INFORMATION

Periodicals

"Analysis: Media Watch - Baseball's steroid scandal has media crying foul on players."*PR Week* (June 24, 2002): 12.

"Back to b(A's)sics." *Sports Illustrated* 86 (February 10, 1997): 14.

"Baseball: No plea agreement for Cansecos." *Sports Network* (August 23, 2002).

Bayless, Skip. "Jose Canseco, simply, may be waxing outrageous." Knight-Ridder/Tribune News Service (May 17, 2002).

Bloom, Barry M. "Monster basher." *Sport* 86 (June 1995): 87.

Fimrite, Ron. "Kiss that one goodbye." *Sports Illustrated* 65 (July 7, 1986): 28.

Gammons, Peter. "The summer of his discontent." *Sports Illustrated* 71 (October 2, 1989): 72.

Hagen, Paul. "Jose Canseco had it all, then lost it, and other notes." Knight-Ridder/Tribune News Service (May 17, 2002).

Herald, Greg. "Canseco needs to exit with class." Knight-Ridder/Tribune News Service (May 14, 2002).

Heredia, Christopher. "Steroids play games with vital hormones." *San Francisco Chronicle* (June 10, 2002): A6.

"Jose Canseco Retires." *New York Times* (May 14, 2002): D6.

Kroichick, Ron. "Jose Canseco." *Sport* 83 (April 1992): 20.

Kurkjian, Tim. "Broken string (Struggles of the Oakland A's)." *Sports Illustrated* 75 (September 30, 1991): 60.

——. "By the numbers." *Sports Illustrated* 77 (August 17, 1992): 98.

——. "Home run derby." *Sports Illustrated* 75 (August 19, 1991): 52.

Montville, Leigh. "Texas-sized trade." *Sports Illustrated* 77 (September 14, 1992): 36.

Olson, Stan. "Jose Canseco delivers in Knights' win." Knight-Ridder/Tribune News Service (April 26, 2002).

Peterson, Gary. "Canseco allowed his star to burn out." Knight-Ridder/Tribune News Service (May 13, 2002).

Price, S.L. "Life Is Beautiful." *Sports Illustrated* 90 (March 22, 1999): 64.

Reilly, Rick. "Whaddya say, Jose?" *Sports Illustrated* 73 (August 20, 1990): 42.

Roderick, Joe. "Canseco's comments bother Bonds." Knight-Ridder/Tribune News Service (May 21, 2002).

Rodriguez, Juan C. "Canseco retires 38 homers short of 500." Knight-Ridder/Tribune News Service (May 13, 2002).

Rogers, Phil. "Like him or not, Jose Canseco creates excitement." Knight-Ridder/Tribune News Service (May 18, 2002).

Scher, Jon. "Bashed." *Sports Illustrated* 76 (February 24, 1992): 89.

Sherrington, Kevin. "Canseco book would shed light on steroids." Knight-Ridder/Tribune News Service (May 26, 2002).

Sorci, Rick. "Jose Canseco 1988 A.L. MVP (Interview)." *Baseball Digest* 61 (June 2002): 61.

Sullivan, Paul. "Canseco performs a Ruthian feat." Knight-Ridder/Tribune News Service (August 1, 2001).

——. "Canseco remains puzzled by release from Angels." Knight-Ridder/Tribune News Service (August
7, 2001).

——. "Was this Canseco's last clout?" Knight-Ridder/
Tribune News Service (October 3, 2001).

Whitley, David. "Canseco ready to bash again with the
truth." Knight-Ridder/Tribune News Service (May
22, 2002).

Sketch by Carol Brennan

Jennifer Capriati

Jennifer Capriati
1976-

American tennis player

Jennifer Capriati took the tennis world by storm in 1990
when she became the youngest player to ever reach a
final of a professional tennis tournament just shy of her
fourteenth birthday. She was the youngest ever player to
reach the semifinals of the major tournaments and the
youngest ever player to be ranked in the top ten. Capriati's
initial success, however, was short-lived. The rebellious
teenager quit tennis at age 17. After battling drugs, legal
problems, and her parents' divorce, a more mature Capriati
returned to the tennis scene in 1996 at age 20. By 2001
Capriati dominated women's tennis, winning two Grand
Slam titles and reaching the number one ranking. Capriati
added a third Grand Slam title to her career in 2002 and
she continues to be a leading player in women's tennis.

Tennis Prodigy

Jennifer Maria Capriati was born on March 29, 1976
in New York, New York. Her mother, Denise, is a New
York native who worked as a flight attendant for Pan Am
airlines. Her father, Stefano, was a professional soccer
player whose career was cut short by a knee injury. He
then taught himself to play tennis. He also moved to
Spain to pursue a career as a stuntman and he appeared in
such films as *Patton, The Last Run,* and *100 Rifles.*
Denise and Stefano Capriati met in Spain when Denise
was there for a layover. They married two years later and
had two children—a daughter, Jennifer, and a son, Steven.

Both Denise and Stefano enjoyed playing tennis and
decided that when they had children, they would also
want them to play tennis. Jennifer Capriati was engulfed
by the tennis world from birth. "Ten days after she was
born, I was back on the court, playing to get back into
shape," Denise Capriati told Bruce Lowitt of the *St. Petersburg Times* in November of 1988. "She was right
there on the court with me. When she started crawling, it
was on the court, pushing a ball around."

At the age of three Capriati began hitting balls with
her father. Even though she did not understand the game
of tennis, she learned to hit the balls back. Although
Capriati was born in New York, she spent her first years
of life living in Spain. However, the family moved to
Lauderhill, Florida, near Fort Lauderdale, in 1980 to
build Jennifer's tennis career. At the age of five Capriati
began taking lessons at Holiday Park with Jimmy Evert,
the father of American tennis sensation **Chris Evert**. Evert
was reluctant to take such a young student, but he was
quickly impressed with her skills.

At the age of nine Capriati started taking lessons with
Rick Macci at the International Tennis Academy in
Grenelefe, Florida so that she could play against other
children. Every weekend her parents would drive three
and a half hours for her training with Macci. After a year
they decided to move to Grenelefe. Capriati attended
public school daily from 8:00 a.m. until 1:00 p.m. and
then practiced tennis from 2:30 p.m. until 6:30 p.m. She
had the weekends to herself, unless she was playing in a
tournament.

Teenage Sensation

Capriati trained with Macci until age 13 when she
began attending the Hopman Tennis Academy at Saddle-
brook resort in Wesley Chapel, Florida. Tom Gullickson
became her next coach. By this time Capriati was already
garnering a lot of attention in the tennis world. In 1988, at

Chronology

1976	Born on March 29 in New York, New York
1981-85	Trains with Jimmy Evert
1985-88	Trains with Rick Macci
1989	Trains with Tom Gullickson
1989	Wins six junior singles titles and two junior doubles titles
1990	Turns professional
1990	Becomes the youngest player ever to reach a professional final
1990	Debuts on the Women's Tennis Association rankings at number 25
1990	Youngest ever semifinalist at the French Open
1990	Youngest ever seed at Wimbledon
1990	Wins first singles title in Puerto Rico
1990	Finishes season ranked number eight and becomes youngest ever player to be ranked in the top ten
1991	Youngest ever semifinalist at Wimbledon
1991	Reaches semifinals at U.S. Open
1991	Finishes season ranked number six
1992	Reaches three Grand Slam quarterfinals
1992	Wins Gold Medal at Olympic Games
1992	Becomes the youngest player to surpass the million-dollar mark in career prize money at age 16
1992	Finishes third season ranked number seven
1993	Drops off of the Women's Tennis Association tour to finish high school
1993	Receives police citation for shoplifting
1994	Arrested in Coral Gables, Florida for possession of marijuana
1994	Enters drug rehabilitation program in Miami Beach, Florida for 28 days
1994	Plays one tournament and loses in the first round
1995	Parents divorce
1996	Returns to the Women's Tennis Association tour
1996	Finishes year ranked number 24
1997	Finishes year ranked number 66
1998	Finishes year ranked number 101
1999	Wins first title in six years in Strasbourg, Germany
1999	Finishes season ranked number 23
2000	Reaches first Grand Slam quarterfinal in nine years at the Australian Open
2000	Finishes season ranked number 14
2001	Wins first Grand Slam title at the Australian Open
2001	Reaches number one ranking for the first time
2001	Wins second Grand Slam title at the French Open
2001	Ends season with over 50 wins for the first time
2001	Finishes season ranked number two
2002	Wins third Grand Slam title at the Australian Open
2002	Reaches the semifinals at the French Open
2002	Reaches the quarterfinals at Wimbledon and the U.S. Open
2002	Finishes season ranked number three

age 12, she won the United States Hard Court and Clay Court junior titles for ages 18 and under. The following year she won the singles junior titles at the French Open and the U.S. Open and the doubles junior titles at Wimbledon and the U.S. Open with Meredith McGrath.

At age 13 Capriati was already talking about turning professional. However, the Women's Tennis Association (WTA) rules did not allow girls to play in professional tournaments until the month of their fourteenth birthday. Even before her first professional match, Capriati had already signed a multimillion-dollar contract with Diadora, an Italian shoe and sportswear company. Capriati made her professional debut just before her fourteenth birthday at the Virginia Slims tournament in Boca Raton, Florida in March of 1990. Although she did not win the tournament, she became the youngest player ever to reach a professional final. She lost to the number three player in the world, **Gabriela Sabatini**.

At five feet seven inches and 130 pounds, Capriati was a teenage sensation who was capable of beating women who were older and more experienced than she was. She debuted on the WTA rankings at number 25. "Jennifer's strengths as a player are her aggressiveness, her unpredictability and her power," wrote Charles Leerhsen and Todd Barre of *Newsweek* in May of 1990. "Her groundstrokes are, as **Billie Jean King** says, too hot for many women to handle; her backhand is superior to [Steffi] Graf's."

Won Olympic Gold

Capriati's break out year left a mark on the tennis world. She became the youngest ever semifinalist at the French Open in Roland Garros and she was the youngest ever seed at Wimbledon. She also won her first WTA singles title that year in Puerto Rico at the $150,000 San Juan Open. She finished the 1990 season ranked number eight in the world and at age 14 she became the youngest ever player to be ranked in the top ten. She earned $80,000 in prize money and signed a million dollar deal with racquet company Prince.

Capriati's success continued the following year. In 1991 she began to beat the top players on the women's tour, including tennis legend **Martina Navratilova** and teen sensation **Monica Seles**. Capriati reached the semifinals of Wimbledon and the U.S. Open. At age 15 she was the youngest semifinalist ever at Wimbledon. She finished the 1991 season ranked number six in the world.

In 1992 Capriati continued to flex her tennis muscle. She reached the quarterfinals of three Grand Slam events and won a Gold Medal at the Olympic Games in Barcelona, Spain. She attracted more endorsements, adding Oil of Olay and Snapple to her product line. At age 16 she became the youngest player to surpass the one million dollar mark in career prize money. She finished the year ranked seven in the world.

Capriati's fourth year on the professional tour in 1993 started off as well as the first three had. She reached the quarterfinals in three of the four Grand Slam tournaments that year. However, she lost in the first round of the U.S. Open. She was also having some physical problems, suffering from tendonitis and bone chips in her elbow. In September of 1993 Capriati announced that she was going to take time off of the WTA tour to finish high school.

Burned Out

Talk of Capriati's potential to burn out early began before the teen phenomenon ever turned professional.

She was continually compared to teen stars Tracy Austin and Andrea Jaeger who had both peaked early, but had short careers due to injuries. However, Capriati's parents were aware of these incidents and they tried to prevent the same thing from happening to their daughter. In particular, they took her to the Virginia Sportsmedicine Institute for physical and psychological testing. They started Jennifer on a special conditioning program to help prevent injuries. They also tried to insulate her from the media and allow her to have a normal teenage life when she was not playing tennis.

Capriati managed to keep up her good grades at the Palmer Academy by doing her homework by fax when she was on the road. However, in 1992 she started to show signs of burn out. Her grades began to slip in school and she was acting rebelliously toward her parents and on the court. Capriati's father was criticized for pushing his daughter too hard at such a young age. He responded by stepping down as her coach and hiring Pavel Slozil to fill that role. "Right now she needs me as a father, not as a coach," Stefano Capriati explained to Sally Jenkins of *Sports Illustrated* in March of 1992. "This way we can keep them separate." Denise Capriati also left her job as a flight attendant so that she could spend more time with her children.

By 1993 Capriati began to feel the pressure of being a top-ranked tennis player. She managed to reach the quarterfinals of three Grand Slam tournaments, but she had hoped to finally win a Grand Slam title. In the fall of 1993 she left the WTA tour to finish high school. In December of that year she received a citation from the Tampa police department for shoplifting a cheap ring from a suburban mall. Although she was a minor and the incident should have been kept confidential, the story was leaked to the media, fueling rumors about her burning out.

After Capriati turned 18 she moved out of her parents home and into her own apartment. By May of 1994 she had left no doubt in her critics' minds that she was indeed burned out. She was arrested in Coral Gables, Florida for possession of marijuana. Two teenage friends who were with her were charged with possession of heroin and suspected crack cocaine. Apparently Capriati had been partying all weekend with friends in a cheap motel and her friends claimed that she had been using drugs for at least a year. Two days after she was arrested, Capriati entered a drug rehabilitation program at Mount Sinai Medical Center in Miami Beach for 28 days.

In September of 1994 the Capriatis moved to Rancho Mirage, California to rebuild their lives and Jennifer's career. "I felt like no one liked me as a person," Capriati told Robin Finn of the *New York Times* in September of 1994. "I felt like my parents and everybody else thought that tennis was the way to make it in life, they thought it was good, but I thought no one knew or wanted to know the person who was behind my tennis life." Capriati played in one tournament in 1994, but she lost in the first round.

Awards and Accomplishments

1988	U.S. Hard Court 18-and-under singles
1988	U.S. Clay Court 18-and-under singles
1989	French Open junior singles title
1989	U.S. Open junior singles title
1989	U.S. Open junior doubles title with Meredith McGrath
1989	Wimbledon junior doubles title with Meredith McGrath
1989	Astrid Bowl junior singles title
1989	Easter Bowl 16-and-under singles title
1989	Named World Tennis and *TENNIS* magazine Junior Player of the Year
1989	Named Athlete of the Year in the Sport of Tennis by the U.S. Olympic Committee
1989	U.S. Wightman Cup Team
1990	First singles title in San Juan, Puerto Rico
1990	Received Sanex Women's Tennis Association Tour Most Impressive Newcomer Award
1990	*TENNIS* magazine/Rolex Watch Female Rookie of the Year
1990-91, 2000	U.S. Fed Cup Team
1991	Two singles titles in San Diego, California and Toronto, Canada
1991	Doubles title with Monica Seles at Italian Open
1991	Named Most Improved Female Player by *TENNIS* magazine
1992	Singles title in San Diego, California
1992	Singles Gold Medal at the Olympic Games in Barcelona, Spain
1993	Singles title in Sydney, Australia
1996	Named Comeback Player of the Year by *TENNIS* magazine
1999	Two singles titles in Strasbourg, Germany and Quebec, Canada
2000	Singles title in Luxembourg
2001	First Grand Slam singles title at Australian Open
2001	Singles title at Charleston, South Carolina
2001	Second Grand Slam singles title at French Open
2001	Ranked number one women's player
2001	Named Sports Woman of the Year by the U.S. Olympic Committee
2001	Named *Sports Illustrated* Sports Woman of the Year
2001	World Singles Champion, International Tennis Federation
2001	Named Associated Press Female Athlete of the Year
2001	Voted Sportswoman of the Year by Reuters
2001	Received Laureus World Comeback of the Year Award
2001	Named Women's Tennis Association Tour Player of the Month in January, April, and June
2002	Third Grand Slam singles title at Australian Open
2002	Received ESPY Award for Best Comeback Athlete
2002	Received Laureus Sports Award for Female Athlete of the Year
2002	Named January Player of the Month by the International Tennis Writer's Association

Returned to Tennis

Capriati stayed away from tennis for the next year and a half. Her parents had divorced in 1995 and rumors began circulating about Capriati's stability and whether she would ever return to tennis. In August of 1996 Capriati did return to the tour, although her performance was lackluster. "If Capriati loves competitive tennis, she has a hard time showing it," wrote Ian O'Connor of the *New York Daily News*. "There were few expressions of misery in defeat, fewer signs of passion." Capriati lost in the first rounds of the French and U.S. Opens. She ended the 1997 season ranked 24 in the world.

Capriati continued to struggle for the next couple of years. She lost in the early rounds of the Grand Slam tournaments. In 1997 she was ranked only 66 in the

Jennifer Capriati

world, and by the end of 1998 her ranking slipped to 101. However, Capriati began to turn her game around by 1999 with the help of a new coach, Harold Solomon. She captured her first title in six years in Strasbourg, and followed up with another title in Quebec City by defeating Chanda Rubin. She also reached the fourth round at the French and U.S. Opens. Capriati's success landed her a lucrative endorsement deal with Fila.

Even though her career was picking up, the media continued to focus on her troubled past. During a press conference for the 1999 U.S. Open, Capriati read from a statement to the press apologizing for the troubles of her youth and requesting the media to focus on her current career rather than the past. The following year marked more successes for Capriati. In 2000 she reached her first Grand Slam semifinal in nine years at the Australian Open, although she lost to Lindsey Davenport. Capriati won a singles title in Luxembourg that year and played singles and doubles for the U.S. Fed Team. She ended the year ranked 17 in the world.

Grand Slam Comeback

Capriati's dream of winning a Grand Slam title finally came true in 2001 when she won the Australian Open. Capriati defeated **Martina Hingis**, the number one player in the world, by a score of 6-4, 6-3. "The motivation was just to live up to my potential," Capriati told Neil Har-

man and Andrew Alderson of the *Sunday Telegraph*. "It was more than just winning a few titles. I wanted the big ones." In order to win the big ones Capriati was committed to get into great shape and to stay focused on her game. "Thanks to a brutal regimen of strength and endurance training, the formerly chunky Capriati had a brand new body, so ripped and muscled it made Hingis look positively waifish," wrote Alex Tresniowski of *People* magazine.

Capriati followed up on her Australian Open title with another Grand Slam victory at the French Open. She defeated Belgian Kim Clijsters in the finals and dedicated her victory to Corina Marariu, an American player who was battling cancer. Capriati became the first American woman to win the French Open since Chris Evert Lloyd in 1986. "I never thought I'd be standing here 11 years later, after playing my first time here when I was 14 years old," Capriati stated after the tournament, as reported by S.L. Price of *Sports Illustrated*. "Really, I'm just waiting to wake up from this dream."

After capturing the first two major titles of the year, speculation began about whether Capriati would make a Grand Slam in 2001 by winning the next two major titles. Unfortunately, that did not happen. Capriati lost in the semifinals of Wimbledon to Belgian Justine Henin. She also lost in the semifinals of the U.S. Open to **Venus Williams**. Capriati finally reached the number one ranking for the first time on October 15, 2001, ending Martina Hingis's 73-week run as number one. She ended the season ranked number two, her first top ten ranking since she left the WTA tour in 1993.

Capriati started 2002 with another win at the Australian Open for her third Grand Slam title. Once again she defeated Martina Hingis in a sweltering final where court temperatures reached 120 degrees. She later reached the semifinals at the French and the quarterfinals at Wimbledon and the U.S. Open, in a year when **Serena Williams** dominated women's tennis. Nonetheless, Capriati still finished out the year ranked number three in the world.

At age 26 Jennifer Capriati has experienced all of the ups and downs of a professional tennis player. At age 14 she accomplished many firsts as the youngest professional tennis player. Despite many successful tournaments, she was not able to capture a Grand Slam title in the early years. By age 17 she had burned out and dropped off of the professional tour. After battling family and legal troubles, Capriati made a slow comeback to professional tennis starting in 1996. By 2001 she had attained her goal of a Grand Slam title and she remains one of the top ranked women's players. "For whatever reason, it wasn't supposed to happen back then," Capriati told Juan C. Rodriguez of *Knight Ridder/Tribune News Service* in October of 2001, "and I would have to say it's definitely been a unique journey for me, unique story, I think, for everyone."

CONTACT INFORMATION

Address: International Management Group, 22 E 71st St, New York, NY, 10021-4975.

FURTHER INFORMATION

Books

Almanac of Famous People, 6th edition. Farmington Hills, MI: Gale Research, 1998.

The Complete Marquis Who's Who. Marquis Who's Who, 2001.

Encyclopedia of World Biography, 2nd edition. Farmington Hills, MI: Gale Research, 1998.

Great Women in Sports. Visible Ink Press, 1996.

Newsmakers 1991, Issue Cumulation. Detroit, MI: Gale Research, 1991.

Periodicals

Arey, Norman, and A.R. Tays. "The Jennifer Capriati Story." *The Atlanta Journal and Constitution* (May 18, 1994): G1.

Atkin, Ronald. "Tennis: Interview Jennifer Capriati." *Independent on Sunday* (May 20, 2001): 15.

Borschke, Margie. "Up From Down Under." *Sports Illustrated for Women* (March/April 2002): 26.

Conlin, Bill. "Capriati Leaves Memories in the Past." *Knight Ridder/Tribune News Service* (June 25, 2001).

Couch, Greg. "The Rise and Fall of Jennifer Capriati." *Chicago Sun-Times* (January 26, 2001): 144.

Degnan, Susan Miller. "Jennifer Capriati Reaches a Huge Milestone in Roller-coaster Life." *Knight Ridder/Tribune News Service* (January 27, 2001).

Finn, Robin. "The Second Time Around for Jennifer Capriati." *The New York Times* (September 26, 1994).

Fins, Antonio N. "Jennifer Capriati, Million-Dollar Baby." *Business Week* (March 26, 1990): 104.

Harman, Neil, and Andrew Alderson. "The Return of Prodigal Tennis Star Jennifer Capriati is Back, Having Beaten the Odds." *Sunday Telegraph* (January 21, 2001): 3.

Harwitt, Sandra. "The Glorious Return of America's Lost Girl." *The Guardian* (June 23, 2001): 2.

Hogan, John. "So Nice to Have You Back, Jennifer." *The Australian* (January 8, 1997): 17.

Howard, Johnette. "This Could Be Capriati's Biggest Victory." *The Sporting News* (February 7, 1994): 8.

Jenkins, Sally. "Teenage Confidential." *Sports Illustrated* (March 30, 1992): 26-29.

"Jennifer Capriati." *U.S. News and World Report* (November 12, 1990): 18.

"Jennifer Capriati: A Teen-ager Tailored for the Tennis Court." *St. Louis Post-Dispatch* (March 25, 1990): 7F.

"Jennifer's World." *Sports Illustrated* (May 16, 1994): 14.

Jones, Malcolm, and Alisha Davis. "Newsmakers." *Newsweek* (June 18, 2001): 62.

Leerhsen, Charles, and Todd Barre. "Teen Queen of Tennis." *Newsweek* (May 14, 1990): 58.

Lowitt, Bruce. "On the Ball: Jennifer Capriati, 12, Can't Wait to Turn Pro." *St. Petersburg Times* (November 13, 1988): 1C.

Lupica, Mike. "She Was an American Girl." *The Sporting News* (May 30, 1994): 8.

O'Connor, Ian. "Capriati Can Still Hit Ball Like a Teen; It's Time She Is Allowed to Live Like One." *Knight Ridder/Tribune News Service* (August 27, 1996).

Ormsby, Mary. "Jennifer Capriati's Return to Greatness." *Toronto Star* (August 11, 2001): S03.

Price, S.L. "Vive L'Amour: At the Love-filled French Open, a Determined Jennifer Capriati and a Dominant Gustavo Kuerten Stole the Fans' Hearts." *Sports Illustrated* (June 18, 2001): 52.

"Reactions to Arrest of Jennifer Capriati." *USA Today* (May 27, 1994): 12 C.

Reed, Susan. "Losing Her Grip: A Teen Star's Arrest Raises Hard Questions About How Fast a Gifted Child Can Be Pushed." *People Weekly* (May 30, 1994): 80-84.

Rodriguez, Juan C. "Capriati Ascends to the Top." *Knight Ridder/Tribune News Service* (October 17, 2001).

Scheiber, Dave. "Tennis' New Legend in the Making (Jennifer Capriati)." *Saturday Evening Post* (July-August 1990): 68-70.

Shaffer, Alyssa. "Jenny's Core Moves." *Sports Illustrated for Women* (May/June 2001): 77.

Tresniowski, Alex, and Dennis Passa. "Jenny, Anyone?" *People* (February 12, 2001): 54.

Viner, Brian. "At 14, Jennifer Capriati Was a Millionaire Tennis Sensation. At 16, She Was a Drug User, Shoplifter and Binge-Eater. Now She's 24, and She May Be About to Win Wimbledon." *The Independent* (June 22, 2001).

Voepel, Michelle. "Capriati's Long Way Back." *Knight Ridder/Tribune News Service* (June 24, 2001).

Wertheim, L. Jon. "The Hard Return." *Sports Illustrated for Women* (December/January 2002): 58.

Wertheim, L. Jon. "How Jenny Got Her Groove Back." *Sports Illustrated for Women* (May/June 2001): 74.

Wertheim, L. Jon. "Jenny Come Lately: A Mature, Resilient Jennifer Capriati Put Her Difficult Past Behind Her and Won Her First Major, While a Focused Andre Agassi Swept to His Third Australian Open Title." *Sports Illustrated* (February 5, 2001): 54.

Wertheim, L. Jon. "A Real Hottie: While Others Were Doing a Fast Fade, Indomitable Jennifer Capriati Took the Heat at the Australian Open and Refused to Wilt." *Sports Illustrated* (February 4, 2002).

Other

The 2002 ESPY Awards. http://espn.go.com/espy2002 /s/02nomineesindex.html (July 11, 2002).

Olympic USA. http://www.olympic-usa.org (January 4, 2003).

TENNIS. http://www.tennis.com (January 3, 2003).

Tennis Corner. http://www.tenniscorner.net (January 4, 2003).

WTA Tour. http://www.wtatour.com (January 3, 2003).

Yahoo! Sports: Tennis. http://sports.yahoo.com/ten/ news/capriati02.html (January 3, 2003).

Sketch by Janet P. Stamatel

Harry Caray

Harry Caray
1914-1998

American sportscaster

Harry Caray changed the world of sports broadcasting forever with a style that reflected his true love of baseball. Caray was a man who spoke his mind. It is this aspect of his personality that endeared him to most, but ostracized him from others. There were many sportscasters who dreaded working with him, because he took over the booth. He was certainly larger than life, and had the life to prove it. He impressed many with his personalized broadcasting style and brought a whole new dimension to the game of baseball. Most say he brought baseball to life.

Growing Up

Harry Carabina started his meager beginnings in St. Louis, Missouri in the year 1914. He was born to Italian-French-Romanian immigrants. His father died before he was two years old and his mother died when he was ten. He went to live with an aunt near by and spent time in several foster homes. It was this start in life that made Caray realize he could never take anything for granted. He worked hard for everything he wanted in life and he enjoyed that life to the fullest.

Cardinal Dreams and Reality

Caray did well in sports, and turned down an athletic scholarship to the University of Alabama in hopes of making it with the St. Louis Cardinals. That dream never came true. He was forced to face the reality he was not going to make it into professional baseball. He took a job as a sales correspondent, which he enjoyed. He would sometimes take afternoons off and go see a ball game. He would come alive at the ballpark; he loved every aspect of the experience. Caray liked the sound of the crowd, the smell of the food in the stands, and anything else that went with a baseball game. A thought occurred to him one day while listening to a game on the radio: either he just happened to attend all the exciting games, or the radio broadcasts were boring. He felt they did not truly convey the excitement of the game. So, he took his correspondence skills and put them to work for his own cause. He wrote to Merle Jones, the general manager of KMOX of St. Louis, and told him how he felt about the baseball broadcasts.

Jones was impressed with what Caray wrote and called him. They discussed the letter and Jones encouraged Caray to get some experience. Caray took his advice, getting a job at WJOL in Joliet, Illinois. Caray said in an interview with Mike Eisenbath of the *St. Louis Post,* "Before the first month was finished, people thought I was pretty good." He went from there to WKZO in Kalamazoo, Michigan, where he worked as a

Chronology

1914	Born March 1, in St. Louis, Missouri
1915	Father dies
1924	Mother dies, moves in with an aunt in Webster Groves
1932	Starts first job as a sales correspondent
1941	Begins broadcasting career with WJOL in Joliet, Illinois
1945	Begins broadcasting for the St. Louis Cardinals on KMOX-TV and Radio
1969	Fired from broadcasting for the Cardinals
1970	Broadcasts for the Oakland A's on KNRB radio
1971	Begins broadcasting for the Chicago White Sox
1975	Fired from White Sox by John Allyn
1975	Marries Delores, also known as "Dutchie"
1976	Bill Veeck buys the White Sox and rehires Caray
1982	Begins broadcasting for the Chicago Cubs on WGN-TV and radio
1987	Opens his restaurant, Harry Caray's, on Kirk Street in Chicago
1987	Suffers from a stroke
1989	Writes book *Holy Cow!*
1989	Inducted into the Baseball Hall of Fame
1995	Suffers a heart attack
1997	Starts only broadcasting for Chicago Cubs home games
1998	Dies from complications resulting from a heart attack

Awards and Accomplishments

1988	Elected to the National Sportscasters and Sportswriters Hall of Fame
1989	Elected to the Baseball Hall of Fame
1989	Awarded the Ford Frick Award
1989	Elected to the National Italian American Sports Hall of Fame

sports editor and news director with Paul Harvey. These positions gave him the experience he needed to break into the broadcasting business.

In 1945 he moved back to St. Louis where he was given the position of broadcaster for the St. Louis Cardinals on KMOX-TV and Radio. At that time he was still Harry Carabina, and the manager asked him to shorten his last name. He legally changed his name to Caray for his broadcasting career. He remained with the Cardinals for twenty-five seasons. Eisenbath stated, "During the height of his time with the Cardinals, Caray could be heard on more than 175 network affiliates ... and fans could pick up KMOX almost everywhere in the country." Dan O'Neill of the *St. Louis Post-Dispatch* stated, "Caray wasn't just the voice of the Cardinals, he was what baseball sounded like." Due to the breadth of the broadcast, as well as Caray's unique style, Eisenbath said, "Caray might strike a familiar chord with more baseball fans than any other sportscaster."

In 1969 Caray was fired from broadcasting for the Cardinals. Some say it was due to a scandalous affair with an executive's wife, others say it was due to him offending someone with his no-nonsense style of broadcasting. Nonetheless he was angered by the decision and to show his disapproval, was seen at his termination press conference holding a Schlitz beer, a competitor to Budweiser, who sponsored the Cardinals.

Moving On and Up

Caray went on to broadcast one season with the Oakland A's, but in 1971 began work with WFLD in Chicago as a broadcaster for the Chicago White Sox. He worked at Comiskey Park for eleven seasons. John M. McGuire

of the *St. Louis Post-Dispatch* wrote, "Caray's firing was the best thing that could have happened to him. Because Chicago and Caray were made for each other." At one point during his tenure with the White Sox, the team's owner fired him because of his tendency to speak his mind on the air. When the White Sox were bought out months later, he was rehired. O'Neill stated, "Flaws in Caray's character are what made him so endearing."

Caray had made quite a name for himself in the broadcasting business. O'Neill explained, "For those who could not get to a game, listening was just as good, maybe better." O'Neill noted that throughout the years, "he became beloved as a symbol." Most people either loved him or hated him. He was one of a kind, and his broadcasts showed that style only he had. Not only that, but "he loved people from all walks of life," long time friend Otis Dunlap stated in an interview with McGuire. Dave Luecking with the *St. Louis Post-Dispatch* stated that "he considered all the fans his best friends." He never held back his disappointment with a player who made a bad move, nor held back praises when a home run was hit. In fact, he coined the phrases "It might be ... it could be ... it is! A homerun!" and "Holy Cow!" "Harry's passion for the game is so real. People identify with that," shared **Bob Costas** in an interview with Luecking.

Caray left the White Sox in 1982 to go across town to start broadcasting for the Chicago Cubs on WGN-TV. It was there he stayed until his death. In fact, according to Rod Beaton of *USA Today,* when asked when he was going to retire, Caray was quoted as saying, "I'll keep going until I die on the job someday." Caray endeared himself to the infamous Cubs fans immediately. One of the traditions was for him to sing "Take Me Out to the Ballgame" at the bottom of the 7th inning. That tradition started when he was singing in the broadcast booth one day and owner Bill Veeck got a kick out of his enthusiasm and turned on the PA system for everyone to hear.

Fun and Family

Caray was known for more than his broadcasting. He was also known for his drinking and socializing after hours. He was dubbed "the mayor of Rush Street" due to his partying nature. He even opened his own restaurant in 1987, aptly named Harry Caray's. But his carefree nature caught up with him, when in that same year he had a stroke. The stroke took him "out of the game" for several months. It was the first time he had missed

Related Biography: Broadcaster Steve Stone

Steve Stone was born July 14, 1947. He made his debut as a pitcher for the San Francisco Giants April 8, 1971, where he remained for an additional season. In 1973 he pitched for the Chicago White Sox, staying only one year, but returning for two more seasons in 1977. From 1974 to 1976 Stone played for the Chicago Cubs, where he was fated to return as a broadcaster with Caray in 1983. He completed his career as a pitcher with the Baltimore Orioles. During his tenure with the Orioles he received the Cy Young Award, and pitched three perfect innings in the All-Star Game in 1980. Stone lead the Orioles to a pennant, before retiring from pitching due to arm problems. Stone worked as a sportscaster with WGN until 2000, working with Chip Caray his final two years after Caray's death. He left WGN for two years to work as a competition consultant in 2000, but returned to broadcasting for the Cubs with Chip Caray in the 2003 season.

Stone put up with Caray's antics for 15 seasons while working for WGN as a baseball analyst. In an interview with Paul Lomartire of the *Palm Beach Post*, Stone said that Caray "was a unique character, charismatic character. People just gravitated towards him." Lomartire surmised that for Stone, "moving to the TV booth alongside Caray was a daily lesson in unpredictability." Stone wrote of Caray's unpredictability and magnetic character in a book titled, *Where's Harry?* The title of the book, Stone explained, came from people always asking him "where's Harry?" whenever Caray was not around. Stone writes, "Harry was more entertaining than 99.99 percent of the people in the business and the fans worshipped him."

an opening game in decades. The Cubs brought in big name celebrities to fill the gap while he was gone, but there was no replacing Caray. When Caray came back to work on May 19, 1987, the mayor announced it to be Harry Caray Day. Caray even received a call from President Ronald Reagan, who expressed how much he missed his broadcasts.

In 1991 he was fortunate enough to broadcast a game with his son, Skip, and grandson, Chip. It was the Cubs against the Braves. Skip was an announcer for the Atlanta Braves and Chip was working with Fox Sports Net. Caray and Chip were to broadcast together again in the 1998 Cubs season. Unfortunately, just six short weeks before their partnership was to begin, Caray passed away.

Caray suffered a heart attack on February 14, 1998, while dining with his wife, Dutchie. He collapsed and was rushed to the hospital. The incident caused brain damage and he was put on life support, but four days later was taken off life support and died on February 18, 1998.

Caray had touched many lives over his career, and thousands mourned his passing. Ned Colletti stated, "The city of Chicago lost an icon. There are thousands of announcers, but only one Harry," in an interview with Rod Beaton of *USA Today*. "Cubs baseball will never be the same," stated Marty Brennaman in the same interview. Mike Littwin of the *Rocky Mountain News* was shocked by Caray's death and stated, "How can Harry Caray be dead if he was bigger than life?" Beaton was equally shocked. He admired Caray and remembered, "Caray made people feel good about themselves, about baseball, even about the often hapless Cubs." When

asked by Beaton, Cubs general manager Ed Lynch said, "He's one of the biggest personalities in baseball in the last 100 years."

The Ultimate Fan

Caray was not only an excellent broadcaster because of his excitement for the game, but also because of the way he truly cared for the fans. Bob Patterson summed it up best in the interview with Beaton, stating, "We always knew that Harry was in our corner. He was really appreciative of the game, the players and the fans." The game of baseball will never be the same without him.

SELECTED WRITINGS BY CARAY:

(With Bob Verdi and David Israel) *Holy Cow!* Random House, 1989.

FURTHER INFORMATION

Books

Caray, Harry, with Bob Verdi and David Israel. *Holy Cow!* New York: Random House, 1989.
Newsmakers. Issue Compilation. Detroit: Gale Group, 1988.
Newsmakers, 1998. Detroit: Gale Group, 1998.
Stone, Steve, with Barry Rozner and Bob Costas. *Where's Harry: Steve Stone Remembers His Years With Harry Caray.* Taylor Publishing, 1999.
Wolfe, Rich, and George Castle. *I Remember Harry Caray.* Sports Publishing, Inc., 1999.

Periodicals

"Baseball loses Harry Caray/Broadcaster dies after suffering brain damage." *Minneapolis Star Tribune* (February 19, 1998): 08C.
Beaton, Ron. "Harry Caray—1920-1998: Baseball loses a legend Cubs announcer to be remember for his love of game." *USA Today* (February 19, 1998): 01C.
Caesar, Dan. "For grandson Chip, Harry's memory is a bittersweet legacy to carry." *St. Louis Post-Dispatch* (August 7, 1998): D3.
Clarke, Norm. "Talk of the town." *Denver Rocky Mountain News* (February 20, 1998): 6A.
Costas, Bob. "Notebook/Eulogy:Eulogy." *Time* (March 2, 1998): 25.
Eisenbath, Mike. "It might be: It could be, it is—Harry Caray!" *St. Louis Post—Dispatch* (May 12, 1994): 01D.
"Fans and friends and family say goodbye to Caray." *Chicago Tribune* (March 1, 1998): F10.
"Harry Caray, Death of a baseball legend: Caray larger than life." *Atlanta Journal and Constitution* (February 19, 1998): E03.
Lomartire, Paul. "Caray memories written in Stone." *Palm Beach Post* (May 12, 1999): 15C.

McGuire, John M. "Caray's resonant voice still has strong echo here." *St. Louis Post-Dispatch* (February 22, 1998): F3.

McGuire, John M. "In new book, people recall Harry Caray Fondly … and sometimes not so fondly." *St. Louis Post-Dispatch* (August 26, 1998): E1.

Moore, Terence. "Harry Caray, Death of a baseball legend: Caray larger than life." *Atlanta Journal and Constitution* (February 19, 1998): E03.

"One-of-a kind Caray was "life of baseball"." *Denver Rocky Mountain News* (February 19, 1998): 17C.

O'Neill, Dan. "Caray was what baseball sounded like." *St. Louis Post-Dispatch* (February 20, 1998): D1.

Rogers, Prentis. "Legacy to Caray on: Family trade: Chip Caray planned to be his grandfather's partner; instead he's his successor." *Atlanta Journal and Constitution* (March 31, 1998): E05.

"Sound off." *St. Louis Post - Dispatch* (February 28, 1998): 4.

Wulf, Steve. "Bonus Piece: As Harry Caray often says, "it might be…. it could be…."," *Sports Illustrated* (November 2, 1992): 74.

Other

"Famed Sportscaster Harry Caray dies." Reuters (February 18, 1998).

Fisher, Janon. "Holy cow! Harry Caray got death threats." APBNews.com. http://www.apbnews.com/media/gfiles/caray/index.html (October27, 2002).

"Harry Caray." National Italian American Sports Hall of Fame. http://www.niashf.org/inductees/caray_harry. html (October27, 2002).

"In memory of the late Harry Caray." Harry Caray Virtual Memorial Web site. http://digitalsol.com/harry caray/ (October 27, 2002).

Sciutto, Jim, Asha Blake. "Legendary sports announcer Harry Caray Dead at 77." ABC World News This Morning (February 19, 1998).

"U.S. Sportscaster Caray's condition still critical." Reuters (February 17, 1998).

Sketch by Barbra J. Smerz

Ricky Carmichael
1979-

American motocross racer

After winning the American Motocross Association (AMA) 125-cc Motocross series for three consecutive years, Ricky Carmichael moved up to the 250-cc class and won that series for the next three years. He is also a two-time champion in the AMA 250-cc Supercross series. In 2002 Carmichael posted an unprecedented perfect record of twelve overall wins in the twelve-race series, winning every heat of every race. He didn't just win, he dominated. And, if Carmichael has anything to say about it, he's not done yet.

Born to Ride

Ricky Carmichael was born on November 27, 1979, in Clearwater, Florida. He was raised in Havana, Florida, by his father, Rick, an electrician known as Big Rick, and mother, Jeannie. Carmichael's first bike was a Yamaha 50 Tri-Zinger that his parents gave him as a Valentine's Day present when he was five years old. Short and stocky with red curly hair and an abundance of freckles, Carmichael didn't always feel comfortable at school so he lost himself in his bike. On his bike he was as tall, strong, and powerful as any athlete. Competing in his first race when he was just five years old, Carmichael had a deep and abiding desire to cross the finish line first, and by the age of sixteen he had a record-setting 67 national amateur titles to prove he could win, and win big.

In 1996, barely seventeen years old, Carmichael turned to the professional ranks, joining the AMA circuit for the last 125-cc Motocross event of the season in Delmont, Pennsylvania. He placed eighth and earned AMA Rookie of the Year honors. For the next couple of years Carmichael raced in the 125-cc division, considered the minor leagues of the sport, before moving up to the 250-cc Supercross in 1999 and the 250-cc Motocross in 2000. In 1997, his rookie season, Carmichael quickly established his dominance as a top motocross contender. Riding for Team Splitfire/Pro Circuit, he took the Eastern Region of the 125-cc Supercross with wins in Atlanta, Georgia; Orlando, Florida; and Charlotte, North Carolina. He was even more impressive in the 125-cc National Motocross series, winning the championship with eight wins and three more podium finishes. He finished the season ranked No. 1 in the 125-cc Motocross and No. 3 in the 125-cc Supercross.

In his sophomore season, Carmichael became the first rider in AMA history to win every round of the 125-cc Eastern Region Supercross series. Taking eight overall wins and an additional podium appearance in 125-cc Mazda Truck Motocross Nationals, Carmichael once again won the 125-cc Motocross championship. Riding for Pro Circuit Kawasaki, he concluded the season ranked No. 1 in both 125-cc Supercross and 125-cc Motocross. Before moving on to the 250-cc class, Carmichael broke every record in the 125-cc division.

Dominates Motocross

Carmichael made the jump to the 250-cc Supercross circuit in 1999, but got off to a difficult start by crashing in the first race of the season, sustaining a mild concussion and a fractured bone in his right hand. He contin-

---

Chronology

1979	Born in Clearwater, Florida
1996	Turns professional, riding in 125cc Motocross
1999	Sustains injury; begins racing 250cc Supercross as well as 125cc Motocross
2001	Dominates the field in 250cc Supercross and 250cc Motocross; becomes winningest rider ever in 125cc motocross with 26 overall victories
2002	Marries; has perfect Motocross season, winning every race

---

Awards and Accomplishments

1996	Named American Motocross Association (AMA) Rookie of the Year
1997	Wins the 125cc National Motocross series with eight overall wins and three podium finishes
1998	Wins the 125cc Mazda Truck Motocross Nationals with eight overall wins and one other podium appearance; wins Eastern Region 125cc Supercross
1999	Wins third consecutive 125cc Motocross championship
2000	Wins 250cc Motocross series championship
2001	Records most wins in one season, fourteen Supercross and eight Motocross; wins both 250cc Supercross and 250cc Motocross championships; named AMA Pro Athlete of the Year
2002	Wins every motocross of the season; wins AMA Supercross championship; named AMA Pro Athlete of the Year; becames all-time winningest rider in AMA history

---

ued to struggle to make the adjustment to the heavier, more powerful bike. Two fourth place finishes were the best Carmichael could do, earning him a season-end ranking of No. 16. Despite his disappointing performance in the 250-cc Supercross, Carmichael once again dominated the 125-cc Motocross season, taking his third consecutive championship with nine overall wins plus two podium finishes.

In 2000 Carmichael earned his first 250-cc Supercross win in Dayton, Ohio, and made five more podium appearances, which moved his ranking up to No. 5. Making the transition into the 250-cc Motocross events was much smoother for Carmichael, who feels more comfortable on the outdoor tracks he grew up with. He took overall nine wins, dominating the season and winning the championship. During 2000 Carmichael participated for the second year on the U.S. Motocross des Nations team, a competition among national teams of racers. In 2000 the U.S. won the competition for the first time in three years.

Driven to win and with little regard for second place, Carmichael was unhappy with his performance in the 250-cc Supercross. On his mother's suggestion, he hired a personal trainer, Aldon Baker, a former mountain-bike racer from South Africa who had recently lost his sponsorship. With Baker's guidance, Carmichael developed an extensive training regiment that included bicycle riding, running, weight lifting, practice riding, and a healthy diet—all of which helped Carmichael slim down twenty pounds. Pudgy at five-feet, six-inches and 170 pounds, he was lean and powerful at 150 pounds. In a sport that has long been characterized by riders who party as hard as they ride, Carmichael became known as the most fit, hardest trainer in Motocross.

Carmichael's hard work paid off in 2001 when he won his first 250-cc Supercross championship, finishing first fourteen times in the sixteen-race series, (with thirteen consecutive wins) and podium finishes in the only two races he didn't win. The championship was especially important to Carmichael because it happened before the impending retirement of racer Jeremy McGrath who, with seven career championships, was the uncontested king of the 250-cc Supercross. Carmichael knew he had beaten the best. He also took the 250-cc Motocross championship for the second consecutive year with seven overall wins in the twelve-race series. With the No. 1 ranking in both the 250-cc Supercross and the 250-cc Motocross, Carmichael was named the AMA Pro Racing Athlete of the Year.

The Perfect Year

In 2002 Carmichael, riding his new red, number 4 Honda CR250R, defended his 250-cc Supercross championship with eleven overall wins, and he made AMA history in the 250-cc Motocross by winning all twelve events. Not only did he sweep the season, he won every qualifying heat, going twenty-four for twenty-four, giving him a perfect season that can only be matched, but never beaten. "With about three races left I figured I could [finish undefeated]," he told *Sports Illustrated*. "There really wasn't much pressure. If I did go undefeated, it was a good thing. If not, it was still a good year." In fact, it was a superb year for Carmichael, who married his girlfriend Ursula in the fall of 2002, was once again named the AMA Pro Racing Athlete of the Year, and headlined in THQ, Inc.'s video game, *MX Superfly Featuring Ricky Carmichael*.

Life in the Lead

Carmichael lives in Havana, Florida, and owns 98 acres in Georgia where he has built three practice courses. His success has earned him long lines of fans waiting for his autograph and, including endorsements, up to $5 million a year. Yet Carmichael's complete dominance has just as many fans awaiting his downfall. When he fell twice in the first 250-cc Supercross of the 2003 season, fans erupted in cheers as he fell into last place. Then again, they cheered just as loudly when he miraculously moved back up to fourth place, threatening to find his way back into the lead before the race ended. A superb recovery, but Carmichael races to win and anything short of an outright victory is certainly a defeat.

With McGrath's retirement after the 2002 season, Carmichael is posed to become the next great king of the sport. Just twenty-three years old, Carmichael plans to race for a long time to come; however, Motocross is a dangerous and daring sport that has crushed its number of competitors, some of whom now live life in a wheelchair. But Carmichael is not worried about getting injured. He explained to CNNSI.com, "It's not the crashing but the losing, because when I lose, I'll retire. And that scares me. I've been doing this since I was five years old. What the hell are you going to do next?" With any luck, he won't have to answer that question for several years to come.

CONTACT INFORMATION

Address: American Honda Motor Co. Inc., Ricky Carmichael, Motorcycle Sports, 100-4C-3B, 1919 Torrance Boulevard, Torrance, California 90501.

FURTHER INFORMATION

Periodicals

Bechtel, Mark. "Just Perfect: Motocross is a Dirty Business, but Ricky Carmichael was Unswerving in his Dash to a Spotless Season." *Sports Illustrated,* (September 23, 2002): 12.

Cote, Alan. "Hey, Skinny." *Bicycling,* (September 2002): 52-55.

Other

Ballard, Chris. "American Idols: Lionized by Teens and Big-Name Athletes Alike, Motocross Stars Like Ricky Carmichael Draw NFL-sized Crowds for a Roaring, Soaring Spectacle." *CNNSI.com,* January 20, 2003. http://www.sportsillustrated.cnn.com/features/siadventure/23/American_idols/ (January 20, 2003).

"Carmichael Ranked No. 1 in ESPN Mag Poll." Racer X Online, November 18, 2002. http://www.racerxill.com (January 20, 2003).

"Carmichael Scores First Win of 2003 AMA Supercross Season." U.S. Motocross.com, January 19, 2003. http://www.usmotocross.com (January 20, 2003).

Cudby, Simon, and Donn Maeda. "Born to Win: A Ricky Carmichael Interview." Transworld Motocross, October 22, 2001. http://www.transworldmotocross.com (January 20, 2003).

Graveline, Eddie. "Interview: Ricky Carmichael." *Motopress.net,* January 5, 2001. http://www.motopress.net/main/riders/rickycarmichael.htm (January 20, 2003).

"Ricky Carmichael." U.S. Motocross.com. http://www.usmotocross.com (January 20, 2003).

"Ricky Carmichael." MXKing.com. http://www.mxking.com/hom.php3 (January 20, 2003).

"Ricky Carmichael Finishes Unprecedented Season!" Motoworld Racing.com, September 1, 2002. http://www.motoworldracing.com/ricky-perfect-season.html (January 20, 2003).

Short, Jim. "Carmichael Rides McGrath's Coattails." *The Press-Enterprise,* January 4, 2003. http://www.pe.com (January 20, 2003).

Short, Jim. "Carmichael Still Favored in the AMA." *The Press-Enterprise,* January 2, 2003. http://wwww.pe.com (January 20, 2003).

Short, Jim. "Carmichael: 'Villain.'" *The Press-Enterprise,* January 5, 2003. http://wwww.pe.com (January 20, 2003).

Sketch by Kari Bethel

Cris Carter
1965-

American football player

When wide receiver Cris Carter, who played most of his career with the Minnesota Vikings, retired after 15 years of playing football, he ranked second all-time in the NFL with 1,096 receptions, 129 of them for touchdowns. Carter, who is an eight-time Pro Bowl athlete, came out of retirement in October of 2002 to join the Miami Dolphins.

Overcame Addiction and Excelled

Carter played his first football game when he was eight years old, in a peewee league in Middletown, Ohio. When his teammates made a feeble attempt at tackling a large opponent, Carter became furious and said he would beat up anyone on his team who didn't play as hard as he did. His older brother, Butch, had to drag him off the field, telling him that this was not how team sports should be played. However, as Jeffri Chadiha noted in *Sports Illustrated,* Carter "was born with talent and a mean streak." Later in life, Carter would tame the mean streak, while retaining the talent.

Carter played for Ohio State University and began his professional career when he was drafted by the Philadelphia Eagles in 1987. His first reception as a pro player was a 22-yard touchdown catch. At the time, however, he was battling addictions to alcohol and cocaine. Carter flunked three drug tests while with the Eagles, who waived him in 1990. He overcame the addictions, turned his life around, and spent the next 12 years playing for the Minnesota Vikings.

Carter, who until then had held a fairly lax notion of training in the off-season—playing pickup basketball and occasional running— started as a backup but was in

Cris Carter

for a big change with the Vikings. Roger Craig, an all-pro running back from the San Francisco 49ers, joined the team, and when Carter asked him how he had become such a good player, Craig told him it was because he took his off-season training seriously. Carter took the hint, and began spending the entire day training. He has continued this regimen throughout his career. "Work is all I know," he told Chadiha. "There are no tricks. Right now I don't even think about football. I just push my body to the limit. When football season comes around, then I put it all together."

The training paid off. While playing with the Vikings, Carter went to the Pro Bowl eight consecutive times from 1993 to 2000. He was known for his avoidance of major injury, playing a full 16 games for 13 seasons. Carter had back-to-back 122-catch seasons in 1994 and 1995 and caught over 90 passes three other times.

In 1996, Carter became an ordained minister; since then, he has frequently testified about his past troubles with addiction and the role of spirituality in helping him overcome them. Carter told Chadiha, "I tell people that when they see alcoholics or drug addicts on the streets, they should think about me. . . . NFL Man of the Year, family man, a man who loves God. Yes, those things are all part of the picture, but so are the other things. They're all part of how I got to where I am now."

In 1998, Carter was devastated when his best chance to play in the Super Bowl slipped away. The Vikings, who had had a stellar season, were beaten by the Atlanta Falcons in overtime in the NFC Championship game. In the locker room after the game, Carter wept, and was unconsoled by teammates who insisted the team would be back and would someday have another chance. But the team made changes in personnel during the off-season, and Carter believed he would not have another chance to win the Super Bowl with the Vikings.

In 1999, Carter was awarded the NFL's Man of the Year Award. In that year, he also became the second player in NFL history to catch 1,000 passes in a career. Only the great **Jerry Rice** caught more passes in his career than Carter.

Talent and Hard Work

Carter has a rigorous workout schedule that includes football drills, speed and strength training, and yoga. He is part-owner of FAST, a speed-agility, and strength fitness center, and works out there. He couples this discipline with natural talent: he has long hands, wears size XX gloves, and is known for his dexterity as a player. In an informal survey in the *Sporting News,* Carter was voted the player with the best hands in the NFL. Carter is able to catch a ball with his fingertips, with one hand while diving to the ground, and, according to Dennis Dillon in the *Sporting News,* "there is his trademark sideline catch, where he stretches like a human rubber band horizontally, his entire body out of bounds except for his tiptoeing feet, and gathers the ball seemingly with his fingernails."

Carter has always practiced difficult catches, trying new and ever more difficult ways to snag a ball. Ohio State University athletics communications director Steve Snapp told Dillon that Carter was the only player he ever knew whose catches during practice would elicit applause from his teammates. In warmups, Carter will run 50 yards down the field and try to catch a pass behind his back; if he succeeds, which he does 50 percent of the time, he believes he will have a good playing day.

To Carter, catching is not just physical, but mental. He told Dillon that a catch is "seeing the point of the ball coming at you (spinning) like a cross, and it's al-

Career Statistics

Yr	Team	Receiving				Rushing				Fumbles	
		REC	YDS	AVG	TD	ATT	YDS	AVG	TD	FUM	LST
1987	PHI	5	84	16.8	2	0	0	0.0	0	0	0
1988	PHI	39	761	19.5	6	1	1	1.0	0	0	0
1989	PHI	45	605	13.4	11	2	16	8.0	0	1	0
1990	MIN	27	413	15.3	3	2	6	3.0	0	0	0
1991	MIN	72	962	13.4	5	0	0	0.0	0	0	0
1992	MIN	53	681	12.8	6	5	15	3.0	0	0	0
1993	MIN	86	1071	12.5	9	0	0	0.0	0	0	0
1994	MIN	22	1256	10.3	7	0	0	0.0	0	4	1
1995	MIN	122	1371	11.2	17	1	0	0.0	0	0	0
1996	MIN	96	1163	12.1	10	0	0	0.0	0	1	1
1997	MIN	89	1069	12.0	13	0	0	0.0	0	3	1
1998	MIN	78	1011	13.0	12	1	-1	-1.0	0	0	0
1999	MIN	90	1241	13.8	13	0	0	0.0	0	0	0
2000	MIN	96	1274	13.3	9	0	0	0.0	0	3	1
2001	MIN	68	811	11.9	6	1	4	4.0	0	1	1
2002	MIA	8	66	8.3	1	0	0	0.0	0	1	1
TOTAL		1101	13889	12.6	130	13	41	3.2	0	17	6

MIA: Miami Dolphins; MIN: Minnesota Vikings; PHI: Philadelphia Eagles.

most in slow motion. And my head is staying on the ball the whole time. That's the perfect catch." Carter visualizes catches, imagining himself running and catching the ball from many different positions and angles.

In addition to his skill in catching, Carter is also known for evading defenders, knocking a defender's hands off him at the line of scrimmage, or grabbing a defender's jersey and pushing him away. According to Dillon, he is so good at these moves that "it's hard to tell he's doing anything illegal." Cardinals cornerback Aeneas Williams told Dillon, "He does it in such a way that it's part of his release pattern—all one motion."

Retires But Returns to Play

In spring of 2002, unable to find a contract to play with a team that suited him, Carter announced his retirement after 15 seasons with the NFL. Sad to leave the Vikings, he told Bob Sansevere of the *Knight Ridder/Tribune News Service*, "I never thought I'd come to this cold place [Minnesota] and feel sad I'm leaving."

Carter accepted an offer to work as an analyst on the HBO program "Inside the NFL." According to Alex Marvez of the *Knight Ridder/Tribune News Service*, Carter told reporters at an HBO media conference, "[My playing career] has been a tremendous ride, and that ride has come to an end. I wanted to play football, but I had to be in the right situation."

In October of 2002, Carter found the right situation. He came out of retirement to join the Miami Dolphins, whose performance had suffered after a series of wide receivers were injured; the team hoped he would improve their performance. Although he was hesitant to return to play, his friend and former Dolphins quarter-

Awards and Accomplishments

1993-2000	Pro Bowl
1999	Wins NFL Man of the Year Award

back **Dan Marino** helped convince him to sign a one-year contract. Marino worked with Carter on "Inside the NFL." In an article on *Allsports.com,* Carter said that Marino told him, "You just have to do it. You can still play." Carter admitted that he missed playing, and noted that HBO would still pay him even if he did sign with Miami.

Carter joined the team on October 21, and was paired with team members in practice so that he could learn the team's offense. Although some of his new teammates were initially upset because Carter was signed as a starter, not a backup, he got along well with them. In the *Knight Ridder/Tribune News Service,* player James McKnight Alex Marvez, "The camaraderie in this locker room is the best I've ever been around." Carter, who appreciated the help and advice that was given to him by veteran players when he began his career, was happy to tutor young players. "I just think you should help people out no matter what profession you are in," he explained to Marvez. "To me, it's a crime for athletes or anyone else that has a talent or a skill when they don't try to share some of that with other people."

Player Bernardo Harris of the Baltimore Ravens told Mike Berardino in the *Knight Ridder/Tribune News Service,* "Cris is coming in, and a lot of pressure is put on him because he's the veteran guy, he's the name guy. The expectations are going to be so high. If he doesn't do anything, it's a letdown. If he does anything, it's expected." And he added, "He came out of retirement to save the team."

Unfortunately, Carter's return was short-lived. On November 9, 2002, Carter was admitted to the hospital and diagnosed with a kidney abnormality and was out of play for the rest of the season. His future in football was in doubt at the end of the 2002 season.

Carter told Sansevere that given the successes of his career, he expected to be inducted into the Pro Football Hall of Fame someday. "I look forward to that day," he said. "It's going to happen. Whenever it happens, I'll be overwhelmed with emotions."

CONTACT INFORMATION

Address: Cris Carter's Fast Program, 499 E. Spanish River Road, Boca Raton, FL. Phone: 1-866-552-5215. Email: info@fastprogram.com. Online: www.fastprogram. com.

FURTHER INFORMATION

Periodicals

Berardino, Mike. "All the Talk Only Motivates Cris Carter While He Regains His Health." *Knight Ridder/ Tribune News Service,* November 17, 2002, K0326.

Chadiha, Jeffri. "Time Trial." *Sports Illustrated,* July 3, 2000, 60.

Cole, Jason. "Cris Carter Out with Kidney Illness." *Knight Ridder/Tribune News Service,* November 9, 2002, K4011.

Dillon, Dennis. "Show of Hands." *Sporting News,* October 30, 2000, 10.

Marvez, Alex. "Cris Carter Chooses Cash Over Game." I. Knight May 25, 2002, K4478.

Marvez, Alex. "Newest Dolphin Cris Carter Has Plenty to Teach—and Learn." *Knight Ridder/Tribune News Service,* October 27, 2002, K4005.

"NFL Football: Cris Carter Leaves Hospital." *Sports Network,* November 16, 2002, 100831S6220.

Sansevere, Bob. "It Appears to Be Time for Cris Carter to Move On." *Knight Ridder/Tribune News Service,* December 23, 2001, K1851.

Other

"Cris Carter," ESPN.com. http://sports.espn.go.com/ (January 2, 2003)

"Inside the NFL: Hosts: Cris Carter," HBO.com. http:// www.hbo.com/ (January 3, 2003).

"WR Cris Carter Signs With Dolphins." Allsports.com. http://www.allsports.com/ (January 3, 2003).

Don Carter
1926-

American bowler

Known as Mr. Bowling, Don Carter was an early professional star in and tireless promoter of the sport of bowling. He was the first to make more than six figures in winnings. With his signature unconventional bowling style, Carter won more than forty individual, double, and team competitions. A founder of the Professional Bowlers Association (PBA) in the mid-1950s, Carter led the PBA twice in earnings and was named bowler of the year six times. He was the only professional bowler to win the Hickok Belt as the professional athlete of the year, in 1962.

Born July 29, 1926, in St. Louis, Missouri, Carter was the son of Gladys Carter. His father abandoned him, his mother, and his brother when he was a baby, and he was raised by his mother. While still in school, he helped support his family by working as a golf caddy and a pinsetter at a bowling alley.

Early Interest in Bowling

Working at the bowling alley peaked Carter's interest in bowling. To become good at the sport, he built a lane in the basement of his home so he could practice. But bowling was not his only sport. At Wellston High School, he was a star athlete in baseball (four varsity letters) and football (three letters).

When Carter graduated from high school in 1944, World War II was still being fought. He enlisted in the U.S. Navy after graduation. Carter served as a radarman, working on a military vessel. By the time he was discharged in 1946, Carter had reached the rank of third-class petty officer.

After his stint in the Navy ended, Carter did not turn to bowling right away, but became a professional baseball player first. In 1947, he signed a contract with the Philadelphia Athletics in the American League. Carter was assigned to their Class D farm team in Red Springs, North Carolina.

Chronology	
1926	Born July 29 in St. Louis, Missouri
1953	Joins Anheuser-Busch-sponsored bowling team; marries LaVerne Haverly, also a professional bowler
1958	Serves as PBA president
1973	Retires from Bowling competition
1976	Marries third wife Paula
1994	Comes out of retirement to compete in the Palm Beach Senior Classic

Don Carter

Carter had a short-lived career in the minor leagues. He played both pitcher and infielder at Red Springs. He had a .302 batting average while playing infield, but had a poor record as a pitcher. Carter decided that he would not make it as a major league baseball player and asked for his release after the season ended.

Returned to St. Louis

After Carter ended his baseball career, he returned to his home town of St. Louis. He found employment at an industrial plant and also worked as the manager of a bowling center. Bowling soon became a focus of his life. Carter bowled in six leagues and was a coach for other players.

By the early 1950s, Carter had become a successful professional bowler, one of the first to dominate the sport. One reason for his popularity was his appearance on early televised bowling shows and matches. This also made the sport more popular.

One aspect of his game that was noticed from his earliest days in the spotlight was Carter's unusual bowling style. As he made his approach, he would crouch lower and lower with each step. When he finally released the ball, it was with a bent elbow. Carter said one contributing factor to this style was that early in his career, he used a ball that was too heavy.

Other factors contributed to Carter's success. He had nerves of steel in competitions. And, as Chuck Pezzano wrote in the *Record*, "He was impressive physically at 6-feet, 200 pounds, and always in top shape. If he felt a certain part of his game needed fine-tuning, he thought nothing of working on it for hours."

Won Championships

Carter began winning professional titles in the early 1950s. In 1952, he won the U.S. All-Star Match-Game Championship (later known as the U.S. Open). He also won this tournament in 1954, 1956, and 1958. The following year, in 1953, he was asked to join the Anheuser-Busch-sponsored bowling team. Carter was important to team's success—included other future PBA Hall of Famers such as Ray Bluth, Pat Patterson, and Tom Hennessey.

Other big wins by Carter included six national titles between 1955 and 1962. In 1957, he won the World's In-

vitational title. Carter won it again each year from 1959 to 1962. For his championships and other professional accomplishments, he was named bowler of the year by the Bowling Writers Association of America in 1953, 1954, 1957, 1958, 1960, and 1962. In 1959, he was named first team All-American by *Bowling* magazine. Carter won this honor again every year through 1963.

Helped Found PBA

In 1958, Carter was a charter member of the PBA and served as the organization's first president. It was organized by Carter and other professional bowlers who wanted the professional tour to have a structure in terms of tournaments, travel, and organization. They modeled it after the Professional Golf Association (PGA) tour.

Carter was instrumental in making the PBA successful. It began sponsoring tournaments in 1959, and Carter was its early dominant bowler. His importance to the sport could be found when in 1961, an upstart rival, the National Bowling Association, was founded to challenge the PBA's dominance. While the National Bowling Association attracted many leading pros of the day, it lasted only a year in part because Carter would not leave the PBA.

Being an early part of the PBA was not Carter's only contribution to the sport. He also helped develop equipment. In 1959, Carter designed the first bowling glove, known as the Don Carter Glove. The glove had a small

Don Carter

pad that filled the space between the palm and the bowling ball that it gripped. It made the wearer feel like they had better control over the ball. Many of Carter's gloves were sold. He also came up with innovations for shoes and bowling bags.

By the 1960s, Carter had cemented his place at the top of his game, both professionally and from a business point of view. In 1960, he led the PBA in money won, and won the All-Star, World's Invitational and the PBA National Championship. Carter again led the PBA in money won in 1962, and became the only bowler to ever win the Hickok Belt as professional athlete of the year.

Carter capitalized on his fame with commercial endorsements. He had a 23-year-long association with Ebonite, including a ten-year deal he signed in the 1960s worth $100,000. At the time, it was the biggest deal for an athlete and one of the biggest ever for a bowler.

Carter understood what it took to become a leader at his sport. He told Pezzano of the *Record*, "To become a great bowler takes temperament and dedication. Bowling

is a very difficult game mentally. In golf, you see all the hazards. In bowling you don't see the slick boards. Every lane is different. You have to adjust for your mistakes. The best bowlers are the ones who are able to adjust."

Retired as Professional

Though Carter continued to bowl in the late 1960s and early 1970s, severe knee problems curtailed his effectiveness. His last professional tournament was at the 1972 Ebonite Open in Coral Gables, Florida. Carter officially retired in 1973.

At the end of his career, Carter had averaged 201 pins over his career. Known as the **Babe Ruth** of bowling, Carter had thirteen perfect games in tournaments and sanctioned events. Fellow PBA Hall of Fame member Dave Davis told Chuck Otterson of the *Palm Beach Post*, "Don had an impact on everybody in this sport. Don had that **Arnold Palmer**-type charisma. He and **Dick Weber** accomplished things using hard black rubber balls that have never been matched, even with today's lane conditions and urethane balls."

Awards and Accomplishments

1952, 1954, **1956, 1958**	U.S. All-Star Match-Game Championship
1953-54, **1957-58,** **1960, 1962**	Named Bowler of the Year by Bowling Writers Association of America
1957, **1959-62**	World's Invitational title
1959-63	Named first team All-American by *Bowling*
1960	Led Professional Bowlers Association in money won; won PBA National Championship
1962	Won Hickok Belt; led Professional Bowlers Association in money won
1970	Named Best Bowler of All Time by *Bowling*; named to the American Bowling Congress Hall of Fame
1975	Named charter member of the Professional Bowlers Association Hall of Fame
1995	Primary honoree at Salute to Champions dinner
1999	Named one of the 20 best bowlers of the 20th century by *Bowling*

CONTACT INFORMATION

Address: c/o 9895 SW 86th St., Miami, FL 33176.

SELECTED WRITINGS BY CARTER:

Ten Secrets of Bowling, Viking Press, 1958.
Bowling the Pro Way, Viking Press, 1975.

FURTHER INFORMATION

Books

Hickok, Ralph. *A Who's Who of Sports Champions.* Boston: Houghton Mifflin Company, 1995.
The Lincoln Library of Sports Champions. 2001.

Periodicals

Heroux Pounds, Marcia. "Sunrise, Fla., Bowling Firm Leader Pursues Younger Generation of Bowlers." Knight Ridder/Tribune Business News (October 18, 2002).
Otterson, Chuck. "Carter Shows Fans He's Still Kingpin." *Palm Beach Post* (October 2, 1994): 1C.
Otterson, Chuck. "Carter to End 22-Year Break from Competition." *Palm Beach Post* (August 17, 1994): 2C.
Pezzano, Chuck. "Carter Receives a Major Salute." *Record* (February 12, 1995): S19.
Pezzano, Chuck. "A Career of Excellence Proves Carter the Greatest." *Record* (October 19, 1994): S22.
Pezzano, Chuck. "Carter Centers: State-of-the-Art." *Record* (November 29, 1987): S19.
Pezzano, Chuck. "Legendary Don Carter Still Going Strong at 74." *Record* (April 29, 2001): S13.
Pezzano, Chuck. "A Vote for Carter As the Best Ever." *Record* (August 13, 1995): S18.

Where Is He Now?

After Carter retired in the early 1970s, he could no longer bowl because of his bad knees but did stay in the business side of bowling. He owned several alleys in St. Louis and other cities, and later founded, with partners, Don Carter Bowling Centers. Located in several states in the sun belt, there were fourteen centers by the mid-1990s. Though the company had problems in the late 1990s, it was reorganized and seven Don Carter Bowling Centers remained by 2002. At one time, Carter also had his own line of bowling apparel, gloves, shirts, and slacks.

Carter retired to Miami, Florida, with his third wife, Paula, and pursued hobbies like golfing and painting. He had knee replacement surgeries in the early 1990s, and began bowling in a scratch league in 1993. Carter then occasionally competed in pro-am bowling tournaments, including the Palm Beach Senior Classic as part of the Professional Bowlers Association Senior Tour in 1994. With wife Paula, Carter also brought Women's Intentional Bowling Council events to south Florida. Outside of bowling, Carter was involved in charity work, especially concerning children that had been abused and neglected.

Pezzano, Chuck. "Weber, Carter, Anthony Head Best of Century." *Record* (August 22, 1999): S17.
"20th Century's Top 20 to be Honored by ABC." *Record* (February 6, 2000): S15.

Sketch by A. Petruso

Vince Carter
1977-

American basketball player

One of the brightest young stars in professional basketball, Vince Carter has helped to popularize basketball in a country that long has focused the bulk of its sports interests on hockey during the fall and winter months. In only his second season with the Toronto Raptors, he led the young franchise to its first-ever appearance in the National Basketball Association (NBA) playoffs. Carter's explosive style of play and dazzling moves on the basketball court have won the hearts of Canadians and gained greater exposure for the Raptors. A member of the U.S. Olympic basketball team that won gold at Sydney, Australia, in 2000, Carter was a basketball star in high school and college, leading the University of North Carolina Tar Heels to the National Collegiate Athletic Association (NCAA) Tournament's Final Four twice during his years at Chapel Hill. Carter was selected fifth in the first round of the 1998 NBA draft by the Golden State Warriors but was traded immediately to the Raptors. In his first four seasons with the Raptors (through 2001-02), Carter averaged 24.1 points and 5.6 rebounds per game.

Vince Carter

Chronology

1977	Born in Daytona Beach, Florida, on January 26
1995-98	Attends University of North Carolina
1998	Picked by Golden State Warriors in first round of NBA draft
1998	Traded by Warriors to Toronto Raptors
2001	Earns bachelor's degree from University of North Carolina

Born in Daytona Beach, Florida

He was born Vincent Lamar Carter in Daytona Beach, Florida, on January 26, 1977. The son of Vince and Michelle Carter, who divorced when Carter was seven years old, he showed an early interest and talent in both music and sports. Although he excelled at basketball as a boy, his mother and stepfather, Harry Robinson, both schoolteachers, endeavored to ensure that Carter had as well-rounded a background as possible, encouraging him to pursue his interest in music as well as sports. As a student at Mainland High School in Daytona Beach, Carter played alto, baritone, and tenor saxophone in the marching band and also led the band as drum major. A talented composer, Carter wrote the school's homecoming song. By the time he reached his junior year in high school, however, Carter found himself focusing more and more of his time and energy on basketball. He led the school's basketball team to the 1994-95 Florida Class 6A championship. In his senior year Carter turned down a music scholarship to nearby Bethune-Cookman College in favor of a basketball scholarship to the University of North Carolina.

After a slow start as a freshman, averaging only 7.5 points per game, Carter began to make a name for himself in Tar Heel basketball during his sophomore year, nearly doubling both his playing time and scoring average. At season's end, he led the Tar Heels squad to the NCAA Tournament's Final Four, where North Carolina lost to the eventual national champion, Arizona. Solidifying his growing reputation as an all-around player, Carter led the Tar Heels back to the NCAA Final Four during his junior year. After a brilliant season as a junior, he declared himself eligible for the NBA draft of 1998. Making good on a promise to his mother and stepfather that he would not abandon his goal of earning a college degree, Carter continued to pursue his studies during summer sessions and eventually received his bachelor's degree in 2001.

Picked Fifth Overall in NBA Draft

Carter was picked fifth overall in the first round of the 1998 NBA draft by California's Golden State Warriors and traded almost immediately to the Toronto Raptors for Antawn Jamison, his former teammate at North Carolina. Although his debut with the Raptors was delayed by a players' strike, his presence seemed to energize the young franchise, which for the first time made a serious challenge for a playoff berth. He also worked to promote not just his team but basketball in general with multiple appearances on ESPN and other sports programming. This was particularly apparent in Canada where interest in professional basketball-and ticket sales-jumped dramatically. Carter's rookie card sold for as much as $10, and sports stores found it almost impossible to keep Carter's number 15 jersey in stock. In an interview with Michael Farber of *Sports Illustrated,* Carter expressed surprise at his impact on the city of Toronto and the NBA. "I didn't plan for it to be this way. My goal was to fit in, gradually work my way to being an impact player. My whole scheme fell through from Day One."

During the 1999-2000 season, Carter's second season with the Raptors, he improved his scoring average to 25.7 points per game from 18.3 points per game in his rookie season. Thanks to his electrifying style of play and spectacular slam dunks, Carter found himself increasingly compared to then-retired NBA superstar **Michael Jordan.** Many touted Carter as the player most likely to succeed Jordan as *the* star of professional basketball. Although such comparisons were pleasing to Carter in some ways, they also created a sense of pressure he could have lived without. As his mother told Mike Wise of the *New York Times,* "the Michael Jordan comparison is something he's been dealing with since high school. On the one hand, it's very flattering. You can't overlook the similarities. By the same token, it gets a little old, too. Vince gets tired of hearing it."

Career Statistics

Yr	Team	GP	PTS	FG%	3P%	FT%	RPG	APG	SPG	BPG
1998-99	TOR	50	18.3	.450	.288	.761	5.7	3.0	1.1	1.5
1999-00	TOR	82	25.7	.465	.403	.791	5.8	3.9	1.3	1.1
2000-01	TOR	75	27.6	.460	.408	.765	5.5	3.9	1.5	1.1
2001-02	TOR	60	24.7	.428	.387	.798	5.2	4.0	1.6	0.7
TOTAL		267	24.1	.451	.372	.779	5.6	5.5	1.4	1.1

TOR: Toronto Raptors.

Emerges into Ranks of NBA Stardom

Carter's emergence into the ranks of NBA stardom was signaled by a last-minute programming change made by NBC Sports one day after Carter won the slam dunk competition during the All-Star Game weekend of his second season. The network shifted a Raptors game into its main programming slot in place of a New York Knicks game originally scheduled to be broadcast. To further showcase Carter, the program featured a pregame introductory piece on Carter, as well as interviews at half time and after the game with the Raptors star. Rising to the occasion, Carter scored a spectacular 51 points during the game. This flattering programming change was followed by a bitter disappointment when Carter was passed over in the selection of players for the U.S. Olympic basketball team. Although he tried not to let his omission from the team bother him, it did cause Carter to focus more on winning play rather than flashy, grandstanding moves on the court. He told the Associated Press: "It has helped me step up. I said, 'OK, you just have to show the world what you can do night in and night out.'" Carter eventually was added to the Olympic squad when one of the original players selected suffered a knee injury.

With Carter focused more intensely on winning play, the Raptors in 2000 made it into the NBA playoffs for the first time in franchise history. Toronto faced off against the Knicks in the first round of the playoffs. Although the Raptors had beaten the Knicks three times during the regular season, the New York team made short work of Toronto in the playoffs, sweeping the series in three games. Shadowed by the Knicks' **Latrell Sprewell** throughout the series, Carter was held to only 15 of 50 field goal attempts.

Joy Disappears from Carter's Game

One of the characteristics that had helped to endear Carter to Canadian basketball fans was the obvious joy he took in the game. Between the end of the Raptors' season in the playoffs and the start of the Olympics, some of that joy seemed to disappear. Contributory factors included a separation between his mother and stepfather, a criminal investigation into the activities of Carter's former agent, Tank Black, legal hassles over termination of a shoe contract, and being passed over in the selection process for the U.S. Olympic team. Added to the Olympic team as a substitute for an injured player, it was a radically different Carter who took the court in the Olympics. Gone was his trademark smile. In its place was a look of grim determination and even rage. But, if anything, this pent-up anger at a whole constellation of real and perceived indignities and injuries only sharpened Carter's play. He quickly emerged as the U.S. basketball team's dominant force, leading the squad in scoring. Finally, in the moments after the team seized gold, all the hurt and frustration of the recent past seemed, at least for the moment, to be shed.

Particularly hurtful to Carter were some of the comments made about him by teammate and distant cousin Tracy McGrady after leaving the Raptors for the Orlando Magic in August 2000. McGrady said publicly that he needed to needed to carve out a niche somewhere for himself, but his mother told the media that her son had grown tired of hearing about Carter constantly. Carter admitted later that McGrady's comments "bothered me for a long time. It was wild. My head was spinning so fast. I read [his mother's quotes]; then people said he was saying the same things on TV. I said, 'Fine. If that's how he feels, so be it.' I couldn't find enough guts to call him and say, 'What's going on?'"

Ranks Fifth in Scoring during 2000-2001

During Carter's 2000-2001 season in the NBA, he averaged 27.6 points per game, ranking fifth in the NBA for scoring. He also ranked sixth in the league in three-point field goals. Despite his continued success on the basketball court, one of Carter's proudest moments in 2001 came in May when he received his bachelor's degree in African-American studies at the University of North Carolina. He hoped to continue his studies over the next few years to earn a master's degree in business administration or communications. Carter's scoring average slipped slightly during the season of 2001-02, falling to 24.7 points per game. He averaged 5.2 rebounds and 4 assists per game for the season and was selected to play in his third consecutive NBA All-Star Game.

Vince Carter

One of Carter's proudest accomplishments off the court has been his Embassy of Hope Foundation, established in 1998 to help needy children and their families in his home state of Florida and adopted hometown of Toronto. The foundation's slogan—"Believing in Your Dreams"—represents Carter's personal approach to success and is intended to serve as inspiration to others that they too can work hard enough to make their dreams come true. For his work with the foundation and other humanitarian efforts, Carter in 2000 was named Child Advocate-of-the-Year by the Children's Home Society. Carter is also actively involved in "Vince's HOOP Group," a program to recognize student achievement in Canadian schools. He also participates in the NBA's Read to Achieve program.

Love of the Game

Carter's career has only just begun. Barring serious injury, he is likely to be playing pro ball a decade or so from now. Whether he ever becomes the NBA's next Michael Jordan, only time will tell. But there can be little doubt that Carter is likely to remain a dominant force in professional basketball for the foreseeable future. As for Carter himself, he seems prepared to face whatever

---

> ### Related Biography: Basketball Player Tracy McGrady
>
> One of Carter's closest friends during his first two seasons in Toronto was his fellow Raptor and distant cousin Tracy McGrady Jr. Carter and McGrady lived in the same Toronto apartment building and spent much of their time off court in each other's company. Over time, however, the warm relationship between the two players chilled somewhat as Carter consistently outpaced McGrady's efforts on the court.
>
> As Carter continued to occupy more and more of the spotlight in Toronto, McGrady began to yearn for some breathing space, hoping that he might develop better on his own. In August 2000 he left the Raptors and signed a lucrative free-agent contract with the Orlando Magic. In announcing his decision to leave the Raptors, McGrady said he wanted to be able carve out his own space somewhere and he hoped that playing for the Magic would afford him that opportunity. McGrady's mother, however, said her son had grown tired of hearing about Carter all the time. Although Carter initially reacted angrily to McGrady's remarks, the two have since patched up their relationship to some degree and look forward to a continuing rivalry between their teams.
>
> McGrady was born in Bartow, Florida, on May 24, 1979. Beginning at the age of five, he participated in a wide variety of sports but had focused largely on basketball by the time he entered high school. He left Auburndale (FL) High School to finish his senior year at Mount Zion Christian Academy in Durham, North Carolina, and entered the NBA draft immediately after high school. He was drafted in 1977 by the Raptors.

comes his way. As he told Bill Harris of the *Toronto Sun,* "I'm ready to take on all challenges. I don't care what it is or what people have to say, bring it. You can say what you want, but I'm going to step in and represent who I am and what I can do."

CONTACT INFORMATION

Address: c/o Toronto Raptors, 150 York St., Toronto, ON M5H 355, Canada. Online: http://www.vince-carter15.com.

FURTHER INFORMATION

Books

"Vince Carter." *Contemporary Black Biography,* Volume 26. Farmington Hills, MI: Gale Group, 2000.

"Vince Carter." *Newsmakers,* Issue 4. Farmington Hills, MI: Gale Group, 2001.

Periodicals

Harris, Bill. "Raptors Are Only as Good as Vince; Superstar Is in the Spotlight." *Toronto Sun* (October 1, 2001): 61.

Price, S. L. "Semi-Tough: The Raptors' Vince Carter Has Star Power to Burn, But Can He Stoke Up the Competitive Fire That Rages in the Game's Elite Players?" *Sports Illustrated* (January 29, 2001): 66.

Ulmer, Mike. "Vince Needs a Makeover; Carter Very Popular But He's Not That Cool." *Toronto Sun* (August 23, 2002): 94.

Other

"#15, Vince Carter." ESPN.com. http://sports.espn.go. com/nba/players/statistics?statsId=3248 (December 10, 2002).

"Tracy McGrady, Jr." *Biography Resource Center Online*. Farmington Hills, MI: Gale Group, 2001.

"Vince Carter." *Biography Resource Center Online*. Farmington Hills, MI: Gale Group, 2001.

"Vince Carter Biography." Vince Carter's Official Web Site. http://www.vincecarter15.com/aboutme/ bio.sps?sid=8819&lid=1&eid=null&aid=0 (December 13, 2002).

Sketch by Don Amerman

Alexander Cartwright

Alexander Cartwright
1820-1892

American baseball pioneer

Ask baseball fans the name of their sport's founder, and most will answer "Abner Doubleday." Yet it was not the Civil War general who laid down the groundwork for America's most popular game. The man who did perhaps the most to formalize and codify modern baseball was one Alexander Cartwright, a New York City banker. Neither Cartwright nor Doubleday can truly be credited with inventing baseball—which traces its roots back to a centuries-old English children's game known as "rounders"—yet it was Cartwright who founded the first official baseball club, the Knickerbockers, in 1845, and who published the first set of formal rules for the game in September of that year.

Formed First Recognized Baseball Team

Alexander Joy Cartwright, Jr., was born on April 17, 1820, in New York City. The son of a marine surveyor and former sea captain, Cartwright grew up in lower Manhattan, where as a boy he played the common children's game known alternately as rounders, base ball, or town ball. He attended school until age 16, when he left to become a bank clerk, and later, a volunteer firefighter. In 1842 he married Eliza Ann Gerrits Van Wie, who hailed from an old Dutch family near Albany.

A strapping, unusually tall man for his day, at 6 feet 2 inches, Cartwright was popular among a crowd of young New York bankers, lawyers, and businessmen, who on fair days after work gathered to play rounders at Parade Ground meadow or at Madison Square. In 1845, 25-year-old Cartwright—known to his friends as Alick—proposed that the group create an organized club. Thus was born the Knickerbocker Base Ball Club, named after a disbanded firefighter company where Cartwright had once volunteered. Cartwright was named secretary and vice-president when the club formed in September of that year.

Perhaps more important than Cartwright's creation of the club was the Knickerbockers' official organization of the game with a constitution and bylaws. The bylaws—some 14 written rules created by Cartwright and his club mates—transformed baseball from a folk sport, with rules passed down orally over the centuries, to a formal, structured sport. The rules also made the game less rough-and-tumble and more genteel, since they abolished the common practice of soaking or plugging—that is, hitting the runner with the ball to make an out. This change made it safer for players to use a harder ball, which led to a faster, more exciting game. Other bylaws Cartwright instituted included the diamond-shaped field, the rules of fair and foul territories, and the 90-foot distance between each of the four bases.

Cartwright is often credited with establishing the rule that nine players compose a baseball team; however, the Knickerbockers were not consistent with their number of players, which, in a given game, ranged from 8 to 12. The position of shortstop—a player between the second and third bases, whose job was mainly to relay throws from the outfield to the infield—was not instituted until 1849. Nor was it Cartwright who established the nine-inning game length, which was created by a convention of players in 1857. In the early days of the sport, the game would end when the first team scored a winning 21 runs.

The first organized baseball team needed an opponent, so the Knickerbockers advertised for games. Stepping up to the challenge was a team called the New York Nine. Since lower Manhattan had become increasingly more urban and there was little space for a baseball diamond, the players had sought out new territory across the Hudson River in then-rural Hoboken, New Jersey. To get there, both clubs crossed the river by ferry, then walked to Elysian Fields, a picturesque park and a popular holiday destination. It is Elysian Fields that takes credit for hosting the first recognized modern baseball game, between the Knickerbockers and the New York Nine, on June 19, 1846.

Spread the Rules of the Game

Cartwright did not remain with the Knickerbockers very long. In March of 1849, the 29-year-old bank clerk, like so many other Americans, followed the California Gold Rush in hopes of making his fortune out west. Yet he did not abandon baseball; rather, he took it with him. A kind of Johnny Appleseed of the sport, Cartwright helped spread the game as he traveled across the country by train, covered wagon, and foot. From Pittsburgh to Cincinnati to the Midwest to San Francisco, he taught the sport to locals and encouraged the creation of formal clubs.

Though the game spread first through the northeastern United States, within 15 years baseball had taken root across the country. While Cartwright played a role in its burgeoning popularity, it was the American Civil War (1861-1865) that prompted the game's growth as a national pastime. Union soldiers formed teams and Confederate prisoners picked up the rules of the game; when the soldiers returned home, they took the sport with them.

When Cartwright arrived in San Francisco, the Gold Rush was over; he stayed only six weeks, but in that short time he did much to spread the word about baseball in that city. Deciding to return to New York, he boarded a ship set to sail across the Pacific, Indian, and Atlantic oceans. Yet water travel did not suit Cartwright, who fell ill and disembarked at the Sandwich Islands-known today as Hawaii. Regaining his health and falling in love with the lush islands, he decided to stay. Cartwright's wife and children joined him in 1851.

Naturally, Cartwright taught baseball to the islanders and formed Hawaiian baseball clubs—which explains why the sport took hold in Honolulu even before it became established in cities like Philadelphia and Chicago. Cartwright is also credited with giving Honolulu its first volunteer fire department, of which he served as chief for ten years. The enterprising man quickly grew prosperous, becoming one of the Honolulu's leading bankers and merchants, and managing the finances of Hawaii's royal family. Cartwright was also active in local government. Among his contributions as a civic leader were the founding of the Hawaiian city's first library and first major hospital.

Recognized for Contribution to Sport

When he died on July 12, 1892, Cartwright was one of Honolulu's most respected citizens. He never returned to the mainland United States to see just how popular his beloved sport had become—and in the world of baseball, his contribution was largely forgotten. It was not until 1938, when a special committee of baseball veterans reviewed his journals, that Cartwright gained proper recognition. That year, he was elected to Baseball's Hall of Fame for originating the sport's basic concepts. Even today, only the most well-versed sports historians and enthusiasts recognize Cartwright as the true father of modern American baseball.

FURTHER INFORMATION

Books

Peterson, Harold. *The Man Who Invented Baseball.* New York: Charles Scribner's Sons, 1973.

Periodicals

"Honolulu's Link to Baseball History." *Travel Weekly* (June 19, 1997): 29.

"Time Trip." *Current Events* (December 7, 2001): 2.

Other

"Alexander Cartwright." BaseballLibrary.com. http://www.pubdim.net/baseballlibrary/ballplayers/C/Cartwright_Alexander.stm (October 4, 2002).

"Alexander Cartwright." Baseball Hall of Fame. http://www.baseballhalloffame.org/hofers_and_honorees/hofer_bios/Cartwright_Alexander.htm (October 3, 2002).

Biography Resource Center. Detroit: The Gale Group, 2002.

"Cartwright, Alexander J." Hickok Sports.com. http://www.hickoksports.com/biograph/cartwrig,shtml (October 4, 2002).

Sketch by Wendy Kagan

Rosemary Casals

Rosemary Casals
1948-

American tennis player

Rosemary Casals teamed with **Billie Jean King** to become one of the top doubles tandems ever in women's tennis. On the court, Casals disdained the conservative, baseline strategy that had been the trademark of the women's game until the late 1960s. Casals, however, may have been most effective as a rebel off-court. She, along with pioneer King and others, fought for better pay and media attention for the women's game and helped originate the separate pro tour in the 1970s.

She won 11 singles and 112 pro doubles titles overall, including 11 Grand Slam doubles titles, primarily with King. "Tiny package, explosive contents. Tennis was no waiting game at the baseline," longtime tennis journalist Bud Collins wrote of Casals on his web site. "She went for the jugular fast, a serve-and-volleying acrobat whose incredible arsenal of strokes and tankful of competitive verve were necessities merely to stay alive among the sisterhood that established female professional tennis during the 1970s."

Rich Game, Poor Background

Casals, born in San Francisco, was a distant relative of famed cellist Pablo Casals, but grew up poor to parents had moved to the United States from El Salvador. They arranged for Manuel and Maria Casals, her great-uncle and great-aunt, to raise her. Rosemary Casals began playing on the city's free tennis courts at Golden Gate Park; Manuel Casals was her only tennis coach. Ambitious, she insisted on playing against older players in junior tournaments.

At 5-foot-2, Casals faced a distinct height advantage on the court, but her biggest battle may have involved class conflict. Her impoverished background sharply contrasted with the affluence of many peers. Casals, however, channeled her aggressions into her play. With such nicknames as "Rosie" and "Rosebud" fast becoming misnomers, Casals earned a reputation, and popularity among many fans, for charging the net and even launching a shot from between her legs. She also won. She was the top junior and women's level player in Northern California by age 16. One year later she was ranked first in the country.

Her best play was in doubles. She and singles standout Billie Jean King teamed up to capture the U.S. hard-court and indoor tournaments in 1966, and in 1967, they prevailed in women's doubles at Wimbledon and the U.S. championships (later the U.S. Open), and also the South African championships. Casals and King became

Chronology

1948	Born November 16 in San Francisco, California
1970	Helped organize threat to boycott traditional tournaments if pay for women's tennis players not increased
1971	Virginia Slims women's tour commences
1972	Wimbledon official orders Casals to change out of purple-lined white dress, citing tournament policy
1973	Network TV commentator on "Battle of the Sexes" exhibition tennis match between King and Bobby Riggs
1974	Appeared in episode of ABC-TV series "Love American Style."

Awards and Accomplishments

1966	Wins U.S. hardcourt and indoor championships with doubles partner Billie Jean King
1967	Casals and King capture Wimbledon and U.S. Open women's doubles championships
1968	Repeats Wimbledon doubles title with King
1970	Wimbledon mixed doubles champion with Ilie Nastase
1970-71	Casals and King win consecutive Wimbledon doubles titles
1971	U.S. Open women's doubles champion with Judy Tegart Dalton
1972	Wimbledon mixed doubles champion with Nastase
1973	Captures fifth Wimbledon's doubles title with King
1973	Wins Family Circle Cup championship and first prize of $30,000, considered major payout at the time
1974	U.S. Open women's doubles champion with King
1982	U.S. Open women's doubles champion with Wendy Turnbull
1990	Wins U.S. Open Seniors' women's doubles title with King
1996	Inducted into International Tennis Hall of Fame

the only tandem to win U.S. titles on grass, clay, indoor and hard surfaces.

But her success as a doubles player meant that Casals's individual play was underappreciated. She rose to third in singles in 1970. Over her 15 years, Casals was 12 times in the top 10. She reached at least the quarterfinals in all four major tournaments.

Fought for Women's Improvements

Casals, drawing on her upbringing, helped lead the crusade to end what she felt was discrimination against players from poorer backgrounds. Major tournaments such as Wimbledon admitted only amateurs, who were independently wealthy, Other players, Casals said, had to take money to keep playing. Pure amateurs were independently wealthy. The "open format" was introduced in 1968, allowing both amateur and professional players to play in the same tournaments. In 1970, Casals and other leading women's players threatened to boycott major tournaments, and after the United States Lawn Tennis Association rebuffed their demands, the women began their own event, the Virginia Slims International.

"Billie Jean King and protege Rosie Casals ... [were] names that went together like wine and roses," Bud Collins wrote in his *Bud Collins' Tennis Encyclopedia* biography, published on the International Tennis Hall of Fame website. "But all the while their influence as pioneering pros ran deeper than the five Wimbledon and two U.S. titles together. Although Rosie, the riveting volleyer, is the smallest modern in the tennis valhalla, she and Billie Jean were giants in launching the long march of the 'Long Way Babies' as the Virginia Slims circuit began to take shape in 1970." The Slims circuit is the forerunner to today's WTA Tour.

"It was becoming increasingly clear that the women players were being left with little more than the crumbs from the way a male-dominated game divided the prize money, as Open tennis, which only began in 1968, began to expand and flourish," wrote John Parsons of the London *Daily Telegraph* on the WTA Tour's Web site. "Matters came to head only a couple of weeks after **Margaret Smith Court** had earned barely one third of the

amount collected by the men's singles champion for winning the women's singles title at the (1970) U.S. Open—and with it the Grand Slam."

Casals also found herself at odds with Wimbledon officials in 1972 when she wore a purple-patterned white dress designed by "The Leaning Tower of Pizzazz," Briton Ted Tinling. Tournament coordinators insisted Casals leave the court and return wearing all-white. Casals later claimed that the dress she wore became so famous that it won a place in the tennis hall of fame before she herself did.

Slims Tour Takes Shape

Gladys Heldman of *World Tennis* magazine, also a Hall of Famer, put up $5,000 of her own money and provided operational help to King and Casals. "B.J. and Rosie were the ringleaders on court, close doubles partners, (and) frequent final-round saleswomen for the emerging tour," Collins wrote. "They were perfect role players, feisty but good-humored kids off the public courts who believed women had a destiny in professional sport."

In 1971, the first full year of the Slims tour, Casals competed in a record 32 tournaments in singles, 31 in doubles-in all, 205 matches. King played in 210. "More than 200 matches in a season? **Steffi Graf** has played as many as 117 only once," Collins wrote. By then, the USTA and other associations had lifted their sanctions. In 1973 Casals, who competed in a record 685 singles and doubles tournaments throughout her career, won the first large-pay tournament, collecting $30,000 with the Family Circle Cup, while defeating King and clay-court specialist Nancy Richey.

Casals won eight of her 10 Grand Slam doubles titles playing with King. She also won the U.S. Open with Judy Tegart Dalton in 1971 and with Ilie Nastase, in mixed doubles, in 1975. She and Nastase took Wimbledon mixed doubles in 1970 and 1972. "For sheer shot-making sorcery, plus merrymaking on one side of the net, the amalgam of Casals and Ilie Nastase, winning the Wimbledon mixed in 1970 and 1972, may never be equalled," Collins wrote.

Casals was also a commentator on the ABC telecast of the "battle of the sexes" exhibition match in September, 1973, between King and Bobby Riggs at Houston's Astrodome. It drew 30,472 spectators, a tennis record. Some media critics railed over the choice of Casals, because of her longstanding affiliation and friendship with King. Riggs was known for trumpeting male athletic superiority. King won 6-4, 6-3, 6-3 in a match seen as a publicity breakthrough for women's sports.

Later Years

In the mid-1970s, Casals also joined another new venture, World Team Tennis, in which teams consisting of two women and four men apiece traveled across the U.S. Casals played for the Detroit Loves and Oakland Breakers and coached the Los Angeles Strings. She retired shortly after having knee surgery in 1978. The International Tennis Hall of Fame inducted her in 1996. "Doubles was her shtick, 56 of them with King," Collins wrote. "But Rosie was a singles contender at all the majors. She just wanted to be the best ever. Inch-for-inch she was—and the fun flowed in all directions from this diminutive dynamo who took such joy from playing, and passed it all along to grateful witnesses."

FURTHER INFORMATION

Books

Altman, Linda Jacobs. *Rosemary Casals: The Rebel Rosebud.* St. Paul: EMC Corp., 1975.

Thacher, Alida M. *Raising a Racket: Rosie Casals.* Chicago: Children's Press, 1976.

Other

Collins, Bud. "Rosie Casals, Class of 1996." International Tennis Hall of Fame, http://www.tennisfame.org/enshrinees/rosie_casals.html, (January 11, 2003).

Gale Group, Women's History Month, http://www.galegroup.com/free_resources/whm/bio/casals_r.htm, (January 6, 2003).

"The Week's Famous and Infamous Women." Women's Stories, http://writetools.com/women/stories/casals_rosemary.html, (January 6, 2003).

Sketch by Paul Burton

Tracy Caulkins
1963-

American swimmer

One of the greatest swimmers ever produced by the United States in terms of her versatility, Tracy Caulkins was at her peak in the late 1970s and early 1980s. Caulkins won a record 48 national championships, and set five world and 62 U.S. records. She was the first American to win a national title and set an American record in each of the four swimming strokes (backstroke, breaststroke, butterfly, and freestyle). Caulkins is also the youngest athlete to ever win the Sullivan Award, awarded each year to the outstanding amateur athlete in the United States.

Caulkins was born January 11, 1963, in Winona, Minnesota, the youngest of three children of Thomas Caulkins and his wife Martha. Her father was a group-testing coordinator for public schools, who later became a part-time swim coach. Her mother was a junior high school art teacher. Caulkins grew up in Waukon, Iowa, until the age of six, when the family moved to Nashville, Tennessee.

Began Swimming

When Caulkins was eight years old, she began swimming at the Seven Hills Swim and Tennis Club, where her older siblings, Amy and Tim, already swam. Originally Caulkins would only swim the backstroke because she did not like getting her face wet. She eventually learned the other strokes, and though she hated the cold water and did not want to practice at first, in a short amount of time she became very good. With the encouragement of her mother and father, Caulkins realized her potential and began to embrace the tougher aspects of swimming.

At the age of ten, Caulkins joined the West Side VC (later known as the Nashville Aquatic Club) and was shortly ranked in the top ten in the nation in a few swimming events. Only two years later, when she was 12 years old, Caulkins qualified for the senior nationals. Some reasons for her success as a swimmer could be

Tracy Caulkins

Chronology

1963	Born January 11, in Winona, Minnesota
1971	Begins swimming with the Seven Hills Club
1973	Joins the West Side VC
1975	Qualifies for and competes in the senior nationals for the first time
1976	Competes at the Summer Olympic Trials
1978	Sets three world records
1980	Makes U.S. Olympic team, but does not compete because the U.S. boycotts the Olympic Games
1981	Enters University of Florida; becomes the only swimmer in U.S. history of the sport to win the greatest number of national titles
1982	Wins 36th title, surpassing record set by Johnny Weismuller
1982-84	Becomes member of Swimming All-American Team
1984	Competes in the Summer Olympic Games; becomes captain of the U.S. swim team; retires from swimming
1985	Graduates from the University of Florida
1991	Marries Australian swimmer Mark Stockwell

found in her body; she had hyperextended knees that gave her leverage and had the ability to do a great kick. She also had a solid stroke and could glide through the water. With her big feet, long arms, and long wingspan, Caulkins's body was built for swimming. At her peak, she was five feet, nine inches tall and 135 lbs.

As Caulkins's swimming training intensified, it began to affect her schooling. Her public junior high school would not accommodate her need to travel for her swimming, so she transferred to Harpeth Hall Academy, a private girl's school. Harpeth was supportive of her swimming, but also was academically demanding.

Won First National Titles

When Caulkins was 13 years old, she competed in the Olympic Trials for the 1976 Summer Olympics. She did not qualify, but within a year, she would have several titles under her belt and an international reputation. In 1977, she won her first national titles in the Amateur Athletic Union (AAU) National Championships in the 100- and 200-meter short course breaststroke, and the 200- and 400-meter long course individual medleys. She also won the 100-meter breaststroke at the U.S. Indoor National Championships that year. Caulkins's international status was cemented at a swim meet between the United States and Germany, when she defeated Andrea Pollock, who had won the gold medal in the 200-meter butterfly at the 1976 Olympics.

Caulkins did not make a big deal of these accomplishments, but remained focused and determined. She trained hard, swimming eight to ten miles a day and lifting weights three days a week. She even swam with a cast when she broke her leg in 1977. Her father told J. D. Reed of *Sports Illustrated,* "Tracy really doesn't believe that she's done anything yet that's worth getting excited about. She never says much about swimming."

Best Year as a Swimmer

Although she was only in her late teens, Caulkins was a dominant force in swimming in the late 1970s. The year 1978 was arguably her best as a swimmer. She won the Sullivan Award for best amateur athlete because of the number of championships she had won and records she had set. Caulkins won world championships in the 200-meter butterfly, 200- and 400-meter individual medleys, and won a silver medal in the 100-meter breaststroke. She also won national championships in the 200-meter long course butterfly, the short course individual medleys, and both the 100- and 200-meter breaststroke. At the AAU National Short Course Championships, she set five U.S. records, winning the 200-meter medley, the 200-meter backstroke, the 100-meter breaststroke, and the 400-meter individual medley. At the AAU Long Course Championships she set two world records and five American records, and also won the 200-meter butterfly. In total, in 1978 she broke or tied 27 records, both world and American records.

In 1979, Caulkins continued to dominate on both the American and international stage. She won two gold medals and two silver medals at the Pan American Games, set five U.S. records at the AAU National Short Course Championships, and won numerous events including the 100-meter breaststroke, 500-meter freestyle, 400-meter individual medley, 400-meter medley relay, 400-meter freestyle relay, and the 200-meter individual medley.

Caulkins also took second in the 800-meter freestyle relay. Although she had been sick with a virus a short time before the event, Caulkins did well there; her great concentration and will to win overcame her bodily weakness.

By this time, Caulkins's dominance was recognized, though her only "weakness" was the backstroke. The University of Southern California's swim coach, Peter Daland, told *Sports Illustrated,* "She's probably the greatest swimmer in the world today, male or female, and her event possibilities are almost unlimited. I'm sure that if she were to train for a month for backstroke that she would be giving the champion here ... all she could handle. We've had some great versatile people, but she probably is as good as anybody we've had. And the thing that's most amazing about her is that she has the speed to go sprints and the stamina to go distance."

Olympic Boycott Affected Caulkins

By the 1980 Summer Olympics, which were held in Moscow, U.S.S.R., Caulkins expected to dominate because she easily made the U.S. team. But the United States decided to boycott the games because of the Soviet Union's invasion of Afghanistan. Though denied a chance at Olympic gold, Caulkins still swam at the National Outdoor Championships, winning four gold medals and one silver, and was named American Swimmer of the Year.

Despite her Olympic disappointment, Caulkins continued to pile up honors in swimming. In 1981, she became the only swimmer in U.S. history to win the greatest number of titles when she bested the records set by Ann Curtis Cuneo. In January at the U.S. Swimming International, she won 200- and 400-meter individual medleys, 100-meter breaststroke, and 100-meter backstroke, setting world records. She also finished second in the 100-meter and 200-meter butterfly, and was part of three winning women's relays. At this meet, she swam against the best swimmers in the world, many of whom competed in the 1980 Olympics, and more than held her own. She also competed in the National Short Course, winning the 200-meter backstroke, setting a national record, and winning three other events in similar fashion.

Began College Career

In 1981, Caulkins entered the University of Florida, where she majored in communications and trained harder in anticipation of the Summer Olympics in 1984. She won 12 NCAA Championships between 1982 and 1984. In 1982 and 1984, she won the Honda Broderick Cup, given to the nation's outstanding female college athlete. In 1982, 1983, and 1984, she also won the Broderick Award, given to the best female college swimmer.

While competing for her college team, Caulkins continued to compete nationally and internationally. In 1982, she won her 36th title, surpassing **Johnny Weis-**

Awards and Accomplishments

1977	Won first national titles in the Amateur Athletic Union National Championships in both the 100- and 200-meter short course breaststroke, and the 200- and 400-meter long course individual medleys; won 100-meter breaststroke at the U.S. Indoor National Championships
1977-78	Named Swimmer of the Year by *Swimming World* magazine
1978	Won Sullivan Award; won world championships in 200-meter butterfly, 200- and 400-meter individual medleys, silver in 100-meter breaststroke; won national championships in 200-meter long course butterfly, short course individual medleys, and 100- and 200-meter breaststroke; won 200-meter butterfly at the Amateur Athletic Union Long Course Championships; named high school All-American; named United Press International's Female Athlete of the Year
1979	Won two gold medals and two silver medals at the Pan American Games; set five records at the Amateur Athletic Union National Short Course Championships, winning 100-meter breaststroke, 500-meter freestyle, 400-meter individual medley, 400-meter medley relay, 400-meter freestyle relay, and 200-meter individual medley
1980	Won four gold medals and one silver medal at the National Outdoor Championships; named American Swimmer of the Year
1980-82	Won J. H. Kiphuth Award
1981	Set world records at the U.S. Swimming International Championships in the 200- and 400-meter individual medleys, 100-meter breaststroke, and the 100-meter backstroke; won 200-meter backstroke and set American record at National Short Course Championships; named American Female Swimmer of the Year by *World* magazine; named WSF Amateur Athlete of the Year; named Sportswoman of the Year by the Women's Sports Foundation
1982	Won 200-meter individual medley and two other events at U.S. Swimming Long Course Championships; won Southland Olympia Award
1982-83	Won Honda Broderick Cup, awarded to the top female college athlete
1982-84	Won Broderick Award; won 12 National Collegiate Athletic Association (NCAA) swimming titles
1983	Won gold medals in both individual medleys at Pan American Games; won Broderick Award
1983-84	Named Academic All-American
1984	Won Honda Broderick Cup; won gold medals at the Summer Olympics in Los Angeles, California, in the 200-meter individual medley, the 400-meter individual medley, and as part of 4 x 100-meter medley relay team; won NCAA Championships in two individual medleys, 100-yard breaststroke and 200-yard butterfly, and in 400- and 800-yard team medleys; won 200-meter individual medley at National Indoor Championships; named Female Athlete of the Year by U. S. Olympic Committee; named Academic All-American; named Swimmer of the Year by the U.S. Swimming Association; named member of the All-Southeastern Conference Academic Honor Roll
1986	Elected to the International Women's Sports Hall of Fame
1990	Inducted into the International Swimming Hall of Fame; inducted into the U.S. Olympic Hall of Fame

---

muller's record for national titles. At the U. S. Swimming Long Course National Championships in 1982, she won the 200-meter medley, and at least two other events. Caulkins did not do as well at the World Championships, where the highest she finished was third. In 1983, she won the individual medleys at the Pan American Games, but her times were slower than in the past. She also did not do well at the World Championships, winning neither gold nor silver medals.

By 1984, although there were doubts about Caulkins's ability to win in big competitions, she proved them wrong. At the NCAA (National Collegiate Athletic Association) competitions that year, she won both of the individual medleys, the 100-yard breaststroke, and the 200-yard butterfly. With other members of the 400-meter freestyle relay team, she set an American record, and set an NCAA record in the 800-yard relay with other team members. Caulkins also set records in the 200-meter individual medley, the 400-meter individual medley, the 100-meter breaststroke, and the 200-meter butterfly. She also did well at the National Indoor Championships where, despite an infection, she won the 200-meter individual medleys.

Finally Won Olympic Gold

Spurred on by those who still counted her out of Olympic contention, Caulkins reacquired her aggressiveness in training and in races. She did well at the Olympics, where she was captain of the swim team. At the Olympic Trials, she set an American record in the 200-meter individual medley. At the 1984 Olympic Games in Los Angeles, she won the 200-meter medley (setting an Olympic record with a time of 2:12.64); the 400-meter medley (with a time of 4.39.4); and with three others as part of 4 x 100-meter medley relay team. Caulkins also placed fourth in the 100-meter breaststroke. The United States Olympic Committee named her Sportswoman of the Year, while the U.S. Swimming Association named her Swimmer of the Year.

After the Olympics ended, the 21-year-old Caulkins retired. Over the course of Caulkins distinguished swimming career, she made swimming look easy. University of Florida Coach Randy Reese told Dave Anderson of the *New York Times,* "She's the greatest swimmer this country has ever had, by far. Her sheer ability, her versatility in all four strokes, and her durability in being so great for so long."

CONTACT INFORMATION

Address: 511 Oman St., Nashville, TN 37203-1234.
Email: info@tracycaulkins.com.

FURTHER INFORMATION

Books

Hickok, Ralph. *A Who's Who of Sports Champions: Their Stories and Records.* Boston: Houghton Mifflin Company, 1995.

Johnson, Anne Janette. *Great Women in Sports.* Detroit: Visible Ink Press, 1996.

Layden, Joe. *Women in Sports: The Complete Book on the World's Greatest Female Athletes.* Santa Monica, CA: General Publishing Group, 1997.

Porter, David L., editor. *Biographical Dictionary of American Sports: Basketball and Other Indoor Sports.* New York: Greenwood Press, 1989.

Sherrow, Victoria. *Encyclopedia of Women and Sports.* Santa Barbara, CA: ABC-CLIO, 1996.

Periodicals

Allen, Karen. "Caulkins' Loyalties Split by Swimmers." *USA Today* (September 15, 2000): 3C.

Anderson, Dave. "Sports of the Times: America's Best Swimmer." *New York Times* (August 3, 1984): B13.

Boswell, Thomas. "Caulkins on Track for Moscow Mission." *Washington Post* (July 3, 1979): E1.

"Caulkins Gave 'em Five." *Sports Illustrated* (April 23, 1979): 90.

"Caulkins Will Retire after Olympics, Father Says." *Associated Press.* (August 3, 1984).

Cress, Doug. "Caulkins Sets U.S. Record in 200 Individual Medley." *Washington Post* (June 30, 1984): D1.

Litsky, Frank. "Backstroke to Miss Caulkins." *New York Times* (April 9, 1981): D27.

Litsky, Frank. "Miss Caulkins Out to Regain Stature." *New York Times* (January 9, 1984): C11.

Litsky, Frank. "Tracy Caulkins Rules Swimming World." *New York Times* (January 7, 1981): B7.

Litsky, Frank. "Tracy Caulkins Sets Mark in Swim Titles." *New York Times* (April 12, 1981): section 5, p. 9.

Moore, Kenny. "Search for Still Water." *Sports Illustrated* (August 3, 1981): 25.

Reed, J. D. "Thank Heaven for Little Girls." *Sports Illustrated* (April 17, 1978): 22.

Sell, Dave. "Caulkins in Swim with New Stroke." *Washington Post* (February 6, 1986): E2.

"Tracy Caulkins Wins Third Gold." *New York Times* (August 21, 1982): section 1, p. 14.

Other

"Tracy Caulkins Stockwell." University of Florida, Alumnae of Outstanding Achievement. http://www.dso.ufl.edu/whm/WHM98/50thYear/Stockwell.html (January 13, 2003).

Sketch by A. Petruso

Wilt Chamberlain
1936-1999

American basketball player

In a 14-year professional career studded with superlatives, Wilt Chamberlain established the centrality of court dominance in basketball, and thus changed the game forever. At seven feet, one inch tall, he was a towering figure, nicknamed "Wilt the Stilt"—a moniker he is said to have despised. Chamberlain was not simply a Goliath, however; he was also extraordinarily coordinated, and seemed to score and rebound almost without effort. Along the way, he racked up countless records, including the highest number of points for a single player in a single game (100), the most rebounds (55), and the greatest number of consecutive field goals (18).

Chamberlain was no stranger to controversy, as when he claimed in 1991 that he had bedded more than 20,000 women. Yet the controversy would hardly have mattered if his performance as a player had not been so extraordinary. At the time of his retirement, Chamberlain had scored more points in his career—31,419—than anyone in NBA history. The only player to exceed that record, **Kareem Abdul-Jabbar,** said at Chamberlain's funeral, "Wilt was one of the greatest ever, and we will never see another like him." Even more poignant were the words of the Boston Celtics' **Bill Russell,** with whom Chamberlain engaged in a celebrated on-court rivalry (and off-court friendship) during the 1960s and 1970s: "He and I will be friends through eternity."

A Giant at an Early Age

Named Wilton after the street on which his parents lived in west Philadelphia, Chamberlain was one of eight children born to William and Olivia Chamberlain. William worked as a porter at a publishing company, and Olivia sometimes cleaned houses to supplement the family's income. Given Chamberlain's size, one might guess that his parents or siblings were tall, but such was not the case. Indeed, none of the other nine Chamberlains exceeded a modest 5'9" in height.

At the age of 10, Wilt was already tall, and he became positively gargantuan after he reached adolescence. In a single summer, he gained four inches, and by the time he began playing for Overbrook High School, he stood 6'11". With his height, he was a natural for basketball, but from the beginning, he was not simply big: he was also graceful, resourceful, and creative as a player.

Recruited by Kansas

Beginning with his 1952-53 varsity year, Chamberlain led the Overbrook team to a series of victories, with season records of 19-2, 19-0, and 18-1. His reputation as a

Wilt Chamberlain

rebounder began at this early stage: the Overbrook high coach actually taught his players to miss free throws so that Chamberlain could rebound them and score more valuable field goals. In those days, goaltending, or hovering over the basket, was still legal, and Chamberlain was known to tip a ball thrown by a teammate into the hoop even when it would have gone in anyway—a practice that irritated his fellow Overbrook players.

At Overbrook, Chamberlain did not confine himself to a single sport, gaining notoriety on the cross country and track and field teams, and even winning a conference title—not surprisingly—in the long jump. It is also not surprising that college recruiters had their eye on Chamberlain, and that the University of Kansas gave him a scholarship. In terms of talent, he qualified for the varsity team, but NCAA (National Collegiate Athletic Association) rules at the time prohibited freshmen from playing varsity basketball, so Chamberlain took his place on the Jayhawks' freshman squad. In a significant showing of his skills, Chamberlain led the freshmen to victory in their first game—which happened to be against their varsity counterparts. Thanks to some 40 points, 30 rebounds, and 15 blocks courtesy of their extraordinary new player, the freshmen trounced the varsity Jayhawks 81-71.

On December 3, 1956, Chamberlain, now a sophomore, played his first game for the Jayhawks' varsity team. In that game, against Northwestern, he set a school record by scoring 52 points, helping to ensure an

Chronology

1936	Born August 21 in Philadelphia, Pennsylvania, to William and Olivia Chamberlain
1955	Finishes high school career with a total of 2,252 points scored in four years, joins the University of Kansas Jayhawks freshman team
1957	Leads Kansas in the NCAA championships against North Carolina, and earns the title of MVP for the tournament
1958	Leaves Kansas in his junior year, and begins a season with the Harlem Globetrotters, earning a then-unheard of $50,000 a year
1959	Begins his professional career with the Philadelphia Warriors
1960	Engages in the first of eight different NBA championship playoffs against Bill Russell and the Boston Celtics
1961	Begins the season in which he becomes the only player in NBA history to score more than 4,000 points in a single season
1962	Scores 100 points, setting an NBA record for the most points by a single player in a single game, against the New York Knicks on March 2
1962	Moves with the Warriors to San Francisco
1965	Two days after the NBA All-Star Game, is traded to the new Philadelphia 76ers
1966	Leads the Sixers to the best record in the league (55-25)
1967	Capping off a year in which the Philadelphia 76ers set a new league record with a 68-13 season, leads the team to victory over Boston in division finals, and over the San Francisco Warriors in the championships
1968	Traded to Los Angeles Lakers
1972	Leads the Lakers to a season record better than that of Philadelphia in 1966-67 (69-13), and to the second of two NBA championship victories, against the Knicks
1973	Retires with what were then all-time records for total points scored (31,419) and average points per game (30.1), as well as number of rebounds (23,924) and average rebounds per game (22.9)
1991	Publishes second autobiography, *A View from Above*, containing controversial boast of 20,000 sexual conquests
1999	Dies of heart attack in his sleep at his home in the Bel-Air section of Los Angeles on October 12

Awards and Accomplishments

1957	NCAA Tournament MVP, unanimous first team all-America
1958	Unanimous first team all-America
1960	NBA rookie of the year and most valuable player; NBA all-star and all-NBA first team; record for most points (2,707, or 37.6 ppg) and rebounds (1,941, or 27.0 rpg) in a rookie year, and for most points by a rookie in a single game (58, on January 25)
1961	NBA all-star and all-NBA first team
1962	NBA all-star, NBA all-star MVP, and all-NBA first team; all-time record for most points scored in a single game (100, on March 2); seasonal records for most minutes (3,338, or 41.7 mpg), most points (4,029, or 50.4 ppg), field goals made (1,597), and field goals attempted (3,159); single-game all-star record for most points (42)
1963-65	NBA all-star and all-NBA second team
1966	NBA most valuable player; NBA all-star and all-NBA first team
1967	NBA championship with the Philadelphia 76ers; NBA most valuable player; NBA all-star and all-NBA first team
1968	NBA most valuable player; NBA all-star and all-NBA first team
1969-71	NBA all-star
1972	NBA championship with the Los Angeles Lakers; NBA all-star and finals MVP; all-NBA second team, NBA all-defensive first team
1973	NBA all-star and all-defensive first team
1978	Elected to Naismith Memorial Basketball Hall of Fame
1980	Named to NBA 35th anniversary all-time team
1996	Named to NBA 50th anniversary all-time team

salary of $50,000. Though hardly impressive in the world of pro basketball today, at the time this was an almost inconceivably large salary for a basketball player.

Chamberlain, who would later tour with the Globetrotters during a few summers in the 1960s, joined his first NBA team in 1959. Thanks to the "territorial" draft rule established by the NBA in 1955, a team could choose a local college player in exchange for its first-round draft pick. Even though Chamberlain had actually played for a school far away, Philadelphia Warriors owner Eddie Gottlieb claimed the Philadelphia native, and since Kansas had no NBA teams, there was no competition for the 7'1" juggernaut. Once again, Chamberlain earned a distinction, in this case as the only player in NBA history to become a territorial pick based on his roots prior to college.

87-69 victory. In 1957, Kansas went to the NCAA championships against the University of North Carolina, and though the Jayhawks lost by a single point in triple overtime, Chamberlain himself earned the title of MVP (most valuable player) for the tournament.

From the Jayhawks to the Globetrotters to the Warriors

During his college years, Chamberlain played for all-conference and all-America teams, and again showed his prowess off the court at the Big Eight track and field championships, in which his 6'6" high jump won. He was eager to get on with his career, however, and for very practical reasons: he wanted to start earning money. Therefore, he finished out his junior year at Kansas and went on to the pros.

An NBA (National Basketball Association) rule at the time forbade professional teams from hiring college players whose class had not yet graduated. Therefore, Chamberlain spent the year 1958-59 on a team quite literally in a league of its own, a spot that earned him a

Beginnings of Rivalry with Bill Russell

During that 1959-60 season, Chamberlain averaged 37.6 points and 27 rebounds per game, and earned the title of NBA rookie of the year, all-star game MVP, and NBA MVP. He was also selected for the All-NBA First Team. Once again, Chamberlain was virtually without equal: other than Wes Unseld nine years later, no other player would win rookie and MVP recognition in a single year.

The Warriors, which Chamberlain propelled from last place to second place, went up against the Celtics in the 1960 NBA playoffs, thus beginning the legendary Chamberlain-Russell rivalry. This was the first of eight years in which a team on which Chamberlain played would meet the Celtics in the playoffs, but only once would Chamberlain's team gain victory over the Celtics.

Career Statistics

Yr	Team	GP	PTS	PPG	FG%	FT%	REB	RPG	APG
1959-60	PHW	72	2707	37.6	.461	.582	1941	27.0	2.3
1960-61	PHW	79	3033	38.4	.509	.504	2149	27.2	1.9
1961-62	PHW	80	4029	50.4	.506	.613	2052	25.7	2.4
1962-63	SF	80	3586	44.8	.528	.593	1946	24.3	3.4
1963-64	SF	80	2948	36.9	.524	.532	1787	22.3	5.0
1964-65	SF/PHI	73	2534	34.7	.510	.464	1673	22.9	3.4
1965-66	PHI	79	2649	33.5	.540	.513	1943	24.6	5.2
1966-67	PHI	81	1956	24.1	.683	.441	1957	24.2	7.8
1967-68	PHI	82	1992	24.3	.595	.380	1952	23.8	8.6
1968-69	LAL	81	1664	20.5	.583	.446	1712	21.1	4.5
1969-70	LAL	12	328	27.3	.568	.446	221	18.4	4.1
1970-71	LAL	82	1696	20.7	.545	.538	1493	18.2	4.3
1971-72	LAL	82	1213	14.8	.649	.422	1572	19.2	4.0
1972-73	LAL	82	1084	13.2	.727	.510	1526	18.6	4.5
TOTAL		1045	31419	30.1	.540	.511	23924	22.9	4.4

LAL: Los Angeles Lakers; PHI: Philadelphia 76ers; PHW: Philadelphia Warriors; SF: San Francisco Warriors.
Traded to 76ers after 1965 all-star game.

After the 4-2 loss to Boston in the series, Chamberlain stunned fans by announcing that he was thinking of retiring after just one season. Precisely because of his size, he was taking too much of a pounding from opposing teams, who worked to level the playing field, on the way committing numereous hard fouls against him. Chamberlain himself never fouled out once in 1,045 regular-season and 160 playoff games, a hallmark of his even temper on the court. Of course, one could argue that he did not have to get angry, given his physical dominance. In any case, all the abuse on the court was taking its toll on his body, and to combat the effects, Chamberlain, who was already strong, made himself even stronger. He worked out with weights, and by the time he reached the peak of his career, he tip the scale at 300 lean, fast, muscular pounds.

Victory over Boston—Finally

Chamberlain's second year with the Warriors was every bit as good as his first, and his third (1961-62) was significantly better, with an average of 50.4 points in a game. That was also the year when he became the only player in NBA history to score more than 4,000 points in a single season, and on March 2, 1962, he did something perhaps even more extraordinary. He had been out partying the previous night, and yet in a game against the New York Knicks in Hershey, Pennsylvania, Chamberlain scored 100 of the Warriors' 169 points against the Knicks' 147. As the minutes ticked by and his teammates became aware that they were witnessing history being made, they began applying the old Overbrook strategy of doing everything in their power to get the ball into Chamberlain's hands, even fouling the Knicks so that the legendary rebounder could take control.

Chamberlain stayed with the Warriors when they moved to San Francisco in 1962, and during the two seasons that followed, he was the leading scorer in the league. Then, just two days after the 1965 NBA All-Star Game, the Warriors traded him to the new Philadelphia 76ers for three players and $150,000.

Twice the Sixers went up against Chamberlain's old nemesis, Boston, only to lose—even in 1966, when they had earned the best record in the league at 55 wins and 25 losses. Then, in the 1966-67 season, Philadelphia earned a 68-13 record, the best in league history up to that time. In the division finals, Philadelphia trounced Boston in five games, ending an eight-year streak of Celtics NBA titles. The championship found him up against his old team, the Warriors. The 76ers came away victorious after six games, giving Chamberlain the first of only two championship wins in his career.

A Team Player

The 1966-67 season would prove to be not only the halfway point of Chamberlain's career, but also the high point. As **Oscar Robertson** once said, when a Philadelphia *Daily News* reporter asked him if Chamberlain was the best player of all time, "The numbers don't lie"—and this was equally true when assessing the relative decline that marked Chamberlain's latter years. Granted, his 20.7 point-per-game average for the period 1967-74 was one for which most NBA players would kill, but it was only a little more than half as good as his 1959-67 record of 39.4 points per game, a showing that only **Michael Jordan** has managed to equal.

A variety of reasons have been offered for Chamberlain's relative decline. Age and the effects of lifestyle (including all those amorous encounters of which he boasted) were obvious possibilities, as was the development of better defenses by opposing teams. Chamberlain, on the other hand, maintained that his coaches—in a reversal of patterns that went back all the way his high-school years—did not want him shooting as much. The fact was that while Chamberlain did well, teams on which he played did not tend to fare as well in the finals. During that winning 1966-67 season, on the other hand, Coach Alex Hannum instructed him to pass more and shoot less, a strategy that obviously worked.

Chamberlain took on his new, more team-oriented role with alacrity, leading the NBA in assists during the 1967-68 season. Traded to the Los Angeles Lakers in 1968, he went on to take his team to the finals four times, and in 1972 won his second and last championship in five games against the Knicks. In his final years in the NBA, Chamberlain distinguished himself as a team player alongside the likes of guard **Jerry West** and others, and in 1971-72 the Lakers went one better than the record set by Chamberlain and the 76ers in 1966-67, with a season record of 69-13.

A Very Busy Retiree

After he retired in 1973, Chamberlain pursued a number of careers. He coached the San Diego Conquistadors of the shortlived American Basketball Association for a season; played tennis, volleyball, and racquetball; and ran the Honolulu marathon. He coached a women's volleyball team, and even challenged **Muhammad Ali** to a fight that never occurred. Despite hints that he might return to basketball, Chamberlain never did.

Even before his retirement, Chamberlain had appeared in *Rowan & Martin's Laugh In,* as well as a memorable Volkswagen commercial that played on the length of his legs in relation to the size of the car. He later did spots for Brut aftershave and Miller Lite, and appeared alongside Arnold Schwarzenegger and Grace Jones in *Conan the Destroyer.* He also served as executive producer for the documentary *Go For It* in 1976.

In 1973, Chamberlain published the first of two autobiographies, *Wilt: Just Like Any Other Seven-Foot Black Millionaire Who Lives Next Door,* later published simply as *Wilt.* Nearly two decades later, a second autobiography, this one called *A View from Above* (1991), caused a much bigger stir with his claim of 20,000 conquests. Nearly coinciding as it did with **Magic Johnson**'s announcement that he was HIV-positive, the boast seemed ill-timed, and many observers criticized Chamberlain for being irresponsible.

During his later years, Chamberlain suffered from heart trouble, and his health declined quickly over a period of just a few weeks in the fall of 1999. He died of a heart attack at his home in the Bel-Air section of Los Angeles at age 63. In addition to Russell and Abdul-Jabbar, mourners at the City of Angels Church of Religious Science in Los Angeles included **Meadowlark Lemon** of the Globetrotters, West, **Bill Walton**, and **Jim Brown**.

The Warrior

Chamberlain earned enemies in the African American community when he condemned the Black Power movement in the late 1960s. He never aligned himself with civil-rights leaders such as Jesse Jackson, and invoked considerable ire when he supported Richard Nixon's campaigns for the presidency in 1968 and 1972. Blacks and whites alike expressed antipathy toward Chamberlain's oft-stated preference for white women.

In the world of basketball, Chamberlain won many a detractor with his candid talk and his outspoken persona. In the mid-1960s, he caused a stir with a *Sports Illustrated* story in which he was quoted as criticizing various coaches and players provided his critics with plenty of ammunition. Yet for all his ability to spark controversy, Chamberlain could get the job done on the court, and the breathtaking scope of his accomplishments will stand long after the disagreements have been forgotten. Said Russell, speaking to *USA Today* at the time of Chamberlain's death (quoted in *Jet*), "I'm one

Wilt Chamberlain, shooting for basket

of the guys who think Wilt was so good that people don't even known how good he was. I remember sitting at home, getting ready to play him one night, and thinking, 'another night in hell.'"

SELECTED WRITINGS BY CHAMBERLAIN:

(With David Shaw) *Wilt: Just Like Any Other Seven-Foot Black Millionaire Who Lives Next Door,* Macmillan, 1973, published as *Wilt,* Warner, 1975.
A View from Above, Villard, 1991.

FURTHER INFORMATION

Books

Chamberlain, Wilt with David Shaw. *Wilt: Just Like Any Other Seven-Foot Black Millionaire Who Lives Next Door.* New York: Macmillan, 1973.
Chamberlain, Wilt. *A View from Above.* New York: Villard, 1991.
Garner, Joe and Bob Costa. *And the Crowd Goes Wild: Relive the Most Celebrated Sports Events Ever Broadcast.* Napierville, IL: Sourcebooks, 1999.
Libby, Bill. *Goliath: The Wilt Chamberlain Story.* New York: Dodd, Mead, 1977.

Periodicals

Achenbach, Joel. "Wilt, Filling a Tall Order; The Hoops Legend Bares His Greatest Stat: 20,000 Women." *Washington Post* (November 1, 1991): B1.
Ryan, Jeff. "A Bum Rap." *Sporting News* 223 (October 25, 1999): 12-14.
"Wilt Chamberlain, 1936-1999: NBA Legend Remembered." *Jet* 96 (November 1, 1999): 51-56.

Other

"NBA History: Wilt Chamberlain." National Basketball Association. http://www.nba.com/chamberlain_bio.html (November 19, 2002).
The Official Web Site of Wilt Chamberlain. http://www.wiltchamberlain.com/ (November 19, 2002).
"Wilt Chamberlain Biography." Basketball Hall of Fame. http://www.hoophall.com/halloffamers/Chamberlain.htm (November 19, 2002).

Sketch by Judson Knight

Michael Chang
1972-

American tennis player

Michael Chang was the youngest tennis player to be ranked among the five best players in the world. Just fifteen years old when he came out from the juniors becoming the youngest player to win a major match at the U.S. Open, and the youngest go to the Tour semifinals, Chang turned pro in 1988. In 1989, at the age of 17, he became the youngest player ever to win the French Open, and the first American to win the event since 1955.

A devout Christian, Chang attributes his success to God. "People need to understand," he told the *San Francisco Chronicle*'s Tim Keown, speaking of his religion, "it's my first priority in life, and I'm going to give glory where glory's due." He acknowledged that his outspoken beliefs "can be a touchy subject. . .but it's something I'm going to speak out about."

Michael Chang was born in Hoboken, New Jersey, just across the Hudson River from New York City, in 1972. His father, Joe, was a refugee from Canton, China during the Chinese revolution in 1948. After first living in Taiwan for 18 years, Joe Chang emigrated to New

Michael Chang

In 1989 Chang became the youngest male to win the French Open. His accomplishments there included defeating Ivan Lendl, who was the number one ranked tennis player in the world, and then besting Stefan Edberg, the then-current Wimbledon champion, in the final to win the Open. Upon winning, Chang said on his Web site, "I thank the Lord Jesus Christ, because without Him, I am nothing."

Chang's family took an active role in his career from the beginning; his brother Carl acted as his coach, and his father managed the finances—a serious business, since Chang eventually earned close to $18 million in tournament purses alone—not including product endorsements. Chang explained his family's close involvement this way to Keown: "That's part of the Chinese culture—Asian families are close-knit. My family's made a lot of sacrifices for me. The first four years I turned pro, my mom quit her job to come and travel with me. That's a great sacrifice, and it was great to have my mom travel with me when I was still a teenager."

Chang became a devout Christian in 1988 when he was 15 years old. As he said on his Web site, "My grandparents had given me a Bible and they wanted me to read it every day. On this one particular evening I didn't have anything else to do so I decided to take a good luck at my Bible." He found much that was relevant to his own life and search for meaning, and he launched a personal study of Christianity. "Eventually, I accepted Him as my Lord and Savior."

Chang's comparatively small stature (five feet, nine inches, 150 pounds) made him an underdog in his own eyes, battling bigger and heavier opponents, who typically outweighed him by 20 pounds. But, this only made him play harder, again taking his inspiration from Christianity. Chang told Keown that although his frame is small, he saw this "as a way to glorify the Lord." Chang took advantage of his smaller size to be quicker on his feet than his opponents, finessing his way through tournaments where other players relied on brute power.

Triumphing at a series of tournaments though the 1990s, Chang became an international tennis sensation. By the end of 2002, he had won a total of 34 titles. Chang's successes made him popular in Asian countries where tennis fans were used to seeing mostly Europeans or European-Americans playing in the major events. "Hopefully," he told Tom Archdeacon in the *St. Louis*

Jersey to pursue a master's degree in chemistry. On a blind date in New York City he met Chang's mother, Betty, also Chinese. "My mom's sister knew my dad's family and decided to do the matchmaking," Chang explained to Tom Archdeacon in the *St. Louis Post-Dispatch.* "It's kind of an old Chinese custom, where families get involved in putting a boy and girl together."

Soon after Chang's birth, his family moved to Minnesota. When Chang was seven years old, and his talent for tennis already apparent, the family moved to Carlsbad, California, where he and his older brother Carl could practice their game year-round. As a child, Chang idolized the top tennis players of the time, "**[John] McEnroe** for his talent," as he told Archdeacon, "**[Jimmy] Connors** for his never-say-die attitude and **[Bjorn] Borg** for his coolness."

Although he began playing tennis at an early age, "I never felt the pressure to play tennis," Chang told Keown. "My parents would tell me I didn't have to be a tennis player, but their message was always the same: Do what you enjoy, but when you choose a profession, be the best at it."

It was advice he took to heart. He worked his way up through the junior tournaments, in the eighth grade, winning the San Diego California Interscholastic Federation Individual Championship, and turning pro just a week before he turned 16. Only a year later, at the age of 17, he won the French Open.

Dispatch, "in the future there will be some Asian tennis players coming on strong like Bjorn Borg made an impact in Sweden."

As 2002 drew to a close and his game began to lose steam, Chang, now 30, began to think about retirement. The decision to retire within the next year or so improved his focus. One of his opponents in 2002, number one ranked Lleyton Hewitt, told Jim Allen of the *Daily Yomiuri,* "In the last few weeks, he's played some of the best tennis he's played in three or four years." Chang agreed, telling Allen, "Strangely I'm more relaxed. My personality is one to work very hard. At times in my career, I've overworked and that's hurt me. . . .There comes a time when it's time to move on and to move on to other things."

Chang gave no hint as to what new career he might pursue after tennis. But he has left no doubt as to what leisure pursuits might be on his horizon; the sport he enjoys most besides tennis is fishing. "Fishing is more difficult than tennis," he told Archdeacon, "It takes more preparation and technique. You have to decide what to fish for, the type of hook, the position of the boat" and what kind of bait to use. "It's such a big challenge."

SELECTED WRITINGS BY CHANG:

With Mike Yorkey. *Holding Serve: Persevering On and Off the Court.* Nashville: T. Nelson, 2002.

FURTHER INFORMATION

Periodicals

Allen, Tim. "Hewitt Hummers Aging Star Chang." (Tokyo) *Daily Yomiuri* (October 3, 2002): 23.
"An American in Paris Wins at Last: Chang Is Champ."*St. Louis Post-Dispatch* (June 12, 1989): 1C.
Archdeacon, Tom. "At 5-Foot-9, Chang Stands Tall in World-Class Tennis." *St. Louis Post-Dispatch* (August 21, 1994): 11F.
Jenkins, Logan. "Chang Stays True to His Faith and Game." *San Diego Union-Tribune* (November 18, 2002): B2.
Keown, Tim. "Keeping the Faith: Change Gets Strength from His Religion." *San Francisco Chronicle* (February 14, 1996): E1.

Other

"Biography Page." mchang.com. http://www.mchang.com/biography.html (December 16, 2002).
"Christianity Page." mchang.com. http://www.mchang.com/christianity.html (December 16, 2002).
"Michael Chang: Time to Retire from Tennis?" Goldsea Asian Air Forum. http://goldsea.com/Air/Issues/Chang/chang.html (December 16, 2002).
"Michael Chang (USA)." ATPtennis.com. http://www.atptennis.com/en/players/playerprofiles/default2.asp?playernumber=C274 (December 16, 2002).

Sketch by Michael Belfiore

Brandi Chastain
1968-

American soccer player

Brandi Chastain became one of the most recognizable figures in American sports when she scored the winning goal at the Women's World Cup soccer tournament final against China on July 10, 1999. In the excitement following her game-winning kick, Chastain whipped off her jersey, exposing her sports bra (which functions as a bra, but looks more like a suit top). The image of Chastain kneeling on the field shirtless, fists raised in victory, graced the covers of *Sports Illustrated, Time,* and *Newsweek* The game provided women's soccer in the United States a much-needed boost, drawing a record 40 million viewers.

Chastain, who grew up in San Jose, California, was inspired by George Best, the European Player of the Year who led Manchester United of England to the 1968 European Cup championship. Best ended his career in Chastain's hometown with the San Jose Earthquakes of the North American Soccer League.

Chastain led Archbishop Mitty High School to three consecutive state championships, then was Soccer American Freshman of the Year at the University of California, Berkeley. She had to sit out the next two sea-

Brandi Chastain

sons, however, after undergoing surgery to reconstruct ligaments in both knees.

Transferring to Santa Clara University in 1989, Chastain returned to soccer and was named First-Team NSCAA All-Far West. The following year, she made First-Team NSCAA All-American. She graduated from Santa Clara with a degree in television and communications.

Chastain made her professional debut on the U.S. national team in 1988, in a game against Japan. She scored her first international goal in April, 1991, against Mexico, scoring five in that game, and played for the 1991 World Cup champion, back when many fans were unaware such a tournament existed. Chastain played professional soccer in Japan for Skiroki Serena in 1993, and was named the team's most valuable player. Also that year, she was the only non-Japanese ranked among that league's top 11 players.

Cut from the 1995 World Cup team because her coach felt she wasn't in good enough shape, Chastain trained hard and switched positions, from striker to defender. She helped the U.S. women's Olympic team win the gold medal in Atlanta in 1996.

Rose Bowl High Drama

Though Chastain was a hero at the end of the 1999 World Cup, she was a central figure in the quarterfinals of that tournament, against Germany. Chastain scored an "own goal," accidentally into her own net, early in the first half. Later that day, Chastain suffered a mild ankle sprain. But she redeemed herself, scoring off a corner kick in the 49th minute to tie the game, and the U.S. rallied to a 3-2 win. Brazil fell 2-0 in the semifinals.

The unforgettable final was at the Rose Bowl in Pasadena, California on July 10, 1999. The U.S. and China went scoreless into extra time. The game came down to a series of five penalty kicks; the team that scored the most would win. Chastain was tapped for the final attempt with the shootout tied 4-4—American goalkeeper **Briana Scurry** had stopped Liu Ying on China's third try while all four U.S. shooters had scored.

Unlike some players who dislike the intense pressure of penalty kicks, Chastain relished the opportunity. Chastain, never been one to avoid the spotlight; had appeared in the German magazine *Gear*, in a photo series before the tournament, with nothing on but her soccer cleats and a "strategically-placed" soccer ball. She had also been a guest on David Letterman's television talk show.

U.S. coach Tony DiCicco had instructed Chastain to train for penalty kicks with her left foot instead of her dominant right so goalies would be less able to predict where the ball would go. Goalkeepers often merely guess in defending penalty kicks; the shooter, in close range and with a yawning net, enjoys a pronounced advantage. After the briefest of pauses to line up her shot, Chastain used her left foot to slam the ball past China's Gao Hong.

"I didn't hear any noise. I didn't get caught up looking at Gao Hong," Chastain said. "I just put it home."

Both Chastain's photo spread in *Gear* and the famous doffing of her shirt raised questions about the appropriateness of such behavior. She brushed off these concerns, saying in the *Atlanta Journal-Constitution* in 2000, "I don't understand what's wrong with attractive, beautiful things. I don't think about sex when I see a beautifully toned athlete. I think of all the hard work they put into getting that way. I can appreciate what that's all about."

It Went Down to the Wire

After 120 minutes, including two overtime periods, victory lay at the feet of 30-year-old Brandi Chastain. . . .

The United States and China were locked in a scoreless tie. U.S. goalkeeper Briana Scurry had made a diving, fingertip save deflecting a Chinese shot. The game . . . had come down to a single penalty kick. Chastain approached the ball and barely hesitated before drilling her shot perfectly into the upper right corner of the net.

As frenzied fans . . . roared, she whipped off her shirt and waved it at the crowd before being buried in celebration by . . . her teammates.

Source: Starr, Mark, Martha Brant and Sam Register. *Newsweek*, July 19,1999.

Still, others questioned just how spontaneous was her celebration. Chastain and nine teammates were wearing Nike's Inner Actives sports bra earmarked for public sale. "After the game, some newspaper and television types wondered if Chastain's shirt-stripping had been orchestrated, in an effort to generate some Nike awareness," Jim Pedley wrote in the *Kansas City Star*. A Nike sportswoman denied the company had scripted Chastain's celebration, but also said Nike "will certainly capitalize on it."

In 1999, there was no U.S. women's soccer league. That changed in 2001 with the launch of the Women's United Soccer Association (WUSA). Chastain immediately joined the new league as a member of the San Jose CyberRays, who won the inaugural championship. In 2002, the WUSA honored its one millionth fan, an achievement that surprised even Chastain.

Chastain is also an assistant coach for the women's soccer team at her alma mater, Santa Clara University. Her husband, Jerry Smith, is the head coach.

She also competed in the 2000 Olympics in Sydney, Australia. She scored one goal in five games as the U.S. earned a silver medal, falling 3-2 in overtime to Norway for the gold.

Chastain's Impact

The World Cup victory propelled women's soccer into the national spotlight at a time when Chastain and her teammates were working hard to bring the sport greater recognition. "For those of us who were involved with it, it's a wonderful thing, considering how we've been clamoring for soccer to be in the public eye for so long," she told the *San Francisco Chronicle* in 2002. "And it's special to have individuals who normally are distinguished by men's sports events think of a women's soccer match that way." The win also helped convince investors that a pro women's soccer league would sell in the United States.

FURTHER INFORMATION

Periodicals

Brant, Martha, Sam Register, and Mark Starr. "It Went Down to the Wire." *Newsweek* (July 19, 1999): 46.

Chapin, Dwight. "Chastain's Winning Moment Takes on Life of Its Own." *San Francisco Chronicle* (July 7, 2002): B10.

Parker, Wendy. "The Liberation of Brandi Chastain." *Atlanta Journal and Constitution* (September 14, 2000): 1F.

Wahl, Grant. " Out of this World: A Last-Second Hunch and a Clutch Left Foot Lifted the U.S. to Victory Over China." *Sports Illustrated* (July 19, 1999).

Other

"10 Burning Questions for . . . Brandi Chastain." ESPN. com.http://espn.go.com/page2/ (February 8, 2003).

"Soccer Profile: Brandi Chastain." SoccerTimes.com. http://www.soccertimes.com/usteams/roster/women/chastain.htm (January 15, 2003).

Pedley, Jim. "How We Did It: Making the call on Cup Photo Play." *Dallas Morning News: Associated Press Sports Editors*. http://apse.dallasnews.com/oct1999/ (February 8, 2003).

Sketch by Michael Belfiore

Chris Chelios
1962-

American hockey player

Chris Chelios

Chris Chelios is one of the best, most seasoned defensemen in the National Hockey League (NHL). He has played in the NHL since 1984, winning three Norris Trophies and two Stanley Cups during that time. Although earlier in his career Chelios was known for his violent style of play and short temper, as he has gotten older he has become a more restrained but no less effective player.

Perseverance

Although Chelios was born in Chicago, a relatively good place for a boy to learn hockey, his family moved to San Diego in 1977. There were few good players for Chelios to compete with and learn from in southern California. He played in a weekly game with a team of Marines for a while, but even this was not enough. During his senior year of high school, Chelios took a bus to Hawkesbury, Ontario to try out for a junior B league team there. He was cut from the Hawkesbury team after one game, so he tried out for another junior B league team, this one in Chatham, Ontario. That didn't work out either, and Chelios found himself in a bus station in Michigan without enough money to make it home. He borrowed the money, returned to California, and began attending the U.S. International University in San Diego, which had inaugurated a hockey program one year earlier. Chelios did not make the team. Finally, he found a place with a junior B team in Moose Jaw, Saskatchewan.

Chelios's career started looking up in 1981, when he was recruited to play for the University of Wisconsin.

Chelios, formerly a forward, credited his time spent playing under famed Wisconsin coach "Badger" Bob Johnson, one of the most successful hockey coaches of all time, with teaching him how to be a solid defensive player. Chelios was drafted by the Montreal Canadiens in 1981, but he remained in college, helping Wisconsin to win the National College Athletic Association (NCAA) hockey championships in 1981 and 1983. Then, after playing with the United States hockey team at the 1984 Olympics, Chelios finally began playing for the Canadiens.

The Big League

Chelios's first National Hockey League (NHL) game was in March of 1984, at Madison Square Garden against the New York Rangers. He remembered it to *Sports Illustrated* reporter Jay Greenberg in 1990: "I was lined up across from James Patrick, whom I had played against at Moose Jaw, then when he was at the University of North Dakota, and then when he played for the Canadian Olympic Team. We were thinking the same thing, because we had these big grins on our faces. I was like a ten-year-old."

Chelios quickly established himself in Montreal, which won the Stanley Cup in his third season there. On the ice, he was known for his daring offensive plays and hard-hitting defensive style. Off of the ice, he was widely credited with a great deal of carousing, although Chelios says that stories of his exploits were greatly exaggerated. Still, by the late 1980s Chelios had settled down, marrying his wife, Tracee, whom he met at the University of Wisconsin, in 1987, and having his first child, a son named Dean, in 1989.

Controversial Shots

In 1990, Chelios was traded to the Chicago Blackhawks. There, he expanded upon his reputation for rough defense, which had been cemented by an incident in a 1989 playoff game against the Philadelphia Flyers. Chelios elbowed Flyers player Brian Propp, driving his face into a metal bar holding up the glass around the rink. He was knocked unconscious, and a riot by Flyers fans nearly followed. However, Chelios was unapologetic. "I'm sorry he got hurt, but if he hit his head on the

Career Statistics

Yr	Team	GP	G	A	PTS	+/−	PIM	SOG	SPCT	PPG	SHG
1982-84	MC	12	0	2	2	−5	12	23	0.0	0	0
1984-85	MC	74	9	55	64	11	87	199	4.5	2	1
1985-86	MC	41	8	26	34	4	67	101	7.9	2	0
1986-87	MC	71	11	33	44	−5	124	141	7.8	6	0
1987-88	MC	71	20	41	61	14	172	199	10.1	10	1
1988-89	MC	80	15	58	73	35	185	206	7.3	8	0
1989-90	MC	53	9	22	31	20	136	123	7.3	1	2
1990-91	CB	77	12	52	64	23	192	187	6.4	5	2
1991-92	CB	80	9	47	56	24	245	239	3.8	2	2
1992-93	CB	84	15	58	73	14	282	290	5.2	8	0
1993-94	CB	76	16	44	60	12	212	219	7.3	7	1
1994-95	CB	48	5	33	38	17	72	166	3.0	3	1
1995-96	CB	81	14	58	72	25	140	219	6.4	7	0
1996-97	CB	72	10	38	48	16	112	194	5.2	2	0
1997-98	CB	81	3	39	42	−7	151	205	1.5	1	0
1998-99	CB-DRW	75	9	27	36	1	93	187	4.8	3	1
1999-00	DRW	81	3	31	34	48	103	135	2.2	0	0
2000-01	DRW	24	0	3	3	4	45	26	0.0	0	0
2001-02	DRW	79	6	33	39	40	126	128	4.7	1	0
TOTAL		1260	174	700	874	291	2556	3187	5.5	68	11

CB: Chicago Blackhawks; DRW: Detroit Red Wings; MC: Montreal Canadiens.

metal, that's just bad luck. I know I'm chippy, but that's when I'm most effective," he told Greenberg.

Chelios also gained notoriety for a thoughtless comment he made during the 1994 lockout, when NHL management refused to let the players play when the two sides could not agree on contract terms. Chelios, worried about his career and about the future of the sport, said to a reporter, "If I was [NHL commissioner] Gary Bettman, I'd be worried about my family, about my well-being right now. Some crazed fan or even a player, who knows, might take it into his own hands and figure that if they get him out of the way this might get settled." Chelios immediately regretted the comment, but it was too late.

In recent years, Chelios has attempted to tone down his aggression on and off the ice. "I want to be a role model for my kids," he told *Sporting News* reporter Larry Wigge in 1996. "I certainly don't want my . . . kids to come up to me or my wife, Tracee, and ask why daddy's such a mean guy." Still, Chelios maintains a tough streak. "He comes to win and he'll pay the price to win, whatever it is," Lou Lamoriello, who coached Chelios in the 1996 World Cup and the 1998 Olympics, told *Sporting News* reporter Helene Elliot. "That's something you don't teach. It has to be within a player."

Another Stanley Cup

In 1999, Chelios was traded to the Detroit Red Wings, the division rival team that he had learned to hate as a boy cheering for the Chicago Blackhawks and as an adult playing for them. He was sorry to leave his hometown, he said, but if he had to be traded he wanted it to be to a team that had a chance of winning the Stanley Cup. Fitting in with his new team was tough at

Awards and Accomplishments

1986, 2002	Stanley Cup
1989, 1993, 1996	Named a first-team all-star
1989, 1993, 1996	Wins Norris Trophy for best defenseman
1989	Prince of Wales Trophy championship
1990	Presidents' Trophy championship
1992	Campbell Bowl championship
1996	Named Man of the Year by Ronald McDonald's Children's Charities for his work with physically challenged children

first—"It's sort of like letting Public Enemy No. 1 free and telling his enemies that they have to make friends with him," Chelios said to *Sporting News* reporter Larry Wigge in 2000—but eventually it all came together. In 2002, Chelios achieved his goal, winning his second Stanley Cup at the age of forty.

FURTHER INFORMATION

Books

Dowbiggin, Bruce. *Of Ice and Men: Steve Yzerman, Chris Chelios, Glen Sather, Dominik Hasek: The Craft of Hockey.* Toronto: Macfarlane, Walter & Ross, 1998.

Periodicals

Elliott, Helene. "Made in the U.S.A." *Sporting News* (January 19, 1998): 27-29.

Falla, Jack. "Alors! Look Who's Coming to Dinner." *Sports Illustrated* (November 19, 1984): 44-47.

Farber, Michael. "Captain America." *Sports Illustrated* (February 15, 2002): 12.

Farber, Michael. "Prince of Darkness." *Sports Illustrated* (May 27, 2002, 2002): 46.

Greenberg, Jay. "Daddy Dearest." *Sports Illustrated* (January 8, 1990): 36-39.

"Looney Goon." *Sports Illustrated* (October 10, 1994): 16.

Myers, Jess. "'Badger Bob' Remembered." *Minnesota Daily* (December 2, 1991).

Simmons, Steve. "'It's a Great Day for Hockey.'" *Toronto Sun* (September 12, 1996).

Swift, E. M. "In a Class by Himself." *Sports Illustrated* (December 9, 1991).

Wigge, Larry. "'A Junk Yard Dog.'" *Sporting News* (January 10, 2000): 56.

Wigge, Larry. "Red Wings Again Champs in Deadline Dealing." *Sporting News* (April 5, 1999): 50.

Wigge, Larry. "Rink Brat?" *Sporting News* (May 6, 1996): 43-44.

Other

"'Badger' Bob Johnson." U.W. Badgers.com. http://www.uwbadgers.com/history/hall_of_fame/1992/johnson_bob.aspx (November 17, 2002).

Finder, Chuck. "10 Years Have Passed, But Memories of Badger Bob Are Still Strong." Finder on the Web. http://www.post-gazette.com/sports/columnists/20011120webfinder1120p4.asp (November 17, 2002).

"Player Bio: Chris Chelios." National Hockey League Players' Association. http://www.nhlpa.com/Content/THE_PLAYERS/player_bio1.asp?ID=939 (November 10, 2002).

"Robert 'Bob' Johnson." U.S. Hockey Hall of Fame. http://ushockeyhall.com/Enshrinees/Robert%20Johnson.htm (November 17, 2002).

Sketch by Julia Bauder

1919 Chicago White Sox
American baseball team

Often dubbed the greatest scandal in sports history, the "Black Sox" story is one of how greed and deception came to rule the diamonds during the 1919 World Series. The Chicago White Sox, a team consisting of some of the greatest players the game had ever known—men like **Shoeless Joe Jackson** and George "Buck" Weaver—seemed a lock to take home the trophy. When they lost, and when it was later revealed that eight men on the team had agreed to "fix" the series for gamblers, the series of events that followed would tarnish the nation's pastime in the public eye. It would also ruin the careers of the players involved, and the 1919 Chicago White Sox would become known to baseball fans everywhere, forever, as the Chicago "Black" Sox.

The Background

By the end of the regular season in 1919, the Chicago White Sox were playing better baseball than anyone had expected. With 88 wins and 52 losses on the year, they'd far surpassed their previous season, when they had finished sixth, near the bottom of the rankings. And yet, they were poised and playing wonderful ball and staring at a postseason that would send them back to the World Series for the second time in three years. The genesis for these triumphant seasons had been set in motion in 1915, when Charles Comiskey, owner of the team, put the pieces in place for what he'd hoped would be one of the greatest teams in baseball. In only two short seasons, he'd built a club that dominated the league and went on to easily win the 1917 World Series.

But then America entered World War I, shortening the 1918 season and sending many ballplayers overseas to fight and leaving many of those who remained to work in shipping yards or steel mills in order to avoid the draft. By the end of the war, in November of 1918, it was time once again for Comiskey to rebuild his team. Though he'd been willing to spend money on the acquisition of good players, he was also well-known for failing to pay his men what they were worth. Unlike in today's game, where teams have payrolls that stagger the mind, in the early 1900s, baseball players, even major stars, were poorly compensated for their talents, and Charles Comiskey was among those whose compensation was the poorest. In one instance, he had promised his team a bonus if they won the pennant in 1919, and after clinching, the White Sox entered the locker room and found only a case of stale champagne—Comiskey's "bonus."

Charles Comiskey often looked the other way when his players complained, in essence biting the hands that fed him—or filled his pockets—and soon he had salary disputes among his players. Robert Cottrell, in his book, *Blackball, the Black Sox and the Babe*, wrote how, "Team dissension and divisions were clearly present among the White Sox." Some of the stars on the team were making less than half that of other players, and Comiskey was only inviting trouble into the team dugout by allowing the money concerns of his players—namely, most of them didn't have any—to affect their attitude about the club. Comiskey chose instead to wine and dine the members of the press, whom he often invited to join him at expensive meals, the liquor flowing freely. All the while, in the White Sox locker room, the players were getting along on the bare minimum.

Eddie Cicotte of the 1919 Chicago White Sox

Chronology

1919	Five to one favorites to win the World Series, the Chicago White Sox lose in eight games (in a best of nine series) to the Cincinnati Reds. Rumors of a "fixed" series spread among diehard baseball fans, but are dismissed as unfounded.
1920	Judge Charles A. McDonald instructs a grand jury in Chicago to open investigation into charges of gambling in the major leagues. On September 28, eight Chicago White Sox players are indicted for conspiring to throw the 1919 World Series.
1921	Fifteen day trial takes place in July, and the grand jury brings back verdict of "not guilty." Ignoring the verdict, however, newly appointed Commissioner of Baseball Kenesaw Mountain Landis will soon ban all eight defendants from baseball for life.

The 1919 World Series

Even so, Chicago's boys of summer headed into October with hot bats and blazing pitching. In spite of their dissatisfaction with management, the fans would have been hard-pressed to find anything wrong. They loved to play baseball, and the Sox had been playing stellar ball all season. They had a pitching staff that seemed unbeatable—Eddie Cicotte, a 29 game winner, and Lefty Williams, who had 23 victories, were the top two men, and they were followed by two other starters who each had over twenty wins. Add to the equation the talented fielding of third baseman Buck Weaver and a hitter like "Shoeless" Joe Jackson, and the best of nine series against the Cincinnati Reds appeared a mere formality. The Reds, coming off of a banner year, had won 96 games and lost only 44 on their way to their first National League pennant. Yet in spite of the Reds' better numbers, they were underdogs. Oddsmakers gave the White Sox a clear advantage; they couldn't see how Comiskey's boys could lose.

But lose they did. From the very first pitch of the series by the White Sox Eddie Cicotte, something seemed off. He hit Maury Rath of the Reds on the first toss of the game, which, it would later be learned, was a signal to the men who'd fixed the World Series that the eight players on the Sox agreed to throw the games. Cicotte allowed the Reds to whallop him in that first game, which Cincinnati won 9-1. William "Kid" Gleason, a first year manager for the Sox and a student of

the game, knew his players too well and suspected something was wrong—the team that he'd coached all summer hadn't shown up. He took his concerns to Comiskey who, in turn, took the issue up with the American League president (who chose to ignore both men's concerns).

And so the games continued. The Cincinnati Reds went on to win the second game by a score of 4-2. The White Sox would win game three, but games four and five went to the Reds. In what reads like a description of a little league game, Eddie Cicotte's fielding was out of sorts—he badly played an infield grounder, then threw the ball over his target and into the outfield, allowing the runner to reach second. A few plays later, he bobbled a throw from the outfield, allowing a Red to score. Cincinnati took four of the first five games in a series that had been pushed from a best of seven series to a best of nine. Although the White Sox would win games six and seven, they would fold in game eight, and the series would be over.

How the Fix Happened

It is difficult to know exactly what happened in the weeks prior to the 1919 World Series. The scheme has been pieced together with details given by some of the conspirators, who said there was an agreement that players who participated in "fixing" the series so that Chicago lost would be paid a total of $100,000 in installments over the course of the games.

The eight men involved had been bought to lose the first three games, but after losing game one, some of the players went looking for their money and were told that it was out on bets. They didn't get paid. The men were disappointed, yet they were in over their heads and stuck to the plan, losing game two. Once again, following the loss, they sought their payment but received only a part of the money. This prompted several of the players to shy away from their agreed upon deal.

The White Sox eventually won games six and seven. The players involved in the fix were frustrated at not getting the money they'd agreed to. However, when a

Team Statistics (1919)

Player	AVG	GP	AB	R	H	HR	RBI	BB	SO	SB
Eddie Cicotte	.202	40	99	5	20	0	8	9	18	0
Eddie Collins	.319	140	515	87	165	4	80	68	27	33
Shano Collins	.279	63	179	21	50	1	16	7	11	0
Dave Danforth	.111	15	9	0	1	0	0	2	2	0
Red Faber	.185	25	54	8	10	0	4	6	20	0
Happy Felsch	.275	135	502	68	138	7	86	40	35	19
Chick Gandil	.290	115	441	54	128	1	60	20	20	10
Joe Jackson	.351	139	516	79	181	7	96	60	10	9
Bill James	.143	5	14	2	2	0	0	0	2	0
Joe Jenkins	.158	11	19	0	3	0	1	1	1	1
Dickie Kerr	.250	39	68	12	17	0	4	9	8	1
Nemo Leibold	.302	122	434	81	131	0	26	72	30	17
Grover Lowdermilk	.088	20	34	1	3	0	1	0	19	1
Byrd Lynn	.227	29	66	4	15	0	4	4	9	0
Erskine Mayer	.000	6	7	0	0	0	0	0	3	0
Harvey McClellan	.333	7	12	2	4	0	1	1	1	0
Tom McGuire	.000	1	1	0	0	0	0	0	1	0
Fred McMullin	.294	60	170	31	50	0	19	11	18	4
Eddie Murphy	.486	30	35	8	17	0	5	7	0	0
Win Noyes	.500	1	2	0	1	0	0	0	0	0
Swede Risberg	.256	119	414	48	106	2	38	35	38	19
Ray Schalk	.282	131	394	57	111	0	34	51	25	11
Frank Shellenback	.091	8	11	0	1	0	0	2	5	0
John Sullivan	.000	4	3	0	0	0	1	1	3	0
Buck Weaver	.296	140	571	89	169	3	75	11	21	22
Roy Wilkinson	.444	4	8	1	3	0	2	1	3	0
Lefty Williams	.181	41	94	10	17	0	10	9	28	0
TOTAL	.287	140	4675	667	1343	25		427	358	150

few members of the White Sox who had agreed to throw the series were threatened by those who'd engineered the fix, the team lost game eight, touching off the flood of events that followed.

A Calm Before the Maelstrom

Corruption in baseball is nothing new. Gambling and the fixing of games had afflicted organized ball since the end of the Civil War, and orchestraters of underhanded ball followed close on the heels of any new league or team that popped up. So when the National League formed in 1876, gambling was prohibited in the rules, but it was a law that never matched up with the practice on the field.

With America's entrance into World War I, wrote Eliot Asinof in his book *Eight Men Out*, gambling's stronghold on baseball became solidified. When the government shut down race tracks, the numbers men looked elsewhere for their fix, and since ballparks remained open during the war, it was the next logical place for gamblers to migrate.

As the 1919 World Series drew to a close, many baseball afficianados had doubts as to the validity of the games they'd witnessed. Those who kept a close eye on White Sox players felt that something was amiss—they just couldn't put their fingers on it.

Rumors soon began to circulate about the possibility of a fix and news reporters mentioned that certain key

players on the White Sox made more than their fair share of mistakes. Hugh Fullerton, a reporter who loved baseball more than life itself, led the post-Series cries of "foul," continuing to raise questions after most other writers let the subject drop. Eventually, the New York *World* ran one of Fullerton's pieces in which he suggested that the 1919 World Series had been tampered with, kicking off speculation that wouldn't reach a fever pitch for almost a year. The 1920 baseball season would continue as scheduled, and Fullerton's articles kept the embers burning. In September of 1920, the story burst into flame.

The Indictment

In early September of 1920 a grand jury was summoned to investigate allegations into the rampant gambling in professional baseball. By the middle of the month, that investigation turned its focus to the 1919 World Series and the play of the Chicago White Sox. On September 28th, the grand jury indicted eight players on the team for "conspiring to defraud the public and injure the business of Charles Comiskey and the American League" (there was no statute on the Illinois books that specifically forbade "fixing" a baseball game). "Chick" Gandil, Eddie Cicotte, "Shoeless" Joe Jackson, George "Buck" Weaver, Charles "Swede" Risberg, Oscar "Happy" Felsch, Claude "Lefty" Williams and utility infielder Fred McMullin were the eight men named on the indictment.

The American public was shocked. Most people were unaware of how deep gambling had sunk its claws into

---

Jury to Probe Charges

Jackson and Felsch and Cicotte and Weaver and the rest of them were heroes to the boys of America. They belonged to the goodly fellowship that includes pirates and Indian fighters, super-detectives and, more recently, aces of the air service. To hear that they sold a world's series is as bad [a] news to the boys of America as if one of our modern historians should discover that Daniel Boone had been bought by the Indians to lose his fights in Kentucky, or that Paul Jones had thrown the Serapis-Bonhomme Richard battle for British gold.

On city corner lots, in small towns and country villages, on diamonds improvised by farm lads in the stubblefield, millions of boys have spent the energy of their growing years in the wild hope that some day they, too, might take their places in the fellowship of the big-league elect. Most of them eventually outgrew the ambition, but it did them no harm. And now they find that some of their heroes were only crooks, and contemptible, whimpering crooks at that. They did it for their wives and children or to lift a mortgage from the old farm. They had scruples about going in, and their guilty knowledge was an awful load on the conscience, but they all kept quiet till they had been found out; then they did what they could to get off easily by betraying each other.

Perhaps the law has no punishment for them. Leave it to a vote of the fans, and they would be punished.

Source: *The New York Times* (September 8, 1920): p. 12.

Eight Men Out

The "Black Sox" scandal was retold in the 1988 film *Eight Men Out*. Starring John Cusack as Buck Weaver and D.B. Sweeney as "Shoeless" Joe Jackson, the movie is sympathetic to the White Sox players involved in the scandal but doesn't absolve them of their responsibilities. In fact, by the end of the movie, the viewer is forced to make the ultimate decision about whether or not these players were guilty or innocent (some players were, of course, more guilty than others). Written and directed by John Sayles, the film closely follows the book upon which it is based: Eliot Asinof's 1963 sweeping treatment of the scandal. Roger Ebert, in a mild criticism of the film, faulted it for being an "insider's movie." Nonetheless, the performances of Cusack as Buck Weaver and David Straithairn as Eddie Cicotte are impressive, showing what it must have been like to wrestle with ethical questions raised by the circumstances leading up to, during, and following the entire "Black Sox" scandal. *Eight Men Out* vividly portrays a pivotal event in our national pastime, and it's rendered with an exacting eye for baseball and the detail of the period.

---

the national pastime, and even those who knew that games were often fixed were shocked that corruption had risen all the way to the ranks of the World Series. A *New York Times* editorial on September 24, 1920, declared that the men involved in fixing the 1919 Series would "undoubtedly be blacklisted…[For] it is a matter of self-preservation as well as of honor and of pride in the national game to stamp out every vestige of crookedness."

After the grand jury's investigation, Cottrell wrote, the story soon broke about Eddie Cicotte and "Shoeless" Joe Jackson "confessing to having received $10,000 and $5,000 respectively to help fix the 1919 World Series." Cicotte, it is said, broke down in front of the grand jury, claiming he'd never regretted anything so much in his life. He blamed Risberg, Gandil, and McMullin for pressuring him the entire week prior to the start of the Series. With a wife and kids and a $4,000 mortgage on a farm in Michigan, Cicotte had reluctantly agreed to the fix.

Sportswriters and many influential people in baseball demanded that another look be taken at baseball's National Commission. This outcry led to the appointment of Judge Kenesaw Mountain Landis as commissioner of major league baseball. When he took office on December 12, 1920, he wielded greater power over the game than the previous three-man commission held. "Landis proved to be a master at working the public relations angle," Cottrell wrote. "[He presented] himself as the repository of the time-honored values associated with the national game." Here was a man who some declared the "Moses of baseball." Stately and intimidating, Landis appeared on the scene when the public needed an arbiter in whom they could rest their faith.

The Trial

The actual trial began on a hot day in June of 1921. The eight White Sox faced the possibility of a five-year prison sentence, as well as fines of up to $10,000 each. In a strange turn of events, all of the official documents relating to the scandal disappeared only days before the court convened. The transcripts of the grand jury testimony were gone, so now any White Sox who had previously confessed proceeded to change their stories. Those who didn't change their stories flat out refused to incriminate themselves on the stand. So when the verdict was read, the eight men indicted for fixing the 1919 World Series discovered they had been acquitted due to a lack of evidence.

That night, they celebrated with a huge dinner down the street from the courthouse. But the celebration would not last long. The very next morning, newspapers bore Judge Kenesaw Mountain Landis' own verdict: he banned the eight men from baseball forever. In a statement issued to the press, Landis said: "Regardless of the verdict of juries, no player that throws a ballgame, no player that entertains proposals or promises to throw a game, no player that sits in conference with a bunch of crooked players and gamblers where the ways and means of throwing games are discussed and does not promptly tell his club about it, will ever play professional baseball."

Eight Men Forever Out

Asinof has said that after the scandal and their banishment from professional baseball, "the eight Black Sox fanned out over the vast expanse of America, but their lives ran in similar patterns." Many would play ball anonymously in small leagues in various towns, and most of them would end up in quiet occupations, trying to forget what happened during those years when they lived their dreams.

In 1956, Chick Gandil finally told his story to *Sports Illustrated*, acknowledging that he was the "first player contacted by gamblers and [brought] together seven other

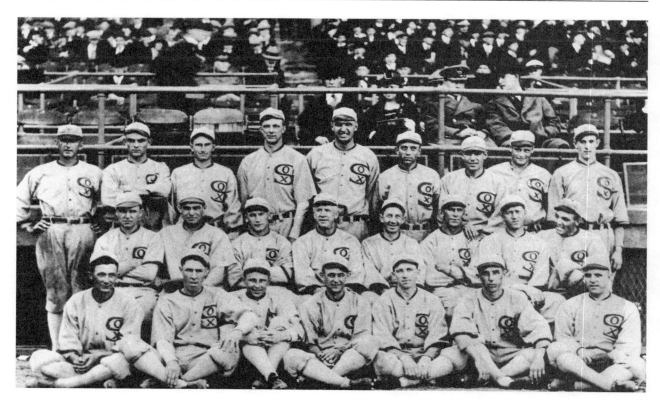

1919 Chicago White Sox

players who initially agreed to rig the series for $20,000 each." When asked if he was one of the ringleaders of the Black Sox Scandal, he said, "It's true, I was." He claimed, however, that the rumors of a "fix" that started soon after the 1919 World Series began scared many of the players who had initially agreed to throw the series. Therefore, Gandil said, the games were played legitimately. He maintained that the way the White Sox lost the series that year "was pure baseball fortune."

Buck Weaver would deny involvement in the scandal until his dying day. True, he was present and knew about the fix, but he never accepted any money and never gave anything but his all in each series game. Weaver batted .324 in the 1919 World Series and had no errors. The September 29, 1920, *New York Tribune* called Weaver "one of baseball's leading third basemen," asserting that his statistics in the series should be "a good enough alibi" to prove his innocence.

Indeed, as Cottrell wrote, Weaver's continued claims of innocence after the trial provoked W.A. Phelon, of *Baseball Magazine*, to examine the Series records. His conclusion: "I'll say close analysis fails to show a darned thing on Weaver." Yet for the next thirty-five years of his life, Weaver worked tirelessly to clear his tarnished name. He sought reinstatement with Landis, sending letters and pleading his case, but his requests were always turned down. Buck Weaver's association with the Black Sox scandal, and his mere presence during the discussions and subsequent failure to do any-

thing about it on his own gave him, in Judge Landis's eyes, a "guilty knowledge."

In later years, **Ty Cobb** would stand up for Weaver, saying, "I can't speak for the others who were involved, but they'll never get me to believe that Buck Weaver was guilty of anything." Weaver died in 1956, never finding peace with the scandal that so dramatically changed his life and the world of baseball.

Ted Williams tried, before his death in 2002, to exonerate "Shoeless" Joe Jackson and get him into the Hall of Fame. Williams made it one of his final ambitions to get Cooperstown to acknowledge that Jackson was innocent, believing Jackson to be one of the best pure hitters the game has ever seen. Williams took up the cause in the late 1990s after conducting some research on the man who named his bat "Black Betsy," calling senators, baseball executives, and even presidents on Jackson's behalf.

Williams died before finding success, though many have taken up the cause and are still trying to vindicate Jackson. In fact, it has become such a mainstream fight that the United States Congress took up the debate in the late 1990s, bitterly divided on the issue. "Shoeless" Joe still waits for the Hall of Fame.

The magnifying lens held up in 1920 on eight men who played baseball—a few of whom were the greatest to ever play the game—only served to show the public what had been going on since the game began. Even today, baseball is far from "clean" in the way the fans thought it was before the Black Sox Scandal. In 1986 a drug scandal erupted in the major leagues, and **Pete Rose** was banished from baseball in 1989 when he was tried, and found guilty, of betting on his own team. Many baseball purists—indeed many of the people who want to see Joe Jackson in the Hall of Fame—point out that the eight men of the 1919 Chicago White Sox were acquitted of all charges.

In the end, the Chicago "Black" Sox showed America how greed and deception could rise all the way to the top in a game that seemed—to most fans—immune to corruption. When eight players agreed to "fix" the 1919 World Series for gamblers, it tarnished the national pastime in the public eye and ruined the careers of all players involved.

FURTHER INFORMATION

Books

Alexander, Charles. *Our Game: An American Baseball History*. New York: Henry Holt and Company, 1991.

Asinof, Elliot. *America's Loss of Innocence*. New York: Donald I. Fine, Inc., 1990.

Asinof, Elliot. *Eight Men Out: The Black Sox and the 1919 World Series*. New York: Henry Holt and Company, 1987.

Cottrell, Robert C. *Blackball, the Black Sox, and the Babe: Baseball's Crucial 1920 Season*. Jefferson, N.C.: McFarland & Company, Inc., 2002.

Discovering U.S. History. Farmington Hills, MI: Gale Research, 1997.

Gropman, Donald. *Say It Ain't So, Joe!: The True Story of Shoeless Joe Jackson*. New York: Carol Publishing Group, 1995.

Gutman, Dan. *Baseball Babylon: From the Black Sox to Pete Rose, the Real Stories behind The Scandals That Rocked the Game*. New York: Penguin Books, 1992.

Katcher, Leo. *The Big Bankroll: The Life and Times of Arnold Rothstein*. New York: Harper and Row, 1959.

Lindberg, Richard Carl. *Stealing First in a Two-Team Town: The White Sox from Comiskey to Reinsdorf*. Champaign, IL: Sagamore Publishing, 1994.

Luhr, Victor. *The Great Baseball Mystery: The 1919 World Series*. South Brunswick, NY: A.S. Barnes and Co., 1966.

Scheiner, Richard. *Field of Screams: The Dark Underside of America's National Pasttime*. New York: Norton, 1994.

Spink, J.G. Taylor. *Judge Landis and Twenty-five Years of Baseball*. New York: Thomas Y. Crowell Co., 1947.

White, G. Edward. *Creating the National Pastime: Baseball Transforms Itself: 1903-1953*. Princeton: Princeton University Press, 1996.

Periodicals

Gee, Michael. "Look through Rose-colored glasses." *The Boston Herald* (November 10, 1999): p. 100.

Gustkey, Earl. "He Maintained Fix Was Never in for '19 Series." *Los Angeles Times* (December 12, 1999): p. D-16.

Jones, David. "Williams' final cause: Going to bat for Shoeless Joe." *Florida Today* (Melbourne, FL) (July 6, 2002): p. 02.

"Lawmakers Urge Selig to Lift Jackson's Ban." *The Cincinnati Post* (Cincinnati, OH) (June 15, 2000): p. 7C.

Other

"Black Sox Scandal." Baseball Library.com. http://www.baseballlibrary.com.

"1919 Chicago White Sox". Baseball-Reference.com. http://www.baseball-reference.com.

"Crisis in Baseball: The 'Black Sox' Scandal of 1919." Your Mining Co. Guide to American History. http://americanhistory.miningco.com/library/weekly/aa092297.htm.

"Kenesaw Mountain Landis." Baseball Library.com. http://www.baseballlibrary.com.

Sketch by Eric Lagergren

Lee-Kyung Chun
1976-

Korean speed skater

As short track speed skating is one of the most popular sports in Korea, it's no wonder South Korea's Lee-Kyung Chun was one of the greatest women's short track speed skaters. Her gold medal in the women's 1,000 meter event at Lillehammer, Norway in 1994 was just the beginning of a sports career highlighted by world records and Olympic records. She is the reigning overall women's world champion short track speed skater. Today, she is a member of the IOC Athletes' Commission.

Olympic Career

Short track speed skating entered the Winter Olympics in 1992. Just two years later, 18-year-old Chun participated in the 1994 Winter Olympics in Lillehammer, Norway. She shined as she won two of the three short track speed skating events. In the 1,000-meter race, she faced veteran skaters such as **Cathy Turner** of the US, and Sylvie Daigle and Nathalie Lambert of

Lee-Kyung Chun

Chronology

1976	Born in South Korea on January 6
1993	World Champion for 1,000m
1994	Participates in Winter Olympics in Lillehammer, wins three gold medals
1998	Participates in Winter Olympics in Nagano, wins three gold medals and one bronze medal
1999	Joins the Korean National Olympic Committee Athletes' Commission
2002	Becomes IOC Athletes' Commission member

Canada. In the final lap of the 1,000m she pulled ahead of Lambert to win the gold by one-tenth of a second, pulling off an Olympic record speed of 1 minute 36.87 seconds. In the 3,000m relay, Chun led her Korean team to a gold medal win.

At the Nagano, Japan Winter Olympics in 1998, Chun surpassed her Lillehammer victories. The short track speed skating venue was marked by a particularly exciting race involving Chun and world champion Yang Yang from China. Yang was eventually disqualified for her attempt to impede Chun during the race. Chun, in the final strides, thrust her foot out at the finish line to win the gold medal by the length of a skate blade.

In addition to the 1,000m at Nagano, Chun earned a bronze medal in the women's 500m race, a vast improvement over the 15th place she garnered in Lillehammer. Chun also repeated her performance at the women's 3,000m relay, leading the Korean team to a gold medal. The 3,000m time achieved a world record at 4:16.260.

Chun has set women's short track speed skating world records in addition to Olympic records. She holds world records in three of four individual events. Her impressive career marks world records in Beijing in 1993 for 1,000m with a time of 1:37.19. In 1995 in Gjvik, she skated 5:02.18 in the 3,000m. That same year, at the Winter University Games in Jaca, Spain, Chun set another world record in the 1,500m in 2:27.38. She and her teammates went on to win the 3,000m relay in 1996 in Beijing with a time of 4:17.63.

Her World Championship wins consist of three gold medals and two silver in 1995, two gold medals and two silver in 1996, and three gold medals and one bronze in 1997. In the Team World Championships, Chun won gold medals overall in 1995 and 1996.

Post Olympic Achievements

Following her years in athletic competition, Chun has held positions in various sports organizations. She is a member of the Women and Sport Working Group and in 1999 joined the Korean National Olympic Committee Athletes' Commission. In 2002, she was one of two women athletes appointed by the International Olympic Committee president to join the elected members of the IOC Athletes Commission. Chun joined Egyptian swimmer Rania Amr Elwan as new members to, as the IOC noted, ensure the commission has a fair balance between continents and gender. In 2002, Chun was named to **Bud Greenspan**'s list of 25 Greatest Winter Olympians.

With a Bachelor's Degree and Master's Degree in physical education, Chun holds a teaching certificate. She is a speed skating lecturer and golf teacher's assistant. Part of the Korean powerhouse that dominates women's short track speed skating, Lee-Kyung Chun is one of only seven women to earn four or more career gold medals in the Winter Olympics. She is a two-time Olympic champion, is ranked first in the world for both the 1,500m and 3,000m short track speed skating distances, and is the defending Olympic champion and the world record holder in the 1,000m.

FURTHER INFORMATION

Books

Chronicle of the Olympics. New York: DK Publishing, 1998.

Other

GM Media Online, http://media.gm.com/events/ olympics/25_greatest.html (November 15, 2002).

Awards and Accomplishments

1993	World record in Beijing for 1,000m, time: 1:37.19
1994	Olympic record in Lillehammer for 1,000m, time: 1:36.87
1995	World record in Gjvik for 3,000m, time: 5:02.18
1995	World record in Jaca, Spain, for 1,500m, time: 2:27.38
1996	World record in Beijing for 3,000m relay, time: 4:17.63
1998	Two gold medals and a bronze medal in Nagano Olympics
1998	World record in Nagano for 3,000m relay, time: 4:16.26
2002	Named to Bud Greenspan's top 25 Greatest Winter Olympians

International Skating Union, www.isu.org/historical/
sthisrecs.html (November 15, 2002).

Official Web Site of the Olympic Movement, http://
www.olympic.org (November 15, 2002).

Official Web Site of the Olympic Movement, http://
multimedia.olympic.org/pdf/en_report_5.pdf (November 15, 2002).

Sketch by Lorraine Savage

Kelly Clark

Kelly Clark
1983-

American snowboarder

American snowboarder Kelly Clark "had such an awesome run," on February 10, 2002, her Olympic teammate Shannon Dunn-Downing told the *Washington Post*. "She just kept going big. She did a super-nice McTwist ... at the end, she just busted out a seven." Translation: Clark won the gold medal in the women's halfpipe competition in the 2002 Olympics in Salt Lake City, Utah. And she did so by soaring higher, and landing more inverted tricks than most of her fellow competitors. Clark's medal was the first American gold in snowboarding, and also the first gold of the 2002 Olympics.

Clark was born July 26, 1983 in Newport, Rhode Island. Her family moved to Mount Snow, Vermont, and her parents, Terry and Cathy Clark, own a tavern in nearby West Dover, Vermont called T.C.'s Family Restaurant. She was a ski racer until the third grade, when she got bored of skiing and tried snowboarding, which had just been allowed at her home mountain. Her parents tried to convince her to stick with skiing, that snowboarding was just a fad. Clark began competing in local contests at age thirteen. In ninth grade, she enrolled in the ski academy at Mount Snow, where students divide their time between academics and ski or snowboarding training. She started training with the U.S. Snowboard Team in 2000. Clark graduated high school in 2001 and was accepted at the University of Rhode Island, but deferred her first year of college to concentrate on her snowboarding. She moved to Mammoth, California to train for the Olympics.

When Clark was in ninth grade, and snowboarding debuted as an Olympic sport in 1998 in Nagano, Japan, not a single woman did what is called an "inverted air," which is a somersault in the air after coming off the wall of the halfpipe. In 2002, many women attempted them, but few landed them as confidently as Clark did. She said fear was her biggest obstacle when she first starting attempting the high-flying tricks. "Once you break through that level of fear, and feel comfortable with yourself, you can push yourself to the limit," she told the *Washington Post.*

Clark entered the U.S. Championships in 1999 and finished third in the snowboardcross event and fourth in the halfpipe. In 2000, she won the World Junior Championships, took second at the Goodwill Games, and took a first in snowboardcross and fourth in halfpipe at the U.S. Championships. In 2001, she swept both events at the U.S. Championships as well as the prestigious U.S. Snowboarding Grand Prix. In addition to her halfpipe gold at the Olympics, Clark took first place at the X Games and U.S. Championships before the year 2002 was through. Though she is a competent snowboardcross rider, Clark gave it up to focus on halfpipe because

Chronology

1983	Born July 26 in Newport, Rhode Island
1985	Starts skiing
1991	Starts snowboarding
1996	Begins competing in local snowboarding contests
2000	Begins training with the U.S. Snowboarding Team
2001	Graduates high school
2002	Wins first American gold at Salt Lake City Olympics

Awards and Accomplishments

1999	Third place in snowboardcross, U.S. Championships
1999-2000	Fourth place in halfpipe, U.S. Snowboarding Championships
2000	First place in halfpipe, World Junior Championships
2000	Second place, Goodwill Games
2000-01	First place in snowboardcross, U.S. Snowboarding Championships
2001	Nineteenth place in halfpipe, World Championships
2001	First place, U.S. Snowboarding Grand Prix
2001-02	First place in halfpipe, U.S. Snowboarding Championships
2002	First place in halfpipe, Salt Lake City Olympics
2002	First place in halfpipe, X Games
2002	Fourth place, U.S. Snowboarding Grand Prix

snowboardcross riders tend to be more prone to injuries. Even though she was a success on the competition circuit, and the prize money was good for her bank account, Clark could just as soon do without competing. "I don't think snowboarding needs contests," she told *WWD*, "but they are fun to participate in."

Clark went into the Olympics with a hairline fracture in her right wrist and pain in her back from a crash in practice only days before the competition. Doctors were consulted, X-rays were taken. "When I was lying ... in bed that night, I was thinking, 'Ohhh, what am I going to do?'" she recalled in the *New York Times*. Clark probably knew that she was going to do what she traveled to Salt Lake City to do: compete in her sport.

"The most impressive thing about her is her incredible attitude," Jake Burton, of the Burton snowboard company, told *WWD*. "Obviously, she's got the skills, but mentally she's unflappable. Nerves are a big part of this, as much as they are for figure skating and golf." In addition to nerve, she is known for being aggressive in the halfpipe, but, off the course, "she is calm and soft-spoken, eschewing the rebel image of snowboarders," Edward Wong noted in the *New York Times*. "She could very well be the fresh-scrubbed Generation Y champion that Olympic officials hope will draw younger fans."

Clark competes wearing her mini-disc headphones and listening to music to drown out distraction. As she hit the wall and sailed upwards of eight to nine feet in the air on her Olympic halfpipe runs, though, even loud music by the rock group Blink 182 could not compete with the roaring crowd. "They were so amazing," she said of the cheering fans in *Teen People*. "I've never heard anything like it." And her competitors—most of whom reach heights of five to six feet in the air—had never seen anything like Clark. "I try to have as much personal style as I can to make the most twists and stand out for the judges," she told *WWD*.

France's Doriane Vidal was in the lead when Clark prepared to make her third and final run in the 426-foot halfpipe on February 10, 2002. Her final Olympic halfpipe competition lasted less than two minutes, but she managed to pack in seven tricks, including a McTwist with an indy grab and a frontside 720. That is, an inverted aerial trick where the rider does a 540-degree rotational flip, followed by a 720-degree spin.

Clark's personal style impressed the five competition judges enough to earn her a gold medal—the first for an American in the 2002 Games—in the halfpipe competition. The judges gave her 47.9 out of 50 points, with the French judge turning in a perfect ten. During the awards ceremony, she pulled silver and bronze-medal winners Vidal and Fabienne Reuteler from Switzerland up to share her top spot on the podium after the playing of "The Star Spangled Banner." "It's unbelievable," Clark told the *Washington Post* after her win. "I've never had a feeling like that in my life. It was so overwhelming, and so rewarding at the same time. It means a lot to me, and all the rest of America."

FURTHER INFORMATION

Periodicals

Anstey, Gabby. "Kelly Clark's new tricks." *Sports Illustrated Women*. (December 2002-January 2003): 27.

Burris, Joe. "Smokin' pipe Vermonter Clark gets first U.S. gold." *Boston Globe*. (February 11, 2002): D1.

Chamberlain, Tony. "Clark gets on board." *Boston Globe*. (March 26, 2001): D7.

Chamberlain, Tony. "Kass, Clark stars of the halfpipe." *Boston Globe*. (March 17, 2002): D3.

Feitelberg, Rosemary. "Kelly Clark: Gnarly and nice." *WWD*. (February 13, 2002): 4.

Howard, Caroline. "Person of the month: Kelly Clark." *Teen People*. (May 2002): 117.

Oberjuerge, Paul. "Women's halfpipe: It's gold for a teen; snowboarder Clark gets first top medal for U.S." *Daily News* (Los Angeles, CA). (February 11, 2002): S12.

Ruibal, Sal. "For U.S. star Clark, the future is now." *USA Today*. (February 11, 2002): D4.

Shipley, Amy. "A golden moment: Snowboarder is first American to win at Games." *Washington Post*. (February 11, 2002): A1.

Wong, Edward. "Clark starts with pain and ends up with gold." *New York Times*. (February 11, 2002): D1.

Kelly Clark

Other

"Athlete profile: Kelly Clark." U.S. Olympic Team homepage. http://www.usolympicteam.com/athlete_profils/k_clark.html (January 15, 2003).

"Kelly Clark." EXPN.com. http://expn.go.com/athletes/bios/CLARK_KELLY.html (January 15, 2003).

Sketch by Brenna Sanchez

Roger Clemens
1962-

American baseball player

His native talents alone would have been enough to make Roger Clemens one of baseball's greats. His six foot four, two hundred and twenty-pound frame is capable of hurling a baseball at speeds approaching one hundred miles per hour. His split-finger fastball—only eight miles per hour—dives away as it reaches the plate, confounding the baseball's best hitters. Oakland Athletics out-fielder **Rickey Henderson** described the experience of facing Roger Clemens's fastball to the *Providence Journal* as being, "as difficult to hit as a marble shot out of a cannon." But add to these natural gifts a phenomenal work ethic, obsessive drive, and profound focus, and Roger Clemens may just possess the combination of qualities to propel him to the top as the greatest pitcher in baseball history.

Child of the Heartland

Clemens was born in Dayton, Ohio, the youngest of Bill and Bess Clemens's five children. Clemens never knew his father. When he was eight weeks old, Clemens's mother left his father, a truck driver. This lack of a father figure would always haunt Clemens. Two years later, his mother married Woody Booher, a tool-and-die maker fifteen years her senior, only to have him die five years later of a heart attack. "I'm sure [his death] was hard on Roger, because Woody was the only father he ever knew," Bess Booher told *Sports Illustrated*. "But if he had any problems, he never showed it. When you have adversities in your life, you have to strive to overcome them."

Early Prodigy

Clemens's prodigious baseball talents showed themselves early. By seven he was the star pitcher in a league of nine- and ten-year-olds and by adolescence he was

Roger Clemens

Chronology

1962	Born August 4 in Dayton Ohio
1976	Moves to Houston to join his older brother Randy
1980	Graduates from Spring Woods High School in Houston
1981	Turns down Minnesota Twins offer and attends San Jacinto Junior College, Pasadena, Texas; drafted by New York Mets.
1982	Attends University of Texas; winning pitcher in College World Series final game
1983	Drafted by the Boston Red Sox; marries wife, Debbie
1984	Major league debut against Cleveland Indians
1984-96	Plays for the Boston Red Sox
1997	Signs with the Toronto Blue Jays
1999	Signs with the New York Yankees and wins first World Series game and title
2000	Wins second World Series title
2002	Turns down Yankees contract option and declares free agency, but finally resigns with Yankees

dominating his peer group to the point where his parents felt the need to seek a more competitive environment for him to develop in. His parents shipped him off to live with his brother Randy, in suburban Houston, home of one of Texas's top high school baseball programs. The transition from being the big fish in a small pond to having to prove himself was instrumental in forming Clemens's character. "It was very intimidating for me," Clemens told the *Boston Globe.* "I was the best player I knew in Dayton. And then suddenly ... I was just the third-best pitcher in the rotation. But I decided I wanted to make it to the top and I set certain rules to follow, and discipline just became a habit."

Despite his talent, Clemens did not get the University of Texas scholarship he had dreamed of upon finishing high school in 1980, nor was he drafted by any major league team, though the Minnesota Twins offered him a contract.

Work Ethic

Clemens, thinking he could do better than the Twins, enrolled at San Jacinto Junior College instead and set about building the body he would need to reach his goals. At age 18 he was six-foot two and 220 pounds, and not in good enough shape to achieve the velocity he needed to be truly competitive. Clemens put himself on a rigorous conditioning and weight training program and lost fifteen pounds. The conditioning program did

the trick, pushing the velocity on his fastball from eighty-six miles per hour to the ninety plus miles per hour he would need to succeed in the pros.

He played well enough as a freshman (with a 9-2 won-loss record) for the New York Mets to pick him in round twelve of the 1981 draft with a $30,000 signing bonus. Just as he was considering the New York deal, the University of Texas finally came through with its scholarship offer to Clemens. Clemens, who was close to signing with the Mets, decided that playing with the powerhouse Longhorns was the better strategy. There he would have several more years to develop fully under the tutelage of Longhorns' legendary pitching guru, coach Cliff Gustafson.

Choosing the Longhorns turned out to be the winning strategy. In his first two years for the Longhorns, Clemens won twenty-five games, and lost just seven, striking out 241 batters in 275 innings, while walking just fifty-six. In June of 1983, he was the winning pitcher in the final game of the College World Series, giving Texas the national college title.

"He was an excellent pitcher in college, improving every year," college and pro teammate Spike Owen told *Sports Illustrated.* "But I don't think anybody could have looked at him then and known what was in store."

Boston Bound

In 1983, Roger Clemens's hard work and foresight paid off when the Boston Red Sox selected him in the first round of the draft. Clemens had a meteoric rise through the Red Sox farm system. Rac Slider, manager of the Red Sox's AA New Britain team declared to the *Boston Globe,* "I haven't seen anyone at the same stage who's got what he's got." Fully grown at 6'4" and 220 pounds, Clemens had the unique combination of one of baseball's best fastballs paired with pinpoint control. Joining the Red Sox midway through the 1984 season, he won nine games and lost four.

Career Statistics

Yr	Team	W	L	ERA	GS	CG	SHO	IP	H	R	BB	SO
1984	BOS	9	4	4.32	20	5	1	133.3	146	64	29	126
1985	BOS	7	5	3.29	15	3	1	98.3	83	36	37	74
1986	BOS	24	4	2.48	33	10	1	254.0	179	70	67	238
1987	BOS	20	9	2.97	36	18	7	281.7	248	93	83	256
1988	BOS	18	12	2.93	35	14	8	264.0	217	86	62	291
1989	BOS	17	11	3.13	35	8	3	253.3	215	88	93	230
1990	BOS	21	6	1.93	31	7	4	228.3	193	49	54	209
1991	BOS	18	10	2.62	35	13	4	271.3	219	79	65	241
1992	BOS	18	11	2.41	32	11	5	246.7	203	66	62	208
1993	BOS	11	14	4.46	29	2	1	191.7	175	95	67	160
1994	BOS	9	7	2.85	24	3	1	170.7	124	54	71	168
1995	BOS	10	5	4.18	23	0	0	140.0	141	65	60	132
1996	BOS	10	13	3.63	34	6	2	242.2	216	98	106	257
1997	TOR	21	7	2.05	34	9	3	264.0	204	60	68	292
1998	TOR	20	6	2.65	33	5	3	234.7	169	69	88	272
1999	NYY	14	10	4.60	30	1	1	187.7	185	96	90	163
2000	NYY	13	8	3.70	32	1	0	204.3	184	84	84	188
2001	NYY	20	3	3.51	33	0	0	220.3	205	86	72	213
2002	NYY	13	6	4.35	29	0	0	180.0	172	87	63	192
TOTAL		293	151	3.15	573	116	45	4067.0	3478	1425	1321	3909

BOS: Boston Red Sox; NYY: New York Yankees; TOR: Toronto Blue Jays.

The Red Sox, plagued by disappointing pitching, and having not won a World Series since 1918, expected the 21-year old Clemens to become even more that a star; in Clemens they saw a savior.

Career Crisis

Midway through the 1985 season, however, Clemens's career was already in danger of being derailed. His shoulder began hurting so much that he could barely lift his pitching arm. Clemens underwent surgery, removing cartilage near his rotator cuff. While some feared that his career might be over, others, like Red Sox pitching coach Bill Fischer speculated that the injury might actually have been a blessing in disguise, scaring Clemens into focusing and working even harder. Fischer told *Newsday* "Maybe it's that arm injury that left him so determined to get the best out of himself. Maybe it scared him to work even harder. A lot of people have athletic ability. But very few make use of every ounce of it the way he does."

Cy Young and MVP

Clemens didn't have to wait long for redemption. In 1986, he roared back to lead the American League in wins (twenty-four with just four losses), winning percentage (.857) and ERA (2.48). He started and won the All-Star game. One memorable night against the Seattle Mariners in May of that year, Clemens struck out twenty batters. No pitcher in 111 years of major league history had ever done that before. "It puts me in the Hall of Fame, at least in one sense," he told the Boston Globe. "Nobody can take that away from me. I just hope people don't think it's a misprint." He won the **Cy Young** Award as the American League's best pitcher and was voted

Most Valuable Player as the Red Sox won the pennant for the first time in eleven seasons. He pitched in two World Series games that October, but won neither.

In the 1987 season, Clemens had another Cy Young-quality season, winning twenty games, striking out 256 batters, and posting a 2.97 ERA, good enough to beat the jinx that traditionally plagues Cy Young winners and giving him his second consecutive award—a feat achieved by only four other pitchers, **Sandy Koufax**, Denny McLain, Jim Palmer, and **Greg Maddux**.

With great achievement and fame comes the potential for great controversy and in this category too Clemens has always been a leader. In 1988 Clemens left training camp in a salary dispute. He criticized team management for its treatment of players and their families, criticism that was largely interpreted as complaints about New England and its baseball fans. Clemens drew the ire of Red Sox fans and heard boos for the first time.

In 1988 and 1989, Clemens was bothered by a strained back which limited his effectiveness. In 1988, won 18 games, lost 12, led the majors strikeouts and shutouts, and had an ERA of 3.13. Boston won the American League East title but was swept in the American League championship series by Oakland. In 1989, he was again off his usual pace, winning only seventeen games, and striking out 231. In 1990, Clemens regained his top-of-the-game form, winning twenty-one games, losing just six, and posting a league-leading 1.93 ERA. A performance brilliant enough to inspire *Sports Illustrated*'s Leigh Montville to rhapsodize, "When he is pitching well, when the control is good, when the speed is up, he is almost untouchable. The best pitcher in base-

Awards and Accomplishments

1986	All-Star game MVP
1986-87,	Cy Young Award
1991,	
1997-98,	
2001	
1986, 1988,	Made All-Star Team
1990-92,	
1997-98,	
2001	
1996	Strikes out 20 in one game for the second time in his career
1998	3,000th strikeout
1999	First World Series title
2000	Second World Series title
2001	Oldest starting pitcher in All-Star game in baseball history

Roger, Over and Out?

Clemens does not accept the idea that he is in some sort of irreversible decline. He argues instead that, with a few runs here and there, everything could have turned out much differently in 1999. "Six games could've gone either way," he says. "I could easily have been a twenty-game winner. And if I did that, there wouldn't be any talk about how I'm losing it." It's true that the Yankees supported him with a mere fifteen runs in his ten losses last year, but how many times did they score by the bushel-load to dig him out of a hole? He just as easily could have been a fifteen-game loser. "Listen, the only downer last season was that I hurt my hamstring and couldn't hold on to some four-to-nothing leads." He hints that for most of season, he pitched while he was in pain. Yankees owner George Steinbrenner had theorized this over the winter. "I was in a defensive mode after the hamstring injury, trying to protect it, trying not to reinjure it," Clemens says. "I didn't want to miss more time. I wanted to answer the bell."

Source: Michael P. Geffner, *Texas Monthly*, August 2000, p. 120.

ball. No debate. The evening sports news will be a collage of strikeouts, batters swinging at air, batters frozen in place, looking at pitches they can't see."

Man of Controversy

It was also a performance that helped propel the 1990 Red Sox to the American League East title and a shot at making the World Series. Only the Oakland Athletics stood in their way. The series did not go well for Boston or Clemens. Boston lost the first three games. Clemens started the must-win fourth game. Down 2-0, in the second inning, Clemens was thrown out of the game by home plate umpire Gerry Cooney, after Cooney claimed that Clemens swore at him. In front of a national television audience Clemens lost his temper, had to be restrained, and was carried off the field. The Red Sox went on to lose the game and Clemens received a five-game suspension and a $10,000 fine. The incident only added to Clemens's growing legend as a fierce competitor to some, and spoiled prima donna to others. "Who is Roger Clemens—a hothead who boiled over in the playoffs or an overgrown kid driven by obsessions?" asked *Sports Illustrated*'s previously enraptured Leigh Montville.

Third Time Cy Young Charm

Whatever the answer, the Red Sox certainly forgave Clemens. Before the 1991 season, the Red Sox signed Clemens to a four-year, $21 million deal confirming Clemens's status at the top of his profession. Clemens returned the confidence in him by winning his third Cy Young award, posting an 18-11 record, leading the majors in strikeouts with 241 and innings pitched (271), as well as the American League in ERA (3.62). The 1992 season saw Clemens turn in another successful 18-11 performance, leading the majors in shutouts with five and the American League in ERA (2.41).

A New Start North of the Border

Clemens's performance in 1992 didn't help the fortunes of his team. The Red Sox slid to the bottom of the American League East with a dismal record of seventy-

three victories. Clemens's fortunes also slid the following year when, bothered once again by shoulder and arm injuries, he suffered his first losing season (11-14). The infamous strike-shortened 1994 season saw Boston still foundering and Clemens posting a 9-7 record. These were not good times for Clemens. Over the next two seasons, he continued to struggle with a groin injury and tendonitis, as well as the knowledge that the Red Sox were no nearer to winning a World Series than when his career had begun. With Clemens and the Red Sox slumping and Clemens becoming a free agent, the big market, big league rumor mill started. Would the Red Sox trade Clemens for new blood or hang on to him? Would Clemens jump to another team for a big payday and the opportunity to pitch for a World Series ring?

The answer came in a $24.75 million, three-year contract to play for the Toronto Blue Jays, who outbid the Texas Rangers and the New York Yankees. This contract made Clemens the highest paid pitcher of the moment. The Blue Jays were counting on Clemens turning around his sub par performances of the past several years and making them a contender. Clemens delivered, turning in a stellar 1997 season where he was easily the most dominating pitcher in baseball, putting together a league leading 21-7 record, 2.05 ERA, and a career-best 297 strikeouts The Rocket was back! Clemens also collected his fourth Cy Young award. Sports Magazine named him one of the ten most dominant athletes of 1997, along with **Michael Jordan, Pete Sampras, Martina Hingis**, and **Tiger Woods**.

Roger, Meet George

The 1998 season with the Blue Jays was equally productive with Clemens adding his 3,000th strikeout and becoming the only pitcher in history to win a fifth Cy Young award. Clemens could have easily stayed where he was, collecting his third year of guaranteed money and forcing an optional fourth year, but whereas Clemens was at the top of his game, Toronto wasn't. Clemens, realizing that the Blue Jays weren't going to

Roger Clemens

be contenders, exercised an option in his contract that put him again on the open market.

George Steinbrenner and the Yankees came calling, trading their star pitcher David Wells, reliever Graeme Lloyd, and second baseman Homer Bush for Clemens. The deal rocked the baseball world. Steinbrenner took a lot of heat for trading hometown hero Wells, who had come off of a great year, as well as having pitched a perfect game, but as Yankee pitcher and Wells's best friend David Cone told *Newsweek*: "When you add the best pitcher in the game, how could it not be a good deal?"

At first it looked like Steinbrenner's bet on Clemens was not going to pay off. Clemens stumbled badly through the 1999 year, leaving many to wonder, especially in the media glare of New York's number one media market, how a five-time Cy Young winner, 41-13 in the past two seasons with the Blue Jays, could be struggling to keep his ERA under 5.00? With Clemens's regular season record being a mediocre 14-10, all the usual questions about Clemens's age and durability surfaced. But Clemens pitched brilliantly in the postseason, helping the Yankees win his first World Series game and his first World Series ring by winning Game Four of the Yankees shocking 4-0 sweep of the Atlanta Braves.

The 2000 season followed pretty much the same pattern with Clemens barely doing better than a .500 winning percentage. But his postseason was brilliant. First he helped shut down the Mariners with a one-hit, 15-strikeout masterpiece in Game 4 of the American League Championship Series. Then in Game 2 of the Subway Series with the New York Mets, Clemens faced **Mike Piazza**, the popular Mets catcher and slugger. What followed was an incident that will be forever replayed in the annals of World Series history. Piazza's bat shattered on one of Clemens's fastballs. Clemens fielded one of the shards and hurled it back towards the first-base sideline missing Piazza by less than a foot. The resulting face-off between Piazza and Clemens emptied the benches, though without incident. On the next pitch, Clemens retired Piazza on a grounder. After that the Mets went down meekly and the Yankees went on to win the game and subsequently the Series in five games.

Still Top of the World

The 2001 season saw Clemens at thirty-nine, long after fastball pitchers are supposed to be spent, reassert his dominance at the top of the game with his sixth Cy Young and a 20-3 record. Even with a heartbreaking loss to the Arizona Diamondbacks in the World Series, Clemens had a year that led *Sports Illustrated* to declare: "Today Woody Booher's son is as close to an unbeatable pitcher as there has ever been in baseball."

The 2002 season was less successful with the Yankees bowing out early in the playoffs to the Anaheim Angels (who went on to beat the San Francisco Giants for the World Series crown) and Clemens posting mediocre stats: 13-6 record; 4.35 ERA, and only 192 strikeouts. Nonetheless Clemens initially felt confident enough in his value to turn down his $10.3 million option with the Yankees, go free agent, and entertain offers from other teams. However, he eventually re-signed with the Yankees.

With his conditioning program, his iron discipline, his fierce competitiveness, a fastball that still pops at ninety-eight miles per hour, and a "splitter" that is still unhittable, who knows how long Roger Clemens can continue to play…and win.

CONTACT INFORMATION

Address: Roger Clemens, c/o Major League Baseball, 75 Ninth Ave., New York, NY 10011. Fax: (212) 485-3456. Phone: (212) 485-3182.

SELECTED WRITINGS BY CLEMENS:

(With Peter Gammons) *Rocket Man: The Roger Clemens Story*, S. Greene Press, 1987.

FURTHER INFORMATION

Periodicals

"Booster Rocket." *Sports Illustrated* (March 1, 1999)

Buckley, Steve. "Rocket Science: behind the scenes with baseball's best pitcher." *Sport* (May 1993): 12.

Callahan, Gerry. "Rocket's red glare." *Sports Illustrated* (Dec 29, 1997).

Costas, Bob. "A pitcher." *Sporting News* (April 19, 1999)

Faulkner, David. "Secrets to success." *Sporting News* (June 27, 1994): 14.

Hille, Bob. "Bombing in the Bronx." *Sporting News* (September 20, 1999)

Knisley, Michael. "A grip on greatness." *Sporting News* (September 24, 2001).

Lazenby, Roland, et al. "Dominators of Sport: 1997." *Sport* (January 1998)

Marantz, Steve. "Count down." *Sporting News* (July 29, 1996).

McAdam, Sean. "The return of Boston's Rocket." *Sporting News* (Mar 7, 1994): 12.

Ribowsky, Mark. "Not so fast." *Sport* (May, 2000)

Schmuck, Peter. "Clemens is winning, but is he happy?" *Sporting News* (August 4, 1997)

Schmuck, Peter. "Star trek: the Rocket fuel Hall trip with his 3000th K." *Sporting News* (July 13,1998).

Schmuck, Peter. "Headed for a new pad, The Rocket in a bargain." *Sporting News* (Dec 14, 1998): D6.

Verducci, Tom. "Roger & Out." *Sports Illustrated* (October 30, 2000)

Verducci, Tom. "Going Batty." *Sports Illustrated* (November 1, 2000)

Verducci, Tom. "Rocket science." *Sports Illustrated* September 10, 2001).

Weinberg, Rick. "Special Delivery." *Sport* (May 1997).

Other

The Roger Clemens Foundation, http://www.roger clemensonline.com/index2.htm (Sept 24, 2001).

Sketch by Gordon Churchwell

Roberto Clemente
1934-1972

American baseball player

Roberto Clemente

Hall of Fame baseball player Roberto Clemente was the first great Hispanic star in major league baseball. Playing for the Pittsburgh Pirates, he had a lifetime average of .317 and 240 home runs; had four seasons with 200 or more hits; and won twelve Gold Gloves in eighteen seasons. He also won the National League Most Valuable Player award in 1966. Clemente's stellar performance helped open the door for other Hispanic players to enter the sport.

Clemente was born in 1934 in Carolina, Puerto Rico, the youngest of seven children, six of whom were boys. His father, Melchor, was a foreman of a sugar plantation and worked long hours in the fields, receiving a dollar a day. When Clemente was young, he worked in the same fields, loading and unloading trucks.

Clemente began playing baseball with his friends at an early age, and continued to play through high school, where he starred in baseball and track. He was such a skilled javelin thrower that some thought he might make Puerto Rico's 1952 Olympic team. However, baseball was his favorite sport, and he devoted most of his free time to it. His high school coach, Robert Marin, told a scout for the Santurce professional baseball team to take a look at Clemente. The scout held tryouts for seventy-one players, and sent seventy of them home after watching Clemente. He offered Clemente a $5,000 bonus, a $60-per-month contract, and a baseball glove.

From 1952 to 1955, Clemente played for Santurce. Although Latin players, like African-American players, had been barred from the U.S. major leagues, this barrier was beginning to break down, and Clemente attracted the attention of major league scouts in the U.S. After he

---

Chronology

1934	Born August 18, in Carolina, Puerto Rico
1952-53	Plays for Santurce, Puerto Rico baseball team
1953	Plays for Brooklyn Dodgers' minor-league team, the Montreal Royals
1954	Drafted by Pittsburgh Pirates
1955	Clemente bats .311, the first of 13 seasons batting at better than .300
1960	Bats .314 with 16 home runs and 94 RBIs, but comes in eighth in MVP voting
1960	Pittsburgh Pirates win World Series
1963	Meets Vera Zabula
1964	Marries Vera Zabula
1966	National League Most Valuable Player
1971	World Series Most Valuable Player
1972	Injured, but still bats .312
1972	In his final at-bat, makes his 3,000th hit
1972	Dies when his plane crashes during a mission to help earthquake victims in Nicaragua
1972	Elected to Baseball Hall of Fame

Clemente

Clemente's life was celebrated in this Fox Sports Net documentary, which originally aired in March of 1998. Narrated by actor Jimmy Smits and combining home movies, media footage, and interviews with Clemente's friends and family members, the documentary provides a well-rounded portrait of Clemente. It also examines the impact of racism on Clemente's career. According to Steve Crowe in *Knight Ridder/Tribune News Service,* this video portrait "soars in capturing the pride of Puerto Rico's baseball grace and demand for dignity."

batted .356 for Santurce during the 1952-1953 winter season, Brooklyn Dodger scout Al Campanis chose him to attend a baseball clinic. In addition, Clemente was paid a $10,000 bonus.

When Clemente graduated from high school, ten teams, including the Dodgers, wanted to recruit him. Clemente, who had promised Campanis he would go with the Dodgers, was true to his word, despite the fact that the Milwaukee Braves had offered him $30,000. In 1953, at the age of 19, Clemente went to the Dodgers' top minor-league team, the Montreal Royals. He then ran into problems with red tape: baseball regulations stated that if a player received a bonus of more than $4,000, he had to be placed on the major league roster after one season. If he was not, another team could draft him for $4,000.

This caused a problem for the Dodgers, as their major-league roster was too crowded for them to use Clemente so soon. Although they tried to hide Clemente from other teams by using him very little, the Pittsburgh Pirates were not fooled, and drafted him on November 22, 1954.

Clemente made his major league debut on April 17, 1955, playing for the Pittsburgh Pirates. At the time, the Pirates were in last place, but by 1956, with Clemente batting .311, the Pirates moved up to seventh place. This was the first of thirteen seasons in which Clemente would bat at better than .300.

In 1958, Clemente made twenty-two assists, the most among outfielders. In 1960, the Pirates won the World Series.

Clemente's Puerto Rican heritage caused a great deal of commentary, much of it negative, despite his playing ability. Because many Americans were uncomfortable with the "foreignness" of Clemente's name, Roberto, he was introduced as Bob Clemente in games. In the press, writers emphasized his origins and appearance, calling

him a "dusky flyer" and a "chocolate-colored islander." In addition, they regularly mocked his imperfect English, reprinting sentences such as "I no run fast cold weather," according to Steve Wulf in *Sports Illustrated.*

Although he constantly battled this prejudice, Clemente retained an inner sense of his own worth as a player. Wulf noted that in 1955, when a radio interviewer told him that he ran, threw, and hit as well as **Willie Mays,** Clemente replied, "Nonetheless, I play like Roberto Clemente." He also said, "Pitch me outside. I will hit .400. Pitch me inside, and you will not find the ball."

Racist feelings against Clemente became even more obvious in 1960, when he hit .314 with 16 home runs and 94 RBIs for the Pittsburgh Pirates. Despite this stellar performance, he came in eighth in the voting for Most Valuable Player. The award was given to Clemente's teammate Dick Groat, who hit .325 but only had two home runs and 50 RBIs.

Sportswriter Phil Musick, who spent years covering Clemente's career, was one of those who focused more on racist characterizations of Clemente than on his skills as a player. However, Musick later apologized in his 2001 book, *Reflections on Roberto,* writing, "There was a racial overtone to much of what was written about Clemente early in his career, and unfortunately it precluded much reporting on his baseball skills and how they were acquired. The author of this work (Musick) bears some of that responsibility."

From 1961 to 1972, Clemente's average season was .331. with seventeen home runs and eighty-one RBIs. Eventually this overwhelming talent became too difficult to ignore, and in 1966 he finally won the Most Valuable Player award.

In 1961, Clemente won the first of four batting titles, batting .351 with 201 hits.

In 1963, Clemente met Vera Zabula in a drugstore; she was 23, and he fell in love at first sight. She told Wulf, "On our first real date, he told me he was going to marry me. On our second date he brought pictures of houses."

Clemente won his second batting title in 1964. On November 14 of that year, he also married Zabula; they would later have three sons, Roberto Jr., Luis Roberto, and Enrique Roberto. He won his third batting title in

Awards and Accomplishments

1960	Pittsburgh Pirates win World Series
1961-72	National League Gold Glove at OF
1966	National League Most Valuable Player
1971	World Series Most Valuable Player
1972	In his final at-bat, makes his 3,000th hit
1972	Elected to Baseball Hall of Fame

Roberto Clemente, at bat

1965 with a batting average of .329, and took his final title in 1967 with .357 and twenty-three home runs. In 1969, the Pirates took the Eastern Division title; Clemente had an average of .352.

In 1970 the Pirates lost the National League playoffs to the Cincinnati Reds, but in 1971 they won both the National League title and the World Series. Clemente was named Most Valuable Player of the World Series.

Clemente was injured in 1972, but still batted .312. The Pirates won the division title, but lost to the Reds in the playoffs.

Clemente's last hit, his 3,000th, was on September 30, 1972. He was only the eleventh player ever to reach that number. After the 1972 championship, Clemente returned to San Juan, Puerto Rico, where he had customarily spent his off-seasons working with youth programs.

Clemente's Personality

Known as a hypochondriac, Clemente frequently suffered from a variety of injuries and ailments: headaches, backaches, stomach pains, malaria, insomnia, bone chips, and pulled muscles. According to Steve Wulf in *Sports Illustrated,* someone once asked Clemente how he was feeling. "Well," Clemente said, "My bad shoulder feels good, but my good shoulder feels bad." However, when he was called a hypochondriac, Clemente replied, "If I was a hypochondriac, I wouldn't be playing," according to another *Sports Illustrated* article by Wulf.

Although he worried about his own health, this did not prevent Clemente from being concerned about others' feelings and welfare. He was notably generous with fans and others. After the Pirates beat the New York Yankees in the 1960 World Series, Clemente did not attend the team party—instead, he walked around Pittsburgh thanking the fans. In *Sports Illustrated,* Steve Wulf quoted his wife, who said, "He would rather be late for a meeting with the governor than pass by a stranger who needed help with a tire."

Clemente's desire to help others would later contribute to his early death, which he often feared. According to Steve Crowe in the *Knight Ridder/Tribune News Service,* Clemente had a deep fear that he would not live to see his children grow up. In early November of 1972,

he dreamed that he was watching his own funeral; the dream would later seem oddly prophetic.

In late December of 1972, an earthquake destroyed most of Managua, Nicaragua; 6,000 people were killed, 20,000 injured, and 250,000 left homeless, without food, clothing, water, or medical supplies. Clemente helped organize relief missions to the survivors in the stricken city. On December 31, 1972, Clemente's plane took off from San Juan, Puerto Rico carrying eight tons of supplies. A few minutes later, it exploded and crashed into the sea. Clemente and the four other people on board were killed in the crash, and although divers searched for his remains, his body was never found. Puerto Rico declared three days of official mourning for its lost hero.

Clemente's Legacy

Shortly after his death, Clemente became the first Hispanic person ever inducted into the Baseball Hall of Fame; the usual rules, which stipulated that a player had to wait five years after ending his career before being inducted, were waived.

After Clemente's death, the Pirates honored him for the next several seasons by wearing patches on their sleeves. The patches had Clemente's uniform number, 21, circled in black. The team also played a series of exhibition games in San Juan in order to make Clemente's dream of a "sports city" in Puerto Rico come true.

Career Statistics

Yr	Team	AVG	GP	AB	R	H	HR	RBI	BB	SO	SB
1955	PIT	.255	124	474	48	121	5	47	18	60	2
1956	PIT	.311	147	543	66	169	7	60	13	58	6
1957	PIT	.253	111	451	42	114	4	30	23	45	0
1958	PIT	.289	140	519	69	150	6	50	31	41	8
1959	PIT	.296	105	432	60	128	4	50	15	51	2
1960	PIT	.314	144	570	89	179	16	94	39	72	4
1961	PIT	.351	146	572	100	201	23	89	35	59	4
1962	PIT	.312	144	538	95	168	10	74	35	73	6
1963	PIT	.320	152	600	77	192	17	76	31	64	12
1964	PIT	.339	155	622	95	211	12	87	51	87	5
1965	PIT	.329	152	589	91	194	10	65	43	78	8
1966	PIT	.317	154	638	105	202	29	119	46	109	7
1967	PIT	.357	147	585	103	209	23	110	41	103	9
1968	PIT	.291	132	502	74	146	18	57	51	77	2
1969	PIT	.345	138	507	87	175	19	91	56	73	4
1970	PIT	.352	108	412	65	145	14	60	38	66	3
1971	PIT	.341	132	522	82	178	13	86	26	65	1
1972	PIT	.312	102	378	68	118	10	60	29	49	0
TOTAL		.317	2433	9454	1416	3000	240	1305	621	1230	83

PIT: Pittsburgh Pirates.

Clemente's wife Vera remembered that for years he had talked about creating a "sports city" for the young people of Puerto Rico, and she spearheaded the effort to build one. Today the Ciudad Deportiva Roberto Clemente, located in Carolina, Puerto Rico, continues to encourage young people to play sports and to succeed at them. Since its beginnings, it has fostered many players who later came to the major U.S. leagues.

In addition to being depicted on almost 100 baseball cards, Clemente was honored in 1982 with a 20-cent stamp issued by Puerto Rico. At the 1994 All-Star game in Pittsburgh, a bronze statue of Clemente was unveiled. Pirates outfielder Orlando Merced told Wulf, "Roberto Clemente means a dream to me, and to a lot of kids and people. . . . He has pushed me to be a better player and a better person. When they unveiled the statue, I was crying. It made me proud to be who I am and to be a Puerto Rican."

When Clemente entered major league baseball, he contended with widespread racism among players, fans, and sports reporters. Partly because of his presence and his talent, baseball teams today spend millions of dollars to recruit and keep talented Hispanic players; by 1998, almost nineteen percent of major-league players were Hispanic. According to Bill Plaschke in *The Sporting News,* Dodger scout Mike Brito said, "Today, the Latin player coming in is treated like a king. If he is any good, he gets everything." Despite this, Latin players still face stereotypes, according to Plaschke, "that they are hotheaded, or that they don't have inner drive." In addition, although Hispanic players are now relatively common, only one of 120 personnel executives is Hispanic. In *The Sporting News,* Richard Lapchick quoted former player agent Joe Masso, who said that

Hispanic players need a transition program to help them understand the language and culture of the United States, and that "The U.S.-born players need a deeper understanding of Latino culture so they can play better as teammates on and off the field."

In *Stamps,* John D. Babbitt quoted Clemente's summation of his life philosophy: "Accomplishment is something you cannot buy. If you have a chance to do something for somebody and you do not make the most of it, you are wasting your time on this earth."

FURTHER INFORMATION

Books

Musick, Phil. *Reflections on Roberto.* Sports Publishing, Inc, 2001.

Periodicals

Babbitt, John S. "Roberto Clement: A Sports Legend." *Stamps* (July 30, 1994): 1.

Crowe, Steve. "'Clemente' Documentary Soars with Pride." *Knight Ridder/Tribune News Service* (March 5, 1998): 305K6854.

Kaplan, Jim. "It's a Dream Come True." *Sports Illustrated* (October 5, 1987): 95.

Lapchick, Richard. "Recalling Roberto." *Sporting News* (October 27, 1997): 7.

Plaschke, Bill. "Lamenting Clemente." *Sporting News* (January 12, 1998): 9.

Wulf, Steve. "Arriba Roberto!" *Sports Illustrated* (December 28, 1992): 114.

Wulf, Steve. "Roberto Clemente." *Sports Illustrated* (September 19, 1994): 110.

Ziegel, Vic. "Remembering Roberto Clemente." *Knight Ridder/Tribune News Service* (December 31, 1997), p. 1231K5142.

Other

"Roberto Walker Clemente." *RobertoClemente21.com.* http://www.robertoclemente21.com/ (November 17, 2002).

Sketch by Kelly Winters

Alice Coachman

Alice Coachman
1923-

American track and field athlete

Alice Coachman became the first black woman of any nationality to win a gold medal at the Olympics with her victory was in the high jump at the 1948 Summer Games in London. Coachman broke jump records at her high school and college, then became the U.S. national high jump champion before competing in the Olympics. She is also the first African-American woman selected for a U.S. Olympic team.

Coachman was born the middle child to a family of ten children in rural Georgia, near the town of Albany. Her parents were poor, and while she was in elementary school, Coachman had to work at picking cotton and other crops to help her family meet expenses.

Her athleticism was evident, but her father would whip her when he caught her practicing basketball or running. "Back then," she told William C. Rhoden of the *New York Times* in 1995, "there was the sense that women weren't supposed to be running like that. My father wanted his girls to be dainty, sitting on the front porch."

Coachman, however, continued to practice in secret. Unable to train at public facilities because of segregation laws and unable to afford shoes, Coachman ran barefoot on the dirt roads near her house, practicing jumps over a crossbar made of rags tied together.

When Coachman was in the seventh grade, she appeared at the U.S. track championships, and Tuskegee Institute Cleveland Abbot noticed her. Abbot convinced Coachman's parents to nurture her rare talent. Reluctantly at first, her parents allowed her to compete in the Tuskegee Institute relay in the 1930s, where she broke first high school, and then collegiate records by the time she was 16 years old. She went on to win the national championships in the high jump, and 50 and 100 meter races as well.

Coachman also sang with the school choir, and played in several other sports just for fun, including soccer, field hockey, volleyball and tennis. She also swam to stay in shape.

Coachman's biggest ambition was to compete in the Olympic games in 1940, when she said, many years later, she was at her peak. But World War II forced the cancellation of those games and those of 1944. The war ended in 1945, clearing the way for the 1948 Summer Games in London. In 1946, Coachman became the first black women selected for a U.S. Olympic team, in the first Olympiad since the 1936 Games in Nazi Germany.

Winner at Wembley

Illness almost forced Coachman to sit out the 1948 Olympics, but sheer determination pulled her through the long boat trip to England. Until Coachman competed, the U.S. women runners and jumpers had been losing event after event.

She made her famous jump on August 7, 1948. At age 25, she launched herself into the record books in front of 83,000 spectators, becoming the first woman of African descent to win an Olympic gold medal.

The English had pinned their hopes on high jumper D. J. Tyler. Both Tyler and Coachman hit the same high-jump mark of five feet, 6 1/4 inches, an Olympic record. But Tyler required two attempts to hit that mark, Coachman one, and so Coachman took the gold, which King George VI presented her. Coachman's record lasted until 1956.

<table>
<tr><td colspan="2">Chronology</td></tr>
<tr><td>1923</td><td>Born November 9 in Albany, Georgia</td></tr>
<tr><td>1996</td><td>Founds Alice Coachman Track and Field Foundation</td></tr>
</table>

<table>
<tr><td colspan="2">Awards and Accomplishments</td></tr>
<tr><td>1939</td><td>Wins her first Amateur Athletic Union competition</td></tr>
<tr><td>1939-48</td><td>Wins national high jump championship every year</td></tr>
<tr><td>1946</td><td>Named to the women's All-America track and field team for 1945</td></tr>
<tr><td>1946</td><td>Becomes first African-American woman selected for an Olympic team</td></tr>
<tr><td>1948</td><td>Wins gold medal in the high jump at the Olympics, becoming the first black woman to win Olympic gold</td></tr>
<tr><td>1975</td><td>Inducted into the National Track & Field Hall of Fame</td></tr>
<tr><td>1996</td><td>Honored as one of the 100 Greatest Olympic Athletes</td></tr>
</table>

Coachman returned home a national celebrity. She was honored in meetings with President Harry Truman and former First Lady Eleanor Roosevelt, and with a parade that snaked 175 miles from Atlanta to Albany, with crowds cheering her in every town in between. She also became the first African-American woman to endorse an international product when the Coca-Cola Company featured her prominently on billboards along the nation's highways. Back in her hometown, meanwhile, Alice Avenue and Coachman Elementary School were named in her honor.

Coachman's Olympic gold medal paved the way for the generations of African-American athletes. "I think I opened the gate for all of them," she told the *Atlanta Journal-Constitution*'s Karen Rosen in 1995. "Whether they think that or not, they should be grateful to someone in the black race who was able to do these things."

After graduating from Albany State College, Coachman worked as an elementary and high school teacher and a track coach. She married and had two children.

In 1994, Coachman founded the Alice Coachman Track and Field Foundation. This organization helps develop young athletes, and to help former Olympic athletes to establish new careers.

Great Olympic Athlete

Choosing to stay largely out of the spotlight in later years, Coachman, nonetheless, was happy to grant media interviews in advance of the 100th anniversary modern Olympic games in 1996, held in Atlanta. She told reporters then that her mother had taught her to remain humble because, as she told William C. Rhoden of the *New York Times* in 1995, "The people you pass on the ladder will be the same people you'll be with when the ladder comes down."

She also advised young people with a dream not to let obstacles discourage them. Instead, she advised, listen to that inner voice that won't take "no" for an answer. "Guts and determination," she told Rhoden, "will pull you through."

FURTHER INFORMATION

Periodicals

"Alice Coachman, 1st Black Woman Gold Medalist, To Be Honored." *Jet* (July 29, 1996): 53.

Cummings, D. L. "An Inspirational Jump Into History." *Daily News* (February 9, 1997): 75.

Danzig, Allison. "83,000 At Olympics." *New York Times* (August 8, 1948): S1.

Deramus, Betty. "Living Legends." *Essence* (February, 1999): 93.

"Georgia's Top 100 Athletes of the 1900s." *Atlanta Journal and Constitution* (December 26, 1999): 4G.

"Miss Coachman Honored: Tuskegee Woman Gains 3 Places on All-America Track Team." *New York Times* (January 11, 1946): 24.

Rhoden, William C. "Sports of the Times; Good Things Happening for the One Who Decided to Wait." *New York Times* (April 27, 1995): B14.

Rosen, Karen. "Olympic Weekly; 343 Days; Georgia's Olympic Legacy." *Atlanta Journal and Constitution* (August 11, 1995): 6D.

Weiner, Jay. "A Place in History, Not Just a Footnote." *Star Tribune* (July 29, 1996): 4S.

Other

"Alice Coachman." Infoplease.com. http://www.info please.com/ipsa/A0771730.html (January 17, 2003).

"Alice Coachman." USA Track & Field. http://www. usatf.org/athletes/hof/coachman.shtml (January 17, 2003).

Sketch by Michael Belfiore

Ty Cobb
1886-1961

American baseball player

Ty Cobb is arguably the greatest baseball player who ever put on spikes. During his 24-year career, he established records in virtually every area of the offensive game. His .367 lifetime average stands as the best in baseball history, a virtually unattainable goal for hitters. He is also number one among all-time runs scored leaders, number two in hits and triples, number three in stolen bases, and number four in runs batted in, doubles, at bats and games played. Cobb was a dazzling player. Nearly impossible to strike out, he was a batter who could hit to all fields, both for power and average, and he could drop bunts with pinpoint accuracy. He drove opponents to distraction in the base paths, always trying for the extra base and stealing almost at will. His approach to baseball was fierce and unrelenting—every game was a war with the diamond its battlefield. This competitive drive was a symptom of other, deeper character flaws. Possessed of a dangerous temper, a racist disposition and a tendency to brutal violence, Cobb alienated family, friends, opponents, and perfect strangers. Besides being supremely talented as a player, he was also supremely difficult as a person.

Tyrus Raymond Cobb was born on December 18, 1886 in Narrows, Georgia, to William Herschel Cobb and Amanda (Chitwood) Cobb. W.H. Cobb invented Tyrus's name himself after reading about the city of Tyre's stubborn resistance to the besieging armies of Alexander the Great. He could have but little suspected its appropriateness for his impulsive, headstrong son. Cobb's father, a school principal who placed a high premium on learning, hoped Tyrus would become a doctor or lawyer. From the time he was a child, however, the boy was infatuated with the game of baseball. As a teen he became the star player for a local team, the Royston Reds. In 1904, when a regular held out for more money, Cobb got to play with the Augusta Tourists of the South Atlantic (Sally) League. He hit a single and double in four at-bats his first game. Within days, however, the holdout was back and Cobb was released.

With the words of his father—"don't come home a failure"—in his ears, Cobb signed on with a team in Anniston, Alabama. A little later Grantland Rice, the sports editor of the Atlanta *Journal,* began receiving letters of praise for young Cobb. Impressed, Rice wrote in his column "over in Alabama there's a young fellow named Cobb who seems to be showing an unusual amount of talent." Years later Cobb would admit that he had written all the letters himself, using a variety of handwriting styles. Cobb did well enough at Anniston, however, that the Augusta team asked him to come back for the rest of the 1904 season, and eventually for the 1905 season as well.

The Detroit Tigers got their first look at Cobb during spring training at Augusta in 1905. After witnessing Cobb's antics on the bases—stealing on nearly every pitch, trying to stretch every single to a double, and running from first to third on sacrifice bunts—second baseman Germany Schaefer described Cobb to Tiger management as "the craziest player I ever saw." Cobb's exhibition play impressed the Tigers and in August the team purchased his contract. By then, he was the best player in the Sally League: He won the batting

Ty Cobb

title with a .326 batting average; he was the first in the league ever to get 100 hits in a season; and his 40 stolen bases was third best in the league. He joined the Tigers for the last month of the season. During the next five years Cobb would single-handedly make Detroit over from the weakest market for baseball to the most lucrative. Cobb's play with the Tigers that year alternated between brilliance, foolhardiness and embarrassment. He lashed hits, ran into foolish outs and interfered with his own fielders. But he brought an element of excitement that few fans had ever experienced in baseball.

Despite being called up to the big leagues, 1905 and 1906 would be among the most difficult years of Cobb's life. In August, when he was preparing to join the Tigers, personal tragedy struck. His father was shot to death, and the killer was Cobb's own mother. Amanda Cobb thought her husband, who was climbing in her bedroom window at night, was a prowler, and in March 1906 she was found not guilty. W.H. Cobb's unexpected death robbed Cobb of the family member he was closest to, and possibly the only one capable of exerting a steadying influence on the headstrong youth. It also denied Cobb the chance to prove to his father that he had made good in baseball.

Cobb's difficulties did not end with his return to the Tigers in spring 1906. At a time when rookie ballplayers were routinely hazed by veteran players, the Tigers'

Chronology

1886	Born in Narrows, Georgia
1904	Joins Augusta Tourists of the South Atlantic League
1905	Joins Detroit Tigers
1905	W.H. Cobb is shot to death by Amanda Cobb
1906	Amanda Cobb found innocent of manslaughter
1907	Tigers win the first of three American League pennants
1907-19	Cobb wins 12 American League batting titles
1908	Marries Charlie Marion Lombard
1909	Causes uproar when he spikes Philadelphia's Frank Baker
1910	Cobb's first child, Tyrus Raymond Cobb Jr., born
1912	Enters stands in New York City to attack heckler Claude Lucker
1912	Plays lead in stage play *The College Widow*
1915	Cobb sets long-standing record of 96 stolen bases in single season
1915	Becomes highest paid player in baseball
1916	Stars in film *Somewhere in Georgia*
1918	Joins Chemical Warfare Service
1921	Becomes player-manager of Detroit Tigers
1926	Resigns as player and manager
1926	Accused of game-fixing and betting on baseball games
1927	Signs with Philadelphia Athletics
1928	Leaves baseball for good
1936	Becomes first player inducted into Baseball Hall of Fame at Cooperstown
1945	Endows the Cobb Memorial Hospital in Royston, Georgia
1947	Divorces Charlie Cobb
1949	Marries Francis Fairburn
1953	Establishes the Cobb Educational Fund
1955	Divorces Francis Fairburn
1960	Starts working on his autobiography with Al Stumpf
1961	Dies in Atlanta

treatment of Cobb was particularly harsh. He was refused his turn at batting practice; he was locked out of bathrooms in the team hotel; he was systematically ignored; his handmade ash bats were sawed in half. Cobb's southern origins did not help among a team of northerners. However, his treatment was exacerbated by his thin skin, hair-trigger temper, well-honed prejudices, and his ability to hold a grudge. By the end of 1906 he was sincerely disliked by most Tiger players. Through his 21 seasons with the team, long after he had established himself as a regular, he was never close to his teammates, who continued to dislike him.

The strain of the hazing eventually took its toll. In July 1906, the nineteen-year-old Cobb suffered a nervous breakdown that took him out of the lineup for nearly two months. He eventually returned to full form on the field, but his confrontations with his teammates continued, frequently concluding in vicious physical brutality on Cobb's part. With so many enemies, both real and imagined, he started a lifelong practice of keeping a loaded pistol nearby at all times. His ball playing performance in his first full season was remarkable. He hit .320—fifth best in the American league—and stole 39 bases. The Tigers as a team had played more disappointingly, finishing in sixth place, with a losing record, 71-78. That would change in

1907, with the first of three consecutive American League championships.

By mid-1907 Cobb was being called "Ty" for the first time in his life. He had developed a recognizable personality on the field too. In the batter's box he swung three bats. Although he threw right-handed, he batted left-handed—he would later say it started him off closer to first base. Playing in the so-called "dead ball" era, when emphasis was on base hits, sacrifice bunts, base running and stealing, Cobb gripped his bat in an unorthodox manner, with his hands about six inches apart, and would slide one hand up or down for better control. On the base paths he was "daring to the point of dementia." His philosophy was the more chances he took, the more likely opponents were to be forced into making an error, and he was usually right.

The 1907 Tigers took the American League pennant with a 92-58 record, before losing the World Series in four games to the Chicago Cubs. Cobb's .350 batting average won him the first of nine consecutive and 12 in total batting titles. He was already recognized around the American League as the finest all-around player in baseball. Secure in his position as one of the game's stars and a genuine box office attraction, Cobb held out for more money in 1908, eventually receiving $4,000 a year from the Tigers. More controversially, he spoke out against the reserve clause, which bound a player to a certain club. Ahead of his time, Cobb proposed an alternative: Limit the term of the reserve to five years, and then let a player freely sell his services to the highest bidder. Predictably, organized baseball considered such propositions radical and dangerous, and did not recognize free agency until the 1970s. Cobb earned his extra pay, winning his second batting title in 1908 and leading the Tigers to their second straight league pennant.

Cobb played with a fervor that has rarely been matched. His rough style on the bases led players, fans, and writers in opposing cities to call him a dirty player. He was accused of deliberately sharpening his spikes to intimidate opposing infielders. Cobb occasionally denied such allegations, but in general he let them stand—they served too well the psychological warfare he practiced on the diamond. Whether or not he sharpened his spikes, Cobb felt no compunction about sliding into base with spikes high, deliberately colliding with a defender to dislodge the baseball. In 1909, for example, Cobb's no-holds-barred play drew him into controversy at the height of a pennant race with the Philadelphia Athletics. Sliding into third, Cobb's spikes caused a small cut in the arm of Athletics third baseman Frank Baker. A fight was averted, but later in the game Cobb knocked over second baseman Eddie Collins. After the Tigers swept the series to take first place from Philadelphia, **Connie Mack**, the normally soft-spoken Athletics' owner, responded by calling

Awards and Accomplishments

1905-27	Stole home 54 times, an all time record; 46 inside-the-park HR, a career AL record
1907	Led American League in RBIs and hits
1907-15, 1917-19	American League batting title
1908	Led American League in triples
1909	Triple Crown, American League, 9 HR, .377 BA, 107 RBI, plus led majors in stolen bases
1911	Chalmers Most Valuable Player Award; batting title, .420 average; led American League in hits, runs, doubles, RBIs, and stolen bases.
1912	Stole home 8 times for a major league record
1915	Led major leagues with 96 stolen bases
1936	First player elected to National Baseball Hall of Fame

Cobb

Ty Cobb's last lonely, bitter years are the subject of the dark 1995 film *Cobb*. *Cobb* is less a traditional baseball movie than a compelling character study of a man who happened to be both the greatest baseball player in history and a monster of epic proportions. Its story describes the experiences of young Al Stump (portrayed by Robert Wuhl), a writer hired by Cobb to put his autobiography onto paper. Expecting to encounter a great old ballplayer when he arrives at Cobb's Nevada home, Stump finds a angry alcoholic with a dangerous penchant for shooting the pistol ever at his side whenever he gets upset. On a long drive from Nevada to Cooperstown, Stump confronts the man and the legend, and must decide how he will eventually tell Cobb's story—the sugar-coated success story or the ugly truth. The film was directed and written by Ron Shelton, who had earlier made another excellent baseball movie, *Bull Durham*. Tommy Lee Jones as Cobb gives the performance of his career, which left many reviewers wondering how he could have been passed over for an Oscar nomination.

Cobb the dirtiest player in the history of the game. As so often happened during his career, the notoriety Cobb gained from the incident only seemed to inspire him to better play. During that period, he hit at a .640 pace and stole one base or more per game. By the end of the season he had racked up an average of .377, hit 107 RBIs and nine home runs, and stolen 76 bases, leading the league in virtually every offensive category. Detroit finished in first place again but it would be the last time Cobb would play for a pennant winner.

Cobb's racism attracted regular, if unwanted, public attention. He instigated nasty fights with blacks. In 1907, for example, he started a slapping match with a black groundskeeper, and then choked the man's wife when she shouted at Cobb to stop. Not long after the Philadelphia incidents, Cobb got into a fight with a black night watchman at a hotel in Cleveland, trying to stab the man with his knife. A warrant was sworn out for Cobb's arrest in Cleveland, and the rest of the season, Cobb had to travel apart from the rest of the Tigers whenever they passed through the city.

Cobb's most infamous instance of ruffianism, one also tinged by his racist prejudice, occurred on May 15, 1912 in New York. Claude Lucker, a spectator behind the Tiger bench, targeted a stream of abuse at Cobb that lasted most of the game. Cobb requested that the man be removed from the park, in vain. When Lucker directed at Cobb a racial epithet normally reserved for blacks, Cobb lost control, charged up into the stands, and commenced to kicking and stomping Lucker, who was little able to defend himself, having lost a hand and three fingers in an industrial accident. The resulting publicity was highly critical of Cobb and the American League suspended him for ten games. Surprisingly, the Tiger players forgot their past animosities with Cobb and supported him, staging a strike that forced the Tiger management to field a team of semi-pros for one game.

Cobb dominated baseball to such an extent between 1910 and 1920 that the period came to be known as the "Cobbian" era, in distinction to the "Ruthian" era of home runs that would follow the First World War (named for baseball great **Babe Ruth**). Between 1910 and 1919, Cobb would win the batting title every year except 1916, including a squeaker over Napoleon Lajoie in 1910 that is still disputed by some fans. In 1911 he hit .420, the second highest season average in modern baseball history. He led the league in stolen bases four times, including 1915 when he stole 96 bases, a record that stood until Maury Wills shattered it in the 1960s. Cobb's presence was felt off the diamond in those years as well. In the winter of 1912 he appeared in a stage play, *The College Widow,* that toured the South, the Midwest and the eastern seaboard. In 1916 he was the first pro athlete to star in a movie, *Somewhere in Georgia*. He counted among his friends presidents William Howard Taft, Woodrow Wilson, and later Warren G. Harding. Beginning in 1915 his $20,000 a year from the Tigers made him the highest paid player in baseball. By that time he hardly needed the money. He had invested shrewdly in real estate ventures and had gotten in on the ground floor with new companies such as General Motors and Coca-Cola that would help make him a millionaire well before his playing days had ended.

By the 1920s, as the home run ball was replacing the era of inside baseball, years of unfettered base-running and abandoned slides had taken their toll on Cobb's legs and knees. He could no longer run like he used to, but he still hit with the best, with a 1920 average of .334. That winter, following the resignation of long-time Tiger manager Hughey Jennings, Cobb was offered the managership of the team. Cobb had reservations about accepting the job, but it was difficult to resist $35,000 a year, a sum that made him the highest paid player or manager in baseball, except for John McGraw. Cobb vowed to bring a new style to managing the Tigers. Rather than the sarcasm and invective that Jennings relied on, Cobb intended to use encouragement and advice. It was a promise that the quick-tempered, demanding Cobb was ill-equipped to keep. Before long, he was belittling and demeaning players who did not play the game his way. He fomented feuds between players. He benched good players against whom he held some grudge. In the end, despite strong hitting by the Tigers, they only finished in sixth place under Cobb. They improved in 1922, finishing third, and second in 1923. That was the best Cobb could achieve in five years as manager. By his last season in 1926, the Tigers were back in sixth place. The fault was not entirely Cobb's though. He was hampered by a poor pitching staff and an owner who refused to spend money to get better players. When he resigned, he quit both as a manager as a player. Ty Cobb said he had played his last game.

Cobb reentered baseball, just months later after being implicated in the biggest scandal of his career. In spring 1926, Dutch Leonard, a former Detroit pitcher, had told league officials that during a Cleveland-Detroit series in September 1919, Indians manager Tris Speaker had arranged with Cobb to deliberately lose a game with the Tigers to help Detroit finish in third place. Moreover, according to Leonard, they arranged to place bets on the game's outcome. At the time of Leonard's allegations, baseball was still reeling from revelations that members of the **1919 Chicago White Sox** had conspired with gamblers to fix the outcome of the 1919 World Series. The Tigers had indeed won the game in question, but questions lingered about whether it was fixed. Cobb had been unable to get a hit, while Speaker hit two triples. Further complicating the matter, it turned out Leonard secretly held Cobb and Speaker responsible for ending his career in the majors. In the fall of 1926, Ban Johnson, the president of the American League, quietly told Cobb and Speaker to leave baseball. Meanwhile the affair came to the attention of the imperious commissioner of baseball, Kenesaw Mountain Landis, who publicly opened his own investigation. Cobb acknowledged writing a letter to Leonard that connected him with bets on the game. However, he insisted that he was only an intermediary, he had not wagered on the game himself. He also insisted that Speaker was not connected with the affair at all. The scandal unleashed a wave of national publicity arguing the comparative merits of Cobb vs. Leonard. Most observers agreed that whatever Cobb's faults as a man, he was not dishonest and he had no history as a gambler. In January 1927, Judge Landis announced that Cobb and Speaker had been completely exonerated, and were restored to the active rosters of their former teams.

When the Tigers released him, Cobb accepted an offer estimated at $70,000 a year to play for Connie Mack's Philadelphia Athletics in 1927. By that time he didn't need the money, but it was certainly an incentive—it made him the highest paid player in the game once again. Above and beyond the money, he was anxious to play with a club that was a pennant contender. He also considered his comeback as a means of vindi-

Ty Cobb

cating his name in the public eye. Lastly, however, baseball had been the central focus of his life since he could lift a bat. Despite his aging legs and accruing injuries, it would have been difficult for him to walk away from the game. His comeback was a total success. In 134 games, Cobb batted a resounding .357, including 32 doubles and 5 home runs. He even managed to steal 22 bases. In 1928, his last year as a player, Cobb hit a respectable .323. He stole only 5 bases, but one was a steal of home, an exploit he had specialized in as a young player. Despite his high hopes, however, the Athletics did not win the American League pennant while Cobb was on their roster.

When Cobb left baseball for good after the 1928 season he had the credentials to demonstrate irrefutably that he had been the greatest all-around player in baseball up to that time. He had the highest lifetime average of any player in history, had more hits, the most runs batted in, the most runs scored, the most stolen bases, the most steals of home, and the season high for stolen bases. He was second in all-time doubles and triples. He had an extremely low strikeout rate, only 357 in 11,429 at bats. These remarkable achievements, together with the excitement he had generated, led the nation's base-

Career Statistics

Yr	Team	AVG	GP	AB	R	H	HR	RBI	BB	SB	E
1905	DET	.240	41	150	19	36	1	15	10	2	4
1906	DET	.320	98	350	45	112	1	41	19	23	9
1907	DET	.350	150	605	97	212	5	116	24	49	11
1908	DET	.324	150	581	88	188	4	108	34	39	14
1909	DET	.377	156	573	116	216	9	107	48	76	14
1910	DET	.385	140	509	106	196	8	91	64	65	14
1911	DET	.420	146	591	147	248	8	144	44	83	18
1912	DET	.410	140	553	119	237	7	90	43	61	22
1913	DET	.390	122	428	70	167	4	67	58	52	19
1914	DET	.368	97	345	69	127	2	57	57	35	10
1915	DET	.369	156	563	144	208	3	99	118	96	18
1916	DET	.371	145	542	113	201	5	68	78	68	17
1917	DET	.383	152	588	107	225	7	102	61	55	11
1918	DET	.382	111	421	83	161	3	64	41	34	10
1919	DET	.384	124	497	92	191	1	70	38	28	8
1920	DET	.334	112	428	86	143	2	63	58	14	9
1921	DET	.389	128	507	124	197	12	101	56	22	10
1922	DET	.401	137	526	99	211	4	99	55	9	7
1923	DET	.340	145	556	103	189	6	88	66	9	12
1924	DET	.338	155	625	115	211	4	74	85	23	6
1925	DET	.378	121	415	97	157	12	102	65	13	15
1926	DET	.339	79	233	48	79	4	62	26	9	6
1927	PHI	.357	134	490	104	175	5	93	67	22	8
1928	PHI	.323	95	353	54	114	1	40	34	5	6
TOTAL		.367	3034	11429	2245	4191	118	1961	1249	892	278

DET: Detroit Tigers; PHI: Philadelphia Athletics.

ball writers to name him, nearly unanimously, as the first player elected to the National Baseball Hall of Fame in 1936.

Ty Cobb's life after baseball was restless and apparently unhappy. Already a millionaire, he did not have to work. He refused offers to become a ball club executive or manager, and opportunities to purchase clubs fell through. He used part of his fortune for philanthropic purposes in his home state of Georgia, funding the construction of the Cobb Memorial Hospital in Royston to perpetuate his parents' names. He also established the Cobb Educational Fund, to provide scholarships-nonathletic scholarships-to worthy Georgia students.

Cobb's relations with his family were less than ideal. He was a strict, demanding, anger-prone husband and father. He was estranged from his first son for most of Tyrus Jr.'s short life—he died of a brain tumor in 1951. After filing for divorce on several occasions, Cobb's wife, Charlie, finally went through with it in 1947. His second marriage in 1949 to Frances Fairburn foundered seven years later, thanks to Cobb's abusive temper, which was fueled by his excessive drinking.

By January 1960, Ty Cobb's health was in rapid decline. He had been diagnosed with diabetes, heart disease, high blood pressure, degenerative kidney disease, and prostate cancer. His last days were spent in loneliness, traveling from hospital to hospital with an envelope containing millions of dollars in negotiable securities and a loaded Luger pistol. His one frequent companion was Al Stump, a writer whom Cobb had contracted to work with him on his autobiography. Stump completed his research just months before Cobb passed away on July 17, 1961 in Atlanta, Georgia. Three ex-ballplayers and a Hall of Fame official were baseball's only representatives at the funeral of the greatest ball player who ever lived.

SELECTED WRITINGS BY COBB:

Busting 'Em Out and Other Stories. New York: Edward J. Clode Publishers, 1914.

"Batting Out Better Boys." *Rotarian* 71 (July 1947): 10-12.

"They Don't Play Baseball Any More." *Life* 32 (March 17, 1952): 136-38f.

"Tricks That Won Me Ball Games." *Life* 32 (March 24, 1952): 63-64f.

(With Al Stump) *My Life in Baseball: The True Record.* Garden City: Doubleday, 1961.

FURTHER INFORMATION

Books

Alexander, Charles C. *Ty Cobb.* New York: Oxford University Press, 1984.

The Baseball Encyclopedia. Tenth edition, New York, Macmillan, 1996.

Cobb, Ty, with Al Stumpf. *My Life in Baseball: The True Record.*Garden City, Doubleday1961.

Stump, Al. *Cobb: A Biography.* Chapel Hill, Algonquin Books, 1994.

Stumpf, Al. "Ty Cobb's Wild Ten-Month Fight to Live," *True.* 14 (December 1961).

"Ty Cobb, Baseball Great, Dies; Still held 16 Big League Marks." *New York Times.* July 18, 1961.

Sketch by Gerald E. Brennan

Derrick Coleman

Derrick Coleman
1967-

American basketball player

Derrick Coleman represents the kind of elite athlete that achieves such success and notoriety so early in his career that he develops a seriously skewed view of his own importance in the world, and even in his sport. The undeniably talented power forward has a record marred by questionable choices that have affected him both on and off the court. Coleman has worn out his welcome with two of the three teams he has played for professionally, and his "bad boy" behavior has landed him in legal trouble as well.

Number One Draft Pick

Coleman was born on June 21, 1967, in Mobile, Alabama, but considers Detroit, Michigan his hometown. Coleman first attracted national attention as the star of the Syracuse University basketball team; he was the number one draft pick for the NBA in 1990, and signed with the New Jersey Nets.

Coleman, who has a rare love of the history of basketball, seemed determined early on to place himself in the pantheon of the game's greats. His professional career started off spectacularly: he won the Rookie of the Year Award in 1991 while playing for the Nets, and was chosen for the Dream Team II, which captured the gold medal at the World Championships in Toronto in 1994. He also played in the All-Star game that year.

Coleman's early fame was sullied by accusations in 1994 that he had raped a woman in Detroit. Although no charges were brought against him, Coleman was embittered by the incident; it proved to him that people were out to get him because of his fame and outstanding talent.

Coleman has a real love and talent for the rhythm and flow of basketball; as Raad Cawthon wrote in the *Sporting News,* "Coleman has an acute understanding of how the game works, of the spacing and geometry of a play, and so can easily spot a breakdown." Sometimes this ability leads Coleman to make the shots, the assists, the rebounds, the three-pointers. Sometimes, though, Coleman's abilities are channeled into deriding his teammates and second-guessing the coaching staff. During his years with the Nets, Coleman's vocalizations about what the team should be doing soured his relationships with teammates and coaches. By 1995, the team was ready to unload him; a former coach told the *Sporting News,* "I did all with Derrick that I could do. But with Derrick, you are only going to get so far, and you might as well understand that."

New Start in Philadelphia

Coleman was traded to the Philadelphia 76ers in 1995, and the season got off to a slow start. Coleman, while maintaining a great respect for the game, seemed to disdain practicing as somehow beneath him. During his last months with the New Jersey team, he was misdiagnosed with a heart ailment and had to sit out two months of the season. He gained weight during his time off the court, and when he got to Philadelphia, he rushed into play before he was back in shape. This anxiousness to get back in the game led to a sprained ankle and more time on the bench.

While 76ers coach John Lucas admired Coleman's talent, he also hated the attitude. He told the *Sporting*

Career Statistics

Yr	Team	GP	PTS	FG%	3P%	FT%	RPG	APG	SPG	BPG	TO	PF
90-91	NJN	74	18.4	.467	.342	.731	10.30	2.2	.96	1.34	2.93	2.90
91-92	NJN	65	19.8	.504	.303	.763	9.50	3.2	.83	1.51	3.82	2.60
92-93	NJN	76	20.7	.460	.232	.808	11.20	3.6	1.21	1.66	3.20	2.80
93-94	NJN	77	20.2	.447	.314	.774	11.30	3.4	.88	1.84	2.70	2.70
94-95	NJN	56	20.5	.424	.233	.767	10.60	3.3	.63	1.68	3.07	2.90
95-96	PHI	11	11.2	.407	.333	.625	6.50	2.8	.36	.91	2.55	2.70
96-97	PHI	57	18.1	.435	.269	.745	10.10	3.4	.88	1.32	3.23	2.90
97-98	PHI	59	17.6	.411	.265	.772	9.90	2.5	.78	1.15	2.66	2.40
98-99	CHA	37	13.1	.414	.212	.753	8.90	2.1	.65	1.14	2.43	2.60
99-00	CHA	74	16.7	.456	.362	.785	8.50	2.4	.46	1.76	2.34	2.60
00-01	PHI	34	8.1	.380	.392	.685	5.40	1.1	.29	.62	1.24	1.60
01-02	PHI	58	15.1	.450	.337	.815	8.80	1.7	.72	.88	2.05	2.70
TOTAL		687	17.6	.448	.298	.768	9.60	2.7	.78	1.40	2.75	2.70

CHA: Charlotte Hornets; NJN: New Jersey Nets; PHI: Philadelphia 76ers.

Chronology

1967	Born June 21 in Mobile, Alabama
1986	Begins playing for Syracuse University
1990	Graduates from Syracuse University
1990	Number one draft pick in NBA, signs to New Jersey Nets
1991	Named Rookie of the Year
1994	Plays in NBA All-Star game
1994	Accused of rape (never charged)
1994	Plays on Dream Team II, wins gold medal
1995	Traded to Philadelphia 76ers
1998	Traded to Charlotte Hornets
1999	Involved in traffic accident, charged with DWI (later acquitted)
2000	Turns himself in on a warrant for driving with suspended license
2001	Traded back to Philadelphia 76ers
2002	Arrested for speeding, DUI in Detroit; pleads no contest

News, "I told [Coleman] no one wanted him any more. I told him if he was unhappy and wanted to get out of Philadelphia, he needed to play to earn back the respect that he thought he deserved." Coleman took Lucas's advice and made the most of ownership and coaching changes on the team to work hard during the next two seasons. Things seemed to be improving for the forward, and in 1998 Coleman signed a five-year, $40 million contract to play with the Charlotte Hornets.

Trouble in Charlotte

In November 1999, Coleman drove his truck through a tractor trailer. His female passenger suffered lacerations, and his teammate Eldridge Recasner sustained a partially collapsed lung and a fractured shoulder socket. Coleman refused to take a Breathalyzer after the accident, claiming that he was being singled out because he was a celebrity. Showing little remorse, he told the press, "People act like nobody ever had an accident be-

fore. I understand that we as athletes are under the microscope, but we're human beings just like everyone else. If one of you guys goes out and has an accident, nothing is ever said. But as soon as one of us does it, it's magnified."

Charlotte fans seemed to have different ideas about the situation. Coleman was enthusiastically booed during the team's season opener, and coach Paul Silas publicly acknowledged that Coleman's attitude and behavior posed problems for the team.

Things didn't improve much for Coleman in Charlotte. When he showed up 30 pounds overweight at training camp in 2000, his coaches were concerned. The extra weight likely contributed to various injuries during the season, including a knee injury that required surgery, a sprained ankle, and a strained back. Coleman had an awful season, and his attitude remained sullen. Some Hornets spoke out publicly, indicating the team would be better without Coleman. Coleman did act as a mentor for some of the younger players on the team, but overall his presence was not appreciated. By 2001, the Charlotte team was looking to dump Coleman.

Back to Philadelphia

In a three-team swap, Coleman was traded back to the Philadelphia 76ers in October 2001. Coach Larry Brown expressed unprecedented support for Coleman, saying, "He's talked to me for two years about coming back here and it's no secret how much I like him, what a terrific player I thought he was."

Coleman's troubles weren't over with the trade to Philadelphia, though. In July 2002, Coleman was pulled over in a Detroit suburb for speeding; he had been clocked going 120 miles per hour on a freeway. He refused the Breathalyzer test, but later pleaded no contest to the DUI charge. Again, Coleman felt singled out because of his celebrity status. After the sentencing (which some felt to be inappropriately light—three days of community service and nine months of no-report probation), Coleman stated publicly, "If I was a regular Joe Schmo, they probably would have just given me a ticket and sent me on my way. We, as athletes, are in the public eye. That's the bad thing about it."

"Bad Boy"

Another basketball player with an uneven reputation, **Charles Barkley**, weighed in on Coleman's "bad boy" reputation. He said, "I don't think anyone has ever questioned the talent he has, but sometimes he has let outside distractions take away from what he is doing on the court." Other commentators, though, have had a different opinion: that Coleman is a narcissist, spoiled by his fame and talent to the point of not noticing anything in the real world. Whatever the cause, Coleman's reputation continues to be problematic, and interferes at times with how well he plays the game that he has such talent for.

CONTACT INFORMATION

Address: Derrick Coleman, Philadelphia 76ers, 3601 S. Broad St., Philadelphia, PA 19148.

FURTHER INFORMATION

Periodicals

Adande, J.A., Gregg Hoffmann, and Raad Cawthon. "Looking Out for No. 1," *Sporting News* (February 10, 1997): 9-13.

"Coleman Returns to 76ers in Trade." *New York Times* (October 26, 2001): 12.

D'Alessandro, Dave. "Coleman Needs to Get a Grip On Himself and Life," *Sporting News* (November 15, 1999): 14.

Lyon, Bill. "Coleman Never Will Be Designated Driver." *Philadelphia Inquirer* (October 5, 2002): S1.

"Nets' Coleman Cleared of Rape Allegation after DNA Test." *Jet* (August 15, 1994): 46.

Smith, Stephen A. "NBA Endures Disastrous Off-Season." *Philadelphia Inquirer* (September 29, 2002): S1.

Wertheim, L. John. "Players and Staff Only." *Sports Illustrated* (May 21, 2001): 52-69.

Sketch by Christine M. Kelley

Colorado Silver Bullets
American baseball team

Hitting the field for the first time in 1994, the Colorado Silver Bullets was the first women's professional baseball team in fifty years. The team, managed by Hall of Fame pitcher Phil Niekro, played men's amateur, college, and Olympic teams for four years. Facing taunts from some, but providing encouragement for the future of women in sports in others, the Silver Bullets represented the United States in tournaments around the world. Following a season that saw a brawl on the field and the eventual loss of its major sponsor, the team disbanded in 1997.

National Sponsorship

Robert Hope, a public relations manager for the Atlanta Braves, had a dream to establish a women's professional baseball team since 1984. He believed that women had a right and a desire to play professional baseball. His persistence in pitching the idea and the 1992 film *A League of Their Own* about women's baseball teams during World War II, which fostered acceptance of women in baseball, finally led to success.

In 1993, Coors Beverage Company, based in Colorado, agreed to sponsor Hope's team. Coincidentally, Coors had been searching for a way to venture into the women's sports market and to promote women's rights. With the help of Hope's agency, Hope-Beckham, and the team named after a Coors' advertising campaign, the Silver Bullets became a sports property for beer brand Coors Light.

With an infusion of $3 million from Coors to get the team started, Hope began forming his staff. He chose Phil Niekro, Baseball Hall of Fame member and former Atlanta Braves pitcher, as team manager. Like Hope, Niekro respected the game of baseball and believed in the drive and determination of women players. "Their attitude [about learning baseball] is absolutely the best I've ever seen," he told the *Christian Science Monitor*. Shereen Samonds was hired as general manager. She was the only female general manager in Double-A baseball and had been named the Rawlings' 1993 Female Executive of the Year.

Next came the selection of the team members. Most hopefuls had come from the realm of softball, since girls and women were still discouraged or banned from playing baseball. The invitation-only tryouts rounded up nearly 3,000 players nationwide, most having been All-American college softball players and all had been recommended by college coaches and scouts. In the end, twenty-four players were chosen.

First Women's Team Since the 1950s

On Mother's Day, May 8, 1994, the Colorado Silver Bullets played their first game. They became the first

Shereen Samonds of the Colorado Silver Bullets, at right, with models and team manager Phil Niekro

pro women's baseball team since the All-American Girls Professional Baseball League, which began in 1943 and disbanded in 1954 when women were officially banned from playing professional baseball.

For a meager $20,000 salary per player, the Silver Bullets' members played against men's amateur, college, Olympic, semi-pro, and military teams, and represented the United States in tournaments around the world. Much media attention surrounded the women's team, which was featured in *Newsweek,* on *NBC Nightly News,* and other media. The team played fifty games per year, held in various cities from Jacksonville, Florida; San Diego, California; Fenway Park in Boston; and even China. Overall, sixty of the team's games were televised.

The Bullets started off unimpressively but progressively improved. They finished their first season with a 6-37 record, with a team batting average of .141 and scoring only eighty-three runs. By the next year they won eleven games, and in 1996, won eighteen games, which included a team record of three home runs that season. In 1997, they got their own field in Albany, New York, where they played fifteen of their fifty games. That same year, they finished above .500 for the first time with a final record of 23-22.

The Silver Bullets gained recognition for their pioneering achievements. The team was sanctioned by the National Association of Professional Baseball Leagues, and in 1995 became part of the Women in Baseball exhibit in the National Baseball Hall of Fame. The team held fund-raisers to fight domestic violence, and with the Southern League of Professional Baseball Clubs, which encourages amateur baseball leagues to let girls play, the Silver Bullets created the Give a Girl a Chance program.

Notable Silver Bullets Players

Bullets' pitcher Gina Satriano, daughter of Tom Satriano of the Boston Red Sox and the California Angels, was one of only two team members who previously had experience in baseball. In fact, her father once sued in California to allow Gina to play in the Little League. Gina commented, "Baseball is a game where size doesn't have to matter."

Kim Braatz hit the first-ever home run by a Silver Bullets player. Outfielder Tammy Holmes, a University of California—Berkeley, four-time All-American college basketball and volleyball player, became the first woman to hit two home runs in a season.

Pitcher Lee Anne Ketcham and first baseman Julie Croteau were the first women to sign with the men's

Career Statistics

Yr	Name	Avg	GP	AB	R	H	HR	RBI	BB	SO	SB
1994	Stacy Sunny	.200	43	110	11	22	0	11	10	21	0
	Michele McAnany	.200	39	100	8	20	0	6	31	22	1
	Jeannette Amado	.200	23	35	4	7	0	1	15	0	2
1995	Stacy Sunny	.246	39	130	10	32	0	17	16	14	2
	Michele McAnany	.230	44	122	22	28	0	9	50	26	1
	Angie Marzetta	.221	40	95	16	21	0	9	20	18	2
1996	Laura Espinoza-Watson	.308	51	214	34	66	1	–	–	–	6
	Michele McAnany	.284	51	155	32	44	0	–	51	–	–
	Stacy Sunny	.260	44	200	32	52	0	–	–	–	3

Statistics represent the top three batters for each year.

Class A and AA Winter Baseball League in Hawaii. Croteau had made headlines in 1989 when she played first base for the otherwise-male Seahawks of St. Mary's College in Maryland, an NCAA Division III baseball team.

On June 4, 1996, Bullets pitcher Pam Davis became the first female to pitch on an affiliated men's professional team when the Class AA Jackson Suns played an exhibition game against the Australian Olympic Club. Davis pitched the fifth inning and struck out one batter.

Slow Downfall, But Still an Inspiration

The Bullets were recognized by Congress for their contributions to women's sports, and even Coors, for its efforts, received the Women's Sports Foundation's Pioneer Award. Dr. Donna Lopiano, president of the Women's Sports Foundation, and herself a Little League all-star pitcher, noted, "It is important not only for women to see women play baseball against men, but it is also important for men to see both women and men competing as equals on the sports field."

Unfortunately a brawl that erupted in 1996 and an inability to win many games were precursors to the team's downfall. After a pitcher for the all-male Americus Travelers team in Georgia spouted slurs against the Bullets and Bullets batter Kim Braatz was hit by a pitch, she charged the mound provoking a brawl involving both sides. Despite the media frenzy that resulted, team owner Hope lauded the incident as a reminder of the team's existence.

The next year, the Bullets eventually found it difficult to schedule games with men's teams. None of their games that year were televised. The decisive factor in the team's demise was the 1997 decision of Coors to pull its sponsorship of the team. Having invested more than $8 million in the team for the past four years, Coors claimed it did not have the money to continue. The novelty of an all-women's team seemed to have faded.

Chronology

1993	Team is officially recognized by the National Association of Professional Baseball Teams on December 10
1994	Plays first game on May 8
1997	Major League Baseball becomes a team sponsor
1997	In August, Coors withdraws as team sponsor and team disbands

The Silver Bullets paved the way for women and girls who want to play baseball. The US Baseball Federation noted that there are twenty-one women's baseball associations and that roughly 300,000 women in all age ranges play baseball, from T-ball for young girls to women in senior leagues. Over one million women and girls now play softball, and as many as 50,000 women play in amateur baseball leagues in the US.

FURTHER INFORMATION

Books

Kindred, Dave. *The Colorado Silver Bullets for the Love of the Game: Women Who Go Toe-To-Toe with the Men*. Atlanta, GA: Longstreet Press, 1995.

Sherrow, Victoria. *Encyclopedia of Women and Sports*. Santa Barbara, CA: ABC-CLIO Inc., 1996.

Periodicals

Atkin, Ross. "Women's baseball makes a pitch for Major League recognition" *Christian Science Monitor* (August 4, 1997): 13.

"Lady Slugger." *Jet* (October 14, 1996): 50.

Other

Biography Resource Center, http://www.galenet.com/servlet/BioRC (January 20, 2003).

Colorado Silver Bullets, http://www.coloradosilverbullets.com (January 20, 2003).

Awards and Accomplishments

1995	Part of National Baseball Hall of Fame's Women in Baseball exhibit
1996	May 13, outfielder Tammy Holmes is first woman to hit two home runs in a season
1996	Selected as the national team by USA Baseball
1997	Bullets manager Phil Niekro inducted into Baseball Hall of Fame

Hope-Beckham Inc., http://www.hopebeckham.com/hbc_cr3.html (January 20, 2003).

Girl Tech, http://www.girltech.com/sports/sp_csb.html (January 20, 2003).

Nando Media, http://cgi.nando.net/newsroom/ap/bbo/1995/mlb/mlb/feat/archive/082197/mbl8957.html (January 20, 2003).

Sketch by Lorraine Savage

Nadia Comaneci

Nadia Comaneci
1961-

Romanian gymnast

Nadia Comaneci made her mark on the gymnastics scene and on the world with her breathtaking performances at the 1976 Olympic Games in Montreal, Canada. At the age of 14 Comaneci became the first gymnast to earn a perfect ten score in Olympic competition. In two Olympic appearances Comaneci earned five gold, three silver, and one bronze medal. After she retired from the sport she immigrated to the United States from Romania. She has remained active in gymnastics as a coach, analyst, magazine publisher, and exhibition athlete.

Nadia Elena Comaneci was born on November 12, 1961, in Onesti (formally known as Gheorghe Gheorghiu-Dej), Romania. She was named after a heroine Nadejda from a Russian film that her parents had seen before her birth. She was the oldest of two children born to Gheorghe and Stefania Comaneci. Her younger brother Adrian was born six years later. Her father worked as an auto mechanic, while her mother was an office employee.

Comaneci was an energetic child who loved to explore new things and to be active. "If ever a child aged its parents overnight, it was me," wrote Comaneci in her 1981 autobiography titled *Nadia*. "I was virtually uncontrollable." Comaneci found an outlet for all of her energy in gymnastics, which she began to learn in kindergarten. When she was six years old, Comaneci and a friend were spotted doing cartwheels by the prominent Romanian gymnastic coach, **Bela Karolyi**. He and his wife Marta were looking for young children to train for the Romanian National Junior Team.

Discovered by Famous Coach

The Karolyis invited Comaneci to train with them. She attended gymnastics lessons two to three hours a day. From the beginning Comaneci showed that she was fearless and willing to try new and difficult moves. She also exhibited a good work ethic and practiced her routines on her own initiative. In 1969 Comaneci entered her first major competition, the Romanian National Junior Championships. She placed thirteenth that year. However, she returned the following year to win the Junior Championships, which was the first of many victories for Comaneci.

Comaneci held her Junior Championship title for the next few years. By the time she was 12 years old she moved into a state-run gymnastics training school where she trained with Karolyi for eight hours a day, six days a week. Comaneci continued to improve her technique, adding increasingly difficult moves to her routines, and she continued to be successful at championships. In 1976 Comaneci won first place for the all around competition, as well as for vault, uneven bars, and balance beam at both the Romanian Championships and the European Championships held in Nor-

Chronology

1961	Born on November 12 in Onesti, Romania
1967	Begins training with Bela and Marta Karolyi
1969	Places 13th in first national competition
1970	Wins Romanian National Junior Championships
1975	Wins five gold medas at European Championships
1976	Scores first perfect ten at Olympic Games in Montreal, Canada
1976	Wins three gold, one silver, and one bronze medal at Olympic Games in Montreal, Canada
1977	Wins two gold medals at European Championships
1978	Wins three gold and one bronze medal at European Championships
1980	Wins two gold and two silver medals at Olympic Games in Moscow, U.S.S.R.
1981	Wins five gold medals at World University Games
1984	Retires from gymnastics
1989	Immigrates to the United States
1996	Marries American gymnast Bart Conner
2001	Becomes a United States citizen

Awards and Accomplishments

1969	Thirteenth place Romanian National Junior Championships
1970-71	First place Romanian National Junior Championship
1971	First place all-around, vault, uneven bars, balance beam, and floor exercise, Cup of the Romanian Gymnastic Federation
1972	First place team and all-around, Romanian National Junior Championship
1972	First place team, Cup of the Romanian Gymnastics Federation
1973	First place all-around, vault, uneven bars, balance beam, and floor exercise, International Championships of Romania
1973	First place team and all-around, Romanian Senior Championships
1974	First place team and all-around, Romania-Poland-USA Junior TriMeet
1975	First place all-around, vault, uneven bars, balance beam, and floor exercise, European Championships
1975	First place team, all-around, vault, uneven bars, balance beam, floor exercise, Romanian Championships
1976	First place all-around, uneven bars, balance beam, and floor exercise, second place team, Olympic Games
1976	Named Associated Press Female Athlete of the Year
1977	First place all-around and uneven bars, European Championships
1977	First place team and all-around, Balkan Championships
1977	First place all-around, International Championship of Romania
1977	First place all-around, Orleans International
1978	First place bars, second place vault and team, World Championships
1979	First place all-around, vault, and floor exercise, third place balance beam, European Championships
1979	First place all-around, International Championship of Romania
1979	First place team, World Championships
1979	First place vault and floor exercise, second place balance beam, World Cup
1979	First place team, all-around, vault, and uneven bars, second place floor exercise, Balkan Championships
1980	First place uneven bars, International Championship of Romania
1980	First place bars and floor exercise, second place team and all-around, Olympic Games
1981	First place team, all-around, vault, uneven bars, and balance beam, University Games
1984	Received Olympic Order Award
1991	Inducted into Sudafed International Women's Sports Hall of Fame
1993	Inducted into International Gymnastics Hall of Fame
1996	Named Honorary President of the Romanian Gymnastics Federation
1996	Honored in Atlanta's Opening Ceremonies as an Unforgettable Olympian
1998	Received Flo Hyman Award celebrating National Girls and Women in Sport Day
2001	Named Sportswoman of the Century, World Sports Awards

way. At the European Championships she upset the two-time defending champion, Lyudmila Turischeva, who was expecting another victory.

Comaneci took the world gymnastics scene by storm with her impeccable technique and her daring moves. However, her stoic style was often compared with the bubbly personality of Russian champion **Olga Korbut**, who won the hearts of the audience with her smiles and her tears. In contrast, Comaneci rarely smiled and was often perceived as cold or sad. Comaneci explained in her autobiography *Nadia* that "a gymnast must always be controlled, during training and, even more importantly, during a performance. The sport demands total concentration, and a gymnast gets used to the idea that any extraneous expression or thought is a waste of energy."

Earned a Perfect Ten at the Olympics

Despite her demeanor Comaneci managed to win over both the judges and the audience at the 1976 Olympic Games in Montreal, Canada. She also made history at these games by becoming the first gymnast to score a perfect ten on an apparatus. The record breaking moment came with Comaneci's performance on the uneven bars. However, the judging equipment was not equipped to display the four digits of a 10.00 score, so the scoreboard simply showed 1.00. The crowd soon understood the meaning of the score when the announcer declared, "Ladies and gentleman, for the first time in Olympic history, Nadia Comaneci has received the score of a perfect ten," reported Septima Green in *Top 10 Women Gymnasts*.

Comaneci earned a total of seven perfect ten scores at those Olympic Games. She won three gold medals for the all-around competition, uneven bars, and balance beam. She also won a silver medal for the team competi-

tion and a bronze medal for the floor exercise. Comaneci became the first Romanian to win the all-around title and she was also the youngest all-around champion at 14 years old. "The technical purity of her performance is her most brilliant characteristic. Physically she has strength, speed, and flexibility. Mentally, she has intelligence, phenomenal powers of concentration—and courage," Bela Karolyi told Peter Bonventre of *Newsweek*.

Comaneci also tried to endear the crowd by smiling and waving more often than she had in other competitions, but this did not change the media's impression of her as an unhappy child. "Here was an example of a dour, cheerless child driven to icy perfection by a totalitarian state," wrote Robert Lindsey of the *New York Times*. After the 1976 Olympics rumors also circulated claiming that Comaneci was no longer a top gymnast because she had gained a lot of weight and had tried to commit suicide. Comaneci denied those rumors and continued to compete internationally.

Returned to the Olympics for More Gold

Comaneci continued to win medals at the European Championships in 1977 and 1979 and the World Championships in 1978. In 1979 she became the only woman to win three European all-around titles. Comaneci returned to the Olympics in 1980 in Moscow, U.S.S.R. The Americans boycotted the event as a political statement against the Soviet invasion of Afghanistan. However, Comaneci's biggest competition came from the Soviets. Unfortunately Comaneci's performance at the 1980 Olympics was not perfect. In fact, she fell off of the uneven bars during the team competition. "More than my dignity had been bruised in that fall, and as I gingerly made my way back to the bench, I was half aware of the sympathetic stares from some of my fellow competitors. At first I felt angry, and then strangely numb, until I sat down when I was furious with myself," Comaneci wrote in her autobiography *Nadia*.

To make matters worse, Comaneci was also not able to defend her all around champion title. Three women, including Comaneci, were in the running for the title when they all went to do their final apparatus. Comaneci gave a spectacular performance on the balance beam, but the judges only awarded her a score of 9.85. This meant that she placed second in the all around, behind Soviet gymnast Yelena Davydova. Coach Karolyi was furious and disputed the score, charging that the host team was influencing the results so that their gymnast became champion. The score remained unchanged and Comaneci had to settle for a silver all-around medal. Despite these difficulties, Comaneci also won gold medals for balance beam and floor exercise, and a team silver medal.

In 1981 Comaneci completed in the World University Games in Bucharest, Romania, where she won first place for the team competition, all around competition, vault, uneven bars, and balance beam. This was her last major competition and she officially retired from gymnastics in 1984. "I regret that from now on I will never know the excitement of competition," Nadia was quoted in the *New York Times*.

Escaped from Communism

The 1980s were a difficult time for Comaneci. She was living in a totalitarian country that was not only politically repressive, but also struggling economically. Coach Karolyi and his wife defected to the United States in 1981. The Romanian government feared that she might do the same so her international travels were restricted and tightly guarded. In many other ways, however, Comaneci was treated as a celebrity. She and her family lived in a large home, she owned a car, and she had many privileges that her fellow countrymen did not enjoy. After retirement she finished college at the University of Physical Education and she worked as a state coach.

Despite her celebrity status Comaneci was unhappy because of the difficult living conditions in her country and because of her lack of personal freedom. In 1989 she decided to defect to the United States with the help of her manager Konstantin Panit, a Romanian expatriate who worked as a roofer in Florida. When she arrived in the United States Comaneci told Sally Jenkins of the *Washington Post,* "I am very happy because I am here in America. I wanted for a long time to come here, but I didn't have anyone to help me."

However, the American media did not exactly welcome Comaneci. Stories circulated that she and Panit were a couple, even though Panit had a wife and children in Florida. Comaneci maintained that she was held hostage by Panit who was trying to exploit Comaneci's fame for his own financial gain. He threatened to send her back to Romania if she did not cooperate. Eventually her gymnast friends and former coach Karolyi intervened on her behalf. Panit fled with Comaneci's money, but she finally had her freedom.

Comaneci spent the following year in Montreal with the family of Alexandru Stefu, a fellow Romanian. She then moved to Norman, Oklahoma to work with coach Paul Ziert. She also developed a strong friendship with American gymnast **Bart Conner**. The two gymnasts performed in exhibitions together an eventually began dating. They married in Romania in 1996. They both work as coaches at the Bart Conner Gymnastics Academy in Norman and they also have several other business ventures together. In 2001 Comaneci became a United States citizen.

For over 40 years Comaneci has managed to captivate the world both as an athlete and in her personal life. She is one of the most memorable Olympic athletes who has dedicated her career to promoting the sport of gymnastics. According to Frank Litsky of the *New York Times,* Comaneci gives the following advice to the young gymnasts that she trains: "If you go for a little gold every day instead of saving that energy for a big championship, that's the best way."

CONTACT INFORMATION

Address: 3206 Bart Conner Dr., Norman, OK 73072-2406. Phone: (405) 447-7500.

SELECTED WRITINGS BY COMANECI:

Nadia, London: Proteus, 1981.

FURTHER INFORMATION

Books

Cohen, Joel. *Superstars of Women's Gymnastics.* New York: Chelsea House Publishers, 1997.

The Complete Marquis Who's Who. Marquis Who's Who, 2001.

Encyclopedia of World Biography. Farmington Hills, MI: Gale Research, 1998.

Great Women in Sports. Visible Ink Press, 1996.

Green, Septima. *Top 10 Women Gymnasts.* Berkeley Heights, NJ: Enslow Publishers, Inc., 1999.

Periodicals

Amdur, Neil. "Miss Comaneci Loses to Russian as Result is Marred by Dispute." *The New York Times* (July 25, 1980): A15.

Atkin, Ross. "Nadia Comaneci Finds Balance Off the Beam." *The Christian Science Monitor* (June 17, 1996): 14.

Bonventre, Peter. "Princess of the Games." *Newsweek* (August 2, 1976): 68.

Brady, Erik. "Tiny Comaneci Was Colossus in '76. At Age 14, Gymnast Spun Perfection to Earn First 10." *USA Today* (July 18, 1996): 10C.

Gray, Kevin. "Head Over Heels: For Gold Medal Gymnasts Nadia Comaneci and Bart Conner, Love Is Something to Flip For." *People Weekly* (March 17, 1995): 105.

"Gymnast Nadia Comaneci Leaps for Freedom and Lands in the Arms of a Married Father of Four." *People Weekly* (December 18, 1989): 116.

Hallman, Charley. "Perfect in the Past, Comaneci Sees a Brighter Future." *Knight Ridder/Tribune News Service* (April 11, 1996).

Heller, Dick. "Comaneci Made Perfection Routine in 1976 Olympics." *The Washington Times* (July 29, 2002): C13.

"Here Flips the Bride." *Sports Illustrated* (May 6, 1996): 22-23.

Jenkins, Sally. "Comaneci Arrives in New York; Ex-Gymnastics Star Gets Refugee Status." *The Washington Post* (December 2, 1989): D1.

Leibowitz, Elissa. "Comaneci Vaults Back into the Spotlight; Olympic Gymnast Receives Women's Sports Foundation Award." *The Washington Post* (February 6, 1998): C02.

Lindsey, Robert. "Nadia Comaneci Still Glows as Images of 1976 Recede." *The New York Times* (July 29, 1984).

Litsky, Frank. "Comaneci's Landing in the West Remains Perfect." *The New York Times* (August 12, 2001).

Lorge, Barry. "Comaneci Finally Wins Two Golds as Judging Controversies Continue." *The Washington Post* (July 26, 1980): F1.

"Nadia Comaneci, Now Married to US Gymnast Bart Conner; Her Two Gold Medals in '80 'Better than any American Did.'" *The Plain Dealer* (September 11, 2000): 9C.

"Nadia Comaneci's Road to Freedom." *USA Today* (December 5, 1989): 9C.

"Nadia Comaneci Takes Gold." *The New York Times* (July 22, 1981): B5.

"Nadia Comaneci Timeline." *The Times-Picayune* (November 28, 1999): C14.

"New Nadia." *U.S. News and World Report* (December 11, 1989): 18.

"Perfection Personified." *Time* (August 5, 1996): 18.

Peter, Josh. "The First to Perfection; Nadia Comaneci's Work Ethic and Technical Genius Made Her the Best." *The Times-Picayune* (November 28, 1999): C14.

Raboin, Sharon. "Comaneci Set the Standard." *USA Today* (July 30, 1999): 9C.

Schmalz, Jeffrey. "Scorn Gives Comaneci a Lesson in Image." *The New York Times* (December 13, 1989): A22.

Schneider, Karen S. "After Escaping Her Romanian Svengali, Nadia Comaneci Tries to Get Her Live Back on the Beam." *People Weekly* (November 26, 1990): 52.

Stoeltje, Melissa Fletcher. "Let's Do Lunch With Bart Conner and Nadia Comaneci." *The Houston Chronicle* (May 20, 1993): 3.

Sullivan, Kevin. "Comaneci Finds Her Balance: Defection in 1989 Leads to New Life." *The Washington Post* (October 12, 1995): D06.

"Tearful Comaneci Farewell." *The New York Times* (May 7, 1984): C10.

Weir, Tom. "Changed Comaneci Eager for Visit Home." *USA Today* (October 18, 1994): 3C.

White, Carolyn. "Comaneci Spreads Gymnastics Word." *USA Today* (February 5, 1998): 6C.

White, Carolyn. "Karolyi Doesn't Doubt Comaneci Charge." *USA Today* (October 17, 1990): 2C.

Other

Gymn Forum. http://www.gymn-forum.com/bios/comaneci.html (December 18, 2002).

International Gymnast Magazine. http://www.intl gymnast.com/magazine.html (December 31, 2002).

Nadia Comaneci Bio. http://www.nadiacomaneci.com/nadia_comaneci_bio.htm (December 31, 2002).

Sketch by Janet P. Stamatel

Bart Conner
1958-

American gymnast

Bart Conner

Bart Conner was the first U.S. male gymnast to receive a gold medal in international competition. He is credited with helping to bring the American men's gymnastics team to a first place finish at the 1984 Olympics and is remembered as the only American male gymnast to win a gold medal at every level of competition.

A Champion is Nurtured

Bart Conner was born on March 28, 1958, in Chicago, the son of Harold and Jackie Conner. Conner's father, an engineer, was the director of the School of Construction Science. Conner was an athletic youngster growing up in Morton Grove, Illinois; he played pee wee football and enjoyed speed skating. His participation in an elementary school gymnastics program at age ten led him to seek further training at the local Young Men's Christian Association (YMCA). He entered regional competition at age eleven, winning medals in pommel horse and tumbling. In 1972 Conner finished in first-place in the all-around competition at the Amateur Athletic Union (AAU) Junior Olympics Junior Nationals.

As a member of the gymnastic team at Niles West High School in Skokie, Illinois, Conner took first place trophies both in all-around competition and on parallel bars, at the Illinois State Championships in 1974. As the U.S. Gymnastics Federation (USGF) elite junior division all-around champion, and AAU junior national champion that year, Conner received recognition as the outstanding high school gymnast in Illinois. In 1975 he tied for first place at the USA Men's (USGF) all-around championship.

Olympic Years

In 1976, after winning the first McDonald's American Cup, Conner was named to the U.S. team for the Montreal Olympics. He finished at forty-sixth place in the all-around preliminaries, but distinguished himself as the youngest member of the team.

At the University of Oklahoma in Norman from 1976-79, Conner trained under Coach Paul Ziert. Oklahoma took the Big Eight and National College Athletic Association (NCAA) gymnastics championships in 1978, and Conner won the NCAA all-around title that year. Also in 1978 he won all-American honors and won a second American Cup. Soon his reputation as the top U.S. male gymnast was rivaled only by his contemporary, Kurt Thomas.

At the World Championships in 1979 Conner placed first on parallel bars, to become the first American man to take the gold in international gymnastics competition. He won the USA Men's all-around championship with a score of 114.25 that year and won gold medals on pommel horse and parallel bars at the World Cup.

Conner was the top qualifier for the 1980 U.S. Olympic team, but an American boycott of the Moscow venue that year kept the team from competition. The boycott provided Conner with ample time to recuperate from a torn right bicep, and he returned to Norman to complete work on an undergraduate degree in journalism and public relations.

After winning American Cup Championships in 1981 and again in 1982, Conner pushed the envelope of his athletic prime when late in 1983, on December 3, a slip

Chronology	
1958	Born March 28 in Chicago, Illinois
1976	Wins a place on U.S. Olympic 7th Team, places 46th in all-around preliminaries
1980	Wins a place on Olympic Team that boycotts games in Moscow
1984	Wins a place on Olympic Team
1985	Publishes memoir
1992	Establishes the Bart Conner Gymnastics Academy
1996	Marries Nadia Comaneci in Bucharest, Romania on April 26-27

during a performance in Japan caused another torn bicep. With only six months remaining before the Olympic trials, he held out hope of making the 1984 team.

Still ailing in May, at the USGF championships in Evanston, Illinois, Conner withdrew from the competition on the second day, despite a strong second place showing in the compulsories. The pullout left him deficient in the qualification points necessary to place on the Olympic team. He petitioned successfully to the Olympic Committee to make an exception because of the circumstance and after a sixth place finish at the subsequent Olympic trials earned a spot on the 1984 team.

At the Olympics in Atlanta, Conner won a gold medal on parallel bars, scoring two perfect tens. The U.S. team won a gold medal in the all-around competition with a score of 591.40, besting China's score of 590.80. Conner expressed his pleasure to the *Omaha World-Herald* and praised his teammates succinctly, "Nothing matches a team victory ... because you have six times as much emotion."

When the hoopla subsided, Conner published a book, *Winning the Gold,* in 1985. He devoted much of his time to bringing professional gymnastics to the level of an art-sport—Just as professional ice skaters move from competition to exhibition and onward, to full-blown paid performances, Conner envisioned a similar career path for professional gymnasts. Endorsements provided him with financial subsidy, and he appeared on television and in movies.

Mr. Nadia Comaneci

Five years after winning the gold, the grit and determination of Olympic competition segued into an international romance for Bart Conner when in 1989 he became personally entwined in the dramatic personal life of gold-medal Romanian gymnast **Nadia Comaneci**. It was some years earlier in 1976 when the two first met at Madison Square Garden, during a pre-Olympic gymnastics exhibition. In the rush of reporters after the program, Comaneci—then an anonymous fourteen-year-old—posed with Conner who kissed her cheek for a promotional photo.

More than ten years passed, and in 1989 Comaneci escaped under cover of night from her homeland, to

Awards and Accomplishments	
1972	Amateur Athletic Union Jr. Olympic Jr. Nationals all-around champion
1974	U.S. Gymnastics Federation elite junior division all-around champion; Amateur Athletic Union junior national champion; State of Illinois high school all-around and parallel bars champion; named outstanding high school gymnast for the State of Illinois
1975	USA Men's all-around co-champion; Amateur Athletic Union national elite all-around champion; national high school all-around champion
1976	American Cup all-around champion; national high school all-around champion
1978	National College Athletic Association all-around champion; USA parallel bars champion
1979	USA Men's all-around champion; wins two gold medals at World Cup: for pommel horse and parallel bars; National College Athletic Association floor exercise champion; US Olympic Festival champion for vault, parallel bars, and high beam; USA Championship: all-around, pommel horse, rings, and parallel bars; USA World Trials all-around champion; World Championship 3rd Team, parallel bars champion; World Cup champion for pommel horse
1981-82	American Cup champion
1983	USA Champion for pommel horse
1984	Wins two Olympic gold medals: for parallel bars and team competition
1991	Inducted into the U.S. Olympic Hall of Fame
1996	Inducted into the USA Gymnastics Hall of Fame
1997	Inducted into the Oklahoma Sports Hall of Fame; inducted into the International Gymnastics Hall of Fame

Conner is the only American to win gold medals at every level of competition.

seek asylum in the United States. Soon, rumors surfaced that she was being held in Florida against her will and Conner contacted her. He offered moral support through her difficult time in a strange country, and in 1991 she joined him at his home in Norman. The friendship flourished, and the following year Conner and Comaneci established a gymnastics academy. Conner proposed marriage to her in 1994; they were married in 1996.

The Conner-Comaneci nuptials were among the most lavish of the decade. Held in Bucharest, the ceremonies spanned two days, beginning on April 26 with a civil ceremony at the Parliamentary Palace. A religious ritual on the following day was held at the historic Casin Monastery. A banquet, hosted by the future president of Romania was attended by dignitaries of the sports world and government officials alike. So elaborate were the national preparations in Romania to honor Comaneci at her wedding, that Conner was left to remark, "Next to her ... I'm going to look like the little guy on top of the wedding cake ... After April 27, I'll be known as Mr. Nadia Comaneci."

Working against painful osteoarthritis in his left elbow, right knee, and lower back, Conner has been on therapy since his 1983 biceps injury. At that time he underwent surgery to re-attach the biceps, and in 1985 he underwent knee reconstruction. Overall he endured a series of nine operations.

español

In the early 2000s, he continues to practice gymnastics in 45-minute sessions daily. Managed by Ziert, Conner maintains a limited agenda on the exhibition circuit where he is known for his artistic pairs performances with Comaneci. Slowed only minimally by the pain of osteoarthritis, that debilitating condition nonetheless creates increasing obstacles as he approaches middle age. His involvement with an osteoarthritis public awareness campaign called Boost Education of Arthritis Treatments (B.E.A.T.) provides a positive outlet for Conner, allowing him to bring awareness of the disease as well as its various remedies into the public domain.

While serving as a color commentator for several news networks, including ESPN, and ABC, Conner additionally operates his own company, Perfect 10 Productions, in partnership with a group of fellow Olympians. He and Comaneci host a fitness program on cable television. He is active as an inspirational speaker and sits on the Executive Board of Special Olympics International. He is a national vice-president of the Muscular Dystrophy Association.

Conner stands 5-feet-5-inches tall and weighs 125 pounds. As a tribute to his historic contributions to men's gymnastics in the United States, he was enshrined in 1991 into the U.S. Olympic Hall Fame. He was inducted to the USA Gymnastics Hall of Fame in 1996, and into the International Gymnastics Hall of Fame in 1997.

CONTACT INFORMATION

Address: c/o IMG Speakers New York, 825 7th Avenue, New York, NY 10019. Fax: (212) 246-1596. Phone: (212) 774-6735. Address: c/o Bart Conner Gymnastics Academy, 3206 Bart Conner Dr., P.O. Box 720217, Norman, Oklahoma 73070-4166. Fax: (405) 447-7600. Phone: (405) 447-7500. Email: speakers@imgworld.com. Online: www.bartconnergymnastics.com/.

SELECTED WRITINGS BY CONNER:

(With Paul Ziert) *Winning the Gold.* New York: Warner Books, 1985.

FURTHER INFORMATION

Books

Eisenhart, Henry A. *Great Athletes* Salem Press/Magill Books, 2001: 477.
Markoe, Arnold, ed., and Kenneth T. Jackson. *Scribner Encyclopedia of American Lives.* New York: Charles Scribner's Sons, 2002.

Periodicals

Atlanta Journal/Atlanta Constitution (April 12, 1996).
New York Times Biographical Service (January, 1984): 776.
Omaha World-Herald (August 1, 1984): 1.
People (August 7, 2000): 131.
Star Tribune (Minneapolis) (April 10, 1996): 3C.

Sketch by G. Cooksey

Maureen Connolly
1934-1969

American tennis player

Maureen "Little Mo" Connolly's career ended prematurely with a freakish accident, and cancer cut short her life. But Connolly, who won all nine of her Grand Slam women's tennis events, still played long enough to make an indelible mark on the game. "Whenever a great player comes long you have to ask, 'Could she have beaten Maureen,'" wrote Lance Tingay, tennis correspondent for the *Daily Telegraph* of London. "In every case the answer is, I think not."

Connolly won her major titles as a teenager. She was the first woman to sweep all four major Grand Slam events in one year, 1953. She took the Wimbledon and U.S. Open three straight years apiece in the early 1950s. She became the youngest U.S. Open champion at 16 years, 11 months, until Tracy Austin broke the record in 1979. She arrived East from San Diego in 1949 and, according to the Hall of Fame, "would soon have the world under her right thumb while technically a junior, not yet 19, an obstreperous intruder overthrowing the established order of older women." A bizarre accident, however, ended Connolly's career. In 1954, a truck struck the back of her leg while she was riding horseback in San Diego, shortly after winning Wimbledon. She died of cancer in 1969, at age 34.

Parents Couldn't Afford Riding

Tennis was actually a backup recreational activity for Connolly, whose divorced mother could not afford horseback riding. Connolly first wielded a racket at age ten and after her first coach, Wilbur Folsom, switched her to right-handed play, she went under the tutelage of Eleanor "Teach" Tennant, who had influenced the Hall of Fame careers of **Helen Wills** (later Helen Wills Moody, eight-time Wimbledon champion) and Alice Marble. Tennant would not let Connolly talk with other women's tennis players. "Maureen approached tennis with an intense hatred for her opponents, a trait that Tennant encouraged," the *Gale Group*'s Women's History Month Web site wrote. "Maureen believed that she could not win if she

Maureen Connolly

did not despise her opponent. Winning became a single-minded pursuit for the talented youngster."

After sweeping tournaments in Southern California, Connolly came to New York and won the U.S. junior titles in 1949 and 1950. She reached the second round of the mainstream U.S. Open tournaments both years.

A sportswriter nicknamed her "Little Mo" for her powerful, accurate strokes, in reference to "Big Mo," the U.S. battleship Missouri. She was not overly strong and disdained the volley, but compensated with a methodical baseline game. "Sportswriters raved about her engaging blend of teenage charm and killer instinct on the court," the Women's History Month web site reported. "Fueled by her intense passion to win, her drive and energy on the court swept her past all of the best women players of her day. Later in life she remarked about the fear that drove her and the talent that she displayed."

Fallout with Coach

During her first major championship run, the 1951 U.S. Open, Tennant had told Connolly that Doris Hart, the tennis star's friend and semifinal opponent, had insulted her. Connolly defeated Hart and then overtook Shirley Fry in a tough, three-set match. After the tournament, Connolly discovered Tennant's misrepresentation and she and Hart resumed their friendship. Connolly split with Tennant for good at Wimbledon when Connolly played despite a shoulder injury when Tennant wanted her to default. After a match, Connolly called a press conference, a rarity for a player in those days, and announced the split.

Connolly once admitted that competitive tennis at such a young age wore on her. "Tennis can be a grind and there is always the danger of going stale, if you think about it too much," she said. "You can get embittered if you train too hard and have nothing else on your mind. You have to be able to relax between matches and between tournaments."

Australian Davis Cup captain Harry Hopman became Connolly's coach and his wife, Nell, her chaperon. With the Hopmans' a stabilizing influence, Connolly's game, already potent, moved up a level in 1953. She joined **Don**

Budge as the only player, man or woman, to capture the Australian Open, French Open, Wimbledon, and U.S. Open the same year. She dropped only one set in the Australian and French tournaments combined, then beat Hart in tough Wimbledon and U.S. Open finals—the 8-6, 7-5 Wimbledon final at the All-England Club was especially memorable.

Career Ends Tragically

Connolly added the French Open and Wimbledon titles to her resume in 1954-by then she had also won seven straight matches in the Wightman Cup international team competition against Britain. But her career then ended "with heartbreaking suddenness" as the International Tennis Hall of Fame described on its Web site. On July 20, 1954—back home in San Diego after capturing Wimbledon—Connolly was riding her thoroughbred colt, Colonel Merryboy, when a cement truck collided with her and the horse. She was thrown from the animal and suffered a broken bone and severed calf muscles in her right leg. "I knew immediately I'd never play again," she said.

She married Norman Brinker of Dallas, a restaurateur and former member of the U.S. equestrian team, and they had two children, Cindy and Brenda. Despite Connolly's inability to play in tournaments, she could still teach children. She worked as a tennis instructor and, with friend Nancy Jeffett, co-founded the Maureen Connolly Brinker

Awards and Accomplishments

1950-51	Won United States junior championships
1951-53	Associated Press Female Athlete of the Year
1951-53	Won three consecutive U.S. Open singles championships
1951-54	Captured all seven singles matches as U.S. defeated Britain in four straight Wightman Cup tournaments
1952-54	Won three straight Wimbledon singles championships
1953	Completed pure Grand Slam, winning all four major tournaments— Australian Open, French Open, Wimbledon and U.S. Open
1968	Inducted into Tennis Hall of Fame

Tennis Foundation in 1968. She died six months later, on the eve of the Wimbledon tournament. She had battled stomach cancer since 1966. The Brinker foundation today sponsors a variety of youth activities, including tournaments such as the Maureen Connolly Challenge trophy and "Little Mo" events for boys and girls.

The Connolly Legacy

Spellbound Pictures of Brooklyn, New York, is working on a documentary film celebrating the 50th anniversary of Connolly's Grand Slam win. In 1978, a feature film, "Little Mo," starring Anne Baxter and Mark Harmon, detailed Connolly's tennis successes and personal tragedies.

"Little Mo was a champion at tennis," nine-time Wimbledon champion **Martina Navratilova** wrote in *Little Mo's Legacy: A Mother's Lessons, a Daughter's Story,* written by Connolly's daughter, Cindy Brinker Simmons. "Had her accident not cut short her remarkable career, we all would have been chasing her records. More importantly, she was a champion at life by affecting others in a positive way."

SELECTED WRITINGS BY CONNOLLY:

Power Tennis. New York: Barnes, 1954.

FURTHER INFORMATION

Books

Simmons, Cindy Brinker and Robert Darden. *Little Mo's Legacy: A Mother's Lessons, a Daughter's Story.* Irving, TX: Tapestry, 2001.

Periodicals

"Maureen Connolly, Tennis Star, Dies." *New York Times,* (January 7, 2003).

Other

Films and TV, http://www.filmsandtv.com, (January 9, 2003).

Handbook of Texas Online, Maureen Catherine Connolly Brinker profile, http://www.tsha.utexas.edu/handbook/online/articles/view/BB/fbr54.html, (December 4, 2002).

Hickok Sports, http://www.hickoksorts.com/biograph/connollym.shtml, (January 8, 2003).

"Maureen Connolly, Class of 1968." International Tennis Hall of Fame, http://www.tennisfame.org/enshrinees/maureen_connolly.html, (January 7, 2003).

Maureen Connolly Brinker Tennis Foundation Inc., http://www.mcbtennis.org, (January 9, 2003).

"Women's History Month: Maureen Connolly." Gale Group, http://www.gale.com, (January 9, 2003).

Sketch by Paul Burton

Jimmy Connors
1952-

American tennis player

Jimmy Connors, has been one of the most recognizable American tennis players for four decades. The left-handed player was known for his two-handed backhand and powerful return-of-serve which helped him win eight Grand Slam championships. In particular, Connors won the U.S. Open championship five times and he is the only player to win this tournament on three different surfaces—grass, clay, and hard court. Connors is the all-time male leader in tournament wins with 109. He also held the number one ranking in men's tennis for a record 160 weeks from 1974 until 1977. Aside from these accomplishments, Connors was known for his emotional outbursts on the court. Connors claimed that his on-court antics added flavor and entertainment to the sport, but his critics considered his actions classless. Whether he was loved or hated by the fans or the media, Connors's passion for the sport brought fans, press, and sponsors to the game of tennis. Connors played professional tennis past his 40th birthday and then he started the Champions Tour for male players over thirty-five years old.

Molded by His Mother To Become a Champion

James Scott Connors, Jr., known to the world simply as Jimmy Connors, was born on September 2, 1952 in East St. Louis, Illinois. His father, "Big Jim" Connors, worked as a toll bridge attendant and he was the son of the mayor of East St. Louis. His mother, Gloria Thompson Connors, was a tennis teacher who learned the sport from her own mother, Bertha Thompson. Gloria was determined to teach her older son, Johnny, and Jimmy to

Chronology

1952	Born September 2 in East St. Louis, Illinois
1960	Plays in first U.S. Championship in the 11-and-under division
1970	Reaches U.S. Open quarterfinals with Pancho Gonzalez
1971	Begins college at the University of California at Los Angeles
1972	Drops out of college to play professional tennis full time
1973	Finishes year ranked number one (tied with Stan Smith)
1974	Wins 99 of 103 matches and 14 out of 20 tournaments
1974	Wins Australian Open, Wimbledon, and U.S. Open on grass court
1976	Wins U.S. Open singles title on clay court
1976	Ranked number one tennis player in U.S. and world
1978	Wins U.S. Open singles title on hard court
1978	Ranked number one tennis player in world
1978	First player to earn over two million dollars in career earnings
1978	Marries former Playboy Playmate-of-the-Year Patti McGuire
1980	Son Brett David is born
1982	Wins U.S. Open singles title on hard court
1983	Wins U.S. Open singles title on hard court
1985	Daughter Aubree Leigh is born
1991	Reaches U.S. Open semifinals at age 39
1992	Coauthors fitness book
1993	Begins Championship Tour for male tennis players over 35
1995	Reaches quarterfinals of ATP tournament in Halle, Germany
2001	Ranked 15 in Championship Tour

Jimmy Connors

play tennis from an early age. When she was pregnant with Jimmy, she even cleared the land behind their house in Belleville, Illinois to build a tennis court.

Gloria Connors expected her older son, Johnny, to become a tennis champion. However, Johnny did not have the same passion for the sport as his younger brother, Jimmy. Johnny, who later became a tennis teaching professional in Atlanta, was raised primarily by his father, while his mother and grandmother groomed Jimmy to become a champion. These two women not only taught Connors how to play the game, but they also molded him into a feisty, passionate player. "We taught him to be a tiger," Gloria Connors told Frank Deford of *Sports Illustrated* in 1978. "'Get those tiger juices flowing!' I would call out, and I told him to try and knock the ball down my throat, and he learned to do this because he found out that if I had the chance, I would knock it down his."

Throughout his career, Gloria Thompson Connors was his primary coach. However, when the family moved to California to support Jimmy's budding tennis career, Connors also trained occasionally with **Pancho Gonzalez** and Pancho Segura. Connors played in his first U.S. Championship in the eleven-and-under division when he was eight years old. By the time he was eighteen he was ready to play against the top professionals. In 1970 he reached the quarterfinals in doubles of the U.S. Open with Gonzalez. As a freshman in college at the University of California at Los Angeles, Connors won the National Intercollegiate singles title. He dropped out of college in 1972 to play tennis full-time.

In the same year he won his first professional title at Jacksonville, Florida. He finished the season ranked number eighty-three.

Became a Grand Slam Champion

Connors continued to win titles at a record pace. In only a year he reached the number one ranking in the United States, tying Stan Smith. In 1973 he also won the Wimbledon doubles title with Ilie Nastase. By 1974, only his second year as a professional, Connors was winning Grand Slam singles events. He began the year by winning the Australian Open, and he then went on to win Wimbledon and the U.S. Open, which was then a grass court at Forest Hills.

Connors had a shot at winning the Grand Slam in 1974 by capturing all four major titles. He only missed the French Open title because he was not allowed to play in that tournament. In 1972 the Association of Tennis Professionals (ATP) became the new union for most male professionals. Connors, however, chose to join the World Team Tennis (WTT) organization instead of the ATP. Because the ATP and the organizers of the French Open did not approve of the WTT, they did not allow WTT players to compete in the tournament that year. Connors and his manager, Bill Riordan, responded by filing a $10 million anti-trust lawsuit against the ATP and its president, **Arthur Ashe**, but the lawsuit was eventually dropped.

Awards and Accomplishments

1971	National Intercollegiate singles title
1971	Named All American
1973	Wimbledon doubles champion with Ilie Nastase
1973	U.S. Pro Championship singles champion
1973-75, 1978-79, 1983-84	U.S. Indoor Open singles champion
1974	Australian Open singles champion
1974	U.S. Indoor Open doubles champion with Frew McMillan
1974	U.S. Clay Court doubles champion with Ilie Nastase
1974	Named Player of the Year
1974, 1976, 1978-79	U.S. Clay Court singles champion
1974, 1976, 1978, 1982-83	U.S. Open singles champion
1974, 1982	Wimbledon singles champion
1975	U.S. Open doubles champion with Ilie Nastase
1975	U.S. Indoor Open doubles champion with Ilie Nastase
1976	Ranked number one tennis player in U.S. and world
1976	Cologne Cup
1976, 1978-80	Pro Indoor singles champion
1976, 1981	Davis Cup Team
1976, 1985	World Cup Team
1977	World Championship Tennis singles
1978	Ranked number one tennis player in world
1991	Reached U.S. Open semifinals at age 39
1991	Included in 25 Most Intriguing People by *People* magazine
1998	Inducted into International Tennis Hall of Fame
2001	Inducted into St. Louis Walk of Fame

"Bad Boy" of American Tennis

Connors gained public attention not only from his powerful two-handed backhand and his excellent return-of-serve, but also for his emotional outbursts and antics on the court. "He has been called tennis champion, punk, maverick, and street fighter rolled into one," wrote Daniel B. Wood of the *Christian Science Monitor* in April of 1985. "When he's up, he struts like a rooster and crows like a bullfinch. When he's down, he grunts and curses like a guttersnipe, wielding his racket switchblade-style toward the crowd."

Connors and American tennis rival **John McEnroe** were easily labeled the "bad boys" of American tennis for their frequent outbursts, arguments with umpires, and playing to the crowds. "They are great characters, American toughs from the 'if-you-don't-like-the-call-kick-dirt-on-the-umpire' school," wrote Sally Jenkins of *Sports Illustrated* in June of 1992. "But for years McEnroe and Connors have unapologetically believed that brazenness could substitute for class." Despite the criticism from the media and sometimes from the fans, both Connors and McEnroe believed that they added personality to the sport and they often claimed that many of the world's best tennis players were simply boring. "I wasn't afraid to wear myself inside out and let you see me," Connors told Bud Geracie of Knight Ridder/Tribune News Service in January of 1994. "See where my heart lies. See where my guts are. See what I'm thinking. I was happy for you to see that. The guys today aren't giving you anything to see."

Connors' passion for tennis did not always translate into tournament wins. After his spectacular performance in the Grand Slam events of 1974, Connors became the number one player in the world. He held this position from 1975 until 1978, which is still the record for the longest continuous streak in men's tennis. However, Connors began to struggle in his matches against other top players, particularly at Grand Slam events. He had a difficult year in 1975, when he ended his relationship with fiancée **Chris Evert** and then lost the Wimbledon finals to Arthur Ashe, the man he was suing for not allowing him to compete at the 1974 French Open. Connors did manage to win the doubles title at the U.S. Open that year, although he lost the singles title in the final. Connors regained the U.S. Open singles title in 1976, when it was a clay court at Forest Hills. He won again in 1978 when the tournament was moved to the hard courts of Flushing Meadows. He is the only tennis player to win the U.S. Open title on three different surfaces.

In the late 1970s Connors became a family man. In 1978 he met Patti McGuire, the 1977 Playboy Playmate-of-the-Year, and the couple was married just three months later. In 1980 they had their first child, Brett David. At first Connors found it difficult to balance his family life with his professional career, and his marriage almost ended in divorce in 1983. However, the couple was able to reconcile and they even had another child, Aubree Leigh, in 1985.

Age-Defying Comebacks

After suffering a drought at the Grand Slams for a few years after he was married, Connors rededicated himself to tennis in the early 1980s. In 1982 he won Grand Slam singles titles at Wimbledon and on the hard courts of the US. Open. He repeated his U.S. Open victory again in 1983, which was his 100th tournament title. In both U.S. Open finals Connors defeated Ivan Lendle. "It wasn't quite as beautiful as some other finals I have played," Connors told Ross Atkin of the *Christian Science Monitor* in September of 1983. "And maybe wasn't the best match to look at, but it got the job done."

Connors continued to play tennis for the next decade, even though most of his peers were retiring. Although it was difficult for Connors to beat the younger generations of tennis greats, he still enjoyed the game. At age thirty-nine he began another tennis comeback after recovering from wrist surgery. In 1991 he returned to the French Open, the only Grand Slam title he had not won. In a thrilling third-round match Connors almost beat American teenage sensation **Michael Chang**. After three and a half hours of play Connors was physically unable

Jimmy Connors

to continue playing and he had to forfeit the match in the fifth set.

Connors' most remarkable performance came during the 1991 U.S. Open, his favorite competition. Connors was ranked 174th in the world and received a wildcard entry for the tournament. He defeated Patrick McEnroe, Aaron Krickstein, and Paul Haarhuis. The four and a half hour match against Krickstein fell on Connors' 39th birthday. Before Haarhuis' match against Connors, Tom Callahan of *U.S. News and World Report* quoted Haarhuis as saying, "My strategy, I guess, is to tire Connors out. He's a great player, and nobody will ever do what he's done. But, after all, he is 39 years old." The strategy was unsuccessful and Connors beat the 25-year-old Haarhuis in the quarterfinals. However, Connors was finally stopped in the semifinals by fellow American **Jim Courier**. Connors referred to his 1991 comeback as "the summer of all summers." "You dream of putting together a streak like that," Connors told *People* in December of 1991.

Organized Champions Tour

While Connors never officially retired from tennis, he did not play full time after 1992. Injuries and age forced Connors to pursue other interests, although he never lost his passion for tennis. In 1995 he played in two ATP tournaments, and he even reached the quarter-

finals in Halle, Germany. Most of the tennis Connors played in the 1990s was on the Champions Tour, the over-35 male tennis tour that he started in 1993. Connors was not only the co-founder with Ray Benton and president of the tour, but he was also often the champion. Although he recruited other top players, such as McEnroe, **Bjorn Borg**, Guillermo Vilas, and Roscoe Tanner to participate, Connors dominated the tour during the early years so much that the press dubbed it the "Connors Tour."

Vanity may have played a role in Connors' motivation to organize the seniors' tour, as did his love for the game. Connors also saw the tour as a vehicle to promote tennis in general, much like the Senior PGA tour for golf. "I wanted tennis to be a sport where everybody could enjoy it … yell and scream and root and cheer and boo like they do at baseball games, football games, basketball games and hockey games," Connors told David Elfin of the *Washington Times* in May of 1996. The tour started with only three tournaments, but grew to over twenty tournaments in eleven countries by 2001.

In the late 1990s Connors suffered from some injuries, including torn stomach muscles, which hampered his play. McEnroe took over as the leader on the seniors' tour, although Connors continued to play some tournaments. In 2001 at the age of 49, he finished 15th in the Tour of Champions standings.

Connors, a brash young American tennis star, who learned the game on public courts, took the elitist, country-club world of tennis by storm with his talent and his emotions. The lefty was known for his two-handed backhand and killer return-of-serve, as well as for his emotional outbursts and arguments with the umpires. Connors won eight Grand Slam titles, including five U.S. Open championships. He has played in more tournaments, won more finals, and won more matches than any other male professional tennis player. His legacy was summed up best by BBC Sports in 2001: "'Jimbo' may have lacked the supreme natural talent of John McEnroe or **Rod Laver**, but there was one area where Connors was streets ahead of the rest—his competitiveness."

CONTACT INFORMATION

Address: Tennis Management Inc., 109 Red Fox Rd, Belleville, IL 62223-2242.

SELECTED WRITINGS BY CONNORS:

(With Neil Gordon). *Don't Count Yourself Out. Staying Fit After 35,* Hyperion, 1992.

FURTHER INFORMATION

Books

Collins, Bud, and Zander Hollander (eds.). *Bud Collins' Tennis Encyclopedia.* Detroit: Visible Ink Press, 1997.

St. James Encyclopedia of Popular Culture. Detroit: St. James Press, 2000.

Periodicals

Atkin, Ronald. "Interview: John McEnroe—First Among Senior Citizens; He's Old, He's Loud and He's Back, Talking Up His Rivalry with Jimmy Connors." *Independent* (November 29, 1998): 8.

Atkin, Ross. "Jimmy Connors Basks in Fifth U.S. Title, 100th Overall Victory." *Christian Science Monitor* (September 13, 1983): 8.

Callahan, Tom. "Jimmy Connors's Wonderful Life." *U.S. News and World Report* (September 16, 1991): 61.

"The Connors Tour." *Sports Illustrated* (May 8, 1995): 15.

Deford, Frank. "He Got Down and Did It. (Jimmy Connors Wins U.S. Open)." *Sports Illustrated* (September 19, 1983): 24-28.

Deford, Frank. "Raised By Women to Conquer Men." *Sports Illustrated* (August 22, 1994): 56-63.

Dwyer III, Joe. "Connor's Aces Off the Court Now Worth $86.3 Million." *St. Louis Business Journal* (June 21, 1993): 1-2.

Elfin, David. "Will Jimmy Connors Hit Another Winner with Over-35 Tour?" *Washington Times* (May 10, 1996): 5.

Geracie, Bud. "Jimmy Connors Laments Absence of Fun, Personality in Men's Pro Tennis." Knight Ridder/Tribune News Service (January 13, 1994).

Hruby, Dan. "Jimmy Connors Next Two-Sport Star?" Knight Ridder/Tribune News Service (January 20, 1994).

Jenkins, Sally. "Gone and Unlamented (John McEnroe and Jimmy Connors, French Open Tennis Tournament)." *Sports Illustrated* (June 8, 1992): 92.

"Jimmy Connors: Tennis's Old Man in a Hurry Smashes Both His Biological Clock and Baffled Young Men Half His Age." *People* (December 30, 1991): 98-99.

Kirkpatrick, Curry. "Open and Shut (1991 U. S. Open Tennis)." *Sports Illustrated* (September 16, 1991): 16-23.

Kirkpatrick, Curry. "Prince Valiant: After Nearly Two Years of Ignoble Tennis, Jimmy Connors at 38 Made a Gallant Stand in Paris." *Sports Illustrated* (June 10, 1991): 32-35.

Lorge, Barry. "Jimmy Connors: The Rude American; Subdued Connors Breezes in First as the Boos Rains Down." *Washington Post* (June 22, 1977): D1.

Newman, Bruce. "Double Faux (Jimmy Connors Defeats Martina Navratilova)." *Sports Illustrated* (October 5, 1992): 9.

Nichols, Bill. "Love Match? Chris Arrives Late—With Friend." *Plain Dealer* (July 25, 1972).

Podolsky, Doug. "The Jimbo Question." *U.S. News and World Report* (September 16, 1991): 13.

Purdy, Mark. "More than a Modest Tennis Proposal for a Worthy Cause." knight Ridder/Tribune News Service (October 19, 2001).

"Reconciled. Jimmy Connors." *Time* (August 29, 1983): 78.

"Seeking Divorce. Patti McGuire, Jimmy Connors." *Time* (May 16, 1983): 70.

Stein, Ruthe. "The Bad Boy, All Grown Up." *San Francisco Chronicle* (January 18, 1993): B3.

Thornley, Gerry. "Happy to Be Out of the Modern Game." *Irish Times* (June 18, 1993): 15.

Turner, Mili. "Connors Savors Taste of Good Competition Again." Knight Ridder/Tribune News Service (August 1, 1995).

Wood, Daniel B. "Jimmy Connors Juggling Tennis Career, Family Responsibilities." *Christian Science Monitor* (April 15, 1985): 22.

Other

ATP Tennis. http://atptennis.com/en/tournaments/championstour/ (January 4, 2003).

BBC Sport. http://news.bbc.co.uk/sport/hi/english/static/in_depth/tennis/2001/wimbledon/legends/connors/stm (December 21, 2002).

International Tennis Hall of Fame. http://www.tennisfame.org/enshrinees/jimmy_connors.html (December 21, 2002).

St. Louis Walk of Fame. http://www.stlouiswalkoffame.org/inductees/jimmy-connors.html (December 21, 2002).

Sketch by Janet P. Stamatel

Jody Conradt
1941-

American basketball coach

Jody Conradt

J ody Conradt, the powerhouse women's basketball coach at the University of Texas-Austin (UT), has won more college women's basketball games than any other coach in history. At a last count just shy of 800 wins, she also holds the record for coaching 1,000 games—the first female coach to do so. She's a five-time Southwest Conference Coach of the Year, multiple National Coach of the Year, and Hall of Famer. As UT's women's athletic director from 1992 to 2001, she grew women's sports at a time when the school was facing the federal government's Title IX.

For the Love of Coaching

Jody Conradt grew up in Goldthwaite, a small town near Austin, Texas, where sports were a way of life for both boys and girls. She attended Goldthwaite High School, where she played for the Eagles basketball team. During her high school career, she was known for her determination and hard work and averaged forty points per game.

In 1959, she entered Baylor University in Waco, Texas, eventually earning a bachelor's and later a master's degree in physical education. The 5'7" athlete played on the school's inaugural varsity team, averaged twenty points per game, and earned four letters. As a teacher at Waco Midway High School, Conradt learned that coaching was where her heart lay when her mentor, M.T. Rice, one of the state's most successful girls' basketball coaches, asked her to help coach his team.

Chronology	
1941	Born May 13 in Goldthwaite, Texas
1955-59	Attended Goldthwaite High School
1963	Earned bachelor's degree in physical education at Baylor University
1963	Taught at Waco Midway High School
1969	Earned master's degree
1969-73	Head basketball coach Sam Houston State (Huntsville, TX)
1973-76	Coached University of Texas at Arlington
1976	Becomes head coach of University of Texas at Austin
1982	Joins National Collegiate Athletic Association
1986	Leads Texas to the NCAA title with a 34-0 record
1992	Becomes University of Texas Women's Athletic Director
2001	Resigns as UT Women's Athletic Director
2001	Recognized by Texas State Senate for her 1,000th game

Conradt began her collegiate coaching career at Sam Houston State in Huntsville, Texas, in 1969. Named head basketball coach, she recorded a school record of 74-23, and also oversaw the women's volleyball and track teams. In 1973, she ventured to the University of Texas-Arlington where she coached basketball, volleyball, and softball and left with an Arlington basketball record of 43-39.

Conradt's career truly exploded in 1976 when she became head coach at the University of Texas-Austin. With women's sports underrepresented, she created a model women's program that propelled the Lady Longhorns to a streak of successful seasons. The team ranked in the Top 20 her first year, followed by a 37-4 finish and Top 15 rank the second year, and Top 5 rank the third year. By 1980, Conradt had led her team to a 33-4 season and she had won National Coach of the Year, a title she would wear four times during her career.

The Longhorns were fast becoming one of the most successful basketball teams in the country winning six consecutive AIAW tournaments. During this time, Conradt's accolades continued to accumulate. She joined the NCAA in 1982 and brought her team to the top four straight years. She became a five-time Southwestern Conference Coach of the Year between 1984 and 1996, and was inducted into the Texas Women's Hall of Fame in 1986.

The Personal Touch

Conradt is known for her personal touch when recruiting players and for her success in building an enthusiastic fan base. She scoured Texas high schools personally to find the best players, learned about their programs, and interacted with players and coaches on a personal level. For the fans, Conradt used her visibility and charismatic personality to increase attendance at games. Growing to hundreds then thousands, fans liked what they were seeing and kept coming back.

Conradt's continued success fueled the excitement. In 1986, Texas had grown into one of the finest teams in

Awards and Accomplishments

1980, 1984, 1986, 1997	National Coach of the Year
1984-85	Southwestern Conference Coach of the Year
1986	Texas Women's Hall of Fame
1987	Carol Eckman Award
1987	Pan American Games gold medal for US team
1987-88	Southwestern Conference Coach of the Year
1991	National Association for Girls and Women in Sports Award
1995	International Women's Sports Hall of Fame
1996	Southwestern Conference Coach of the Year
1997	December 18 became the 8th coach in history to win 700 games
1997	Recipient of the inaugural John and Nellie Wooden Award as the women's basketball national Coach of the Year
1998	Naismith National Memorial Basketball Hall of Fame October 2
1998	Texas Sports Hall of Fame
1998	One of the Top 50 Women's Sports Executives
1999	Women's Basketball Hall of Fame
1999	Finalist for Naismith Women's Basketball Coach of the Century
1999	Finalist for John and Nellie Wooden National Coach of the Year Award
2001	First woman to coach 1,000 games in a career

basketball and proved it by winning the NCAA national championship with a record 34-0, the first unbeaten season in NCAA women's history. Conradt led her team to the 1986 and 1987 Final Four.

The year 1987 was a busy one, as Conradt not only received the Women's Basketball Coaches Association's Carol Eckman Award, but also managed the US team to a gold medal at the 1987 Pan American Games. By 1990, she would dominate the Southwest Conference by winning 183 consecutive league games during the twelve-year stretch since 1978, one of the longest win streaks for any sport in college history.

The Athletic Director

Conradt became UT-Austin's Women's Athletic Director in 1992, replacing Dr. Donna Lopiano, who had held the seat for the past eighteen years. At the time, the school was facing mandated compliance with Title IX, a federal law that required equality between men's and women's athletic programs at public universities. Now as director, Conradt oversaw the school's newly installed varsity soccer, softball, and rowing programs.

Despite her numerous accomplishments, the achievement that put her in the record books was on December 18, 1997, becoming the first female collegiate coach to win 700 games when Texas defeated Northwestern 89-86. Her 500th win, out of 589 games, had been the fastest achieved at one school by a women's college coach, and her 600th win, out of 753 games, had been the second fastest.

Not surprisingly, these honors were followed by Conradt's naming to the Texas Sports Hall of Fame in 1998, the Basketball Hall of Fame, and a spot in the Top 50

Women's Sports Executives by Street & Smith's *Sports Business Journal,* all in 1998, and the Women's Basketball Hall of Fame a year later.

By 1999, with her college coaching record of 766 wins, Conradt ranked ninth all-time in men's and women's collegiate basketball victories, and second best among all active collegiate basketball coaches. Rapidly approaching the 800 mark by December 2002, Conradt, with 793 wins, was neck-in-neck competition with University of Tennessee coach **Pat Summitt** with 796 wins.

In 2000, Conradt was the first woman, and one of only seventeen coaches, to coach 1,000 games in the NCAA Division One. On May 18, 2001, the Texas State Senate passed a resolution recognizing Jody Conradt's perseverance, honesty, and dedication, and her contribution to women's sports in response to coaching her 1,000th game.

Conradt resigned her post as athletic director of UT in 2001 to concentrate on coaching. During her tenure as director, Texas teams won six NCAA national championships (track and field and tennis) and thirty-nine conference championships. The women's program grew to eleven varsity sports. Between 1992 and 2001 she had overseen ten NCAA Championship caliber, women's athletics programs.

In an article in the *Daily Texan* following her 1,000th game, Conradt noted that she never wanted to continue on in the administrative role but to return to what she loved most, coaching young women. "This has always been my dream job. What gets me excited and motivates me is working with young people," she said.

During her career, Conradt has coached four Olympians, twenty-nine All-Americans (NCAA and AIAW), six SWC Players of the Year, two National Players of the Year, three Wade Trophy National Players of the Year winners, one Broderick National Female Athlete of the Year Award winner (Kamie Ethridge), forty-nine All-Conference honor winners, twenty-one players who went to the pros, and Clarissa Davis, the NCAA 1980s Player of the Decade.

Conradt is active with community and charitable institutions, such as Girl Scouts, the Susan B. Komen Foundation, and Coaches vs. Cancer. She conducted a lecture in November 2001 at the University of Texas' Lyndon B. Johnson School of Public Affairs, speaking about her experiences with team building and leadership during her tenure as basketball coach and administrator.

FURTHER INFORMATION

Periodicals

Lawlor, Chris. "The ayes of Texas are upon her." *Scholastic Coach & Athletic Director* (March 1998): 52.

Patrick, Dick. "800 wins." *USA Today* (December 20, 2002) 11.

Other

Basketball Hall of Fame. http://www.hoophall.com/halloffamers/conradt.htm (January 15, 2003).

Daily Texan. http://tspweb02.tsp.utexas.edu/webarchive/04-06-01/2001040601_s06_Conradt.html (January 15, 2003).

Sports Illustrated. http://sportsillustrated.cnn.com/basketball/college/women/news/2001/04/05/conradt_ad_ap/ (January 15, 2003).

Texas Longhorns. http://www.texassports.com (January 15, 2003).

Texas State Capitol. http://www.capitol.state.tx.us/tlo/77R/billtext/SR01094F.htm (January 15, 2003).

University of Texas. http://www.utexas.edu/lbj/news/S2001/conraddt.html (January 15, 2003).

Sketch by Lorraine Savage

Cynthia Cooper

Cynthia Cooper
1963-

American basketball player

After being a standout player in college and in European basketball leagues, Cynthia Cooper finally achieved her dream of being able to play professional basketball in the United States when the Women's National Basketball Association (WNBA) debuted in 1997. She was the star of the Houston Comets for the next four years, leading them to four straight WNBA championships and being named the most valuable player of the championship series four times before retiring at the end of the 2000 season.

Early Successes

Cooper didn't learn how to play basketball until the summer before she started high school. That spring she saw a girl in her junior high gym pass the ball around behind her back before making a layup and thought to herself that she'd like to be able to do that. Cooper pleaded with an acquaintance of hers who was also an assistant basketball coach at her future high school to teach her how to play. They met at the high school gym every day that summer, and by the fall Cooper was good enough to make the high school varsity team.

After joining her high school's starting lineup as a sophomore and leading them to the California girls' high school basketball championships in her senior year, in the fall of 1981 Cooper began attending the University of Southern California (USC) on a basketball scholarship. Cooper, who prior to this had lived in poverty in the infamous Watts neighborhood of Los Angeles, recalls in her autobiography that the culture shock she felt at the university was intense. Her success on the court helped her to adjust, but then in the fall of her junior year Cooper suffered a major setback: she was ruled ineligible to play on the team because of poor grades. Cooper brought her grades up, rejoined the team after the fall semester, and helped the Lady Trojans to win their second NCAA championship in two years.

Cooper's academic problems prevented her from playing again during her senior year, and in frustration she quit school early in 1985. Hoping to help her single-parent mother with the family's financial worries, Cooper found a job as a bank teller. Within months, she had been promoted to head teller, but Cooper missed basketball. She reenrolled at USC later in 1985. The team made it to the NCAA championships again that season, but lost the championship game to the University of Texas.

Playing on the World Stage

That summer, Cooper tried out for the U.S. National women's basketball team. Three hundred players came to Colorado Springs at their own expense to compete with thirty invited athletes for twelve spots on the team.

Career Statistics

Yr	Team	GP	PTS	FG%	3P%	FT%	RPG	APG	SPG	BPG	TO	PF
1997	HOU	28	621	.470	.414	.864	4.0	4.7	2.11	.21	109	68
1998	HOU	30	680	.446	.400	.854	3.7	4.4	1.60	.37	95	65
1999	HOU	31	686	.463	.335	.891	2.8	5.2	1.39	.35	104	61
2000	HOU	31	643	.459	.355	.875	2.7	5.0	1.26	.19	99	61
TOTAL		120	2630	.496	.377	.871	3.3	4.7	1.58	.28	407	255

HOU: Houston Comets.

Of the three hundred walk-on players, only one made the final cut: Cooper. With the U.S. National team, Cooper made her second trip abroad (she had participated in the Jones Cup in Taiwan in the summer of 1981), competing in the Goodwill Games in Moscow and the World Championships in Vilnius, U.S.S.R. The U.S. team won both events.

Late in 1985, Cooper was offered a job playing in a professional league in Valencia, Spain, which she took eagerly. After playing there for a year, she was offered a spot on a team in the Italian league, which was more competitive and prestigious than the Spanish league. Cooper packed up and moved to Parma, Italy. She now describes the city as her second home, although language problems made playing on the Parma team difficult until she became fluent in Italian. Under Cooper's leadership, the Parma team became one of the dominant ones in the Italian league, and Cooper wound up playing there for the seven seasons. She left Parma to play for a Sicilian team for two seasons after that, but in 1996 she returned to Parma. This would be her final season playing in Europe: in 1997 the WNBA would open, and Cooper would finally get to play professional basketball on her home soil.

Home at Last

Despite having played professionally in Europe for so long, Cooper was not unknown to American fans. She had played for the U.S. National team in the World Championships and the Goodwill Games in 1986 and 1990, and on the gold medal-winning team in the 1988 Olympics and the bronze medal-winning one in 1992. This and her dominance in the Italy—she was that league's leading scorer eight times—guaranteed her a marquee spot in the new WNBA. Cooper was assigned to the Houston Comets, along with 1996 Olympian and former Texas Tech star **Sheryl Swoopes**. Swoopes was out on maternity leave the first half of the season, but with Cooper and other excellent players the Comets still managed to make an impact. They eventually caught up to their division's early leaders, the New York Liberty, and on the penultimate day of the season they clinched the Eastern Division title.

The Comets went on to become the first dynasty in the WNBA, winning the WNBA championships that year and for the next three years as well. Cooper was named the most valuable player of the championship series every one of those four years. She became a celebrity, appearing on the Rosie O'Donnell and David Letterman shows after that first championship. Nike even created a shoe, called the C-14, in honor of her. She also became a spokesperson for General Motors' Concept Cure program, a charity focused on preventing and curing breast cancer. This cause is particularly dear to Cooper: her mother was diagnosed with breast cancer early in 1997 and passed away from the disease in 1999.

Retirement

Cooper retired as a WNBA player at the end of the 1999-2000 season, after the Comets won their fourth straight championship. Midway through the 2001-02 season, Cooper became the head coach of another WNBA team, the Phoenix Mercury, but she retired from that job only ten games into her second season there in order to spend more time with her growing family: Cooper's twin children were born June 14, 2002.

Shortly after retiring as coach of the Phoenix Mercury in June, 2002, Cooper was tapped by the administration of President George W. Bush to co-chair a fifteen-member panel that studied the impact of Title IX, the federal law which mandated gender equity in federally-funded education activities, including college sports. Cooper and her husband, Brian Dykes (a sports agent), live in Sugar Land, Texas, where they are raising their twins, Brian Jr. and Cyan, as well as Tyquon, Anthony, and Tyrone, the sons of one of Cooper's sisters whom Cooper has adopted.

The WNBA and the success of female basketball players such as Cooper have inspired thousands of girls to follow their dreams of making a living as a professional athlete. Even though Cooper is no longer competing, her incredible feats during the four years she played in the WNBA contributed greatly to the success of the fledgling league. By the time Cooper retired as a player, the WNBA had expanded from its original eight teams to sixteen, giving 176 women the opportunity to play professional basketball in the United States and millions more the ability to cheer for these dedicated female athletes.

CONTACT INFORMATION

Address: c/o Author Mail, Warner Books, 1271 Avenue of the Americas, New York, NY 10020.

SELECTED WRITINGS BY COOPER:

She Got Game: My Personal Odyssey, Warner Books, 1999.

FURTHER INFORMATION

Books

Cooper, Cynthia. *She Got Game: My Personal Odyssey.* New York: Warner Books, 1999.

Periodicals

Anderson, Kelli. "Coop De Grace." *Sports Illustrated* (September 13, 1999): 56.

Calkins, Laurel Brubaker, and Nick, Charles. "In Good Hands." *People* (June 22, 1998): 203.

Cooper, Cynthia. "Welcome to Coop's Scoop." *Houston Chronicle* (July 10, 1997): 3.

Falduto, Brad. "Cooper Stuns Team, Steps Down." Knight Ridder/Tribune News Service (June 30, 2002): K4084.

"Former WNBA Star to Chair Title IX Review Panel." *Black Issues in Higher Education* (August 1, 2002): 19.

"Houston Comets Win Fourth Straight WNBA Championship." *Jet* (September 11, 2000): 54.

Howard, Johnette. "Comet's Tale." *Sports Illustrated* (August 25, 1997): 34-35.

Karkabi, Barbara. "This Comet's Not Flashy." *Houston Chronicle* (September 14, 1999): 1.

Liebowitz, Julie. "New Horizons." *Sport* (November, 1998): 96-97.

Racine, Marty. "Coop in Charge!" *Houston Chronicle* (September 4, 1997): 4.

"Ten Greatest Women Athletes." *Ebony* (March, 2002): 74-77.

Terry, Mike. "Cloud Hangs over Cooper's Departure." *Los Angeles Times* (July 2, 2002): D-7.

"Transition Game." *Sports Illustrated for Women* (March 1, 2001): 26.

Other

WNBA.com. http://www.wnba.com (November 27, 2002).

Sketch by Julia Bauder

Jim Corbett
1866-1933

American boxer

Heavyweight champion boxer "Gentleman" Jim Corbett forever changed his sport's image as a brawling ground for hooligans, and legitimized it as a professional sport. Before Corbett won his championship bout in 1892, boxing was perceived as mainly a test of raw power. Corbett brought strategy to the game, beating his heavier, stronger opponent, **John L. Sullivan,** with skill and agility. That, combined with his penchant for elegant clothes, and his refined manner, earned him his nickname. As former featherweight boxing champion and commentator Barry McGuigan put it in his introduction to Patrick

Jim Corbett

Myler's book *Gentleman Jim Corbett,* "He wrote the original boxing textbook for the others to follow."

A Born Fighter

James Corbett was born to Irish immigrant parents in San Francisco, California in 1866. His parents were devout Catholics, and they envisioned a life in the priesthood for their son, who was named after his father's brother, a Catholic priest back in the old country. (Corbett's parents met a tragic end when, on August 16, 1898, Corbett's father, who had been in declining mental health for some time, murdered Corbett's mother with a revolver and then shot and killed himself in their home in San Francisco.).

Corbett's father supported his family, ten children in all, by running a livery stable. Corbett, in later years, would describe the street of his childhood home as a dirt track whose major businesses were saloons.

Corbett first realized his calling when he took on his parochial school bully. Although the bully was older and stronger than Corbett, Corbett began to get the better of him, instinctively stepping out of the way of his blows, and looking at one part of the other boy's body to distract him, while attacking another. Corbett later wrote in his autobiography, *The Roar of the Crowd,* that he would have won the fight if the bully had not sat on him to pin him down before pummeling him.

Both boys were expelled from their school for fighting, but the encounter was to have a lasting impression on the future boxer. He learned, among other things, that he could beat a bigger and stronger opponent by being light on his feet, and quick.

After their son was expelled from his next school, again for fighting, Corbett's parents finally had to admit that their boy was not a scholar. So, at the age of 14, Corbett was sent to work as a clerk for a local company. He did well at this job, and when the opportunity came to work for one of his father's customers, a banker, he jumped at the chance. Starting out as a messenger, he rose through the company ranks over the next six years to become a bank teller.

From Bank Teller to Professional Boxer

While working as a bank teller, Corbett practiced in amateur boxing matches, first with some of his fellow bank clerks on their lunch break, and then at scheduled matches at sporting establishments. Although a right-hander, Corbett developed the power of his left punch, and many an opponent found his then-unusual left jab devastating.

The young boxer began his career in earnest when he joined San Francisco's Olympic Athletic Club. Initially, the coaches at the club steered the young Corbett into playing baseball, which he did until a serious hand injury forced him out of the game. He then returned to boxing. Under the tutelage of Olympic's boxing coach, Corbett soon became the club's middleweight champion, and by the time he turned 18, became the club's heavyweight champion.

At the top of his game as an amateur boxer, Corbett nevertheless still worked as a bank clerk, and he longed to make more money. During this time, when he was just 19 years old, in 1886, Corbett and Olive Lake eloped to Salt Lake City, Utah and were married. It was in Utah that Corbett fought his first bout as a professional. The heavyweight champion of Utah, Frank Smith, issued a challenge, and Corbett responded under the name of Jim Dillon, to avoid tipping off his family back in San Francisco that he was in Salt Lake City. Corbett won the match, earning a prize of $460 in the process—money that Corbett and his bride desperately needed to pay the rent.

After fighting another professional match in Evanston, Wyoming (accounts differ as to the results of that fight), Corbett returned to San Francisco, where he got a job as a clerk at an insurance company and moonlighted as a boxing instructor at the Olympic Athletic Club.

Corbett made his pro boxing debut near his hometown on May 30, 1889. This was when he and fighter Joe Choynski met for a "fight to the finish" This meant that the match would last until one of them could no longer go on, or until they both agreed to a draw. Promoters of the fight emphasized the combatants' ethnic differences (Choynski was Jewish), and local authorities forbade the fight on the grounds that it might start a riot. So Corbett and Choynski had to box unadvertised in a barn in remote Marin County. Nevertheless, word got around, and hundreds of spectators turned out to watch the fight.

The boxers went five rounds before the sheriff showed up to stop the proceedings. Corbett and Choynski met for a rematch a week later, this time on a barge north of San Francisco Bay, safely out of the jurisdiction of local police. The fight lasted a punishing 28 rounds. The deck of the barge grew slick with the combatant's blood, and sawdust had to be laid down so that they wouldn't slip in it. Corbett at last won the fight with a knock-out punch. Corbett himself was so dazed that he had to be told that he had won the fight.

Rise of a Champion

Now firmly established as a professional boxer, Corbett was able to quit his job at the insurance company and devote himself full time to boxing. After fighting in matches in the San Francisco area and in Portland, Oregon, his fame spread to New Orleans, where he met the challenge of New Yorker Jake Kilrain, who had previously fought England's champion to a draw in 106 rounds. After Corbett won the match against Kilrain, word of Corbett's victory spread to New York, where he was courted by boxing promoters there. His career was assured after he defeated Dominick McCaffrey at Brooklyn's Casino Rink in April, 1890.

Returning in triumph to San Francisco, Corbett took up his old job as coach at the Olympic Athletic Club and fought often in exhibition matches. He also began a parallel career that was to carry him into his later years; in 1890, he was cast in his first play, in a small role alongside the famous actor Maurice Barrymore. Corbett found acting a natural extension of his desire to be in the spotlight as a boxer, and he eagerly pursued other acting opportunities, eventually becoming a stage and screen celebrity.

Corbett now had his sights on the world championship, and his first step in that direction came with his bout against Peter Jackson. Jackson was Australia's champion, and the reigning world champion, John L. Sullivan, had refused to fight with him because Jackson was black. Corbett, however, fought him for 61 rounds in San Francisco on May 21, 1891. The fight was ended only after both combatants were too tired and battered to swing effectually at each other, and the match was declared to be a "no contest." The fight lasted about four hours, and supporters of Jackson, who was favored to win by 2 to 1 odds, were shocked. Corbett became a challenger Sullivan could not refuse.

After his fight with Jackson, Corbett took on a new manager, William A. Brady, who saw Corbett's boxing successes merely as a prelude to his acting career, and began booking him in plays in New York City. One play, *Gentleman Jack,* was written specially for Corbett by Charles T. Vincent, and featured the future champion in the lead role. Advertising posters for the play promoted Corbett as the boxing champion of the world, *before* his bout with Sullivan.

The gamble did pay off before the play opened, however, and Corbett become heavyweight champion of the world on September 7, 1892 when he defeated John L. Sullivan in New Orleans. Corbett was the first world heavyweight champion under Marquis of Queensberry Rules. These rules insisted on the use of boxing gloves; before these were enacted, boxing matches were commonly fought with bare fists.

Corbett had had an opportunity to size up his opponent first-hand at an exhibition bout in San Francisco, during which both boxers sparred in full evening dress, at Sullivan's insistence. The combatants fought half-

---

Gentleman Jim

Gentleman Jim, released in 1942 by Warner Brothers, starred Errol Flynn in the title role. Based on Corbett's autobiography, *The Roar of the Crowd*, it was timed to coincide with the 50th anniversary of Corbett's championship victory over John L. Sullivan. It was said that of the more than 60 films made by Flynn, this one was his favorite.

Directed by Raoul Walsh, the film portrayed Corbett as a devil-may-care, happy-go-lucky fighter who never lost his nerve or confidence in his own abilities. It also evoked the rough-and-tumble San Francisco of the late 1800s.

Memorable scenes included an enactment of the Corbett-Choynski barge fight, and, of course, the climatic fight for the title with Sullivan. Sullivan was played by Ward Bond, who had been an accomplished boxer in college. The filmmakers took some artistic license in adding a fictitious scene in which Sullivan hands over his championship belt to Corbett, telling him that it was time for him (Sullivan) to make way for a new breed of fighter.

Flynn was a good choice to play Corbett, since he was about the same height and weight as the famous boxer, and had been something of an amateur boxer himself. The film star found the role extremely taxing however; a heart condition rendered him unable to shoot fight scenes for more than a minute at a time. But fight trainer Mushy Callahan, charged with getting Flynn in shape for the movie, found Flynn a quick study. Primary among his tasks was to train Flynn to make extensive use of his left punch, the way Corbett did.

Gentleman Jim opened to strong reviews, and was a box office success. Boxing great Mike Tyson later said that the film was the best boxing movie he had ever seen.

---

heartedly, but Corbett had an excellent chance to take the measure of the man he would later battle for the title of world heavyweight champion.

The fateful day arrived in New Orleans with thousands of spectators from all over the country crowded into the newly-completed Olympic Club. Reporters from around the world covered the fight, and 50 Western Union telegraph operators sat ringside to deliver blow-by-blow accounts. Sullivan was favored to win with 4-to-1 odds, and even Corbett's manager bet some money on Sullivan "just in case."

He need not have worried. Corbett successfully evaded most of Sullivan's blows in the first two rounds, and scored a devastating hit to Sullivan's face in the third, breaking his nose. Although Sullivan was larger and stronger than Corbett, Corbett wore his opponent down, dancing around him, and dashing in to place well-aimed blows before Sullivan could react. Corbett wore out his opponent over 21 rounds, finally finishing him off with a knockout when Sullivan was too tired and beaten to put up much of a fight.

An International Sensation

Corbett was celebrated around the world, and especially in his hometown of San Francisco, and immediately began to cash in; his stage career took off when *Gentleman Jack* opened in Elizabeth, New Jersey, and from there toured the country. Corbett held his own on the stage, regularly selling out houses. Exhibition matches and even product endorsements followed, mak-

ing Corbett and his manager, now equal partners in the firm of Corbett and Brady, wealthy men. Corbett had by now moved with his wife to the New York City area, where they owned more than one home.

But in order to keep the money flowing, Corbett was obliged, sooner or later, to defend his championship title; it was, after all, his major draw. Corbett got his first chance to defend his title when he was challenged by Englishman Charley Mitchell. On January 25, 1894, in Jacksonville, Florida, Corbett knocked Mitchell out in three rounds.

More exhibition matches and stage appearances followed through the 1890s, including a European tour of *Gentleman Jack*. In the mid-1890s, Corbett left his wife, and married his mistress, Vera Stanwood. Not long after, Corbett had to accept a challenge of his heavyweight title from Bob Fitzsimmons, the reigning middleweight champion of the world. After unsuccessful attempts to stage the fight in Texas and, later, Arkansas (the governors in both states refused to allow boxing on moral grounds), the combatants finally squared off in Carson City, Nevada on March 17, 1897.

Loses His Title in the World's First Feature Film

The Fitzsimmons fight was filmed by pioneering film director Enoch J. Rector, who captured the entire bout with three separate cameras. The event was staged in a specially erected ring just for the occasion, and it took place during daylight hours to accommodate the movie cameras. Since the fight lasted more than 90 minutes, Rector created the first known feature-length film in the process of filming the fight.

Corbett got the better of his challenger for six rounds, bloodying his face, and neatly avoiding the worst that Fitzsimmons could dish out. In the sixth round, Corbett knocked Fitzsimmons down for a nine-count, very nearly winning the match. But Fitzsimmons rallied, finally wearing the champion down with body blows, and scoring a knockdown in the 14th round with a devastating blow to Corbett's solar plexus. Fitzsimmons rejected all future challenges by Corbett, and so Corbett was not able to attempt to regain his title until after Fitzsimmons lost the title to James J. Jeffries.

Out with a Bang

Corbett and Jeffries fought at Coney Island, New York, on May 11, 1900. Many observers agreed that this fight was Corbett's finest, and a brilliant demonstration of "scientific" boxing over brute power. Jeffries was bigger, stronger, and nine years younger, but Corbett got the better of him for 22 rounds, consistently avoiding his opponent's boilermakers, and dancing in for quick jabs that soon bloodied his face. Clearly far ahead in points, Corbett had only to last the required 25 rounds to regain his championship title, but it was not to be. Jeffries finally managed to land one of his powerful blows, knocking Corbett out cold.

Corbett made one more attempt to regain the title from Jeffries three years later, at the age of 37, but he lost this match in the tenth round, and afterwards vowed to retire from boxing and devote himself full time to his acting career. Thereafter, he appeared regularly on Broadway, in theatrical tours around the United States and Europe, and in films as a popular box office draw. Corbett spent his final years with his wife Vera in Bayside, New York, where he died on February 18, 1933 of liver cancer. He had no children.

Credited with being the first to bring strategy, dexterity, and analytical thought to his sport, Corbett forever changed the nature of boxing. Often elegantly dressed and always well-mannered, Corbett attracted many new fans to boxing, including women. He brought a sense of refinement to a sport that had been seen simply as a contest between brutes. Such twentieth-century boxing greats as **Jack Dempsey**, **Rocky Marciano**, and **Mike Tyson** all followed in Corbett's footsteps.

FURTHER INFORMATION

Books

Myler, Patrick. *Gentleman Jim Corbett: The Truth Behind a Boxing Legend.* London: Robson Books Ltd., 1989.

Periodicals

Mee, Bob. "Book Review: Shadows Behind a Boxing Legend: Gentleman Jim Corbett by Patrick Myler." *Independent* (January 17, 1999).

Other

"Biography—Jim Corbett." HickokSports.com. http://www.hickoksports.com/biograph/corbettj.shtml (October 4, 2002).
"Gentleman Jim (1942)." Internet Movie Database. http://us.imdb.com/Title?0034778 (October 7, 2002).
"James J. Corbett." International Boxing Hall of Fame. http://www.ibhof.com/corbett.htm (September 27, 2002).
"James J. Corbett." Internet Movie Database. http://us.imdb.com/Name?Corbett,%20James%20J. (October 4, 2002).
"The Marquis of Queensberry Rules." HickokSports.com.http://www.hickoksports.com/history/marqrule.shtml (October 4, 2002).
"The Plot Summary for Corbett-Fitzsimmons Fight." Internet Movie Database. http://us.imdb.com/Plot?0000147 (October 4, 2002).

Sketch by Michael Belfiore

Howard Cosell
1918-1995

American sportscaster

Sportscasting had never before known the likes of Howard Cosell, nor is it likely to see another like him again. He became an enormous figure despite the fact that he was verbose, egotistical, decidedly untelegenic, outspoken about controversial issues, and oblivious to the feelings of others. These negative attributes were almost equally balanced by his intelligence, work ethic, social commitment, and ability to entertain. As a radio and television commentator, Cosell became one of the best-known voices and faces in the United States in the 1970s and 1980s, during which time he was loved and hated in seemingly equal measure. The highest point in his career came when he appeared on ABC television's *Monday Night Football,* helping to establish it as one of the most successful shows in television history. But Cosell did more than increase ratings for televised sports, he also introduced a journalistic approach to the subject. Most notably, he addressed the issue of race in sports and became a vocal supporter of boxer **Muhammad Ali** when he was censured for evading the draft. The sportscaster's inability to temper his criticisms ultimately shortened his career, however. His 1985 autobiography *I Never Played the Game* contained such harsh appraisals of his ABC colleagues that it effectively ended his television career.

Family Influence

Born Howard William Cohen on March 25, 1918 in Winston-Salem, North Carolina, Cosell grew up in Brooklyn, New York. When he chose to study law at New York University, he was following the wishes of his parents, Isidore and Nellie Cohen, rather than his own interest in newspaper reporting. After serving as editor of the Law Review and making Phi Beta Kappa, he graduated in 1940 and took a job with a successful law firm. However, he was soon called to serve in World War II. He enlisted in the Army and was stationed at the New York Port of Embarkation in Brooklyn, where he became one of the youngest in the Army to earn the rank of major during the war. Having legally changed his name while a law student, Cosell also met and married WAC sergeant Mary Edith "Emmy" Abrams while he served at the Port. The Cosells would have a long and devoted marriage, in which Emmy served as Howard's emotional bedrock.

After leaving the Army, Cosell somewhat reluctantly returned to practicing law. For eight years he had his own private practice in Manhattan, serving clients including actors and athletes. He worked for the Little League of New York, a connection that led to his being

Howard Cosell

asked in 1953 to line up Little League players for an ABC radio show in which kids would ask questions of major league players. Cosell was soon cast as the show's unpaid host, and he became involved in snagging star players as well as making sure they were asked the right questions. On one program, Hank Bauer complained about having been benched by coach **Casey Stengel**, proving that players were responding to questions that they would have balked at if asked by a reporter. The success of the approach earned Cosell a longer time slot and extended the show's proposed six-week run into six years.

Career at ABC

In 1956 Cosell left his law practice to do five-minute weekend radio broadcasts for ABC. With Emmy's support, he quit a job that earned him almost $30,000 a year to take a six-week, two hundred-and-fifty dollar contract. Cosell's prospects horrified his father, who, until his death in 1957, pleaded with his daughter-in-law to convince Howard to return to the law. Indeed his son was an unusual figure in the broadcast ranks, in both appearance and behavior. Rather homely and balding, Cosell put on a toupee for his television broadcasts. As Myron Cope reported in a 1967 *Sports Illustrated* article, the toupee stayed in Cosell's coat pocket until he arrived at the studio. Cosell's voice, which would become widely imitated by entertainers and viewers, was nasal, harsh, and staccato. But if Cosell's first impression

paled in comparison to those of his more polished colleagues, he soon overshadowed them in his pursuit of sports stories.

When Cosell entered the profession, the "rip-and-read" style of sportscasting was common, in which the sportscaster read statistics and facts as provided by the wire services. Cosell, however, was determined to provide more commentary and in-depth coverage. He would become famous for telling viewers that he would "tell it like it is." For his radio programs, Cosell began taping interviews on location before the advent of the cassette recorder. That meant carrying a thirty-pound tape recorder on his back. Cope noted that such determined behavior was rare; he wrote, "Cosell's forward progress stems from the fact that, alone among sportscasters of national stature, he works at his trade. He goes out and looks for news and personalities, instead of waiting for gossip at Toots Shor's." Within a year, Cosell was appearing in *Sports Focus,* a commentary program on evening television that was introduced as a summer replacement for *Kukla, Fran, and Ollie.* In 1961 he was made the evening sports reporter on New York's WABC-TV. Soon thereafter Cosell began announcing boxing matches for ABC's *Wide World of Sports.* He was quickly making his way up the ladder at the network, despite the fact that he was disliked by some at ABC and faced racial prejudice as a Jew.

A big part of Cosell's success was his revolutionary use of the interview format. He asked difficult questions, as well as gave athletes the opportunity to make personal observations. He also created additional drama by using an accusatory tone. Chet Forte, a Columbia basketball star who would later work with Cosell as a producer for ABC, remembered Cosell telling him not to worry about what he would be asked in an interview. But as Forte recalled in *Sports Illustrated,* Cosell's first question was "Chet, is it true that some of your teammates hate to pass to you because you shoot so much?" He was also notorious for listening carefully to responses and pressing the interviewee to elaborate on ambiguous or half-hearted comments. Being interviewed by Cosell was often a daunting prospect. On other occasions, the sportscaster's unconventional style was a welcome change. Olympic gold medalist **Tommie Smith** went to Cosell after giving the "Black Power" salute on the medal stand in 1968, knowing that he would have a chance to comment on his highly controversial action. "He asked questions that gave a young athlete like myself enough space to say what I felt," Smith explained years later in *Multichannel News.*

Controversial Commentary

Cosell's most famous interviews were with Muhammad Ali. The verbally precocious pair developed a friendship that was strengthened by controversy. Cosell was the first sportscaster to call the heavyweight champion, originally known as Cassius Clay, by his new

Muslim name. This act alone was scandalous to many Americans. In 1967 when Ali refused for religious reasons to be drafted to fight in Vietnam, Cosell was irate about the New York State Boxing Commission taking away his championship. "What the government did to this man was inhuman and illegal under the Fifth and Fourteenth Amendments," he was quoted in a *Washington Post* obituary; "Nobody says a damned word about the professional football players who dodged the draft. But Muhammad was different; he was black and he was boastful." Some would discount the relationship between the two men by saying that Cosell knowingly rode to fame on Ali's coattails. Looking back decades later, essayist Stanley Crouch listed it among Ali's major accomplishments, asserting in *Time Atlantic* that "in his relationship with the Jewish sportscaster Howard Cosell, Ali realized the ongoing dream of our society—and perhaps the world—that people of different colors and religious backgrounds can disagree, taunt each other, support each other and at almost every point so purely recognize the humanity of each other that a transcendent friendship can emerge."

It was important for Cosell to show the same issues that trouble the world at large were also to be found inside sports. "I have sought to bring to the American people a sense of the athlete as a human being and not as a piece of cereal-box mythology," he told *Playboy*. He wanted dispel the idea that "sport is somehow different, that it's a privileged sanctuary from real life, a looking-glass world unto itself." Racism and drug use were two of the "real world" issues Cosell explored. The ABC radio sports director Shelby Whitfield commented in a *People* magazine retrospective, "When Howard came on the scene … no one criticized referees

or coaches or players or anybody. But he was a lawyer, and that went to the core of everything." Other legal issues that Cosell weighed in on were Curt Flood's challenge of baseball's reserve clause and the 1986 USFL lawsuit against the NFL.

Monday Night Football

When Roone Arledge made the daring move to broadcast NFL games in the evening, he chose Cosell as part of a three-man team of announcers. His presence drew a flood of hate mail from racist fans who despised his support of black athletes, but also increased the network's audience by 50 percent. The original *Monday Night Football* broadcasts featured play-by-play announcer **Frank Gifford** and color analyst Don Meredith, both former athletes, and Cosell. According to Bruce Newman in *Sports Illustrated*, Cosell's role was "blowhard" and that "for 14 seasons Cosell amused, amazed, outraged, annoyed and attracted audiences, building the Monday-night broadcast into something that was often bigger than the game itself." Dave Kindred explained in *Sporting News* how Cosell had transformed the broadcast: "Then on MNF came Cosell. With that Brooklyn nasal voice. That melodramatic delivery. All those opinions, many harsh, all made at great volume in tones brooking no argument. Cosell commanded attention." Thus a new phenomenon was born. *Monday Night Football* would go on to become the most successful show in prime-time history. It was also important in increasing the NFL's marketing edge over other sports, including major league baseball.

In a few years Cosell was probably the most recognizable man in America, according to Cosell's former producer Peter Bonventre. "You couldn't walk down the street anywhere with him and not have everybody know him—kids of 5 or 6 and little old ladies. They would scream, 'Howie, tell it like it is,'" Bonventre recalled in *People*. Cosell was all over the television and not just on sports programs. He acted as guest host on several popular programs, including *The Dick Cavett Show* and *The Tonight Show*. Among other appearances, Cosell was seen on the television series *The Odd Couple, The Flip Wilson Show,* and *Laugh-In,* and in the motion pictures *Sleeper* (1973) and *The World's Greatest Athlete* (1973). ABC even tried Cosell as the host of his own variety series in 1975; however, *Saturday Night Live with Howard Cosell* only lasted for half a season. In the late 1970s, a *TV Guide* poll rated Cosell as both the favorite and most-disliked sportscaster of the day.

Howard Cosell

Bars began holding contests during *Monday Night Football* in which the winner had the honor of throwing a brick through a television with Cosell's face on it. Following a 1970 World Series broadcast, the broadcaster's limousine was rocked by angry Baltimore fans until he was rescued by the police.

Criticism hurt Cosell deeply, but his responses did little to win him sympathy. When others derided him, he defended himself loudly, which drew still more criticism from within the industry. "There's one thing about this business: There is no place in it for talent. That's why I don't belong. I lack sufficient mediocrity," he once said in *Sports Illustrated*. His long-winded, accusatory, egotistical style appalled many sports reporters. He earned the nick names "The Mouth that Bored," "The Hanging Judge," and "The Martha Mitchell of Sportscasting." Sports columnist Jimmy Cannon was outraged that Cosell sold himself as a truth-teller and writer David Halberstam called him a bully. Such criticisms increased as the years passed and Cosell's ego grew, but as early as 1967 members of the press were pointing out his tendency to grandstand. "He asks better questions than the other radio and TV interviewers," *New York Daily News* columnist Dick Young was quoted in *Sports Illustrated;* "but he hokes up his questions so that they sound better than they are. 'Now truthfully'—it's always 'truthfully,' as if it's a question the guy on the other end has been ducking." Similarly, *New York Post* writer Larry Merchant observed that

Cosell made "the world of fun and games sound like the Nuremberg trials." Responding to such criticisms, Cosell would boastfully agree in *Cosell:* "Arrogant, pompous, obnoxious, vain, cruel, verbose, a showoff. I have been called all of these. Of course, I am."

Broken Ties

During the 1980s, Cosell's strong opinions eroded his presence on television. In 1982 he decided on the air that he would no longer announce boxing matches, while he watched Larry Holmes pulverize Randall "Tex" Cobb in a heavyweight title fight. Suddenly appalled by professional boxing's viciousness, he would later call for an end to the sport altogether. In 1984, he made an equally dramatic departure from *Monday Night Football,* calling it a "stagnant bore." This decision followed complaints about Cosell saying "look at that little monkey run" to describe black receiver Alvin Garrett in a Washington Redskins game. The remark was condemned as racist, despite Cosell's long record of supporting black athletes and the fact that he had previously used the same words regarding white players. Cosell created the sports newsmagazine *Sportsbeat* in 1985, which opened to strong reviews. The show was cancelled after just three months when Cosell released his autobiography, *I Never Played the Game,* a volume filled with negative appraisals of his ABC colleagues. He would never work in television again.

The rupture with ABC television left Cosell doing interviews and commentary on the radio. He was exceedingly bitter and, already reputed to be a heavy drinker, was said to be turning more frequently to alcohol. Sports writer Frank Deford suggested in *People* that Cosell did not sour until, after fifty-four years of marriage, his wife Emmy died in 1990. Emmy has been described as the one person to whom Howard would listen and, at home with their daughters Jill and Hilary, he was said to have been a different man, quiet and kind. In his book *Cosell,* he once wrote, "Emmy's my life.... I go nowhere without her. I wouldn't do 'Monday Night Football,' I wouldn't travel, I wouldn't cross the Triboro Bridge without Emmy." Both, his own health and his career faltered in her absence. A year after Emmy's death, Cosell had a cancerous tumor surgically removed from his chest and in 1992 he retired from broadcasting. His few remaining years were spent in near isolation.

Howard Cosell was seventy-seven when he died of a heart embolism at the Hospital for Joint Diseases in Manhattan on April 23, 1995. His death was met with an odd mix of responses, comprising both testimonies to his tremendous impact and a decided lack of emotion. William Nack noted in *Sports Illustrated,* "None inspired a sense of ambivalence that ran quite as deep and powerful as did Howard Cosell, in life and in death, and this was nowhere more evident than in the eulogies served up on Sunday with a side of ice." He described

Roone Arledge as being without emotion when he said, "Howard Cosell was one of the most original people to appear on American television.... He became a giant by telling the truth in an industry that was not used to hearing it and considered it revolutionary." An obituary writer for *The Economist* looked for Cosell's place in history and noted that "Mr Cosell's decline owed something to an early skirmish in the political-correctness wars," referring to his comment about Alvin Garrett. The writer concluded, "Probably, there will never be another sportscaster like him: not because he symbolized a bygone era, but because he was himself such an extraordinary human being. He was a genius, a braggart, a cynic and a boor. And if few tears were shed at his death, he will be missed just the same." A rare, warm comment came from filmmaker Woody Allen, who featured Cosell in several of his productions. He said in *Entertainment Weekly,* "He was in a class by himself as a sportscaster ... with an urgent voice, wit, and first-rate intelligence. And most importantly, he was his own man."

During the decade after Cosell's death several film projects reflected the high drama of Cosell's life. The HBO documentary *Howard Cosell: Telling it Like It Is* was both a tribute and an exploration of his great contradictions. The film detailed the kinds of discrimination that Cosell faced as a Jew during his childhood and television career. Interviews include Cosell's children, Muhammad Ali, comedian Billy Crystal, and colleagues from ABC televsion. Notably, sportscasters Frank Gifford and Al Michaels still had positive comments to make about Cosell despite his harsh treatment of them in his autobiography. As portrayed by actor Jon Voight, he was an important figure in the motion picture *Ali* (2001). Soon thereafter, TNT's cable-television movie *Monday Night Mayhem* (2002) was dominated by Cosell's presence as recreated by John Turturro. According to Dave Kindred in the *Sporting News,* the film proved that Cosell was "still news" seven years after his death. While the film is ostensibly about the larger issue of creating *Monday Night Football,* Kindred suggested that the film "succeeds because it gives us a Howard Cosell so complex as to be respected and despised, deplored and admired. Just as in life."

Time will tell how long Howard Cosell's notoriety will survive beyond living memory. He has been much imitated for comic effect but rarely emulated. When Bruce Newman reviewed Cosell's career in *Sports Illustrated* shortly before his death, he noted, "when Cosell decided to leave the broadcast booth after 38 years, he was still the only one doing whatever it was he did." Sportscaster Keith Olbermann would later echo this sentiment when he said in the *Sporting News,* "There have been doors opened, but we have not followed in Howard's lead.... We have not been the provocateurs ... not been the journalists that Howard demanded we should be."

Cosell's quotes and videotaped television appearances still shock, still interest, and still entertain. If he remains unchallenged as the most daring and outrageous of sportscasters, he has nevertheless set the standard for that title.

SELECTED WRITINGS BY COSELL:

Great Moments in Sport: A Sport Magazine Anthology, Macfadden-Bartell, 1964.
Cosell, Pocket Books, 1973.
I Never Played the Game, Morrow, 1985.
What's Wrong With Sports, 1991.

FURTHER INFORMATION

Books

Cosell, Howard. *Cosell.* New York: Pocket Books, 1974.
Newsmakers 1995, Issue 4. Detroit: Gale, 1995.
St. James Encyclopedia of Popular Culture. Detroit: St. James Press, 2000.

Periodicals

Cope, Myron. "Would You Let This Man Interview You?" *Sports Illustrated* (March, 21, 1994): 94.
Crouch, Stanley. "An American Original." *Time Atlantic* (January 28, 2002): 50.
Demenchuk, Michael. "HBO Documentary Tells It Like It Is." *Multichannel News* (October 25, 1999): 24.
Kindred, Dave. "Telling It Like It Was." *Sporting News* (January 21, 2002): 64.
Nack, William. "Telling It Like It Is." *Sports Illustrated* (May 1, 1995): 120.
Newman, Bruce. "Howard Cosell." *Sports Illustrated* (September 19, 1994): 104.
Playboy (May, 1972).
Plummer, William and Mary Huzinec. "The Mouth That Roared." *People* (May 8, 1995): 244.
Washington Post (April 24, 1995): A1, C1, C10.

Sketch by Paula Pyzik Scott

Bob Costas

Bob Costas
1952-

American sportscaster

Bob Costas has turned the broadcasting world upside down with his impeccable style. He is known for his ability to memorize trivial facts and insert them with precision timing when broadcasting. Costas is also known for his ability to hold his own when situations occur on a live broadcast. The thing he is most known for, however, is his love of baseball. Not the present baseball, but the heroic baseball of the past. Costas hopes that perhaps one day his children can see the kind of baseball he grew up listening to on the radio, and watching on a black and white screen.

Living and Breathing Baseball

Costas had early aspirations for becoming a broadcaster. Growing up listening to people like **Harry Caray** and **Howard Cosell** inspired him to walk in their paths. Costas stated in an article for the *Philadelphia Daily News:* "I always thought the broadcaster was as much a part of the game as the game itself." His father was a sports fan, which helped to fuel the fire. It was his father who taught Costas about baseball and shared his love for **Mickey Mantle**. Costas carries that admiration of

Chronology

1952	Born in Queens, New York
1970	Graduates from Commack South High School
1970	Enrolls in Syracuse University
1974	Lands job in Syracuse with WSYR-TV and Radio
1974	Hired to broadcast games in St. Louis at KMOX-AM
1976	Begins working freelance for CBS
1980	Moves to working for NBC
1982	Offered a job hosting NBC pre-game show called "NFL 82" which he declines
1983	Teams up with Tony Kubek to broadcast the for the national baseball game of the week
1983	Marries Randi Krummenmacher
1984	Offered and accepts a job hosting NBC pre-game show called "NFL 84"
1986	Welcomes his first child Keith into the world
1988	Breaks into commentating for the Summer Olympics in Seoul, South Korea
1988	Launches show *Later with Bob Costas*
1992	Broadcasts the Summer Olympics from Barcelona, Spain
1996	Broadcasts Olympics in Atlanta, Georgia
2000	Testifies before Senate Judiciary Committee talking about the revenue and competition gap between large market teams and small market teams in Major League Baseball
2000	Publishes his first book *Fair Ball: A Fan's Case for Baseball*
2001	Files for divorce from his wife Randi

Mantle with him to this day, symbolized by Mantle's 1958 baseball card he keeps in his wallet.

In Costas's senior year in high school, he applied to Syracuse University, because he knew that is where broadcast greats Marty Glickman and **Marv Albert** had gone to school. In 1970 he began attendance at Syracuse University as a journalism major. Stan Alten, one of Costas's professors, stated to *USA Today,* "Bob is one of those natural talents that doesn't come along that often, just like a great poet. When those come your way, the best thing to do is make sure you don't screw him up by trying to change his style." In 1974, his final year of college, Costas was offered a job at KMOX-AM. He had submitted an application with them using a tape he had doctored by turning up the base, as his voice at the time did not sound very mature. Costas never dreamed that the stunt would actually work. He packed up his things and left immediately to go become the voice for the St. Louis Spirits of the American Basketball Association. Broadcasting on KMOX-AM was a dream for Costas. He recalls picking up the signal on a good night when he was young, and listening to Harry Caray broadcast in his phenomenal fashion. Costas admitted to the *Rochester Times-Union,* "I thought I was in way over my head. I only hoped to be adequate enough not to embarrass myself."

Bigger and Better

Costas got himself noticed by the executives at CBS, as the broadcasting system was affiliated with KMOX. In 1976 he began doing freelance work for CBS, going on the air for basketball and football. In 1980, NBC took

---

Bob Costas

At the young age of 34, sportscaster Bob Costas was cited by his colleagues as the best in his profession. It was heady stuff for a guy who, just a decade earlier had doctored his radio audition tape so he would sound older. But Costas, combining a witty irreverence with top-notch reportage, mixing a deep affection for sports with an off-the-wall demeanor, was the hottest name in sports broadcasting by the mid-eighties. His style appealed to both old-timers and baby-boomers, earned him jobs broadcasting baseball and hosting football afternoons for NBC, and brought him a $550,000-a-year contract. "I would have been willing to pay my dues," he told *Sports Illustrated*. "But nobody ever made me."

Source: *Contemporary Newsmakers 1986*, Issue Cumulation. Gale Research, 1987.

Awards and Accomplishments

1985	Named Sportscaster of the Year by National Sportscasters and Writers Association

---

Costas on, where he again covered basketball and football, but truly longed to cover baseball. His life changed in many ways in the year of 1980, as it was also the year he met his wife, Randi. He was speaking to a classroom about broadcasting and ended up falling in love with the teacher. They eventually married in 1983. In 1983 he also began to work alongside Tony Kubek for the national baseball game of the week. Costas really admired Kubek, for his knowledge of the mechanics of the game. He shared with the *Detroit News:* "I lean toward anecdotes, interesting facts and statistics that illustrate a particular part of the game." Glad to be covering the game he loves, Costas admitted to *USA Today,* "Baseball is an ongoing love affair. All the other sports are one-night stands by comparison."

Not everyone likes Costas's style though. Many people tire of the endless facts he regurgitates during numerous broadcasts. Mike Weisman, an NBC producer, told *Sports Illustrated,* "I still think he is too talkative.... Instead of letting a thought sink in, he tends to hit the audience with another good point." Most people do embrace Costas's style, and the majority of his colleagues really admire his work. So much so, that in 1985 he was named the Sportscaster of the Year. Costas was honored to simply be nominated to run with some of his greatest idols, like Vin Scully and Dick Enberg. It was moments like that when he realized he was glad he stuck with his style, knowing it was different. Costas expressed to *Sports Illustrated,* "if you don't take a risk, you'll never be any good."

Challenges Broadcaster Stereotypes

The biggest cause Costas has championed is for the arena of professional baseball. He wrote a book on the topic to get people thinking and to throw out some of his own ideas for changes to the grand old game. A writer for Hollywood.com wrote that the book shows Costas "offering carefully considered views on the ramifications of the 1994 baseball strike." Jerry Gladman with the *Toronto Sun* surmises that "Costas has written this book solely as someone seeking solutions.... In the hopes someone is listening and can help return the game

to full health." Costas made his effort and will continue to pursue a better world for baseball.

Costas has challenged the broadcasting circuit to throw away the cookie cutter sportscasters. He has pushed for his colleagues to consider breaking out of their shells to bring life and vitality to the broadcast again. He doesn't want everyone to be like him, but does want to inspire fellow broadcasters to renew a passion for the sports they are reporting. Robert Bianco, reporting for *USA Today,* believes "Costas was everything you'd want in an anchor: smart and witty, without being intrusive or smug or losing his sense of occasion." Bianco continued, "Pay Costas whatever he wants."

CONTACT INFORMATION

Address: Bob Costas, c/o NBC Sports, 30 Rockefeller Plaza, New York, NY 10112.

SELECTED WRITINGS BY COSTAS:

Bob Costas on Sports. Bantam Doubleday Dell Publishing, 1997.
Fair Ball: A Fan's Case for Baseball. New York: Broadway Books, 2000.
St. Louis: For the Record (Urban Tapestry Series). Towery Publications, 2000.

FURTHER INFORMATION

Books

"Bob Costas." *St. James Encyclopedia of Popular Culture*. 5 vols. St. James Press, 2000.
"Bob Costas." *Contemporary Newsmakers 1986*. Issue Cumulation. Gale Research, 1987.

Periodicals

Berger, Jerry. "Bob Costas Says That He and His Wife, Randi, are Getting a Divorce." *St. Louis Post-Dispatch*. (August 31, 2001): A2.
Bianco, Robert. "How to Mine More Gold from the Olympics Mix in More Live Events, Ditch the Packaging - and keep Bob Costas." *USA Today,* (October 02, 2000): 01D.
"Bob Costas...Take two." *St. Louis Post-Dispatch,* (August 4, 1996): 04F.
Gladman, Jerry. "Costas Calls 'Em as He Sees 'Em." *Toronto Sun,* (May 13, 2001): S32

Thompson, Kevin. "For the Record, Costas Among the Best." *Palm Beach Post,* (February 11, 2001): 2J.

Walters, John. "Features/Atlanta 1996: Master of Ceremonies from the Center Spot On 'The Hollywood Squares' to Center Stage at the Atlanta Games - Bob Costas Makes it all Look Easy." *Entertainment Weekly,* (July 19, 1996): 30.

Other

"Bob Costas." MSNBC. http://www/msnbc.com/onair/bios/b_costas.asp. (January 4, 2003).

"Bob Costas." Hollywood.com. http://www.hollywood.com/celebs/bio/celeb/1673835. (January 4, 2003).

Costas, Bob. "Bob Costas' Eulogy for Mickey Mantle." http://members.aol.com/mindycpa/Eulogy.htm. (January 4, 2003).

Fendrich, Howard. "Costas to stay with NBC." AP Sports Writer. AP Online. (January 4, 2003).

Marin, Drake. "Bob Costas." The BOB COSTAS Page. http://drake.marin.k12.ca.us/students/friedmad/announce/Costas.html. (January 4, 2003).

McDermid, Brendan. "Bob Costas Appears Before the Senate Judiciary Committee." Reuters News Pictures Service. (November 11, 2000).

Sketch by Barbra J. Smerz

Jim Courier

Jim Courier
1970-

American tennis player

Jim Courier, arguably the world's best men's tennis player for one all-too-brief period in the early 1990s, has always managed to keep things in perspective. Although he has not been the toast of the tennis world since the beginning of the first Clinton administration, Courier, who won both the French Open and Australian Open twice, has found a comfortable role on and off the court. He is again involved with the game he once dominated, while still pursuing other passions such as rock music.

Despite retiring from competitive tennis in 2000 at age 29—following a successful 12-year career—the temperamental and tenacious Courier continues to stay in the public eye. Courier introduced himself to the newest generation of tennis fans in summer 2001 when he signed a multi-year deal with Turner Sports to work as a television analyst, initially covering Wimbledon. Courier, about a year later, increased his tennis world profile when he agreed to assist U.S. Davis Cup captain Patrick McEnroe.

Courier finished with a 506-237 record, 23 singles titles and the four Grand Slams. He earned more than $13.5 million in prize money and was ranked No. 1 in 1992. He also sported a 16-10 record in seven years in Davis Cup competition for the United States.

Raised in Florida

Courier had the benefit of working for responsive coaches. By age 11, he decided to forsake a promising Little League pitching career for tennis. He attended a tennis camp in Bardmoor, Florida, run by Harry Hopman, the successful coach of strong Australian Davis Cup teams in the 1950s and 1960s. Impressed by Courier's tenacity, Hopman convinced him to enroll for two years.

Growing up in Dade City, Florida, Courier was introduced to tennis by Emma Spencer, a great aunt who ran Dreamworld Tennis Club out of her home in Sanford. She was a former women's tennis coach at the University of Southern California. Courier inherited a strong arm from his father, an executive of a juice processing plant who had spent his college years pitching on a scholarship at Florida State University.

In 1986, Courier—a banger, not a finesse player—made good on Hopman's training and won the 14-and-under Orange Bowl championship, the World Series of junior tennis. That victory brought a invitation for Courier to train at the famed Nick Bollettieri Tennis Academy in Bradenton, Florida, a hothouse for budding American tennis stars such as **Andre Agassi** (the teacher's

---

Chronology

1970	Born August 17 in Sanford, Florida
1983-90	Trained at Nick Bollettieri's training camp in Bradenton, Florida
1988	Joins men's professional tennis tour
1990	Begins training with Jose Higueras
1992	Competes in Summer Olympic Games in Barcelona, Spain
1993	Loses French Open, Wimbledon finals; ranking drops to third
2000	Retires from competitive tennis
2001	Signs multi-year agreement with Turner Sports as analyst for Wimbledon coverage
2002	Named coach of U.S. Davis Cup team; Americans reach semifinals

Awards and Accomplishments

1986	Wins 14-and-under Orange Bowl championship, the World Series of junior tennis
1991	Ranked No. 2 among men worldwide at end of year
1991-92	Back-to-back French Open champion
1992	Ranked No. 1 most of year; named ATP Tour Player of the Year, Florida Pro Athlete of the Year and Jim Thorpe Player of the Year
1992	Competes on Davis Cup champion U.S. team
1992-93	Back-to-back Australian Open champion

pet and at one time Courier's roommate). Under Bollettieri's tutelage, Courier went on to win junior championships in 1986 and 1987, turning pro in 1988 at the Via del Mar Challenger event.

Soars to No. 1

When Courier dropped in rankings to No. 25 in the world in 1990, he teamed that November with Jose Higueras, then working with the U.S. Tennis Association player development program. Higueras, twice a French Open semifinalist, addressed the mental as well as physical parts of Courier's game. "Jose helped me see the game differently. He calmed me down a bit," Courier told the *New York Times*.

Courier became the world's top ranked tennis player for 58 weeks beginning on February 10, 1992, the peak of his career. "Are we surprised? Yes to put it mildly. You never allow yourself to look too far ahead. Even when he made the top 50, we didn't think of him becoming No. 1," Courier's father, Jim, told *The New York Times* when his son's top ranking was imminent.

His biggest victories were four Grand Slams, specifically the French Open in 1991 (defeating one-time camp roommate, Andre Agassi) and 1992 and the Australian Open in 1992 and 1993. He placed second in 1991 at the U.S. Open and at Wimbledon, as well as the 1993 French Open, which he captured the two prior years. "Courier is 110 days younger than Agassi, and he's nearly as crass, sassy and satorially dyslexic," *Sports Illustrated*'s Curry Kirkpatrick said in his report on the 1991 French Open final. Courier, whose record in Grand Slam matches was 118-38, also represented the United States in the 1992 Summer Olympic Games in Barcelona, Spain, and collected more than $13.5 million in prize money while on the professional circuit.

Dropoff in Play

However, his performance on the professional circuit fell into a steep, uncharacteristic dive following a strong start in 1993. Following the 1993 French Open in Paris, Courier "suddenly lost his edge. Despite taking frequent breaks to get his head and his game back together,

Courier rarely has been a threat during the last five years, although he did comeback somewhat to reach the world's eight ranking in 1995," Hickok Sports wrote. To resurrect his career, Courier in 1997 parted ways with longtime coach Jose Higueras and decided to train with Harold Solomon, a former Top 10 player later credited with saving the career of **Jennifer Capriati**.

Courier excelled late his career on the Davis Cup team. By winning the deciding fifth sets of five-set matches in 1998 and 1999, he became the first American to do so since the competition originated in 1900. Other noteworthy twilight career achievements include winning the U.S. Men's Clay Court Championship in 1998 and a quarterfinalist showing at the duMaurier Open in Canada in 1999. But about nine months later, on May 8, 2000, Courier announced that he was retiring from professional tennis.

After retiring, Courier became coach of the U.S. Davis Cup team. "I think the players are happy, especially the younger players, to have Jim Courier around and have his insight and experience. When he talks, they listen," U.S. Captain Patrick McEnroe told the Associated Press upon Courier's appointment. "We want the guys to do well individually, but this is about the U.S. team, and who better epitomizes what the team is about than Courier?" McEnroe asked rhetorically.

Brief but Noteworthy Reign

Courier's intensity may have contributed to the burnout that marked the beginning of his downfall. His reign at No. 1 was relatively brief, but noteworthy. Americans saw him as a standard-bearer, and one more than willing to represent his country in Davis Cup competition (an event some tennis stars avoid).

FURTHER INFORMATION

Periodicals

"For Courier, If It's Monday, It's Almost Time to be No. 1," *New York Times* (February 3, 1992).

Kirkpatrick, Curry. "It's Hammer Time." *Sports Illustrated* (June 17, 1991): 34-36.

Lidz, Franz. "Top Hat," *Sports Illustrated* (February 24, 1992).

Other

"Courier Glad to be Helping Out," Slam!Sports, http://www.canoe.ca, (January 20, 2003).

Courier, Jim. "Wimbledon Still Stirs the Emotion of Its Players," USA Today, http://www.usatoday.com, (July 3, 2001).

Hickok Sports, http://www.hickoksports.com, (January 20, 2003).

"Jim Courier Biographical Essay." Biography Resource Center, http://galenet.galegroup.com, (January 20, 2003).

"Jim Courier Leaves Tennis." WBUR-FM, http://www.onlyagame.com, (May 11, 2000).

Jim Courier Profile, http://www.davidfosterfoundation.org, (January 21, 2003).

"Turner Sports Names Jim Courier Wimbledon Television Analyst," CNN-Sports Illustrated, http://www.sportsillustrated.cnn.com, (August 9, 2001).

Sketch by Paul Burton

Margaret Smith Court

Margaret Smith Court
1942-

Australian tennis player

Australian Margaret Smith Court was a dominant woman's tennis player in the 1960s and early 1970s. Over the course of her career, she won a total of sixty-two Grand Slam women's singles events, more than anyone in the history of women's tennis, and seventy-nine total singles titles. The first Australian to win Wimbledon, Court won the second Grand Slam in women's singles in 1970. (**Maureen Connolly** did it in 1953, when it was an all amateur affair). Court also won mixed doubles Grand Slam in 1963. She was the only player to win a Grand Slam in both singles and in doubles. In the days before big prize money, however, Court only earned about a half million dollars for her professional victories.

Court's amazing success led to her becoming the first female tennis player from Australia who had a following. She was known for her great fitness, athleticism, and endurance, and had a game that featured a dominant forehand, good volleying skills, and an attacking style of play. Though her game spoke volumes, Court herself was somewhat media shy and she did not really seek publicity. As Bud Collins and Zander Hollander wrote in *Bud Collins'*

Modern Encyclopedia of Tennis, "For sheer strength of performance and accomplishment there has never been a tennis player to match Margaret Smith Court."

Court's background was not indicative of her future success. Born on July 16, 1942, in Albury, New South Wales, Australia, she was the youngest of four children born into a working class family. Her father worked in a cheese and butter processing plant as a foreman. No one in her family was interested or played the game of tennis (though two siblings were competitive cyclists), though they lived opposite Border Tennis Association.

Early Interest in Tennis

When Court was a child, about age eight or so, she would sneak into the club using empty courts. Her first racquet was a used piece of equipment given to her by a neighbor. She, sometimes with other children in the neighborhood, would play on the courts until they were kicked out. This happened repeatedly until Court was about ten years old.

By that time, Wally Rutter, the owner of the club (or janitor according to some sources), gave Court a membership and tennis lessons. He and his wife had no children, and gave the young self-motivated athlete what her parents could not. When she became old enough, Court also worked there part time to earn her court time.

Chronology

1942	Born July 16 in Albury, New South Wales, Australia
1961	Becomes professional tennis player
1966-68	Briefly retires as professional tennis player
1967	Marries Barry Court on October 28
1968	Returns to professional tennis
1971-72	Misses parts of seasons to have child
1977	Retires as a professional tennis player
1991	Ordained as a minister

Related Biography: Coach Frank Sedgman

The coach who had arguably the most influence on Court's development as a young player was Frank Sedgman. Sedgman had had a great playing career of his own in the 1940s and 1950s, when events were all amateur. He was a great volleyer with a strong forehand. He won a number of Grand Slam Events, including the Australian Open men's singles titles in 1949-50 and doubles in 1951-52, Wimbledon singles in 1952 and doubles in 1948, 1951, and 1952, the U.S. Open singles in 1951-52 and doubles in 1950-51, and the French Open doubles in 1951-52. He also represented Australia in Davis Cup play from 1949-52, leading his country to victory over the United States in 1950. Sedgman played professional tennis in the 1950s and 1960s, and played on a Grand Masters (senior) tour in the 1970s. He was inducted in the International Tennis Hall of Fame in 1979.

Even at an early age, Court showed promise as a tennis player. She could hit harder than any girl, and repeatedly won many tournaments for her age groups. Tennis was not her only focus. She often played sports with boys, including cricket and soccer, as well as basketball and softball.

Court was not only a gifted tennis player, but a track star in the 400 meter and 800 meter races. As a teenager, she was in training to be on the Australian Olympic team for the 400 meter and 800 meter races, but gave them up because she believed that the training was negatively affected her tennis game. By the time she was fifteen, had won sixty trophies for tennis.

Trained in Melbourne

By the time Court was in her late teens, Rutter and the local coaches believed that she needed better training. To that end, they contacted world champion Frank Sedgman who had a club in Melbourne, Australia. With her parents' approval, Court moved there and began training with him and other members of his staff. To pay for the training, she worked as a receptionist for the squash courts and gymnasium.

Sedgman and his group gave Court a wide-range of training experiences. Stan Nicholls worked with her inherent athletic ability to give her more fitness than had often been seen in female athletes of the time. Coach Keith Rogers helped her with her strokes. Sedgman worked on tactics and the game as a whole.

The tennis game Court and her coaches developed relied on her athleticism. She had strong volleying abilities, in part because of her childhood days playing with boys. She also played an attacking game that relied on her serve and volley, only using ground strokes when needed. She had a great serve, which she worked on, as well as endurance. The most unusual aspect of the game they developed was playing tennis right-handed, though she was left-handed, something done to a number of lefties in this era.

Early Victories

When Court was seventeen years old, she lost in the finals of the Australian Junior Open Championship, but she also made the finals of the main draw, the Australian Open. Thus, Court won her first Grand Slam (defeating Jan Lehane) when she was only seventeen years and six months old. She was the youngest to ever win the Australian Open.

Court was still an amateur, and though she could have gone to Europe and played on the women's tennis circuit, she did not think she had the stamina nor the speed yet. After winning in the Australian Open, she played in New Zealand and did not do well. For the next year, she worked harder in her training and learned how to deal with the press despite her shyness.

Turned Professional

In 1961, Court won her second Australian Open, against defeating Lehane. She also won the women's doubles championship there. After the victory, Court turned professional, and was able to travel abroad for the first time. She did not go alone or with her family, but with several other Australian women tennis players under the captaincy of Nell Hopman.

In her first year, Court did not do exceptionally well. Though she won the Kent All-Comers Championship, defeating Ann Haydon, she also lost in the quarterfinals of the French Open and Wimbledon. She suffered from nervousness and was not prepared. She also had problems with the schedule and the rules Hopman dictated. The following year, Court refused to travel with them in the 1962 season. Instead, she traveled with an American player and had two friends serve as chaperones. This situation created tension with the official Australian team, but led to more victories for Court.

In 1962, Court won both the women's singles and doubles championship at the Australian Open, the women's singles title at the French Open, and the women's singles and mixed doubles title at the U.S. Open. Her only failure came at Wimbledon where she lost in the first round to Billie Jean Moffitt (later known as **Billie Jean King**). This was the first year that Court was ranked the number one player in the world. (Court was ranked number one in 1963-65, 1969-70, and 1973.).

Awards and Accomplishments

1960	Women's singles championship at Australian Open—youngest woman to win title
1961	Women's singles championship and women's doubles championship at Australian Open; mixed doubles championship at U.S. Open; Kent All-Comers Championship
1962	Women's singles championship and mixed doubles championship at U.S. Open; women's singles championship at French Open; women's singles championship and women's doubles championship at Australian Open
1963	Women's singles championship at Wimbledon; women's singles championship and women's doubles championship at Australian Open; women's double championship at U.S. Open; mixed doubles Grand Slam (with Ken Fletcher)
1963-65, 1969-70, 1973	Ranked number one in world
1964	Women's singles championship, women's doubles championship, and mixed doubles championship at French Open; women's singles championship and mixed doubles championship at Australian Open; mixed doubles championship at U.S. Open; women's double championship at Wimbledon; helped Australia win Federation Cup
1965	Women's singles championship, women's doubles championship, and mixed doubles championship at Wimbledon; women's singles championship and mixed doubles championship at U.S. Open; women's singles championship and women's doubles championship at Australian Open; women's doubles championship and mixed doubles championship at French Open; helped Australia win Federation Cup
1966	Women's singles championship at Australian Open; women's doubles championship at French Open; mixed doubles championship at Wimbledon
1968	Women's double championship at U.S. Open; mixed doubles championship at Wimbledon; helped Australia win Federation Cup
1969	Women's singles championship and mixed doubles championship at U.S. Open; women's singles championship and mixed doubles championship at French Open; women's singles championship and women's doubles championship at Australian Open; women's doubles championship at Wimbledon
1970	Women's singles championship at Wimbledon; women's singles championship, women's double championship, and mixed doubles championship at U.S. Open; women's singles championship at French Open; women's double championship at Australian Open
1971	Women's singles championship and women's doubles championship at Australian Open; helped Australia win Federation Cup
1972	Mixed doubles championship at U.S. Open
1973	Women's singles championship and women's double championship at U.S. Open; women's singles championship and women's double championship at French Open; women's singles championship and women's doubles championship at Australian Open
1975	U.S. Open doubles championship; mixed doubles championship at Wimbledon
1979	Inducted into the Tennis Hall of Fame
1986	Inducted into the Women's Sports Hall of Fame

Won Mixed Doubles Grand Slam

In 1963, Court avenged her loss to King at Wimbledon, defeating her for the victory. This was the first time an Australian won the tournament. King became Court's main rival throughout her career, and whenever Court was not ranked number one, King was. While Court also

won women's singles at the Australian Open in 1963 and was the number one ranked woman, the year was important because she completed a Grand Slam in mixed doubles with Ken Fletcher. They won the Australian, French, and U.S. Opens as well as Wimbledon in one calendar year.

Despite her tensions with the other Australian players, Court was emerging as a dominant force. To that end, she agreed to begin playing for Australia in Federation Cup play in 1963. Though Australia lost to the United States in the final round that year, Court helped Australia win the Fed Cup in 1964, 1965, 1968, and 1971.

In the mid-1960s, Court continued to win multiple Grand Slam championships in women's singles and doubles as well as mixed doubles. She repeated her victory at Wimbledon in 1965, defeating rival King, as well as at the U.S. Open and the Australian Open, but lost in the finals of the French Open to Lesley Turner.

Retired Briefly from Tennis

After reaching the finals of women's singles and winning the mixed doubles tournament at Wimbledon in 1966, Court decided to retire. For the previous year or two, she had become bored by tennis, the practice, and the travel. Court had won everything and found she no longer needed to compete. Instead she decided to make up for the fun she missed as a teenager.

Court returned home to Western Australia. She lived in Perth with a friend and opened a boutique named Peephole. Tennis was the furthest thing from her mind, though she did learn how to play squash. She also was married to Barry Court, a wealthy wool broker, yachtsman, whose father was a politician, in 1967, and became known Margaret Smith Court.

Returned to Professional Tennis

It was Court's husband who sparked her interest in returning to tennis. She wanted to show him her life in tennis around the world. Court began training hard and returned to the circuit in 1968. Though it took a while for her to regain her form, Court was not as nervous as she had been in the first part of her career. She did not win a singles title until 1969, when she won the Australian, U.S., and French Opens, but lost Wimbledon in the finals to Ann Jones.

The best year of Court's career came in 1970, when she won the women's singles titles in all four Grand Slam events and eighteen of twenty-five tournaments she entered. She was only the second woman ever to win the women's singles Grand Slam. The hardest victory was Wimbledon, where she again faced King in the finals. Court injured her ankle in her quarterfinal match against Helga Niessen, and suffered through the semifinals to make the finals. The final match lasted a record forty-six games and 148 minutes with Court winning 14-12, 11-9. Court was not the only one in pain; King had cramps too. Observers later believed that this was one of the best matches played by two women ever. Nerves became an issue at the last tournament in the slam, the U.S. Open. She defeated **Rosemary Casals**, 6-2, 2-6, 6-1.

Though Court remained dedicated to her tennis career. She missed parts of the 1971 and 1972 season because she had a baby, but returned in late 1972 to win the mixed doubles championship at the U.S. Open. While she won both women's singles and doubles championships at the Australian, French, and U.S. Opens in 1973, that year she made what she considered a big mistake in her career.

Lost Battle of the Sexes

In 1973, Court accepted the challenge to play male tennis player Bobby Riggs. King had already turned him down. Riggs, who was fifty-five years old at the time, had won Wimbledon in 1939 and believed that any male tennis player could beat the best woman tennis player in the world because men were superior to women. The match was a television event that would benefit charity.

Court agreed to play Riggs because she did not believe King was the best player of the time. However, she did not take the match seriously, was ill-prepared for the kind of game Riggs played, and lost badly 6-2, 6-1. She was not sure why she lost. She later told Jon Henderson of the *Observer,* "I wasn't ready for the showbiz side of it which I would have been if I'd played team tennis by then. I was used to playing at places like Wimbledon where you could hear a pin drop." The loss was embarrassing, though King later beat Riggs.

Despite the Riggs fiasco, 1973 turned out to be the last best year of Court's career. She won eighteen of twenty-five tournaments she entered. Her last victory in a Grand Slam event came in 1975, when she won the U.S. Open doubles championship. When she became pregnant with her third child in 1977, Court decided to permanently retire from professional tennis.

Margaret Smith Court

Over the course of their rivalry, Court won twenty-two of thirty-two matches against King, who nicknamed her "The Arm." She might have won more championships overall if she had not had her problem with nerves. As Gwilym S. Brown wrote in *Sports Illustrated* in 1970, of Court's strong tennis game, "It is powerful, destructive, relentless and seemingly without a flaw. Definitely not on the sweet side. She is a superbly athletic animal, the physical equal of a great many men, but determination is really Margaret Court's chief trademark. For almost 10 years ... this passion to excel has made her the dominating figure in women's tennis."

CONTACT INFORMATION

Address: c/o Victory Life Centre, PO Box 20, Osborne Park, Western Australia 6917 Australia; c/o Margaret Court Ministries, 37 Florence Rd., Nedlands, Western Australia 6009 Australia.

SELECTED WRITINGS BY COURT:

(With Don Lawrence) *The Margaret Smith Story, as Told to Don Lawrence,* S. Paul, 1965.
(With George McGunn) *Court on Court, a Life in Tennis,* Dodd, Mead, 1975.

FURTHER INFORMATION

Books

Arnold, John, and Deidre Morris, eds. *Monash Biographical Dictionary of 20th Century Australia.* Reed Reference Publishing, 1994.

Athletes and Coaches of Summer. Detroit: Macmillan Reference USA, 2000.

Christensen, Karen, et al., eds. *International Encyclopedia of Women and Sports.* New York: Macmillan Reference USA, 2001.

Collins, Bud, and Zander Hollander, eds. *Bud Collins' Modern Encyclopedia of Tennis.* Detroit: Gale, 1992.

Davidson, Owen, and C. M. Jones. *Great Women Tennis Players.* Pelham Books, 1971.

Johnson, Anne Janette. *Great Women in Sports.* Detroit: Visible Ink Press, 1996.

Parry, Melanie, ed. *Chambers Biographical Dictionary.* Chambers, 1997.

Periodicals

Brown, Gwilym S. "Fierce lass in quest of an elusive title." *Sports Illustrated* (September 14, 1970): 94.

"A powerful athlete subject to jitters." Agence France Presse (December 6, 1999).

"Youngest female grand slam champions." *USA Today* (June 11, 1990): 7C.

Other

"Frank Sedgman." International Tennis Hall of Fame. http://www.tennisfame.org/enshrinees/frank_sedgman.html (January 5, 2003).

"Margaret Court." http://www.aftour10s.com/aftour10s%20web/archives/margaret_court (January 1, 2003).

"Margaret Smith Court, 1979 Enshrinee: International Tennis Hall of Fame." International Tennis Hall of Fame. http://www.tennisfame.org/enshrinees/margaret_smith.html (January 1, 2003).

"Who2 Profile: Margaret Smith Court." Who2. http://www.who2.com/margaretsmithcourt.html (January 1, 2003).

"Word of God is holding Court." Guardian.com. http://www.guardian.co.uk/Print/0,3858,4036131,00.html (January 1, 2003).

Sketch by A. Petruso

Bob Cousy
1928-

American basketball player

Bob Cousy

Bob Cousy was one of greatest passers and playmakers in NBA history. A showman with flair and an entertainer as much as he was a basketball player, Cousy was a renegade in an era of rather conventional league play. He helped to build one of the revolutionary teams in the history of professional basketball. His contribution is as great as—if not greater than—any other single player who helped the Boston Celtics dominate the 1950s and 1960s. Cousy cared about basketball. He was the catalyst that turned the game into the popular modern spectacle that fans know it as today.

Growing Up

Bob Cousy was born August 9, 1928, to Joseph and Julliette Cousy, poor French immigrants who lived on Manhattan's East side. Cousy grew up a "ghetto rat," and while young played stickball and boxball and stole hubcaps for some occasional quick change.

Eventually his father was able to save up $500 from his job driving a cab and working for an airline, and the family moved into their own house in the St. Alban's neighborhood of Queens, Long Island. His mother worked days as a secretary and language teacher, and to keep himself occupied after school, Cousy discovered the game of basketball. Though early on he would have some basketball disappointments, getting cut twice from the Andrew Jackson High School junior varsity team.

Chronology

1928	Born August 9 to Joseph and Julliette Cousy
1940	Moves from Manhattan to St. Albans, Queens
1941	Learns the game of basketball for first time
1941	Breaks arm in fall from tree; learns how to dribble and shoot with other arm
1942	Invited back on high school team by coach
1945-46	Wins city scoring championship as a high school senior
1946	Enters Holy Cross as scholarship player
1947-48	Becomes known as one of best-known players in college basketball
1949-50	Plays on Holy Cross team that wins 26 straight games
1950	Graduates from Holy Cross with a B.S. in business
1950	Drafted in first round by Tri-Cities Blackhawks, traded immediately to Chicago Stags; ends up with Boston Celtics when Stags disband
1950-51	Helps Celtics improve from one of worst teams to a team with a winning record
1956	Becomes first NBA player to appear on cover of *Sports Illustrated*
1956-57	Wins first NBA Championship with the Celtics
1962-63	Retires from game at age 35
1963	Takes position as head coach of Boston College, where he remains until 1969
1969	Hired by Cincinnati Royals (later the Kansas City Kings). Plays for one season as player coach
1974	Retires from coaching
1974	Begins long run as color commentator for the Celtics
1974-79	Serves as commissioner of the American Soccer League
1989	Named president of Boston Celtics
1994	Appears in movie *Blue Chips*, a film about corruption in recruitment of college basketball players

Related Biography: Basketball Player K.C. Jones

K.C. Jones was an integral member of the Boston Celtics during their reign over professional basketball in the 1950s and 1960s. With Bob Cousy as their conductor, Jones, who played on the U.S. Olympic basketball team in 1956, was a welcome addition to a glorious supporting cast that included his college teammate, roommate, and best friend Bill Russell, Tommy Heinsohn, Frank Ramsey and Jim Loscutoff. He helped make an already-dominant Celtics team even more so.

Born on May 25, 1932, in Tyler, Texas, Jones was a bit suspicious of basketball as a child. But when his father abandoned the family, Jones's mother moved to San Francisco, where Jones would play every day at the recreation center. When he got into high school, he broke the Triple A prep league scoring record, and earned All-Star football honors.

Known for his deadly set shot on the basketball court, Jones was a master at passing the ball, and his constant hustle wore opponents down. He never stood still. After he retired, Jones would first work as an assistant coach at Harvard, then move on to coach the Washington Bullets. He eventually moved back to his basketball home, taking the helm of the Celtics in 1983. He led the team to two World Championships.

As a head coach, K.C. Jones won 522 regular season games and finished with a .647 winning percentage.

K.C. Jones was elected into the Basketball Hall of Fame in 1983.

The Incident

There seems to be one pivotal moment or incident for most professional athletes, that time from which they can pinpoint their rise into greatness. Cousy is no exception. In what seems like the biography of a superhero, one afternoon when Cousy was thirteen, he fell from a tree and broke his right arm. Never dissuaded after being cut from the high school team, he still practiced daily. Since he was right-handed, he learned to dribble and shoot with his left. That season, when coach Lou Grummond saw Cousy played equally as well with either hand, he asked him to come back on the team—the high school team lacked a guard who could make important plays, and Cousy, able now to go either way and confuse opponents, fit the bill.

His rise to prominence happened quickly. In only a year and a half on the varsity squad, Cousy became something of a local celebrity. As a senior, he won the city scoring championship and helped lead his team to one of their best seasons.

The College Years

After seeing his success on the high school court, Holy Cross, a smaller school in Worcester, Massachusetts—less than an hour's drive from Boston—offered him a scholarship. This was in 1946, and in 1946 the style of basketball that was played at both the college and pro levels was not like it is today. The teams were much slower, playing a methodical and deliberate ball, their shots of choice typically were two-handed set shots.

But that was not Cousy's style of play, and Holy Cross was not ready for what Coach Alvin "Doggie" Julian saw as "showboating." Holy Cross was a powerful school, and they won the national championship in the 1946-47 season—without Cousy as a starter. He would win the spot his second year, but the coach, still fearful of his hotdogging, limited his playing time.

Given the circumstances, Cousy considered transferring, but the coach at St. John's actually convinced Cousy to stay at Holy Cross. He would be given his opportunity in a game against Loyola of Chicago played at Boston Garden (Holy Cross had an old, small gym). With less than five minutes left, Holy Cross was trailing. The crowd was aware of Cousy's style, and they enjoyed watching him play. They began chanting "We want Cousy! We want Cousy!" The coach had no choice left. Cousy was put into the game, and in the last few minutes of play, Cousy scored eleven points. He topped it off by putting down a buzzer-beating lefthanded hook, moving past a much larger player with his behind-the-back-dribble.

Cousy would earn All-American status three times while in college. He became the biggest name in college hoops. Under Cousy's floor leadership, Holy Cross won twenty-six straight games.

Cousy graduated in 1950 with a degree in business, but he would be known as one of the standout college players to ever come through the system.

Career Statistics

Yr	Team	GP	MIN	PTS	FGM	FGA	FG%	FTM	FTA	FT%	AST	PF
50-51	BOS	69	—	1078	401	1138	.352	276	365	.756	341	185
51-52	BOS	66	2681	1433	512	1388	.369	409	506	.808	441	190
52-53	BOS	71	2945	1407	464	1320	.352	479	587	.816	547	227
53-54	BOS	72	2857	1383	486	1262	.385	411	522	.787	518	201
54-55	BOS	71	2747	1504	522	1316	.397	460	570	.807	557	165
55-56	BOS	72	2767	1356	440	1223	.360	476	564	.844	642	206
56-57	BOS	64	2364	1319	478	1264	.378	363	442	.821	478	134
57-58	BOS	65	2222	1167	445	1262	.353	277	326	.850	463	136
58-59	BOS	65	2403	1297	484	1260	.384	329	385	.855	557	135
59-60	BOS	75	2588	1455	568	1481	.384	319	403	.792	715	146
60-61	BOS	76	2468	1378	513	1382	.371	352	452	.779	587	196
61-62	BOS	75	2114	1175	462	1181	.390	251	333	.754	584	135
62-63	BOS	76	1975	1003	392	988	.397	219	298	.735	515	175
TOTAL		917	30,131	16,955	6167	16,465	.375	4621	5753	.803	6945	2231

BOS: Boston Celtics.

Basketball or The Road?

It wasn't a foregone conclusion that Cousy would play professional basketball. The salary wasn't all that much, and Cousy could have easily made more money putting his business degree to use. In addition to entering the draft, he also contemplated opening up a driving school. Cousy opted to try his luck with the draft, and was picked up by Tri-Cities Blackhawks. He was then traded to the Chicago Stags, but that team folded before the season ever began.

A new team, however, the Boston Celtics, had been playing for three years in the Basketball Association of America, but had recently joined the NBA in the 1949-50 season. Since they had finished last in the eastern division, they were the team with the first pick in draft. They had not, however, chosen Cousy. When the Stags folded, Cousy's name, along with two other players, was thrown into a hat. The Celtics wound up with him anyway, with a contract for $9,000 a year.

In his first year with the Celtics, they had a winning record. Cousy averaged 15.6 points and 4.9 assists per game. People were drawn from all over the New England coast to the Garden to watch Cousy and his style of play. Just as in college, however, Celtics' coach **Arnold "Red" Auerbach** was not yet sold on the Cousy showmanship, but it was hard to overlook his excellent timing, outstanding reflexes and deft touch.

By his third season, Cousy would win his first of eight straight assists titles, averaging 7.7 assists per game (remarkable in an era before the shot clock). In Game two of the 1952-53 season's division semifinals against the Syracuse Nationals, Cousy played a game that would become one of the most talked-about of his career. With a bad leg giving him trouble, he scored twenty-five points in regulation, tying the game at seventy-seven with a free throw. In the first overtime, he scored six of the team's nine points, then in the second extra period, scored all four points for the Celtics. In a game that didn't seem to want to end, Cousy found eight points in the third overtime, tying it yet again with a twenty-five-foot jumper in the final seconds.

Down 104-99 in the fourth overtime, The Cooz put in five straight points, and the Celtics would finally defeat the Nationals 111-105 in a game that went three hours and eleven minutes. Cousy finished with fifty points, including a record setting thirty free throws in thirty-two attempts.

The Dominant Era

As the fifties progressed, the Celtics acquired a supporting cast that would become one of the most fabled in NBA history, adding the likes of **Bill Russell**, Tommy Heinsohn, K.C. Jones, Frank Ramsey, and Jim Loscutoff to a team that was already dominant. Although the Celtics won the 1956-57 NBA Championship, their first ever, they would lose the next year to the St. Louis Hawks. However, it would be the last time any team but the Celtics would touch the title for the next eight years, all helped in part by Cousy's masterful performances.

"Cooz was the absolute offensive master," Heinsohn told the Boston Herald in 1983. He was known as the "Houdini of the Hardwood. What Russell was on defense, that's what Cousy was on offense—a magician. Once that ball reached his hands, the rest of us just took off, never bothering to look back. We didn't have to. He'd find us. When you got into a position to score, the ball would be there."

After his retirement, Cousy coached for Boston College, leading them to a 117-38 record over six years, but he grew to hate the recruiting game, and feeling that he

Awards and Accomplishments

1951	NBA Rookie of the Year Award
1952-61	All-NBA First Team
1953	Set playoff record for most free throws made (30) and attempted (32)
1953-60	Led NBA in assists
1954, 1957	NBA All-Star Game Most Valuable Player
1957	NBA Most Valuable Player
1959	Single game record for most assists (19) in one half
1962-63	All-NBA Second Team
1970	Inducted into Basketball Hall of Fame
1974	All-NBA Silver Anniversary Team
1984	All-NBA 35th anniversary team
1999	ESPN selects Cousy as #94 on Sports Century top 100 athletes list
1999	All-NBA 50th anniversary team

Bob Cousy

could do more elsewhere, left after the 1968-69 season to join the pro ranks as coach of the Cincinnati Royals. He remained with the team until 1974, and even returned to the court as a player for seven games in his first year as coach.

The Cousy Legacy

Cousy retired at age thirty-five. The last game ceremony has since become known as "the Boston Tear Party," with a sold out Garden sitting in rapt silence as Cousy spoke his final farewell. In 1960, as Cousy was winding down his career, former Knicks coach Joe Lapchick said Cousy was the best player he'd ever seen. Celtics owner Walter Brown told a Boston Newspaper that "the Celtics wouldn't be here without him. If he had played in New York, he would have been as big as **Babe Ruth**. I think he is anyway."

He left the team having scored 16,955 points (18.5 points per game), 6,945 assists (7.6 assists per game), and an .803 free-throw percentage in 917 games. In 109 playoff games he averaged 18.5 points and 8.6 assists. In thirteen All-Star Games the two-time game MVP averaged 11.3 points and 6.6 assists. He has since been named to the NBA's 25th, 35th, and 50th Anniversary teams. In 1970 he was inducted into the Basketball Hall of Fame. Bob Cousy would be the first NBA player to appear on the cover of *Sports Illustrated*. In 1999, ESPN selected Cousy as #94 on the Sports Century top 100 athletes list.

When he retired from the Celtics in 1963, he was making $30,000 a year. He went out at what appeared to be the top of his game. Fans thought he had many more years left in him, and he probably did. But he told Tom Callahan of *Time* magazine, "I was very conscious of my skills eroding ... The minute there is even a subtle diminishment of legs, you're the first to know. I became aware of when I should stop wanting the ball in key situations. For a couple of years, I decoyed myself at those moments, making

sure Sam Jones, Tommy Heinsohn—or whoever—ended up with the shot." Cousy opted to retire when he did because, as a man with a degree in business hanging on his wall, he knew something about marketing himself after basketball, something that agents do for players these days but which Cousy would have to do by himself to earn a living. "I knew I'd be exploiting this notoriety for 20 years," he said. "If it had been $300,000, chances are I would have played until 1969."

Bob Cousy was one of the greatest passers and playmakers in NBA history. A showman with flair and an entertainer as much as a basketball player, Cousy was a renegade in an era of rather conventional league play. He helped to build one of the most revolutionary teams in the history of professional basketball. His contribution is as great as—if not greater than—any other single player who helped the Boston Celtics dominate the 1950s and 1960s. Cousy drew audiences to the arenas where a new and struggling NBA was trying to get off the ground. Watching Cousy was fun, and the fans wanted fun, not fundamentals. He was the catalyst that turned the game into the popular modern spectacle that fans know it as today.

CONTACT INFORMATION

Address: Bob Cousy, c/o CMG Worldwide, 8560 Sunset Boulevard 10th Floor Penthouse, West Hollywood, CA 90069.

FURTHER INFORMATION

Books

"Bob Cousy." *Encyclopedia of World Biography Supplement, Volume 21*. Detroit: Gale, 2001.

Hickock, Ralph. *The Encyclopedia of North American Sports History*. New York: Facts on File, 1992.

Ryan, Bob. *The Boston Celtics: The History, Legends, and Images of America's Most Celebrated Team*. New York: Addison-Wesley Publishing Co, 1989.

Periodicals

"Bob Cousy spans the ages." Knight Ridder/Tribune News Service (February 8, 1997).

Boston Globe (May 26, 1999).

Boston Globe (August 27, 1999).

Entertainment Weekly (March 4, 1984).

"Just one more season: if legs go first, how soon will pride follow?" *Time* (December 24, 1984).

MacMullan, Jackie. "Catching up with . . . Boston Celtics guard Bob Cousy." *Sports Illustrated*, (November 11, 1996): 4.

Other

"NBA Legends: Bob Cousy." http://www.nba.com/history/cousybio_html/ (November 6, 2002).

"The Official Bob Cousy Webpage." http://www.cmgww.com/sports/cousy/ (November 6, 2002).

Schwartz, Larry, "Celtics tried to pass on ultimate passer." *ESPN.com*. http:/espn.go.com/sportscentury/features/00014144.html/ (November 6, 2002).

Sketch by Eric Lagergren

Tom Curren
1964-

American surfer

Tom Curren was the American surfing icon of the 1980s. As the first American to find success on the Australian-dominated Association of Surfing Professionals tour, he gave hope to hundreds of young would-be competitors across the country. Between his fame, his success, and his clean-living Christian lifestyle, Curren was a role model for thousands of young surfers.

The First Legendary Curren

Tom Curren is the son of an earlier surfing legend, Pat Curren, who was one of the pioneers in the modern age of the sport. The elder Curren started surfing in California in 1950, at the age of eighteen. In 1955 Curren moved to Hawaii to surf the larger waves of the North Shore of the island of Oahu. He continued to shape surfboards there as he had in California, but the larger surf required a different style of board. Curren's designs, known as Elephant Guns since they were designed for hunting the biggest waves, had more of a rocker or curve than standard boards and went very quickly. Curren also made a name for himself in Hawaii for being one of six men who pioneered surfing in the Waimea part of the island, where the waves can be particularly dangerous.

In 1961 Pat Curren married a surfer named Jeanine. A year later the two of them moved to Santa Barbara, California, where Jeanine ran a bikini shop and Pat made a living by shaping surfboards, diving for abalone, and designing bikinis for Jeanine's shop. Tom Curren, the first of their three children, was born in 1964, and almost as soon as he could walk he was in the water. He got his first surfboard, a present from his father, when he was six. But Pat was discontented with this domesticated life, and eventually he and Jeanine began to fight. Tommy, caught in the middle, began drinking, running away, and smoking marijuana as a sixth- and seventh-grader. Jeanine, at her wits end, hardly ever let him out of her sight. She took Curren to church with her, inculcating the Christianity that would later become an important part of his life, and she drove him to surfing competitions all along the West Coast. By the time he was fourteen, he was winning major championships.

Taking on the World

After winning two U.S. junior national championships, one world junior championship, and one amateur world championship, Curren was ready to try his luck on the professional tour. The Association of Surfing Professionals (ASP) world tour was only in its seventh season when Curren joined in 1982, but the Australian and to a lesser extent South African surfers had already established their dominance. As a teenaged American, Curren might not have merited much respect from the other surfers, except for one thing: he won events, three in his first season alone. The next season, Curren became the first American to complete the four-event Australian Grand Slam, a feat which he repeated in 1985. Curren was handicapped in his quest to win a world title because he boycotted the competitions which were held in South Africa to protest that country's apartheid system. Despite this, he captured the ASP championship in 1985 and in 1986.

Curren's most memorable single event from these years may have been the 1986 Op Pro. The Op Pro, which is held at Huntington Beach, California, has always been a good event for Curren: it provided him with his first professional victory in 1982, and he won the event again in 1985. In 1986, Curren was undefeated going into the event. He faced perennial rival Mark Occhilupo in a preliminary round. Curren took the lead early, but Occhilupo caught two great waves to catch up in the second half of their thirty-minute heat. With only minutes left to go in the heat, the two had a paddling race to the priority buoy, which would determine which of them would get first choice of waves. Occhilupo won by mere inches, forcing Curren to move closer to the shore and take a less desirable wave. This gave Occhilupo the victory in that heat, and he went on to win the entire event. The American crowd, looking forward to watching Curren win, was furious with this outcome, and some of the 50,000 spectators began to riot, even overturning and burning a police car.

Comebacks

Curren took some time off from surfing in the late 1980s, but he returned in 1990 to win an unprecedented third world title. He continued to compete through the early 1990s, but after 1992 he spent less and less time competing and more time doing other things. As he had throughout his career, Curren continued to appear in surfing cult-flick films, including *The Endless Summer II* in 1994. He also became even more famous through an ad series called The Search, featuring Curren searching the world for the perfect wave, produced by his sponsor Rip Curl.

After having been out of competition completely for several years, Curren mounted another comeback in 1997. Occhilupo made a comeback around the same time, and crowds were thrilled to see these two masters surfing against each other again. Curren quickly made it back into the upper ranks of surfers in the world, winning or finishing in the top three in several events in 1998. His wins in seasons since include the 2001 Quiksilver Pro at Lower Trestles, where he won his first professional competition ever in 1982. At the latter competition, even Curren's board was loaded with nostalgia: it was a replica of his famous Black Beauty board of the mid-1980s.

Curren remains an inspiration to thousands of young surfers, although he is uncomfortable about being given too much credit for influencing today's competitors. "Sometimes I feel old out there. . . . No, most of the time," he told *Los Angeles Times* reporter Erik Hamilton in 1999. "[S]urfing is changing. There's more of a technical aspect to it. I can't do the stuff these kids are doing." But those kids might not be competing with the spectacular aerial tricks that they perform today if Curren had not paved the way for Americans to be champions on the world tour.

FURTHER INFORMATION

Periodicals

Anderson, Bruce. "Getting Amped on the Coast." *Sports Illustrated*, (September 8, 1986): 12-17.

Arritt, Dan. "Surf Event Is More Like Festival." *Los Angeles Times*, (July 26, 2002): D-7.

"Back for More: Tom Curren Takes the Cake at Trestles . . . Again." *Surfer*, (October, 2001): 242.

"Curren Passes Beschen to Win Surfing Title." *Los Angeles Times*, (August 31, 1998): 3.

Hamilton, Erik. " Dream Heat Looms as Contest Starts." *Los Angeles Times*, (July 28, 1999): 1.

Hamilton, Erik. "Katin Challenge: San Clemente's Lopez Is Second and Two-Time Event Champion Curren Is Third." *Los Angeles Times*, (July 28, 1997): 3.

Hamilton, Erik. "Surfing: Favorites Curren and Oc-chilupo Need to Advance Through One More Heat to Meet in Quarterfinals." *Los Angeles Times,* (July 25, 1999): 3.

Hamilton, Erik. "Surfing: Former World Champion Edges Dorian with Ride in Final Minute." *Los Angeles Times,* (July 31, 1999): 2.

Hamilton, Erik. "Surfing: His Loss to Neco Padaratz Dashes Hopes for Match Against Curren at Huntington Beach Event." *Los Angeles Times,* (July 30, 1999).

Hamilton, Erik. "Surfing: Santa Barbara Veteran Looks as Good as He Ever Did While Winning First-Round Heat." *Los Angeles Times,* (July 29, 1999): 1.

Hynd, Derek. "Where's Curren?" *Surfer,* (February, 2002): 62-63.

Keteyian, Armen. "Riding the Wave of the Future." *Sports Illustrated,* (July 8, 1985): 38-43.

Pasillas, Gena. "Catch a Flick About Surfing That Has a Christian Theme." *Los Angeles Times,* (February 26, 2000): B-8.

"Surfing." *Advertiser,* (Adelaide, Australia) (April 4, 1998): 144.

"Twenty Years Later, Curren Wins Again at Trestles." *Los Angeles Times,* (April 29, 2001): D-14.

Weyler, John. "Making Waves at Lower Trestles." *Los Angeles Times,* (April 25, 2001): D-9.

Other

Kampion, Drew. Op: A Brief History of the Surf Culture Icon. Op. http://www.op.com/History.asp (January 15, 2003).

Pat Curren, King of the Bay. Legendary Surfers. http://www.legendarysurfers.com/surf/legends/lsc203.shtml (January 21, 2003).

Pat Curren. Surfline. http://content.surfline.com/sw/content/surfaz/curren_pat.jsp (January 21, 2003).

Profile: Tom Curren. Surfhistory.com. http://www.surfhistory.com/html/profiles/curren.html (January 21, 2003).

Tom Curren. Surfline. http://content.surfline.com/sw/content/surfaz/curren_tom.jsp (January 21, 2003).

Tom Curren Wins at the Seventh Annual Donnie Solomon Memorial Event. Transworld Surf. http://www.transworldsurf.com/surf/competition/article/0,15337,406749,00.html (January 21, 2003).

Sketch by Julia Bauder

Chuck Daly
1930-

American basketball coach

Charles J. "Chuck" Daly is the only coach in the Basketball Hall of Fame to win both an Olympic gold medal and a National Basketball Association (NBA) championship. Lauded as a player's coach, Daly worked his way up from college player to high school coach to college coach, then moved on to coach NBA teams. He is perhaps best known for his work with the Detroit Pistons, which he led to nine straight winning seasons. His career successes and ability to meld diverse players into a successful team landed him the job of coach of basketball's Dream Team for the 1992 Olympics in Barcelona. During his 30 years of coaching, he was known as one of the most respected coaches in the NBA.

Moving through the Ranks

Daly attended Kane Area High School in Kane, Pennsylvania, from 1944-48, becoming a four-year letter winner and named All Conference in 1947-48. He was a student first at St. Bonaventure University in New York in 1948 for one year, then moved to and graduated from Bloomsburg State College in Pennsylvania. He played on the teams of both schools during his time as a student.

Truly moving his way up the ranks, Daly began his coaching career in 1955 when he led the Punxsutawney (PA) High School basketball team. He served there until 1963. As coach he was able to achieve a 11-70 (.613) record. His collegiate career began as assistant coach at Duke University in 1963. He headed to Boston College in 1969, where he compiled a 26-24 record. From 1971 to 1977 he coached at the University of Pennsylvania, where he led the team to four straight Ivy League championships from 1972 to 1975, and four NCAA Tournament appearances those same years. In eight college seasons, he compiled a 151-62 record, including four straight 20-win seasons at Penn.

Daly's professional coaching career began in 1978 when he was named to the NBA's Philadelphia 76ers

Chuck Daly

as assistant coach to Billy Cunningham. During his three-year stint, the team won two Eastern Division titles and four post-season berths. In 1981, he moved to the Cleveland Cavaliers, but a 9-32 record ended his tenure that season.

Turning around the Detroit Pistons

It was with the Detroit Pistons (beginning in 1983 and running through 1992) that Daly achieved both success and notoriety. Although the Pistons had never before achieved back-to-back winning seasons, under Daly's leadership the team won three Eastern and Central Division titles, two World Championships, saw nine straight winning seasons, and scored five 50-plus wins between 1988 and 1990. Daly became the fifth NBA coach to achieve back-to-back NBA championships.

The Pistons racked up some impressive stats during Daly's stint as coach. In his first year, the Pistons participated in the highest scoring game in NBA history, winning the 186-184 triple-overtime game. The team's 1989 record of 63-19 was the best in the history of the franchise, followed in 1990 by a record of 59-23 that was second best in franchise history. The team's 25-1 streak in 1990 was the third best in NBA history. The Pistons were the top defensive team in 1990, holding opponents to 98.3 points per game and 47.7 field-goal percentage.

In 1992, Daly became coach of the New Jersey Nets. Although he served only two years, he led the team to the playoffs in both seasons, giving the Nets their best record since 1983.

Olympic Victory and Retirement

Daly's success with the Pistons and Nets helped him land his history making job—coaching the US's first Dream Team basketball team in the 1992 Barcelona Olympics. With players such as **Michael Jordan**, **Magic Johnson**, and **Larry Bird**, the Dream Team won the gold medal.

In the 1993-94 season, Daly announced his retirement from coaching. He was soon honored on May 9, 1994 with enshrinement as a coach in the Basketball Hall of Fame. He is renowned as the only Hall of Fame coach to win both an Olympic gold medal and an NBA championship.

Daly's professed retirement didn't last long. On June 4, 1997, he was named coach for the Orlando Magic for two years. As reported in *Sports Illustrated,* although he was making $5 million, one reason he may have retired was to avoid hassles with player **Penny Hardaway**, who claimed he got no respect from Daly.

This may have been a surprising turn, since during his career, Daly was often praised for his respectful stance with players, for giving of himself, and for turning a group of diverse players into a winning team. In an example of his character, Daly has been quoted as saying, "It's discouraging to make a mistake, but it's humiliating when you find out you're so unimportant that nobody noticed it."

In an interview for ESPN's Page 2, Daly talked about the most important lesson he learned about coaching. In his first year of college coaching, he told players that they had to be tough in the game, but once they step outside the lines, everything goes back to normal. A football player questioned this idea, saying that you can't be two different people. That was when Daly learned that coaches and players must discover who they really are, what motivates them, and to be true to themselves at all times.

Following his second and final retirement, Daly has remained in the sports field. He served as a special consultant for the Grizzlies, and an NBA analyst with Turner Network Television. In 1996, he provided the keynote graduation speech at his alma mater, Kane Area Senior High School. In October 2002, the Michigan Basketball Coaches Clinic, a training session open to coaches at all levels, featured Daly as a guest speaker.

Daly still promotes basketball through multimedia. He appeared as an instructor on the All Pro Basketball Superstar Series of videos in the volume *Chuck Daly: The Coach—Offensive Plays, Defense & Motivation*. In the 50-minute video, he demonstrates offensive plays, discusses winning strategies, and shares the story of his success. Daly also made an appearance in the NBA Comic Relief video *The Great Blooper Caper* (1991) which focused on a fanciful basketball game. On the serious side, Daly wrote introductions to a series of books released in the late 1990s focusing on the top players in basketball history.

Daly's overall statistics give him a respectable place in basketball coaching history. He compiled a 564-379 (.598) career record—13th best among all coaches, and

9th best by percentage. Daly's 564 wins ranks 17th all-time on the combined NBA/ABA victory list. His 74-48 playoff record with the Detroit Pistons ranks 4th best in NBA history by wins and 8th best by percentage (.607).

FURTHER INFORMATION

Books

Heeren, Dave. *The Basketball Abstract*. Edgewood Cliffs, NJ: Prentice Hall, 1988.

Hickok, Ralph. *Encyclopedia of North American Sports History*. New York, NY; Facts on File, 1992.

Hickok, Ralph. *Who's Who of Sports Champions*. Boston, MA; Houghton Mifflin, 1995.

Other

Basketball Hall of Fame, www.hoophall.com/hallof-famers/daly.htm (December 15, 2002).

Detroit Pistons Bad Boys, www.smackbomb.com/bad-boys/daly.html (December 15, 2002).

ESPN, http://espn.go.com/page2/s/coaches/daly.html (December 15, 2002).

Hickoksports, www.hickoksports.com/biograph/daly-chuc.shtml (December 15, 2002).

Sports Illustrated, http://sportsillustrated.cnn.com/inside_game/magazine/basketball/nba/news/1999/05/2 5/nba/0531 (December 15, 2002).

Sketch by Lorraine Savage

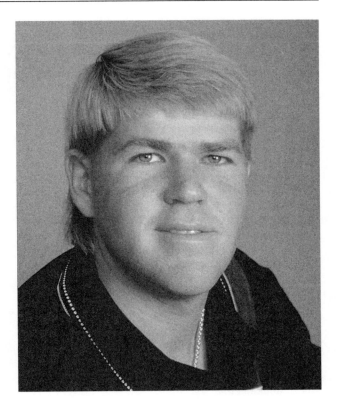

John Daly

John Daly
1966-

American golfer

John Daly has won two major golf tournaments, one of them against unspeakable odds. He has also self-destructed through substance abuse, only to repeatedly bounce back. People admire his personal tenacity as much as his towering tee shots; many fans see Daly as one of them. "They've stuck by him through two PGA Tour suspensions, two trips to alcohol rehab centers, three failed marriages and countless embarrassing moments," Bob Carter wrote for ESPN.com.

Family Moved to Arkansas

Daly moved from California to Arkansas when his father, Jim, landed a job with a nuclear power plant in Dardanelle. John Daly hit golf balls at age four, but also began drinking at age nine. He won the adult club championship at Lake of the Woods in Virginia when he was still underage and was miffed when the club's sponsors refused to give him the trophy.

Daly was a prized recruit when he came to the University of Arkansas in 1984, but also weighed 235 pounds. Coach Steve Loy wanted the golfer to lose 60 pounds and insisted on a restrictive diet and daily weigh-ins. Daly dropped the weight using a liquid diet of his own devising—Jack Daniels, right out of the bottle. "A fifth a day," Daly told Mark Seal of *Golf Digest*.

In 1987 Daly dropped out of Arkansas and turned pro. He competed in mini-tournaments, winning $6,300 in his pro debut, the Missouri Open—after borrowing $300 from his mother. Daly estimates he won $40,000 before even enrolling in PGA Tour school. But he still drank heavily, often carrying whiskey with him in his golf cart. Sometimes his drinking led to violence. Nicknamed "Wild Thing," Daly destroyed a hotel in South Africa in 1990 while on the verge of divorcing his first wife, Dale.

Cinderella PGA Champ

His life turned in 1991 at the PGA Championship, one of golf's four Grand Slam events. Daly, the ninth and final alternate, got to play when Nick Price was scratched, his wife about to give birth. Upon getting the news, Daly drove all night from Memphis to Crooked Stick Golf Club outside Indianapolis. He played without a practice round and won the tournament.

Dan Davies, writing for the British Web site Rivals.net, said the Sunday gallery served to inspire Daly, not intimidate him. "They simply loved Daly's 'Grip it and rip it' mentality, the way he walked after his ball, sent it into orbit and then walked after it again." Daly, inspired by a good-luck note on his locker from the redoubtable Jack Nicklaus, overcame a first-hole bogey and some jitters on the final three holes to claim the $230,000 first prize and an avalanche of endorsement deals. The money went to his head and contributed to his quick decline.

Problems Eclipse Success

Though Daly landed about $10 million worth of endorsement deals, earned the PGA Tour's Rookie of the Year award for 1991, and won the B.C. Open a year later, his life was sliding down a slippery slope. He was disqualified from two international events over scorecard-signing procedures, and was charged with assaulting his second wife, Bettye, at a Christmas party (he pled the charge down to harassment) in Denver and entered his first rehab. While not drinking for a while, Daly admitted to heavy gambling, saying he was cross-addicted.

Commissioner Deane Beman suspended him for three months after he walked off the Kapalua International. He rebounded to win the BellSouth Classic the following year. But Reebok suspended his endorsement deal after he resumed heavy drinking. Gambling problems also mounted.

The final shining moment of Daly's career came in the 1995 British Open at storied St. Andrew's golf course. The wide fairways suited Daly's hard-driving game. Daly, a 66-1 long shot, won an 18-hole playoff against Constantino Rocca by four stokes, one day after Rocca had forced the playoff by making a 70-foot putt from the "Valley of Sin" on hole number 18. Daly's game and life, however, backslid again. St. Andrews was his last pro victory.

"When the downward spiral revived, all the old nightmares, plus a few new ones, came calling," Carter wrote. Daly threw clubs, withdrew prematurely from tournaments, battled depression and even suicide attempts, after he escaped from the Betty Ford Clinic in Rancho Mirage, California. He also amassed $2.6 million in gambling debts and lost the sponsorship of Calloway Golf, for whom he endorsed Big Bertha drivers. His third wife, Paulette, left him.

Feels Alone

Daly, in a commentary in *Sports Illustrated* in March, 2001, wrote about feelings of abandonment. "I'm the Tour's forgotten man—not by the fans, who have been awesome although I've had five rough years—but by the sponsors and some of the players I considered friends. From 1991 to 1998 they begged me to play in their off-season events. Now they don't want anything to do with me."

Daly rebounded with an upbeat 2001, finishing 66th in money winnings on the Tour. He also wed Sherrie Miller that summer, his fourth marriage. In addition, he founded his own business, John Daly Enterprises. Playing in a tournament in the Australian PGA Championship in November 2002, shortly after his mother died, Daly was disqualified after he threw his putter into the lake and did not sign his scorecard.

Despite Daly's problems, *Golf Weekly* writer Lance Cagle says no golfer is more loved. "Not **Tiger [Woods]**, not **Greg Norman**, and certainly not one of the countless Orlando/Phoenix robots with their perfect swings and perfect portfolios," Cagle wrote. "When fans look at Daly, we see both the talent we wish we had and the insecurities that we cannot shake.... Here's hoping John Daly's movie ends the way Rocky Balboa's did. Here's hoping John Daly is well enough to deal with it."

SELECTED WRITINGS BY DALY:

(With John Andrisani) *Grip It and Rip It,* New York: HarperCollins, 1992.

FURTHER INFORMATION

Books

Wartman, William. *John Daly: Wild Thing.* New York: Harper Paperbacks, 1966.

Other

Cagle, Lance. "Why You Have to Love John Daly." eGolf Weekly, http://www.egolfweekly.com/daly. html (November 15, 2001).

Carter, Bob. "Excesses Undermine Daly's Potential." ESPN.com, http://espn.go.com/classic/biography/s/ daly_john.html (January 14, 2003).

Daly, John. "My Shot." *Sports Illustrated*, http://sports illustrated.cnn.com/golf/news/2001/03/13/my_shot (March 13, 2001).

Davies, Dan. "Crooked Stick and the Birth of a Legend." Rivals.net, http://ukgolf.rivals.net (August 14, 2001).

"John Daly—Biographical Information." PGA Tour, http://www.pgatour.com/players/00/12/49bio.html (January 14, 2003).

Mack, James. "Exit Daly with Club in Lake." *The Guardian,* http://www.sport.guardian.co.uk/golf/ story/0.10069,851032,00.html (November 30, 2002).

Seal, Mark. "Still Afloat." *Golf Digest*, http://www. golfdigest.com/features/index.ssf?/features/gd20010 8daly.html (August, 2001).

Voepel, Mechelle. "Daly's Big Hitting and Big Personality Part of Children's Mercy Field." *Kansas City Star,* http://www.kansascity.com/mld/kansascity/ sports/4870043.htm (January 4, 2003).

Sketch by Paul Burton

Fabiola da Silva
1979-

Brazilian inline skater

One of the most popular and respected inline skaters in the world, Fabiola da Silva has dominated women's aggressive skating competitions from 1996 through the early 2000s. As the first female to compete among men in the "vert" field (where skaters perform tricks inside a half-pipe), da Silva has lifted women's inline skating to a new level. Her many titles have included the 2002 EXPN Invitational, the 2001 ASA World Championships, and five ESPN X Games. Petite yet powerful, da Silva has become sort of a cover girl for inline skating, and has received more media exposure than perhaps any other athlete in the sport. Da Silva actively promotes women's participation in extreme and alternative sports.

Growing up in Sao Paulo, Brazil, young da Silva was a thrill-seeker who enjoyed extreme sports; she and her sister, Fabiona, were junior kick-boxing champions. Her first love was skateboarding. "I started skateboarding first, but I hurt my ankle," da Silva told Cindy Rhodes of the *Press-Enterprise* of Riverside, California. "I had rollerblades and I would put them on and skate up and down my street. Then I started bringing my blades to the park and learning tricks."

After only a year of learning tricks, da Silva met American inline skaters Chris Edwards and Arlo Eienberg. The former X Games medalists were giving a demonstration in a Sao Paulo skate park near da Silva's home. Edwards and Eienberg exchanged addresses with da Silva, who a few weeks later received an invitation to compete in the 1996 ESPN X Games in Providence, Rhode Island.

Overnight Skating Sensation

When da Silva, then 17, showed up in Providence for the X Games, a nationally known, ESPN-sponsored extreme-sports competition, no one had heard of the Brazilian skater. But by the end of the games, everyone in inline skating would know her name. The 5-foot-2, 112-pound skater stole the show in the women's vert competition, soaring high into the air and turning flips. With few women attempting vert tricks, da Silva was largely regarded as a novelty. "When I first came to America, they all thought I was crazy," she told Scott Bernarde of the *Atlanta Journal-Constitution.* "I went so high, did a back flip. They thought, 'Where's this girl coming from?'"

Da Silva's first high-profile win earned her the attention of Team Rollerblade, a sponsored team comprised of inline skating's premier athletes. As the only woman invited to join Team Rollerblade, da Silva was an instant media sensation. Her next step, after graduating from high school, was to move to the United States, the center of competitive inline skating. Her parents, Claudette and Ernesto, supported their teenage daughter's decision to take up residence in Santa Ana, California. Claudette often travels with her daughter when she attends skating competitions, even internationally.

Dominates Women's Inline Skating

After making her grand entrance to inline skating in 1996, da Silva became a standard participant on the Aggressive Skating Association (ASA) professional tour. No other female skater, it seemed, could beat her in the vert competition, where she executed 720s (two complete turns in the air) with skill and flair. While da Silva's talent was initially for vert competitions, she gradually improved her performance in street events. Within two years she had become a force in the street competition; at the close of the 1998 season, ASA ranked her No. 1 in women's street and vert.

Meanwhile, da Silva had become inline skating's most visible promoter, and one of the most talked-about athletes in extreme sports. In addition to Team Rollerblade, her sponsors included Fifty-50, Harbinger, Athletes Direct, The Gap, and Levi's. Money from these

Chronology	
1979	Born June 18 in Sao Paulo, Brazil
1995	Hones rollerblading skills in a Sao Paulo skate park
1996	Invited to join Team Rollerblade
1997	Graduates from high school; moves to California to participate in pro skating tour
1997-98	Defends championship title in women's vert at ESPN X Games
2000	Becomes only woman qualified to compete with men in vert field
2001	Begins competing in men's vert field

Awards and Accomplishments	
1996-97	First, women's vert, ESPN X Games
1998	First, women's vert; fourth, women's street, ESPN X Games
1999	Second, women's vert; sixth, women's street, ESPN X Games
1999	First, women's vert; third, women's street, ASA World Championships
1999	First, women's vert; first, women's street, NBC Gravity Games
2000	First, women's vert; first, women's street, ESPN X Games
2000	Ranked no. 1 in women's vert and street by ASA
2001	First, women's vert; fourth, women's street, ESPN X Games
2001	Second, women's vert; second, women's street, NBC Gravity Games
2001	First, women's vert; second, women's street, ASA World Championships
2001	Ranked no. 1 in women's vert and street by ASA
2002	Second, men's vert, Latin America X Games qualifiers (Rio de Janeiro)
2002	First, women's street; sixth, men's vert, EXPN Invitational (Grand Prairie, TX)
2002	Second, women's street; seventh, men's vert, ASA (Del Mar, CA)
2002	Ranked no. 2 in women's street by ASA

endorsements, as well as prize money from competitions, supported da Silva in her professional skating career. As she traveled to compete on the tour circuit, the popular Brazilian skater often visited local skate parks to meet fans and offer advice. Publicizing the sport among girls has become a mission for da Silva. "I like helping everyone," she told Brad Weinstein of the *San Francisco Chronicle*. "I don't like to hide my tricks. We should all try and help each other, because then we can have a great competition."

While da Silva continued to dominate women's inline skating, some female skaters posed a formidable challenge. These included Ayumi Kawasaki of Japan, who won the vert competition at the 1999 X Games, and Martina Svobodova of Slovakia, who sometimes edged out da Silva in street competitions in the early 2000s.

Skated with Men

After the 2001 season, the ASA eliminated the women's vert field due to a lack of participants. Yet in 2000 the association had allowed women to compete in the men's vert field if they qualified among the top ten. Since da Silva was the only woman qualifier, the new regulation became known as the Fabiola Rule. Da Silva welcomed the opportunity to compete with men in the half-pipe. "I think it helps a lot to show that girls can do it," she told Bernarde. "I love skating with the guys. It helps me improve. I want to be as good as they are."

Da Silva quickly proved herself at least as good as most male skaters. At the 2001 X Trial in Grand Prairie, Texas, she finished fourth in men's vert, and at the 2002 Latin America X Games qualifiers in Rio de Janeiro, she was second. In the women's street competition, meanwhile, da Silva slipped to No. 2 behind Slovoboda in the 2002 year-end ASA ranking.

Da Silva turned 23 in 2002, and showed no signs of retiring from skating. "I'm young, doing what I love to do," she told Shalise Manza Young of the *Providence Journal-Bulletin*. "It's great, (but) Rollerblading isn't going to last forever. I want to enjoy it now. Hopefully I'll have a family by the time I'm retired, and maybe I'll start college. College is always there. It's never too late."

FURTHER INFORMATION

Periodicals

Bernarde, Scott. "Extreme Sports: She Soars with the Big Boys." *Atlanta Journal-Constitution* (May 19, 2002): 18D.

Rhodes, Cindy. "Xtremely Fabulous." *Press-Enterprise* (Riverside, CA; August 16, 2001): D11.

Weinstein, Brad. "Da Silva an Inspiration on Wheels." *San Francisco Chronicle* (July 3, 1999): E8.

Young, Shalise Manza. "Gravity Games 2001: Da Silva, Queen of the Inline Event, Competes Against Men and Often Wins." *Providence Journal-Bulletin* (September 8, 2001): C1.

Other

"Fabiola." Team Rollerblade Official Web Site. http://www.rollerblade.com/skate/aggressive/bios/fabiola_int.html (January 20, 2003).

"Fabiola da Silva." EXPN.com. http://expn.go.com/athletes/bios/DASILVA_FABIOLA.html (January 20, 2003).

"Martina Svobodova." EXPN.com. http://expn.go.com/athletes/bios/SVOBODOVA_MARTINA.html (January 20, 2003).

Sketch by Wendy Kagan

Lindsay Davenport
1976-

American tennis player

L indsay Davenport has won three Grand Slam women's tennis tournaments—all but the French Open. Davenport, who rose to a No. 1 ranking with little of the fanfare of some of her peers, looked to return to top form after missing much of 2002 to knee surgery.

Playing in her first big test of 2003, Davenport reached the fourth round of the Australian Open. She found herself adjusting from a No. 1 rank more than a year earlier to just barely in the top ten. Davenport's Grand Slam victories are the U.S. Open (1998), Wimbledon (1999) and the Australian Open (2000). She has never made it past the quarterfinals in the French Open.

Athletic Family

Davenport's father, Wink, played on the 1968 U.S. Olympic volleyball team and her mother, Ann, served on the board of the U.S. Volleyball Association. Both were tall and Lindsay grew to 6-foot-2. (She has worn a size 10 men's tennis shoe.) She broke from her family's volleyball tradition, took up tennis, and played under the tutelage of the U.S. Tennis Association as a pre-teen. She captured singles and doubles championships at the 18-and-under national tournament in 1991 and a year later at the Junior U.S. Open. One week after turning pro in 1993, Davenport upset fifth-ranked **Gabriela Sabatini** in Delray Beach, Florida. The sudden media attention overwhelmed her.

Despite her rising status, however, some journalists made issue of her weight. She battled injuries and pneumonia, and once reached 200 pounds. Some players called her "Dump Truck" behind her back. And she had the added emotional baggage of her parents' divorce in 1995. The resulting stress isolated Davenport even from her sisters.

Breaks Through in 1996

She lost weight, however, and regained confidence. 1996 was a breakthrough year. Davenport won the Olympic gold medal in Atlanta, defeating Spain's **Arantxa Sanchez Vicario** in the final, and was one of only four players to defeat **Steffi Graf**. In addition, she helped the U.S. capture the Federation Cup tournament.

Davenport finally won her first major, at the U.S. Open in New York in 1998. She became the first American-born woman in 16 years to win the event when she defeated **Martina Hingis,** 6-3, 7-5. The following summer, Davenport prevailed at Wimbledon, offsetting a history of struggles on its grass court. "When I won I was almost more numb than in shock," she told *CNN-Sports Illustrated* online after beating Graf 6-4, 7-5. "I never thought that it would be my Wimbledon because I had struggled on this surface before." She also won the doubles title there; she and Corina Morariu toppled Mariaan De Swardt and Elena Tatarkova, 6-4, 6-4.

Davenport added a third Grand Slam in January, 2000, when she beat No. 1 Hingis 6-1, 7-5 to win the Australian Open. Davenport broke Hingis's 27-match, three-title win streak at the Open and became the first American to win there since **Chris Evert** in 1984.

Knee Surgery in 2002

Davenport, who injured her right knee at the season-ending championships in 2001, underwent arthroscopic surgery in January, 2002, to correct a full-thickness cartilage defect; she missed the first half of the year. In the U.S. Open, she lost in the semifinals to eventual champion **Serena Williams**.

In the 2003 Australian Open, Davenport struggled at times but reached the fourth round before losing a three-hour, 13-minute match to Justine Henin-Hardenne of Belgium. Henin-Hardenne overcame leg cramps to win the marathon match. ESPN commentator and former star player Pam Shriver saw Davenport improve during the tournament. "It was great to see Davenport's attitude adjustment from her second-round match where she was way too negative," Shriver wrote on the ESPN.com web site. Davenport is engaged to Jon Leach, the brother of her coach, Rick Leach.

Davenport's Impact

She is self-effacing, lacks the dominance of Serena and **Venus Williams**, the stridency of Hingis and the sex appeal of **Anna Kournikova**. Some in women's tennis and media circles feel Davenport has been shortchanged in publicity, particularly in June, 2000, when *Sports Illustrated* ran on its cover a photo of Kournikova, who has never won a professional tournament, in a sexually suggestive pose.

"Top-ranked Lindsay Davenport is too gawky and pudgy to grace the cover of SI, which could stand for Sexist Illustrated," Michael Muldoon wrote in the Lawrence, Massachusetts *Eagle-Tribune*. "Kournikova, [soccer star] **Brandi Chastain**, soccer star **Mia Hamm** and WNBA standout/model **Lisa Leslie** are very attractive, making them the darlings of Madison Avenue. Davenport, tennis all-time great **Martina Navratilova** and long-time golf champion Laura Davies are considered rather plain, so their phones never ring." Davenport, however, is popular with the media. Journalists honored her at the 2000 French Open as "friendliest and most approachable player on Tour."

FURTHER INFORMATION

Books

McCann, John T. *Lindsay Davenport*. Philadelphia: Chelsea House Publishers, 2001.

Periodicals

Barovick, Harriet, "Who Are You Calling an Old Lady?" *Time* (September 7, 1998): 68.
"Davenport Out to Reclaim Winning Form." *New York Times* (January 17, 2003): 5.
Dillman, Lisa. "Davenport Planning Her Own Ring Ceremony." *Los Angeles Times* (November 1, 2002): D3.
"Justine Gets Up to Floor Lindsay." *New York Daily News* (January 24, 2003): 65.

Other

Biography Resource Center, Lindsay Davenport Profile. http://galenet.galegroup.com (January 25, 2003).
"Changing of the Guard: Davenport Breaks Hingis' Australian Open Stranglehold," *CNN-Sports Illustrated,* http://sportsillustrated. cnn.com/tennis/2000/australian_open/news/2000/01/28/final_davenport_a p/ (January 30, 2000).
"Lindsay Sends Steffi Packing." *CNN-Sports Illustrated.* http://media.cnnsi.com/tennis/1999/Wimbledon (August 6, 1999).
"Sexism Is Alive and Well in World of Sports." *Lawrence Eagle- Tribune.* http://www.eagletribune.com/news/stories/20000602/SP_002.htm (June 2, 2000).
Shriver, Pam. "Davenport Has to Keep Her Attitude Up." ESPN.com. Http://www.espn.go.com/tennis (January 17, 2003).
"Sports Illustrated Feeling Heat from Steamy Kournikova Cover." SportsForWomen.com. http://www.caaws.

ca/Whats_New/jun00/sicover_jun10.htm (June 5, 2000).
"Tennis Star Lindsay Davenport." *CBS SportsLine.* http://cbssportsline.com/u/chat/1999/women/davenport040199.htm (April 1, 1999).
WTA Tour, Lindsay Davenport Profile, http://www.wtatour.com (January 24, 2003).

Sketch by Paul Burton

Al Davis
1929-

American football executive

As owner of the National Football League's (NFL) Oakland Raiders, Al Davis has been both vilified and admired by his colleagues. Davis has created a team in his own image, both arrogant and mysterious, determined and successful. His unorthodox approach to the game on the field, and the equally interesting one played in the league's back rooms, has won him Super Bowls, a place in the Pro Football Hall of Fame, and most importantly to him, the respect and admiration of his players. He has revolutionized the sport and set a standard that has influenced the league for forty years.

Growing Up

Born Allen Davis on July 4, 1929 in Massachusetts, his family soon moved to Crown Heights, Brooklyn. As a child Davis dreamed of owning and managing a franchise more than he did of playing the game. Raised in the World War II era, Davis was fascinated by military principles and history and would eventually marry his strategic mind to his lust for power. His goal was to run the greatest sports organization in history.

During his college career he didn't excel on the field but was immediately recognized for his ability to motivate the other players. This talent paid off when he was hired, without any coaching experience, to be the line and baseball coach at Adelphi College. After a stint in the United States Army, where he coached the military team, Davis became a scout for the Baltimore Colts before moving on to coach line at the University of Southern California.

Davis and the AFL

Davis entered professional football in the sixties as the offensive end coach with the Los Angeles Chargers of the newly formed American Football League (AFL). During his stay with the Chargers, his recruitment tech-

Chronology

1929	Born July 4 in Brockton, Massachusetts
1957	Coaches line at the University of Southern California
1963	Hired as coach and general manager of the Oakland Raiders
1963	Named AFL Coach of the Year
1966	Named AFL commissioner
1969	Returns to Oakland as managing general partner
1977	Wins first Super Bowl with the Raiders
1977	Named NFL Executive of the Year
1980	Wins second Super Bowl with the Raiders
1982	Moves team from Oakland to Los Angeles
1984	Wins third Super Bowl
1992	Inducted into Pro Football Hall of Fame
1995	Moves Raiders back to Oakland

Al Davis

niques would become notorious. Unafraid to approach the opposing teams' players, Davis was always trying to lure players to his team. He also made waves with a passing attack that was responsible for elevating the Chargers' offensive rank.

The Black and Silver

In 1963, Davis was hired by the AFL's Oakland Raiders as the head coach and general manager. He was the youngest man to ever hold both positions. That year the rookie head coach would transform a 1-13 team into a 10-4 contender and win the AFL's Coach of the Year award. His innovative ideas, such as bump and run pass coverage, would become staples of the NFL in years to come. He redesigned the team's image, changing their colors to black and silver, and gave them a motto, "Pride and Poise." With the relentless passing attack and intimidating defense that would become their trademark, the Raiders were on the verge of becoming one of the AFL's most dominant teams.

In 1966, Davis was named the AFL's commissioner. In direct competition with the NFL, the AFL chose Davis in hopes of forcing a merger. They had hoped his ruthless tactics would eventually weaken their rival. Davis immediately set out to lure unhappy NFL players to the AFL. Their strategy worked and the two leagues merged following the 1969 Super Bowl. **Pete Rozelle** took over as commissioner and Davis went back to Oakland, but the hostility that festered between the two would last for decades.

The Glory Years

Gathering unwanted players from around the league, Davis continued to build on the Raiders' powerful reputation. Throughout the 1970s and 1980s, the Raiders and Davis were despised for dirty play and even dirtier business tactics. Davis, on the other hand, had by now adopted his "just win, baby" attitude and continued unfazed by the criticism. Rumors spread that not only had Davis bugged the opposing team's locker room but that

he had an army of unofficial scouts spying on other teams and luring their players away from them. "I'd run into some high school coach and he'd tell me he was a Raider scout," said former player, Gene Upshaw. "Everybody was a Raider scout." Davis was also rumored to have been seen at a celebrity golf tournament hoping to find an unhappy player to steal. "Al can steal your eyeballs and convince you that you look better without them," said former Cleveland Brown's coach Sam Rutigliano. Inside the organization, however, Davis's players regarded him as a hero and remained loyal to the black and silver. His treatment of players was unparalleled in the league. The NFL even had to impose a maximum on the amount spent on Super Bowl rings after Davis's diamond studded design following the Raiders' 1980 victory.

Turmoil and Relocation

His reputation for upsetting the NFL establishment was solidified in 1982 when he sued the NFL for the opportunity to move his franchise from Oakland to Los Angeles. His victory cost the NFL $50 million dollars and led to a period of expansion and relocation that had more to do with money and less to do with loyalty to the fans. Davis's reputation took a beating in the press but privately other NFL owners took notice. Leading the opposition, Art Modell of the Cleveland Browns, soon changed his tune and went on a similar search for the sweetest deal. Davis, however, didn't stop there, eventually moving his team back to Oakland in 1995 because, among other reasons, he believed the L.A. Coliseum's size and lack of fan support was costing his team four to six points a game.

Death and a Legacy

Throughout the turmoil and the rumors of relocation, Davis has remained an intriguing figure. His obsession with death and his nearly supernatural record of reviving loved ones the medicine had given up on, only reinforces this image. In 1979, when his wife went into cardiac arrest and eventually a coma, her doctors told him that she would be a vegetable if she even woke up at all. Davis, unconvinced, stayed by her bed around the clock and seemingly willed her back to life in less than a week and a half.

A mythic figure in the NFL, Davis's pompadour and white Raiders jump suit doesn't instill fear in his opponents the way it did in his Raider glory days. It isn't that he has become any less radical but he is no longer alone on the frontier, owners like Jerry Jones and Daniel Snyder have adopted Davis's hands on approach, and in the process made him seem more like the old guard he spent his career battling. His teams, however, are still the result of instinctive scouting and discarded players and remain fiercely loyal to the black and silver.

FURTHER INFORMATION

Books

Biography Resource Center. Detroit: Gale Group, 2002.

Periodicals

"Al to World: Get Out of Our Way." *Sports Illustrated* (September 5, 1984): 86.

"A Commitment to Cynicism." *Sports Illustrated* (September 17, 1990): 102.

"It's Never Really Over." *Sports Illustrated* (September 24, 1990): 88.

"Just Move, Baby." *Sports Illustrated* (July 3,1995): 26.

"Lord of the Rings." *Sports Illustrated* (December 11, 1989): 104.

Lord of the Rings

For an owner, Davis has always been strangely considerate of labor. He flew former Raiders to Super Bowl games, back when the team was in them, and continues to fly former players to home games throughout the season. Whenever a Raider is inducted into the Hall of Fame—there have been six, and they have all asked for Davis to present them—he arranges for former teammates to be on hand. One former Raider, long since traded away, got into trouble with drugs, and Davis secretly financed his rehabilitation. And, said [Gene] Upshaw, "If a player passes away, like Dan Birdwell did in 1978, he flies us all in for the funeral. . . ."

[He] defers as much acclaim as possible to the players. He rarely goes to awards banquets for fear of denying the players their proper due. The gesture occasionally backfires. He got some heat in 1983 when he stiffed the Los Angeles Press Club; friends say he was just being careful not to steal attention away from the team.

When Upshaw and Davis visited Irwindale, Calif., to see one of several proposed sites for a new Raider stadium, Upshaw asked if it would be named Al Davis Stadium. Davis was surprised at the suggestion. "Not in a million years," he said, adding that the hall of fame he intends to build with the stadium will be devoted entirely to players.

Source: Richard Hoffer, *Sports Illustrated,* December 11, 1989, p. 104.

"No Pride, No Poise." *Sporting News* (December 22, 1997): 9.

"The Raid-Uh Rules." *Esquire* (January, 1996): 41.

Sketch by Aric Karpinski

Terrell Davis
1972-

American football player

Terrell Davis's exuberant seven year NFL career was marked by record-breaking accomplishments and debilitating migraines and injuries. Davis's speed and tenacity helped **John Elway** and the Denver Broncos win two consecutive Super Bowl titles, first in 1998, then again in 1999. Among his many feats are an amazing 2,008 rushing yard season in 1998 and a Super Bowl MVP. In August 2002, Davis retired due to an arthritic condition in his left knee.

In the Lincoln Park neighborhood of San Diego, California, rife with crime, gangs and drugs, Davis learned to keep hope alive. He suffered migraines from the age of seven. "There wasn't medication or anything we could give him, just the tea," Kateree Davis confided to the *Sporting News*. "I knew he was strong, but he was so brave, too. After a while, he learned he just had to be patient until the pain went away." Davis's patience proved to be a great asset to his record-setting career in the

Terrell Davis

NFL. His seven year NFL career with the Denver Broncos was marked by spectacular plays and crippling injuries.

As a kid Davis played in the Pop Warner youth football league. He was such an enthusiast that he continued playing with them until he was a freshman in high school, often going to extreme measures to stay under the weight limit. However, when Davis was in the ninth grade, he lost his father to lupus, an immune deficiency disease, and for a time his love of the sport was extinguished. He had a hard time keeping up with his school work, even flunking gym class, in the first two years of high school. As a junior, Davis transferred from Morse High School to Lincoln High School, the same school from which legendary running back **Marcus Allen** graduated. The new environment lifted his spirits somewhat and by the next year he was a star football player dominating the fullback, nose guard, and kicker positions.

Davis's older brother, Reggie Webb, was a tailback at U.C. Long Beach and convinced his coaches to offer Terrell a football scholarship. At that time the former Washington Redskins coach George Allen was coaching the Long Beach team. Davis had the opportunity to work with the legendary coach for only one season. When Allen died, the Long Beach campus eliminated its football organization and Davis transferred to the University of Georgia. Due to a twice-torn hamstring, Davis's college statistics didn't reflect his ability. During the 1995 NFL draft, Davis played board games at his girlfriend's house while 21 running backs were chosen ahead of him. When the Denver Broncos picked him in the sixth round (he was the 196th player overall) he took the news as a challenge.

With no injuries holding him back and a long way to go to earn his coaches' respect, Davis started Broncos training camp hungry to show everyone that he belonged in the starting lineup. "Being drafted in the sixth-round was like a slap in the face for me," Davis admitted in the *Atlanta Journal-Constitution*. "But deep down I knew I wasn't a sixth-round pick. I came here [to training camp] with something to prove." Bobby Turner, the Broncos running back coach, told *Sporting News*, "If there had been 20 running backs he would have been 20th." By the end of training season, Broncos coach Mike Shanahan told the *Atlanta Journal-Constitution*, "Davis has surprised me. He is really competing right now for a starting job, and that doesn't happen that often with a sixth-round draft choice and a guy who really didn't carry the ball a lot his senior year."

Denver played Davis as a starting running back and he finished the 1995 season with 1,117 yards on the ground, to become the lowest draft pick ever to rush for over 1,000 yards. His teammates voted him most valuable offensive player over their celebrated quarterback, **John Elway**. At the end of the 1995 season the Broncos rewrote Davis's $131,000-a-year rookie contract, raising it to $6.8 million for five years.

In the 1996 season Davis rushed for an incredible 1,538 yards, second in the league. He missed part of the

Career Statistics

Yr	Team	Rushing				Receiving			
		Att	Yds	Avg	TD	Rec	Yds	Avg	TD
1995	DEN	237	1117	4.7	7	49	367	7.5	1
1996	DEN	345	1538	4.5	13	36	310	8.6	2
1997	DEN	369	1750	4.7	15	42	287	6.8	0
1998	DEN	392	2008	5.1	21	25	217	8.7	2
1999	DEN	67	211	3.1	2	3	26	8.7	0
2000	DEN	78	282	3.6	2	2	4	2.0	0
2001	DEN	167	701	4.2	0	12	69	5.8	0
2002	DEN	0	0	0.0	0	0	0	0.0	0
TOTAL		1655	7607	4.6	60	169	1280	7.6	5

DEN: Denver Broncos.

Awards and Accomplishments

1995	Named Rookie of the Year by *Football Digest.* Voted Broncos' Offensive MVP by teammates
1997-99	Pro Bowl selection
1998	Super Bowl MVP
1999	NFL MVP

following season with a separated right shoulder but returned to help the Broncos beat the Jacksonville Jaguars in a wild card game for a play-off spot. The Broncos went on to win Super Bowl XXXII, hosted in San Diego, Davis's hometown.

Davis etched his name in Super Bowl history, rushing for a record 157 yards and scoring three touchdowns. However, he was almost sidelined with a crushing migraine that blurred his vision. Davis took a newly released migraine medication and was able to play again. He was named the Super Bowl MVP.

After the Super Bowl, Davis appeared in his second consecutive Pro Bowl. In July of 1998, he re-signed his contract with the Broncos, becoming the highest paid running back in the NFL at $56.1 million over nine years.

In 1998, The Broncos were unstoppable, winning Super Bowl XXXIII. Davis was named the season MVP and top offensive player of year. He had a record setting season, becoming only the fourth player in history to rush for over 2,000 yards in a single season. Davis appeared in his third straight Pro Bowl.

Several injuries, including a torn knee ligament, put Davis out of commission for much of the 1999 and 2000 seasons. He rushed for a career low 211 yards in 1999. In the 2001 season Davis recuperated somewhat rushing for 701 yards. However, his knee injury was diagnosed as a degenerative condition that despite numerous operations did not show signs of improving. "It is tough to re-

alize I am not going to play anymore," Davis said in an August 2002 interview. "My mind is telling me one thing, but my knees are telling me something else." "It's very unfortunate that Terrell hurt his knees because he could have been one of the best, if not the best, running backs in NFL history," former Broncos quarterback John Elway told the *Denver Post*. In August 2002 Davis was put on the injured reserve list and decided to officially retire.

Terrell Davis had a brilliant if short career. He had a three-year streak from 1995 to 1998 that puts him among the top running backs in NFL history. There is no question that he is one of the most talented players ever to play the position. However, the jury is still very much out on whether he warrants a spot in the Hall of Fame. Many argue that the numbers speak for themselves: a 2,008 yard season in 1997, two Super Bowl rings, and 4.87 yards per carry when he was uninjured added to his MVP award make him a shoo-in for the Hall.

Others contend that the mark of a Hall of Famer is longevity and that Davis, despite his exuberant performances during his three uninjured seasons, does not qualify. However, no one can debate Davis's spirit.

FURTHER INFORMATION

Periodicals

"Davis Holds Out Hope for One More Comeback." *Columbian* (August 21, 2002): B6.

Other

CBSSportsline.com. http://www.cbs.sportsline.com/ (December 3, 2002).

DenverPost.com. "Terrell Davis: 'Keep Hope Alive.'" http://www.denverpost.com/ (December 3, 2002).

Galenet.com. Biography Resource Center. http://galenet.galegroup.com/ (December 3, 2002).

The Official Terrell Davis Website. http://www.td30. com/bio.html (December 02, 2002).

Sketch by Paulo Nunes-Ueno

Dominique Dawes
1976-

American gymnast

Dominique Dawes changed U.S. amateur sports forever by becoming the first African American to represent the United States in Olympic gymnastics. Her lifetime achievements are impressive, including a clean sweep at the 1994 U.S. National Championships and three appearances in the Olympic Games (1992, 1996, and 2000). Her reputation has been defined by powerful and risky performances that raise the bar for her competitors. Her famous move of tumbling up and back from one corner of the mat to the other without stopping originated when her coaches asked her to do a full maneuver on the tiny mat in her gym; a fitting signature for a young woman who overcame many obstacles to accomplish things no one else had before.

Determination

Dominique Dawes was born in 1976 in Silver Spring, Maryland. From an early age, she displayed the energy required to be a future gymnast. At six years old she had made a hobby of cart wheeling around the house. Her parents were impressed by her talent but also wanted to give her an outlet to express herself away from their more delicate items. "I had a lot of energy around the house, so my parents thought it would be good to put me in a gym," she told CBS Sportsline. They found a trainer with a good reputation in nearby Gaithersburg, Maryland at Hill's Gymnastics. Kelli Hill, the owner, immediately spotted talent. "There are other people with God-given ability, but it takes a very special person to pursue it day after day," Hill told *People.* Dawes didn't know a thing about the sport of gymnastics but she immediately took to the discipline and hard work. While other children bowed out, she stuck with it.

When Dawes began to compete in local meets at the age of nine, she would write the word "determination" on the mirror in shaving cream. "[At that age] I was amazed she even knew how to spell it," her father told *People,* "but it worked." She began her amateur career as a gymnast in 1991 at the age of fifteen when she joined the U.S. Senior National team. By the end of the year she was ranked ninth in the nation, making a distinct im-

Dominique Dawes

pression for a young girl from a small town and an unknown gym.

With a strong performance at the Olympic trials and a blossoming reputation for unusual strength and poise, Dawes became a member of the Olympic team in Barcelona's 1992 games. This is noteworthy because she became the very first African American woman to represent the U.S. Gymnastics Team. When asked about her place in history by Susan Stamberg, Dawes was humble but showed the wisdom of a young woman who had seen racism up close. "I think [my attitude] has to do with having a good outlook on things … And, you know, that's what I constantly try to tell young kids.… You know there's going to be negative things there and they're going to get you down.… But you need to think positive and think that there's a brighter side to everything." Hopes were high for the 1992 team and they managed to take home the bronze medal. But there were even more incredible accomplishments ahead for the young talent.

The following year proved to be as successful when Dawes pulled off a solid performance at the 1993 World Gymnastics Championships in Birmingham, Great Britain. Her two silver medals in the uneven bars and balance beam were a personal best and a first for a black gymnast in a world championship competition. Dawes's reputation was being built on solid and risky performances across all different gymnastic events.

USA Gymnastics named Dawes the 1993 Athlete of the Year.

Awesome Dawesome Struts Her Stuff

But it was the 1994 Coca-Cola U.S. National Championships in Nashville where "Awesome Dawesome" earned her nickname. She won first in all the main events. Her clean sweep easily gave her the coveted First All-Around to top it off. The accomplishment was the first of its kind in twenty-five years. Once again, *USA Gymnastics* named Dawes 1994 Athlete of the Year.

In high school, she practiced seven times a day; two hours before school and five hours after and still managed to maintain an A average. Like any other young woman in her teens, college beckoned. She had her pick of many great schools with her combination of accomplishments and hunger for self-improvement. Stanford offered a scholarship, but she deferred twice due to the strong draw of her favorite sport.

After a wrist injury sidelined her in 1995, Dawes returned with a tremendous effort at the 1996 Coca-Cola U.S. National Championships in Knoxville. Reminiscent of the 1994 Nationals, she took first in a number of events. At twenty, an age when most gymnasts consider retiring, Dawes looked like she was just getting started.

The Magnificent Seven

Dawes excelled at the 1996 Olympic trials and joined six talented young women, penned as the "Magnificent Seven," for the 1996 Olympic Games. The potential that the team displayed made all of the gymnasts household names overnight. Expectations were high for the female team since it was made up of promising talents; un-

knowns and veterans alike. The Magnificent Seven delivered. As a team they won the gold medal for the U.S. while Dawes, with one stumble in the floor exercise, fought back from disappointment to grab the bronze. She cried as she left the mat, which many took to mean she was disappointed that she didn't win the gold.

Retiring to College

Dawes retired from amateur gymnastics at the end of 1996 and found a number of outlets for her talents. She appeared in the Broadway production of *Grease* and also danced for a Prince video. She attended college at University of Maryland where she considered a career in medicine as well as law enforcement. But competitive gymnastics beckoned. Only a few months before the 2000 Olympic trials she began to train for a third appearance in the Games. The comeback was primarily due to a discomfort with life outside the sport. "It was very boring having a non-gymnastics life," she told Paula Parrish of the *Gazette*. "I would wake up and I wouldn't be nervous and I didn't have to go and do anything. I just kind of made up my schedule as I went along." She might have woken up nervous on the morning of the 2000 trials, but she didn't show it. Dawes stunned everyone with a seventh place finish, proving her veteran ability to stay calm under pressure.

Her climb back to the top was not without controversy. The Selection Committee, which decides who will attend the Olympics, changed an old policy and based their decisions on a gymnast's specific abilities, instead of overall performance. However, they allotted two spots for strong performers. Considering this criterion and her stunning performance in the trials, Dawes was chosen to go to her third Olympics; even though she was picked over Vanessa Atler, who finished one spot ahead in the trials. The controversy that followed could have been huge, but Atler exited gracefully. "I wasn't having fun," she told the *Cincinnati Enquirer.* "When my name wasn't called, I almost had a sense of relief because deep down, I knew I shouldn't be going."

Time to Move On

Dawes's performance at the 2000 games was disappointing. The U.S. team struggled to avoid being eliminated in the early rounds. Eventually, they ended up in fourth place and Dawes, the sentimental favorite to win gold, went home empty-handed. But she insists she's been made stronger by this and finds comfort in her curiosity, her optimism, and her religious faith.

Many consider Dawes a primary example of the new generation of athlete. She exemplified the surge of powerful and innovative sports figures who proliferated in the 1990s. Her consistently powerful performances through some of the highest drama in recent sports memory, endeared her to millions of Americans and her fellow competitors. The fact that she broke down a stubborn wall for African American gymnasts adds to her already impressive legacy.

CONTACT INFORMATION

Address: Dominique Dawes, USA Gymnastics, Pan American Plaza, Suite 300, 201 S. Capitol Avenue, Indianapolis, IN 46225.

FURTHER INFORMATION

Periodicals

"Cincinnati's White makes Olympic team." *Cincinnati Enquirer* (August 21, 2000).
"Gym Dandy." *People* (November 14, 1994): 64.
Parrish, Paula. "Dawes earns one more shot at the Gold." *Gazette* (September 10, 2000).
Swift, E.M. "Flips and Flops." *Sports Illustrated* (July 6, 1996): 34.

Other

"Dominique Dawes." CBS Sportsline. http://cbs.sports line.com/u/gymnastics/0597cbs/dawes.htm.
"Dominique Dawes." USA Gymnastics Official Biography. http://www.usa-gymnastics.org/athletes/bios/d/ddawes.html
Stamberg, Susan. "Olympic gymnast Dominique Dawes talks about her experiences in the last three Olympic Games." *NPR*. http://cbs.sportsline.com/u/gymnastics/ 0597cbs/dawes.htm.
"Teenwire.com Talks with Dominique Dawes." *Teenwire.com*. http://www.teenwire.com/index.asp? taStrona=http://www.teenwire.com/takingac/articles/ta_20021029p065_self-esteem.asp

Sketch by Andrew Zackheim

Dizzy Dean
1910-1974

American baseball player

During the 1930s, baseball fans flocked to stadiums across the United States to get a peek of Dizzy Dean, the anchor of the St. Louis Cardinals' pitching staff. Dean was a dominant pitcher, to be sure—with his intimidating fastball, Dean hurled his way to four consecutive strikeout titles (1932-1935) and had four seasons with 20 or more wins. Over his career, Dean struck out 1,163 batters in 1,967 innings. Along with his fastball, Dean served up plenty of shenanigans, making him one of baseball's premier gate attractions. Once, he brought a black cat into the stadium and pretended to put a hex on the rival team. Other times, he joked around on the loudspeaker before the game. Dean was also a beloved braggart. Time and again, Dean predicted the impossible, then stepped to the mound and made it come true. To spectators suffering from the hardships of the Depression, the fun-loving, fastball-pitching Dean served as a beacon of hope. He was the uncultured country boy made good, a hero who had somehow escaped the hardships they could not.

Born to Sharecroppers

Dizzy Dean was born Jay Hanna Dean on January 16, 1910, in Lucas, Arkansas, to sharecroppers Alma and Albert Dean. In 1918, Dean's mother died of tuberculosis, leaving Albert Dean with three sons to raise. Dean had an older brother, Elmer, and a younger broth-

Dizzy Dean

Chronology

1910	Born Jay Hanna Dean on January 16 in Lucas, Arkansas
1926	Joins the U.S. Army
1930	Makes debut in baseball with St. Louis Cardinals farm team in St. Joseph, Missouri
1930	Makes major league debut for Cardinals, gets 3-1 win over Pittsburgh Pirates on September 28, but is sent back down to minor leagues
1931	Marries Patricia Nash on June 10
1932	Spends first full season in the major league
1934	Enjoys season with brother (Paul Dean) joining him on Cardinals pitching staff
1935	Stars in Warner Bros. movie *Dizzy and Daffy,* a comedy based on the pitching lives of Dizzy and Paul Dean
1937	Fractures toe pitching in All-Star Game
1938	Traded to Chicago Cubs
1941	Retires from baseball and embarks on radio career as broadcaster for the St. Louis Browns and St. Louis Cardinals
1947	Makes last major league appearance pitching for the St. Louis Browns on September 28
1950	Becomes TV announcer for New York Yankees
1952	Film biography, *The Pride of St. Louis,* is released
1955-65	Works as announcer for CBS-TV's *Game of the Week*
1974	Dies on July 17, in Reno, Nevada, following a heart attack

er, Paul. When they weren't picking cotton or working the fields, the Dean boys amused themselves playing baseball with their homespun ball—often a rock tightly wrapped with yarn from an old sock.

In 1925, the Deans moved to Spaulding, Oklahoma, where Dizzy and Paul Dean's baseball abilities became well-known. The boys didn't attend school regularly because their father kept them home to work. On Fridays, however, the town's baseball-fanatic farmers made sure the scruffy boys showed up at school so they could help deliver a win for the school baseball team.

Honed Pitching Skills in Army

In 1926, the lean and lanky 16-year-old Dean was looking for a better life. He persuaded the U.S. Army that he was 18 and enlisted. For Dean, Army life was good. He got paid, he got food, and his first pair of new shoes.

Dean, however, proved to be a dismal soldier at Fort Sam Houston, Texas. The only place he stood out was as a pitcher for the base's baseball team. It was during his Army years that Dean earned the nickname "Dizzy." A sergeant called him Dizzy once after he'd done something stupid. Also, his fastballs made batters dizzy. The name was so perfect, it stuck, and Dean was more than happy to play the part.

In March 1929, Dean left the Army. He signed with the St. Louis Cardinals and spent 1930 in their farm sys-

tem. In 1932, Dean experienced his first full major league season. The rookie led the league in strikeouts (191) and innings pitched (286), ending the season with 18 wins. In 1933, he won 20 games and set a new major league record with 17 strikeouts in one game.

Along with his fastball, Dean's personality stood out. He was a born actor, who used the baseball diamond as his stage. One sweltering July afternoon, Dean built a pretend fire in front of the dugout, then sat under a wool blanket, mocking the 105-degree heat. Perched at hotel windows, he and teammate Pepper Martin dropped bags of water on walkers below.

Pitched Way to World Series

In 1934, Dean's kid brother, Paul, joined the Cardinals' pitching staff. Dean bragged about his little brother's talent and predicted that they would win 45 games between them. Dizzy Dean won 30 that season, while his little brother won 19, for a total of 49. The Cardinals also won the pennant and ended up in the World Series playing the Detroit Tigers. Once again, the immodest Dizzy Dean spouted off, saying that he and his kid brother would win the series for the Cardinals. Again, he was right. The Dean brothers each won two games apiece in the series, giving the Cardinals the championship. It was a phenomenal season for Dizzy Dean, who led the National League in wins (30), complete games (24), shutouts (7), and strikeouts (195). He was named the National League Most Valuable Player (MVP), as well as World Series MVP.

At the start of 1935, Dizzy Dean once again boasted that "me 'n Paul" would win 45 games—and they did.

Career Statistics

Yr	Team	W	L	ERA	GS	CG	SHO	IP	H	R	BB	SO
1930	STL	1	0	1.0	1	1	0	9	3	1	3	5
1932	STL	18	15	3.30	33	16	4	286	280	105	102	191
1933	STL	20	18	3.04	34	26	3	293	279	99	64	199
1934	STL	30	7	2.66	33	24	7	311.2	288	92	75	195
1935	STL	28	12	3.04	36	29	3	325.1	324	110	77	190
1936	STL	24	13	3.17	34	28	2	315	310	111	53	195
1937	STL	13	10	2.69	25	17	4	197.1	206	59	33	120
1938	CHI	7	1	1.81	10	3	1	74.2	63	15	8	22
1939	CHI	6	4	3.36	13	7	2	96.1	98	36	17	27
1940	CHI	3	3	5.17	9	3	0	54	68	31	20	18
1941	CHI	0	0	18.0	1	0	0	1	3	2	0	1
1947	STL-B	0	0	0.00	1	0	0	4	3	0	1	0
TOTAL		150	83	3.02	230	154	26	1967.1	1925	661	453	1163

CHI: Chicago Cubs; STL: St. Louis Cardinals; STL-B: St. Louis Browns.

Dizzy Dean was a braggart, but a braggart people loved. As teammate Bill Hallahan told Curt Smith, author of *America's Dizzy Dean,* "When you have a person that says, 'I can do this or that. Just watch me,' that's being a braggart. But when you say that and keep doing what you say, that's something."

The allure of the baseball-throwing brothers, however, was short-lived. In 1936, Paul Dean developed a sore arm from overuse and in 1937, Dizzy Dean broke a toe, but refused to rest so it could heal. Dizzy Dean never recovered, and in 1938 was dealt to the Chicago Cubs. Dean kept trying to pitch, but his well of fastballs had run dry. Finally, in 1941, he retired.

Became Beloved Baseball Broadcaster

Dean soon took his act to the Cardinals' broadcast booth, where the ungrammatical, chatty farm boy was an instant success. For Dean, slide became "slid, slide, slud." Fielders "threwed" the ball, and runners returned to their "respectable" bases. English teachers cringed, but fans roared. Dean later did network telecasts and turned the CBS-TV *Game of the Week* into a household favorite. In 1953, Dean was elected to the Baseball Hall of Fame.

Dean retired from broadcasting in the late 1960s and settled with his wife, Patricia Nash, in Bond, Mississippi. The couple, who had no children, had wed in 1931, during Dean's minor league years. Dean died on July 17, 1974. During his funeral in Bond, Mississippi, the Rev. Bill Taylor summed up Dean's life this way, according to Vince Staten's book, *Ol' Diz:* "He has left us, but he has not left us empty. Few men will be remembered as he will be, a man of kindness and good will. He was an institution it would have been a tragedy to institutionalize…. His speech didn't always follow the rules, but he was better understood that our best grammarian."

Awards and Accomplishments

1930	Won first major league start on September 28
1932	Led National League in strikeouts (191) and innings pitched (286)
1933	Struck out 17 batters in one game to set a new league record
1933	Led National League in strikeouts (199)
1934	Pitched to a record of 30-7; led National League in strikeouts (195), wins (30), and shutouts (7); named National League Most Valuable Player and Associated Press Male Athlete of the Year
1934	Won final game of the World Series with an 11-0 rout over Detroit on October 9
1934-37	Named to the All-Star team
1935	Led National League in strikeouts (190) and wins (28)
1953	Elected to the Baseball Hall of Fame

Dean ended his career with a record of 150 wins to 83 losses.

FURTHER INFORMATION

Books

Golenbock, Peter. *The Spirit of St. Louis: A History of the St. Louis Cardinals and Browns.* New York: Avon Books, 2000.

Gregory, Robert. *Diz: Dizzy Dean and Baseball During the Great Depression.* New York: Viking, 1992.

Kavanagh, Jack. *Dizzy Dean.* New York: Chelsea House Publishers, 1991.

Smith, Curt. *America's Dizzy Dean.* St. Louis: Bethany Press, 1978.

Staten, Vince. *Ol' Diz: A Biography of Dizzy Dean.* New York: HarperCollins Publishers, 1992.

Other

"Dizzy Dean Statistics." Baseball-Reference.com. http://www.baseball-reference.com/d/deandi/01.shtml (November 18, 2002).

Sketch by Lisa Frick

Mary Decker
1958-

American track and field athlete

Mary Decker is remembered by many for what she did not do, rather than what she did. Although Decker, who started her impressive career as a pre-teen, is one of the world's fastest middle-distance runners ever, bad circumstances interfered in Decker's attempts to win an Olympic gold medal. Throughout her long running career, Decker pushed her body past its breaking point, courting the spotlight and injuries with her intensity and drive. Unfortunately, this determination and relentless commitment to her sport led to related injuries that kept her out of the 1976 Olympics. In 1980, when it looked like she would get a second chance, the American government—caught up in Cold War politics—boycotted the Olympic games, which were held in Moscow. In 1984, Decker made it to the Games, and was in good shape to win the 3,000-meter event, when she was tripped by another runner and knocked out of the race. In 1988 and 1996, Decker qualified for the Olympics again, but failed to medal each time.

Little Mary

Mary Decker was born on August 4, 1958, in Bunnvale, New Jersey, although her family moved to Southern California ten years later. It was in California that Decker first got interested in running. At age eleven, a year after taking up running, Decker won her first local racing competition. She immersed herself in running, competing in several other local and regional events. She also joined a running club and ran for her school teams. Decker showed an amazing determination and pushed herself to the limits of her endurance. During one week when she was twelve, Decker completed a marathon and four middle- and long-distance races, ending the week with a trip to the hospital to get an appendectomy.

By the time she was in her early teens, Decker had won enough competitions and posted low-enough times that she was recognized as a world-class runner. Despite this fact, Decker, nicknamed Little Mary (because she was under five feet tall and weighed only eighty pounds) was ineligible to attend the 1972 Olympic trials, since she was too young. This did not stop Decker from competing with Olympians, however. Decker won the 800-meter event in her first international competition later that year—beating the silver-medal winner from the 1972 Olympics in the process.

By 1973, Decker was ranked first in the United States and fourth in the world in the 800-meter race. The same year, she scored her first record, by running an indoor mile in 4:40.1. A year later, thanks in part to a tremen-

Mary Decker

dous growth spurt, Decker developed a case of compartment syndrome, a muscle condition. In 1978, Decker had leg surgery to correct this problem, and the surgery kept her out of competition temporarily.

Olympic Struggles

By 1980, however, Decker had recovered from her surgery and was running in top form, setting several records in the process, including an American record in the 800-meter race and world records in the 880-yard and 1,500-meter races. At the Olympic trials for the 1980 Moscow Olympics, Decker qualified and was expected to medal, but never even had the chance to try. United States President Jimmy Carter authorized an American boycott of the Olympics. This political decision meant that Decker would miss her chance for an Olympic medal once again. Decker set her sights on the 1984 Olympics in Los Angeles, and qualified for both the 1,500-meter and the 3,000-meter races—the latter being a new Olympic event. Since the two events overlapped on the schedule, she chose to run the 3,000-meter race.

Decker was in the best shape of her life and she was competing in her hometown of Los Angeles. She—and the general public—felt that this would be her time to shine. The 3,000-meter finals race was very dramatic. Although Decker led from the beginning, setting a world-record pace at the start, a tight pack of competitors trailed just behind her. Just past the midpoint of the race, the second-place competitor, Zola Budd, pulled slightly

Chronology

1958	Born August 4 in Bunnvale, New Jersey
1968	The Decker family relocates to southern California
1969	Enters and wins her first running competition, a parks board cross-country race
1972	Recognized as a world-class runner, but is too young to try out for the 1972 Olympics
1974	X-rays reveal several improperly healed stress fractures in her lower legs
1976	As a high school senior, misses the chance to compete in the 1976 Olympics due to her stress fractures
1977-78	Attends University of Colorado at Boulder on a track scholarship
1980	Sets American record in the 800-meter race and world records in the 880-yard and 1,500-meter races
1980	Qualifies for and is favored to medal at the 1980 Moscow Olympics, which she misses due to the American boycott of the Games
1981	Marries Ron Tabb
1983	Divorces Ron Tabb
1984	Favored to medal in the 3,000-meter event at the Los Angeles Olympics, but gets her feet tangled with South African runner, Zola Budd; Decker stumbles over the railing into the infield, pulling a hip muscle and falling out of the race
1984	Unable to compete for the rest of the year due to hip injury sustained at the Olympics
1985	Marries Richard Slaney
1986	Misses the 1986 indoor and outdoor running seasons due to the birth of her daughter, Ashley
1987	Misses 1987 outdoor season because of injuries
1988	Misses 1988 indoor season because of injuries
1988	Qualifies for the 1988 Olympic team, but does not medal
1992	Fails to qualify for the 1992 Olympic team
1996	Qualifies for the 1996 Olympic team, but does not medal
1997	At the age of 38, in her first appearance at the U.S. Indoor Championships in 23 years, wins the women's 1,500-meter run
1998	Tests positive for a high level of testosterone, and undergoes a series of related court hearings to determine if she is on steroids
1999	Her name is cleared by the U.S. Track Federation, but the International Federation removes her name from all post-1996 records

Awards and Accomplishments

1972	Set an age-group world record in the 800-meter race
1972	Won an international race in the 800-meters
1973	Set three world records: the outdoor 800-meter, the indoor 880 yards, and the indoor 1,000 yards
1973	Ranked first in the United States and fourth in the world in the 800-meter race
1974	Set a U.S. high school record of 2:02.29 in the 800-meter run
1979	Gold medal in the 1500-meter race at the Pan American Games
1980	Set a world record in the mile, with a time of 4:17.55, becoming the first woman to break the 4:20 barrier
1982	Set seven world records
1982	Won Sullivan Award for best amateur athlete
1982	Became first woman to win the Jesse Owens award, presented annually to the best American track and field athlete
1982	Named Associated Press Female Athlete of the Year
1983	Becomes first woman to run 880 yards in less than two minutes
1983	Gold medals in 1,500 meter and 3,000 meter races at the inaugural World Track and Field Championships
1983	Named *Sports Illustrated*'s 1983 Sportsman of the Year
1984	Held American record at every distance between 800 and 10,000 meters
1985	Set a world record in the mile
1985	Set a world record in the indoor 2,000-meter race
1985	Named Sportswoman of the Year by the United States Olympic Committee
1997	Set a new record in the 1,500-meter event in masters competition

In her prime in the early 1980s, Decker compiled 36 American and 17 world records in running

Decker still holds four American records, all set between 1983 and 1985

From 1980 to 1984, Decker won every middle-distance race she entered, with the exception of the Olympics

ahead of Decker and tried to cut in on her. In the resulting collision, both runners lost their balance, but it was Decker who ultimately fell, tumbling over the infield barrier and pulling a hip muscle in the process, knocking her out of the race that she was favored to win—and bringing the total of failed Olympic attempts to three.

Repairing the Damage

Following the Olympics, Decker underwent six weeks of therapy to heal her injuries, which included a pulled hip muscle. Once her body was healed, Decker started training again. At the same time, she married Richard Slaney—a former discus thrower—and tried to move on with her life. Unfortunately, it was not that easy. Besides working to repair the physical injuries she sustained in the Los Angeles Olympics and build up her family life, Decker also worked to repair her image. Although many initially felt bad for Decker after her collision with Budd, public attitude soon changed when Decker refused to ac-

knowledge Budd's apology and maintained her own innocence in the incident. Decker earned the reputation as a bad loser, and received criticism from fellow runners and the news media. Some speculated that Decker's harsh treatment of Budd also cost the runner additional endorsement contracts from major sponsors.

In January 1985, Decker competed at the Sunkist Invitational indoor track meet in Los Angeles—her first race since the Olympic accident. Some of the public still rankled over Decker's unwillingness to apologize, as was evidenced by the combination of boos and cheers that greeted Decker's pre-race introduction. Still, at this event Decker began repairing the damage to her reputation, and her runner's ego. Throughout the 2,000-meter race, Decker steadily increased the lead between her and Ruth Wysocki—who had trounced Decker's attitude in the press in the weeks leading up to the race. By the time the race was over, Decker had broken the world record and finished nearly twelve seconds ahead of Wysocki.

While this race was a crowd pleaser, nothing matched the hype drummed up for the 3,000-meter rematch with Budd, nearly a year after their collision at the Olympics. The event took place at London's Crystal Palace in July

---

Triumph and Tragedy in Los Angeles

Decker sensed Budd drifting to the inside. "She tried to cut in without being, basically, ahead," Decker would say. But Decker didn't do what a seasoned middle-distance runner would have done. She didn't reach out to Budd's shoulder to let her know she was there, too close behind for Budd to move to the pole.

Instead, Decker shortened her stride for a couple of steps. There was contact. Decker's right thigh grazed Budd's left foot. Budd took five more strides, slightly off balance. Trying to regain control, she swayed in slightly to the left. Decker's right foot struck Budd's left calf, low, just above the Achilles tendon. Budd's left leg shot out, and she was near falling.

But Decker was falling, tripped by that leg all askew. "To keep from pushing her, I fell," she would say. She reached out after Budd, inadvertently tearing the number from her back and went headlong across the rail onto the infield.

Decker's competitiveness is without limit. "My first thought was, 'I have to get up.'" she said. But when she tried, "It felt like I was tied to the ground." She had a pulled gluteus, the hip stabilizer muscle. . . . Hers was the horrible realization that once again, in the race she'd been denied by injury and boycott for eight years, she was being denied any chance of a conclusion of her own making.

Source: Moore, Kenny. *Sports Illustrated* (August 20, 1984): 22.

1985. Although Decker and Budd had privately resolved their issues with each other, they both looked forward to the rematch, so they could put the track issue to rest, too. In this memorable race, Decker ran strong from the beginning, and although Budd tried to keep up, Decker buried her after the 2,000-meter mark—and everybody else for that matter. Decker's time was nearly six seconds faster than the second-place finisher, and nearly thirteen seconds faster than Budd's time.

Over the next two decades, Decker continued to surprise the world by remaining competitive despite frequent injuries and the effects of aging. Decker qualified for two more Olympic teams, in 1988 and 1996—the latter when she was 38 years old—although she failed to medal in either of them.

Decker's Legacy

While many will undoubtedly remember Decker for the medals that got away, her consistent and impressive record for middle-distance running has made her a star—Olympic medal or not. Decker started her career at the ripe age of eleven and began setting world records in her teens. More than three decades later, with a teenage daughter of her own, Decker continued to impress her peers with her relentless drive. Decker remained competitive in her sport despite her advancing age, a host of injuries, more than twenty operations and exercise-induced asthma. Decker will long be remembered for her determination and never-wavering commitment to running, as well as her sheer athletic talent. Decker is the rare athlete who is born with both stunning natural ability and limitless drive, a potent combination which, for Decker, led to countless records and a hard-won respect.

CONTACT INFORMATION

Address: Mary Decker-Slaney, 2923 Flintlock St., Eugene, OR 97401-4660.

FURTHER INFORMATION

Books

Christensen, Karen, Allen Guttmann, and Gertrud Pfister, eds. *International Encyclopedia of Women and Sports*. Detroit: Macmillan Reference USA, 2001.
Great Women in Sports. Detroit: Visible Ink Press, 1996.
Layden, Joe. *Women In Sports: The Complete Book on the World's Greatest Female Athletes*. Los Angeles: General Publishing Group, 1997.
Lincoln Library of Sports Champions. The Frontier Press Company, 1989.
St. James Encyclopedia of Popular Culture, five volumes. Detroit: St. James Press, 2000.

Periodicals

Brownlee, Shannon. "Moms in the fast lane." *Sports Illustrated* (May 30, 1988): 56.
Kardong, Don. "Elusive dream." *Runner's World* (July 1992): 102.
Moore, Kenny. "Sweet, sweet revenge." *Sports Illustrated* (July 29, 1985): 34.
Neff, Craig. "Mary, Mary quite contrary." *Sports Illustrated* (January 28, 1985): 50.
Neill, Michael. "Hail Mary: stunning the skeptics, Mary Decker Slaney is Olympic-bound again." *People* (July 1, 1996): 95.
Noden, Merrell. "Don't count her out; beset by injuries and bad luck, Mary Slaney still harbors Olympian aspirations." *Sports Illustrated* (July 29, 1991): 52.
Reed, Susan. "Going the distance: ten years after her fall, runner Mary Decker Slaney aims for a comeback." *People* (October 17, 1994): 59.
Zoglin, Richard. "The way it might have been; a year later, Mary Decker Slaney puts away Zola Budd." *Time* (July 29, 1985): 76.

Sketch by Ryan D. Poquette

Brian Deegan
1975-

American motocross racer

Brian Deegan is a champion freestyle motocross (FMX) rider, the gold medal winner of his event at the 2002 Winter X Games. A medalist in each X Games from 1999 to 2002, Deegan is a member of the Metal Mulisha, a team of riders that includes Deegan, Mike Jones and Tommy Clowers. These riders take even extreme games to the extreme, dressing in black leather with spikes, cultivating bad boy attitudes, and developing death-defying stunts to match.

Deegan was born in Omaha, Nebraska, and later settled in Temecula, California. He was drawn to freestyle motocross, the sport of motorcycle stunt riding at an early age, carefully marking "Metal Mulisha" on his bike in magic marker. The dream became a reality when he and fellow bikers Mike Jones and Tommy Clowers formed the Metal Mulisha to push the sport of FMX to new limits, specializing in aerial acrobatics atop, or even briefly separated from, their motorcycles in mid-air. With names such as the Coffin, Sterilizer, and the Superman Seat Grab, these stunts have helped to make FMX one of the most popular extreme sporting events, as fans come to see competitors wipe out—often spectacularly—as often as they manage to complete their stunts.

"We formed the Mulisha because we wanted to have our own group of guys who stood up against the (motocross industry) establishment," Deegan told Phil Bartsch of the *Courier Mail* of Australia. "We're against people trying to make you do things you don't want to do, like dress and look how you don't want to look."

After first competing in the ESPN-sponsored X Games (formerly the Extreme Games), in 1999, and in each X Games through 2002, Deegan took home the gold medal for the first time at the Winter 2002 X Games. He won the medal for the Big Air competition with a stunt of his own invention, which he dubbed the Mandatory Suicide. This involved a 100-foot jump over a snow-covered track, in mid-air leaping from the seat of his bike to twist his body through the air, and landing seated sideways. Commentators were thrilled by the new stunt, and judges promptly awarded Deegan the gold medal. Deegan's fellow Metal Mulishamen, Jones and Clowers, took home silver and bronze medals, respectively.

Deegan went into the competition with his new stunt a carefully guarded secret—not even the name, Mandatory Suicide, was announced until after he had pulled it off. He named the stunt after a song by his favorite band, Slayer. After the competition, Deegan crowed over the

Brian Deegan

Metal Mulisha's sweep of the X Games over younger competitors, according to the EXPN Web site, saying, "That's what separates us old-school guys from the new kids. Us old-school guys have it in us to pull it out when it gets gnarly. It's inside us."

In keeping with his bad-boy image—Deegan, on the Gravity Games Web site, listed Charles Manson as the person who most inspired him—he was charged with assaulting a police officer outside a night club in Cleveland. In the early morning hours of August 1, 2002, Deegan was thrown out of the club by the establishment's security detail, and then he got into a fight with an officer outside, according to the Cleveland *Plain Dealer,* which quoted police.

Deegan has also started a film career as a stunt biker—he doubled for Vin Diesel in the action film *XXX.* The film called for its hero to perform a death-defying motorcycle jump while at the same time shooting bad guys. It was just another day's work for Deegan, who later told Chris Madigan of the *Independent,* "Vin Diesel isn't hardcore. He's an actor. Actors were drama geeks at school. We're the real deal."

Broken bones are also all part of a day's work for Deegan. One crash broke ribs, tore his knee and shoulder and "knocked me out for a while," he told Michael Bodey in the *Daily Telegraph* of Sydney. He cites respect from his peers and his fans as one of his main motivations early in his career. That, and the fact that his

Awards and Accomplishments

1999	Named number one rider by the World Freeride Association
1999	Wins bronze medal for the Freestyle motocross competition at the summer X Games
2000	Wins bronze medal for the Freestyle motocross competition at the summer X Games
2000	Wins bronze medal for the Step Up motocross competition at the summer X Games
2001	Wins bronze medal at the Big Air motocross competition at the summer X Games
2002	Wins gold medal for the Freestyle motocross competition at the winter X Games

sport allows him to blow off steam like nothing else can. "If I didn't have dirt biking I'd probably go nuts," Deegan told Bodey. "It's the way to release my energy; it's the only way I know how."

In a sport that thrives on danger, the only way to continue to push the envelope is to attempt more and more dangerous stunts. Stunts like the mid-air backflip have resulted in more than a few broken bones for Deegan, but he relishes each new challenge.

Now that he's well established as one of the best in the business, he admits the money is a primary motivator. "I created a job for myself and now the money is good I've got to do it, make the money while I can and try not to end up in a wheelchair," he told Bartsch. That money has bought him a lakeside house, several vehicles, and everything else he has ever wanted, but, as he told Bartsch, "Who knows how long it's going to last?"

Never content to be part of any establishment, including the one he helped to create with competitive stunt biking, Deegan had his sights set at the end of 2002 on bringing his sport to a new level. "The next level," he told Bodey, "is watching a show, a theatrical show that's almost like a concert or club, with you on the edge of your seat the whole time. It's not a contest where the lights are on and you're watching the guys do the same (stuff) over and over. This is entertainment."

Accordingly, Deegan and a team of riders dubbed the Crusty Demons launched a theatrical FMX tour in Australia in 2002, called the Global Assault tour, with one of its first stops at the Sydney Superdome. Their goal was nothing less than to achieve the enormous box-office receipts and tremendous popularity enjoyed in the past by the World Wrestling Federation, complete with onstage pyrotechnics, scantily clad women in cages, and guys with mean attitudes astride meaner machines.

Deegan's Impact

Deegan, for sure, represents a different breed of athlete in an alternative form of sports. "Sport(s) realized it was entertainment decades ago," Bodey wrote. "Yet some pursuits continue to astound with how they can morph themselves into new and extreme forms of entertainment."

FURTHER INFORMATION

Periodicals

Bartsch, Phil. "Dirt Demons." *Courier Mail* (May 23, 2001): Features, 17.

Bodey, Michael. "Dare Devils." *Daily Telegraph* (December 20, 2002): Features, 93.

Madigan, Chris. "Winter Pursuits: 'X' Marks the Spot." *Independent* (December 28, 2002): Metro, 3.

Mitchell, Elvis. "Film Review: This Skateboard Uses High Octane." *New York Times* (August 9, 2002): E1.

Treffinger, Sarah. "Manson-Fan Games Biker Is Charged with Assault." *Plain Dealer* (August 3, 2002): Metro, 3.

Other

"Athlete Bio: Brian Deegan." EXPN.com. http://expn. go.com/athletes/bios/DEEGAN_BRIAN.html (January 20, 2003).

"Winter X Games VI—Deegan Takes Over." EXPN. com. http://expn.go.com/xgames/wxg/2002/s/ motoair.html (January 20, 2003).

"Winter X Games VI—Q&A with Brian Deegan." EXPN.com. http://expn.go.com/xgames/wxg/2002/s/ deeganq&a.html (January 20, 2003).

Sketch by Michael Belfiore

Anita DeFrantz
1952-

American athletic administrator

In 1986 Anita DeFrantz became the first American woman and first African American to serve on the International Olympic Committee (IOC). Her inclusion was considered groundbreaking in an institution that has been dominated by white men and non-athletes. DeFrantz was a former rower, who first became involved in organized sports when she was in college. She competed in the 1976 Olympics in Montreal, the first Olympic Games to include rowing, where her team won the bronze medal. After completing law school, DeFrantz protested the U.S. boycott of the 1980 Olympics in the Soviet Union, where she had also hoped to compete. Despite the unpopularity of this challenge, she was soon working for the U.S. Olympic Committee (USOC), starting with the 1984 Olympics in Los Angeles. De-

Chronology

1952	Born October 4 in Philadelphia, Pennsylvania to Anita P. and Robert D. DeFrantz
1974	Graduates from Connecticut College with a B.A. in political philosophy
1976	Wins Olympic bronze medal as member of the U.S. women's rowing team
1977	Graduates from the University of Pennsylvania Law School
1977-79	Works as attorney at the Juvenile Law Center of Philadelphia
1978	Wins silver medal in rowing at the World Championships
1979-81	Administrator at Princeton University
1980	Sues U.S. Olympic Committee to stop boycott of Olympics in Moscow
1980-81	Serves as counsel to the Corporation for Enterprise Development
1981-85	Serves as vice president for the Los Angeles Olympic Organizing Committee
1986	Named to the International Olympic Committee
1987	Named president of the Amateur Athletic Foundation of Los Angeles
1992	Named to the IOC executive board
1997-2001	Serves as first female vice president of IOC
2001	Makes unsuccessful bid to become IOC president

Anita DeFrantz

Frantz has been the president of the Amateur Athletic Foundation of Los Angeles since 1987 and serves on the boards of numerous sports organizations. She made an unsuccessful bid to become the first female president of the IOC in 2002. An advocate for athletes including children, women, and minorities, she is one of the most influential women in sports.

Growing up in Indianapolis, Indiana, DeFrantz watched her brothers play basketball but did not have similar opportunities to compete. As a student at Connecticut College, her five foot-eleven figure made her a welcome candidate for the rowing team. Her aptitude for the sport put her on the U.S. women's team at the Montreal Olympics in 1976. The team was awarded the bronze medal in the first Olympic event of its kind, placing behind East German and Soviet teams. DeFrantz continued to row while in law school at the University of Pennsylvania, and would be part of every national team from 1975 to 1980, including the silver medal-winning team at the 1978 World Championships.

In 1976 DeFrantz became an advocate for athletes when she joined the U.S. Olympic Committee's Athletes Advisory Council. She would testify before the Senate to support the Amateur Sports Act of 1978, which reworked how Olympic sports were governed in the United States. In order to prepare for the 1980 Olympics, DeFrantz took a leave of absence from her job at a public interest law firm in Philadelphia. She was horrified when, in January 1980, President Jimmy Carter spoke out against U.S. participation in the Olympics in the Soviet Union, following that country's invasion of Afghanistan. After failing to persuade the USOC to reject Carter's request, DeFrantz was a plaintiff in an unsuccessful lawsuit challenging the boycott. These efforts made DeFrantz unpopular with some, including individuals who sent her hate mail. However, she was also awarded the Bronze Medal of the Olympic Order for her support of the 1980 Olympic Games.

DeFrantz would not be ostracized by the USOC for her challenge to the boycott. She was hired by Peter Ueberroth as a vice president of the 1984 Olympic Games in Los Angeles, where she served as chief administrator for the Olympic Village. When she was elected to the IOC in 1986, she was selected over Ueberroth, who was the commissioner of Major League Baseball at the time, and swimming champion/sports reporter Donna de Varona. This made DeFrantz just the fifth woman on the 93-member IOC, as well as the first African American and first American woman on the committee. The appointment is for life and makes DeFrantz a voting member until she is 75. In 1997 she became the organization's first female vice president, a position she held until 2001.

While she serves on the boards of several organizations, one of DeFrantz's larger responsibilities is serving as president and board member of the Amateur Athletic Foundation of Los Angeles (AAFLA). The Los Angeles Olympic Games had a $230 million profit, from which $93 million went to form the AAFLA.

Awards and Accomplishments	
1976	Olympic bronze medal in rowing
1978	Silver medal in rowing at the World Championships
1980	Awarded Bronze Medal of the Olympic Order
1986	Became first American woman and African American to be selected to the International Olympic Committee
1988	Awarded U.S. Olympic Committee Olympic Torch Award
1991	Received Honor Award from the National Association of Women Collegiate Athletic Administrators
1993	Received Turner Broadcasting Trumpet Award
1996	Awarded Billie Jean King Contribution Award

The foundation grants funds to youth sports organizations and has created the largest sports library in North America. At the same time, DeFrantz's work with the IOC and USOC has made her an important figure in Olympic planning and management for nearly two decades. For the 1992 games in Barcelona she was in charge of the Olympic Village housing project and served on the program and eligibility commissions. She would later be part of the Atlanta Committee for the Olympic Games and the Salt Lake City Olympic Organizing Committee.

Throughout her work, DeFrantz has tried to create gender equity for female athletes and sports managers. She helped put women's soccer and softball in the Olympics and led the way in creating an IOC policy requiring that women make up at least ten percent of the board and national Olympic committees. In 2001, with the endorsement of the USOC, she sought to become the first female and black president of the IOC. Despite being arguably the most influential female administrator in sports, DeFrantz was considered a long shot and was eliminated in the first round of voting. News reports explained that she lost votes because some members wanted to block the election of controversial candidate Kim Un-Yong of South Korea, who was said to have been shopping for votes. Jacques Rogge of Belgium was elected to replace **Juan Antonio Samaranch** as president.

Having begun her involvement in sports in rowing, a field dominated by whites, and then making an unpopular challenge to the U.S. boycott of the 1980 Olympics, Anita DeFrantz started her career as an outsider. She has since been highly successful in advancing the rights of all athletes and widening opportunities for children, women, and minorities in sports. Although she has sought to upset the status quo in sports, DeFrantz has been happy working within some of the oldest and most tradition-bound institutions. As a member of the IOC and the USOC, as well as many other sports organizations, she has been involved in a staggering number of athletic events and a wide range of policy developments. Her achievements make her a pioneer among American women and African Americans.

CONTACT INFORMATION

Address: Amateur Athletic Foundation of Los Angeles, 2141 W. Adams Blvd., Los Angeles, CA 90018. Phone: (213) 730-9614.

FURTHER INFORMATION

Books

Encyclopedia of World Biography, 2nd edition. Detroit: Gale Group, 1998.
Who's Who Among African Americans, Detroit: Gale Group, 2001.

Periodicals

Collier, Aldore. "Olympic Power." *Ebony* (July 1992): 76.
Fischman, Josh. "A rower's Olympic dream." *U.S. News & World Report* (March 12, 2001): 17.
Meyer, John. "DeFrantz: Voting impacted by Kim." *Denver Post* (July 17, 2001): D-08.
Moore, Kenny. "An advocate for athletes; Anita De-Frantz is an unlikely member of the powerful IOC." *Sports Illustrated* (August 29, 1988): 134.
Sharp, Kathleen. "Unsung Heroes." *Women's Sports & Fitness* (July-August 1996): 64.
Sullivan, Robert. "New Blood in the IOC." *Sports Illustrated* (October 27, 1986): 13.
Warner, Adrian. "Olympic Games: DeFrantz to run for IOC Presidency." *Independent* (February 6, 2001): 23.

Other

"Americans lose influence in IOC leadership." Associated Press File (August 25, 2001).

Sketch by Paula Pyzik Scott

Oscar De La Hoya
1973-

American boxer

Called the "Golden Boy" since he became the only American boxer to win a gold medal at the 1992 Barcelona Olympics, Oscar De La Hoya has always had a simple plan in the ring: "You should hit but not get hit," as he once explained it to a *Sports Illustrated* reporter. The plan seems to be working. By the time of the Olympics, De La Hoya's amateur record stood at 223 wins and 5 losses, with 153 knockouts. His professional record has been equally successful, at 27-0, with 22 knockouts. He has captured three titles and many observers think that, pound-for-pound, De La Hoya is the best boxer out there.

Chronology

1973	Born February 4, in East Los Angeles, California
1979	First boxing match
1990	Mother dies, from breast cancer, in October
1992	Fires longtime trainer Al Stankie
1992	Wins gold medal at Barcelona Olympics
1992	Makes his professional debut, beating Lamar Williams, November
1994	Wins WBO junior lightweight championship, with technical knockout of Jimmi Bredahl, March
1994	Wins WBO lightweight title by knocking out Jorge Paez, July
1995	Becomes IBF junior lightweight champion, defeating John Molina, February
1995	Fires trainer Robert Alcazar, hires Jesus "the Professor" Rivero
1995	Wins IBF lightweight championship, knocking out Rafael Ruelas, May
1996	Becomes WBC super lightweight champion by defeating legendary Julio Cesar Chavez, June
1997	Wins WBC welterweight title, defeating Pernell "Sweet Pea" Whittaker, April
2000	Loses WBC welterweight title, to Shane Mosley, June
2001	Fires Alcazar, hires Floyd Mayweather
2001	Wins WBC superwelterweight title, defeating Javier Castillejo, June

Oscar De La Hoya

At the same time, his good looks have made him a media favorite, unusually so for anyone outside the heavyweight division. They have also propelled him to the top ranks of earners, ranking third in *Forbes* magazine's list of the world's highest paid athletes. Just as importantly, De La Hoya is often seen as an exemplar for Hispanic Americans, a kid from the barrio who made it, with fortitude and very much on his own terms. The strain of being a role model has sometimes taken its toll.

Poor Boy

Oscar De La Hoya was born on February 4, 1973, in East Los Angeles, California, to Joel and Cecilia De La Hoya, both immigrants to the United States from Mexico. The family, including an older brother, Joel Jr., and a sister, Ceci, did not always have money for food, and to this day De La Hoya carries a food stamp in his wallet to remember where he came from. The neighborhood was tough, with street gangs and drug dealers an everyday menace. Like most kids, Oscar got into fights, and sometimes got beat up, so his father decided to get him some boxing lessons. Actually, boxing was in the De La Hoya blood. His grandfather had fought as an amateur in the 1940s and his father had boxed professionally in the 1960s. Oscar's uncles and cousins as well as his brother had also taken up the sport.

De La Hoya recalled those early years to *Los Angeles Magazine* reporter Bill Davidson. "My first boxing match came when I was six. On Sundays Dad would take me to the Pico Rivera Sports Arena, where there was a kind of boys' club.... One day there was a boxing tournament for kids in the arena, and Dad entered me in it. They put me in the ring with another kid, and I won. The referee stopped it. It was pretty one-sided."

By the age of ten, Oscar was working out at the Resurrection Boy's Club Gym, a former church. Soon he was going religiously, and by the time he got to junior high, he was entering amateur boxing tournaments. By the time he graduated from high school, he had amassed 225 wins and only five losses. He had also become a national Junior Olympic champion. Immediately he began training for the Olympics, with Al Stankie. Before long, he had earned a place on the Olympic team by defeating Patrice Brooks for the 132-pound gold medal at the 1991 U.S. Olympic Festival. He had already won a gold medal at the Goodwill Games.

But it had not all been smooth sailing for De La Hoya. Al Stankie had a serious drinking problem, and when he was arrested for drunk driving, De La Hoya had to fire him. He hired his father's friend Robert Alcazar, as a replacement. Then a much harder blow fell. In October 1990, his mother and "biggest fan" passed away from breast cancer. Often, it had been his mother who made him go to the gym when he would rather be home or with his friends. "You'll be a champion," she told him. Before she died, she asked her son to win a gold medal at the Olympics. It was a terrible time for De La Hoya, but it gave him incredible motivation.

Golden Boy

At the 1992 Summer Olympics, in Barcelona, Spain, De La Hoya was widely expected to do well, but he never got overconfident. In the first bout, he went up

Awards and Accomplishments

1988	Won National Junior Olympic 119-pound championship
1989	Won National Junior Olympic 125-pound championship
1990	Gold medal, Goodwill Games
1991	Won National Golden Gloves 125-pount title
1991	First place, U.S. Amateur Boxing 132-pound tournament
1991	Gold medal, Olympic Festival 132-pound tournament
1991	Named Boxer of the Year by USA Boxing
1992	Gold medal, Barcelona Olympics, lightweight boxing
1994	WBO junior lightweight, then lightweight champion
1994	IBF junior lightweight champion
1995	IBF lightweight champion
1996	WBC super lightweight champion
1996	WBC welterweight champion
2001	WBC super welterweight champion

against Cuban Julio Gonzalez, a four-time World Amateur Junior Lightweight champion. De La Hoya, the underdog, dispatched him in a 7-2 decision. The next victory, against the Korean champion, was closer: 11-10. The last match, against Marco Rudolph of Germany, actually turned out to be surprisingly easy, and with a 7-2 decision, De La Hoya had become a gold medallist, the only American boxer to win gold at Barcelona. At the medals ceremony, De La Hoya carried two flags. "The American flag was for my country; the Mexican flag was for my heritage," he told Davidson. The newly christened "Golden Boy" returned to a hero's welcome in East Los Angeles, where he paid tribute to his mother by laying the medal on her grave.

Shortly thereafter he turned pro, hiring the management team of Robert Mittleman and Steve Nelson. On November 23, 1992, his first professional match against Lamar Williams ended in a first round knockout. In December of that year, he repeated the same feat against Cliff Hicks. Over the next few months, he fought Paris Alexander, Curtis Strong, Jeff Mayweather, and Mike Grable. Only Grable proved able to go the distance against De La Hoya, who nonetheless knocked him down seven times in their eight-round match. He finished out the year with knockouts against Frank Avelar, Troy Dorsey, Renaldo Carter, Angelo Nunez, and Narciso Alenzuela. And in December of that year, he became his own manager, dismissing Mittelman and Nelson.

Champion

De La Hoya had certainly been racking up the victories, but he had yet to win a title. He yearned for a title, saying, "I won the gold for my mother. Now the championship will be for me." In March 1994, he finally got one when he defeated Danish fighter Jimmi Bredahl to win the World Boxing Organization (WBO) Junior Lightweight championship. That July, he took the WBO Lightweight title from Jorge Paez, knocking him out in

the second round. On February 18, 1995, De La Hoya took on the International Boxing Federation (IBF) Junior Lightweight Champion, John Molina. It was a grueling struggle, and led to a realization. As *Sports Illustrated* reporter Richard Hoffer noted, "De La Hoya won the decision but was appalled when he looked for instructions in the tough middle rounds and got none. Alcazar later explained to his fighter that he had felt nervous. That was not a confidence builder."

After the fight, De La Hoya told his manager, Mike Hernandez, and his promoter, Bob Arum, that he needed better training if he was to reach his potential. After scouting around for a while, they settled on a Mexican, Jesus Rivero, nicknamed "the Professor," who had helped Mexican flyweight Miguel Angel Canto to a record 14 title defenses. (To keep some semblance of continuity, and to keep peace with De La Hoya's father, they retained Alcazar as a cornerman, giving him a five-year contract.) The Professor believed in a more holistic approach, training the mind as well as the body. In addition to teaching some new moves, he introduced De La Hoya to Shakespeare and classical music, and encouraged him in his architectural interests. Some in the De La Hoya camp were nervous about this new direction, but their doubts were stilled when De La Hoya knocked out his next opponent, Rafael Ruelas, in less than five minutes. With that victory, on May 6, 1995, De La Hoya added the IBF belt to his growing collection. He followed this up with victories over Genaro Hernandez, "Jesse" James Leija, and Darryl Tyson.

At this point, De La Hoya stood undefeated, with 21 victories and four titles. But many fans, particularly Hispanic fans, felt he hadn't really been tested. In June 1996, he changed that by facing the legendary Mexican fighter Julio Cesar Chavez. The crowd at Caesar's Palace that night were behind Chavez, but De La Hoya had all the energy, as he repeatedly laid stinging blows on the old warrior. In the fourth round, the referee stepped in to end the fight, giving the World Boxing Council (WBC) super lightweight title to De La Hoya. He followed this up by taking on Pernell "Sweet Pea" Whittaker in April 1997. Whittaker was a former gold medallist and a champion in four weight classes, and this time De La Hoya had difficulty laying a glove on his opponent. And in the ninth round, De La Hoya found himself on the mat, though briefly. He got back up and performed just well enough to win a unanimous decision, but it had been a near miss. This time he took home the WBC Welterweight title.

In September 1999, De La Hoya suffered his first loss, to fellow welterweight **Felix Trinidad**. After starting strong in the first few rounds, but having decided the fight was "in the bank" as he admitted to *Sports Illustrated* "he simply circled without jabbing or doing anything else risky." The judges gave the match to Trinidad, a decision disputed by a number of observers. Then, in June of 2000, he lost his WBC Welterweight title to Shane Mosley in a hard-fought 12-round match. A disappointed De La Hoya announced his retirement, saying, "It's tough to live with what goes on around boxing."

Instead of retiring, De La Hoya decided to make a few personnel changes that year. He replaced his long-time trainer, Robert Alvarez, with Floyd Mayweather, Sr., oddly enough the father of a boxer De La Hoya had defeated a few years earlier. Prior to coming to De La Hoya, Mayweather had worked for and been fired by his own son. That same year, he ended his relationship with Bob Arum, who had been promoting him almost from the beginning. That split actually proved temporary. Uncharacteristically, he also began badmouthing former trainers to the press, blaming them for his losses to Trinidad and Mosley. He also put his boxing career on hold temporarily, to focus on a new interest, music. He even released a CD, which was nominated for a Latin Grammy.

Still the Champion

De La Hoya has continued his highly successful boxing career. In June 2001, he got his fifth title when he defeated Javier Castillejo in a 12-round unanimous decision to win the WBC Super Welterweight crown. De La Hoya had bulked up to 154 pounds for the match—unfamiliar territory for him—and even he admitted, "I have a lot of room for improvement" after the match. The win did put him in exclusive company, making him one of only three boxers to win five championships in five weight classes.

Oscar De La Hoya has sometimes been accused of forgetting his roots, of turning his back on his community. He has moved out of Los Angeles, to a house he designed himself in the mountain resort of Montebello, California. He also has a mansion in Bel Air. And with $110 million in earnings, he certainly leads a different lifestyle from the one he grew up in. But he continues to take a keen interest in his old community. Through the Oscar De La Hoya Foundation he sponsors Olympic hopefuls and provides educational sponsorships. And in 1997, he bought the Resurrection Gym where he used to train for $500,000. Renamed the Oscar De La Hoya Youth Boxing Center, it provides a place for students to go after school and, of course, a boxing program.

That is why it stung him when rival boxer Fernando Vargas accused De La Hoya of selling out, of turning his back on his barrio beginnings and of going soft. In September 2002 the two boxers met, and De La Hoya found his 11th round technical knockout of Vargas deeply satisfying. "He got under my skin, but I let my fists do the talking," said De La Hoya after the match.

De La Hoya's long-term goal is to win titles in seven weight classes, and he is well on his way. And many have noticed his skill. In May 2002 *Sports Illustrated* asked **George Foreman** who he thought was the best fight-

---

A Little Bit of Tarnish on the Gold

Oscar De La Hoya's looks, charm, and "good guy" reputation have garnered him lucrative endorsement contracts and favorable press attention. But in the area of personnel, this has been tempered with harsh criticism of his ruthlessness. De La Hoya has gone through a string of managers and trainers, starting with the well-respected Shelly Finkel, who had also managed Evander Holyfield. Brought in to help usher De La Hoya into pro boxing, Finkel had invested a great deal of money into the youth, even paying for his mother's chemotherapy and later her funeral. "But after Oscar kept the promise he'd made to his mother and won the 1992 gold medal, becoming the most marketable face boxing had seen in more than a decade, he signed with little-known managers Robert Mittelman and Steve Nelson. Finkel still hasn't gotten over it," wrote *Sports Illustrated* reporter S.L. Price.

Mittelman and Nelson didn't fare much better. In December of 1993, he broke with them "in an abrupt and muddled bid to seize 'full control' of his career," wrote another *Sports Illustrated* reporter. That same year, De La Hoya brought on Mike Hernandez as his business manager. In 1999, De La Hoya fired him, and accused him of skimming. Hernandez in turn has sued Oscar for breach of contract and defamation.

In 2001, De La Hoya himself turned to the courts to end his longtime association with promoter Bob Arum, claiming that he had been badly promoted. He also began telling reporters that he had been badly trained by such well-respected names as Gil Clancy and Emanuel Steward. Few would dispute De La Hoya's natural talent, but there are some who wish he would remember the help he has received along the way.

---

er in the world. "Oscar De La Hoya," he replied. "And we haven't seen the best of him yet."

CONTACT INFORMATION

Address: Oscar De La Hoya Enterprises, 2401 South Atlantic Blvd., Monterey Park, CA 91754-6807.

FURTHER INFORMATION

Periodicals

Davidson, Bill. "Golden Boy." *Los Angeles Magazine* (March 1994): 74.

Fernandez, Bernard. "De La Hoya gains sense of satisfaction against Vargas." *Knight Ridder/Tribune News Service* (September 17, 2002): K3021.

Fernandez, Bernard. "Oscar De La Hoya moving on up." *Knight Ridder/Tribune News Service* (June 25, 2001): K2374.

Heater, Jay. "New man enters Oscar De La Hoya's corner." *Knight Ridder/Tribune News Service* (February 9, 2001): K3176.

Hoffer, Richard. "Ringing in the New, Again." *Sports Illustrated* (April 2, 2001): R2.

Hoffer, Richard. "Dissing match: these guys hate each other." *Sports Illustrated* (September 16, 2002): 58.

Hoffer, Richard. "The pugilist and the professor." *Sports Illustrated* (June 10, 1996): 80.

Hoffer, Richard. "Class dismissed: Oscar De La Hoya gave Felix Trinidad a boxing lesson—and his share of the title." *Sports Illustrated* (September 27, 1999): 56.

"Interview with Oscar De La Hoya." *Hispanic* (October 1995)

Kriegel, Mark. "The great (almost) white hope." *Esquire* (November 1996): 78.

LeBreton, Gil. "Oscar shows he is still golden." *Knight Ridder/Tribune News Service* (September 14, 2002): K2289.

LeBreton, Gil. "Boxing's best are no longer heavyweights." *Knight Ridder/Tribune News Service* (September 16, 2002): K2639.

McAlpine, Ken. "The golden boy." *Sports Illustrated for Kids* (January 1997): 32.

O'Brien, Richard. "Arriving with a bang." *Sports Illustrated* (December 7, 1992): 78.

Price, S. L. "He Says He's a Gladiator." *Sports Illustrated* (June 19, 2000): 80.

Smith, Tim. "De La Hoya savors his whine." *Knight Ridder/Tribune News Service* (June 18, 2000): K2196.

Smith, Tim. "Oscar De La Hoya wins fifth title." *Knight Ridder/Tribune News Service* (June 23, 2001): K2005.

"Tarnished Gold." *Sports Illustrated* (December 20, 1993): 13.

Sketch by Robert Winters

Jack Dempsey

Jack Dempsey
1895-1983

American boxer

William "Jack" Harrison Dempsey ushered in the age of big-time sports. His rise from hobo to heavyweight champion to Hollywood celebrity not only gave boxing the stamp of legitimacy, but became the prototype for every superstar athlete that followed. His popularity during and after his boxing career overshadowed all of his contemporaries, including **Babe Ruth**. Dempsey's ventures in films, on Broadway and in the restaurant business were made possible because of the American public's unchecked adoration for him.

The Early Years

Born into a family of thirteen in Manassa, Colorado, Dempsey's mother read to her son from *Modern Gladiator,* a book about fighter **John L. Sullivan,** the first champion of the modern era. Growing up listening to stories of Sullivan and watching his two older brothers become fighters, Dempsey, at age eleven, decided he would become the heavyweight champion of the world. After completing the eighth grade, Dempsey left his large poor family to follow the rumor of work from town to town. Working as a miner, dishwasher, farm hand and cowboy, he would use his spare time to indulge his passion for boxing. With a high-pitched voice, the skinny kid with blue-black hair would challenge anybody he could for a few dollars and bragging rights. He was known as "Kid Blackie" during the early years of his career but would eventually become the "Manassa Mauler." He once walked across the Nevada desert from Tonopah to Goldfield for a $20 purse. The fight, against "One-Punch" Hancock was held in the back of a bar. Lasting only fifteen seconds, Dempsey floored "One-Punch" with one punch and then took on Hancock's brother, who suffered a similarly embarrassing fate. "When I got five bucks for thirty-five seconds of fighting," said Dempsey. "I felt I was on my way."

Chronology

1895	Born June 24 in Manassa, Colorado
1910	Begins training with brother Bernie
1914	Fights in first recorded professional bout
1915	First uses name "Jack Dempsey"
1916	Marries Maxine Cates
1917	Meets manager Jack "Doc" Kearns
1917	Younger brother Bruce stabbed to death in a street fight
1919	Divorces Maxine Cates
1919	Wins heavyweight championship against Jess Willard
1920	Acquitted of draft evasion charges
1921	Successfully defends title against Georges Carpentier
1923	Fights Luis Firpo
1926	Marries Estelle Taylor
1926	Loses title to Gene Tunney
1927	Loses rematch to Tunney in "The Battle of the Long Count"
1928	Stars in *The Big Fight* with his wife, Taylor
1929	Promoter "Tex" Rickard dies
1933	Marries singer Hannah Williams
1936	Opens Jack Dempsey's Restaurant in New York City
1943	Divorces Williams
1954	Charter inductee into Boxing Hall of Fame
1958	Marries fourth wife Deanna Piatelli
1963	Jack "Doc" Kearns dies
1974	Closes Dempsey's restaurant
1983	Dies at age 87
1990	Hall of Fame induction

Related Biography: Manager John "Doc" Kearns

"Doc" Kearns was born John Patrick Leo McKernan in 1882 on a farm in Michigan. He worked as everything from a fighter to a cemetery plot salesman before becoming a manager. It wasn't his work experience, however, that led to his success. Kearns's success was due in large part to his lack of ethics. He was a loud and flamboyant man and the exact opposite of his most successful fighter. A master of hype, he was pushy and irresponsible with his fighter's money. Not many people trusted "Doc" Kearns, but he was respected for his ability to do his job and get his fighters where they needed to be. Kearns and Dempsey maintained a business relationship for eight years that took them both to the top of their chosen profession. It is doubtful they could have accomplished as much on their own. Their differences, however, kept them from becoming close friends and eventually led to the dissolution of their relationship. Kearns went on to manage many boxers, but never another Jack Dempsey. He played an important role in bringing big-time boxing to Las Vegas and managed into the twilight of his life. He died of pneumonia on July 7, 1963. He was memorialized with the traditional final 10-count before the second Liston-Patterson heavyweight championship, the first genuine championship to be held in Kearns' adopted town, Las Vegas.

Dempsey soon developed a reputation for his menacing style and powerful punch that would make it difficult for him to find fights. Meeting manager Jack Price would change that. Dempsey and his new manager traveled to New York armed with press clippings of his twenty-six knockouts and dreams of fame. Without the polish and training of a fighter from the big city, however, Dempsey didn't get much attention. He did manage to catch the eye of an interested fight man named John "the barber" Reisler after one particular bout at the Fairmont Fight Club. Reisler then set up a fight with a superior veteran heavyweight named John Lester Johnson. Knowing his limitations, Dempsey reluctantly agreed to fight. With twenty pounds on Dempsey, Johnson delivered a beating that left three fractured ribs and two black eyes in its wake. Although he was recognized for his flair, style and courage, Dempsey headed back west to regroup.

It was during this trip home that Dempsey met and married a piano-playing prostitute fifteen years his senior named Maxine Cates. The two endured a tumultuous relationship that was marked by his long trips away from home and her reluctance to give up her way of life. At nineteen, Dempsey was struggling to provide for his wife and continuing to dream of fame and fortune. In San Francisco, he met the flamboyant manager that would help him take the next step. John Leo McKernan, known as "Doc" Kearns, had been a welterweight fighter, minor league ballplayer, faro dealer, bouncer and bartender before he settled in as a fight manager. His flashy style—including jewelry and strong cologne—clashed with Dempsey's. Ultimately, though, the match would be fruitful. Kearns got the fights and Dempsey the knockouts. In the spring of 1917, they began a string of fights that would pave the way to his first title fight.

Heavyweight Champion

Jess Willard was one of the many boxers who had been to referred to as the "White Hope." He was thirty-seven when he met Dempsey in the ring. Six-feet-six-inches tall, and 245 pounds, he made the 195 pound Dempsey sign an agreement that he would not be held responsible if Dempsey was killed or seriously injured in the ring. The fight, promoted by George L. "Tex" Rickard, was held in Toledo, Ohio, at an outdoor arena specifically built for the title fight. In the 100 degree heat on July 4, 1919, Dempsey knocked Willard down seven times in the first round. Badly battered, Willard couldn't come out for the fourth round and Dempsey became, at twenty-four, the heavyweight champion of the world.

With his newfound fame, Dempsey became a magnet for publicity both good and bad. Kearns wanted to capitalize on the champ's instant celebrity and began signing Dempsey for everything from Vaudeville appearances to a fifteen episode serial, Daredevil Jack. Although Dempsey had planned on enjoying the fame and fortune he now had, the press came after him just as quickly. The day after his championship fight with Willard a story in the *New York Tribune* alleged that Dempsey was a draft dodger. He would be eventually acquitted of the charges, by the San Francisco US District Court in 1920, but the story, and the testimony of his ex-wife Cates, would plague Dempsey for nearly six years.

Dempsey's 1921 match against French war hero Georges Carpentier was called the "Battle of the Century." The fight took on international significance because of Dempsey's sullied reputation and Carpentier's as a French war hero. It was the first fight ever to be broad-

Jack Dempsey

cast on radio and the first to gross over one million dollars. Held at Boyle's Thirty Acres in Jersey City, the fight drew the largest crowd ever at a sporting event and forced Dempsey to defend his reputation during the short four round fight. He was given a cold reception in comparison to the loud ovation that greeted Carpentier upon entering the ring. But Dempsey's knockout of the French hero proved too much for the patriotic crowd who cheered his victory wildly.

Dempsey would successfully defend his title over the next few years, but it was his battle with the "Wild Bull of the Pampas," Argentinean Luis Firpo, that would become his next big fight. On September 14, 1923, at the Polo Grounds in New York, Dempsey took Firpo in four-and-a-half of the most intense minutes in boxing history. The crowd of 88,000, including many top celebrities like Babe Ruth and Ethel Barrymore, witnessed Dempsey knocking Firpo down seven times before Firpo landed a powerful right that threw him clear out of the ring. Landing on the press table he was thrown back in the ring by journalists and spectators only to lay Firpo out in the second. The fight's few minutes were of such ferocity that one man in the cheap seats died of heart failure.

The Hollywood Years

Dempsey's star had eclipsed his desire and following the Firpo fight the champ took time off to enjoy the

fruits of his labor. The highly paid fighter moved to Hollywood and in 1926 married silent film actress Estelle Taylor. In his years away from the ring, his public image softened as he attempted to live the life of the nouveau riche. He even went as far as to have his fight-flattened nose remodeled. When Dempsey was invited to Calvin Coolidge's White House, it signaled boxing's arrival and solidified its star's position as ambassador. It was during this time, however, that his relationship with longtime manager "Doc" Kearns ended. Living on opposite ends of the country, Kearns could not exercise his influence over Dempsey. Disapproving of his romantic inclinations and marriage Kearns was powerless to stop them. Dempsey's wife was equally skeptical of Kearns and her influence on the champ only exacerbated the cracks that had already formed in the men's relationship.

Back in the Ring

After three years off, Dempsey was itching to get back in the ring. His much anticipated return came against **Gene Tunney** in September 1926. Tunney represented a shift in boxing strategy. While Dempsey was from the hit and be hit school of bar room boxing, Tunney was a more defensive fighter. Tunney's popularity suffered because of his "hit and run" style, but was chosen because of "Tex" Rickard's reluctance to promote a mixed race title fight. While there were many black fighters who deserved a shot at the champion, Rickard believed it would be financially disastrous. Of the two worthy heavyweights between 1923 and 1926, Harry Wills and Gene Tunney, Dempsey fought Tunney, not because he was the top contender, but because he was white.

Held at Philadelphia's Sesquicentennial Stadium and broadcast on radio by the newly formed National Broadcasting Company, a visibly slower Dempsey was defeated in the driving rain. Dempsey's many fans were quick to excuse the fighter's disappointing loss. Among the many explanations were his three years out of boxing. However disappointing, the fight would set the stage for the controversial rematch at Chicago's Soldier Field on September 22, 1927. The rematch set a new record with its $2.3 million gate. The radio broadcast was said to have reached three of every four Americans. This was Dempsey's opportunity to prove his worth and regain his title. Trailing in the seventh, Dempsey landed a combination of powerful punches that floored Tunney. Rather than return to a neutral corner, however, Dempsey lingered over the downed boxer and delayed the referee's count. Tunney rose on the nine count, that with the delay, had actually been closer to eighteen, and held on to defeat Dempsey. It would be Dempsey's final title fight and the "Battle of the Long Count" would be debated for a generation.

Dempsey accepted his loss gracefully and never publicly debated or excused himself. His defeats only seemed to make him more popular with the adoring

---

Awards and Accomplishments

1919	Won heavyweight title against Jess Willard
1920	Defended title successfully against Billy Miske
1920	Defended title successfully against Bill Brennan
1921	Defended title successfully against Georges Carpentier
1923	Defended title successfully against Tommy Gibbons
1923	Defended title successfully against Luis Angel Firpo
1926	Lost title to Gene Tunney
1950	Named greatest boxer of the half-century by the Associated Press
1954	Charter inductee to Boxing Hall of Fame
1990	Inducted officially to Boxing Hall of Fame

Dempsey retired with a career record of eighty total bouts, sixty wins, six losses, eight draws, fifty knockouts and six no decisions.

Jack Dempsey, 87, Is Dead

To many, Mr. Dempsey always remained the champion, and he always comported himself like one. He was warm and generous, a free spender when he had it and a soft touch for anybody down on his luck. After retirement from the ring, he made his headquarters in New York at Jack Dempsey's Restaurant, first at the corner of 50th Street across Eighth Avenue from the old Madison Square Garden and later at 1919 Broadway, where his partner was Jack Amiel, whose colt, Count Turf, won the Kentucky Derby. . . .

Grantland Rice said Mr. Dempsey was perhaps the finest gentleman, in the literal sense of gentle man, he had met in half a century of writing sports; Mr. Dempsey never knowingly hurt anyone except in the line of business.

Source: Smith, Red. *New York Times*, June 1, 1983.

---

public, however, and he was quick to capitalize. In 1928, he starred with his wife in *The Big Fight* , produced by David Belasco of Broadway fame. When his former promoter "Tex" Rickard died in 1929, Dempsey got back into the fight game as a promoter, but the collapse of the stock market, the Depression and his divorce bankrupted the champ and he began to consider a return to fighting. After a few exhibitions and a loss to Kingfish Levinsky he retired for good at the age of thirty-six.

Retirement and Beyond

Dempsey married third wife singer Hannah Williams in 1933 and had two daughters. He joined the coast guard during World War II and generally kept to himself. In 1936, he opened Jack Dempsey's Restaurant in New York City, which would remain open for over thirty years. His third marriage, like the previous two, ended in divorce in 1943 and he eventually married for the fourth and final time in 1958, to Deanna Piatelli. His retirement was marked by many awards and accolades, including induction to the Boxing Hall of Fame and a seventy-fifth birthday party at Madison Square Garden. He died in 1983, after a series of heart problems, at the age of eighty-seven.

Jack Dempsey's career is remembered not only for his achievements but for the precedents he set. He came to represent the boom of the 1920s and the rugged determination of the American dream during the golden age of sports. His is the prototypical boxing story and there are shades of Dempsey in every great boxer that followed. He single-handedly moved boxing from the back rooms of saloons to the forefront of American society and his life outside of the ring continues to serve as a blueprint for retired superstars in every corner of the sporting world.

SELECTED WRITINGS BY DEMPSEY:

Jack Dempsey: The Manassa Mauler, Louisana State University Press, 1979.

The 100 Greatest Boxers of All Time, Bonanza, 1984.
Champions of the Ring, Robson, 1992.
The Boxing Register, McBooks Press, 1997.
A Flame of Pure Fire, Harcourt Brace, 1999.

FURTHER INFORMATION

Books

Kahn, Roger. *A Flame of Pure Fire*. New York: Harcourt Brace, 1999.

Roberts, James and Alexander Skutt. *The Boxing Register*. Ithaca, NY: McBooks Press,1997.

Roberts, Randy. *Jack Dempsey: The Manassa Mauler*. Baton Rouge: Louisiana State University Press, 1979.

The Scribner Encyclopedia of American Lives, Volume 1. New York: Charles Scribner's Sons, 1998.

Sugar, Bert. *The 100 Greatest Boxers of All Time*. New York: Bonanza Books, 1984.

Suster, Gerald. *Champions of the Ring*. London: Robson, 1992.

Sketch by Aric Karpinski

Donna de Varona
1947-

American swimmer

When she qualified for the U.S. swim team for the 1960 Summer Olympic Games in Rome, Donna de Varona was only 13 years old, the youngest member of the Games that year. Four years later she won two gold medals at the Tokyo Olympics. She remains a world record holder in numerous events, including the sport's most challenging one, the 400-meter individual

Donna de Varona

Chronology

1947	Born in San Diego, California
1950	Learns to swim
1956	Enters first competition
1964	Retires from competitive swimming after Olympics
1965-76	Becomes sportscaster for ABC, *Wide World of Sports*, Olympic coverage (1968, 1972, 1976)
1966-68, 1984-88	Named member of the President's Council on Physical Fitness & Sport
1969-88	Sits on founding board of Special Olympics
1974	Co-founds the Women's Sports Foundation
1974-76	Appointed to President Ford's Commission on Olympic Sports
1976-80	Named member of President Carter's Women's Advisory Commission
1978-83	Hired by NBC for *Sports World, Today Show* (sports programs)
1983-97	Promoted to ABC commentator, consultant, writer, co-producer to *Wide World of Sports, ABC News, Good Morning America*, ESPN, ABC Radio
1986	Graduates UCLA with Bachelor of Arts degree
1988	Appointed member of President Reagan's Olympic delegation to Seoul, South Korea
1989	Joins U.S. Olympic Foundation
1991-94	Voted board member of World Cup Organizing Committee
1997, 1999	Named chairman of Women's World Cup
1998	Advises White House's Office of National Drug Control Policy (ONDCP); named member of World Anti-Doping Agency Committee on Ethics and Education; covers Olympic Games in Nagano, Japan, for TNT; hired as sports commentator for Sporting News Radio (to present)
1998	Sues ABC for age and gender discrimination
1999	Becomes member U.S. Soccer Foundation
2000	Covers Olympic Games in Sydney, Australia, for NBC Cable
2001-02	Chosen senior advisor to U.S. Olympic Committee (USOC) President; co-chairs USOC Government Relations Committee and joins International Relations Committee; advises ONDCP on anti-doping

medley, and the 100-meter backstroke. The individual medley requires enormous strength, flexibility, and endurance; competitors must swim four 100-meter laps, one for each stroke, including backstroke, freestyle (crawl), butterfly, and breast. Always up for a challenge, it is no surprise that the individual medley was always de Varona's favorite event. De Varona went on to become ABC's first full-time female sportscaster. In a controversial legal dispute, de Varona sued ABC Sports, charging age and gender discrimination. That battle won, she continues her award-winning career as a broadcast sports journalist.

Team Member "0"

De Varona was raised in Southern California by a family she has characterized as tightly knit and supportive. Her father, David, was an insurance salesman and a former All-American football player and rower At the University of California who encouraged his four children in athletics. De Varona's sister, Joanna Kerns, (best known for her role as the mother on ABC's *Growing Pains*) studied gymnastics until she took up acting, as did sister Sandra. Brother David joined Little League until a knee jury sidelined him and he took up swimming.

Young Donna had been eager to play baseball with her brother and the neighborhood boys but was denied the chance due to her gender. "I spent all my money on

bubble gum so I could bribe my way into the Little League," she said in an interview with *Women's Sports & Fitness* magazine. But all she got for her effort was a uniform with the number "0" on it and the privilege of retrieving the team's bats. She stored that memory, which motivated her to fight for equality later.

Swimming gave the spirited youth the outlet she needed. "I got in trouble until I started to swim," de Varona admitted to *Women's Sports & Fitness*. As an adolescent, she trained with some of the sport's top coaches, including George Haines, the legendary coach of seven U.S. Olympic teams between 1960 and 1984. She was soon committed athletically and academically, maintaining a B average while training up to six hours a day.

When de Varona returned to the Olympic team in 1964, the 17-year-old had broken 18 world swimming records and ten American records while capturing two gold medals at the Summer Games in Tokyo. In winning the 400-meter individual medley, de Varona set a world record of 5:18.7. She and teammates Sharon Stouder, Pokey Watson and Kathy Ellis won the gold in the 400-meter freestyle relay, another record-breaking achievement at 4:03.8. But even before the Olympics, the blonde de Varona had come to define swimming in

America. She had appeared on the cover of newspapers and magazines such as *Life, Time, Saturday Evening Post,* and *Sports Illustrated.*

She enrolled in the University of California, Los Angeles (UCLA), and majored in political science. Like most colleges of the time, UCLA had no women's athletics department. Seeing that she couldn't compete for a college team, de Varona formally retired from swimming. This freed her to accept a job with ABC, which had previously consulted the young student about where they should focus their cameras. While under contract with ABC and while still at UCLA, de Varona volunteered in the government-funded program Operation Champ, which worked with inner-city children. De Varona testified before Congress advocating government's continued and increased funding of programs for kids. Suddenly, she realized she was learning so much outside of college that she left, two finals short of her degree.

Broadcasting Beckons

In 1964, the Associated Press and United Press International voted de Varona most outstanding female athlete in the world. At the 1965 men's Amateur Athletic Union national championships, she made her debut in swimming commentary for ABC's *Wide World of Sports* with Jim McKay. She was a trailblazer at age 17, the first female network television sportscaster.

She became host, special reporter, and analyst for many of the network's high-profile programs, including ABC Sports and ABC News. She covered the Summer Olympics for ABC from 1968 to 1976, and again in 1984 and 1996, and the Winter Olympics in 1984, 1988, and 1994. From 1978 to 1983, she worked for the NBC network on *Sportsworld* and the sports segments of the *Today Show.* As part of the team of journalists telecasting the 1998 Nagano Winter Olympics for Turner Network Television, de Varona, who presented feature stories on female athletes, was instrumental in the cable network's exceptional ratings.

The former Olympic champion received a prestigious Emmy Award, for her coverage of an athlete competing in the 1991 Special Olympics. Seven years later she received an Emmy nomination for *Keepers of the Flame,* an ABC Olympic television special, which she co-produced, wrote, and narrated.

De Varona in 1994 provided extensive coverage of the feud between American figure skaters **Tonya Harding** and **Nancy Kerrigan**. (In January, Harding's boyfriend, Jeff Gillooly, clubbed Kerrigan in the knees in an attempt to eliminate her from the 1994 Winter Olympics in Lillehammer, Norway. Harding claimed to have no foreknowledge of the event.) De Varona appeared on ABC's *World News Tonight, Good Morning America, Weekend News,* ABC's *Wide World of Sports,* and various talk shows. She also followed the story to Norway, and covered the athletic events. Two years later, when

Awards and Accomplishments	
1960	Youngest member of U.S. Olympic team at Rome
1960-64	37 national swimming championships
1963	Two gold medals at Pan American Games
1964	Two gold medals at Tokyo Olympics; named Most Outstanding Female Athlete by Associated Press and United Press International; world record holder in 400-meter individual medley and 100-meter backstroke
1969	International Swimming Hall of Fame
1983	Women's Sports Hall of Fame
1986	Yale Kephuth Fellowship and New York State Board of Regents' Medal of Excellence
1987	Girl Scouts Humanitarian Award, U.S. Olympic Hall of Fame; Bay Area Sports Hall of Fame
1988	Member of National Women's Law Center advisory board; receives Honorary Doctor of Humane Letters, Drury College, Springfield, Missouri; receives Lifetime Fitness Award from National Fitness Foundation
1989	Outstanding Mother of the Year from Mother's Day Committee; receives Woman of the Year Award from Mew York Athletic League
1990	National Handicapped Sports Hero Award
1991	Gold Medallion Award from International Swimming Hall of Fame
1991	Emmy Award as producer of Special Olympics feature
1992	American Woman Award for Leadership from Women's Research and Education Institute; receives Olympia Award from U.S. Olympic Committee
1995	Ellis Island Medal of Honor
1995	Flo Hyman Award from Women's Sports Foundation
1997	HOBY International Award for youth leadership from the Hugh O'Brien Youth Leadership Organization
1998	Honorary Doctor of Humane Letters, St. Joseph College, West Hartford, Connecticut
1998	Emmy Award nomination for *Keepers of the Flame,* as co-producer and co-writer
1999	Honorary Doctor of Humane Letters, Springfield College, Springfield, Massachusetts; Thurman Munson Award
2000	Gracie Award, American Women in Radio and Television, for excellence in broadcasting; Honorary Doctorate, United States Sports Academy; Olympic Order for leadership and service
2001	Gracie Award; Susan B. Anthony "Trailblazer" Award from University of Rochester; Albert Schoenfield Journalism Award; led the delegation accompanying US Women's National Soccer Team to China
2002	Overcoming Obstacles Achievement Award from Community for Education Foundation
2003	Theodore Roosevelt Award, highest honor from the National Collegiate Athletic Association

the Summer Olympics were in Atlanta, de Varona anchored *Good Morning America*'s Olympic coverage, while broadcasting the days' results on ABC Radio.

Since 1998, de Varona has been a weekly commentator for Sporting News Radio, a 24-hour sports radio network. De Varona covered her 12th Olympic Games in 2000 when she signed on with NBC for the Games in Sydney, Australia. At those Games, the International Olympic Committee presented de Varona with its highest award, the Olympic Order.

Asterisk After Her Name

De Varona has been active in a variety of organizations and committees. She has been an adviser to Presi-

Where Is She Now?

These days, de Varona balances her life between broadcasting, family, and women's advocacy. She has been writing commentary for Sporting News Radio, and working as a sports and organizational consultant for the ABC, ESPN, and Disney networks.

The former Olympian chaired the 1999 Women's World Cup Soccer Organizing Committee, which resulted in what some have called "the most successful women's sporting event ever," according to Marty Benson of the National Collegiate Athletic Association (NCAA). Still, de Varona believes the media gives women short shrift. "I thought as cable permeated the airwaves that women's sports would get a better piece of the action," she told NCAA's Benson, adding, "I'm frustrated that we don't read, hear, and see more about women's sports." De Varona, who remains active as chair of the Women's Sports Foundation's Board of Stewards, is still an honorary trustee for the Foundation. Most recently, de Varona was awarded the Overcoming Obstacles award from the Community for Education Foundation, given to those who have achieved professional excellence and fostered growth within their sphere of expertise.

De Varona and her husband, John Pinto, a lawyer, live in Greenwich, Connecticut. The couple have two teenage children, John David and Joanna, both of whom participate in sports.

dent Ford's Commission on Olympic Sports and President Carter's Women's Advisory Commission, and served five terms on the President's Council on Physical Fitness and Sports. From its inception in 1969, to 1988, de Varona has sat on the board of the Special Olympics. She was also consultant on Title IX legislation, which became law in 1972 and prohibits sex discrimination in sports. She finally earned her degree in 1986 upon completion of two assignments: one on the history of amateur sports legislation and the other on the impact on women's sports of Title IX.

Shortly after the adoption of Title IX, de Varona and tennis champion **Billie Jean King** founded the Women's Sports Foundation in 1974, de Varona serving as its first president. "The effort I had put forth in my swimming career gave me the stamina to become an activist for Olympic athletes and women, raising money and awareness," de Varona told *USA Swimming online*. "The world is political and you have to fight. Once you've been able to reach goals, like winning Olympic gold medals, no one can take that effort away. That accomplishment opens doors. It's like having an asterisk after your name." De Varona has received dozens of honorary degrees and awards, including the National Collegiate Athletic Association's highest honor, the Theodore Roosevelt Award.

A $50 Million Lawsuit

In April 1998, ABC did not renew de Varona's contract. Their reason for firing her was, allegedly, her "failing to appeal to a male demographic of ages eighteen to thirty-nine." Charging age and gender discrimination under federal law, de Varona shot back with a $50 million lawsuit. In her complaint, de Varona asserted that male veteran colleagues, such as **Frank Gifford**, then 69,

received preferential assignments. "It took a lot of soul-searching," de Varona told *People*. "It would have been much easier to walk away, but I felt I had to do it."

The suit was settled out of court in 2002, and de Varona rejoined ABC Sports as a commentator and reporter.

Fights for Women's Sports

De Varona left ABC once before, in 1976, after facing what she termed "discriminatory barriers" as a female sportscaster. The NBC network soon swept her up. ABC Sports enticed her back in 1983, when de Varona assumed a management position and went on to cover such events as the Harding-Kerrigan scandal, the New York City Marathon, the Indianapolis 500 auto race, and several Olympic Games.

De Varona has never backed down from supporting justice for women in amateur and professional athletics. "I will always be an activist," she told *Women's Sports and Fitness*. "That is a lifetime commitment."

CONTACT INFORMATION

Address: c/o Women's Sports Foundation, Eisenhower Park, East Meadow, NY 11554. Fax: 1-800-227-3988. Email: wosportpr@aol.com. Online: www.womenssportsfoundation.org.

SELECTED WRITINGS BY DE VARONA:

(With Barry Tarshis) *Donna de Varona's Hydro-Aerobics,* New York: Fawcett, 1986.

FURTHER INFORMATION

Books

Johnson, Anne Janette. *Great Women in Sports,* Detroit: Visible Ink Press, 1996.

Pemberton, Cynthia Lee A. *More Than a Game: One Woman's Fight for Gender Equity in Sport.* Boston: Northeastern University Press, 2002.

Periodicals

"Donna de Varona Receives NCAA's Highest Honor; 2003 Theodore Roosevelt Award." *PR Newswire* (December 5, 2002).

Grossman, Andrew. "De Varona Plans to Return to ABC as Lawsuit Is Settled." *Hollywood Reporter* (October 1, 2002): 4.

"Making Waves: Olympian Donna de Varona Charges ABC Fired Her because of Her Age." *People* (May 15, 2000): 89.

Schneider, Michael. "De Varona Accuses ABC of Bias." *Variety* (April 17, 2000): 47.

Other

"Donna de Varona Receives NCAA's Highest Honor: 2003 Theodore Roosevelt Award." NCAA. www.ncaa.org/ (December 30, 2002).

"Donna de Varona Rejoins ABC Sports." ABC Sports. espn.go.com/ (December 30, 2002).

Geocities.com. www.geocities.com/ (January 10, 2003).

Hickok Sports.com. www.hickoksports.com/ (December 30, 2002).

Hiss & Pop. www.hissandpop.com/ (January 10, 2003).

HOBY Organization. www.hoby.org/ (January 13, 2003).

Hollywood.com. www.hollywood.com/ (January 10, 2003).

Internet Movie Database. www.imdb.com/ (January 10, 2003).

Olympic Aid. www.olympicaid.org/ (January 10, 2003).

Rogers, Roger. "The Players Who Are the NSA." Women's Soccer World, www.womensoccer.com/ (January 11, 2003).

Schwimmverein Limmat. www.svl.ch/ (January 11, 2003).

Sporting News Radio. radio.sportingnews.com/ (December 30, 2002).

Swingin Chicks. www.swinginchicks.com/ (December 30, 2002).

USA Swimming. www.usa-swimming.org/ (December 30, 2002).

Women's Sports Foundation. www.womenssportsfoundation.org/ (January 13, 2003).

Yahoo! Movies, movies.yahoo.com/ (January 10, 2003).

Sketch by Jane Summer

Gail Devers

Gail Devers
1966-

American track and field athlete

Gail Devers will go down as one of the fastest female combination sprinters and hurdlers in history, as well as one of the greatest track and field athletes. While her awards and accomplishments, including setting several American and world records in various indoor and outdoor events, are impressive, they are only half the story. Devers's triumph over Graves' disease—a debilitating and potentially dangerous thyroid condition—early in her career is the stuff of legend. The disease and the treatments that she pursued made Devers so ill that she had to be carried around by her family. At one point, doctors almost amputated her feet because they were so swollen. Devers's professional comeback, which began in 1991 after years of sedentary living with her condition, was extraordinary, and included gold medals in the 100-meter dash in both the 1992 and the 1996 Olympics.

A Born Competitor

Yolanda Gail Devers was born on November 19, 1966, in Seattle, Washington, although her family relocated to National City, California, a small town near San Diego. From an early age, Devers's brother, Parenthesis, would race Gail, always making fun of her when she lost. Devers decided that she did not want to lose anymore, and began training. She beat her brother in their next race. From that point, Devers steadily increased her competitive arena, moving from the neighborhood races against her brother to the races at Sweetwater High School.

Throughout school, Devers continued to improve, and her stellar performances helped the team win the San Diego sectional track and field team title. In 1984, her senior year at Sweetwater, Devers went to the state championships, where she won the 100-meter dash and 100-meter hurdles, and placed second in the long jump. All of these accomplishments attracted attention from major universities, who heavily courted Devers with offers of athletic scholarships. Devers chose the University of California at Los Angeles, where she trained under coach Bob Kersee, the future husband of fellow track star, **Jackie Joyner-Kersee**. Bob Kersee was the first coach who pushed Devers harder than she pushed herself, and

Chronology

1966	Born November 19 in Seattle, Washington
1984	Enrolls at University of California, Los Angeles, on a track scholarship, and begins training with Bob Kersee; Devers is the first female athlete from her high school to earn an athletic scholarship from a major university
1988	Graduates from University of California, Los Angeles with a degree in Sociology
1988	Marries Ron Roberts, the captain of the UCLA men's track team
1988	While training for the 1988 Summer Olympics, Devers's health begins to deteriorate
1988	Competes at the 1988 Summer Olympics, finishing eighth in her qualifying heat for the 100-meter dash
1988	Becomes violently ill
1990	Diagnosed with Graves' disease; she opts to undergo radiation treatment as opposed to taking a medication that is on the banned medications list for the Olympics
1991	Two days before her feet are set to be amputated, doctors realize that Devers's radiation treatments are the cause of her dangerously swollen feet
1991	Begins her track and field comeback by walking around a track with socks on her feet, since her feet are still too tender to wear shoes
1991	Gets divorced from Ron Roberts
1992	Less than seventeen months after doctors almost amputate her feet, she wins the gold medal in the 100-meter dash in the 1992 Summer Olympics; she also leads the race for the 100-meter hurdles event, but trips over the last hurdle, falling to a fifth-place finish
1994	Misses most competitions this year, due to a hamstring injury and back problems that result from a car accident
1996	Wins gold medal in the 100-meter dash in the 1996 Summer Olympics
1996	Marries American Olympic gold medalist and triple jumper, Kenny Harrison
2000	Forced to drop out of the 100-meter hurdle race at the 2000 Summer Olympics, due to Achilles tendon and hamstring injuries

Awards and Accomplishments

1984	Won 100-meter dash and 100-meter hurdles, and places second in long jump in California high school state championships
1987	Gold medal in the 100-meter dash at the 1987 Pan-American Games
1988	Set an American record in the 100-meter hurdles
1988	NCAA champion in the 100-meter dash
1988	Member of U.S. Olympic Team
1992	Silver medal in 100-meter hurdles at the World Track & Field Championships
1992	Gold medal in 100-meter dash at 1992 Summer Olympics
1992-93	Ran world's fastest time in 100-meter hurdles
1993	Gold medal in 60-meter dash at the World Indoor Track & Field Championships
1993	Gold medals in 100-meter dash and 100-meter hurdles at World Track & Field Championships, the first woman to do this in international competition in 45 years
1993	Set American indoor record in 60-meter dash
1993	Won 21 of 23 races in hurdles and sprints
1993	Ran world's fastest time in 100-meter dash
1994	Named one of two top athletes in 1993 (along with fellow track and field star, Michael Johnson) by the U.S. Olympic Committee
1995	Won the 100-meter hurdles at the World Track & Field Championships
1996	Gold medal in 100-meter dash at the 1996 Summer Olympics, becoming only the second woman in history (the other is Wyomia Tyus) to win back-to-back Olympic golds in the 100-meter dash; also won a gold medal as part of the 4 x 100-meter relay at the 1996 Olympics
1997	Gold medal for the 4 x 100-meter relay at the World Track & Field Championships
1999	Gold medal and sets national record in 100-meter hurdles at the World Track & Field Championships
2000	Broke her own national record in 100-meter hurdles at the U.S. Olympic trials

his difficult training methods—which included entering Devers in six or seven track-and-field events in some meets—paid off. Devers advanced rapidly, even in events like the 100-meter hurdles, which she had always felt were out of her reach due to her small size.

A Mysterious Affliction

In 1988, Devers was in top form. She set a national record of 12.61 seconds in the 100-meter hurdles and qualified for the American track-and-field team for the 1988 Summer Olympics in Seoul, South Korea. While training for the Olympics, however, Devers began to experience a host of physical problems, including fatigue, muscle pulls, bouts of insomnia, fainting spells, migraine headaches, and various other ailments. Nevertheless, Devers pushed herself, and at the Olympics she had her worst competition performance since high school. She did not qualify for the finals, and many experts assumed that Devers had pushed herself too hard under Kersee.

Devers's symptoms worsened, and included memory and hair loss, skin discoloration, and near-constant menstruation. In 1990, after two years of suffering, doctors finally realized that Devers had Graves' disease, a thyroid disorder. Although she was miserable, Devers opted not to take the standard medication treatment for the disease, since this drug was on the list of mediations banned by the International Olympic Committee. Even as she was bed-ridden, Devers never gave up hope that she would someday return to the Olympics, and she did not want to take the chance of becoming ineligible for competition. Instead of medication, Devers opted for painful radiation therapy, which destroyed the cyst on her thyroid gland, but which also obliterated her thyroid gland itself in the process.

Her symptoms disappeared for a short while, and Devers thought she was cured. In 1991, however, Devers experienced new disturbing symptoms, including severe blood blisters on her feet, which doctors misdiagnosed as athlete's foot. Devers's feet swelled up to a dangerous size, and began oozing yellow fluid. Devers was in so much pain that she could not walk. At one point, the pain and swelling were so bad that doctors were ready to amputate both of her feet. Fortunately, Devers's doctors realized that the symptoms were the result of the athlete's radiation therapy. As soon as they stopped this treatment, her condition rapidly improved. As soon as she was able to walk, Devers began training again, starting with a single walk around the UCLA track—in socks, because her feet were still too tender to wear shoes. These were her first tentative steps in what is generally acknowledged as one of the most notable comebacks in sports history.

Back, and Better Than Ever

Now that her feet had been spared, Devers put them to good use. In March 1991, mere months after stopping the radiation treatment, Devers qualified for The Athletics Congress (TAC) meet, a prestigious event where she won the 100-meter hurdles. Devers's performance continued to improve, and in 1992, at the World Track and Field Championships in Tokyo, Devers won a silver medal in the 100-meter hurdles. Under the coaching of Kersee, who encouraged Devers to focus on her performance in the 100-meter dash, Devers qualified for the 1992 Barcelona Olympics in the 100-meter dash *and* in the 100-meter hurdles. During the qualifying races for the finals of the 100-meter dash, Devers temporarily lost feeling in her feet while she was waiting in the starting blocks.

She shook it out, however, and made it to the finals, which featured one of the closest finishes in Olympic history. Devers crossed the finish line at almost exactly the same time as her four competitors, which included fellow American, **Gwen Torrence**. Judges analyzed the photo finish, and Devers was declared the victor, despite accusations from other competitors that Devers might have been using performance-enhancing drugs—rumors that were quickly shown to be unfounded. Devers had successfully come back from her debilitating bout with Graves' disease to win an Olympic gold medal. She was not done, however. Several days later, Devers competed in the finals of the 100-meter hurdles, a race that she dominated from the beginning. Unfortunately, Devers's tremendous speed worked against her, and she came up too fast on the final hurdle, hitting it with her lead foot. Devers tripped and fell, stumbling across the finish line in fifth place.

Devers bounced back quickly from this latest setback, and in 1993, she set several indoor track records, including an American record of 6.99 seconds in the 60-meter dash. She also pulled a hamstring muscle, but was healed in time for the World Track and Field Championships in Stuttgart, Germany, where she won both the 100-meter dash and the 100-meter hurdles, something that she had been unable to do in Barcelona. Devers continued to have a strong year, and ultimately finished 1993 with twenty-one wins out of twenty-three races, plus three titles. For this reason, the United States Olympic Committee named Devers the U.S. Female Athlete of the Year.

In 1994, Devers's hamstring injury returned, and she was out of competition for most of the year. Over the next two years, Devers mainly concentrated on training for the 1996 Atlanta Olympics, although she did win the

---

Dash to Glory

Ninety-five meters into the [1992 Summer] Olympic women's 100-meter dash, the crowd had quit cheering. The sprinters crossed the finish line to exhalations of disbelief, to stunned muttering. The question of who was the fastest woman in the world had just been decided. But no one could tell who she was. She herself didn't know. Here, in a heavenly grove atop Barcelona's Montjuic, five sprinters had expected to reach a lonely pinnacle. Instead, they found themselves on a plateau crowded with virtual equals. ...

Five meters from the finish, Devers was passing [Russian Irina] Privalova, [Jamaican Juliet] Cuthbert was catching Devers, [Jamaican Merlene] Ottey was catching Cuthbert, and [American Gwen] Torrence was catching Ottey. The five seemed to merge at the line. Even the blurry, warped finish photo on the scoreboard, freezing the sprinters in the throes of their final efforts, was of no immediate help. But wait. If it's a sentimental favorite you want, look again at Devers, leaning there in lane 2, and listen to what she has endured over the last Olympiad.

Source: Moore, Kenny. *Sports Illustrated* (August 10, 1992): 12.

100-meter hurdles at the 1995 World Track and Field Championships. At the Olympics, Devers once again qualified for both the 100-meter dash and the 100-meter hurdles. As in the 1992 Olympics, the finals race was a photo finish, and Devers was once again declared the winner—becoming only the second woman to win consecutive 100-meter titles in the Olympics. At the same time, Devers's fiancee, American triple-jumper Kenny Harrison, also won the gold medal in his event.

Devers also made it to the finals in the 100-meter hurdles. Determined not to make the same mistake she made at the 1992 Olympics, Devers nevertheless came too slow out of the blocks and did not turn in a good performance, finishing fourth. This time around, however, Devers did take home a second gold medal—as part of American women's 4 x 100-meter relay team. Four years later, Devers stunned the track and field world by qualifying for her fourth Olympics, in Sydney, Australia in both the 100-meter hurdles and the 4 x 100 meter relay. Unfortunately, Devers injured a hamstring muscle before the Olympics, and was forced to drop out of the competition. Devers continues to compete, and 2002 featured one of her best seasons yet. After she retires, Devers plans to devote her endless energy and determination to community outreach projects, something that she already does on a part-time basis through her company, Gail Force, Inc.

Devers's Legacy

Most people acknowledge Devers's extraordinary comeback from Graves' disease, which sports commentators often discuss even more than her three Olympic gold medals. Since 1991 when she returned to competition, however, Devers has consistently proven that, while her illness and subsequent comeback is compelling and even miraculous, it is only a small testament to her greatness as a sports figure. Devers has not only returned to her pre-disease state of athletic fitness, she has surpassed it, again and again, sometimes breaking her own records in the process. Paradoxically, she just keeps on improving as she gets older. Now in her mid-thirties, the time when many professional track-and-field athletes start to consider retirement, Devers continues to compete and is stronger than ever. How long will Devers remain competitive? If she continues to push her body to its limits, using the same mind-over-matter willpower that helped her battle Graves' disease, there's no telling how long she may compete. One thing's for certain, though: Devers is already a legend. And until the day arrives when she launches out of the starting blocks for the last time, Devers's competitors will know not to make the mistake of underestimating her abilities or determination.

CONTACT INFORMATION

Address: Gail Devers, Elite International Sports and Management, 1034 Brentwood Blvd., Suite 1530, Saint Louis, MO 63117-1215.

FURTHER INFORMATION

Books

Contemporary Black Biography, Vol. 7. Detroit: Gale, 1994.

Great Women in Sports. Detroit: Visible Ink Press, 1996.

Gutman, Bill. *Gail Devers: Overcoming the Odds.* Bt Bound, 1999.

Layden, Joe. *Women In Sports: The Complete Book on the World's Greatest Female Athletes.* Los Angeles: General Publishing Group, 1997.

Mead, Katherine. *Gail Devers: A Runner's Dream (Young Biographies).* Raintree/Steck-Vaughn, 1998.

Plowden, Martha Ward. *Olympic Black Women.* Gretna: Pelican Publishing Company, 1996.

St. James Encyclopedia of Popular Culture. five volumes. Detroit: St. James Press, 2000.

Who's Who Among African Americans. 14th ed. Detroit: Gale, 2001.

Worth, Richard. *Gail Devers (Overcoming Adversities).* Philadelphia: Chelsea House, 2001.

Periodicals

Cazeneuve, Brian. "Inside Track and Field." *Sports Illustrated* (July 29, 2002): 84.

"Gail Devers story tells how sprinter overcame illness to win Olympic gold." *Jet* (June 3, 1996): 52.

Leavy, Walter. "Athlete: Gail Devers." *Ebony* (March 1997): 90.

Moore, Kenny. "Dash to glory." *Sports Illustrated* (August 10, 1992): 12.

Other

Gail Devers's Home Page. http://www.gaildevers.com. (January 20, 2003).

Run for the Dream: The Gail Devers Story, Videocassette. Hallmark Home Entertainment, 1996.

Sports Stars Series 1–4. U•X•L, 1994-98. Reproduced in *Biography Resource Center.* Detroit: Gale Group. 2003. http://www.galenet.com/servlet/BioRC (January 24, 2003).

Sketch by Ryan D. Poquette

Eric Dickerson
1960-

American football player

During his professional football career, running back Eric Dickerson more often resembled a thoroughbred than a human being. Game after game, Dickerson electrified fans as he tucked the football under his arm, then sprinted down the field with all the beauty and grace of a well-groomed racehorse. Dickerson also possessed an uncanny ability to read the defense and knew which holes he could burst through to score. Because of these talents, Dickerson enjoyed many record-setting seasons in the National Football League (NFL) and was undoubtedly the most productive ball carrier of his time. Over the course of his eleven-year career, Dickerson set the NFL record for most yards rushed in a single season-2,105 yards. He also became the first player in NFL history to gain more than 1,000 yards in seven consecutive seasons. When he retired in 1993, his 13,259 career rushing yards was the second best of all time.

Raised in the Lone Star State

Eric Demetric Dickerson was born September 2, 1960, in Sealy, Texas, a small town about fifty miles west of Houston. Dickerson was raised by his great-aunt and great-uncle, Viola and Kary Dickerson, and spent the first part of his life believing Viola was his mother. Dickerson was a teenager when he discovered that his birth mother was actually a woman named Helen, whom he believed was his older sister. Helen, just seventeen when Dickerson was born, decided not to marry Dickerson's father, Richard Seal. Giving the child over to Viola seemed like the best option. Dickerson likely inherited some of his athletic ability from his father, Richard, who was a running back at Prairie View College in Texas.

Because he was terribly skinny and wore glasses, Dickerson endured teasing from his the neighborhood kids. That all changed, however, once he began playing football. Dickerson's success on the football field was almost instant. By seventh and eighth grade, Dickerson was making a name for himself as a running back. "I'll

Eric Dickerson

never forget our first game," Dickerson recalled in Nancy J. Nielsen's book *Eric Dickerson*. "I was absolutely terrified, really just running for my life, but I guess my fear was a pretty good motivator. I wound up scoring four touchdowns that day. . . . Suddenly people were looking at me differently. Their eyes showed respect."

Entering Sealy High School, Dickerson starred on the football and track teams, winning the state 100-yard dash championship with a lightening-quick time of 9.4 seconds. The sport he really stood out in, however, was football.

Even in high school, Dickerson's coaches could tell he had natural instincts as a running back. His senior year, Dickerson rushed for 2,642 yards and thirty-seven touchdowns to lead Sealy to the state high school Class AA championship. He was named a 1978 *Parade* magazine All-American.

Played Football at Southern Methodist University

Following high school, Dickerson entered Southern Methodist University (SMU) in Dallas because his mother, Viola, wanted him to stay close to home. Dickerson, however, had wanted to play for the Oklahoma Sooners. Injuries plagued Dickerson his freshman year, and the "hometown" boy didn't make much of an impact. His sophomore year, however, Dickerson rushed for more than 100 yards in five different games. His junior year, Dickerson moved the ball 1,428 yards to score nineteen touchdowns and was selected as the Southwest Conference Player of the Year. While Dickerson was at SMU, he and running mate Craig James were dubbed "The Pony Express."

During Dickerson's senior year, he gained 1,617 yards and scored seventeen touchdowns, while helping his team to a Cotton Bowl victory. That year, Dickerson rushed for an average of 147 yards per game-third best in the nation. Dickerson was chosen as an All-American, was voted Southwest Conference Offensive Player of the Year, and came in third in Heisman trophy balloting.

Drafted by Los Angeles Rams

During the April 1983 NFL draft, the Los Angeles Rams selected Dickerson. He was the second player selected in the draft, behind quarterback **John Elway**.

Dickerson's start in the pros, however, was not nearly as smooth as his stride. His first game, a scrimmage game against the Dallas Cowboys, was a near disaster. "I was so jittery my mind went completely blank," he recalled in Nielsen's book. "I couldn't remember a thing—not a play, not a formation, not anything."

Dickerson's jitters plagued him at the start of his rookie year. In his first three pro game appearances, Dickerson fumbled the ball six times. One of the fumbles led to a game-winning field goal by the opponent. Dickerson soon calmed down and in his fourth game, he made an 85-yard touchdown run against the New York Jets. Later, he rushed for 199 yards against the Detroit Lions. Despite his shaky start, Dickerson ended up rewriting the NFL rookie record book. He ended the season as the NFL's top rusher with 1,808 yards, beating out all of the other veteran players. He scored eighteen touchdowns rushing and gained 100 or more yards in nine games. That season, he set rookie records for rushing yards (1,808), rushing attempts (390), and rushing touchdowns (18) to earn NFL Rookie of the Year honors.

Broke NFL's Single-Season Rushing Record

By 1984, Dickerson's second season, he'd gained enough confidence to calm down. He became choosier about which holes he would try to slip through. That season, Dickerson had twelve 100-yard games. As the end of the season approached, it looked as if Dickerson

Career Statistics

		Rushing				Receiving				
Yr	Team	ATT	YDS	AVG	TD	REC	YDS	AVG	TD	FUM
1983	RAMS	390	1808	4.6	18	51	404	7.9	2	13
1984	RAMS	379	2105	5.6	14	21	139	6.6	0	14
1985	RAMS	292	1234	4.2	12	20	126	6.3	0	10
1986	RAMS	404	1821	4.5	11	26	205	7.9	0	12
1987	RAMS/IND	283	1288	4.6	6	18	171	9.5	0	7
1988	IND	388	1659	4.3	14	36	377	10.5	1	5
1989	IND	314	1311	4.2	7	30	211	7.0	1	10
1990	IND	166	677	4.1	4	18	92	5.1	0	0
1991	IND	167	536	3.2	2	41	269	6.6	1	6
1992	LA	187	729	3.9	2	14	85	6.1	1	1
1993	ATL	26	91	3.5	0	6	58	9.7	0	0
TOTAL		2996	13259	4.4	90	281	2137	7.6	6	78

ATL: Atlanta Falcons; IND: Indianapolis Colts; LA: Los Angeles Raiders; RAMS: Los Angeles Rams.

might be able to break **O.J. Simpson**'s single-season rushing record of 2,003 yards, set in 1973. The pressure mounted, and during a December 2 game against New Orleans, Dickerson gained only 149 yards. He blamed the disappointing numbers on mounting pressure from the press and fans. A few days later, Dickerson said he was having nightmares. According to *Sports Illustrated,* Dickerson told the press: "I didn't sleep well last night. I was trying to sleep, and I had a dream about getting 2,001 yards." That's exactly where his dream ended—at 2,001 yards—three shy of breaking Simpson's record. Dickerson, however, pulled it together later in the month during the second to last game of the regular season. Playing the Houston Oilers, Dickerson gained 215 yards in twenty-seven carries to break Simpson's single-season rushing record. Dickerson ended the season with 2,105 rushing yards and fourteen touchdowns. He also caught twenty-one passes for 139 yards.

When Dickerson broke Simpson's single-season rushing record in 1984, he found himself thrust into the spotlight. Dickerson, however, gave his teammates plenty of credit for his success. The humble Dickerson didn't forget the ten offensive linemen who made his record-shattering possible. In appreciation, Dickerson gave them each a diamond-studded gold ring etched with the number 2,105.

In each of his first four years with the Rams, Dickerson delivered his team to the playoffs. In 1986, Dickerson set a new record for rushing yardage in a playoff game by gaining 248 yards against the Dallas Cowboys.

Following a salary dispute, Dickerson was traded to the Indianapolis Colts in 1987. It was one of the biggest deals in NFL history. The trade involved three teams and 10 players, as well as draft-choice swapping. The trade proved good for the Colts, and in 1988, Dickerson earned his fourth rushing title, leading the league with

1,659 yards. Dickerson spent four seasons with the Colts before joining the Los Angeles Raiders in 1992 and the Atlanta Falcons in 1993. He retired in 1993 without ever making it to the Super Bowl.

Nicknamed 'Mr. Fourth Quarter'

While Dickerson had natural athletic abilities, part of his success came from his year-round training program. Strength training and sprinting programs were a staple in his life. Over the course of his career, Dickerson earned the nickname "Mr. Fourth Quarter" because he could turn it up a notch as the others were winding down.

This stamina also helped Dickerson become the seventh back in NFL history to hit the 10,000-yard milestone. Though others had reached that mark, Dickerson did it in the fewest games—ninety-one.

Besides his workhorse mentality, Dickerson was also well-known for his signature prescription goggles, which he wore on the field to correct poor vision. He never seemed to have trouble finding holes in the defense, however.

Off the field, Dickerson involved himself with many youth programs. In 1984, he formed Dickerson's Rangers, a Los Angeles-area youth club for boys and girls aimed at providing an alternative to streets, gangs, and drugs.

Remembered as Potent, Graceful Runner

While it is feasible that another NFL player could match Dickerson's records, no one will surely match his style. A potent and graceful runner, Dickerson stands in a league of his own. In the forward to his book, *Eric Dickerson's Secrets of Pro Power,* Indianapolis Colts coach Ron Meyer described Dickerson's distinctive running style this way: "He has the power to run right over would-be tacklers, the moves to leave them flatfooted, and the speed to run away from them. He's like a lion on

Awards and Accomplishments

1978	Named *Parade* magazine All-American
1982	Named to *Sporting News* All-America team
1983	Set NFL rookie record for most yards rushing (1,808) and led NFL and NFC (National Football Conference) in rushing yards (1,808)
1983	Named Associated Press Offensive Rookie of the Year, Pro Football Writers Association Rookie of the Year, United Press International NFC Rookie of the Year, *Sporting News* MVP/Player of the Year; and NFL Rookie of the Year; selected for the NFL All-Pro team, as well as the Pro Bowl
1984	Set NFL single-season rushing record with 2,105 yards, earning both the NFL and NFC rushing titles; named to the NFL All-Pro team and the Pro Bowl
1986	Set NFL record for most yards rushed in a playoff game (248); earned NFL and NFC rushing titles with a league-leading 1,821 yards
1986	Named Associated Press Offensive Player of the Year
1986-88	Named to the NFL All-Pro team
1986-89	Named to the Pro Bowl
1987	Earned AFC rushing title with 1,288 yards
1988	Earned NFL and AFC rushing titles with 1,659 yards
1999	Inducted into the Pro Football Hall of Fame

Where Is He Now?

Dickerson resides in Calabasas, California. Since leaving pro football, he's devoted a lot of time to various charity events. Over the past few years, he's sponsored fund-raisers for the American Diabetes Association and for a local leukemia patient. Dickerson plays golf five or six times a week and has even sponsored his own celebrity golf tournament.

In addition to his fund-raising, Dickerson has worked as a sports analyst. He joined the ABC *Monday Night Football* broadcasting team in 2000.

"Eric Dickerson-Highlights." Pro Football Hall of Fame. http://www.profootballhof.com/players/highlights/edickerson.cfm (January 2, 2003).

"Eric Dickerson-Statistics." Pro Football Hall of Fame. http://www.profootballhof.com/players/statistics/edickerson.cfm (January 2, 2003).

Sketch by Lisa Frick

the prowl with a football, hunting for the end zone, or like a thoroughbred in shoulder pads, sprinting down the home stretch. Give him a step and he'll take 6 points." Statistics aside, if just for his running style, Dickerson will forever be rated as one of the best running backs in the NFL simply because he was so magnificent to watch.

SELECTED WRITINGS BY DICKERSON:

(With Steve Delsohn) *On the Run,* McGraw-Hill, 1986.
(With Richard Graham Walsh) *Eric Dickerson's Secrets of Pro Power,* Warner Books, Inc., 1989.

FURTHER INFORMATION

Books

Dickerson, Eric, with Richard Graham Walsh. *Eric Dickerson's Secrets of Pro Power.* New York: Warner Books, Inc., 1989.

Nielsen, Nancy J. *Eric Dickerson.* Mankato, Minnesota: Crestwood House, 1988.

Periodicals

Dingus, Anne. "Eric Dickerson." *Texas Monthly* (September 1999): 216.

Nack, William. "He Put the Squeeze on the Juice." *Sports Illustrated* (December 17, 1984): 16.

"NFL Career Rushing Leaders." *St. Louis Post-Dispatch* (September 8, 2002).

Other

"Eric Dickerson-Biography." Pro Football Hall of Fame. http://www.profootballhof.com/players/mainpage.cfm?cont_id=99899 (January 2, 2003).

Joe DiMaggio
1914-1999

American baseball player

One of the greatest of all baseball players, Joe DiMaggio played the game with grace (one of his nicknames was the Yankee Clipper), power (the other nickname was Joltin' Joe), and an all-around level of skill that few others have approached. His talent, combined with his desire to win and his team's sustained success, led to him become an icon of popular culture—the man who was considered baseball's greatest living player after his retirement.

The son of Sicilian immigrant parents, Joseph Paul DiMaggio was born in Martinez, California, a tiny East Bay village, on November 25, 1914. Named for his father, Giuseppe, he was the eighth of nine children. Not long after DiMaggio's birth the family moved to San Francisco where Giuseppe continued to ply his trade as a fisherman. DiMaggio grew up in the Italian neighborhood of North Beach, not far from Fisherman's Wharf where his father docked his boat. He attended public schools until age 16 whereupon he dropped out of Gallileo High School. By then he was already showing prowess as a baseball player as had his older brother, Vince. In fact, the last three DiMaggio siblings—Vince, Joe, and Dominic—would all become major league baseball players.

Hometown Sensation

From 1930 to 1932 DiMaggio resisted working on his father's boat, and after numerous odd jobs and a growing

Joe DiMaggio

and won the league's second-half pennant. (The Angels won the first half). The Seals then went on to win the league championship against the Angels, four games to two. DiMaggio was the league's most valuable player (MVP) with a .398 batting average, 34 home runs and 173 RBIs. He had an astounding 270 hits. He was more than ready to join the Yankees.

Off to a Fabulous Start

If the Rookie of the Year award had existed in 1936, there is no doubt that DiMaggio would have won it in the American League (AL). DiMaggio joined a Yankee team that had not won the league pennant since 1932 and was now led by first baseman **Lou Gehrig**. The sportswriters, always in search of a colorful angle, dubbed DiMaggio as the next Ruth on the strength of his incredible 1935 PCL season. But when the Yankees season opened, DiMaggio was on the disabled list with an injured foot—in later years, bone chips and botched surgery on his heels would prove to be DiMaggio's physical undoing. He played his first regular season game for the Yankees on May 3, 1936, against the St. Louis Browns (since relocated and renamed the Baltimore Orioles) at Yankee Stadium. DiMaggio went three for six with a triple, an RBI, and three runs scored.

His rookie season pretty much kicked into gear then and he finished the year with 29 home runs, 125 RBIs, and a .323 average—all very good statistics but all far behind Gehrig, who won the AL MVP award that year. Still, DiMaggio was the final component in the powerful Yankee club—he was the first rookie to play in the All-Star Game. The Yankees not only won the league pennant, but defeated their city archrivals, the New York Giants, four games to two in the World Series. DiMaggio hit .346 in his first World Series. Furthermore, he proved, throughout that first season and during the World Series, to be a graceful outfielder. Unfortunately the Gold Glove Award, given to players in each league for defensive prowess, was not instituted until 1957, six years after DiMaggio retired.

There proved to be no sophomore jinx for DiMaggio. As good as he was in his rookie season, he was better in nearly every offensive category in his second year, including leading the AL in home runs in 1937 with 46. He also led the league in runs scored, total bases, and slugging percentage. That season DiMaggio became the fourth player in the history of the game—after **Shoeless Joe Jackson**, Lloyd Waner, and Johnny Frederick—to record at least 200 base hits in his first two seasons. The feat has since been accomplished by Johnny Pesky, Harvey Kuenn, and **Ichiro Suzuki**. The Yankees again won the league pennant and the World Series. The team was now in the midst of a tear, winning the World Series four years in a row, 1936-1939.

Prior to the 1938 season DiMaggio held out for more than the $25,000 per season offered by the Yankees.

reputation in San Francisco as a semi-pro baseball player, he signed late in the 1932 season to play for the San Francisco Seals of the Pacific Coast League (PCL). At that time the PCL was not a minor league but a highly regarded independent league, just a half-step below the major leagues. He joined his older brother, Vince, who had already signed with the Seals earlier in the year. He appeared in the final three games at shortstop and hit for a .222 average. The next season, 1933, DiMaggio's greatness on the diamond first shone. Replacing his brother as the team's slugging star and center fielder, he hit for a .340 average with 28 home runs and 169 runs batted in (RBIs). More importantly he put together a 61-game hitting streak that was only stopped by the outstanding effort of Ed Walsh, Jr. of the cross-bay rival Oakland Oaks who pitched a no-hitter. Vince DiMaggio, meanwhile, caught on with the Los Angeles Angels.

Following the 1934 season the New York Yankees decided to purchase DiMaggio's contract from the Seals. (1934 was **Babe Ruth**'s last season with the Yankees.) Unfortunately for Seals owner Charley Graham, DiMaggio injured his knee and the original sale price of $75,000 was cut to $25,000. However, both teams publicly announced the higher figure. Furthermore, DiMaggio spent the 1935 season with the Seals.

DiMaggio's final season with his hometown team was another memorable one. The Seals had brought in former major leaguer Lefty O'Doul as a player-manager

With the nation still staggering through the Great Depression public feeling was not on his side, and DiMaggio eventually signed for the amount offered. In 1939 the Yankees officially became DiMaggio's team. Gehrig, suffering from amyotrophic lateral sclerosis, or ALS (from which he died two years later), retired prematurely and DiMaggio had to carry a heavier load. He responded by winning the AL batting championship with a .381 average, hitting 30 home runs and driving in 126 runs. DiMaggio was named AL MVP that season, and the Yankees swept the Cincinnati Reds in the World Series. Perhaps the biggest DiMaggio news of the year occurred on November 19, 1939 when he married actress Dorothy Arnold in the Church of Sts. Peter and Paul in San Francisco. Thousands turned out to see the wedding of their hometown hero, or at least glimpse DiMaggio and Arnold as they emerged from the church.

The 1940 season was an "off" year for the Yankees—they fell to third place—but not for DiMaggio, who still put up excellent numbers at the plate; he repeated as the AL batting champion with a .352 average. Although not involved in postseason play, the urbane DiMaggio was by then a regular in the café society that dominated Manhattan night life.

The Streak

DiMaggio was one of the leading performers, if not *the* leading performer of the incredible 1941 season. The Yankees won the AL pennant and went on to defeat the Brooklyn Dodgers in the World Series four games to one. (Within ten years Brooklyn would replace the New York Giants as National League archrival to the Yankees, before both NL teams decamped to the West Coast in 1958.) DiMaggio hit .357 in 1941 with 30 home runs and a league-leading 125 RBIs. He again led the league in total bases and was second in slugging percentage and runs scored, but he did not win the league batting title. That honor went to DiMaggio's hitting rival, **Ted Williams**, who that season hit .406—that last man in major league baseball to bat over .400 for an entire season. DiMaggio, however led his team to the pennant and for that, and other exploits on the field he won his second MVP award.

The other exploits during the 1941 season included what is known simply as The Streak, which many baseball experts and fans consider the one baseball mark that will never be surpassed. Beginning on May 15th and continuing until July 16th DiMaggio hit safely in 56 consecutive games. Against the Boston Red Sox (Williams's team) on July 2nd, DiMaggio hit a home run to break Wee Willie Keeler's record; it was the 45th consecutive game in which he got a least a hit. The streak was finally halted two weeks later in Cleveland by Indians pitchers Al Smith and Jim Bagby and two outstanding defensive plays by third baseman Ken Keltner. DiMaggio then hit safely in 16 consecutive games beginning with the game after the streak ended. In that

Chronology

1914	Born November 25 in Martinez, California
1932	Signs first professional contract with San Francisco Seals of the Pacific Coast League
1933	Hits in 61 consecutive games for the Seals
1934	Contract sold to the New York Yankees
1936	Begins his major league career
1936-42, 1946-51	American League All-Star Team
1939	Wins his first American League MVP award
1941	Sets major league record with 56-game hit streak
1941	Wins his second American League MVP award
1941	Son Joseph DiMaggio, III born
1943	Enlists in the U.S. Army
1944	Dorothy Arnold divorces DiMaggio
1946	Returns to baseball
1947	Wins his third American League MVP award
1951	Retires from baseball
1954	Marries and is divorced from actress Marilyn Monroe
1955	Elected to Baseball Hall of Fame
1962	Arranges funeral of Marilyn Monroe
1968	Becomes coach of the Oakland Athletics
1969	Is named baseball's Greatest Living Player
1999	Dies March 8 in Hollywood, Florida

run he hit in 72 out of 73 games. The only sad note for the Yankees during the streak was Lou Gehrig's death from ALS on June 2nd. When the season was over the Associated Press named DiMaggio as Athlete of the Year. To top off his year, Joe DiMaggio, III was born on October 23, 1941.

The 1942 season was DiMaggio's last for the Yankees for a long time. His offensive numbers were down from the previous few years, but only slightly—he still finished in the top ten or even the top five in most important hitting categories—and the powerful Yankees again won the AL pennant, though were defeated by the St. Louis Cardinals in the World Series. But in 1942 war, which had been raging in Europe and Asia for years, finally embroiled the United States. Like many ballplayers of the era, DiMaggio volunteered for the military, though grudgingly. A few, such as Williams, actually saw combat action, but most were ensconced on military bases playing exhibition baseball games to lift the morale of the servicemen. DiMaggio, who enlisted in 1943 and held the rank of sergeant in the Army Air Corps, fell into the latter category. During these years the DiMaggios' shaky marriage fell apart. They were divorced in May 1944. Dorothy Arnold was granted custody of their two-and-a-half-year old son, and thereafter the extremely private DiMaggio's relationship with Joe III was strained, even into adulthood.

Postwar Comeback

DiMaggio was stationed first in Southern California and later Hawaii and all told missed three full seasons from his prime athletic years, 1943-45. The Yankees still managed to win the AL pennant the first year he was gone and took sweet revenge on the Cardinals in the

Awards and Accomplishments

1936-42, 1946-51	American League All-Star Team
1939	American League MVP
1941	American League MVP
1941	Associated Press Athlete of the Year
1947	American League MVP
1955	Baseball Hall of Fame
1969	Baseball's Greatest Living Player
1999	Major League Baseball All-Century Team

The DiMaggio Nobody Knew

Joe DiMaggio was our first modern media star, an athlete of extraordinary gifts and grace, a personage of regal dignity, an icon of American glamour. He was also the loneliest hero we have ever had.

In the end, he was free of the crowds that cheered and revered him, the crowds that made his fortune and that he detested. He always hated it when fans would interrupt him in restaurants, stop him on the street, ask him to sign. Now, at last, with the help of a roaring squadron of San Francisco motorcycle cops, Joe DiMaggio would make his last trip on earth nonstop, beyond all annoyance, in perfect privacy. Perfection was always the goal. Joe's brother Dominic, the old Red Sox center fielder, ruled that only family could say goodbye in the grand old church. Dom said that's what Joe would have wanted. Yet even among those 60 mourners, there were many whom Joe had pushed away in life.... That pallbearer with the gray ponytail—that was Joe DiMaggio Jr., whom Big Joe bitterly cut out of his life. Father and son never spoke. Even Dommie, the youngest and sole surviving brother, didn't speak with Joe for years. Only as lung cancer was killing Joe at 84 did the brothers try to repair the breach....

That was the point: he died as he lived ... without intimates of any sort, an object of feverish curiosity, in impenetrable secrecy, swaddled in myth, without even a formalistic nod to the public's right to know. Dominic was correct: that's what Joe would have wanted ... as the family in the church, the fans in the morning chill on the street who politely applauded his casket, as the nation as a whole looking in on TV ... said goodbye to the loneliest hero we have ever had.

Source: Richard Ben Cramer. *Newsweek,* March 22, 1999, p. 52.

World Series. DiMaggio did not return until 1946 and when he did he was obviously rusty—or perhaps merely mortal. His batting average was .290, the first time in his major league career he hit under .300. He hit only 25 home runs and drove in 95 runs, both numbers were also career lows. However, his outfield play remained superb.

Without a doubt the 1947 season was DiMaggio's comeback year. His offensive numbers were still down from his prewar years, though he did hit .315. Prior to the season DiMaggio had two surgeries on his left heel: the first to remove a bone spur, the second a skin graft. Still he answered the bell for most of the season and led the Yankees to another pennant and a World Series victory over the Dodgers, against whom he hit two home runs and drove in five runs. At season's end DiMaggio was awarded with his third AL MVP.

In 1948 DiMaggio discovered the quirkiness of the game, or rather, the fickleness of the writers who vote for postseason awards. His offensive statistics were much better than they had been the previous season, and a fairly healthy DiMaggio resembled his prewar self. For the season he batted .320 and led the American League in home runs (39), RBIs (155), and total bases (355). He was second in slugging percentage and fourth in number of hits, but he came in second in the MVP voting to Lou Boudreau whose team, the Cleveland Indians, won the pennant that year.

In 1949 the Yankee Clipper signed a contract that made him the first ballplayer to earn $100,000, topping Babe Ruth's historic $80,000 annual salary. 1949 also was the year DiMaggio proved what a champion he really was. Out with illness and injuries (his heel again) for most of the season—he played in only 76 games—he still managed to hit for a .346 average and drive in 67 runs, including four home runs at Fenway Park late in the season that broke the hearts of the Boston faithful who, nevertheless, gave him a standing ovation. On October 1st the Yankees celebrated "Joe DiMaggio Day" at the Stadium, but more importantly they played their archrivals, the Boston Red Sox, who held a one-game lead over the Yankees with just two games left in the season. The Red Sox not only featured Williams but their center fielder was DiMaggio's brother Dominic.

DiMaggio was determined to play despite a recent battle with viral pneumonia, which had kept him out of the lineup for almost two weeks. In that first game DiMaggio had told manager **Casey Stengel** that he expected to play only three innings, but as the game wore on and the Yankees chipped away at a Boston lead he managed to play all nine; he collected two hits. The next day, the final game of the season a noticeably ill DiMaggio played for eight and one third innings, but took himself out of the game with one out in the ninth when a ball was hit over his head for triple that drove in two runs and cut the Yankee lead. The Yankees held on to win the game, the pennant and the World Series, in five games, against the Brooklyn Dodgers. It was the start of their most amazing championship run of all—five in a row.

Age and injury were now creeping up on DiMaggio, yet he was still the most celebrated man in the game. He turned in a respectable year in 1950 with a .301 average, 32 home runs and 122 RBIs, while leading the league in slugging percentage. In 1951, though, he knew he was finished. He missed 38 games and when he played his performance was subpar. The World Series against the New York Giants was DiMaggio's swan song in which he hit a home run and drove in 5 runs. After 13 years in the major leagues Joe DiMaggio hung up his spikes for good; he relinquished the coveted center field position to the young **Mickey Mantle**. Announcing his retirement at a press conference DiMaggio said, "When baseball is no longer fun it's no longer a game. And so, I've played my last game of ball.... I feel I have reached the stage where I can no longer produce for my ballclub, my man-

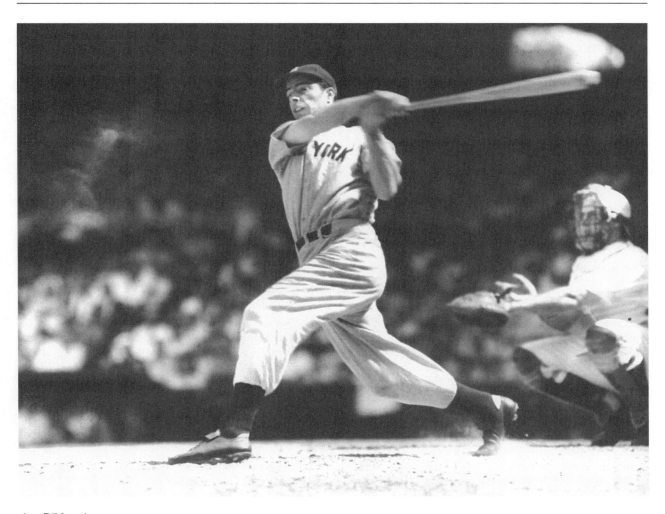

Joe DiMaggio

ager, my teammates, and my fans the sort of baseball their loyalty to me deserves."

Marriage to Marilyn Monroe

DiMaggio was an extremely private man who was nevertheless in the public eye. After retiring as a ballplayer he briefly worked as a Yankee announcer. In the late 1960s he served as a coach for the Oakland Athletics. In the 1970s he gained celebrity with a new generation as a spokesman for Mr. Coffee and the Bowery Savings Bank. DiMaggio was celebrated in song and literature both during his career and after. Ernest Hemingway referred to him in his 1954 Nobel Prize-winning novel, *The Old Man and the Sea,* as did Paul Simon in the 1968 Grammy-winning song, "Mrs. Robinson," which plaintively asked, "Where have you gone Joe DiMaggio?/Our nation turns its lonely eyes to you." In 1941, the year of his 56-game hitting streak, radios throughout America played "Joltin' Joe DiMaggio," a swing paean to the Yankee Clipper. DiMaggio was a frequent visitor at Yankee Stadium through the years, especially at the annual old-timers'

game where he was the last person introduced and the one who received the loudest applause.

Despite his baseball heroics and the adulation he received from fans and the media, DiMaggio remained aloof throughout most of his career and afterward. He was a man with few friends, even becoming estranged for many years from his brother Dominic. The one thing that made him seem mortal was his love affair with, marriage to, divorce from, and ongoing relationship with Marilyn Monroe. During the 1950s Monroe was Hollywood's biggest female star. Twelve years younger than DiMaggio and almost his polar opposite in temperament—she sought the kind of personal adulation and contact with crowds that he shied away from—they nevertheless fell in love after a blind date in 1952. They were married in a civil ceremony in San Francisco's City Hall on January 14, 1954. The conservative DiMaggio was looking for more of a stay-at-home type of wife, which Marilyn was anything but, and consequently the marriage lasted only nine months. During their honeymoon in Japan, Monroe made a side trip to Korea to entertain the troops. As Roger Kahn described

Career Statistics

Yr	Team	AVG	GP	AB	R	H	HR	RBI	BB	SO	SB	SLG
1936	NYY	.323	138	637	132	206	29	125	24	39	4	.576
1937	NYY	.346	151	621	151	215	46	167	64	37	3	.673
1938	NYY	.324	145	599	129	194	32	140	59	21	6	.581
1939	NYY	.381	120	462	108	176	30	126	52	20	3	.671
1940	NYY	.352	132	508	93	179	31	133	61	30	1	.626
1941	NYY	.357	139	541	122	193	30	125	76	13	4	.643
1942	NYY	.305	154	610	123	186	21	114	68	36	4	.498
1946	NYY	.290	132	503	81	146	25	95	59	24	1	.511
1947	NYY	.315	141	534	97	168	20	97	64	32	3	.522
1948	NYY	.320	153	594	110	190	39	155	67	30	1	.598
1949	NYY	.346	76	272	58	94	14	67	55	18	0	.596
1950	NYY	.301	139	525	114	158	32	122	80	33	0	.585
1951	NYY	.263	116	415	72	109	12	71	61	36	0	.422
TOTAL		.325	1736	6821	1390	2214	361	1537	790	369	30	.579

NYY: New York Yankees.

it in *Joe and Marilyn: A Memory of Love,* "When she was reunited with DiMaggio she described the crowds and then burst out, 'Joe, you never heard such cheering.' 'Yes I have,' DiMaggio said.... He told her not to take the cheers seriously because he knew from his own life that they could quickly turn to boos."

Magazine and newspaper writers of the time attributed their breakup to one incident in particular—the famous scene from the *Seven Year Itch* in which Marilyn's skirt was blown up from the wind coming through a New York subway grate. DiMaggio was present and witnessed the crowd's reaction. That incident—her exhibitionism and his shyness turned to anger—epitomized their relationship. Monroe subsequently married playwright Arthur Miller; DiMaggio never remarried. Indeed, he carried a torch for Monroe and never ruled out reconciliation, especially since they continued seeing each other. Following her August 1962 suicide, it was DiMaggio who took charge of her funeral arrangements.

DiMaggio's own last years were spent going to baseball memorabilia shows, old-timers games and other events related to his greatness as a player. He died of cancer on March 8, 1999, in Hollywood, Florida.

As the best ballplayer on the best baseball team (at a time when baseball itself was far and away the primary sporting attraction) in the largest market and media center of the country, Joe DiMaggio was a natural to become the first sports superstar. Arguably, he was the first athlete to transcend his sport and every sports superstar since his time has emulated his combination of grace, power and a will to dominate his opponents. In fact, his name remained a byword for success in heroism long after he retired. Joe DiMaggio's career statistics for what amounts to less than 13 years are a .325 batting average, 2,214 hits, 361 home runs, 1,537 RBIs, and .579 slugging percentage. Incredibly, DiMaggio struck out only 369 times in his career. He led the Yankees to nine world championships in 10 appearances and was a member of the American League All-Star team 13 times. He was elected to the Baseball Hall of Fame in 1955. In 1969, as part of baseball's centenary celebration, Joe DiMaggio was voted baseball's greatest living player.

SELECTED WRITINGS BY DIMAGGIO:

Lucky to Be a Yankee, New York: R. Field; Greenberg, 1946.
Baseball for Everyone, New York: Whittlesey House, 1948.

FURTHER INFORMATION

Books

Cramer, Richard Ben. *Joe DiMaggio: The Hero's Life,* New York: Simon & Schuster, 2000.
Halberstam, David, *Summer of '49,* New York: William Morrow and Company, Inc., 1989.
Johnson, Dick, ed. *DiMaggio: An Illustrated Life,* New York: Walker and Company, 1995.
Kahn, Roger. *Joe & Marilyn: A Memory of Love,* New York: William Morrow and Company, Inc., 1986.
New York Daily News. Joe DiMaggio: An American Icon, New York: Sports Publishing, Inc., 1999.

Periodicals

Newsweek (March 22, 1999): 52.
Seattle Times (September 23, 2002): D14.

Other

"AP Athlete of the Year," http://www.hickoksports.com/history/apathloy.shtml (October 8, 2002).

"Joe DiMaggio," www.baseball-reference.com (September 23, 2002).

"Timeline of Joe DiMaggio's Life," http://www.pbs.org/wgbh/amex/dimaggio/timeline/index.html (September 26, 2002).

"When Joe Was a Seal," http://www.tdl.com/~thawley/dimag.html (October 7, 2002)

Sketch by F. Caso

Uschi Disl
1970-

German biathlete

Uschi Disl

Germany's Uschi Disl has won more Olympic medals in the biathlon than any other competitor, male or female, in the sport. A curious blend of cross-country skiing and sharpshooting, the biathlon presents unique challenges for its devotees; many, like Disl, serve in the military or as border guards in their home countries, where biathletes are able to train as part of a special unit. During the 2002 Winter Olympics in Salt Lake City, Utah, Disl helped bring her team the gold medal against some impressive competition from Russia and Norway, and with it gained the eighth Olympic win of her career, more than any other biathlete in history.

Trained as Teen

Born Ursula Disl in 1970, the future Olympic star grew up in an area known as the "Foothills of the Alps," in Bad Tölz, Bavaria. She began cross-country skiing at age 10, and took up the biathlon in 1986. Germany is home to some of the best athletes in the sport, which dates back centuries as standard practice for hunters in wintry northern climates. The biathlon as a sport formally originated in the early twentieth century as a showcase for military teams. Skiers take off racing on the skis, then must halt to shoot at a small, coin-sized target at a 50-meter distance. Pausing to steady themselves takes precious seconds off the finish time. As *Maclean's* writer Mary Nemeth remarked, "few sports exact the physical toll of biathlon." The route can be up to 20 kilometers in length, and targets number as many as 20; the competitions are over in roughly 20 minutes. A writer for *Sports Illustrated,* Robert Sullivan, explained that in this sport, "the difficult part of the sport consists not of skiing fast or shooting well, but of doing both in concert." When biathletes miss a target, they are penalized with additional time or penalty laps. "It is the sports world's Dr. Jekyll: a thing painfully at odds with itself," Sullivan noted. "In other compound sports, for example the decathlon and pentathlon, events are approached in sequence—the third effort doesn't really affect the fourth, apart from increasing the athlete's fatigue. Not so in biathlon: When the skier glides into the range he starts shooting, and when he has squeezed off five shots he immediately skis on."

Disl first rose to prominence in the sport in 1991 at her debut in the World Championships, held in Finland that year. She anticipated competing in her first Olympic biathlon the following year. It had been a men's medal competition event since the Squaw Valley, Idaho, Games in 1960, but women's World Cup races had taken place only since 1984, and it became a women's medal event in the Olympics at the 1992 Albertville, France Winter Games. The Olympic biathlon featured three separate categories for men and women: a 15-kilometer individual race, the 7.5-kilometer sprint, and a team relay. At Albertville, Disl and her team won the silver medal for Germany in the relay, but she placed poorly in the sprint, finishing eleventh. She fared better at the Lillehammer Winter Games in Norway in 1994, taking a bronze in the 15-kilometer individual, and again helping the German women's biathlon team take a silver in the relay. The sprint again proved Disl's toughest challenge, and this year she finished in thirteenth place.

Won First Olympic Gold

Four years later, at the 1998 Winter Games in Nagano, Japan, Disl won gold, silver, and bronze medals.

Awards and Accomplishments

1990	Gold medal in team event, Junior World Championships, Sodankyla, Finland
1991	Bronze medal in 7.5-kilometer team relay, World Championships, Lahti, Finland
1992	Gold medal in team relay, World Championships, Novosibirsk, Russia
1992	Silver medal, 7.5-kilometer team relay, Albertville Winter Olympic Games
1994	Silver medal, 7.5-kilometer team relay; bronze medal, individual, Lillehammer Winter Olympic Games
1995	Gold medal in 7.5-kilometer team relay, silver medals in sprint, individual, and team events, World Championships, Antholz, Italy
1996	Gold medal in 7.5-kilometer team relay, World Championships, Ruhpolding, Germany
1997	Gold medal in 7.5-kilometer team relay, World Championships, Osrblie, Slovakia
1998	Gold medal, 7.5-kilometer team relay; silver medal, sprint; bronze medal, individual, Nagano Winter Olympic Games
1999	Gold medal in 7.5-kilometer team relay, World Championships, Kontiolahti, Finland
2000	Silver medal in pursuit and 7.5-kilometer team relay, World Championships, Holmenkallen, Norway
2001	Silver medal in sprint and 7.5-kilometer team relay, World Championships, Bled-Pokljuka, Slovenia
2002	Gold medal, 7.5-kilometer team relay; silver medal, sprint, Salt Lake City Winter Olympic Games

She won a silver in the sprint, and the bronze for her time in the 15-kilometer individual event. The gold-medal winner of the individual was another formidable Slavic athlete, Ekaterina Dafovska of Bulgaria. Disl's skiing in the relay—even though at one point she lost a pole, and had to return and dig it out of the snow where others had skied over it—helped Germany take the gold medal in the relay. It was her sixth career Olympic medal, but her first-ever gold, and she described it as "the greatest thing one can have in one's life in sport," a report in the *Fresno Bee* quoted her as saying. Disl and the other German women again bested some impressive competition from the Russians and Scandinavians. Press reports mentioned that Disl had attempted to have her brown hair dyed gold as a good-luck gesture, but the process did not take and she emerged a redhead instead.

Readying for the 2002 Winter Olympics in Salt Lake City, Utah, Disl faced tough competition from Sweden's **Magdalena Forsberg**, pegged as the top woman biathlete. But Disl bested Forsberg in the 7.5-kilometer sprint, taking the silver, with Disl's German teammate Kati Wilhelm winning the gold. The German women again took the gold medal in the relay event, though another teammate, Katrin Apel, had missed some shots and the team sank to sixth place; again, Disl's quick skiing helped them gain points, and at the finish, Disl won her eighth career medal, giving her more Olympic wins than any other male or female biathlete in the world.

Disl again made an impressive finish in the World Cup event, held in Oberhof, Germany, in January of 2003. In the women's 12.5-kilometer race, she had four shooting mistakes, but finished ahead of Bulgaria's Dafovska by three seconds. Disl trains near her home in the Austrian Tyrol, in Kössen and Tux, and has worked as a border guard and a bank clerk.

CONTACT INFORMATION

Address: Moserbergweg 6, 6345 Kössen, Austria. Online: http://www.uschi-disl-fanclub.de/.

FURTHER INFORMATION

Periodicals

"Bjoerndalen Wins Third Straight." *New York Times* (January 13, 2003): D9.

Deacon, James. "Queens of winter." *Maclean's* 106 (February 22, 1993): 55.

"Disl Finally Gets Biathlon Gold." *Fresno Bee* (February 20, 1998): D4.

"Germany Rallies In Women's Biathlon." *St Louis Post-Dispatch* (February 20, 2002): D8.

Gordon, Jeff. "Tipsheet: Looking at Who's In and Who's Out in the World of Sports." *St. Louis Post-Dispatch* (February 20, 1998): D2.

Heika, Mike. "Athletes to watch in women's biathlon." Knight Ridder/Tribune News Service (January 31, 2002).

Hillenbrand, Barry. "Have Gun, Will Triumph." *Time International* 159 (February 25, 2002): 48.

Nemeth, Mary. "Pursuing the agony of victory." *Maclean's* 107 (February 14, 1994): 58.

"Olympic Digest: Disl Wanted Golden Hair, Gets Gold Medal Instead." *Seattle Times* (February 19, 1998): D6.

Reed, J.D. "Marching to their own beat." *Time* 123 (January 30, 1984): 50.

"Russian Biathlete Wins at the Wire." *Rocky Mountain News* (February 15, 1998): 20C.

Sullivan, Robert. "She turns rabbits into rocks." *Sports Illustrated* 59 (November 28, 1983): 104.

"Winter Olympics: Monday's Medal Winners." *Los Angeles Times* (February 19, 2002): U2.

"Winter Olympics: Tuesday's Medal Winners." *Los Angeles Times* (February 19, 2002): U2.

Other

"Dafovska wins first Olympic gold for Bulgaria." http://www.shinmai.co.jp/oly-eng/19980209/0005.htm (January 31, 2003).

Uschi Disl Fan Club, http://www.uschi-disl-fanclub.de/
    (January 31, 2003).

Sketch by Carol Brennan

Mike Ditka
1939-

American football coach

Football coach Mike Ditka, known as "Iron Mike" and "Da Coach," was a star tight end for the Chicago Bears from 1961 through 1966, before finishing his playing career with the Philadelphia Eagles and Dallas Cowboys. After retiring from play in 1972, he became an assistant coach of the Dallas Cowboys. He then worked as head coach of the Bears for 11 years, during which he had a 112-68 record and led Chicago to victory in the Super Bowl. Ditka subsequently became coach of the New Orleans Saints, and is now retired. A successful player and coach, he is now a member of the Pro Football Hall of Fame.

"You Could Hear the House Rock"

The son of a steelworker from Aliquippa, Pennsylvania, Ditka was large and strong even as a child. In *People,* Jack Friedman quoted Ditka's father, Mike Sr., who said that when Ditka did pushups, "You could hear the house rock."

Ditka went on to play football at the University of Pittsburgh, where, as an end, he was an All-American. However, in his senior year, he also showed the anger that would later get him in trouble as a coach: at the halftime of a game, he slammed a teammate into a locker because the teammate had missed a tackle. A week later, he apologized.

In 1961, Ditka was drafted by the Chicago Bears, and spent six years playing with them as a tight end. Although he was not fast, he was unstoppable once he had the ball. He was the NFL Rookie of the Year for 1961, and played in the Pro Bowl from 1961 through 1966. Ditka was also willing to play through pain; in 1964 he played most of the season with a separated shoulder. He could not lift his left hand higher than his shoulder, but caught balls by swatting them with his right hand and pinning them to his chest.

In 1967, Ditka was traded to the Philadelphia Eagles, and played two years with them before being traded to the Dallas Cowboys, with whom he played four more seasons. With the Cowboys, Ditka won the Super Bowl in 1972, catching a touchdown pass in the Cowboys'

Mike Ditka

24-3 victory over the Miami Dolphins. He retired from playing football after that season. During his career he caught 427 passes, 43 for touchdowns. He averaged 13.6 yards per catch

Ditka did not remain unemployed for long. He was soon hired by **Tom Landry**, the Cowboys' head coach, as an offensive assistant and special teams coach. He helped guide Dallas to a Super Bowl win in 1977, a 27-10 victory over the Denver Broncos.

Head Coach of the Chicago Bears

In 1982, the Chicago Bears' famed coach, **George Halas**, who had drafted Ditka as a player, brought him back to Chicago, this time as head coach of the Bears. He would coach the Bears for 11 seasons, period of time that would bring him lasting fame in football.

In the 1980s, the Bears were a strong team; from 1985 to 1988, they had 52 regular-season victories, the most ever by an NFL team in any four-year period. Their success hinged largely on one player, running back **Walter Payton**. Ditka told Mike Sager in *Esquire* that other teams "tried to stop our running game, and it didn't matter if they did stop it, because we kept trying to run the football, and eventually we made it work. And we made it work because of one guy—Walter Payton." Payton would eventually set a new career rushing record, with 16,726 yards in his 13-year career.

Chronology	
1939	Born in Carnegie, Pennsylvania
1961	Drafted by Chicago Bears
1967	Traded to Philadelphia Eagles
1969	Traded to Dallas Cowboys
1972	Retires from playing football
1972	Becomes offensive assistant and special teams coach for Dallas Cowboys
1982	Becomes head coach of Chicago Bears
1986	Leads Bears to victory in Super Bowl over the New England Patriots
1992	Fired by Bears owner Mike McCaskey
1997	Hired as head coach of New Orleans Saints
2000	Retired from coaching

Awards and Accomplishments	
1961	NFL Rookie of the Year
1961-66	Pro Bowl player
1972	Dallas Cowboys win Super Bowl
1977	Dallas Cowboys win Super Bowl
1985-86, 1998	Sporting News Coach of the Year
1986	Chicago Bears win Super Bowl
1988	Inducted into Pro Football Hall of Fame

In 1985, Ditka was named the Sporting News Coach of the Year as the Bears went 15-1 and won the Super Bowl 46-10 over the New England Patriots in 1986 with, as Paul Attner wrote in the *Sporting News,* "some of the toughest, most aggressive, hard-nosed football you could ever want." The Bears played relentlessly, with drive and flair, and Ditka was credited for bringing that out in them. It was the team's first championship since 1963.

The Bears failed to repeat as championships, losing early in the playoffs to the Washington Redskins. Their victory in 1986, however, brought the team fame. As Friedman pointed out, the Bears led the NFL in endorsements at that time; several, including Ditka, owned restaurants; and 13, including Ditka, had their own radio or television shows. Ditka was appearing on both television and radio.

In 1988, Ditka was inducted into the Pro Football Hall of Fame. That season he led the Bears to a 12-4 record and was named *Sporting News* Coach of the Year for the second time. Chicago came up one game short of the Super Bowl, losing in the NFC Championship Game to the San Francisco 49ers.

During the 1992 season, Ditka's desire to coach began to wane, and he reached a breaking point on October 4, when the Bears were leading the Minnesota Vikings 20-0 in the first quarter. This was a great beginning, but the Bears played so badly the rest of the way that they lost the game 21-20. After the game, Ditka, veins protruding in his neck, screamed at quarterback Jim Harbaugh. Morale on the team suffered, and the Bears slid to 5-11 for the season. According to Peter King in *Sports Illustrated,* critics contended that Ditka was burned out and had lost his love of football, citing his bad temper and numerous outbursts directed at players, fans and Bears owner Mike McCaskey. Ditka denied this for many years, but eventually admitted to King, "They spoke the truth. I totally lost my desire. The best thing for me was to do something else, and it was best for the Bears, too."

McCaskey fired Ditka, and Ditka spent most of the next four years golfing, traveling, and working as a mo-

tivational speaker and as an analyst on NBC's "NFL Live." However, as he told King, "Getting up and going to the golf course is not life." And he remarked to Paul Attner in the *Sporting News,* "I was figuring out what color shirt I was going to wear instead of reading a good book or doing something constructive." He began looking for something to do that would give him direction.

New Orleans Saints Head Coach

When the New Orleans Saints offered him a job as head coach, he was skeptical about whether they would actually give it to him and whether he should take it. But when he talked to Saints owner Tom Benson, he became excited about the idea. "I firmly believe everything happens for a reason, and as I sat in that room, I began to think this was where I was meant to be." Ironically, the Saints' previous coach, Jim Mora, had quit after a disastrous game, just as Ditka had.

The Saints needed to improve: they were playing so badly that their fans called them "the Ain'ts," showed up at games with paper bags over their heads, and called the New Orleans Superdome, where the Saints played, the "House of Blues." They had not had a winning season since 1992, and fan morale was so bad that in 1996, the average home game attendance was only 37,750, the worst in the team's 30-year history.

On January 28, 1997, Ditka was announced as the new coach of the New Orleans Saints. His first two seasons with the Saints produced a 12-20 record. In 1999, Ditka traded several draft picks to earn the right to draft Texas running back Ricky Williams. The choice was controversial. "A lot of people think I'm nuts," Ditka told Sager. "People ask me if by giving away our entire draft I'm ransoming the whole future of the Saints. Well, let me tell you: There is no future. This game is about winning. It's about trying to get as good as you can as soon as you can."

Citing the example of Walter Payton, who was such a large part of the Bears' success in the 1980s, he said, "Maybe that's old-fashioned and maybe the new gurus of football don't see it that way, but I don't really care." In 2000 Benson, evidently feeling that the Saints had not improved enough, fired 22 employees, including Ditka. Since that time, he has been retired from coaching.

Career Statistics

Yr	Team	Receiving			
		REC	YDS	AVG	TD
1961	CHI	56	1076	19.2	12
1962	CHI	58	904	15.6	5
1963	CHI	59	794	13.5	8
1964	CHI	75	897	12.0	5
1965	CHI	36	454	12.6	2
1966	CHI	32	378	11.8	2
1967	PHI	26	274	10.5	2
1968	PHI	13	111	8.5	2
1969	DAL	17	268	15.8	3
1970	DAL	8	98	12.2	0
1971	DAL	30	360	12.0	1
1972	DAL	17	198	11.6	1
TOTAL		427	5812	13.6	43

CHI: Chicago Bears; DAL: Dallas Cowboys; PHI: Philadelphia Eagles.

As he grew older, Ditka's health began to deteriorate; he suffered a heart attack in 1998 and had an angioplasty. He takes heart medication, and he has had two hip replacements. He told Sager, "The things that seemed so important when you were young don't seem so important anymore. You realize that the greatest gifts you've got are life, health, friends, your spiritual beliefs." Ditka summed up his often-opinionated coaching methods when he told Attner, "There is a reason I do everything. You'll learn that. If I don't say anything for any other reason but effect. If it gets the right effect, then I have said the right thing."

CONTACT INFORMATION

Address: c/o Nationwide Speaker Bureau, Inc., 120 El Camino Drive, Beverly Hills, CA 90212; Mike Ditka's Restaurant, 100 E. Chestnut Street, Chicago, IL 60611. Fax: 310-273-5928. Phone: 310-273-8807. Online: www.nationwidespeakers.com; mikeditkaschicago.com.

SELECTED WRITINGS BY DITKA:

(With Don Pierson) *Ditka: An Autobiography,* Bonus Books, 1987.

FURTHER INFORMATION

Periodicals

Attner, Paul. "Everything's Going My Way." *Sporting News,* July 14, 1997, 38.
Friedman, Jack. "Staring Down His Rowdy Ruffians, Chicago Coach Mike Ditka Prods the Bears to the Super Bowl." *People,* January 5, 1987, 66.
King, Peter. "The Ditka Dilemma." *Sports Illustrated,* July 30, 1990, 44.

Where Is He Now?

Since leaving the Saints, Ditka has continued to work as a motivational speaker, television commentator on CBS Sports, and also as an actor in commercials. He enjoys playing golf, collecting antique cars, and riding motorcycles. He is the owner of Mike Ditka's Restaurant, which has branches in Chicago, Illinois; Naples, Florida; and New Orleans, Louisiana, and is also involved in numerous charitable and nonprofit organizations. He sponsors a scholarship at his alma mater, the University of Pittsburgh. Ditka has been married to his wife Diana since 1977; they have four children from Ditka's previous marriage.

King, Peter. "Touch Down." *Sports Illustrated,* April 14, 1997, 46.
Lamb, Kevin. "Ditka is TSN's Coach of the Year." *Sporting News,* January 27, 1986, 14.
"Once a Bear, Always a Bear." *Sports Illustrated.* December 16, 1985, 78.
Pierson, Don. "'Da Coach' and 'Da Stoic.'" *Knight Ridder/Tribune News Service,* December 8, 2001, K3903.
Sager, Mike. "Is Ditka Nuts?" *Esquire,* October 1999, 126.

Other

Mike Ditka's Restaurant, http://www.mikeditkaschicago.com/ (January 5, 2003).
New Orleans Saints Web site, http://www.neworleanssaints.com/ (January 5, 2003).

Sketch by Kelly Winters

Larry Doby
1924-2003

American baseball player

Larry Doby is the invisible man in the struggle to bring black players into major league baseball. For most of his career Doby lived in the long shadow cast by **Jackie Robinson**, the first African-American to play major league baseball. Doby, who joined the Cleveland Indians just eleven weeks after Robinson made his debut with Brooklyn was the *second* black player to enter the majors. He was the *second* black, after **Frank Robinson**, to manage a major league club , he was even the *second* major league player to play in Japan. Doby can lay claim to a number of important firsts however: he was the first African-American to jump directly from the Negro Leagues into the majors, the first to play in the American League, the first to play on a championship club, the first to hit a home run in the World Series, and the first black home run champion. Doby was also one of the first African-Americans to

Larry Doby

coach at the major league level and to enter the rank of major league executives. Like Jackie Robinson, in realizing these accomplishments Doby had to overcome the ugly racism that was permeated many facets of American life. He did it with courage and dignity. Along the way, Doby proved himself one of the most potent hitters in baseball.

Early Life

Lawrence Eugene Doby was born in 1923 in Camden, South Carolina. His father, David Doby, was a professional horse groom whose long trips to racetracks in the North led to the breakup of his marriage while Larry was still a child. When his mother, the former Etta Brooks, went North looking for work for herself, Larry was put in the care of others, first his grandmother and then his aunt and uncle. While in their care, Doby attended a school in Camden run by the Methodist Church, where he played organized sports for the first time. When he was ready to attend high school, he joined his mother in Paterson, New Jersey. At Eastside High in Paterson, New Jersey, he quickly proved himself a talented athlete, earning eleven varsity letters, in football, baseball, basketball and track. Foreshadowing his early experience in professional baseball, Doby was the sole black player on the school's football team.

Just before his graduation from high school, Doby played his first professional baseball game for the Newark Eagles of the Negro National League—under the name Larry Walker to protect his amateur status. After a year of college in 1942-43 at Long Island University and Virginia Union, he was drafted into the Navy. When he returned to the States in 1946, Jackie Robinson had been signed by the National League's Brooklyn Dodgers. Doby's future abruptly changed. "I felt I had a chance to play major league baseball," he revealed to his biographer Joseph Thomas Moore. "My main thing was to become a teacher and coach somewhere in New Jersey, but when I heard about Jackie, I decided to concentrate on baseball. I forgot about going back to college."

Enters Major Leagues

Doby, a 22-year-old second baseman, rejoined the Newark Eagles in 1946, hitting .348 and helping the Eagles to a victory over the Kansas City Monarchs in the Negro World Series. Then fate intervened in the person of Cleveland Indian owner Bill Veeck. Veeck was looking for a black player for the Indians. He had good reports on Doby, who in addition to boasting a .414 batting average and 14 home runs for the first half of 1947, neither smoked, drank, nor swore. Veeck bought Doby's contract from the Eagles. On July 3, while the Indians were playing in Chicago, Larry Doby made his debut as the American League's first black player.

Career Statistics

Yr	Team	AVG	GP	AB	R	H	HR	RBI	BB	SO	SB	E
1947	CLE	.156	29	32	3	5	0	2	1	11	0	0
1948	CLE	.301	121	439	83	132	14	66	54	77	9	14
1949	CLE	.280	147	547	106	153	24	85	91	90	10	9
1950	CLE	.326	142	503	110	164	25	102	98	71	8	5
1951	CLE	.295	134	447	84	132	20	69	101	81	4	8
1952	CLE	.276	140	519	104	143	32	104	90	111	5	6
1953	CLE	.263	149	513	92	135	29	102	96	121	3	6
1954	CLE	.272	153	577	94	157	32	126	85	94	3	2
1955	CLE	.291	131	491	91	143	26	75	61	100	2	2
1956	CWS	.268	140	504	89	135	24	102	102	105	0	5
1957	CWS	.288	119	416	57	120	14	79	56	79	2	4
1958	CLE	.283	89	247	141	70	13	45	26	49	0	0
1959	DET	.218	18	55	5	12	0	3	8	9	0	1
1959	CWS	.241	21	58	1	14	0	9	2	13	1	4
TOTAL		.283	1533	5348	960	1515	253	969	871	1011	47	64

CLE: Cleveland Indians; CWS: Chicago White Sox; DET: Detroit Tigers.

Veeck expected Doby—like Robinson in Brooklyn—to comport himself by a different set of rules from other players: Doby was told not to react to the inevitable racial insults he would encounter. He must not fight back on the field. He could not disagree with umpires or react to fans. Doby was glad to submit. "He said this was the price I'd have to pay for being a part of baseball history. I was not worried about being a part of baseball history. All I wanted to do was play," Doby explained to Burt Graeff of the *Cleveland Plain Dealer*. His resolve was put to the test from the time he entered the Indians clubhouse. Introduced to the team, some Cleveland players refused to shake Doby's hand. On the field before the game, he stood alone for five minutes before second baseman Joe Gordon finally threw him a ball and warmed up with him.

Those were just the beginning of the indignities. Hotels across the country refused to let Doby room with his Indian teammates. He was denied service in restaurants. He was barred from entering ball parks in the South during spring training. On the field he was thrown at by opposing pitchers and spat on when he slid into base. He received hate mail from all over the country. With no other blacks on the Indians during his first year, Doby was forced to spend hours on the road by himself. Forty years after the fact some thought that Robinson's earlier entry into the big leagues would have made things easier for Doby. "To say I had it easy because of him is silly," he recalled to Burt Graeff, "I came in 11 weeks after he did. Eleven weeks did not alter the course of race relations in this country. We still have problems 50 years later. Jack and I went through a lot of the same things."

Doby struck out in his first at bat, and sat on the bench for most of the remainder of the 1947 season. Realizing he was unlikely to replace either Joe Gordon or Lou Boudreau—both All-Stars—in the infield, the Indians converted Doby to an outfielder in 1948. He had never played there before, but within a couple years he made himself into one of the finest defensive center-fielders in baseball.

Becomes a Star

Doby started to come into his own in 1948. He had hit 14 homers, knocked in 66 runs and finished with a .301 average that year, helping the Indians to a World Series victory over the Boston Braves along the way. Over the following years, he was named to seven consecutive American League All-Star teams. In 1952 and 1954 he was the American league home run champ, he led the league in RBIs in 1954, and in runs in 1952. In 1950, the *Sporting News* named Doby the best center fielder in baseball, over **Joe DiMaggio**. Those years were not without pain, however. Segregation from his teammates during many road trips continued. After a bad slump in September 1951, he was blamed for the Indians failure to beat the Yankees for the American League pennant, and the Cleveland papers called for him to be traded.

By 1952 with a salary of $28,000, Larry Doby was the highest paid player on the Cleveland team with the exception of star pitcher Bob Feller. Doby led the Indians to another pennant in 1954, but the team was beaten in the World Series by the New York Giants. His performance fell off in 1955 because of injuries. At the end of the 1955 season, Doby was traded to the Chicago White Sox. He played well in 1956, but injuries were beginning to take their toll on the 30-year-old player. He went on to play with the Baltimore Orioles, Cleveland, the Detroit Tigers, and the White Sox, before breaking his ankle in a game with the San Diego Padres of the Pacific Coast League in 1959. The injury spelt the end of Larry Doby's major league career.

Awards and Accomplishments

1949-55	American League All-Star
1950	Named best centerfielder in major leagues by *Sporting News*
1951	Named Baseball Man of the Year by Cleveland sports writers
1987	Awarded Doctorate of Humane Letters by Montclair State College
1987	July 15, 1987 designated "Larry Doby Day" by New Jersey Legislature
1993	Inducted into New Jersey Hall of Fame
1994	Number retired by Cleveland Indians
1997	Throws out first pitch at All-Star Game
1998	Inducted into National Baseball Hall of Fame

In 1962 he and former Dodger Don Newcombe joined the Chunichi Dragons for a season, becoming the first former major leaguers to play baseball in Japan. On his return from Japan, Doby moved to Newark New Jersey, where in the summer of 1967 he experienced first-hand the race riot that wracked the city. Early in 1968 he told an interviewer that blacks would probably have to burn down a stadium before there would be any African-American managers or coaches in the big leagues. The comment touched a nerve in Commissioner Bowie Kuhn's office and in 1969 Kuhn arranged for Doby to be hired as a scout by the Montreal Expos. By 1971 Doby won praise as Montreal's batting coach. "There are few great hitters who can communicate," Expo manager Gene Mauch told Joseph Thomas Moore. "Larry Doby has sound theories and he can get the message across to the players. He is articulate and can communicate."

Seeks Manager's Job

Doby had his sights set on becoming a manager. After a season managing winter ball, he had let it be known that he was available for a job. "I give myself five years," Joseph Thomas Moore quotes Doby as saying. "If I don't make it by then, I'll give up on the idea and get out of baseball altogether." Unfortunately baseball in the 1970s seemed as unwilling to admit a black manager as it had been in the 1940s to admit black players. Doby took a coaching job in Cleveland with an understanding that he would be in line for the manager's job there. When the manager was sacked, however, Doby was passed over in favor of another African-American, Frank Robinson. Returning to a coaching position with the Expos, he was passed over two more times within one season for the manager's job. Discouraged, he considered leaving baseball for good.

In 1977, however, Doby's old mentor, Bill Veeck, offered him a coaching job with the Chicago White Sox. When the team got off to a slow start in 1978, Veeck made Doby another offer—to manage the team. It was a bittersweet opportunity for Doby. He would be replacing Bob Lemon, a friend and teammate from the Indi-

ans. Veeck not only wanted Doby to turn the club around in the standings, but also to attract more black fans to Comiskey Park. When neither materialized, Doby was replaced. He had become the second black major league manager, but he was never given a fair opportunity to show what he could do.

After leaving the White Sox, Doby became the Director of Community Relations for the New Jersey Nets of the NBA. In the 1990s, he later became a special assistant for licensing matters to the president of the American League.

In 1997 Larry Doby began to receive some of the long-overdue recognition for his pioneering efforts to integrate major league baseball. He threw out the ceremonial first pitch at that year's All-Star Game in Cleveland, followed by a week of celebrations honoring Doby. In August 1998 he was elected to Baseball's Hall of Fame. Despite the trials he had to suffer as a player and coach, Doby was not bitter. Far from feeling baseball had particular problems with race, he believes it led the way for American society. "A lot of people are complaining that baseball hasn't come along fast enough. And there is much more work to be done," Doby admitted to David Maraniss of the *Washington Post*. "But if you look at baseball, we came in 1947, before Brown versus the Board of Education [the 1954 Supreme Court decision integrating public schools], before anyone wrote a civil rights bill saying give them the same opportunities everyone else has. So whatever you want to criticize baseball about-it certainly needs more opportunities for black managers, black general managers, black umpires-remember that if this country was as far advanced as baseball it would be in much better shape."

Doby died on June 17, 2003, in his home in Montclair, New Jersey, after a long illness. "He had been ill for some time," his son told the Associated Press. He is survived by his five children.

FURTHER INFORMATION

Books

Moffi, Larry and Jonathan Kronstadt. *Crossing the Line: Black Major Leaguers, 1947-1959*. McFarland & Company, Inc., Publishers, 1994.

Moore, Joseph Thomas. *Pride Against Prejudice: The Biography of Larry Doby*.Westport, CT: Greenwood Press, 1988.

Tygiel, Jules. *Baseball's Great Experiment*. New York: Oxford Univ. Press, 1997.

Veeck, Bill. *Veeck—As in Wreck: The Autobiography of Bill Veeck*. New York: G. P. Putnam's Sons, 1962.

Periodicals

"American League wins 3-1 at All-Star Game Dedicated to Larry Doby." *Jet*, July 28, 1997 v92 n10: 46.

"Baseball legend Larry Doby, First Black in American League, Selected for Hall of Fame." *Jet,* March 23, 1998 v93 n17: 47(1).

Berkow, Ira. "He Crossed Color Barrier, But In Another's Shadow." *New York Times,* February 23, 1997: A1.

Dolgan, Bob. "Barrier Buster." *Cleveland Plain Dealer,* June 5, 2001: 1D.

Graeff, Burt. "Doby Getting His Due; First Black Player In American League Faced Same Racism As Jackie Robinson." *Cleveland Plain Dealer,* July 3, 1997: 1D.

Grossi, Tony. "The Debt Owed To Larry Doby; Segregation And Ignorance Couldn't Deter Black All Star." *Cleveland Plain Dealer,* July 3, 1994: 1A.

"Larry Doby in Good Spirits While Recovery from Surgery." *Jet,* Dec 1, 1997 v93 n2: 50(1).

Maraniss, David. "Neither a Myth Nor a Legend; Larry Doby Crossed Baseball's Color Barrier — After Robinson." *Washington Post,* July 08, 1997: A01.

Sketch by Mike Pare

Tom Dolan

Tom Dolan
1975-

American swimmer

Tom Dolan is a swimmer who has overcome serious breathing problems to become a national and world champion. Although he was diagnosed with exercise-induced asthma at age fourteen, Dolan continues to swim competitively. In 1994 he became a national collegiate champion at the University of Michigan. In 1996 and 2000 he won Olympic gold medals for the 400-meter individual medley event. He also set the world record for that event twice. Dolan still swims competitively and he is also a spokesperson for the American Lung Association.

A Young Competitor

Tom Dolan was born on September 15, 1975 in Arlington, Virginia. His father, William, is a civil trial attorney and his mother, Jef, is a communications professor at Marymount University. Dolan was active in a variety of sports when he was a child, including soccer, basketball, golf, and tennis. He became interested in swimming at age five when he noticed that his older sister, Kathleen, was really involved in the sport.

Dolan began swimming competitively at the Washington Golf and Country Club in Arlington when he was seven years old. He was a fierce competitor who would push his body to its limit. He began competing in the breast stroke; however, he would sometimes have trouble breathing in this position. Rather than stop swimming, Dolan would simply flip onto his back and continue swimming the backstroke because it allowed him to breathe more easily. When Dolan was fourteen, his doctors diagnosed him with exercise-induced asthma and allergies.

Despite this diagnosis Dolan continued to compete in club-team swimming along with his sister. He began training with coach Rick Curl at the Curl-Burke Swim Club. Curl was the coach of the 1992 Olympic gold medallist swimmer Mike Barrowman. Dolan graduated with honors from Yorktown High School. He then went to college at the University of Michigan in 1993 where he won a swimming scholarship.

Quickly Became a Collegiate Champion

Dolan immediately proved that he was able to compete at the college-level. In 1993 he won silver medals in the 400-meter individual medley at both the United States Summer Nationals and the Pan-Pacific Games. The individual medley is one of the most difficult competitions because it consists of the butterfly, backstroke, breaststroke, and freestyle. He also won the bronze medal in the 800-meter freestyle at the United States Spring Nationals. In 1994 Dolan won first place in the 800-meter freestyle relay at the National Collegiate Athletic Association (NCAA) meet. He also won second place for the 500-meter freestyle and the 400-meter individual medley and third place for the 1,650 freestyle. With Dolan's successes, the University of Michigan won its first NCAA swim title in thirty-four years.

In 1994 Dolan also won four gold medals for the 400-meter, 800-meter, and 1,500-meter freestyle and the 400-meter individual medley at the United States Spring Nationals. He was the first collegiate swimmer to win four events since **Mark Spitz**, the legendary champion swimmer of the 1972 Olympics. Dolan added to his medal collection by winning a gold for the 800-meter freestyle at the United States Summer Nations.

At age eighteen Dolan became the youngest member of the United States Swimming Team and he represented his country at the World Swimming Championship in Rome, Italy. Dolan not only won the gold medal for the 400-meter individual medley, but he also set the world record at four minutes and 12.30 seconds. Dolan was named 1994 Swimmer of the Year by both the NCAA and United States Swimming.

Battled Breathing Problems

Despite his success at competition, Dolan continued to have problems breathing. In 1994 doctors discovered that Dolan had an unusually narrow esophagus. At times Dolan only gets twenty percent of the oxygen intake of an average person. Dolan would often hyperventilate during practice and occasionally faint. To make matters worse, Dolan could not treat his breathing problems with many of the medications that are available for asthma or allergies because of the strict doping rules in competitive swimming. "I'd rather not have asthma," Dolan told Christine Brennan of the *Washington Post* in July of 1996. "But it has made me tougher, made me stronger."

In 1995 Dolan won three more gold medals, two silvers, and one bronze at the United States Summer Nationals. He also set three American records at the NCAA Championships and was named Swimmer of the Year for the second year in a row. These successes, however, were only a prelude to the Olympic Games. In 1996 Dolan trained relentlessly for the Olympics in Atlanta.

"Tom just doesn't know how to slow down," University of Michigan swimming coach John Urbanchek told Gerry Callahan of *Sports Illustrated* in July of 1996. "This is what makes him great and also what gets him in trouble. He can push his psychological limits almost as far as his physiological limits."

Olympic Champion

Dolan's hard work paid off and he was the first American athlete to win a gold medal at the XXVI Olympic Games. Dolan won the 400-meter individual medley, beating University of Michigan teammate Eric Namesnik by only .35 of a second. The victory seemed to sap Dolan's strength, however, and he did not do as well in his other two events, the 200-meter individual medley and the 400-meter freestyle. Nonetheless, Dolan became one of the media stars of the Olympic games. Sporting a perfectly lean swimmer's body, decorated with an earring and a tattoo, and battling his physical limitations, Dolan represented the heart and soul of the Olympics. He even made the cover of both *Sports Illustrated* and Wheaties cereal boxes.

After the 1996 Olympics there was much speculation as to whether Dolan would retire. Dolan considered the option, however, his competitive spirit was still eager for more victories. Dolan continued to compete in and win at the United States swimming championships. In 1998 he became the first male swimmer since **Johnny Weissmuller** in the 1920s to win four events at two United States National Championships. Dolan underwent knee surgery in 1999, but he returned to the pool to prepare for the Olympics again.

Dolan had to fight off a lung virus that had him breathing from an oxygen tank only a week before the Olympics in Australia. He not only managed to repeat his gold medal win in the 400-meter individual medley, but he also broke his own world record in the event. He completed the race in four minutes and 11.76 seconds, a half-second faster than his previous Olympic run.

After the 2000 Olympics Dolan traveled the country as a motivational speaker and spokesperson for the American Lung Association. He still swims at special events. In 2001 he organized a relay swim to raise money for the facilities of the victims of the September 11, 2001 terrorist attacks on the Pentagon and the World Trade Center. He also participated in the 2001 Holiday Invitational swim meet at George Mason University.

CONTACT INFORMATION

Address: USA Swimming, 1 Olympic Plaza, Colorado Springs, CO, 80909-5746.

FURTHER INFORMATION

Books

Newsmakers, Issue 2. Detroit: Gale Group, 2001.
Sports Stars, Series 1-4. Detroit: U•X•L, 1994-1998.

Periodicals

Adelman, Ken. "A Place of Calm." *Washingtonian* (May 2001): 31.
Allen, Karen. "Dolan Organizes Swim to Benefit Victims' Families." *USA Today* (September 27, 2001): 14C.
Allen, Karen. "USA Gets Back in the Swim Dolan, Bennett, Malchow Lead Rival in Water." *USA Today* (September 18, 2000): 3E.
Barnas, Jo-Ann. "Dolan Digs Deep for Return Trip to Games." *Detroit Free Press* (August 11, 2000).
Barnas, Jo-Ann. "Men's Swimming: Tom Dolan the Pool Shark Wears His Age Well." *Detroit Free Press* (September 14, 2000).
Brant, Martha, and Mark Starr. "Gills Are All He Lacks." *Newsweek* (March 11, 1996): 66-67.
Brennan, Christine. "Dolan Pools Swimmer's Body, Mind; Long, Lean Local is Gold Meal Hope." *Washington Post* (July 14, 1996): D01.
Callahan, Gerry. "Gasp!" *Sports Illustrated* (July 22, 1996): 98-101.
Callahan, Gerry. "A Breath of Fresh Air." *Sports Illustrated* (April 3, 1995): 62-63.
Clock, Michele. "Swimmers Set Pace at Holiday Invite." *The Washington Post* (December 20, 2001): T26.
Frey, Jennifer. "Dolan's Race of a Lifetime Ends in 1st U.S. Gold." *The Washington Post* (July 22, 1996): A01.
Henderson, John. "U.S. Splashes Back at Hosts. Six Medals Taking Edge Off Thorpe." *Denver Post* (September 18, 2000): C15.
Hoffer, Richard. "Day 3: A Duel in the Pool." *Sports Illustrated* (August 1996): 28-33.
Hohlfeld, Neil. "Countdown to Back in the Swim." *Houston Chronicle* (June 4, 2000): 4.
Montville, Leigh. "Go Blue!" *Sports Illustrated* (July 29, 1996): 40-45.
Plummer, William. "Fighting to Inhale." *People Weekly* (April 22, 1996): 141-142.
Shipley, Amy. "Arlington's Dolan Grabs Gold." *Washington Post* (September 18, 2000): A01.
Stevens, Doug. "Dolan Will Not Swim for Blue in '96-'97." *Michigan Daily* (April 11, 1996).
Van Dyne, Larry. "How Do You Become Good Enough to Swim in the Olympics?" *Washingtonian* (June 1995).

Other

Curl-Burke Swim Club. http://home.att.net/~curlburke/main (January 20, 2003).
FINA - Biographies - Tom Dolan. http://www.fina/org/bio_Dolan.html (January 20, 2003).
Sports Illustrated For Kids Olympics 2000. http://sikids.com/olympics2000/reports/dolan_qa.html (January 20, 2003).
"Tom Dolan's Story: An Olympian's Victory Over Asthma." American Lung Association. http://lungusa/org/press/association/january96/dolan.html (January 20, 2003).
USA Swimming Official Web site. http://www.usswim.org (January 20, 2003).

Sketch by Janet P. Stamatel

Tony Dorsett
1954-

American football player

At just five-feet-ten-inches and 188 pounds dripping wet, Tony Dorsett didn't appear cut out to be a good running back. However, he spent four spectacular years at the University of Pittsburgh and twelve seasons

Tony Dorsett

Chronology

1954	Born April 7 in Rochester, Pennsylvania
1970-73	Star running back at Hopewell High School in Hopewell Township, Pennsylvania, near Aliquippa
1973-77	Star running back at the University of Pittsburgh
1977	Drafted by the Dallas Cowboys
1977-87	Star running back for the Cowboys
1981	Marries wife, Julie Ann
1984	Divorces
1988	Traded to the Denver Broncos
1989	Knee injury forces retirement
2002	Introduces, with Thomas Foods, a line of sauces and marinades

in the National Football League (NFL) proving that he wasn't only good, he was great. Combining lightning speed with agility that allowed him to change directions without losing momentum, Dorsett was an elusive runner with an uncanny ability to find a path down the field. His college record of 6,082 rushing yards stood for twenty-two years before being surpassed by Ricky Williams. His 12,739 rushing yards in the NFL was second only to **Walter Payton**.

Steel Mill Town

Tony Dorsett was born on April 7, 1954 in Rochester, Pennsylvania. He was the sixth of seven children in the family. Dorsett's father, West, worked in the steel mills for thirty years. Dorsett was very attached to his mother, Myrtle, who ran the household and carted the children to the Methodist church every Sunday. After his older brothers got into trouble for being out late drinking, Dorsett's parents laid down the law with him, and he avoided much of the trouble so readily available in the neighborhood. Although the family lived in a government-funded project called Plan 11, the housing development was clean and well-kept.

All his siblings were known for their speed, and Dorsett was no exception. His older brothers were track and football stars before him, and they served as Dorsett's role models and motivators. Upon entering high school Dorsett followed his brothers to Hopewell High School, located in a predominately white neigh-

borhood, where a small number of black kids from the projects were bussed. Dorsett was determined that he would not end up working in the steel mills. Finding a better life was always in his mind.

As a sophomore Dorsett made the varsity football team, despite the fact that he only weighed 130 pounds. He played the season as a defensive back, and he quickly proved that he had the speed expected from a Dorsett boy. As a junior, Dorsett moved to the running back position. Over the next two years he scored forty-two touchdowns and led his team to consecutive 9-1 seasons. During high school Dorsett's reputation as being hot-tempered grew as fast as his reputation as an excellent football player. He was involved in numerous fights and was once briefly suspended from sports.

By his senior year Dorsett was drawing the attention of college scouts. Although he was recruited by more than one hundred colleges, Dorsett, who wanted to stay near his family, chose the University of Pittsburgh. It was risky move, considering Pitt had gone 1-10 the previous season and did not have the national media coverage of other top programs knocking on Dorsett's door. But Dorsett put his trust in the university's new coach, Johnny Majors, and his assistant Jackie Sherrill. On February 17, 1973, Dorsett signed a letter of intent to attend Pitt.

University of Pittsburgh

Many at Pitt were skeptical that Dorsett, at just 157 pounds, was the answer to anyone's prayer. But the skinny, shy freshman was soon to prove them wrong. On his first play from scrimmage the first day of practice, Dorsett ran the ball for an 80-yard touchdown. Initially named to the third team, by the third day of practice, he was listed as the team's starting tailback.

Successful from the start as a football player, Dorsett was not always happy after he arrived in Pittsburgh. He had to adjust to being away from his family, living in a much larger city, and the increasing "fishbowl" nature of his existence. The Pitt sports information office began to refer to him as Tony, but until his junior year Dorsett, who had always been called Anthony, continued to sign autographs as Anthony Dorsett. His spot in limelight in-

Awards and Accomplishments

1973-77	First Team All-American
1976	Heisman Trophy Award; won national championship as a member of the University of Pittsburgh Panthers
1977	*Sporting News* Rookie of the Year; set an all-time National Collegiate Athletic Association rushing record of 6,082 total yards, which stood for 22 years
1978	Won Super Bowl as a member of the Dallas Cowboys
1978-81, 1983	Selected to National Football League (NFL) Pro Bowl
1981	Named National Football Conference (NFC) Player of the Year; named All-NFL.
1982	Set unbreakable record of a 99-yard touchdown run; NFC rushing champion
1988	Surpassed Jim Brown's rushing record; ended career with 12,739 yards rushing
1994	Elected to the Pro Football Hall of Fame

Dorsett was the first player to gain more than 1,000 yards each of his four college seasons and the first to accumulate more than 6,000 yards during his college career. He also set a record for three seasons with over 1,500 yards.

Related Biography: Football Player Herschel Walker

Herschel Walker won the Heisman Trophy as a junior at the University of Georgia in 1982. After establishing ten National Collegiate Athletic Association records in three years of play, Walker opted out of his senior year of college to join the upstart United States Football League (USFL). When the USFL folded in 1985 the Dallas Cowboys added Walker to the roster. At six-feet-one-inch, 223 pounds, Walker was a physical, straight-up-the-field runner with excellent skills as a receiver. He led the NFL in rushing in 1988.

When the Cowboys franchise was sold to Jerry Jones in 1989, the team was restructured to emphasize its passing game. As a result, Walker was traded to the Minnesota Vikings. After three seasons in Minnesota, he was traded to the Philadelphia Eagles, where he remained three seasons. Although he played an additional three seasons (one with the New York Giants and two again with the Dallas Cowboys), Walker's last season of major production was 1994. Over his career, he recorded 8,225 rushing yards and 4,859 receiving yards.

tensified after his girlfriend, Karen Casterlow, gave birth to the couple's son, Anthony, on September 14, 1973, the day Dorsett played in his first game as a Pitt Panther. The two never married, but Dorsett remained involved with his son throughout his childhood.

Unhappy and homesick, Dorsett almost gave up on college during his freshman year. Only after being encouraged by his mother and his coaches, did he agree to stick it out. After a freshman season with 1,686 yards rushing, Dorsett no longer had any doubts about his place. During his sophomore year, he was slowed by double- and triple-team defenses, but still managed to gain over 1,000 yards. During his junior and senior seasons, Dorsett, who bulked up to 185 pounds by his senior year, continued to improve, as did the Pitt team record. By the fall of 1976, Dorsett's final college season, Pitt was vying for the number one ranking in the nation, and Dorsett was vying for the Heisman.

During his senior year Dorsett rushed for 1,948 yards, scored twenty-one touchdowns, and set an all-time National Collegiate Athletic Association (NCAA) record of 6,082 yards. Along with winning the Heisman Trophy in 1976, Dorsett ended his storybook college career with fifty-five touchdowns, an average of 5.7 yards per attempt, a national championship, and his jersey was retired. He had also been named an All-American all four years. He was ready for the pros.

Becomes a Dallas Cowboy

In 1977 the Seattle Seahawks had first pick in the draft and planned on selecting Dorsett; however, Dorsett made it clear that he did not want to play for the Seahawks organization, which was at the time struggling through its infancy as an NFL expansion team, even bluffing that he may decide to play in Canada if the Seahawks took him. Ultimately the Dallas Cowboys stepped in, trading Seattle its first round pick plus three second round picks for a chance to take Dorsett.

During his first pro season, Dorsett rushed for more than 1,000 yards, averaged 4.8 yards per carry, and scored twelve touchdowns. For his efforts, he was named the NFL Rookie of the Year. Dorsett and the Cowboys went all the way to the 1978 Super Bowl, beating the Denver Broncos, 27-10. The following season Dorsett was equally impressive, posting 1,325 rushing yards, plus an additional 378 yards receiving. Each year Dorsett methodically moved the ball down the field, rushing for 1,000-plus yards eight of his first nine seasons. Only in 1982, which was shortened by a players' strike, did he fail to achieve 1,000 yards. He reached the pinnacle of his career in 1981, his fifth season in the NFL, rushing for a team-record 1,646 yards.

Life in the Fast Lane

Dorsett, living in the limelight, decided to take full advantage of his status as a superstar. The same explosive personality that drove him on the field also characterized his life off the field. He became notorious for his extravagant and frequent parties. He frequented the local clubs, and more than once became involved in a scuffle. He lived the high life, filled with women, alcohol, and plenty good times—a stark contrast to his aloof, all-about-business, church-going coach **Tom Landry**. However, by the mid-1980s Dorsett was suffering some personal and professional setbacks.

Dorsett's marriage ended in 1984, followed closely by his father's death. Then in 1985 the Internal Revenue Service (IRS) came knocking, garnishing his wages and placing a lien on his two Dallas homes to satisfy more than $400,000 owed in back taxes after a tax shelter Dorsett had invested in was disallowed. Dorsett had other concurrent financial troubles. He had made numerous poor investments, costing him much of his money. Because of his wild lifestyle and unproven, but widely rumored, drug use, Dorsett secured few endorsement deals to supplement his player's pay check.

Career Statistics

Yr	Team	Rushing					Receiving			
		GP	ATT	YDS	AVG	TD	REC	YDS	AVG	TD
1977	Dallas	14	208	1007	4.8	12	29	273	9.4	1
1978	Dallas	16	290	1325	4.6	7	37	378	10.2	2
1979	Dallas	14	250	1107	4.4	6	45	375	8.3	1
1980	Dallas	15	278	1185	4.3	11	34	263	7.7	0
1981	Dallas	16	342	1646	4.8	4	32	325	10.2	2
1982	Dallas	9	177	745	4.2	5	24	179	7.5	0
1983	Dallas	16	289	1321	4.6	8	40	287	7.2	1
1984	Dallas	16	302	1189	3.9	6	51	459	9.0	1
1985	Dallas	16	305	1307	4.3	7	46	449	9.8	3
1986	Dallas	13	184	748	4.1	5	25	267	10.7	1
1987	Dallas	12	130	456	3.5	1	19	177	9.3	1
1988	Denver	16	181	703	3.9	5	16	122	7.6	0
TOTAL		173	2936	12739	4.3	77	398	3554	8.9	13

Dallas: Dallas Cowboys; Denver: Denver Broncos.

A Relationship Gone Bad

Prior to the 1985 season things began to sour between Dorsett and the Cowboys organization. Dorsett decided to hold out, demanding that his contract be renegotiated. Dorsett was angry because he believed that the Cowboys management was responsible for the public airing of his financial problems, and because Randy White, the Cowboys' celebrated defensive tackle, had been awarded a larger contract than Dorsett. When the Cowboys brought on running back Herschel Walker, Dorsett went on a tirade because Walker's $5 million five-year contract exceeded his own $4.5 million five-year contract.

The signing of Walker proved to be the beginning of the end for Dorsett's days in Dallas. Although Dorsett personally liked Walker, the younger running back was everything that Dorsett had never been: bigger, younger, and in possession of a gentler nature that fit the all-American image of Dallas Cowboy football. Suddenly Dorsett was sharing time in the back field, and it deeply bruised his ego. On November 22, 1987, in a game against the Miami Dolphins, for the first time in his career, Dorsett was listed in the stats as DNP (Did Not Play). It was an embarrassment and an insult that Dorsett could not stomach. He began loudly demanding to be traded.

Dorsett eventually got his wish, and after eleven seasons in a Cowboy uniform, he was traded to the Denver Broncos. After a long, frustrating season in Dallas, Dorsett told *Sports Illustrated* that he was excited about the change, remarking, "Mentally, I couldn't feel better. As far as my reputation for being a troublemaker, well, I don't back off. The Cowboys try to mold everyone in their image, and I couldn't be molded." Despite his positive outlook, injuries limited Dorsett's playing time with the Broncos during the 1988 season. When he suffered from torn knee ligaments during training camp the following year, Dorsett was forced to retire.

At the age of thirty-four, when Dorsett joined the Broncos, he could still run forty yards in 4.3 seconds. According to the Pro Football Hall of Fame's tribute to Dorsett, "[He] was a player who had it all ... the swift, smooth strides; the sharp, crisp cuts; the uncanny knack of finding daylight in the chaos along the line of scrimmage. Every time he touched a football, opponents shuddered. He turned small gainers into big gainers and routine plays into touchdowns." In 1994 Dorsett, in his first year of eligibility, was inducted into the Pro Football Hall of Fame.

SELECTED WRITINGS BY DORSETT:

(With Harvey Frommer) *Running Tough: Memoirs of a Football Maverick,* Doubleday, 1989.

FURTHER INFORMATION

Books

Dorsett, Tony, and Harvey Frommer. *Running Tough: Memoirs of a Football Maverick.* New York: Doubleday, 1989.

Markoe, Arnold, ed. *The Scribner Encyclopedia of American Lives: Sports Figures.* Vol. 1. New York: Charles Scribner's Sons, 2002.

Who's Who Among African Americans, 14th ed. Detroit: Gale Group, 2001.

Periodicals

"Dustbin." *Sporting News* (October 23, 2000): 7.

Looney, Douglas S. "Thrown for Some Big Losses." *Sports Illustrated* (August 12, 1985): 22-27.

Telander, Rick. "Walker and Dorsett." *Sports Illustrated* (November 17, 1986): 76.

"Tony Dorsett Talks About Tax Problems, Divorce and the Death of his Dear Dad." *Jet* (October 28, 1985): 48-49.

Zimmerman, Paul. "Goodbye, Big D, Hello Denver." *Sports Illustrated* (August 1, 1988): 36-40.

Other

"Tony Dorsett." Dallas Cowboys Fan Club.com. http://www.dallascowboysfanclub.com/dorsett.htm (December 28, 2002)

"Tony Dorsett." Pro Football Hall of Fame. http://www.profootballhof.com/players/enshrinees/tdorsett.cfm/ (December 28, 2002)

Sketch by Kari Bethel

Dave Dravecky

Dave Dravecky
1956-

American baseball player

Fate has been both kind and cruel to baseball's Dave Dravecky. First he was gifted with a talent for pitching that led him to the major leagues and two All-Star games. Then that same gift was cruelly taken away as cancer destroyed Dravecky's left arm—his throwing arm. But Dravecky, whose Christian faith led him through the hard times, has devoted his post-baseball life to helping others who have faced the ravages of cancer and amputation.

A native of Youngstown, Ohio, Dravecky "seemed like the ultimate, all-American, clean-cut athlete," according to an essay for *Contemporary Heroes and Heroines*. He graduated from his hometown Youngstown State University, then was drafted by the Pittsburgh Pirates to play Double-A ball, honing his game in such towns as Buffalo, New York, and Amarillo, Texas. Called to the majors in 1982, Dravecky took the mound for the San Diego Padres, serving as both starting and relief pitcher. The left-hander reached an early peak; in 1984, Dravecky threw more than ten scoreless innings of relief in postseason play, first in the National League playoffs versus the Chicago Cubs, and then during the World Series against the Detroit Tigers.

Getting the Bad News

Traded to the San Francisco Giants in 1987, Dravecky continued to show the form that won him acclaim. He again pitched in the postseason and went on to gain a shutout during the Giants' opening day in 1988. But something was amiss with Dravecky's left arm. He initially experienced stiffness in his shoulder, which led to a three-week stint on the disabled list. Doctors detected a lump, but told Dravecky that it was only a harmless cyst. But the pitcher suspected a deeper problem.

Dravecky and his wife, Jan, left San Francisco in September 1988, returning home to Ohio where he could have more tests done. According to a *Newsmakers* essay, "he and his wife were waiting for the news when they heard the doctors discussing his case through an open door. The diagnosis of cancer was almost certain, and major surgery was inevitable. The Draveckys heard the worst before the doctors could break it to them gently." A biopsy had revealed a rare form of cancer known as a desmoid tumor. The malignancy was positioned on Dravecky's left deltoid muscle, a crucial muscle that allows pitchers to wind up and extend the arm during a throw. To save Dravecky's arm—and his life—the tumor would have to be removed, along with a large portion of the patient's arm.

On October 7, 1988—the Dravecky's wedding anniversary—Dave Dravecky underwent surgery at Ohio's Cleveland Clinic. Doctors removed the tumor and most of the deltoid muscle that surrounded it. To combat the cancer's return, the doctors froze Dravecky's upper arm bone where the tumor had been, leaving a fist-sized pit in the front of his upper arm. From the beginning, Dravecky had been advised that he would never pitch again. But he had other plans.

A Brief, Bright Comeback

Sessions of painful physical therapy followed as Dravecky learned a new way to maneuver his left arm. "I

Career Statistics

Yr	Team	W	L	ERA	GS	CG	SHO	IP	H	R	BB	SO
1982	SDP	5	3	2.57	10	0	0	105.0	86	8	33	59
1983	SDP	14	10	3.58	28	9	1	183.7	181	18	44	74
1984	SDP	9	8	2.93	14	3	2	156.7	125	12	51	71
1985	SDP	13	11	2.93	31	7	2	214.7	200	18	57	105
1986	SDP	9	11	3.07	26	3	1	161.3	149	17	54	87
1987	SDP	3	7	3.76	10	1	0	79.0	71	10	31	60
1987	SFG	7	5	3.20	18	4	3	112.3	115	8	33	78
1988	SFG	2	2	3.16	7	1	0	37.0	33	4	8	19
1989	SFG	2	0	3.46	2	0	0	13.0	8	2	4	5
TOTAL		64	57	3.13	146	28	9	1062.7	968	97	315	558

SDP: San Diego Padres. SFG: San Francisco Giants.

started tossing a football in January, picked up my first baseball in March, and by June I was able to throw batting practice" at San Francisco's Candlestick Park, noted Dravecky in a *People* interview with Liz MacNeil. "I had very little velocity, but just being able to throw from the mound to home plate was a thrill." Dravecky returned to the minors, throwing innings for the Phoenix Firebirds, augmenting his recovery with running and weight training to build strength and stamina. Finally in the summer of 1989 Dravecky was called back to the Giants.

The publicity surrounding the pitcher's return to the big leagues came to a head when Dravecky stepped to the mound on August 10, to riotous ovations by the crowd. He had not pitched a big-league game in fourteen months. More than two hours later he had made his mark with a 4-3 victory over the Cincinnati Reds. Dravecky had hurled five strikeouts and only one walk. According to Craig Neff's *Sports Illustrated* report, Dravecky's throws reached speeds of 88 miles per hour. When a relief pitcher was put in during the eighth inning, the crowd of 34,810 called Dravecky back for one of his many standing ovations. "I've been in five World Series," Giants manager Roger Craig told the *Los Angeles Times,* "and this is my biggest thrill. I've never been involved with something like this."

The thrill felt by Craig and baseball fans was short-lived, however. In his second comeback game, on August 15, 1989, Dravecky was pitching in Montreal against the Expos. During the sixth inning, he wound up to hurl a fastball to batter Tim Raines. As Dravecky released the ball, a loud *crack* emanated—a sound so sharp it was heard in the stands. The next image was of Dravecky collapsing on the mound. The pitch had broken his left humerus bone. "My immediate reaction was to grab my arm because I thought it had left my body," Dravecky recalled in the *People* article.

Dravecky again faced a long and painful rehabilitation. But this time recovery didn't make itself apparent. The former All-Star suffered strep and staph infections; meanwhile, his once-golden left arm had become "a nuisance," as Dravecky told *Sports Illustrated* contributor William Nack. "A pest. It became 'The Thing.' It got to the point where the only thing I could use it for was to put my socks on." The final blow came in May 1990, when the simple act of putting his left hand down for balance caused another blow to his humerus. The cancer had returned.

Life Goes On

After a series of operations and radiation treatments, Dravecky after ten months came to the conclusion that there was only one viable option left. On June 18, 1991, Dravecky's left arm and shoulder were amputated. "I felt like I lost a real good buddy," the pitcher told Nack. "You know, this friend that has been attached to me all those years; that allowed me to do something that I enjoyed more than just about anything on this earth ... that friend is gone." What remained was "phantom pain," a medical phenomenon that causes an amputee to feel pain where a limb has been removed. "It burns," he explained to Nack. "Very hot and painful. A constant burn. Not a throb, but a burning in the fingers and the palm, like someone is taking a match and sticking it right at the end of my fingertips."

Still, the amputation gave Dravecky a new chance for life. As he recovered, he found joy in being able to get a full night's sleep, or to play with his children without fear of further injury. Throughout the entire ordeal, Dravecky and his family have relied on their devout Christianity to help both Dave and Jan deal with severe depression. Dravecky spoke frankly about his life in his book *When You Can't Come Back: A Story of Courage and Grace.* "I used to feel [my condition] was tragic," wrote the onetime pitcher. "I used to be preoccupied with my own needs; now I am learning compassion for others. I used to depend on myself; now I lean more on God." In his retirement from baseball, Dravecky wasn't forgotten by his fans. Pitching "righty," he threw out the first ceremonial ball at a 1998 Giants game.

Dave Dravecky is one of 7.4 million cancer survivors in the United States. In 1991 he and his wife, Jan, founded Outreach of Hope (formerly the Dave Dravecky Foundation), a nonprofit organization that provides sup-

<table>
<tr><td colspan="2">

Chronology

</td></tr>
</table>

1956	Born February 14, in Youngstown, Ohio
1978	Drafted by Pittsburgh Pirates
1982	Made professional debut with San Diego Padres
1987	Traded to San Francisco Giants
1988	Named starting pitcher for Giants opening day
1988	Discovered malignant growth on left shoulder
1988	Cancerous tumor removed in operation, October 7
1989	Returns to baseball, August 10
1989	Pitching arm breaks in second comeback game
1989	Ends baseball career
1990	Becomes a motivational speaker and author
1991	Left arm and shoulder amputated
1991	Founds Outreach of Hope Ministries

Awards and Accomplishments

1978	Graduated Youngstown State University
1984	Pitched in National League playoffs and World Series
1987	Tied the record for fewest hits given up in a playoff game
1989	Won Willie McCovey Award
1990	Won American Cancer Society's Courage Award
1991	"Dave Dravecky Day" at Candlestick Park, San Francisco
1998	Threw out first pitch for Giants game versus Montreal Expos
1998	Given Lou Gehrig Ironman Award
1999	Named to Giants' Team of the Decade for 1980s.

port to cancer patients and their families, as well as others facing adversity. An author affiliated with the Christian publisher Zondervan, Dravecky is also a professional speaker, touching on points inspirational, motivational, and evangelical.

"If you can't admire Dave Dravecky," Giants teammate Terry Kennedy told the *San Francisco Herald* during the pitcher's 1989 comeback attempt, "then something is wrong with you. He's an example for people who have cancer especially, and for people who have major afflictions in general. It's something that he can throw a ball at all. This is a guy who wasn't supposed to be able to comb his hair."

CONTACT INFORMATION

Email: zauthor@zondervan.com. Online: http://www.out reachofhope.com.

SELECTED WRITINGS BY DRAVECKY:

Comeback, Zondervan, 1990.
When You Can't Come Back: A Story of Courage and Grace, Cahners, 1992.
(With C. W. Neal) *The Worth of a Man.* Zondervan, 1996.

FURTHER INFORMATION

Books

Contemporary Heroes and Heroines, Book III. Detroit: Gale, 1998.
Dravecky, Dave. *Comeback.* Grand Rapids, MI: Zondervan, 1990.
Dravecky, Dave. *Dave Dravecky.* Grand Rapids, MI: Zondervan, 1992.
Dravecky, Dave. *When You Can't Come Back: A Story of Courage and Grace.* Grand Rapids, MI: Zondervan, 1992.
Dravecky, Dave, and C. W. Neal*The Worth of a Man.* Zondervan, 1996.

Gire, Judy. *A Boy and His Baseball: The Dave Dravecky Story.* Grand Rapids, MI: Zondervan, 1992.
Newsmakers. Detroit: Gale, 1992.

Periodicals

Jaffe, Michael. "Recovering." *Sports Illustrated.* (July 1, 1991): 11.
Los Angeles Times. (August 11, 1989).
McNeil, Liz. "After a Courageous Comeback, a Star Pitcher Breaks His Arm but Keeps His Faith Intact." *People* (September 11, 1989): 69.
Nack, William. "'Let's Make the Best of It.'" *Sports Illustrated.* (July 22, 1991): 34.
Neff, Craig. "A Broken Comeback."*Sports Illustrated.* (August 28, 1989).
Neff, Craig. "Armed with a Miracle." *Sports Illustrated.* (August 21, 1989): 18.
San Francisco Herald. (August 17, 1989).
Zoller, Harriet. "Pitcher Dave Dravecky Captures Courage Award." *Cancer News.* (Summer, 1990): 4.

Sketch by Susan Salter

Ken Dryden
1947-

Canadian hockey player

While many consider Ken Dryden to be one of the best goalies who ever played in the National Hockey League (NHL), he was considered odd, even for a goalie (who in hockey circles are often regarded as eccentric individuals), in part because of his intellectual, non-hockey pursuits. While he won five Stanley Cups in the 1970s with the Montreal Canadiens, he also took a year out of his prime playing career to complete the requirements of his law degree. Dryden retired from professional hockey in his early thirties, but later returned to become the president of the Toronto Maple Leafs.

Ken Dryden

Dryden was born on August 8, 1947 in Islington, Ontario, Canada, the son of Murray and Margaret Dryden. His father sold bricks and building materials. Both Dryden and his elder brother Dave were goalies. (Dave Dryden also played in the NHL for the Chicago Blackhawks, and completed his education while playing professional hockey.) The brothers had a year round rink at home because their father paved the backyard with asphalt. Because of all the shots that broke glass, the windows of the family home had to boarded up.

Drafted by Boston; Traded to Montreal

After a successful career playing Junior B hockey in Toronto, Dryden was selected by the Boston Bruins in the 1964 amateur draft in the third round with the fourteenth pick. After the draft, Boston traded his rights to the Montreal Canadiens. Dryden had made it clear that he wanted to attend college, and while Montreal was willing to let him do that, they had their own plan for him. The team wanted him to play junior A in Peterborough and attend Trent University. Dryden, ever the individual, forged his own path.

Attended Cornell University

Dryden decided to play college hockey in the United States at Cornell University, where he received a college scholarship. He faced quality competition and was an outstanding college player. While earning his B.A. in history, Dryden was an All-American three times and had a goals against average of 1.65 in seventy-one games. Cornell won the Division I title in 1967; in 1969, it was second in Division I.

After Dryden graduated in 1969, Montreal sent him to play for Canada in the World Championships in Stockholm, Sweden, so he could gain more experience. Dryden played in two games, including a 1-0 shutout against the Americans. Dryden then signed a three-year deal to play for Canada's national team as a way of developing his goalie skills. Soon this contract was negated as the program was in turmoil, and he left the national team in the summer of 1970. Dryden also attended law school at the University of Manitoba during this time.

Dryden's next career move was to sign with the Montreal Canadiens. He was assigned to their minor league system, playing for the Montreal Voyageurs in the American Hockey League (AHL) for the 1970-71 season. His coach there, Floyd Curry knew he was good enough to play for the Canadiens—Dryden had proved it by playing well in an exhibition game. In thirty-three games with the Voyageurs, Dryden had a goals against of 2.68 and three shutouts. But hockey was not his only focus. Dryden also began attending law school at Montreal's McGill University.

Called up by the Canadiens

At the end of the 1970-71 season, Dryden was called up from the minors to play for the Canadiens. He was the first Ivy League graduate to play in the NHL. He started in six games at the end of the season, and gave up only nine goals. Dryden was played to give their veteran number one goaltender Rogie Vachon a break—he had not played consistently through the season—and test Dryden's mettle. Because of Dryden's success in those games, he was picked to start in goal in the playoffs by coach Al MacNeil.

Career Statistics

Yr	Team	GP	W	L	T	GAA	SHO
1970-71	Montreal	6	6	0	0	1.65	0
1971-72	Montreal	64	39	8	15	2.24	8
1972-73	Montreal	54	33	7	13	2.26	6
1974-75	Montreal	56	30	9	16	2.69	4
1975-76	Montreal	62	42	10	8	2.03	10
1976-77	Montreal	56	41	6	8	2.14	5
1977-78	Montreal	52	37	7	7	2.05	5
1978-79	Montreal	47	30	10	7	2.30	5
TOTAL		397	258	57	74	2.24	46

Montreal: Montreal Canadiens (NHL).

Awards and Accomplishments

1967	Backstopped Cornell to the Division I title
1971	Won Conn Smythe Trophy as Playoff MVP; Won Stanley Cup
1972	Won the Calder Trophy as Rookie of the Year; All-Star (second team)
1973	All-Star (first team)
1973, 1976-79	Vezina Trophy
1976-79	Won Stanley Cup

MacNeil made a wise choice. Dryden helped the Canadiens defeat the Boston Bruins in a tough seven game series. They then defeated the Minnesota North Stars in six games and the Chicago Blackhawks in seven games. Though Dryden had some rough patches, he and the Canadiens went on to win the Stanley Cup. In twenty playoff games, Dryden posted a 3.00 goals against average, the highest of his career. He was also awarded the Conn Smythe Trophy as the most valuable player in the playoffs.

After winning the Cup, Dryden continued to forge his own path. He went to Washington D.C. to be one of Ralph Nader's Raiders, fighting for fisherman who wanted clean water. Dryden continued to do this in other ways in Canada when he returned to the Canadiens in the fall.

Became Canadiens' number one goaltender

At the beginning of the 1971-72, Dryden was named the number one goaltender for the Canadiens. Because of the limited number of games he had appeared in the previous season, this was technically his rookie year. He played in sixty-four games with a 2.24 goals against average, and won the Calder Trophy as rookie of the year. This marked the first time a player was named playoff MVP before being named rookie of the year.

Dryden continued to play well in goal in the 1972-73 season, winning the Vezina Trophy as best goaltender in the league. In fifty-four games, he had a record of 33-7-13 with a goals against of 2.26. He also graduated from McGill University's law school in 1973. To complete the requirements of his degree and practice law, he had to begin "articling" within two years. Articling was doing a year's clerkship at a law firm.

Quits Hockey for Year

In September 1973, Dryden announced that he would not play in the 1973-74 season so he could article for the firm of Osler, Hoskin and Harcourt in Toronto. He made this decision not just because his degree required it, but also because the Canadiens would not meet his financial demands. Dryden believed he was one of the best goalies in the NHL and wanted to be paid like it.

While living in Toronto, Dryden remained connected to hockey by playing defense in an industrial league in Toronto and doing television commentary for the World Hockey Association's Toronto Toros. The Canadiens suffered in Dryden's absence. They played horribly behind three different goalies, Wayne Thomas, Michel Plasse, and Michel "Bunny" Larocque. Though the team made the playoffs, Montreal lost in the first round.

Returned to the Canadiens

In May 1974, Dryden signed a big contract to return to play for the Canadiens, giving him something in the neighborhood of $450,000-600,000 over three years. He had considered playing for the World Hockey Association, and had a significant offer. But Dryden decided he was better off with the Canadiens. It took some time for him to regain his form. While the Canadiens did make the playoffs, his goals against during the regular season was a career-high 2.69. The team did not make it to the finals.

Though some in Montreal wondered if the team had made a mistake in re-signing Dryden, he proved his worth during each of the next four seasons. From 1976-79, he won the Vezina Trophy every year, and the Canadiens won the Stanley Cup every year. In 1975-76, he had a goals against of 2.03. His best season was arguably 1976-77, where in fifty-six games, Dryden had a goals against of 2.14 with ten shutouts. In the playoffs, had a goals against of 1.56 with four shutouts in fourteen games.

Retired at Early Age

After winning the Stanley Cup in 1979, Dryden retired permanently. Over the course of eight seasons with Montreal, he had a record of 258-57-74, with forty-six shutouts and a career 2.24 goals against average. His playoff record was equally impressive: eighty wins in 112 games, with 2.40 goals against average and ten shutouts. He also had nineteen assists in the regular season and four assists in the playoffs. As Douglas Hunter wrote in *A Breed Apart,* "Ken Dryden is remembered, above all, for The Stance: hands atop his stick, chin atop his hands, one knee flexed, more contemplative of the spectacle of the game than the spectators on the other side of the boards. Goaltending, ultimately, is a reactive discipline, and it has been Ken Dryden's metier to react as arrestingly on the ice as off." He was elected to the Hockey Hall of Fame in 1983.

CONTACT INFORMATION

Address: c/o Toronto Maple Leafs, Air Canada Centre, 40 Bay St., Suite 400, Toronto, Ontario M4J 2X2 Canada.

SELECTED WRITINGS BY DRYDEN:

(With Mark Mulvoy) *Faceoff at the Summit,* Little Brown, 1973.
The Game: A Thoughtful and Provocative Look at a Life in Hockey, New York: Times Books, 1983.
In School: Our Kids, Our Teaching, Our Classrooms, McClelland & Stewart, 1995.
Finding a Way: Legacy of the Past, Recipe for the Future, University of Ottawa Press, 2002.

FURTHER INFORMATION

Books

Fischler, Stan. *The All-New Hockey's 100.* Toronto: McGraw-Hill Ryerson Ltd., 1988.
Fischler, Stan, and Shirley Fischler. *Fischlers' Hockey Encyclopedia.* New York: Thomas Y. Crowell Company, 1975.
Hickock, Ralph. *A Who's Who of Sports Champions.* Boston: Houghton Mifflin Company, 1995.
Hunter, Douglas. *A Breed Apart: An Illustrated History of Goaltending.* Chicago: Triumph Books, 1995.

Periodicals

Deacon, James. "Aiming for the Stanley Cup." *Maclean's* (June 23, 1997): 43.
"Four-Story Goalie." *Newsweek* (May 17, 1971): 62.
Lapointe, Joe. "Dryden's Drive for Success in Toronto." *New York Times* (May 23, 1999): section 8, p. 1.
Mulvoy, Mark. "Ken Dryden on Trial." *Sports Illustrated* (November 24, 1974): 24.
Swift, E.M. "Tough Saves." *Sports Illustrated* (December 8, 1997): 70.

Vecesey, George. "Ken Dryden Scores." *New York Times* (April 16, 1984): C8.

Other

"Ken Dryden." http://www.hockeysandwich.com/ kdryden.html (December 14, 2002).

Sketch by A. Petruso

Tim Duncan
1976-

American basketball player

Combining skills as a passer, rebounder, shooter, scorer, dribbler, and defender, Tim Duncan is one of the best all-round players in the NBA. Winner of the National Basketball Association's (NBA) Most Valuable Player honors in 2002, Duncan is no stranger to awards; his resume has a long list of well-earned basketball achievements. Yet despite all the accolades continually heaped upon him, Duncan remains the quiet, intense young man who grew up in the Virgin Islands and dreamed of becoming an Olympic swimmer.

Life on the Island

Timothy Theodore Duncan was born on April 25, 1976, on St. Croix, U.S. Virgin Islands, an 82-square-mile island in the eastern Caribbean Sea. He was the third of four children born to William and Ione Duncan. His father, a mason, worked a variety of jobs, and his mother was a midwife. Both Duncan and his sister Tricia were talented swimmers. Tricia represented the Virgin Islands in the 100- and 200- meter backstroke in the 1988 Olympics, and Duncan holds the Virgin Islands record in the 50- and 100-meter freestyle events and was a nationally ranked swimmer in the United States in the 400-meter freestyle by the age of thirteen.

Duncan's mother encouraged and supported her children. She attended all Duncan's swim meets, usually yelling loud enough for Duncan to hear her above the crowd. His mother instilled a strong work ethic in her children, and Duncan still repeats her motto to himself: "Good, better, best. Never let it rest, until your good is better and your better is best." Duncan expected to pursue his swimming career to the next Olympics, but Hurricane Hugo hit St. Croix in 1989, destroying the only Olympic-sized pool on the island. With no place to train, Duncan tried swimming in the ocean, but was not thrilled with sharing the water with the sharks that inhabited the waters around St. Croix. If the hurricane took away Duncan's place to swim,

Tim Duncan

Chronology	
1976	Born April 25 on St. Croix, U.S. Virgin Islands
1989	Hurricane Hugo hits St. Croix
1990	Duncan's mother loses her fight with breast cancer
1993-97	Star player for the Wake Forest Demon Deacons
1997	Graduates with a degree in psychology; drafted by the San Antonio Spurs
1999	Wins National Basketball Association (NBA) championship with the Spurs
2000	Re-signs with Spurs
2002	Named NBA Player of the Year

his mother's death from breast cancer just one day before his fourteenth birthday took away Duncan's desire to swim. Duncan's older sister, Cheryl, who had been studying nursing in the United States, returned to the island with her husband to help care for the devastated family.

Cheryl's husband, Ricky Lowry, who had played basketball at Capital University, a small college in Ohio, encouraged Duncan to pursue basketball. In 1988 Cheryl had shipped a pole and basketball backboard from Ohio to her younger brother as a Christmas present. Planted deep in the ground by his father, it was one of the few things left standing after Hugo passed through. In the days that followed his mother's death, Duncan's brother-in-law encouraged him to play hoops. Duncan complied, and later told *Sports Illustrated,* "I remember thinking that after basketball season ended, I'd go back to swimming, but then basketball season never ended." Not knowing that Duncan would grow ten inches in the next few years, Lowry taught his then-six-foot pupil the perimeter game, lessons that provided Duncan with ball-handling skills and a court awareness that set him apart from other big men in the game.

By the time he was a senior, Duncan was averaging twenty-five points, twelve rebounds, and five blocked shots per game at St. Dunstan's Episcopal High School. Despite glowing write-ups in the local St. Croix sports pages, Duncan received relatively little interest from colleges. When a group of NBA rookies toured the Vir-

gin Islands, Chris King, who played college ball at Wake Forest University, was impressed by Duncan's performance against Alonzo Mourning. King called his old coach, Dave Odom, who made the trip to St. Croix to see Duncan play. During the visit, reticent and shy, Duncan watched television as Odom spoke until the coach finally asked if he might turn it off so he could have Duncan's full attention. To Odom's astonishment, Duncan repeated back the entire discussion, making the coach quickly realized that Duncan's distracted look did not translate into distracted attention.

Goes to School, Takes Opponents to School

Arriving as a seventeen-year-old freshman at Wake Forest in 1993, Duncan was expected to spend most of his time on the bench his first season, but when the team's starting center was declared ineligible, Duncan was called upon to contribute right away. His first college game was played against the University of Alaska in Anchorage; it was the first time Duncan had ever seen snow. Although he didn't score during his first outing, it didn't take long for Duncan to establish himself on the defensive end. As a freshman, he averaged 9.8 points, 9.6 rebounds, and 3.8 blocks per game and set a new Demon Deacon record for total single-season blocked shots.

During his sophomore year Duncan averaged 16.8 points and 12.5 rebounds per game. He was named the National Defensive Player of the Year, First Team All-Atlantic Coast Conference (ACC), and Third Team All-American. Increasing his offensive production in his junior year Duncan continued to earn honors, including consecutive years as Defensive Player of the Year and First Team All-ACC. Also as a junior he was named First Team All-American and the ACC Player of the Year. During his final year of college ball, Duncan led the nation in rebounds per game (14.7) and upped his scoring average to 20.8 points per game. Along with once again being named Defensive Player of the Year (for an unmatched third straight year), ACC Player of the Year, and First Team All American, Duncan was also selected as the National Player of the Year.

Duncan's talent was obvious to everyone, but for a long while his personality remained a mystery to many, includ-

Career Statistics

Yr	Team	GP	PTS	PPG	FG%	3P%	FT%	RPG	APG	BPG	TO
1998	SA	82	1731	21.1	.549	.000	.622	11.9	2.7	2.5	279
1999	SA	50	1084	21.7	.495	.143	.690	11.4	2.4	2.5	146
2000	SA	74	1716	23.2	.490	.091	.761	12.4	3.2	2.2	242
2001	SA	82	1820	22.2	.499	.259	.618	12.2	3.0	2.3	242
2002	SA	82	2089	25.5	.508	.100	.799	12.7	3.7	2.5	263
TOTAL		370	8440	22.8	.509	.154	.711	12.2	3.1	2.4	1172

SA: San Antonio Spurs.

ing his teammates. His subdued nature, which bordered on aloofness, could be misconstrued as lack of intensity. But soon both his fans and foes realized that Duncan was extremely dedicated, focused, and enjoying himself, even if he didn't always look the part. Although he took winning and losing seriously, he refused to be goaded into confrontations on the court or in the media. He took care of business and proved himself with his play.

Although he would have likely been the number one pick in the 1995 NBA draft, to the delight of Demon Deacon fans, nineteen-year-old Duncan decided to pass up the possibility of a $3 million a year NBA contract to remain in college for his junior and senior years. Hopeful of their chances in the NCAA tournament, the Demon Deacons made it to the East Regional Finals in 1996 and suffered a disappointing second-round loss in 1997. Nonetheless, Duncan had established himself as one of the best to ever play four years of college ball. According to *Sports Illustrated,* in 1997 Wofford coach Richard Johnson, whose well-overmatched team would face Duncan and the Demon Deacons the following day, told his players: "Let me tell you guys about who you're playing tomorrow. Someday your six-year-old kid will ask you for a Tim Duncan jersey for Christmas. This is your chance to play a future NBA Hall of Famer, your turn to face the greatest player any of you will ever meet."

Spurs, Title, and MVP

As expected Duncan was selected as the first overall pick of the 1997 draft by the San Antonio Spurs. The Spurs, who had gone 20-62 the previous year, were a deceptively good team. Their pathetic showing in the 1996-97 season was due primarily to the absence of star **David Robinson**, who sat out all but six games due to injury. But Robinson was once again healthy for the 1997-98 season, and Spurs Coach Greg Popovich considered Duncan as icing on the cake. If there was any doubt that Duncan was tough enough to compete at the next level, he spent his rookie year proving just how well he could play. He averaged 21.1 points, 11.9 rebounds, 2.5 blocks, and .549 field goal percentage, leading all NBA rookies in all categories and finishing third in the nation in rebounding. Named NBA Rookie of the Year in 1998, Duncan was also selected to the First Team All-NBA and was the only rookie to play in the 1998 All Star Game.

Duncan helped the Spurs rebound from a twenty-win year to post a record turnaround of fifty-six wins for the 1997-98 season. Injury struck Duncan in the playoffs, and despite hopes of an NBA title, the Spurs fell to the Utah Jazz in the second round. The following season was shortened to fifty games because of a player lockout, but when play resumed in January of 1999, Duncan and the Spurs were ready. After sweeping **Shaquille O'Neal** and the Los Angeles Lakers in four games, the Spurs beat the New York Knicks in five games to win the NBA title. Duncan, who was named the Most Valuable Player of the finals, averaged 27.4 points, 14.0 rebounds, and 2.2 blocks per game.

After finishing the 1999-2000 season averaging 23.2 points, 12.4 rebounds, and 2.2 blocks per game, Duncan watched his team lose in the first round of the playoffs as he sat on the bench, sidelined by injury. He then became a free agent and the Spurs scrambled to convince their young star to stay in San Antonio. Although the Orlando Magic made a strong bid, ultimately Duncan decided with remain with the Spurs.

The 2001-02 season proved to be the best of Duncan's career. After leading the Spurs to fifty-eight wins, and averaging 25.5 points, 12.7 rebounds, and 2.5 blocks per game, Duncan was named the 2002 NBA Most Valuable Player. With the Spurs beginning to rebuild their aging team, and anticipating the retirement of "The Admiral" David Robinson after the 2002-03 season, Duncan has found himself in a new leadership role on the team. As a result, he has worked to increase his emotional demonstrations on the court to help inspire his teammates. Spurs forward Malik Rose told *Basketball Digest,* "He's always trying to get us pumped up. And we get real inspired by it because we know how tough it is for him. He's such a quiet kid." Quiet or not, Duncan continues to make a loud statement as one of the finest players in the NBA.

CONTACT INFORMATION

Address: San Antonio Spurs, 600 E. Market Street, San Antonio, Texas 78205. Phone: (210) 554-7773.

Awards and Accomplishments

1994	Named to the Atlantic Coast Conference (ACC) All-Rookie Team
1995-96	National Collegiate Athletic Association (NCAA) National Defensive Player of the Year
1995-97	First Team All-ACC
1996-97	NCAA First Team All American
1997	NCAA National Player of the Year and ACC Player of the Year; selected first overall in the 1997 National Basketball Association (NBA) draft by the San Antonio Spurs
1998	Rookie of the Year and NBA All Star
1998-2002	First Team All NBA
1999	NBA championship as member of the San Antonio Spurs; selected Most Valuable Player of the NBA finals
2002	Named NBA's Most Valuable Player and received the IBM Award

FURTHER INFORMATION

Books

Contemporary Black Biography, Volume 20. Detroit: Gale Group, 1998.
Newsmakers 2000, Issue 1. Detroit: Gale Group, 2000.
Sports Stars. Series 5. Detroit: U•X•L, 1999.
Who's Who Among African Americans, 14th ed. Detroit: Gale Group, 2001.

Periodicals

Crothers, Tim. "Demon Deacon." *Sports Illustrated* (February 17, 1997): 28.
Crothers, Tim. "Out of Nowhere: Tim Duncan, an Unassuming Basketball Prodigy from, of All Places, St. Croix, Has Taken the NBA by Storm." *Sports Illustrated* (July 7, 1999): 77.
Crothers, Tim. "Slam Duncan." *Sports Illustrated* (November 27, 1995): 78.
Howerton, Darryl. "Tim Duncan." *Sport* (January 2000): 46.
Kertes, Tom. "He's Got the Game, and 'The Stuff.'" *Basketball Digest* (Summer 2002): 26.
Smith, Sam. "Star Speaking Up: Quiet Duncan Making Loud MVP Statement." Knight Ridder/Tribune News Service (March 3, 2002).
Soonachan, Irwin. "Duncan Signs." *Basketball Digest* (November 2000): 50.
Steinmetz, Matt. "Kidd Deserved the MVP Award, But so did Duncan." Knight Ridder/Tribune News Service (May 12, 2002).

Other

"Tim Duncan." National Basketball Association. http://www.nba.com/ (December 11, 2002)
"Tim Duncan." Sports Stats.com. http://www.sportsstats.com (December 10, 2002.

Sketch by Kari Bethel

Related Biography: Coach Greg Popovich

Greg Popovich, known as "Pop," became the coach of the San Antonio Spurs during the 1997-98 season. During his time in San Antonio, Pop has won more than any coach in the franchise's history. His career winning percentage of .631 puts him sixth all-time among NBA coaches, and his playoff record of 31-22 ranks third among all active coaches. A great part of Popovich's success is due to his management of the Spurs twin towers, David Robinson and Tim Duncan. He is the only coach in the NBA that Duncan has ever played for. The fact the Duncan re-signed with the Spurs in 2000 and will likely re-sign again in 2003 is a tribute to his excellent skills both on and off the court.

Popovich played basketball for four years at the U.S. Air Force Academy. After graduating in 1970 he fulfilled a five-year service commitment in the Air Force, during which time he played for the U.S. Armed Forces Team. He returned to the Air Force Academy as an assistant coach. In 1979 he became the head coach at Pomona-Pitzer Colleges in Claremont, California. In 1988 he moved to the NBA as a Spurs assistant coach under Larry Brown. In the summer of 1992 he became an assistant coach for the Golden State Warriors under Don Nelson. Popovich returned to San Antonio in 1994 when he was named the Spurs general manager.

Leo Durocher
1905-1991

American baseball player

Leo ("The Lip") Durocher will be forever identified with the phrase "nice guys finish last," which was the title of his autobiography and is in Bartlett's *Familiar Quotations.* Durocher is also famous for having said he would trip his own mother if she were rounding third base and he could prevent her from scoring a run. *New York Times* sportswriter Arthur Daley once called Durocher "the most hated man in baseball." He was known for his combative nature on the field and was constantly getting into arguments and fistfights with umpires, opposing players, and fans. Durocher was an outstanding shortstop with the St. Louis Cardinals and Brooklyn Dodgers (among other teams) and the manager of four National League teams. He ranks seventh among baseball managers in career wins, with 2,009.

Hardscrabble Childhood

Leo Ernest Durocher was born on July 25, 1905 in West Springfield, Massachusetts, the son of George Durocher, a railroad worker. Durocher stopped attending school regularly when he was around age twelve and spent a lot of time as a youth hanging out in local pool halls, becoming a consummate pool player and local pool hall hustler. Durocher claimed in his autobiography, *Nice Guys Finish Last,* that he forfeited a college scholarship because of an incident in which he punched a high school teacher. His biographer, Gerald Eskenazi, states, however, that "it is unlikely he even attended high school, and if he did, it wasn't for long."

Leo Durocher

Durocher played baseball and football for amateur teams in West Springfield and later played for a baseball team sponsored by the Wico Electric Company, where he worked as a mechanic in his teens. Durocher's father was employed intermittently and the family eked out a living, with Durocher's mother, Clara, taking in boarders and earning money by stitching baseballs for Spalding, a manufacturer of baseballs in the nearby town of Chicopee.

Early Career

Durocher began his professional baseball career as a shortstop with the Hartford Senators in the Eastern League. His defensive play attracted the attention of the New York Yankees, who purchased Durocher's contract in 1925. Durocher spent two years playing for minor league teams in Atlanta and St. Paul and was promoted to the Yankees roster in 1928. Durocher was a favorite of Yankee manager Miller Huggins, but was unpopular with his teammates and with Yankee general manager Ed Barrow for a variety of reasons, including his foul mouth, his expensive clothes, his nightlife, and his penchant for running up debts and writing bad checks. After Huggins's untimely death in 1929, Durocher was sold to a second division National League club, the Cincinnati Reds, for the waiver price and a player to be named later. Durocher stated in his autobiography that a dispute with Barrow over salary caused the Yankees to get rid of him. The final straw came when Durocher stormed out of Barrow's office after cursing at him. He spent the rest

of his playing career in the National League and compiled a lifetime batting average of .247. He was an outstanding defensive player but a weak hitter.

Captain of Gashouse Gang

In 1933, the Reds traded Durocher to the St. Louis Cardinals, who were in need of a shortstop to team up with second baseman Frankie Frisch after an offseason injury to the team's regular shortstop, Charley Gelbert. Durocher solidified the Cardinals' infield. He was captain of the 1934 Cardinals team immortalized as the "Gashouse Gang," which was known for its rough and ready play and antics on and off the field (the Gashouse Gang appellation has been credited to Durocher), and starred in the 1934 World Series against the Detroit Tigers, which the Cardinals won in seven games.

The general manager of the Cardinals at the time, **Branch Rickey**, was quoted at a later date as saying of Durocher (who later managed under Rickey in Brooklyn) that he had "an infinite capacity for making a bad situation worse." While with the Cardinals, Durocher had already proven the truth of this observation. In 1934, Durocher was involved in contentious divorce proceedings with his first wife, Ruby Marie Hartley, that involved charges of infidelity on both sides and abuse by Durocher. In the same year, he married a glamorous fashion designer, Grace Dozier (whom he divorced in 1943). In April 1935, he was the cause of a dispute that erupted with St. Louis area trade unions which voted to boycott Cardinals games because Durocher had taken actions that seemed to be antiunion in an incident that began when Durocher's wife crossed a picket line. Sportsman's Park, the Cardinals' stadium, was subsequently picketed in a protest action by the unions.

In May 1936, during a game against the Brooklyn Dodgers at Ebbets Field, Durocher got into a shouting match with Dodgers manager **Casey Stengel**. Stengel and Durocher met under the stands and engaged in a brief fight. Durocher also had a falling out with his player-manager and second base partner, Frankie Frisch, who may have feared that Durocher was after his job as manager. Frisch ultimately demanded of management that Durocher be traded, saying it's "either him or me." The Cardinals accommodated Frisch by trading Durocher in 1937 to the Dodgers for four players.

Becomes Player-Manager

Durocher was named player-manager of the Dodgers, a hapless perennial second division team, at the end of the 1938 season, replacing Burleigh Grimes, who, suspecting that he would be fired, suggested to Durocher that he apply for the job. Durocher managed the Dodgers to a third place finish in 1939, to second in 1940, to a pennant in 1941 (the team's first in twenty-one years), and to a strong second place finish in 1942 (when the Dodgers won 104 games). In 1941, Durocher

Career Statistics

Yr	Team	AVG	GP	AB	R	H	HR	RBI	BB	SO	SB	E
1925	NY-A	.000	2	1	1	0	0	0	0	0	0	0
1928	NY-A	.270	102	296	46	80	0	31	22	52	1	25
1929	NY-A	.246	106	341	53	84	0	32	34	33	3	23
1930	Cin	.243	119	354	31	86	3	32	20	45	0	24
1931	Cin	.227	121	361	26	82	1	29	18	32	0	20
1932	Cin	.217	143	457	43	99	1	33	36	40	3	30
1933	Cin	.216	16	51	6	11	1	3	4	5	0	5
	StL-N	.258	123	395	45	102	2	41	26	32	3	24
1934	StL-N	.260	146	500	62	130	3	70	33	40	2	33
1935	StL-N	.265	143	513	62	136	8	78	29	46	4	28
1936	StL-N	.286	136	510	57	146	1	58	29	47	3	21
1937	StL-N	.203	135	477	46	97	1	47	38	36	6	28
1938	Bklyn	.219	141	479	41	105	1	56	47	30	3	24
1939	Bklyn	.277	116	390	42	108	1	34	27	24	2	25
1940	Bklyn	.231	62	160	10	37	1	14	12	13	1	11
1941	Bklyn	.286	18	42	2	12	0	6	1	3	0	4
1943	Bklyn	.222	6	18	1	4	0	1	1	2	0	0
1945	Bklyn	.200	2	5	1	1	0	2	0	0	0	0
TOTAL		.247	1637	5350	575	1320	24	567	377	480	31	325

Bklyn: Brooklyn Dodgers; Cin: Cincinnati Reds; NY-A: New York Yankees; StL-N: St. Louis Cardinals.
Managed, but did not play, in 1942 and 1944 seasons.

handed the starting shortstop job to **Pee Wee Reese** and from that point on made infrequent appearances as a player. The Dodgers were a lackluster team during the war years, when their stock of players was depleted, but in 1946, Durocher managed them to a tie for first place, losing to the Cardinals in a three-game playoff.

Creates Controversy

Durocher's tenure with the Dodgers was marked by a seemingly never-ending series of feuds. During the 1938 season (his first with the Dodgers), for example, Durocher got into a clubhouse fight with **Babe Ruth**, who was serving for a season as a Dodger coach. The incident appears to have involved Durocher insulting the intelligence of Ruth, who was hoping to become the Dodgers' manager. (The job instead went to Durocher a few months later.) In July 1943, Durocher made a remark critical of a Dodger player, Bobo Newsom, to a reporter that almost caused a revolt by disgruntled Dodger players and led to Newsom being traded to the St. Louis Browns. Durocher was constantly feuding with Dodger management, notably the team's flamboyant and tempestuous general manager, Larry MacPhail, who "fired" and "rehired" Durocher, it was said, hundreds of times because of disagreements between the two. In 1943, Durocher was quoted in the *Daily Worker* as saying that there were "about a million" blacks who could play in the major leagues if it were not for baseball's unwritten policy barring black players. The remark got Durocher into hot water with baseball commissioner Kenesaw Mountain Landis, who issued a statement denying (falsely) that any such policy existed.

Defends Robinson

The 1947 season was a watershed one for both Durocher and the Dodgers. It was the year that **Jackie Robinson**, the first black player in the modern major leagues, was called up to the Brooklyn club. As former Dodger broadcaster Red Barber has noted in his book *1947: When All Hell Broke Loose in Baseball,* the Dodgers' general manager, Branch Rickey, knew that he could count on Durocher's support in calling up Robinson. "Rickey knew Durocher would fight for Robinson," Barber wrote. "… The rest of the league would be against the black man. Leo relished such a fight."

During spring training in 1947, the Dodgers were playing an exhibition series in Panama. Durocher was alerted to a petition that had been drawn up by a group of Dodger players who were opposed to the call-up of Robinson and who, refusing to play with Robinson because of his race, indicated they would rather be traded. Durocher said he would play an elephant "if he can do the job" and that anyone who did not want play with Robinson could take off his uniform and leave the team, putting an end to the uprising. "This fellow is a great ballplayer," Durocher added. "He's going to win pennants for us. He's going to put money in your pockets and money in mine."

Suspended from Baseball

The year 1947 was also notable because on April 9 (the day before Robinson's promotion to the Dodgers), it was announced, six days before the start of the baseball season, that Durocher had been suspended from baseball for one year by baseball commissioner Albert B. (Happy) Chandler for an "accumulation of unpleas-

Chronology

1905	Born July 25 in West Springfield, Massachusetts
1925	Signed by Hartford of Eastern League
1925	New York Yankees purchase Durocher's contract and is called up by Yankees at end of season. Gets into two games and bats once
1926	Optioned to Atlanta in Southern League
1927	Promoted to St. Paul of American Association
1928-29	Plays shortstop and second base for Yankees
1930	Sold to Cincinnati Reds for waiver price
1933	Traded to St. Louis Cardinals
1937	Traded to Brooklyn Dodgers
1938	Named Dodgers player-manager
1947	Marries motion picture actress Laraine Day
1947	Is suspended by baseball commissioner Chandler for entire season for "an accumulation of unpleasant incidents" (which are not specified) considered detrimental to baseball
1948	Returns as manager of Dodgers
1948	Obtains release from Brooklyn and replaces Mel Ott as manager of New York Giants
1955	Resigns as manager of Giants
1956-60	Works as announcer for NBC's "Game of the Week"
1961-64	Third base coach for Los Angeles Dodgers
1966	Named manager of Chicago Cubs
1972	Steps down as Cubs manager
1972	Named manager of Houston Astros
1973	Quits as Astros manager at end of season
1991	Dies October 7 in Palm Springs, California

ant incidents in which he has been involved which the commissioner construes as detrimental to baseball." Chandler's action was greeted with shock and disbelief by Durocher and Dodger fans. The *Times*'s Arthur Daley wrote: "Leo Durocher is like the man who is hailed into a traffic court for passing through a red light and then is sentenced to the electric chair. In this instance, the penalty does not fit the crime and is much too severe."

Triumphant Return to Baseball

Durocher was reinstated as manager by the Dodgers (who won the pennant in 1947 under a replacement manager, Burt Shotton) in 1948 after serving his suspension, but in midseason he obtained his release from Brooklyn and became manager of the Dodgers' archrivals, the New York Giants, in a move that stunned New York baseball fans, who could not conceive of Durocher managing the Giants, with whom he and the Dodgers were continually feuding. Durocher replaced the popular Mel Ott, whose team had occasioned Durocher's "nice guys finish last" remark to a sportswriter, Frank Graham.

The Giants steadily improved under Durocher, from fifth place finishes in 1948 and 1949 (Durocher's first full year with the team) to third place in 1950. In 1951, Durocher insisted that the Giants call up rookie sensation **Willie Mays** from their Minneapolis farm club. Durocher was a virtual godfather to Mays, who started slowly and became despondent. Durocher kept Mays in the lineup and treated him like a son, nurturing Mays to greatness. The Giants battled the Dodgers for the pennant all sea-

son, and in an amazing stretch run during which they won thirty-seven of their last forty-four games, tied the Dodgers for the pennant. They won the pennant in the third and final playoff game on Bobby Thomson's ninth-inning game-winning homer off the Dodgers' Ralph Branca. It is one of the most famous moments in sports history. Years later, it was revealed that Durocher's Giants had been stealing signs for the last three months of the season and using a relay system including an electronic device connected to the bullpen to give batters advance knowledge of what type of pitch was coming. In 1954, the Giants under Durocher won the National League pennant and swept a favored Cleveland Indians team in the World Series, with Mays as the star.

Despite his success as a manager, Durocher's years with the Giants were by no means placid. In April 1949, he was suspended "indefinitely" by baseball commissioner Chandler (who feared a race riot) for hitting and kicking a 22-year-old Puerto Rican fan at the Polo Grounds. The Giants front office made strenuous efforts to discredit the victim's version of events and support Durocher's. Chandler rescinded the suspension after four days because of "insufficient" evidence. In June 1949, Durocher was suspended for five days and fined by the National League for bumping an umpire and using abusive language. In 1952, he was suspended and fined three times for run-ins with umpires and for a beanball incident involving a Giants pitcher.

Leaves Baseball Temporarily

Disagreements with the team's owner, Horace Stoneham, led Durocher to resign as Giants manager at the end of the 1955 season. He spent several years as a color announcer for NBC's *Game of the Week* and also appeared in episodes of television series such as *Mister Ed* and *The Beverly Hillbillies*. (In the 1940s, he had often appeared on radio with the likes of Jack Benny and Milton Berle.) Durocher was divorced from Laraine Day in 1960. He had attained celebrity status and was known as a charming and dapper man off the field. He was proud of his friendships with entertainers such as Danny Kaye and Frank Sinatra.

Durocher was back in baseball as third base coach with the Los Angeles Dodgers from 1961 to 1964. He often questioned the moves of Dodger manager Walter Alston, sometimes publicly, leading to controversy.

Later Years

Durocher was hired by Chicago Cubs owner Phil Wrigley in 1966 to manage the Cubs, who had been a second division team for over twenty years. After finishing tenth in Durocher's first season as manager, the Cubs finished third for two straight seasons in 1967 and 1968. In 1969, Durocher married his fourth wife, Lynn Walker Goldblatt, a Chicago media personality from whom he was divorced in 1981.

Awards and Accomplishments

1936, 1938, 1940	National League All Star team
1939	*Sporting News* Manager of the Year
1941	Manages Dodgers to first pennant in 21 years
1946	Manages Dodgers to tie for first place in National League. Dodgers are beaten by St. Louis Cardinals in three-game playoff
1951	Bobby Thomson's "shot heard round the world" off Ralph Branca sends Giants, managed by Durocher, to World Series. Giants lose to Yankees in six games. Durocher is named *Sporting News* Manager of the Year
1954	Leads Giants to pennant. Giants sweep World Series against Cleveland Indians. Named *Sporting News* Manager of the Year
1994	Inducted into National Baseball Hall of Fame

Durocher ranks seventh among Major League managers in career wins, with 2,009.

The 1969 Cubs team was in first place in the National League for most of the season and was expected to win the pennant, but the team came apart down the stretch and collapsed, finishing second to the New York Mets. The Cubs' collapse led to bitter criticism being directed at Durocher because of his handling of the team and other matters (such as his leaving the team for two days in midseason to visit one of his stepsons at summer camp). While near the end of his tenure as Cubs manager, Durocher was said to have lost control of the team, with some players being in open revolt against him. He found himself increasingly out of touch and at odds with a newer, younger generation of ballplayers, many of whom resented Durocher's autocratic managerial style.

In August 1972, Durocher replaced Harry Walker as manager of the Houston Astros. It was only the second time that someone had managed two National League teams in a season. The first time was in 1948, when Durocher had managed the Dodgers and the Giants. Durocher quit as Astros manager at the end of the 1973 season, begging off for health reasons.

Durocher was bitter about not being elected to the National Baseball Hall of Fame during his lifetime and told his friends not to accept a posthumous induction into the Hall on his behalf. Nevertheless, he was elected to the Hall of Fame by the Veterans Committee in 1993, two years after his death in Palm Springs, California, and the induction was not refused.

Leo Durocher's notoriety, celebrity, and Hollywood connections made him into a larger than life figure, a sort of renegade pop culture icon. He was also one of the first sports figures to become a prominent radio and TV personality and a media figure in his own right. But Durocher is known primarily for the traits he embodied and the "rules" he played by: a take-no-prisoners, win-at-any-cost ethos that has molded athletes from **Ty Cobb** to **Pete Rose** (two of Durocher's favorite sayings were "I come to kill you" and "stick it in his ear") and an adver-sarial stance toward authority figures. Durocher was known for his fiery nature and brilliant strategic moves, and always seemed to be embroiled in controversy with the front office.

It should also be noted that Durocher was ahead of his time in being an "equal opportunity employer" who was without prejudice when it came to winning ballgames. He deserves credit and a footnote in sports history for the supporting role he played in facilitating Jackie Robinson's acceptance by his teammates and entrance into major league baseball.

SELECTED WRITINGS BY DUROCHER:

(With Ed Linn) *Nice Guys Finish Last,* New York: Simon & Schuster, 1975.

FURTHER INFORMATION
Books

Barber, Red. *1947: When All Hell Broke Loose in Baseball.* New York: Chelsea House, 1991.

Bouton, Jim with Neil Offen. *I Managed Good, But Boy Did They Play Bad.* Chicago: Playboy Press, 1973.

Chandler, Albert B. with Vance H. Trimble. *Heroes, Plain Folks, and Skunks: The Life and Times of Happy Chandler.* Chicago: Bonus Books, 1989.

Claerbaut, David. *Durocher's Cubs: The Greatest Team That Didn't Win.* Dallas: Taylor, 2000.

Cohen, Stanley. *Dodgers! The First One-Hundred Years.* New York: Carol Publishing Group, 1990.

Dewey, Donald, and Nicholas Acocella. *Encyclopedia of Major League Baseball Teams.* New York: HarperCollins, 1993.

Eskenazi, Gerald. *The Lip: A Biography of Leo Durocher.* New York: William Morrow, 1993.

Frommer, Harvey. *Baseball's Greatest Managers.* New York: Chelsea House, 1991.

Gold, Eddie, and Art Ahrens. *The New Era Cubs, 1941-1985.* Chicago: Bonus Books, 1985.

Holmes, Tommy. *The Dodgers.* New York: Macmillan, 1975.

Kahn, Roger. *The Era, 1947-1957: When the Yankees, the Giants, and the Dodgers Ruled the World.* New York: Ticknor & Fields, 1993.

Kelley, Brent. *The Case For: Those Overlooked by the Baseball Hall of Fame.* Jefferson, N.C., McFarland, 1992.

Keyes, Ralph. *"Nice Guys Finish Seventh": False Phrases, Spurious Sayings and Familiar Misquotations.* New York: HarperCollins, 1992.

Koppett, Leonard. *The Man in the Dugout: Baseball's Top Managers and How They Got That Way.* Philadelphia: Temple University Press, 2000.

Powers, Jimmy. *Baseball Personalities.* New York: Rudolph Field, 1949.

Prince, Carl E. *Brooklyn's Dodgers: The Bums, the Borough, and the Best of Baseball, 1947-1957*. New York: Oxford University Press, 1996.

Periodicals

Anderson, Dave. "Leo the Lip Was Baseball in New York." *New York Times* (October 9, 1991): B11.

Prager, Joshua Harris. "Giants' 1951 Comeback, the Sport's Greatest, Wasn't All It Seemed." *Wall Street Journal* (January 31, 2001): A1, A14.

Rogers, Thomas. "Leo Durocher, Fiery Ex-Manager, Dies at 86." *New York Times* (October 8, 1991): D25.

Other

"Baseball Library.com: Leo Durocher." http://www.pubdim.net/baseballlibrary/ballplayers/D/Durocher_Leo.stm (November 29, 2002).

"The BASEBALL page.com: Leo Durocher." http://www.thebaseballpage.com/past/pp/durocherleo/default.htm (November 29, 2002).

"National Baseball Hall of Fame: Leo Durocher." http://www.baseballhalloffame.org/hofers_and_honorees/hofer_bios/durocher_leo.htm (November 29, 2002).

Sketch by Roger W. Smith

Camille Duvall
1960-

American waterskier

Camille Duvall, "The Golden Goddess" of professional water skiing, holds more titles in slalom than all other women waterskiers combined. Her nearly thirty year dominance in the sport is unprecedented, and her impact on the public's perception of water skiing helped it gain recognition and popularize the sun-drenched water sport. Her impact is so great that it is difficult to pinpoint just where the legend of Camille Duvall can be separated from the sport of professional water skiing.

Growing Up

Camille Duvall started water skiing when she was only four. Born July 11, 1960, to Sam and Diane Duvall, Camille and her brother were provided every opportunity to achieve success as a professional waterskiers. The single-mindedness with which the family went about their pursuit of excellence was stunning. Camille won her first tournament when she was six years old, and her determination to be better than everyone else was already apparent. She practiced near Greenville, South Carolina, on a private lake that her father, an executive with a construction company, leased for the sole use of his two athletically gifted children.

For hours on end each day, Camille worked with private coaches on courses that had been set up for her and her brother, complete with ramps and a variety of boats to simulate any of the variables they might face in a competition. It has been estimated that Duvall's father spent nearly $25,000 a year, for ten years, on his children. His intense desire to see his children succeed at any cost helped mold Camille into one of the best talents the world of water skiing has ever known.

Family Affair

Duvall's brother Sam also happened to be one of the sport's fiercest competitors. Perhaps one of the most talented sister-brother duo in any sport, Sam and Camille Duvall early on earned the nicknames "Golden Boy" and "Golden Girl."

As Camille matured, her popularity increased at the same rate, if not faster, as her skills on the water. Many believe her rising fame was due in no small part to her beauty. Duvall matured into a tall, statuesque woman whose physical presence, many said, was as impressive as her skiing feats. Her looks earned her the moniker "The Golden Goddess."

But her records clearly indicate that she came to win, not to show off for the crowd. In fact, Duvall was often unhappy—and rightly so—about the attention paid to her appearance. She wanted the emphasis on her achievements and what she could accomplish as an athlete. After high school, Duvall returned to Florida (the family had moved to Dallas during Camille's high school years) to concentrate solely on her skiing. She soon suffered a knee injury that, though not serious, pushed her away from the sport for a few years.

After a brief hiatus from water skiing, Duvall returned to the sport in 1981 and surpassed her former accomplishments. She rejoined the U.S. Elite Water Ski Team, and from 1983 to 1987 she helped that team to world championship victories. She also won the 1985 Women's World Slalom Championships, going on to capture many national, professional and Masters titles in the process.

Olympics Only A Dream

Unfortunately the sport of water skiing would not become an Olympic event until 1996—a few years after Duvall left the spotlight due to neck injuries and after her decision to retire in 1993. Camille Duvall would not be able to add Olympic gold to her list of accomplishments, but that did not lessen the impact of her phenomenal achievements, including being cited in 2000 as one of *Sports Illustrated*'s Top 100 Female Athletes of the Century.

Duvall's reach as a human being extends beyond the world of water sports and her three-decade tenure as the

Chronology

1960	Born July 11 to Sam and Dianne Duvall
1964	Gets on water skis for the first time
1966	Wins her first water ski tournament
1973	Jumps 100 feet for the first time (105 feet measured)
1975	Family moves to Dallas, participates in horse riding and other sports while still skiing
1978	Moves back to Florida after graduating to focus on skiing
1979	Injures knee in a fall, drops out of skiing for 2 years.
1979	Marries for the first time. Will divorce a few years later when she decides to focus on skiing
1981	Gets back into skiing at the urging of her family
1982	Starts competing once again, goes on the road on a tournament tour
1986	Father dies of a heart attack at 49
1992	Publishes her book, *Camille Duvall's Instructional Guide to Water Skiing*
1994	Retires from a thirty year water skiing career while still ranked #1 in the world
2000	*Sports Illustrated* names her #91 on the 20th century's Top 100 athletes
2003	Inducted into the American Water Ski Hall of Fame

Awards and Accomplishments

1975-78	Member of Undefeated World Champion U.S. Elite Water Ski Team
1983-87	Member of Undefeated World Champion U.S. Elite Water Ski Team
1984-85	Women's Slalom Champion
1984-88	Wins Pro World Slalom Championships
1985	Women's World Slalom Champion
2003	Inducted into American Water Ski Hall of Fame

most dominant female athlete water skiing ever knew. She graduated from New York University's School of Broadcasting and used her communications skills in multiple arenas. She has been a television reporter and producer for various networks, including such sports powerhouses as ESPN and Fox Sports, as well as lesser known but still important venues such as MSG Network and Oxygen Sports. Duvall also published a book in 1992, *Camille Duvall's Instructional Guide To Water Skiing*.

After her retirement from the world of professional water skiing, Duvall—who has added her husband Byron Hero's last name to her own—has been a fixture in New York City's Upper East Side, where she has been for the past 14 years. She is a mother of two who wears many hats. Some of the work with which she is currently involved includes coaching the U.S. National Water Ski team (the first woman to hold that position); serving on the Board of Directors for New York City's 2012 bid for the Olympic Games; and serving as a member of the New York City Sports Commission. She is also the co-founder and marketing director for Duvall Competition Skis. In 2003, Duvall-Hero became the 47th person elected into the Water Ski Hall of Fame.

CONTACT INFORMATION

Address: Camille Duvall-Hero, 1356 Third Ave, New York, NY 10021.

SELECTED WRITINGS BY DUVALL:

Camille Duvall's Instructional Guide to Water Skiing, Fireside Press, 1992.

FURTHER INFORMATION

Books

"Camille Duvall." *Great Women in Sports.* Detroit: Visible Ink Press, 1996.
"Camille Duvall." *Newsmakers,* Issue Cumulation. Detroit, MI: Gale Research, 1996.
Duvall, Camille. *Camille Duvall's Instructional Guide to Water Skiing.* Fireside Press, 1992.

Periodicals

Falla, Jack. "Wild, Wet and Wondrous." *Sports Illustrated* (August 5, 1985).
Neil, Mike and Linda Marx. "No one beats slalom champ Camille Duvall at making waves where the buoys are." *People Weekly* (July 13, 1987).

Other

Announcement of Duvall's induction into Hall of Fame. http://www.usawaterski.org/pages/Current%20News/CN2003DuvallHallofFame.htm (January 29, 2003).
"Camille Duvall-Hero: Trailblazing in Action." Women's Sports Foundation. http://www.womenssportsfoundation.org/cgi-bin/iowa/athletes/article.html?record=27 (January 29, 2003).

Sketch by Eric Lagergren

Becky Dyroen-Lancer
1971-

American synchronized swimmer

Considered one of the most decorated synchronized swimmers and one of the best in the sport, Becky Dyroen-Lancer won championship awards and Olympic gold medals throughout the 1990s. Starting out life with a heart condition, Lancer recovered and came to dominate her sport, achieving consecutive grand slam titles in

Becky Dyroen-Lancer

solo, duet, figures, and team events in synchronized swimming. A member of the Santa Clara Aquamaids, Lancer is known as a dedicated athlete who practices more than six hours a day.

A String of Championships

Becky Dyroen-Lancer overcame a tough-and-go beginning to become an incredible athlete. She has joked that she was born to be a swimmer and hold her breath underwater because she was born a blue baby who was not breathing after birth. She was diagnosed with a heart defect and at age five had open heart surgery. Once she recovered, her parents were eager to see her do the same activities as other children. At age ten, Lancer delved into the same sport as her mother, Paula, who had been a synchronized swimmer. So did Lancer's sister, Suzannah Dyroen Bianco.

Lancer grew up in Campbell, California, attended West Valley College, and studied secondary education at De Anza College. In 1984, synchronized swimming entered the Olympic Games as a Summer event, just in time for Lancer, who in 1989 had won the first in a long string of titles—Junior World Solo, Duet and Team champion. The next year she received the silver medal at the Moscow Invitational Duet and began a five-year streak as USSS All-American.

The year 1991 held not only a gold medal solo performance at the Pan American Games and recognition as

Coca-Cola Athlete of the Day, but four more championships in solo, duet, and team competitions, including the FINA World Cup, French Open, and World Aquatics Team. In both 1991 and 1992, Lancer received a silver medal at the US National. She also placed second at the 1992 US Olympic Trials solo event.

On January 9, 1993, Lancer married Kevin Lancer, a retired ballet dancer, who helps with her choreography. That same year, she was part of the US team that swept all the events at the Synchronized Swimming World Cup.

Lancer, who represented the synchronized swimming category, was one of fifty nominees for the 1993 Amateur Athletics Union's Sullivan Award for top amateur athlete in the country. Although she didn't receive the award, there were plenty of others that graced her mantle. Some of her numerous accomplishments that year were USOC Top Ten SportsWoman of the Year, German Open, World Cup, and *Swimming World*'s World Synchronized Swimmer of the Year. For three consecutive years from 1993 to 1995, Lancer received the Edna Hines Award and the Kay Vilen High Point Individual Award, and was named USSS Athlete of the Year.

Synchronized swimming incorporates elements of gymnastics, figure skating, and aerobics all performed in water. Lancer practices six to eight hours a day, six days a week to perfect her grace and strength in the sport, as well as her concentration. Her coach Chris Carver noted in *The Olympic Fact Book*, "I always knew that Becky was good, but you never know about the mind. She has that, too. She's amazing, because she continues to grow. That's a coach's dream."

World and Olympic Gold Medals

In the 1994 Goodwill Games, Lancer won the silver medal as a soloist, won the figures portion, and with teammate Jill Sudduth, she earned the gold medal for the duet event. Lancer continued to strike gold at the 1994 World Aquatic Championships in Rome by winning three gold medals, more than any other American, for the solo, duet, and team titles. This performance made her the first American in more than twenty years to win all three events at the world championships. Not since Tracie Ruiz in 1982 had a U.S. synchronized swimmer won the solo event. Incidentally, the U.S. team that year swept all the events, which included swimming, diving, and water polo.

Lancer saw another prolific award season in 1994 with championships in the French Open, French Winter Nationals, Jantzen Nationals, and World championships. Repeat performances included two more USOC Top Ten SportsWoman of the Year award and *Swimming World's* World Synchronized Swimmer of the Year for years 1994 and 1995. She was also a three-time Women's Sports Foundation SportsWoman of the Year finalist.

In 1995, among even more championships in the US and around the world, including the Pan American Games, Lancer won the FINA Prize, the highest award given to an aquatics sports participant. In the Nations-Bank Synchronized Swimming World Cup in Atlanta, Team USA swept the events and Lancer achieved her ninth consecutive grand slam since 1992 in solo, duet, team, and figures events. In the US Olympic Team trials that year, Lancer won first place by receiving a perfect score of ten 10s, an American record and the first for a competitor in a major international competition.

Beginning with the 1996 Olympics in Atlanta, the Olympics Committee eliminated the synchronized swimming solo, duet, and figures competitions and settled for a single 10-member team competition. Under the new rules, Lancer lost her chance to win gold in solo and duet, yet she was delighted when her sister, Suzannah Bianco, earned the 10th and final spot on the team. As expected, the US Team won the Olympic gold medal.

Lancer is still active in her sport and in community projects. She coaches the Cerritos Synchronettes synchronized swimming club team in Southern California for girls aged six to seventeen. She is an Avon Products representative who has appeared in print ads for the beauty products company. Having undergone open heart surgery as a child, she now volunteers for the American Heart Association.

She has been a member of USSS Executive Committee, and on July 20, 2000, Lancer participated with other champion female athletes in the Women Sports Foundation's second annual awards luncheon in Hollywood. She continues to be a member of the Santa Clara Aquamaids.

Dipping her toe into pop culture, Lancer is credited as the synchronized swimming choreographer for the 1998 movie *Austin Powers: The Spy Who Shagged Me,* and she was a member of the cast of Cirque Du Soleil's water performance *O.* Her hobbies include ballet, art, costume design, bicycling, and horticulture.

Whether she's performing solo, with a teammate in a duet, or sharing the spotlight as a member of a group,

Awards and Accomplishments	
1989	Junior World Solo, Duet, and Team champion
1990	Moscow Invitational Duet silver medal
1990-95	USSS All-American
1991	FINA World Cup Team champion
1991	French Open Solo, Duet, and Team champion
1991	Mallorca Open Duet and Team champion
1991	Pan American Games Solo gold medal
1991	World Aquatics Team champion
1991-92	U.S. National Solo, Duet, and Team silver medal
1992	Loano Cup Duet silver medal
1992	Swiss Open Solo, Duet, Team, and Figures champion
1992	U.S. Olympic Trials Solo silver medal
1993	Nominee for the Sullivan Award
1993	German Open Solo and Duet champion
1993	May USOC Athlete of the Month
1993	U.S. National Solo, Duet, and Team champion
1993	World Cup Solo, Duet, Team, and Figures champion
1993-94	Synchronized Swimming World Cup Solo, Duet, Team, and Figures gold medal
1993-95	Edna Hines Award
1993-95	Kay Vilen High Point Individual Award
1993-95	Swimming World's World Synchronized Swimmer of the Year
1993-95	USOC Top Ten SportsWoman of the Year
1993-95	USSS Athlete of the Year Women's Sports Foundation
1993-95	Women's Sports Foundation SportsWoman of the Year finalist
1994	French Open Solo, Duet, Team, and Figures champion
1994	French Winter Nationals Solo and Duet champion
1994	Goodwill Games Solo silver medal, Duet gold medal
1994	May and September USOC Athlete of the Month
1994	World Aquatic Championships
1994	World Solo, Duet, Team, and Figures champion
1994-95	Jantzen Nationals Solo, Duet, Team, and Figures champion
1995	FINA Prize
1995	NationsBank World Cup Solo, Duet, Team, and Figures champion, Lancer's 9th consecutive grand slam
1995	Pan American Games Solo, Duet, Team, and Figures champion
1995	U.S. Olympic Team Trials first place
1996	Atlanta Olympic Team gold medal

Becky Dyroen-Lancer dominated the sport of synchronized swimming.

FURTHER INFORMATION

Books

Nelson, Rebecca. *Olympic Fact Book.* Detroit: Visible Ink Press, 1996.

Sherrow, Victoria. *Encyclopedia of Women and Sports.* Santa Barbara, CA: ABC-CLIO Inc., 1996.

Periodicals

Lazzeretti, Craig. "They say Becky Dyroen-Lancer was born to be a synchronized swimmer." *Contra Costa Times* (July 13, 1996): 713.

Other

Cerritos Synchronettes, http://www.angelfire.com/ca2/cerritossynchroteam/teaminfo.html (January 15, 2003).

Washington Post. http://www.washingtonpost.com/
    wp-srv/sports/olympics/longterm/synchro/dyroen.
    htm (January 15, 2003).

Sketch by Lorraine Savage

Dale Earnhardt, Sr.
1951-2001

American race car driver

Seven-time Winston Cup champion Dale Earnhardt Sr. collected a huge following of fans during his 28-year career on the circuit of the National Association for Stock Car Racing (NASCAR). Driving a black #3 Chevrolet sedan and dressed in black, he was nicknamed the Intimidator for his bullish driving behavior on the track. He died when his car crashed and hit the side wall on the final turn of the Daytona 500 in 2001.

What Makes a Champ?

Born in Kannapolis in south central North Carolina, on April 29, 1951, Earnhardt was the oldest son of Ralph and Martha Earnhardt. With two older sisters and two younger brothers, he fell in the middle of his four siblings. The Earnhardts were known as lint heads in their regional slang—a lint head being anyone from Kannapolis, which is the mill town headquarters of Cannon Mills. With a population of 36,000, Kannapolis is a suburb to the northeast of Charlotte and is the largest unincorporated population center in the area. The name Kannapolis is Greek for the "City of Looms," and it is an unwritten tradition among the residents that everyone in the town works at the mill at one time or another.

The mills and looms notwithstanding, Earnhardt's heritage was much larger than lint town. The red dirt countryside where he was raised falls on a terrain called the Piedmont that stretches northward from Birmingham, Alabama, and into Virginia. The landscape of the Piedmont encompasses a vast bed of fine red clay where dirt-road racers are nurtured.

Dale Earnhardt held a great admiration for his father, a sixth-grade dropout who quit the mills at a young age and went on to become a hall-of-fame NASCAR driver. In the early days, with a wife and a family to support, Ralph Earnhardt worked in an auto garage to supplement his income, and Dale Earnhardt and his brothers

Dale Earnhardt, Sr.

spent a good deal of time in the shop. They learned to maintain and care for the cars, and in 1956 they cheered their father's victory in the NASCAR Sportsman series championship. Earnhardt, who was much like his father, quit school at age sixteen, married young, and fathered a son named Kerry.

Unlike his father, Earnhardt was soon divorced and living alone. He began his career as a dirt-road racer, driving a 1956 Ford Club Sedan as his first bona fide race car. The six-cylinder Ford was nothing remarkable. Earnhardt had ordered it painted purple, although it ended up an un-macho pink. He drove it regardless. His first race was on the Concord Speedway, a local track owned by a man named Henry Furr.

By 1973 Earnhardt was working in Concord, at Punch Whitaker's wheel alignment shop on Route 9. He had married again—this time to Brenda Gee. Their daughter, Kelley, was born in 1972. After a while Earnhardt found a cache of old Ford Falcons and selected one to be his new race car. He made a project out of fixing it up in his spare time and supported his family by working as a welder for the Great Dane Trucking Company.

The family lived poorly in assorted apartments and trailers, and Earnhardt was sometimes slow in paying his bills. They all rode around in old fixer-upper cars, and all the while he kept a steady stream of race cars moving through the garage at the old Earnhardt family home on Sedan Avenue in Kannapolis. Earnhardt and Gee soon had a son, Dale Jr., born in 1974. That same year Earnhardt Sr. switched from dirt racing to asphalt. He picked up a used race car and drove in local races as part of the old Sportsman division which later became the Busch circuit.

He made his debut on the Winston Cup circuit at the Charlotte Motor Speedway, driving in the Charlotte 600 on Memorial Day 1975. He drove car number 8, a Dodge belonging to Ed Negré and his mechanic son, Norman. Earnhardt finished at twenty-second place in the race and pocketed $2,425.

Guts Make a Champ

From 1976-79 Earnhardt drove in eight Winston Cup races altogether. Sponsors agreed that he was an excellent driver. He possessed the natural grit and calm demeanor to be a champion driver. Earnhardt was fearless, in fact, to a fault. He crashed and flipped cars as if they were old soda pop cans. As a result his potential went largely untapped because he could not find sponsors willing to subsidize the cost of repairing his cars.

With the failure of his second marriage in 1977 he returned home briefly and lived with his mother. He stopped racing on the asphalt circuit and drove the dirt-road tracks again. He worked for Chrysler Motors, testing so-called kit cars.

In 1978 Earnhardt crossed paths with an investor named Rod Osterlund who was putting together a Winston Cup team in an old garage in Derita, near Charlotte. Earnhardt drove two races for Osterlund and finished second and fourth respectively. The following year, at age twenty-nine, Earnhardt joined Osterlund's team as one of two drivers. With Osterlund's help Earnhardt purchased a home on Lake Norman near the Frog Creek Campground, where Osterlund's crew housed and maintained their cars at the Car-o-Winds trailer park.

On April 1 of his rookie year, Earnhardt won his first Winston Cup race. The race, at Bristol, was the Southeastern 500, the seventh on the circuit. Earnhardt led for 160 laps and beat Bobby Allison to the finish. Earnhardt was only the fourth rookie in the history of NASCAR to win a race. With winnings of $264,086 that year, he was named NASCAR's Rookie of the Year and signed to drive for five more years with Osterlund.

For a no-holds-barred driver like Earnhardt, of course, winning came at a price. He lost four weeks to recuperation that season after a severe crash at Pocono. Earnhardt, who blew a tire and hit the wall, suffered two broken collarbones, a concussion, and severe bruises. This extreme style paid off in 1980, however, when he won his first Winston Cup at age twenty-nine. He took the trophy by a nineteen-point margin, his winnings for the season totaling more than one-half million dollars.

In 1981 Osterlund sold the Winston Cup operation to J. D. Stacy and moved to the West Coast. Unhappy with the change of operations, Earnhardt drove only four races for Stacy then quit. He completed the 1981 season by driving ten races for Bud Moore Engineering, but altogether that year finished only twelve of thirty races.

Earnhardt signed with Richard Childress in August of 1981. Childress was a would-be driver himself who, like Earnhardt, had dropped out of school at a young age. Then thirty-six years old, Childress was wheeling and dealing in earnest to build a racing car empire. At the time that he hooked up with Earnhardt he had a parts deal underway with General Motors (GM) at Talladega (in Anniston, Alabama). A tire deal with Goodyear was

Dale Earnhardt, Sr.

already signed and sealed. Earnhardt in turn brought sizable funding with him in the form of a sponsorship contract from Wrangler Jeans.

Still driving Ford cars, Earnhardt finished in twelfth place in points in 1982; he finished eighth in 1983. He renewed his deal with Childress who—through deals with GM, Goodyear, and others—was crafting entire cars in the shop. Earnhardt began driving the sturdier Childress chasses and won two Winston circuit races in 1984, to finish in fourth place in points. Ricky Rudd joined the Childress team as a driver around that time.

In 1985, Earnhardt ranked eighth in points for the season. His family by that time had grown to include four children and a new wife. With a larger family to support, Earnhardt pulled out all of the stops, and his reckless competition style emerged with a vengeance. In three out of his four wins that year he bumped other drivers from his path.

At the second Winston Cup race of the 1986 season, at Richmond, Earnhardt knocked Darrell Waltrip's car so hard in the final lap that both drivers spun out. The officials slapped Earnhardt with a $5,000 fine and one year of probation. Although the probation was lifted, the incident sparked an intense rivalry that season between the two drivers. In the end it was Earnhardt, with five wins, who took home the Winston Cup.

Around that time an entrepreneur named Hank Jones had dubbed Earnhardt the Dominator and had printed t-shirts and souvenirs with the moniker. Although the Dominator merchandise never sold well, Jones followed a new hunch and reordered more Earnhardt souvenir merchandise with a different nickname, calling Earnhardt the Intimidator instead. The new name hit pay dirt, and Jones made $180,000 selling Intimidator souvenirs from a trackside trailer in 1985. Before long the name and the logos were registered

Related Biography: Winston Cup Driver Neil Bonnett

Neil Bonnett of Hueyville, Alabama, was born in 1946. He worked as a pipe fitter in high-rise construction before entering the race car circuit. After driving for Butch Nelson in 1972, Bonnett joined the Winston Cup circuit in 1974, winning his first event in 1977 and taking a total of eighteen Winston Cup races during his career.

Despite shattering his leg in a crash in Charlotte in 1987, Bonnett returned to the circuit three months later with a plate in his hip. In 1988 he won three races, but he crashed again in 1989 and broke his sternum. A crash at Darlington in 1990 left Bonnett with severe amnesia and effectively ended his career.

Bonnett and Earnhardt were close friends, and it was the memory of bagging a prize buck with Earnhardt that snapped Bonnett from the amnesia. Recovered, he retired from auto racing to become a color commentator and host of his own show on The Nashville Network (TNN).

Like Earnhardt, Bonnett earned a reputation for no-holds-barred auto racing, and in 1993 he opted to return to the Winston Cup circuit. After testing some Monte Carlos for Childress, he was set to race at Talladega on July 25. He crashed that day, but walked away unhurt. After scheduling a five-race farewell tour, Bonnett crashed and died on February 11, 1994, at the fourth turn at Daytona, while practicing for the first race of his farewell tour.

On July 12, 1993, just months before his own death, it was Bonnett who pulled Davey Allison from the wreckage of a helicopter crash that caused Allison's death. Bonnett was inducted into the International Motor Sports Hall of Fame in 2001.

with the copyright office, and sales outlets were expanded to include a cable television shopping network. Earnhardt created his own marketing company, Sports Image Incorporated, to handle the business, and the name of Dale Earnhardt Sr. became synonymous with the new alias, the Intimidator.

When his seven-year sponsorship arrangement with Wrangler came to a premature conclusion in 1987, Earnhardt turned to GM Goodwrench for funding and used the opportunity to purchase his car number. Thus the familiar black Chevrolet sedan with a big white "3" on the top became Earnhardt's trademark on the track. After winning six of the first eight races in 1987, he finished the season with eleven wins, clinching the Winston Cup with two races still in the offing.

Earnhardt earned a reputation for highly emotional displays and outbursts while driving. He was a moody, aggressive competitor who went after the competition by making physical contact between the cars. It was midway through the 1987 season when he accomplished what will be remembered as his remarkable Pass-in-the-Grass chase at the Charlotte speedway. A skirmish/collision (between Bill Elliott, Geoff Bodine, and Earnhardt) sent Earnhardt skidding onto the grassy bank of the race course. Without missing a lap, the Intimidator stayed the course and kept driving; he returned to the asphalt and continued the race. All three drivers—Elliott, Bodine, and Earnhardt—were fined after the race.

Although tire problems plagued Earnhardt's car during the 1988 season, he bounced back to a second-

place finish in 1989. He won his fourth Winston Cup in 1990 and a fifth in 1991. Faced with replacing his crew chief in 1992, Earnhardt slumped into a twelfth place finish. He brought Andy Petree into the organization in 1993, won six of his first eighteen races, and ended the season with a sixth Winston Cup in hand. A third consecutive championship in 1994 came as a result of a consistently winning season wherein he took first place in four races, second place in seven, and third place in six. It was Earnhardt's seventh Winston Cup overall, to tie **Richard Petty**'s record for most Winston Cup championships.

The death of Neil Bonnett in a crash in 1994 had a profound effect on Earnhardt as the two had been very close. They were hunting buddies and confidants, and had helped each other through difficult times. That year Earnhardt moved his family from Lake Norman to a two-story house in Mooresville, North Carolina. The estate, situated on 900 acres, included a 108,000-foot garage.

Showing no less mercy on the track than before, the Intimidator continued his rule of the asphalt track. A horrific crash at Talladega in 1996 left him with a broken collarbone and sternum, and with a bruised pelvis. Overall he was lucky, but he expressed some concern over a memory blackout during a race at Darlington the following season.

Earnhardt, with an annual income approaching $24.5 million in the late 1990s, sold the Sports Image venture for $30 million in 1996. By 2000 he ranked at number forty on the *Forbes* list of 100 wealthiest celebrities. In addition to his new home with its so-called Garage Mahal car maintenance facility, he owned a helicopter, a Leer Jet, numerous ATVs, and an oversized trailer, plus he kept a fully staffed yacht moored in Florida.

Death at Daytona

In nearly two decades of Winston Cup competition, including seven championship seasons, Earnhardt met his nemesis every year at Florida's Daytona Speedway. With eighteen career losses on record at Daytona Beach, his determination to win the 500-mile classic approached fanaticism. In 1997 he flipped his car but managed to walk away from the crash. He headed for a waiting ambulance as his head cleared, suddenly realizing that all four wheels and tires on his car remained intact. He beat the wrecker crew back to his car, slid into the cab, and finished the race—albeit in thirty-first place.

One year later, in 1998, Earnhardt took the theretofore elusive first prize at Daytona. It was a hard-earned win. Three years passed again, until 2001 when Earnhardt lost the race and his life in one final instant. The drive that day had progressed with Earnhardt leading in laps number 27 through 31. He was back in front on the eighty-third and eighty-fourth laps. Some time later a 19-car pile up and crash on lap number 174 caused a ruckus but little injury. Flamboyantly, Earnhardt flipped an obscene gesture with his finger to Kurt Bursch when they pinged bumpers during the course.

The number 3 sedan with its cocksure driver regained the lead in lap number 183. In the final lap Earnhardt approached the finish on a wild drive. He was in third place and blocking for two members of his team who held the lead. The trio was poised for a memorable three-way win, but the victory stalled with only seconds left to the finish. Earnhardt's car, clipped from behind, went out of control and careened into a car driven by Kenny Schrader. Both cars left the track and nosed into the wall on the final turn of the race. Schrader emerged from his car without help while Earnhardt remained motionless in the wreck. Earnhardt was pronounced dead at 5:16 p.m. at the Halifax Medical Center, from a basal skull fracture.

Earnhardt over the years had matured into a devoted family man. After the 1980 Winston Cup season, having divorced Gee and assumed custody of their two children, he married Teresa Houston in November of 1982. Their daughter, Taylor Nicole, was born in 1985. He took custody of his older son Kerry as well. He loved the wilderness and was an avid hunter and fisherman.

At the time of his death Earnhardt remained tied with Richard Petty for the most Winston Cups in history. In *At the Altar of Speed,* Leigh Montville said of Earnhardt, "He was the bridge, the connector," between the old world of auto racing and modern high-stakes game at the turn of the twenty-first century.

FURTHER INFORMATION

Books

Benson, Michael. *Race Car Legends: Dale Earnhardt.* New York: Chelsea House Publishers, 1998.

Montville, Leigh. *At the Altar of Speed: The Fast Life and Tragic Death of Dale Earnhardt.* New York: Doubleday, 2001.

Periodicals

Independent (London, England) (February 20, 2001): 6.

St. Louis Post-Dispatch (February 20, 2001): C1.

Other

"Neil Bonnett - International Motorsports Hall of Fame Member," *International Motor Sports Hall of Fame.* http://www.motorsportshalloffame.com/halloffame/2001/Neil_Bonnett_main.htm (January 27, 2003).

Sketch by G. Cooksey

Teresa Edwards

Teresa Edwards
1964-

American basketball player

S he is the most decorated Olympic basketball player ever, male or female, and has a street named after her in her hometown. But Teresa Edwards is often overlooked among women's greats in the sport, having played before the boom in media and fan interest. "She played many of (her) games before her sport caught the public's attention," the Associated Press wrote after Edwards won her fourth Olympic gold medal, as the United States prevailed at the 2000 Games in Sydney, Australia. "Women's basketball had just some [teams] under the NCAA['s auspices] when she started at Georgia. The fan support and media coverage weren't close to what they are now."

Raised in Jackie's Hometown

Edwards grew up as the oldest of four children, and the only girl, in Cairo, Georgia, hometown of baseball legend **Jackie Robinson**. She said she took up basketball because it was the only sport in which she could beat boys head-to-head. During Edwards' four years at the University of Georgia, the Bulldogs sported a 116-17 record, and played in the NCAA tournament each time.

Chronology

1964	Born July 19 in Cairo, Georgia
1987-88	Plays pro basketball in Vicenza and Magenta, Italy
1989-93	Plays pro basketball in Nagoya, Japan
1994	Plays pro basketball in Valencia, Spain and Tarbes, France
1996	Signs with Atlanta Glory of fledgling American Basketball League
1996	Takes Olympic oath at Atlanta Summer Games
1997	Named Atlanta Glory player-coach
1998	Traded to ABL's Philadelphia Rage
1998	ABL folds on December 23

Awards and Accomplishments

1980	Wins high jump in Georgia state high school track and field championships
1982	High school All-America at Cairo (Ga.) High School
1983	Leads University of Georgia to Final Four semifinals
1983	Leads University of Georgia to Final Four championship game
1983	Freshman All-America
1984	Gold medalist, Los Angeles Olympic Games
1984-86	All Southeastern Conference first team selection three straight seasons
1985-86	All-American selection two successive seasons
1987	USA Basketball Female Athlete of the Year
1987	University of Georgia retires her number (5)
1988	Gold medalist, Seoul Olympic Games
1990	USA Basketball Female Athlete of the Year
1992	Bronze medalist and co-captain, Barcelona Olympic Games
1996	Gold medalist, Atlanta Olympic Games
1996	USA Basketball Female Athlete of the Year
1998	Names All-ABL First Team
2000	Gold medalist, Sydney Olympic Games

They played in the Final Four in 1983 and in 1985, when they lost to Old Dominion in the championship game. Edwards scored eleven points in the final but fouled out early. Georgia was Southeastern Conference champion in three of her four seasons. She was all-SEC three times, and became one of only three Georgia women's basketball players to have her jersey number (#5) retired. Lacking the professional outlet women have today, Edwards went overseas for nine seasons, competing for teams in Vicenza and Magenta, Italy; Nagoya, Japan; Valencia, Spain; and Tarbes, France.

Olympic Glory

Edwards began her Olympic run in 1984, following her freshman year at Georgia, when she was the youngest member of the U.S. team that won easily in Los Angeles. Four years later, in Seoul, South Korea, Edwards helped spark the Americans to a second-half comeback in their opening game against Czechoslovakia, scoring 24 points overall in an 87-81 triumph. She added 23 points against Yugoslavia in a 101-74 win and contributed 12 points and six assists in the semifinal as the U.S. beat the Soviet Union for the first time, 102-88. In the gold medal contest, a rematch against Yugoslavia, Edwards scored 14 of her game-high 18 points in the second half, and broke open a tense game with three consecutive fast-break baskets to put the U.S. up by 12. The Americans prevailed, 77-70.

After settling for a bronze at the Barcelona games in 1992 (Edwards averaged 12.6 points per game), the Americans were determined to win back the gold as host nation in 1996, in Atlanta. The Olympic team captains voted for Edwards, also a basketball co-captain, to take the oath during opening ceremonies. On the basketball court, the Americans reclaimed the gold, and culminated a historic 60-0 record during international competition in 1995-96. Later-round games were played at the Georgia Dome before crowds of bigger than 30,000. **Lisa Leslie** and **Sheryl Swoopes** attracted the biggest headlines, but Edwards drew raves for a 20-point, 15-assist effort in a 96-76 trouncing of Australia in the preliminary round. The U.S. routed Brazil 111-87 in the gold medal game, atoning for losses to the South American nation in

the semifinals of the 1994 World Championship and 1991 Pan Am Games.

ABL, All Too Briefly

Playing for the Atlanta Glory when the women's professional American Basketball League began in 1996-97, Edwards made the all-league first team and was runner-up to 1996 Olympic teammate **Nikki McCray** in the voting for most valuable player. Four times in two seasons, she scored more than 40 points in a game. A year later, with the added responsibilities of player-coach, Edwards again made all-league first team and led the ABL in assists (6.7).

After the 1997-98 season, she was traded to the Philadelphia Rage, but the league folded right before Christmas, unable to compete financially with the fledgling Women's National Basketball Association (WNBA). Edwards had been the league's leader in scoring (21.0 points per game) at the time it dissolved. She felt she could have done well in the WNBA, but they could not meet her financial demands .

One More Gold

Edwards, however, was ready for one last Olympic attempt—the 2000 Games in Sydney. She announced that this would be her final international competition, and got in playing shape with daily workouts and games against men in an Atlanta gym. "It seems like she's older than she is because she's been playing so long," said Olympic teammate Ruthie Bolton-Holifield in a biography of Edwards published on the University of Georgia Athletic Association's web site. "But she's only three years older than me. Thirty-six is not crazy. To me, she's got some more years left in her." Edwards exited with her last gold as the Americans won all eight games

Career Statistics

Yr	Team	GP	Pts	FG%	FT%	RPG	APG	SPG
1983	GA	33	430	.459	.634	2.2	4.8	2.12
1984	GA	33	465	.524	.785	2.5	4.1	2.45
1984	US	6	15	.273	.333	2.0	1.3	1.2
1985	GA	30	464	.527	.734	2.8	4.8	3.33
1986	GA	32	630	.558	.788	4.6	4.1	2.84
1988	US	5	83	.579	.810	1.8	3.4	4.6
1992	US	5	63	.371	.600	0.4	5.4	3.6
1996	US	8	55	.600	.462	3.8	8.0	1.0
1997	ATL	40	842	.423	.852	6.7	5.6	0.5
1998	ATL	44	899	.419	.858	6.4	6.7	0.3
1999	PHI	14	294	.498	.345	4.8	6.5	0.3
2000	US	8	49	.613	.800	1.9	3.4	0.4

ATL: Atlanta Glory; GA: University of Georgia; PHI: Philadelphia Rage; US: United States Olympic Team.

and dominated Australia 76-54 in the championship game. She totaled 2,008 points overall for the U.S. in international competition and is the Americans' all-time Olympic career leader for games played (32), assists (143) and steals (59).

While retired as an active player, Edwards is still involved with the U.S. basketball program. The four-time Olympic gold medalist was the keynote speaker at the 2002 USA Basketball Women's Youth Development Festival. Edwards made her national debut at the event's forerunner, the U.S. Olympic Sports Festival, in 1981.

Edwards, asked why she enjoyed talking to the youth on the USA Basketball Women's Youth Development Festival web site, cited "the importance of respecting each other's talents because they're all on the same page, on the same level." She added: "Being there to answer questions that they may have at this time of their life, they're so young. If they can stay on the right path then I've done something to help somebody. So I think that, for me to give and for them to get something out of it is important."

"I'm At Peace"

Edwards missed out on big professional dollars because the WNBA arrived after the prime of her career. She had to play abroad for several seasons and her one pro league in the U.S. folded. Ironically, the WNBA, which put Edwards's ABL out of business, has begun to struggle financially as the NBA has begun to distance itself. "A cynic might argue the (NBA) lost interest in the women once a potential entertainment competitor, the ABL, went out of business," Filip Bondy wrote in the New York *Daily News* in January, 2003.

But Edwards, known as "T" to her friends, has no regrets. "I played when I was supposed to," she told the online journal *Canoe*. "I'm very happy with the process. I'm at peace with where I am. If somehow my abilities and talents have been used to further the game, then it feels good."

FURTHER INFORMATION

Books

Johnson, Anne Janette. *Great Women in Sports*. Detroit: Visible Ink Press, 1996.

Periodicals

Adande, J.A. "When Dreams Become Just That; The ABL's Demise Makes Playing Pro Basketball in This Country Tougher for Some and Impossible for Others." *Los Angeles Times* (December 24, 1998).

Bondy, Filip. "Risky WNBA Business: Its Alliance with Casino Big Gamble." *New York Daily News* (January 29, 2003).

Solomon, Alisa. "Ready, Willing, and ABL." *Village Voice* (November 24, 1998).

Other

"Edwards Bids Farewell after Stellar Career," *Canoe*, http:/www.canoe.ca/2000GamesBasketball/oct1_usa-ap.html, (October 1, 2000).

"Edwards Remains World's Most Decorated Player," CNN-Sports Illustrated, http://sportsillustrated.cnn.com/olympics/news/2000/06/29/update_edwards/, (June 30, 2000).

Leaders in Sport, http://www.sd83.bc.ca/stu/9701/w3ejg1.htm, (January 26, 2003).

"Teresa Edwards Imparts Words of Wisdom to the Young," USA Basketball, http://www.usabasketball.com/women/02_wydf_edwards.html, (January 26, 2003).

University of Georgia Athletic Association, bio of Teresa Edwards, http://georgiabulldogs.ocsn.com/

traditions/olympians/edwards_shtml, (January 21, 2003).

USA Basketball, Teresa Edwards Profile, http://www. usabasketball.com/bioswomen/teresa_edwards_bio. html, (January 25, 2003).

Sketch by Paul Burton

Krisztina Egerszegi
1974-

Hungarian swimmer

Krisztina Egerszegi

Hungarian swimmer Krisztina Egerszegi is the youngest to ever win a gold medal in the Olympic Games. She won this medal at the 1988 Summer Games in Seoul, South Korea, in the 200 meter backstroke. Egerszegi won the gold in the same event in two subsequent Olympics, marking only the second time an athlete won golds in three consecutive games in the same event. She is also the only woman to win five gold medals in individual swimming events. Egerszegi was an expert in the backstroke, dominating women's events from the late 1980s through the mid-1990s.

Egerszegi was born August 16, 1974, in Budapest, Hungary. She began swimming at the age of four. Her first coach was Miklos Kiss, who taught children to swim, in addition to his primary occupation as an engineer at a factory. Kiss noticed early on that she had talent, especially in the backstroke. He brought her talent to the attention of Laszlo Kiss (no relation)—the head coach of the Budapest Swim Club and trainer of the Hungarian women's team—when she was five. Laszlo Kiss sent Egerszegi to another top notch coach, Gyorgy Thury, to be trained when she was six.

In 1986, Laszlo Kiss himself began training Egerszegi. Though she was taught in all four swimming strokes (freestyle, breast, butterfly, and backstroke), she had the ideal physique for the backstroke. Laszlo Kiss refined her abundant natural ability and already solid technique. Egerszegi proved easy to train, and appreciated his tutelage.

Won First Olympic Golds

Egerszegi broke out in international competition at the Summer Olympics in Seoul in 1988. She was only fourteen years old and weighed ninety-nine pounds, forty-four pounds less than the next smallest competitor. Despite her youth and small stature, Egerszegi won a gold in the 200 meter backstroke—setting an Olympic record in the process—and a silver in the 100 meter backstroke. She lost the gold in the 100 meter race by less than a second.

In 1991, Egerszegi continued to show her prowess in the backstroke. She set world records in two events at the European and World Championships. At the worlds, she won gold medals in the 200 meter backstroke and the 100 meter backstroke, setting the world record in the 200 meter backstroke. At the European Championships, Egerszegi set the world record with a time of 1:00.31 in the 100 meter backstroke, winning gold in this race. She also won gold in the 200 meter backstroke and 400 meter individual medley at that competition. The value of her training showed through at the European Championships. Craig Lord of the *Times* wrote "Egerszegi's ability to endure the pain of hard training was said by [Laszlo] Kiss to be one of the key reasons why she was so far ahead of her rivals."

Queen of the Olympics

Egerszegi was still powerful swimming force at the 1992 Summer Olympics in Barcelona, Spain, as a veteran eighteen-year-old. By this time, she was a star in Hungary, and was dubbed the "Queen" of these Olympics. She was the only female athlete to win three individual events at these games. She won one gold medal in the 400 meter individual medley, though she was not expected to, nor did think she would. Egerszegi's primary concern was the 200 meter backstroke,

Chronology

1974	Born on August 16 in Budapest, Hungary
c. 1978	Begins swimming
c. 1986	Begins being coached by Laszlo Kiss
1988, 1992, 1996	Wins gold medals at the Summer Olympic Games
1996	Retires as a competitive swimmer

which she also won gold in as well as the 100 meter backstroke. She set Olympic records in both the 100 meter and 200 meter backstroke.

The following year, Egerszegi continued to prove her dominance and improvement as a swimmer. At the European swimming championships, she won four gold medals in the 100 and 200 meter backstroke, 400 meter individual medley, and 200 meter butterfly. Her win in the butterfly marked the first time she won the event in a major competition. By this time, Egerszegi had good backing from sponsors in Switzerland and was considered the most multitalented swimmer in the world.

In 1994 and 1995, Egerszegi did not do as well at the World and European Championships as she had in recent years. At the 1994 World Championships, she only medaled in the 200 meter backstroke, and it was a silver. Egerszegi had actually planned on retiring after this competition, but because of the loss to China's He Cihong, she decided to continue training. However she chose to stop competing in the 100 meter backstroke at this time, in part because she believed that her technique helped her win over younger swimmers and this worked best in the longer races. At the European Championships in 1995, she won gold in the 200 meter backstroke and 400 meter individual medley.

Egerszegi competed at her third Summer Olympics at the 1996 games in Atlanta, Georgia. She again won in the 200 meter backstroke. She also won a bronze in the 400 meter individual medley. Though she did not enter the 100 meter backstroke competition, her backstroke time in the individual medley—which was 100 meters in length—would have won the gold in the event. Egerszegi's gold in the 200 meter backstroke was her fifth gold medal, the most won by an individual swimmer.

Retired from Swimming

Immediately after the 1996 Olympics, the swimmer nicknamed "Mouse" (because the first four letters of her last name translates to the word in Hungarian) retired from competition. She planned on training progressively down in order to not shock her body. Referring to her win in the 200 meter backstroke at the Summer Games, she told Julian Linden of *United Press International*, "I love all my medals, but I think this one is the best. I'm not going to swim at the next world championships; I'm just going to swim for fun now."

Awards and Accomplishments

1988	Gold medal in the 200 meter backstroke (set Olympic record) and silver in the 100 meter backstroke at the Summer Olympics
1989	Silver medal in the 400 individual medley at the European Championships
1990	Named European Female Swimmer of the Year
1991	Gold medals in the 200 meter backstroke (setting world record) and 100 meter backstroke at the World Championships; gold medals in the 100 meter backstroke (breaking world's record), 200 meter backstroke and 400 meter individual medley at the European Championships; named world female swimmer of the year by *Swimming World*; named European Swimmer of the Year
1992	Won gold medal in the 200 meter backstroke (set Olympic record), 100 meter backstroke (set Olympic record), and 400 meter individual medley at the Summer Olympic Games; named European Swimmer of the Year; named European Sportswoman of the Year
1993	Gold medal in the 100 meter and 200 meter backstroke, 200 meter butterfly, and 400 meter individual medley at the European Championships
1994	Silver medal in the 200 meter backstroke at the World Championships
1995	Gold medal in the 200 meter backstroke and 400 individual medley at the European Championship
1996	Gold medal in the 200 meter backstroke and bronze in the 400 meter individual medley at the Summer Games
2001	Named Female Athlete of the Century by the Hungarian Olympic Committee

FURTHER INFORMATION

Books

The Women's Sports Encyclopedia. New York: Henry Holt and Company, 1997.

Periodicals

Bondy, Filip. "In Final Race, Sanders Wins Her Test of Nerves." *New York Times* (August 1, 1992): section 1, p. 31.

"Ferenc Puskas and Kriszstina Egerszegi named Athletes of the Century." Global News Wire (January 28, 2001).

"Golden van Almsick and Egerszegi triumph in Sheffield." Agence France Presse (August 8, 1993).

Hodgson, Guy. "Swimming: Duo maintain their dominance." *Independent* (August 9, 1993): 25.

Knack, Marty. "Mouse leads record haul Canadians shut out of swimming finals." *Gazette* (July 27, 1992): D1.

Linden, Julian. "Egerszegi joins exclusive swim club." *United Press International* (July 25, 1996).

Lord, Craig. "Egerszegi the class act in swimming's great show." *Times* (August 3, 1992).

Lord, Craig. "Kiss eases Egerszegi's pain." *Times* (August 23, 1991).

Porter, Anne. "Swimming: Hungarian gold levels rising." *Independent* (January 10, 1991): 32.

Porter, Anne. "Swimming: Hungary's gold rush." *Independent* (August 23, 1991): 27.

Strange, Mike. "Hungarian Steals Evans' Script." *Cincinnati Post* (July 26, 1996): 1C.

Other

"Heroes: Krisztina Egerszegi." International Olympic Committee. http://www.olympic.org (January 29, 2003).

"Krisztina Egerszegi: The Development of a World Champion Backstroker." *Swimming Technique.* http://www.swiminfo.com (January 29, 2003).

"Krisztina Egerszegi (HUN)." International Swimming Hall of Fame. http://www.ishof.org/01kegerszegi. html (January 29, 2003).

Sketch by A. Petruso

John Elway
1960-

American football player

John Elway

John Elway is arguably one of the best quarterbacks in football history. He retired after sixteen seasons and two Super Bowl championships as the winningest starting quarterback in the history of the National Football League (NFL).

Two Sports

John Elway was born on June 28, 1960 in Port Angeles, Washington. He grew up in a happy home with his twin sister Jana, older sister Lee Ann, and his parents. His father, Jack, was a college football coach, and the family followed his coaching jobs from Washington, to Montana, to Los Angeles, where Elway attended Granada Hills High School. With his father as his mentor and ad hoc coach, Elway learned the basic elements of throwing, running, and reading defenses, as well as the values of hard work and sportsmanship. In his first football game as a sixth-grader, Elway ran for six touchdowns in the first half.

Elway was talented in football, basketball, and baseball. Washington State University basketball coach George Raveling, who saw Elway at a basketball camp, thought he showed significant promise as a basketball player. As a senior he batted .491, had a pitching record of 4-2, led his team to the Los Angeles City championship, and was named Southern California's player of the year. In his final season on the football field at Granada Hills, he completed 129 passes on 200 attempts for 1,837 yards and nineteen touchdowns. His athletic abilities earned the attention of an array of college football and baseball scouts, as well as professional baseball scouts. The Kansas City Royals selected him in the eighteenth round of the 1979 draft; however, Elway, opting to play college football, signed a letter of intent with Stanford University.

During his four years at Stanford, from 1979 to 1983, Elway set five major National Collegiate Athletic Association (NCAA) records as well as nine major Pac-10 conference records. He completed 774 of 1,243 pass attempts (62.1 percent) for 9,349 yards and seventy-seven touchdowns. Elway also played baseball at Stanford for two years. In his last season as a sophomore, he batted .349 with nine home runs and fifty runs batted in (RBI) in forty-nine games. He was drafted by the New York Yankees and played a summer with the Yankees' single-A farm club in Oneonta, New York. His batting average was .349, and he had a team-high twenty-four RBIs.

Joins the Broncos

Graduating with a degree in economics in 1983, Elway entered the NFL draft with several other celebrated college quarterbacks, including **Jim Kelly** and **Dan Marino**. The Baltimore Colts had first pick and selected Elway. However, Elway made it clear that he did not want to play for the Colts, a team characterized by their dictatorial coach, Frank Kush. He also wanted to play closer to home and even considered opting for a professional baseball contract rather than play football in Baltimore. Accordingly,

Chronology

1960	Born June 28 in Port Angeles, Washington
1979-83	Star quarterback for Stanford University
1982	Spends summer playing baseball for a New York Yankees' farm team
1983	Drafted by the Baltimore Colts and then traded to the Denver Broncos
1984	Marries wife, Janet
1997	Creates the Elway Foundation to fight child abuse
1999	Announces retirement; joins Wayne Gretzky and Michael Jordan in forming MVP.com
2002	Becomes co-owner, president, and chief executive officer of Arena Football League team, the Colorado Crush; separates from wife

Awards and Accomplishments

1983	Received second most votes in bid for the Heisman Memorial Trophy
1986-87, 1989, 1991, 1993-94, 1996-98	NFL Pro Bowl
1987	NFL Player of the Year
1993	American Football Conference's (AFC) Player of the Year
1998	Won Super Bowl XXXII over the Green Bay Packers; 31-24; selected as game's Most Valuable Player
1999	Won Super Bowl XXXIII over the Miami Dolphins, 38-3; inducted into Colorado Sports Hall of Fame
2000	Inducted into the College Football Hall of Fame

the Colts worked a deal to trade Elway to the Denver Broncos, whose generous contract made the rookie the second highest paid quarterback in the NFL.

Elway's entrance into the NFL proved to be a rocky road. A superstar at Stanford, he was expected by fans to be an instant success in Denver. It was the first time Elway had ever heard booing directed at him. In his regular season debut he completed just one of eight pass attempts for fourteen yards, threw one interception, and was sacked four times before injuring his elbow and being replaced by veteran quarterback Dan DeBerg. After the first five games Elway was benched, but started the last five games of the season after De-Berg was injured. Working much of the year with a sore elbow and a porous offensive line that offered little protection, Elway ended his first season with a completion rate of just 47.5 percent with seven touchdown passes and fourteen interceptions.

Following his rookie year, Elway married his college sweetheart, Janet. They have four children, three daughters and a son. With his feet more firmly under him during his sophomore season, Elway began to improve his performance. In fifteen games Elway led the team to twelve wins. He completed 214 of 380 passes for 2,598 yards, was third on the team in rushing with 237 yards, and improved his completion rate to 56.3 percent. With an overall team record of 13-3, the Broncos were the American Football Conference (AFC) Western Division champions. Elway and his team strolled into the postseason, but lost in the first round to the Pittsburgh Steelers.

Hits His Stride

Better in his second year than his first, Elway began to shine in 1985, his third season. No booing could be heard as Elway broke nearly every Broncos record on the books and knocked at the door of several NFL records. He led the league with 605 pass attempts, a Bronco record and just four shy of the all-time NFL record of 609 set by Dan Fouts. Other franchise records set included pass completions (327, second in the NFL), passing yards (3891, sec-

ond in the NFL), and total offense (4,414, first in the NFL). He threw twenty-two touchdowns, but also threw a career-high twenty-three interceptions, the one blemish on his otherwise incredible season.

In 1986 the Broncos repeated as the AFC champions in dramatic fashion. Locked in a tight game with the Cleveland Browns, Elway took the Broncos from their own two-yard line, in what became known as simply "The Drive," to score a game-tying touchdown with just thirty-seven seconds left on the clock. The Broncos won in overtime on a field goal, 23-20, and Elway was poised to appear in his first Super Bowl. Although he threw for 304 yards against the New York Giants, the Giants came from behind, outscoring Denver 30-20 in the second half, to defeat the Broncos, 39-20. Despite losing the Super Bowl, Elway earned his first trip to the Pro Bowl.

In a season shortened by a players' strike, Elway still managed to pass for over 3,000 yards in twelve games in 1987, and, in another thrilling AFC championship game, the Broncos once again defeated the Browns. Appearing in his second straight Super Bowl, this time facing the Washington Redskins, Elway threw a 55-yard touchdown pass on Denver's first play from scrimmage, setting a record for the earliest touchdown ever scored in a Super Bowl game. Unfortunately, that was the first and last of the Broncos' highlights on the day as Elway threw three interceptions and the Broncos were stomped by the Redskins, 42-10. Despite his final performance, Elway was named the NFL's Most Valuable Player.

Super Bowls: 0-3

Missing the playoffs in 1989, Elway led his team back to the AFC championship for the third time in four years in 1990, once again sending the Browns home in the AFC championship game. Facing **Joe Montana** and the San Francisco 49ers in the Super Bowl, Elway and the Broncos were embarrassed by the 49ers, losing 55-10. Elway passed for just 108 yards and threw two interceptions; his Super Bowl record fell to 0-3. The following season Elway experienced his first losing season as the Broncos posted a record of 5-11, but in 1991

Career Statistics

| Yr | Team | GP | Passing | | | | | | | Rushing | | | |
			ATT	COM	YDS	COM%	TD	INT	SK	RAT	ATT	YDS	TD
1983	Den	11	259	123	1663	47.5	7	14	28	54.9	28	146	1
1984	Den	15	380	214	2598	56.3	18	15	24	76.8	56	237	1
1985	Den	16	605	327	3891	54.0	22	23	38	70.0	51	253	0
1986	Den	16	504	280	3485	55.6	19	13	32	79.0	52	257	1
1987	Den	12	410	224	3198	54.6	19	12	20	83.4	66	304	4
1988	Den	15	496	274	3309	55.2	17	19	30	71.3	54	234	1
1989	Den	15	416	223	3051	53.6	18	18	35	73.7	48	244	3
1990	Den	16	502	294	3526	58.6	15	14	43	78.5	50	258	3
1991	Den	16	451	242	3253	53.7	13	12	45	68.3	55	255	6
1992	Den	12	316	174	2242	55.1	10	17	36	65.7	34	94	2
1993	Den	16	551	348	4030	63.2	25	10	39	92.8	44	153	0
1994	Den	14	494	307	3490	62.1	16	10	46	85.7	58	235	4
1995	Den	16	542	316	3970	58.3	26	14	22	86.3	41	176	1
1996	Den	15	466	287	3328	61.6	26	14	26	89.2	50	249	4
1997	Den	16	502	280	3635	55.8	27	11	34	87.5	50	218	1
1998	Den	13	356	210	2806	59.0	22	10	18	93.0	37	94	1
TOTAL		234	7250	4123	51475	56.9	300	226	516	79.8	774	3407	33

Den: Denver Broncos.

the team bounced back to win eleven games, winning the AFC Western Division title before being beaten by the Buffalo Bills in the conference championship.

By the early 1990s Elway's relationship with head coach Dan Reeves was becoming increasingly tense. Depending on the viewpoint, Elway came off looking a bit like a spoiled brat, or Reeves appeared to be a stiff-necked, control freak. The conflict boiled over into the press after Reeves fired offensive coach Mike Shanahan, Elway's close personal friend. After finishing the 1992 season with a record of 8-8, Elway was intimating that it was going to be either him or Reeves. The Broncos organization chose Elway, and Reeves' contract was not renewed after the end of the season.

Elway entered the 1993 season with renewed focus. He threw 551 passes, completing 348 (63.2 percent), for 4,030 yards, twenty-five touchdowns and only ten interceptions, but the Broncos struggled in 1994, and Shanahan was invited to return to Denver as the head coach in 1995. After two years of rebuilding, the Broncos, who had added sensational running back **Terrell Davis** to its roster, posted a record of 13-3 in 1996, and Elway became just the fourth player in NFL history to throw for more than 45,000 career yards. The Broncos made their first appearance in postseason play since 1993, but were upset at home in the first round by the Jacksonville Jaguars.

In 1997 Elway threw twenty-seven touchdown passes, a career high, and led the Broncos to a 12-4 regular season record. Reaching his fourth Super Bowl, Elway, already considered one of the game's greatest quarterbacks, was under serious scrutiny regarding his ability to perform in the big game. Although Elway only threw for

123 yards in the Super Bowl against the Pittsburgh Steelers, the Broncos' win, 31-24, quieted his detractors and Elway, now with a Super Bowl title, finally got the monkey off his back.

The Broncos came back strong in 1998, and Elway joined Marino as the only quarterbacks to pass for more than 50,000 yards. On January 16, 1999, Elway played his last game at Mile High Stadium, earning his fifth trip to the Super Bowl. In a made-for-television match-up, Elway and the Broncos squared off in the Super Bowl against the Atlanta Falcons, coached by Dan Reeves. The Broncos prevailed, and Elway won his second consecutive Super Bowl.

Having reached the mountaintop twice, 38-year-old Elway, who was suffering from some nagging injuries, announced his retirement in May 2000. After sixteen years of play, he walked away with a career record of 142-82-1 (.643), making him the NFL's all-time winningest starting quarterback. With two Super Bowl titles, the Comeback Kid had made the biggest comeback of them all.

FURTHER INFORMATION

Books

Newsmakers 1990, Issue 3. Detroit: Gale Group, 1990.
Sports Stars. Series 1-4. Detroit: U•X•L, 1994-98.
St. James Encyclopedia of Popular Culture. five volumes. Detroit: St. James Press, 2000.

Periodicals

Attner, Paul. "Smart. Very Smart." *Sporting News* (May 3, 1999): 12.

Bechtel, Mark. "The King of the Comeback." *Sports Illustrated* (February 10, 1999): 22.

Elliott, Josh. "Back in the Game." *Sports Illustrated* (June 24, 2002)

King, Peter. "Where Does He Stand?" *Sports Illustrated* (February 10, 1999): 84.

Looney, Douglas S. "Elway on Elway." *Christian Science Monitor* (January 22, 1998).

Reilly, Rick. "Welcome to the Real World." *Sports Illustrated* (August 19, 2002): 80.

Silver, Michael. "Champions At Last." *Sports Illustrated* (February 10, 1999): 50.

Silver, Michael. "Last Call." *Sports Illustrated* (May 3, 1999): 52.

Other

Carter, Bob. "Elway Led Broncos on 'The Drive.'" ESPN Classic. http://www.espn.com (December 28, 2002)

"Football Scrapbooks: John Elway." *Sporting News.* http://www.sportingnews.com/archives/elway/timeline.html/ (December 28, 2002)

"John Elway." Denver Broncos.com. http://www.denverbroncos.com/history/ringoffame/elway/php3/ (December 28, 2002)

"John Elway: President and Chief Executive Officer." Colorado Crush Arena Football. http://www.coloradocrush.com (December 28, 2002)

"QB Club: John Elway." National Football League. http://www.nfl.com/qbclub/elway.html/ (December 28, 2002)

Knisley, Michael. "Elway-Reeves Power Struggle Threatens Broncos' Success." *Sporting News.com.* http://www.sportingnews.com/archives/elway/article13.html/ (December 28, 2002)

Sketch by Kari Bethel

Julius Erving

Julius Erving
1950-

American basketball player

Julius Erving, commonly referred to as Dr. J, made his mark in the National Basketball Association (NBA) with the grace he displayed on and off the court and by playing an instrumental role in the creation of the league as it's known today. As the lone superstar of the ABA, the professional basketball league in direct competition with the more established NBA during the 1970s, his presence was a major factor in the decision to merge the two leagues. He is also credited with putting the slam in slam dunk and being one of the games great ambassadors who, along with superstars such as **Magic Johnson** and **Larry Bird**, elevated the game's popularity in the late 1970s and early 1980s. Although he was originally recognized for his flamboyant play and oversized afro, it was his reserved manner and generous spirit that endeared him to the public and his peers.

In the Beginning

Born Julius Winfield Erving II on February 22, 1950, in Roosevelt, New York, his father abandoned the family when he was only three. At the age of seven his father was hit and killed by a car, forever erasing any possibili-

Chronology

1950	Born February 22 in Roosevelt, New York
1967	Named All-Conference at Roosevelt High
1968	Enrolled at University of Massachusetts
1970	Scores career high 37 points twice in one season
1970	Named All-America and All-Yankee Conference
1971	Decides to turn professional
1971	Joins the Virginia Squires
1971	Leads ABA in playoff scoring with a 33 point average per game
1972	Marries wife Turqouise
1973	Moves to the New York Nets of the ABA
1974	Named the ABA's MVP
1974	Wins first ABA championship with the Nets
1975	Scores career high 63 points in a game for the Nets
1976	Named ABA's MVP again
1976	Wins second ABA championship with the Nets
1976	Joins Philadelphia 76ers
1977	Named All-star Game MVP
1978	Named to the All-NBA First Team
1980	Named to NBA's 35th Anniversary All-time Team
1981	Named NBA MVP
1983	Awarded Walter J. Kennedy Citizenship Award
1983	Wins NBA championship with 76ers
1984	Scores 34 points in All-star Game
1987	Retires from basketball
1993	Enshrined in Basketball Hall of Fame
1996	Named to NBA's 50th Anniversary All-time Team

Awards and Accomplishments

1974, 1976	ABA Most Valuable Player
1974, 1976	ABA championship
1975	ABA co-Most Valuable Player
1977, 1983	Named All-Star Game Most Valuable Player
1981	NBA Most Valuable Player
1983	Wins NBA championship with the 76ers
1983	Named to NBA 35th Anniversary Team
1983	Walter J. Kennedy Citizenship Award
1983	Jackie Robinson Award from Ebony Magazine
1985	American Express Man of the Year
1993	Inducted into the Basketball Hall of Fame
1996	Named to NBA 50th Anniversary Team

ty of having a father figure in his life. His mother raised her three kids on her own working as a house cleaner. Erving was withdrawn as a child but did well in school and athletics. He picked up basketball at the age of nine and was immediately successful on the court. At the age of ten, he led his team to the Inter-County Basketball Association championship. It was during these early years in his New York neighborhood that Erving was first called the Doctor, a name that would stick with him for the rest of his life. "Whether basketball chose me, or I chose it, I still don't know," he later recalled. "I think it's the former—it chose me."

After graduating high school he was offered many basketball scholarships and eventually decided to attend the University of Massachusetts at Amherst. In his first year, he broke the school's records for scoring and rebounding for a freshman and led his team to an undefeated season. After his junior season, Erving decided to turn professional. He made the controversial decision in 1971 after being lured by lucrative offers from the American Basketball Association (ABA). Signing with the Virginia Squires for $500,000, he would stay with the team for two years before moving to the New York Nets.

The ABA

In his first season with the Nets, the young Erving won his second straight league scoring championship, averaging 27.4 points per game, and led his team to the championship against the Utah Stars. After that championship season, the Nets would struggle while their star's popularity continued to swell. In the less recognized league, Erving's presence would draw a crowd no matter where his team would play. ABA commissioner, and Hall of Fame forward, Dave DeBusschere once commented, "Plenty of guys have been 'The Franchise.' For us, Dr. J is 'The League.'"

The Greatest Game in Basketball History

It became increasingly more evident that the two competing leagues would merge by the 1975-76 season, but not before Erving played what is commonly considered one of the greatest games in basketball history. The ABA's final championship series between the New York Nets and the Denver Nuggets would come down to a final game in which the Nets would trail by twenty points but come back due in large part to the individual performance of Erving. Erving averaged 37.7 points in that championship series which would serve as his farewell to the ABA and his introduction to the newly expanded NBA. He won the Most Valuable Player (MVP) award for the season and ranked first in scoring, fifth in rebounding, seventh in assists, third in steals and seventh in blocked shots. In short, Erving did it all, even becoming the first player to win a league wide slam dunk contest that year.

Offered a contract with the Nets, Erving turned it down and held out for a better offer before landing in Philadelphia with the 76ers. The 76ers were a talented team full of self-serving egos and little regard for team play. In his first year there, Philadelphia would go to the finals and lose to the Portland Trailblazers after winning the first two games of the series. It was after two disappointing seasons that the 76ers' management decided to unload their highly priced stars and build the team around Erving.

The NBA Championship

Very shortly afterward, the 76ers would become perennial contenders on a heartbreaking streak of near misses and no championships. Although Erving was continually recognized for his artistic play and gravity defying moves, he was ultimately concerned with win-

Career Statistics

Yr	Team	GP	PTS	FG%	3P%	FT%	RPG	APG	SPG	BPG	TO
1971-72	VA	84	2,290	.498	.188	.745	1,319	335	—	—	342
1972-73	VA	71	2,268	.496	.208	.776	867	298	181	127	326
1973-74	NYN	84	2,299	.512	.395	.766	899	434	190	204	341
1974-75	NYN	84	2,343	.506	.333	.799	914	462	186	157	301
1975-76	NYN	84	2,462	.507	.330	.801	925	423	207	160	307
1976-77	Phil	82	1,770	.499	—	.777	695	306	159	113	—
1977-78	Phil	74	1,528	.502	—	.845	481	279	135	97	238
1978-79	Phil	78	1,803	.491	—	.745	564	357	133	100	315
1979-80	Phil	78	2,100	.519	.200	.787	576	355	170	140	284
1980-81	Phil	82	2,014	.521	.222	.787	657	364	173	147	266
1981-82	Phil	81	1,974	.546	.273	.763	557	319	161	141	214
1982-83	Phil	72	1,542	.517	.286	.759	491	263	112	131	196
1983-84	Phil	77	1,727	.512	.333	.754	532	309	141	139	230
1984-85	Phil	78	1,561	.494	.214	.765	414	233	135	109	208
1985-86	Phil	74	1,340	.480	.281	.785	370	248	113	82	214
1986-87	Phil	60	1,005	.471	.264	.813	264	191	76	94	158
TOTAL		1,243	30,026	.504	.271	.827	10,525	5,176	2,272	1,941	3,940

NYN: New York Nets; Phil: Philadelphia 76ers; VA: Virginia Squires.

ning an NBA championship. After losing repeatedly in the playoffs and finals to NBA powerhouses, Boston and Los Angeles, the 76ers signed **Moses Malone** for the 1982-83 season. He provided the missing link and Erving and the 76ers won their first and last NBA title together against the Los Angeles Lakers. During his career, Erving was in the finals four times total with this the one and only NBA championship for the superstar.

Erving retired from basketball in 1987 after becoming only the third player to score 30,000 career points. His feat would go largely unnoticed because he played in the less recognized ABA and their statistics are not included in the NBA record books. Erving, along with the rest of the former ABA players, quietly accept this fact while privately feeling that their accomplishments deserve equal billing in the history of professional basketball.

Retirement and Beyond

After basketball, however, he would go on to become a successful business man and analyst with NBC sports. He was inducted into the Basketball Hall of Fame in 1993 and recognized as one of the forty greatest athletes of all time by *Sports Illustrated* the following year. In 1997, he was named executive vice-president of the NBA's Orlando Magic.

Married to Turquoise Erving since 1972, with four children, his reputation was slightly tarnished in 1999 when it was revealed he fathered a child in 1980 with a freelance writer who covered the 76ers in their heyday. The daughter he fathered out of wedlock turned out a surprising prospect in the world of women's tennis, taking Wimbledon by storm in 1999. In 2000, Erving's youngest son Cory went missing and was tragically

Dr. J: Getting Straight to the Point

Erving's nickname, "Dr. J," is a nom de guerre more widely recognized than any other in sport. Picked up years ago in the macho games of his youth, "Dr. J" has become the code word for a certain thunderous, awesome elegance on the basketball court.

Such is the distinction with which Erving ... plays the game. Even his own teammates have been known to pause in wonderment at his airborne exploits. Many players nowadays can dunk the ball. Few, if any, can do so with Erving's flair. With hands so large they seem to reduce the basketball to grapefruit size, he can leave his feet far from the basket and float, angling as he goes, to jam the ball through the hoop.

Source: Barry Jacobs, *Saturday Evening Post*, November 1983, p. 64.

found drowned in his car in a pond only a mile away from his family's Florida home.

Erving continues to be one of the games most recognized personalities because of his role in creating the modern game. During the late 1970s and early 1980s, Erving. and his peers brought the league new popularity with their grace, improvisation and high-flying technique. So well known for his fluidity on the court he was granted an honorary doctorate in dance from Temple University, Erving is also considered a gentleman and ambassador of the game. "He's got one of the most beautiful hearts in the world," said former player Gene Banks. "He's what the NBA is all about."

FURTHER INFORMATION

Books

Contemporary Black Biography, Vol. 18. Detroit: Gale, 1998.

Encyclopedia of World Biography, 2nd ed. Detroit: Gale, 1998.

St. James Encyclopedia of Popular Culture Detroit: St. James Press, 2000.

Periodicals

"Dr. J: Getting Straight to the Point." *Saturday Evening Post* (November, 1983): 64.

"Dr. J's Daughter, Alexandra Stevenson, Speaks Out for First Time in ABC-TV Interview." *Jet* (August 16, 1999): 51.

"Julius Erving." *Sports Illustrated* (September 19,1994): 146.

"Julius Erving: Doctor of Fillosophy in Hoops." *Philadelphia Daily News* (February 7, 2002).

"No Turning Back: The Slam Dunk." *European Intelligence Wire* (October 13, 2002).

"Preliminary Findings Suggest No Foul Play in Death of Erving's Son." *Miami Herald* (July 7, 2000).

"Previous Lakers-Sixers Showdowns Ran the Full Spectrum of Drama." *Philadelphia Inquirer* (June 4, 2001).

"Pro Basketball's Five-Tool Players." *Basketball Digest* (February, 2002): 30.

"Smashing Debut: Found: Mr. Mystery, the Dad Behind Wimbledon Star Alexandra Stevenson." *People* (July 19, 1999): 73.

"The Doctor's Daughter: An 18-Year-Old Tennis Phenom Turns Out to Have a Most Spectacular Athletic Bloodline." *Time* (July 12, 1999): 62.

Sketch by Aric Karpinski

Phil Esposito

Phil Esposito
1942-

Canadian hockey player

Considered by many to be one of the greatest centers to play the game, Phil Esposito won numerous scoring titles, primarily during his tenure with the Boston Bruins. He was the first player to score 100 points in a season, but one example of his scoring touch. After retiring as a player, he was a hockey executive who helped expand the league into the Sun Belt by being a force behind the expansion Tampa Bay Lightning.

Esposito was born on February 20, 1942, in Sault Ste. Marie, Ontario, the son of Patrick and Frances Esposito. His younger brother **Tony Esposito**, also played in the NHL as a goalie. It was the elder Esposito who forced his little brother to play goal for him when they were kids.

Part of Blackhawks Program

Because the Chicago Blackhawks sponsored the youth hockey program in Sault Ste. Marie, of which Esposito was a part, he was chosen by them as a player. Esposito took hockey seriously enough to drop out of high school to play junior hockey. In 1961, he turned professional when he began playing for the Blackhawks' minor league affiliate.

During the 1963-64 season, Esposito was called up to the Blackhawks, but he only had three goals in 27 games. Though never a great skater, Esposito was good because of his strength. He continued to play for the Chicago Blackhawks for three seasons. Over those years, he scored only seventy-one goals. Esposito played on a line with **Bobby Hull**. Many of Esposito's goals were considered easy because of who he played with—Hull was a gifted goal scorer—though he helped Hull's scoring proficiency as well.

Traded to Boston

In 1967, Esposito was traded to the Boston Bruins because Chicago needed a defenseman and he had not played well in the playoffs before that date. It was in Boston that Esposito had his best years as a player and Boston had some of its best years as a franchise. During his six years in Boston, he won or finished second in the scoring title race each year. Esposito also became an all-around player, who was used in every situation.

Chronology

1942	Born February 20 in Sault Ste. Marie, Ontario, Canada
1961	Turns pro as a hockey player
1963	Is called up by the Chicago Blackhawks
1963-67	Plays with the Chicago Blackhawks
1967	Traded to Boston Bruins
1969	First player to score more than 100 points in a season
1970	Wins Stanley Cup with the Boston Bruins
1972	Wins Stanley Cup with the Boston Bruins; plays for Team Canada in the Summit Series
1975	Traded to New York Rangers on November 7
1981	Retires as a player in mid-season, becomes coach (January)
1984	Elected to the Hockey Hall of Fame
1986	Named general manager of the New York Rangers
1989	Fired as general manager of Rangers in May
1990	Part of team that gets expansion franchise Tampa Bay Lightning admitted to NHL for 1992-93 season
1992	Is general manager and president when Tampa Bay joins the NHL
1998	Fired as general manager of Tampa Bay Lightening
1998-99	Works as analyst for Fox Sports
2000	Buys (with partners) the Cincinnati Cyclones, a minor league hockey team

Awards and Accomplishments

1968	All-Star (second team)
1969, 1971-74	Art Ross Trophy as NHL's leading scorer
1969, 1971-75	All-Star (first team)
1969, 1974	Hart Trophy
1972	Won Stanley Cup with the Boston Bruins; played for Team Canada in the Summit Series
1974	Lester B. Pearson Award
1978	Awarded the Lester Patrick Trophy for his contributions to U.S. hockey
1984	Elected to the Hockey Hall of Fame

In his second season with Boston after the trade, Esposito became the first player to score more than 100 points in a season. He followed that up with a 99 point season in 1969-70, and 152 points—including seventy-six goals—in 1970-71. In 1972-73, Esposito had fifty-five goals and seventy-five assists. In 1973-74, he had sixty-eight goals and seventy-seven assists. From 1969-73, he scored at least fifty goals in a season. These were amazing numbers for the time. Esposito also won the Stanley Cup with Boston in 1970 and 1972.

Traded to New York Rangers

Esposito suffered a knee injury in 1973, after which some believed he was not the same player. This became true after he was traded to the New York Rangers in November 1975. He was not nearly as effective of a player for the last part of his career. Though he became a popular player in New York, the adjustment was hard. He also had problems with injuries and did not have the same touch he had in Boston. Esposito abruptly retired in the middle of the 1980-81 season.

Over course of his playing career, Esposito scored 717 goals and 873 assists. He scored at least thirty goals in thirteen consecutive seasons. Though Esposito's strengths were often overshadowed by high profile teammates like Hull and **Bobby Orr**, he still had a number of significant goals. Esposito was elected to the Hall of Fame in 1984.

Remained Connected to Hockey

Though Esposito was finished as a player, his career in professional hockey remained. The day after he retired, he became an assistant coach for the Rangers. The following season, he worked as a color commentator for the Madison Square Garden Network.

Esposito continued his association with the Rangers when he was hired as general manager and vice president in 1986. He controlled all players and coaches for the Rangers and the minor league system. The team was not doing well when he took over, but it did better with him the first year. But Esposito was sometimes impatient with the progress. He fired two head coaches and named himself head coach just before the playoffs in 1987 and 1989. Esposito had paid a hefty price in draft picks to acquire Michel Bergeron, the coach he fired in 1989. When Esposito took the helm in 1989, the team never won again. Shortly after playoffs ended in 1989, Esposito himself was fired. He had done forty-three trades in three years.

Soon after his dismissal, in 1990, Esposito began working on getting a new NHL franchise accepted in Florida, the Tampa Bay Lightning. This would bring NHL hockey back to the Sun Belt (it had previously been in Atlanta). He lined up Japanese investors and Yankees owner **George Steinbrenner** among other American investors, and promised the league that a $90 million hockey arena would be built. The Lightning began playing in the 1992-93 season. When the project started, Esposito had been a partner in franchise, but by the time the team began playing, he was only the president and general manager. Esposito was criticized for some of his actions while the franchise was being developed, but the team survived. Esposito guided the team until he was fired in October 1998 by its new owner, Art Williams.

After his dismissal, Esposito remained in hockey as a commentator for Fox Sports Net for one season and for Tampa Bay Lightning radio for several seasons. He also worked for the Lightning as a promotions employee. He also was owner and director of the Cincinnati Cyclones, a minor league hockey team that he bought with other investors in 2000.

While Esposito's front office accomplishments were important, it was his skills as a player, especially in Boston, that were his legacy. Describing his comple-

Career Statistics

Yr	Team	GP	G	AST	PTS	PIM
1963-64	Chicago	27	3	2	5	2
1964-65	Chicago	70	23	32	55	44
1965-66	Chicago	69	27	26	53	49
1966-67	Chicago	69	21	40	61	40
1967-68	Boston	74	35	49	84	21
1968-69	Boston	74	49	77	126	7
1969-70	Boston	76	43	56	99	50
1970-71	Boston	78	76	76	152	71
1971-72	Boston	76	66	67	133	76
1972-73	Boston	78	55	75	130	87
1973-74	Boston	78	68	77	145	58
1974-75	Boston	79	61	66	127	62
1975-76	Boston	12	6	10	16	8
1975-76	New York	62	29	38	67	28
1976-77	New York	80	34	46	80	52
1977-78	New York	79	38	43	81	53
1978-79	New York	80	42	36	78	37
1979-80	New York	80	34	44	78	73
1980-81	New York	41	7	13	20	20
TOTAL		1282	717	873	1590	910

Boston: Boston Bruins (NHL); Chicago: Chicago Blackhawks (NHL); New York: New York Rangers (NHL).

ness at the time, Stan and Shirley Fischler in the *Hockey Encyclopedia* quoted an unnamed scout as saying, "Esposito combines reach, strength, intelligence, and competitiveness to the degree that the only way he can be countered is with superbly coordinated defensive play."

CONTACT INFORMATION

Address: c/o BCE Place, 30 Yonge St., Toronto, Ontario M5E 1X8 Canada. Online: www.legendsofhockey.com.

SELECTED WRITINGS BY ESPOSITO:

(With Tony Esposito and Tim Moriarty) *Brothers Esposito,* Hawthorn Books, 1971.

(With Gerald Estenazi) *Hockey Is My Life,* Dodd Mead, 1972.

(With Tony Esposito and Kevin Walsh) *We Can Teach You To Play Hockey,* Hawthorn Books, 1972.

(With Dick Dew) *Phil Esposito's Winning Hockey for Beginners,* H. Regency, 1976.

FURTHER INFORMATION

Books

Diamond, Dan, and Joseph Romain. *Hockey Hall of Fame: The Official History of the Game and Its Greatest Stars.* New York: Doubleday, 1988.

Fischler, Stan. *The All-New Hockey's 100.* Toronto: McGraw-Hill Ryerson, Ltd., 1988.

Fischler, Stan and Shirley. *Fischlers' Hockey Encyclopedia.* New York: Thomas Y. Crowell, 1975.

Hickok, Ralph. *A Who's Who of Sports Champions: Their Stories and Records.* Boston: Houghton Mifflin Company, 1995.

Hollander, Zander, and Hal Bock, eds. *The Complete Encyclopedia of Ice Hockey.* Englewood Cliffs: Prentice-Hall, Inc., 1974.

Periodicals

Associated Press (May 25, 1989).

"Coming of Age: Who will ever forget The Goal?" *Maclean's* (July 1, 1999): 42.

Dupont, Kevin. "Big Heart and Big Memories." *New York Times* (September 25, 1984): B8.

Erlendsson, Erik. "Andreychuk Sets Mark." *Tampa Tribune* (November 16, 2002): 7.

"Esposito Brothers Dismissed." *New York Times* (October 14, 1998): D6.

Finn, Robin. "Esposito Expected to Beat Odds." *New York Times* (December 10, 1990): C3.

Finn, Robin. "Esposito Is Replacing Patrick as General Manager." *New York Times* (July 15, 1986): A25.

Finn, Robin. "Esposito Timetable Moving Too Slowly." *New York Times* (November 30, 1987): C1.

Frayne, Trent. "A deal that saved the Lightning." *Maclean's* (January 13, 1992): 44.

"Inside the NHL." *Sports Illustrated* (October 26, 1998): 86.

Lapointe, Joe. "Less Clout for Esposito Means More for Steinbrenner." *New York Times* (December 17, 1991): B15.

Scher, Jon. "Snow job in Tampa." *Sports Illustrated* (November 2, 1992): 65.

Sexton, Joe. "Candid Esposito Itemizes a Long List of Complaints on Bergeron." *New York Times* (April 12, 1989): A19.

Sexton, Joe. "Esposito Replaces Bergeron." *New York Times* (April 2, 1989): section 8, p. 1.

Sexton, Joe. "Rangers Pull a Surprise: Esposito Is Dismissed." *New York Times* (May 25, 1989): D23.

Vecsey, George. "The Big Man's Final Shot." *New York Times* (January 10, 1981): section 1, p. 17.

Wolff, Craig. "Esposito Casts His Spell Over Rangers." *New York Times* (February 23, 1987): C1.

Wolff, Craig. "Esposito Is Moving Quickly in Bid to Take Rangers to Top." *New York Times* (September 8, 1986): C14.

Wolff, Craig. "Esposito Rushes In, Drops Sator and Takes Over." *New York Times* (November 22, 1986): section 1, p. 15.

Other

"Five Questions With Phil Esposito." *Cincinnati Enquirer* (October 20, 2002). http://enquirer.com/editions/2002/10/20/spt_five_questions_with.html (December 16, 2002).

"Phil Esposito Awards." Legends of Hockey. http://www. legendsofhockey.com/Phil%Esposito/ape-awards. htm (December 16, 2002).

"Phil Esposito Stats." Legends of Hockey. http://www. legendsofhockey.com/Phil%Esposito/ape-stats.htm (December 16, 2002).

Sketch by A. Petruso

Tony Esposito
1943-

Canadian hockey player

Tony Esposito

Nicknamed "Tony O," Tony Esposito was a Hall of Fame goaltender who was an early proponent of the modern style of butterfly goaltending and the use of an unorthodox, sprawling style to make saves. Younger brother of fellow Hall of Famer **Phil Esposito**, a forward, Esposito won three Vezina Trophies as the best goaltender in the NHL (National Hockey League) playing primarily for the Chicago Blackhawks. Despite his success, Esposito claimed he didn't really enjoy being a goaltender. After retiring from playing, Esposito and his brother ran the front office of the expansion Tampa Bay Lightening for the first six years of the franchise's existence.

Esposito was born on April 23, 1943, in Sault Ste. Marie, Ontario, where he and his elder brother Phil were raised. Their father, Pat, was a construction worker. Phil Esposito was the first to play hockey as a skater, and he often joked that as the younger brother, he forced Tony to play goalie for him. As a child, Esposito learned the position by stopping shots in the driveway and in the basement. While he wanted to be a forward, but he was always put in net in pickup games.

In high school at St. Mary's College, Esposito also played football, track and field, and softball. Some believed that he was a better fullback in football than a hockey player. He quit playing goalie when he was seventeen years old to play football, but returned when asked to play junior hockey for the Sault Ste. Marie Greyhounds.

Played Junior and College Hockey

After graduating from high school, Esposito was enlisted to play goal for the junior A hockey team in Sault Ste. Marie for the 1962-63 season. The team was founded by his father and other parents. This led to a scholarship at Michigan Technical University, where Esposito played goalie for the Huskies. In his four years there, he was in goal for three seasons, beginning in 1964. He was an All-America every year, and won an NCAA championship. Esposito also earned a degree in business administration.

While playing for Michigan Tech, Esposito would visit his brother Phil, who was then playing professional hockey in the NHL for the Chicago Blackhawks. There, Esposito talked about his position with the great goaltender **Glenn Hall**, who taught him a great deal. Hall used a version of the butterfly style of goaltending which influenced Esposito's own approach. When Esposito graduated in 1967, he immediately signed with the NHL's Montreal Canadians who loaned him to the Western Hockey League's Vancouver Canucks for the rest of the 1967-68 season.

For the 1968-69 season, Esposito played on the Houston Apollos of the Central Hockey League, a farm team of the Canadiens. In nineteen games, he had a 2.42 goals against average. By this time, Esposito already had his distinctive style of goaltending. He was an early proponent of the butterfly style of goaltending. That is, he would drop to his knees to block shots and make saves. Unlike other early butterfliers, like Hall, Esposito would drop before the shot fired and stayed there after.

This was not the only aspect of Esposito's goaltending style. He would also sprawl on the ice, roam from his net, scramble—anything to make saves. He did whatever was necessary to get the job done, no matter how unorthodox. Esposito also had a quick glove. As a

Chronology

1943	Born on April 23 in Sault Ste. Marie, Ontario, Canada
1962-63	Plays for the Junior A Sault Ste. Marie Greyhounds
1963-67	Attends Michigan Technical University as scholarship athlete
1967	Graduates from Michigan Tech with degree in business; turns professional as a hockey player; plays for the Vancouver Canucks in the Western Hockey League
1968-69	Plays in 19 games for the Houston Apollos of the Central Hockey League; Joins the Montreal Canadiens for 13 games
1969	Picked up by Chicago Blackhawks in the intraleague draft
1969-84	Appears in post-season every year with the Blackhawks
1984	Retires from professional hockey after being released by the Blackhawks
1988	Becomes general manager of the Pittsburgh Penguins
1989	Fired as general manager of the Pittsburgh Penguins
1992	Becomes director of hockey operations and assistant general manager of the Tampa Bay Lightening
1998	Fired from Tampa Bay Lightening

Awards and Accomplishments

1965	Won NCAA championship with Michigan Tech; NCAA West First All-American Team; WCHA First Team All-Star; NCAA Championship All-Tournament Team
1966-67	WCHA First Team All-Star; NCAA West First All-American Team
1970	Won Vezina Trophy as NHL's best goaltender; Won Calder Trophy as best rookie; All-Star (first team); appeared in All-Star game
1971	Played in All-Star Game
1972	Won Vezina Trophy (with Gary Smith); All-Star (first team); played in All-Star Game
1973	All-Star (second team); played in All-Star Game
1974	Won Vezina Trophy (tied with Philadelphia Flyer Bernie Parent); All-Star (second team); played in All-Star game
1980	All-Star (first team); played in All-Star game
1988	Inducted into the Hockey Hall of Fame; his number 35 was retired by the Chicago Blackhawks

Newsweek contributor wrote of a game in 1970, "Against Boston last week, the pudgy, heavily padded Esposito whirled around the goal like a pirouetting pachyderm, deflecting shots with his elbows, knees, and shoulders. Occasionally he even used his stick."

Picked up by the Blackhawks

Esposito finally was called up to the Montreal Canadiens early in the 1968-69 season. He appeared in thirteen games beginning on November 29. Though he played well, Esposito was left unprotected by the Canadiens in the June intraleague draft and was picked up by the Chicago Blackhawks before the 1969-70 season.

In 1969-70, Esposito's true rookie season, Coach Billy Reay had confidence in the young netminder, making veteran Denis DeJordy his backup. Though Esposito lost the season opener in St. Louis, 7-2, he went on to win the Calder Trophy as rookie of the year and the Vezina Trophy as best goaltender. Esposito had a great rookie season—one of the best ever for a rookie goaltender. He won 38 games, 15 by shutout. The Blackhawks made it to the Stanley Cup semifinals against Boston Bruins, for which his brother Phil played, but the Blackhawks were swept in four games.

Proving his rookie season was no fluke, Esposito almost repeated as the Vezina Trophy winner in 1970-71, but missed it by seven goals. He and the Blackhawks appeared in the Stanley Cup finals that season, but lost. In 1971-72, Esposito again won Vezina Trophy with Gary Smith. They had a combined 2.12 goal against average. Esposito's own was 1.76 goals against average in the forty-eight games in which he played.

Played in Summit Series

In 1972, Esposito played in the famous Summit Series, Team Canada vs. Team USSR, on Team Canada with his brother. This was one of the only times they played to-

gether after their youth. While Esposito was supposed to be backup to number one goalie **Ken Dryden**, he ended up playing in games two, three, five, and seven. He won games two and seven, tied game three, and lost game five.

While Esposito remained a top-level goalie for the rest of his career, the Blackhawks began to slip after the 1972-73 season. That season, the team appeared in the Stanley Cup finals, but again lost. This would be the last time that Esposito would be close to winning the Cup. In 1974, he won the Vezina Trophy (tying with Bernie Parent of the Philadelphia Flyers). By the 1979-80 season, Esposito was still appearing in nearly every game for the Blackhawks, with a goals against of 2.25, but was not really happy with the team and its direction.

Esposito continued to play almost all the games in 1980-81, though the demands of travel and the games themselves were hard on his 38-year-old body. He wanted to play, and he played well. However, he had a high goals against of 3.06 because of the ineffective Chicago defense. By the 1982 season, the team improved slightly, and Esposito's play did as well. He was also involved as the head of the NHL Player's Association.

Retired as a Player

During his last season in the NHL, 1983-84, Esposito was one of the oldest players in the league, and had problems with his coach, Orval Tessier. Esposito refused to play in the last game of the regular season, after being benched when he lost on February 5. Esposito was not invited to the Chicago Blackhawks' training camp in September 1984, then was released by the team.

After the release, Esposito retired as a player. When he retired, his regular season record was 423-307-151, with seventy-six shutouts and a 2.92 goals against average. In ninety-nine playoff games, he had a 3.07 goals against average and six shutouts. While he played with the Blackhawks, the team made the playoffs every sea-

Career Statistics

Yr	Team	GP	W	L	T	GAA	TGA	SO
1968-69	Montreal	13	5	4	4	2.73	34	2
1969-70	Chicago	63	38	17	8	2.17	136	15
1970-71	Chicago	57	35	14	7	2.27	126	6
1971-72	Chicago	48	31	10	6	1.77	82	9
1972-73	Chicago	56	32	17	7	2.51	140	4
1973-74	Chicago	70	34	14	21	2.04	141	10
1974-75	Chicago	71	34	30	7	2.74	193	6
1975-76	Chicago	68	30	23	13	2.97	198	4
1976-77	Chicago	69	25	36	8	3.47	235	2
1977-78	Chicago	64	28	22	14	2.63	168	5
1978-79	Chicago	63	24	28	11	3.27	206	4
1979-80	Chicago	69	31	22	16	2.97	205	6
1980-81	Chicago	66	29	23	14	3.75	246	0
1981-82	Chicago	52	19	25	8	4.52	231	1
1982-83	Chicago	39	23	11	5	3.46	135	1
1983-84	Chicago	18	5	10	3	4.82	88	1
Total		886	423	306	151	2.92	2563	76

Chicago: Chicago Blackhawks (NHL); Montreal: Montreal Canadiens (NHL).

son. In 1988, Esposito was elected to the Hockey Hall of Fame, the same year his number was retired by the Chicago Blackhawks.

Worked as Hockey Executive

After retiring from the Blackhawks, Esposito remained connected to hockey. In his first post, he spent time with the NHL Players Association as an official. But he soon returned to more direct involvement, working in the front office of several teams.

In April 1988, Esposito was hired as director of hockey operations for the Pittsburgh Penguins. He ran the club on a day to day basis, and later named himself general manager for the struggling Penguins. During the 1988-89 season, Esposito's team was in a battle for playoff spot with his brother's team. (Phil Esposito was the general manager of the New York Rangers, in the same division as Pittsburgh). When the team continued to struggle, Esposito was fired in December 1989.

By 1992, Esposito was the director of hockey operations and assistant general manager for Tampa Bay Lightening, an expansion team. His brother was the team's general manager. The brothers were fired together in October 1998 by the team's new owner, Art Williams. It had proven hard to get the team going with money limitations imposed by the previous owners, and the Lightening had struggled since its inception.

Though Esposito had been a relatively unsuccessful hockey executive, his stylistic contributions as a goaltender and his success with the Blackhawks distinguished him. Ironically, Esposito did not enjoy his job as a professional hockey player. As he was quoted in *A Breed Apart* by Douglas Hunter, "It's a job, that's what it is, a job. I have to do it. But it's tough. I don't like it. To be playing well as a goalkeeper, you have to be afraid. Not afraid that you'll get hurt, but afraid that they're going to score on you. Every time they come down the ice with that puck, I'm afraid the puck is going to go in."

CONTACT INFORMATION

Address: 418 55th Ave., St. Petersburg. Florida 33706. Online: http://www.legendsofhockey.com (with brother, Phil Esposito).

SELECTED WRITINGS BY ESPOSITO:

(With Phil Esposito and Tim Moriarty), *The Brothers Esposito,* Hawthorn Books, 1971.
(With Phil Esposito and Kevin Walsh) *We Can Teach You To Play Hockey,* Hawthorn Books, 1972.

FURTHER INFORMATION

Books

Fischler, Stan and Shirley. *Fischlers' Hockey Encyclopedia.* New York: Thomas Y. Crowell Company, 1975.
Fischler, Stan, and Shirley Walton Fischler. *The Hockey Encyclopedia.* New York: MacMillan Publishing Company, 1984.
Hickok, Ralph. *A Who's Who of Sports Champions: Their Stories and Records.* Boston: Houghton Mifflin Company, 1995.
Hunter, Douglas. *A Breed Apart: An Illustrated History of Goaltending.* New York: Penguin Books, 1998.
Kariher, Harry C. *Who's Who in Hockey.* New Rochelle: Arlington House, 1973.

McGovern, Mike. *The Encyclopedia of Twentieth-Century Athletes.* New York: Facts on File, Inc., 2001.

Periodicals

Chia, Ken. "Esposito Likes Kodiaks' Blend." *Wisconsin State Journal* (October 22, 1999): 5B.

Clark, Cammy. "NHL's family tree has deep roots: Shinny siblings share tales of rink rivalry." *Calgary Herald* (February 23, 1997): B4.

Cummings, Roy. "Tony Esposito Might Be Moving to Phoenix." *Tampa Tribune* (May 16, 1996): 1.

Kaufman, Ira. "Bolts had Their Phil." *Tampa Tribune* (October 14, 1998): 1.

Kaufman, Ira. "Espositos' firings come as surprise." *Tampa Tribune* (October 14, 1998): 8.

Kaufman, Ira. "Espositos hold little animosity a year after their abrupt firing." *Tampa Tribune* (October 12, 1999): 5.

Minkoff, Randy. "Tony Esposito Is Ironman Goalie." *United Press International* (April 4, 1981).

"Newcomer at the Net." *Time* (March 9, 1970): 58.

"N.H.L.: Roundup-Tampa Bay; Esposito Brothers Dismissed." *New York Times* (October 14, 1998): D6.

Panaccio, Tim. "Espositos last too long in Tampa." *Florida Times-Union* (October 18, 1998): C7.

"Penguins Clean House and Bring in Patrick." *New York Times* (December 6, 1989): D31.

Rappoport. Associated Press (November 19, 1998).

"Sports People: Esposito Era Ends." *New York Times* (September 7, 1984): A18.

"Sports People: Shake-Up for Penguins." *New York Times* (April 15, 1988): D23.

"Sports People: An Unhappy Goalie." *New York Times* (April 3, 1984): B10.

Swift, E.W. "Seems Like Old Times." *Sports Illustrated* (February 20, 1995): 58.

Yannis, Alex. "Pro Hockey; Esposito Brothers Facing Off Again." *New York Times* (April 9, 1989): section 8, p. 5.

Other

"Anthony James (Tony) 'Tony O' Esposito." http://uscu.colorado.edu/~norrisdt/bio/esposito.html (November 2, 2002).

"The Legends: Players: Tony Esposito: Biography." Legends of Hockey. http://www.legendsofhockey.net:8080/LegendsOfHockey/jsp/LegendMember.jsp?type=Player&mem=P198801&list=ByName#photo (November 2, 2002).

"#35 Tony Esposito." September to Remember. http://www.1972summitseries.com/tesposito.html (November 2, 2002).

"Tony Esposito." http://www.hockeysandwich.com/tesposito.html (November 2, 2002).

"Tony Esposito Biography." http://www.legendsofhockey.com/Tony%20Esposito/ate-bio.html (November 2, 2002).

Sketch by A. Petruso

Janet Evans
1971-

American swimmer

The first American woman to win four individual Olympic gold medals in swimming, Janet Evans first took to the water while still in diapers. At the very tender age of one, Evans went into the water at the North Orange County YMCA pool, not far from her home in Placentia, California. By the time the diminutive (5 feet, 4 inches and 99 pounds) Evans was 17, she had set three world records. At the 1988 Summer Olympic Games in Seoul, South Korea, her trademark bursts of speed in the pool carried her to gold in three individual Olympic swimming events: the 400-meter and 800-meter freestyle swims and the 400-meter individual medley. Towards the end of each race, Evans would rapidly increase her stroke rate to propel her to a winning finish, often besting competitors as much as 60 pounds heavier and with longer arms and bodies. Evans, who qualified for the U.S. swim team at three successive Olympics (in 1988, 1992, and 1996), captured another gold medal at the 1992 Olympics in Barcelona and in the process became the first woman to win the 800-meter freestyle in two consecutive Olympics. Although she qualified for the American swim team at Atlanta in 1996, Evans never came close to medaling and retired from competitive swimming not long thereafter.

Born in Fullerton, California

Evans was born in Fullerton, California, on August 28, 1971. The youngest of the three children of Paul (a veterinarian) and Barbara (a homemaker) Evans, she grew up in nearby Placentia. She was walking by the time she was eight months old, and she first hit the water at the age of one, taking a brief dip in the swimming pool at the nearby North Orange County YMCA. Her mother enrolled Evans in swimming classes, and by the time she

Janet Evans

was 3 years old she was able to do both the breaststroke and the butterfly. Barbara Evans kept a close eye on her daughter's development, making sure that she ate right, got to bed on time, and adhered to her swimming practice schedule. Full of energy, Janet was always on the go, even away from the pool, tagging along with her older brothers, David and John. Of her daughter's high energy level, Barbara told *Sports Illustrated*: "When Janet was 2, she would stand in the middle of the kitchen, doing the hula hoop for 20 minutes nonstop. The only thing that seemed to calm her down was being in the water."

As a member of the Swim Team of Placentia, 10-year-old Evans broke the national record for children 10-and-under in the 200-meter freestyle. The following year she qualified for the U.S. Junior Olympics and finished 47th out of 81 swimmers participating. Officials wanted Evans to compete against younger swimmers because she was small for her age, but she refused to do so. "Janet fought and fought with one official," her mother recalled in *Sports Illustrated*. "He said, 'I think you belong with the 10-year-olds'; she said, 'I think you're wrong. This is my race.'" To compensate for her smaller stature, Evans moved her arms and legs faster than her opponents. "I never saw myself as being small," she told *Sports Illustrated*. "Size doesn't matter as long as you can get to the end of the pool faster than everybody else." To be sure she could do this, Evans threw herself into training with a vengeance. She got up each morning at five to practice before attending classes at El Dorado High School. After school, she lifted weights and rode an exercise bike before hitting the pool once again in the late afternoon.

Hard Work Pays Off

All of Evans' hard work paid off. In 1986 she qualified to compete in the Goodwill Games, held in Moscow, where she finished third in both the 800-meter and 1500-meter freestyle events. At the U.S. Open, later in the year, she won the 400- and 800-meter freestyle events, as well as the 400-meter individual medley. The following year at the U.S. Long Course Championship, Evans set world records in both the 800- and 1500-meter freestyle events. Not long thereafter, competing in the U.S. Indoor Championships, she set a new world record

in the 400-meter freestyle race. At the 1988 U.S. Olympic Trials, Evans won the 400- and 800-meter freestyle events and the 400-meter individual medley while breaking her own records in the 800- and 1500-meter freestyle events.

At 17, Evans was the youngest and smallest member of the U.S. women's swim team at the Seoul Olympics in 1988. But neither her youth nor her diminutive stature in any way kept her from turning in a stellar performance in the Olympic pool. Evans won gold in the 400-meter freestyle, setting a new world record. She also won the 800-meter freestyle race, setting a new Olympic record. Evans' third gold medal came in the 400-meter individual medley, in which she set a new American record. Her performance made her only the fifth woman ever to have won three or more gold medals in individual (as opposed to team) swimming events. As the only member of the U.S. Olympic women's swim team to win a medal in an individual event, she became an overnight star. "I'm proud of myself for not giving in," Evans told reporters. "I didn't skip workouts. I couldn't have won a gold medal if I did that. Not to be boastful or anything like that, but you have to be proud of yourself if you win an Olympic gold medal. To know all the work paid off. I accomplished my goal."

Continues to Break Records

Evans continued to break records after her brilliant performance at the Seoul Olympics. At the Pan Pacific

---

Related Biography: Coach Richard Quick

An important force in Evans' swimming career was Richard Quick, a longtime Olympic coach and the coach of the women's swimming and diving programs at Stanford University for more than 15 years. Quick was the head coach of the men's and women's swim teams at the 1988 Olympics in Seoul, South Korea, assistant coach of the women's team in 1992 in Barcelona, Spain, and head coach of the women's team in Atlanta, Georgia, the three Olympics in which Evans participated. In addition Quick was assistant coach of the men's and women's swim teams at the 1984 Olympics and head coach of the women's team at the 2000 Olympics.

Born in Akron, Ohio, Quick was raised mostly in Austin, Texas, where he learned to swim under the tutelage of coach Bill Crenshaw at the Austin Aquatics Club. After graduating from high school, Quick attended Southern Methodist University (SMU), where he was an All-American swimmer in 1965 and 1966. He began his coaching career at Spring Branch Memorial High School in Houston, Texas, where he guided the school's swim team to six state championships. Quick next served as assistant coach for the men's team at SMU, his alma mater. In 1976 he launched the women's swimming program at SMU. He later served as head coach at Iowa State University, Auburn, and the University of Texas. In the fall of 1988, he took over as head coach of the women's team at Stanford, guiding the team to multiple NCAA national titles.

Awards and Accomplishments

1984	Wins 1500-meter freestyle at U.S. Junior Nationals
1986	Finishes third in 800- and 1500-meter freestyle events at Goodwill Games
1987, 1989-90	Named World Swimmer of the Year
1988	Wins gold in 400- and 800-meter freestyle and 400-meter individual medley at Seoul Olympics
1989	Sets new world record in 800-meter freestyle at Pan Pacific Games
1992	Wins gold in 800-meter freestyle and silver in 400-meter freestyle at Barcelona Olympics
1996	Finishes sixth in 800-meter freestyle at Atlanta Olympics

---

Games in 1989, she broke her own world record in the 800-meter freestyle. At the 1992 Goodwill Games, she won the 400-, 800-, and 1500-meter freestyle races and finished second in the 400-meter individual medley. At the 1992 Olympic trials for the summer games in Barcelona, Evans handily qualified for the 400- and 800-meter freestyle events but failed to qualify for the 400-meter individual medley. At the Barcelona games themselves, Evans won gold in the 800-meter freestyle but had to settle for silver in the 400-meter freestyle event. With her gold medal-winning victory in the 800-meter event, she became only the third American woman to win four gold Olympic medals (the others being sprinter **Evelyn Ashford** and diver **Pat McCormick**). Their record for gold medals was eventually broken by speed skater **Bonnie Blair**, who won a total of five.

Although Evans continued to compete after the Barcelona Olympics, few observers of the swimming scene expected her to be able to qualify for the 1996 Olympics. To their surprise, she once again qualified to compete for the United States in both the 400- and 800-meter freestyle, despite torn ligaments in her left foot. However, the competition at Atlanta proved too tough for her, and she finished sixth in the 800-meter event and failed to qualify for the finals in the 400-meter freestyle. Following her last Olympic performance, Evans told reporters, "I had my highs and lows, but I wouldn't give it [her swimming career] up for the world." Shortly thereafter, she announced her retirement from competitive swimming. In an interview with the *Chicago Tribune,* Evans admitted there were some things she wouldn't miss. "The chlorine makes my feet sore and dries all my skin, and I hate that. My hair sometimes gets yucky. I always wanted long hair, but I could never have it. I can do everything I wanted to do as a kid after I quit."

Named in her honor, the Janet Evans Invitational is sponsored by the University of Southern California. The event annually draws up to 800 of the best swimmers in the United States. Although she has not actively competed for several years, Evans will be forever remembered as one of the greatest female distance swimmers in American history.

CONTACT INFORMATION

Address: Janet Evans, 8 Barneburg, Dove Canyon, CA 92679-4210.

FURTHER INFORMATION

Books

"Janet Evans." *Great Women in Sports.* Visible Ink Press, 1996.
"Janet Evans." *Newsmakers 1989,* Issue 4. Gale Research, 1989.
"Janet Evans." *Sports Stars,* Series 1-4. U•X•L, 1994-1998.

Periodicals

Dugard, Martin. "No Fish Out of Water." *Runner's World,* (March 1994): 36.
Skow, John. "One Last Splash." *Time,* (Summer 1996): 60.

Other

"Evans, Janet: Swimming." HickokSports.com. http://www.hickoksports.com/biograph/evansjanet.shtml (January 27, 2003).
"Janet Evans (USA)." International Swimming Hall of Fame. http://www.ishof.org/01jevans.html (January 27, 2003).
"The Perfect Race: Janet Evans." USA Swimming. http://www.usswim.org/superstars/template.pl?opt=news&pubid=2405 (January 27, 2003).
"Richard Quick: Profile." Stanford Cardinal. http://gostanford.ocsn.com/sports/w-swim/mtt/quick_richard00.html (January 27, 2003).

"Richard Quick (USA)." International Swimming Hall of Fame. http://www.ishof.org/00rquick.html (January 27, 2003).

Sketch by Don Amerman

Chris Evert

Chris Evert
1954-

American tennis player

In the 1970s and 1980s, Chris Evert was one of the most dominant and popular women's tennis players in the United States and the world, influencing many young players to try the game. Over the course of her professional tennis career, she won 157 titles and 1300 matches, including eighteen singles titles at Grand Slam events. She had a winning percentage of more than 90 percent. Evert was the first woman tennis player to win $1 million playing professional tennis, and went on to earn over $9 million before she retired in 1989. As Janet Woolum wrote in *Outstanding Women Athletes,* "She symbolized the best of women's athletics in America: drive, determination, skill, professionalism, and grace."

Evert was born on December 21, 1954, in Fort Lauderdale, Florida, the second child of Jimmy and Colette Evert. Jimmy Evert had been a decent tennis player in his day, winning as a junior and in some single men's tournaments. He was employed as a teaching tennis professional and tennis park manager in Florida. Evert began playing tennis at the age of six at Holiday Park Tennis Center where her father was the teaching pro. Her two brothers and two sisters also played, though only her younger sister Jeanne became a ranked professional player.

Early Promise

Evert was a good tennis player from an early age, and her father, who served as a coach for much of her career (late in her career she turned to Dennis Ralston), had her practicing every day from the time she was a young child. She primarily played on clay courts, a surface on which she would dominate as an adult.

By the time Evert was ten years old, she was winning local junior tournaments. Evert's style of play already had many of the trademarks of her adult game. She played from the baseline, focusing on groundstrokes that were carefully placed and strongly hit. Because she was such a small child (and only 5'5" and 115 lbs as an adult) and did not have the strength to use

a one-handed backhand, she developed her own two-handed backhand. Because of her success with the stroke, her father/coach did not change it. It became trademark of her game. She later became a better volleyer than she was often given credit for, but she had to learn to like coming to the net.

Because Evert was not a very athletic person, she practiced hard, working especially to enhance her mental focus and great concentration so she could outwit her competition. This focus also gave her the ability to outlast her opponents. Her father taught her not to show a lot of emotion on the court because it would intimidate her opponent. Her coolness on the court became a another trademark of her adult game. While it lead to nicknames like "The Ice Maiden," her real personality was very different. Evert's smart game was considered boring but influential in how others played tennis.

Teenage Victory over Court

By the time Evert was a teenager, she competed in a number of junior tournaments in singles as well as doubles and did well. At the age of fifteen, Evert defeated arguably the best female tennis player at the time, the number one ranked **Margaret Smith Court** (who had just completed the Grand Slam), during a ladies' clay court tournament in North Carolina, the Carolinas, in the semifinals. Evert lost to Nancy Richey in the finals.

Chronology

1954	Born December 21 in Fort Lauderdale, Florida
1971	Makes the semifinals of the U.S. Open, losing to Billie Jean King
1972	Makes the semifinals of Wimbledon—losing to Evonne Goolagong; wins the Virginia Slims championship as an amateur
1973	Turns professional as a tennis player
1973-79	From August 1973 to May 1979, does not lose a clay court match
1976-77	Plays World Team Tennis for Phoenix
1979	Marries tennis player John Lloyd on April 17
1983	Elected president for the first of nine terms of the Women's International Tennis Association
1986	Suffers knee injury
1987	Divorces John Lloyd in April
1988	Plays on the U.S. Olympic Tennis Team; marries Andy Mill
1989	Retires as a professional tennis player
1991	Son Alexander James born on October 12

Related Biography: Coach Dennis Ralston

One of the few coaches that Chris Evert worked with in addition to her father was Dennis Ralston. Ralston had impressive tennis credentials of his own. As a player, he played college tennis for the University of Southern California, and won several Grand Slams in men's doubles. He won Wimbledon with Rafe Osuna in 1960, and three U.S. Opens with Chuck McKinley in 1961, 1963 and 1964. As a singles player, Ralston was ranked in the top ten in the United States from 1960-67, and went to the finals of Wimbledon in 1966. He played Davis Cup tennis as both a player (winning in 1963) and a coach (winning in 1968-72). He later was an influential varsity tennis coach at Southern Methodist University. Ralston was inducted into the International Tennis Hall of Fame in 1987.

When Evert was sixteen, she began playing on the women's tennis circuit as an amateur. Though tennis was her focus, she continued to attend high school at St. Thomas Aquinas High School in Fort Lauderdale, Florida, from which she later graduated. She had no social life outside of school and tennis. Before she played in the U.S. Open in 1971, she won forty-six straight singles titles. Her first victory came in the Virginia Slims Master's Tournament in St. Petersburg, Florida, in 1972. Evert would later win the tournament as a professional in 1973, 1975, and 1977.

Played in Grand Slams as Amateur

In 1971, when Evert was only sixteen, she played in her first Grand Slam, appearing the U.S. Open. Evert defeated four ranked players to make it to the semifinals, where she lost to **Billie Jean King**. The following year, Evert played in her first Wimbledon. She again lost in the semifinals, losing to **Evonne Goolagong**.

Evert's talent led her to international play for the United States. In 1971, she was selected to play Wightman Cup tennis. When she began, she was one of the youngest on the team. Evert ended up playing on the 1971-73, 1975, and 1977 through 1985 teams, winning the twenty-six singles matches she played. The U.S. team won the Cup eleven times during her tenure. Evert also played Federation Cup tennis from 1977 to 1980, 1982, and 1989.

Turned Professional

On her eighteenth birthday, Evert turned professional, beginning her career on the United States Lawn Tennis Association (USLTA) circuit. She won their championship from 1975-78, and in 1980 and 1982. Though she was young, tennis was the defining aspect of her life. She told Sally Jenkins of *Sports Illustrated*

in 1992, "I was very insecure when I was young. I was shy and introverted. When I went out on the tennis court, I could express myself. It was a way of getting reactions from people, like my father. I really admired my dad and put him on a pedestal, and I wanted his attention. Whether it's ego or insecurity or whatever, when you start winning and getting attention, you like it, and that feeling snowballs. You start to feel good about yourself. You feel complete and proud of yourself." As Evert told Christopher Whipple of *Life* in 1986, "When I was younger I was a little robot: Wind her up and she plays tennis."

Evert dominated on the court from earliest days as a professional. From August 1973 through May 1979, she did not lose one match on clay courts. This was 125 straight matches on the surface best suited to her game. During this span, she won the French Open, which was played on clay, in 1974, 1975, and 1979. It was in 1974 that she began to blossom as a professional. In addition to winning the French Open, her first Grand Slam win, she won Wimbledon, and the Italian and Canadian championships.

Evert played many of these early matches on television, the beginnings of when some women's sports began to air. One aspect of the 1974 win at Wimbledon was made for television. At the time, she was engaged to men's tennis star **Jimmy Connors**, who won the men's singles title. It was dubbed the "summer of love." Evert's first career year was also highlighted by the fact that she was ranked number one on the USLTA, the youngest woman to be number one in decades.

After her 1974 wins at the French Open and Wimbledon, Evert won at least one Grand Slam women's singles title until 1986. In the mid-1970s, she won at least two, as well as a number of women's doubles titles, and was ranked number one in the world from 1975-77. In 1976, Evert was named *Sports Illustrated*'s sportswoman of the year. In 1977, she was named the Associated Press's Female Athlete of the Year. In this time, Evert also played World Team Tennis for Phoenix, from 1976-77. She later won a World Team Tennis championship with Los Angeles.

Chris Evert

Awards and Accomplishments

1971	Lebair Sportsmanship Trophy
1972	Won the Virginia Slims championship as an amateur
1973	Won the Virginia Slims championship
1974	Won the French Open and Wimbledon; won French Open doubles with Olga Morozova; named Associated Press Female Athlete of the Year
1975	Won the French Open; won the U.S. Open; won the Virginia Slims championship ranked number one player in the world; won both French Open and Wimbledon doubles tournament with Martina Navratilova; Associated Press Female Athlete of the Year
1976	Won Wimbledon; won the U.S. Open; named *Sports Illustrated*'s sportswoman of the year; ranked number one player in the world
1977	Won the U.S. Open; won the Virginia Slims championship; ranked number one player in the world; Associated Press Female Athlete of the Year
1978	Won the U.S. Open; ILTA (International Lawn Tennis Association) World Champion; won World Team Tennis Championship with Los Angeles
1979	Won the French Open; Women's International Tennis Association (WITA) Karan Krantzcke Sportsmanship Award
1980	Won the French Open; won the U.S. Open; ranked number one player in the world; Associated Press Female Athlete of the Year; ILTA World Champion
1981	Won Wimbledon; ranked number one player in the world; ILTA World Champion; named Sportswoman of the Year, Women's Sports Foundation; inductee, International Women's Sports Hall of Fame; Women's International Tennis Association Player Service Award winner
1982	Won the Australian Open; won the U.S. Open; USLTA Service Bowl winner
1983	Won the French Open
1984	Won the Australian Open
1985	Won the French Open
1986	Won the French Open; WITA Player Service Award
1987	WITA Player Service Award
1989	Won five singles matches in Federation Cup competition, as U.S. won the Cup
1990	Won the Flo Hyman Award from the Women's Sports Foundation
1995	Elected into the International Tennis Hall of Fame
1997	Awarded ITF Phillippe Chartier Award for lifetime contribution to the game

Rivalry with Navratilova

By the late 1970s and into the early 1980s, Evert had a foe whose talent matched hers on the court. **Martina Navratilova** was a Czechoslovakian who had emigrated to the United States in the early 1970s. Unlike Evert, Navratilova played a serve-and-volley game and had more potent athletic skills. Their rivalry began in 1973, but Evert dominated many of their matches through the late 1970s. The pair often faced each other at Grand Slam and other big tournaments. Navratilova's first significant victory came when she defeated Evert at the Wimbledon finals in 1978. Navratilova went to defeat her in four additional Wimbledon finals. By the mid to late 1980s, Navratilova began to dominate Evert.

Over the course of their rivalry, Navratilova won forty of seventy-six singles matches, but lost twenty of the first twenty-four. Off the court, the pair were actual-ly friends. They even won the French Open and Wimbledon doubles title in 1975. Evert said that near the end of the career, it was her rivalry with Navratilova kept her playing for five or six more years. As Frank Deford wrote in *Sports Illustrated* in 1986, "Chris, the more consistent, casts the longer shadow, while Martina, the more sensational, shines the brighter light. Together, they form a complete whole. There never has been a rivalry like it in women's sports."

Married John Lloyd

Evert's personal life also changed in this time period. She was married to John Lloyd, a British tennis player, in 1979, and was known as Chris Evert-Lloyd until their divorce in 1987. There were problems in marriage in part because she wanted to continue her career in earnest and he did not. Winning was more important to her than Lloyd, and she felt she had more game in her.

In the early part of her marriage, Evert's victories proved this to be true. In 1980, she was again the number one ranked player in the world, winning both the French and U.S. Opens. In 1981, she was again the number one player in the world, and won Wimbledon. But there was a fall-off in the early part of the 1980s after this. She lost

Where Is She Now?

After retiring, Evert remained connected to tennis by serving as a commentator for NBC sports for Wimbledon and French Open and the BBC and other networks for major tennis events. She also served on the boards of the International Tennis Hall of Fame and the Women's Sports Foundation. In 1997, she, her father, and brother John founded the Evert Tennis Academy in which Evert was actively involved. She was also named publisher of *Tennis Magazine* in 2000. Though she occasionally played on the Virginia Slims Legends Tour, she avoided the senior tournament circuit. She was inducted into the International Tennis Hall of Fame in 1995.

Evert focused much of her time raising her three sons with Andy Mill, Alexander, Nicholas, and Colton, and doing charity work. In 1989, she founded Chris Evert Charities, Inc., and served on the boards of numerous charitable foundations. In addition, Evert was in demand for commercials endorsements and did them for such companies as Nike, Wavex, and Rolex.

in the third round of Wimbledon in 1983, the first time she had lost before the semifinals in her thirty-four Grand Slam appearances as a professional. Though she had a stomach virus, her game was not as potent this time period as the players she faced were more athletic. At that time, Evert changed her training to work on the weak parts of her game (second services, attacking shortballs) and included weight work and aerobics. Her game soon improved. Even during this transition, however, Evert did win at least one Grand Slam, including three French Opens in 1983, 1985, and 1986.

By 1988, Evert was nearing the end of her playing career. She married Andy Mill, an American downhill skier that year, and also played for the U.S. Olympic tennis team, though she did not medal. Evert did not play well during her last two years on the women's tennis tour. She even skipped the French Open in 1989 because she was not playing up to her standards.

Retired as Tennis Player

Evert's last official tournament was the 1989 U.S. Open. She lost in the quarterfinals to Zina Garrison. Evert found it to be mentally tiring to play through early rounds, though physically, she was fitter than ever. By this point, she had wanted to retire for the two previous years, but could not. She told Robin Finn of the *New York Times,* "Until this year I always had the feeling that I was going for the grand slam tournaments and that I had a chance to be No. 1. But this year I felt, 'Well, it's tough,' and I didn't want to make that emotional commitment, and even if I did, I knew there'd be no guarantee." After the U.S. Open, she played for her country in Federation Cup competition. The U.S. won the Cup, and Evert won all the singles matches she played. After this, the only tennis she played in were some exhibition matches with Navratilova.

When Evert retired in 1989, she never was ranked lower than four as a singles player. (She was number four when she retired.) She had won more than $9 million in money, and was the first player ever to win 157

tournaments and 1000 matches—the best at the time. As George Vecsey wrote in the *New York Times,* "If there was one thing Christine Marie Evert never was, it was average. She stood apart, cool and methodical as a teenager, poised and commanding as a young woman, and then, best of all, she re-created herself through exercise and more daring strokes in her final years, just to stay close to **[Steffi] Graf** and Navratilova. If she hadn't, it would have ended years ago."

CONTACT INFORMATION

Address: c/o Evert Tennis Academy, 10334 Diego Dr. South, Boca Raton, FL 33428.

SELECTED WRITINGS BY EVERT:

(With Neil Amdur) *Chrissie, My Own Story,* Simon & Schuster, 1982.
(With John Lloyd and Carol Thatcher) *Lloyd on Lloyd,* Beaufort Books, 1986.
(Curry Kirkpatrick) "Tennis was my showcase." *Sports Illustrated* (August 28, 1989): 72.

FURTHER INFORMATION

Books

Christensen, Karen, et al., eds. *International Encyclopedia of Women and Sports.* New York: Macmillan Reference USA, 2001.
Collins, Bud, and Zander Hollander, eds. *Bud Collins' Modern Encyclopedia of Tennis.* Detroit: Gale, 1992.
Johnson, Anne Janette. *Great Women in Sports.* Detroit: Visible Ink Press, 1996.
Parry, Melanie, ed. *Chambers Biographical Dictionary.* Chambers, 1997.
Sherrow, Victoria. *Encyclopedia of Women and Sports.* ABC-CLIO, 1996.
Woolum, Janet. *Outstanding Women Athletes: Who They Are and How They Influenced Sports in America.* Oryx Press, 1992.

Periodicals

Alfano, Peter. "Evert's Retirement Plan Includes a Cutback in her Schedule." *New York Times* (January 28, 1989): section 1, p. 47.
Berkow, Ira. "The Lady Was Deadly." *New York Times* (August 31, 1989): D19.
Callahan, Tom. "Fire over ice, in three sets." *Time* (July 15, 1985): 66.
Cunningham, Kim. "Where the boy is?." *People* (April 8, 1996): 132.
Deford, Frank. "The Day Chrissie reclaimed Paris." *Sports Illustrated* (June 17, 1985): 28.

Deford, Frank. "A pair beyond compare." *Sports Illustrated* (May 26, 1986): 70.

"Evert to Serve as Tennis Publisher." *Mediaweek* (December 11, 2000): 56.

Finn, Robin. "Back to Where It All Began." *New York Times* (August 28, 1989): C7.

Finn, Robin. "Evert Bows out as Garrison Prevails, 7-6, 6-2." *New York Times* (September 6, 1989): D21.

Finn, Robin. "Legendary Rivals and Close Friends." *New York Times* (May 6, 1998): C1.

Grant, Meg. "It's game, set, love match for Chris Evert and skier Andy Mill." *People* (August 15, 1988): 96.

Jenkins, Sally. "I've lived a charmed life." *Sports Illustrated* (May 25, 1992): 60.

Johnson, Bonnie, and Meg Grant. "Special delivery." *Sports Illustrated* (November 25, 1991): 114.

Kirkpatrick, Curry. "A stunning string is broken." *Sports Illustrated* (July 4, 1983): 54.

Navratilova, Martina. "A great friend and foe." *Sports Illustrated* (August 28, 1989): 88.

PR Newswire, July 11, 1997.

"Tennis great never wants to feel the pressure again." *Minneapolis Star Tribune* (October 11, 1996): 2C.

Time (April 13, 1987): 74.

Vecsey, George. "Game, Set, Match, Career." *New York Times* (September 6, 1989): D21.

Whipple, Christopher. "Chrissie." *Life* (June 1986): 64.

Other

"Chris Evert." BBC Sport/Tennis/Wimbledon/BBC coverage. http://news.bbc.co.uk/sport1/hi/tennis/ wimbledon/bbc_coverage/20 (January 1, 2003).

"Chris Evert Tennis Academy." http://www.evertacademy. com/ (January 1, 2003).

"Dennis Ralston." International Tennis Hall of Fame. http://www.tennisfame.org/enshrinees/dennis_ ralston.html (January 5, 2003).

"Evert Tennis Academy-The Vision." http://www. evertacademy.com/vision/htm (January 1, 2003).

Sketch by A. Petruso

Weeb Ewbank

Weeb Ewbank
1907-1998

American football coach

Weeb Ewbank was small in stature, and could often get lost on the sideline among the players he coached. But he had a large heart and was well liked by most everyone he encountered. As head coach with the Baltimore Colts (1954-1962) and then with the New York Jets (1963-1973), he would mentor some of the great names in professional football. He also coached the winning team in two of most famous games in NFL history, the 1958 NFL Championships and Super Bowl III. Ewbank spent forty-six years in football and coached at every level. He was the only coach to win championships in both NFL (2 with the Colts) and AFL (with Jets). He died at the age of ninety-one in 1998.

Growing Up

Charles "Weeb" Ewbank was born on May 6, 1907, in Richmond, Indiana, to Mr. and Mrs. Charles Ewbank, and would grow up in the Fairview area of Richmond, the son of a grocery store owner. At nine, Weeb was delivering orders for his father in a horse-drawn wagon. As a teenager, he would find his way to Dayton, Ohio, to watch **Jim Thorpe** play for the Canton Bulldogs.

At Oliver P. Morton High School, Ewbank was a three-sport star. He married his wife Lucy—whom he would remain married to for sixty-nine years—while still attending high school. In order to earn extra money, he played semi-pro ball. He went on to play football and baseball in college.

The Early Years

After Ewbank graduated from college, he taught and coached at Van Wert High School in Ohio. He made only $2000 a year for his position, since he took the job as the Depression hit, and he learned lessons about frugality that would stick with him the rest of his life. When he made it into professional football and earned a pretty good living, he was never flashy, and he often told his players with bigger contracts to keep quiet about them. He was embarrassed by all the money in the game, and didn't want the lower-paid players to find out (salaries weren't as public then as they are now).

Later he would coach at Oxford-McGuffey High School and lead his team to seventy-one wins and only twenty-one losses in thirteen years. This included a twenty-one game winning streak, where his team outscored their opponents 270 to 0.

Football is like a family in Ohio, and Ewbank was a member of a pretty important family. During the war he had served as an assistant coach for **Paul Brown** during his time in the armed forces at the Great Lakes Naval Training Base outside of Chicago. In 1949, Paul Brown hired Ewbank to serve as his assistant in charge of tacklers and kickers for the Cleveland Browns. Weeb was uneasy about such specialization, but Brown convinced him, and he excelled at line coach. Ewbank, like Brown, had played quarterback in high school and college, stressed pass protection. He revolutionized pass blocking.

The Baltimore Colts were founded in 1953, and Ewbank would soon take over, leaving the Browns to become the Colts head coach in 1954. He had quite a task in front of him. Art Donovan would say that most of the team was "awful," and claim there were guys on that club who "couldn't make a good high school team." Ewbank's first task was to find a quarterback, and he signed **Johnny Unitas** in 1955.

Coached in Memorable Games

Ewbank had the distinction of coaching in history-making games. He coached the first sudden death overtime victory title game, in 1958, as coach of the Colts. When the game ended in a 17-17 tie at the end of regulation, no one knew what to do, but they eventually figured it out, setting a precedent for the league.

He also coached in the "Heidi Bowl." On an NBC televised game, with sixty-five seconds remaining, Ewbank's Jets kicked a field goal to take a 32-29 lead over the Raiders in Oakland. At that point, it was 7 p.m. EST, and NBC cut off its coverage of the game with fifty seconds remaining (except on the West Coast) to begin the two-hour children's movie "Heidi." Jets fans were livid, especially when they learned that the Raiders came back to score two touchdowns in nine seconds to win 43-32.

Ewbank was with the Cleveland Browns in their 1950 NFL debut against the Philadelphia Eagles. And then, in what was probably his sweetest victory, coached the Jets, with **Joe Namath** at the helm, to an upset in Super Bowl III over his former team, the Baltimore Colts. Ewbank was also on the sidelines in the 1970 debut of Monday Night Football, picking up a win against Cleveland.

Though he won a championship with Unitas, Ewbank was fired after the 1962 season, to be replaced by thirty-three-year-old coach **Don Shula**. When he went to the New York Jets as head coach and general manager in 1963, he needed just five seasons to take Jets to the Super Bowl. Jets owner Sonny Werblin had signed Joe Namath to a $400,000 contract-the richest in team sports at the time. Namath proved to be the catalyst the team needed.

The Later Years

Ewbank retired in 1974. A quiet man, he seldom got angry with his players, and he didn't do much boat-rocking, so the media rarely paid him much attention. Ewbank just happened to be in the right place when major events took place. He helped shape the game of football, helping make it what it is today. The "no-huddle" offense can be attributed to Ewbank. He was known for working with a simple offense, making it only as complicated as need be to cover all necessary tasks.

Weeb Ewbank had a big heart. He remained married to Lucy for sixty-nine years, had three daughters, many grandchildren and great-grandchildren. Over half a century later, Weeb could still remember the names and positions of the players he coached back in Ohio. When he passed away on November 17, 1998, at his home in Oxford, Ohio, Ewbank left behind quite a legacy. At his funeral, many of his former players were there—including Namath—but were too choked up to make any comments.

SELECTED WRITINGS BY EWBANK:

Football Greats, Chalice Press, 1977.

FURTHER INFORMATION

Books

Ewbank, Weeb. *Football Greats*. Chalice Press, 1977.
Hickok, Ralph. *A Who's Who of Sports Champions.* New York: Houghton Mifflin, Co., 1995.
Mendell, Ronald L., and Timothy Phares. *Who's Who in Football*. New Rochester, New York, 1974.
Zimmerman, Paul. *Last Season of Weeb Ewbank*. New York: Farrar Straus & Giroux, 1974.

Periodicals

Clark, Jan. "Wilbur 'Weeb' Ewbank." (obituary) *Palladium-Item* (Ohio) (November 18, 1998): 34.
Mravic, Mark and Kostya Kennedy. "A Coach with Nothing To Hide." *Sports Illustrated* (November 30, 1998): 34.
Time (November 30, 1998): 35.

Other

Didinger, Ray. "Weeb Ewbank." http://www.superbowl. com/xxxvi/insider/weeb_xxx.html/ (October 25, 2002).
Wallace, Bill. "Remembering Weeb: Slightly unconventional, Ewbank was loved by his players." http:// archive.profootballweekly.com/content/archives/ features_1998/wallace_112398.asp (October 25, 2002).

Sketch by Eric Lagergren

Patrick Ewing
1962-

American basketball player

Patrick Ewing

Named in 1996 one of the top NBA players of all time, Patrick Ewing was an NBA All-Star eleven times, including for ten seasons in a row, from 1988-97. A center for the New York Knicks for fifteen years starting in 1986, Ewing set team records for the most games played, (1,039), most points scored (23,665), most rebounds (10,759), most steals (1,061), and most blocked shots (2,758). Ewing is also an Olympic gold medalist, helping Team USA to victory in the 1984 and 1992 Olympic games.

Born in Jamaica

Patrick Ewing was born in Kingston, Jamaica in 1962. His father, Carl, was a mechanic at the time, and his mother, Dorothy, was a homemaker. Dorothy conceived of a better life for her children in the United States, and she moved to Cambridge, Massachusetts in 1971 to pave the way for a family move there. She took a job as a kitchen worker in a hospital, and brought her family over one by one. In 1975, at twelve years of age, Patrick Ewing joined his mother and four of his siblings who had immigrated before him. His father eventually found work in a rubber hose factory.

Ewing had never even seen a basketball before his arrival in the United States, much less played the game that was later to make him famous. Soccer is the sport most played in Jamaica, and that was the game he played as a youngster. But he became fascinated by

Chronology

1962	Born August 5 in Kingston, Jamaica
1975	Moves to Cambridge, Massachusetts
1984	Son Patrick Ewing Jr. is born
1984	Wins gold medal on the U.S. Olympic basketball team in Los Angeles
1985	Graduates from Georgetown University with a B.A. degree
1985	Signs as a player for the New York Knicks basketball team
1986	Named NBA Rookie of the Year
1992	Winds gold medal on the U.S. Olympic basketball team in Barcelona
1996	Named one of the top 59 players in NBA history
2000	Leaves the Knicks for the Seattle Supersonics
2001	Leaves the Supersonics for the Orlando Magic
2002	Retires from playing, signs as assistant coach with the Washington Wizards

Awards and Accomplishments

1984	Plays on gold-medal-winning U.S. Olympic basketball team
1984	Plays on NCAA-championship-winning team, the Georgetown Hoyas
1985-86	Named to the All-Rookie First Team
1985-86, 1988-89, 1991-92	Named to the NBA All-Defensive Second Team
1986	Named Rookie of the Year
1987-89, 1990-93, 1996-97	Named to the All-NBA Second Team
1989-90	Named to the All-NBA First team
1992	Played on gold-medal-winning U.S. Olympic basketball team
1996	Named among the top 59 players in NBA history
1996	Inducted into the Madison Square Garden Walk of Fame

basketball only weeks into his new life as an American. Walking past a playground where other children played basketball, he would often stop and watch. One day, he was asked by the other kids if he wanted to join a game, and he began what was to become a career. Playing basketball did not come easily for the future superstar. "I knew that it was something I'd have to work at," he later told Roy S. Johnson in the *New York Times*.

"Something I'd Have to Work At"

Hard work did indeed become the mainstay of Ewing's early basketball career. Ewing attended high school at Latin High School in Cambridge, where he reached his full height of seven feet, and played on the school basketball team under coach Mike Jarvis. Jarvis, and his later college coach, John Thompson, both later recalled for reporters that they often tried to curtail Ewing's unusually long and hard practice sessions for fear that he would hurt himself or a teammate out of sheer exhaustion.

Ewing also had to overcome the racist attitudes of some of his opposing team members and those who were jealous of his success. Coach Jarvis helped him through the worst of it, drawing on his own experience of growing up black in America. "You have to understand how it hits you," Jarvis told Jackie MacMullan in the *Boston Globe*. "I can still remember the first time someone called me that. I was riding my bicycle, and I heard it. …You don't ever forget that. But if you are Patrick, you start to realize very early in life it's part of the territory."

Through it all, Ewing learned to grow a thick skin, developing a reputation for being unemotional and ruthless on the court, and reluctant to give interviews. As he told MacMullan in the *Boston Globe* of this time, "Everyone looked at me like some kind of freak. The older guys taunted me. They told me I would never be anything. They said I would never learn the game. At first, I couldn't understand why they said those things. But I got used to it. And I learned not to let what anyone said affect me."

Basketball's "Most Important Figure"

By the time he was in college at Georgetown University, Ewing was already being called by Roy S. Johnson of *New York Times* basketball's "most important figure for the future." Ewing excelled on the Georgetown basketball team, helping his team to three NCAA championship games, one of which they won. Ewing's mother never got to see her son's championship game, which took place in 1984; she died in 1983 at the age of fifty-five. She had worked at her job in the hospital kitchen up until two days before her death.

With pro basketball offers pouring in while he was still at Georgetown, Ewing could have easily dropped out of school and immediately become a millionaire. But his mother had always felt that the key realizing the opportunities she felt America had to offer was to get a college degree, and so, Ewing stayed in school. Also, as he explained at the time to Johnson in the *New York Times*, "Money's never been the most important thing in my life."

In 1984, while he was still in college, Ewing played on the U.S. men's basketball team in the Olympic games, which took place in Los Angeles. His team took home the gold medal. It was a big year for Ewing; he also fathered a son by a girlfriend, Sharon D. Stanford. Patrick Ewing Jr. was born May 20, 1984, and he too went on to become an outstanding basketball player.

At the Top of His Game

Ewing graduated from Georgetown in 1985 with a bachelor of arts degree in theology. In attendance were his father Carl and his siblings. The New York Knicks were given first pick of players in a lottery for new players in May, 1985, and as was widely expected, they chose Ewing.

Career Statistics

Yr	Team	GP	PTS	FG%	3P%	FT%	RPG	APG	SPG	BPG	TO	PF
1985-86	NY	50	20.0	.474	.000	.739	9.0	2.0	1.08	2.06	3.44	3.80
1986-87	NY	63	21.5	.503	.000	.713	8.8	1.7	1.41	2.33	3.63	3.90
1987-88	NY	82	20.2	.555	.000	.716	8.2	1.5	1.27	2.99	3.50	4.00
1988-89	NY	80	22.7	.567	.000	.746	9.2	2.4	1.46	3.51	3.33	3.90
1989-90	NY	82	28.6	.551	.250	.775	10.9	2.2	.95	3.99	3.39	4.00
1990-91	NY	81	26.6	.514	.000	.745	11.2	3.0	.99	3.19	3.59	3.50
1991-92	NY	82	24.0	.522	.167	.738	11.2	1.9	1.07	2.99	2.55	3.40
1992-93	NY	81	24.2	.503	.143	.719	12.1	1.9	.91	1.99	3.27	3.50
1993-94	NY	79	24.5	.496	.286	.765	11.2	2.3	1.14	2.75	3.29	3.50
1994-95	NY	79	23.9	.503	.286	.750	11.0	2.7	.86	2.01	3.24	3.40
1995-96	NY	76	22.5	.466	.143	.761	10.6	2.1	.89	2.42	2.91	3.30
1996-97	NY	78	22.4	.488	.222	.754	10.7	2.0	.88	2.42	3.45	3.20
1997-98	NY	26	20.8	.504	.000	.720	10.2	1.1	.62	2.23	2.96	2.80
1998-99	NY	38	17.3	.435	.000	.706	9.9	1.1	.79	2.63	2.61	2.80
1999-00	NY	62	15.0	.466	.000	.731	9.7	0.9	.58	1.35	2.29	3.20
2000-01	SEA	79	9.6	.430	.000	.685	7.4	1.2	.67	1.15	1.91	2.90
2001-02	ORL	65	6.0	.444	.000	.701	4.0	0.5	.34	0.69	1.00	2.00
TOTAL		1183	21.0	.504	.152	.740	9.8	1.9	.96	2.45	2.99	3.40

NY: New York Knicks; ORL: Orlando Magic; SEA: Seattle Supersonics.

Beginning in 1986, after his graduation from college, Ewing played center with the New York Knicks. His initial six-year contract was said to have been worth $17 million. He was named Rookie of the year during his first year, and he was named one of the top fifty-nine players in NBA history in 1996. He stayed with the team for a total of fifteen years, after which he played briefly with the Seattle Supersonics and the Orlando Magic before retiring from playing at the age of forty. He retired from playing with a career total of 24,815 points and 11,607 rebounds.

Coach Ewing

It was in September of 2002 that Ewing announced that he would retire from playing basketball. He also announced that he would take a job as an assistant coach for the Washington Wizards, working alongside the legendary **Michael Jordan**.

Said Abe Pollin, the owner of the Wizards, about signing Ewing as coach, "It will be a unique opportunity for our players to be tutored by three of the 50 greatest players of all time—Michael Jordan, Wes Unseld and now, Patrick Ewing."

Ewing's old high school coach, Mike Jarvis turned out for a news conference Ewing held to say goodbye as a player. When asked how he thought how should be remembered as a player, Ewing responded, quoted on ESPN.com, "As a hard hat. A hard nose. The work ethic I brought, I gave it 110 percent. I thought I had a great career. I have no regrets. I wouldn't trade it anything. I enjoyed every minute." His only disappointment, he said, was not wining a professional championship. "We did the best we could to help the franchise win one," he said. "It didn't happen. That's life. You've got to move on."

FURTHER INFORMATION

Periodicals

Elderkin, Phil. "Rookie Pat Ewing: a 7-ft. Silver Lining in Knicks' Cloudy Season." *Christian Science Monitor* (January 29, 1986): Sports, 16.

"Ewing Has a 1-Year-Old Son." *Washington Post* (May 16, 1985): A30.

Gallo, Jon. "A Chip Off the Old Blocker of Shots: Basketball Player Patrick Ewing Jr. Comes to Town." *Washington Post* (August 6, 2002): D1.

Johnson, Roy S. "Class of '85." *New York Times* (May 27, 1985): A30.

Johnson, Roy S. "Man in the News; Biggest Court Prize: Patrick Ewing." *New York Times* (May 13, 1985): C6.

MacMullan, Jackie. "As the Misperceptions that Alienated Him and Boston Begin to Fade, Patrick Ewing Is Getting Closer to Home." *Boston Globe* (April 11, 1993): Sports, 41.

Other

"Biography—Patrick Ewing." HickokSports.com. http://www.hickoksports.com/biograph/ewingpatr.shtml. (December 3, 2002).

"Ewing Retires, Accepts Coaching Job with Wizards." ESPN.com. http://espn.go.com/nba/news/2002/0917/1432895.html (December 3, 2002).

"Patrick Ewing Player Info." NBA.com. http://www.nba.com/playerfile/patrick_ewing/ (December 3, 2002).

"Patrick Ewing Player Profile." Yahoo! Sports. http://sports.yahoo.com/nba/players/1/106/ (December 3, 2002).

Sketch by Michael Belfiore